German
School
Dictionary

Published by Collins
An imprint of HarperCollins Publishers
Westerhill Road
Bishopbriggs
Glasgow G64 2QT

HarperCollins Publishers
Macken House
39/40 Mayor Street Upper
Dublin 1, D01 C9W8, Ireland

Third Edition 2025

10 9 8 7 6 5 4 3 2 1

© HarperCollins Publishers 2010, 2015, 2025

ISBN 978-0-00-871832-9

Collins® and Collins Gem® are registered trademarks of HarperCollins Publishers Limited

www.collins.co.uk/dictionaries

Typeset by Davidson Publishing Solutions, Glasgow

Printed in India

All rights reserved. No part of this book may be reproduced, stored in a retrieval system, or transmitted in any form or by any means, electronic, mechanical, photocopying, recording or otherwise, without the prior permission in writing of the Publisher. This book is sold subject to the conditions that it shall not, by way of trade or otherwise, be lent, re-sold, hired out or otherwise circulated without the Publisher's prior consent in any form of binding or cover other than that in which it is published and without a similar condition including this condition being imposed on the subsequent purchaser.

Entered words that we have reason to believe constitute trademarks have been designated as such. However, neither the presence nor absence of such designation should be regarded as affecting the legal status of any trademark.

The contents of this publication are believed correct at the time of printing. Nevertheless the Publisher can accept no responsibility for errors or omissions, changes in the detail given or for any expense or loss thereby caused.

HarperCollins does not warrant that any website mentioned in this title will be provided uninterrupted, that any website will be error free, that defects will be corrected, or that the website or the server that makes it available are free of viruses or bugs. For full terms and conditions please refer to the site terms provided on the website.

A catalogue record for this book is available from the British Library.

If you would like to comment on any aspect of this book, please contact us at the given address or online.
E-mail: dictionaries@harpercollins.co.uk

Acknowledgements
We would like to thank those authors and publishers who kindly gave permission for copyright material to be used in the Collins Corpus. We would also like to thank Times Newspapers Ltd for providing valuable data.

EDITOR
Susie Beattie

CONTRIBUTORS
Joyce Littlejohn
Horst Kopleck
Maggie Seaton
Anna Stevenson
Silke Zimmerman

FOR THE PUBLISHER
Kerry Ferguson
Michelle I'Anson

TECHNICAL SUPORT
Agnieszka Urbanowicz

CONTENTS

v–vii
Using this dictionary

viii
Abbreviations used in this dictionary

ix
Time

x
Dates

xi–xii
Numbers

1–275
German – English dictionary

277–528
English – German dictionary

1–98
Verb tables

Acknowledgements
We are grateful to all those teachers and students who have contributed to the development of the *Collins German School Dictionary* by advising us on how to tailor it to their needs. We also gratefully acknowledge the help of the examining boards.

USING THIS DICTIONARY

The *Collins German School Dictionary* is designed specifically for anyone starting to learn German, and has been carefully researched with teachers and students. It is very straightforward, with an accessible layout that is easy on the eye, guiding students quickly to the right translation. It also offers essential help on German culture.

This section gives useful tips on how to use the *Collins German School Dictionary* effectively.

▷ Make sure you look in the right side of the dictionary

There are two sides in a bilingual dictionary. Here, the **German–English** side comes first, and the second part is **English–German**. At the top of each page there is a reminder of which side of the dictionary you have open. The middle pages of the book have a grey border so you can see where one side finishes and the other one starts.

▷ Finding the word you want

To help you find a word more quickly, use the **alphabet tabs** down the side of the page, then look at the words in **black** at the top of pages. They show the first and last words on the two pages where the dictionary is open.

▷ Make sure you use the right part of speech

Some entries are split into several parts of speech. For example '**glue**' can either be a noun ("Can I borrow your **glue**?") or a verb ("**Glue** this into your exercise book"). Parts of speech within an entry are separated by a black triangle ▶ and are given on a new line. They are given in their abbreviated form (*n* for noun, *adj* for adjective, etc). For the full list of abbreviations, look at page viii.

> **glue** *n* Klebstoff *m* (*pl* Klebstoffe)
> ▶ *vb* kleben [**38**] ▷ *to glue something together* etwas zusammenkleben

v

▷ Choosing the right translation

The main translation of a word is underlined and is shown after the part of speech. If there is more than one main translation for a word, each one is numbered. You may also sometimes find bracketed words in *italics* which give you some context. They help you choose the translation you want.

> **pool** n ❶ *(puddle)* <u>Pfütze</u> f ❷ *(pond)*
> <u>Teich</u> m *(pl* Teiche*)* ❸ *(for swimming)*
> <u>Schwimmbecken</u> nt *(pl*

Often you will see phrases in *italics*, preceded by a white triangle ▷. These are examples of the word being used in context.

> **kaum** adv <u>hardly</u> ▷ *Ich habe kaum*
> *geschlafen.* I hardly slept.

Phrases in **bold type** are phrases which are particularly common and important. Sometimes these phrases have a totally different translation.

> **Besserung** f improvement; **Gute**
> **Besserung!** Get well soon!

Once you have found the right translation, remember that you may need to adapt the German word you have found. You may need to make a **noun** feminine or plural or genitive. Remember that the feminine form is given for nouns and that irregular plurals and genitive forms are also given.

> **dancer** n Tänzer m *(pl* Tänzer*)*, Tänzerin f

> **zip** n Reißverschluss m *(gen*
> Reißverschlusses, *pl* Reißverschlüsse*)*

You may also need to adapt the **verb**. Verbs are given in the infinitive form, but you may wish to use them in the present, past or future tense. To do this, use the **verb tables** in the last section of the dictionary. Many German verbs on both sides are followed by a number in square brackets. This number corresponds to a verb table number in the verb tables at the back of the dictionary.

In the example below, **kauen** follows the same pattern as **holen**, which is verb number **38** in the verb tables.

> **kauen** *vb* [**38**] to chew

Verbs which have no number are followed by the main forms in brackets, but some irregular verbs have both a number and show the main forms, for clarity.

▷ **Find out more**

In the *Collins German School Dictionary*, you will find lots of extra information about the German language. These **usage notes** help you understand how the language works, draw your attention to false friends (words which look similar to English words but have a different meaning), and give you some word-for-word translations.

> **entgegen** *prep*
> ▮ entgegen takes the dative.
>
> **Chips** *pl* crisps *pl*
> ▮ Be careful! The German word **Chips** does not mean **chips**.
>
> **Wörterbuch** (*pl* **Wörterbücher**) *nt*
> dictionary
> ▮ Word for word, **Wörterbuch** means 'word book'.

You can also find out more about life in Germany and German-speaking countries by reading the **cultural notes**.

> **A levels** *npl* Abitur *nt sg*
> • Germans take their **Abitur** at the age
> • of 19. The students sit examinations in
> • a variety of subjects to attain an
> • overall grade. If you pass, you have the
> • right to apply for a place at university.

▷ **Remember!**

Never take the first translation you see without looking at the others. Always look to see if there is more than one translation, or more than one part of speech.

ABBREVIATIONS USED IN THIS DICTIONARY

abbr	abbreviation
adj	adjective
adv	adverb
art	article
conj	conjunction
excl	exclamation
f	feminine
gen	genitive
imperf	imperfect tense
m	masculine
mf	masculine and feminine
n	noun
nt	neuter
num	number
perf	perfect tense
pl	plural
prep	preposition
pres	present tense
pron	pronoun
sing	singular
vb	verb

SYMBOLS

▷	example
▶	new part of speech
●	new meaning
[38]	verb table number (see Verb Tables section at the back of the dictionary)
accident	Key words which you need for your GCSE or other exams of a similar level are highlighted in light grey throughout both sides of the dictionary to help you find them more easily.

TIME

Wie spät ist es? What time is it?

ein Uhr

zehn nach eins

Viertel nach eins

halb zwei

zwanzig vor zwei

Viertel vor zwei

Um wie viel uhr? At what time?

um Mitternacht

um Mittag

um ein Uhr (nachmittags)

um acht Uhr (abends)

um 11:15 Uhr *or* elf Uhr fünfzehn

um 20:45 Uhr *or* zwanzig Uhr fünfundvierzig

DATES

▷ Days of the week

Montag	Monday
Dienstag	Tuesday
Mittwoch	Wednesday
Donnerstag	Thursday
Freitag	Friday
Samstag	Saturday
Sonntag	Sunday

▷ Months of the year

Januar	January	**Juli**	July
Februar	February	**August**	August
März	March	**September**	September
April	April	**Oktober**	October
Mai	May	**November**	November
Juni	June	**Dezember**	December

▷ Wann?

im Februar
am 1. Dezember
am ersten Dezember 2025

zweitausendneunzehn

▷ When?

in February
on 1 December
on the first of December in 2025

in two thousand and nineteen

▷ Der Wievielte ist heute?

Heute ist...
Sonntag, der 1. Oktober or
Sonntag, der erste Oktober
Monntag, der 10. Februar or
Monntag, der zehnte Februar

▷ What day is it?

It's...
Sunday 1 October or
Sunday, the first of October
Monday 10 February or
Monday, the tenth of February

NUMBERS

▷ **Ordinal numbers**

1st	erste(r, s)
2nd	zweite(r, s)
3rd	dritte(r, s)
4th	vierte(r, s)
5th	fünfte(r, s)
6th	sechste(r, s)
7th	siebte(r, s)
8th	achte(r, s)
9th	neunte(r, s)
10th	zehnte(r, s)
11th	elfte(r, s)
12th	zwölfte(r, s)
13th	dreizehnte(r, s)
14th	vierzehnte(r, s)
15th	fünfzehnte(r, s)
16th	sechzehnte(r, s)
17th	siebzehnte(r, s)
18th	achtzehnte(r, s)
19th	neunzehnte(r, s)
20th	zwanzigste(r, s)
21st	einundzwanzigste(r, s)
22nd	zweiundzwanzigste(r, s)
30th	dreißigste(r, s)
100th	(ein)hundertste(r, s)
101st	(ein)hundert(und)erste(r, s)
1000th	(ein)tausendste(r, s)

NUMBERS

▷ **Cardinal numbers**

0	null	20	zwanzig
1	eins	21	einundzwanzig
2	zwei	22	zweiundzwanzig
3	drei	30	dreißig
4	vier	40	vierzig
5	fünf	50	fünfzig
6	sechs	60	sechzig
7	sieben	70	siebzig
8	acht	80	achtzig
9	neun	90	neunzig
10	zehn	100	(ein)hundert
11	elf	101	(ein)hundert(und)eins
12	zwölf		
13	dreizehn	200	zweihundert
14	vierzehn	300	dreihundert
15	fünfzehn	301	dreihundert(und)eins
16	sechzehn		
17	siebzehn	1000	(ein)tausend
18	achtzehn	2000	zweitausend
19	neunzehn	1,000,000	eine Million

▷ **Fractions etc**

1/2	ein halb	1/5	ein Fünftel
1/3	ein Drittel	0.5	null Komma fünf (1,5)
2/3	zwei Drittel	10%	zehn Prozent
1/4	ein Viertel	100%	hundert Prozent
3/4	drei Viertel		

DEUTSCH - ENGLISCH | GERMAN - ENGLISH

ab prep, adv

▪ The preposition **ab** takes the dative. ① from ▷ Kinder ab zwölf Jahren children from the age of twelve ▷ ab morgen from tomorrow ② off ▷ Die Straße geht nach links ab. The road goes off to the left. ▷ Der Knopf ist ab. The button has come off. ▷ Ab nach Hause! Off you go home!; **ab sofort** as of now; **ab und zu** now and then

abbiegen (imperf **bog ab**, perf **ist abgebogen**) vb ① to turn off ▷ Sie bog an der Kreuzung nach links ab. At the crossroads she turned off to the left. ② to bend ▷ Die Hauptstraße biegt nach rechts ab. The main road bends to the right.

Abbildung f illustration

abbrechen vb [11] ① to break off ▷ Sie brach einen blühenden Zweig ab. She broke off a flowering branch. ② to pull down ▷ Das alte Gebäude muss abgebrochen werden. The old building will have to be pulled down. ③ to stop ▷ Es ist schon spät, wir sollten abb... It's late now; we ought to stop. ④ ... abort ▷ Das dauert zu lang, du solltest... Programm abbrechen. It's taking too long; you should abort the program.

Abend (pl **Abende**) m evening ▷ Sie macht jeden Abend einen Spaziergang. She goes for a walk every evening. ▷ guten Abend good evening; **zu Abend essen** to have dinner; **heute Abend** this evening

Abendbrot nt supper

Abendessen (pl **Abendessen**) nt dinner ▷ Zum Abendessen gibt es Spaghetti. There's spaghetti for dinner.

abends adv in the evening

Abenteuer (pl **Abenteuer**) nt adventure

aber conj, adv ① but ▷ Er wollte mit uns mitkommen, aber seine Eltern haben es nicht erlaubt. He wanted to come with us, but his parents wouldn't let him. ② however ▷ Ich möchte nach Ägypten reisen. Ich habe aber kein Geld. I'd like to go to Egypt. However, I haven't got any money.; **Das ist aber schön!** That's really nice.; **Nun ist aber Schluss!** Now that's enough!

abfahren vb [21] to leave ▷ Wir fahren morgen sehr früh ab. We're leaving very early tomorrow. ▷ Wann fährt dein Zug ab? When does your train leave?

Abfahrt f departure

Abfall (pl **Abfälle**) m rubbish

Abfalleimer (pl **Abfalleimer**) m rubbish bin

abfliegen vb [25] to take off ▷ Die Maschine ist mit Verspätung abgeflogen. The plane was late taking off.; **Um wie viel Uhr fliegt ihr ab?** What time does your plane leave?

Abflug (pl **Abflüge**) m ① departure ▷ Wir müssen eine Stunde vor Abflug am Flughafen sein. We have to be at the airport one hour before departure.

Abgas | 2

❷ takeoff ▷ *Die Maschine stürzte kurz nach dem Abflug ab.* The plane crashed shortly after takeoff.

Abgas (gen **Abgases**, pl **Abgase**) nt exhaust fumes pl

abgeben vb [28] ❶ to hand in ▷ *Die Klassenarbeiten müssen am Ende der Stunde abgegeben werden.* Tests must be handed in at the end of the lesson. ❷ to pass ▷ *Er gab den Ball an den Mittelstürmer ab.* He passed the ball to the centre-forward.; **sich mit jemandem abgeben** to associate with somebody; **sich mit etwas abgeben** to bother with something; **jemandem etwas abgeben** to let somebody have something

abgelegen adj remote

abgemacht adj agreed ▷ *Wir trafen uns zur abgemachten Zeit.* We met at the agreed time.; **Abgemacht!** OK!

abgesehen adj **es auf jemanden abgesehen haben** to be out to get somebody; **es auf etwas abgesehen haben** to be after something; **abgesehen von ...** apart from ...

abgewöhnen vb [38] **sich etwas abgewöhnen** to give something up

Abhang (pl **Abhänge**) m slope

abhängen (1) (perf **hat abgehängt**) vb [4] ❶ to take down ▷ *Weil ihr das Bild nicht mehr gefiel, hängte sie es ab.* She took the picture down because she didn't like it any more. ❷ to unhitch ▷ *Er hängte den Wohnwagen ab, bevor er in die Stadt fuhr.* He unhitched the caravan before he drove into town. ❸ to shake off ▷ *Den Räubern gelang es, die Polizei abzuhängen.* The robbers managed to shake off the police.

abhängen (2) (imperf **hing ab**, perf **hat abgehangen**) vb [35] **von jemandem abhängen** to depend on somebody; **von etwas abhängen** to depend on something

abhängig adj **abhängig von** dependent on

abheben (imperf **hob ab**, perf **hat abgehoben**) vb [4] ❶ to answer ▷ *Es scheint niemand zu Hause zu sein, es hebt nämlich keiner ab.* There doesn't seem to be anyone at home as nobody's answering the phone. ❷ to withdraw ▷ *Ich muss Geld vom Sparbuch abheben.* I'll have to withdraw some money from my savings account. ❸ to take off ▷ *Wir sahen zu, wie das Flugzeug abhob.* We watched the plane take off. ❹ to lift off ▷ *Die Rakete hob senkrecht ab.* The rocket lifted off vertically.; **sich von etwas abheben** to stand out against something

abholen vb [4] ❶ to collect ▷ *Der Müll wird einmal in der Woche abgeholt.* Rubbish is collected once a week. ❷ to pick up ▷ *Ich hole dich um sieben ab.* I'll pick you up at seven.

Abitur nt A levels

Abiturient (gen **Abiturienten**, pl **Abiturienten**) m A level student

Abiturientin f A level student

abkürzen vb [36] to abbreviate ▷ *Man kann 'bitte wenden' mit b. w. abkürzen.* You can abbreviate 'please turn over' to PTO.; **den Weg abkürzen** to take a short cut

Abkürzung f ❶ abbreviation ▷ *Die Abkürzung für Europäische Union ist EU.* The abbreviation for European Union is EU. ❷ short cut ▷ *Wir haben eine Abkürzung genommen.* We took a short cut.

abladen (pres **lädt ab**, imperf **lud ab**, perf **hat abgeladen**) vb to unload

ablaufen vb [43] ❶ to expire ▷ *Ihr Pass ist leider abgelaufen.* Unfortunately, your passport has expired. ❷ to drain away ▷ *Der Abfluss ist verstopft, und deshalb läuft das Wasser nicht ab.* The waste pipe is blocked, and that's why the water won't drain away.

ablehnen vb [4] ❶ to turn down ▷ *Sie hat das Amt der Klassensprecherin abgelehnt.* She turned down being class representative. ▷ *Mein Antrag auf ein Stipendium wurde abgelehnt.* My application for a grant was turned down. ❷ to disapprove of ▷ *Ich lehne eine solche Arbeitseinstellung ab.* I disapprove of such an attitude to work.

ablenken vb [4] ❶ to distract ▷ *Lenk ihn nicht von seiner Arbeit ab.* Don't distract him from his work.; **vom Thema ablenken** to change the subject

abliefern vb [88] ❶ to drop off ▷ *Wir haben die Kinder wieder wohlbehalten zu Hause abgeliefert.* We dropped the children off at home safe and sound. ❷ to hand in ▷ *Bis wann musst du das Referat abliefern?* When do you have to hand your assignment in by?; **etwas bei jemandem abliefern** to take something to somebody

abmachen vb [4] ❶ to take off ▷ *Weißt du, wie man den Deckel abmacht?* Do you know how to take the lid off? ❷ to agree ▷ *Wir haben abgemacht, dass wir uns um sieben Uhr treffen.* We agreed to meet at seven. ❸ to sort out ▷ *Ihr solltet das untereinander abmachen, wer heute aufräumt.* Sort out amongst yourselves who's going to clear up today.

Abmachung f agreement

Abnahme f decrease ▷ *eine weitere Abnahme der Teilnehmerzahlen* a further decrease in attendance

abnehmen vb [52] ❶ to remove ▷ *Bei diesem Auto kann man das Verdeck abnehmen.* You can remove the hood on this car.; **Als das Telefon klingelte, nahm sie ab.** When the telephone rang, she answered it.; **jemandem etwas abnehmen** to take something away from somebody ❷ to decrease ▷ *Die Zahl der Teilnehmer hat stark abgenommen.* The number of participants has decreased dramatically. ❸ to lose weight ▷ *Ich muss dringend abnehmen.* I really must lose weight. ▷ *Ich habe schon zwei Kilo abgenommen.* I've already lost two kilos. ❹ to buy ▷ *Wenn Sie mehr als zehn Stück abnehmen, bekommen Sie einen Rabatt.* If you buy more than ten you get a discount. ▷ *Hat sie dir diese Geschichte wirklich abgenommen?* (informal) Did she really buy that story?

abonnieren vb [76] to subscribe to

abräumen vb [4] to clear away ▷ *Sie räumte die Teller ab.* She cleared away the plates.; **den Tisch abräumen** to clear the table

Abreise f departure

abreisen (perf **ist abgereist**) vb [4] to leave

Absage f refusal

absagen vb [4] ❶ to call off ▷ *Die Vorstellung wurde abgesagt, weil ein Schauspieler krank war.* The performance was called off because one of the actors was ill. ❷ to turn down ▷ *eine Einladung absagen* to turn down an invitation

Absatz (gen **Absatzes**, pl **Absätze**) m ❶ heel ▷ *Die Absätze von deinen Schuhen sind ganz schief.* The heels of your shoes are worn down. ❷ paragraph ▷ *Hier solltest du einen Absatz machen.* You need to start a new paragraph here. ❸ sales pl ▷ *Der Absatz an elektrischen Geräten ist gestiegen.* Sales of electrical appliances have risen.

abschaffen vb [4] ❶ to abolish ▷ *Wann wurde in Deutschland die Todesstrafe abgeschafft?* When was the death sentence abolished in Germany? ❷ to get rid of ▷ *Ich werde mein Auto abschaffen.* I'm going to get rid of my car.

abscheulich adj abominable

abschicken vb [4] to send off

Abschied (pl **Abschiede**) m parting; **von jemandem Abschied nehmen** to say goodbye to somebody

abschleppen vb [4] ❶ to tow ▷ *ein Auto abschleppen* to tow a car; **jemanden abschleppen** (informal) to pick somebody up

abschließen (imperf **schloss ab**, perf **hat abgeschlossen**) vb ❶ to lock ▷ *Ich schließe meinen Schreibtisch immer ab.* I always lock my desk. ❷ to conclude ▷ *einen Vertrag abschließen* to conclude a contract

abschließend adj, adv in conclusion ▷ *Abschließend möchte ich noch Folgendes sagen: ...* In conclusion I would like to say this: ...

Abschluss (gen **Abschlusses**) m ❶ conclusion (of contract) ❷ leaving certificate (school) ❸ degree (college, university) ▷ *Sie hat einen guten Abschluss.* She's got a good degree.

Abschlussprüfung f final exam

abschneiden vb [60] ❶ to cut ▷ *Kannst du mir bitte eine Scheibe Brot abschneiden?* Can you cut me a slice of bread, please? ❷ to do ▷ *Sie hat in der Prüfung sehr gut abgeschnitten.* She did very well in the exam.

abschrecken vb [4] to deter ▷ *Diese Maßnahmen sollen Jugendliche davon abschrecken, Drogen zu nehmen.* These measures are intended to deter young people from taking drugs.

abschreiben vb [61] to copy ▷ *Er wurde dabei erwischt, wie er von seinem Nachbarn abgeschrieben hat.* He was caught copying from his neighbour. ▷ *Schreibt diesen Satz bitte in eure Hefte ab.* Please copy this sentence into your exercise books.

absehbar adj foreseeable ▷ *in absehbarer Zeit* in the foreseeable future; **Das Ende ist absehbar.** The end is in sight.

abseits adv apart ▷ *Sie stand etwas abseits von den anderen.* She was standing somewhat apart from the others.

Absender (pl **Absender**) m sender

absetzen vb [36] ❶ to drop off ▷ *Ich setze dich am Bahnhof ab.* I'll drop you off at the station. ❷ to take off ▷ *Willst du nicht deinen Motorradhelm absetzen?* Don't you want to take your helmet off? ❸ to drop ▷ *Dieser Sprachkurs musste vom Programm abgesetzt werden.* This language course has had to be dropped from the syllabus.; **die Pille absetzen** to stop taking the pill

Absicht f intention ▷ *Das war nicht meine Absicht.* That was not my intention.; **mit Absicht** on purpose

absichtlich adj, adv deliberate ▷ *eine absichtliche Beleidigung* a deliberate insult; **etwas absichtlich tun** to do something deliberately

absolut adj, adv absolute; **Das ist absolut unmöglich.** That's absolutely impossible.

abspülen vb [4] to rinse ▷ *Er spülte die Teller ab.* He rinsed the plates.; **Geschirr abspülen** to wash up

Abstand (pl **Abstände**) m distance ▷ *Abstand halten* to keep one's distance

abstellen vb [4] ❶ to put down ▷ *Der Koffer ist so schwer, ich muss ihn kurz abstellen.* The case is so heavy that I'll have to put it down for a moment. ❷ to park ▷ *Wir haben das Auto am Stadtrand abgestellt.* We parked the car on the outskirts of town. ❸ to switch off ▷ *Kannst du bitte das Radio abstellen?* Can you switch the radio off, please?

Abstimmung f vote

abstreiten (imperf **stritt ab**, perf **hat abgestritten**) vb to deny

abstürzen (perf **ist abgestürzt**) vb [36] ❶ to fall ▷ *Mathis ist beim Klettern abgestürzt.* Mathis fell while climbing.

❷ to crash ▷ *Die Maschine ist kurz nach dem Start abgestürzt.* The plane crashed shortly after takeoff.
Abteil (*pl* **Abteile**) *nt* compartment
Abteilung *f* ❶ department ▷ *Sie wurde in eine andere Abteilung versetzt.* She was transferred to another department.
❷ ward ▷ *In welcher Abteilung liegt Mathis?* Which ward is Mathis in?
Abtreibung *f* abortion
abtrocknen *vb* [53] to dry
abwärts *adv* down
Abwasch *m* washing-up ▷ *den Abwasch machen* to do the washing-up
abwaschen *vb* [89] ❶ to wash ▷ *Wer muss heute das Geschirr abwaschen?* Who's turn is it to wash the dishes today? ❷ to wash off ▷ *Wasch dir mal die Soße vom Gesicht ab!* Wash that gravy off your face.
Abwechslung *f* change ▷ *zur Abwechslung* for a change
abwerten *vb* [2] to devalue
abwertend *adj, adv* derogatory ▷ *sich abwertend über etwas äußern* to talk in a derogatory way about something
abwesend *adj* absent
Abwesenheit *f* absence
abzählen *vb* [4] to count
Abzeichen (*pl* **Abzeichen**) *nt* badge
abziehen *vb* [96]

> For the perfect tense use **haben** when the verb has an object and **sein** when there is no object.

❶ to take out ▷ *Er zog den Zündschlüssel ab.* He took out the ignition key. ❷ to withdraw ▷ *Sie haben ihre Truppen aus der Stadt abgezogen.* They have withdrawn their troops from the town. ❸ to deduct ▷ *Die Steuer wird vom Gehalt abgezogen.* Tax is deducted from earnings.; **Er ist beleidigt abgezogen.** (*informal*) He went away in a huff.
ach *excl* oh!

Achsel *f* shoulder
acht *num* eight; **acht Tage** a week
Acht *f* eight ▷ *Schreibe eine Acht.* Write the figure eight.; **sich in Acht nehmen** to beware; **etwas außer Acht lassen** to disregard something; **Acht geben** *see* **achtgeben**
achte *adj* eighth ▷ *Sie wiederholte den Satz ein achtes Mal.* She repeated the sentence for an eighth time. ▷ *Er kam als Achter.* He was the eighth to arrive.
achten *vb* [2] to respect ▷ *Ich achte deine Meinung.* I respect your opinion. ▷ *Sie ist sehr geachtet.* She's highly respected.;
auf etwas achten to pay attention to something; **auf jemanden achten** to take notice of somebody
achtgeben *vb* [28] to pay attention ▷ *Du solltest etwas mehr auf die Rechtschreibung achtgeben!* You should pay a bit more attention to spelling.;
auf jemanden achtgeben to keep an eye on somebody; **Gib acht!** Look out!
achtmal *adv* eight times
Achtung *f* respect ▷ *Ich habe große Achtung vor ihr.* I've great respect for her.; **Achtung!** Look out!; **Achtung Stufe!** Mind the step.; **Achtung, Achtung, hier eine Durchsage!** Your attention, please. Here is an announcement.; **Alle Achtung!** Well done!
achtzehn *num* eighteen
achtzig *num* eighty
Acker (*pl* **Äcker**) *m* field
addieren *vb* [76] to add
Adel *m* nobility
Ader *f* vein
ADHS *abbr* (= Aufmerksamkeitsdefizit-Hyperaktivitätsstörung) ADHD
Adjektiv (*pl* **Adjektive**) *nt* adjective
Adler (*pl* **Adler**) *m* eagle
adlig *adj* noble
adoptieren *vb* [76] to adopt
Adoptiveltern *pl* adoptive parents *pl*

Adoptivkind (pl **Adoptivkinder**) nt adopted child

Adresse f address

adressieren vb [76] to address ▷ *An wen soll ich den Brief adressieren?* To whom should I address the letter?

Adventskalender (pl **Adventskalender**) m Advent calendar

Adverb (pl **Adverbien**) nt adverb

Affe (gen **Affen**, pl **Affen**) m monkey

Afrika nt Africa

Afrikaner (pl **Afrikaner**) m African

Afrikanerin f African

afrikanisch adj African

Ägypten nt Egypt

Ägypter (pl **Ägypter**) m Egyptian

Ägypterin f Egyptian

ägyptisch adj Egyptian

ähneln vb [34] jemandem ähneln to resemble somebody; **Sie ähneln sich.** They are alike.

ahnen vb [38] ❶ to know ▷ *Ich habe geahnt, dass er nicht kommen würde.* I knew he wouldn't come. ▷ *Das konnte ich doch nicht ahnen!* How was I supposed to know that? ❷ to sense ▷ *Das Tier hat die Gefahr geahnt und ist schnell verschwunden.* The animal sensed the danger and quickly disappeared.

ähnlich adj similar ▷ *Unsere Kleider sind sehr ähnlich.* Our dresses are very similar.; **Sein Auto sieht ähnlich aus wie meines.** His car looks like mine.; **Er ist seinem Vater sehr ähnlich.** He's very like his father.; **Das sieht ihr ähnlich!** That's typical of her.

Ähnlichkeit f similarity

Ahnung f ❶ idea ▷ *Ich habe keine Ahnung, ob er kommt.* I've no idea whether he's coming.; **Er hat von Computern keine Ahnung.** He doesn't know the first thing about computers. ❷ hunch ▷ *Er hatte eine Ahnung, dass etwas Schlimmes geschehen würde.* He had a hunch that something terrible would happen.

ahnungslos adj unsuspecting

Aids (gen **Aids**) nt AIDS sg (= Acquired Immune Deficiency Syndrome) ▷ *Gerd ist an Aids gestorben.* Gerd died of AIDS.

Akademiker (pl **Akademiker**) m university graduate

Akademikerin f university graduate

Akkusativ (pl **Akkusative**) m accusative

Akne f acne ▷ *Sie hat Akne.* She's got acne.

Akte f file; **etwas zu den Akten legen** to file something away

Aktentasche f briefcase

Aktie f share ▷ *in Aktien investieren* to invest in shares

Aktion f ❶ campaign ▷ *eine Aktion für den Frieden* a campaign for peace ❷ operation ▷ *Wir alle nahmen an der Aktion teil.* We all took part in the operation.; **in Aktion treten** to go into action

> Word for word, **in Aktion treten** means 'to step into action'.

aktiv adj active

Aktivität f activity

aktuell adj ❶ topical ▷ *ein aktuelles Thema* a topical issue ❷ up-to-date ▷ *ein aktueller Fahrplan* an up-to-date timetable

Akzent (pl **Akzente**) m ❶ accent ▷ *Sie spricht mit einem amerikanischen Akzent.* She speaks with an American accent. ❷ emphasis ▷ *Der Akzent liegt auf Benutzerfreundlichkeit.* The emphasis is on user-friendliness.

akzeptieren vb [2] to accept

albern adj silly; **sich albern benehmen** to act silly

Albtraum (pl **Albträume**) m nightmare

Album (pl **Alben**) nt album

Alkohol m alcohol

alkoholfrei adj nonalcoholic

Alkoholiker (pl **Alkoholiker**) m alcoholic

GERMAN > ENGLISH

Alkoholikerin f alcoholic
alkoholisch adj alcoholic
All nt space ▷ *Sie haben eine Rakete ins All geschossen.* They've sent a rocket into space.
alle adj, pron ❶ all the ▷ *Alle Schüler sollten kommen.* All the pupils should come. ❷ all ▷ *Nicht alle Kinder mögen Schokolade.* Not all children like chocolate. ❸ all of them ▷ *Wir haben alle gesehen.* We saw all of them.; **Sie kamen alle.** They all came.; **wir alle** all of us; **Ich habe alle beide eingeladen.** I've invited both of them. ❹ every ▷ *alle vier Jahre* every four years ▷ *alle fünf Meter* every five metres; **Die Milch ist alle.** The milk's all gone.; **etwas alle machen** to finish something up
Allee (pl **Alleen**) f avenue
allein adj, adv, conj ❶ alone ▷ *Sie lebt allein.* She lives alone. ▷ *Du allein kannst das entscheiden.* You alone can decide. ❷ on one's own ▷ *Sie hat das ganz allein geschrieben.* She wrote that all on her own. ▷ *Seit ich allein bin, habe ich mehr Zeit.* Since I've been on my own, I've had more time.; **Er fühlt sich allein.** He feels lonely.; **nicht allein** not only
alleinstehend adj single

> Word for word, **alleinstehend** means 'standing alone'.

allerdings adv ❶ though ▷ *Der Urlaub war schön, allerdings etwas kurz.* The holiday was nice, though it was rather short. ❷ certainly ▷ *Das ist allerdings schwierig.* That's certainly difficult.
Allergie f allergy
allergisch adj allergic ▷ *Sie ist allergisch gegen Katzen.* She's allergic to cats.
Allerheiligen nt All Saints' Day
  * Allerheiligen (November 1st) is a
  * public holiday in those parts of
  * Germany where most of the
  * population are Roman Catholics.

allerlei adj all sorts of ▷ *allerlei Sachen* all sorts of things
alles pron everything ▷ *Sie haben alles aufgegessen.* They've eaten everything up.; **alles, was er sagt** everything he says; **alles in Allem** all in all; **Alles Gute!** All the best!
allgemein adj general; **im Allgemeinen** in general
allmählich adj, adv ❶ gradual ▷ *eine allmähliche Besserung* a gradual improvement ❷ gradually ▷ *Es wird allmählich wärmer.* It's gradually getting warmer.; **Allmählich solltest du das wissen.** You should know that by now.
Alltag m everyday life
allzu adv all too ▷ *allzu oft* all too often; **allzu viel** far too much
Alm f alpine pasture
Alpen fpl Alps pl
Alphabet (pl **Alphabete**) nt alphabet
alphabetisch adj alphabetical ▷ *alphabetisch geordnet* arranged in alphabetical order
Alptraum (pl **Alpträume**) m nightmare
als conj ❶ when ▷ *Als ich ein Kind war ...* When I was a child ... ❷ as ▷ *Sie kam, als ich gerade gehen wollte.* She arrived as I was about to leave. ▷ *Ich als Lehrerin weiß, ...* As a teacher, I know ...; **gerade, als ...** just as ...; **als ob** as if ❸ than ▷ *Sie ist älter als ich.* She's older than me. ▷ *Ich kam später als er.* I came later than he did.; **lieber als ...** rather than ...; **nichts als Ärger** nothing but trouble
also adv, conj, excl ❶ then ▷ *Was sollen wir also tun?* What shall we do, then? ▷ *Du willst also nicht mit.* You don't want to come along, then. ▷ *Du hast es also gewusst.* You did know then. ❷ so ▷ *Es war schon spät, also bin ich nach Hause gegangen.* It had got late, so I went home. ❸ well ▷ *Also ich gehe jetzt!* Well, I'm off now. ▷ *Also, Sie fahren immer*

alt | 8   GERMAN > ENGLISH

geradeaus ... Well, keep going straight on ...; **Also gut!** Okay then.; **Also, so was!** Well really!; **Na also!** There you are then!

> Be careful! The German word **also** does not mean **also**.

alt adj old ▷ *Wie alt bist du?* How old are you? ▷ *Felix ist zehn Jahre alt.* Felix is ten years old. ▷ *Sein Auto ist älter als unseres.* His car is older than ours.; **meine ältere Schwester** my elder sister; **alles beim Alten lassen** to leave everything as it was
Altar (pl **Altäre**) m altar
Alter (pl **Alter**) nt ❶ age ▷ *In deinem Alter sollte man das wissen.* You ought to know that at your age. ❷ old age ▷ *Im Alter sind die Menschen oft einsam.* People are often lonely in old age.; **im Alter von** at the age of
Alternative f alternative
Altglas (gen **Altglases**) nt used glass
Altglascontainer (pl **Altglascontainer**) m bottle bank
altmodisch adj old-fashioned
Altpapier nt waste paper
Altstadt (pl **Altstädte**) f old town
Alufolie f tinfoil
Aluminium nt aluminium
am = **an dem**; **am fünften März** on the fifth of March; **am höchsten** the highest; **am schönsten** the most beautiful
Ameise f ant
Amerika nt America
Amerikaner (pl **Amerikaner**) m American
Amerikanerin f American
amerikanisch adj American
Ampel f traffic lights pl ▷ *Die Ampel ist grün.* The traffic lights are at green.
Amsel f blackbird
Amt (pl **Ämter**) nt office ▷ *Welches Amt ist für Kindergeld zuständig?* Which office deals with child benefit?
amtlich adj official
amüsant adj amusing
amüsieren vb [76] to amuse ▷ *Diese Geschichte hat uns sehr amüsiert.* The story amused us very much.; **sich amüsieren** to enjoy oneself
an prep, adv

> Use the accusative to express movement or a change of place. Use the dative when there is no change of place.

❶ on ▷ *Das Wort stand an der Tafel.* The word was written on the blackboard. ▷ *Der Lehrer schrieb das Wort an die Tafel.* The teacher wrote the word on the blackboard. ▷ *Köln liegt am Rhein.* Cologne is on the Rhine. ▷ *Christoph hat am neunten November Geburtstag.* Christoph's birthday is on the ninth of November. ▷ *an diesem Tag* on this day ❷ to ▷ *Er ging ans Fenster.* He went to the window. ▷ *Wir waren gestern am Meer.* We went to the seaside yesterday. ▷ *Wir wollen morgen ans Meer fahren.* We want to go to the seaside tomorrow. ▷ *Ich habe einen Brief an meine Mutter geschrieben.* I've written a letter to my mother. ❸ by ▷ *Ihr Haus liegt an der Autobahn.* Their house is by the motorway.; **an Ostern** at Easter; **an etwas denken** to think of something; **reich an Nährstoffen** rich in nutrients; **an etwas sterben** to die of something; **an und für sich** actually; **an die hundert** about a hundred; **von heute an** from today onwards; **Das Licht ist an.** The light's on.; **ohne etwas an** with nothing on; **eine Frage an dich** a question for you; **an diesem Ort** in this place; **unten am Fluss** down by the river
Ananas (pl **Ananas**) f pineapple
anbauen vb [4] ❶ to build on ▷ *eine Garage ans Haus anbauen* to build a garage onto the house ❷ to cultivate ▷ *Reis anbauen* to cultivate rice

anbei adv enclosed

anbieten vb [8] to offer ▷ Ich bot ihr eine Tasse Kaffee an. I offered her a cup of coffee.; **anbieten, etwas zu tun** to volunteer to do something

Anblick (pl **Anblicke**) m sight

anbrechen vb [11]

For the perfect tense use **haben** when the verb has an object and **sein** when there is no object.

❶ to break into ▷ Für den Kauf müsste ich meine Ersparnisse anbrechen. To buy it, I'd have to break into my savings. ❷ to break ▷ wenn der Tag anbricht when day breaks ❸ to dawn ▷ Ein neues Zeitalter ist angebrochen. A new age has dawned.

andauernd adj, adv ❶ continual ▷ diese andauernden Unterbrechungen these continual interruptions ❷ constantly ▷ Er stört andauernd. He's constantly interrupting.

Andenken (pl **Andenken**) nt ❶ memory ▷ zum Andenken an eine schöne Zeit in memory of a wonderful time ❷ souvenir ▷ Ich habe mir aus dem Urlaub einige Andenken mitgebracht. I brought a few souvenirs back from my holiday.

andere adj, pron ❶ other ▷ Nein, nicht dieses Buch, gib mir bitte das andere. No, not that book, please give me the other one. ❷ different ▷ Er hat jetzt eine andere Freundin. He's got a different girlfriend now. ❸ another ▷ ein anderes Mal another time ▷ Wir werden das an einem anderen Tag machen. We'll do that another day.; **kein anderer** nobody else; **die anderen** the others; **etwas anderes** something else

andererseits adv on the other hand ▷ Einerseits ..., andererseits ... On the one hand ..., on the other hand ...

ändern vb [88] to alter ▷ Ich habe das Kleid ändern lassen. I've had the dress altered.; **sich ändern** to change

anders adv differently ▷ So geht das nicht, du musst das anders machen. Not like that – you have to do it differently.; **anders als** different from; **Wer anders?** Who else?; **jemand anders** somebody else; **irgendwo anders** somewhere else; **anders aussehen** to look different

anderthalb adj one and a half

Änderung f alteration

andeuten vb [2] to hint ▷ Sie hat angedeutet, dass sie weiß, wer es war. She's hinted that she knows who it was.

Andeutung f hint ▷ Sie hat eine Andeutung gemacht, dass sie es weiß. She hinted that she knew.

anerkennend adj, adv appreciative

Anerkennung f ❶ appreciation ▷ Ihre Leistung fand nicht die entsprechende Anerkennung. Her work didn't get the appreciation it deserved. ❷ recognition ▷ Dieser neue Staat hofft auf Anerkennung durch die Bundesrepublik. This new country is hoping for recognition by the Federal Republic.

Anfall (pl **Anfälle**) m fit ▷ Sie hatte einen epileptischen Anfall. She had an epileptic seizure. ▷ Wenn er das erfährt, bekommt er einen Anfall. (informal) If he finds out, he'll have a fit.

Anfang (pl **Anfänge**) m beginning ▷ von Anfang an right from the beginning ▷ am Anfang at the beginning ▷ Anfang Mai at the beginning of May; **zu Anfang** first

anfangen vb [23] ❶ to begin ▷ Es fängt an zu regnen. It's beginning to rain. ❷ to start ▷ Der Film hat schon angefangen. The film's already started. ▷ Hast du den Aufsatz schon angefangen? Have you already started your essay?; **Damit kann ich nichts anfangen.** It doesn't mean anything to me.; **Das fängt ja gut an!** That's a good start!

Anfänger (pl **Anfänger**) m beginner
anfassen vb [31] ① to touch ▷ *Fass den Hund besser nicht an!* You'd better not touch the dog. ② to treat ▷ *Du solltest die Kinder nicht immer so rau anfassen!* You shouldn't treat the children so roughly.; **mit anfassen** to lend a hand; **sich anfassen** to feel
sich **anfreunden** vb [4] ① to make friends ▷ *Ich habe mich in den Ferien mit einer Engländerin angefreundet.* I made friends with an English girl during the holidays. ② to become friends ▷ *Die beiden haben sich angefreundet.* The two of them have become friends.
Angabe f ① information ▷ *Die Angaben waren falsch.* The information was wrong. ② (tennis) serve ▷ *Wer hat Angabe?* Whose serve is it?; **Das ist doch alles nur Angabe!** That's nothing but show.
angeben vb [28] ① to give ▷ *Geben Sie bitte Ihre Personalien an.* Please give your personal details. ② to state ▷ *Sie hat angegeben, dass sie zu dem Zeitpunkt zu Hause war.* She stated that she was at home at the time. ③ to indicate ▷ *Alle Raststätten sind auf der Karte angegeben.* All service areas are indicated on the map. ④ to show off ▷ *Glaub ihm kein Wort, er gibt nur an.* Don't believe a word he says – he's just showing off.
Angeber (pl **Angeber**) m (informal) show-off
angeblich adj, adv ① alleged ▷ *Sie ist die angebliche Täterin.* She's the alleged culprit. ② allegedly ▷ *Angeblich hat sie es getan.* Allegedly, she did it.
Angebot (pl **Angebote**) nt offer ▷ *Ich nehme dein Angebot an.* I accept your offer.; **ein Angebot an etwas** a selection of something; **Angebot und Nachfrage** supply and demand

angehen vb [29]

> For the perfect tense use **haben** when the verb has an object and **sein** when there is no object.

① to concern ▷ *Diese Angelegenheit geht mich nichts an.* This matter doesn't concern me.; **Was geht dich das an?** What business is it of yours?; **was ... angeht** as regards ... ② to tackle ▷ *Ich weiß noch nicht so richtig, wie ich das Thema angehen soll.* I'm not really sure how to tackle the subject. ③ to go on ▷ *Das Licht ging an.* The light went on.
Angehörige (gen **Angehörigen**, pl **Angehörigen**) mf relative ▷ *Er ist ein Angehöriger von mir.* He's a relative of mine.
Angel f ① fishing rod ② (of door) hinge

> Be careful! The German word **Angel** does not mean angel.

Angelegenheit f ① matter ▷ *Ich werde diese Angelegenheit prüfen.* I'll look into the matter. ② affair ▷ *Das ist meine Angelegenheit.* That's my affair.
angeln vb [34] ① to catch ▷ *Er hat eine große Forelle geangelt.* He caught a large trout. ② to fish ▷ *Sonntags geht Alex immer angeln.* Alex always goes fishing on Sundays.
angenehm adj, adv pleasant; **Angenehm!** Pleased to meet you.
angesehen adj respected
Angestellte (gen **Angestellten**, pl **Angestellten**) mf employee ▷ *Er ist nur ein kleiner Angestellter.* He's just a lowly employee.
angewiesen adj **auf jemanden angewiesen sein** to be dependent on somebody; **auf etwas angewiesen sein** to be dependent on something
angewöhnen vb [38] **jemandem etwas angewöhnen** to teach somebody something; **sich etwas angewöhnen** to get into the habit of doing something

GERMAN > ENGLISH   11 | **Anlage**

Angewohnheit f habit ▷ *Das ist so eine Angewohnheit von ihr.* That's a habit of hers.

angreifen (*imperf* **griff an**, *perf* **hat angegriffen**) *vb* ❶ to attack ▷ *Ich wurde von einem Hund angegriffen.* I was attacked by a dog. ❷ to criticize ▷ *Sie wurde wegen dieser Aussage von ihren Freunden angegriffen.* She was criticized by her friends for what she said.

Angriff (*pl* **Angriffe**) *m* attack; **etwas in Angriff nehmen** to make a start on something

Angst (*pl* **Ängste**) f fear; **vor jemandem Angst haben** to be afraid of somebody; **vor etwas Angst haben** to be afraid of something; **Ich habe Angst vor der Prüfung.** I'm worried about the exam.; **Angst um jemanden haben** to be worried about somebody; **jemandem Angst machen** to scare somebody

ängstlich *adj, adv* ❶ scared ▷ *Nun sei doch nicht so ängstlich, der Hund tut dir nichts!* There's no need to be scared, the dog won't harm you. ❷ anxious ▷ *'Wird er wieder gesund?', fragte sie ängstlich.* 'Will he get well again?', she asked anxiously.

anhaben *vb* (**32**) to have on ▷ *Sie hatte heute das rote Kleid an.* She had her red dress on today.; **jemandem nichts anhaben können** to have nothing on somebody

anhalten *vb* (**33**) ❶ to stop ▷ *Können wir bitte anhalten, mir ist schlecht.* Can we stop please? I feel sick. ▷ *Kannst du bitte das Auto anhalten?* Can you stop the car please? ❷ to last ▷ *Das wird nicht lange anhalten.* It won't last long.; **die Luft anhalten** to hold one's breath

Anhalter (*pl* **Anhalter**) *m* hitchhiker; **per Anhalter fahren** to hitchhike

anhand *prep*
> The preposition **anhand** takes the genitive.

with the help of ▷ *Wir werden das anhand der Unterlagen prüfen.* We'll check that with the help of the documents.

Anhang (*pl* **Anhänge**) *m* appendix

Anhänger (*pl* **Anhänger**) *m* ❶ supporter ▷ *Er ist Anhänger von Schalke.* He's a Schalke supporter. ❷ (*on car*) trailer ❸ label ▷ *Mach einen Anhänger mit deinem Namen und deiner Adresse an deinen Koffer.* Put a label with your name and address on your case. ❹ pendant ▷ *Sie trug eine Kette mit Anhänger.* She was wearing a chain with a pendant.

Anhängerin f supporter ▷ *Sie ist Anhängerin von Schalke.* She's a Schalke supporter.

anhören *vb* [**4**] to listen to ▷ *Wir haben CDs angehört.* We listened to CDs.; **jemandem etwas anhören** to hear something in somebody's voice; **sich anhören** to sound

Anker (*pl* **Anker**) *m* anchor

anklicken *vb* [**4**] (*computer*) to click on ▷ *ein Icon anklicken* to click on an icon

ankommen *vb* [**40**] to arrive ▷ *Wir kommen morgen Nachmittag an.* We'll arrive tomorrow afternoon. ▷ *Ist der Brief schon angekommen?* Has the letter arrived yet?; **bei jemandem gut ankommen** to go down well with somebody; **bei jemandem schlecht ankommen** to go down badly with somebody; **es kommt darauf an** it depends; **wenn es darauf ankommt ...** when it really matters ...; **es darauf ankommen lassen** to wait and see

ankreuzen *vb* [**36**] to mark with a cross

ankündigen *vb* [**4**] to announce

Ankunft (*pl* **Ankünfte**) f arrival

Anlage f ❶ gardens *pl* ▷ *Wir sind in der Anlage spazieren gegangen.* We went for a walk in the gardens. ❷ plant ▷ *Das ist eine neuartige Anlage zum Recycling von Kunststoff.* That's a new plastics

Anlass | 12   GERMAN > ENGLISH

recycling plant. ❸ investment ▷ *Wir raten zu einer Anlage in Immobilien.* We would advise investment in real estate.

Anlass (*gen* **Anlasses**, *pl* **Anlässe**) *m* occasion ▷ *ein festlicher Anlass* a festive occasion; **ein Anlass zu etwas** cause for something; **aus Anlass** on the occasion of; **Anlass zu etwas geben** to give cause for something

Anleitung *f* instructions

Anlieger (*pl* **Anlieger**) *m* resident ▷ *'Anlieger frei'* 'residents only'

anmachen *vb* [4] ❶ to put on ▷ *Mach bitte das Licht an.* Please put the light on. ❷ to light ▷ *Wir haben ein Feuer angemacht.* We lit a fire. ❸ to dress ▷ *Sie macht den Salat immer mit Zitrone an.* She always dresses her salads with lemon. ❹ (*informal*) to chat up ▷ *Ich glaube, der Typ versucht, dich anzumachen.* I think that bloke is trying to chat you up.

anmelden *vb* [54] ❶ to announce ▷ *Sie hat für morgen ihren Besuch angemeldet.* She's announced that she'll visit us tomorrow.; **jemanden anmelden (1)** to make an appointment for somebody ▷ *Er hat seinen Sohn für morgen beim Zahnarzt angemeldet.* He's made a dental appointment for his son for tomorrow. **(2)** to put somebody's name down ▷ *Habt ihr Max schon im Gymnasium angemeldet?* Have you already put Max's name down for grammar school?; **sich anmelden (1)** to make an appointment ▷ *Ich muss mich beim Zahnarzt anmelden.* I must make an appointment with the dentist. **(2)** to put one's name down ▷ *Sie hat sich für einen Judokurs angemeldet.* She's put her name down for a judo course. ❷ to report ▷ *Alle Besucher müssen sich beim Pförtner anmelden.* All visitors must report to the gatehouse. ❸ to register ▷ *Haben Sie sich schon beim Einwohnermeldeamt angemeldet?* Have you already registered with the residents' registration office?
: Anyone moving to a new address in
: Germany is required by law to
: register (**sich anmelden**) at the
: residents' registration office
: (**Einwohnermeldeamt**).

Anmeldung *f* registration ▷ *Schluss für Anmeldungen ist der erste Mai.* The deadline for registrations is the first of May.

annehmen *vb* [1] ❶ to accept ▷ *Sie wollte das Geschenk nicht annehmen.* She didn't want to accept the present. ▷ *Danke für die Einladung, ich nehme gerne an.* Thank you for the invitation, which I'm happy to accept. ❷ to take ▷ *Er hat den Namen seiner Frau angenommen.* He took his wife's name.; **ein Kind annehmen** to adopt a child ❸ to believe ▷ *Die Polizei nimmt an, dass er der Täter war.* The police believe he did it. ❹ to suppose ▷ *Nehmen wir einmal an, es wäre so.* Let's suppose that was the case.; **angenommen ...** supposing ...

anordnen *vb* [53] ❶ to arrange ▷ *Er ordnete die Blumen zu einem hübschen Gesteck an.* He arranged the flowers into a pretty bouquet. ❷ to order ▷ *Wer hat das angeordnet?* Who ordered that?

anprobieren *vb* [76] to try on

Anrede *f* form of address ▷ *Für verheiratete und unverheiratete Frauen benutzt man die Anrede 'Frau'.* 'Frau' is the form of address used for married and unmarried women.

Anruf (*pl* **Anrufe**) *m* phone call

anrufen *vb* [56] to phone ▷ *Hat jemand angerufen?* Did anyone phone? ▷ *Ich muss mal eben meine Eltern anrufen.* I must just phone my parents.

ans = **an das**

anschalten *vb* [2] to switch on

anschauen vb [4] to look at ▷ *Schau mich an!* Look at me.; **sich anschauen** ❶ to look at ▷ *Willst du dir mal die Fotos anschauen?* Do you want to look at the photos? ❷ to see ▷ *Den Film will ich mir unbedingt anschauen.* I must go and see that film.

anscheinend adv apparently

Anschlag (pl **Anschläge**) m ❶ notice ▷ *Sie machte einen Anschlag am Schwarzen Brett.* She put a notice on the notice board. ❷ attack ▷ *Es gab einen Anschlag auf den Präsidenten.* There's been an attack on the President.

anschließen (imperf **schloss an**, perf **hat angeschlossen**) vb to connect ▷ *Der Computer ist noch nicht angeschlossen.* The computer hasn't been connected yet.; **sich jemandem anschließen** to join somebody; **Ich schließe mich dieser Meinung an.** I endorse this view.

anschließend adj, adv ❶ subsequent ▷ *die daran anschließende Diskussion* the subsequent discussion ❷ adjacent ▷ *das anschließende Grundstück* the adjacent plot of land ❸ afterwards ▷ *Wir waren essen, und anschließend sind wir ins Kino gegangen.* We had a meal and afterwards went to the cinema.

Anschluss (gen **Anschlusses**, pl **Anschlüsse**) m connection ▷ *Sie haben Anschluss an einen Zug nach Paris.* You have a connection with a train to Paris.; **im Anschluss an** following; **Anschluss finden** to make friends

> Word for word, **Anschluss finden** means 'to find a connection'.

sich anschnallen vb [4] to fasten one's seat belt

Anschrift f address

ansehen vb [64] ❶ to look at ▷ *Sieh mich an!* Look at me. ❷ to regard ▷ *Sie wird als eine Expertin auf diesem Gebiet angesehen.* She's regarded as an expert in this field.; **sich ansehen** ❶ to look at ▷ *Willst du dir mal die Fotos ansehen?* Do you want to look at the photos? ❷ to see ▷ *Den Film will ich mir unbedingt ansehen.* I must go and see that film. ▷ *Man hat ihr ihre Enttäuschung angesehen.* You could see the disappointment in her face.

Ansehen nt ❶ respect ▷ *Sie genießt großes Ansehen bei ihren Kollegen.* She enjoys great respect among her colleagues. ❷ reputation ▷ *Ein solches Benehmen könnte unserem Ansehen schaden.* Behaviour like that could damage our reputation.

Ansicht f view ▷ *eine Postkarte mit der Ansicht des Matterhorns* a postcard with a view of the Matterhorn ▷ *Wenn Sie meine Ansicht in dieser Sache hören wollen ...* If you want to hear my view on this business ... ▷ *meiner Ansicht nach* in my view; **zur Ansicht** on approval

Ansichtskarte f picture postcard

ansprechen vb [70] ❶ to approach ▷ *Mich hat ein wildfremder Mann angesprochen.* I was approached by a complete stranger. ❷ to appeal to ▷ *Diese Art von Malerei spricht mich nicht an.* This style of painting doesn't appeal to me. ❸ to ask ▷ *Ich werde Herrn Arnold ansprechen, ob er uns vielleicht hilft.* I'll ask Mr Arnold if he'll maybe help us. ❹ to mention ▷ *Sie hat dieses Problem bis jetzt noch nicht angesprochen.* She hasn't mentioned this problem yet.; **auf etwas ansprechen** to respond to something

Anspruch (pl **Ansprüche**) m demand ▷ *Sie war den Ansprüchen ihres Berufs nicht gewachsen.* She wasn't up to the demands of her job.; **hohe Ansprüche haben** to demand a lot; **hohe Ansprüche an jemanden stellen** to demand a lot of somebody; **Anspruch auf etwas haben** to be entitled to

anständig | 14   **GERMAN > ENGLISH**

something; **etwas in Anspruch nehmen** to take advantage of something; **Ihr Beruf nimmt sie sehr in Anspruch.** Her job's very demanding.

anständig adj decent ▷ *ein anständiges Essen* a decent meal; **sich anständig benehmen** to behave oneself

anstatt prep, conj
> The preposition **anstatt** takes the genitive.

instead of ▷ *Sie kam anstatt ihres Bruders.* She came instead of her brother.

anstecken vb [4] **Er hat die halbe Klasse mit seiner Grippe angesteckt.** He gave half the class his flu.; **Lachen steckt an.** Laughter is infectious.; **sich anstecken** to catch something

ansteckend adj infectious ▷ *eine ansteckende Krankheit* an infectious disease

anstelle prep
> The preposition **anstelle** takes the genitive.

instead of ▷ *Anstelle der Mutter hat seine Tante unterschrieben.* His aunt has signed instead of his mother. ▷ *Pralinen anstelle von Blumen* chocolates instead of flowers

anstellen vb [4] ❶ to turn on ▷ *Kannst du mal bitte den Fernseher anstellen?* Can you turn the television on, please? ❷ to employ ▷ *Sie ist bei einem Versandhaus angestellt.* She's employed by a mail-order company. ❸ to do ▷ *Wie soll ich es bloß anstellen, dass er es erlaubt?* What can I do to get him to allow it? ▷ *Was stellen wir denn heute Nachmittag an?* What shall we do this afternoon? ❹ (informal) to be up to ▷ *Was hat der Lümmel denn schon wieder angestellt?* What has that rascal been up to this time?; **sich anstellen** (1) to queue ▷ *Musstet ihr euch für die Karten lange anstellen?* Did you have to queue for long for the tickets? (2) to act ▷ *Sie hat* *sich wirklich dumm angestellt.* She acted really stupidly.; **Stell dich nicht so an.** Don't make such a fuss.

anstrengen vb [4] **Die Reise hat mich sehr angestrengt.** The journey took a lot out of me.; **Streng deinen Kopf an!** Use your head!; **sich anstrengen** to make an effort

anstrengend adj tiring

Anstrengung f effort

Antarktis f the Antarctic ▷ *in der Antarktis* in the Antarctic

Anteil (pl **Anteile**) m share ▷ *Ich möchte meinen Anteil am Gewinn haben.* I would like to have my share of the profit.; **Anteil nehmen an** to sympathize with

Antenne f aerial

antiautoritär adj anti-authoritarian

antik adj antique

Antiquitäten fpl antiques pl

Antrag (pl **Anträge**) m ❶ application ▷ *Sie stellte einen Antrag auf Arbeitslosenunterstützung.* She put in an application for unemployment benefit. ❷ motion ▷ *der Antrag der Opposition* the motion put by the opposition

antun vb [81] **jemandem etwas antun** to do something to somebody; **jemandem ein Unrecht antun** to wrong somebody; **sich Zwang antun** to force oneself; **sich etwas antun** to kill oneself

Antwort f answer ▷ *jemandem eine Antwort geben* to give somebody an answer

antworten vb [2] to answer ▷ *Antworte bitte!* Please answer.; **auf etwas antworten** to answer something; **jemandem antworten** to answer somebody

Anwalt (pl **Anwälte**) m lawyer

Anwältin f lawyer

Anweisung f instruction ▷ *Folgen Sie bitte den Anweisungen Ihres Führers.* Please follow your guide's instructions.

▷ *Anweisung haben, etwas zu tun* to have instructions to do something
anwenden (*imperf* **wendete an** *or* **wandte an**, *perf* **hat angewendet** *or* **angewandt**) *vb* ❶ to use ▷ *Welche Software wenden Sie an?* What software do you use? ▷ *Gewalt anwenden* to use violence ❷ (*law, rule*) to apply
Anwendung *f* application
anwesend *adj* present
Anwesenheit *f* presence
Anzahl *f* number ▷ *je nach Anzahl der Teilnehmer* according to the number of participants ▷ *eine große Anzahl an Fehlern* a large number of mistakes
anzahlen *vb* [4] fünfzig Euro anzahlen to pay fifty euros deposit; **ein Auto anzahlen** to put down a deposit on a car
Anzahlung *f* deposit ▷ *eine Anzahlung leisten* to pay a deposit
Anzeichen (*pl* **Anzeichen**) *nt* sign
Anzeige *f* advertisement ▷ *Ich habe ihn über eine Anzeige kennengelernt.* I met him through an advertisement.; **Anzeige gegen jemanden erstatten** to report somebody to the police; **Ich möchte Anzeige wegen Diebstahls erstatten.** I wish to report a theft.
anzeigen *vb* [4] ❶ to show ▷ *Der Tachometer zeigt die Geschwindigkeit an.* The speedometer shows the speed. ❷ to report ▷ *Ich werde Sie wegen Ruhestörung anzeigen!* I'll report you for breach of the peace. ▷ *Ich habe einen Diebstahl anzuzeigen.* I wish to report a theft.
anziehen *vb* [96] ❶ to put on ▷ *Ich muss mir nur noch die Schuhe anziehen.* I just have to put my shoes on. ❷ to dress ▷ *Kannst du bitte die Kinder anziehen?* Can you dress the children, please? ❸ to attract ▷ *Der Zoo zieht viele Besucher an.* The zoo attracts a lot of visitors.; **sich von jemandem angezogen fühlen** to feel attracted to somebody ❹ (*screw*) to tighten; **sich anziehen** to get dressed
Anzug (*pl* **Anzüge**) *m* suit
anzünden *vb* [54] to light ▷ *Ich habe eine Kerze angezündet.* I lit a candle.
Apfel (*pl* **Äpfel**) *m* apple
Apfelmus (*gen* **Apfelmuses**) *nt* apple purée
Apfelsaft (*pl* **Apfelsäfte**) *m* apple juice
Apfelsine *f* orange
Apotheke *f* chemist's ▷ *in der Apotheke* at the chemist's
Apotheker (*pl* **Apotheker**) *m* pharmacist ▷ *Er ist Apotheker.* He's a pharmacist.
App (*pl* **Apps**) *f* app (*for mobile*) ▷ *eine Handy-App* a mobile app
Apparat (*pl* **Apparate**) *m* ❶ gadget ▷ *Mit diesem Apparat kann man Dosen zerkleinern.* You can crush tins with this gadget. ❷ camera ❸ telephone ▷ *Wer war am Apparat?* Who was on the telephone?; **Am Apparat!** Speaking! ❹ (*TV*) set
Appetit *m* appetite; **Ich habe keinen Appetit.** I'm not hungry.

> Word for word, **Ich habe keinen Appetit** means 'I don't have an appetite'.

Guten Appetit! Enjoy your meal!

> Word for word, **Guten Appetit!** means 'Good appetite!'.

Aprikose *f* apricot
April (*gen* **April** *or* **Aprils**, *pl* **Aprile**) *m* April ▷ *im April* in April ▷ *am dritten April* on the third of April ▷ *Ulm, den 3. April 2024* Ulm, 3 April 2024 ▷ *Heute ist der dritte April.* Today is the third of April.; **April, April!** April Fool!
Araber (*pl* **Araber**) *m* Arab
Araberin *f* Arab
arabisch *adj* **arabische Länder** Arab countries; **die arabische Sprache** Arabic

Arbeit f ❶ job ▷ *Das ist eine sehr anstrengende Arbeit.* That's a very tiring job. ▷ *Er sucht eine Arbeit auf dem Bau.* He's looking for a job on a building site. ❷ work ▷ *Ich habe im Moment viel Arbeit.* I've got a lot of work at the moment. ▷ *Sie hat keine Arbeit.* She's out of work. ▷ *Das war eine Arbeit!* That was hard work. ❸ dissertation ▷ *Sie schreibt eine Arbeit über englische Ortsnamen.* She's writing a dissertation on English place names. ❹ test ▷ *Ich habe in der Arbeit eine Fünf geschrieben.* I got an 'E' in the test. ▷ *Morgen schreiben wir in Mathe eine Arbeit.* We've got a maths test tomorrow.; **in Arbeit sein** to be in hand

arbeiten vb [2] to work ▷ *Sie arbeitet hart.* She works hard. ▷ *Sie arbeitet als Elektrikerin bei der Firma Müller.* She works as an electrician for Müller's. ▷ *Seine Nieren arbeiten nicht richtig.* His kidneys don't work properly.; **sich durch etwas arbeiten** to work one's way through something

Arbeiter (pl **Arbeiter**) m worker

Arbeiterin f worker

Arbeitgeber (pl **Arbeitgeber**) m employer

Arbeitnehmer (pl **Arbeitnehmer**) m employee ▷ *Als Arbeitnehmer hat man gewisse Rechte.* As an employee you have certain rights.

Arbeitsamt (pl **Arbeitsämter**) nt job centre

Arbeitserlaubnis (pl **Arbeitserlaubnisse**) f work permit

arbeitslos adj unemployed

Arbeitslose (gen **Arbeitslosen**, pl **Arbeitslosen**) mf unemployed person ▷ *Ein Arbeitsloser hat die Stelle bekommen.* An unemployed person got the job.; **die Arbeitslosen** the unemployed

Arbeitslosigkeit f unemployment

Arbeitsort (pl **Arbeitsorte**) m place of work

Arbeitsplatz (gen **Arbeitsplatzes**, pl **Arbeitsplätze**) m ❶ job ▷ *Suchen Sie einen neuen Arbeitsplatz?* Are you looking for a new job? ❷ desk ▷ *Frau Marr ist im Moment nicht an ihrem Arbeitsplatz.* Ms Marr isn't at her desk at the moment.

Arbeitszeit f working hours pl; **gleitende Arbeitszeit** flexitime

> Word for word, **gleitende Arbeitszeit** means 'gliding working hours'.

Arbeitszimmer (pl **Arbeitszimmer**) nt study

Architekt (gen **Architekten**, pl **Architekten**) m architect ▷ *Er ist Architekt.* He's an architect.

Architektur f architecture

Argentinien nt Argentina

Ärger m ❶ anger ▷ *Er hat seinen Ärger über die Verspätung an mir ausgelassen.* He took out his anger at the delay on me. ❷ trouble ▷ *Wenn du das machst, bekommst du Ärger.* If you do that, you'll get into trouble.; **Ärger mit etwas haben** to have trouble with something

ärgerlich adj ❶ annoying ▷ *Diese dauernden Störungen sind sehr ärgerlich.* These constant interruptions are very annoying. ❷ angry ▷ *Ich bin auf ihn ärgerlich.* I'm angry with him. ▷ *Er ist über die Verzögerung ärgerlich.* He's angry at the delay.; **jemanden ärgerlich machen** to annoy somebody

ärgern vb [88] to annoy ▷ *Du sollst deine Schwester nicht immer ärgern!* Don't keep annoying your sister.; **sich ärgern** to be annoyed

Arktis f the Arctic ▷ *in der Arktis* in the Arctic

arm adj poor ▷ *Er ist ärmer als ich.* He's poorer than me.

Arm (pl **Arme**) m arm; **jemanden auf den Arm nehmen** (informal) to pull somebody's leg

Armband (pl **Armbänder**) nt bracelet

Armbanduhr f wristwatch
Armee f army
Ärmel (pl **Ärmel**) m sleeve
Ärmelkanal m the English Channel
Armut f poverty
arrangieren vb [76] to arrange ▷ Sie hat ein Treffen der beiden arrangiert. She arranged for them both to meet.
Art (pl **Arten**) f ❶ way ▷ Ich mache das auf meine Art. I do that my way. ❷ kind ▷ Ich mag diese Art Obst nicht. I don't like this kind of fruit. ▷ Häuser aller Art all kinds of houses ❸ species ▷ Diese Art ist vom Aussterben bedroht. This species is in danger of extinction.; **Es ist nicht seine Art, das zu tun.** It's not like him to do that.
Artikel (pl **Artikel**) m article
Arzneimittel (pl **Arzneimittel**) nt (medicine) drug
Arzt (pl **Ärzte**) m doctor ▷ Helmut ist Arzt. Helmut's a doctor.
Ärztin f doctor ▷ Jutta ist Ärztin. Jutta's a doctor.
ärztlich adj medical; **Die Wunde muss ärztlich behandelt werden.** The wound will have to be treated by a doctor.
As nt see **Ass**
Asche (pl **Aschen**) f ash
Aschenbecher (pl **Aschenbecher**) m ashtray
Aschermittwoch m Ash Wednesday ▷ am Aschermittwoch on Ash Wednesday
Asiat (gen **Asiaten**, pl **Asiaten**) m Asian
Asiatin f Asian
asiatisch adj Asian
Asien nt Asia
aß vb see **essen**
Ass (gen **Asses**, pl **Asse**) nt ace ▷ das Herzass the ace of hearts
Assistent (gen **Assistenten**, pl **Assistenten**) m assistant
Assistentin f assistant

Ast (pl **Äste**) m branch
Asthma nt asthma ▷ Sie hat Asthma. She's got asthma.
Astrologie f astrology
Astronaut (gen **Astronauten**, pl **Astronauten**) m astronaut ▷ Er ist Astronaut. He's an astronaut.
Astronomie f astronomy
Asyl (pl **Asyle**) nt asylum ▷ um Asyl bitten to ask for asylum; **ein Obdachlosenasyl** a hostel for the homeless
Asylbewerber (pl **Asylbewerber**) m asylum seeker
Asylbewerberin f asylum seeker
Atem m breath ▷ außer Atem out of breath
atemlos adj breathless
Atlantik m the Atlantic ▷ eine Insel im Atlantik an island in the Atlantic
Atlas (gen **Atlasses**, pl **Atlasse** or **Atlanten**) m atlas
atmen vb [3] to breathe
Atmosphäre f atmosphere
Atom (pl **Atome**) nt atom
Atombombe f atom bomb
Atomwaffen fpl atomic weapons pl
attraktiv adj attractive ▷ attraktiv aussehen to look attractive
ätzend adj ❶ (informal) rubbish ▷ Die Musik ist ätzend. The music's rubbish. ❷ corrosive ❸ caustic
auch adv ❶ also ▷ Wir verkaufen auch Gummienten. We also sell rubber ducks. ❷ too ▷ Das ist auch schön. That's nice, too. ▷ Ich auch. Me too.; **Ich auch nicht.** Me neither.; **auch nicht** not ... either; **Auch das noch!** That's all we needed! ❸ even ▷ Auch wenn das Wetter schlecht ist. Even if the weather's bad. ▷ ohne auch nur zu fragen without even asking; **wer auch** whoever; **was auch** whatever; **wie dem auch sei** be that as it may; **wie sehr er sich auch bemühte** however much he tried

auf prep, adv ❶ **on**

Use the accusative to express movement or a change of place. Use the dative when there is no change of place.

▷ *Stell die Suppe bitte auf den Tisch.* Please put the soup on the table. ▷ *Die Suppe steht auf dem Tisch.* The soup's on the table.; **auf dem Land** in the country; **auf der ganzen Welt** in the whole world; **auf Deutsch** in German; **bis auf ihn** except for him; **auf einmal** at once; **auf seinen Vorschlag hin** at his suggestion ❷ **open** ▷ *Das Fenster ist auf.* The window's open. ▷ *Die Geschäfte sind am Sonntag nicht auf.* The shops aren't open on Sunday. ❸ **up** ▷ *Ist er schon auf?* Is he up yet? ▷ *Ich bin schon seit sieben Uhr auf.* I've been up since seven.; **auf und ab** up and down; **auf und davon** up and away

aufatmen vb [4] **to heave a sigh of relief**

aufbauen vb [4] **to build up**

aufbekommen vb [40] ❶ **to get open** ▷ *Ich bekomme das Fenster nicht auf.* I can't get the window open. ❷ **to be given homework** ▷ *Wir haben heute nichts aufbekommen.* We weren't given any homework today.

aufbewahren vb [38] **to keep** ▷ *Sie bewahrt ihre Ersparnisse in einer Blechdose auf.* She keeps her savings in a tin.

aufbleiben vb [10] ❶ **to stay open** ▷ *Heute bleiben die Geschäfte länger auf.* The shops stay open longer today. ❷ **to stay up** ▷ *Heute dürft ihr ausnahmsweise länger aufbleiben.* Today you can stay up late for once.

aufbrechen vb [11]

For the perfect tense use **haben** when the verb has an object and **sein** when there is no object.

❶ **to break open** ▷ *Die Diebe haben den Safe aufgebrochen.* The thieves broke the safe open. ❷ **to open up** ▷ *Die Wunde ist wieder aufgebrochen.* The wound has opened up again. ❸ **to set off** ▷ *Wann seid ihr aufgebrochen?* When did you set off?

aufbringen vb [13] ❶ **to open** ▷ *Ich bringe das Konservenglas nicht auf.* I can't open the jar. ❷ **to raise** ▷ *Wie soll ich nur das Geld für die Reparatur aufbringen?* However am I going raise the money for the repairs?; **Verständnis für etwas aufbringen** to be able to understand something

aufeinander adv **on top of each other** ▷ *Leg die Handtücher aufeinander.* Put the towels on top of each other.; **aufeinander schießen** to shoot at one another; **aufeinander vertrauen** to trust each other

Aufenthalt (pl **Aufenthalte**) m ❶ **stay** ▷ *Während unseres Aufenthalts in London* … During our stay in London … ❷ **stop** ▷ *Der Zug hat fünf Minuten Aufenthalt in Ulm.* The train has a five-minute stop in Ulm.

aufessen vb [20] **to eat up**

auffallen vb [22] **to be conspicuous**; **jemandem auffallen** to strike somebody

auffällig adj **conspicuous**; **auffällig gekleidet sein** to be dressed strikingly

auffangen vb [23] **to catch**

aufführen vb [4] ❶ **to perform** ▷ *ein Stück aufführen* to perform a play ❷ **to list** ▷ *Alle Fachausdrücke sind im Anhang aufgeführt.* All technical terms are listed in the appendix.; **sich aufführen** to behave

Aufführung f **performance**

Aufgabe f ❶ **task** ▷ *Vier Kinder zu erziehen ist eine schwierige Aufgabe.* Bringing up four children is a difficult task. ❷ **question** ▷ *Ich konnte die zweite Aufgabe in der Mathearbeit nicht lösen.* I couldn't solve the second question in the maths test. ❸ **homework** ▷ *Hast du*

deine Aufgaben schon gemacht? Have you done your homework yet?

aufgeben vb [28] ❶ to give up ▷ *Du solltest das Rauchen aufgeben.* You should give up smoking. ❷ to post ▷ *Ich habe das Paket an dich vor drei Tagen aufgegeben.* I posted the parcel to you three days ago. ❸ to check in ▷ *Du kannst den Koffer ja vor der Reise aufgeben.* You can check in your suitcase before you travel.; **eine Anzeige aufgeben** to place an advertisement; **Ich gebe auf!** I give up!

aufgehen vb [29] ❶ to rise ▷ *Der Mond ist aufgegangen.* The moon has risen. ❷ to open ▷ *Die Tür ging auf, und Christoph kam herein.* The door opened and Christoph came in.; **Zwanzig durch sechs geht nicht auf.** Six into twenty doesn't go.

aufgeregt adj excited

aufgrund prep

The preposition **aufgrund** takes the genitive.

❶ because of ▷ *Das Spiel ist aufgrund des schlechten Wetters ausgefallen.* The game was cancelled because of the bad weather. ❷ on the basis of ▷ *Sie wurde aufgrund von Indizien überführt.* She was convicted on the basis of circumstantial evidence.

aufhaben vb [32] ❶ to have on ▷ *Sie hatte einen roten Hut auf.* She had a red hat on. ❷ to have homework to do ▷ *Wir haben heute in Englisch nichts auf.* We haven't got any English homework to do today.

aufhalten vb [33] ❶ to detain ▷ *Ich möchte dich nicht aufhalten.* I don't want to detain you. ❷ to check ▷ *Wie kann die Vergrößerung des Ozonlochs aufgehalten werden?* How can the growth of the ozone hole be checked? ❸ to hold open ▷ *Kannst du mir bitte die Tür aufhalten?* Can you hold the door open for me, please?; **Sie hielt die Hand auf.** She held out her hand.; **sich aufhalten** (1) to live ▷ *Sie hat sich lange im Ausland aufgehalten.* She lived abroad for a long time. (2) to stay ▷ *Ich möchte mich nicht lange aufhalten.* I don't want to stay long.; **sich mit etwas aufhalten** to waste time over something ▷ *Mit solchen Kinderspielen halte ich mich doch nicht auf.* I'm not wasting my time over such childish games.

aufhängen vb [35] (washing) to hang up; **sich aufhängen** to hang oneself

aufheben (imperf **hob auf**, perf **hat aufgehoben**) vb ❶ to pick up ▷ *Sie hob das Heft, das auf den Boden gefallen war, auf.* She picked up the exercise book which had fallen on the floor. ❷ to keep ▷ *Sie hat alle seine Briefe aufgehoben.* She's kept all his letters.; **gut aufgehoben sein** to be well looked after

aufhören vb [4] to stop ▷ *Der Regen hat aufgehört.* The rain's stopped.; **aufhören, etwas zu tun** to stop doing something

Aufkleber (pl **Aufkleber**) m sticker

aufladen (pres **lädt auf**, imperf **lud auf**, perf **hat aufgeladen**) vb ❶ to load ▷ *Wir müssen die Möbel auf den Lastwagen aufladen.* We have to load the furniture onto the truck. ❷ to charge ▷ *Wo kann ich mein Handy aufladen?* Where can I charge my phone?

auflassen vb [42] ❶ to leave open ▷ *Lass bitte das Fenster auf.* Please leave the window open. ❷ to keep on ▷ *Kann ich meine Mütze auflassen?* Can I keep my hat on?

auflegen vb [4] to hang up ▷ *Sie hat einfach aufgelegt.* She simply hung up.

auflösen vb [4] ❶ to dissolve ▷ *Du solltest die Tablette in Wasser auflösen.* You should dissolve the tablet in water. ❷ to break up ▷ *Die Polizei hat die Demonstration aufgelöst.* The police broke up the demonstration.; **sich auflösen** to dissolve; **wenn sich der Nebel aufgelöst hat** when the fog has lifted; **in Tränen aufgelöst sein** to be in tears

aufmachen vb [4] ❶ to open ▷ *Kannst du bitte die Tür aufmachen?* Can you open the door, please? ▷ *Wann machen die Geschäfte auf?* When do the shops open? ❷ to undo ▷ *Ich schaffe es nicht, den Reißverschluss aufzumachen.* I can't undo the zip.; **sich aufmachen** to set out

aufmerksam adj attentive; **jemanden auf etwas aufmerksam machen** to point something out to somebody

Aufmerksamkeit f attention ▷ *Darf ich um Ihre Aufmerksamkeit bitten!* May I have your attention?; **Wir sollten ihnen eine kleine Aufmerksamkeit mitbringen.** We ought to take them a little something.

Aufnahme f ❶ welcome ▷ *Wir fanden eine sehr freundliche Aufnahme in unserer Partnerstadt.* We were given a very friendly welcome in our town. ❷ recording ▷ *Wir haben uns die Aufnahme des Konzerts angehört.* We listened to a recording of the concert. ❸ photograph ▷ *Möchtest du die Aufnahmen sehen, die ich in den Ferien gemacht habe?* Would you like to see the photographs I took on holiday?

Aufnahmeprüfung f entrance test

aufnehmen vb [52] ❶ to take ▷ *Wie hat sie die Nachricht aufgenommen?* How did she take the news? ❷ to record ▷ *eine Sendung aufnehmen* to record a programme ❸ to photograph ▷ *Diesen tollen Sonnenuntergang muss ich aufnehmen.* I must photograph this wonderful sunset. ❹ to admit ▷ *Was muss man tun, um in den Tennisklub aufgenommen zu werden?* What do you have to do to be admitted to the tennis club?; **es mit jemandem aufnehmen können** to be able to compete with somebody

aufpassen vb [31] to pay attention ▷ *Ich habe heute im Unterricht nicht aufgepasst.* I didn't pay attention in class today.; **auf jemanden aufpassen** to look after somebody; **auf etwas aufpassen** to look after something; **Aufgepasst!** Look out!

aufräumen vb [4] to tidy up ▷ *Ich darf erst raus, wenn ich mein Zimmer aufgeräumt habe.* I can't go out until I've tidied up my room.

aufrecht adj upright

aufregen vb [4] to excite; **sich aufregen** to get excited

aufregend adj exciting

aufs = **auf das**

Aufsatz (gen **Aufsatzes**, pl **Aufsätze**) m essay ▷ *Wir haben heute in Deutsch einen Aufsatz geschrieben.* We wrote an essay in today's German lesson.

aufschieben (imperf **schob auf**, perf **hat aufgeschoben**) vb ❶ to push open ▷ *Man kann diese Tür aufschieben.* You can push this door open. ❷ to put off ▷ *Wir haben unsere Abreise noch einmal aufgeschoben.* We put off our departure once again.

aufschlagen vb [59] ❶ to open ▷ *ein Buch aufschlagen* to open a book ▷ *Schlagt Seite 111 auf.* Open your books at page 111. ❷ to pitch ▷ *Sie schlugen ihre Zelte auf.* They pitched their tents. ❸ (prices) to go up ▷ *Butter ist wieder aufgeschlagen.* The price of butter has gone up again. ❹ (tennis) to serve ▷ *Du schlägst auf.* It's your turn to serve.

aufschließen (imperf **schloss auf**, perf **hat aufgeschlossen**) vb to unlock ▷ *Schließ bitte die Tür auf!* Please unlock the door. ▷ *Sie schloss auf und ging hinein.* She unlocked the door and went in.

aufschlussreich adj informative

Aufschnitt (pl **Aufschnitte**) m cold meat

aufschreiben vb [61] to write down

Aufsehen nt stir ▷ *Ihre Kleidung hat Aufsehen erregt.* Her outfit caused a stir.

aufsehenerregend adj sensational

auf sein vb [65] see **auf**

aufsetzen vb [36] to put on ▷ *Setz dir eine Mütze auf!* Put a hat on.; **Ich setze das Teewasser auf.** I'll put the kettle on.; **sich aufsetzen** to sit up

Aufsicht f supervision; **die Aufsicht haben** to be in charge

aufstehen vb [72]

Use **sein** for 'to get up' and **haben** for 'to be open'.

① to get up ▷ *Wann bist du heute Morgen aufgestanden?* When did you get up this morning? ▷ *Sie stand auf und ging.* She got up and left. ② to be open ▷ *Die Tür hat aufgestanden, also ging ich hinein.* The door was open, so I went in.

aufstellen vb [4] ① to put up ▷ *Wir haben unser Zelt am Waldrand aufgestellt.* We pitched our tent at the edge of the woods. ② to stand up ▷ *Der Sonnenschirm ist umgefallen, ich muss ihn wieder aufstellen.* The sunshade has fallen over. I'll have to stand it up again. ③ to set up ▷ *Sie stellte die Schachfiguren auf.* She set up the chess pieces.; **eine Liste aufstellen** to draw up a list; **einen Rekord aufstellen** to set a record; **jemanden für ein Spiel aufstellen** to pick somebody for a game; **sich aufstellen** to line up

auftauchen (perf **ist aufgetaucht**) vb [4] to appear

auftauen (perf **hat/ist aufgetaut**) vb [4]

For the perfect tense use **haben** when the verb has an object and **sein** when there is no object.

① to thaw ▷ *Der Schnee taute auf.* The snow thawed. ② to defrost ▷ *Ich habe die Pizza im Mikrowellenherd aufgetaut.* I've defrosted the pizza in the microwave.

Auftrag (pl **Aufträge**) m orders pl ▷ *Ich habe den Auftrag, Sie davon zu unterrichten, dass ...* I have orders to inform you that ...; **im Auftrag von** on behalf of

auftreten vb [79] ① to appear ▷ *Dieser Schauspieler tritt erst im dritten Akt auf.* This actor doesn't appear until the third act. ② to occur ▷ *Sollten Probleme auftreten, wende dich an uns.* If any problems occur, get in touch with us. ③ to behave ▷ *Er ist ziemlich unbeliebt, weil er immer so überheblich auftritt.* He's quite unpopular because he always behaves so arrogantly.

aufwachen (perf **ist aufgewacht**) vb [4] to wake up

aufwachsen vb [87] to grow up

aufwecken vb [4] to wake up

Aufzug (pl **Aufzüge**) m lift ▷ *Wir sind mit dem Aufzug nach oben gefahren.* We went up in the lift.

Auge (pl **Augen**) nt eye ▷ *Sie hat dunkle Augen.* She's got dark eyes.; **unter vier Augen** in private

Augenblick (pl **Augenblicke**) m moment; **im Augenblick** at the moment

Augenbraue f eyebrow

August (gen **Augustes** or **August**, pl **Auguste**) m August ▷ *im August* in August ▷ *am fünften August* on 5 August ▷ *Ulm, den 5. August 2024* Ulm, 5 August 2024 ▷ *Heute ist der fünfte August.* Today is the fifth of August.

Aula (pl **Aulen**) f assembly hall

aus prep, adv

The preposition **aus** takes the dative.

① out of ▷ *Sie nahm ein Bonbon aus der Tüte.* She took a sweet out of the bag.

▷ **aus dem Fenster** out of the window ❷ from ▷ *Wenn er aus der Schule kommt, ist er immer sehr müde.* When he comes home from school he's always very tired. ▷ *Ich komme aus Deutschland.* I come from Germany. ▷ *Er ist aus Berlin.* He's from Berlin. ❸ made of ▷ *Die Vase ist aus Porzellan.* The vase is made of china.; **aus Erfahrung** from experience; **aus Spaß** for fun; **aus Freundschaft** out of a sense of friendship ❹ finished ▷ *wenn das Kino aus ist* when the film's finished ▷ *Komm sofort nach Hause, wenn die Schule aus ist.* Come straight home when school has finished.; **Wann ist die Schule aus?** When does school finish? ❺ off ▷ *Der Fernseher ist aus.* The television's off.; **Licht aus!** Lights out!; **Sie können meinen Mann nicht sprechen, er ist aus.** You can't speak to my husband. He's out.; **von sich aus** of one's own accord; **von ihm aus** as far as he's concerned

ausatmen vb [2] to breathe out
ausbilden vb [54] to train ▷ *Er bildet Lehrlinge aus.* He trains apprentices. ▷ *Sie ist ausgebildete Krankenschwester.* She's a qualified nurse.
Ausbildung f training ▷ *eine solide Ausbildung* a decent training
Ausbildungsplatz (gen **Ausbildungsplatzes**, pl **Ausbildungsplätze**) m training job
Ausdauer f stamina
ausdenken vb [14] **sich etwas ausdenken** to think something up
Ausdruck (1) (pl **Ausdrücke**) m expression ▷ *Sie hat in der Schule ein paar schlimme Ausdrücke gelernt.* She's learned a few nasty expressions at school. ▷ *Als Ausdruck meiner Dankbarkeit habe ich ihr Blumen geschenkt.* I gave her flowers as an expression of my gratitude. ▷ *Ich kann am Ausdruck in deinem Gesicht sehen, dass dir das nicht passt.* I can see by your expression that it doesn't suit you.
Ausdruck (2) (pl **Ausdrucke**) m printout ▷ *Kannst du mir von der Datei einen Ausdruck machen?* Can you do me a printout of the file?
ausdrucken vb [4] to print out ▷ *Soll ich dir die Namen ausdrucken?* Shall I print out the names for you?
ausdrücken vb [4] to express ▷ *Ich weiß nicht, wie man das auf Englisch ausdrückt.* I don't know how to express it in English.
ausdrücklich adj explicit ▷ *Sie hat dir das ausdrücklich verboten.* She explicitly forbade you to do it.
auseinander adv apart ▷ *weit auseinander* far apart
Ausfahrt f exit ▷ *Wir müssen an der nächsten Ausfahrt raus.* We have to take the next exit.
ausfallen (perf ist ausgefallen) vb [22] ❶ to be cancelled ▷ *Der Sportunterricht fällt heute aus.* PE has been cancelled today. ❷ to break down ▷ *Die Heizung ist mal wieder ausgefallen.* The heating has broken down again.; **Wenn der Strom ausfällt, ...** If there's a power cut ... ❸ to fall out ▷ *Ihm sind die Haare ausgefallen, als er noch ziemlich jung war.* His hair fell out when he was still quite young.; **Die Arbeit ist sehr schlecht ausgefallen.** The results of the test were awful.
Ausflug (pl **Ausflüge**) m outing ▷ *einen Ausflug machen* to go on an outing
ausfragen vb [4] to question
Ausfuhr f export
ausführen vb [4] ❶ to carry out ▷ *Sie hat ihren Plan ausgeführt.* She carried out her plan. ❷ to export ▷ *Waren ausführen* to export goods; **jemanden ausführen** to take somebody out; **einen Hund ausführen** to take a dog for a walk

ausführlich adj, adv ❶ detailed ▷ *ein ausführlicher Bericht* a detailed report ❷ in detail ▷ *Sie hat mir ausführlich erzählt, wie es in den Ferien war.* She told me in detail what her holidays were like.

ausfüllen vb [4] to fill in ▷ *Füllt bitte die Lücken im Text aus.* Please fill in the gaps in the text. ▷ *Hast du den Antrag schon ausgefüllt?* Have you filled in the application form yet?

Ausgabe f ❶ expenditure ▷ *Wir hatten in der letzten Zeit viele Ausgaben.* We've had a lot of expenditure recently. ❷ edition ▷ *Sie hat eine sehr alte Ausgabe von Goethes Werken.* She's got a very old edition of Goethe's works. ❸ issue ▷ *Ich habe das in der letzten Ausgabe meines Computermagazins gelesen.* I read it in the last issue of my computer magazine.

Ausgang (pl **Ausgänge**) m ❶ exit ▷ *Ich warte dann am Ausgang auf euch.* I'll wait for you at the exit, then.; **'Kein Ausgang'** 'No exit' ❷ ending ▷ *Der Film hat einen sehr traurigen Ausgang.* The film has a very sad ending. ❸ result ▷ *Welchen Ausgang hatte das Spiel?* What was the result of the match?

ausgeben vb [28] ❶ to spend ▷ *Wir haben auf dem Volksfest hundert Euro ausgegeben.* We spent a hundred euros at the fair. ❷ to distribute ▷ *Du musst dich da vorn anstellen, da werden die Karten ausgegeben.* You have to queue at the front there. That's where the tickets are being distributed.; **einen ausgeben** (*informal*) to stand a round; **sich für jemanden ausgeben** to pass oneself off as somebody; **sich als etwas ausgeben** to pretend to be something

ausgehen vb [29] ❶ to go out ▷ *Sollen wir heute Abend ausgehen?* Shall we go out this evening? ▷ *Fritz will mit dir ausgehen.* Fritz wants to go out with you. ▷ *Plötzlich ging das Licht aus.* Suddenly the light went out. ❷ to run out ▷ *Wir sollten tanken, bevor das Benzin ausgeht.* We ought to fill up before we run out of petrol. ▷ *Mir ging das Benzin aus.* I ran out of petrol.; **Wie ist das Spiel ausgegangen?** How did the game end?; **schlecht ausgehen** to turn out badly; **Wir können davon ausgehen, dass ...** We can assume that ...

ausgelassen adj exuberant

ausgenommen conj except ▷ *Alle kamen, ausgenommen Günter.* Everyone came except Günter.; **Anwesende sind ausgenommen.** Present company excepted.

ausgerechnet adv ausgerechnet heute today of all days; ausgerechnet du you of all people

ausgeschlossen adj impossible ▷ *Ich halte das für ausgeschlossen.* I think that's impossible.

ausgezeichnet adj, adv ❶ excellent ▷ *Werner ist ein ausgezeichneter Koch.* Werner's an excellent cook. ❷ excellently ▷ *Sie hat es ausgezeichnet gemacht.* She did it excellently.

aushalten vb [33] **Ich halte diese Hitze nicht aus!** I can't stand this heat.; **Das ist nicht zum Aushalten.** It's unbearable.

sich **auskennen** vb [39] ❶ to know about ▷ *Sie kennt sich mit Kindern gut aus.* She knows a lot about children. ❷ to know one's way around ▷ *Er kennt sich in Stuttgart aus.* He knows his way around Stuttgart.

auskommen vb [40] **mit jemandem auskommen** to get on with somebody; **mit etwas auskommen** to manage on something

Auskunft (pl **Auskünfte**) f ❶ information ▷ *Nähere Auskunft*

auslachen | 24   GERMAN > ENGLISH

erhalten Sie unter der folgenden Nummer. For further information ring the following number. ❷ information office ▷ *Fragen Sie bei der Auskunft, wann der nächste Zug nach Bremen geht.* Ask at the information office when the next train leaves for Bremen.; **Telefonauskunft** directory inquiries pl

auslachen vb [4] to laugh at ▷ *Sie hat mich nur ausgelacht.* She just laughed at me.

Ausland nt **im Ausland** abroad; **ins Ausland** abroad

Ausländer (pl **Ausländer**) m foreigner ▷ *Ihr Mann ist Ausländer.* Her husband's a foreigner.

Ausländerin f foreigner ▷ *Seine Frau ist Ausländerin.* His wife's a foreigner.

ausländisch adj foreign

Auslandsgespräch (pl **Auslandsgespräche**) nt international call

auslassen vb [42] ❶ to leave out ▷ *Die nächste Übung können wir auslassen.* We can leave out the next exercise.; **Ich lasse heute das Mittagessen aus.** I'm skipping lunch today. ❷ to leave off ▷ *Heute lass ich den Fernseher aus.* I'm leaving the television off today. ▷ *Bei der Hitze kannst du die Jacke auslassen.* You can leave your jacket off in this heat.; **seine Wut an jemandem auslassen** to take one's anger out on somebody

ausleihen (imperf **lieh aus**, perf **hat ausgeliehen**) vb [4] to lend ▷ *Kannst du mir dein Moped ausleihen?* Can you lend me your moped?; **sich etwas ausleihen** to borrow something

ausloggen vb [4] (computer) to log off

ausmachen vb [48] ❶ to turn off ▷ *Mach bitte das Radio aus, die Musik stört mich.* Please turn the radio off. The music's disturbing me.; **das Licht ausmachen** to switch off the light ❷ to put out ▷ *Du solltest deine Zigarette ausmachen, bevor du hineingehst.* You should put your cigarette out before you go in. ❸ to arrange ▷ *Habt ihr schon einen Termin für das Fest ausgemacht?* Have you arranged a date for the party yet? ▷ *Ich habe mit ihr ausgemacht, dass wir uns um fünf Uhr treffen.* I've arranged to meet her at five. ❹ to settle ▷ *Macht das unter euch aus.* Settle the matter between you. ❺ to mind ▷ *Es macht mir nichts aus, wenn ich allein gehen muss.* I don't mind having to go alone. ▷ *Macht es Ihnen etwas aus, wenn ...?* Would you mind if ...?

Ausnahme f exception

ausnahmsweise adv for once

ausnützen vb [4] to use

auspacken vb [4] to unpack

ausprobieren vb [4] to try out

Auspuff (pl **Auspuffe**) m exhaust

ausrechnen vb [4] to calculate

Ausrede f excuse

ausreichen vb [4] to be enough

ausreichend adj ❶ sufficient ▷ *ausreichend Geld* sufficient money ❷ adequate
    German marks range from one (**sehr gut**) to six (**ungenügend**).

Ausreise f departure; **bei der Ausreise** when leaving the country

ausrichten vb [4] ❶ to tell ▷ *Ich werde es ihm ausrichten.* I'll tell him.; **Richte bitte an deine Eltern schöne Grüße aus.** Please give my regards to your parents. ❷ to gear to ▷ *Wir müssen unser Veranstaltungsangebot mehr auf Jugendliche ausrichten.* We must gear our events more to young people.

ausrufen vb [56] to cry out; **jemanden ausrufen lassen** to page somebody

Ausrufezeichen (pl **Ausrufezeichen**) nt exclamation mark

sich **ausruhen** vb [4] to rest

ausrüsten vb [4] to equip

Ausrüstung f equipment

ausschalten vb [2] to switch off

ausschlafen vb [58] to have a good sleep; **Morgen kann ich ausschlafen.** I can have a lie-in tomorrow.; **Ich bin nicht ausgeschlafen.** I didn't get enough sleep.

ausschließlich adv, prep ❶ exclusively ▷ *Der Schulhof ist ausschließlich für Schüler dieser Schule.* The school yard is exclusively for pupils of this school. ❷ except ▷ *Wir haben jeden Tag geöffnet ausschließlich Sonntag.* We're open every day except Sunday.

ausschneiden vb [60] to cut out

aussehen vb [64] to look ▷ *Sie sieht sehr hübsch aus.* She looks very pretty. ▷ *Wie siehst du denn aus?* What do you look like! ▷ *Es sieht nach Regen aus.* It looks like rain. ▷ *Es sieht schlecht aus.* Things look bad.

Aussehen nt appearance

aus sein vb [65] see **aus**

außen adv on the outside ▷ *Außen ist es rot.* It's red on the outside.

Außenseiter (pl **Außenseiter**) m outsider

außer prep, conj

The preposition **außer** takes the dative.

❶ apart from ▷ *Außer dir haben das alle verstanden.* Everyone has understood apart from you. ▷ *Wer war noch außer Horst?* Apart from Horst, who was there?; **außer Haus** out; **außer Landes** abroad; **außer Gefahr** out of danger; **außer Betrieb** out of order; **außer sich sein** to be beside oneself ❷ if ... not ▷ *Wir machen morgen ein Picknick, außer es regnet.* We're having a picnic tomorrow if it doesn't rain.

außerdem conj in addition

äußere adj ❶ outer ▷ *Sie bildeten einen äußeren und einen inneren Kreis.* They formed an outer and an inner circle. ❷ external ▷ *Nur zur äußeren Anwendung.* For external use only.

außergewöhnlich adj unusual

außerhalb prep, gen

The preposition **außerhalb** takes the genitive.

❶ outside ▷ *Es liegt außerhalb der Stadt.* It's outside the town. ❷ out of town ▷ *Sie wohnt nicht in Ulm, sondern ziemlich weit außerhalb.* She doesn't live in Ulm, but quite a way out of town.; **außerhalb der Saison** out of season

äußern vb [88] to express ▷ *Sie hat den Wunsch geäußert, allein in die Ferien fahren zu dürfen.* She's expressed the wish to be allowed to go on holiday alone.; **eine Meinung äußern** to give an opinion; **sich äußern** to comment

äußerst adv extremely

äußerste adj utmost ▷ *Diese Sache ist von äußerster Wichtigkeit.* This matter is of the utmost importance.

Äußerung f remark

Aussicht f ❶ view ▷ *Vom Hotel aus hat man eine schöne Aussicht aufs Meer.* You have a wonderful view of the sea from the hotel. ❷ prospect ▷ *Die Aussicht auf diese Stelle hat ihr neuen Mut gegeben.* The prospect of this job gave her new hope. ▷ *Das sind ja schöne Aussichten!* What a prospect!; **etwas in Aussicht haben** to have the prospect of something

ausspannen vb [4] to relax

Aussprache f ❶ pronunciation ▷ *Die Aussprache der Wörter ist mit phonetischen Zeichen angegeben.* The pronunciation of the words is shown by phonetic symbols. ❷ frank discussion ▷ *Ich hatte gestern eine lange Aussprache mit ihm.* I had a long, frank discussion with him yesterday.

aussprechen vb [70] to pronounce ▷ *Wie spricht man dieses Wort aus?* How do you pronounce this word?; **sich mit jemandem aussprechen** to talk things out with somebody; **sich gegen etwas aussprechen** to speak out against something; **sich für etwas aussprechen** to speak out in favour of something; **Lass ihn doch aussprechen!** Let him finish.

aussteigen vb [74] to get off ▷ *Ich sah, wie sie aus der Straßenbahn ausstieg.* I saw her get off the tram.

ausstellen vb [4] ❶ to exhibit ▷ *Im Museum werden zurzeit Bilder von Chagall ausgestellt.* Pictures by Chagall are currently being exhibited in the museum. ❷ to be on display ▷ *Im Schaufenster war exotisches Obst ausgestellt.* Exotic fruit was on display in the window. ❸ to switch off ▷ *Die Heizung wird im Mai ausgestellt.* The heating's switched off in May. ❹ to write ▷ *Die Lehrerin hat ihm ein gutes Zeugnis ausgestellt.* The teacher wrote him a good report. ❺ to issue ▷ *Auf welchem Amt werden Pässe ausgestellt?* Which office issues passports?

Ausstellung f exhibition

aussterben vb [75] to die out

Ausstieg m ❶ exit ▷ *Der Ausstieg ist hinten.* The exit is at the back. ❷ abandonment ▷ *der Ausstieg aus der Atomenergie* abandonment of nuclear energy

aussuchen vb [4] to choose ▷ *Such dir ein Eis aus.* Choose yourself an ice cream.

Austausch (gen **Austausches**) m exchange ▷ *ein Schüleraustausch* a school exchange

austauschen vb [4] ❶ to replace ▷ *Ich habe die Festplatte ausgetauscht.* I've replaced the hard disk. ❷ to substitute ▷ *Der Mittelstürmer wurde ausgetauscht.* The centre-forward was substituted.

austeilen vb [4] to give out

austragen vb [77] ❶ to deliver ▷ *Morgens trägt er immer die Post aus.* In the morning he always delivers the post. ❷ to hold ▷ *Der Wettkampf wird im Olympiastadion ausgetragen.* The competition will be held in the Olympic® stadium.

Australien nt Australia

Australier (pl **Australier**) m Australian

Australierin f Australian

australisch adj Australian

austreten vb [79] **aus etwas austreten** to leave something; **Ich muss mal austreten.** (informal) I need to go to the loo.

austrinken vb [80] ❶ to drink up ▷ *Er trank aus und ging.* He drank up and left. ❷ to finish ▷ *Lass mich noch schnell meinen Saft austrinken.* Let me just quickly finish my juice.

Ausverkauf (pl **Ausverkäufe**) m clearance sale

ausverkauft adj ❶ sold out ▷ *Die Vorstellung ist leider ausverkauft.* The performance is sold out, I'm afraid. ❷ full ▷ *Das Kino war ausverkauft.* The cinema was full.

Auswahl f selection ▷ *Sie haben eine große Auswahl an Schuhen.* They have a large selection of shoes.

auswählen vb [4] to select

auswandern vb [88] to emigrate ▷ *Sie sind nach Australien ausgewandert.* They emigrated to Australia.

auswärts adv ❶ in another town ▷ *Sie wohnt in Calw, arbeitet aber auswärts.* She lives in Calw but works in another town. ❷ away ▷ *Unsere Mannschaft spielt nächste Woche auswärts.* Our team's playing away next week.; **auswärts essen** to eat out

Ausweis (pl **Ausweise**) m ❶ identity card ▷ *Der Polizist wollte meinen Ausweis sehen.* The police officer wanted to see my identity card. ❷ card ▷ *Wenn du Schüler bist und deinen Ausweis zeigst, bekommst du Ermäßigung.* If you're a student and show them your card, you get a reduction.

auswendig *adv* by heart ▷ *etwas auswendig lernen* to learn something by heart

ausziehen *vb* [96]

For the perfect tense use **haben** when the verb has an object and **sein** when there is no object.

❶ to take off ▷ *Sie hat ihren Mantel nicht ausgezogen.* She didn't take off her coat. ❷ to undress ▷ *Kannst du bitte die Kinder ausziehen und ins Bett bringen?* Can you undress the children and put them to bed, please?; **sich ausziehen** to undress ❸ to move out ▷ *Meine Nachbarn sind letzte Woche ausgezogen.* My neighbours moved out last week.

Auszubildende (*gen* **Auszubildenden**, *pl* **Auszubildenden**) *mf* trainee

autistisch *adj* autistic

Auto (*pl* **Autos**) *nt* car; **Auto fahren** to drive

Autobahn *f* motorway

Autobus (*gen* **Autobusses**, *pl* **Autobusse**) *m* bus

Autofahrer (*pl* **Autofahrer**) *m* motorist

Autogramm (*pl* **Autogramme**) *nt* autograph

Automat (*gen* **Automaten**, *pl* **Automaten**) *m* machine

automatisch *adj* automatic ▷ *Die Türen schließen automatisch.* The doors close automatically.

Autor (*pl* **Autoren**) *m* author

Autoradio (*pl* **Autoradios**) *nt* car radio

Autorin *f* author

autoritär *adj* authoritarian

Autorität *f* authority

Autounfall (*pl* **Autounfälle**) *m* car accident

Axt (*pl* **Äxte**) *f* axe

Baby (*pl* **Babys**) *nt* baby

babysitten (*perf* **hat gebabysittet**) *vb* [2] to babysit

Babysitter (*pl* **Babysitter**) *m* babysitter

Babysitterin *f* babysitter

Bach (*pl* **Bäche**) *m* stream

Backe *f* cheek

backen (*pres* **bäckt**, *imperf* **backte** or **buk**, *perf* **hat gebacken**) *vb* to bake

Bäcker (*pl* **Bäcker**) *m* baker ▷ *beim Bäcker* at the baker's ▷ *zum Bäcker* to the baker's

Bäckerei *f* baker's

Backofen (*pl* **Backöfen**) *m* oven

Bad (*pl* **Bäder**) *nt* bath; **ein Bad im Meer** a swim in the sea

Badeanzug (*pl* **Badeanzüge**) *m* bathing suit

Badehose *f* swimming trunks *pl*

baden *vb* [54] to have a bath; **jemanden baden** to bath somebody; **sich baden** to have a bath

Baden-Württemberg

Baden-Württemberg nt Baden-Württemberg ▷ Baden-Württemberg is one of the 16 **Länder**. Its capital is Stuttgart. Baden-Württemberg is home to the cuckoo clock and to Mercedes-Benz and Porsche.

Badewanne f bath (tub)

Badezimmer (pl **Badezimmer**) nt bathroom

Baguette (pl **Baguettes**) nt ▷ You can also say **die Baguette**. baguette

Bahn (pl **Bahnen**) f ❶ railway ▷ Er arbeitet bei der Bahn. He works for the railway.; **mit der Bahn fahren** to go by train ❷ tram ❸ lane ▷ Die Schwimmerin auf Bahn drei liegt in Führung. The swimmer in lane three is in the lead.; **auf die schiefe Bahn geraten** to go off the rails

Bahnfahrt f railway journey

Bahnhof (pl **Bahnhöfe**) m station ▷ auf dem Bahnhof at the station

Bahnhofshalle f station concourse

Bahnsteig (pl **Bahnsteige**) m platform

bald adv ❶ soon ▷ Es wird bald Frühling. It'll soon be spring.; **Bis bald!** See you later. ❷ almost ▷ Ich hätte bald was gesagt. I almost said something.; **Wird's bald!** Get a move on!

Balken (pl **Balken**) m beam

Balkon (pl **Balkons** or **Balkone**) m balcony

Ball (pl **Bälle**) m ball ▷ Die Kinder spielen mit dem Ball. The children are playing with the ball. ▷ Mit wem kommst du zum Ball? Who are you going to the ball with?

Ballett (pl **Ballette**) nt ballet

Ballon (pl **Ballons** or **Ballone**) m balloon

Bambus (gen **Bambusses**, pl **Bambusse**) m bamboo

Banane f banana

band vb see **binden**

Band (1) (pl **Bände**) m volume ▷ ein Lexikon in fünf Bänden an encyclopedia in five volumes

Band (2) (pl **Bands**) f band ▷ Sie spielt Gitarre in einer Band. She plays the guitar in a band.

Band (3) (pl **Bänder**) nt ❶ ribbon ▷ Sie hatte ein rotes Band im Haar. She had a red ribbon in her hair. ❷ production line ▷ Mein Vater arbeitet am Band. My father works on the production line.; **am laufenden Band** nonstop

Bank (1) (pl **Bänke**) f bench ▷ Sie saß auf einer Bank im Park. She was sitting on a park bench.

Bank (2) (pl **Banken**) f bank ▷ Ich muss Geld von der Bank holen. I'll have to get money from the bank.

Bankkonto (pl **Bankkonten**) m bank account

Bankleitzahl f bank sort code

bankrott adj bankrupt ▷ Die Firma ist bankrott. The firm is bankrupt.; **Bankrott machen** to go bankrupt

bar adj bares Geld cash; **etwas bar bezahlen** to pay cash for something

Bar (pl **Bars**) f bar

Bär (gen **Bären**, pl **Bären**) m bear

barfuß adj barefoot

Bargeld nt cash

Barren (pl **Barren**) m parallel bars pl

Bart (pl **Bärte**) m beard

bärtig adj bearded

Basis (pl **Basen**) f basis

Basketball m basketball

Bass (gen **Basses**, pl **Bässe**) m bass

basteln vb [34] to make things ▷ Ich bastle gern. I like making things.; **etwas basteln** to make something

bat vb see **bitten**

Batterie f battery

Bau (pl **Bauten**) m ❶ construction ▷ Das Haus ist noch im Bau befindlich. The house is still under construction. ❷ building ▷ In New York gibt es viele

GERMAN > ENGLISH

beeindruckende Bauten. There are many impressive buildings in New York. ❸ **building site** ▷ *In den Ferien arbeitet er auf dem Bau.* He works on a building site in the holidays.

Bauarbeiter (*pl* Bauarbeiter) *m* building worker

Bauarbeiterin *f* building worker

Bauch (*pl* Bäuche) *m* stomach ▷ *Mir tut der Bauch weh.* My stomach's sore.

Bauchnabel (*pl* Bauchnabel) *m* belly button

Bauchschmerzen *pl* stomachache *sg*

bauen *vb* [38] to build ▷ *Meine Eltern haben das Haus gebaut, in dem wir wohnen.* My parents built the house we live in.

Bauer (*gen* Bauern, *pl* Bauern) *m* ❶ **farmer** ▷ *Friedas Vater ist Bauer.* Frieda's father is a farmer. ❷ **pawn** ▷ *Sie zog mit dem Bauer.* She moved the pawn.

Bäuerin *f* ❶ **farmer** ▷ *Sie möchte Bäuerin werden.* She would like to be a farmer. ❷ **farmer's wife**

Bauernhof (*pl* Bauernhöfe) *m* farm

baufällig *adj* dilapidated

Baum (*pl* Bäume) *m* tree

Baumwolle *f* cotton ▷ *eine Tischdecke aus Baumwolle* a cotton tablecloth

Baustelle *f* building site

Bayer (*gen* Bayern, *pl* Bayern) *m* Bavarian

Bayerin *f* Bavarian

Bayern *nt* Bavaria
* Bayern is one of the 16 Länder. Its
* capital is München (Munich).
* Bavaria has the longest cultural
* tradition of any of the Länder, and
* since 1945 has developed into an
* important industrial region.

bayrisch *adj* Bavarian

beabsichtigen (*perf* hat beabsichtigt) *vb* [7] to intend ▷ *Ich beabsichtige, ins Ausland zu fahren.* I intend to go abroad.

29 | Becher

beachten (*perf* hat beachtet) *vb* [2] ❶ **to pay attention to** ▷ *Beachte ihn nicht!* Don't pay any attention to him. ▷ *Du solltest den Hinweis auf der Packung beachten.* You should pay attention to the instructions on the packet. ❷ **to obey** ▷ *Man muss die Verkehrsregeln beachten.* You have to obey the traffic regulations. ❸ **to observe** ▷ *Sie hat die Vorfahrt nicht beachtet.* She didn't observe the right of way.

Beamte (*gen* Beamten, *pl* Beamten) *m* ❶ **official** ▷ *Der Beamte stempelte meinen Pass ab.* The official stamped my passport. ❷ **civil servant**
* In Germany, traditionally all public
* employees are civil servants. They
* enjoy many privileges.
▷ *Deutsche Lehrer sind Beamte.* German teachers are civil servants. ▷ *Er ist nur ein kleiner Beamter.* He's just a lowly civil servant.

Beamtin *f* civil servant ▷ *Meine Mutter ist Beamtin.* My mother's a civil servant.

beantragen (*perf* hat beantragt) *vb* [7] to apply for

beantworten (*perf* hat beantwortet) *vb* [2] to answer

bearbeiten (*perf* hat bearbeitet) *vb* [2] ❶ **to deal with** ▷ *Welches Thema hat sie in ihrer Diplomarbeit bearbeitet?* What subject did she deal with in her dissertation? ❷ **to process** ▷ *Wir haben Ihren Antrag noch nicht bearbeitet.* We haven't processed your application yet. ❸ **to treat** ▷ *Sie hat den Fleck mit Fleckenmittel bearbeitet.* She treated the stain with stain remover.; **jemanden bearbeiten** (*informal*) to work on somebody

Becher (*pl* Becher) *m* ❶ **mug** ▷ *Auf ihrem Schreibtisch stand ein Becher mit Kaffee.* There was a mug of coffee on her desk. ❷ **carton** ❸ **tub**

Becken (pl **Becken**) nt ① sink ▷ *Er ließ Wasser ins Becken laufen.* He ran water into the sink. ② pool; **ein breites Becken** broad hips

sich bedanken (perf **hat sich bedankt**) vb [7] to say thank you ▷ *Hast du dich auch bedankt?* Did you say thank you?; **sich bei jemandem bedanken** to say thank you to somebody

Bedarf m demand ▷ *je nach Bedarf* according to demand; **bei Bedarf** if necessary; **Bedarf an etwas haben** to be in need of something

bedauerlich adj regrettable

bedauern (perf **hat bedauert**) vb [88] ① to be sorry for ▷ *Wir bedauern es sehr, dass wir nicht kommen können.* We're very sorry that we can't come.; **Ich bedaure!** I'm sorry!; **Ich bedaure kein Wort.** I don't regret a single word! ② to pity ▷ *Ich bedaure dich wirklich!* I really pity you!

Bedenken pl doubts pl ▷ *Ich habe Bedenken, ob das klappt.* I have my doubts as to whether it'll work.; **Hast du keine Bedenken, wenn du deine Eltern so anlügst?** Don't you feel bad about lying to your parents like that?

bedenklich adj ① dubious ▷ *Das sind sehr bedenkliche Methoden.* These are very dubious methods. ② dangerous ▷ *Die Lage ist bedenklich.* The situation is dangerous.; **Ihr Gesundheitszustand ist bedenklich.** Her state of health is giving cause for concern.

bedeuten (perf **hat bedeutet**) vb [2] to mean ▷ *Was bedeutet dieser Ausdruck?* What does this expression mean? ▷ *Was hat das zu bedeuten?* What's that supposed to mean? ▷ *Er bedeutet mir sehr viel.* He means a lot to me.

bedeutend adj ① important ▷ *Er ist ein bedeutender Wissenschaftler.* He's an important scientist. ② considerable ▷ *Sie haben eine bedeutende Summe dafür bezahlt.* They paid a considerable sum for it.; **bedeutend besser** considerably better; **bedeutend schlechter** considerably worse

Bedeutung f ① meaning ▷ *die Bedeutung eines Worts* the meaning of a word ② importance ▷ *eine Erfindung von großer Bedeutung* an invention of great importance

bedienen (perf **hat bedient**) vb [7] ① to serve ▷ *Wir wurden sehr schnell bedient.* We were served very quickly. ② to operate ▷ *Er bedient die Druckmaschine.* He operates the printing press.; **sich bedienen** to help oneself

Bedienung f ① service ▷ *In diesem Geschäft ist die Bedienung schlecht.* The service is very poor in this shop. ② waiter, waitress ▷ *Wir haben bei der Bedienung ein Bier bestellt.* We ordered a beer from the waitress. ③ shop assistant ▷ *Die Bedienung im Kaufhaus war äußerst unfreundlich.* The shop assistant in the department store was extremely unfriendly. ④ service charge ▷ *Die Bedienung ist im Preis enthalten.* The service charge is included in the price.

Bedingung f condition ▷ *unter der Bedingung, dass ...* on condition that ...

bedrohen (perf **hat bedroht**) vb [7] to threaten

Bedürfnis (gen **Bedürfnisses**, pl **Bedürfnisse**) nt need

sich beeilen (perf **hat sich beeilt**) vb [7] to hurry

beeindrucken (perf **hat beeindruckt**) vb [7] to impress

beeindruckend adj impressive

beeinflussen (pres **beeinflusst**, imperf **beeinflusste**, perf **hat beeinflusst**) vb [7] to influence

beenden (perf **hat beendet**) vb [54] to end

Beerdigung f funeral

Beere f ① berry ② grape

Befehl (pl **Befehle**) m command
befehlen (pres **befiehlt**, imperf **befahl**, perf **hat befohlen**) vb ❶ to order ▷ *Der General hat den Rückzug befohlen.* The general ordered his men to retreat. ❷ to give orders ▷ *Du hast hier nicht zu befehlen!* You're not the one who gives the orders here!; **jemandem etwas befehlen** to order somebody to do something
befestigen (perf **hat befestigt**) vb [7] to fix ▷ *Die Regalbretter sind mit Schrauben an der Wand befestigt.* The shelves are fixed to the wall with screws.
sich **befinden** (imperf **befand sich**, perf **hat sich befunden**) vb [24] to be ▷ *Er befindet sich zurzeit im Ausland.* He's abroad at the moment.
befolgen (perf **hat befolgt**) vb [7] to obey
befördern (perf **hat befördert**) vb [88] ❶ to carry ▷ *Die städtischen Busse befördern täglich viele Menschen.* The municipal buses carry many people every day. ❷ to promote ▷ *Sie ist zur Abteilungsleiterin befördert worden.* She's been promoted to head of department.
Beförderung f ❶ transport ▷ *Das Rote Kreuz übernimmt die Beförderung der Hilfsgüter.* The Red Cross undertakes the transport of emergency supplies. ❷ promotion ▷ *Bei einer Beförderung bekommt man auch mehr Geld.* Promotion also means more money.
befragen (perf **hat befragt**) vb [7] to question
befreien (perf **hat befreit**) vb [7] ❶ to set free ▷ *Die Geiseln sind noch nicht befreit.* The hostages haven't been set free yet. ❷ to exempt ▷ *Sie ist vom Sportunterricht befreit.* She's exempt from PE lessons.
befreundet adj **mit jemandem befreundet sein** to be friends with somebody

befriedigen (perf **hat befriedigt**) vb [7] to satisfy
befriedigend adj satisfactory
● German marks range from one (**sehr**
● **gut**) to six (**ungenügend**).
befürchten (perf **hat befürchtet**) vb [2] to fear
begabt adj talented
Begabung f talent
begann vb see **beginnen**
begegnen (perf **ist begegnet**) vb [53] **jemandem begegnen** to meet somebody
begehen (imperf **beging**, perf **hat begangen**) vb [29] to commit ▷ *Er hat einen Mord begangen.* He committed a murder.
begehren (perf **hat begehrt**) vb [7] to desire
begehrt adj ❶ in demand ❷ eligible
begeistern (perf **hat begeistert**) vb [88] to thrill ▷ *Der Film hat mich begeistert.* I was thrilled with the film.; **sich für etwas begeistern** to get enthusiastic about something
begeistert adj enthusiastic
Beginn m beginning ▷ *zu Beginn* at the beginning
beginnen (imperf **begann**, perf **hat begonnen**) vb [5] to start
begleiten (perf **hat begleitet**) vb [2] to accompany ▷ *Er hat mich zum Ball begleitet.* He accompanied me to the ball.
beglückwünschen (perf **hat beglückwünscht**) vb [7] to congratulate ▷ *Alle meine Freunde haben mich zur bestandenen Prüfung beglückwünscht.* All my friends congratulated me on passing the exam.
begonnen vb see **beginnen**
begraben (pres **begräbt**, imperf **begrub**, perf **hat begraben**) vb to bury
begreifen (imperf **begriff**, perf **hat begriffen**) vb to understand

Begriff (pl **Begriffe**) m term ▷ *Das ist ein Begriff aus der Architektur.* That is an architectural term.; **im Begriff sein, etwas zu tun** to be about to do something; **schwer von Begriff** slow on the uptake; **sich einen Begriff von etwas machen** to imagine something

begründen (perf **hat begründet**) vb [54] to justify

Begründung f justification

begrüßen (perf **hat begrüßt**) vb [31] to welcome ▷ *Ich begrüße diese Änderung sehr.* I very much welcome this change.; **herzlich begrüßt werden** to receive a warm welcome

Begrüßung f welcome

behaglich adj cosy

behalten (pres **behält**, imperf **behielt**, perf **hat behalten**) vb [33] ❶ to keep ▷ *Kann ich das Buch noch ein paar Tage behalten?* Can I keep the book for another couple of days? ❷ to remember ▷ *Ich kann ihren Namen nie behalten.* I can never remember her name.

Behälter (pl **Behälter**) m container

behandeln (perf **hat behandelt**) vb [34] ❶ to treat ▷ *Wir wurden sehr freundlich behandelt.* We were treated in a very friendly manner. ▷ *Die Wunde muss behandelt werden.* The wound will have to be treated. ▷ *Welcher Arzt behandelt Sie?* Which doctor is treating you? ❷ to deal with ▷ *Der Film behandelt das Thema Jugendkriminalität.* The film deals with the subject of juvenile delinquency.

Behandlung f treatment

behaupten (perf **hat behauptet**) vb [2] to claim

beherrschen (perf **hat beherrscht**) vb [7] ❶ to master ▷ *Ich beherrsche diese Technik noch nicht.* I haven't mastered this technique yet. ❷ to control ▷ *Er konnte seine Wut nicht mehr beherrschen.* He couldn't control his anger any longer.; **sich beherrschen** to control oneself

behilflich adj helpful; **jemandem bei etwas behilflich sein** to help somebody with something

behindern (perf **hat behindert**) vb [88] to hinder

behindert adj disabled

Behinderte (gen **Behinderten**, pl **Behinderten**) mf disabled person; **die Behinderten** people with disabilities

Behinderung f ❶ obstruction ❷ disability ▷ *Sie hat gelernt, mit ihrer Behinderung zu leben.* She's learned to live with her disability.

Behörde f authorities pl

bei prep

The preposition **bei** takes the dative.

❶ near ▷ *Unser Haus ist beim Bahnhof.* Our house is near the station. ▷ *bei München* near Munich ❷ at ▷ *Felix ist zurzeit bei seiner Großmutter.* Felix is at his grandmother's at the moment. ▷ *Wenn man bei fremden Leuten zu Besuch ist ...* When you're at other people's houses ... ▷ *beim Friseur* at the hairdresser's ▷ *bei Nacht* at night ▷ *bei uns* at our place ❸ with ▷ *bei seinen Eltern wohnen* to live with one's parents ▷ *Wenn du bei mir bist, habe ich keine Angst.* When you're with me, I'm not afraid.; **Ich habe kein Geld bei mir.** I don't have any money on me.; **bei einer Firma arbeiten** to work for a firm; **beim Militär** in the army ❹ on ▷ *bei meiner Ankunft* on my arrival ▷ *bei der Abreise* on departure ❺ during ▷ *beim Abendessen* during dinner; **beim Fahren** while driving; **bei solcher Hitze** in such heat; **bei Nebel** in fog; **bei Regen** if it rains

beibringen (imperf **brachte**, perf **hat beigebracht**) vb [13] jemandem

etwas beibringen to teach somebody something

beide *adj, pron* both ▷ *Ich habe beide Bücher gelesen.* I've read both books. ▷ *Ich will beide.* I want both of them. ▷ *jeder der beiden* both of them ▷ *Meine Eltern haben das beide verboten.* Both my parents have forbidden it.; **meine beiden Brüder** both my brothers; **die ersten beiden** the first two; **wir beide** we two; **einer von beiden** one of the two

beides *pron* both ▷ *Ich möchte beides.* I want both of them. ▷ *Beides ist schön.* Both of them are lovely.; **alles beides** both of them

beieinander *adv* together

Beifall *m* applause; **Beifall spenden** to applaud

beige *adj* beige

Beil (*pl* **Beile**) *nt* axe

Beilage *f* ① supplement ▷ *eine Beilage zur Samstagszeitung* a supplement in Saturday's paper ② side dish

beilegen (*perf* **hat beigelegt**) *vb* [4]
① to enclose ▷ *Ich lege ein Foto bei.* I enclose a photo. ② to settle ▷ *Der Streit war schnell beigelegt.* The argument was quickly settled.

Beileid *nt* sympathy ▷ *Wir haben ihr unser Beileid ausgesprochen.* We offered her our sympathy.; **herzliches Beileid** deepest sympathy

beim = **bei dem**

Bein (*pl* **Beine**) *nt* leg

beinahe *adv* almost

beisammen *adv* together

beiseite *adv* to one side ▷ *Sie schob ihren Teller beiseite.* She pushed her plate to one side.

beiseiteschaffen *vb* [4] to put by ▷ *Er hat sehr viel Geld beiseitegeschafft.* He's put a lot of money by.

Beispiel (*pl* **Beispiele**) *nt* example; **sich an jemandem ein Beispiel nehmen** to take a leaf out of somebody's book; **zum Beispiel** for example

beispielsweise *adv* for example

beißen (*imperf* **biss**, *perf* **hat gebissen**) *vb* [6] ① to bite ▷ *Mein Hund beißt nicht.* My dog doesn't bite. ▷ *Sie biss in den Apfel.* She bit into the apple. ② to burn ▷ *Der Rauch beißt mich in den Augen.* The smoke's burning my eyes.; **sich beißen** to clash

Beitrag (*pl* **Beiträge**) *m* ① contribution ▷ *einen Beitrag zu etwas leisten* to make a contribution to something; **Beiträge für die Zeitung** articles for the newspaper ② membership fee ▷ *Der Beitrag für den Klub wird am Monatsanfang fällig.* Membership fees for the club are due at the beginning of the month. ③ premium ▷ *die Beiträge zur Krankenversicherung* the health insurance premiums

beitragen (*pres* **trägt bei**, *imperf* **trug bei**, *perf* **hat beigetragen**) *vb* [77] **zu etwas beitragen** to contribute to something

bekämpfen (*perf* **hat bekämpft**) *vb* [7] to fight ▷ *ein Feuer bekämpfen* to fight a fire; **sich bekämpfen** to fight

bekannt *adj* ① well-known ▷ *Sie ist eine bekannte Schauspielerin.* She's a well-known actress. ② familiar ▷ *Bekannte Wörter brauche ich nicht nachzuschlagen.* I don't have to look up familiar words. ▷ *Sie kommt mir bekannt vor.* She seems familiar. ▷ *Das kommt mir bekannt vor.* That sounds familiar.; **mit jemandem bekannt sein** to know somebody; **für etwas bekannt sein** to be known for something; **Das ist mir bekannt.** I know that.; **etwas bekannt geben** to announce something publicly; **etwas bekannt machen** to announce something

Bekannte (*gen* **Bekannten**, *pl* **Bekannten**) *mf* ① friend ▷ *Ein*

Bekannter von mir hat mir das erzählt. A friend of mine told me. ❷ acquaintance ▷ *Sie hat viele Bekannte, aber wenig Freunde.* She has a lot of acquaintances but few friends.

bekanntgeben vb [28] *see* **bekannt**

bekanntlich adv as you know ▷ *Rauchen macht bekanntlich süchtig.* As you know, smoking is addictive.

bekanntmachen vb [48] *see* **bekannt**

sich **beklagen** (*perf* **hat sich beklagt**) vb [7] to complain ▷ *Die Schüler haben sich darüber beklagt, dass sie Hausaufgaben aufbekommen haben.* The pupils complained about being given homework.

Bekleidung f clothing

bekommen vb [40] ❶ to get ▷ *Was hast du zum Geburtstag bekommen?* What did you get for your birthday? ▷ *Sie hat in Englisch eine schlechte Note bekommen.* She got bad marks in English. ▷ *Wir haben nichts zu essen bekommen.* We didn't get anything to eat.; **Hunger bekommen** to feel hungry; **Durst bekommen** to feel thirsty; **Angst bekommen** to become afraid; **ein Kind bekommen** to have a baby ❷ to catch ▷ *Ich habe den letzten Bus gerade noch bekommen.* I just caught the last bus.; **Das fette Essen ist ihm nicht bekommen.** The fatty food didn't agree with him.; **Was bekommen Sie?** What would you like?; **Bekommen Sie schon?** Are you being served?; **Was bekommen Sie dafür?** How much do I owe you?

> Be careful! **bekommen** does not mean **to become**.

belasten (*perf* **hat belastet**) vb [2] ❶ to burden ▷ *Ich möchte dich nicht mit meinen Problemen belasten.* I don't want to burden you with my problems. ❷ to load ▷ *Der Aufzug darf mit maximal zehn Personen belastet werden.* The lift's maximum load is ten people. ❸ to pollute ▷ *Unsere Umwelt ist mit zu vielen Schadstoffen belastet.* The environment is polluted by too many harmful substances. ❹ to debit ▷ *Wir werden Ihr Konto mit diesem Betrag belasten.* We will debit this amount from your account. ❺ to incriminate ▷ *Die Zeugin hat den Angeklagten belastet.* The witness incriminated the accused.

belästigen (*perf* **hat belästigt**) vb [7] to pester; **jemanden sexuell belästigen** to sexually harass somebody

belegt adj **ein belegtes Brot** an open sandwich; **belegt sein** to be engaged ▷ *Die Nummer ist belegt.* The number's engaged.

beleidigen (*perf* **hat beleidigt**) vb [7] to insult

Beleidigung f insult

Belgien nt Belgium

Belgier (pl **Belgier**) m Belgian

Belgierin f Belgian

belgisch adj Belgian

beliebig adj, adv ❶ any you like ▷ *in beliebiger Reihenfolge* in any order you like ▷ *eine beliebige Anzahl* any number you like ❷ as you like ▷ *beliebig oft* as often as you like ▷ *beliebig viel* as much as you like ▷ *beliebig viele* as many as you like

beliebt adj popular ▷ *sich bei jemandem beliebt machen* to make oneself popular with somebody

Beliebtheit f popularity

bellen vb [38] to bark

belohnen (*perf* **hat belohnt**) vb [7] to reward

Belohnung f reward ▷ *zur Belohnung* as a reward

belügen (*imperf* **belog**, *perf* **hat belogen**) vb [47] to lie to

bemerken (*perf* **hat bemerkt**) vb [7] to notice ▷ *Ich habe keine Änderung bemerkt.* I haven't noticed any change.

Bemerkung f remark
bemitleiden (perf **hat bemitleidet**) vb [7] to pity
sich **bemühen** (perf **hat sich bemüht**) vb [7] to make an effort ▷ *Er hat sich bemüht, höflich zu bleiben.* He made an effort to remain polite.; **Bemühen Sie sich nicht.** Don't trouble yourself.; **sich um eine neue Arbeit bemühen** to try and find a new job; **Ich werde mich bemühen!** I'll do my best!
benachrichtigen (perf **hat benachrichtigt**) vb [7] to inform
benachteiligt adj disadvantaged
sich **benehmen** (pres **benimmt sich**, imperf **benahm sich**, perf **hat sich benommen**) vb [52] to behave ▷ *sich anständig benehmen* to behave properly ▷ *Sie haben sich furchtbar benommen.* They behaved terribly. ▷ *Benimm dich!* Behave yourself!
Benehmen nt behaviour
beneiden (perf **hat beneidet**) vb [54] to envy ▷ *Er ist nicht zu beneiden.* I don't envy him.; **jemanden um etwas beneiden** to envy somebody something
beneidenswert adj, adv enviable; **Sie ist beneidenswert reich.** She's enviably rich.
benoten (perf **hat benotet**) vb [2] to mark
benutzen (perf **hat benutzt**) vb [36] to use
Benutzer (pl **Benutzer**) m user
benutzerfreundlich adj user-friendly
Benutzung f use
Benzin nt petrol
beobachten (perf **hat beobachtet**) vb [2] to observe
bequem adj ❶ comfortable ▷ *ein bequemer Stuhl* a comfortable chair; **eine bequeme Ausrede** a convenient excuse ❷ lazy ▷ *Er ist zu bequem, sich selbst etwas zu kochen.* He's too lazy to cook himself something.

beraten (pres **berät**, imperf **beriet**, perf **hat beraten**) vb [7] ❶ to give advice ▷ *Der Mann vom Arbeitsamt hat mich gut beraten.* The man at the job centre gave me good advice.; **Lassen Sie sich von Ihrem Arzt beraten.** Consult your doctor. ❷ to discuss ▷ *Wir müssen das weitere Vorgehen beraten.* We have to discuss further action.; **gut beraten sein** to be well advised; **schlecht beraten sein** to be ill advised
berauben (perf **hat beraubt**) vb [7] to rob
berechnen (perf **hat berechnet**) vb [53] to charge ▷ *Was berechnen Sie für eine Beratung?* What do you charge for a consultation?
bereit adj ready ▷ *Wir sind bereit abzufahren.* We're ready to leave. ▷ *Das Essen ist bereit.* Dinner's ready.; **bereit sein, etwas zu tun** to be prepared to do something; **etwas bereit haben** to have something ready
bereiten (perf **hat bereitet**) vb [2] to cause ▷ *Das hat mir einige Schwierigkeiten bereitet.* That caused me some problems.; **Die Kinder bereiten mir sehr viel Freude.** The children give me a great deal of pleasure.
bereits adv already
bereuen (perf **hat bereut**) vb [7] to regret
Berg (pl **Berge**) m ❶ mountain ▷ *Im Winter fahren wir in die Berge zum Skifahren.* In winter we go skiing in the mountains. ❷ hill ▷ *Hinter unserem Haus ist ein kleiner Berg.* There's a small hill behind our house.
Bergsteigen nt mountaineering ▷ *Bergsteigen ist ihr Hobby.* Her hobby's mountaineering. ▷ *Sie ist beim Bergsteigen verunglückt.* She had a mountaineering accident.
Bergsteiger (pl **Bergsteiger**) m mountaineer

Bergwerk (pl **Bergwerke**) nt mine
Bericht (pl **Berichte**) m report
berichten (perf **hat berichtet**) vb [2] to report ▷ *Die Zeitungen haben nichts über diesen Zwischenfall berichtet.* The newspapers didn't report anything about this incident.
Berlin nt Berlin
- Berlin is one of the 16 **Länder**. It is a 'city-state' like Bremen and Hamburg. From 1963 to 1989 it was divided by the Berlin Wall. Now it is again the German capital.

Berliner (pl **Berliner**) m ❶ person from Berlin ❷ jam-filled doughnut
Berlinerin f person from Berlin
- A person from Berlin would say **Ich bin Berliner** (I'm a Berliner), NOT **Ich bin ein Berliner** (I'm a doughnut). In German you don't translate the indefinite article 'a/an' when describing where someone is from.

berücksichtigen (perf **hat berücksichtigt**) vb [7] to bear in mind
Beruf (pl **Berufe**) m occupation ▷ *Welchen Beruf hat dein Vater?* What's your father's occupation?; **Sie ist Lehrerin von Beruf.** She's a teacher by profession.
beruflich adj professional; **beruflich unterwegs sein** to be away on business
Berufsberater (pl **Berufsberater**) m careers adviser
Berufsschule f technical college
berufstätig adj working ▷ *Seit wann ist deine Mutter wieder berufstätig?* When did your mother start working again?
beruhigen (perf **hat beruhigt**) vb [18] to calm down ▷ *Dem Lehrer gelang es nicht, die Klasse zu beruhigen.* The teacher didn't manage to calm the class down. ▷ *Beruhige dich doch!* Calm down!; **sich beruhigen** to calm down

Beruhigungsmittel (pl **Beruhigungsmittel**) nt tranquillizer
berühmt adj famous
berühren (perf **hat berührt**) vb [18] ❶ to touch ▷ *Er berührte meinen Arm.* He touched my arm. ❷ to affect ▷ *Die Armut der Menschen hat mich sehr berührt.* The poverty of the people affected me deeply. ❸ to touch on ▷ *Ich kann diese Frage heute nur berühren.* I can only touch on this question today.; **sich berühren** to touch
Berührung f contact ▷ *mit etwas in Berührung kommen* to come into contact with something
beschädigen (perf **hat beschädigt**) vb [7] to damage
beschaffen (perf **hat beschafft**) vb [7] to get ▷ *Ich muss mir ein Visum beschaffen.* I have to get a visa. ▷ *Können Sie mir nicht einen Job beschaffen?* Can't you get me a job?
beschäftigen (perf **hat beschäftigt**) vb [18] ❶ to occupy ▷ *Kannst du nicht irgendwie die Kinder beschäftigen?* Can't you occupy the children somehow? ▷ *Diese Frage beschäftigt mich seit Langem.* This question has been occupying me for a long time. ❷ to employ ▷ *Unsere Firma beschäftigt zweihundert Leute.* Our company employs two hundred people.; **sich beschäftigen** to occupy oneself; **sich beschäftigen mit** to deal with
beschäftigt adj busy
Beschäftigung f work ▷ *Er sucht eine Beschäftigung.* He's looking for work.; **Sie ist zurzeit ohne Beschäftigung.** She is unemployed at the moment.
Bescheid (pl **Bescheide**) m information ▷ *Ich warte auf den Bescheid des Konsulats.* I'm waiting for information from the consulate.; **Bescheid wissen** to know; **über etwas**

Bescheid wissen to know a lot about something; **jemandem Bescheid sagen** to let somebody know
bescheiden adj modest
Bescheinigung f certificate ▷ *Du brauchst eine Bescheinigung über die Teilnahme am Kurs.* You need a certificate showing that you attended the course. ▷ *eine Bescheinigung des Arztes* a doctor's certificate
Bescherung f giving out of Christmas presents; **Da haben wir die Bescherung!** What did I tell you!
beschimpfen (perf **hat beschimpft**) vb [18] to swear at
beschleunigen (perf **hat beschleunigt**) vb [7] ❶ to increase ▷ *Wir müssen das Arbeitstempo beschleunigen.* We have to increase our work rate. ❷ to accelerate ▷ *Das Auto vor mir beschleunigte.* The car in front of me accelerated.
beschließen (imperf **beschloss**, perf **hat beschlossen**) vb to decide ▷ *Wir haben beschlossen, nach Spanien zu fahren.* We decided to go to Spain.
Beschluss (gen **Beschlusses**, pl **Beschlüsse**) m decision
beschränken (perf **hat beschränkt**) vb [18] to limit ▷ *Wir müssen unsere Ausgaben beschränken.* We have to limit our spending.; **sich auf etwas beschränken** to restrict oneself to something
beschränkt adj ❶ limited ▷ *Diese Regel hat nur beschränkte Gültigkeit.* This regulation has only limited validity. ❷ stupid ▷ *Wie kann man nur so beschränkt sein?* How can anyone be so stupid?
beschreiben (imperf **beschrieb**, perf **hat beschrieben**) vb [61] to describe ▷ *Können Sie den Täter beschreiben?* Can you describe the culprit?
Beschreibung f description

beschützen (perf **hat beschützt**) vb [7] to protect ▷ *Ich möchte euch vor diesen Gefahren beschützen.* I want to protect you from these dangers.
Beschwerde f complaint ▷ *Wenn Sie eine Beschwerde haben, dann wenden Sie sich an den Geschäftsführer.* If you have a complaint, then please contact the manager.; **Beschwerden** trouble
sich beschweren (perf **hat sich beschwert**) vb [18] to complain ▷ *Deine Lehrerin hat sich über dich beschwert.* Your teacher has complained about you.
beseitigen (perf **hat beseitigt**) vb [7] to remove
Besen (pl **Besen**) m broom
besetzen (perf **hat besetzt**) vb [7] ❶ to occupy ▷ *Napoleons Truppen haben weite Teile Deutschlands besetzt.* Napoleon's troops occupied large areas of Germany. ❷ to fill ▷ *Der Posten soll mit einer Frau besetzt werden.* The position is to be filled by a woman. ▷ *Die Stelle ist noch nicht besetzt.* The position hasn't been filled yet.
besetzt adj ❶ full ▷ *Der Zug war voll besetzt.* The train was full. ❷ engaged ▷ *Es ist besetzt.* It's engaged. ❸ taken ▷ *Ist der Platz hier besetzt?* Is this seat taken?
besichtigen (perf **hat besichtigt**) vb [18] to visit
Besichtigung f visit
besitzen (imperf **besaß**, perf **hat besessen**) vb [68] ❶ to own ▷ *Sie besitzen ein Haus am Meer.* They own a house by the seaside. ❷ to have ▷ *Sie besitzt das Talent, sich mit allen zu zerstreiten.* She has the talent of quarrelling with everyone.
Besitzer (pl **Besitzer**) m owner
besondere adj special ▷ *Das sind besondere Umstände.* Those are special circumstances.; **keine besonderen Kennzeichen** no distinguishing features

besonders adv particularly ▷ Es hat mir nicht besonders gefallen. I didn't particularly like it.

besorgen (perf **hat besorgt**) vb [18] to get ▷ Kannst du mir nicht einen Ferienjob besorgen? Can't you get me a holiday job? ▷ Soll ich dir ein Taxi besorgen? Shall I get you a taxi? ▷ Ich muss Milch und Eier besorgen. I'll have to get milk and eggs.

besorgt adj worried ▷ Sie ist sehr besorgt um dich. She's very worried about you.

besprechen (pres **bespricht**, imperf **besprach**, perf **hat besprochen**) vb [70] to discuss ▷ Das muss ich mit deiner Mutter besprechen. I'll have to discuss it with your mother.

Besprechung f ❶ meeting ▷ Frau Airlie ist in einer Besprechung. Ms Airlie is in a meeting. ❷ review ▷ Hast du die Besprechung dieses Films gelesen? Have you read the review of this film?

besser adj, adv better ▷ eine bessere Note a better mark ▷ Du gehst jetzt besser nach Hause. You'd better go home now.; **Es geht ihm besser.** He's feeling better.; **je schneller, desto besser** the quicker the better

sich bessern vb [88] to improve ▷ Das Wetter hat sich gebessert. The weather's improved.

Besserung f improvement; **Gute Besserung!** Get well soon!

bestätigen (perf **hat bestätigt**) vb [18] ❶ to confirm ▷ Ich kann bestätigen, dass sie die Wahrheit gesagt hat. I can confirm that she told the truth. ❷ to acknowledge ▷ Hiermit bestätigen wir den Erhalt Ihres Briefes. We hereby acknowledge receipt of your letter.; **sich bestätigen** to prove to be true

beste adj best ▷ Sie ist die beste Schülerin der Klasse. She's the best pupil in the class. ▷ So ist es am besten. It's best that way.; **Am besten gehst du gleich.** You'd better go at once.; **jemanden**

zum Besten haben to pull somebody's leg; **einen Witz zum Besten geben** to tell a joke; **Es ist nur zu deinem Besten.** It's for your own good.

bestechen (pres **besticht**, imperf **bestach**, perf **hat bestochen**) vb to bribe

Bestechung f bribery

Besteck (pl **Bestecke**) nt cutlery

bestehen (imperf **bestand**, perf **hat bestanden**) vb [72] ❶ to be ▷ Es besteht die Möglichkeit, einen Sprachkurs zu belegen. There's the chance of registering for a language course. ▷ Es besteht keine Hoffnung mehr, sie jemals wiederzusehen. There's no more hope of ever seeing her again. ❷ to exist ▷ Die Firma besteht seit hundert Jahren. The firm has existed for a hundred years.; **etwas bestehen** to pass something; **auf etwas bestehen** to insist on something; **bestehen aus** to consist of

bestehlen vb [73] **jemanden bestehlen** to rob somebody

bestellen (perf **hat bestellt**) vb [7] ❶ to order ▷ Ich habe ein Kleid online bestellt. I've ordered a dress online. ▷ Haben Sie schon bestellt? Have you ordered yet? ▷ Wir sollten ein Taxi bestellen. We should order a taxi. ❷ to reserve ▷ Ich habe einen Tisch beim Chinesen bestellt. I've reserved a table at the Chinese restaurant. ❸ to send for ▷ Der Direktor hat mich zu sich bestellt. The headmaster sent for me.; **Bestell deiner Mutter schöne Grüße.** Give my regards to your mother.; **Soll ich ihr etwas von dir bestellen?** Shall I give her a message from you?

Bestellung f order; **auf Bestellung** to order

bestimmen (perf **hat bestimmt**) vb [7] to decide ▷ Du kannst bestimmen, wer mitkommen soll. You can decide who's coming. ▷ Wer bestimmt hier, was

GERMAN > ENGLISH — **Betragen**

gemacht werden muss? Who decides what has to be done?; **Du hast hier nichts zu bestimmen!** You're not the one who decides here!; **für jemanden bestimmt sein** to be meant for somebody; **für etwas bestimmt sein** to be intended for something

bestimmt *adj, adv* ① certain ▷ *Wir treffen uns immer zu einer bestimmten Zeit.* We always meet at a certain time. ▷ *Die Teilnehmer sollten eine bestimmte Anzahl nicht überschreiten.* The participants shouldn't exceed a certain number. ② particular ▷ *Ich suche ein ganz bestimmtes Buch.* I'm looking for a particular book.; **Suchen Sie etwas Bestimmtes?** Are you looking for something in particular?; **der bestimmte Artikel** the definite article; **Ich habe ihn bestimmt gesehen.** I'm sure I've seen him.; **Das hat er bestimmt nicht so gemeint.** I'm sure that's not how he meant it.; **Das hat sie bestimmt vergessen.** She's bound to have forgotten.

bestrafen *(perf* **hat bestraft***) vb* **[7]** to punish

Besuch *(pl* **Besuche***) m* ① visit ▷ *Deutschland bereitet sich auf den Besuch der Königin vor.* Germany's preparing for the Queen's visit.; **bei unserem Besuch in London** during our visit to London; **Der Schulbesuch ist Pflicht.** School attendance is compulsory. ② visitor ▷ *Ist euer Besuch noch da?* Is your visitor still there? ▷ *Besuch haben* to have visitors; **bei jemandem einen Besuch machen** to pay somebody a visit; **bei jemandem zu Besuch sein** to be visiting somebody; **zu Besuch kommen** to come for a visit

besuchen *(perf* **hat besucht***) vb* **[7]** ① to visit ▷ *Hast du schon das Planetarium besucht?* Have you visited the planetarium yet?; **Besuch uns mal wieder!** Come again! ② to attend ▷ *Sie besucht das Gymnasium.* She attends grammar school. ▷ *Der Vortrag war sehr gut besucht.* The lecture was very well attended.; **Wir haben ein Konzert besucht.** We went to a concert.

Besucher *(pl* **Besucher***) m* visitor

Besucherin *f* visitor

betätigen *(perf* **hat betätigt***) vb* **[7] die Hupe betätigen** to sound the horn; **einen Schalter betätigen** to press a switch; **die Bremse betätigen** to apply the brakes; **Du solltest dich sportlich betätigen.** You should do some sport.

beteiligen *(perf* **hat beteiligt***) vb* **[7] sich an etwas beteiligen** to take part in something; **Alle werden am Gewinn beteiligt.** Everyone will share in the winnings.

beten *vb* **[2]** to pray

Beton *(pl* **Betons***) m* concrete

betonen *(perf* **hat betont***) vb* **[7]** to stress

Betonung *f* stress ▷ *Wo liegt die Betonung bei diesem Wort?* Where's the stress in this word?

betrachten *vb* **[2]** ① to look at ▷ *Sie hat das Bild lange betrachtet.* She looked at the picture for a long time. ② to consider ▷ *Ich betrachte ihn als Freund.* I consider him a friend.

beträchtlich *adj, adv* ① considerable ▷ *eine beträchtliche Summe* a considerable amount ② considerably ▷ *Es hat beträchtlich länger gedauert.* It took considerably longer.

Betrag *(pl* **Beträge***) m* amount

betragen *(pres* **beträgt***, imperf* **betrug***, perf* **hat betragen***) vb* **[77]** to come to ▷ *Die Reparatur betrug dreihundert Euro.* The repair came to three hundred euros.; **sich betragen** to behave

Betragen *nt* behaviour ▷ *Ich werde mich über dein schlechtes Betragen beschweren.* I'm going to complain about your bad behaviour.

betreffen (pres **betrifft**, imperf **betraf**, perf **hat betroffen**) vb [78] to concern; **was mich betrifft** as far as I'm concerned

betreten (pres **betritt**, imperf **betrat**, perf **hat betreten**) vb [79] to enter ▷ *Sie klopfte, bevor sie das Zimmer betrat.* She knocked before entering the room.; **'Betreten verboten'** 'Keep out'

Betreuer (pl **Betreuer**) m carer

Betreuerin f carer

Betrieb (pl **Betriebe**) m ❶ firm ▷ *Unser Betrieb beschäftigt dreihundert Menschen.* Our firm employs three hundred people. ❷ operation ▷ *Die Maschine ist jetzt in Betrieb.* The machine is now in operation.; **In der Stadt war heute viel Betrieb.** It was really busy in town today.; **außer Betrieb sein** to be out of order

sich **betrinken** (imperf **betrank sich**, perf **hat sich betrunken**) vb [80] to get drunk

betroffen adj ❶ full of concern ▷ *Sie machte ein betroffenes Gesicht.* Her face was full of concern. ❷ affected ▷ *von etwas betroffen sein* to be affected by something ▷ *Wir sind über diese Nachricht zutiefst betroffen.* We are deeply affected by the news.

betrügen (imperf **betrog**, perf **hat betrogen**) vb ❶ to cheat ▷ *Der Händler hat dich betrogen.* The dealer's cheated you. ❷ to defraud ▷ *Er hat seinen Arbeitgeber um Millionen betrogen.* He defrauded his employer of millions. ❸ to be unfaithful to ▷ *Hast du deine Freundin schon mal betrogen?* Have you ever been unfaithful to your girlfriend?

betrunken adj drunk

Bett (pl **Betten**) nt bed ▷ *ins Bett gehen* to go to bed ▷ *das Bett machen* to make the bed

Bettdecke f blanket

betteln vb [34] to beg

Bettlaken (pl **Bettlaken**) nt sheet

Bettler (pl **Bettler**) m beggar

Betttuch (pl **Betttücher**) nt sheet

Bettwäsche f bed linen

beugen vb [38] to bend ▷ *Ich kann den Arm nicht beugen.* I can't bend my arm.; **sich beugen** to bow

Beule f ❶ bump ▷ *eine Beule am Kopf* a bump on the head ❷ dent ▷ *Das Auto hat eine Beule.* The car has a dent in it.

beunruhigen (perf **hat beunruhigt**) vb [7] to alarm

beurteilen (perf **hat beurteilt**) vb [7] to judge ▷ *Ich beurteile die Leute nicht nach ihrem Aussehen.* I don't judge people on their appearance.

Beutel (pl **Beutel**) m ❶ bag ▷ *Sie tat die Einkäufe in den Beutel.* She put the shopping in the bag. ❷ purse ▷ *Er nahm einen Euro aus dem Beutel.* He took a euro from the purse.

Bevölkerung f population

bevor conj before ▷ *Sie war gegangen, bevor ich es ihr sagen konnte.* She left before I could tell her.

bevorstehen (imperf **stand bevor**, perf **hat bevorgestanden**) vb [72] to be imminent ▷ *Die Prüfung steht bevor.* The exam's imminent.; **jemandem bevorstehen** to be in store for somebody

sich **bewähren** (perf **hat sich bewährt**) vb [7] to prove oneself ▷ *Er hat sich als mein Freund bewährt.* He proved himself to be my friend. ▷ *Diese Methode hat sich bewährt.* This method has proved itself.

bewährt adj tried and tested ▷ *Das ist eine bewährte Methode.* That's a tried and tested method.; **Sie ist eine bewährte Mitarbeiterin.** She's a reliable colleague.

bewegen (perf **hat bewegt**) vb [7] to move; **sich bewegen** to move; **jemanden zu etwas bewegen** to persuade somebody to do something

beweglich adj ① movable ▷ *Die Puppe hat bewegliche Beine.* The doll has movable legs. ② agile ▷ *Sie ist trotz ihres Alters noch sehr beweglich.* She's still very agile despite her age.

bewegt adj ① eventful ▷ *Sie hatte ein bewegtes Leben.* She had an eventful life. ② touched ▷ *Wir waren von seinen Worten sehr bewegt.* We were very touched by his words.

Bewegung f ① movement ▷ *Mir fällt jede Bewegung schwer.* Every movement is difficult for me. ② motion ▷ *Er setzte das Fahrzeug in Bewegung.* He set the vehicle in motion. ③ exercise ▷ *Du brauchst mehr Bewegung.* You need more exercise.

Beweis (pl **Beweise**) m ① proof ▷ *Die Polizei hat keine Beweise.* The police don't have any proof. ② sign ▷ *als Beweis meiner Freundschaft* as a sign of my friendship

beweisen (imperf **bewies**, perf **hat bewiesen**) vb ① to prove ▷ *Ich kann nicht beweisen, dass sie das gesagt hat.* I can't prove that she said it. ▷ *Die Polizei kann nichts beweisen.* The police can't prove anything. ② to show ▷ *Er hat sehr viel Mut bewiesen.* He showed great courage.

sich **bewerben** (pres **bewirbt sich**, imperf **bewarb sich**, perf **hat sich beworben**) vb [90] to apply ▷ *Es haben sich dreißig Kandidaten beworben.* Thirty candidates have applied. ▷ *Sie hat sich bei Siemens um einen Ausbildungsplatz beworben.* She applied to Siemens for an apprenticeship.

Bewerber (pl **Bewerber**) m applicant

Bewerbung f application

bewerten (perf **hat bewertet**) vb [2] to assess ▷ *Der Lehrer hat unsere Aufsätze zu bewerten.* The teacher has to assess our essays.

bewirken (perf **hat bewirkt**) vb [7] ① to bring about ▷ *Dieses Medikament wird eine schnelle Besserung bewirken.* This medicine will bring about a rapid improvement. ② to achieve ▷ *Meine Bitte hat nichts bewirkt.* My request didn't achieve anything.; **Ich konnte bei ihm nichts bewirken.** I couldn't get anywhere with him.

bewohnen (perf **hat bewohnt**) vb [7] to live in ▷ *Das Haus wird von drei Familien bewohnt.* Three families live in the house.

Bewohner (pl **Bewohner**) m ① inhabitant ▷ *die Bewohner des Landes* the inhabitants of the country ② resident ▷ *die Bewohner des Hauses* the residents of the house

bewölkt adj cloudy

Bewölkung f clouds pl

bewundern (perf **hat bewundert**) vb [88] to admire

Bewunderung f admiration

bewusst adj ① conscious ▷ *umweltbewusst* environmentally conscious ② deliberate ▷ *Er hat ganz bewusst gelogen.* He lied quite deliberately.; **sich einer Sache bewusst sein** to be aware of something; **Ihr wurde plötzlich bewusst, dass ...** She suddenly realized that ...

bewusstlos adj unconscious; **bewusstlos werden** to lose consciousness

Bewusstlosigkeit f unconsciousness

bezahlen (perf **hat bezahlt**) vb [7] to pay ▷ *Er bezahlte die Rechnung.* He paid the bill.

Bezahlung f payment

bezeichnen (perf **hat bezeichnet**) vb [53] ① to mark ▷ *Bezeichnen Sie die Stelle mit einem Kreuz.* Mark the spot with a cross. ② to call ▷ *Sie hat mich als Lügnerin bezeichnet.* She called me a liar.

bezeichnend adj typical ▷ *Das ist bezeichnend für sie!* That's typical of her!

beziehen (*imperf* **bezog**, *perf* **hat bezogen**) *vb* [**96**] ❶ to cover ▷ *Sie beschloss, alle Kissen zu beziehen.* She decided to cover all the cushions.; **das Bett beziehen** to change the bed ❷ to move into ▷ *Wann könnt ihr euer neues Haus beziehen?* When can you move into your new house? ❸ to get ▷ *Wir beziehen unsere Kartoffeln direkt vom Bauern.* We get our potatoes straight from the farm. ▷ *Sie beziehen Arbeitslosenhilfe.* They get unemployment benefit. ❹ to subscribe to ▷ *Ich beziehe eine Tageszeitung.* I subscribe to a daily newspaper.; **sich beziehen** to cloud over; **sich auf etwas beziehen** to refer to something

Beziehung *f* ❶ relationship ▷ *Er hat eine Beziehung mit einer verheirateten Frau.* He has a relationship with a married woman. ❷ relations *pl* ▷ *unsere Beziehungen zu dieser Firma* our relations with this company ▷ *diplomatische Beziehungen* diplomatic relations ❸ connection ▷ *Es besteht eine Beziehung zwischen den beiden Straftaten.* There's a connection between the two crimes.; **in dieser Beziehung** in this respect; **Beziehungen haben** to have contacts; **eine Beziehung zu etwas haben** to be able to relate to something

Bezirk (*pl* **Bezirke**) *m* district

Bezug (*pl* **Bezüge**) *m* cover ▷ *Das Sofa hatte einen bunten Bezug.* The sofa had a brightly-coloured cover.; **in Bezug auf** regarding; **Bezug nehmen auf** to refer to

bezweifeln (*perf* **hat bezweifelt**) *vb* [**34**] ▷ *Ich bezweifle das.* I doubt it.

BH (*pl* **BHs**) *m* (= *Büstenhalter*) bra

bi *adj* (= *bisexuell*) bi (= *bisexual*)

Bibel *f* Bible

Bibliothek (*pl* **Bibliotheken**) *f* library

biegen (*imperf* **bog**, *perf* **hat gebogen**) *vb* ❶ to bend ▷ *Sie bog den Draht zur Seite.* She bent the wire to one side. ❷ to turn ▷ *Du musst an der Ampel rechts in die Seitenstraße biegen.* You have to turn right at the lights, into the side street.; **sich biegen** to bend

Biene *f* bee

Bier (*pl* **Biere** *or* **Bier**) *nt* beer ▷ *Zwei Bier, bitte!* Two beers, please!

bieten (*imperf* **bot**, *perf* **hat geboten**) *vb* [**8**] ❶ to offer ▷ *Dieser Job bietet mir die Möglichkeit, meine Englischkenntnisse anzuwenden.* This job offers me the chance to use my knowledge of English. ❷ to bid ▷ *Sie hat zweihundert Euro für den Stuhl geboten.* She bid two hundred euros for the chair. ▷ *Wer bietet mehr?* Any more bids?; **sobald sich die Gelegenheit bietet** as soon as the opportunity arises; **sich etwas bieten lassen** to put up with something

Bild (*pl* **Bilder**) *nt* ❶ picture ▷ *ein Bild von Picasso* a picture by Picasso.; **ein Bild der Verwüstung** a scene of destruction ❷ photo ▷ *Hast du ein Bild von deinem Freund?* Have you got a photo of your boyfriend?

bilden *vb* [**54**] ❶ to form ▷ *Bildet einen Kreis.* Form a circle. ▷ *Wie wird der Plural dieses Worts gebildet?* How do you form the plural of this word? ❷ to set up ▷ *Sie haben einen Ausschuss gebildet.* They set up a committee.; **sich eine Meinung bilden** to form an opinion; **sich bilden** (1) to form ▷ *Am Himmel bildeten sich dunkle Wolken.* Dark clouds formed in the sky. (2) to educate oneself ▷ *Sie macht Kurse, um sich zu bilden.* She attends courses in order to educate herself.

Bildschirm (*pl* **Bildschirme**) *m* screen

Bildschirmschoner (*pl* **Bildschirmschoner**) *m* screen saver

Bildung *f* ❶ education ▷ *Sie hat eine gute Bildung.* She has a good education. ❷ formation ▷ *Die Bildung des Plurals im*

Englischen ist ziemlich regelmäßig. The formation of the plural in English is quite regular. ▷ die Bildung der Regierung the formation of the government

billig adj cheap

Billigflieger (pl **Billigflieger**) m low-cost airline

bin vb see **sein**

binär adj binary ▷ nicht binär non-binary

Binde f ① bandage ▷ eine elastische Binde an elastic bandage ② sanitary towel ▷ Sie benützt lieber Binden als Tampons. She prefers sanitary towels to tampons.

binden (imperf **band**, perf **hat gebunden**) vb ① to tie ▷ Die Tomaten werden an einen Stock gebunden. The tomatoes are tied to a cane. ▷ Sie band die Haare zu einem Pferdeschwanz. She tied her hair back into a ponytail.; **ein Buch binden** to bind a book; **sich binden** to get involved

Bindestrich (pl **Bindestriche**) m hyphen

Bindfaden (pl **Bindfäden**) m string

Bio- prefix organic

Biologie f biology

biologisch adj biological

Birke f birch

Birne f ① pear ▷ Zum Nachtisch gab es Birnen mit Schokoladensoße. There were pears with chocolate sauce for dessert. ② bulb ▷ Die Lampe funktioniert nicht, weil die Birne kaputt ist. The lamp isn't working because the bulb's gone.

bis prep, conj

The preposition **bis** takes the accusative.

① until ▷ Sie bleibt bis Ende August in England. She's staying in England until the end of August. ▷ Du hast bis Montag Zeit. You have until Monday. ▷ bis es dunkel wird until it gets dark; **bis auf weiteres** until further notice ② by ▷ Das Referat muss bis nächsten Montag fertig sein. The assignment must be finished by next Monday.; **bis in die Nacht** into the night; **bis bald** see you later; **bis gleich** see you soon ③ as far as ▷ Ich fahre bis Köln. I'm going as far as Cologne.; **bis hierher** this far; **von ... bis ...** from ... to ... ④ up to ▷ Kinder bis drei fahren umsonst. Children up to three travel free. ▷ bis zu dreißig Grad up to thirty degrees; **zehn bis zwanzig** ten to twenty; **bis zu** up to; **bis auf** apart from

bisher adv up to now

bisherig adj previous

biss vb see **beißen**

Biss (gen **Bisses**, pl **Bisse**) m bite

bisschen adj, adv bit ▷ ein bisschen a bit

bissig adj ① vicious; **Vorsicht, bissiger Hund!** Beware of the dog! ② cutting ▷ Er machte eine bissige Bemerkung. He made a cutting remark.

bist vb see **sein**

bitte excl ① please ▷ Kann ich bitte noch etwas Saft haben? Can I have some more juice, please? ▷ Darf ich? — Bitte! May I? — Please do.; **Wie bitte?** Pardon?; **Hier bitte!** Here you are.; **Bitte warten.** Please hold the line. (phone) ② don't mention it ▷ Vielen Dank für die Hilfe! — Bitte! Many thanks for your help! — Don't mention it!; **Bitte schön!** It was a pleasure.; **Bitte sehr!** You're welcome.

Bitte f request ▷ Ich habe eine Bitte. I have a request.; **auf seine Bitte hin** at his request

bitten (imperf **bat**, perf **hat gebeten**) vb [9] **jemanden um etwas bitten** to ask somebody for something

bitter adj bitter

blamieren (perf **hat blamiert**) vb [76] **sich blamieren** to make a fool of oneself; **jemanden blamieren** to let somebody down

Blase f ① bubble ▷ *Die Blase platzte.* The bubble burst. ② blister ▷ *Ich habe Blasen an den Füßen.* I've got blisters on my feet. ③ bladder ▷ *Sie hat eine schwache Blase.* She has a weak bladder.

blasen (*pres* **bläst**, *imperf* **blies**, *perf* **hat geblasen**) *vb* to blow

Blasinstrument (*pl* **Blasinstrumente**) *nt* wind instrument

Blasmusik f brass band music

blass *adj* pale ▷ *Als sie das hörte, wurde sie blass.* When she heard that, she turned pale.

Blatt (*pl* **Blätter**) *nt* ① leaf ▷ *Im Herbst fallen die Blätter von den Bäumen.* In autumn, the leaves fall from the trees. ② sheet ▷ *ein Blatt Papier* a sheet of paper ③ newspaper ▷ *In welchem Blatt hast du die Anzeige aufgegeben?* Which newspaper did you place the advertisement in?

blau *adj* ① blue ▷ *Er hat blaue Augen.* He has blue eyes. ② (*informal*) sloshed ▷ *Gestern Abend warst du ganz schön blau.* You were absolutely sloshed yesterday evening.; **ein blaues Auge** a black eye

> Word for word, **ein blaues Auge** means 'a blue eye'.

ein blauer Fleck a bruise

> Word for word, **ein blauer Fleck** means 'a blue spot'.

eine Fahrt ins Blaue a mystery tour

Blech (*pl* **Bleche**) *nt* ① sheet metal ② baking tray

Blei *nt* lead

bleiben (*imperf* **blieb**, *perf* **ist geblieben**) *vb* [**10**] ① to stay ▷ *Wie lange bleiben Sie hier?* How long are you staying here? ▷ *Hoffentlich bleibt das Wetter schön.* I hope the weather will stay fine.; **bei etwas bleiben** to stick to something ② to be left ▷ *Vom Kuchen war nur noch ein Stück für mich geblieben.* There was only one piece of cake left for me.; **Bleibt es bei morgen zehn Uhr?** Is ten o'clock tomorrow morning still on?; **Wo bleibt sie denn?** Where's she got to?

bleich *adj* pale ▷ *Als er das hörte, wurde er bleich.* When he heard that, he turned pale.

bleifrei *adj* unleaded

Bleistift (*pl* **Bleistifte**) *m* pencil

Blick (*pl* **Blicke**) *m* ① glance ▷ *Ich habe mit einem Blick gesehen, dass das nicht gut gehen kann.* I saw at a glance that it couldn't work.; **Er warf einen Blick auf die Uhr.** He glanced at the clock. ② look ▷ *Sie warf mir einen verzweifelten Blick zu.* She gave me a desperate look. ③ view ▷ *Das Zimmer hat einen herrlichen Blick auf die Berge.* The room has a wonderful view of the mountains.; **auf den ersten Blick** at first glance

blicken *vb* [**48**] to look ▷ *Sie blickte zur Seite.* She looked to one side.; **sich blicken lassen** to show one's face ▷ *Er hat sich hier nie wieder blicken lassen.* He's never shown his face here again.; **Das lässt tief blicken!** That's very revealing!

blieb *vb see* **bleiben**

blind *adj* ① blind ▷ *Er ist auf einem Auge blind.* He's blind in one eye. ② tarnished ▷ *Der Spiegel war blind geworden.* The mirror had become tarnished

Blinddarm (*pl* **Blinddärme**) *m* appendix ▷ *Er wurde am Blinddarm operiert.* He had his appendix out.

blinzeln *vb* [**88**] to blink

Blitz (*pl* **Blitze**) *m* lightning ▷ *Der Blitz schlug in den Baum ein.* The tree was struck by lightning.

blitzen *vb* [**36**] **Es blitzt.** There's a flash of lightning.

Blitzlicht (*pl* **Blitzlichter**) *nt* flashlight

Block (*pl* **Blöcke**) *m* ① block ▷ *Unsere Nachbarn aus dem nächsten Block haben uns gestern besucht.* Our neighbours from the next block visited us yesterday. ② pad ▷ *Er riss ein Blatt vom*

GERMAN > ENGLISH

Block und fing an zu schreiben. He tore a sheet from the pad and began to write.

Blockflöte f recorder

blöd adj stupid ▷ *Du bist blöd!* You're stupid!; **blöd fragen** to ask stupid questions

Blödsinn m nonsense

Blog (pl **Blogs**) nt blog

bloggen vb [4] to blog

blond adj ❶ blond ▷ *Er hat blonde Haare.* He has blond hair. ❷ blonde ▷ *Meine Schwester ist blond.* My sister's blonde. ▷ *Sie hat ihre Haare blond gefärbt.* She dyed her hair blonde.

bloß adv, adj only ▷ *Er hat bloß einen Fehler gemacht.* He only made one mistake. ▷ *Wenn das bloß schon fertig wäre!* If only it was finished.; **Lass das bloß!** Don't do that!; **Wie ist das bloß passiert?** How on earth did that happen?; **Wo ist er bloß?** Where's he got to?; **mit bloßem Auge** with the naked eye; **der bloße Gedanke** the very thought; **bloßer Neid** sheer envy

blühen vb [38] to be in bloom ▷ *Zurzeit blüht der Flieder.* The lilac's in bloom at the moment.

Blume f flower ▷ *Sie hat mir einen Strauß Blumen mitgebracht.* She brought me a bunch of flowers.

Blumenbeet (pl **Blumenbeete**) nt flowerbed

Blumenkohl (pl **Blumenkohle**) m cauliflower

Bluse f blouse

Blut nt blood

Blutdruck m blood pressure

Blüte f blossom

bluten vb [2] to bleed ▷ *Meine Nase blutet.* My nose is bleeding.

Blutprobe f blood test

Bock m **Bock haben, etwas zu tun** (*informal*) to fancy doing something

Bockwurst (pl **Bockwürste**) f frankfurter

Boden (pl **Böden**) m ❶ soil ▷ *Der Boden ist in dieser Gegend sehr fruchtbar.* The soil in this area is very fertile. ▷ *auf deutschem Boden* on German soil ❷ floor ▷ *Wir haben auf dem Boden gesessen.* We sat on the floor. ❸ bottom ▷ *Das Schiff sank auf den Boden des Meeres.* The ship sank to the bottom of the sea. ▷ *Das Fass hat einen hölzernen Boden.* The barrel has a wooden bottom. ❹ attic ▷ *Wir haben die alten Möbel auf den Boden gebracht.* We put the old furniture into the attic.

Bodensee m Lake Constance ▷ *eine Stadt am Bodensee* a town on Lake Constance

Bohne f bean

bohren vb [38] ❶ to bore ▷ *Sie bohrte ein Loch in das Brett.* She bored a hole in the shelf. ❷ to drill ▷ *Der Zahnarzt musste nicht bohren.* The dentist didn't have to drill. ▷ *In der Nordsee wird nach Erdöl gebohrt.* They're drilling for oil in the North Sea.; **in der Nase bohren** to pick one's nose

Bohrer (pl **Bohrer**) m drill

Bohrmaschine f drill

Bombe f bomb

Bonbon (pl **Bonbons**) m sweet

Boot (pl **Boote**) nt boat

Bord (1) m an Bord on board

Bord (2) (pl **Borde**) nt shelf ▷ *Er brachte über dem Schreibtisch ein Bord für seine Bücher an.* He put up a shelf on his desk for his books.

borgen vb [38] to borrow ▷ *Das gehört nicht mir, das habe ich mir geborgt.* That doesn't belong to me, I borrowed it.; **jemandem etwas borgen** to lend somebody something

Börse f ❶ purse ▷ *Sie nahm zehn Euro aus ihrer Börse.* She took ten euros out of her purse. ❷ stock exchange ▷ *Diese Aktien werden an der Börse gehandelt.* These shares are traded on the stock exchange.

böse adj ❶ bad ▷ *Er ist ein böser Mensch.* He's a bad man. ▷ *Die Kinder waren böse.* The children were bad. ▷ *Sie hat eine böse Erkältung.* She has a bad cold. ❷ angry ▷ *Ich habe ihm einen bösen Brief geschrieben.* I wrote him an angry letter.; **böse werden** to get angry ▷ *Wenn du das noch einmal tust, werde ich böse.* If you do that again, I'll get angry. ▷ *Bist du mir noch böse?* Are you still angry with me?; **auf jemanden böse sein** to be angry with somebody ▷ *Ich bin böse auf Martin, weil er nicht gekommen ist.* I'm angry with Martin because he didn't come.; **eine böse Überraschung** a nasty shock; **Mit ihm sieht es böse aus.** It doesn't look too good for him.

Bosnien nt Bosnia
bot vb see **bieten**
Botschaft f ❶ message ▷ *Kannst du ihm eine Botschaft übermitteln?* Can you give him a message? ❷ embassy ▷ *Sie müssen das Visum auf der Botschaft beantragen.* You have to apply to the embassy for a visa.
boxen vb [48] to box
Boxer (pl **Boxer**) m boxer
brach vb see **brechen**
brachte vb see **bringen**
Brand (pl **Brände**) m fire
Brandenburg nt Brandenburg
- Brandenburg is one of the 16 Länder.
- Its capital is Potsdam, and is
- famous as Frederick the Great's
- residence. Agriculture and forestry
- are still important parts of the
- economy.

Brasilien nt Brazil
braten (pres **brät**, imperf **briet**, perf **hat gebraten**) vb ❶ to roast ▷ *Wir haben das Hähnchen im Backofen gebraten.* We roasted the chicken in the oven. ❷ to fry ▷ *Sie briet die Kartoffeln in der Pfanne.* She fried the potatoes in the frying pan.

Braten (pl **Braten**) m roast
Brathähnchen (pl **Brathähnchen**) nt roast chicken
Bratkartoffeln fpl fried potatoes pl
Bratwurst (pl **Bratwürste**) f fried sausage
Brauch (pl **Bräuche**) m custom
brauchbar adj ❶ usable ▷ *Dieses alte Gerät ist nicht mehr brauchbar.* The old appliance is no longer usable. ❷ capable ▷ *Sie ist eine sehr brauchbare Mitarbeiterin.* She's a very capable colleague.
brauchen vb [48] ❶ to need ▷ *Wir brauchen noch Brot und Butter.* We still need bread and butter. ▷ *Dazu brauche ich mindestens zwei Tage.* I'll need at least two days. ❷ to have to ▷ *Du brauchst heute nicht zu kommen.* You don't have to come today. ▷ *Du brauchst nur Bescheid zu sagen, dann helfe ich dir.* You only have to let me know and I'll help you.; **Das kann ich gut brauchen.** I could really do with that.
Brauerei f brewery
braun adj ❶ brown ▷ *Sie hat braune Haare und braune Augen.* She has brown hair and brown eyes. ❷ tanned ▷ *Wir kamen ganz braun aus den Ferien zurück.* We came back all tanned from our holidays.
Braut (pl **Bräute**) f bride
Bräutigam (pl **Bräutigame**) m bridegroom
Brautpaar (pl **Brautpaare**) nt bride and groom pl
brav adj good ▷ *Die Kinder waren brav.* The children were good.; **Er ist ganz brav ins Bett gegangen.** He went to bed as good as gold.

Be careful! **brav** does not mean brave.

bravo! excl well done!
BRD f (= Bundesrepublik Deutschland) Federal Republic of Germany

GERMAN > ENGLISH | 47 | **Briefträgerin**

brechen (pres **bricht**, imperf **brach**, perf **hat/ist gebrochen**) vb [11]

> For the perfect tense use **haben** when the verb has an object and **sein** when there is no object. Use **haben** for 'to vomit'.

❶ to break ▷ *Der Zweig ist gebrochen*. The branch broke. ▷ *Ich habe den Stock in zwei Teile gebrochen*. I broke the stick in two. ▷ *Ich habe mir den rechten Arm gebrochen*. I've broken my right arm. ▷ *Sie hat ihr Versprechen gebrochen*. She broke her promise. ▷ *einen Rekord brechen* to break a record ❷ to vomit ▷ *Ihm wurde schlecht, und er musste brechen*. He felt ill and had to vomit.

breit adj wide ▷ *Das ist ein breiter Fluss.* That's a wide river. ▷ *Das Brett ist fünfzehn Zentimeter breit.* The plank is fifteen centimetres wide.

Breitband nt broadband

Breitbandanschluss (pl **Breitbandanschlüsse**) m broadband connection

Breite f width ▷ *die Breite des Tisches* the width of the table

Bremen nt Bremen
- The 'Free Hanseatic City of Bremen' is
- one of the 16 **Länder**. It is a 'city-state'
- like Berlin and Hamburg, and is
- made up of the cities Bremen and
- Bremerhaven. It is the smallest **Land**,
- but the second-oldest city-republic in
- the world.

Bremse f ❶ brake ▷ *Sie trat auf die Bremse.* She stepped on the brakes. ❷ horsefly ▷ *Wir sind von Bremsen gestochen worden.* We were bitten by horseflies.

bremsen vb [36] to brake ▷ *Als er das Kind sah, bremste er.* When he saw the child, he braked.; **Sie versuchte, das Auto zu bremsen.** She tried to stop the car.; **Sie ist nicht zu bremsen.** There's no stopping her.

brennen (imperf **brannte**, perf **hat gebrannt**) vb [12] ❶ to burn ▷ *Das Holz ist zu nass, es brennt nicht.* The wood's too wet, it won't burn. ▷ *Im Wohnzimmer brennt Licht.* There's a light burning in the living room. ▷ *Der Schnaps brennt auf der Zunge.* The schnapps burns your tongue. ▷ *ein Loch in etwas brennen* to burn a hole in something ❷ to be on fire ▷ *Das Haus brannte.* The house was on fire.; **sich brennen** to burn oneself; **darauf brennen, etwas zu tun** to be dying to do something

Brennnessel f stinging nettle

Brett (pl **Bretter**) nt ❶ board ▷ *Die Hütte bestand aus ein paar zusammengenagelten Brettern.* The hut consisted of a few boards nailed together. ▷ *Sie stellte die Schachfiguren aufs Brett.* She set the chessmen on the board. ❷ shelf ▷ *Die Gewürze stehen auf einem Brett über dem Herd.* The spices are on a shelf above the cooker.; **das Schwarze Brett** the notice board

> Word for word, **das Schwarze Brett** means 'the black board'.

Ich hatte ein Brett vor dem Kopf. My mind went blank.

Brezel f pretzel

bricht vb see **brechen**

Brief (pl **Briefe**) m letter

Brieffreund (pl **Brieffreunde**) m pen friend

Brieffreundin f pen friend

Briefkasten (pl **Briefkästen**) m ❶ letterbox ❷ postbox

Briefmarke f stamp

Brieftasche f wallet

Briefträger (pl **Briefträger**) m postman ▷ *Günter ist Briefträger.* Günter's a postman.

Briefträgerin f postwoman ▷ *Meine Tante ist Briefträgerin.* My aunt's a postwoman.

Briefumschlag (pl **Briefumschläge**) m envelope

brief vb see **braten**

Brille f ❶ glasses pl ▷ *Lesley trägt eine Brille.* Lesley wears glasses. ▷ *eine Brille a pair of glasses* ❷ goggles pl ▷ *Beim Schweißen sollte man eine Brille tragen.* You should wear goggles when welding. ❸ toilet seat ▷ *Ich hasse es, wenn Männer die Brille oben lassen.* I hate it when men leave the toilet seat up.

bringen (imperf **brachte**, perf **hat gebracht**) vb [13] ❶ to bring ▷ *Unsere Gäste haben uns einen schönen Blumenstrauß gebracht.* Our guests have brought us a lovely bunch of flowers. ▷ *Kann ich meine Schwester mit zur Party bringen?* Can I bring my sister to the party? ❷ to take ▷ *Meine Freunde haben mich zum Flughafen gebracht.* My friends took me to the airport. ▷ *jemanden nach Hause bringen* to take somebody home ❸ to bring in ▷ *Diese Anlage bringt fünf Prozent Zinsen.* This investment brings in five per cent interest. ❹ to publish ▷ *Alle Zeitungen brachten diese Geschichte auf der ersten Seite.* All the newspapers published this story on the first page. ❺ to be on ▷ *Sieh mal in der Zeitung nach, was das Theater bringt.* Look in the paper to see what's on at the theatre.; **jemanden zu etwas bringen** to make somebody do something; **jemanden dazu bringen, etwas zu tun** to get somebody to do something; **es über sich bringen, etwas zu tun** to bring oneself to do something; **jemanden um etwas bringen** to cheat somebody out of something; **jemanden in Gefahr bringen** to put somebody in danger; **Unser Computer bringt's nicht.** (informal) Our computer's rubbish.; **Das bringt nichts!** That's no use!

Brite (gen **Briten**, pl **Briten**) m Briton; **die Briten** the British

Britin f Briton
britisch adj British
Brombeere f blackberry
Broschüre f brochure
Brot (pl **Brote**) nt ❶ bread ▷ *Haben wir noch Brot im Haus?* Do we still have some bread in the house? ❷ loaf ▷ *Kannst du für die Party drei Brote holen?* Can you get three loaves for the party?

Brötchen (pl **Brötchen**) nt roll
browsen (perf **hat gebrowst**) vb [38] to browse

Bruch (pl **Brüche**) m ❶ fracture ▷ *Sie wurde mit einem Bruch ins Krankenhaus eingeliefert.* She was taken to hospital with a fracture.; **zu Bruch gehen** to get broken ❷ hernia ▷ *Trag das nicht allein, du hebst dir sonst einen Bruch!* Don't carry that on your own, you'll give yourself a hernia! ❸ fraction ▷ *Das Rechnen mit Brüchen haben wir noch nicht gelernt.* We haven't learned fractions yet.

Brücke f bridge
Bruder (pl **Brüder**) m brother
brüllen vb [38] ❶ to roar ▷ *Der Löwe brüllte.* The lion roared.; **Er brüllte vor Schmerz.** He screamed with pain.
brummen vb [38] ❶ to growl ▷ *Der Bär brummte.* The bear growled. ❷ to buzz ▷ *Eine dicke Fliege brummte durchs Zimmer.* A huge fly buzzed around the room.; **etwas brummen** to mumble something

Brunnen (pl **Brunnen**) m ❶ fountain ▷ *Am Marktplatz steht ein Brunnen.* There's a fountain in the market square. ❷ well ▷ *Wasser aus dem Brunnen* water from the well

Brust (pl **Brüste**) f breast ▷ *Sie hat kleine Brüste.* She has small breasts.
brutal adj brutal
Brutalität f brutality
brutto adv gross
Buch (pl **Bücher**) nt book

buchen vb [48] to book ▷ *Wir haben eine Reise nach Kreta gebucht.* We've booked a trip to Crete.

Bücherei f library

Bücherregal (pl **Bücherregale**) nt bookcase

Buchhalter (pl **Buchhalter**) m accountant

Buchhandlung f bookshop

Buchladen (pl **Buchläden**) m bookshop

Büchse f tin ▷ *Sie bewahrt den Tee in einer Büchse auf.* She keeps her tea in a tin.

Büchsenöffner (pl **Büchsenöffner**) m tin opener

Buchstabe (gen **Buchstabens**, pl **Buchstaben**) m letter of the alphabet

buchstabieren (perf **hat buchstabiert**) vb [76] to spell

sich **bücken** vb [48] to bend down

Bude f stall ▷ *Die Buden auf dem Jahrmarkt* the stalls at the fair; **Kommt ihr noch mit auf meine Bude?** Do you want to come back to my place?

Bügel (pl **Bügel**) m hanger

Bügeleisen (pl **Bügeleisen**) nt iron ▷ *Ich habe mir die Hand am Bügeleisen verbrannt.* I burnt my hand on the iron.

bügeln vb [34] to iron

Bühne f stage ▷ *auf der Bühne stehen* to be on stage

buk vb see **backen**

Bulgarien nt Bulgaria

Bummel (pl **Bummel**) m stroll ▷ *Wir machten einen Bummel an der Donau entlang.* We went for a stroll along the Danube.

bummeln vb [88]

> Use **sein** to form the perfect tense for 'to stroll' and **haben** for 'to dawdle'.

① to stroll ▷ *Wir sind durch die Stadt gebummelt.* We strolled through the town. ② to dawdle ▷ *Heute hast du auf dem Heimweg aber gebummelt.* You've really been dawdling on your way home today.

Bund (pl **Bünde**) m ① association ▷ *Die Bauern schlossen sich zu einem Bund zusammen.* The farmers formed an association.; **Bund und Länder** the Federal Government and the Länder ② waistband ▷ *Die Hose ist am Bund zu eng.* The trousers are too tight at the waistband.

Bundes- prefix Federal

Bundeskanzler (pl **Bundeskanzler**) m Federal Chancellor

Bundeskanzlerin f Federal Chancellor

Bundesland (pl **Bundesländer**) nt state

Bundesliga f Premier League

Bundesrat m upper chamber of the German Parliament

- The **Bundesrat** is not directly elected,
- but is made up of representatives of
- the 16 **Länder**. In many cases,
- **Bundesrat** approval is required
- before laws (particularly amendments
- to the constitution) can be passed.

Bundesregierung f Federal government

Bundesrepublik f Federal Republic ▷ *die Bundesrepublik Deutschland* the Federal Republic of Germany

Bundestag m German Parliament

- The **Bundestag** is the German
- parliamentary assembly, elected
- every four years.

Bundeswehr f German Armed Forces pl

bunt adj ① brightly-coloured ▷ *Sie hatte ein buntes Kleid an.* She was wearing a brightly-coloured dress. ② mixed ▷ *Unsere Klasse ist ein buntes Häufchen.* Our class is a mixed bunch.; **Mir wird es zu bunt.** It's getting too much for me.

> Word for word, **Mir wird es zu bunt** means 'It's getting too colourful for me'.

Burg (*pl* **Burgen**) *f* castle
Bürger (*pl* **Bürger**) *m* citizen
Bürgerin *f* citizen
bürgerlich *adj* ❶ civil ▷ *bürgerliche Rechte* civil rights ❷ middle-class ▷ *eine gute bürgerliche Familie* a good middle-class family
Bürgermeister (*pl* **Bürgermeister**) *m* mayor
Bürgermeisterin *f* mayor
Bürgersteig (*pl* **Bürgersteige**) *m* pavement
Büro (*pl* **Büros**) *nt* office
Büroklammer *f* paper clip
Bürste *f* brush
bürsten (*perf* **hat gebürstet**) *vb* [2] to brush
Bus (*gen* **Busses**, *pl* **Busse**) *m* bus ▷ *mit dem Bus fahren* to go by bus
Busbahnhof (*pl* **Busbahnhöfe**) *m* bus station
Busch (*pl* **Büsche**) *m* bush
Busen (*pl* **Busen**) *m* bosom
Busfahrer (*pl* **Busfahrer**) *m* bus driver
Bushaltestelle *f* bus stop
Buslinie *f* bus route
Bußgeld (*pl* **Bußgelder**) *nt* fine
Büstenhalter (*pl* **Büstenhalter**) *m* bra
Butter *f* butter
Butterbrot (*pl* **Butterbrote**) *nt* bread and butter

C

Café (*pl* **Cafés**) *nt* café ▷ *Sonntags gehen wir immer ins Café.* On Sundays we always go to a café.
Cafeteria (*pl* **Cafeterias**) *f* cafeteria
Callcenter (*pl* **Callcenter**) *nt* call centre
campen *vb* [**38**] to camp
Campingplatz (*gen* **Campingplatzes**, *pl* **Campingplätze**) *m* campsite
CD (*pl* **CDs**) *f* CD
CD-Spieler (*pl* **CD-Spieler**) *m* CD player
Cent (*pl* **Cents**) *m* cent
Champignon (*pl* **Champignons**) *m* button mushroom
Chance *f* chance
Chaos (*gen* **Chaos**) *nt* chaos
chaotisch *adj* chaotic
Charakter (*pl* **Charakter**) *m* character
charmant *adj* charming
Charterflug (*pl* **Charterflüge**) *m* charter flight
Chat (*pl* **Chats**) *m* (internet) chat
Chatroom (*pl* **Chatrooms**) *m* chat room

chatten vb [**2**] to chat ▷ *Wir haben den ganzen Abend über gechattet.* We chatted all evening.

Chef (pl **Chefs**) m ❶ head ▷ *Er ist Chef einer großen Firma.* He's the head of a large company. ❷ boss ▷ *Da muss ich den Chef fragen.* I'll have to ask my boss.

Chefin f boss

Chemie f chemistry

Chemiker (pl **Chemiker**) m industrial chemist

chemisch adj chemical; **chemische Reinigung** dry cleaning

Chile nt Chile

China nt China

Chinese (gen **Chinesen**, pl **Chinesen**) m Chinese; **die Chinesen** the Chinese

Chinesin f Chinese

chinesisch adj Chinese

Chips pl crisps pl

> Be careful! The German word **Chips** does not mean chips.

Chirurg (gen **Chirurgen**, pl **Chirurgen**) m surgeon

Chirurgie f surgery

Chirurgin f surgeon

Chor (pl **Chöre**) m choir ▷ *Sie singt im Chor.* She sings in a choir.

Christ (gen **Christen**, pl **Christen**) m Christian ▷ *Er ist Christ.* He's a Christian.

Christin f Christian ▷ *Sie ist Christin.* She's a Christian.

christlich adj Christian

Club (pl **Clubs**) m club

cm abbr (= Zentimeter) cm

Cola (pl **Colas**) f Coke®

Computer (pl **Computer**) m computer

Computerspiel (pl **Computerspiele**) nt computer game

cool adj cool

Cousin (pl **Cousins**) m cousin

Cousine f cousin

Covid-19 nt Covid

Creme (pl **Cremes**) f ❶ cream ▷ *eine Handcreme* a hand cream ❷ polish ▷ *Hast du schwarze Schuhcreme?* Do you have any black shoe polish? ❸ mousse ▷ *eine Zitronencreme* a lemon mousse

Curry m curry powder

Currywurst (pl **Currywürste**) f curried sausage

Cyberkriminalität f cybercrime

d

da *adv, conj* ❶ there ▷ *Da ist es schön.* It's beautiful there. ▷ *da draußen* out there ▷ *Da haben wir Glück gehabt.* We were lucky there.; **da sein** to be there ❷ here ▷ *Da liegt meine Brille ja.* Here are my glasses. ▷ *Da bin ich.* Here I am.; **Ist noch Milch da?** Is there any milk left? ❸ since ▷ *Da du gerade hier bist ...* Since you're here ...

dabei *adv* nahe dabei close by; **Sie hatten ihren Hund dabei.** They had their dog with them.; **Was ist schon dabei?** What of it?; **Es ist doch nichts dabei, wenn ...** It doesn't matter if ...; **Bleiben wir dabei.** Let's leave it at that.; **Es bleibt dabei.** That's settled.; **dabei sein** to be there; **Er war gerade dabei, zu gehen.** He was just about to leave.

Dach (*pl* **Dächer**) *nt* roof
Dachboden (*pl* **Dachböden**) *m* attic
dachte *vb see* **denken**
Dackel (*pl* **Dackel**) *m* dachshund
dadurch *adv, conj* ❶ through it ▷ *Er muss dadurch gekrochen sein.* He must have crawled through it. ❷ that's why ▷ *Dadurch habe ich mich verspätet.* That's why I was late. ❸ as a result

dafür *adv* ❶ for it ▷ *Was hast du dafür bezahlt?* How much did you pay for it? ▷ *Was bekomme ich dafür?* What will I get for it?; **Er ist bekannt dafür.** He's well-known for that. ❷ instead ▷ *Wenn du nicht mit ins Schwimmbad kannst, dann komm dafür doch mit ins Kino.* If you can't come with us to the swimming pool, then come along to the cinema instead.; **Er kann nichts dafür.** He can't help it.

dagegen *adv, conj* ❶ against it ▷ *Was hast du dagegen?* What have you got against it? ▷ *Ich war dagegen.* I was against it.; **Ich habe nichts dagegen.** I don't mind.; **Dagegen kann man nichts tun.** You can't do anything about it. ❷ into it ▷ *Er sah den Baum nicht und rannte dagegen.* He didn't see the tree and ran into it. ❸ for it ▷ *Das ist jetzt mein Ball, ich habe meine Murmeln dagegen getauscht.* This is my ball now — I swapped my marbles for it. ❹ by comparison ▷ *Dagegen ist unser Haus klein.* Our house is small by comparison. ❺ however ▷ *Sie wollte gehen, er dagegen wollte bleiben.* She wanted to leave; however he wanted to stay.

daheim *adv* at home
daher *adv, conj* ❶ from there ▷ *Daher komme ich gerade.* I've just come from there. ❷ that's where ▷ *Das war ein schwerer Unfall; daher hat er sein kaputtes Bein.* It was a serious accident; that's where he got his bad leg. ❸ that's why ▷ *Sie war krank und konnte daher nicht mitkommen.* She was ill, and that's why she couldn't come.
dahin *adv* there ▷ *Dahin gehe ich jetzt.* I'm going there now.
dahinten *adv* over there

GERMAN > ENGLISH

dahinter adv behind it ▷ *Er versteckte sich dahinter.* He hid behind it.

damals adv in those days

Dame f ❶ lady ❷ *(chess, cards)* queen ❸ draughts sg ▷ *Dame ist mein Lieblingsspiel.* Draughts is my favourite game.

damit adv, conj ❶ with it ▷ *Wisch damit den Tisch ab.* Wipe the table with it. ❷ by that ▷ *Was meint er damit?* What does he mean by that?; **Was willst du damit sagen?** What are you getting at?; **Genug damit!** That's enough of that!; **Damit eilt es nicht.** There's no hurry. ❸ so that ▷ *Ich sage dir das, damit du das weißt.* I'm telling you so that you know.

Dampf m steam

dampfen vb [48] ❶ to vape ❷ to puff

Dampfer (pl **Dampfer**) m steamer ▷ *mit dem Dampfer fahren* to go by steamer; **Du bist auf dem falschen Dampfer.** *(informal)* You've got the wrong idea.

> Word for word, **Du bist auf dem falschen Dampfer** means 'You're on the wrong steamer'.

danach adv ❶ afterwards ▷ *Ich habe etwas getrunken, und danach fühlte ich mich besser.* I had something to drink and afterwards felt much better. ❷ accordingly ▷ *Verhalte dich bitte danach.* Please behave accordingly.

Däne (gen **Dänen**, pl **Dänen**) m Dane

daneben adv ❶ beside it ❷ by comparison

Dänemark nt Denmark

Dänin f Dane

dänisch adj Danish

dank prep

> **dank** takes the genitive or dative.

thanks to ▷ *Dank meiner Schwester habe ich noch rechtzeitig davon erfahren.* Thanks to my sister I found out about it in time.

Dank m thanks pl ▷ *Unser Dank gilt vor allem Herrn Morris.* Our thanks to Mr Morris in particular.; **Vielen Dank!** Many thanks.

dankbar adj grateful ▷ *Ich bin dir sehr dankbar.* I'm very grateful to you.; **eine dankbare Aufgabe** a rewarding task

danke excl thank you; **Danke sehr!** Thank you.; **Danke schön!** Thank you very much.; **Nein, danke!** No, thanks.

danken vb [38] to thank ▷ *Ich möchte dir dafür danken.* I'd like to thank you for that.; **Nichts zu danken!** Don't mention it!

dann adv then; **dann und wann** now and then

daran adv ❶ on it ▷ *ein Päckchen mit einem Zettel daran* a parcel with a label on it ❷ of it ▷ *Er ist daran gestorben.* He died of it. ▷ *Ich habe nicht daran gedacht.* I didn't think of it.; **Es liegt daran, dass ...** This is because ...; **das Beste daran** the best thing about it; **Ich war nahe daran, zu gehen.** I was on the point of going.

darauf adv ❶ on it ▷ *Nimm einen Untersetzer und stelle den Topf darauf.* Take a mat and put the pan on it. ❷ afterwards ▷ *kurz darauf* shortly afterwards; **die Tage darauf** the following days; **am Tag darauf** the next day; **Er ging darauf zu.** He walked towards it.; **Es kommt ganz darauf an, ob ...** It all depends whether ...

daraus adv ❶ out of it ▷ *Sie nahm einen Keks daraus.* She took a biscuit out of it. ❷ of it ▷ *Was ist daraus geworden?* What became of it?; **Daraus geht hervor, dass ...** This means that ...

darf vb see **dürfen**

darin adv in it ▷ *eine Dose mit Keksen darin* a tin with biscuits in it; **Darin sehe ich kein Problem.** I don't see any problem there.

Darm (pl **Därme**) m intestine

darstellen (perf **hat dargestellt**) vb [4] to portray ▷ *etwas in einem günstigen*

Licht darstellen to portray something in a good light

darüber adv ❶ over it ▷ *ein Tisch mit einer Lampe darüber* a table with a light over it ▷ *Da war eine Brücke, wir aber nicht darüber gefahren.* There was a bridge, but we didn't drive over it. ❷ about it ▷ *Wir haben darüber gesprochen.* We talked about it. ▷ *Denk mal darüber nach.* Think about it. ❸ more ▷ *Sie verdient fünftausend oder vielleicht sogar darüber.* She earns five thousand or maybe even more.

darum adv, conj ❶ round it ▷ *Sie machte ein rotes Band darum.* She put a red ribbon round it.; **Es geht darum, dass ...** The important thing is to ...; **Er würde viel darum geben, wenn ...** He would give a lot to ... ❷ that's why ▷ *Darum bin ich nicht gekommen.* That's why I didn't come.; **Ich tue es darum, weil ...** I'm doing it because ...

darunter adv ❶ under it ▷ *Der Topf ist heiß, leg einen Untersetzer darunter.* The pot's hot, put a mat under it.; **ein Stockwerk darunter** one floor below ❷ less ▷ *Er verdient nur dreitausend Euro oder vielleicht sogar darunter.* He earns only three thousand euros or maybe even less.; **Was verstehst du darunter?** What do you understand by that?

das art, pron
■ *das* is the definite neuter article.
❶ the ▷ *das Auto* the car; *das Leben* life; **Er hat sich das Knie verletzt.** He's hurt his knee. ❷ who ▷ *das Kind, das dir das gesagt hat* the child who told you; **das Kind, das du gesehen hast** the child you saw ❸ which ▷ *das Fahrrad, das du da siehst* the bike which you can see over there; **das mit dem roten Sattel** the one with the red saddle ❹ that ▷ *Das habe ich nicht gehört.* I didn't hear that.; **das da** that one

dasjenige pron the one (who/that) ▷ *dasjenige, das ich ausgesucht habe* the one that I chose

dass conj that ▷ *Ich bin böse, dass er nicht gekommen ist.* I'm annoyed that he didn't come. ▷ *Ich weiß, dass du besser in Mathe bist als ich.* I know you're better at maths than me.

dasselbe pron the same ▷ *dasselbe Kind* the same child

dastehen (*imperf* **stand da**, *perf* **hat dagestanden**) vb [72] to stand there

Datei f file

Daten ntpl data pl

Datenbank (pl **Datenbanken**) f database

Datenverarbeitung f data processing

Dativ (pl **Dative**) m dative

Datum (pl **Daten**) nt date

Dauer f ❶ duration ▷ *für die Dauer meines Aufenthalts* for the duration of my stay ❷ length ▷ *die Dauer einer Reise* the length of a journey ▷ *die Dauer eines Anrufs* the length of a call; **von Dauer sein** to be permanent; **Ihr Glück war nur von kurzer Dauer.** Their happiness was only short-lived.; **auf die Dauer (1)** in the long run ▷ *Auf die Dauer wird ihm das langweilig werden.* He'll get bored with it in the long run. **(2)** indefinitely ▷ *Auf die Dauer geht das aber nicht.* That can't go on indefinitely.

dauern vb [88] to last ▷ *Der Krieg hat zehn Jahre gedauert.* The war lasted ten years.; **lange dauern** to take a long time; **Wie lange dauert das denn noch?** How much longer is this going to take?

dauernd adj, adv constant ▷ *Ich konnte sein dauerndes Stöhnen nicht ertragen.* I couldn't stand his constant moaning.; **Musst du mich dauernd stören?** Do you have to constantly interrupt me?

Daumen (pl **Daumen**) m thumb; **Ich drücke dir die Daumen.** I'll keep my fingers crossed for you.

davon adv ❶ of them ▷ *Sie nahm zwei davon.* She took two of them.; **Sie nahm hundert Gramm davon.** She took a hundred grams. ❷ away ▷ *Er lief davon.* He ran away. ❸ from it ▷ *Sie hat den Knopf davon abgetrennt.* She removed the button from it.; **Sie bekommt Kopfschmerzen davon.** It gives her a headache.; **davon abgesehen** apart from that ❹ about it ▷ *davon sprechen* to talk about it ▷ *Sie weiß nichts davon.* She doesn't know anything about it.; **Was habe ich davon?** What's the point?; **Das kommt davon!** That's what you get.

davonkommen (*imperf* **kam davon**, *perf* **ist davongekommen**) vb [40] to escape ▷ *Wir sind noch einmal davongekommen.* We've had a lucky escape.

davor adv ❶ in front of it ▷ *Ich stellte mich davor.* I stood in front of it. ❷ first ▷ *Du solltest davor aber noch zum Friseur.* You ought to go to the hairdresser's first.; **Ich habe dich davor gewarnt.** I warned you about it.

dazu adv with it ▷ *Was sollen wir dazu trinken?* What shall we drink with it?; **ein Beispiel dazu** an example of this; **seine Gedanken dazu** his thoughts on this; **dazu fähig sein** to be capable of it; **und dazu noch** and in addition

dazwischen adv ❶ in between ▷ *Wir können dazwischen ja eine Pause machen.* We can have a break in between. ❷ between them ▷ *Siehst du die beiden Pfosten, stell dich dazwischen.* You see the two posts? Go and stand between them. ▷ *der Unterschied dazwischen* the difference between them

DDR (*gen* **DDR**) f (= *Deutsche Demokratische Republik*) GDR ▷ *die ehemalige DDR* the former GDR

Decke f ❶ ceiling ▷ *Wir haben die Decke des Kinderzimmers gestrichen.* We've painted the ceiling of the children's room. ❷ blanket ▷ *eine Wolldecke* a woollen blanket; **eine Tischdecke** a tablecloth

Deckel (pl **Deckel**) m lid

decken vb [38] to cover ▷ *Er deckte die Hand über seine Augen.* He covered his eyes with his hand.; **den Tisch decken** to lay the table

dehnen vb [38] to stretch ▷ *Er dehnte sich und gähnte.* He stretched and yawned.

dein adj ❶ your ▷ *Dein Englischlehrer ist nett.* Your English teacher's nice. ▷ *Hat deine Mutter das erlaubt?* Did your mother let you? ▷ *Ist das dein Buch?* Is that your book? ▷ *Wo sind deine Eltern?* Where are your parents? ❷ yours ▷ *Der Bleistift hier, ist das deiner?* Is this pencil yours? ▷ *Meine Mutter heißt Ulla, wie heißt deine?* My mother's called Ulla; what's yours called? ▷ *Mein Fahrrad ist kaputt, kann ich deins benutzen?* My bike's broken; can I use yours?

deinetwegen adv ❶ for your sake ▷ *Ich habe deinetwegen darauf verzichtet.* I did without for your sake. ❷ on your account ▷ *Er hat sich deinetwegen aufgeregt.* He got upset on your account.

deklinieren (*perf* **hat dekliniert**) vb [76] to decline

Delphin (pl **Delphine**) m dolphin

dem *art*, *pron*
■ **dem** is the dative of **der** and **das**.
the ▷ *auf dem Tisch* on the table; **Gib es dem Mann.** Give it to the man.; **der Mann, dem ich es gegeben habe** the man I gave it to

demnächst adv shortly

Demokratie f democracy

demokratisch adj democratic

Demonstration f demonstration

demonstrieren | 56

demonstrieren (*perf* hat demonstriert) *vb* [76] to demonstrate

den *art, pron*
▌ **den** is the accusative of **der**.
① the ▷ *Ich sehe den Mann.* I can see the man. ▷ *durch den Wald* through the wood; **Er hat sich den Fuß verletzt.** He's hurt his foot.; **der Mann, den ich gesehen habe** the man I saw

denen *pron*
▌ **denen** is the dative of **die** (plural).
① whom; **die Leute, denen ich die Bücher gegeben habe** the people I gave the books to; **die Leute, denen ich helfen wollte** the people I wanted to help ② which ▷ *Probleme, denen wir nicht gewachsen sind* problems which we can't cope with

denkbar *adj* conceivable

denken (*imperf* dachte, *perf* hat gedacht) *vb* [14] to think; **an jemanden/etwas denken** to think of someone/something; **sich etwas denken** ▷ *Das kann ich mir denken.* I can imagine.

Denkmal (*pl* Denkmäler) *nt* monument

denn *conj, adv* ① because ▷ *Ich habe sie nicht gesehen, denn sie war schon weg.* I didn't see her because she had already left. ② than ▷ *besser denn je* better than ever; **es sei denn ...** unless ...; **Warum denn?** But why?

dennoch *conj* nevertheless

der *art, pron*
▌ **der** is the definite masculine article and genitive and dative of **die**.
① the ▷ *der Mann* the man; **der Tod** death; **das Auto der Frau** the woman's car; **Gib es der Frau.** Give it to the woman. ② who ▷ *der, der dir das gesagt hat* the person who told you that; **die Frau, der ich es gegeben habe** the woman I gave it to ③ which ▷ *der Computer, der mir gehört* the computer which belongs to me; **der mit der Brille** the one with glasses; **der da** that one

deren *pron*
▌ **deren** is the genitive singular of **die**.
whose ▷ *meine Freundin, deren Mutter letzte Woche gestorben ist* my friend whose mother died last week

derjenige *pron* the one (who/that) ▷ *Derjenige, der das getan hat, soll sich entschuldigen.* The one who did it should apologize.

derselbe *pron* the same ▷ *derselbe Mann* the same man

deshalb *adv* that's why

dessen *pron*
▌ **dessen** is the genitive of **der** and **das**.
whose ▷ *mein Freund, dessen Schwester krank ist* my friend whose sister is ill

deswegen *conj* that's why ▷ *Hat er deswegen so geschimpft?* Is that why he was so mad?; **Es ist spät, deswegen gehen wir jetzt.** It's late, so we're leaving.; **Ich sage das deswegen, weil ...** The reason I'm saying this is that ...

deutlich *adj, adv* ① clear ▷ *mit deutlicher Stimme* in a clear voice ② clearly ▷ *Drück dich bitte deutlicher aus.* Please speak more clearly. ▷ *Es war deutlich zu sehen.* It was clearly visible.; **ein deutlicher Unterschied** a distinct difference

deutsch *adj* German

Deutsch (*gen* Deutschen) *nt* German ▷ *Er lernt Deutsch in der Schule.* He's learning German at school.; **auf Deutsch** in German

Deutsche (*gen* Deutschen, *pl* Deutschen) *mf* German; **Ich bin Deutscher.** I'm German.

Deutschland *nt* Germany

Dezember (*gen* Dezember *or* Dezembers, *pl* Dezember) *m* December ▷ *im Dezember* in December ▷ *am vierten Dezember* on the fourth of

December ▷ Ulm, den 5. Dezember 2025 Ulm, 5 December 2025 ▷ Heute ist der sechste Dezember. Today is the sixth of December.

d. h. abbr (= das heißt) i.e.

Dia (pl **Dias**) nt slide

Dialekt (pl **Dialekte**) m dialect

Diamant (gen **Diamanten**, pl **Diamanten**) m diamond

Diät f diet ▷ Sie muss Diät halten. She has to stick to a strict diet.

dich pron ❶ you ▷ Ich habe dich gesehen. I saw you. ❷ yourself ▷ Sieh dich mal im Spiegel an. Look at yourself in the mirror.

dicht adj, adv ❶ dense ▷ dichte Wälder dense woods ❷ thick ▷ dichter Nebel thick fog ❸ watertight ▷ Ist der Behälter dicht? Is the container watertight?; **Die Gasleitung war nicht dicht.** There was a leak in the gas pipe.; **dichter Verkehr** heavy traffic; **dicht an** close to

Dichter (pl **Dichter**) m poet

dick adj ❶ thick ▷ Das Brett ist drei Zentimeter dick. The plank's three centimetres thick. ❷ fat ▷ Ich bin zu dick. I'm too fat.

die art, pron

die is the definite feminine article and the definite article plural.

❶ the ▷ die Frau the woman ▷ die Kinder the children; **die Liebe** love; **Er hat sich die Hand verletzt.** He's hurt his hand. ❷ who ▷ die, die dir das gesagt hat the person who told you that; **die Frau, die du gesehen hast** the woman you saw ❸ which ▷ die Uhr, die mir gehört the watch which belongs to me; **die mit der Brille** the one with glasses; **die da** that one

Dieb (pl **Diebe**) m thief

Diebstahl (pl **Diebstähle**) m theft

diejenige pron the one (who/that) ▷ Gerade diejenige, die mir helfen kann, ist verschwunden. The only one who can help me has disappeared.

Diele f hall ▷ Sie stand vor dem Spiegel in der Diele. She stood in front of the mirror in the hall.

dienen (perf **hat gedient**) vb [38] to serve ▷ Es dient einem guten Zweck. It serves a useful purpose.; **Womit kann ich Ihnen dienen?** What can I do for you?

Dienst (pl **Dienste**) m service; **Dienst haben** to be on duty

Dienstag (pl **Dienstage**) m Tuesday ▷ am Dienstag on Tuesday

dienstags adv on Tuesdays

dies pron ❶ this ▷ Dies ist unser Haus. This is our house. ❷ these ▷ Dies sind meine Bücher. These are my books.

diese pron ❶ this ▷ diese Woche this week ▷ dieser Monat this month ▷ dieses Jahr this year ❷ these ▷ diese Bücher these books ❸ this one ▷ Ich möchte diesen hier. I'd like this one.; **Ich suche ein Paar Sandalen, kann ich diese anprobieren?** I'm looking for a pair of sandals; can I try these ones on?

Diesel m diesel

dieselbe pron the same ▷ dieselbe Frau the same woman

diesmal adv this time

digital adj digital ▷ die digitale Revolution the digital revolution

Diktat (pl **Diktate**) nt dictation

Ding (pl **Dinge**) nt thing

Diplom (pl **Diplome**) nt diploma

Diplomatie f diplomacy

diplomatisch adj diplomatic

dir pron

dir is the dative of du.

❶ you ▷ Ich habe es dir doch gesagt. I told you so. ❷ to you ▷ Ich habe es dir gestern gegeben. I gave it to you yesterday.

direkt adj direct ▷ Der Flug geht direkt. It's a direct flight.

Direktor (pl **Direktoren**) m ❶ director ▷ der Direktor der Firma the director of the company ❷ head teacher ▷ Mein

Bruder musste gestern zum Direktor. My brother was sent to the head teacher yesterday.

Direktorin f ❶ director ❷ head teacher

Diskothek f disco

Diskussion f discussion; **zur Diskussion stehen** to be under discussion

Diskuswerfen nt throwing the discus

diskutieren (perf **hat diskutiert**) vb [76] to discuss ▷ *Wir haben über Politik diskutiert.* We discussed politics.

Diversität f diversity

doch adv, conj ❶ after all ▷ *Sie ist doch noch gekommen.* She came after all. ❷ anyway ▷ *Du machst ja doch, was du willst.* You do what you want anyway. ❸ but ▷ *Ich habe ihn eingeladen, doch er hatte keine Lust.* I invited him, but he didn't feel like it. ▷ *Sie ist doch noch so jung.* But she's still so young. ❹ yes

doch is used to contradict a negative statement.
▷ *Du magst doch keine Süßigkeiten.* — Doch! You don't like sweets. — Yes I do. ▷ *Das ist nicht wahr.* — Doch! That's not true. — Yes it is!; **Komm doch.** Do come.; **Lass ihn doch.** Just leave him.

Doktor (pl **Doktoren**) m doctor ▷ *Er ist Doktor der Philosophie.* He's a doctor of philosophy.

Doktorin f doctor

Dokument nt document

Dokumentarfilm (pl **Dokumentarfilme**) m documentary

dolmetschen vb [48] to interpret

Dolmetscher (pl **Dolmetscher**) m interpreter

Dom (pl **Dome**) m cathedral

Donau f Danube

Donner (pl **Donner**) m thunder

donnern vb [88] to thunder ▷ *Es donnerte.* It was thundering.

Donnerstag (pl **Donnerstage**) m Thursday ▷ *am Donnerstag* on Thursday

donnerstags adv on Thursdays

doof adj (informal) thick

Doppelbett (pl **Doppelbetten**) nt double bed

Doppelfenster ntpl double glazing sg

Doppelhaus (gen **Doppelhauses**, pl **Doppelhäuser**) nt semidetached house

Doppelpunkt (pl **Doppelpunkte**) m colon

Doppelstunde f double period

doppelt adj ❶ double ▷ *die doppelte Menge* double the amount ❷ twice the ▷ *der doppelte Preis* twice the price ▷ *die doppelte Geschwindigkeit* twice the speed; **doppelt so viel** twice as much; **in doppelter Ausführung** in duplicate

Doppelzimmer (pl **Doppelzimmer**) nt double room

Dorf (pl **Dörfer**) nt village

dort adv there; **dort drüben** over there

dorther adv from there

dorthin adv there ▷ *Wir gehen jetzt dorthin.* We're going there now.

Dose f tin

Dosenöffner (pl **Dosenöffner**) m tin opener

Dr m (= Doktor) Dr. (= Doctor)

Draht (pl **Drähte**) m wire; **auf Draht sein** to be on the ball

drahtlos adj wireless

Drama (pl **Dramen**) nt drama

dran adv Jetzt bin ich dran! It's my turn now.; **Wer ist dran?** Whose turn is it?; **gut dran sein** to be well-off; **schlecht dran sein** to be in a bad way

drauf adv see **darauf**

draußen adv outside

Dreck m dirt

dreckig adj dirty ▷ *Mach deine Kleider nicht dreckig.* Don't get your clothes dirty.

drehen vb [38] to turn ▷ *Dreh mal deinen Kopf zur Seite.* Turn your head to one side. ▷ *Du musst an dem Rad drehen.* You have to turn the wheel.; **eine Zigarette drehen** to roll a cigarette; **einen Film drehen** to shoot a film; **sich drehen** to turn; **Es dreht sich um ...** It's about ...

drei num three

Drei f ❶ three ❷ satisfactory
* German marks range from one (**sehr gut**) to six (**ungenügend**).

Dreieck (pl **Dreiecke**) nt triangle

dreihundert num three hundred

dreimal adv three times

dreißig num thirty

Dreiviertelstunde f three-quarters of an hour ▷ *Eine Dreiviertelstunde war vergangen.* Three-quarters of an hour had passed.

dreizehn num thirteen

drin adv see **darin**

dringend adj urgent

drinnen adv inside

dritt adj third ▷ *Sie kamen zu dritt.* The three of them came together.

dritte adj third ▷ *Sie antwortete beim dritten Klingeln ab.* She answered on the third ring. ▷ *Er kam als Dritter.* He was the third to arrive.; **die Dritte Welt** the Third World; **das Dritte Reich** the Third Reich

Drittel (pl **Drittel**) nt third

Droge f drug

drogenabhängig adj addicted to drugs

Drogerie f chemist's shop

Drogist (gen **Drogisten**, pl **Drogisten**) m pharmacist

Drogistin f pharmacist

drohen vb [38] to threaten ▷ *jemandem drohen* to threaten somebody

drüben adv over there

drüber adv see **darüber**

Druck (pl **Drucke**) m ❶ pressure ▷ *Der Behälter muss viel Druck aushalten.* The container has to withstand a lot of pressure.; **jemanden unter Druck setzen** to put pressure on somebody ❷ printing ▷ *der Druck eines Buches* the printing of a book ❸ print ▷ *An der Wand hingen Drucke.* There were prints on the wall.

drücken vb [38] ❶ to press ▷ *Er drückte auf den Knopf.* He pressed the button.; **Sie drückte ihm die Hand.** She squeezed his hand. ❷ to pinch ▷ *Meine Schuhe drücken.* My shoes pinch.; **sich vor etwas drücken** to get out of something

Drucker (pl **Drucker**) m printer

Drucksache f printed matter

Dschungel (pl **Dschungel**) m jungle

du pron you ▷ *Hast du das gesehen?* Did you see that?; **du sagen** to use the 'du' form of address
* Only use **du** when speaking to one
* person, and when the person is your
* own age or younger. Use **ihr** for
* several people of your own age or
* younger. If in doubt use the polite
* form **Sie**.

Dudelsack (pl **Dudelsäcke**) m bagpipes pl ▷ *Er spielt Dudelsack.* He plays the bagpipes.

Duft (pl **Düfte**) m scent

duften vb [2] to smell ▷ *Hier duftet es nach Kaffee.* It smells of coffee here.

dumm adj ❶ stupid ▷ *Das ist die dümmste Ausrede, die ich je gehört habe.* That's the stupidest excuse I've ever heard. ❷ bad ▷ *Es ist wirklich zu dumm, dass du nicht gekommen bist.* It's really too bad that you didn't come.; **der Dumme sein** to draw the short straw

dummerweise adv stupidly

Dummheit f ❶ stupidity ▷ *Deine Dummheit ist wirklich grenzenlos.* Your stupidity really knows no bounds. ❷ stupid mistake ▷ *Es war eine Dummheit, ihr das zu erzählen.* It was a stupid mistake telling her that.; **Dummheiten machen** to do something stupid

Dummkopf (pl **Dummköpfe**) m idiot
dunkel adj dark ▷ *Im Zimmer war es dunkel.* It was dark in the room.; **eine dunkle Stimme** a deep voice; **eine dunkle Ahnung** a vague idea; **dunkle Gestalten** sinister figures; **dunkle Geschäfte** shady dealings; **im Dunkeln tappen** to grope about in the dark; **ein Dunkles** a dark beer
Dunkelheit f dark ▷ *Er hat Angst vor der Dunkelheit.* He's afraid of the dark.
dünn adj thin
Dunst (pl **Dünste**) m haze
durch prep, adv

> The preposition **durch** takes the accusative.

❶ through ▷ *durch den Wald* through the wood ▷ *Ich habe die Stelle durch meinen Onkel bekommen.* I got the job through my uncle. ▷ *durch seine Bemühungen* through his efforts ❷ throughout ▷ *die ganze Nacht durch* throughout the night ▷ *den Sommer durch* throughout the summer ❸ owing to ▷ *Durch die Verspätung haben wir den Anschluss verpasst.* Owing to the delay we missed our connection.; **Tod durch Herzschlag** death from a heart attack; **durch die Post** by post; **durch und durch** completely
durcharbeiten (perf **hat durchgearbeitet**) vb [15] to work without a break
durcheinander adv ❶ in a mess ▷ *Warum ist dein Zimmer so durcheinander?* Why is your room in such a mess? ❷ confused ▷ *Ich war völlig durcheinander.* I was completely confused.; **Du bringst mich ganz durcheinander.** You completely confuse me.
Durcheinander nt mess ▷ *In ihrem Zimmer war ein völliges Durcheinander.* Her room was in a complete mess.
durchfahren (pres **fährt durch**, imperf **fuhr durch**, perf **ist durchgefahren**) vb [21] ❶ to drive through ▷ *Wir sind durch einen Tunnel durchgefahren.* We drove through a tunnel. ❷ to drive without a break ▷ *Wir sind die ganze Nacht durchgefahren.* We drove all night without a break.; **Der Zug fährt bis Hamburg durch.** The train runs direct to Hamburg.
Durchfahrt (pl **Durchfahrten**) f way through ▷ *auf unserer Durchfahrt durch Frankreich* on our way through France; **'Durchfahrt verboten'** 'no through road'
Durchfall m diarrhoea
durchfallen (pres **fällt durch**, imperf **fiel durch**, perf **ist durchgefallen**) vb [22] ❶ to fall through ▷ *Die Münze ist durch dieses Gitter durchgefallen.* The coin fell through this grating. ❷ to fail ▷ *Sie ist in der Prüfung durchgefallen.* She failed the exam.
durchführen (perf **hat durchgeführt**) vb [4] to carry out
durchgehen (imperf **ging durch**, perf **ist durchgegangen**) vb [29] ❶ to go through ▷ *durch einen Tunnel durchgehen* to go through a tunnel ❷ to break loose ▷ *Das Pferd ist durchgegangen.* The horse has broken loose.; **jemandem etwas durchgehen lassen** to let somebody get away with something; **ein durchgehender Zug** a through train
durchkommen (imperf **kam durch**, perf **ist durchgekommen**) vb [40] ❶ to get through ▷ *Obwohl die Öffnung sehr schmal war, sind wir durchgekommen.* Although the opening was very narrow, we got through. ❷ to pass ▷ *Es war knapp, aber ich bin durchgekommen.* It was a close shave, but I passed. ❸ to pull through ▷ *Er war schwer verletzt, ist aber durchgekommen.* He was seriously injured, but he pulled through.

GERMAN > ENGLISH

durchlassen (pres **lässt durch**, imperf **ließ durch**, perf **hat durchgelassen**) vb [42] to let through ▷ *Der Ordner wollte uns nicht durchlassen.* The steward didn't want to let us through.; *Der Behälter lässt Wasser durch.* The container isn't watertight.

durchlesen (pres **liest durch**, imperf **las durch**, perf **hat durchgelesen**) vb [45] to read through

Durchmesser (pl **Durchmesser**) m diameter

durchnehmen (pres **nimmt durch**, imperf **nahm durch**, perf **hat durchgenommen**) vb [52] to do ▷ *Wir nehmen gerade Shakespeare durch.* We're doing Shakespeare just now.

Durchreise f journey through ▷ *die Durchreise durch die Schweiz* the journey through Switzerland; *Ich bin nur auf der Durchreise.* I'm just passing through.

durchs = **durch das**

Durchschnitt m average ▷ *über dem Durchschnitt* above average ▷ *unter dem Durchschnitt* below average; *im Durchschnitt* on average

durchschnittlich adj, adv ❶ average ▷ *Ich habe durchschnittliche Noten.* My marks are average. ❷ on average ▷ *Durchschnittlich brauche ich eine Stunde für die Hausaufgaben.* On average, my homework takes me an hour.

durchsetzen (perf **hat durchgesetzt**) vb [15] **sich durchsetzen** to assert oneself; *Du solltest dich mehr durchsetzen.* You should be more assertive.; *seinen Kopf durchsetzen* to get one's way

durchsichtig adj transparent

durchsuchen (perf **hat durchsucht**) vb [18] to search

dürfen (pres **darf**, imperf **durfte**, perf **hat gedurft** or **dürfen**) vb [16] to be allowed to ▷ *Ich darf das.* I'm allowed to

do that. ▷ *Er darf das nicht.* He's not allowed to do that. ▷ *Ich habe leider nicht gedurft.* Unfortunately, I wasn't allowed.; *Darf ich?* May I?; *Darf ich ins Kino?* Can I go to the cinema?

> The past participle **dürfen** is used when **dürfen** is a modal auxiliary.

Ich habe das nicht tun dürfen. I wasn't allowed to do that.; *darf nicht* must not; *Da darf sie sich nicht wundern.* That shouldn't surprise her.; *Das darf nicht wahr sein!* I don't believe it!; *Darf ich Sie bitten, das zu tun?* Could I ask you to do that?; *Was darf es sein?* What can I do for you?; *Das dürfen Sie mir glauben.* You can take my word for it.; *Das dürfte genug sein.* That should be enough.; *Es dürfte Ihnen bekannt sein, dass ...* As you will probably know ...

Durst m thirst; **Durst haben** to be thirsty

durstig adj thirsty

Dusche f shower

duschen vb [48] to have a shower; **sich duschen** to have a shower

düster adj ❶ dark ▷ *Hier drin ist es so düster.* It's so dark in here. ❷ gloomy

Dutzend (pl **Dutzende** or **Dutzend**) nt dozen ▷ *zwei Dutzend Bücher* two dozen books

duzen vb [36] to address someone as 'du'

- Only use **du** when speaking to one
- person, and when the person is your
- own age or younger. Use **ihr** for
- several people of your own age or
- younger. If in doubt use the polite
- form **Sie**.

DVD-Player (pl **DVD-Player**) m DVD player

D-Zug (pl **D-Züge**) m through train

e

E-Auto (pl **E-Autos**) nt electric vehicle
Ebbe f low tide ▷ *bei Ebbe* at low tide
eben adj, adv ❶ flat ▷ *eine ebene Fläche* a flat surface ❷ just ▷ *Er ist eben erst gegangen.* He's just gone. ❸ exactly ▷ *Eben, das sage ich ja.* That's exactly what I'm saying.; **eben deswegen** that's precisely why
Ebene f ❶ plain ▷ *Wir sahen auf die Ebene hinunter.* We looked down onto the plain. ❷ level ▷ *Das muss auf höherer Ebene entschieden werden.* That has to be decided at a higher level.
ebenfalls adv likewise
ebenso adv just as ▷ *Sie ist ebenso groß wie ihr Bruder.* She's just as tall as her brother.
Echo (pl **Echos**) nt echo
echt adj, adv ❶ real ▷ *echtes Gold* real gold; **Der Geldschein ist nicht echt.** That banknote's a fake. ❷ really ▷ *Die Party war echt gut.* The party was really good.; **Echt?** Really?
Ecke f corner ▷ *um die Ecke* round the corner

Edelstein (pl **Edelsteine**) m precious stone
EDV f (= *elektronische Datenverarbeitung*) electronic data processing
egal adj all the same **Es ist mir egal.** It's all the same to me.; **Das ist egal.** That makes no difference.; **Egal, ob ...** It doesn't matter whether ...
egoistisch adj selfish
ehe conj before ▷ *Ehe ich es vergesse, ...* Before I forget, ...
Ehe f marriage
Ehefrau f wife
ehemalig adj former
Ehemann (pl **Ehemänner**) m husband
Ehepaar (pl **Ehepaare**) nt married couple pl
eher adv sooner ▷ *Das hättest du eher sagen müssen.* You should have said that sooner.; **Das kommt schon eher der Wahrheit nahe.** That's more like the truth.
Ehre f honour
ehrgeizig adj ambitious
ehrlich adj honest
Ehrlichkeit f honesty
Ei (pl **Eier**) nt egg
Eiche f oak
Eichhörnchen (pl **Eichhörnchen**) nt squirrel
Eid (pl **Eide**) m oath ▷ *einen Eid schwören* to swear an oath
Eid al-Fitr nt Eid
Eifersucht f jealousy
eifersüchtig adj jealous ▷ *Er ist eifersüchtig auf seine kleine Schwester.* He's jealous of his little sister.
eifrig adj eager
Eigelb (pl **Eigelb**) nt egg yolk
eigen adj own ▷ *meine eigene Meinung* my own opinion
Eigenart f peculiarity ▷ *Wir haben alle unsere Eigenarten.* We all have our own peculiarities.
eigenartig adj peculiar

Eigenschaft f quality
eigensinnig adj obstinate
eigentlich adj, adv ① actual ▷ *Er ist der eigentliche Besitzer.* He's the actual owner. ② actually ▷ *Eigentlich wollte ich heute nicht weggehen.* Actually I didn't want to go out today.; **Eigentlich nicht.** Not really.
Eigentum nt property
Eigentümer (pl **Eigentümer**) m owner
sich **eignen** vb [53] to be suited ▷ *Er eignet sich nicht für diese Stelle.* He's not suited to this position.
eilen vb [38] to be urgent ▷ *Das eilt nicht.* It's not urgent.
eilig adj urgent ▷ *Ich muss zuerst die eiligen Dinge erledigen.* I'll have to do the urgent things first.; **es eilig haben** to be in a hurry
Eilzug (pl **Eilzüge**) m fast stopping train
Eimer (pl **Eimer**) m bucket
ein num, art ① one ▷ *Es war nur ein Kind da.* There was only one child there. ▷ *Ich möchte nur einen.* I only want one. ② somebody ▷ *Wenn einer dir das sagt, glaube es nicht.* If somebody tells you that, don't believe it. ③ you ▷ *Da kann einem die Lust vergehen.* It's enough to put you off. ④ a ▷ *ein Mann* a man ▷ *eine Frau* a woman ▷ *ein Kind* a child ▷ *an Ei* an egg ▷ *eine Stunde* an hour
einander pron each other
einatmen (perf **hat eingeatmet**) vb [3] to breathe in
Einbahnstraße f one-way street
einbilden (perf **hat eingebildet**) vb [54] **sich etwas einbilden** to imagine something
einbrechen (pres **bricht ein**, imperf **brach ein**, perf **ist eingebrochen**) vb [11] to break in ▷ *Bei ihnen wurde eingebrochen.* Their house has been broken into. ▷ *Er ist in das Haus eingebrochen.* He broke into the house.

Einbrecher (pl **Einbrecher**) m burglar
Einbruch (pl **Einbrüche**) m break-in ▷ *In dieser Gegend gibt es häufige Einbrüche.* There are a lot of break-ins in this area.; **bei Einbruch der Nacht** at nightfall; **vor Einbruch der Nacht** before nightfall
eindeutig adj clear ▷ *eine eindeutige Antwort geben* to give a clear answer
Eindruck (pl **Eindrücke**) m impression
eindrucksvoll adj impressive
eine see **ein**
einer see **ein**
einerseits adv on the one hand ▷ *Einerseits ..., andererseits ...* On the one hand ..., on the other hand ...
einfach adj, adv ① easy ▷ *Das war eine einfache Frage.* That was an easy question. ▷ *Das ist nicht einfach.* That isn't easy. ② simple ▷ *aus dem einfachen Grund* ... for the simple reason ... ▷ *Sie leben in sehr einfachen Verhältnissen.* They live very simple lives. ③ single ▷ *eine einfache Fahrkarte* a single ticket ④ simply ▷ *Ich will das einfach nicht.* I simply don't want it. ▷ *Er wollte einfach nicht begreifen.* He simply didn't want to understand.
Einfachheit f simplicity
Einfahrt f entrance
Einfall (pl **Einfälle**) m idea ▷ *Das war so ein Einfall von mir.* It was just an idea. ▷ *Du hast manchmal Einfälle!* You do come up with strange ideas sometimes!
einfallen (pres **fällt ein**, imperf **fiel ein**, perf **ist eingefallen**) vb [22] **jemandem einfallen** to occur to somebody; **Das fällt mir gar nicht ein.** I wouldn't dream of it.; **sich etwas einfallen lassen** to come up with a good idea
einfarbig adj plain
Einfluss (gen **Einflusses**, pl **Einflüsse**) m influence ▷ *Er hat einen schlechten Einfluss auf dich.* He has a bad influence on you.

Einfuhr f import
Einführung f introduction
Eingang (pl **Eingänge**) m entrance
eingeben (pres **gibt ein**, imperf **gab ein**, perf **hat eingegeben**) vb [28] to enter ▷ *Beate hat den Text in den Computer eingegeben.* Beate entered the text into the computer.
eingebildet adj conceited ▷ *Sie ist furchtbar eingebildet.* She's terribly conceited.; **Ihre Krankheit ist nur eingebildet.** Her illness is all in the imagination.
eingehen (imperf **ging ein**, perf **ist eingegangen**) vb [29] ❶ to die ▷ *Mir ist schon wieder eine Pflanze eingegangen.* Another of my plants has died. ❷ to shrink ▷ *Der Pulli ist in der Wäsche eingegangen.* The pullover shrank in the wash.; **auf etwas eingehen** to comment on something
eingenommen adj **eingenommen von** taken with
eingestellt adj **auf etwas eingestellt sein** to be prepared for something
eingreifen (imperf **griff ein**, perf **hat eingegriffen**) vb to intervene
Einheimische (gen **Einheimischen**, pl **Einheimischen**) mf local ▷ *Wir sollten einen Einheimischen fragen.* We should ask a local.
einholen (perf **hat eingeholt**) vb [4] ❶ to catch up with ▷ *Wir werden euch sicher bald einholen.* We'll soon catch up with you. ❷ to make up ▷ *Wir haben die Verspätung nicht mehr eingeholt.* We didn't make up the delay.
einhundert num a hundred
einig adj **sich einig sein** to be in agreement; **einig werden** to reach an agreement
einige adj, pron ❶ some ▷ *einige Bücher* some books ▷ *einige von uns* some of us; **einiges** quite a lot of things ❷ several ▷ *Wir sind dort einige Tage geblieben.* We stayed there several days. ▷ *Bei dem Konzert sind einige früher gegangen.* Several people left the concert early.
sich einigen vb [38] to agree ▷ *Wir haben uns auf diesen Termin geeinigt.* We agreed on this date.
einigermaßen adv ❶ somewhat ▷ *Ich war einigermaßen erstaunt.* I was somewhat surprised. ❷ reasonably ▷ *Diesmal hast du dich wenigstens einigermaßen angestrengt.* At least this time you've tried reasonably hard. ▷ *Das Wetter war einigermaßen trocken.* The weather was reasonably dry.
Einigung f agreement
Einkauf (pl **Einkäufe**) m purchase; **Einkäufe machen** to go shopping
einkaufen (perf **hat eingekauft**) vb [4] ❶ to buy ▷ *Wir müssen Brot einkaufen.* We'll have to buy bread. ❷ to shop ▷ *Wir kaufen meist samstags ein.* We usually shop on Saturdays.; **einkaufen gehen** to go shopping
Einkaufsbummel (pl **Einkaufsbummel**) m shopping spree
Einkaufswagen (pl **Einkaufswagen**) m shopping trolley
Einkaufszentrum (pl **Einkaufszentren**) nt shopping centre
Einkaufszettel (pl **Einkaufszettel**) m shopping list
Einkommen (pl **Einkommen**) nt income
einladen (pres **lädt ein**, imperf **lud ein**, perf **hat eingeladen**) vb ❶ to invite ▷ *Sie hat mich zu ihrer Party eingeladen.* She's invited me to her party.; **jemanden ins Kino einladen** to take somebody to the cinema; **Ich lade dich ein.** I'll treat you. ❷ to load ▷ *Kannst du bitte die Koffer ins Auto einladen?* Can you load the cases into the car, please?
Einladung f invitation
einlaufen (pres **läuft ein**, imperf **lief ein**, perf **ist eingelaufen**) vb [43] ❶ to

GERMAN > ENGLISH   65 | **einschränken**

come in ▷ *Das Schiff läuft in den Hafen ein.* The ship is coming into the harbour. ❷ to shrink ▷ *Mein Pullover ist eingelaufen.* My jumper has shrunk.

Einleitung f introduction

einleuchten (*perf* hat eingeleuchtet) *vb* [4] jemandem einleuchten to make sense to somebody

einleuchtend *adj* clear

einloggen (*perf* hat eingeloggt) *vb* [4] (computer) to log on

einlösen *vb* [4] ❶ to cash ▷ *Kann ich diesen Scheck einlösen?* Can I cash this cheque?; **ein Versprechen einlösen** to keep a promise

einmal *adv* ❶ once ▷ *Wenn du das erst einmal begriffen hast ...* Once you've understood it ...; **Es war einmal ...** Once upon a time there was ...; **noch einmal** once more; **auf einmal** all at once ❷ one day ▷ *Das wirst du schon einmal begreifen.* You'll understand it one day.; **Nehmen wir einmal an: ...** Let's just suppose: ...; **nicht einmal** not even

einmalig *adj* ❶ unique ▷ *Das ist eine einmalige Gelegenheit.* This is a unique opportunity. ❷ single ▷ *Das erfordert nur eine einmalige Überprüfung.* That requires only a single check. ❸ fantastic ▷ *Das war eine einmalige Party.* That was a fantastic party.

einpacken (*perf* hat eingepackt) *vb* [4] to pack ▷ *Hast du deine Zahnbürste eingepackt?* Have you packed your toothbrush?

Einreise f entry; **bei der Einreise** when entering the country

einreisen (*perf* ist eingereist) *vb* [4] **in ein Land einreisen** to enter a country

einrichten (*perf* hat eingerichtet) *vb* [2] ❶ to furnish ▷ *Sie haben ihr Haus antik eingerichtet.* They've furnished their house with antiques. ❷ to set up ▷ *Die Stadt hat eine Beratungsstelle eingerichtet.* The town has set up an advice bureau.; **sich auf etwas einrichten** to prepare for something

Einrichtung f ❶ furnishings *pl* ▷ *Die moderne Einrichtung gefiel mir gut.* I liked the modern furnishings. ❷ facility ▷ *städtische Einrichtungen* municipal facilities

eins *num* one ▷ *Ich habe nur eins bekommen.* I only got one.; **Es ist mir alles eins.** It's all the same to me.

Eins f (*pl* **Einsen**) ❶ one ❷ very good
  ⁂ German marks range from one (**sehr gut**) to six (**ungenügend**).

einsam *adj* ❶ lonely ▷ *Ich fühle mich einsam.* I'm feeling lonely. ❷ remote ▷ *eine einsame Gegend* a remote area

einsammeln (*perf* hat eingesammelt) *vb* [4] to collect

einschalten (*perf* hat eingeschaltet) *vb* [2] to switch on ▷ *Schalt mal das Radio ein.* Switch the radio on.

einschlafen (*pres* schläft ein, *imperf* schlief ein, *perf* ist eingeschlafen) *vb* [58] to fall asleep

einschließen (*imperf* schloss ein, *perf* hat eingeschlossen) *vb* [4] ❶ to lock in ▷ *Sie hat mich im Badezimmer eingeschlossen.* She locked me in the bathroom. ❷ to lock away ▷ *Du solltest die Wertsachen einschließen.* You should lock away the valuables. ❸ to include ▷ *Der Preis schließt die Verpflegung ein.* The price includes all meals.; **sich einschließen** to lock oneself in

einschließlich *adv, prep*
  ▮ The preposition **einschließlich** takes the genitive.
  ❶ inclusive ▷ *Wir sind vom zehnten bis einschließlich fünfzehnten Juni weg.* We're away from the tenth to the fifteenth of June inclusive. ❷ including ▷ *Das macht zwanzig Euro einschließlich Bedienung.* That's twenty euros including service.

einschränken (*perf* hat eingeschränkt) *vb* [4] ❶ to restrict

▷ Dadurch wurde unsere Freiheit eingeschränkt. This restricted our freedom. ❷ **to reduce** ▷ Wir müssen die Kosten einschränken. We'll have to reduce costs.; **sich einschränken** to cut down

sich **einschreiben** (imperf **schrieb sich ein**, perf **hat sich eingeschrieben**) vb [61] ❶ to register ▷ Hast du dich für den Kurs eingeschrieben? Have you registered for the course? ❷ to enrol ▷ sich an der Universität einschreiben to enrol at university

Einschreiben (pl **Einschreiben**) nt recorded delivery

einsehen (pres **sieht ein**, imperf **sah ein**, perf **hat eingesehen**) vb [64] to see ▷ Siehst du das nicht ein? Don't you see that?

einseitig adj one-sided

einsenden (imperf **sendete ein** or **sandte ein**, perf **hat eingesendet** or **hat eingesandt**) vb to send in

einsetzen (perf **hat eingesetzt**) vb [36] ❶ to put in ▷ Setzt das richtige Wort ein. Put in the correct word. ❷ to bet ▷ Wie viel Geld hast du eingesetzt? How much money did you bet? ❸ to use ▷ An den Schulen werden immer mehr Computer eingesetzt. More and more computers are being used in schools. ❹ to set in ▷ Wenn der Winter einsetzt ... When winter sets in ...; **sich einsetzen** to work hard; **einsetzen für jemanden** to support somebody

einsperren (perf **hat eingesperrt**) vb [4] to lock up

einsprachig adj monolingual

Einspruch (pl **Einsprüche**) m objection

einsteigen (imperf **stieg ein**, perf **ist eingestiegen**) vb [74] ❶ to get on ▷ Wir sind in den Bus eingestiegen. We got on the bus.; **Bitte einsteigen!** All aboard! ❷ to climb in ▷ Wir sind durchs Kellerfenster ins Haus eingestiegen. We climbed into the house through the cellar window.

einstellen (perf **hat eingestellt**) vb [4] ❶ to adjust ▷ den Spiegel einstellen to adjust the mirror; **eine Kamera einstellen** to focus a camera ❷ to tune in to ▷ Welchen Sender hast du da eingestellt? Which station have you tuned in to? ❸ to stop ▷ Sie haben die Produktion eingestellt. They've stopped production. ❹ to employ ▷ Sie wurde als Sekretärin eingestellt. She was employed as a secretary.; **sich auf etwas einstellen** to prepare oneself for something

Einstellung f attitude ▷ Ich mag deine Einstellung nicht. I don't like your attitude.

Einstieg m entrance ▷ Der Einstieg ist vorn. The entrance is at the front.

einstimmen (perf **hat eingestimmt**) vb [4] to join in ▷ Alle stimmten in das Lied ein. Everyone joined in the singing.; **sich auf etwas einstimmen** to get oneself in the right mood for something

eintägig adj one-day

eintausend num a thousand

eintönig adj monotonous

Eintopf (pl **Eintöpfe**) m stew

Eintrag (pl **Einträge**) m entry ▷ ein Eintrag im Wörterbuch a dictionary entry

eintragen (pres **trägt ein**, imperf **trug ein**, perf **hat eingetragen**) vb [77] to write ▷ Tragt die Vokabeln in euer Heft ein. Write the vocabulary in your exercise book.; **sich eintragen** to put one's name down

eintreffen (pres **trifft ein**, imperf **traf ein**, perf **ist eingetroffen**) vb [78] ❶ to arrive ▷ Sobald die Gäste eintreffen ... As soon as the guests arrive ... ❷ to come true ▷ Die Prophezeiung ist tatsächlich eingetroffen. The prophecy actually came true.

GERMAN > ENGLISH

eintreten (pres **tritt ein**, imperf **trat ein**, perf **ist eingetreten**) vb [**79**] eintreten in (1) to enter ▷ *Er ist ins Zimmer eingetreten.* He entered the room. (2) to join ▷ *Wann bist du in den Tennisklub eingetreten?* When did you join the tennis club?; **Es ist eine Verzögerung eingetreten.** There has been a delay.

Eintritt (pl **Eintritte**) m admission ▷ *Wie viel kostet der Eintritt?* How much does the admission cost?; **'Eintritt frei'** 'Admission free'

Eintrittsgeld (pl **Eintrittsgelder**) nt admission charge

Eintrittskarte f admission ticket

einverstanden adj einverstanden sein to agree; **Einverstanden!** Okay!

Einwanderer (pl **Einwanderer**) m immigrant

einwandern (perf **ist eingewandert**) vb [**88**] to immigrate

Einwegflasche f nonreturnable bottle

einweihen (perf **hat eingeweiht**) vb [**4**] to open ▷ *Morgen wird die neue Brücke eingeweiht.* The new bridge is being opened tomorrow.; **jemanden in etwas einweihen** to initiate somebody into something; **jemanden in ein Geheimnis einweihen** to let somebody into a secret

einwerfen (pres **wirft ein**, imperf **warf ein**, perf **hat eingeworfen**) vb [**92**] to smash ▷ *Ich habe eine Scheibe eingeworfen.* I've smashed a pane.; **einen Brief einwerfen** to post a letter; **Geld einwerfen** to insert money

Einwohner (pl **Einwohner**) m inhabitant

Einwohnermeldeamt (pl **Einwohnermeldeämter**) nt residents' registration office

* Anyone moving to a new address
* in Germany is required by law to
* register (**sich anmelden**) at the
* residents' registration office
* (**Einwohnermeldeamt**).

Einwurf (pl **Einwürfe**) m ① slot ▷ *Sie steckte den Brief in den Einwurf.* She put the letter through the slot. ② (sport) throw-in ▷ *Der Schiedsrichter gab einen Einwurf.* The referee gave a throw-in.

Einzahl f singular

einzahlen (perf **hat eingezahlt**) vb [**4**] to pay

Einzelbett (pl **Einzelbetten**) nt single bed

Einzelfahrschein (pl **Einzelfahrscheine**) m single ticket

Einzelheit f detail

Einzelkind (pl **Einzelkinder**) nt only child

einzeln adj, adv ① single ▷ *Jeder einzelne Schüler wurde befragt.* Every single pupil was asked. ② odd ▷ *Ich habe ein paar einzelne Socken.* I've got a couple of odd socks. ③ one at a time ▷ *Bitte einzeln eintreten.* Please come in one at a time.; **einzeln angeben** to specify; **der Einzelne** the individual; **ins Einzelne gehen** to go into details

Einzelteil (pl **Einzelteile**) nt component

Einzelzimmer (pl **Einzelzimmer**) nt single room

einziehen (imperf **zog ein**, perf **ist/hat eingezogen**) vb [**96**]

> For the perfect tense use **haben** when the verb has an object and **sein** when there is no object.

① to retract; **den Kopf einziehen** to duck one's head ② to collect ③ to move in ▷ *Wann sind die neuen Nachbarn eingezogen?* When did the new neighbours move in?

einzig adj only ▷ *Er ist unser einziges Kind.* He's our only child.; **das Einzige** the only thing; **der Einzige** the only one

einzigartig adj unique

Eis (pl **Eis**) nt ① ice ▷ *Es war Eis auf dem See.* There was ice on the lake. ② ice

cream ▷ *Möchtest du ein Eis?* Would you like an ice cream?
Eisbär (*gen* **Eisbären**, *pl* **Eisbären**) *m* polar bear
Eisberg (*pl* **Eisberge**) *m* iceberg
Eisen (*pl* **Eisen**) *nt* iron ▷ *Die Brücke ist aus Eisen.* The bridge is made of iron.
Eisenbahn *f* railway
eisern *adj* iron ▷ *eine eiserne Stange* an iron rod; **die eiserne Reserve** emergency reserves
Eishockey *nt* ice hockey
eisig *adj* icy
eiskalt *adj* ❶ ice-cold ▷ *ein eiskaltes Getränk* an ice-cold drink ❷ icy cold ▷ *In diesem Zimmer ist es eiskalt.* This room's icy cold.
Eiswürfel (*pl* **Eiswürfel**) *m* ice cube
eitel *adj* vain
Eiter *m* pus
Eiweiß (*pl* **Eiweiße**) *nt* ❶ egg white ▷ *Das Eiweiß zu Schnee schlagen.* Whisk the egg whites until stiff. ❷ protein ▷ *eine eiweißreiche Diät* a diet rich in protein
Ekel *m* disgust
ekelhaft *adj* disgusting
sich **ekeln** *vb* [**34**] to disgust; **sich vor etwas ekeln** to find something disgusting
Elefant (*gen* **Elefanten**, *pl* **Elefanten**) *m* elephant
elegant *adj* elegant
Elektriker (*pl* **Elektriker**) *m* electrician
elektrisch *adj* electric
Elektrizität *f* electricity
Elektroauto (*pl* **Elektroautos**) *nt* electric vehicle
Elektrogerät *nt* electrical appliance
Elektroherd (*pl* **Elektroherde**) *m* electric cooker
Elektronik *f* electronics *sg* ▷ *Er studiert Elektronik.* He's studying electronics. ▷ *Die Elektronik am Auto ist kaputt.*

There's something wrong with the electronics in the car.
elektronisch *adj* electronic
▷ *elektronische Post* electronic mail
▷ *elektronischer Briefkasten* electronic mailbox
Element (*pl* **Elemente**) *nt* element
elend *adj* miserable ▷ *Ich fühle mich so elend.* I feel so miserable.
Elend *nt* misery
elf *num* eleven ▷ *Sie ist elf.* She's eleven.
Elfmeter (*pl* **Elfmeter**) *m* penalty

⬛ Word for word, **Elfmeter** means 'eleven metres'.

▷ *einen Elfmeter schießen* to take a penalty
Ellbogen (*pl* **Ellbogen**) *m* elbow
Eltern *pl* parents *pl*
Elterngeld (*pl* **Elterngelder**) *nt* child benefit
Elternschaft *f* parenthood
Elternteil (*pl* **Elternteile**) *m* parent ▷ *beide Elternteile* both parents
E-Mail (*pl* **E-Mails**) *f* email ▷ *Meine E-Mail-Adresse ist ...* My email address is ...
Emoticon (*pl* **Emoticons**) *nt* smiley
Empfang (*pl* **Empfänge**) *m*
❶ reception ▷ *Wart ihr auch bei dem Empfang?* Were you at the reception too? ❷ receipt ▷ *Bitte bestätigen Sie den Empfang der Ware.* Please acknowledge receipt of the goods.; **in Empfang nehmen** to receive
empfangen (*pres* **empfängt**, *imperf* **empfing**, *perf* **hat empfangen**) *vb* [**23**] to receive
Empfänger (*pl* **Empfänger**) *m* receiver
Empfängnisverhütung *f* contraception
empfehlen (*pres* **empfiehlt**, *imperf* **empfahl**, *perf* **hat empfohlen**) *vb* [**17**] to recommend ▷ *Dieses Restaurant ist zu empfehlen.* This restaurant is to be recommended.

empfinden (imperf **empfand**, perf **hat empfunden**) vb [24] to feel ▷ *Ich empfinde nichts für sie.* I don't feel anything for her.

empfindlich adj ❶ sensitive ▷ *Er ist ein sehr empfindlicher Mensch.* He's very sensitive. ❷ touchy ▷ *Sie ist schrecklich empfindlich.* She's terribly touchy.

empfohlen vb see **empfehlen**

Ende (pl **Enden**) nt end; **am Ende (1)** at the end ▷ *am Ende des Zuges* at the end of the train **(2)** in the end ▷ *Am Ende ist er dann doch mitgekommen.* He came in the end.; **zu Ende gehen** to come to an end; **zu Ende sein** to be finished; **Ende Dezember** at the end of December

enden vb [54] to end

endgültig adj definite

endlich adv finally ▷ *Ich bin endlich fertig.* I've finally finished. ▷ *Hast du das endlich begriffen?* Have you finally understood it?; **Endlich!** At last!; **Komm endlich!** Come on!

endlos adj endless

Endspiel (pl **Endspiele**) nt final

Endstation f terminus

Endung f ending

Energie f energy ▷ *seine ganze Energie für etwas einsetzen* to devote all one's energies to something

energisch adj energetic

eng adj ❶ narrow ▷ *ein enger Durchgang* a narrow passageway ❷ tight ▷ *Die Hose ist mir zu eng.* The trousers are too tight for me. ❸ close ▷ *Wir sind eng befreundet.* We are close friends.

Enge f narrowness; **jemanden in die Enge treiben** to drive somebody into a corner

Engel (pl **Engel**) m angel

England nt England

Engländer (pl **Engländer**) m Englishman; **Er ist Engländer.** He's English.; **die Engländer** the English

Engländerin f Englishwoman; **Sie ist Engländerin.** She's English.

englisch adj English

Englisch (gen **Englischen**) nt English ▷ *Er lernt Englisch in der Schule.* He's learning English at school.

Enkel (pl **Enkel**) m grandson; **alle ihre Enkel** all her grandchildren

Enkelin f granddaughter

Enkelkind (pl **Enkelkinder**) nt grandchild

enorm adj enormous ▷ *Er verdient enorm viel Geld.* He earns an enormous amount of money.

entdecken (perf **hat entdeckt**) vb [18] to discover

Ente f duck

entfernen (perf **hat entfernt**) vb [18] to remove

entfernt adj distant ▷ *ein entfernter Verwandter* a distant relative; **weit entfernt** far away; **weit davon entfernt sein, etwas zu tun** to be far from doing something; **nicht im Entferntesten** not in the slightest

Entfernung f distance

entführen (perf **hat entführt**) vb [18] to kidnap

entgegen prep

entgegen takes the dative.

contrary to ▷ *entgegen meinen Anweisungen* contrary to my instructions

entgegenkommen (imperf **kam entgegen**, perf **ist entgegengekommen**) vb [40] ❶ to come towards ▷ *Uns kam ein Lastwagen entgegen.* A lorry came towards us. ❷ to meet half way ▷ *Ich werde Ihnen entgegenkommen, sagen wir zwanzig Euro.* I'll meet you half way, let's say twenty euros.

entgehen (imperf **entging**, perf **ist entgangen**) vb [29] **jemandem entgehen** to escape somebody's

enthalten (pres **enthält**, imperf **enthielt**, perf **hat enthalten**) vb [33] to contain ▷ *Dieses Fass enthält radioaktiven Müll.* This drum contains radioactive waste.; **sich enthalten** to abstain

entkommen (imperf **entkam**, perf **ist entkommen**) vb [40] to escape

entlang prep

▍ **entlang** takes the accusative or the dative.

along ▷ *Entlang der Mauer wuchs Efeu.* Ivy was growing along the wall. ▷ *Wir gingen den Fluss entlang.* We walked along the river.

entlassen (pres **entlässt**, imperf **entließ**, perf **hat entlassen**) vb [42] ❶ to release ▷ *Er wurde aus dem Gefängnis entlassen.* He was released from prison. ❷ to make redundant ▷ *500 Arbeiter mussten entlassen werden.* 500 workers had to be made redundant.

entrüstet adj outraged

entschädigen (perf **hat entschädigt**) vb [18] to compensate ▷ *jemanden für etwas entschädigen* to compensate somebody for something

entscheiden (imperf **entschied**, perf **hat entschieden**) vb to decide; **sich entscheiden** to make up one's mind

entscheidend adj decisive

Entscheidung f decision

entschieden adj ❶ decided ▷ *Es ist entschieden, wir fahren nach Rom.* It's been decided that we're going to Rome. ❷ resolute ▷ *ein sehr entschiedener Mensch* a very resolute person

sich **entschließen** (imperf **entschloss sich**, perf **hat sich entschlossen**) vb to decide

entschlossen adj determined

Entschluss (gen **Entschlusses**, pl **Entschlüsse**) m decision

entschuldigen (perf **hat entschuldigt**) vb [18] ❶ to excuse ▷ *Entschuldige bitte die Verspätung.* Please excuse the delay. ❷ to apologize ▷ *Du solltest dich besser bei ihm entschuldigen.* You'd better apologize to him.

Entschuldigung f ❶ apology ▷ *Hat er deine Entschuldigung angenommen?* Did he accept your apology?; **jemanden um Entschuldigung bitten** to apologize to somebody ❷ excuse ▷ *Krankheit ist keine Entschuldigung.* Illness is no excuse.; **Entschuldigung!** Sorry.

entsetzlich adj dreadful

entsetzt adj, adv horrified

Entsorgung f waste disposal

sich **entspannen** (perf **hat sich entspannt**) vb [18] ❶ to relax ▷ *Entspann dich!* Relax! ❷ to ease ▷ *Die Lage hat sich entspannt.* The situation has eased.

entspannend adj relaxing

entsprechen (pres **entspricht**, imperf **entsprach**, perf **hat entsprochen**) vb [70] ❶ to meet ▷ *Sie hat den Anforderungen nicht entsprochen.* She didn't meet the requirements. ❷ to comply with ▷ *Dieses Gerät entspricht nicht den Normen.* This appliance doesn't comply with the standards.

entsprechend adj, adv ❶ appropriate ▷ *Die entsprechende Antwort ankreuzen.* Tick the appropriate answer. ❷ accordingly ▷ *Benimm dich entsprechend.* Behave accordingly.

entstehen (perf **ist entstanden**) vb [72] to originate ▷ *Die Legende ist in der Schweiz entstanden.* The legend originated in Switzerland.

enttäuschen (perf **hat enttäuscht**) vb [18] to disappoint

enttäuschend adj disappointing

Enttäuschung f disappointment

entweder conj either; **entweder ... oder ...** either ... or ...

entwerten vb [**18**] to cancel ▷ *Du musst die Fahrkarte erst entwerten.* You have to cancel your ticket first.

Entwerter (pl **Entwerter**) m ticket stamping machine

- When you travel by train or tram
- (and sometimes by bus) you often
- have to stamp your ticket in an
- **Entwerter**. The machines are on
- the platforms or inside the vehicles.

entwickeln (perf **hat entwickelt**) vb [**34**] ❶ to develop ▷ *Fähigkeiten entwickeln* to develop skills ▷ *einen Film entwickeln* to develop a film ❷ to show ▷ *Sie hat eine enorme Energie entwickelt.* She showed terrific energy.; **sich entwickeln** to develop

Entwicklung f development

Entwicklungsland (pl **Entwicklungsländer**) nt developing country

sich entzünden (perf **hat sich entzündet**) vb [**18**] to become inflamed ▷ *Die Wunde hat sich entzündet.* The wound has become inflamed.

Entzündung f inflammation

entzwei adv broken ▷ *Die Vase ist entzwei.* The vase is broken.

er pron ❶ he ▷ *Er ist größer als ich.* He's taller than me. ❷ it ▷ *Schöner Ring, ist er neu?* Lovely ring, is it new? ❸ him ▷ *Er ist es.* It's him. ▷ *Er war es nicht, ich war's.* It wasn't him, it was me.

erben vb [**38**] to inherit

erbrechen (pres **erbricht**, imperf **erbrach**, perf **hat erbrochen**) vb [**11**] to vomit

Erbse f pea

Erdbeben (pl **Erdbeben**) nt earthquake

Erdbeere f strawberry

Erde f earth; **zu ebener Erde** at ground level; **auf der ganzen Erde** all over the world

Erdgas (gen **Erdgases**) nt natural gas

Erdgeschoss (gen **Erdgeschosses**, pl **Erdgeschosse**) nt ground floor ▷ *im Erdgeschoss* on the ground floor

Erdkunde f geography

Erdnuss (pl **Erdnüsse**) f peanut

Erdöl nt mineral oil

sich ereignen (perf **hat sich ereignet**) vb [**53**] to happen

Ereignis (gen **Ereignisses**, pl **Ereignisse**) nt event

erfahren (pres **erfährt**, imperf **erfuhr**, perf **hat erfahren**) vb [**21**] ❶ to hear ▷ *Ich habe erfahren, dass du heiraten willst.* I've heard that you want to get married. ❷ to experience ▷ *Sie hat im Leben viel Gutes erfahren.* She's experienced a lot of good things in her life.
▶ adj experienced ▷ *Er ist ein erfahrener Lehrer.* He's an experienced teacher.

Erfahrung f experience

erfassen (perf **hat erfasst**) vb [**31**] ❶ to understand ▷ *Ich habe den Text noch nicht erfasst.* I haven't understood the text yet. ❷ to register ▷ *Alle AIDS-Fälle werden erfasst.* All AIDS cases are registered.

erfinden (imperf **erfand**, perf **hat erfunden**) vb [**24**] to invent

Erfinder (pl **Erfinder**) m inventor

Erfindung f invention

Erfolg (pl **Erfolge**) m success; **Erfolg versprechend** promising; **Viel Erfolg!** Good luck!

erfolglos adj unsuccessful

erfolgreich adj successful

erforderlich adj necessary

erfreut adj pleased ▷ *Über mein gutes Zeugnis bin ich sehr erfreut.* I was very pleased with my good report.

erfrieren (imperf **erfror**, perf **ist erfrieren**) vb [**15**] to freeze to death ▷ *Er ist erfroren.* He froze to death.; **Die Pflanze ist erfroren.** The plant was killed by frost.

Erfrischung f refreshment
erfüllen (perf **hat erfüllt**) vb [7] to fulfil ▷ *Er hat ihr den Wunsch erfüllt.* He fulfilled her wish.; **sich erfüllen** to come true
ergänzen (perf **hat ergänzt**) vb [36] to complete ▷ *Ergänzt den Satz.* Complete the sentence.; **sich ergänzen** to complement one another
Ergebnis (gen **Ergebnisses**, pl **Ergebnisse**) nt result
ergreifen (imperf **ergriff**, perf **hat ergriffen**) vb ❶ to seize ▷ *Er ergriff meine Hand.* He seized my hand. ▷ *die Gelegenheit ergreifen* to seize the opportunity; **einen Beruf ergreifen** to take up a profession; **Maßnahmen gegen etwas ergreifen** to take measures against something ❷ to move ▷ *Ihr Schicksal hat uns sehr ergriffen.* Her fate moved us deeply.
ergreifend adj moving
ergriffen adj deeply moved
erhalten (pres **erhält**, imperf **erhielt**, perf **hat erhalten**) vb [33] ❶ to receive ▷ *Sie hat den ersten Preis erhalten.* She received first prize. ❷ to preserve ▷ *Das Gebäude sollte erhalten werden.* The building should be preserved.; **gut erhalten** in good condition

> Word for word, **gut erhalten** means 'well preserved'.

erhältlich adj obtainable
erhitzen (perf **hat erhitzt**) vb [7] to heat
erhöhen (perf **hat erhöht**) vb [19] to raise ▷ *Sie erhöhten ihr Jahresgehalt um 2.000 € auf 40.000 €.* They raised her salary by £2,000 to £40,000 a year.
sich erholen (perf **hat sich erholt**) vb [19] ❶ to recover ▷ *Der Patient muss sich nach der Operation erholen.* The patient needs to recover after the operation. ❷ to have a rest ▷ *Wir haben uns in den Ferien gut erholt.* We had a good rest when we were on holiday.

erholsam adj restful
Erholung f rest ▷ *Wir fahren zur Erholung ans Meer.* We're going to the sea for a rest.
erinnern (perf **hat erinnert**) vb [88] **erinnern an** to remind of; **sich erinnern** to remember; **sich an jemanden/etwas erinnern** to remember somebody/something
Erinnerung f ❶ memory ▷ *Wir haben Erinnerungen ausgetauscht.* We swapped memories. ❷ souvenir ▷ *eine Erinnerung an meinen Finnlandaufenthalt* a souvenir of my stay in Finland
erkältet adj **erkältet sein** to have a cold
Erkältung f cold
erkennbar adj recognizable
erkennen (imperf **erkannte**, perf **hat erkannt**) vb [39] ❶ to recognize ▷ *Ich hätte dich fast nicht erkannt.* I would hardly have recognized you. ❷ to see ▷ *Jetzt erkenne ich, dass es ein Fehler war.* I see now that it was a mistake.
erklären (perf **hat erklärt**) vb [19] to explain; **sich erklären** to declare oneself ▷ *Sie erklärte sich für die EU.* She declared herself pro-EU.
Erklärung f explanation; **eine Liebeserklärung** a declaration of love
sich erkundigen (perf **hat sich erkundigt**) vb [19] **sich erkundigen nach** to inquire about; **Er hat sich nach dir erkundigt.** He was asking about you.
erlauben (perf **hat erlaubt**) vb [19] **jemandem etwas erlauben** to allow somebody to do something; **sich etwas erlauben** to allow oneself something; **Was erlaubst du dir denn eigentlich?** How dare you!
Erlaubnis (pl **Erlaubnisse**) f permission
erleben (perf **hat erlebt**) vb [19] ❶ to experience ▷ *Eine solche Frechheit habe ich selten erlebt.* I've seldom experienced

such cheek.; **Wir haben in den Ferien viel Schönes erlebt.** We had a lovely time on holiday.; **Sie hat viel Schlimmes erlebt.** She's had a lot of bad experiences. ❷ to live through ▷ *Mein Opa hat den Zweiten Weltkrieg erlebt.* My grandpa lived through the Second World War. ❸ to see ▷ *Ich möchte die Geburt deines Kindes noch erleben.* I would like to live to see the birth of your child.

Erlebnis (gen **Erlebnisses**, pl **Erlebnisse**) nt experience

erledigen (perf **hat erledigt**) vb [19] ❶ to see to ▷ *Ich habe heute noch viel zu erledigen.* I've a lot to see to today. ❷ to do ▷ *Hast du deine Hausaufgaben schon erledigt?* Have you done your homework already? ❸ to wear out (informal) ▷ *Die Wanderung hat mich ziemlich erledigt.* The hike's really worn me out.

Erleichterung f relief ▷ *Das war eine Erleichterung!* That was a relief!

erlösen (perf **hat erlöst**) vb [7] to save ▷ *Sie erlöste ihn aus einer gefährlichen Lage.* She saved him from a dangerous situation.

Ermahnung f admonition

Ermäßigung f reduction

ermöglichen (perf **hat ermöglicht**) vb [7] **jemandem etwas ermöglichen** to make something possible for somebody

ermorden (perf **hat ermordet**) vb [53] to murder

ermüdend adj tiring

ermutigen (perf **hat ermutigt**) vb [7] to encourage

ernähren (perf **hat ernährt**) vb [19] to support ▷ *Er hat eine Familie zu ernähren.* He has a family to support.; **sich von etwas ernähren** to live on something

Ernährung f ❶ food ❷ diet ▷ *die pflanzliche Ernährung* plant-based diet

ernennen (imperf **ernannte**, perf **hat ernannt**) vb to appoint

erneuerbar adj renewable ▷ *erneuerbare Energie* renewable energy

erneuern (perf **hat erneuert**) vb [88] to renew

ernst adj serious

Ernst m seriousness; **Das ist mein Ernst.** I'm quite serious.; **im Ernst** in earnest

ernsthaft adj, adv serious ▷ *ein ernsthaftes Gespräch* a serious talk ▶ seriously ▷ *Glaubst du das ernsthaft?* Do you seriously believe that?

ernstlich adj, adv serious; **ernstlich besorgt** seriously concerned

Ernte f harvest

ernten vb [2] to harvest ▷ *Es ist Zeit, die Kirschen zu ernten.* It's time to harvest the cherries.; **Lob ernten** to earn praise

erobern (perf **hat erobert**) vb [88] to conquer

eröffnen (perf **hat eröffnet**) vb [7] to open ▷ *Die Ausstellung wurde gestern vom Künstler eröffnet.* The exhibition was opened yesterday by the artist.

erotisch adj erotic

erpressen (perf **hat erpresst**) vb [7] ❶ to blackmail ▷ *Du willst mich wohl erpressen?* Are you trying to blackmail me? ❷ to extort ▷ *Er hat von ihm Geld erpresst.* He extorted money from him.

erraten (pres **errät**, imperf **erriet**, perf **hat erraten**) vb to guess

Erregung f excitement

erreichen (perf **hat erreicht**) vb [19] ❶ to reach ▷ *Wir haben Hamburg am späten Nachmittag erreicht.* We reached Hamburg in the late afternoon. ❷ to catch ▷ *Wir haben den Zug nicht mehr erreicht.* We didn't manage to catch the train. ❸ to achieve ▷ *seinen Zweck erreichen* to achieve one's purpose ▷ *Was willst du damit erreichen?* What do you aim to achieve by this?; **So erreichst du bei mir gar nichts.** You won't get anywhere with me by doing that.

Ersatzteil (pl **Ersatzteile**) nt spare part

erschaffen (imperf **erschuf**, perf **hat erschaffen**) vb to create

erscheinen (imperf **erschien**, perf **ist erschienen**) vb [57] to appear

erschießen (imperf **erschoss**, perf **hat erschossen**) vb to shoot dead

erschöpft adj exhausted

erschrecken (1) (perf **hat erschreckt**) vb [19] to frighten ▷ *Hast du mich erschreckt!* You really frightened me!

erschrecken (2) (pres **erschrickt**, imperf **erschrak**, perf **ist erschrocken**) vb to be frightened ▷ *Ich bin furchtbar erschrocken, als plötzlich das Licht ausging.* I was terribly frightened when the light suddenly went out.

erschreckend adj alarming

erschrocken adj frightened

ersetzen (perf **hat ersetzt**) vb [36] to replace ▷ *Du musst die Vase ersetzen.* You'll have to replace that vase.; **jemandem die Unkosten ersetzen** to pay somebody's expenses

erst adv ❶ first ▷ *Erst will ich wissen, was das kostet.* First I want to know what it costs.; *Mach erst mal die Arbeit fertig.* Finish your work first.; **Wenn du das erst mal hinter dir hast, ...** Once you've got that behind you, ... ❷ only ▷ *Das ist erst gestern passiert.* That happened only yesterday. ▷ *Er ist gerade erst angekommen.* He's only just arrived. ❸ not until ▷ *Er hat es erst gemacht, als ich es ihm befohlen habe.* He didn't do it until I told him. ▷ **erst morgen** not until tomorrow ▷ **erst um 5 Uhr** not until 5 o'clock

erstaunlich adj astonishing

erstaunt adj astonished

erste adj first ▷ *Ich habe gerade mein erstes Auto gekauft.* I've just bought my first car. ▷ *Er kam als Erster.* He was the first to arrive.; **Erste Hilfe** first aid

erstechen (pres **ersticht**, imperf **erstach**, perf **hat erstochen**) vb to stab to death

erstens adv firstly

erstklassig adj first-class

erstmals adv for the first time

ertragen (pres **erträgt**, imperf **ertrug**, perf **hat ertragen**) vb [77] to stand ▷ *Ich kann die Schmerzen kaum ertragen.* I can hardly stand the pain. ▷ *Sie erträgt es nicht, wenn man ihr widerspricht.* She can't stand being contradicted.

erträglich adj bearable

ertrinken (imperf **ertrank**, perf **ist ertrunken**) vb [80] to drown

erwachsen adj grown-up

Erwachsene (gen **Erwachsenen**, pl **Erwachsenen**) mf adult ▷ *Erwachsene können das nicht verstehen.* Adults can't understand that. ▷ *Kinder glauben, dass ein Erwachsener alles kann.* Children think an adult can do anything.

erwähnen (perf **hat erwähnt**) vb [19] to mention

erwarten (perf **hat erwartet**) vb [2] to expect ▷ *Er erwartet zu viel von uns.* He's expecting too much of us.; **Wir können es kaum erwarten, dass die Ferien beginnen.** We can hardly wait for the holidays to begin.

erweisen (imperf **erwies**, perf **hat erwiesen**) vb sich erweisen als to prove to be

erwerben (pres **erwirbt**, imperf **erwarb**, perf **hat erworben**) vb [90] to acquire

erzählen (perf **hat erzählt**) vb [19] to tell

Erzählung f story

erzeugen (perf **hat erzeugt**) vb [19] ❶ to produce ▷ *In dieser Gegend wird Wein erzeugt.* Wine is produced in this region. ❷ to generate ▷ *Strom erzeugen* to generate electricity

GERMAN > ENGLISH

Erzeugnis (gen **Erzeugnisses**, pl **Erzeugnisse**) nt produce ▷ ausländische Erzeugnisse foreign produce

erziehen (imperf **erzog**, perf **hat erzogen**) vb [96] to bring up ▷ Sie hat fünf Kinder erzogen. She brought up five children. ▷ Sie sollte ihre Kinder zu etwas mehr Höflichkeit erziehen. She should bring her children up to be more polite.

Erziehung f education

es pron it ▷ Es ist rot. It's red. ▷ Ich habe es nicht gesehen. I didn't see it. ▷ Es schneit. It's snowing.

Esel (pl **Esel**) m donkey

essbar adj edible

essen (pres **isst**, imperf **aß**, perf **hat gegessen**) vb [20] to eat

Essen (pl **Essen**) nt ❶ meal ▷ Komm doch am Freitag zum Essen. Why don't you come for a meal on Friday?. ❷ food ▷ Das Essen war lecker. The food was delicious.

Essig (pl **Essige**) m vinegar

Esszimmer (pl **Esszimmer**) nt dining room

Etage f floor ▷ Wir wohnen in der dritten Etage. We live on the third floor.

Etikett (pl **Etikette** or **Etiketten**) nt label ▷ Lies mal, was auf dem Etikett steht. Read what's on the label.

etliche pron pl quite a few ▷ etliche Leute quite a few people

Etui (pl **Etuis**) nt case ▷ ein Brillenetui a glasses case

etwa adv ❶ about ▷ Es waren etwa zwanzig. There were about twenty. ❷ for instance ▷ Leute wie etwa Jochen wissen das eben nicht. People like Jochen, for instance, just don't know that.; **Soll das etwa heißen, dass ...** Is that supposed to mean that ...; **Du willst doch nicht etwa schon gehen.** You're not going already, are you?

etwas pron, adv ❶ something ▷ Wir sollten ihr etwas schenken. We should

75 | evangelisch

give her something. ❷ anything ▷ Hast du nicht etwas gehört? Haven't you heard anything? ❸ a little ▷ Wir sollten uns etwas ausruhen. We should have a little rest. ▷ Nur etwas Milch bitte. Just a little milk, please.

EU f (= Europäische Union) EU (= European Union)

euch pron
euch is the accusative and dative of ihr.
❶ you ▷ Ich habe euch gesehen. I saw you. ▷ Ich komme mit euch. I'll come with you. ❷ yourselves ▷ Seht euch mal im Spiegel an. Look at yourselves in the mirror. ❸ to you ▷ Sie hat es euch gegeben. She gave it to you.

euer adj, pron ❶ your ▷ Euer Deutschlehrer ist nett. Your German teacher is nice. ▷ Wenn das eure Mutter erlaubt. If your mother lets you. ▷ Ist das euer Haus? Is that your house? ❷ yours ▷ Das ist nicht unser Computer, das ist euer. That's not our computer, that's yours. ▷ Unsere Mutter heißt Ulla, wie heißt eure? Our mother's called Ulla, what's yours called? ▷ Wenn es in unserem Haus nicht geht, feiern wir in eurem. If it's not OK in our house, then we'll celebrate in yours.

Eule f owl

eure see **euer**

eures see **euer**

euretwegen adv ❶ for your sakes ▷ Wir sind euretwegen nicht in Urlaub gefahren. We didn't go on holiday for your sakes. ❷ on your account ▷ Er hat sich euretwegen aufgeregt. He got upset on your account.

Euro (pl **Euros** or **Euro**) m euro ▷ Das kostet fünf Euro. It costs five euros.

Europa nt Europe

Europäer (pl **Europäer**) m European

Europäerin f European

europäisch adj European

evangelisch adj Protestant

eventuell *adv, adj* perhaps ▷ *Eventuell komme ich später nach.* Perhaps I'll come on later.; **Eventuelle Fragen wird mein Kollege gerne beantworten.** My colleague will be pleased to answer any questions you may have.

> Be careful! **eventuell** does not mean **eventual**.

ewig *adj* eternal
Ewigkeit *f* eternity
Examen (*pl* **Examen**) *nt* exam
existieren (*perf* **hat existiert**) *vb* [76] to exist
Experte (*pl* **Experten**) *m* expert
Expertin *f* expert
explodieren (*perf* **ist explodiert**) *vb* [76] to explode
Explosion *f* explosion
exportieren (*perf* **hat exportiert**) *vb* [76] to export
extra *adv, adj* ❶ separately ▷ *Schicke den USB-Stick lieber extra.* It'd be better to send the USB stick separately. ❷ specially ▷ *Das wurde extra für sie angefertigt.* That was made specially for her. ▷ *Ich bin extra wegen dir gekommen.* I came specially because of you. ❸ on purpose ▷ *Das hat er extra gemacht.* He did that on purpose. ❹ extra ▷ *Ich habe das extra schnell gemacht.* I did it extra quickly. ▷ *Das sind extra starke Pfefferminzbonbons.* These are extra strong peppermints.
extrem *adj* extreme

f

Fabrik *f* factory

> Be careful! **Fabrik** does not mean **fabric**.

Fach (*pl* **Fächer**) *nt* ❶ shelf ▷ *Das ist mein Fach im Schrank.* This is my shelf in the cupboard. ❷ pigeonhole ▷ *Jeder Lehrer hat im Lehrerzimmer ein Fach.* Every teacher has a pigeonhole in the staff room. ❸ subject ▷ *In welchem Fach bist du am besten?* What subject are you best at?
Facharzt (*gen* **Facharztes**, *pl* **Fachärzte**) *m* specialist (doctor)
Fachärztin *f* specialist (doctor)
Fachfrau *f* expert
Fachhochschule *f* college
Fachmann (*pl* **Fachleute**) *m* expert
Fachschule *f* technical college
Fackel *f* torch
Faden (*pl* **Fäden**) *m* thread
fähig *adj* capable ▷ *Sie ist eine sehr fähige Lehrerin.* She's a very capable teacher.; **fähig sein, etwas zu tun** to be capable of doing something

GERMAN > ENGLISH

Fähigkeit f ability
Fahne f flag
Fahrausweis (gen **Fahrausweises**, pl **Fahrausweise**) m ticket ▷ *Die Fahrausweise, bitte.* Tickets, please.
Fahrbahn f carriageway
Fähre f ferry
fahren (pres **fährt**, imperf **fuhr**, perf **ist/hat gefahren**) vb [21]

> For the perfect tense use **haben** when the verb has an object and **sein** when there is no object.

① to drive ▷ *Er hat mich nach Hause gefahren.* He drove me home. ▷ *Er ist sehr schnell gefahren.* He drove very fast.; **ein Rennen fahren** to drive in a race ② to go ▷ *Der Intercity fährt stündlich.* The Intercity train goes every hour. ③ to leave ▷ *Wann seid ihr gefahren?* When did you leave? ④ to sail ▷ *Das Schiff fährt nach Amerika.* The ship's sailing to America. ▷ *Wir sind mit dem Schiff nach Amerika gefahren.* We sailed to America.; **Rad fahren** to cycle; **mit dem Auto fahren** to go by car; **mit dem Zug fahren** to go by train
Fahrer (pl **Fahrer**) m driver
Fahrerin f driver
Fahrgast (pl **Fahrgäste**) m passenger
Fahrgeld (pl **Fahrgelder**) nt fare ▷ *Bitte das Fahrgeld abgezählt bereithalten.* Please have exact fare ready.
Fahrkarte f ticket ▷ *Die Fahrkarten, bitte.* Tickets, please.
Fahrkartenautomat (gen **Fahrkartenautomaten**, pl **Fahrkartenautomaten**) m ticket machine
Fahrkartenschalter (pl **Fahrkartenschalter**) m ticket office
fahrlässig adj negligent
Fahrplan (pl **Fahrpläne**) m timetable
Fahrpreis (gen **Fahrpreises**, pl **Fahrpreise**) m fare
Fahrprüfung f driving test

77 | fallenlassen

Fahrrad (pl **Fahrräder**) nt bicycle
Fahrradweg (pl **Fahrradwege**) m cycle lane
Fahrschein (pl **Fahrscheine**) m ticket ▷ *Die Fahrscheine, bitte.* Tickets, please.
Fahrschule f driving school
Fahrstuhl (pl **Fahrstühle**) m lift
Fahrt f ① journey ▷ *Am Wochenende haben wir eine Fahrt in den Schwarzwald gemacht.* We went on a trip to the Black Forest at the weekend.; **Gute Fahrt!** Have a good journey.
Fahrtkosten pl travelling expenses pl
Fahrzeug (pl **Fahrzeuge**) nt vehicle
fair adj fair ▷ *Das ist nicht fair!* That's not fair!
Faktor (pl **Faktoren**) m factor
Fakultät f faculty
Falke (gen **Falken**, pl **Falken**) m falcon
Fall (pl **Fälle**) m case ▷ *Die Polizei untersucht den Fall.* The police are investigating the case. ▷ *In diesem Fall mache ich eine Ausnahme.* I'll make an exception in this case. ▷ *Welcher Fall steht nach 'außer'?* Which case does 'außer' take?; **auf jeden Fall** definitely; **für alle Fälle** just in case; **Auf keinen Fall!** No way!
Falle f trap
fallen (pres **fällt**, imperf **fiel**, perf **ist gefallen**) vb [22] to fall; **etwas fallen lassen** (1) to drop something ▷ *Lass es nicht fallen!* Don't drop it! (2) to abandon something ▷ *Wir haben die Idee, in Frankreich Ferien zu machen, wieder fallen lassen.* We've abandoned the idea of spending our holidays in France.; **eine Bemerkung fallen lassen** to make a remark
fällen vb [38] **einen Baum fällen** to fell a tree; **ein Urteil fällen** to pronounce judgement
fallenlassen vb [42] see **fallen**

fällig adj due
falls adv if
Fallschirm (pl **Fallschirme**) m parachute
falsch adj ❶ wrong ▷ *Die Antwort war falsch.* The answer was wrong.; **jemanden falsch verstehen** to get somebody wrong ❷ false ▷ *falsche Zähne* false teeth
fälschen vb [38] to forge
Fälschung f forgery
Falte f ❶ fold ▷ *eine Falte im Papier* a fold in the paper ❷ crease ▷ *Die Hose ist voller Falten.* The trousers are all creased. ❸ wrinkle ▷ *Ihr Gesicht ist voller Falten.* Her face is all wrinkled. ❹ pleat ▷ *eine Rockfalte* a pleat in a skirt
falten vb [2] to fold
faltig adj ❶ wrinkled ▷ *Er hat ein faltiges Gesicht.* He's got a wrinkled face. ❷ creased ▷ *Deine Hose ist ganz faltig.* Your trousers are all creased.
Familie f family
Familienname (gen **Familiennamens**, pl **Familiennamen**) m surname
Fan (pl **Fans**) m fan ▷ *Sie ist ein Fan von Ariana Grande.* She's an Ariana Grande fan.
fand vb see **finden**
fangen (pres **fängt**, imperf **fing**, perf **hat gefangen**) vb [23] to catch
Fantasie f imagination
fantasieren (perf **hat fantasiert**) vb [76] to fantazise
fantastisch adj fantastic
Farbe f ❶ colour ▷ *Rosa ist Beates Lieblingsfarbe.* Pink is Beate's favourite colour. ❷ paint ▷ *Hast du Farben, ich möchte was malen?* I'd like to do some painting, have you got any paints?
farbecht adj colourfast
färben vb [38] to dye ▷ *Sie hat ihre Haare gefärbt.* She's dyed her hair.
farbenblind adj colour-blind
Farbfilm (pl **Farbfilme**) m colour film

Farbfoto (pl **Farbfotos**) nt colour photograph
farbig adj coloured
farblos adj colourless
Farbstift (pl **Farbstifte**) m coloured pencil
Farbstoff (pl **Farbstoffe**) m dye
Farbton (pl **Farbtöne**) m shade
Fasan (pl **Fasane** or **Fasanen**) m pheasant
Fasching (pl **Faschinge**) m carnival
- The German carnival season lasts
- from 11 November to Shrove Tuesday
- but most events, fancy-dress
- processions and parties take place
- in the week leading up to Ash
- Wednesday.

Faser f fibre
Fass (gen **Fasses**, pl **Fässer**) nt barrel ▷ *ein Weinfass* a wine barrel; **ein Ölfass** an oil drum; **Bier vom Fass** draught beer
fassen (perf **hat gefasst**) vb [31] ❶ to grasp ▷ *Er fasste mich am Arm.* He grasped my arm. ❷ to hold ▷ *Der Behälter fasst zwanzig Liter.* The container holds twenty litres. ❸ to understand ▷ *Ich kann es nicht fassen, dass du das noch immer nicht gemacht hast.* I can't understand why you still haven't done it.; **nicht zu fassen** unbelievable; **sich fassen** to calm down
Fassung f ❶ composure ▷ *Sie hat die Fassung verloren.* She lost her composure.; **jemanden aus der Fassung bringen** to upset somebody ❷ version ▷ *der Text in einer neuen Fassung* the text in a new version
fassungslos adj speechless
fast adv almost

Be careful! The German word **fast** does not mean **fast**.

fasten vb [2] to fast
Fastenzeit f Lent

Fast Food nt fast food

Fastnacht f carnival
- The German carnival season lasts from 11 November to Shrove Tuesday
- but most events, fancy-dress processions and parties take place in the week leading up to Ash Wednesday.

faul adj ① rotten ▷ *Der Apfel ist faul.* The apple's rotten. ② lazy ▷ *Er ist der faulste Schüler.* He's our laziest pupil.; **eine faule Ausrede** a lame excuse; **Daran ist etwas faul.** (informal) There's something fishy about it.

faulen vb [38] to rot

faulenzen vb [36] to laze about

Faust (pl **Fäuste**) f fist; **auf eigene Faust** off one's own bat

faxen vb [36] to fax ▷ *jemandem etwas faxen* to fax something to somebody

FCKW m (= Fluorchlorkohlenwasserstoff) CFC (= chlorofluorocarbon)

Februar (gen **Februar** or **Februars**, pl **Februare**) m February ▷ *im Februar* in February ▷ *am dritten Februar* on the third of February ▷ *Bonn, den 3. Februar 2025* Bonn, 3 February 2025 ▷ *Heute ist der zweite Februar.* Today is the second of February.

fechten (pres **ficht**, imperf **focht**, perf **hat gefochten**) vb to fence

Feder f ① feather ▷ *Er hatte eine Feder am Hut.* He had a feather in his hat. ② spring ▷ *Die Federn des Betts sind ausgeleiert.* The bed springs have worn out.

Federbett (pl **Federbetten**) nt continental quilt

fegen vb [38] to sweep

fehl adj **fehl am Platz** out of place

fehlen vb [38] ① to be absent ▷ *Er hat gestern in der Schule gefehlt.* He was absent from school yesterday. ② to be missing ▷ *Da fehlt ein Knopf.* There's a button missing. ▷ *Wer fehlt?* Is anyone missing?; **Mir fehlt das nötige Geld.** I haven't got the money.; **Du fehlst mir.** I miss you.; **Was fehlt ihm?** What's wrong with him?

Fehler (pl **Fehler**) m ① mistake ▷ *Wie viele Fehler hast du gemacht?* How many mistakes did you make? ② fault ▷ *Sein einziger Fehler ist, dass er den Mund nicht halten kann.* His only fault is that he can't keep his mouth shut.

Feier f celebration

Feierabend (pl **Feierabende**) m clocking-off time; **Feierabend machen** to clock off; **Wann hat dein Vater Feierabend?** When does your father finish work?

feierlich adj solemn

Feierlichkeit f festivity

feiern vb [88] to celebrate

Feiertag (pl **Feiertage**) m holiday ▷ *ein öffentlicher Feiertag* a public holiday

feige adj cowardly

Feige f fig

Feigling (pl **Feiglinge**) m coward

Feile f file ▷ *eine Nagelfeile* a nailfile

fein adj ① fine ▷ *feiner Sand* fine sand ② refined ▷ *feine Leute* refined people; **Fein!** Great!

Feind (pl **Feinde**) m enemy

feindlich adj hostile

Feindschaft f hostility

Feld (pl **Felder**) nt ① field ▷ *Auf diesem Feld wächst Hafer.* There are oats growing in this field. ② pitch ▷ *ein Fußballfeld* a football pitch ③ square ▷ *Er rückte mit seinem Bauern ein Feld vor.* He moved his pawn forward one square.

Fels (gen **Felsen**, pl **Felsen**) m rock; **die weißen Felsen von Dover** the white cliffs of Dover

feminin adj feminine

Fenster (pl **Fenster**) nt window

Fensterscheibe f windowpane

Ferien pl holidays pl; **Ferien haben** to be on holiday

Ferienjob (pl **Ferienjobs**) m holiday job
Ferienkurs (gen **Ferienkurses**, pl **Ferienkurse**) m vacation course
Ferienlager (gen **Ferienlagers**, pl **Ferienlager**) nt holiday camp
fern adj, adv distant ▷ *in ferner Zukunft* in the distant future; **fern von hier** a long way from here
Fernbedienung f remote control
Fernglas (gen **Fernglases**, pl **Ferngläser**) nt binoculars pl ▷ *ein Fernglas* a pair of binoculars
Fernsehapparat (pl **Fernsehapparate**) m television set
fernsehen (pres **sieht fern**, imperf **sah fern**, perf **hat ferngesehen**) vb [64] to watch television
Fernsehen nt television ▷ *im Fernsehen* on television
Fernseher (pl **Fernseher**) m television set
Fernsehsendung f TV programme
Fernsehserie f TV series
Fernsteuerung f remote control
Ferse f heel ▷ *Ich habe eine Blase an der Ferse.* I've got a blister on my heel.
fertig adj ❶ ready ▷ *Das Essen ist fertig.* Dinner's ready. ❷ finished ▷ *Der Aufsatz ist fertig.* The essay's finished. ▷ *Bist du mit deinen Hausaufgaben fertig?* Have you finished your homework?; **etwas fertig machen** to finish something; **sich fertig machen** to get ready
fertigbringen (imperf **brachte fertig**, perf **hat fertiggebracht**) vb [13] **es fertigbringen, etwas zu tun** to bring oneself to do something
Fertiggericht (pl **Fertiggerichte**) nt ready meal
fertigmachen vb [48] jemanden fertigmachen (1) to wear somebody out ▷ *Die Radtour hat mich fertiggemacht.* The cycling trip wore me out. (2) (informal) to tear somebody off a strip ▷ *Meine Englischlehrerin hat mich heute fertiggemacht.* My English teacher tore me off a strip today.
fesselnd adj captivating
fest adj, adv firm ▷ *Er hielt sie mit festem Griff.* He had a firm grip of her. ▷ *Er hat einen festen Händedruck.* He has a firm handshake.; **ein festes Einkommen** a regular income; **fest schlafen** to sleep soundly; **feste Nahrung** solids pl
Fest (pl **Feste**) nt ❶ party ▷ *Fritz macht am Samstag ein Fest.* Fritz is having a party on Saturday. ❷ festival ▷ *das Backnanger Straßenfest* the Backnang Street Festival; **Frohes Fest!** Happy Christmas!
festhalten (pres **hält fest**, imperf **hielt fest**, perf **hat festgehalten**) vb [33] to keep hold of ▷ *Du musst das Steuer festhalten.* You must keep hold of the wheel.; **sich festhalten an** to hold on to
festlegen (perf **hat festgelegt**) vb [4] to fix ▷ *einen Termin festlegen* to fix a date; **sich festlegen** to commit oneself
festlich adj festive
festmachen (perf **hat festgemacht**) vb [48] ❶ to fix ▷ *Habt ihr den Termin schon festgemacht?* Have you fixed the date yet? ❷ to moor ▷ *Wir haben das Boot im Hafen festgemacht.* We moored the boat in the harbour.
festnehmen (pres **nimmt fest**, imperf **nahm fest**, perf **hat festgenommen**) vb [52] to arrest
Festplatte f hard disk
feststehen (imperf **stand fest**, perf **hat festgestanden**) vb [72] to be certain ▷ *So viel steht fest:* ... This much is certain: ...
feststellen (perf **hat festgestellt**) vb [4] ❶ to establish ▷ *Wir konnten nicht feststellen, wer das geschrieben hatte.* We couldn't establish who'd written it. ❷ to see ▷ *Ich stelle fest, dass du schon wieder nicht aufgepasst hast.* I see that

GERMAN > ENGLISH

you haven't been paying attention again. ③ to detect ▷ *Wir haben da einen Fehler festgestellt.* We've detected an error.

Festtag m special day

fett adj ① fat ▷ *Er ist zu fett.* He's too fat.; **fettes Essen** greasy food; **fette Schrift** bold type

Fett (pl **Fette**) nt fat

fettarm adj low-fat

fettig adj greasy

Fetzen (pl **Fetzen**) m scrap ▷ *ein Fetzen Papier* a scrap of paper

feucht adj ① damp ▷ *etwas mit einem feuchten Tuch abwischen* to wipe something with a damp cloth ② humid ▷ *Das Klima ist sehr feucht.* The climate's very humid.

Feuchtigkeit f ① moisture ▷ *Salz zieht Feuchtigkeit an.* Salt attracts moisture. ② humidity ▷ *hohe Luftfeuchtigkeit* high humidity

Feuer (pl **Feuer**) nt fire

Feuerlöscher (pl **Feuerlöscher**) m fire extinguisher

Feuerwehr (pl **Feuerwehren**) f fire brigade

Feuerwehrauto (pl **Feuerwehrautos**) nt fire engine

Feuerwehrfrau f firefighter

Feuerwehrmann (pl **Feuerwehrleute** or **Feuerwehrmänner**) m firefighter

Feuerwerk (pl **Feuerwerke**) nt fireworks pl ▷ *Wir waren beim Feuerwerk.* We went to the fireworks.

Feuerzeug (pl **Feuerzeuge**) nt lighter

Fieber (pl **Fieber**) nt ① fever ▷ *Das Fieber wird sich in ein paar Tagen senken.* The fever will pass in a couple of days. ② temperature ▷ *Hast du Fieber?* Have you got a temperature?

fiel vb see **fallen**

fies adj nasty

Figur f ① (body) figure ② (in book) character

81 | Fitness

Filiale f branch

Film (pl **Filme**) m film

filmen vb [38] to film

Filter (pl **Filter**) m filter

Filzstift (pl **Filzstifte**) m felt-tip pen

Finanzamt (pl **Finanzämter**) nt tax office

finanziell adj financial

finanzieren (perf **hat finanziert**) vb [76] to finance

finden (imperf **fand**, perf **hat gefunden**) vb [24] ① to find ▷ *Hast du deinen Radiergummi gefunden?* Have you found your rubber? ② to think ▷ *Ich finde, er sieht gut aus.* I think he's good-looking. ▷ *Ich finde sie nicht attraktiv.* I don't think she's attractive.; **Ich finde nichts dabei, wenn ...** I don't see what's wrong with ...; **Das wird sich finden.** Things will work out.

fing vb see **fangen**

Finger (pl **Finger**) m finger

Fingerabdruck (pl **Fingerabdrücke**) m fingerprint; **genetische Fingerabdrücke** genetic fingerprinting

Fingernagel (pl **Fingernägel**) m fingernail

Finne (gen **Finnen**, pl **Finnen**) m Finn

Finnin f Finn

finnisch adj Finnish

Finnland nt Finland

finster adj ① dark ▷ *Hier ist es aber finster.* It's dark in here. ② sinister ▷ *finstere Gestalten* sinister figures; **ein finsteres Gesicht** a grim face

Finsternis f darkness

Firma (pl **Firmen**) f firm

Fisch (pl **Fische**) m fish; **Fische** Pisces sg

fischen vb [48] to fish ▷ *Sonntags geht Alex immer fischen.* Alex always goes fishing on Sundays.

Fischer (pl **Fischer**) m fisherman

fit adj fit ▷ *Ich halte mich mit Schwimmen fit.* I keep fit by swimming.

Fitness f fitness

Fitnessstudio (pl **Fitnessstudios**) nt gym

fix adj fix und fertig (1) finished ▷ *Alles war fix und fertig.* Everything was finished. (2) (informal) all in ▷ *Ich bin fix und fertig.* I'm all in.

flach adj ❶ flat ▷ *Norddeutschland ist flach.* North Germany's flat. ❷ shallow ▷ *Ich brauche eine flache Schale.* I need a shallow bowl.

Flachbildschirm (pl **Flachbildschirme**) m flat screen ▷ *ein Fernseher mit Flachbildschirm* a flatscreen TV

Fläche f area ▷ *eine Fläche von hundert Quadratkilometern* an area of a hundred square kilometres

flackern vb [88] to flicker

Flagge f flag

Flamme f flame

Flasche f bottle ▷ *eine Flasche Mineralwasser* a bottle of mineral water

Flaschenöffner (pl **Flaschenöffner**) m bottle-opener

Fleck (pl **Flecke**) m ❶ stain ▷ *Der Wein hat einen Fleck auf dem Teppich gemacht.* The wine left a stain on the carpet. ❷ spot ▷ *Das ist ein hübscher Fleck.* This is a beautiful spot.

fleckig adj ❶ spotted ▷ *Ein Dalmatiner hat ein fleckiges Fell.* A Dalmatian has a spotted coat. ❷ stained ▷ *Die Tischdecke ist ganz fleckig.* The tablecloth's all stained.

Fledermaus (pl **Fledermäuse**) f bat

Fleisch nt meat ▷ *Ich esse kein Fleisch.* I don't eat meat.

Fleischer (pl **Fleischer**) m butcher

Fleischerei f butcher's

Fleiß (gen **Fleißes**) m hard work ▷ *Mit etwas Fleiß könntest du deine Noten verbessern.* With a bit of hard work you could improve your marks.

fleißig adj hard-working ▷ *Silke ist eine fleißige Schülerin.* Silke's a hard-working pupil.; *Ich war heute schon fleißig.* I've already done quite a bit of work today.

flexibel adj flexible

flicken vb [48] to mend

Fliege f ❶ fly ▷ *Er tut keiner Fliege etwas zuleide.* He wouldn't hurt a fly. ❷ bow tie ▷ *Er trug eine Fliege.* He was wearing a bow tie.

fliegen (imperf **flog**, perf **ist geflogen**) vb [25] to fly

fliehen (imperf **floh**, perf **ist geflohen**) vb [26] to flee

Fliese f tile

Fließband (pl **Fließbänder**) nt assembly line

fließen (imperf **floss**, perf **ist geflossen**) vb [27] to flow

fließend adj, adv ❶ running ▷ *fließendes Wasser* running water ❷ fluent ▷ *Sie spricht fließend Englisch.* She is fluent in English.

flink adj nimble

Flitterwochen fpl honeymoon sg

flitzen (perf **ist geflitzt**) vb [48] to dash

Flocke f flake ▷ *eine Schneeflocke* a snowflake

flog vb see **fliegen**

Floh (pl **Flöhe**) m flea

Flohmarkt (pl **Flohmärkte**) m flea market

floss vb see **fließen**

Flosse f ❶ fin ▷ *die Flosse eines Hais* a shark's fin ❷ flipper ▷ *Er hat seine Flossen mit ins Schwimmbad genommen.* He took his flippers with him to the swimming baths.

Flöte f ❶ flute ▷ *Cordula spielt Flöte.* Cordula plays the flute. ❷ recorder ▷ *Phil spielt Flöte.* Phil plays the recorder.

fluchen vb [38] to curse

flüchtig adj at large ▷ *Der Einbrecher ist noch flüchtig.* The burglar's still at large.; *jemanden nur flüchtig kennen* to know somebody only superficially

GERMAN > ENGLISH

Flüchtling (pl **Flüchtlinge**) m refugee
Flug (pl **Flüge**) m flight ▷ *Der Flug nach Atlanta ist verspätet.* The flight to Atlanta's been delayed.
Flugbegleiter (pl die **Flugbegleiter**) m flight attendant
Flugbegleiterin f flight attendant
Flugblatt (pl **Flugblätter**) nt leaflet
Flügel (pl **Flügel**) m ① wing ▷ *die Flügel des Adlers* the eagle's wings ② grand piano ▷ *Im Musikzimmer steht ein Flügel.* There's a grand piano in the music room.
Fluggast (pl **Fluggäste**) m airline passenger
Fluggesellschaft f airline
Flughafen (pl **Flughäfen**) m airport
Fluglotse (gen **Fluglotsen**, pl **Fluglotsen**) m air traffic controller
Flugplan (pl **Flugpläne**) m flight schedule
Flugplatz (gen **Flugplatzes**, pl **Flugplätze**) m ① airport ▷ *Wir bringen dich zum Flugplatz.* We'll take you to the airport. ② airfield ▷ *Dieser Flugplatz ist nur für Privatflugzeuge.* This airfield is only for private planes.
Flugticket (pl **Flugtickets**) nt plane ticket
Flugzeug (pl **Flugzeuge**) nt aeroplane
Flugzeugentführung f hijacking
Flur (pl **Flure**) m corridor

> Be careful! **Flur** does not mean floor.

Fluss (gen **Flusses**, pl **Flüsse**) m river
flüssig adj liquid
Flüssigkeit f liquid
flüstern vb [88] to whisper
Flut (pl **Fluten**) f ① flood ▷ *Wir haben eine Flut von Briefen bekommen.* We received a flood of letters. ② high tide ▷ *Das Schiff läuft bei Flut aus.* The ship sails at high tide.
Flutlicht (pl **Flutlichter**) nt floodlight
Föhn (pl **Föhne**) m ① (*warm dry alpine wind*) foehn ② hair dryer

83 | **formulieren**

föhnen vb [38] to blow-dry
Folge f ① result ▷ *Er starb an den Folgen des Unfalls.* He died as a result of the accident.; **etwas zur Folge haben** to result in something; **Folgen haben** to have consequences ② episode ▷ *Hast du die letzte Folge der 'Lindenstraße' gesehen?* Did you see the latest episode of 'Lindenstraße'?; **ein Roman in Folgen** a serialized novel
folgen (perf **ist gefolgt**) vb [38] to follow ▷ *Uns ist ein grünes Auto gefolgt.* We were followed by a green car. ▷ *Folgen Sie dem Wagen da.* Follow that car. ▷ *Ich konnte ihm nicht folgen.* I couldn't follow what he was saying.; **Meine Kinder folgen nicht immer.** My children don't always do what they're told.
folgend adj following
Folgerung f conclusion
folglich adv consequently
folgsam adj obedient
Folie f foil
foltern vb [88] to torture
Fön® (pl **Föne**) m hair dryer
fordern vb [88] to demand
Forderung f demand
Forelle f trout ▷ *drei Forellen* three trout
Form (pl **Formen**) f ① shape ▷ *Das Auto hat eine elegante Form.* The car has an elegant shape.; **in Form sein** to be in good shape ▷ *Sie war in bester Form.* She was in great shape. ② mould ▷ *Das Metall wird in eine Form gegossen.* The metal is poured into a mould. ③ baking tin
Format (pl **Formate**) nt format
formatieren (perf **hat formatiert**) vb [76] to format
Formel f formula
formen vb [38] to form
förmlich adj formal
Formular (pl **Formulare**) nt form ▷ *ein Formular ausfüllen* to fill in a form
formulieren (perf **hat formuliert**) vb [76] to formulate

Forscher (*pl* **Forscher**) *m* ❶ research scientist ▷ *Die Forscher haben noch keinen Impfstoff dagegen entwickelt.* Research scientists have still not developed a vaccine for it. ❷ explorer ▷ *Ein Gruppe von Forschern ist im Amazonasgebiet verschollen.* A group of explorers is missing in the Amazon region.

Forschung *f* research

fort *adv* gone ▷ *Mein Geldbeutel ist fort.* My purse is gone.; **und so fort** and so on; **in einem fort** on and on; **Fort mit dir!** Away with you!

sich fortbewegen (*perf* **hat sich fortbewegt**) *vb* [4] to move

fortbleiben (*imperf* **blieb fort**, *perf* **ist fortgeblieben**) *vb* [10] to stay away

fortfahren (*pres* **fährt fort**, *imperf* **fuhr fort**, *perf* **ist fortgefahren**) *vb* [21] ❶ to leave ▷ *Sie sind gestern fortgefahren.* They left yesterday. ❷ to continue ▷ *Er fuhr in seiner Rede fort.* He continued with his speech.

fortgeschritten *adj* advanced

Fortschritt (*pl* **Fortschritte**) *m* progress ▷ *Fortschritte machen* to make progress

fortschrittlich *adj* progressive

fortsetzen (*perf* **hat fortgesetzt**) *vb* [15] to continue

Fortsetzung *f* ❶ continuation ▷ *die Fortsetzung des Krieges* the continuation of the war ❷ sequel ▷ *Hast du die Fortsetzung gelesen?* Have you read the sequel?; **Fortsetzung folgt** to be continued

Foto (*pl* **Fotos**) *nt* photo

Fotoapparat (*pl* **Fotoapparate**) *m* camera

Fotograf (*gen* **Fotografen**, *pl* **Fotografen**) *m* photographer

Be careful! **Fotograf** does not mean photograph.

Fotografie *f* ❶ photography ▷ *Die Fotografie ist sein Hobby.* His hobby is photography. ❷ photograph ▷ *Ich habe eine Fotografie davon gesehen.* I've seen a photograph of it.

fotografieren (*perf* **hat fotografiert**) *vb* ❶ to take a photo of ▷ *Kannst du uns mal fotografieren?* Can you take a photo of us? ❷ to take photographs ▷ *Ich fotografiere in den Ferien nie.* I never take photographs on holiday.

Fotohandy (*pl* **Fotohandys**) *nt* camera phone

Fotokopie *f* photocopy

Fracht *f* freight ▷ *Frachtkosten* freight charges

Frage *f* question ▷ *Könntest du bitte meine Frage beantworten?* Could you please answer my question? ▷ *jemandem eine Frage stellen* to ask somebody a question; **in Frage kommen/stellen** *see* **infrage**

Fragebogen (*pl* **Fragebogen**) *m* questionnaire

fragen *vb* [38] to ask ▷ *Kann ich dich was fragen?* Can I ask you something?; **sich fragen** to wonder ▷ *Das frage ich mich auch.* That's just what I was wondering.

Fragezeichen (*pl* **Fragezeichen**) *nt* question mark

fraglich *adj* doubtful ▷ *Es ist sehr fraglich, ob wir kommen können.* It's very doubtful whether we can come.

Franken (*pl* **Franken**) *m* franc ▷ *Er bezahlte 50 Franken.* He paid 50 francs.; **der Schweizer Franken** the Swiss franc

frankieren (*perf* **hat frankiert**) *vb* [76] **einen Brief frankieren** to put a stamp on a letter; **ein frankierter Briefumschlag** a stamped self-addressed envelope

Frankreich *nt* France

Franzose (*gen* **Franzosen**, *pl* **Franzosen**) *m* Frenchman; **Er ist Franzose.** He's French.; **die Franzosen** the French

GERMAN > ENGLISH

Französin f Frenchwoman; **Sie ist Französin.** She's French.
französisch adj French
Französisch (gen **Französischen**) nt French ▷ *Er lernt Französisch in der Schule.* He's learning French at school.
fraß vb see **fressen**
Frau f ① woman ▷ *Sie ist eine kluge Frau.* She's a clever woman. ② wife ▷ *Herr Arnold ist mit seiner Frau gekommen.* Mr Arnold came with his wife.; **Sehr geehrte Frau Braun (1)** Dear Mrs Braun **(2)** Dear Ms Braun
• Generally **Frau** is used to address all
• women whether married or not.
• **Frau Doktor** Doctor
Frauenarzt (gen **Frauenarztes**, pl **Frauenärzte**) m gynaecologist
Fräulein (pl **Fräulein**) nt Miss ▷ *Liebes Fräulein Dümmler* Dear Miss Dümmler
• **Fräulein** is hardly ever used nowadays
• and **Frau** is used instead to address
• all women whether married or not.
frech adj cheeky
Frechheit f cheek
frei adj free; **Ist der Platz hier frei?** Is this seat taken?; **Soll ich einen Platz für dich frei halten?** Shall I keep a seat for you?; **'Einfahrt frei halten'** 'Keep clear'; **Wir haben im Moment keine freien Stellen.** We haven't got any vacancies at the moment.; **ein freier Mitarbeiter** a freelancer; **im Freien** in the open air
Freibad (pl **Freibäder**) nt open-air swimming pool ▷ *Im Sommer gehe ich gern ins Freibad.* I like going to the open-air swimming pool in the summer.
freigebig adj generous
freihalten vb [33] see **frei**
Freiheit f ① freedom ② liberty ▷ *sich Freiheiten herausnehmen* to take liberties
freilassen (pres **lässt frei**, imperf **ließ frei**, perf **hat freigelassen**) vb [42] to free

85 | **Freund**

Freiminuten pl free minutes
Freitag (pl **Freitage**) m Friday ▷ *am Freitag* on Friday
freitags adv on Fridays
freiwillig adj voluntary
Freizeit f spare time ▷ *Was machst du in deiner Freizeit?* What do you do in your spare time?
Freizeitbeschäftigung f leisure activity
fremd adj ① strange ▷ *eine fremde Umgebung* strange surroundings ② foreign ▷ *fremde Länder und Sprachen* foreign countries and languages; **Ich bin in London fremd.** I'm a stranger to London.
Fremdenverkehr m tourism
Fremdenzimmer (pl **Fremdenzimmer**) nt guest room
Fremdsprache f foreign language
fressen (pres **frisst**, imperf **fraß**, perf **hat gefressen**) vb to eat ▷ *Er frisst wie ein Schwein.* He eats like a pig.
Freude f ① joy ▷ *Welche Freude!* What joy! ② delight ▷ *Zu meiner Freude hatten wir gestern keine Schule.* To my delight we didn't have any school yesterday.; **Er hat viel Freude an seinem Mountainbike.** He's delighted with his mountain bike.; **Das wird den Kindern Freude machen.** That'll please the children.; **Ich wollte dir eine Freude machen.** I wanted to make you happy.
freuen vb [38] **sich freuen** to be glad; **sich auf etwas freuen** to look forward to something; **sich über etwas freuen** to be pleased with something; **Dein Brief hat mich sehr gefreut.** Your letter made me very happy.; **Freut mich!** Pleased to meet you.
Freund (pl **Freunde**) m ① friend ▷ *Alle meine Freunde waren da.* All my friends were there. ② boyfriend ▷ *Hast du einen Freund?* Have you got a boyfriend?

Freundin f ▶ friend ▷ *Wiltrud kommt mit ihrer Freundin.* Wiltrud's coming with her friend. ❷ girlfriend ▷ *Tobias hat keine Freundin.* Tobias hasn't got a girlfriend.

freundlich adj ❶ friendly ▷ *Die Leute waren sehr freundlich.* The people were very friendly. ▷ *ein freundliches Lächeln* a friendly smile ❷ kind ▷ *Das ist sehr freundlich von Ihnen.* That's very kind of you.

Freundlichkeit f friendliness

Freundschaft f friendship

Frieden (pl **Frieden**) m peace; **im Frieden** in peacetime

Friedhof (pl **Friedhöfe**) m cemetery

friedlich adj peaceful

frieren (imperf **fror**, perf **hat gefroren**) vb to freeze ▷ *Ich friere.* I'm freezing.; **Es friert mich.** I'm freezing.; **Letzte Nacht hat es gefroren.** It was frosty last night.

Frikadelle f rissole

frisch adj fresh ▷ *frische Milch* fresh milk ▷ *ein frischer Wind* a fresh wind ▷ *Nimm ein frisches Blatt.* Take a fresh sheet of paper.; **Frisch gestrichen!** Wet paint!; **sich frisch machen** to freshen oneself up

Friseur m hairdresser

Friseuse f hairdresser

frisieren (perf **hat frisiert**) vb [76] **jemanden frisieren** to do somebody's hair; **sich frisieren** to do one's hair

frisst vb see **fressen**

Frist f deadline ▷ *eine Frist einhalten* to meet a deadline

Frisur f hairdo

froh adj happy ▷ *frohe Gesichter* happy faces; **Ich bin froh, dass ...** I'm glad that ...

fröhlich adj cheerful

fromm adj devout

fror vb see **frieren**

Frosch (pl **Frösche**) m frog

Frost (pl **Fröste**) m frost ▷ *ein strenger Frost* a hard frost

frösteln vb [88] to shiver

Frucht (pl **Früchte**) f fruit

fruchtbar adj ❶ fruitful ▷ *ein fruchtbares Gespräch* a fruitful conversation ❷ fertile ▷ *fruchtbarer Boden* fertile soil

Fruchtsaft (pl **Fruchtsäfte**) m fruit juice

früh adj, adv early ▷ *Komm lieber etwas früher.* It's better if you come a bit earlier.; **heute früh** this morning

früher adj, adv ❶ former ▷ *eine frühere Schülerin unserer Schule* a former pupil of our school ❷ once ▷ *Hier stand früher ein Haus.* A house once stood here.; **Früher war das anders.** That used to be different.

Frühjahr (pl **Frühjahre**) nt spring ▷ *im Frühjahr* in spring

Frühling (pl **Frühlinge**) m spring ▷ *im Frühling* in spring

Frühstück nt breakfast

frühstücken vb [38] to have breakfast

frustrieren (perf **hat frustriert**) vb [76] to frustrate

Fuchs (gen **Fuchses**, pl **Füchse**) m fox

fühlen vb [38] to feel ▷ *Fühl mal, wie weich das ist.* Feel how soft it is. ▷ *Ich fühle mich wohl.* I feel fine.

fuhr vb see **fahren**

führen vb [38] ❶ to lead ▷ *Sie führte uns nach draußen.* She led us outside.; **ein Geschäft führen** to run a business ❷ to be winning ▷ *Welche Mannschaft führt?* Which team's winning?

Führer (pl **Führer**) m ❶ leader ▷ *der Parteiführer* the party leader ❷ guide ▷ *Unser Führer zeigte uns alle Sehenswürdigkeiten.* Our guide showed us all the sights. ❸ guidebook ▷ *Hast du einen Führer von Rom?* Have you got a guidebook of Rome?

Führerschein (pl **Führerscheine**) m driving licence; **den Führerschein machen** to take one's driving test

Führung f ❶ lead ▷ *Unsere Mannschaft liegt in Führung.* Our team is in the lead. ❷ leadership ▷ *Er übernahm die Führung der Partei.* He took over the leadership of the party. ❸ management ▷ *Das Geschäft hat unter neuer Führung wiedereröffnet.* The business has reopened under new management. ❹ guided tour ▷ *Führungen durchs Museum finden stündlich statt.* There are guided tours of the museum every hour.

füllen vb [38] ❶ to fill ▷ *Sie füllte das Glas bis zum Rand.* She filled the glass to the brim. ❷ to stuff ▷ *Heute gibt es gefüllte Paprika.* We're having stuffed peppers today.

Füller (pl **Füller**) m fountain pen

Füllung f filling

Fundament (pl **Fundamente**) nt foundations pl

Fundbüro (pl **Fundbüros**) nt lost property office

fundiert adj sound ▷ *fundierte Englischkenntnisse* a sound knowledge of English

fünf num five

Fünf f ❶ five ❷ poor
: German marks range from one (**sehr gut**) to six (**ungenügend**).

fünfte adj fifth ▷ *Ich erkläre dir das jetzt zum fünften Mal.* This is the fifth time I've explained this to you. ▷ *Er kam als Fünfter.* He was the fifth to arrive.

fünfzehn num fifteen

fünfzig num fifty

Funke (gen **Funkens**, pl **Funken**) m spark

funkeln vb [88] to sparkle

Funkloch (pl **Funklöcher**) nt (mobile phone) dead spot

Funktion f function

funktionieren (perf **hat funktioniert**) vb [76] to work

Funktionstaste f function key

für prep
▌ The preposition **für** takes the accusative.
for ▷ *Das ist für dich.* This is for you.; **was für** what kind of; **das Für und Wider** the pros and cons
▌ Word for word, **das Für und Wider** means 'the for and against'.

Furcht f fear

furchtbar adj terrible

fürchten vb [2] to be afraid ▷ *Ich fürchte mich vor diesem Mann.* I'm afraid of that man.

fürchterlich adj awful

fürs = für das

Fuß (gen **Fußes**, pl **Füße**) m ❶ foot ▷ *Mir tun die Füße weh.* My feet hurt. ❷ leg ▷ *Der Tisch hat vier Füße.* The table's got four legs.; **zu Fuß** on foot

Fußball (pl **Fußbälle**) m football

Fußballplatz (gen **Fußballplatzes**, pl **Fußballplätze**) m football pitch

Fußballspiel (pl **Fußballspiele**) nt football match

Fußballspieler (pl **Fußballspieler**) m footballer

Fußboden (pl **Fußböden**) m floor

Fußgänger (pl **Fußgänger**) m pedestrian

Fußgängerzone f pedestrian precinct

Fußweg (pl **Fußwege**) m footpath

Futter (pl **Futter**) nt ❶ feed ▷ *BSE entstand durch verseuchtes Futter.* BSE was the result of contaminated feed. ❷ food ▷ *Hast du Futter für die Katze gekauft?* Have you bought cat food? ❸ lining ▷ *Der Mantel hat ein Futter aus Pelz.* The coat has a fur lining.

füttern vb [88] ❶ to feed ▷ *Kannst du bitte das Baby füttern?* Can you feed the baby, please? ❷ to line ▷ *Der Mantel ist gefüttert.* The coat's lined.

Futur (pl **Future**) nt future

g

g abbr (= Gramm) g
gab vb see **geben**
Gabel f fork
gähnen vb [38] to yawn
Galerie f gallery
gamen vb [48] to game (on computer)
Gamer (pl **Gamer**) m gamer (on computer)
Gamerin f gamer (on computer)
Gaming nt gaming (on computer)
Gang (pl **Gänge**) m ❶ corridor ▷ *Häng deinen Mantel im Gang auf.* Hang your coat up in the corridor. ❷ aisle ▷ *Ich hätte gern einen Platz am Gang.* I'd like an aisle seat. ❸ gear ▷ *Mein Fahrrad hat zehn Gänge.* My bike has ten gears. ❹ course ▷ *Das war erst der zweite Gang, und ich bin schon satt.* That was only the second course and I'm full already. ▷ *der Gang der Dinge* the course of events; **etwas in Gang bringen** to get something off the ground
Gans (pl **Gänse**) f goose
Gänseblümchen (pl **Gänseblümchen**) nt daisy
Gänsehaut f goose pimples pl
ganz adj, adv ❶ whole ▷ *die ganze Welt* the whole world ▷ *ganz Europa* the whole of Europe; **sein ganzes Geld** all his money ❷ quite ▷ *ganz gut* quite good; **ganz und gar nicht** not at all; **Es sieht ganz so aus.** It really looks like it.
ganztags adv full time ▷ *ganztags arbeiten* to work full time
gar adj, adv done ▷ *Die Kartoffeln sind gar.* The potatoes are done.; **gar nicht** not at all; **gar nichts** nothing at all; **gar niemand** nobody at all
Garage f garage (for parking)
garantieren (perf **hat garantiert**) vb [76] to guarantee; **Er kommt garantiert.** He's sure to come.
Garderobe f cloakroom ▷ *Ich habe meinen Mantel an der Garderobe abgegeben.* I left my coat in the cloakroom.
Gardine f curtain ▷ *die Gardinen zuziehen* to shut the curtains
Garten (pl **Gärten**) m garden
Gas (gen **Gases**, pl **Gase**) nt gas ▷ *Wir kochen mit Gas.* We cook with gas.; **Gas geben** to accelerate
Gasherd (pl **Gasherde**) m gas cooker
Gaspedal (pl **Gaspedale**) nt accelerator
Gasse f lane ▷ *die schmalen Gassen der Altstadt* the narrow lanes of the old town
Gast (pl **Gäste**) m guest ▷ *Wir haben Gäste aus England.* We've got guests from England.; **bei jemandem zu Gast sein** to be somebody's guest
gastfreundlich adj hospitable
Gastfreundschaft f hospitality
Gastgeber (pl **Gastgeber**) m host
Gastgeberin f hostess
Gasthaus (gen **Gasthauses**, pl **Gasthäuser**) nt inn
Gasthof (pl **Gasthöfe**) m inn

Gaststätte f pub
* In Germany there's practically no difference between pubs and restaurants. You can eat or drink in a **Gaststätte**, families are welcome and the opening hours are flexible.

gay adj gay

Gebäck (pl **Gebäcke**) nt pastry ▷ *Kuchen und Gebäck* cakes and pastries

gebären (pres **gebiert**, imperf **gebar**, perf **hat geboren**) vb to give birth to

Gebäude (pl **Gebäude**) nt building

geben (pres **gibt**, imperf **gab**, perf **hat gegeben**) vb [28] to give ▷ *Gib ihm bitte das Geld.* Please give him the money. ▷ *Kannst du dieses Buch bitte deiner Mutter geben.* Could you give this book to your mother, please.; **Karten geben** to deal

> Word for word, **Karten geben** means 'to give cards'.

es gibt there is; ▷ *Hier gibt es ein schönes Freibad.* There's a lovely open-air pool here. ▷ *In Stuttgart gibt es viele Parks.* There are many parks in Stuttgart. **es gab** there was ▷ *Es gab ein kleines Problem.* There was a small problem. ▷ *Es gab letztes Jahr viele Äpfel.* There were a lot of apples last year. **Was gibt's?** What's up?; **Was gibt es im Kino?** What's on at the cinema?; **sich geschlagen geben** to admit defeat; **Das wird sich schon geben.** That'll sort itself out.

Gebet (pl **Gebete**) nt prayer

gebeten vb see **bitten**

Gebiet (pl **Gebiete**) nt ❶ area ▷ *ein bewaldetes Gebiet* a wooded area ❷ field ▷ *Er ist Experte auf diesem Gebiet.* He's an expert in this field.

gebildet adj cultured

Gebirge (pl **Gebirge**) nt mountain chain ▷ *Die Alpen sind ein großes Gebirge.* The Alps are a large mountain chain.; **ins Gebirge fahren** to go to the mountains

Gebiss (gen **Gebisses**, pl **Gebisse**) nt ❶ teeth pl ▷ *Sie hat ein gesundes Gebiss.* She's got healthy teeth. ❷ dentures pl ▷ *Opas Gebiss lag auf dem Tisch.* Grandpa's dentures were lying on the table.

gebissen vb see **beißen**

geblieben vb see **bleiben**

geboren vb see **gebären**
▷ adj ❶ born ▷ *Wann bist du geboren?* When were you born? ❷ née ▷ *Frau Dümmler, geborene Schnorr* Mrs Dümmler, née Schnorr

geboten vb see **bieten**

gebracht vb see **bringen**

gebraten adj fried

gebrauchen (perf **hat gebraucht**) vb [48] to use

Gebrauchsanweisung f directions for use pl ▷ *Wo ist die Gebrauchsanweisung?* Where are the directions for use?

gebraucht adj used

Gebrauchtwagen (pl **Gebrauchtwagen**) m second-hand car

gebrochen vb see **brechen**

Gebühr f fee

Gebühreneinheit f unit (telephone)

gebührenpflichtig adj subject to a charge; **eine gebührenpflichtige Verwarnung** a fine

gebunden vb see **binden**

Geburt f birth ▷ *bei der Geburt* at the birth

gebürtig adj native of ▷ *ein gebürtiger Schweizer* a native of Switzerland

Geburtsdatum (pl **Geburtsdaten**) nt date of birth

Geburtsort (pl **Geburtsorte**) m birthplace

Geburtstag (pl **Geburtstage**) m birthday ▷ *Herzlichen Glückwunsch zum Geburtstag!* Happy Birthday!

gedacht vb see **denken**

Gedächtnis (gen **Gedächtnisses**, pl **Gedächtnisse**) nt memory ▷ *Ich habe ein schlechtes Gedächtnis.* I've got a bad memory.

Gedanke (gen **Gedankens**, pl **Gedanken**) m thought; **sich über etwas Gedanken machen** to think about something

gedeihen (imperf **gedieh**, perf **ist gediehen**) vb to thrive

Gedicht (pl **Gedichte**) nt poem

Gedränge nt crush ▷ *Vor der Kinokasse herrschte großes Gedränge.* There was a huge crush at the cinema box office.

Geduld f patience

sich gedulden (perf **hat sich geduldet**) vb [7] to be patient

geduldig adj patient

gedurft vb see **dürfen**

geehrt adj Sehr geehrter Herr Butterfeld Dear Mr Butterfeld

geeignet adj suitable

Gefahr f ❶ danger ▷ *in Gefahr schweben* to be in danger ❷ risk ▷ *Gefahr laufen, etwas zu tun* to run the risk of doing something ▷ *auf eigene Gefahr* at one's own risk

gefährden (perf **hat gefährdet**) vb [7] to endanger

gefährlich adj dangerous

Gefälle (pl **Gefälle**) nt gradient

gefallen (1) vb [22] see **fallen**

gefallen (2) (pres **gefällt**, imperf **gefiel**, perf **hat gefallen**) vb [22] to like ▷ *Es gefällt mir.* I like it. ▷ *Das Geschenk hat ihr gefallen.* She liked the present. ▷ *Er gefällt mir.* I like him. ▷ *Das gefällt mir an ihm.* That's one thing I like about him.; **sich etwas gefallen lassen** to put up with something

Gefallen (pl **Gefallen**) m favour ▷ *Könntest du mir einen Gefallen tun?* Could you do me a favour?

gefangen vb see **fangen**; **jemanden gefangen nehmen** to take somebody prisoner

Gefangene (gen **Gefangenen**, pl **Gefangenen**) mf prisoner ▷ *Ein Gefangener ist geflohen.* A prisoner has escaped.

gefangennehmen vb [52] see **gefangen**

Gefangenschaft f captivity

Gefängnis (gen **Gefängnisses**, pl **Gefängnisse**) nt prison

Gefängnisstrafe f prison sentence

Gefäß (gen **Gefäßes**, pl **Gefäße**) nt container

gefasst adj composed ▷ *Sie war sehr gefasst.* She was very composed.; **auf etwas gefasst sein** to be prepared for something

geflogen vb see **fliegen**

geflossen vb see **fließen**

Geflügel nt poultry

gefragt adj in demand ▷ *Er ist ein sehr gefragter Künstler.* He's an artist very much in demand. ▷ *Handwerker sind sehr gefragt.* Tradesmen are in great demand.

gefräßig adj greedy

Gefrierfach (pl **Gefrierfächer**) nt icebox

Gefriertruhe f deep-freeze

gefroren adj frozen

Gefühl (pl **Gefühle**) nt feeling ▷ *Sie hat ein Gefühl für Kunst.* She's got a feeling for art.; **etwas im Gefühl haben** to have a feel for something

gefüllt adj stuffed ▷ *gefüllte Auberginen* stuffed aubergines

gefunden vb see **finden**

gegangen vb see **gehen**

gegeben vb see **geben**

gegen prep

The preposition **gegen** takes the accusative.

❶ against ▷ *Ich bin gegen diese Idee.* I'm against this idea. ▷ *nichts gegen jemanden haben* to have nothing against somebody; **ein Mittel gegen**

GERMAN > ENGLISH

Schnupfen something for colds; **Maske gegen Botha** Maske versus Botha ❷ towards ▷ *gegen Osten* towards the east ▷ *gegen Abend* towards evening; **gegen einen Baum fahren** to drive into a tree ❸ round about ▷ *gegen drei Uhr* round about three o'clock

Gegend f area ▷ *die Gegend um Ulm* the area around Ulm

Gegensatz (gen **Gegensatzes**, pl **Gegensätze**) m contrast; **Im Gegensatz zu mir ist er gut in Mathe.** Unlike me, he's good at maths.

gegenseitig adj mutual ▷ *gegenseitiges Vertrauen* mutual trust; **sich gegenseitig helfen** to help each other

Gegenstand (pl **Gegenstände**) m object

Gegenteil nt opposite ▷ *Das ist das Gegenteil von schön.* That's the opposite of lovely.; **im Gegenteil** on the contrary

gegenüber prep, adv

> The preposition **gegenüber** takes the dative.

❶ opposite ▷ *Die Apotheke ist gegenüber.* The chemist's is opposite. ▷ *Er saß mir gegenüber.* He sat opposite me.
❷ towards ▷ *Sie waren mir gegenüber sehr freundlich.* They were very friendly towards me.

Gegenverkehr m oncoming traffic

Gegenwart f present ▷ *in der Gegenwart leben* to live in the present

gegessen vb see **essen**

Gegner (pl **Gegner**) m opponent

Gegnerin f opponent

Gehackte (gen **Gehackten**) nt mince ▷ *Ein Kilo Gehacktes, bitte.* A kilo of mince, please.

Gehalt (pl **Gehälter**) nt salary ▷ *Er verdient ein gutes Gehalt.* He earns a good salary.

gehässig adj spiteful

91 | Gehweg

geheim adj secret ▷ *geheim halten* to keep secret

Geheimnis (gen **Geheimnisses**, pl **Geheimnisse**) nt ❶ secret ▷ *Kannst du ein Geheimnis behalten?* Can you keep a secret? ❷ mystery ▷ *die Geheimnisse der Erde* the Earth's mysteries

geheimnisvoll adj mysterious

Geheimnummer f ex-directory number; **Wir haben eine Geheimnummer.** We're ex-directory.

gehen (imperf **ging**, perf **ist gegangen**) vb [29] ❶ to go ▷ *Wir gehen jetzt.* We're going now. ▷ *schwimmen gehen* to go swimming ❷ to walk ▷ *Sollen wir gehen oder den Bus nehmen?* Shall we walk or go by bus?; **Wie geht es dir?** How are you?; **Wie geht's?** How are things?; **Es geht mir gut.** I'm fine.; **Mir/Ihm geht's gut.** I'm/He's fine.; **Es geht.** Not bad.; **Geht das?** Is that possible?; **Geht's noch?** Can you manage?; **Das geht.** That's fine. ▷ *Das geht, dass wir uns morgen treffen.* That's fine to meet up tomorrow. **Das geht nicht.** That's not on.; **um etwas gehen** to be about something; **Hier geht es um sehr viel Geld.** There's a lot of money at stake here.

Gehirn (pl **Gehirne**) nt brain

Gehirnerschütterung f concussion

gehoben vb see **heben**

geholfen vb see **helfen**

gehorchen (perf **hat gehorcht**) vb [48] to obey ▷ *Du solltest deinem Vater gehorchen.* You should obey your father. ▷ *Ein Hund sollte lernen zu gehorchen.* A dog should learn to obey.

gehören (perf **hat gehört**) vb [38] **jemandem gehören** to belong to somebody; **Das gehört sich einfach nicht.** That just isn't done.

gehorsam adj obedient

Gehorsam m obedience

Gehweg (pl **Gehwege**) m pavement

Geier (pl **Geier**) m vulture
Geige f violin ▷ *Wiltrud spielt Geige.* Wiltrud plays the violin.
geil adj ❶ (informal) horny ▷ *Wenn er das sieht, wird er geil.* When he sees that, he'll get horny. ❷ (informal) cool ▷ *Das war eine geile Party.* That was a cool party. ▷ *ein geiler Song* a cool song
Geisel f hostage
Geist (pl **Geister**) m ❶ ghost ❷ mind ▷ *Er hat einen regen Geist.* He has a lively mind.; *Seine Rede sprühte vor Geist.* His speech was very witty.
geisteskrank adj mentally ill
Geisteskrankheit f mental illness
geistig adj intellectual; **geistig behindert** learning-disabled
Geiz (gen **Geizes**) m meanness
Geizhals (gen **Geizhalses**, pl **Geizhälse**) m miser
geizig adj mean
gekannt vb see **kennen**
gekonnt vb see **können**
▶ adj skilful
Gel (pl **Gele**) nt gel
Gelächter nt laughter
geladen vb see **laden**
▶ adj ❶ loaded ▷ *eine geladene Waffe* a loaded weapon ❷ invited ▷ *geladene Gäste* invited guests; **geladen sein** to be furious
gelähmt adj paralysed
Gelände (pl **Gelände**) nt ❶ grounds pl ▷ *auf dem Gelände der Schule* on the school grounds ❷ terrain ▷ *unwegsames Gelände* difficult terrain; **durchs Gelände fahren** to go cross-country; **ein Baugelände** a building site
gelangweilt adj bored
gelassen vb see **lassen**
▶ adj calm ▷ *Sie blieb gelassen.* She remained calm.
geläufig adj common ▷ *ein geläufiger Begriff* a common term; **Das ist mir nicht geläufig.** I'm not familiar with that.

gelaunt adj **gut gelaunt** in a good mood; **schlecht gelaunt** in a bad mood; **Wie ist er gelaunt?** What sort of mood's he in?
gelb adj ❶ yellow ❷ amber ▷ *Die Ampel war gelb.* The traffic lights were at amber.
Geld (pl **Gelder**) nt money; **etwas zu Geld machen** to sell something off
Geldautomat (gen **Geldautomaten**, pl **Geldautomaten**) m cash machine
Geldschein (pl **Geldscheine**) m banknote
Geldstrafe f fine
Geldstück (pl **Geldstücke**) nt coin
Geldwechsel m changing of money ▷ *Beim Geldwechsel muss man eine Gebühr bezahlen.* There is a charge for changing money.; **'Geldwechsel'** 'bureau de change'
gelegen vb see **liegen**
Gelegenheit f ❶ opportunity ▷ *Sobald ich eine Gelegenheit bekomme ...* As soon as I get an opportunity ... ▷ *bei jeder Gelegenheit* at every opportunity ❷ occasion ▷ *Bei dieser Gelegenheit trug sie das blaue Kostüm.* On this occasion she wore her blue suit.
gelegentlich adv ❶ occasionally ▷ *Gelegentlich gehe ich ganz gern ins Kino.* I occasionally like going to the cinema. ❷ some time or other ▷ *Ich werde mich gelegentlich darum kümmern.* I'll do it some time or other.
Gelenk (pl **Gelenke**) nt joint (in body)
gelenkig adj supple
gelernt adj skilled
geliehen vb see **leihen**
gelingen (imperf **gelang**, perf **ist gelungen**) vb to succeed ▷ *Sein Plan ist ihm nicht gelungen.* His plan didn't succeed.; **Es ist mir gelungen, ihn zu überzeugen.** I succeeded in convincing him.; **Der Kuchen ist gelungen.** The cake turned out well.

gelten (pres **gilt**, imperf **galt**, perf **hat gegolten**) vb to be valid ▷ *Dein Ausweis gilt nicht mehr.* Your passport is no longer valid.; **es gilt, etwas zu tun** it's necessary to do something; **jemandem gelten** to be aimed at somebody; **etwas gelten lassen** to accept something; **Was gilt die Wette?** What do you bet?

gelungen vb see **gelingen**
▶ adj successful

Gemälde (pl **Gemälde**) nt painting ▷ *ein Gemälde von Rembrandt* a painting by Rembrandt

gemein adj mean ▷ *Das war gemein!* That was mean!; **etwas gemein haben mit** to have something in common with

gemeinsam adj, adv ❶ joint ▷ *gemeinsame Anstrengungen* joint efforts ❷ together ▷ *Wir sind gemeinsam zum Lehrer gegangen.* We went together to the teacher. ▷ *ein gemeinsames Abendessen* dinner together; **etwas gemeinsam haben** to have something in common

gemischt adj mixed

gemocht vb see **mögen**

Gemüse (pl **Gemüse**) nt vegetables pl ▷ *Gemüse ist gesund.* Vegetables are healthy.

gemusst vb see **müssen**

gemütlich adj ❶ cosy ▷ *eine gemütliche Wohnung* a cosy flat; **ein gemütlicher Abend** a pleasant evening ❷ good-natured ▷ *Sie ist ein gemütlicher Mensch.* She's good-natured.

Gen (pl **Gene**) nt gene

genannt vb see **nennen**

genau adj, adv ❶ exact ▷ *Ich brauche genaue Zahlen.* I need exact figures. ❷ accurate ▷ *Diese Übersetzung ist nicht sehr genau.* This translation isn't very accurate. ❸ exactly ▷ *Genau das habe ich auch gesagt.* That's exactly what I said. ▷ *Sie hatte genau dasselbe Kleid an.* She was wearing exactly the same dress. ▷ *Das ist genau anders herum.* That's exactly the opposite.; **etwas genau nehmen** to take something seriously; **genau genommen** strictly speaking

genauso adv genauso gut just as good

genehmigen (perf **hat genehmigt**) vb [7] to approve; **sich etwas genehmigen** to treat oneself to something

Genehmigung f ❶ permission ▷ *Für den Umbau brauchen wir eine Genehmigung.* We need permission for the conversion. ❷ permit ▷ *Hier ist meine Genehmigung.* Here's my permit.

Generation f generation

generell adj, adv ❶ general (rule, principle) ❷ generally ▷ *Das ist generell ein Problem.* That is generally a problem.

Genf nt Geneva; **der Genfer See** Lake Geneva

genial adj brilliant

Genick (pl **Genicke**) nt back of the neck; **sich das Genick brechen** to break one's neck

Genie (pl **Genies**) nt genius

genießen (imperf **genoss**, perf **hat genossen**) vb to enjoy ▷ *Wir haben die Ferien genossen.* We enjoyed our holidays.

genmanipuliert adj genetically modified ▷ *genmanipulierte Lebensmittel* genetically modified food

genommen vb see **nehmen**

genug adj enough ▷ *Wir haben genug Geld.* We've got enough money. ▷ *gut genug* good enough

genügen (perf **hat genügt**) vb [38] to be enough ▷ *Das genügt noch nicht.* That isn't enough.; **jemandem genügen** to be enough for somebody

genügend adj sufficient

Genuss (gen **Genusses**, pl **Genüsse**) m ❶ pleasure ▷ *Es war ein Genuss!* That was sheer pleasure! ❷ <u>consumption</u> ▷ *der Genuss von Alkohol* the consumption of alcohol; **in den Genuss von etwas kommen** to receive the benefit of something

geöffnet *adj* <u>open</u>
Geografie *f* <u>geography</u>
Geometrie *f* <u>geometry</u>
Gepäck *nt* <u>luggage</u>
Gepäckannahme *f* <u>luggage office</u>
Gepäckausgabe *f* <u>baggage reclaim</u>
gepflegt *adj* ❶ <u>well-groomed</u>
▷ *gepflegte Hände* well-groomed hands
❷ <u>well-kept</u> ▷ *ein gepflegter Park* a well-kept park
gerade *adj, adv* ❶ <u>straight</u> ▷ *eine gerade Strecke* a straight stretch ❷ <u>upright</u>
▷ *eine gerade Haltung* an upright posture; **eine gerade Zahl** an even number ❸ <u>just</u> ▷ *Du kommst gerade richtig.* You've come just at the right time. ▷ *Das ist es ja gerade!* That's just it! ▷ *Er wollte gerade aufstehen.* He was just about to get up.; **gerade erst** only just; **gerade noch** only just; **gerade deshalb** that's exactly why; **gerade du** you of all people; **nicht gerade** not exactly
geradeaus *adv* <u>straight ahead</u>
gerannt *vb see* **rennen**
Gerät (*pl* **Geräte**) *nt* ❶ <u>gadget</u> ▷ *ein Gerät zum Papierschneiden* a gadget for cutting paper ❷ <u>appliance</u> ▷ *ein Haushaltsgerät* a household appliance ❸ <u>tool</u> ▷ *ein Gartengerät* a garden tool ❹ <u>apparatus</u> ▷ *Wir haben heute an den Geräten geturnt.* We did gymnastics on the apparatus today. ❺ <u>equipment</u> ▷ *Gerät zum Angeln* fishing equipment
geraten (*pres* **gerät**, *imperf* **geriet**, *perf* **ist geraten**) *vb* ❶ <u>to thrive</u> ▷ *Hier geraten die Pflanzen.* Plants thrive here. ❷ <u>to turn out</u> ▷ *Ihre Kinder sind alle gut geraten.* All their children have turned out well. ▷ *Der Kuchen ist mir nicht geraten.* The cake hasn't turned out well.; **in etwas geraten** to get into something; **in Angst geraten** to get frightened; **nach jemandem geraten** to take after somebody

geräuchert *adj* <u>smoked</u>
Geräusch (*pl* **Geräusche**) *nt* <u>sound</u>
gerecht *adj* <u>fair</u> ▷ *Das ist nicht gerecht!* That's not fair!
Gerechtigkeit *f* <u>justice</u>
Gerede *nt* <u>gossip</u> ▷ *Das ist alles nur Gerede.* That's all just gossip.
gereizt *adj* <u>irritable</u>
Gericht (*pl* **Gerichte**) *nt* ❶ <u>court</u>
▷ *Wir sehen uns vor Gericht.* I'll see you in court. ❷ <u>dish</u> ▷ *ein leckeres Gericht* a tasty dish; **das Jüngste Gericht** the Last Judgement
gerieben *vb see* **reiben**
gering *adj* ❶ <u>small</u> ▷ *eine geringe Menge* a small amount ❷ <u>low</u> ▷ *geringe Beteiligung* low participation; **eine geringe Zeit** a short time
geringste *adj* <u>least</u> ▷ *Das ist meine geringste Sorge.* That's the least of my worries.
geritten *vb see* **reiten**
gern *adv* <u>gladly</u> ▷ *Das habe ich gern getan.* I did it gladly.; **gern mögen** to like; **etwas gern tun** to like doing something; **Das würde ich sehr gerne tun.** I'd really love to do that.; **Ich hätte gern ...** I'd like ...; **Ja, gern!** Yes, please.; **Gern geschehen!** It's a pleasure.
gerochen *vb see* **riechen**
Geruch (*pl* **Gerüche**) *m* <u>smell</u>
Gerücht (*pl* **Gerüchte**) *nt* <u>rumour</u>
gesalzen *vb see* **salzen**
▷ *adj* **gesalzene Preise** (*informal*) <u>hefty prices</u>

> Word for word, **gesalzene Preise** means 'salted prices'.

gesamt *adj* <u>whole</u> ▷ *die gesamte Klasse* the whole class; **die gesamten Kosten**

the total cost; **gesamte Werke** complete works; **im Gesamten** all in all

Gesamtschule f comprehensive school
* **Gesamtschulen** are the exception rather than the rule in Germany.

gesandt vb see **senden**

Geschäft (pl **Geschäfte**) nt ❶ shop ▷ In welchem Geschäft hast du das gekauft? Which shop did you buy that in? ❷ business ▷ Die Geschäfte gehen gut. Business is good. ❸ deal ▷ Ich schlage dir ein Geschäft vor. I'll make a deal with you. ▷ Das war ein gutes Geschäft. That was a good deal.

Geschäftsfrau f businesswoman

Geschäftsmann (pl **Geschäftsmänner**) m businessman

geschehen (pres **geschieht**, imperf **geschah**, perf **ist geschehen**) vb to happen ▷ Was ist geschehen? What's happened? ▷ Was ist mit ihm geschehen? What's happened to him?

gescheit adj clever

Geschenk (pl **Geschenke**) nt present

Geschichte f ❶ story ▷ eine lustige Geschichte a funny story ❷ history ▷ die deutsche Geschichte German history ❸ business ▷ die Geschichte mit dem verschwundenen Pass the business of the missing passport

geschickt adj skilful

geschieden vb see **scheiden**
▷ adj divorced

geschienen vb see **scheinen**

Geschirr nt crockery ▷ In welchem Schrank steht das Geschirr? What cupboard is the crockery kept in?; **das Geschirr spülen** to do the dishes

Geschirrspülmaschine f dishwasher

Geschirrtuch (pl **Geschirrtücher**) nt dish cloth

Geschlecht (pl **Geschlechter**) nt ❶ sex ▷ ein Kind weiblichen Geschlechts a child of the female sex ❷ gender ▷ Welches Geschlecht hat dieses Substantiv? What gender is this noun?

Geschlechtskrankheit f sexually transmitted disease

geschlossen vb see **schließen**
▷ adj shut; '**Geschlossen**' 'Closed'

Geschmack (pl **Geschmäcke**) m taste ▷ Das ist nicht nach meinem Geschmack. This is not to my taste.; **Geschmack an etwas finden** to come to like something

geschmacklos adj ❶ tasteless ▷ Die Suppe war ziemlich geschmacklos. The soup was pretty tasteless. ❷ in bad taste ▷ Das war ein geschmackloser Witz. That joke was in bad taste.

geschmackvoll adj tasteful

geschnitten vb see **schneiden**

geschossen vb see **schießen**

geschrieben vb see **schreiben**

geschrien vb see **schreien**

geschützt adj protected

Geschwätz nt chatter

geschwätzig adj talkative

Geschwindigkeit f speed

Geschwindigkeitsbeschränkung f speed limit

Geschwister pl brothers and sisters pl

geschwommen vb see **schwimmen**

gesellig adj sociable

Gesellschaft f ❶ society ▷ die Gesellschaft verändern to change society ❷ company ▷ jemandem Gesellschaft leisten to keep somebody company

gesellschaftlich adj social

gesessen vb see **sitzen**

Gesetz (gen **Gesetzes**, pl **Gesetze**) nt law

gesetzlich adj legal; **gesetzlicher Feiertag** public holiday

Gesicht (pl **Gesichter**) nt face

gespannt adj ❶ strained ▷ Die Lage im Nahen Osten ist gespannt. The situation in the Middle East is strained. ❷ eager ▷ gespannte Zuhörer eager listeners; **Ich**

bin gespannt, ob ... I wonder whether ...; **auf etwas gespannt sein** to look forward to something

Gespenst (pl **Gespenster**) nt ghost

gesperrt adj closed off

Gespräch (pl **Gespräche**) nt ❶ conversation ▷ *ein langes Gespräch* a long conversation ❷ call ▷ *Frau Morris, ein Gespräch für Sie.* Mrs Morris, there's a call for you.

gesprächig adj talkative

gesprochen vb see **sprechen**

gesprungen vb see **springen**

Gestalt f ❶ shape ▷ *die Gestalt der Skulptur* the shape of the sculpture; **Gestalt annehmen** to take shape ❷ figure ▷ *Ich konnte eine dunkle Gestalt im Garten erkennen.* I could see a dark figure in the garden.; **in Gestalt von** in the form of

gestalten (perf **hat gestaltet**) vb [2] to lay out ▷ *Wer hat euren Garten gestaltet?* Who laid out your garden?; **Wie gestaltest du deine Freizeit?** How do you spend your spare time?

gestanden vb see **stehen**

Geständnis (gen **Geständnisses**, pl **Geständnisse**) nt confession

Gestank m stench

gestatten (perf **hat/ist gestattet**) vb [2] to allow; **Gestatten Sie?** May I?

gestattet adj permitted ▷ *Das ist nicht gestattet.* That is not permitted.

Geste f gesture

gestehen (imperf **gestand**, perf **hat gestanden**) vb [72] to confess

gestern adv yesterday; **gestern Abend** yesterday evening; **gestern Morgen** yesterday morning

gestohlen vb see **stehlen**

gestorben vb see **sterben**

gestört adj disturbed

gestreift adj striped

gestresst adj stressed ▷ *Meine Eltern sind gestresst.* My parents are stressed.

gesund adj healthy; **wieder gesund werden** to get better

Gesundheit f health; **Gesundheit!** Bless you!

gesungen vb see **singen**

getan vb see **tun**

Getränk (pl **Getränke**) nt drink

Getreide (pl **Getreide**) nt cereals pl

getrennt adj separate

Getriebe (pl **Getriebe**) nt gearbox

getrieben vb see **treiben**

getroffen vb see **treffen**

getrunken vb see **trinken**

geübt adj experienced

gewachsen vb see **wachsen**
▶ adj **jemandem gewachsen sein** to be a match for somebody; **Sie ist den Kindern nicht gewachsen.** She can't cope with the children.; **einer Sache gewachsen sein** to be up to something

gewagt adj risky

Gewalt f ❶ force ▷ *die Gewalt des Aufpralls* the force of the impact ❷ power ▷ *die staatliche Gewalt* the power of the state ❸ violence ▷ *Gewalt gegen Kinder* violence against children; **mit aller Gewalt** with all one's might

gewaltig adj tremendous ▷ *eine gewaltige Menge* a tremendous amount; **Sie hat sich gewaltig angestrengt.** She tried tremendously hard.; **ein gewaltiger Irrtum** a huge mistake

gewalttätig adj violent

gewann vb see **gewinnen**

Gewässer (pl **Gewässer**) nt waters pl

Gewebe (pl **Gewebe**) nt ❶ fabric ▷ *ein feines Gewebe* a fine fabric ❷ tissue ▷ *Die Gewebeprobe hat ergeben, dass alles in Ordnung ist.* The tissue samples showed that there's nothing wrong.

Gewehr (pl **Gewehre**) nt gun

GERMAN > ENGLISH

Gewerkschaft f trade union
- Unions in Germany are mainly organized within the **Deutscher Gewerkschaftsbund (DGB)**.

gewesen vb see **sein**
Gewicht (pl **Gewichte**) nt weight ▷ *das Gewicht meines Koffers* the weight of my case
Gewinn (pl **Gewinne**) m profit ▷ *Wir haben dieses Jahr einen Gewinn gemacht.* We've made a profit this year. ▷ *etwas mit Gewinn verkaufen* to sell something at a profit
gewinnen (imperf **gewann**, perf **hat gewonnen**) vb [30] to win ▷ *Sie hat den ersten Preis gewonnen.* She won first prize.; **im Lotto gewinnen** to have a win on the lottery; **an etwas gewinnen** to gain in something
Gewinner (pl **Gewinner**) m winner
gewiss adj, adv certain ▷ *Zwischen den beiden besteht eine gewisse Ähnlichkeit.* There's a certain similarity between them.; **Das weiß ich ganz gewiss.** I'm certain about that.; **Das hat sie gewiss vergessen.** She must have forgotten.
Gewissen (pl **Gewissen**) nt conscience
gewissenhaft adj conscientious
Gewitter (pl **Gewitter**) nt thunderstorm
gewöhnen (perf **hat gewöhnt**) vb [75] **sich an etwas gewöhnen** to get used to something; **jemanden an etwas gewöhnen** to teach somebody something
Gewohnheit f habit ▷ *Es ist so eine Gewohnheit von mir, morgens Kaffee zu trinken.* It's a habit of mine to drink coffee in the morning.; **zur Gewohnheit werden** to become a habit; **aus Gewohnheit** from habit
gewöhnlich adj ❶ usual ▷ *Ich bin heute früh zu der gewöhnlichen Zeit aufgestanden.* I got up at my usual time

this morning.; **Ich stehe gewöhnlich um sieben Uhr auf.** I usually get up at seven o'clock. ❷ ordinary ▷ *Das sind ganz gewöhnliche Leute.* They're quite ordinary people.; **wie gewöhnlich** as usual
gewohnt adj usual ▷ *Mir fehlt die gewohnte Umgebung.* I miss my usual surroundings.; **etwas gewohnt sein** to be used to something
gewonnen vb see **gewinnen**
geworden vb see **werden**
geworfen vb see **werfen**
Gewürz (gen **Gewürzes**, pl **Gewürze**) nt spice
gewusst vb see **wissen**
Gezeiten pl tides pl
gezogen vb see **ziehen**
gezwungen vb see **zwingen**
gibt vb see **geben**
Gier f greed
gierig adj greedy ▷ *gierig nach Geld* greedy for money
gießen (imperf **goss**, perf **hat gegossen**) vb [30] to pour ▷ *Sie goss mir Wein ins Glas.* She poured wine into my glass.; **die Blumen gießen** to water the flowers; **Es gießt in Strömen.** It's pouring.
Gießkanne f watering can
Gift (pl **Gifte**) nt poison

   Be careful! The German word **Gift** does not mean **gift**.

giftig adj poisonous ▷ *eine giftige Pflanze* a poisonous plant
ging vb see **gehen**
Gipfel (pl **Gipfel**) m ❶ peak ▷ *die schneebedeckten Gipfel* the snow-covered peaks ❷ height ▷ *Das ist der Gipfel der Unverschämtheit.* That's the height of impudence.
Giraffe f giraffe
Girokonto (pl **Girokonten**) nt current account
Gitarre f guitar ▷ *Ich spiele Gitarre.* I play the guitar.

glänzen vb [36] to shine ▷ *Ihr Gesicht glänzte vor Freude.* Her face shone with joy.

glänzend adj ❶ shining ▷ *ein glänzendes Metall* shining metal ❷ brilliant ▷ *Das war eine glänzende Leistung.* That was a brilliant achievement.

Glas (gen **Glases**, pl **Gläser**) nt glass

Glasscheibe f pane

glatt adj ❶ smooth ▷ *Der Tisch hat eine glatte Oberfläche.* The table has a smooth surface. ❷ slippery ▷ *Pass auf, die Straßen sind glatt.* Be careful, the streets are slippery.; **eine glatte Absage** a flat refusal; **eine glatte Lüge** a downright lie; **Das habe ich glatt vergessen.** It completely slipped my mind.

Glatteis (gen **Glatteises**) nt black ice ▷ *Bei Glatteis sollte man vorsichtig fahren.* When there's black ice, you have to drive carefully.

glauben vb [38] ❶ to believe ▷ *Ich habe kein Wort geglaubt.* I didn't believe a word. ❷ to think ▷ *Ich glaube, wir sind hier nicht willkommen.* I don't think we're welcome here.; **jemandem glauben** to believe somebody; **an etwas glauben** to believe in something

glaubwürdig adj ❶ credible ▷ *Das ist keine besonders glaubwürdige Geschichte.* That story's not particularly credible. ❷ trustworthy ▷ *Er ist ein glaubwürdiger Mensch.* He's a trustworthy person.

gleich adj, adv ❶ same ▷ *Wir haben das gleiche Problem.* We have the same problem. ❷ identical ▷ *Bei einem Würfel sind alle Seiten gleich.* All the sides of a cube are identical. ❸ the same ▷ *Ich behandle alle meine Kinder gleich.* I treat all my children the same. ▷ *Sie waren genau gleich angezogen.* They were dressed exactly the same.; **gleich groß** the same size ❹ equal ▷ *Wir wollen für die gleiche Arbeit auch die gleiche Bezahlung.* We want equal pay for equal work. ❺ straight away ▷ *Ich werde ihn gleich anrufen.* I'll call him straight away.; **Ich bin gleich fertig.** I'll be ready in a minute.; **Es ist mir gleich.** It's all the same to me.; **Zwei mal zwei gleich vier.** Two times two equals four.; **gleich nach** right after; **gleich neben** right next to

gleichaltrig adj of the same age ▷ *gleichaltrige Schüler* pupils of the same age ▷ *Sie sind gleichaltrig.* They're the same age.

gleichartig adj similar

Gleichberechtigung f equal rights pl ▷ *die Gleichberechtigung der Frau* equal rights for women

gleichen (imperf glich, perf hat geglichen) vb jemandem gleichen to be like somebody; **einer Sache gleichen** to be like something; **sich gleichen** to be alike

gleichfalls adv **Danke gleichfalls!** The same to you.

Gleichgewicht nt balance

gleichgültig adj ❶ indifferent ▷ *Er zeigte sich ihr gegenüber ziemlich gleichgültig.* He seemed to be quite indifferent to her. ❷ not important ▷ *Es ist doch gleichgültig, wie wir das machen.* It's not important how we do it.

gleichzeitig adv at the same time ▷ *Ich kann doch nicht drei Dinge gleichzeitig tun.* I can't do three things at the same time.

Gleis (gen **Gleises**, pl **Gleise**) nt ❶ line ▷ *die Straßenbahngleise* the tram lines ❷ platform ▷ *Achtung auf Gleis drei.* Attention on platform three.

Gletscher (pl **Gletscher**) m glacier

gliedern vb [88] to structure ▷ *Du musst deinen Aufsatz besser gliedern.* You must structure your essay better.

glitzern vb [88] ❶ to glitter ▷ *Das Wasser glitzerte in der Sonne.* The water glittered in the sun. ❷ to twinkle ▷ *Die Sterne glitzerten.* The stars twinkled.

global *adj* global

Globalisierung *f* globalization

Glocke *f* bell; **etwas an die große Glocke hängen** to shout something from the rooftops

> Word for word, **etwas an die große Glocke hängen** means 'to hang something from the big bell'.

Glück *nt* ❶ luck ▷ *Ein vierblättriges Kleeblatt bringt Glück.* A four-leaf clover brings good luck.; **Glück haben** to be lucky; **Viel Glück!** Good luck!; **zum Glück** fortunately ❷ happiness ▷ *Sie strahlte vor Glück.* She was beaming with happiness.

glücklich *adj* ❶ happy ▷ *Ich bin sehr glücklich mit ihm.* I'm very happy with him. ▷ *Das waren glückliche Tage.* Those were happy days. ❷ lucky ▷ *Das war ein glücklicher Zufall.* That was a lucky coincidence.

glücklicherweise *adv* fortunately

Glückwunsch (*pl* **Glückwünsche**) *m* congratulations *pl* ▷ *Herzlichen Glückwunsch zur bestandenen Prüfung.* Congratulations on passing your exam.; **Herzlichen Glückwunsch zum Geburtstag.** Happy Birthday.

Glühbirne *f* light bulb

Gluten *nt* gluten

glutenfrei *adj* gluten-free

GmbH *abbr* (= *Gesellschaft mit beschränkter Haftung*) limited company

Gold *nt* gold

golden *adj* golden

Goldfisch (*pl* **Goldfische**) *m* goldfish ▷ *Ich habe zwei Goldfische.* I've got two goldfish.

Golf (*pl* **Golfe**) *m* gulf ▷ *der Persische Golf* the Persian Gulf
▶ *nt* golf ▷ *Mein Vater spielt Golf.* My father plays golf.

Golfplatz (*gen* **Golfplatzes**, *pl* **Golfplätze**) *m* golf course

Golfstrom *m* the Gulf Stream

gönnen *vb* [38] **sich etwas gönnen** to treat oneself to something; **Sie gönnt mir meinen Erfolg nicht.** She begrudges me my success.

Gott (*pl* **Götter**) *m* god; **Mein Gott!** For heaven's sake!; **Um Gottes willen!** For heaven's sake!; **Grüß Gott!** Hello!; **Gott sei Dank!** Thank God!

Göttin *f* goddess

Grab (*pl* **Gräber**) *nt* grave

graben (*pres* **gräbt**, *imperf* **grub**, *perf* **hat gegraben**) *vb* to dig

Graben (*pl* **Gräben**) *m* ditch

Grad (*pl* **Grad**) *m* degree ▷ *dreißig Grad im Schatten* thirty degrees in the shade

Grafikkarte *f* graphics card ▷ *Welche Grafikkarte hast du in deinem PC?* What graphics card do you have in your PC?

grafisch *adj* graphic

Gramm (*pl* **Gramme** *or* **Gramm**) *nt* gram ▷ *hundert Gramm Käse* a hundred grams of cheese

Grammatik *f* grammar

Gras (*gen* **Grases**, *pl* **Gräser**) *nt* grass

Gräte *f* bone ▷ *Dieser Fisch hat zu viele Gräten.* This fish has too many bones in it.

gratis *adv* free of charge

gratulieren (*perf* **hat gratuliert**) *vb* [76] **jemandem gratulieren** to congratulate somebody; **Gratuliere!** Congratulations!

grau *adj* grey

Graubrot (*pl* **Graubrote**) *nt* brown bread

Gräuel (*pl* **Gräuel**) *m* horror ▷ *die Gräuel des Bürgerkriegs* the horrors of civil war; **Das ist mir ein Gräuel.** I loathe it.

grauenhaft *adj* horrible

grausam *adj* cruel

Grausamkeit *f* cruelty

greifen (*imperf* **griff**, *perf* **hat gegriffen**) *vb* **nach etwas greifen** to reach for something; **um sich greifen** to spread

grell adj harsh ▷ *eine grelle Farbe* a harsh colour; **ein greller Schrei** a piercing scream

Grenze f ❶ border ▷ *Wir sind an der Grenze kontrolliert worden.* Our papers were checked at the border. ❷ boundary ▷ *Der Zaun ist die Grenze zum Grundstück des Nachbarn.* The fence marks the boundary with our neighbour's property. ❸ limit ▷ *die Grenzen des guten Geschmacks* the limits of good taste

grenzen vb [36] **an etwas grenzen** to border on something; **Das grenzt an Wahnsinn.** It verges on madness.

grenzenlos adj boundless

Greuel m see **Gräuel**

Grieche (gen **Griechen**, pl **Griechen**) m Greek

Griechenland nt Greece

Griechin f Greek

griechisch adj Greek

Griff (pl **Griffe**) m ❶ handle ▷ *Halte dich da an dem Griff fest.* Hold on to the handle. ❷ hold ▷ *Ich habe Judogriffe geübt.* I've been practising judo holds.

griffbereit adj handy ▷ *etwas griffbereit halten* to keep something handy

Grill (pl **Grills**) m grill

grillen vb [48] ❶ to grill ▷ *gegrillter Fisch* grilled fish ❷ to have a barbecue ▷ *Wir wollen am Sonntag grillen.* We'd like to have a barbecue on Sunday.

grinsen vb [38] to grin

Grippe f flu

grob adj ❶ coarse ▷ *grober Sand* coarse sand ❷ rough ▷ *Sei nicht so grob zu deiner Schwester.* Don't be so rough with your sister. ❸ serious ▷ *ein grober Fehler* a serious mistake

groß adj, adv ❶ big ▷ *Das war mein größter Fehler.* That was my biggest mistake. ▷ *Sie haben ein großes Haus.* They have a big house. ❷ tall ▷ *Mein Bruder ist viel größer als ich.* My brother is much taller than me. ❸ **Wie groß bist du?** How tall are you? ❹ great ▷ *Das war eine große Leistung.* That was a great achievement. ▷ *Er war ein großer Politiker.* He was a great politician.; **großen Hunger haben** to be very hungry; **die großen Ferien** the summer holidays; **Er hat sich nicht groß angestrengt.** He didn't try very hard.; **im Großen und Ganzen** on the whole

großartig adj splendid

Großbritannien nt Great Britain

Größe f ❶ size ▷ *Welche Schuhgröße hast du?* What size shoes do you take? ❷ height ▷ *Im Pass steht bei den Angaben zur Person auch die Größe.* Your height's also included in your passport under personal details.

Großeltern pl grandparents pl

Großmutter (pl **Großmütter**) f grandmother

großschreiben (imperf **schrieb groß**, perf **hat großgeschrieben**) vb [61] to write in capitals

Großstadt (pl **Großstädte**) f city

größtenteils adv for the most part

Großvater (pl **Großväter**) m grandfather

großzügig adj, adv generous ▷ *Meine Eltern sind sehr großzügig.* My parents are very generous. ▷ *Sie hat großzügig darauf verzichtet.* She generously did without.

grün adj green ▷ *Die Ampel ist grün.* The traffic lights are at green.

Grund (pl **Gründe**) m ❶ reason ▷ *Nenn mir einen Grund, warum wir das nicht so machen können.* Give me one reason why we can't do it like this.; **Aus welchem Grund ist er so böse?** Why is he so angry? ❷ ground ▷ *Das Haus ist auf felsigem Grund gebaut.* The house is built on rocky ground. ❸ bottom ▷ *Das*

Schiff sank auf den Grund des Meeres. The ship sank to the bottom of the sea.; **im Grunde genommen** basically; **auf Grund** see **aufgrund**; **zu Grunde** see **zugrunde**

gründen vb [54] to found ▷ *Wir haben einen Fanklub gegründet.* We've been a fan club.

gründlich adj, adv thorough ▷ *eine gründliche Vorbereitung zur Prüfung* thorough preparation for the exam ▷ *Wir haben das Haus gründlich geputzt.* We cleaned the house thoroughly.; **Ich habe mich gründlich geirrt.** I was completely wrong.

Grundsatz (gen **Grundsatzes**, pl **Grundsätze**) m principle

grundsätzlich adj, adv ① fundamental ▷ *Es bleibt die grundsätzliche Frage, ob das erlaubt werden soll.* The fundamental question remains: should it be allowed? ② basically ▷ *Grundsätzlich bin ich ja dafür, aber ...* Basically I'm in favour, but ... ③ on principle ▷ *Ich bin grundsätzlich gegen die Prügelstrafe.* I'm against corporal punishment on principle.

Grundschule f primary school

Grüne f die Grünen the Greens pl

grunzen vb [36] to grunt

Gruppe f group

Gruß (gen **Grußes**, pl **Grüße**) m greeting; **viele Grüße** best wishes; **mit freundlichen Grüßen** yours sincerely; **Grüße an** regards to

grüßen vb [31] to say hello ▷ *Sie hat mich nicht gegrüßt.* She didn't say hello to me.; **Grüß Lorna von mir.** Give Lorna my regards.; **Lorna läßt dich grüßen.** Lorna sends her regards.

gucken vb [38] (informal) ① to look ▷ *Guck mal!* Look! ② to watch ▷ *einen Krimi im Fernsehen gucken* to watch a crime drama on TV

Gulasch (pl **Gulaschs**) m goulash

gültig adj valid

Gummi (pl **Gummis**) nt
You can also say **der Gummi**.
rubber ▷ *Die Reifen sind aus Gummi.* The tyres are made of rubber.

Gummiband (pl **Gummibänder**) nt elastic band ▷ *Sie machte ein Gummiband um das Geschenk.* She put an elastic band round the present.

günstig adj convenient ▷ *Morgen wäre günstig.* Tomorrow would be convenient.; **eine günstige Gelegenheit** a favourable opportunity.; **Das habe ich günstig bekommen.** It was a bargain.

Gurke f cucumber ▷ *Sie mag Gurkensalat nicht.* She doesn't like cucumber salad.; **saure Gurke** gherkin

Gurt (pl **Gurte**) m belt

Gürtel (pl **Gürtel**) m belt

gut adj, adv ① good ▷ *Ich habe gute Noten bekommen.* I got good marks. ▷ *Sie ist ein guter Mensch.* She's a good person. ▷ *Das ist ein guter Witz.* That's a good joke.; **In Englisch habe ich 'gut'.** I got a B in English.

German marks range from one (**sehr gut**) to six (**ungenügend**).

Alles Gute! All the best.; **das Gute** pl the good thing ▷ *Das ist das Gute an meiner Familie.* That's the good thing about my family. **also gut** all right then ② well ▷ *Sie hat das gut gemacht.* She did it well. ▷ *Ich kenne ihn gut.* I know him well.; **gut schmecken** to taste good; **gut drei Stunden** a good three hours.; **Das kann gut sein.** That may well be.; **Gut, aber ...** OK, but ...; **Lass es gut sein.** That'll do.; **Es ist zum Glück gut gegangen.** Fortunately it came off.; **Mir geht's gut.** I'm fine.; **gut gemeint** well-meant; **gut tun** see **guttun**

Güter ntpl goods pl

gutgehen vb [29] see **gut**

gütig adj kind

gutmütig adj good-natured

Gutschein (pl **Gutscheine**) m voucher
guttun (imperf **tat gut**, perf **hat gutgetan**) vb [81] jemandem guttun to do somebody good
Gymnasium (pl **Gymnasien**) nt grammar school
Gymnastik f keep-fit ▷ *Ich mache einmal in der Woche Gymnastik.* I do keep-fit once a week.

Haar (pl **Haare**) nt hair ▷ *Sie hat dunkle Haare.* She's got dark hair.; **um ein Haar** nearly
haben (pres **hat**, imperf **hatte**, perf **hat gehabt**) vb [32] to have ▷ *Ich habe einen neuen Pulli.* I've got a new pullover. ▷ *Sie hat ihn nicht gesehen.* She hasn't seen him.; **Welches Datum haben wir heute?** What's the date today?; **Hunger haben** to be hungry; **Angst haben** to be afraid; **Woher hast du das?** Where did you get that from?; **Was hast du denn?** What's the matter with you?; **Ich hätte gern ...** I would like ...
Hackfleisch nt mince
Hafen (pl **Häfen**) m harbour
Hafenstadt (pl **Hafenstädte**) f port
Hafer m oats pl
Haferflocken fpl porridge oats pl
haftbar adj responsible ▷ *Eltern sind für ihre Kinder haftbar.* Parents are responsible for their children.
haften vb [2] to stick ▷ *Der Klebstreifen haftet nicht.* The adhesive tape isn't

GERMAN > ENGLISH

sticking.; **haften für** to be responsible for
Haftpflichtversicherung f third party insurance
Hagel m hail
hageln vb [88] **Es hagelt.** It's hailing.
Hahn (pl **Hähne**) m ❶ cock ▷ *Der Hahn krähte.* The cock crowed. ❷ tap ▷ *Der Hahn tropft.* The tap's dripping.
Hähnchen (pl **Hähnchen**) nt chicken ▷ *Heute gibt es Hähnchen.* We're having chicken today.
Hai (pl **Haie**) m shark
Haken (pl **Haken**) m ❶ hook ▷ *Häng deine Jacke an den Haken.* Hang your jacket up on the hook. ❷ catch ▷ *Die Sache hat einen Haken.* There's a catch.
halb adj half ▷ *ein halber Kuchen* half a cake ▷ *eine halbe Stunde* half an hour; **halb eins** half past twelve
halbieren (perf **hat halbiert**) vb [76] to halve
Halbjahr (pl **Halbjahre**) nt six months pl
halbtags adv **halbtags arbeiten** to work part-time
Halbtagsarbeit f part-time job
half vb see **helfen**
Hälfte f half
Halle f hall ▷ *eine Messehalle* an exhibition hall
Hallenbad (pl **Hallenbäder**) nt indoor swimming pool
hallo excl hello!
Hals (gen **Halses**, pl **Hälse**) m ❶ neck ▷ *Ich habe einen steifen Hals.* I've got a stiff neck. ❷ throat ▷ *Mir tut der Hals weh.* My throat's sore.; **Hals über Kopf** in a rush
Halskette f necklace
Halsschmerzen pl sore throat sg ▷ *Ich habe Halsschmerzen.* I've got a sore throat.
Halstuch (pl **Halstücher**) nt scarf
halt excl stop!
haltbar adj durable ▷ *Das ist ein sehr haltbares Material.* That's a very durable

103 | **Handbuch**

material.; **Butter ist nur begrenzt haltbar.** Butter only keeps for a limited time.; **'Mindestens haltbar bis ...'** 'Best before ...'
halten (pres **hält**, imperf **hielt**, perf **hat gehalten**) vb [33] ❶ to hold ▷ *Er hielt sie an der Hand.* He held her by the hand. ▷ *Kannst du das mal halten?* Can you hold that for a moment? ❷ to keep ▷ *Obst hält nicht lange.* Fruit doesn't keep long. ❸ to last ▷ *Ihre Freundschaft hat lange gehalten.* Their friendship has lasted a long time. ❹ to stop ▷ *Der Bus hielt vor dem Rathaus.* The bus stopped in front of the town hall.; **halten für** to regard as; **Ich habe sie für deine Mutter gehalten.** I took her for your mother.; **halten von** to think of; **sich rechts halten** to keep to the right
Haltestelle f stop ▷ *die Haltestelle der Straßenbahn* the tram stop
haltmachen vb [48] to stop
Haltung f ❶ posture ▷ *Er hat eine aufrechte Haltung.* He has an upright posture. ❷ attitude ▷ *Ich bewundere deine Haltung in dieser Frage.* I admire your attitude in this issue.
Hamburg nt Hamburg
- The 'Free and Hanseatic City of
- Hamburg' is one of the 16 **Länder**.
- It is a 'city-state' like Bremen and
- Berlin, and is Germany's principal
- seaport.

Hammer (pl **Hämmer**) m hammer
Hand (pl **Hände**) f hand
Handarbeit f ❶ manual work ▷ *Handarbeit macht ihm mehr Spaß als geistige Arbeit.* He enjoys manual work more than intellectual work. ❷ needlework ▷ *In Handarbeit hat sie eine Zwei.* She got a B in needlework.
Handball m handball
Handbremse f handbrake
Handbuch (pl **Handbücher**) nt manual

Handel m ❶ trade ▷ *der Handel mit Osteuropa* trade with Eastern Europe; *Dieses Gerät ist überall im Handel erhältlich.* This appliance is available in all shops and retail outlets. ❷ deal ▷ *Wir haben einen Handel abgeschlossen.* We have concluded a deal.

handeln vb [34] ❶ to act ▷ *Wir müssen schnell handeln.* We'll have to act quickly. ❷ to trade ▷ *Er handelt mit Gebrauchtwaren.* He trades in second-hand goods.; **mit jemandem handeln** to bargain with somebody; **Es handelt sich um ...** It's about ...; **handeln von** to be about

Handelsschule f business school

Handgepäck nt hand luggage

Händler (pl **Händler**) m dealer ▷ *Ich habe meinen Computerhändler danach gefragt.* I asked my computer dealer about it.

handlich adj handy

Handlung f ❶ act ▷ *Das war eine unüberlegte Handlung.* That was a rash act. ❷ plot ▷ *Ich habe die Handlung des Buches nicht genau verstanden.* I didn't really understand the plot of the book. ❸ shop ▷ *eine Eisenwarenhandlung* an ironmonger's shop

Handschrift f handwriting

Handschuh (pl **Handschuhe**) m glove

Handtasche f handbag

Handtuch (pl **Handtücher**) nt towel

Handy (pl **Handys**) nt mobile phone

Hang (pl **Hänge**) m slope

hängen (1) (imperf **hängte**, perf **hat gehängt**) vb [48] to hang ▷ *Sie hat die Wäsche auf die Leine gehängt.* She hung her washing on the line. ▷ *Sie hängten den Verbrecher.* They hanged the criminal.

hängen (2) (imperf **hing**, perf **hat gehangen**) vb [35] to hang ▷ *An der Wand hing ein Bild von Picasso.* A painting by Picasso was hanging on the wall.; **hängen an** to be attached to

harmlos adj harmless

harmonisch adj harmonious

hart adj hard ▷ *hart wie Stein* as hard as stone ▷ *Wir haben hart gearbeitet.* We worked hard.; **harte Worte** harsh words; **Das ist hart.** That's tough.; **ein hart gekochtes Ei** a hard-boiled egg

hartnäckig adj stubborn

Haschisch (gen **Haschisch**) nt hashish

Hase (gen **Hasen**, pl **Hasen**) m hare

Haselnuss (pl **Haselnüsse**) f hazelnut

Hass (gen **Hasses**) m hatred

hassen (perf **hat gehasst**) vb [31] to hate

hässlich adj ❶ ugly ▷ *Sie ist das hässlichste Mädchen der Klasse.* She's the ugliest girl in the class. ❷ nasty ▷ *Es ist hässlich, so etwas zu sagen.* It's nasty to say things like that.

hast vb see **haben**

hastig adj hasty

Haufen (pl **Haufen**) m heap ▷ *In ihrem Schlafzimmer lag ein Haufen schmutziger Wäsche.* There was a heap of dirty washing lying in her bedroom.; **ein Haufen ...** (informal) heaps of ...

häufig adj, adv ❶ frequent ▷ *sein häufiges Fehlen* his frequent absences ❷ frequently ▷ *Er fehlt häufig.* He is frequently absent.

Hauptbahnhof (pl **Hauptbahnhöfe**) m main station

Hauptfach (pl **Hauptfächer**) nt main subject

Hauptgericht (pl **Hauptgerichte**) nt main course

Hauptsache f main thing ▷ *Hauptsache, du bist gesund.* The main thing is that you're healthy.

Hauptschule f secondary school

Hauptstadt (pl **Hauptstädte**) f capital ▷ *Berlin ist die Hauptstadt von Deutschland.* Berlin's the capital of Germany.

Hauptstraße f main street

GERMAN > ENGLISH

Hauptverkehrszeit f rush hour
Hauptwort (pl **Hauptwörter**) nt noun
Haus (gen **Hauses**, pl **Häuser**) nt house; **nach Hause** home; **zu Hause** at home
Hausarbeit f ❶ housework ▷ *Meine Mutter erledigt immer noch die Mehrheit der Hausarbeit.* My mother still does the majority of the housework. ❷ homework ▷ *Wir haben eine Hausarbeit zum Thema Umweltverschmutzung auf.* We've got homework on the subject of pollution.
Hausarzt (gen **Hausarztes**, pl **Hausärzte**) m family doctor
Hausaufgaben fpl homework ▷ *Heute waren die Hausaufgaben nicht schwierig.* Our homework wasn't difficult today.
Hausfrau f housewife
Haushalt (pl **Haushalte**) m ❶ household ▷ *den Haushalt führen* to run the household ❷ budget ▷ *der Haushalt für 2025* the 2025 budget
Hausmeister (pl **Hausmeister**) m caretaker
Hausnummer f house number
Hausschlüssel (pl **Hausschlüssel**) m front-door key
Hausschuh (pl **Hausschuhe**) m slipper
Haustier (pl **Haustiere**) nt pet
Haustür f front door
Haut (pl **Häute**) f skin
Hbf. abbr (= Hauptbahnhof) central station
Hebel (pl **Hebel**) m lever
heben (imperf **hob**, perf **hat gehoben**) vb to lift
Hecke f hedge
Hefe f yeast
Heft (pl **Hefte**) nt ❶ exercise book ▷ *Schreibt die Verbesserung in euer Heft.* Write the correction in your exercise books. ❷ issue ▷ *Hast du noch das letzte Heft von 'Geo'?* Have you got the latest issue of 'Geo'?
Heftklammer f paper clip

105 | **Heiserkeit**

Heftpflaster (pl **Heftpflaster**) nt sticking plaster
Heide f moor ▷ *Wir haben einen Spaziergang durch die Heide gemacht.* We went for a walk over the moor.; **die Lüneburger Heide** Lüneburg Heath
Heidekraut nt heather
Heidelbeere f blueberry
heilbar adj curable
heilen (perf **hat/ist geheilt**) vb [38]
For the perfect tense use **haben** when the verb has an object and **sein** when there is no object.
❶ to cure ▷ *Viele Arten von Krebs kann man heilen.* Many kinds of cancer can be cured. ❷ to heal ▷ *Die Wunde ist schnell geheilt.* The wound healed quickly.
heilig adj holy; **Heiliger Abend** Christmas Eve
Heiligabend (pl **Heiligabende**) m Christmas Eve
Heilmittel (pl **Heilmittel**) nt remedy
heim adv home ▷ *Ich muss jetzt heim.* I'll have to go home now.
Heim (pl **Heime**) nt home ▷ *ein Heim für Kinder mit Lernschwierigkeiten* a home for children with learning difficulties
Heimat f homeland ▷ *Deutschland ist meine Heimat.* Germany's my homeland.
heimatlos adj homeless
Heimfahrt f journey home
heimgehen (imperf **ging heim**, perf **ist heimgegangen**) vb [29] to go home
heimlich adj secret ▷ *Er hat das heimlich gemacht.* He did it secretly.
Heimreise f journey home
Heimweg (pl **Heimwege**) m way home
Heimweh nt homesickness
Heirat f marriage
heiraten vb [2] to get married ▷ *Sie heiraten morgen.* They're getting married tomorrow.; **jemanden heiraten** to marry somebody
heiser adj hoarse
Heiserkeit f hoarseness

heiß adj hot ▷ *Mir ist heiß.* I'm hot. ▷ *heiße Schokolade* hot chocolate

heißen (imperf **hieß**, perf **hat geheißen**) vb ❶ to be called ▷ *Er heißt Marek.* He's called Marek. ❷ to mean ▷ *Das heißt, dass wir morgen früh aufstehen müssen.* That means that we'll have to get up early tomorrow.; **Es heißt ...** It is said ...; **das heißt** that is to say

heiter adj ❶ cheerful ▷ *Ich war in heiterer Laune.* I was in a cheerful mood. ❷ bright ▷ *Das Wetter wird heiter bis bewölkt.* The weather will be cloudy with bright spells.

heizen vb [36] to heat

Heizung f heating

hektisch adj hectic

Held (gen **Helden**, pl **Helden**) m hero

Heldin f heroine

helfen (pres **hilft**, imperf **half**, perf **hat geholfen**) vb [37] to help ▷ *Kann ich dir helfen?* Can I help you? ▷ *Die Tablette hat geholfen.* The pill helped. ▷ *jemandem bei etwas helfen* to help somebody with something; **sich zu helfen wissen** to be resourceful; **Es hilft nichts, du musst ...** It's no use, you'll have to ...

hell adj bright ▷ *Hier ist es schön hell.* It's nice and bright here. ; **Sie hat einen hellen Teint.** She has a clear complexion.; **eine helle Farbe** a light colour; **ein Helles** a light beer

hellblond adj ash-blond

Helm (pl **Helme**) m helmet

Hemd (pl **Hemden**) nt shirt; **ein Unterhemd** a vest

Hemmung f inhibition ▷ *Er hat furchtbare Hemmungen.* He has terrible inhibitions.

Henne f hen

her adv ago ▷ *Das ist fünf Jahre her.* That was five years ago.; **von ... her** from ...; **Wo bist du her?** Where do you come from?; **Komm her zu mir.** Come here.; **Her damit!** Hand it over!

herab adv down

heran adv **Näher heran!** Come closer!

herauf adv up ▷ *Komm hier herauf.* Come up here.

heraus adv out

herausfordern (perf **hat herausgefordert**) vb [15] to challenge

Herausforderung f challenge

herauskommen (imperf **kam heraus**, perf **ist herausgekommen**) vb [40] to come out ▷ *Die Maus ist aus ihrem Loch herausgekommen.* The mouse came out of its hole.; **Dabei kommt nichts heraus.** Nothing will come of it.

herausnehmen (pres **nimmt heraus**, imperf **nahm heraus**, perf **hat herausgenommen**) vb [52] to take out ▷ *Sie hat das Lesezeichen aus dem Buch herausgenommen.* She took the bookmark out of the book.; **sich etwas herausnehmen** to take liberties

herausziehen (imperf **zog heraus**, perf **hat herausgezogen**) vb [96] to pull out

herb adj bitter ▷ *eine herbe Enttäuschung* a bitter disappointment ▷ *ein herber Geschmack* a bitter taste

herbei adv over ▷ *Alle eilten herbei.* Everyone hurried over.

Herbergseltern pl wardens pl (in youth hostel)

herbringen (imperf **brachte her**, perf **hat hergebracht**) vb [13] to bring here

Herbst (pl **Herbste**) m autumn ▷ *im Herbst* in autumn

Herbstferien pl autumn holidays pl

herbstlich adj autumnal

Herd (pl **Herde**) m cooker ▷ *ein Herd mit vier Platten* a cooker with four rings

Herde f herd ▷ *eine Herde Kühe* a herd of cows; **eine Schafherde** a flock of sheep

herein adv in ▷ *Noch mehr Menschen drängten herein.* Even more people pushed their way in. ▷ *Das Wasser*

strömte herein. The water poured in.; **Herein!** Come in!

hereinfallen (pres **fällt herein**, imperf **fiel herein**, perf **ist hereingefallen**) vb [22] **auf etwas hereinfallen** to fall for something

hereinkommen (imperf **kam herein**, perf **ist hereingekommen**) vb [40] to come in

hereinlassen (pres **lässt herein**, imperf **ließ herein**, perf **hat hereingelassen**) vb [42] to let in

hereinlegen (perf **hat hereingelegt**) vb [4] **jemanden hereinlegen** (informal) to take somebody for a ride

hergeben (pres **gibt her**, imperf **gab her**, perf **hat hergegeben**) vb [28] to hand over ▷ *Gib das Buch her!* Hand over the book!; **sich zu etwas hergeben** to lend one's name to something

hergehen (imperf **ging her**, perf **ist hergegangen**) vb [29] **hinter jemandem hergehen** to follow somebody; **Es geht hoch her.** (informal) There are a lot of goings-on.

Hering (pl **Heringe**) m herring

herkommen (imperf **kam her**, perf **ist hergekommen**) vb [40] to come ▷ *Komm mal her!* Come here!

Herkunft (pl **Herkünfte**) f origin

Heroin nt heroin

Herr (gen **Herrn**, pl **Herren**) m ❶ gentleman ▷ *Meine Herren!* Gentlemen! ❷ Lord ▷ *Herr, gib uns Frieden!* Lord, give us peace. ❸ Mr ▷ *Herr Mosbacher* Mr Mosbacher; **Mein Herr!** Sir!

herrlich adj marvellous

herrschen vb [48] ❶ to reign ▷ *Wann hat Karl der Große geherrscht?* When did Charlemagne reign? ❷ to be ▷ *Hier herrschen ja schöne Zustände.* This is a fine state of affairs. ▷ *Es herrscht noch Ungewissheit, wann das gemacht werden soll.* It's still uncertain when it's to be done.

herstellen (perf **hat hergestellt**) vb [4] to manufacture

Hersteller (pl **Hersteller**) m manufacturer

Herstellung f manufacture

herüber adv ❶ over here ▷ *Er kam langsam zu uns herüber.* He came slowly over to us. ❷ across ▷ *Sie versuchte, zu uns herüberzuschwimmen.* She tried to swim across to us.

herum adv round ▷ *Mach ein rotes Band herum.* Tie a red band round it.; **um etwas herum** round something

herumführen (perf **hat herumgeführt**) vb [4] to show around

herumgehen (imperf **ging herum**, perf **ist herumgegangen**) vb [29] to walk about ▷ *Wir sind ein paar Stunden in der Stadt herumgegangen.* We walked about the town for a couple of hours.; **um etwas herumgehen** to walk round something

sich **herumsprechen** (pres **spricht sich herum**, imperf **sprach sich herum**, perf **hat sich herumgesprochen**) vb [70] to get around

herunter adv down

herunterkommen (imperf **kam herunter**, perf **ist heruntergekommen**) vb [40] ❶ to come down ▷ *Sie ist zu uns heruntergekommen.* She came down to us. ❷ to come run-down ▷ *Das Haus ist in den letzten Jahren ziemlich heruntergekommen.* The house has become rather run-down in the past few years.

herunterladen (pres **lädt herunter**, imperf **lud herunter**, perf **hat heruntergeladen**) vb (computer) to download ▷ *eine Datei herunterladen* to download a file

hervorbringen (imperf **brachte hervor**, perf **hat hervorgebracht**) vb [13] to produce

hervorragend adj excellent

hervorrufen (imperf **rief hervor**, perf **hat hervorgerufen**) vb [56] to cause

Herz (gen **Herzens**, pl **Herzen**) nt ❶ heart ▷ *Es bricht mir fast das Herz.* It almost breaks my heart. ❷ hearts sg ▷ *Herz ist Trumpf.* Hearts are trumps.

Herzinfarkt (pl **Herzinfarkte**) m heart attack

herzlich adj warm ▷ *ein herzlicher Empfang* a warm welcome; **Wir wurden herzlich begrüßt.** We were warmly welcomed.; **Herzlich willkommen in Bamberg.** Welcome to Bamberg.; **Herzlichen Glückwunsch!** Congratulations.; **Herzliche Grüße.** Best wishes.

herzlos adj heartless

Herzschlag (pl **Herzschläge**) m ❶ heartbeat ▷ *bei jedem Herzschlag* with every heartbeat ❷ heart attack ▷ *Er hat einen Herzschlag bekommen.* He had a heart attack.

Hessen nt see **Hesse**

* Hessen is one of the 16 Länder. Its
* capital is Wiesbaden, yet its biggest
* city is Frankfurt am Main, which is
* Germany's principal financial centre
* and home to the Bundesbank.

hetero adj (informal) straight

heterosexuell adj heterosexual

Heu nt hay; **Geld wie Heu** stacks of money

heulen vb [38] ❶ to howl ▷ *Die Wölfe heulten.* The wolves were howling. ❷ to cry ▷ *Jetzt fang nicht gleich an zu heulen.* Now don't start crying.

Heuschnupfen m hay fever ▷ *Sie leidet an Heuschnupfen.* She suffers from hay fever.

heute adv today; **heute Abend** this evening; **heute Morgen** this morning; **heute früh** this morning

heutig adj today's ▷ *die heutige Jugend* today's youth

heutzutage adv nowadays

Hexe f witch

hielt vb see **halten**

hier adv here ▷ *hier drinnen* in here; **Hier spricht Lisa.** This is Lisa.; **hier bleiben** to stay here

hierher adv here

hiesig adj local ▷ *die hiesige Bevölkerung* the local population

hieß vb see **heißen**

Hilfe f help; **Erste Hilfe** first aid; **Hilfe!** Help!

hilflos adj helpless

hilfreich adj helpful

hilfsbereit adj ready to help

hilft vb see **helfen**

Himbeere f raspberry

Himmel (pl **Himmel**) m ❶ sky ▷ *ein wolkenloser Himmel* a cloudless sky ❷ heaven ▷ *in den Himmel kommen* to go to heaven

Himmelsrichtung f **die vier Himmelsrichtungen** the four points of the compass

hin adv **hin und zurück** there and back; **hin und her** to and fro; **Wo ist er hin?** Where has he gone?; **auf meine Bitte hin** at my request

hinab adv down

hinauf adv up

hinaufsteigen (imperf **stieg hinauf**, perf **ist hinaufgestiegen**) vb [74] to climb ▷ *Wir sind auf den Berg hinaufgestiegen.* We climbed up the mountain.

hinaus adv out

hinausgehen (imperf **ging hinaus**, perf **ist hinausgegangen**) vb [29] to go out ▷ *Sie ist kurz hinausgegangen.* She's gone out for a minute.; **über etwas hinausgehen** to exceed something

hinausschieben (imperf **schob hinaus**, perf **hat hinausgeschoben**)

GERMAN > ENGLISH

vb to put off ▷ *Sie haben die Entscheidung hinausgeschoben.* They put the decision off.

hindern vb [88] **jemanden an etwas hindern** to prevent somebody from doing something

Hindernis (gen **Hindernisses**, pl **Hindernisse**) nt obstacle

Hindu (pl **Hindus**) m/f Hindu

hinein adv in ▷ *Hinein mit dir!* In you go!

hineingehen (imperf **ging hinein**, perf **ist hineingegangen**) vb [29] to go in ▷ *Geh doch hinein.* Go in.; **hineingehen in** to go into

Hinfahrt f outward journey

hinfallen (pres **fällt hin**, imperf **fiel hin**, perf **ist hingefallen**) vb [22] to fall ▷ *Sie stolperte und fiel hin.* She stumbled and fell.

Hinflug (pl **Hinflüge**) m outward flight

hinhalten (pres **hält hin**, imperf **hielt hin**, perf **hat hingehalten**) vb [33] to hold out ▷ *Sie hielt ihren Teller hin.* She held out her plate.; **jemanden hinhalten** to put somebody off

hinken vb [38] to limp

hinlegen (perf **hat hingelegt**) vb [4] to put down ▷ *Leg das Buch dort drüben hin.* Put the book down over there.; **sich hinlegen** to lie down

hinnehmen (pres **nimmt hin**, imperf **nahm hin**, perf **hat hingenommen**) vb [52] to put up with ▷ *Das kann ich nicht länger hinnehmen.* I can't put up with this any longer.

Hinreise f outward journey

sich hinsetzen (perf **hat sich hingesetzt**) vb [15] to sit down

hinstellen (perf **hat hingestellt**) vb [4] to put ▷ *Wo soll ich die Vase hinstellen?* Where shall I put the vase?; **Er stellte sich vor den Lehrer hin.** He went and stood in front of the teacher.

hinten adv at the back ▷ *Er sitzt ganz hinten.* He sits at the very back.

109 | Hitparade

hinter prep

Use the accusative to express movement or a change of place. Use the dative when there is no change of place.

❶ behind ▷ *Stell dich hinter deine Schwester.* Stand behind your sister. ▷ *Ich saß hinter ihr.* I was sitting behind her. ❷ after ▷ *Wir hatten kurz hinter Köln eine Panne.* We broke down just after Cologne.

hintere adj back ▷ *die hinteren Reihen* the back rows; **der hintere Reifen** the rear tyre

hintereinander adv one after the other; **dreimal hintereinander** three times in a row

Hintergrund (pl **Hintergründe**) m background

hinterher adv afterwards

Hintern (gen **Hintern**, pl **Hintern**) m bottom

Hinterrad (pl **Hinterräder**) nt back wheel

hinüber adv over

hinübergehen (imperf **ging hinüber**, perf **ist hinübergegangen**) vb [29] to go over

hinunter adv down

Hinweis (gen **Hinweises**, pl **Hinweise**) m ❶ hint ▷ *Er hat mir nicht den kleinsten Hinweis gegeben, wie ich das machen soll.* He didn't give me the slightest hint as to how I was supposed to do it. ❷ instruction ▷ *Hinweise zur Bedienung* operating instructions

hinweisen (imperf **wies hin**, perf **hat hingewiesen**) vb **jemanden auf etwas hinweisen** to point something out to somebody

hinzufügen (perf **hat hinzugefügt**) vb [15] to add

Hirn (pl **Hirne**) nt brain

Hirsch (pl **Hirsche**) m stag

historisch adj historic

Hitparade f charts pl

Hitze f heat
hitzefrei adj **hitzefrei haben** to have time off school because of excessively hot weather
- If the temperature reaches 28°C – 30°C at 10 a.m., then German children are sent home early and any afternoon lessons are cancelled.

Hitzschlag (pl **Hitzschläge**) m heatstroke
hoch adj high ▷ *zehn Meter hoch* ten metres high

> Before a noun or after an article, use **hohe**.

▷ *ein hoher Zaun* a high fence; **Das ist mir zu hoch.** That's beyond me.

> Word for word, **Das ist mir zu hoch** means 'It's too high for me'.

Hoch (pl **Hochs**) nt ❶ cheer ▷ *Ein Hoch auf die Gastgeber!* Three cheers for the hosts! ❷ area of high pressure ▷ *ein Hoch über dem Atlantik* an area of high pressure over the Atlantic
hochachtungsvoll adv yours faithfully
hochbegabt adj extremely talented
Hochhaus (gen **Hochhauses**, pl **Hochhäuser**) nt multistorey building
hochheben (imperf **hob hoch**, perf **hat hochgehoben**) vb to lift up
hochladen (pres **lädt hoch**, imperf **lud hoch**, perf **hat hochgeladen**) vb to upload (computer) ▷ *eine Datei hochladen* to upload a file
Hochsaison (pl **Hochsaisons**) f high season
Hochschulbildung f higher education
Hochschule f ❶ college ❷ university
Hochsommer (pl **Hochsommer**) m high summer
Hochsprung (pl **Hochsprünge**) m high jump
höchst adv extremely
höchste adj highest ▷ *Die Zugspitze ist der höchste Berg Deutschlands.* The Zugspitze is the highest mountain in Germany.; **am höchsten** the highest
höchstens adv at most
Höchstgeschwindigkeit f maximum speed
Hochzeit f wedding
Hochzeitstag (pl **Hochzeitstage**) m ❶ wedding day ▷ *An ihrem Hochzeitstag trug sie ein wunderschönes Kleid.* She wore a beautiful dress on her wedding day. ❷ wedding anniversary ▷ *Morgen ist ihr zehnter Hochzeitstag.* It's their tenth wedding anniversary tomorrow.
Hocker (pl **Hocker**) m stool
Hof (pl **Höfe**) m ❶ yard ▷ *Die Kinder spielen im Hof.* The children are playing in the yard. ❷ farm ▷ *Dieser Bauer hat den größten Hof im Dorf.* This farmer has the largest farm in the village.
hoffen vb [38] to hope ▷ *Ich hoffe, er kommt noch.* I hope he's coming.; **auf etwas hoffen** to hope for something
hoffentlich adv hopefully ▷ *Hoffentlich kommt er bald.* Hopefully he'll come soon. ▷ *Das passiert hoffentlich nie wieder.* Hopefully that won't happen again.; **Hoffentlich nicht.** I hope not.
Hoffnung f hope
hoffnungslos adj hopeless
hoffnungsvoll adj hopeful
höflich adj polite
Höflichkeit f politeness
hohe adj

> **hohe** is the form of **hoch** used before a noun.

high ▷ *ein hoher Zaun* a high fence
Höhe f height
Höhepunkt (pl **Höhepunkte**) m climax ▷ *der Höhepunkt des Abends* the climax of the evening
höher adj, adv higher
hohl adj hollow
Höhle f cave

holen vb [38] ❶ to get ▷ *Ich hole ihn.* I'll get him.; **jemanden holen lassen** to send for somebody

Holland nt Holland

Holländer (pl **Holländer**) m Dutchman; *Er ist Holländer.* He's Dutch.; **die Holländer** the Dutch

Holländerin f Dutchwoman; *Sie ist Holländerin.* She's Dutch.

holländisch adj Dutch

Hölle f hell

Holz (gen **Holzes**, pl **Hölzer**) nt wood

Holzkohle f charcoal

Homeoffice nt working from home; *Zweimal pro Woche arbeite ich im Homeoffice.* I work from home twice a week.

homosexuell adj homosexual

Honig (pl **Honige**) m honey

Hopfen (pl **Hopfen**) m hops pl

hörbar adj audible

Hörbuch (pl **Hörbücher**) nt audio book

horchen vb [48] ❶ to listen ▷ *Er horchte auf das kleinste Geräusch.* He listened for the slightest noise. ❷ to eavesdrop ▷ *Du hast an der Tür gehorcht!* You've been eavesdropping at the door!

hören vb [38] to hear ▷ *Ich höre dich nicht.* I can't hear you.; **Musik hören** to listen to music; **Radio hören** to listen to the radio; **auf jemanden/etwas hören** to listen to someone/something ▷ *Hör auf deine Mutter!* Listen to your mother!

Hörer (pl **Hörer**) m receiver ▷ *Sie hat einfach den Hörer aufgelegt.* She simply put down the receiver.

Horizont (pl **Horizonte**) m horizon ▷ *am Horizont* on the horizon

horizontal adj horizontal

Horn (pl **Hörner**) nt horn

Horror m horror

Horrorfilm (pl **Horrorfilme**) m horror film

Hose f trousers pl ▷ *eine Hose* a pair of trousers

Be careful! The German word **Hose** does not mean hose.

Hosentasche f trouser pocket

Hosenträger (pl **Hosenträger**) m braces pl

Hotel (pl **Hotels**) nt hotel

hübsch adj pretty

Hubschrauber (pl **Hubschrauber**) m helicopter

Hufeisen (pl **Hufeisen**) nt horseshoe

Hüfte f hip

Hügel (pl **Hügel**) m hill

Huhn (pl **Hühner**) nt chicken ▷ *Huhn mit Reis* chicken with rice

Hummel f bumblebee

Humor m humour; **Humor haben** to have a sense of humour

humorvoll adj humorous

Hund (pl **Hunde**) m dog

hundert num a hundred

Hunger m hunger; **Hunger haben** to be hungry

hungrig adj hungry

Hupe f horn ▷ *auf die Hupe drücken* to sound the horn

hupen vb [38] to sound the horn

hüpfen (perf ist gehüpft) vb [38] to hop

husten vb [2] to cough

Husten m cough ▷ *Sie hat Husten.* She has a cough.

Hut (pl **Hüte**) m hat

Hut f **auf der Hut sein** to be on one's guard

Hütte f hut

Hybridauto (pl **Hybridautos**) nt hybrid car

hygienisch adj hygienic

hysterisch adj hysterical ▷ *Sie wurde hysterisch.* She became hysterical.

ICE abbr (= Intercityexpress) Intercity Express train
ich pron ▷ *Ich weiß nicht.* I don't know.; *Ich bin's!* It's me!
ideal adj ideal
Ideal (pl **Ideale**) nt ideal
Idee f idea
identifizieren (perf **hat identifiziert**) vb [76] to identify
identisch adj identical
Ideologie f ideology
Idiot (gen **Idioten**, pl **Idioten**) m idiot
idiotisch adj idiotic
Igel (pl **Igel**) m hedgehog
ihm pron

ihm is the dative of **er** and **es**.

❶ him ▷ *Kannst du ihm sagen, wie spät es ist?* Can you tell him what the time is?
❷ to him ▷ *Gib es ihm!* Give it to him.
❸ it ▷ *Das Meerschweinchen hat Hunger, gib ihm was zu essen.* The guinea pig's hungry, give it something to eat.
ihn pron

ihn is the accusative of **er**.

him ▷ *Ich habe ihn gesehen.* I saw him.
ihnen pron

ihnen is the dative of **sie** (plural).

❶ them ▷ *Ich sage es ihnen.* I'll tell them.
❷ to them ▷ *Gib es ihnen.* Give it to them.
Ihnen pron

Ihnen is the dative of **Sie**.

❶ you ▷ *Darf ich Ihnen etwas zu trinken anbieten?* May I offer you something to drink? ❷ to you ▷ *Darf ich Ihnen das geben?* May I give this to you?
ihr pron ❶ you ▷ *Habt ihr das gesehen?* Did you see that?

- The familiar form of address **ihr**
- (singular **du**) is used when
- addressing family members, friends,
- children under 16 and pets.

▷ *Ihr seid es.* It's you.

ihr is also the dative of **sie** (singular).

❷ her ▷ *Kannst du ihr das bitte ausrichten?* Can you please tell her? ▷ *Er steht neben ihr.* He's standing beside her. ❸ to her ▷ *Gib es ihr.* Give it to her.
▷ adj ❶ her ▷ *Ihr Vater ist nett.* Her father's nice. ▷ *Ihre Mutter hat mir das gesagt.* Her mother told me. ▷ *Das ist ihr Fahrrad.* That's her bike. ❷ hers ▷ *Das ist nicht ihr Füller, ihrer ist schwarz.* That's not her pen, hers is black. ▷ *Meine Mutter heißt Ulla, ihre auch.* My mother's called Ulla, so is hers. ▷ *Mein Fahrrad war kaputt, also habe ich ihres genommen.* My bike was broken, so I took hers. ❸ their ▷ *Das ist ihr Lehrer.* That's their teacher. ▷ *Ihre Englischlehrerin ist netter als unsere.* Their English teacher's nicer than ours. ▷ *Ihr Haus liegt gleich neben unserem.* Their house is right next door to ours. ❹ theirs ▷ *Das ist nicht ihr Lehrer, ihrer heißt Herr Schulz.* That's not their teacher, theirs is called Mr Schulz. ▷ *Unsere Schule macht einen Wandertag, ihre nicht.* Our school is going rambling, theirs isn't.

Ihr adj ❶ your ▷ *Ihr Vater ist nett.* Your father's nice. ▷ *Ihre Mutter hat mir das gesagt.* Your mother told me. ▷ *Ist das Ihr Fahrrad?* Is that your bike? ▷ *Leben Ihre Eltern noch?* Are your parents still alive? ❷ yours ▷ *Das ist nicht Ihr Füller, Ihrer ist hier.* That's not your pen, yours is here. ▷ *Meine Mutter heißt Ulla, wie heißt Ihre?* My mother's called Ulla, what's yours called? ▷ *Mein Fahrrad ist kaputt, kann ich Ihres nehmen?* My bike's broken, can I take yours?

ihretwegen adv

> ihretwegen refers to **sie** (singular or plural).

❶ for her sake ▷ *Ich habe ihretwegen auf den Urlaub verzichtet.* I went without a holiday for her sake. ❷ on her account ▷ *Er hat sich ihretwegen furchtbar aufgeregt.* He got terribly upset on her account. ❸ as far as she's concerned ▷ *Sie sagt, dass du ihretwegen ruhig gehen kannst.* She says that as far as she's concerned you can go. ❹ for their sake ▷ *Wir haben ihretwegen auf den Urlaub verzichtet.* We went without a holiday for their sake. ❺ on their account ▷ *Er hat sich ihretwegen furchtbar aufgeregt.* He got terribly upset on their account. ❻ as far as they're concerned ▷ *Sie sagen, dass du ihretwegen ruhig gehen kannst.* They say that as far as they're concerned you can go.

Ihretwegen adv

> Ihretwegen refers to **Sie**.

❶ for your sake ▷ *Ich habe Ihretwegen auf den Urlaub verzichtet.* I went without a holiday for your sake. ❷ on your account ▷ *Er hat sich Ihretwegen furchtbar aufgeregt.* He got terribly upset on your account.

Illustrierte (gen **Illustrierten**) f magazine

im = in dem

Imbiss (gen **Imbisses**, pl **Imbisse**) m snack

Imbissstube f snack bar

immatrikulieren, **sich** (perf **hat immatrikuliert**) vb [76] to register (at university)

immer adv always ▷ *Du kommst immer zu spät.* You're always late.; **immer wieder** again and again; **immer noch** still; **immer noch nicht** still not; **für immer** forever; **immer wenn ich** ... every time I ...; **immer schöner** more and more beautiful; **immer trauriger** sadder and sadder; **wer auch immer** whoever; **was auch immer** whatever

immerhin adv at least

Imperfekt (pl **Imperfekte**) nt imperfect

impfen vb [38] to vaccinate ▷ *jemanden gegen etwas impfen* to vaccinate somebody against something

Impfstoff (pl **Impfstoffe**) m vaccine

Impfung f vaccination

Import (pl **Importe**) m import

importieren (perf **hat importiert**) vb [76] to import

imstande adj **imstande sein, etwas zu tun** to be able to do something

in prep

> Use the accusative to express movement or a change of place. Use the dative when there is no change of place.

❶ in ▷ *Es ist im Schrank.* It's in the cupboard. ▷ *Sie ist in der Stadt.* She's in town. ▷ *Sie wurde rot im Gesicht.* She went red in the face. ❷ into ▷ *Lege es in diese Schublade.* Put it into this drawer. ▷ *Sie geht in die Stadt.* She's going into town.; **in der Schule sein** to be at school; **in die Schule gehen** to go to school; **in diesem Jahr** this year; **heute in zwei Wochen** two weeks today; **in sein** to be in

inbegriffen adv included

indem conj while; **indem man etwas macht** by doing something ▷ *Sie* *bedankte sich, indem sie mir Blumen schickte.* She thanked me by sending me flowers.

Inder (*pl* **Inder**) *m* Indian

Inderin *f* Indian

Indianer (*pl* **Indianer**) *m* Native American

Indianerin *f* Native American

indianisch *adj* Native American

Indien *nt* India

indisch *adj* Indian

individuell *adj, adv* ❶ individual (*distinctive*) ▷ *Ihr Stil ist sehr individuell.* She has a very individual style. ❷ individually ▷ *Jede Bewerbung wird individuell geprüft.* Each application will be considered individually.

Industrie *f* industry

Industriegebiet (*pl* **Industriegebiete**) *nt* industrial area

Infektion *f* infection

Infinitiv (*pl* **Infinitive**) *m* infinitive

infizieren (*perf* **hat infiziert**) *vb* [**76**] to infect ▷ *Sie hat ihren Bruder infiziert.* She infected her brother.; **sich bei jemandem infizieren** to catch something from somebody

Inflation *f* inflation

infolge *prep*

The preposition **infolge** takes the genitive.

as a result of

infolgedessen *adv* consequently

Informatik *f* computer science

Informatiker (*pl* **Informatiker**) *m* computer scientist

Information *f* information ▷ *Weitere Informationen lassen wir Ihnen zukommen.* We will send you further information.

informieren (*perf* **hat informiert**) *vb* [**76**] to inform; **sich über etwas informieren** to find out about something; **sich über jemanden informieren** to make enquiries about somebody

infrage *adv* **etwas infrage stellen** to question something; **nicht infrage kommen** to be out of the question

Ingenieur (*pl* **Ingenieure**) *m* engineer

Ingenieurin *f* engineer

Ingwer *m* ginger

Inhaber (*pl* **Inhaber**) *m* owner ▷ *Wir müssen den Inhaber des Hauses fragen, ob das geht.* We'll have to ask the owner of the house if it's all right.; **der Inhaber einer Lizenz** the licence holder

Inhalt (*pl* **Inhalte**) *m* ❶ contents *pl* ▷ *Der Inhalt der Flasche war grün.* The contents of the bottle were green. ❷ content ▷ *Fasse den Inhalt dieser Geschichte zusammen.* Summarize the content of this story. ❸ volume ▷ *Berechne den Inhalt des Würfels.* Calculate the volume of the cube.

Inhaltsangabe *f* summary

Inhaltsverzeichnis (*gen* **Inhaltsverzeichnisses**, *pl* **Inhaltsverzeichnisse**) *nt* table of contents

inklusive *prep, adv*

The preposition **inklusive** takes the genitive.

❶ inclusive of ▷ *ein Computer inklusive Bildschirm* a computer inclusive of monitor ❷ included ▷ *Die Bedienung ist inklusive.* Service is included.

Inland *nt* **im In- und Ausland** at home and abroad

innen *adv* inside

Innenstadt (*pl* **Innenstädte**) *f* town centre

innere *adj* internal ▷ *innere Blutungen* internal bleeding ▷ *die inneren Angelegenheiten des Landes* the internal matters of the country

innerhalb *adv, prep*

The preposition **innerhalb** takes the genitive.

❶ within ▷ *Die Hochzeit wird innerhalb der nächsten zwei Jahre stattfinden.* The wedding will take place within the next two years. ▷ *Das muss innerhalb von zwei Tagen gemacht werden.* That must be done within two days. ❷ during ▷ *Der Bus fährt nur innerhalb der Woche, nicht an Wochenenden.* The bus only runs during the week, not at the weekend. ❸ inside (of) ▷ *Innerhalb des Hauses ist es wärmer als draußen.* Inside the house is warmer than outside.

inoffiziell *adj* unofficial
ins = in das
insbesondere *adv* particularly
Insekt (*pl* **Insekten**) *nt* insect
Insel *f* island
insgesamt *adv* in all ▷ *Er hat insgesamt drei Fahrräder.* He has three bikes in all. ▷ *Insgesamt waren dreihundert Leute gekommen.* In all, three hundred people came.
Instinkt (*pl* **Instinkte**) *m* instinct
Instrument (*pl* **Instrumente**) *nt* instrument
intelligent *adj* intelligent
Intelligenz *f* intelligence
intensiv *adj* intensive
Intercityexpress (*gen* **Intercityexpresses**, *pl* **Intercityexpresse**) *m* Intercity Express train
interessant *adj* interesting
Interesse (*pl* **Interessen**) *nt* interest; **Interesse haben an** to be interested in
interessieren (*perf* **hat interessiert**) *vb* [76] to interest ▷ *Es interessiert mich, was du in den Ferien erlebt hast.* I'm interested to know what you did in your holidays.; **sich interessieren für** to be interested in
Internat (*pl* **Internate**) *nt* boarding school
international *adj* international
Internet *nt* internet
Internet-Anbieter (*pl* **Internet-Anbieter**) *m* Internet Service Provider
Internetbenutzer (*pl* **Internetbenutzer**) *m* internet user
Internetbenutzerin *f* internet user
Internetseite (*pl* **Internetseiten**) *f* web page
interpretieren (*perf* **hat interpretiert**) *vb* [76] to interpret
Interview *nt* interview
intransitiv *adj* intransitive
inzwischen *adv* meanwhile
Irak *m* Iraq
irakisch *adj* Iraqi
Iran *m* Iran
iranisch *adj* Iranian
Ire (*gen* **Iren**, *pl* **Iren**) *m* Irishman; **die Iren** the Irish
irgend *adv* at all ▷ *Komm, wenn es irgend geht.* Come if it's at all possible.
irgendein *adj* ❶ some ▷ *Irgendein Mann hat mir das gesagt.* Some man told me. ▷ *Irgendeine Ausrede wird dir schon einfallen.* You'll think of some excuse. ❷ any ▷ *Ich will nicht irgendeinen Computer.* I don't just want any computer. ▷ *Gibt es nicht irgendeine Möglichkeit?* Isn't there any chance? ▷ *Welchen Kuli willst du?* — *Irgendeinen.* Which pen do you want? — Any one.
irgendetwas *pron* ❶ something ▷ *irgendetwas Schönes* something nice ❷ anything ▷ *Hast du irgendetwas gehört?* Did you hear anything?
irgendjemand *pron* ❶ somebody ▷ *Das hat mir irgendjemand gesagt.* Somebody told me. ❷ anybody ▷ *Hast du irgendjemanden gesehen?* Did you see anybody?
irgendwann *adv* sometime
irgendwas *pron* ❶ something ▷ *Er murmelte irgendwas.* He murmured something. ❷ anything ▷ *Was soll ich anziehen?* — *Irgendwas.* What shall I wear? — Anything.
irgendwie *adv* somehow
irgendwo *adv* somewhere

Irin f Irishwoman
irisch adj Irish
Irland nt Ireland
Ironie f irony
ironisch adj ironic ▷ *Das war ironisch gemeint.* That was meant to be ironic.
irre adj, adv ❶ mad ▷ *Wer ist denn auf diese irre Idee gekommen?* Who thought up this mad idea? ❷ fantastic ▷ *Das war ein irres Konzert.* That was a fantastic concert. ❸ incredibly ▷ *Er ist irre schnell gefahren.* He drove incredibly fast. ▷ *Die Party war irre gut.* The party was incredibly good.
irreführen (*perf* **hat irregeführt**) *vb* [4] to mislead
irren *vb* [38]

> Use **haben** to form the perfect tense for 'to be mistaken' but **sein** for 'to wander about'.

to wander about ▷ *Sie ist durch die Straßen geirrt.* She wandered about the streets.; **sich irren** to be mistaken ▷ *Du hast dich geirrt.* You were mistaken.
Irrtum (*pl* **Irrtümer**) *m* mistake
Islam *m* Islam
Island *nt* Iceland
Israel *nt* Israel
Israeli (*pl* **Israelis**) *mf* Israeli ▷ *Sie ist mit einem Israeli verheiratet.* She is married to an Israeli.
israelisch adj Israeli
isst *vb* see **essen**
ist *vb* see **sein**
Italien *nt* Italy
Italiener (*pl* **Italiener**) *m* Italian
Italienerin f Italian
italienisch adj Italian

ja adv ❶ yes ▷ *Hast du das gesehen? — Ja.* Did you see that? — Yes, I did.; **Ich glaube ja.** I think so. ❷ really? ▷ *Ich habe mir ein neues Auto gekauft. — Ach ja?* I've bought a new car. — Really?; **Du kommst, ja?** You're coming, aren't you?; **Sei ja vorsichtig!** Do be careful.; **Sie wissen ja, dass …** As you know, …; **Tu das ja nicht!** Don't you dare do that!; **Ich habe es ja gewusst.** I just knew it.; **ja, also …** well … ▷ *Ja, also wenn ihr alle geht, dann gehe ich mit.* Well, if you're all going, then I'm going too.
Jacht f yacht
Jacke f ❶ jacket ▷ *Sie trug einen blauen Rock und eine schwarze Jacke.* She was wearing a blue skirt and a black jacket. ❷ cardigan ▷ *Wenn es dir kalt ist, solltest du eine Jacke anziehen.* If you're cold, you should put on a cardigan.
Jackett (*pl* **Jacketts**) *nt* jacket
Jagd (*pl* **Jagden**) f ❶ hunt ▷ *Er fiel während der Jagd vom Pferd.* He fell off his horse during the hunt. ❷ hunting

▷ Alan geht ab zur Jagd. Alan often goes hunting.

jagen vb [38]

Use **haben** to form the perfect tense for 'to hunt' or 'to chase' but **sein** for 'to race'.

① **to hunt** ▷ Sonntags gehen sie jagen. They go hunting on Sundays. ▷ Meine Katze jagt Mäuse. My cat hunts mice. ② **to chase** ▷ Die Polizei hat die Bankräuber gejagt, aber nicht eingeholt. The police chased the bank robbers but didn't catch them. ③ **to race** ▷ Wir sind mit ihr ins Krankenhaus gejagt. We raced with her to the hospital.; **Damit kann man mich jagen.** I can't stand that.

Jahr (pl **Jahre**) nt year ▷ Ich bin vierzehn Jahre alt. I'm fourteen years old.; **die Neunzigerjahre** the nineties

Jahreszeit f season; **zu jeder Jahreszeit** throughout the year

Jahrhundert (pl **Jahrhunderte**) nt century

-jährig adj -year-old ▷ ein Fünfjähriger a five-year-old

jährlich adj, adv yearly

Jahrmarkt (pl **Jahrmärkte**) m funfair

Jahrtausend (pl **Jahrtausende**) nt millennium

Jalousie f Venetian blind

jammern vb [88] to whine ▷ Hör auf zu jammern! Stop whining.

Januar (gen **Januars** or **Januar**, pl **Januare**) m January ▷ im Januar in January ▷ am dritten Januar on the third of January ▷ Ulm, den 3. Januar 2025 Ulm, 3 January 2025 ▷ Heute ist der dritte Januar. Today is the third of January.

Japan nt Japan

Japaner (pl **Japaner**) m Japanese

Japanerin f Japanese

japanisch adj Japanese

jawohl adv yes

je adv, conj ① **ever** ▷ Warst du je in Italien? Have you ever been to Italy? ▷ Hast du so was je gesehen? Did you ever see anything like it? ▷ besser denn je better than ever ② **each** ▷ Wir haben je zwei Stück bekommen. We got two pieces each. ▷ Sie zahlten je zehn Euro. They paid ten euros each.; **je nach** depending on; **je nachdem** it depends; **je nachdem, ob ...** depending on whether ...; **je ... umso ...** the ... the ...; **je eher, desto besser** the sooner the better

Jeans (pl **Jeans**) f jeans pl; **eine Jeans** a pair of jeans

jede adj, pron ① **every** ▷ Jeder Schüler bekommt ein Zeugnis. Every pupil receives a report. ▷ Ich besuche sie jede Woche. I visit her every week. ▷ Er gab jedem Mädchen ein Bonbon. He gave every girl a sweet.; **jeder** everybody ② **each** ▷ Jeder von euch bekommt ein Stück. Each of you will get a piece. ▷ Jede seiner Freundinnen war anders. Each of his girlfriends was different. ▷ Jedes der Kinder hat mir etwas geschenkt. Each child gave me something.; **jedes Mal** every time

jedenfalls adv in any case

jederzeit adv at any time

jedoch adv however

jemals adv ever

jemand pron ① **somebody** ▷ Jemand hat mir gesagt, dass du krank bist. Somebody told me that you were ill. ▷ Ich brauche jemanden, der mir das Fenster repariert. I need somebody to repair my window. ▷ Ich treffe mich morgen mit jemandem, der auch dort arbeitet. I'm meeting somebody tomorrow who also works there. ② **anybody** ▷ War jemand zu Hause? Was anybody at home?

jene adj, pron ① **that** ▷ in jener Zeit at that time ② **those** ▷ in jenen Tagen in those days

jetzt adv now ▷ Sie ist jetzt in der Schweiz. She's in Switzerland now.

jeweils adv jeweils zwei zusammen two at a time; **zu jeweils fünf Euro** at five euros each

Job (pl **Jobs**) m (informal) job
Jod nt iodine
joggen vb [48]

> Use **haben** for the perfect tense when you describe the activity and **sein** when you describe the motion.

to jog ▷ *Früher habe ich oft gejoggt.* I used to jog a lot. ▷ *Wir sind durch den Wald gejoggt.* We jogged through the woods.
Jogging nt jogging
Jogginganzug (pl **Jogginganzüge**) m tracksuit
Joghurt (pl **Joghurts**) m yogurt
Jogurt (pl **Jogurts**) m yogurt
Johannisbeere f redcurrant ▷ *Johannisbeeren sind mir zu sauer.* Redcurrants are too sour for me.; **Schwarze Johannisbeere** blackcurrant
Journalist (gen **Journalisten**, pl **Journalisten**) m journalist
Journalistin f journalist
jubeln vb [34] to rejoice
Jubiläum (pl **Jubiläen**) nt anniversary ▷ *Nächstes Jahr feiert unsere Schule ihr zwanzigjähriges Jubiläum.* Our school's celebrating its twentieth anniversary next year.
jucken vb [38] to be itchy ▷ *Meine Nase juckt.* My nose is itchy. ▷ *Es juckt mich am Arm.* My arm's itchy.
Jude (gen **Juden**, pl **Juden**) m Jew
Jüdin f Jew
jüdisch adj Jewish
Jugend f youth ▷ *In meiner Jugend habe ich Fußball gespielt.* I used to play football in my youth. ▷ *die Jugend von heute* the youth of today
Jugendherberge f youth hostel
Jugendklub (pl **Jugendklubs**) m youth club
jugendlich adj youthful ▷ *Er hat ein jugendliches Gesicht.* He has a youthful face. ▷ *Sie sieht sehr jugendlich aus.* She looks very youthful.

Jugendliche (gen **Jugendlichen**, pl **Jugendlichen**) mf teenager ▷ *Ein Jugendlicher wurde gestern wegen Diebstahl verhaftet.* A teenager was arrested yesterday for theft.
Jugendzentrum (pl **Jugendzentren**) nt youth centre
Juli (gen **Juli** or **Julis**, pl **Julis**) m July ▷ *im Juli* in July ▷ *am dritten Juli* on the third of July ▷ *Ulm, den 3. Juli 2025* Ulm, 3 July 2025 ▷ *Heute ist der dritte Juli.* Today is the third of July.
jung adj young ▷ *Er ist drei Jahre jünger als ich.* He's three years younger than me.
Junge (gen **Jungen**, pl **Jungen**) m boy ▷ *In unserer Klasse gibt es zehn Jungen und fünfzehn Mädchen.* There are ten boys and fifteen girls in our class.
▶ nt young animal; **eine Löwin mit ihren Jungen** a lioness with her young
Jungfrau f ❶ virgin ❷ Virgo ▷ *Veronika ist Jungfrau.* Veronika's Virgo.
jüngste adj ❶ youngest ▷ *Er ist der jüngste Schüler der Klasse.* He's the youngest pupil in the class. ❷ latest ▷ *die jüngsten Entwicklungen* the latest developments
Juni (gen **Juni** or **Junis**, pl **Junis**) m June ▷ *im Juni* in June ▷ *am fünfzehnten Juni* on the fifteenth of June ▷ *Ulm, den 3. Juni 2025* Ulm, 3 June 2025 ▷ *Heute ist der dritte Juni.* Today is the third of June.

k

Kabel (pl **Kabel**) nt ❶ wire ▷ *Das Kabel des Telefons ist zu kurz.* The telephone wire is too short. ❷ cable ▷ *Das Kabel der Seilbahn muss regelmäßig überprüft werden.* The cable on the cable car has to be checked regularly.

Kabelfernsehen nt cable television

Kabine f ❶ cabin ▷ *Wir hatten zu zweit eine Kabine auf dem Schiff.* The two of us shared a cabin on the ship. ❷ cubicle ▷ *Sie können das Kleid dort hinten in der Kabine anprobieren.* You can try the dress on in the cubicle over there.

Käfer (pl **Käfer**) m beetle

Kaffee (pl **Kaffees** or **Kaffee**) m coffee ▷ *Herr Ober, zwei Kaffee bitte.* Two coffees please, waiter.

Kaffeekanne f coffeepot

Kaffeepause f coffee break ▷ *Wir machten Kaffeepause.* We had a coffee break.

Käfig (pl **Käfige**) m cage

kahl adj bald ▷ *sein kahler Kopf* his bald head; **die kahlen Bäume im Winter** the bare trees in winter; **kahl geschoren** shaven

Kakao (pl **Kakaos** or **Kakao**) m cocoa ▷ *Herr Ober, zwei Kakao bitte.* Two cups of cocoa please, waiter.

Kalb (pl **Kälber**) nt calf (animal)

Kalbfleisch nt veal

Kalender (pl **Kalender**) m ❶ calendar ▷ *An der Wand hing ein Kalender mit Bildern von Picasso.* A calendar with pictures by Picasso was hanging on the wall. ❷ diary ▷ *Sie holte ihren Kalender aus der Tasche.* She got her diary out of her bag.

Kalorie f calorie

kalorienarm adj low in calories

kalt adj cold ▷ *Heute ist es kälter als gestern.* It's colder today than yesterday. ▷ *Mir ist kalt.* I'm cold.; **etwas kalt stellen** to chill something

Kälte f ❶ cold ▷ *Bei dieser Kälte gehe ich nicht raus.* I'm not going out in this cold. ❷ coldness ▷ *Die Kälte des Wassers hat uns vom Baden abgehalten.* The coldness of the water stopped us from bathing.

kam vb see **kommen**

Kamera (pl **Kameras**) f camera

Kamerad (gen **Kameraden**, pl **Kameraden**) m friend

Kamin (pl **Kamine**) m open fire; **Wir saßen am Kamin.** We sat by the fire.

Kamm (pl **Kämme**) m comb

kämmen vb [38] to comb ▷ *Sie kann es nicht leiden, wenn man sie kämmt.* She can't stand having her hair combed. ▷ *Ich muss meiner kleinen Schwester die Haare kämmen.* I have to comb my little sister's hair.; **sich kämmen** to comb one's hair

Kampf (pl **Kämpfe**) m ❶ fight ▷ *der Kampf zwischen Usyk und Fury* the fight between Usyk and Fury ❷ contest ▷ *Dieses Jahr findet der Kampf um den Pokal in Großbritannien statt.* The contest for the cup is taking place in Great Britain this year. ❸ struggle ▷ *Ich habe die Prüfung geschafft, aber es war ein Kampf.* I passed the exam but it was a struggle.

kämpfen vb [38] to fight
Kanada nt Canada
Kanadier (pl **Kanadier**) m Canadian
Kanadierin f Canadian
kanadisch adj Canadian
Kanal (pl **Kanäle**) m ❶ canal ▷ *Diese beiden Flüsse sind durch einen Kanal verbunden.* These two rivers are connected by a canal. ❷ drain
Kanarienvogel (pl **Kanarienvögel**) m canary
Kandidat (gen **Kandidaten**, pl **Kandidaten**) m candidate
Känguru (pl **Kängurus**) nt kangaroo
Kaninchen (pl **Kaninchen**) nt rabbit
Kanister (pl **Kanister**) m ▷ *ein Benzinkanister* a petrol can
kann vb see **können**
Kanne f ❶ (for coffee) pot ❷ (for milk) churn ❸ watering can
Kante f edge
Kantine f canteen ▷ *Mittags isst sie in der Kantine.* She eats in the canteen at lunchtime.
Kanu (pl **Kanus**) nt canoe; **Kanu fahren** to go canoeing
Kanzler (pl **Kanzler**) m chancellor
Kanzlerin f chancellor
Kapital nt capital (money)
Kapitän (pl **Kapitäne**) m captain
Kapitel (pl **Kapitel**) nt chapter
Kappe f cap
kaputt adj ❶ broken ▷ *Mein Computer ist kaputt.* My computer's broken.; **Am Auto ist etwas kaputt.** There's something wrong with the car.; **kaputt machen** to break ❷ (informal) knackered ▷ *Ich bin von der Wanderung total kaputt.* I'm completely knackered after the walk.

kaputtgehen (imperf **ging kaputt**, perf **ist kaputtgegangen**) vb [29] ❶ to break ▷ *Mein Computer ist gestern kaputtgegangen.* My computer broke yesterday. ❷ (material) to wear out ❸ (plant) to die ❹ (relationship) to break up
kaputtmachen (perf **hat kaputtgemacht**) vb [48] to wear out ▷ *Die viele Arbeit macht mich noch kaputt.* All this work is wearing me out.; **sich kaputtmachen** to wear oneself out
Kapuze f hood ▷ *eine Jacke mit Kapuze* a jacket with a hood
Karfreitag m Good Friday
kariert adj ❶ checked ▷ *Sie hatte ein kariertes Kleid an.* She was wearing a checked dress. ❷ squared ▷ *Für Mathe brauchst du ein Heft mit kariertem Papier.* You need an exercise book with squared paper for maths.
Karies f tooth decay ▷ *Sie hat Karies.* She has tooth decay.
Karneval (pl **Karnevale** or **Karnevals**) m carnival

* The German carnival season lasts
* from 11 November to Shrove Tuesday
* but most events, fancy-dress
* processions and parties take place
* in the week leading up to Ash
* Wednesday.

Karo (pl **Karos**) nt ❶ square ▷ *Das Muster bestand aus kleinen Karos.* The pattern was made up of little squares. ❷ diamonds sg ▷ *Karo ist Trumpf.* Diamonds is trumps.
Karotte f carrot
Karriere f career; **Karriere machen** to get on
Karte f ❶ card ▷ *Sie hat uns aus dem Urlaub eine Karte geschickt.* She sent us a card from her holiday. ▷ *Ich weiß nicht, welche Karte ich ausspielen soll.* I don't know which card I should play.; **die Gelbe Karte** the yellow card; **die Rote**

Karte the red card ❷ map ▷ *Sieh mal auf der Karte nach, wie weit wir noch fahren müssen.* Look on the map to see how far we still have to go. ❸ menu ▷ *Der Ober brachte uns die Karte.* The waiter brought us the menu. ❹ ticket ▷ *Kannst du Karten fürs Konzert besorgen?* Can you get us tickets for the concert? ▷ *Ich fahre morgen nach Bonn, die Karte habe ich schon gekauft.* I'm going to Bonn tomorrow, I've already bought my ticket.; **alles auf eine Karte setzen** to put all one's eggs in one basket

> Word for word, **alles auf eine Karte setzen** means 'to bet everything on one card'.

Kartenspiel (*pl* **Kartenspiele**) *nt* ❶ card game ▷ *Ich habe ein neues Kartenspiel gelernt.* I've learned a new card game. ❷ pack of cards ▷ *Hast du ein Kartenspiel da?* Have you got a pack of cards?

Kartoffel *f* potato

Kartoffelbrei *m* mashed potatoes *pl*

Kartoffelsalat (*pl* **Kartoffelsalate**) *m* potato salad

Karton (*pl* **Kartons**) *m* ❶ cardboard ▷ *Wir haben das Bild auf Karton aufgezogen.* We mounted the picture on cardboard. ❷ cardboard box ▷ *Sie packte die Bücher in einen Karton.* She packed the books in a cardboard box.

Karussell (*pl* **Karussells**) *nt* roundabout ▷ *Ich möchte Karussell fahren.* I'd like to go on the roundabout.

Käse (*pl* **Käse**) *m* cheese

Käsekuchen (*pl* **Käsekuchen**) *m* cheesecake

Kaserne *f* barracks *pl* ▷ *In unserer Nähe gibt es eine Kaserne.* There's a barracks near us.

Kasse *f* ❶ till ▷ *Die meisten Geschäfte haben elektronische Kassen.* Most shops have electronic tills. ❷ checkout ▷ *An der Kasse war nur eine von fünf Kassen besetzt.* Only one of the five checkouts was open. ❸ box office ▷ *Sie können Ihre Karten telefonisch vorbestellen und an der Kasse abholen.* You may order your tickets in advance and collect them from the box office. ❹ ticket office ▷ *Karten fürs Fußballspiel bekommen Sie auch an der Kasse des Stadions.* You can also get tickets for the football match at the ticket office in the stadium. ❺ cash box ▷ *Alle Barbeträge bewahren wir in dieser Kasse auf.* We keep all the cash in this cash box. ❻ health insurance ▷ *Bei welcher Kasse sind Sie versichert?* What health insurance have you got?

* Germany's national service for health
* is available to all and is provided
* through a number of public health
* insurers.

gut bei Kasse sein (*informal*) to be in the money

Kassenzettel (*pl* **Kassenzettel**) *m* receipt

kassieren (*perf* **hat kassiert**) *vb* [**76**] to take ▷ *Die Polizei hat seinen Führerschein kassiert.* The police took his driving licence.; **Der Parkwächter hat zehn Euro Parkgebühren kassiert.** The parking attendant charged us ten euros to park the car.; **Darf ich kassieren?** Would you like to pay now?

Kastanie *f* ❶ chestnut ❷ chestnut tree

Kasten (*pl* **Kästen**) *m* ❶ box ▷ *Er warf den Brief in den Kasten.* He put the letter in the box. ❷ case ▷ *Sie packte die Geige zurück in den Kasten.* She put the violin back in its case.; **ein Kasten Bier** a crate of beer

Katalog (*pl* **Kataloge**) *m* catalogue

Katalysator (*pl* **Katalysatoren**) *m* ❶ catalytic converter ▷ *ein Auto mit Katalysator* a car with catalytic converter

katastrophal *adj, adv* catastrophic; **katastrophal schlecht** appallingly bad

Katastrophe f disaster
Kategorie f category
Kater (pl **Kater**) m ① tomcat ▷ *Wir haben einen Kater und eine Katze.* We have a tomcat and a female cat. ② hangover ▷ *Nach der Party hatte ich einen furchtbaren Kater.* I had a terrible hangover after the party.
katholisch adj Catholic
Katze f cat; **für die Katz** for nothing
kauen vb [38] to chew
Kauf (pl **Käufe**) m purchase ▷ *der Kauf eines Autos* the purchase of a car; **ein guter Kauf** a bargain
kaufen vb [38] to buy
Käufer (pl **Käufer**) m buyer
Kauffrau f businesswoman
Kaufhaus (gen **Kaufhauses**, pl **Kaufhäuser**) nt department store
Kaufmann (pl **Kaufleute**) m ① businessman ▷ *ein erfolgreicher Kaufmann* a successful businessman ② grocer ▷ *zum Kaufmann gehen* to go to the grocer's
Kaugummi (pl **Kaugummis**) m chewing gum
kaum adv hardly ▷ *Ich habe kaum geschlafen.* I hardly slept.
Kehle f throat
Keil (pl **Keile**) m wedge
Keim (pl **Keime**) m ① shoot ▷ *Eine Woche nach der Aussaat zeigen sich die ersten Keime.* The first shoots appear a week after sowing. ② germ ▷ *Das Mittel tötete die Keime ab.* The medicine killed the germs.; **etwas im Keim ersticken** to nip something in the bud
kein adj, pron

> When combined with a noun, **kein** is used for masculine and neuter nouns, **keine** for feminine and plural nouns. On its own **keiner** is used for masculine, **keine** for feminine and plural, and **keines** or **keins** for neuter.

① not ... any ▷ *Ich habe keine Geschwister.* I don't have any brothers or sisters. ▷ *Ich will keinen Streit.* I don't want any quarrelling. ▷ *Er zeigt kein Interesse an Computern.* He doesn't show any interest in computers. ▷ *Von den Autos hat mir keines gefallen.* I didn't like any of the cars. ▷ *Kein Tier könnte in diesem Klima überleben.* No animal could survive in this climate.; **'Kein Zutritt'** 'No entry'; **Ich habe keine Lust.** I don't feel like it.; **Ich habe keinen Hunger.** I'm not hungry. ② no ③ nobody ▷ *Alle waren eingeladen, es ist aber keiner gekommen.* Everybody was invited but nobody came.; **Ich kenne hier keinen.** I don't know anybody here.
Keks (pl **Kekse**) m biscuit
Keller (pl **Keller**) m cellar
Kellner (pl **Kellner**) m waiter
Kellnerin f waitress
kennen (imperf **kannte**, perf **hat gekannt**) vb [39] to know ▷ *Ich kenne ihn nicht.* I don't know him. ▷ *Ich kenne London gut.* I know London well.
kennenlernen vb [4] ① to meet ▷ *Sie hat ihren Freund bei einem Fußballspiel kennengelernt.* She met her boyfriend at a football match. ② to get to know ▷ *Ich würde ihn gern besser kennenlernen.* I'd like to get to know him better.; **sich kennenlernen (1)** to meet ▷ *Wir haben uns auf einer Party kennengelernt.* We met at a party. **(2)** to get to know each other ▷ *Wir haben uns im Laufe der Zeit immer besser kennengelernt.* We got to know each other better and better as time went on.
Kenntnis (pl **Kenntnisse**) f knowledge ▷ *Deutschkenntnisse wären von Vorteil.* Knowledge of German would be an advantage.; **etwas zur Kenntnis nehmen** to note something; **jemanden in Kenntnis setzen** to inform somebody

Kennzeichen (pl **Kennzeichen**) nt ① mark ▷ *unveränderliche Kennzeichen* distinguishing marks ② registration ▷ *das Auto mit dem Kennzeichen S-MJ 2714* the car with the registration S-MJ 2714

Kerl (pl **Kerle**) m bloke; **Sie ist ein netter Kerl.** She's a good sort.

Kern (pl **Kerne**) m ① pip ▷ *Klementinen haben keine Kerne.* Clementines don't have any pips. ② stone ▷ *der Kern der Kirsche* the cherry stone ③ (of nut) kernel ④ nucleus ⑤ core ▷ *der Reaktorkern* the reactor core; **Wir sollten zum Kern des Problems kommen.** We should get to the heart of the problem.

Kernenergie f nuclear energy

Kernkraftwerk (pl **Kernkraftwerke**) nt nuclear power station

Kerze f ① candle ▷ *Sie zündete eine Kerze an.* She lit a candle. ② plug ▷ *Bei der Inspektion werden die Kerzen erneuert.* The plugs are changed while the car is being serviced.

Kette f chain

Keuchhusten m whooping cough ▷ *Meine Schwester hat Keuchhusten.* My sister has whooping cough.

Keule f ① club ▷ *Er schlug ihm mit einer Keule über den Kopf.* He hit him over the head with a club. ② leg ▷ *Beim Hähnchen mag ich am liebsten die Keule.* My favourite part of a chicken is the leg.

kg abbr (= Kilogramm) kg

KI abbr (= künstliche Intelligenz) AI

kichern vb [88] to giggle

Kiefer (pl **Kiefer**) m jaw
▶ f pine tree

Kies m gravel

Kilo (pl **Kilos** or **Kilo**) nt kilo ▷ *Ich muss ein paar Kilos loswerden.* I need to lose a couple of kilos. ▷ *Ich hätte gern zwei Kilo Tomaten.* Can I have two kilos of tomatoes. ▷ *Ich wiege fünfzig Kilo.* I weigh eight stone.

Kilogramm (pl **Kilogramme** or **Kilogramm**) nt kilogram ▷ *zwei Kilogramm Äpfel* two kilograms of apples

Kilometer (pl **Kilometer**) m kilometre ▷ *mit achtzig Kilometern pro Stunde* at fifty miles per hour

Kind (pl **Kinder**) nt child; **von Kind auf** from childhood; **ein Kind bekommen** to have a baby

Kindergarten (pl **Kindergärten**) m kindergarten

Kindergärtnerin f kindergarten teacher

Kindergeld nt child benefit

Kinderkrippe f crèche

Kinderlähmung f polio ▷ *Sie hatte als Kind Kinderlähmung.* She had polio as a child.

Kindertagesstätte f day nursery

Kinderwagen (pl **Kinderwagen**) m pram

Kindheit f childhood

kindisch adj childish; **sich kindisch benehmen** to behave childishly

Kinn (pl **Kinne**) nt chin

Kino (pl **Kinos**) nt cinema ▷ *ins Kino gehen* to go to the cinema

Kiosk (pl **Kioske**) m kiosk

Kirche f church

Kirmes (pl **Kirmessen**) f funfair

Kirsche f cherry

Kissen (pl **Kissen**) nt ① cushion ▷ *Auf dem Sofa lagen bunte Kissen.* There were brightly-coloured cushions on the sofa. ② pillow ▷ *Er schläft ohne Kissen.* He sleeps without a pillow.

kitschig adj kitschy

kitzeln vb [34] to tickle

kitzlig adj ticklish ▷ *Ich bin kitzlig an den Füßen.* My feet are ticklish. ▷ *Das ist eine ganz kitzlige Angelegenheit.* That's a very ticklish matter.

klagen vb [38] ① to wail ▷ *'Hätte ich doch nur auf dich gehört', klagte er.* 'If only I had listened to you', he wailed. ❷ **to complain** ▷ *Sie klagt dauernd über ihre Kinder.* She's constantly complaining about her children. ▷ *Sie klagt in letzter Zeit oft über Kopfschmerzen.* She's been complaining of headaches a lot recently. ❸ **to sue** ▷ *Wir werden gegen ihn klagen.* We're going to sue him.; **Sie hat mir ihr Leid geklagt.** She poured out her sorrows to me.

Klammer (pl **Klammern**) f ❶ **bracket** ▷ *Sie schrieb in Klammern eine Erklärung dazu.* She wrote an explanation in brackets. ❷ (clothes peg) **peg** ❸ (for teeth) **brace** ▷ *Viele Kinder müssen eine Klammer tragen.* Many children have to wear a brace.

Klang (pl **Klänge**) m **sound**

Klappe f ❶ **flap** ▷ *Über dem Briefkasten ist eine Klappe.* There's a flap over the letterbox. ❷ **valve** ▷ *Die Klappe an seinem Herzen hat ein Loch.* His heart valve has a hole in it. ❸ (informal) **trap** ▷ *Er soll die Klappe halten.* He should keep his trap shut.; **Sie hat eine große Klappe.** She's got a big mouth.

klappen vb [48] ❶ **to work** ▷ *Das kann ja nicht klappen.* That won't work. ▷ *Das Experiment hat geklappt.* The experiment worked. ❷ **to tip** ▷ *Sie klappte den Sitz nach oben.* She tipped up the seat. ▷ *Er klappte den Deckel der Kiste nach hinten.* He tipped the lid of the chest back.

klappern vb [88] **to rattle**

klar adj **clear** ▷ *Das Wasser ist sehr klar.* The water is very clear. ▷ *Ich brauche einen klaren Kopf.* I need a clear head. ▷ *eine klare Antwort* a clear answer ▷ *Mir ist nicht klar, was er eigentlich will.* I'm not clear about what he really wants.; **sich über etwas im Klaren sein** to be clear about something; **Na klar!** Of course!; **Alles klar** OK ▷ *Alles klar (bei dir)?* Everything OK (with you)?

klären vb [38] ❶ **to clarify** ▷ *Wir sollten diese Frage klären.* We should clarify this matter. ❷ **to purify** ▷ *In dieser Anlage wird das Abwasser geklärt.* The sewage is purified in this plant.; **sich klären** to clear itself up

Klarheit f ❶ **clarity**; *Wir brauchen in dieser Sache Klarheit.* This matter must be clarified. ❷ **clearness** ▷ *die Klarheit des Wassers* the clearness of the water

Klarinette f **clarinet** ▷ *Oliver spielt Klarinette.* Oliver plays the clarinet.

klarstellen (perf **hat klargestellt**) vb [4] **to make clear** ▷ *Ich möchte doch mal klarstellen, dass ich das nie gesagt habe.* I would like to make it quite clear that I never said that.

klasse adj (informal) **smashing** ▷ *Er ist ein klasse Lehrer.* He's a smashing teacher.

Klasse f **class** ▷ *Wir sind in der ersten Klasse gefahren.* We travelled first class. ▷ *Unsere Klasse fährt nach England.* Our class is going to England.; **große Klasse sein** to be great

Klassenarbeit f **test**
- The **Klassenarbeit** is the main form of assessment in German schools.
- Over the school year, German pupils write between 6 and 8 **Klassenarbeiten**, usually 45 minutes long, in every subject (except practical ones like art or drama).

▷ *Wir schreiben morgen in Englisch eine Klassenarbeit.* We've got a written English test tomorrow.

Klassenbuch (pl **Klassenbücher**) nt **class register**

Klassenkamerad (gen **Klassenkameraden**, pl **Klassenkameraden**) m **classmate**

Klassenkameradin f **classmate**

Klassenlehrer (pl **Klassenlehrer**) m **class teacher**

Klassenlehrerin f class teacher
Klassensprecher (pl **Klassensprecher**) m class representative
Klassensprecherin f class representative
Klassenzimmer (pl **Klassenzimmer**) nt classroom
klassisch adj classical
Klatsch (gen **Klatsches**) m gossip ▷ Hast du schon den neuesten Klatsch gehört? Have you heard the latest gossip?
klauen (perf **hat geklaut**) vb [**38**] (informal) to pinch
Klavier (pl **Klaviere**) nt piano ▷ Bettina spielt Klavier. Bettina plays the piano.
kleben vb [**38**] to stick ▷ Ich habe die zerbrochene Vase wieder geklebt. I've stuck the broken vase together again. ▷ Das klebt nicht. It doesn't stick.; **etwas an etwas kleben** to stick something on something; **an etwas kleben** to stick to something; **jemandem eine kleben** (informal) to thump somebody one
klebrig adj sticky
Klebstoff (pl **Klebstoffe**) m glue
Klee m clover
Kleid (pl **Kleider**) nt dress ▷ Sie trug ein rotes Kleid. She was wearing a red dress.; **Kleider** clothes pl
Kleiderbügel (pl **Kleiderbügel**) m coat hanger
Kleiderschrank (pl **Kleiderschränke**) m wardrobe
Kleidung f clothing
klein adj small ▷ ein kleines Kind a small child ▷ ein kleiner Betrag a small amount; **als ich klein war** when I was little
Kleingeld nt small change
Klempner (pl **Klempner**) m plumber
klettern (perf **ist geklettert**) vb [**88**] to climb
klicken vb [**48**] (computer) to click ▷ mit der Maus klicken to click on the mouse

Klima (pl **Klimas**) nt climate
Klimaanlage f air conditioning
Klimakrise f climate crisis
Klimanotstand (pl **Klimanotstände**) m climate emergency
Klimawandel m climate change
Klingel f bell
klingeln vb [**34**] to ring; **Es klingelte.** The doorbell rang.
Klingelton (pl **Klingeltöne**) m (of mobile phone) ringtone
klingen (imperf **klang**, perf **hat geklungen**) vb to sound ▷ Das Klavier klingt verstimmt. The piano sounds out of tune. ▷ Der Vorschlag klingt gut. The suggestion sounds good. ▷ Du klingst deprimiert. You sound depressed.
Klinik f clinic
Klinke f handle (of door)
Klippe f cliff
Klo (pl **Klos**) nt (informal) loo
klonen vb [**38**] to clone ▷ ein geklontes Schaf a cloned sheep
klopfen vb [**38**] ❶ to knock ▷ Sie klopfte an die Tür. She knocked on the door.; **Es klopft.** There's somebody knocking on the door. ❷ to pound ▷ Mein Herz klopfte vor Aufregung. My heart was pounding with excitement.; **jemandem auf die Schulter klopfen** to tap somebody on the shoulder
Kloster (pl **Klöster**) nt ❶ monastery ❷ convent
Klub (pl **Klubs**) m club
klug adj intelligent
km abbr (= Kilometer) km
knabbern vb [**88**] to nibble ▷ Sie knabberte an einem Keks. She nibbled a biscuit.
Knäckebrot nt crispbread
Knall (pl **Knalle**) m bang ▷ Die Tür schlug mit einem lauten Knall zu. The door closed with a loud bang.
knapp adj ❶ tight ▷ Sie hatte einen sehr knappen Pulli an. She was wearing a very

tight pullover. ❷ scarce ▷ *Benzin ist knapp.* Petrol is scarce.; **knapp bei Kasse** short of money ❸ just ▷ *Sie ist knapp fünfzehn Jahre alt.* She has just turned fifteen. ▷ *Wir haben knapp verloren.* We only just lost.; **eine knappe Stunde** just under an hour; **knapp unter** just under

kneifen (*imperf* **kniff**, *perf* **hat gekniffen**) *vb* ❶ to pinch ▷ *Er hat mich in den Arm gekniffen.* He pinched my arm. ❷ to back out ▷ *Als er springen sollte, hat er gekniffen.* When it was his turn to jump, he backed out.

Kneipe f pub

Knie (*pl* **Knie**) *nt* knee

Knoblauch *m* garlic

Knöchel (*pl* **Knöchel**) *m* ❶ knuckle ▷ *Ich habe mir die Knöchel an der rechten Hand geschürft.* I've scraped the knuckles of my right hand. ❷ ankle ▷ *Bei dem Sprung habe ich mir den Knöchel verstaucht.* I sprained my ankle when I jumped.

Knochen (*pl* **Knochen**) *m* bone

Knödel (*pl* **Knödel**) *m* dumpling

Knopf (*pl* **Knöpfe**) *m* button

Knoten (*pl* **Knoten**) *m* ❶ knot ▷ *Sie machte einen Knoten in die Schnur.* She tied a knot in the string. ❷ bun ▷ *Sie trug das Haar in einem Knoten.* She wore her hair in a bun. ❸ lump ▷ *Sie hat einen Knoten in der Brust entdeckt.* She noticed a lump in her breast.

Knüppel (*pl* **Knüppel**) *m* ❶ cudgel ▷ *Die Robbenbabys werden mit Knüppeln erschlagen.* The baby seals are beaten with cudgels. ❷ truncheon ▷ *Die Polizisten gingen mit Knüppeln gegen die Demonstranten vor.* The police used truncheons against the demonstrators. ❸ joystick

Koch (*pl* **Köche**) *m* cook

kochen *vb* [48] ❶ to cook ▷ *Was kochst du heute?* What are you cooking today?

▷ *Ich koche gern.* I like cooking.; **Sie kann gut kochen.** She's a good cook. ❷ to boil ▷ *Das Wasser kocht.* The water's boiling.

Köchin f cook

Kochtopf (*pl* **Kochtöpfe**) *m* saucepan

Koffer (*pl* **Koffer**) *m* suitcase

Kofferraum (*pl* **Kofferräume**) *m* boot (*of car*)

Kohl *m* cabbage

Kohle f ❶ coal ▷ *Wir heizen mit Kohle.* We use coal for heating. ❷ charcoal ▷ *Wir brauchen noch Kohle zum Grillen.* We need charcoal for the barbecue. ❸ (*money*) dough; **Ich habe keine Kohle.** (*informal*) I'm broke.

Kohlensäure f carbon dioxide; **Mineralwasser mit Kohlensäure** sparkling mineral water

Kokosnuss (*pl* **Kokosnüsse**) f coconut

Kollege (*gen* **Kollegen**, *pl* **Kollegen**) *m* colleague

Kollegin f colleague

Köln *nt* Cologne

Komfort *m* luxury ▷ *ein Auto mit allem Komfort* a luxury car

Komfortzone f comfort zone

Komiker (*pl* **Komiker**) *m* comedian

komisch *adj* funny ▷ *ein komischer Film* a funny film ▷ *ein komisches Gefühl* a funny feeling

Komma (*pl* **Kommas**) *nt* comma; **zwei Komma drei (2,3)** two point three (2.3)

kommen (*imperf* **kam**, *perf* **ist gekommen**) *vb* [**40**] ❶ to come ▷ *Wann ist der Brief gekommen?* When did the letter come? ▷ *Kommst du auch zur Party?* Are you coming to the party too?; **Komm gut nach Hause!** Safe journey home. ❷ to get ▷ *Wie komme ich zum Bahnhof?* How do I get to the station?; **unter ein Auto kommen** to be run over by a car ❸ to appear ▷ *Es wird Frühling, die Schneeglöckchen kommen schon.* Spring is coming, the snowdrops

GERMAN > ENGLISH

are appearing. ❹ to go ▷ *Er ist gestern ins Krankenhaus gekommen.* He went into hospital recently. ▷ *Das kommt in den Schrank.* That goes in the cupboard.; **Mit sechs kommt man in die Schule.** You start school at six.; **Wer kommt zuerst?** Who's first?; **Jetzt kommst du an die Reihe.** It's your turn now.; **kommenden Sonntag** next Sunday; **kommen lassen** to send for; **auf etwas kommen** to think of something; **Wie kommst du auf die Idee?** What gave you that idea?; **Ich komme nicht auf seinen Namen.** His name escapes me.; **Er kommt aus Bayern.** He comes from Bavaria.; **Sie ist durchs Abitur gekommen.** She got through her Abitur.; **ums Leben kommen** to lose one's life; **Das kommt davon!** That's what you get!; **zu sich kommen** to come round; **zu etwas kommen (1)** to get something ▷ *Wie bist du zu dem Computer gekommen?* How did you get the computer? **(2)** to get round to something ▷ *Ich mache das, sobald ich dazu komme.* I'll do it as soon as I get round to it.

Kommunikation f communication
Kommunismus (gen **Kommunismus**) m communism
Komödie f comedy
kompatibel adj compatible
Kompliment (pl **Komplimente**) nt compliment ▷ *Er hat ihr zu ihrer Übersetzung ein Kompliment gemacht.* He complimented her on her translation.
kompliziert adj complicated
Komponist (gen **Komponisten**, pl **Komponisten**) m composer
Kompott (pl **Kompotte**) nt compote
Konditor (pl **Konditoren**) m pastry cook
Konditorei f cake shop
Kondom (pl **Kondome**) nt condom
Konflikt (pl **Konflikte**) m conflict

127 | können

König (pl **Könige**) m king
Königin f queen
Konjugation f conjugation
konjugieren (perf **hat konjugiert**) vb [76] to conjugate
Konjunktion f conjunction
Konjunktiv (pl **Konjunktive**) m subjunctive
Konkurrenz f ❶ competition ▷ *Auf diesem Sektor ist die Konkurrenz groß.* Competition is keen in this sector. ❷ competitors pl ▷ *Sie ist zur Konkurrenz gegangen.* She's gone over to our competitors.

können (pres **kann**, imperf **konnte**, perf **hat gekonnt** or **können**) vb [41]

The past participle **können** is used when **können** is a modal auxiliary.

❶ can ▷ *Kannst du schwimmen?* Can you swim? ▷ *Sie kann keine Mathematik.* She can't do mathematics. ▷ *Sie hat nicht früher kommen können.* She couldn't come earlier. ▷ *Kann ich mit?* Can I come with you? ▷ *Ich kann nicht ...* I can't ... ❷ to be able to ▷ *Morgen werde ich nicht kommen können.* I won't be able to come tomorrow.; **Ich kann nicht mehr. (1)** I can't go on. ▷ *Ich mache jetzt Schluss, ich kann nicht mehr.* I'll have to stop now, I can't go on. **(2)** I'm full up. ▷ *Willst du noch ein Stück Kuchen?* — *Nein danke, ich kann nicht mehr.* Would you like another piece of cake? — No thanks, I'm full up. ❸ may ▷ *Kann ich gehen?* May I go? ▷ *Sie könnten recht haben.* You may be right.; **Es kann sein, dass ...** It may be that ... ▷ *Es kann sein, dass ich etwas später komme.* It may be that I'll come a little later.; **Ich kann nichts dafür.** It's not my fault.; **Das kann sein.** That's possible. ❹ to know ▷ *Er kann viele Geschichtszahlen.* He knows a lot of historical dates.; **Können Sie Deutsch?** Can you speak German?

Können nt ability ▷ *Sie hat ihr Können bewiesen.* She has proved her ability.

konnte vb see **können**

Konsequenz (pl **Konsequenzen**) f consequence

konservativ adj conservative

Konserve f tinned food

Konsonant (gen **Konsonanten**, pl **Konsonanten**) m consonant

Kontakt (pl **Kontakte**) m contact

Kontaktlinsen fpl contact lenses pl

Kontinent (pl **Kontinente**) m continent

Konto (pl **Konten**) nt account ▷ *Geld auf ein Konto einzahlen* to pay money into an account

Kontrolle f control ▷ *die Passkontrolle* passport control ▷ *Sie hat die Kontrolle über das Fahrzeug verloren.* She lost control of the vehicle. ▷ *etwas unter Kontrolle haben* to have something under control

Kontrolleur (pl **Kontrolleure**) m inspector

kontrollieren (perf **hat kontrolliert**) vb [76] to check ▷ *Kann ich bitte Ihre Fahrkarten kontrollieren?* May I check your tickets please?

Konzentration f concentration

sich konzentrieren (perf **hat sich konzentriert**) vb [76] to concentrate ▷ *Ich kann mich nicht konzentrieren.* I can't concentrate.

Konzept nt ❶ concept ❷ plan ▷ *Sie hat ein klares Konzept für das neue Projekt.* She has a clear plan for the new project.

Konzert (pl **Konzerte**) nt ❶ concert ▷ *Wir waren gestern Abend im Konzert.* We were at a concert yesterday evening. ❷ concerto ▷ *ein Konzert für Klavier und Violine* a concerto for piano and violin

Kopf (pl **Köpfe**) m head

Kopfhörer (pl **Kopfhörer**) m headphones pl

Kopfkissen (pl **Kopfkissen**) nt pillow

Kopfsalat (pl **Kopfsalate**) m lettuce

Kopfschmerzen pl headache sg ▷ *Ich habe Kopfschmerzen.* I've got a headache.

Kopie f copy

kopieren (perf **hat kopiert**) vb [76] to copy ▷ *kopieren und einfügen* to copy and paste

Kopiergerät (pl **Kopiergeräte**) nt photocopier

Korb (pl **Körbe**) m basket; **jemandem einen Korb geben** to turn somebody down

> Word for word, **jemandem einen Korb geben** means 'to give somebody a basket'.

Korken (pl **Korken**) m cork

Korkenzieher (pl **Korkenzieher**) m corkscrew

Korn (pl **Körner**) nt corn

Körper (pl **Körper**) m body

körperlich adj, adv ❶ physical ▷ *körperliche Gesundheit* physical health ❷ physically ▷ *Sie war körperlich sehr fit.* She was physically very fit.

korrigieren (perf **hat korrigiert**) vb [76] to correct

Kosmetik f cosmetics pl

Kost f ❶ food ▷ *Sie ernährt sich von gesunder Kost.* She eats healthy food. ❷ board ▷ *Für Kost und Unterkunft ist gesorgt.* Board and lodging will be provided.

kostbar adj precious ▷ *Du vergeudest meine kostbare Zeit.* You're wasting my precious time.

kosten vb [2] ❶ to cost ▷ *Mein Fahrrad hat zweitausend Euro gekostet.* My bike cost two thousand euros.; **Was kostet ...?** How much is ...? ❷ to taste ▷ *Willst du die Soße mal kosten?* Would you like to taste the sauce? ▷ *Koste mal, ob das schmeckt.* Taste it and see if it's good.

Kosten pl ① costs pl ▷ *die Kosten tragen* to bear the costs ② expense ▷ *Bei vielen Kindern hat man auch viele Kosten.* Lots of children mean a lot of expense.; **auf jemandes Kosten** at somebody's expense

kostenlos adj free of charge

köstlich adj ① hilarious ▷ *Das war ein köstlicher Film.* That was a hilarious film. ▷ *ein köstlicher Witz* a hilarious joke ② (food) delicious; **sich köstlich amüsieren** to have a marvellous time

Kostüm (pl **Kostüme**) nt costume; **ein Damenkostüm** a ladies' suit

Kotelett (pl **Koteletts**) nt chop

krabbeln (perf ist gekrabbelt) vb [88] to crawl

Krach m ① crash ▷ *Die Vase fiel mit einem lauten Krach zu Boden.* The vase fell on the ground with a loud crash. ② noise ▷ *Unsere Nachbarn machen viel Krach.* Our neighbours make a lot of noise. ③ row ▷ *Sie hat Krach mit ihrem Freund.* She had a row with her boyfriend.

Kraft (pl **Kräfte**) f strength ▷ *Samson hat seine Kraft verloren.* Samson lost his strength.; **Er hat viel Kraft.** He's very strong.; **mit aller Kraft** with all one's might; **Kinder kosten viel Kraft.** Children require a lot of energy.; **Sie scheint magische Kräfte zu haben.** She seems to have magic powers.; **Das Gesetz tritt am ersten August in Kraft.** The law comes into effect on the first of August.

Kraftfahrzeug (pl **Kraftfahrzeuge**) nt motor vehicle

kräftig adj, adv ① strong ▷ *Er ist ein kräftiger Junge.* He is a strong boy. ② hard ▷ *ein kräftiger Schlag* a hard blow ▷ *kräftig schütteln* to shake hard; **kräftig üben** to practise a lot

Kraftwerk (pl **Kraftwerke**) nt power station

Kragen (pl **Kragen**) m collar

Kralle f ① claw ▷ *die Krallen der Katze* the cat's claws ② talon ▷ *die Krallen des Vogels* the bird's talons

krank adj ill ▷ *Ich bin krank.* I'm ill. ▷ *Ich habe eine kranke Mutter.* My mother's ill.

Krankenhaus (gen **Krankenhauses**, pl **Krankenhäuser**) nt hospital

Krankenkasse f health insurance
- Germany's national service for health
- is available to all and is provided
- through a number of public health
- insurers.

Krankenpfleger (pl **Krankenpfleger**) m nurse

Krankenpflegerin f nurse

Krankenschein (pl **Krankenscheine**) m health insurance card

Krankenschwester f nurse

Krankenwagen (pl **Krankenwagen**) m ambulance

Krankheit f illness

kratzen vb [36] to scratch; **sich kratzen** to scratch oneself

Kraut (pl **Kräuter**) nt ① herb ▷ *eine Salatsoße mit frischen Kräutern* a salad dressing with fresh herbs ② sauerkraut ▷ *Heute gibt es Würstchen mit Kraut.* We're having sausages and sauerkraut today.

Krawatte f tie

kreativ adj creative

Krebs (gen **Krebses**, pl **Krebse**) m ① crab ▷ *Krebse bewegen sich seitlich voran.* Crabs move sideways. ② cancer ▷ *Sie ist an Krebs gestorben.* She died of cancer. ③ Cancer ▷ *Beate ist Krebs.* Beate's Cancer.

Kredit (pl **Kredite**) m credit ▷ *auf Kredit* on credit

Kreditkarte f credit card

Kreide f chalk

Kreis (gen **Kreises**, pl **Kreise**) m ① circle ▷ *Stellt euch im Kreis auf.* Form a circle. ▷ *mein Freundeskreis* my circle of friends ▷ *im Kreis gehen* to go round in circles

❷ district ▷ *Blaubeuren liegt im Kreis Ulm.* Blaubeuren is in the district of Ulm.

kreischen vb [38] to shriek ▷ *Sie kreischte laut.* She shrieked loudly.

Kreislauf m circulation ▷ *Er hat einen labilen Kreislauf.* She has bad circulation.

Kreisverkehr (pl **Kreisverkehre**) m roundabout

Kreuz (gen **Kreuzes**, pl **Kreuze**) nt ❶ cross ▷ *Sie markierte die Stelle mit einem Kreuz.* She marked the place with a cross. ❷ back ▷ *Mir tut das Kreuz weh.* My back's sore. ❸ clubs sg ▷ *Kreuz ist Trumpf.* Clubs is trumps.

Kreuzung f ❶ crossroads sg ▷ *An der Kreuzung fährst du links.* You go left at the crossroads. ❷ cross ▷ *Das ist eine Kreuzung zwischen Pferd und Esel.* It's a cross between a horse and a donkey.

Kreuzworträtsel (pl **Kreuzworträtsel**) nt crossword puzzle

kriechen (imperf **kroch**, perf **ist gekrochen**) vb ❶ to crawl ▷ *Das Baby kroch zur Tür.* The baby crawled towards the door. ▷ *Der Verkehr kriecht.* The traffic is crawling. ❷ to grovel ▷ *Er kriecht vor seinem Chef.* He's grovelling to his boss.

Krieg (pl **Kriege**) m war

kriegen vb [38] to get ▷ *Ich kriege einen Schnupfen.* I'm getting a cold.; **Sie kriegt ein Kind.** She's going to have a baby.

Krimi (pl **Krimis**) m thriller

Kriminalfilm (pl **Kriminalfilme**) m crime thriller

Kriminalroman (pl **Kriminalromane**) m detective story

kriminell adj criminal

Krise f crisis

Kritik (pl **Kritiken**) f ❶ criticism no pl ▷ *Er kann keine Kritik vertragen.* He can't stand criticism. ❷ review ▷ *Sie hat nur schlechte Kritiken bekommen.* All her reviews were bad.

kritisch adj critical

kritisieren (perf **hat kritisiert**) vb [76] to criticize

Krone f crown

Krug (pl **Krüge**) m ❶ jug ▷ *Sie stellte einen Krug Saft auf den Tisch.* She put a jug of juice on the table. ❷ beer mug ▷ *Er trinkt sein Bier immer aus einem Krug.* He always drinks his beer out of a beer mug.

krumm adj ein krummer Rücken a hunched back; **Mach nicht so einen krummen Rücken.** Don't slouch.; **Sitz nicht so krumm.** Sit up straight.

Küche f ❶ kitchen ❷ cooking ▷ *die französische Küche* French cuisine

Kuchen (pl **Kuchen**) m ❶ cake ▷ *ein Marmorkuchen* a marble cake ❷ flan ▷ *ein Obstkuchen* a fruit flan

kucken vb [38] see **gucken**

Kuckuck (pl **Kuckucke**) m cuckoo

Kuckucksuhr f cuckoo clock

Kugel f ❶ bullet ▷ *Er wurde von einer Kugel getroffen.* He was hit by a bullet. ❷ ball ▷ *Die Wahrsagerin hat eine Kugel aus Glas.* The fortune teller has a crystal ball.

Kugelschreiber (pl **Kugelschreiber**) m Biro®

Kuh (pl **Kühe**) f cow

kühl adj cool ▷ *Abends wurde es kühl.* In the evenings it got cool.

Kühler (pl **Kühler**) m radiator (in car)

Kühlschrank (pl **Kühlschränke**) m fridge

Kühltruhe f freezer

kühn adj bold

Kuli (pl **Kulis**) m Biro®

Kultur f ❶ culture; Kultur haben to be cultured ❷ civilization ▷ *die abendländische Kultur* Western civilization

kulturell adj cultural

Kummer m sorrow; **Hast du Kummer?** Have you got problems?

kümmern vb [38] to concern ▷ *Was kümmert mich seine Kritik?* Why should his criticism concern me?; **Das kümmert mich nicht.** That doesn't worry me.; **sich um jemanden kümmern** to look after somebody; **sich um etwas kümmern** to see to something

Kunde (gen **Kunden**, pl **Kunden**) m customer

kündigen vb [38] ① to hand in one's notice ▷ *Die Arbeit gefällt mir nicht, ich werde kündigen.* I don't like the job, I'm going to hand in my notice.; **Der Chef hat ihr gekündigt.** The boss gave her her notice.; **die Wohnung kündigen** to give notice on one's flat ② to cancel ▷ *Ich habe mein Abonnement gekündigt.* I've cancelled my subscription.

Kündigung f notice ▷ *Er reichte seine Kündigung ein.* He handed in his notice.

Kundin f customer

Kundschaft f customers pl

künftig adj future ▷ *künftige Generationen* future generations

Kunst (pl **Künste**) f ① art ▷ *Sie interessiert sich für Kunst.* She's interested in art. ② knack ▷ *Er beherrscht die Kunst, andere zu überzeugen.* He's got the knack of persuading others.; **Das ist doch keine Kunst.** It's easy.

> Word for word, **Das ist doch keine Kunst** means 'It's not an art'.

Künstler (pl **Künstler**) m artist

Künstlerin f artist

künstlerisch adj artistic ▷ *künstlerisch begabt sein* to have artistic talents

künstlich adj artificial

Kunststoff (pl **Kunststoffe**) m synthetic material

Kunststück (pl **Kunststücke**) nt trick

Kunstwerk (pl **Kunstwerke**) nt work of art

Kupfer nt copper (metal)

Kupplung f clutch ▷ *Bei Automatikwagen gibt es keine Kupplung.* Automatic cars don't have a clutch.

Kur f health cure ▷ *eine Kur machen* to take a health cure

Kurs (gen **Kurses**, pl **Kurse**) m ① course ▷ *Ich mache einen Kurs, um Spanisch zu lernen.* I'm doing a course to learn Spanish. ② rate ▷ *Wie ist der Kurs des Pfunds?* What's the rate for the pound?

Kurve f ① bend ▷ *Ein Auto bog um die Kurve.* A car came round the bend. ② curve ▷ *die Kurve eines Schaubilds* the curve on a graph

kurz adj short ▷ *Sie hat kurze Haare.* She has short hair. ▷ *Sie hat eine kurze Rede gehalten.* She made a short speech.; **kurz gesagt** in short; **zu kurz kommen** to come off badly; **den Kürzeren ziehen** to get the worst of it

> Word for word, **den Kürzeren ziehen** means 'to pull the shorter one'.

Kürze f shortness

kürzen vb [36] ① to shorten ▷ *Du solltest den Aufsatz etwas kürzen.* You should shorten your essay a little. ② to cut ▷ *Mein Vater hat mir das Taschengeld gekürzt.* My father has cut my pocket money.

Kurzgeschichte f short story

kürzlich adv recently

kurzsichtig adj short-sighted

Kusine f cousin

Kuss (gen **Kusses**, pl **Küsse**) m kiss

küssen vb [48] to kiss ▷ *Sie hat mich geküsst.* She kissed me.; **sich küssen** to kiss

Küste f coast

L

Labor (pl **Labore** or **Labors**) nt lab
lächeln vb [34] to smile
Lächeln nt smile
lachen vb [48] to laugh
lächerlich adj ridiculous
Lachs (gen **Lachses**, pl **Lachse**) m salmon ▷ *drei Lachse* three salmon
Lack (pl **Lacke**) m ① varnish ▷ *Er hat das Holz mit Lack behandelt.* He treated the wood with varnish. ② paint ▷ *Der Lack an meinem Auto ist stumpf geworden.* The paint on my car has become dull.
laden (pres **lädt**, imperf **lud**, perf **hat geladen**) vb ① to load ▷ *Wir haben das Gepäck ins Auto geladen.* We loaded the luggage into the car. ▷ *Das Programm wird geladen.* The program is being loaded. ▷ *eine Waffe laden* to load a weapon ② to charge ▷ *eine Batterie laden* to charge a battery ③ to summon ▷ *Ich wurde als Zeugin geladen.* I was summoned as a witness.
Laden (pl **Läden**) m ① shop ▷ *In welchem Laden hast du das gekauft?* Which shop did you buy it in? ② shutter ▷ *Im Sommer machen wir tagsüber die Läden zu.* In summer we close the shutters during the day.
Ladung f ① cargo ▷ *Das Flugzeug hatte zu viel Ladung an Bord.* The plane had too much cargo on board. ② loading ▷ *Ein Arbeiter ist bei der Ladung des Schiffes verunglückt.* A worker was injured while loading the ship. ③ summons sg ▷ *Wenn Sie eine Ladung als Zeuge bekommen, müssen Sie erscheinen.* If you receive a summons to appear as a witness, you have to attend. ④ charge ▷ *eine Ladung Dynamit* a charge of dynamite
Lage f ① situation ▷ *Die politische Lage auf dem Balkan ist brisant.* The political situation in the Balkans is explosive. ② layer ▷ *Die Torte bestand aus mehreren Lagen.* The gateau was made up of several layers.; **in der Lage sein, etwas zu tun** to be in a position to do something
Lager (pl **Lager**) nt ① camp ▷ *Er fährt im Sommer in ein Lager der Pfadfinder.* He's going to a scout camp in the summer. ② warehouse ▷ *Die Fabrik hat ein eigenes Lager.* The factory has its own warehouse. ③ stockroom ▷ *Die Verkäuferin hat im Lager nachgesehen.* The sales assistant looked in the stockroom.
lagern vb [88] ① to store ▷ *kühl lagern* to store in a cool place ▷ *trocken lagern* to store in a dry place ② to lay down ▷ *Der Verletzte sollte auf der Seite gelagert werden.* The injured person should be laid down on his side. ③ to camp ▷ *Die Indianer lagerten am Fluss.* The Indians camped by the river.
lahm adj ① lame ▷ *Das Pferd ist lahm.* The horse is lame. ② slow ▷ *Er ist furchtbar lahm.* He is terribly slow.
lähmen vb [38] to paralyse
Lähmung f paralysis

Laken (pl **Laken**) nt sheet (on bed)
Lamm (pl **Lämmer**) nt lamb
Lammfleisch nt lamb (meat)
Lampe f lamp
Land (pl **Länder**) nt ① country ▷ *Italien ist ein schönes Land.* Italy is a beautiful country. ▷ *Am Wochenende fahren wir aufs Land.* We're going to the country at the weekend.; **auf dem Land** in the country; **an Land** on land ② state ▷ *Die Bundesrepublik besteht aus sechzehn Ländern.* The Federal Republic consists of sixteen states.
Landebahn f runway
landen (perf **ist gelandet**) vb [**54**] to land
Landeskunde f regional and cultural studies pl
Landkarte f map
Landkreis (gen **Landkreises**, pl **Landkreise**) m administrative district
- The German administrative
- hierarchy starts with the **Stadt/**
- **Gemeinde** (town/community),
- and continues via the **Landkreis**
- (administrative district) and **Land**
- (federal state) to the **Bund**
- (federation).

ländlich adj rural
Landschaft f ① countryside ▷ *Die toskanische Landschaft ist sehr schön.* The Tuscan countryside is very beautiful. ② landscape ▷ *Turner hat viele Landschaften gemalt.* Turner painted many landscapes.
Landstraße f country road
Landung f landing ▷ *Das Flugzeug verunglückte bei der Landung.* The plane crashed on landing.
Landwirtschaft f agriculture
lang adj ① long ▷ *Sie hat lange Haare.* She has long hair. ▷ *Das war eine lange Rede.* That was a long speech. ▷ *Sie war länger als erwartet weg.* She was away longer than expected. ▷ *Es wird nicht lang*

dauern. It won't take long. ② tall ▷ *Mathis ist der Längste in unserer Klasse.* Mathis is the tallest in our class.
lange adv for a long time ▷ *Sie war lange krank.* She was ill for a long time.; **lange dauern** to last a long time; **lange brauchen** to take a long time
Länge f length ▷ *Sie hat die Länge und Breite des Zimmers ausgemessen.* She measured the length and breadth of the room. ▷ *die Länge eines Films* the length of a film
langen vb [**38**] to be enough ▷ *Das Fleisch hat nicht für alle gelangt.* There wasn't enough meat to go round. ▷ *Meinst du das Geld langt?* Do you think we have enough money?; **Es langt mir.** I've had enough.; **nach etwas langen** to reach for something
Langeweile f boredom
langfristig adj, adv long-term ▷ *eine langfristige Besserung* a long-term improvement ▷ *Wir müssen langfristig planen.* We have to plan long-term.
länglich adj longish
langsam adj, adv ① slow ② slowly ▷ *langsam fahren* to drive slowly; **Das wird langsam langweilig.** This is getting boring.
längst adv **Das ist längst fertig.** That was finished a long time ago.; **Das weiß ich längst.** I've known that for a long time.; **Er ist längst nicht so gescheit wie seine Schwester.** He's far from being as bright as his sister.
längste adj longest ▷ *der längste Tag des Jahres* the longest day of the year
langweilen vb [**38**] to bore ▷ *Langweile ich dich?* Am I boring you?; **sich langweilen** to be bored
langweilig adj boring
Lappen (pl **Lappen**) m rag ▷ *mit einem feuchten Lappen* with a damp rag
Laptop (pl **Laptops**) m laptop
Lärm m noise

Laser (pl **Laser**) m laser

lassen (pres **lässt**, imperf **ließ**, perf **gelassen** or **lassen**) vb [42]

The past participle **lassen** is used when **lassen** is used as a modal auxiliary. ❶ to stop ▷ *Du solltest das Rauchen lassen.* You should stop smoking. ▷ *Er kann das Trinken nicht lassen.* He can't stop drinking. ▷ *Sie kann's nicht lassen.* She won't stop doing it.; **Lass das!** Stop that! ❷ to leave ▷ *Kann ich die Kinder hier lassen?* Can I leave the children here? ▷ *jemanden allein lassen* to leave somebody alone ▷ *Wir haben das Auto zu Hause gelassen.* We left the car at home. ▷ *etwas lassen, wie es ist* to leave something as it is ▷ *Lass mal, ich mache das schon.* Leave it, I'll do it.; **Lassen wir das!** Let's leave it.; **Lass mich!** Leave me alone.; **jemanden irgendwohin lassen** to let somebody go somewhere; **sich etwas machen lassen** to have something done; **jemanden etwas tun lassen** to let somebody do something; **jemanden warten lassen** to keep somebody waiting; **Das lässt sich machen.** That can be done.; **Lass uns gehen.** Let's go.

lässig adj casual

Last f load ▷ *Er stöhnte unter der schweren Last.* He groaned under the heavy load.; **jemandem zur Last fallen** to be a burden to somebody

lästig adj tiresome

Lastwagen (pl **Lastwagen**) m lorry

Latein nt Latin

Lateinamerika nt Latin America

Laterne f ❶ lantern ❷ streetlamp

Lauch (pl **Lauche**) m leek

Lauf (pl **Läufe**) m ❶ run ▷ *Er machte einen Lauf durch den Wald.* He went for a run through the forest. ❷ race ▷ *Sie hat den Lauf über vierhundert Meter gewonnen.* She won the four-hundred-metre race. ❸ course ▷ *der Lauf des Flusses* the course of the river ▷ *im Laufe der Woche* in the course of the week ▷ *einer Sache ihren Lauf lassen* to let something take its course ❹ barrel ▷ *Er richtete den Lauf seiner Pistole auf mich.* He aimed the barrel of his pistol at me.

laufen (pres **läuft**, imperf **lief**, perf **ist gelaufen**) vb [43] ❶ to run ▷ *Sie liefen so schnell sie konnten.* They ran as fast as they could. ▷ *Er läuft Marathon.* He runs marathons. ❷ to walk ▷ *Wir mussten nach Hause laufen.* We had to walk home.

laufend adj, adv ❶ running ▷ *bei laufendem Motor* with the engine running ❷ current ▷ *die laufenden Ausgaben* current expenses; **auf dem Laufenden sein** to be up to date; **auf dem Laufenden halten** to keep up to date ❸ always ▷ *Musst du mich laufend stören?* Do you always have to interrupt me?

Läufer (pl **Läufer**) m ❶ runner ▷ *Die Läufer standen am Start.* The runners were at the start. ▷ *Im Flur liegt ein roter Läufer.* There's a red runner in the hall. ❷ bishop ▷ *Sie zog mit dem Läufer.* She moved her bishop.

Läuferin f runner

Laufwerk (pl **Laufwerke**) nt disk drive ▷ *Die Diskette in Laufwerk A einlegen.* Put the diskette in disk drive A.

Laune f mood ▷ *Was hat sie für eine Laune?* What kind of mood is she in? ▷ *Ich habe gute Laune.* I'm in a good mood. ▷ *Er hat schlechte Laune.* He's in a bad mood. ▷ *Ich bin deine Launen leid.* I'm fed up with your moods.

launisch adj ❶ temperamental ▷ *Sie ist ein sehr launischer Mensch.* She's very temperamental. ❷ bad-tempered ▷ *Er war heute schrecklich launisch.* He was terribly bad-tempered today.

Laus (pl **Läuse**) f louse

laut adj, adv, prep ❶ loud ▷ *Ich mag laute Musik nicht.* I don't like loud music.

❷ noisy ▷ *Hier ist es schrecklich laut.* It's terribly noisy here. ❸ loudly ▷ *Sie schrie so laut sie konnte.* She screamed as loudly as she could.; **laut lesen** to read aloud ❹ according to ▷ *Laut unserem Vertrag ...* According to our contract ...

Laut (pl **Laute**) m sound

lauten vb [2] ❶ to go ▷ *Wie lautet die zweite Strophe des Lieds?* How does the second verse of the song go? ❷ to be ▷ *Das Urteil lautete auf zehn Jahre Gefängnis.* The sentence was ten years' imprisonment.

läuten vb [2] to ring ▷ *Die Glocken läuten.* The bells are ringing. ▷ *Ich habe geläutet, es hat aber niemand aufgemacht.* I rang but nobody answered.

lauter adv nothing but ▷ *Sie hat lauter Lügen erzählt.* She told nothing but lies.

Lautschrift f phonetics pl

Lautsprecher (pl **Lautsprecher**) m loudspeaker

Lautstärke f volume

lauwarm adj lukewarm

Lawine f avalanche

leben vb [38] to live

Leben (pl **Leben**) nt life; **ums Leben kommen** to lose one's life

lebend adj living

lebendig adj ❶ alive ▷ *Er konnte lebendig aus den Trümmern geborgen werden.* He was rescued from the ruins alive. ❷ lively ▷ *Sie ist ein sehr lebendiges Kind.* She's a very lively child.

Lebensgefahr f mortal danger ▷ *Die Geiseln waren in Lebensgefahr.* The hostages were in mortal danger.; '**Lebensgefahr!**' 'danger!'

lebensgefährlich adj ❶ dangerous ▷ *eine lebensgefährliche Kurve* a dangerous corner ❷ critical ▷ *eine lebensgefährliche Krankheit* a critical illness ▷ *lebensgefährlich verletzt* critically injured

lebenslänglich adj for life; *Er hat eine lebenslängliche Gefängnisstrafe bekommen.* He received a life sentence.

Lebenslauf (pl **Lebensläufe**) m CV (= curriculum vitae)

Lebensmittel ntpl food sg

Lebensmittelgeschäft (pl **Lebensmittelgeschäfte**) nt grocer's shop

Lebensversicherung f life insurance

Leber f liver

Leberwurst (pl **Leberwürste**) f liver sausage

Lebewesen (pl **Lebewesen**) nt creature

lebhaft adj lively

Lebkuchen (pl **Lebkuchen**) m gingerbread

lecken vb [48] ❶ to leak ▷ *Der Behälter leckt.* The container's leaking. ❷ to lick ▷ *Die Katze leckte sich das Fell.* The cat licked its fur. ▷ *Sie leckte am Eis.* She licked her ice cream.

lecker adj delicious ▷ *lecker schmecken* to taste delicious

Leder (pl **Leder**) nt leather

Lederhose f leather trousers pl
- **Lederhosen** are the traditional dress
- in South Germany and Austria.

ledig adj single ▷ '*Familienstand: ledig*' 'Marital status: single'

leer adj empty ▷ *eine leere Flasche* an empty bottle ▷ *leere Drohungen* empty threats; **ein leeres Blatt Papier** a blank sheet of paper; **ein leerer Blick** a vacant expression; **leer machen** to empty

Leere f emptiness

leeren vb [38] to empty

legal adj legal

legen vb [38] ❶ to put ▷ *Sie legte das Kind ins Bett.* She put the child to bed. ▷ *Leg das Besteck in die Schublade.* Put the cutlery in the drawer. ▷ *Er legte das Buch aus der Hand.* He put the book down.

❷ to lay ▷ Sie legten den Verletzten auf eine Decke. They laid the injured man on a blanket. ▷ Sie legte ihren Mantel über den Stuhl. She laid her coat over the chair. ▷ ein Ei legen to lay an egg; **sich legen (1)** to lie down ▷ Sie legte sich auf das Sofa. She lay down on the sofa. ▷ Ich lege mich ins Bett. I'm going to bed. **(2)** to drop ▷ Der Wind hat sich gelegt. The wind has dropped.; **Das wird sich legen.** That will sort itself out.

Lehne f ❶ arm ▷ Sie saß auf der Lehne des Sofas. She sat on the arm of the sofa. ❷ back ▷ Der Sessel hat eine hohe Lehne. The chair has a high back.

lehnen vb [38] to lean

Lehnstuhl (pl **Lehnstühle**) m armchair

Lehre f ❶ apprenticeship ▷ bei jemandem in die Lehre gehen to serve one's apprenticeship with somebody ❷ lesson ▷ Lass dir das eine Lehre sein! Let that be a lesson to you!

Lehrer (pl **Lehrer**) m teacher

Lehrerin f teacher

Lehrerzimmer (pl **Lehrerzimmer**) nt staff room

Lehrling (pl **Lehrlinge**) m apprentice

Lehrplan (pl **Lehrpläne**) m syllabus

Lehrstelle f apprenticeship

Leiche f corpse

leicht adj ❶ light ▷ leichtes Gepäck light luggage ❷ easy ▷ Die Klassenarbeit war leicht. The class test was easy.; **es sich leicht machen** to make things easy for oneself

Leichtathletik f athletics sg

leichtfallen vb [22] jemandem leichtfallen to be easy for somebody

leichtmachen vb [48] see **leicht**

leichtsinnig adj careless

leid adj etwas leid sein to be tired of something

Leid nt sorrow

leiden (imperf **litt**, perf **hat gelitten**) vb [44] to suffer ▷ Sie leidet an Asthma. She suffers from asthma. ▷ Wir leiden unter der Hitze. We're suffering from the heat.; **jemanden gut leiden können** to like somebody; **Ich kann ihn nicht leiden.** I can't stand him.

leider adv unfortunately ▷ Ich kann leider nicht kommen. Unfortunately I can't come.; **Ja, leider.** Yes, I'm afraid so.; **Leider nicht.** I'm afraid not.

leidtun (imperf **tat leid**, perf **leidgetan**) vb [81] **Es tut mir leid.** I'm sorry.; **Er tut mir leid.** I'm sorry for him.

leihen (imperf **lieh**, perf **hat geliehen**) vb to lend ▷ Kannst du mir fünfzig Euro leihen? Can you lend me fifty euros?; **sich etwas leihen** to borrow something

Leim (pl **Leime**) m glue

Leine f ❶ line ▷ Sie hängte die Wäsche auf die Leine. She hung the washing on the line. ❷ lead ▷ Hunde müssen an der Leine geführt werden. Dogs must be kept on a lead.

Leinen (pl **Leinen**) nt linen

leise adj, adv ❶ quiet ▷ Seid bitte leise. Please be quiet. ❷ quietly ▷ Sie sprach mit leiser Stimme. She spoke quietly. ▷ Sie kam ganz leise ins Zimmer. She came into the room very quietly.

leisten vb [2] ❶ to do ▷ Du hast gute Arbeit geleistet. You've done a good job. ❷ to achieve ▷ Sie hat viel geleistet im Leben. She's achieved a lot in her life.; **jemandem Gesellschaft leisten** to keep somebody company; **sich etwas leisten** to treat oneself to something; **sich etwas leisten können** to be able to afford something

Leistung f ❶ performance ▷ Sie haben die Leistung des Motors verbessert. They've improved the performance of the engine.; **schulische Leistungen** school results ❷ achievement ▷ eine sportliche Leistung a sporting achievement ▷ Das

leiten vb [2] ① to direct ▷ *Das Wasser wird durch Rohre geleitet.* The water is directed through pipes. ② to lead ▷ *eine Partei leiten* to lead a party ③ to run ▷ *Wer leitet diese Firma?* Who runs this company? ④ to chair ▷ *Wer hat die Versammlung geleitet?* Who chaired the meeting?; **Metall leitet Strom besonders gut.** Metal is a good conductor of electricity.

Leiter (*pl* **Leiter**) *m* head ▷ *Der Leiter des Museums* the head of the museum
▶ *f* ladder ▷ *eine Leiter hinaufklettern* to climb a ladder

Leitung *f* ① management ▷ *Ihr wurde die Leitung der Abteilung übertragen.* She was entrusted with the management of the department. ② direction ▷ *der Jugendchor unter Leitung von ...* the youth choir under the direction of ... ③ pipe ▷ *In unserer Straße werden neue Leitungen für Wasser und Gas verlegt.* They're laying new water and gas pipes in our road. ④ cable ▷ *Die Leitung steht unter Strom.* The cable is live. ⑤ line ▷ *Alle Leitungen waren besetzt.* All the lines were busy.; **eine lange Leitung haben** to be slow on the uptake

Lektion *f* lesson

Lektüre *f* ① reading ▷ *Stör sie nicht bei der Lektüre.* Don't disturb her while she's reading. ② reading matter ▷ *Das ist die richtige Lektüre für die Ferien.* That's the right reading matter for the holidays. ③ set text ▷ *Welche Lektüre habt ihr dieses Jahr in Englisch?* What are your set texts in English this year?

> Be careful! **Lektüre** does not mean **lecture**.

lenken vb [38] to steer ▷ *ein Fahrzeug lenken* to steer a car

Lenkrad (*pl* **Lenkräder**) *nt* steering wheel

lernen vb [38] to learn

Lernplattform *f* VLE, virtual learning environment

Lesbe (*gen* **Lesben**, *pl* **Lesben**) *f* lesbian

Lesebuch (*pl* **Lesebücher**) *nt* reading book

lesen (*pres* **liest**, *imperf* **las**, *perf* **hat gelesen**) vb [45] to read

Leser (*pl* **Leser**) *m* reader

Leserin *f* reader

leserlich *adj* legible ▷ *eine leserliche Handschrift* legible handwriting
▷ *leserlich schreiben* to write legibly

letzte *adj* ① last ▷ *In der letzten Arbeit habe ich eine Zwei geschrieben.* I got a 'B' in the last test. ▷ *Ich habe noch einen letzten Wunsch.* I have one last wish. ▷ *letzte Woche* last week ▷ *das letzte Mal* (the) last time ▷ *zum letzten Mal* for the last time; **als Letzter** last ② latest ▷ *Laut letzten Informationen kam es zu schweren Unruhen.* According to the latest reports there were serious riots.

letztens *adv* lately

leuchten vb [2] to shine ▷ *jemandem ins Gesicht leuchten* to shine a light in somebody's face

Leuchter (*pl* **Leuchter**) *m* candlestick

Leuchtstift (*pl* **Leuchtstifte**) *m* highlighter

Leute *pl* people *pl*

Lexikon (*pl* **Lexika**) *nt* encyclopedia

Licht (*pl* **Lichter**) *nt* light

Lid (*pl* **Lider**) *nt* eyelid

Lidschatten (*pl* **Lidschatten**) *m* eyeshadow

lieb *adj* dear ▷ *Liebe Bettina* Dear Bettina ▷ *Lieber Herr Schlüter* Dear Mr Schlüter; **Das ist lieb von dir.** That's nice of you.; **jemanden lieb haben** to be fond of somebody

Liebe *f* love

lieben vb [38] to love

liebenswürdig *adj* kind

lieber *adv* rather ▷ *Ich hätte jetzt lieber einen Kaffee.* I'd rather have a coffee just now. ▷ *Ich gehe lieber nicht.* I'd rather not go.; **Lass das lieber!** I'd leave that if I were you.; **etwas lieber haben** to prefer something

Liebesbrief (pl **Liebesbriefe**) m love letter

Liebeskummer m **Liebeskummer haben** to be lovesick

Liebesroman (pl **Liebesromane**) m romantic novel

liebevoll adj loving

liebhaben vb [**32**] see **lieb**

Liebling (pl **Lieblinge**) m darling

Lieblings- prefix favourite ▷ *Was ist dein Lieblingsfach?* What's your favourite subject?

liebste adj favourite ▷ *Der Winter ist meine liebste Jahreszeit.* Winter is my favourite season.; **am liebsten** best

Lied (pl **Lieder**) nt song

lief vb see **laufen**

liefern vb [**88**] ❶ to deliver ▷ *Wir liefern die Möbel ins Haus.* We deliver the furniture to your door. ❷ to supply ▷ *Das Kraftwerk liefert den Strom für die ganze Gegend.* The power station supplies electricity to the whole area.; **den Beweis liefern** to produce proof

Lieferwagen (pl **Lieferwagen**) m van

liegen (imperf **lag**, perf **hat gelegen**) vb [**46**] ❶ to lie ▷ *Sie lag auf dem Bett.* She lay on the bed. ▷ *Wir haben den ganzen Tag am Strand gelegen.* We lay on the beach all day. ▷ *Auf meinem Schreibtisch liegt eine Menge Papier.* There's a lot of paper lying on my desk.; **Es lag viel Schnee.** There was a lot of snow. ❷ to be ▷ *Unser Haus liegt sehr zentral.* Our house is very central. ▷ *Ulm liegt an der Donau.* Ulm is on the Danube.; **nach Süden liegen** to face south; **Mir liegt viel daran.** It matters a lot to me.; **Mir liegt nichts daran.** It doesn't matter to me.; **Es liegt bei dir, ob ...** It's up to you whether ...; **Sprachen liegen mir nicht.** Languages are not my thing.; **Woran liegt es?** How come?; **Das liegt am Wetter.** It's because of the weather.; **liegen bleiben** (1) to lie in ▷ *Morgen ist Sonntag, da kann ich liegen bleiben.* It's Sunday tomorrow, so I can lie in. **(2)** not to get up ▷ *Der verletzte Spieler blieb liegen.* The injured player didn't get up. **(3)** to be left behind ▷ *Der Schirm ist liegen geblieben.* The umbrella's been left behind.; **etwas liegen lassen** to leave something ▷ *Ich muss diese Arbeit liegen lassen.* I'll have to leave this job. ▷ *Ich habe meinen Schirm liegen lassen.* I've left my umbrella.

Liegestuhl (pl **Liegestühle**) m deck chair

Lift (pl **Lifte** or **Lifts**) m lift (elevator)

Liga (pl **Ligen**) f league

lila adj purple ▷ *Sie hatte einen lila Hut auf.* She was wearing a purple hat.

Limo (pl **Limos**) f lemonade

Limonade f lemonade

Lineal (pl **Lineale**) nt ruler ▷ *einen Strich mit dem Lineal ziehen* to draw a line with a ruler

Linie f line

linke adj left ▷ *In Großbritannien fährt man auf der linken Seite.* In Great Britain they drive on the left. ▷ *Mein linkes Auge tut weh.* My left eye's hurting. ▷ *Er hat sich den linken Arm gebrochen.* He broke his left arm.

Linke (gen **Linken**) f ❶ left ▷ *Zu Ihrer Linken sehen Sie das Rathaus.* On your left you'll see the town hall. ❷ left hand ▷ *Er schlug mit der Linken zu.* He hit out with his left hand.

links adv left ▷ **links abbiegen** to turn left; **links überholen** to overtake on the left; **Er schreibt mit links.** He writes with his left hand.; **Links sehen Sie das Rathaus.** On the left you'll see the town hall.; **links von der Kirche** to the left of the church; **links von mir** on my left; **links wählen** to vote for a left-wing party; **etwas mit links machen** to do something easily

Linkshänder (pl **Linkshänder**) m **Er ist Linkshänder.** He's left-handed.

Linkshänderin f **Sie ist Linkshänderin.** She's left-handed.

Linse f ① lentil ▷ *Linsensuppe* lentil soup ② lens ▷ *die Linse der Kamera* the camera lens

Lippe f lip

Lippenstift (pl **Lippenstifte**) m lipstick

Liste f list

Liter (pl **Liter**) m

▌ You can also say **das Liter**.

litre

Literatur f literature

Lizenz f licence

Lkw (gen **Lkw** or **Lkws**, pl **Lkws**) m (= *Lastkraftwagen*) lorry

Lob nt praise

loben vb [38] to praise

Loch (pl **Löcher**) nt hole

locker adj ① loose ▷ *ein lockerer Zahn* a loose tooth ② relaxed ▷ *eine lockere Atmosphäre* a relaxed atmosphere

Löffel (pl **Löffel**) m spoon; **ein Löffel Zucker** a spoonful of sugar

logisch adj logical

Lohn (pl **Löhne**) m ① wages pl ▷ *Freitags wird der Lohn ausbezahlt.* The wages are paid on Fridays. ② reward ▷ *Das ist jetzt der Lohn für meine Mühe!* That's the reward for my efforts.

lohnen vb [38] **Das lohnt sich.** It's worth it.

▌ Word for word, **Das lohnt sich** means 'It rewards itself'.

lohnend adj worthwhile

Lohnsteuer f income tax

lokal adj local ▷ *die lokalen Nachrichten* the local news

Lokal (pl **Lokale**) nt pub

Lokomotive f locomotive

los adj loose ▷ *Die Schraube ist los.* The screw's loose.; **Dort ist viel los.** There's a lot going on there.; **Dort ist nichts los.** There's nothing going on there.; **Was ist los?** What's the matter?; **Los! Go on!**

Los (gen **Loses**, pl **Lose**) nt lottery ticket ▷ *Mein Los hat gewonnen.* My lottery ticket has won.

losbinden (imperf **band los**, perf **hat losgebunden**) vb to untie

löschen vb [48] ① to put out ▷ *ein Feuer löschen* to put out a fire ▷ *das Licht löschen* to put out the light; **den Durst löschen** to quench one's thirst; **eine Datei löschen** to delete a file

Löschtaste f delete key

lose adj loose ▷ *lose Blätter* loose sheets ▷ *etwas lose verkaufen* to sell something loose; **ein loses Mundwerk** a big mouth

lösen vb [38] ① to solve ▷ *ein Rätsel lösen* to solve a puzzle ▷ *ein Problem lösen* to solve a problem ② to loosen ▷ *Kannst du diesen Knoten lösen?* Can you loosen the knot?; **etwas von etwas lösen** to remove something from something ▷ *Sie löste das Etikett vom Glas.* She removed the label from the jar.; **sich lösen** (1) to come loose ▷ *Eine Schraube hatte sich gelöst.* A screw had come loose. (2) to dissolve ▷ *Die Tablette löst sich in Wasser.* The pill dissolves in water. (3) to resolve itself ▷ *Das Problem hat sich inzwischen gelöst.* The problem has resolved itself in the meantime.; **eine Fahrkarte lösen** to buy a ticket

losfahren (pres **fährt los**, imperf **fuhr los**, perf **ist losgefahren**) vb [21] to leave

loslassen (pres **lässt los**, imperf **ließ los**, perf **hat losgelassen**) vb [42] to let go of

löslich adj soluble

Lösung f solution ▷ *Weißt du die Lösung des Rätsels?* Do you know the solution to the puzzle?

Lotto (pl **Lottos**) nt National Lottery
Lottozahlen fpl winning lottery numbers pl
Löwe (gen **Löwen**, pl **Löwen**) m ❶ lion ❷ Leo ▷ *Manfred ist Löwe.* Manfred's Leo.
Lücke f gap
Luft (pl **Lüfte**) f air ▷ *Ich brauche frische Luft.* I need some fresh air.; **in der Luft liegen** to be in the air; **jemanden wie Luft behandeln** to ignore somebody

> Word for word, **jemanden wie Luft behandeln** means 'to treat somebody like air'.

Luftballon (pl **Luftballons** or **Luftballone**) m balloon
Luftdruck m atmospheric pressure
Luftmatratze f air bed
Luftpost f airmail ▷ *per Luftpost* by airmail
Luftverschmutzung f air pollution
Lüge f lie
lügen (imperf **log**, perf **hat gelogen**) vb [47] to lie ▷ *Ich müsste lügen, wenn ...* I would be lying if ...; **Er lügt ständig.** He's always telling lies.
Lügner (pl **Lügner**) m liar
Lunge f lung
Lungenentzündung f pneumonia
Lupe f magnifying glass; **unter die Lupe nehmen** to scrutinize
Lust f **Lust haben, etwas zu tun** to feel like doing something; **keine Lust haben, etwas zu tun** not to feel like doing something; **Lust auf etwas haben** to feel like something
lustig adj funny ▷ *eine lustige Geschichte* a funny story
lutschen vb [48] to suck ▷ *am Daumen lutschen* to suck one's thumb
Lutscher (pl **Lutscher**) m lollipop
Luxemburg nt Luxembourg
Luxus (gen **Luxus**) m luxury

m

machen vb [48] ❶ to do ▷ *Hausaufgaben machen* to do one's homework ▷ *etwas sorgfältig machen* to do something carefully ▷ *Was machst du heute Nachmittag?* What are you doing this afternoon?; **eine Prüfung machen** to sit an exam; **den Führerschein machen** to take driving lessons ❷ to make ▷ *aus Holz gemacht* made of wood ▷ *Kaffee machen* to make coffee ▷ *einen Fehler machen* to make a mistake ▷ *Krach machen* to make a noise ▷ *jemanden traurig machen* to make somebody sad ▷ *Das macht müde.* It makes you tired.; **Schluss machen** to finish; **ein Foto machen** to take a photo ❸ to cause ▷ *Das hat mir viel Mühe gemacht.* This caused me a lot of trouble. ▷ *viel Arbeit machen* to cause a lot of work; **Das macht die Kälte.** It's the cold that does that. ❹ to be ▷ *Drei und fünf macht acht.* Three and five is eight. ▷ *Was macht das?* How much is that? ▷ *Das macht acht Euro.* That's eight euros.; **Was macht**

die Arbeit? How's the work going?; **Was macht dein Bruder?** How's your brother doing?; **Das macht nichts.** That doesn't matter.; **Die Kälte macht mir nichts.** I don't mind the cold.; **sich machen** to come on; **sich nichts aus etwas machen** not to be very keen on something; **Mach's gut!** Take care!; **Mach schon!** Come on!

Macht (pl **Mächte**) f power

Mädchen (pl **Mädchen**) nt girl

mag vb see **mögen**

Magazin (pl **Magazine**) nt magazine ▷ Ich habe das in einem Magazin gelesen. I read it in a magazine.

Magen (pl **Magen** or **Mägen**) m stomach

Magenschmerzen pl stomachache sg ▷ Ich habe Magenschmerzen. I've got a stomachache.

mager adj ❶ lean ▷ mageres Fleisch lean meat ❷ thin ▷ Sie ist furchtbar mager. She's terribly thin.

Magnet (gen **Magnets** or **Magneten**, pl **Magneten**) m magnet

magnetisch adj magnetic

Mahlzeit f meal ▷ Wir essen drei Mahlzeiten am Tag. We eat three meals a day.

Mai (gen **Mai** or **Mais**, pl **Maie**) m May ▷ im Mai in May ▷ am sechsten Mai on 6 May ▷ Ulm, den 6. Mai 2024 Ulm, 6 May 2024 ▷ Heute ist der sechste Mai. Today is the sixth of May.; **der Erste Mai** May Day

mailen (perf **hat gemailt**) vb [38] to email ▷ Hast du es gemailt? Did you email it?

Mailingliste (pl **Mailinglisten**) f mailing list

Mais (gen **Maises**) m maize

Majonäse f mayonnaise

mal adv times ▷ zwei mal fünf two times five ▷ Wir haben sechsmal geklingelt. We rang six times.; **Warst du schon mal in Paris?** Have you ever been to Paris?

Mal (pl **Male**) nt ❶ time ▷ das fünfte Mal the fifth time ▷ zum ersten Mal for the first time ▷ Wie viele Male hast du es versucht? How many times have you tried? ❷ mark ▷ Sie hat ein rotes Mal im Gesicht. She has a red mark on her face.

malen vb [38] to paint

Maler (pl **Maler**) m painter

malerisch adj picturesque

Mallorca nt Majorca

malnehmen (pres **nimmt mal**, imperf **nahm mal**, perf **hat malgenommen**) vb [52] to multiply

Malz (gen **Malzes**) nt malt

Mama (pl **Mamas**) f (informal) mum

man pron you ▷ Man kann nie wissen. You never know. ▷ Wie schreibt man das? How do you spell that?; **man sagt, ...** they say ...; **Man hat mir gesagt ...** I was told that ...

Manager (pl **Manager**) m manager

manche pron some ▷ Manche Bücher sind langweilig. Some books are boring.

manchmal adv sometimes

Mandarine f mandarin orange

Mandel f ❶ almond ▷ ein Kuchen mit Nüssen und Mandeln a cake with nuts and almonds ❷ tonsil ▷ Sie hat entzündete Mandeln. Her tonsils are inflamed.

Mangel (pl **Mängel**) m ❶ lack ▷ Schlafmangel lack of sleep ❷ shortage ▷ Der Mangel an Arbeitsplätzen führt zu immer größerer Arbeitslosigkeit. The shortage of jobs is causing rising unemployment. ❸ fault ▷ Das Gerät weist mehrere Mängel auf. The appliance has several faults.

mangelhaft adj ❶ poor ▷ Er hat mangelhaft bekommen. He got a poor mark.

⁑ German marks range from one (**sehr gut**) to six (**ungenügend**).

❷ faulty ▷ Mangelhafte Waren kann man zurückgehen lassen. You can return faulty goods.

mangels prep

The preposition **mangels** takes the genitive.

for lack of ▷ *Er wurde mangels Beweisen freigesprochen.* He was acquitted for lack of evidence.

Manieren pl manners pl ▷ *Sie hat keine Manieren.* She doesn't have any manners.

Mann (pl **Männer**) m ❶ man ▷ *Es war ein Mann am Telefon.* There was a man on the phone. ❷ husband ▷ *Frau Maier kam mit ihrem Mann.* Mrs Maier came with her husband.; **seinen Mann stehen** to hold one's own; **Alle Mann an Deck!** All hands on deck!

männlich adj ❶ male ▷ *meine männlichen Kollegen* my male colleagues; **eine männliche Person** a man ❷ masculine ▷ *ein männliches Substantiv* a masculine noun

Mannschaft f ❶ team ▷ *die deutsche Mannschaft* the German team ❷ crew ▷ *der Kapitän und seine Mannschaft* the captain and his crew

Mantel (pl **Mäntel**) m coat ▷ *Er hatte einen Mantel an.* He was wearing a coat.

Mappe f ❶ briefcase ❷ folder

Be careful! **Mappe** does not mean map.

Märchen (pl **Märchen**) nt fairy tale

Margarine f margarine

Marine f navy ▷ *Er ist bei der Marine.* He's in the navy.

Marke f ❶ brand ▷ *Für diese Marke sieht man in letzter Zeit viel Werbung.* There's been a lot of advertising for this brand recently. ❷ make ▷ *Welche Marke fährt dein Vater?* What make of car does your father drive? ❸ voucher; **eine Briefmarke** a postage stamp

markieren (perf **hat markiert**) vb [76] to mark ▷ *Sie hat die Stelle mit Leuchtstift markiert.* She marked the place with a highlighter.

Markt (pl **Märkte**) m market

Marktplatz (gen **Marktplatzes**, pl **Marktplätze**) m market place

Marmelade f jam ▷ *Erdbeermarmelade* strawberry jam; **Orangenmarmelade** marmalade

Marmor (pl **Marmore**) m marble

März (gen **März** or **Märzes**, pl **Märze**) m March ▷ *im März* in March ▷ *am dritten März* on the third of March ▷ *Ulm, den 3. März 2025* Ulm, 3 March 2025 ▷ *Heute ist der dritte März.* Today is the third of March.

Masche f ❶ mesh ▷ *Das Netz hatte feine Maschen.* The net had a very fine mesh. ❷ stitch; **Das ist die neueste Masche.** That's the latest thing.

Maschine f ❶ machine ▷ *Werkzeug wird heutzutage von Maschinen hergestellt.* Nowadays tools are manufactured by machines. ▷ *Kannst du die schmutzige Wäsche bitte in die Maschine tun?* Can you put the dirty washing in the machine? ❷ engine ▷ *Dieses Motorrad hat eine starke Maschine.* This motorbike has a powerful engine. ❸ typewriter ▷ *Sie hat ihr Referat mit der Maschine geschrieben.* She typed her assignment. ❹ plane

Maschinengewehr (pl **Maschinengewehre**) nt machine gun

Masern pl measles sg ▷ *Masern sind bei Erwachsenen ziemlich gefährlich.* Measles is quite dangerous for adults.

Maske f mask

Maß (1) (gen **Maßes**, pl **Maße**) nt ❶ measure ▷ *In Deutschland werden metrische Maße verwendet.* Metric measures are used in Germany.; **Wie sind die Maße des Zimmers?** What are the measurements of the room? ❷ extent ▷ *Sie war zu einem hohen Maß selbst schuld.* To a large extent she had only herself to blame.

Maß (2) (gen **Maß**, pl **Maß** or **Maßen**) f litre of beer

Massage f massage
Masse f mass
massenhaft adj (informal) masses of ▷ Du hast massenhaft Fehler gemacht. You've made masses of mistakes.
Massenmedien ntpl mass media sg
mäßig adj moderate
Maßnahme f step ▷ Maßnahmen ergreifen to take steps
Maßstab (pl **Maßstäbe**) m ❶ standard ▷ Dieses Gerät setzt neue Maßstäbe. This appliance sets new standards. ❷ scale ▷ In welchem Maßstab ist diese Karte? What's the scale of this map?
Mast (pl **Maste** or **Masten**) m ❶ mast ▷ Am Mast hing die britische Fahne. The Union Jack was hanging from the mast. ❷ pylon ▷ Neben unserem Garten steht ein Hochspannungsmast. There's a high-tension pylon beside our garden.
Material (pl **Materialien**) nt material ▷ Aus welchem Material ist das gemacht? What material is it made of? ▷ Ich sammle Material für mein Referat. I'm collecting material for my assignment.
Mathe f (informal) maths sg
Mathematik f mathematics sg ▷ Mathematik ist mein Lieblingsfach. Mathematics is my favourite subject.
Matratze f mattress
Matrose (gen **Matrosen**, pl **Matrosen**) m sailor
Matsch m ❶ mud ▷ Deine Schuhe sind voller Matsch. Your shoes are covered in mud. ❷ slush
matschig adj ❶ muddy ▷ Nach dem Regen war der Weg sehr matschig. The path was very muddy after the rain. ❷ slushy ▷ Bei matschigem Schnee macht das Skifahren keinen Spaß. Skiing isn't fun when the snow is slushy.
matt adj ❶ weak ▷ Bei der Hitze fühle ich mich so matt. I feel so weak in this heat. ❷ dull ▷ Ihre Augen waren ganz matt. Her eyes were really dull. ❸ matt ▷ Möchten Sie die Abzüge Hochglanz oder matt? Would you like the prints glossy or matt? ❹ mate ▷ Schach und matt checkmate
Matte f mat
Mauer f wall
Maul (pl **Mäuler**) nt mouth ▷ Die Katze hatte einen Vogel im Maul. The cat had a bird in its mouth.; **Halt's Maul!** (informal) Shut your face!
Maulkorb (pl **Maulkörbe**) m muzzle
Maulwurf (pl **Maulwürfe**) m mole
Maurer (pl **Maurer**) m bricklayer
Maus (pl **Mäuse**) f mouse ▷ Sie hat Angst vor Mäusen. She's afraid of mice. ▷ Du musst zweimal mit der Maus klicken. You have to click the mouse twice.
Mausefalle f mousetrap
Mausklick (pl **Mausklicks**) m mouse click; **per Mausklick** by clicking the mouse
maximal adj, adv ❶ maximum ▷ der maximale Betrag the maximum amount ❷ at most ▷ Wir können maximal eine Woche wegfahren. We can go away for a week at most.
Mayonnaise f mayonnaise
Mechaniker (pl **Mechaniker**) m mechanic
Mechanikerin f mechanic
mechanisch adj, adv ❶ mechanical ▷ Das Gerät hat einen mechanischen Schaden. The appliance has a mechanical fault. ❷ mechanically ▷ etwas mechanisch tun to do something mechanically
meckern vb [88] to moan ▷ Müsst ihr über alles meckern? Do you have to moan about everything?
Mecklenburg-Vorpommern nt Mecklenburg-Western Pomerania
- Mecklenburg-Vorpommern is
- one of the 16 **Länder**. Its capital is
- Schwerin. It is Germany's most rural

and thinly populated **Land**, and is becoming increasingly popular with tourists.

Medaille f medal

Medien ntpl media pl

Medikament (pl **Medikamente**) nt drug ▷ *verschreibungspflichtige Medikamente* prescribed drugs

Medizin f medicine

medizinisch adj medical

Meer (pl **Meere**) nt sea ▷ *Wir wohnen am Meer.* We live by the sea.

Meerschweinchen (pl **Meerschweinchen**) nt guinea pig

Mehl (pl **Mehle**) nt flour

mehr adj, adv more

mehrere adj several

mehreres pron several things

mehrfach adj, adv ❶ many ▷ *Dieses Gerät hat mehrfache Verwendungsmöglichkeiten.* This gadget has many uses. ❷ repeated ▷ *Es ist mir erst nach mehrfachen Versuchen gelungen.* I only managed after repeated attempts. ▷ *Ich habe mehrfach versucht, dich zu erreichen.* I've tried repeatedly to get hold of you.

Mehrheit f majority

mehrmalig adj repeated

mehrmals adv repeatedly

Mehrwertsteuer f value added tax

Mehrzahl f ❶ majority ▷ *Die Mehrzahl der Schüler besitzt einen Computer.* The majority of pupils have a computer. ❷ plural ▷ *Wie heißt die Mehrzahl von 'woman'?* What's the plural of 'woman'?

meiden (imperf **mied**, perf **hat gemieden**) vb to avoid

mein adj, pron ❶ my ▷ *Mein Englischlehrer ist nett.* My English teacher's nice. ▷ *Meine Mutter erlaubt es nicht.* My mother won't allow it. ▷ *Ich finde mein Buch nicht.* I can't find my book. ❷ mine ▷ *Das ist nicht mein Füller, meiner ist blau.* That's not my pen, mine's blue. ▷ *Seine Mutter heißt Anne, meine auch.* His mother's called Anne, so's mine. ▷ *Wenn dein Fahrrad kaputt ist, kannst du meins nehmen.* If your bike's broken you can use mine.

meinen vb [38] ❶ to think ▷ *Ich meine, wir sollten jetzt gehen.* I think we should go now. ▷ *Was meint deine Mutter zu deinem Freund?* What does your mother think about your boyfriend? ▷ *Sollen wir sie zur Party einladen, was meinst du?* Should we invite her to the party, what do you think? ❷ to say ▷ *Unser Lehrer meint, wir sollten am Wochenende keine Aufgaben machen.* Our teacher says that we shouldn't do any homework at the weekend. ❸ to mean ▷ *Was meint er mit diesem Wort?* What does he mean by this word? ▷ *Ich verstehe nicht, was du meinst.* I don't understand what you mean. ▷ *So habe ich das nicht gemeint.* I didn't mean it like that.; **Das will ich meinen!** I should think so.

meinetwegen adv ❶ for my sake ▷ *Ihr müsst meinetwegen nicht auf euren Urlaub verzichten.* You don't have to do without your holiday for my sake. ❷ on my account ▷ *Hat er sich meinetwegen so aufgeregt?* Did he get so upset on my account? ❸ as far as I'm concerned ▷ *Meinetwegen kannst du gehen.* As far as I'm concerned you can go. ❹ go ahead ▷ *Kann ich das machen? — Meinetwegen.* Can I do that? — Go ahead.

Meinung f opinion ▷ *Er hat mich nach meiner Meinung zu diesem Punkt gefragt.* He asked for my opinion on this subject.; **meiner Meinung nach** in my opinion; **Ganz meiner Meinung!** I quite agree.; **jemandem die Meinung sagen** to give somebody a piece of one's mind

> Be careful! **Meinung** does not mean **meaning**.

meist adv usually ▷ *Samstags bin ich meist zu Hause.* I'm usually at home on Saturdays.

GERMAN > ENGLISH

meiste adj most ▷ *Die meisten Bücher habe ich schon gelesen.* I've already read most of the books. ▷ *Hast du die Bücher alle gelesen? — Ja, die meisten.* Have you read all the books? — Yes, most of them. ▷ *Die meisten von euch kennen dieses Wort sicher.* Most of you must know this word.; **am meisten (1)** most ▷ *Darüber hat sie sich am meisten aufgeregt.* This upset her most. **(2)** the most ▷ *Er hat am meisten gewonnen.* He won the most.

meistens adv usually ▷ *Samstags bin ich meistens zu Hause.* I'm usually at home on Saturdays.

Meister (pl **Meister**) m ❶ champion ▷ *Er ist deutscher Meister im Ringen.* He's the German wrestling champion. ❷ master craftsman ▷ *Der Meister bildet Lehrlinge aus.* The master craftsman trains apprentices.

Meisterschaft f championship ▷ *Wer hat die Meisterschaft gewonnen?* Who won the championship?

melden vb [54] to report ▷ *Er meldete den Diebstahl bei der Polizei.* He reported the theft to the police.; **sich melden (1)** to answer (phone) ▷ *Es meldet sich niemand.* There's no answer. **(2)** to put one's hand up (in school); **sich polizeilich melden** to register with the police

Melodie f tune

Melone f ❶ melon ❷ bowler hat ▷ *Er trug eine Melone.* He was wearing a bowler hat.

Menge f ❶ quantity ▷ *etwas in großen Mengen bestellen* to order a large quantity of something ❷ crowd ▷ *Ich habe ihn in der Menge verloren.* I lost him in the crowd.; **eine Menge** a lot of

Mensch (gen **Menschen**, pl **Menschen**) m human being ▷ *Es heißt, dass sich der Mensch durch die Sprache vom Tier unterscheidet.* It's said that what distinguishes human beings from animals is language.; **Wie viele Menschen?** How many people?; **kein Mensch** nobody

Menschheit f mankind

menschlich adj human

Menü (pl **Menüs**) nt set meal

merken vb [38] to notice ▷ *Hat sie gemerkt, dass ich gefehlt habe?* Did she notice that I wasn't there? ▷ *Ich habe den Fehler nicht gemerkt.* I didn't notice the mistake.; **sich etwas merken** to remember something; **Das werd' ich mir merken!** I won't forget that in a hurry!

merkwürdig adj odd; **sich merkwürdig benehmen** to behave strangely

Messe f ❶ fair ▷ *Auf der Messe wurden die neuesten Modelle gezeigt.* The latest models were shown at the fair. ❷ mass ▷ *Sie geht jeden Sonntag zur Messe.* She goes to mass every Sunday.

messen (pres **misst**, imperf **maß**, perf **hat gemessen**) vb to measure ▷ *Hast du die Länge gemessen?* Have you measured the length?; **bei jemandem Fieber messen** to take somebody's temperature; **Mit ihm kannst du dich nicht messen.** You're no match for him.

Messer (pl **Messer**) nt knife

Messgerät (pl **Messgeräte**) nt gauge

Metall (pl **Metalle**) nt metal

Meter (pl **Meter**) nt metre

Methode f method

Metzger (pl **Metzger**) m butcher ▷ *Er ist Metzger.* He's a butcher. ▷ *beim Metzger* at the butcher's

Metzgerei f butcher's

mich pron

　mich is the accusative of **ich**.

　❶ me ▷ *Er hat mich zu seiner Party eingeladen.* He's invited me to his party. ❷ myself ▷ *Ich sehe mich im Spiegel.* I can see myself in the mirror.

Miene f look; **eine finstere Miene machen** to look grim

mies adj (informal) lousy ▷ *Mir geht's mies.* I feel lousy.

Miete f rent; **zur Miete wohnen** to live in rented accommodation

mieten vb [2] ❶ to rent
- It is far more usual to live in rented accommodation in Germany than it is in Britain. Flats are mainly rented unfurnished.
- ▷ *Wir haben eine Ferienwohnung gemietet.* We've rented a holiday flat. ❷ to hire ▷ *Man kann am Flughafen ein Auto mieten.* You can hire a car at the airport.

Mietshaus (gen **Mietshauses**, pl **Mietshäuser**) nt block of rented flats

Mietvertrag (pl **Mietverträge**) m lease

Mietwagen (pl **Mietwagen**) m rental car

Mikrofon (pl **Mikrofone**) nt microphone

Mikroskop (pl **Mikroskope**) nt microscope

Mikrowelle f microwave

Milch f milk

mild adj ❶ mild ▷ *eine milde Seife* a mild soap ▷ *mildes Wetter* mild weather ❷ lenient ▷ *ein mildes Urteil* a lenient sentence ▷ *ein milder Richter* a lenient judge

Militär nt army ▷ *zum Militär gehen* to join the army

militärisch adj military

Milliarde f billion

Millimeter (pl **Millimeter**) m millimetre

Million f million

Millionär (pl **Millionäre**) m millionaire ▷ *Er ist Millionär.* He's a millionaire.

Minderheit f minority ▷ *in der Minderheit sein* to be in the minority

Minderjährige (gen **Minderjährigen**, pl **Minderjährigen**) mf minor

▷ *Minderjährige dürfen keinen Alkohol kaufen.* Minors are not allowed to buy alcohol.

minderwertig adj inferior

mindeste adj **das Mindeste** the least; **nicht im Mindesten** not in the least; **zum Mindesten** at least

mindestens adv at least

Mineral (pl **Minerale** or **Mineralien**) nt mineral

Mineralwasser (pl **Mineralwasser**) nt mineral water

Minister (pl **Minister**) m minister (in government)

Ministerium (pl **Ministerien**) nt ministry

Minute f minute

Mio. abbr (= Million(en)) m (= million(s))

mir pron
- **mir** is the dative of **ich**.
- ❶ me ▷ *Kannst du mir sagen, wie spät es ist?* Can you tell me the time? ❷ to me ▷ *Gib es mir!* Give it to me.; **mir nichts, dir nichts** just like that

mischen vb [48] to mix

Mischung f mixture

miserabel adj dreadful ▷ *Mir geht's miserabel.* I feel dreadful.

Missbrauch m abuse

Misserfolg (pl **Misserfolge**) m failure

misshandeln (perf **hat misshandelt**) vb [88] to ill-treat

missmutig adj sullen

misstrauen (perf **hat misstraut**) vb [49] jemandem misstrauen to mistrust somebody

Misstrauen nt suspicion

misstrauisch adj suspicious

Missverständnis (gen **Missverständnisses**, pl **Missverständnisse**) nt misunderstanding

missverstehen (imperf **missverstand**, perf **hat missverstanden**) vb [72] to misunderstand

Mist m ❶ manure ▷ *Im Frühling werden die Felder mit Mist gedüngt.* The fields are fertilized with manure in the spring. ❷ *(informal)* rubbish ▷ *Warum isst du so einen Mist?* Why do you eat such rubbish? ▷ *Heute kommt wieder nur Mist im Fernsehen.* There's nothing but rubbish on TV again today. ▷ *Du redest Mist.* You're talking rubbish.; **Mist!** Blast!

> Be careful! The German word **Mist** does not mean **mist**.

mit *prep, adv*

> The preposition **mit** takes the dative.

❶ with ▷ *Er ist mit seiner Freundin gekommen.* He came with his girlfriend. ▷ *mit Filzstift geschrieben* written with a felt-tip pen ❷ by ▷ *mit dem Auto* by car ▷ *mit der Bahn* by train ▷ *mit dem Bus* by bus; **mit zehn Jahren** at the age of ten; **Sie ist mit die Beste in ihrer Klasse.** She is one of the best in her class.; **Wollen Sie mit?** Do you want to come along?

Mitarbeiter (*pl* **Mitarbeiter**) m ❶ colleague ▷ *meine Mitarbeiter und ich* my colleagues and I ❷ collaborator ▷ *die Mitarbeiter an diesem Projekt* the collaborators on this project ❸ employee ▷ *Die Firma hat 500 Mitarbeiter.* The company has 500 employees.

Mitarbeiterin f ❶ colleague ❷ collaborator ❸ employee

mitbringen (*imperf* **brachte mit**, *perf* **hat mitgebracht**) *vb* [13] to bring along ▷ *Kann ich meine Freundin mitbringen?* Can I bring my girlfriend along?

miteinander *adv* with each another

mitfahren (*pres* **fährt mit**, *imperf* **fuhr mit**, *perf* **ist mitgefahren**) *vb* [21] to come too ▷ *Wir fahren nach Berlin. Willst du mitfahren?* We're going to Berlin. Do you want to come too?; **Ich fahre nicht mit.** I'm not going.; **Willst du mit uns im Auto mitfahren?** Do you want a lift in our car?

mitgeben (*pres* **gibt mit**, *imperf* **gab mit**, *perf* **hat mitgegeben**) *vb* [28] to give

Mitglied (*pl* **Mitglieder**) *nt* member

mitkommen (*imperf* **kam mit**, *perf* **ist mitgekommen**) *vb* [40] ❶ to come along ▷ *Willst du nicht mitkommen?* Wouldn't you like to come along? ❷ to keep up ▷ *In Mathe komme ich nicht mit.* I can't keep up in maths.

Mitleid *nt* ❶ sympathy; **Ich habe wirklich Mitleid mit dir.** I really sympathize with you. ❷ pity ▷ *Er kennt kein Mitleid.* He knows no pity.

mitmachen (*perf* **hat mitgemacht**) *vb* [48] to join in

mitnehmen (*pres* **nimmt mit**, *imperf* **nahm mit**, *perf* **hat mitgenommen**) *vb* [52] ❶ to take ▷ *Kannst du den Brief zur Post mitnehmen?* Can you take the letter to the post office? ▷ *Ich habe meine Freundin zur Party mitgenommen.* I took my girlfriend to the party. ❷ to take away ▷ *Die Polizei ist gekommen und hat ihn mitgenommen.* The police came and took him away. ❸ to affect ▷ *Die Scheidung ihrer Eltern hat sie sehr mitgenommen.* Her parents' divorce really affected her.; **zum Mitnehmen** to take away

Mitschüler (*pl* **Mitschüler**) *m* schoolmate

Mitschülerin *f* schoolmate

mitspielen *vb* [4] to join in ▷ *Willst du nicht mitspielen?* Don't you want to join in?; **Wer hat bei dem Match mitgespielt?** Who played in the match?

Mittag (*pl* **Mittage**) *m* midday ▷ *gegen Mittag* around midday; **zu Mittag essen** to have lunch; **heute Mittag**

at lunchtime; **morgen Mittag** tomorrow lunchtime; **gestern Mittag** yesterday lunchtime
Mittagessen (pl **Mittagessen**) nt lunch
mittags adv at lunchtime
Mittagspause f lunch break
Mitte f middle
mitteilen vb [4] jemandem etwas mitteilen to inform somebody of something
Mitteilung f communication
Mittel (pl **Mittel**) nt means sg ▷ Wir werden jedes Mittel einsetzen, um die Genehmigung zu bekommen. We will use every means to gain approval. ▷ ein Mittel zum Zweck a means to an end; **ein Mittel gegen Husten** something for a cough; **ein Mittel gegen Flecken** a stain remover; **öffentliche Mittel** public funds
Mitteleuropa nt Central Europe
mittelmäßig adj mediocre
Mittelmeer nt the Mediterranean
Mittelpunkt (pl **Mittelpunkte**) m centre
Mittelstürmer (pl **Mittelstürmer**) m centre-forward
Mitternacht f midnight ▷ um Mitternacht at midnight
mittlere adj ❶ middle ▷ Das mittlere von den Fahrrädern ist meins. The bike in the middle is mine. ▷ Der mittlere Teil des Buches ist langweilig. The middle section of the book is boring. ❷ average ▷ Die mittleren Temperaturen liegen bei zwanzig Grad. The average temperature is twenty degrees.; **mittleren Alters** middle-aged; **mittlere Reife** O-levels pl
Mittwoch (pl **Mittwoche**) m Wednesday ▷ am Mittwoch on Wednesday
mittwochs adv on Wednesdays
Mobbing nt workplace bullying
Möbel ntpl furniture sg

Möbelwagen (pl **Möbelwagen**) m removal van
Mobiltelefon (pl **Mobiltelefone**) nt mobile phone
möchte vb see **mögen**
Mode f fashion
Modell (pl **Modelle**) nt model
modern adj modern
modernisieren (perf hat **modernisiert**) vb [76] to modernize
modisch adj fashionable ▷ Jane trägt sehr modische Kleidung. Jane wears very fashionable clothes.
mogeln vb [88] to cheat
mögen (pres **mag**, imperf **mochte**, perf **hat gemocht** or **mögen**) vb [50]
The past participle **mögen** is used when **mögen** is a modal auxiliary.
to like ▷ Ich mag Süßes. I like sweet things. ▷ Ich habe sie noch nie gemocht. I've never liked her.; **Ich möchte ...** I'd like ...; **Ich möchte nicht, dass du ...** I wouldn't like you to ...; **Ich mag nicht mehr.** I've had enough.; **etwas tun mögen** to like to do something; **etwas nicht tun mögen** not to want to do something
möglich adj possible ▷ Das ist gar nicht möglich! That's not possible. ▷ so viel wie möglich as much as possible
möglicherweise adv possibly
Möglichkeit f possibility; **nach Möglichkeit** if possible
möglichst adv as ... as possible ▷ Komm möglichst bald. Come as soon as possible.
Möhre f carrot
Moment (pl **Momente**) m moment ▷ Wir müssen den richtigen Moment abwarten. We have to wait for the right moment.; **im Moment** at the moment; **Moment mal!** Just a moment.
momentan adj, adv ❶ momentary ▷ Das ist nur eine momentane Schwäche. It's only a momentary weakness.

❷ at the moment ▷ *Ich bin momentan sehr beschäftigt.* I'm very busy at the moment.

Monarchie f monarchy

Monat (pl **Monate**) m month

monatlich adj, adv monthly

Monatskarte f monthly ticket

Mond (pl **Monde**) m moon

monetarisieren vb [76] to monetize

Montag (pl **Montage**) m Monday ▷ *am Montag* on Monday

montags adv on Mondays

Moor (pl **Moore**) nt moor

Moral f ❶ morals pl ▷ *Er hat keine Moral.* He hasn't got any morals. ❷ moral ▷ *Und die Moral der Geschichte ist: …* And the moral of the story is: …

moralisch adj moral

Mord (pl **Morde**) m murder

Mörder (pl **Mörder**) m murderer

> Be careful! **Mörder** does not mean **murder**.

Mörderin f murderer

morgen adv tomorrow; **morgen früh** tomorrow morning; **Bis morgen!** See you tomorrow!

Morgen (pl **Morgen**) m morning ▷ *Wir haben den ganzen Morgen Unterricht.* We've got lessons all morning.; **Guten Morgen!** Good morning.

morgens adv in the morning ▷ *Morgens bin ich immer müde.* I'm always tired in the morning.; **von morgens bis abends** from morning to night

Moschee f mosque

Mosel f Moselle

Motiv (pl **Motive**) nt motive ▷ *Was war sein Motiv?* What was his motive?

Motor (pl **Motoren**) m ❶ engine ▷ *Das Auto hat einen starken Motor.* The car has a powerful engine. ❷ motor ▷ *ein Außenbordmotor* an outboard motor

Motorboot (pl **Motorboote**) nt motorboat

Motorrad (pl **Motorräder**) nt motorcycle

Möwe f seagull

MRT abbr (= **Magnetresonanztomographie**) MRI

Mücke f midge

müde adj tired ▷ *Ich bin sehr müde.* I'm very tired.

Müdigkeit f tiredness

Mühe f ❶ trouble ▷ *Das macht gar keine Mühe.* That's no trouble.; **mit Müh und Not** with great difficulty; **sich Mühe geben** to go to a lot of trouble; **sich mehr Mühe geben** to try harder

Mühle f mill ▷ *In dieser Mühle wird Korn gemahlen.* Corn is ground in this mill. ▷ *Hast du eine Mühle, um den Kaffee zu mahlen?* Do you have a coffee mill?

mühsam adj, adv ❶ arduous ❷ with difficulty

Müll m refuse

Müllabfuhr f ❶ disposal of rubbish ▷ *Die Gebühren für die Müllabfuhr sollen erhöht werden.* The charges for the disposal of rubbish are to be increased. ❷ dustmen pl ▷ *Morgen kommt die Müllabfuhr.* The dustmen come tomorrow.

Mülleimer (pl **Mülleimer**) m rubbish bin

Mülltonne f dustbin

multikulturell adj multicultural

multiplizieren (perf **hat multipliziert**) vb [76] to multiply

München nt Munich

Mund (pl **Münder**) m mouth; **Halt den Mund!** (informal) Shut up!

Mundharmonika f mouth organ

mündlich adj oral ▷ *eine mündliche Prüfung* an oral exam

Munition f ammunition

Münster (pl **Münster**) nt cathedral

munter adj lively

Münze f coin

murmeln vb [34] to mumble ▷ *Er murmelte irgendwas vor sich hin.* He mumbled something.

mürrisch adj sullen

Muschel f ❶ mussel ▷ *Ich esse gern Muscheln.* I like mussels. ❷ shell ▷ *Wir haben am Strand Muscheln gesammelt.* We collected shells on the beach. ❸ receiver ▷ *Du musst in die Muschel sprechen.* You have to speak into the receiver.

Museum (pl **Museen**) nt museum

Musik f music

musikalisch adj musical ▷ *musikalisch begabt sein* to be musically gifted

Musiker (pl **Musiker**) m musician

Musikerin f musician

Musikinstrument (pl **Musikinstrumente**) nt musical instrument

Muskel (pl **Muskeln**) m muscle

Müsli (pl **Müsli**) nt muesli

Muslim (pl **Muslime**) m Muslim

Muslima (pl **Muslimas**) f Muslim (female)

Muslimin f Muslim

müssen (pres **muss**, imperf **musste**, perf **hat gemusst** or **müssen**) vb [51]

> The past participle **müssen** is used when **müssen** is a modal auxiliary.

❶ must ▷ *Ich muss es tun.* I must do it. ❷ to have to ▷ *Er hat gehen müssen.* He had to go. ▷ *Ich musste es tun.* I had to do it. ▷ *Er muss es nicht tun.* He doesn't have to do it. ▷ *Muss ich?* Do I have to?; **Muss das sein?** Is that really necessary?; **Es muss nicht wahr sein.** It needn't be true.; **Sie hätten ihn fragen müssen.** You should have asked him.; **Es muss geregnet haben.** It must have rained.; **Ich muss mal.** (informal) I need the loo.

Muster (pl **Muster**) nt ❶ pattern ▷ *ein Kleid mit einem geometrischen Muster* a dress with a geometric pattern ❷ sample ▷ *Lass dir von dem Stoff doch ein Muster geben.* Ask them to give you a sample of the material.

Mut m courage; **Nur Mut!** Cheer up!; **jemandem Mut machen** to encourage somebody; **zu Mute** see **zumute**

mutig adj courageous

Mutter (1) (pl **Mütter**) f mother ▷ *Meine Mutter erlaubt das nicht.* My mother doesn't allow that.

Mutter (2) (pl **Muttern**) f nut ▷ *Hast du die Mutter zu dieser Schraube gesehen?* Have you seen the nut for this bolt?

Muttersprache f mother tongue

Muttertag (pl **Muttertage**) m Mother's Day

Mutti (pl **Muttis**) f (informal) mummy

Mütze f cap

n

Nabel (pl **Nabel**) m navel
nach prep, adv

The preposition **nach** takes the dative.

❶ to ▷ *nach Berlin* to Berlin ▷ *nach Italien* to Italy; **nach Süden** south; **nach links** left; **nach rechts** right; **nach oben** up; **nach hinten** back ❷ after ▷ *Ich fange nach Weihnachten damit an.* I'll start on it after Christmas. ▷ *die nächste Straße nach der Kreuzung* the first street after the crossroads ▷ *einer nach dem anderen* one after the other ▷ *Nach Ihnen!* After you! ▷ *Ihm nach!* After him! ❸ past ▷ *zehn nach drei* ten past three ❹ according to ▷ *Nach unserer Englischlehrerin wird das so geschrieben.* According to our English teacher, that's how it's spelt.; **nach und nach** little by little; **nach wie vor** still

Nachbar (gen **Nachbarn**, pl **Nachbarn**) m neighbour
Nachbarin f neighbour
Nachbarschaft f neighbourhood

nachdem conj ❶ after ▷ *Nachdem er gegangen war, haben wir Witze erzählt.* After he left we told jokes. ❷ since ▷ *Nachdem du sowieso zur Post gehst, könntest du meine Päckchen aufgeben?* Since you're going to the post office anyway, could you post my parcel?; **je nachdem** it depends; **je nachdem, ob** depending on whether

nachdenken (imperf **dachte nach**, perf **hat nachgedacht**) vb [14] **nachdenken über** to think about

nacheinander adv one after the other

nachgeben (pres **gibt nach**, imperf **gab nach**, perf **hat nachgegeben**) vb [28] ❶ to give way ▷ *Das Brett hat nachgegeben.* The plank gave way. ❷ to give in ▷ *Ich werde nicht nachgeben.* I won't give in.

nachgehen (imperf **ging nach**, perf **ist nachgegangen**) vb [29] **jemandem nachgehen** to follow somebody; **einer Sache nachgehen** to look into something; **Die Uhr geht nach.** The clock is slow.

nachhaltig adj sustainable (growth, development)
Nachhaltigkeit f sustainability
nachher adv afterwards
Nachhilfeunterricht m extra tuition
nachholen (perf **hat nachgeholt**) vb [4] ❶ to catch up on ▷ *Weil er gefehlt hat, muss er jetzt viel nachholen.* As he was absent, he's got a lot to catch up on. ❷ to make up for ▷ *Wir konnten meinen Geburtstag nicht feiern, werden das aber nachholen.* We weren't able to celebrate my birthday, but we'll make up for it.; **eine Prüfung nachholen** to do an exam at a later date

nachkommen (imperf **kam nach**, perf **ist nachgekommen**) vb [40] to come later ▷ *Wir gehen schon mal, du kannst ja später nachkommen.* We'll go on and you can come later.; **einer Verpflichtung nachkommen** to fulfil an obligation

nachlassen (pres **lässt nach**, imperf **ließ nach**, perf **hat nachgelassen**) vb [42] ❶ to deteriorate ▷ *Seine Leistungen haben merklich nachgelassen.* His marks have deteriorated considerably.; **Ihr Gedächtnis lässt nach.** Her memory is going.; **Er hat nachgelassen.** He's got worse. ❷ to ease off ▷ *Die Schmerzen haben nachgelassen.* The pain has eased off. ❸ to die down ▷ *sobald der Sturm nachlässt* as soon as the storm dies down

nachlässig adj careless; **etwas nachlässig machen** to do something carelessly

nachlaufen (pres **läuft nach**, imperf **lief nach**, perf **ist nachgelaufen**) vb [43] **jemandem nachlaufen** to run after somebody to chase ▷ *Er läuft allen Mädchen nach.* He chases all the girls.

nachmachen (perf **hat nachgemacht**) vb [4] ❶ to copy ▷ *Macht alle meine Bewegungen nach.* Copy all my movements. ❷ to imitate ▷ *Sie kann unsere Mathelehrerin gut nachmachen.* She's good at imitating our maths teacher. ❸ to forge ▷ *ein Gemälde nachmachen* to forge a painting; **Das ist nicht echt, sondern nachgemacht.** This isn't genuine, it's a fake.

Nachmittag (pl **Nachmittage**) m afternoon ▷ *am Nachmittag* in the afternoon; **heute Nachmittag** this afternoon

nachmittags adv in the afternoon

Nachname (gen **Nachnamens**, pl **Nachnamen**) m surname ▷ *Wie heißt du mit Nachnamen?* What's your surname?

nachprüfen (perf **hat nachgeprüft**) vb [4] to check ▷ *nachprüfen, ob* to check whether

Nachricht f ❶ news sg ▷ *Wir haben noch keine Nachricht von ihr.* We still haven't had any news of her.; **die Nachrichten** the news ❷ message ▷ *Kannst du ihm eine Nachricht von mir übermitteln?* Can you give him a message from me?

nachschlagen (pres **schlägt nach**, imperf **schlug nach**, perf **hat nachgeschlagen**) vb [59] to look up (in dictionary)

nachsehen (pres **sieht nach**, imperf **sah nach**, perf **hat nachgesehen**) vb [64] ❶ to check ▷ *Sieh mal nach, ob noch genügend Brot da ist.* Check whether we've still got enough bread. ▷ *Ich habe im Wörterbuch nachgesehen.* I've checked in the dictionary. ▷ *Mein Vater sieht immer meine Englischaufgaben nach.* My father always checks my English homework.; **jemandem etwas nachsehen** to forgive somebody something; **das Nachsehen haben** to come off worst

nachsichtig adj lenient

nachsitzen (imperf **saß nach**, perf **hat nachgesessen**) vb [68] **nachsitzen müssen** to be kept in

Nachspeise f pudding ▷ *Was gibt's als Nachspeise?* What's for pudding?

nächste adj ❶ next ▷ *Wir nehmen den nächsten Zug.* We'll take the next train. ▷ *Beim nächsten Mal pass du besser auf.* Be more careful next time. ▷ *nächstes Jahr* next year; **am nächsten** (the) next ▷ *am nächsten Morgen* (the) next morning; **als Nächstes** next; **Der Nächste bitte!** Next, please! ❷ nearest ▷ *Wo ist hier die nächste Post?* Where's the nearest post office?

Nacht (pl **Nächte**) f night; **Gute Nacht!** Good night.

Nachteil (pl **Nachteile**) m disadvantage

Nachthemd (pl **Nachthemden**) nt nightshirt

Nachtisch m pudding ▷ *Was gibt's zum Nachtisch?* What's for pudding?

Nachtklub (pl **Nachtklubs**) m night club

Nachtruhe f sleep ▷ *Ich brauche meine Nachtruhe.* I need my sleep.
nachts adv at night
Nacken (pl **Nacken**) m nape of the neck
nackt adj naked ▷ *Er war nackt.* He was naked.; **nackte Arme** bare arms; **nackte Tatsachen** plain facts
Nadel (pl **Nadeln**) f ❶ needle ▷ *Ich brauche Nadel und Faden.* I need a needle and thread. ❷ pin ▷ *Ich habe mich an der Nadel des Ansteckers gestochen.* I've pricked myself on the pin of my badge.
Nagel (pl **Nägel**) m nail
Nagellack (pl **Nagellacke**) m nail varnish
nagelneu adj brand-new
nagen vb [38] to gnaw ▷ *an etwas nagen* to gnaw on something
nahe adj, adv, prep ❶ near ▷ *in der nahen Zukunft* in the near future; **nahe bei** near ❷ close ▷ *Der Bahnhof ist ganz nah.* The station's quite close. ▷ *nahe Verwandte* close relatives ▷ *nahe Freunde* close friends ▷ *Unser Haus ist nahe der Universität.* Our house is close to the university. ▷ *den Tränen nahe* close to tears ▷ *mit jemandem nah verwandt sein* to be closely related to somebody; **der Nahe Osten** the Middle East; **Die Prüfungen rücken näher.** The exams are getting closer.; **nahe daran sein, etwas zu tun** to be close to doing something
Nähe f in der Nähe near; **aus der Nähe** close up
nähen vb [38] to sew
näher adj, adv nearer ▷ *Die Straßenbahnhaltestelle ist näher als die Bushaltestelle.* The tram stop is nearer than the bus stop.; **Näheres** details pl; **näher kommen** to get closer
sich nähern vb [88] to get closer ▷ *Wir näherten uns dem Bahnhof.* We were approaching the station.
nahm vb see **nehmen**

Nähmaschine f sewing machine
nahrhaft adj nourishing
Nahrung f food ▷ *feste Nahrung* solid food
Nahrungsmittel (pl **Nahrungsmittel**) nt foodstuffs pl
Naht (pl **Nähte**) f seam ▷ *Die Hose ist an der Naht geplatzt.* The trousers have split along the seam.
Nahverkehr m local traffic
Nahverkehrszug (pl **Nahverkehrszüge**) m local train
Name (gen **Namens**, pl **Namen**) m name ▷ *Mein Name ist ...* My name is ...; **im Namen von** on behalf of
nämlich adv ❶ you see ▷ *Sie ist nämlich meine beste Freundin.* You see, she's my best friend. ❷ that is to say ▷ *Nächstes Jahr, nämlich im März ...* Next year, that is to say in March ...
nannte vb see **nennen**
Narbe f scar
Narkose f anaesthetic
naschen vb [48] **Sie nascht gern.** She's got a sweet tooth.; **Wer hat von der Torte genascht?** Who's been at the cake?
Nase f nose ▷ *Meine Nase blutet.* My nose is bleeding.
Nasenbluten nt nosebleed ▷ *Ich hatte Nasenbluten.* I had a nosebleed.
nass adj wet ▷ *Nach dem Regen war die Wäsche noch nässer.* After the rain, the washing was even wetter.
Nässe f wetness
Nation f nation
national adj national
Nationalhymne f national anthem
Nationalität f nationality
Natur f ❶ country ▷ *Wir gehen gern in der Natur spazieren.* We like to go for a walk in the country. ❷ constitution ▷ *Sie hat eine robuste Natur.* She's got a strong constitution.
natürlich adj, adv ❶ natural ▷ *Das ist ihre natürliche Haarfarbe.* That's her

natural hair colour. ❷ of course ▷ *Wir kommen natürlich.* Of course we'll come. ▷ *Sie hat das natürlich wieder vergessen.* She's forgotten it again, of course. ▷ *Ja, natürlich!* Yes, of course.

Naturschutzgebiet (*pl* **Naturschutzgebiete**) *nt* nature reserve

Naturwissenschaft *f* natural science

Navi *m* GPS, sat nav

Nebel (*pl* **Nebel**) *m* ❶ mist ❷ fog

nebelig *adj* ❶ misty ❷ foggy

neben *prep*

> Use the accusative to express movement or a change of place. Use the dative when there is no change of place.

❶ next to ▷ *Dein Rad steht neben meinem.* Your bike's next to mine. ▷ *Stell dein Rad neben meines.* Put your bike next to mine. ❷ apart from

> **neben** takes the dative in this sense.

▷ *Neben den Sehenswürdigkeiten haben wir uns auch ein Theaterstück angesehen.* Apart from the sights, we also saw a play.

nebenan *adv* next door

nebenbei *adv* ❶ at the same time ▷ *Ich kann nicht Hausaufgaben machen und nebenbei fernsehen.* I can't do my homework and watch TV at the same time. ❷ on the side ▷ *Sie hat nebenbei noch einen anderen Job.* She has another job on the side.; **Sie sagte ganz nebenbei, dass sie nicht mitkommen wollte.** She mentioned quite casually that she didn't want to come along.; *Nebenbei bemerkt, ...* Incidentally, ...

nebeneinander *adv* side by side

Nebenfach (*pl* **Nebenfächer**) *nt* subsidiary subject

Nebenfluss (*gen* **Nebenflusses**, *pl* **Nebenflüsse**) *m* tributary

Nebenstraße *f* side street

neblig *adj* ❶ misty ❷ foggy

nee *adv* (*informal*) no ▷ *Nee, das mache ich lieber später.* No, I'd rather do that later.

Neffe (*gen* **Neffen**, *pl* **Neffen**) *m* nephew

negativ *adj* negative ▷ *HIV-negativ* HIV-negative

Negativ (*pl* **Negative**) *nt* negative ▷ *Kann ich von den Bildern das Negativ haben?* Can I have the negatives of these pictures?

nehmen (*pres* **nimmt**, *imperf* **nahm**, *perf* **hat genommen**) *vb* [52] to take ▷ *Sie nahm fünf Euro aus dem Geldbeutel.* She took five euros out of her purse. ▷ *Wir nehmen besser den Bus in die Stadt.* We'd better take the bus into town. ▷ *Hast du deine Medizin genommen?* Have you taken your medicine? ▷ *Nimm ihn nicht ernst!* Don't take him seriously.; **Ich nehme ein Erdbeereis.** I'll have a strawberry ice cream.; **Nimm dir doch bitte!** Please help yourself.

Neid *m* envy

neidisch *adj* envious ▷ *Sie ist neidisch auf ihren Bruder.* She's envious of her brother.

nein *adv* no ▷ *Hast du das gesehen?* — *Nein. Did you see that?* — No, I didn't.; **Ich glaube nein.** I don't think so.

Nelke *f* ❶ carnation ▷ *Er brachte mir einen Strauß Nelken.* He brought me a bunch of carnations. ❷ clove ▷ *Zum Glühwein braucht man Nelken.* You need cloves to make mulled wine.

nennen (*imperf* **nannte**, *perf* **hat genannt**) *vb* ❶ to call ▷ *Sie haben ihren Sohn Rafael genannt.* They called their son Rafael. ▷ *Die Band nennt sich 'Die Zerstörer'.* The band call themselves 'The Destroyers'. ▷ *Wie nennt man ...?* What do you call ...? ❷ to name ▷ *Kannst du mir einen Fluss in England nennen?* Can you name a river in England?

Nerv (*pl* **Nerven**) *m* nerve; **jemandem auf die Nerven gehen** to get on somebody's nerves

Nervenzusammenbruch (pl **Nervenzusammenbrüche**) m nervous breakdown

nervös adj nervous

Nervosität f nervousness

Nest (pl **Nester**) nt ❶ nest ▷ *Der Vogel hat ein Nest gebaut.* The bird has built a nest. ❷ (informal) dump ▷ *Wiblingen ist ein Nest.* Wiblingen is a dump.

nett adj ❶ lovely ▷ *Vielen Dank für den netten Abend.* Thanks for a lovely evening. ❷ nice ▷ *Wir haben uns nett unterhalten.* We had a nice talk. ❸ kind ▷ *Wären Sie vielleicht so nett, mir zu helfen?* Would you be so kind as to help me? ▷ *Das war sehr nett von dir.* That was very kind of you.; **etwas Nettes** something nice ▷ *Sie wollte ihm etwas Nettes sagen.* She wanted to say something nice to him.

netto adv net ▷ *Sie verdient dreitausend Euro netto.* She earns three thousand euros net.

Netz (gen **Netzes**, pl **Netze**) nt ❶ net ▷ *Die Fischer werfen ihre Netze aus.* The fishermen cast their nets. ▷ *Der Ball ging ins Netz.* The ball went into the net. ❷ string bag ▷ *Sie packte die Einkäufe ins Netz.* She packed her shopping into a string bag. ❸ network ▷ *ein weitverzweigtes Netz an Rohren* an extensive network of pipes ▷ *einen Computer ans Netz anschließen* to connect a computer to the network

Netzwerk (pl **Netzwerke**) nt network

neu adj new ▷ *Ist der Pulli neu?* Is that pullover new? ▷ *Sie hat einen neuen Freund.* She's got a new boyfriend. ▷ *Ich bin neu hier.* I'm new here.; **neue Sprachen** modern languages; **neueste** latest; **seit Neuestem** recently; **neu schreiben** to rewrite; **Das ist mir neu!** That's news to me.

neuartig adj new kind of ▷ *ein neuartiges Wörterbuch* a new kind of dictionary

Neugier f curiosity

neugierig adj curious

Neuheit f new product ▷ *Auf der Messe werden alle Neuheiten vorgestellt.* All new products are presented at the trade fair.

Neuigkeit f news sg ▷ *Gibt es irgendwelche Neuigkeiten?* Is there any news?

Neujahr nt New Year

neulich adv the other day

neun num nine

neunte adj ninth ▷ *Heute ist der neunte Juni.* Today is the ninth of June.

neunzehn num nineteen

neunzig num ninety

neurodivers adj neurodivergent

Neuseeland nt New Zealand

Neuseeländer (pl **Neuseeländer**) m New Zealander

Neuseeländerin f New Zealander

neutral adj neutral

Neutrum (pl **Neutra** or **Neutren**) nt neuter

nicht adv not ▷ *Ich bin nicht müde.* I'm not tired. ▷ *Er ist es nicht.* It's not him. ▷ *Es regnet nicht mehr.* It's not raining any more.; **Er raucht nicht. (1)** He isn't smoking. **(2)** He doesn't smoke.; **Ich kann das nicht. — Ich auch nicht.** I can't do it. — Neither can I.; **Nicht!** Don't!; **Nicht berühren!** Do not touch!; **Du bist müde, nicht wahr?** You're tired, aren't you?; **Das ist schön, nicht wahr?** It's nice, isn't it?; **Was du nicht sagst!** You don't say!

Nichte f niece

Nichtraucher (pl **Nichtraucher**) m nonsmoker

nichts pron nothing ▷ *nichts zu verzollen* nothing to declare ▷ *nichts Neues* nothing new; **Ich habe nichts gesagt.** I didn't say anything.; **Nichts ist so wie früher.** Things aren't what they used to be.; **Das macht nichts.** It doesn't matter.; **für nichts und wieder nichts** for nothing

nicken vb [48] to nod

nie adv never ▷ *Das habe ich nie gesagt.* I never said that. ▷ *Das werde ich nie vergessen.* I'll never forget that. ▷ *Das habe ich noch nie gehört.* I've never heard that. ▷ *Ich war noch nie in Indien.* I've never been to India.; **nie wieder** never again; **nie mehr** never again; **nie und nimmer** no way

Niederlage f defeat

Niederlande ntpl the Netherlands pl; **aus den Niederlanden** from the Netherlands; **in den Niederlanden** in the Netherlands; **in die Niederlande** to the Netherlands

Niederländer (pl **Niederländer**) m Dutchman; **Er ist Niederländer.** He's Dutch.

Niederländerin f Dutchwoman; **Sie ist Niederländerin.** She's Dutch.

niederländisch adj Dutch

Niedersachsen nt Lower Saxony
* **Niedersachsen** is one of the 16
* **Länder**. Its capital is Hannover. Its
* most important industries are
* mining and car manufacturing
* (Volkswagen). The Hannover
* Industrial Fair is the largest in the
* world.

Niederschlag (pl **Niederschläge**) m precipitation; **heftige Niederschläge** heavy rain; **radioaktiver Niederschlag** radioactive fallout

niedlich adj sweet ▷ *niedlich aussehen* to look sweet

niedrig adj ❶ low ▷ *Die Decke ist sehr niedrig.* The ceiling is very low. ▷ *niedrige Temperaturen* low temperatures ❷ shallow ▷ *Hier ist der Fluss niedriger.* The river is shallower here. ❸ base ▷ *niedrige Motive* base motives

niemals adv never

niemand pron ❶ nobody ▷ *Niemand hat mir Bescheid gesagt.* Nobody told me. ❷ not ... anybody ▷ *Ich habe niemanden gesehen.* I haven't seen anybody. ▷ *Sie hat mit niemandem darüber gesprochen.* She hasn't mentioned it to anybody.

Niere f kidney

nieseln vb [**88**] to drizzle

niesen vb [**38**] to sneeze

Niete f ❶ stud ▷ *Jeans mit Nieten* jeans with studs ❷ blank ▷ *Ich habe eine Niete gezogen.* I've drawn a blank. ❸ In **Mathe ist er eine Niete.** He's useless at maths.

nimmt vb see **nehmen**

nirgends adv ❶ nowhere ❷ not ... anywhere

nirgendwo adv see **nirgends**

nö adv (informal) no ▷ *Nö, ich habe keine Lust.* No, I can't be bothered.

noch adv, conj still ▷ *Ich habe noch Hunger.* I'm still hungry. ▷ *Das kann noch passieren.* That might still happen. ▷ *Das ist noch besser.* That's better still.; **Bleib doch noch ein bisschen!** Stay a bit longer.; **Das wirst du noch lernen.** You'll learn.; **Er wird noch kommen.** He'll come.; **heute noch** today; **noch am selben Tag** the very same day; **noch vor einer Woche** only a week ago; **Wer noch?** Who else?; **Was noch?** What else?; **noch nicht** not yet; **noch nie** never; **immer noch** still; **noch einmal** again; **noch dreimal** three more times; **noch einer** another one; **noch größer** even bigger; **Geld noch und noch** (informal) loads of money; **weder ... noch ...** neither ... nor ...

nochmal adv again

Nominativ (pl **Nominative**) m nominative

Nordamerika nt North America

Norden m north

Nordirland nt Northern Ireland

nördlich adj, prep, adv northerly ▷ *Wir fuhren in nördlicher Richtung.* We drove in a northerly direction.; **nördlich einer Sache** to the north of something; **nördlich von** north of

Nordpol m North Pole ▷ *am Nordpol* at the North Pole

Nordrhein-Westfalen nt North Rhine-Westphalia
* **Nordrhein-Westfalen** is one of the 16 **Länder**. Its capital is Düsseldorf. It is Germany's most densely populated state, and includes the Ruhr district.

Nordsee f North Sea ▷ *Wir fahren an die Nordsee.* We're going to the North Sea. ▷ *Wir waren an der Nordsee.* We've been to the North Sea.

Norm f standard ▷ *Für die meisten technischen Geräte gibt es Normen.* There are set standards for most technical equipment.

normal adj normal

Normalbenzin nt regular petrol

normalerweise adv normally

Norwegen nt Norway

Norweger (pl Norweger) m Norwegian

Norwegerin f Norwegian

norwegisch adj Norwegian

Not f zur Not if necessary

Notausgang (pl Notausgänge) m emergency exit

Notbremse f emergency brake

Notdienst (pl Notdienste) m emergency service

Note f ❶ mark ▷ *Max hat gute Noten.* Max has got good marks. ❷ note ▷ *Welche Note hast du eben gespielt?* What note did you just play?

Notfall (pl Notfälle) m emergency

notfalls adv if need be

notieren (perf **hat notiert**) vb [76] to note down

nötig adj necessary ▷ *wenn nötig* if necessary; **etwas nötig haben** to need something

Notiz f ❶ note ▷ *Sein Kalender ist voller Notizen.* His diary is full of notes. ❷ item ▷ *Das stand heute in einer kleinen Notiz in der Zeitung.* There was a short item on it in the newspaper today.; **Notiz nehmen von** to take notice of

Notizbuch (pl Notizbücher) nt notebook

notlanden (perf **ist notgelandet**) vb [54] to make an emergency landing

Notruf (pl Notrufe) m emergency call

notwendig adj necessary

November (gen November or Novembers, pl November) m November ▷ *im November* in November ▷ *am neunten November* on the ninth of November ▷ *Freiburg, den 9. November 2025* Freiburg, 9 November 2025 ▷ *Heute ist der neunte November.* Today is the ninth of November.

nüchtern adj ❶ sober ▷ *Nach drei Gläsern Wein bist du nicht mehr nüchtern.* After three glasses of wine you aren't sober any more. ▷ *nüchterne Tatsachen* sober facts ❷ with an empty stomach ▷ *Kommen Sie nüchtern ins Krankenhaus.* Come to the hospital with an empty stomach.; **auf nüchternen Magen** on an empty stomach; **eine Lage nüchtern betrachten** to look at a situation rationally

Nudel f noodle ▷ *Es waren Nudeln in der Suppe.* There were noodles in the soup.; **Nudeln** pasta sg

null num ❶ nil ▷ *Sie haben eins zu null gespielt.* They won one nil. ❷ no ▷ *Ich hatte null Fehler.* I had no mistakes.; **null Uhr** midnight; **null und nichtig** null and void

Null f ❶ zero ▷ *Du musst zuerst eine Null wählen.* You have to dial zero first. ❷ nonentity ▷ *Er ist doch eine völlige Null.* He's a complete nonentity.

Nullerjahre pl 2000s, noughties

Nummer f ❶ number ▷ *Ich kann seine Nummer auswendig.* I know his number by heart. ❷ size ▷ *Die Schuhe sind eine Nummer zu groß.* These shoes are a size too big.

nummerieren (perf hat nummeriert) vb [**76**] to number

Nummernschild (pl **Nummernschilder**) nt number plate

nun adv, excl ❶ now ▷ von nun an from now on ❷ well ▷ Nun, was gibt's Neues? Well, what's new?; **Das ist nun mal so.** That's the way it is.

nur adv only ▷ Das hat nur zwanzig Euro gekostet. It only cost twenty euros. ▷ Es sind nur fünf Leute da gewesen. There were only five people there.; **Wo bleibt er nur?** Where on earth can he be?; **Was hat sie nur?** What on earth's wrong with her?

Nuss (pl **Nüsse**) f nut

nutzen vb [**36**] to help ▷ Sprachkenntnisse können dir im Ausland viel nutzen. Knowing a language can help you a lot abroad.; **etwas nutzen** to make use of something; **Das nutzt ja doch nichts.** That's pointless.; **Es nutzt alles nichts, wir müssen …** There's no getting around it, we'll have to …

Nutzen m von Nutzen useful; **Das ist zu deinem Nutzen.** It's for your own good.

nützen vb [**36**] see **nutzen**

nützlich adj useful ▷ sich nützlich machen to make oneself useful

nutzlos adj useless

Oase f oasis

ob conj ❶ whether ▷ Ich weiß nicht, ob ich kommen kann. I don't know whether I can come. ❷ if ▷ Sie fragt, ob du auch kommst. She wants to know if you're coming too.; **Ob das wohl wahr ist?** Can that be true?; **Und ob!** You bet!

obdachlos adj homeless

oben adv on top ▷ oben auf dem Schrank on top of the cupboard; **oben auf dem Berg** up on the mountain; **Die Schlafzimmer sind oben.** The bedrooms are upstairs.; **nach oben** up; **von oben** down; **oben ohne** topless; **Befehl von oben** orders from above

Ober (pl **Ober**) m waiter; **Herr Ober!** Waiter!

obere adj upper ▷ die oberen Stockwerke the upper floors; **die oberen Klassen** the senior classes

Oberfläche f surface

Obergeschoss (gen **Obergeschosses**, pl **Obergeschosse**) nt upper storey

Oberschenkel (pl **Oberschenkel**) m thigh

oberste adj topmost ▷ *Das Buch steht auf dem obersten Regalbrett.* The book is on the topmost shelf.; **Sie ist in der obersten Klasse.** She's in the top class.

Oberstufe f upper school

obgleich conj although ▷ *Obgleich sie müde war, blieb sie lange auf.* Although she was tired, she stayed up late.

Objekt (pl **Objekte**) nt object

objektiv adj objective

Objektiv (pl **Objektive**) nt lens (of camera)

Obst nt fruit

Obstkuchen (pl **Obstkuchen**) m fruit tart

obwohl conj although ▷ *Obwohl sie müde war, blieb sie lange auf.* Although she was tired, she stayed up late.

Ochse (gen **Ochsen**, pl **Ochsen**) m ox

öde adj dull ▷ *eine öde Landschaft* a dull landscape; **Diese Arbeit ist echt öde.** (informal) This job's really the pits.

oder conj or ▷ *entweder ich oder du* either me or you; **Das stimmt, oder?** That's right, isn't it?

Ofen (pl **Öfen**) m ① oven ▷ *Der Kuchen ist im Ofen.* The cake's in the oven. ② heater; **Mach bitte den Ofen an, mir ist kalt.** Put the fire on, I'm cold.

offen adj open ▷ *Das Fenster ist offen.* The window's open. ▷ *Die Banken sind bis sechzehn Uhr offen.* The banks are open until four o'clock. ▷ *Sie ist ein sehr offener Mensch.* She's a very open person.; **offen gesagt** to be honest; **Ich gebe dir eine offene Antwort.** I'll be frank with you.; **eine offene Stelle** a vacancy

offenbar adj, adv ① apparent ▷ *Die E-Mail machte offenbar, dass sie gelogen hatten.* It was apparent from the email that they had lied. ② apparently ▷ *Sie kommen offenbar später.* Apparently they're coming later.

offensichtlich adj, adv ① obvious ▷ *ein offensichtlicher Fehler* an obvious mistake ② obviously ▷ *Er ist offensichtlich nicht zufrieden.* He's obviously dissatisfied.

öffentlich adj public ▷ *öffentliche Verkehrsmittel* public transport

Öffentlichkeit f public ▷ *Die Öffentlichkeit wurde nicht informiert.* The public were not informed. ▷ *in aller Öffentlichkeit* in public

offiziell adj official

öffnen vb [53] to open ▷ *jemandem die Tür öffnen* to open the door for somebody

Öffner (pl **Öffner**) m opener

Öffnung f opening

Öffnungszeiten fpl opening times pl

oft adv often ▷ *Wie oft warst du schon in London?* How often have you been to London?

öfter adv more often ▷ *Ich würde dich gern öfter besuchen.* I would like to visit you more often.; **Sie war in letzter Zeit öfter krank.** She's been ill a lot recently.

öfters adv often

ohne prep, conj

> The preposition **ohne** takes the accusative.

without ▷ *Ich fahre ohne meine Eltern in Ferien.* I'm going on holiday without my parents. ▷ *Ich habe das ohne Wörterbuch übersetzt.* I translated it without a dictionary.; **ohne ... zu ...** ▷ *Sie ist gegangen, ohne Bescheid zu sagen.* She left without telling anyone. ▷ *ohne zu fragen* without asking; **Das ist nicht ohne.** (informal) It's not half bad.; **ohne weiteres** easily; **Du kannst doch nicht so ohne weiteres gehen.** You can't just leave.

ohnmächtig adj **ohnmächtig werden** to faint; **Sie ist ohnmächtig.** She's fainted.

Ohr (pl **Ohren**) nt ear; *Er hat sehr gute Ohren.* His hearing is very good.
Ohrenschmerzen pl earache sg ▷ *Sie hat Ohrenschmerzen.* She's got earache.
Ohrfeige f slap across the face
ohrfeigen vb [38] jemanden ohrfeigen to slap somebody across the face
Ohrhörer (pl **Ohrhörer**) m earbud ▷ *Ich habe neue Ohrhörer gekauft.* I bought new earbuds.
Ohrring (pl **Ohrringe**) m earring
okay adj, adv (informal) okay
ökologisch adj ecological
Oktober (gen **Oktober** or **Oktobers**, pl **Oktober**) m October ▷ *im Oktober* in October ▷ *am dritten Oktober* on the third of October ▷ *Ulm, den 3. Oktober 2025* Ulm, 3 October 2025. ▷ *Heute ist der dritte Oktober.* Today is the third of October.
Oktoberfest (pl **Oktoberfeste**) nt Munich beer festival
Öl (pl **Öle**) nt oil
ölig adj oily
oliv adj olive-green
Olive f olive
Ölsardine f sardine
Ölwechsel (pl **Ölwechsel**) m oil change
Olympiade f Olympic Games pl
Olympiasieger (pl **Olympiasieger**) m Olympic® champion
Olympiasiegerin f Olympic® champion
olympisch adj Olympic®
Oma (pl **Omas**) f (informal) granny
Omelett (pl **Omeletts**) nt omelette
Onkel (pl **Onkel**) m uncle
online adv online
Opa (pl **Opas**) m (informal) grandpa
Oper f ❶ opera ▷ *eine Oper von Verdi* an opera by Verdi ❷ opera house ▷ *Die Mailänder Oper ist berühmt.* The Milan opera house is famous.
Operation f operation

Operationssaal (pl **Operationssäle**) m operating theatre
Operette f operetta
operieren (perf **hat operiert**) vb [76] to operate on ▷ *jemanden operieren* to operate on somebody; *Sie muss operiert werden.* She has to have an operation.; *Sie wurde am Auge operiert.* She had an eye operation.
Opfer (pl **Opfer**) nt ❶ sacrifice ▷ *Das war ein großes Opfer für ihn.* It was a great sacrifice for him. ❷ victim ▷ *Der Unfall hat viele Opfer gefordert.* The accident claimed a lot of victims.
Opposition f opposition
Optiker (pl **Optiker**) m optician
optimal adj, adv optimum ▷ *Das ist die optimale Lösung.* That's the optimum solution.; *Sie hat das optimal gelöst.* She solved it in the best possible way.; *Wir haben den Platz optimal genutzt.* We made the best possible use of the space available.
Optimismus (gen **Optimismus**) m optimism
Optimist (gen **Optimisten**, pl **Optimisten**) m optimist
optimistisch adj optimistic
orange adj orange
Orange f orange
Orangensaft (pl **Orangensäfte**) m orange juice
Orchester (pl **Orchester**) nt orchestra
ordentlich adj, adv ❶ tidy ▷ *Seine Wohnung ist sehr ordentlich.* His flat's very tidy. ▷ *Ich bin ein ordentlicher Mensch.* I'm a tidy person. ❷ decent ▷ *Das sind ordentliche Leute.* They're decent people. ▷ *Das ist doch kein ordentliches Gehalt.* That's not a decent wage. ▷ *eine ordentliche Portion* a decent portion; *Ich brauche jetzt etwas Ordentliches zu essen.* Now I need a decent meal. ❸ respectable ▷ *Das ist eine ordentliche Leistung.* That's a respectable

GERMAN > ENGLISH

achievement. ▷ *Du solltest dir einen ordentlichen Beruf aussuchen.* You ought to look for a respectable job. ❶ neatly ▷ *Du solltest ordentlicher schreiben.* You should write more neatly. ❷ properly ▷ *Kannst du dich nicht ordentlich benehmen?* Can't you behave properly?; **Es hat ordentlich geschneit.** There's been a fair bit of snow.; **Sie haben ihn ordentlich verprügelt.** *(informal)* They beat him up good and proper.

ordnen vb [53] to put in order

Ordner (pl **Ordner**) m file

Ordnung f order ▷ *Ruhe und Ordnung* law and order; **Sie liebt Ordnung.** She likes everything to be in its place.; **Das hat schon alles seine Ordnung.** Everything is as it should be.; **Ordnung machen** to tidy up; **Mit meinem Auto ist etwas nicht in Ordnung.** Something's wrong with my car.; **etwas wieder in Ordnung bringen** to repair something; **Ist alles in Ordnung?** Is everything okay?; **In Ordnung!** Okay!

Organ (pl **Organe**) nt organ ▷ *die inneren Organe* internal organs; **Er hat ein lautes Organ.** He's got a loud voice.

Organisation f organization

organisch adj organic

organisieren (perf **hat organisiert**) vb [76] to organize ▷ *Wer hat das Fest organisiert?* Who organized the party?

Orgel f organ ▷ *Sie spielt Orgel.* She plays the organ.

sich **orientieren** (perf **hat sich orientiert**) vb [76] ❶ to find one's way around ▷ *Ich brauche einen Stadtplan, um mich besser orientieren zu können.* I need a city map to be able to find my way around better. ❷ to find out ▷ *Ich muss mich orientieren, wie das gehandhabt wird.* I'll have to find out what the procedure is.

originell adj original ▷ *ein origineller Einfall* an original idea

Orkan (pl **Orkane**) m hurricane

161 | **Ozonschicht**

Ort (pl **Orte**) m place; **an Ort und Stelle** on the spot

Orthografie f spelling

örtlich adj local

Ortsgespräch (pl **Ortsgespräche**) nt local phone call

Osten m east

Osterei (pl **Ostereier**) nt Easter egg

Osterferien pl Easter holidays pl

Ostern (pl **Ostern**) nt Easter ▷ *an Ostern* at Easter

Österreich nt Austria

Österreicher (pl **Österreicher**) m Austrian

Österreicherin f Austrian

österreichisch adj Austrian
- People in Austria speak a dialect of German.

östlich adj, prep, adv easterly ▷ *Wir fuhren in östlicher Richtung.* We drove in an easterly direction.; **östlich einer Sache** to the east of something; **östlich von** east of

Ostsee f Baltic (Sea) ▷ *Wir fahren an die Ostsee.* We're going to the Baltic (Sea). ▷ *Wir waren an der Ostsee.* We've been to the Baltic (Sea).

oval adj oval

Ozean (pl **Ozeane**) m ocean

Ozon nt ozone

Ozonloch (pl **Ozonlöcher**) nt ozone hole

Ozonschicht f ozone layer

P

Paar (pl **Paare**) nt ① pair ▷ Ich habe ein Paar Schuhe gekauft. I've bought a pair of shoes. ② couple ▷ Sie sind ein sehr glückliches Paar. They're a very happy couple.; **ein paar** a few

paarmal adv **ein paarmal** a few times

Päckchen (pl **Päckchen**) nt ① small parcel ▷ Wie viel kostet ein Päckchen ins Ausland? How much does it cost to post a small parcel abroad? ② packet ▷ Sie raucht ein Päckchen pro Tag. She smokes a packet a day.

packen vb [38] ① to pack ▷ Hast du deinen Koffer schon gepackt? Have you already packed your suitcase? ② to grasp ▷ Sie packte mich am Arm. She grasped my arm.; **Er hat die Prüfung nicht gepackt.** He didn't manage to get through the exam.

Packung f ① packet ▷ eine Packung Tee a packet of tea ▷ eine Packung Zigaretten a packet of cigarettes ② box ▷ eine Packung Pralinen a box of chocolates

Paket (pl **Pakete**) nt ① packet ▷ Ich habe ein Paket Waschpulver gekauft. I bought a packet of washing powder. ② parcel ▷ Die Gebühren für Pakete stehen in dieser Liste. Parcel rates are in this list.

Palast (pl **Paläste**) m palace

Palme f palm tree

Pampelmuse f grapefruit

Panik f panic

panisch adj **panische Angst vor etwas haben** to be terrified of something; **panisch reagieren** to panic

Panne f ① breakdown ▷ Wir hatten eine Panne auf der Autobahn. We had a breakdown on the motorway. ② slip ▷ Mir ist da eine kleine Panne passiert. I made a slight slip.

Panzer (pl **Panzer**) m ① tank ▷ Die Armee setzte Panzer ein. The army used tanks. ② shell ▷ der Panzer einer Schildkröte a tortoise's shell

Papa (pl **Papas**) m (informal) daddy

Papagei (pl **Papageien**) m parrot

Papier (pl **Papiere**) nt paper

Papierkorb (pl **Papierkörbe**) m wastepaper basket

Papiertüte f paper bag

Pappe f cardboard

Paprika (pl **Paprikas**) m ① paprika ▷ Ich habe das Hähnchen mit Paprika gewürzt. I've seasoned the chicken with paprika. ② pepper ▷ Heute gibt es gefüllte Paprikas. We're having stuffed peppers today.

Papst (pl **Päpste**) m pope

Paradies (gen **Paradieses**, pl **Paradiese**) nt paradise

parallel adj parallel

paralympisch adj Paralympic

Pärchen (pl **Pärchen**) nt couple ▷ Auf der Parkbank saß ein Pärchen. There was a couple sitting on the bench in the park.

Parfüm (pl **Parfüms** or **Parfüme**) nt perfume

Park (pl **Parks**) m park
parken vb [38] to park
Parkett (pl **Parkette** or **Parketts**) nt stalls pl (theatre)
Parkhaus (gen **Parkhauses**, pl **Parkhäuser**) nt multistorey car park
Parkplatz (gen **Parkplatzes**, pl **Parkplätze**) m car park
Parkscheibe f parking disc
Parkschein m car-park ticket
Parkuhr f parking meter
Parkverbot (pl **Parkverbote**) nt Hier ist Parkverbot. You're not allowed to park here.
Parlament (pl **Parlamente**) nt parliament
Partei f party (political); **Partei für jemanden ergreifen** to take somebody's side
Parterre (pl **Parterres**) nt ❶ ground floor ▷ Wir wohnen im Parterre. We live on the ground floor. ❷ stalls pl (theatre)
Partner (pl **Partner**) m partner
Partnerin f partner
Partnerstadt (pl **Partnerstädte**) f twin town
Party (pl **Partys**) f party ▷ eine Party veranstalten to have a party
Pass (gen **Passes**, pl **Pässe**) m ❶ passport ▷ Für Indien brauchst du einen Pass. You need a passport for India. ❷ pass ▷ Im Winter ist der Pass gesperrt. The pass is closed in winter.
Passage f passage; **eine Einkaufspassage** a shopping arcade
Passagier (pl **Passagiere**) m passenger
passen vb [31] ❶ to fit ▷ Die Hose passt nicht. The trousers don't fit. ▷ Es ist zu groß und passt nicht in meinen Koffer. It's too big and doesn't fit in my suitcase. ❷ to suit ▷ Passt dir Dienstag? Does Tuesday suit you? ▷ Dieser Termin passt mir nicht. That date doesn't suit me.; **Es passt mir nicht, dass du so frech bist.** I don't like you being so cheeky.; **zu**
etwas passen to go with something; **zu jemandem passen** to be right for somebody ❸ to pass ▷ Auf die Frage muss ich passen. I'll have to pass on that question.
passend adj ❶ matching ▷ Ich muss jetzt dazu passende Schuhe kaufen. I now must buy some matching shoes. ❷ appropriate ▷ Sie hat ein paar passende Worte gesprochen. She said a few appropriate words. ❸ convenient ▷ Das ist nicht die passende Gelegenheit. This isn't a convenient time.
passieren (perf **ist passiert**) vb [76] to happen ▷ Was ist passiert? What happened? ▷ Mir ist etwas Lustiges passiert. Something funny happened to me.
passiv adj, adv passive ▷ passives Rauchen passive smoking ▷ passiv zusehen to watch passively
Passiv (pl **Passive**) nt passive
Passivrauchen nt passive smoking
Passkontrolle f passport control
Passwort (pl **Passwörter**) nt password
Pastete f pie (savoury)
Pate (gen **Paten**, pl **Paten**) m godfather
Patenkind (pl **Patenkinder**) nt godchild
Patent (pl **Patente**) nt patent
Patient (gen **Patienten**, pl **Patienten**) m patient
Patientin f patient
Patin f godmother
Patrone f cartridge
pauken vb [38] ❶ (informal) to swot ▷ Vor der Arbeit habe ich ziemlich gepaukt. I swotted quite a lot before the test. ❷ (informal) to swot up ▷ Ich muss Vokabeln pauken. I have to swot up my vocabulary.
Pauschalreise f package tour
Pause f ❶ break ▷ eine Pause machen to have a break ▷ die große Pause the long

break ❷ interval ▷ *In der Pause haben wir über das Stück gesprochen.* We talked about the play during the interval.

Pazifik m Pacific

Pech nt bad luck ▷ *Das war Pech!* That was bad luck.; **Pech haben** to be unlucky; **Pech!** Hard luck!

Pedal (pl **Pedale**) nt pedal

peinlich adj ❶ embarrassing ▷ *eine peinliche Frage* an embarrassing question ❷ awkward ▷ *eine peinliche Angelegenheit* an awkward situation; **Das ist mir aber peinlich.** I'm dreadfully sorry.; **peinlich genau** painstakingly

Peitsche f whip

Pelle f skin

Pelz (gen **Pelzes**, pl **Pelze**) m fur

Pendel (pl **Pendel**) nt pendulum

pendeln (perf **ist gependelt**) vb [34] to commute ▷ *Er pendelt zwischen Tübingen und Stuttgart.* He commutes between Tübingen and Stuttgart.

Pendelverkehr m ❶ shuttle service ▷ *Die Fluggesellschaft hat einen Pendelverkehr zwischen Köln und Berlin eingerichtet.* The airline set up a shuttle service between Cologne and Berlin. ❷ commuter traffic ▷ *Zwischen Tübingen und Stuttgart besteht ein reger Pendelverkehr.* There is heavy commuter traffic between Tübingen and Stuttgart.

Pendler (pl **Pendler**) m commuter

Penis (gen **Penis**, pl **Penisse**) m penis

pennen vb [48] (informal) to kip ▷ *Ich habe auf dem Fußboden gepennt.* I kipped on the floor.; **Er pennt.** He's having a kip.

Penner (pl **Penner**) m (informal) dosser

Pension f ❶ pension ▷ *Er bezieht eine ordentliche Pension.* He gets a decent pension.; **in Pension gehen** to retire ❷ guesthouse ▷ *Wir haben in einer Pension übernachtet.* We stayed overnight in a guesthouse.

perfekt adj perfect ▷ *ein perfektes Alibi* a perfect alibi ▷ **perfekt passen** to fit perfectly

Perfekt (pl **Perfekte**) nt perfect

Periode f period

Perle f pearl

Person f person; **ich für meine Person ...** personally I ...

Personal nt staff ▷ *das Personal der Firma* the staff of the company ▷ *das Hotelpersonal* the hotel staff

Personalausweis (gen **Personalausweises**, pl **Personalausweise**) m identity card

Personenzug (pl **Personenzüge**) m passenger train

persönlich adj, adv ❶ personal ▷ *das persönliche Fürwort* the personal pronoun ▷ **persönlich werden** to get personal ❷ in person ▷ *persönlich erscheinen* to appear in person ❸ personally ▷ *jemanden persönlich kennen* to know somebody personally ▷ *Das war nicht persönlich gemeint.* It wasn't meant personally.

Persönlichkeit f personality

Perücke f wig

Pessimist (gen **Pessimisten**, pl **Pessimisten**) m pessimist

pessimistisch adj pessimistic

Pest f plague; **jemanden wie die Pest hassen** to loathe somebody

Petersilie f parsley

Pfad (pl **Pfade**) m path

Pfadfinder (pl **Pfadfinder**) m boy scout

Pfadfinderin f girl guide

Pfand (pl **Pfänder**) nt ❶ deposit ▷ *Auf der Flasche ist ein Pfand von siebzig Cent.* There's a deposit of seventy cents on the bottle. ❷ forfeit ▷ *Wer die Frage nicht beantworten kann, muss ein Pfand geben.* Anyone who cannot answer the question must pay a forfeit.

Pfandflasche f returnable bottle

Pfanne f frying pan

Pfannkuchen (pl **Pfannkuchen**) m pancake
Pfarrer (pl **Pfarrer**) m parish priest
Pfeffer (pl **Pfeffer**) m pepper
Pfefferkorn (pl **Pfefferkörner**) nt peppercorn
Pfefferminzbonbon (pl **Pfefferminzbonbons**) nt peppermint
Pfeife f ❶ whistle ▷ *die Pfeife des Schiedsrichters* the referee's whistle ❷ pipe ▷ *Mein Bruder raucht Pfeife.* My brother smokes a pipe.
pfeifen (imperf **pfiff**, perf **hat gepfiffen**) vb to whistle
Pfeil (pl **Pfeile**) m arrow
Pferd (pl **Pferde**) nt horse
Pferderennen (pl **Pferderennen**) nt ❶ race meeting ▷ *Er geht regelmäßig zu Pferderennen.* He regularly goes to race meetings. ❷ horse-racing ▷ *Ich interessiere mich nicht für Pferderennen.* I'm not interested in horse-racing.
Pferdeschwanz (gen **Pferdeschwanzes**, pl **Pferdeschwänze**) m ponytail

> Word for word, **Pferdeschwanz** means 'horse's tail'.

Pferdestall (pl **Pferdeställe**) m stable
Pfingsten (gen **Pfingsten**, pl **Pfingsten**) nt Whitsun ▷ *an Pfingsten* at Whitsun
Pfirsich (pl **Pfirsiche**) m peach
Pflanze f plant
pflanzen vb [36] to plant
pflanzlich adj plant-based
Pflaster (pl **Pflaster**) nt ❶ plaster ▷ *Sie klebte ein Pflaster auf die Wunde.* She put a plaster on the cut. ❷ paving stones pl ▷ *Jemand hatte das Pflaster in der Fußgängerzone bemalt.* Somebody had been painting on the paving stones in the pedestrian precinct.
Pflaume f plum
Pflege f ❶ care ▷ *Diese Pflanze braucht nicht viel Pflege.* This plant doesn't need much care. ▷ *ein Mittel zur Pflege von Leder* a leather-care product ❷ nursing ▷ *Ein krankes Baby braucht viel Pflege.* A sick baby needs a lot of care.; **ein Kind in Pflege geben** to have a child fostered
Pflegeeltern pl foster parents pl
pflegen vb [38] ❶ to nurse ▷ *Sie pflegt ihre kranke Mutter.* She's nursing her sick mother. ❷ to look after ▷ *Briten pflegen ihren Rasen.* The British look after their lawns.; **gepflegte Hände** well-cared-for hands; **gepflegt aussehen** to look well-groomed
Pfleger (pl **Pfleger**) m male nurse
Pflicht f duty ▷ *Es ist deine Pflicht, dich darum zu kümmern.* It's your duty to take care of it.
pflichtbewusst adj conscientious
Pflichtfach (pl **Pflichtfächer**) nt compulsory subject
pflücken vb [48] to pick ▷ *Wir haben Himbeeren gepflückt.* We picked raspberries. ▷ *einen Strauß pflücken* to pick a bunch of flowers
Pförtner (pl **Pförtner**) m doorman
Pfosten (pl **Pfosten**) m post ▷ *Der Ball traf den Pfosten.* The ball hit the post.
Pfote f paw ▷ *Der Hund hat schmutzige Pfoten.* The dog's paws are dirty.
pfui excl ugh!
Pfund (pl **Pfunde** or **Pfund**) nt pound ▷ *drei Pfund Äpfel* three pounds of apples ▷ *dreißig britische Pfund* thirty pounds sterling
pfuschen vb [38] (informal) to be sloppy; **Die Handwerker haben gepfuscht.** The craftsmen produced sloppy work.; **jemandem ins Handwerk pfuschen** to stick one's nose into somebody's business
Pfütze f puddle
Phantasie f see **Fantasie**
phantasieren vb see **fantasieren**
phantastisch adj see **fantastisch**

Philosophie f philosophy
Photo nt see **Foto**
Physik f physics ▷ *Physik ist mein Lieblingsfach.* Physics is my favourite subject.
Physiker (pl **Physiker**) m physicist
Pickel (pl **Pickel**) m ❶ pimple ▷ *Du hast einen Pickel auf der Nase.* You've got a pimple on your nose. ❷ pickaxe ▷ *Die Arbeiter haben die Straßenbelag mit Pickeln aufgeschlagen.* The workers broke up the road surface with pickaxes. ❸ ice axe ▷ *Die Bergsteiger hatten Seile und Pickel dabei.* The mountaineers had ropes and ice axes with them.
Picknick (pl **Picknicks**) nt picnic ▷ *Picknick machen* to have a picnic
Piepser (pl **Piepser**) m (informal) bleeper
Pik (pl **Pik**) nt spades sg ▷ *Pik ist Trumpf.* Spades is trumps.
pikant adj spicy
Pille f pill ▷ *Sie nimmt die Pille.* She's on the pill.
Pilot (gen **Piloten**, pl **Piloten**) m pilot
Pils (gen **Pils**, pl **Pils**) nt Pilsner lager
Pilz (gen **Pilzes**, pl **Pilze**) m ❶ mushroom ▷ *eine Soße mit Pilzen* a mushroom sauce ❷ toadstool ▷ *Der Fliegenpilz ist giftig.* The fly agaric is a toadstool.
pinkeln vb [88] (informal) to pee
Pinsel (pl **Pinsel**) m paintbrush
Pinzette f tweezers pl ▷ *eine Pinzette* a pair of tweezers
Pirat (gen **Piraten**, pl **Piraten**) m pirate
Piste f ❶ run ▷ *Wir sind die blaue Piste runtergefahren.* We skied down the blue run. ❷ runway ▷ *Das Flugzeug stand auf der Piste und wartete auf die Starterlaubnis.* The plane stood on the runway waiting for clearance for takeoff.
Pistole f pistol
Plakat (pl **Plakate**) nt poster

Plan (pl **Pläne**) m ❶ plan ▷ *Unser Plan war, vor ihm da zu sein.* Our plan was to arrive before him. ❷ map ▷ *Hast du einen Plan von München?* Have you got a map of Munich?
planen vb [38] to plan ▷ *Wir planen unseren nächsten Urlaub.* We're planning our next holiday.; **einen Mord planen** to plot a murder
Planet (gen **Planeten**, pl **Planeten**) m planet
planmäßig adj ❶ according to plan ▷ *Alles verlief planmäßig.* Everything went according to plan. ❷ scheduled ▷ *planmäßige Ankunft* scheduled arrival ❸ on time ▷ *Die Maschine ist planmäßig gelandet.* The plane landed on time.
Plastik nt plastic ▷ *Die meisten Spielzeuge sind heute aus Plastik.* Most toys these days are made of plastic.
▶ f sculpture
Plastikbeutel (pl **Plastikbeutel**) m plastic bag
Plastiktüte f plastic bag
platt adj flat ▷ *ein platter Reifen* a flat tyre ▷ *plattes Land* flat country; **etwas platt drücken** to flatten something; **Ich bin platt!** (informal) I'm flabbergasted!
plattdeutsch adj low German
Platte f ❶ plate ▷ *Sie stellte den Topf auf die Platte.* She put the saucepan on the plate.; **eine Platte mit Käseaufschnitt** a platter of assorted cheeses ❷ record ▷ *Sie hat alle Platten der Beatles.* She's got all the Beatles' records.
Plattenspieler (pl **Plattenspieler**) m record player
Platz (gen **Platzes**, pl **Plätze**) m ❶ place ▷ *Das ist ein schöner Platz zum Zelten.* That's a good place to pitch a tent. ▷ *Das Buch steht nicht an seinem Platz.* The book isn't in its place. ▷ *der erste Platz* the first place ❷ seat ▷ *Wir hatten Plätze in der ersten Reihe.* We had seats in the front row. ▷ *Ist hier noch ein Platz frei?*

Are all these seats taken?; **Platz nehmen** to take a seat ▷ *Das Sofa braucht zu viel Platz.* The sofa takes up too much room. ▷ *jemandem Platz machen* to make room for somebody ❹ square ▷ *Auf dem Platz vor der Kirche ist zweimal die Woche Markt.* There's a market twice a week on the square in front of the church. ❺ playing field; *Der Schiedsrichter schickte ihn vom Platz.* The referee sent him off.

Plätzchen (pl **Plätzchen**) nt ❶ spot ▷ *ein hübsches Plätzchen* a beautiful spot ❷ biscuit ▷ *Zum Kaffee gab es Plätzchen.* There were biscuits with the coffee.

platzen (perf **ist geplatzt**) vb [36] ❶ to burst ▷ *Der Luftballon ist geplatzt.* The balloon has burst. ❷ to explode ▷ *In der Innenstadt ist gestern eine Bombe geplatzt.* A bomb exploded in the town centre yesterday.; **vor Wut platzen** (informal) to be livid

Platzkarte f seat reservation
plaudern vb [88] to chat
pleite adj (informal) broke ▷ *Ich bin total pleite.* I'm stony-broke.
Pleite f ❶ bankruptcy ▷ *die Pleite einer Firma* the bankruptcy of a company; **Pleite machen** (informal) to go bust ❷ (informal) flop ▷ *Die Veranstaltung war eine Pleite.* The event was a flop.

Plombe f filling ▷ *Ich habe noch keine einzige Plombe.* I still haven't got a single filling.
plötzlich adj, adv ❶ sudden ▷ *ihr plötzliches Erscheinen* her sudden appearance ❷ suddenly ▷ *Sie war plötzlich weg.* Suddenly she was gone.
plump adj clumsy ▷ *plumpe Bewegungen* clumsy movements; *ein plumper Körper* a shapeless body; *eine plumpe Lüge* a blatant lie
Plural (pl **Plurale**) m plural
Plutonium nt plutonium
Po (pl **Pos**) m (informal) bum
Pokal (pl **Pokale**) m ❶ cup ▷ *Welche Mannschaft hat den Pokal gewonnen?* Which team won the cup? ❷ goblet ▷ *Sie tranken Wein aus Pokalen.* They drank wine out of goblets.

Pokalspiel (pl **Pokalspiele**) nt cup tie
Pol (pl **Pole**) m pole ▷ *am Pol* at the Pole
Pole (gen **Polen**, pl **Polen**) m Pole; **Er ist Pole.** He's Polish.
Polen nt Poland
Police f insurance policy
polieren (perf **hat poliert**) vb [76] to polish
Polin f Pole; **Sie ist Polin.** She's Polish.
Politik f ❶ politics sg ▷ *Politik interessiert mich nicht.* Politics doesn't interest me. ❷ policy ▷ *die Politik Großbritanniens in Bezug auf Immigration* Great Britain's policy on immigration
Politiker (pl **Politiker**) m politician
Politikerin f politician
politisch adj political
Polizei f police

> Note that **Polizei** is used with a singular verb and 'police' with a plural verb.

▷ *Die Polizei ist noch nicht da.* The police haven't arrived yet.
Polizeibeamte (gen **Polizeibeamten**, pl **Polizeibeamten**) m police officer ▷ *Wir wurden von einem Polizeibeamten angehalten.* We were stopped by a police officer.
Polizeibeamtin f police officer ▷ *Sie ist Polizeibeamtin.* She's a police officer.
polizeilich adj *Er wird polizeilich gesucht.* The police are looking for him.
Polizeirevier (pl **Polizeireviere**) nt police station
Polizeiwache f police station
Polizist (gen **Polizisten**, pl **Polizisten**) m policeman ▷ *Cenk ist Polizist.* Cenk's a policeman.
Polizistin f policewoman ▷ *Ursula ist Polizistin.* Ursula's a policewoman.
polnisch adj Polish

Pommes fpl chips ▷ *Pommes mit Mayonnaise* chips with mayonnaise
Pommes frites fpl chips pl ▷ *Würstchen mit Pommes frites* sausages and chips
Pony (pl **Ponys**) nt pony ▷ *Wir sind auf Ponys geritten.* We rode ponies.
▶ m fringe ▷ *Sie trägt einen Pony.* She's got a fringe.
Pop m pop
Popmusik f pop music
Pore f pore
Pornografie f pornography
porös adj porous
Porree (pl **Porrees**) m leek
Portemonnaie (pl **Portemonnaies**) nt purse
Portier (pl **Portiers**) m porter
Portion f portion ▷ *eine große Portion* a big portion ▷ *Zwei Portionen Pommes frites, bitte.* Two portions of chips, please.; *Dazu gehört eine ordentliche Portion Mut.* You need quite a bit of courage for that.
Portmonee (pl **Portmonees**) nt purse
Porto (pl **Portos**) nt postage
Portugal nt Portugal
Portugiese (gen **Portugiesen**, pl **Portugiesen**) m Portuguese
Portugiesin f Portuguese
portugiesisch adj Portuguese
Porzellan nt ❶ porcelain ▷ *eine Figur aus Porzellan* a porcelain figurine ❷ china ▷ *Das Porzellan habe ich von meiner Oma geerbt.* I inherited the china from my grandma.
positiv adj positive ▷ *HIV-positiv* HIV-positive
Post f ❶ post office ▷ *Bring bitte das Päckchen zur Post.* Please take the parcel to the post office. ❷ mail ▷ *Ist Post für mich gekommen?* Was there any mail for me?
Postamt (pl **Postämter**) nt post office
Postausgang (pl **Postausgänge**) m outbox

Postbote (gen **Postboten**, pl **Postboten**) m postman
Postbotin f postwoman
Posteingang (pl **Posteingänge**) m inbox
Posten (pl **Posten**) m ❶ post ▷ *Sie hat einen guten Posten als Psychologin.* She's got a good post as a psychologist. ❷ sentry ▷ *Die Armee hat vor dem Gebäude Posten aufgestellt.* The army posted sentries in front of the building. ❸ item ▷ *Dieser Posten ist nicht auf der Preisliste aufgeführt.* This item doesn't appear on the price list.
Postfach (pl **Postfächer**) nt post office box
Postkarte f postcard
Postleitzahl f postcode
Pracht f splendour
prächtig adj, adv ❶ magnificent ▷ *ein prächtiges Haus* a magnificent house ❷ marvellous ▷ *Wir haben uns prächtig amüsiert.* We had a marvellous time.
prachtvoll adj splendid
Prädikat (pl **Prädikate**) nt predicate ▷ *Subjekt und Prädikat eines Satzes* subject and predicate of a sentence
prahlen vb [38] to brag
Praktikant (gen **Praktikanten**, pl **Praktikanten**) m trainee
Praktikantin f trainee
Praktikum (gen **Praktikums**, pl **Praktika**) nt practical training ▷ *Sie absolviert ihr Praktikum.* She's doing her practical training.
praktisch adj ❶ practical ▷ *ein praktischer Mensch* a practical person ▷ *eine praktische Lösung* a practical solution ▷ *praktische Erfahrung* practical experience ❷ handy ▷ *ein praktisches Gerät* a handy gadget; **praktischer Arzt** general practitioner; **praktisch begabt sein** to be good with one's hands
Praline f chocolate

Präposition f preposition
Präsens (gen **Präsens**) nt present tense
Präsident (gen **Präsidenten**, pl **Präsidenten**) m president
Präsidentin f president
Praxis (pl **Praxen**) f ① practical experience ▷ *Ihr fehlt die Praxis.* She lacks practical experience.; **etwas in die Praxis umsetzen** to put something into practice ② surgery ▷ *Kommen Sie zur Behandlung in die Praxis.* Come to the surgery for treatment. ③ practice ▷ *Mein Anwalt hat seine eigene Praxis aufgemacht.* My solicitor has opened his own practice.
Preis (gen **Preises**, pl **Preise**) m ① price ▷ *Die Preise für Computer sind gefallen.* Computer prices have fallen. ② prize ▷ *Ihr Hund hat einen Preis gewonnen.* Her dog's won a prize.; **um keinen Preis** not at any price
preisgünstig adj inexpensive
Preislage f price range
Preisschild (pl **Preisschilder**) nt price tag
Preisträger (pl **Preisträger**) m prizewinner
preiswert adj inexpensive
Prellung f bruise
Premierminister (pl **Premierminister**) m prime minister
Presse f press
pressen vb [31] to press
Priester (pl **Priester**) m priest
prima adj super ▷ *Es ist ein prima Hotel.* It's a super hotel.
Prinz (gen **Prinzen**, pl **Prinzen**) m prince
Prinzessin f princess
Prinzip (pl **Prinzipien**) nt principle; **aus Prinzip** as a matter of principle
privat adj private
Privatschule f fee-paying school
pro prep

The preposition **pro** takes the accusative.

per ▷ *zehn Euro pro Person* ten euros per person; **einmal pro Woche** once a week
Probe f ① test ▷ *Wir haben in Englisch morgen eine Probe.* We've got an English test tomorrow. ② sample ▷ *Die Probe wird im Labor untersucht.* The sample's being examined in the laboratory. ③ rehearsal ▷ *die letzte Probe vor der Aufführung* the final rehearsal before the performance; **jemanden auf die Probe stellen** to test somebody
probieren (perf **hat probiert**) vb [76] ① to try ▷ *Probier mal eine andere Methode.* Try a different method. ▷ *Willst du mal von dem Käse probieren?* Would you like to try some of the cheese? ② to taste ▷ *Ich werde probieren, ob ich das kann.* I'll give it a try.
Problem (pl **Probleme**) nt problem ▷ *Kein Problem!* No problem.
Produkt (pl **Produkte**) nt product
Produktion f ① production ▷ *die Produktion von Luxusautos* the production of luxury cars ② output ▷ *Wir müssen unsere Produktion erhöhen.* We must increase our output.
produzieren (perf **hat produziert**) vb [76] to produce
Professor (pl **Professoren**) m professor
Profi (pl **Profis**) m (informal) pro ▷ *Er spielt wie ein Profi.* He plays like a pro.
Profit (pl **Profite**) m profit
profitieren (perf **hat profitiert**) vb [76] to profit
Programm (pl **Programme**) nt ① programme ▷ *das Programm des heutigen Abends* this evening's programme ② program ▷ *Für die Kalkulation arbeite ich mit einem anderen Programm.* I've got a different program for spreadsheets.
programmieren (perf **hat programmiert**) vb [76] to program
Programmierer (pl **Programmierer**) m programmer

Projekt (pl **Projekte**) nt project
Promi mf celebrity
Promille (pl **Promille**) nt alcohol level ▷ *Er hatte drei Promille.* He had an alcohol level of three hundred milligrams in a hundred millilitres of blood.
Pronomen (pl **Pronomen**) nt pronoun
Prospekt (pl **Prospekte**) m brochure

> Be careful! **Prospekt** does not mean prospect.

prost excl cheers!
Prostituierte (gen **Prostituierten**) f prostitute
Prostitution f prostitution
Protest (pl **Proteste**) m protest
protestantisch adj Protestant
protestieren (perf **hat protestiert**) vb [76] to protest ▷ *Wir protestieren gegen diese Maßnahmen.* We're protesting against these measures.
Protokoll (pl **Protokolle**) nt ❶ minutes pl ▷ *Wer schreibt das Protokoll der heutigen Besprechung?* Who is taking the minutes of today's meeting? ❷ statement ▷ *Bitte unterschreiben Sie das Protokoll.* Please sign the statement.
Proviant (pl **Proviante**) m provisions pl
provisorisch adj provisional
provozieren (perf **hat provoziert**) vb [76] to provoke
Prozent (pl **Prozente**) nt per cent ▷ *zehn Prozent* ten per cent
Prozess (gen **Prozesses**, pl **Prozesse**) m trial ▷ *der Prozess gegen die Terroristen* the trial of the terrorists; **einen Prozess gewinnen** to win a case
prüfen vb [38] ❶ to test ▷ *Wir werden morgen in Chemie geprüft.* We're having a chemistry test tomorrow. ❷ to check ▷ *Vor der Reise sollte man den Ölstand prüfen.* You should check the oil before your journey.
Prüfer (pl **Prüfer**) m examiner
Prüfung f ❶ examination ▷ *Sie hat die Prüfung bestanden.* She's passed the examination. ❷ check ▷ *Bei der Prüfung der Bremsen haben wir einen Defekt festgestellt.* During a check of the brakes we found a fault.
Prügel (pl **Prügel**) m stick ▷ *Er schlug ihn mit einem Prügel.* He hit him with a stick.; **Prügel bekommen** (informal) to get a hiding; **Er hat von seinen Freunden Prügel bekommen.** His friends beat him up.
prügeln vb [34] to beat ▷ *Eltern sollten ihre Kinder nicht prügeln.* Parents shouldn't beat their children.; **sich prügeln** to fight; **Die beiden haben sich in der Pause geprügelt.** The two of them had a fight in the break.
psychisch adj psychological
Psychologe (gen **Psychologen**, pl **Psychologen**) m psychologist ▷ *Ihr Vater ist Psychologe.* Her father is a psychologist.
Psychologie f psychology
psychologisch adj psychological
Pubertät f puberty ▷ *während der Pubertät* during puberty
Publikum nt audience ▷ *Am Ende des Stückes klatschte das Publikum.* The audience clapped at the end of the play.
Pudding (pl **Puddinge** or **Puddings**) m blancmange
Puder (pl **Puder**) m powder
Pullover (pl **Pullover**) m pullover
Puls (gen **Pulses**, pl **Pulse**) m pulse; **jemandem den Puls fühlen** to take somebody's pulse
Pult (pl **Pulte**) nt desk
Pulver (pl **Pulver**) nt powder
Pumpe f pump
pumpen vb [38] ❶ to pump ▷ *Das Öl wird durch die Pipeline gepumpt.* The oil's pumped along the pipeline. ❷ to lend ▷ *Kannst du mir mal dein iPad® pumpen?* Can you lend me your iPad®? ❸ to borrow ▷ *Ich habe mir das Rad meiner*

Schwester gepumpt. I've borrowed my sister's bike.

Punkt (*pl* **Punkte**) *m* ❶ full stop ▷ *Am Satzende steht ein Punkt.* A full stop goes at the end of a sentence. ❷ point ▷ *In diesem Punkt gebe ich dir recht.* On this point I agree with you. ❸ dot ▷ *Sie trug ein rotes Kleid mit weißen Punkten.* She was wearing a red dress with white dots.

pünktlich *adj, adv* ❶ punctual ▷ *Sie ist nicht sehr pünktlich.* She's not very punctual. ❷ on time ▷ *Der Zug kam pünktlich an.* The train arrived on time.

Puppe *f* doll

pur *adj* pure ▷ *Das ist pures Gold.* That's pure gold. ▷ *Das ist doch der pure Wahnsinn.* But that's pure madness.; **etwas pur trinken** to drink something neat; **Whisky pur** neat whisky

Pute *f* turkey

Puter (*pl* **Puter**) *m* turkey

putzen *vb* [36] ❶ to clean ▷ *Sie putzt jeden Samstag das Haus.* She cleans the house every Saturday. ❷ to wipe ▷ *Putz dir die Schuhe, bevor du reinkommst.* Wipe your shoes before you come in.; **sich die Nase putzen** to blow one's nose; **sich die Zähne putzen** to brush one's teeth

Putzfrau *f* cleaner

Putzmann (*pl* **Putzmänner**) *m* cleaner

Pyramide *f* pyramid

q

Quadrat (*pl* **Quadrate**) *nt* square

Quadratmeter (*pl* **Quadratmeter**) *m* square metre ▷ *eine Wohnung von achtzig Quadratmetern* a flat of eighty square metres

Qual *f* ❶ agony ▷ *Treppensteigen ist für sie eine Qual.* Climbing the stairs is agony for her. ❷ anguish ▷ *Die Qualen, die ich bei dieser Prüfung ausgestanden habe ...* The anguish I went through in that exam ...

quälen *vb* [38] to treat cruelly ▷ *Tiere quälen* to treat animals cruelly; **sich quälen (1)** to struggle ▷ *Sie quälte sich die Treppe hinauf.* She struggled up the steps. **(2)** to torment oneself ▷ *Quäl dich nicht so!* Don't torment yourself like that.; **Er muss sich in der Schule ziemlich quälen.** School's quite a trial for him.

Qualität *f* quality

Qualle *f* jellyfish ▷ *zwei Quallen* two jellyfish

Qualm *m* thick smoke

qualmen vb [**38**] to smoke ▷ *Der Schornstein qualmt.* The chimney is smoking.
Quark m quark
Quarz (gen **Quarzes**) m quartz
Quatsch m (informal) rubbish ▷ *Erzähl keinen Quatsch.* Don't talk rubbish.; **Quatsch machen** to fool around; **Mach keinen Quatsch!** Don't be foolish!
quatschen vb [**48**] (informal) to natter
Quelle f ❶ spring ▷ *heiße Quellen* hot springs ❷ source ▷ *aus zuverlässiger Quelle* from a reliable source
quer adv ❶ diagonally ▷ *Die Streifen auf dem Stoff verlaufen quer.* The stripes run diagonally across the material.; **quer auf dem Bett** across the bed ❷ at right angles ▷ *Die Mannstraße verläuft quer zur Müllerstraße.* Mann Street runs at right angles to Müller Street.
Querflöte f flute ▷ *Cordula spielt Querflöte.* Cordula plays the flute.
querschnittsgelähmt adj paraplegic
Querstraße f eine Straße mit vielen Querstraßen a road with a lot of side streets off it; **Biegen Sie an der zweiten Querstraße links ab.** Take the second street on the left.
quetschen vb [**48**] ❶ to squash ▷ *Pass auf, dass die Tomaten nicht gequetscht werden.* Mind the tomatoes don't get squashed. ❷ to cram ▷ *Sie quetschte das Kleid noch in ihren Koffer.* She crammed the dress into her case.; **Ich habe mir den Finger in der Tür gequetscht.** I trapped my finger in the door.
Quetschung f bruise
quitt adj quits ▷ *Jetzt sind wir quitt.* We're quits now.
Quittung f receipt ▷ *Brauchen Sie eine Quittung?* Do you need a receipt?

Rabatt (pl **Rabatte**) m discount
Rache f revenge
Rad (pl **Räder**) nt ❶ wheel ❷ bike ▷ *Wir sind mit dem Rad gekommen.* We came by bike.; **Rad fahren** to cycle
Radarkontrolle f radar-controlled speed check
radfahren vb [**21**] see **Rad**
Radfahrer (pl **Radfahrer**) m cyclist
Radfahrweg (pl **Radfahrwege**) m cycle track
Radiergummi (pl **Radiergummis**) m rubber
Radieschen (pl **Radieschen**) nt radish
Radio (pl **Radios**) nt radio
radioaktiv adj radioactive
Radioaktivität f radioactivity
Radrennen (pl **Radrennen**) nt ❶ cycle race ▷ *Er hat an dem Radrennen teilgenommen.* He took part in the cycle race. ❷ cycle racing ▷ *Sie begeistert sich für Radrennen.* She's a cycle racing fan.
Rahm m cream

Rahmen (pl **Rahmen**) m frame ▷ *der Rahmen eines Bildes* the frame of a picture; **im Rahmen des Möglichen** within the bounds of possibility

Rakete f rocket

Rand (pl **Ränder**) m ❶ edge ▷ *Er stand am Rand des Schwimmbeckens.* He stood on the edge of the swimming pool. ❷ rim ▷ *der Rand der Tasse* the rim of the cup; **eine Brille mit Goldrand** a pair of gold-rimmed glasses ❸ margin ▷ *Lass an der Seite des Blattes einen Rand.* Leave a margin at the edge of the page. ❹ ring ▷ *In der Badewanne waren dunkle Ränder.* There were dark rings in the bath tub. ❺ verge ▷ *Die Firma steht am Rand des Bankrotts.* The company's on the verge of bankruptcy.; **außer Rand und Band** out of control

Rang (pl **Ränge**) m ❶ rank (military) ▷ *Sie steht im Rang eines Hauptmanns.* She has the rank of captain. ❷ circle (theatre) ▷ *erster Rang* dress circle ▷ *zweiter Rang* upper circle

Rappen (pl **Rappen**) m rappen ▷ *Der Schweizer Franken hat hundert Rappen.* There're one hundred rappen in a Swiss franc.

* In the French-speaking part of Switzerland you talk about **centime** rather than **Rappen**.

rasch adj, adv quick ▷ *Das war rasch gemacht.* That was quickly done.; **Ich gehe noch rasch beim Bäcker vorbei.** I'll just pop round to the baker's.

rasen (perf **ist gerast**) vb [**88**] to race ▷ *Wir sind durch die engen Straßen gerast.* We raced along the narrow streets.

Rasen (pl **Rasen**) m lawn

Rasenmäher (pl **Rasenmäher**) m lawnmower

Rasierapparat (pl **Rasierapparate**) m shaver

Rasiercreme (pl **Rasiercremes**) f shaving cream

rasieren (perf **hat rasiert**) vb [**76**] to shave; **sich rasieren** to shave

Rasiermesser (pl **Rasiermesser**) nt razor

Rasse f ❶ (often offensive) race ▷ *Rassenunruhen* race riots ❷ breed ▷ *Welche Rasse ist Ihr Hund?* What breed is your dog?

Rassismus (gen **Rassismus**) m racism

Rast f rest; **Rast machen** to stop for a break

rasten vb [**2**] to rest

Rasthof (pl **Rasthöfe**) m services pl (motorway)

Raststätte f service area

Rasur f shaving

Rat (pl **Ratschläge**) m advice ▷ *Ich habe viele Ratschläge bekommen.* I've been given a lot of advice.; **ein Rat** a piece of advice; **Ich weiß keinen Rat.** I don't know what to do.; **jemanden zu Rate ziehen** to consult somebody

Rate f instalment

raten (pres **rät**, imperf **riet**, perf **hat geraten**) vb to guess ▷ *Rat mal, wie alt ich bin.* Guess how old I am.; **jemandem raten** to advise somebody

Rathaus (gen **Rathauses**, pl **Rathäuser**) nt town hall

rationalisieren (perf **hat rationalisiert**) vb [**76**] to rationalize

ratlos adj at a loss ▷ *Ich bin ratlos, was ich tun soll.* I'm at a loss as to what to do.; **Sie sah mich ratlos an.** She gave me a helpless look.

Ratschlag (pl **Ratschläge**) m piece of advice ▷ *Ich habe viele Ratschläge bekommen.* I've been given a lot of advice.

Rätsel (pl **Rätsel**) nt ❶ puzzle ▷ *Sie löst gern Rätsel.* She likes solving puzzles. ❷ mystery ▷ *Das ist mir ein Rätsel.* It's a mystery to me.

rätselhaft adj mysterious; **Es ist mir rätselhaft ...** It's a mystery to me ...

Ratte f rat

rau adj ❶ rough ▷ *raue Haut* rough skin ❷ husky ▷ *eine raue Stimme* a husky voice ❸ sore ▷ *ein rauer Hals* a sore throat ❹ harsh ▷ *raues Wetter* harsh weather ▷ *ein rauer Wind* a harsh wind; **Hier herrschen raue Sitten.** People here have rough-and-ready ways.

Raub m robbery

Raubtier (pl **Raubtiere**) nt predator

Rauch m smoke

rauchen vb [48] to smoke ▷ *Er raucht Pfeife.* He smokes a pipe.; **'Rauchen verboten'** 'No smoking'

Raucher (pl **Raucher**) m smoker

räuchern vb [88] to smoke ▷ *Fisch räuchern* to smoke fish

rauh adj see **rau**

Raum (pl **Räume**) m ❶ space ▷ *Sie haben eine Rakete in den Raum geschossen.* They launched a rocket into space. ▷ *Raum und Zeit* space and time ❷ room ▷ *Eine Wohnung mit vier Räumen ist nicht groß genug für uns.* A four-roomed flat isn't big enough for us. ▷ *Dieses Gerät braucht wenig Raum.* This appliance doesn't take up much room. ❸ area ▷ *Im Raum Stuttgart kommt es morgen zu Gewittern.* There will be thunderstorms in the Stuttgart area tomorrow.

räumen vb [38] ❶ to clear ▷ *Die Polizei hat das besetzte Haus geräumt.* The police cleared the squat. ❷ to vacate ▷ *Bitte räumen Sie Ihr Zimmer bis spätestens zehn Uhr.* Please vacate your room by ten o'clock at the latest. ❸ to clear away ▷ *Könnt ihr bitte das Geschirr vom Tisch räumen?* Could you clear away the dishes, please? ❹ to put away ▷ *Räum bitte deine Spielsachen in den Schrank.* Please put your toys away in the cupboard.

Raumfähre f space shuttle

Raumfahrt f space travel

räumlich adj spatial

Raumschiff (pl **Raumschiffe**) nt spaceship

Rausch (pl **Räusche**) m **einen Rausch haben** to be drunk; **seinen Rausch ausschlafen** to sleep it off

Rauschgift (pl **Rauschgifte**) nt drug

Rauschgiftsüchtige (gen **Rauschgiftsüchtigen**, pl **Rauschgiftsüchtigen**) mf drug addict

sich **räuspern** vb [88] to clear one's throat

reagieren (perf **hat reagiert**) vb [76] ❶ to react ▷ *Wie hat sie auf diesen Vorwurf reagiert?* How did she react to the allegation? ❷ to respond ▷ *Die Bremsen haben nicht reagiert.* The brakes didn't respond.

Reaktion f reaction

Reaktor (pl **Reaktoren**) m reactor

realisieren (perf **hat realisiert**) vb [76] ❶ to fulfil ▷ *Sie hat ihre Träume realisiert.* She's fulfilled her dreams. ❷ to carry out ▷ *Wir sollten diese Pläne realisieren.* We ought to carry out these plans. ❸ to realize ▷ *Sie hat gar nicht realisiert, dass er schon längst weg war.* She simply didn't realize that he had long since left.

realistisch adj realistic

Realityshow f reality show

Realschule f secondary school
- Pupils enter **Realschule** at the age of
- about ten, and leave after six years. It
- is not as academically oriented as the
- **Gymnasium**.

rechnen vb [53] to work out ▷ *Lass mich rechnen, wie viel das wird.* Let me work out how much that's going to be.; **gut rechnen können** to be good at arithmetic; **Özil wird zu den besten Fußballspielern gerechnet.** Özil is regarded as one of the best footballers.; **rechnen zu** to class as; **rechnen mit (1)** to reckon with ▷ *Mit wie vielen Besuchern können wir rechnen?* How many visitors can we reckon with? **(2)** to reckon on ▷ *Mit dieser Reaktion hatte ich nicht gerechnet.* I hadn't reckoned on this reaction.; **rechnen auf** to count on

Rechnen nt arithmetic ▷ *Bettina ist gut im Rechnen.* Bettina's good at arithmetic.

Rechner (pl **Rechner**) m ❶ calculator ▷ *Ich habe das mit meinem Rechner nachgerechnet.* I've checked it with my calculator. ❷ computer ▷ *Er hat sich für seinen Rechner einen neuen Prozessor gekauft.* He's bought a new CPU for his computer.

Rechnung f ❶ calculations pl ▷ *Meine Rechnung ergibt, dass wir noch zweihundert Euro haben.* According to my calculations, we still have two hundred euros left. ❷ invoice ▷ *Die Rechnung liegt der Sendung bei.* The invoice is enclosed.

recht adj, adv ❶ right ▷ *Es war nicht recht, dass du sie belogen hast.* It wasn't right of you to lie to her. ▷ *Dies ist nicht der rechte Moment, um darüber zu sprechen.* This isn't the right moment to talk about it.; **Wenn ich dich recht verstehe ...** If I understand you correctly ...; **Das geschieht dir recht!** Serves you right! ❷ quite ▷ *Das scheint nicht recht einfach.* It seems quite simple.; **jemandem recht sein** to be all right with somebody; **Das ist mir recht.** That suits me.; **es jemandem recht machen** to please somebody; **recht haben** to be right; **jemandem recht geben** to agree with somebody; **Jetzt erst recht!** Now more than ever.

Recht (pl **Rechte**) nt ❶ right ▷ *Es ist mein Recht, das zu erfahren.* It's my right to know that. ▷ *Ich habe ein Recht auf eine Erklärung.* I've got a right to an explanation.; **im Recht sein** to be in the right; **etwas mit Recht tun** to be right to do something ❷ law ▷ *Sie wurde nach deutschem Recht zu zehn Jahren Gefängnis verurteilt.* She was sentenced under German law to ten years' imprisonment.; **Recht sprechen** to administer justice

rechte adj right ▷ *In Deutschland fährt man auf der rechten Seite.* They drive on the right in Germany. ▷ *Mein rechtes Auge tut weh.* My right eye's hurting. ▷ *Er hat sich den rechten Arm gebrochen.* He broke his right arm.

Rechte (gen **Rechten**) f ❶ right ▷ *Zu Ihrer Rechten sehen Sie das Rathaus.* On your right you'll see the town hall. ❷ right hand ▷ *Er schlug mit der Rechten zu.* He hit out with his right hand. ❸ right-wing ▷ *eine Partei der Rechten* a right-wing party
▶ nt right thing ▷ *Pass auf, dass du das Rechte sagst.* Make sure you say the right thing.

rechteckig adj rectangular

rechtfertigen vb [38] to justify ▷ *Wie kannst du dein Verhalten rechtfertigen?* How can you justify your behaviour?; **sich rechtfertigen** to justify oneself

rechtmäßig adj lawful

rechts adv right ▷ **rechts abbiegen** to turn right; **rechts überholen** to overtake on the right; **Er schreibt mit rechts.** He writes with his right hand.; **Rechts sehen Sie das Rathaus.** On the right you'll see the town hall.; **rechts von der Kirche** to the right of the church; **rechts von mir** on my right; **rechts wählen** to vote for a right-wing party

Rechtsanwalt (pl **Rechtsanwälte**) m lawyer

Rechtsanwältin f lawyer

Rechtschreibung f spelling

Rechtshänder (pl **Rechtshänder**) m **Er ist Rechtshänder.** He's right-handed.

Rechtshänderin f Sie ist Rechtshänderin. She's right-handed.
rechtzeitig adj, adv in time ▷ Ich bitte um rechtzeitige Benachrichtigung. Please let me know in time. ▷ Wir sind rechtzeitig angekommen. We arrived in time.
recyceln (perf **hat recycelt**) vb [**7**] to recycle
Recycling nt recycling
Redakteur (pl **Redakteure**) m editor
Redaktion f ❶ editorial staff ▷ Die Redaktion hat das Manuskript abgelehnt. The editorial staff rejected the manuscript. ❷ editorial office ▷ Er arbeitet in unserer Redaktion. He works in our editorial office.
Rede f speech ▷ Er hat eine witzige Rede gehalten. He made an amusing speech.; **jemanden zur Rede stellen** to take somebody to task
reden vb [**54**] ❶ to talk ▷ Wir haben über das Wetter geredet. We talked about the weather. ▷ Du redest Unsinn. You're talking nonsense. ❷ to speak ▷ Ich werde mit deiner Mutter reden. I'll speak to your mother. ▷ Ich rede nicht gern vor so vielen Menschen. I don't like speaking in front of so many people. ❸ to say ▷ Was reden die Leute über uns? What are people saying about us?
Redewendung f expression
Redner (pl **Redner**) m speaker
reduzieren (perf **hat reduziert**) vb [**76**] to reduce
Referat (pl **Referate**) nt ❶ assignment ▷ Ich muss in Geografie ein Referat schreiben. I have to write an assignment in geography. ❷ paper ▷ Sie hat ein Referat über Shakespeare gehalten. She gave a paper on Shakespeare. ❸ section ▷ Er ist Leiter des Referats Umweltschutz. He's head of the environmental protection section.
reflexiv adj reflexive

Reform f reform
Regal (pl **Regale**) nt ❶ bookcase ▷ In ihrem Regal stehen viele Krimis. There are a lot of detective stories in her bookcase. ❷ rack ▷ ein Regal für Weinflaschen a wine rack ❸ shelf ▷ Auf dem Regal standen Kräuter. There were herbs on the shelf.
Regel f ❶ rule ▷ Keine Regel ohne Ausnahme. The exception proves the rule. ❷ period ▷ Meine Regel ist ausgeblieben. I've missed a period.
regelmäßig adj, adv regular ▷ in regelmäßigen Abständen at regular intervals ▷ Die Busse verkehren regelmäßig. The buses run regularly.
Regelmäßigkeit f regularity
regeln vb [**34**] ❶ to direct ▷ Ein Polizist regelte den Verkehr. A police officer was directing the traffic. ❷ to control ▷ die Lautstärke regeln to control the volume ❸ to settle ▷ Ich habe da noch eine Sache mit ihm zu regeln. I've still got something to settle with him. ❹ to arrange ▷ Wir haben das so geregelt, dass er abwäscht und ich putze. We've arranged things so that he washes the dishes and I do the cleaning.; **sich von selbst regeln** to take care of itself
Regen (pl **Regen**) m rain
Regenbogen (pl **Regenbogen**) m rainbow
Regenmantel (pl **Regenmäntel**) m raincoat
Regenschauer (pl **Regenschauer**) m shower
Regenschirm (pl **Regenschirme**) m umbrella
regieren (perf **hat regiert**) vb [**76**] ❶ to govern ▷ Wer regiert zurzeit Russland? Who governs Russia nowadays? ❷ to reign ▷ Wann hat Elisabeth die Erste regiert? When did Elizabeth the First reign?
Regierung f ❶ government ▷ die deutsche Regierung the German

government ❷ reign ▷ *England unter der Regierung von Elisabeth der Zweiten* England during the reign of Elisabeth the Second

Region f region

regnen vb [53] to rain ▷ *Es regnet.* It's raining.

regnerisch adj rainy

Reh (pl **Rehe**) nt deer

reiben (imperf **rieb**, perf **hat gerieben**) vb ❶ to rub ▷ *Warum reibst du dir die Augen?* Why are you rubbing your eyes? ❷ to grate ▷ *Er rieb Käse über die Kartoffeln.* He grated cheese over the potatoes.

Reibung f friction

reich adj rich; **die Reichen** the rich

reichen vb [48] ❶ to be enough ▷ *Der Kuchen wird nicht für alle reichen.* There won't be enough cake for everybody. ❷ to give ▷ *Sie reichte mir die Hand.* She gave me her hand.; **jemandem etwas reichen** to pass somebody something; **Nur ein Salat reicht ihm nicht.** A salad won't be enough for him.; **Mir reicht's!** I've had enough.

reif adj ❶ ripe ▷ *Die Äpfel sind noch nicht reif.* The apples aren't ripe yet. ❷ mature ▷ *Für sein Alter ist er schon sehr reif.* He's very mature for his age.

Reifen (pl **Reifen**) m ❶ tyre ▷ *Mir ist ein Reifen geplatzt.* I've got a burst tyre. ❷ hoop ▷ *ein Hula-Hoop-Reifen* a hula hoop

Reifenpanne f puncture

Reihe f row ▷ *Stellt euch in einer Reihe auf.* Stand in a row. ▷ *Wir saßen in der zweiten Reihe.* We sat in the second row.; **der Reihe nach** in turn; **Er ist an der Reihe.** It's his turn.; **an die Reihe kommen** to have one's turn

Reihenfolge f order ▷ *alphabetische Reihenfolge* alphabetical order

Reihenhaus (gen **Reihenhauses**, pl **Reihenhäuser**) nt terraced house

rein adj, adv ❶ pure ▷ *Das ist reines Gold.* That's pure gold. ▷ *reine Seide* pure silk ❷ clean ▷ *Damit wird die Wäsche rein.* This will get the washing clean. ▷ *reine Luft* clean air ▷ *reine Haut* clear skin ❸ sheer ▷ *Das ist der reine Wahnsinn.* That's sheer madness. ▷ *Das ist das reinste Vergnügen.* It's sheer pleasure. ❹ purely ▷ *Rein technisch ist das machbar.* From a purely technical point of view it's feasible.; **rein gar nichts** absolutely nothing; **etwas ins Reine schreiben** to make a fair copy of something; **etwas ins Reine bringen** to clear something up ❺ in ▷ *Deckel auf und rein mit dem Müll.* Off with the lid and in with the rubbish. ▷ *Los rein mit dir, Zeit fürs Bett!* Come on, in you come, it's time for bed.

Reinheit f purity ▷ *die Reinheit des Biers* the purity of beer; **für die Reinheit Ihrer Wäsche ...** To get your washing really clean ...

reinigen vb [38] to clean

Reinigung f ❶ cleaning ▷ *ein Mittel zur Reinigung der Polster* an cleaning agent for upholstery ❷ cleaner's sg ▷ *Bring bitte meine Hose in die Reinigung.* Please take my trousers to the cleaner's.; **chemische Reinigung (1)** dry cleaning ▷ *Bei diesem Stoff empfehlen wir eine chemische Reinigung.* We recommend dry cleaning for this material. **(2)** dry cleaner's ▷ *Im Einkaufszentrum gibt es auch eine chemische Reinigung.* There's also a dry cleaner's in the shopping mall.

Reis (pl **Reise**) m rice

Reise f journey ▷ *Auf meiner letzten Reise durch Ägypten habe ich viel gesehen.* I saw a lot on my last journey through Egypt.; **Reisen** travels; **Gute Reise!** Have a good journey.

Reiseandenken (pl **Reiseandenken**) nt souvenir

Reisebüros (pl **Reisebüros**) nt travel agency

Reiseführer (*pl* **Reiseführer**) *m*
① guidebook ▷ *Ich habe einen Reiseführer für Griechenland gekauft.* I've bought a guidebook to Greece. ② travel guide ▷ *Unser Reiseführer hat uns alles erklärt.* Our travel guide explained everything to us.

Reiseleiter (*pl* **Reiseleiter**) *m* courier

reisen (*perf* **ist gereist**) *vb* [36] to travel ▷ *Ich reise gern.* I like travelling.; **reisen nach** to go to

Reisende (*gen* **Reisenden**, *pl* **Reisenden**) *mf* traveller ▷ *Ein Reisender hat sich verirrt.* A traveller has got lost.

Reisepass (*gen* **Reisepasses**, *pl* **Reisepässe**) *m* passport

Reiseziel (*pl* **Reiseziele**) *nt* destination

reißen (*imperf* **riss**, *perf* **hat/ist gerissen**) *vb*

> Use **haben** to form the perfect tense. Use **sein** to form the perfect tense for 'to break'.

① to tear ▷ *Er riss ihren Brief in tausend Stücke.* He tore her letter into a thousand pieces. ▷ *Sie riss sich die Kleider vom Leib.* She tore her clothes off. ② to break ▷ *Das Seil ist gerissen.* The rope has broken. ③ to snatch ▷ *Er hat mir den Geldbeutel aus der Hand gerissen.* He snatched my purse from my hand. ④ to drag ▷ *Sie hat ihn zu Boden gerissen.* She dragged him to the floor. ⑤ to wrench ▷ *Er riss das Steuer nach links.* He wrenched the steering wheel to the left. ⑥ to tug ▷ *Er riss an der Leine.* He tugged at the rope.; **Witze reißen** to crack jokes; **etwas an sich reißen** to seize something; **sich um etwas reißen** to scramble for something

Reißverschluss (*gen* **Reißverschlusses**, *pl* **Reißverschlüsse**) *m* zip

reiten (*imperf* **ritt**, *perf* **ist geritten**) *vb* to ride

Reiter (*pl* **Reiter**) *m* rider

Reiz (*gen* **Reizes**, *pl* **Reize**) *m* ① charm ▷ *der Reiz dieser Stadt* the charm of this town ② appeal ▷ *der Reiz der Großstadt* the appeal of the big city

reizen *vb* [36] ① to appeal to ▷ *Diese Arbeit reizt mich sehr.* The work greatly appeals to me. ▷ *Es würde mich reizen, mal nach Kreta zu fahren.* The idea of going to Crete appeals to me. ② to annoy ▷ *Du musst den Hund nicht reizen.* Don't annoy the dog. ③ to irritate ▷ *Der Rauch reizt die Augen.* Smoke irritates the eyes.

reizend *adj* charming

reizvoll *adj* attractive

Reklame *f* ① advertising ▷ *Im Fernsehen gibt es viel zu viel Reklame.* There's far too much advertising on television. ② advertisement ▷ *zehn Seiten Reklame* ten pages of advertisements

Rekord (*pl* **Rekorde**) *m* record ▷ *Der Rekord liegt bei zehn Metern.* The record is ten metres. ▷ *einen neuen Rekord aufstellen* to set a new record

Rektor (*pl* **Rektoren**) *m* ① head teacher ▷ *Der Rektor ist bei uns für die Stundenpläne zuständig.* At our school, the head teacher's in charge of timetables. ② vice-chancellor ▷ *Zu Semesterbeginn hält der Rektor eine Rede.* At the beginning of term the vice-chancellor gives a speech.

relativ *adv* relatively ▷ *Das ist relativ einfach.* That's relatively easy.

relaxt *adj* relaxed

Religion *f* religion

religiös *adj* religious

Rendezvous (*gen* **Rendezvous**, *pl* **Rendezvous**) *nt* date ▷ *Sie hatte gestern Abend ein Rendezvous mit Michael.* She had a date with Michael last night.

rennen (*imperf* **rannte**, *perf* **ist gerannt**) *vb* [55] to run

Rennen (*pl* **Rennen**) *nt* race ▷ *ein Pferderennen* a horse race ▷ *ein Autorennen* a motor race

Rennfahrer (pl **Rennfahrer**) m racing driver

Rennwagen (pl **Rennwagen**) m racing car

renovieren (perf **hat renoviert**) vb [76] to renovate

rentabel adj ① lucrative ▷ *eine rentable Arbeit* a lucrative job ② profitable ▷ *Das wäre nicht rentabel.* That wouldn't be profitable.

Rente f pension; **in Rente gehen** to retire

> Be careful! **Rente** does not mean **rent**.

sich **rentieren** (perf **hat sich rentiert**) vb [76] to be profitable ▷ *Das Geschäft rentiert sich nicht mehr.* The business is no longer profitable.; **Das hat sich rentiert.** That was worthwhile.

Rentner (pl **Rentner**) m pensioner

Rentnerin f pensioner

Reparatur f repair

Reparaturwerkstatt (pl **Reparaturwerkstätten**) f garage (repair shop)

reparieren (perf **hat repariert**) vb [76] to repair

Reportage f ① report ▷ *Ich habe eine Reportage über die Zustände in Rumänien gelesen.* I read a report about conditions in Romania. ② live commentary ▷ *Hast du im Radio die Reportage des Europapokalspiels gehört?* Did you hear the live commentary on the European cup game on the radio?

Reporter (pl **Reporter**) m reporter

Reporterin f reporter

Republik f republic

Reserve f reserve

Reserverad (pl **Reserveräder**) nt spare wheel

reservieren (perf **hat reserviert**) vb [76] to reserve ▷ *Ich habe einen Tisch für heute Abend reservieren lassen.* I've reserved a table for this evening.

Reservierung f reservation

Respekt m respect

respektieren (perf **hat respektiert**) vb [76] to respect

respektlos adj disrespectful

respektvoll adj respectful

Rest (pl **Reste**) m ① rest ▷ *Den Rest bezahle ich später.* I'll pay the rest later. ▷ *Die meisten sind früher gegangen, der Rest hat noch lange gefeiert.* Most left early, but the rest carried on celebrating for a long time. ② left-over ▷ *Heute gab's die Reste von gestern.* Today we had yesterday's left-overs.; **die Reste** the remains

Restaurant (pl **Restaurants**) nt restaurant

restlich adj remaining

Restmüll m non-recyclable waste

Resultat (pl **Resultate**) nt result

retten vb [2] to rescue

Rettich (pl **Rettiche**) m radish

Rettung f ① rescue ▷ *Alle zeigten bei der Rettung großen Mut.* They all showed great courage during the rescue. ② salvation ▷ *Das war meine Rettung.* That was my salvation. ③ hope ▷ *seine letzte Rettung* his last hope

Rettungsboot (pl **Rettungsboote**) nt lifeboat

Rettungsdienst (pl **Rettungsdienste**) m rescue service

Rettungsring (pl **Rettungsringe**) m lifebelt

Rettungswagen (pl **Rettungswagen**) m ambulance

Reue f remorse ▷ *Der Täter zeigte keine Reue.* The culprit doesn't show any remorse.

Revier (pl **Reviere**) nt ① police station ▷ *Der Polizist nahm ihn mit aufs Revier.* The police officer took him to the police station. ② territory ▷ *Das männliche Tier verteidigt sein Revier.* The male animal defends his territory.

Revolution f revolution ▷ *die Revolution von 1789* the revolution of 1789

Revolver (pl **Revolver**) m revolver

Rezept (pl **Rezepte**) nt ❶ recipe ▷ *Kannst du mir mal das Rezept von deinem Käsekuchen geben?* Can you give me your cheesecake recipe? ❷ prescription ▷ *Dieses Medikament bekommt man nur auf Rezept.* You can only get this medicine on prescription.

Rezeption f reception

rezeptpflichtig adj available only on prescription; **rezeptpflichtige Medikamente** prescribed drugs

Rhabarber m rhubarb

Rhein m Rhine

- The Rhine is 1320 km long and the entire 865 km which flows through Germany is navigable, making it an important inland waterway. It flows past such important cities as Karlsruhe, Mannheim, Ludwigshafen, Mainz, Cologne, Düsseldorf and Duisburg.

Rheinland-Pfalz nt Rhineland-Palatinate

- Rheinland-Pfalz is one of the 16 **Länder**. Its capital is Mainz. It is home to the BASF chemicals giant and to Germany's biggest television network, ZDF (Channel 2).

Rheuma nt rheumatism ▷ *Meine Oma hat Rheuma.* My granny's got rheumatism.

Rhythmus (gen **Rhythmus**, pl **Rhythmen**) m rhythm

richten vb [2] ❶ to point ▷ *Er richtete das Fernrohr zum Himmel.* He pointed the telescope at the sky.; **eine Waffe auf jemanden richten** to aim a weapon at somebody; **etwas an jemanden richten** to address something to somebody ▷ *Der Brief war an meine Eltern gerichtet.* The letter was addressed to my parents.; **Ich richte mich ganz nach dir.** I'll do whatever you want.; **sich nach etwas richten (1)** to conform to something ▷ *Auch du solltest dich danach richten, wie wir das hier machen.* You should conform to our way of doing things. **(2)** to be determined by something ▷ *Das Angebot richtet sich nach der Nachfrage.* Supply is determined by demand.

Richter (pl **Richter**) m judge

richtig adj, adv ❶ right ▷ *Es war nicht richtig von dir, ihn zu belügen.* It wasn't right of you to lie to him. ▷ *Das war nicht die richtige Antwort.* That wasn't the right answer.; **Bin ich hier richtig?** Have I come to the right place?; **der Richtige** the right person; **das Richtige** the right thing ❷ correctly ▷ *Du hast das nicht richtig geschrieben.* You haven't written that correctly. ❸ proper ▷ *Ich will ein richtiges Motorrad und kein Moped.* I want a proper motorbike, not a moped. ❹ really ▷ *Wir waren richtig froh, als es vorbei war.* We were really glad when it was over.

Richtung f direction ▷ *Wir gehen in die falsche Richtung.* We are going in the wrong direction. ▷ *in östlicher Richtung* in an easterly direction

rieb vb see **reiben**

riechen (imperf **roch**, perf **hat gerochen**) vb to smell ▷ *Ich rieche Gas.* I can smell gas. ▷ *Das riecht gut.* That smells good. ▷ *Ich kann nichts riechen.* I can't smell anything.; **an etwas riechen** to smell something; **nach etwas riechen** to smell of something; **Ich kann ihn nicht riechen.** I can't stand him.

> Word for word, **Ich kann ihn nicht riechen** means 'I can't smell him'.

rief vb see **rufen**

Riegel (pl **Riegel**) m ❶ bolt ▷ *Sie schob den Riegel vor die Tür.* She bolted the door. ❷ bar ▷ *Für unterwegs haben wir* einen Schokoriegel mitgenommen. We've brought a bar of chocolate to eat on the way.

Riese (gen Riesen, pl Riesen) m giant

riesengroß adj gigantic

riesig adj huge

riet vb see **raten**

Rind (pl **Rinder**) nt ❶ (male) ox ❷ (female) cow; **Rinder** cattle ❸ beef ▷ Wir essen kaum noch Rind. We hardly eat beef any more.

Rinde f ❶ rind ▷ Er schnitt die Rinde vom Käse ab. He cut the rind off the cheese. ❷ crust ▷ frisches Brot mit knuspriger Rinde fresh crusty bread ❸ bark ▷ Er ritzte ihren Namen in die Rinde einer Eiche. He carved her name into the bark of an oak tree.

Rindfleisch nt beef

Ring (pl **Ringe**) m ring

Ringbuch (pl **Ringbücher**) nt ring binder

Ringen nt wrestling ▷ Ringen ist sein Hobby. His hobby is wrestling.

Ringkampf (pl **Ringkämpfe**) m wrestling bout

Rippe f rib

Risiko (pl **Risiken**) nt risk

riskant adj risky

riskieren (perf hat riskiert) vb [76] to risk

Riss (gen Risses, pl Risse) m ❶ crack ▷ Die Maus verschwand durch einen Riss in der Mauer. The mouse disappeared into a crack in the wall. ▷ Der trockene Boden war voller Risse. The dry soil was full of cracks. ❷ tear ▷ Er hatte einen Riss in der Hose. There was a tear in his trousers.

rissig adj ❶ cracked ▷ Von der Trockenheit ist die Erde rissig geworden. The soil is cracked as a result of the drought. ❷ chapped ▷ Vom vielen Waschen hat sie ganz rissige Hände. Her hands are all chapped from doing so much washing.

ritt vb see **reiten**

Robbe f seal ▷ ein Robbenbaby a seal pup

Roboter (pl **Roboter**) m robot

roch vb see **riechen**

Rock (pl **Röcke**) m skirt

Roggen m rye

roh adj ❶ raw ▷ rohes Fleisch raw meat ▷ Karotten esse ich am liebsten roh. I like carrots best raw. ❷ callous ▷ Sei nicht so roh. Don't be so callous. ❸ rough ▷ Er hat sie ziemlich roh mit sich gezogen. He dragged her off pretty roughly.

Rohr (pl **Rohre**) nt ❶ pipe ▷ Das Abwasser wird durch Rohre in die Kanalisation geleitet. Sewage is fed into the sewer via pipes. ❷ cane ▷ ein Stuhl aus Rohr a cane chair ❸ reeds pl ▷ In dem Teich wuchs Rohr. Reeds were growing in the pond.

Rohstoff (pl **Rohstoffe**) m raw material

Rollbrett (pl **Rollbretter**) nt skateboard

Rolle f ❶ role ▷ Der Schauspieler hat die Rolle des Königs gut gespielt. The actor was good in the role of the king. ▷ Die Rolle der Frau hat sich geändert. The role of women has changed. ❷ castor ▷ ein Stuhl mit Rollen a chair with castors ❸ roll ▷ eine Rolle Toilettenpapier a roll of toilet paper ❹ reel ▷ Sie hat den Faden von der Rolle abgewickelt. She unwound the thread from the reel.; **keine Rolle spielen** not to matter; **eine wichtige Rolle spielen bei** to play a major role in

rollen (perf hat/ist gerollt) vb [38]

> For the perfect tense use **haben** when the verb has an object and **sein** when there is no object.

to roll ▷ Sie haben den Stein der Berg hinuntergerollt. They rolled the stone down the hill. ▷ Der Ball ist direkt vor ihn auf gerollt. The ball rolled right in front of a car.

Roller (pl **Roller**) m scooter

Rollladen (pl **Rollläden**) m shutter

Rollschuh (pl **Rollschuhe**) m roller skate
Rollstuhl (pl **Rollstühle**) m wheelchair
Rolltreppe f escalator
Rom nt Rome
Roman (pl **Romane**) m novel
romantisch adj romantic
röntgen vb [54] to X-ray
rosa adj pink ▷ *Sie hatte ein rosa Kleid an.* She was wearing a pink dress.
Rose f rose
Rosenkohl m Brussels sprouts pl ▷ *Rosenkohl ist mein Lieblingsgemüse.* Brussels sprouts are my favourite vegetable.
Rosine f raisin
Rost (pl **Roste**) m rust ▷ *An diesem Auto ist viel Rost.* This car has a lot of rust on it.; **ein Bratrost** a grill
rosten (perf **ist gerostet**) vb [2] to rust
rösten vb [2] ❶ to roast ▷ *geröstete Erdnüsse* roasted peanuts ❷ to toast ▷ *Brot rösten* to toast bread ❸ to grill ▷ *Würstchen auf dem Grill rösten* to grill sausages
rostig adj rusty
rot adj red ▷ *Sein Gesicht wurde immer röter.* His face got redder and redder.; **in den roten Zahlen** in the red; **das Rote Meer** the Red Sea
Röteln pl German measles sg ▷ *Röteln sind für schwangere Frauen gefährlich.* German measles is dangerous for pregnant women.
rothaarig adj red-haired
Rotkohl m red cabbage
Rotwein (pl **Rotweine**) m red wine
Roulade f beef olive
Route f route
Routenplaner (pl **Routenplaner**) m route planner
Router m router
Rowdy (pl **Rowdys**) m hooligan
RSI-Syndrom nt (= *Repetitive-Strain-Injury-Syndrom*) RSI

Rübe f beet ▷ *Der Bauer füttert die Kühe mit Rüben.* The farmer feeds his cows with beet.; **Gelbe Rübe** carrot; **Rote Rübe** beetroot
rüber adv over ▷ *Komm hier rüber, du siehst du besser.* Come over here, you'll get a better view. ▷ *Ich geh mal zu den Nachbarn rüber.* I'm just going over to our neighbours.
rücken (perf **ist/hat gerückt**) vb [38]
  For the perfect tense use **haben** when the verb has an object and **sein** when there is no object.
  ❶ to move over ▷ *Rück mal ein bisschen.* Move over a bit. ❷ to shift ▷ *Sie rückten den Schrank zur Seite.* They shifted the cupboard to one side.
Rücken (pl **Rücken**) m back ▷ *Er schläft auf dem Rücken.* He sleeps on his back.
Rückenschmerzen pl backache sg
Rückfahrkarte f return ticket
Rückfahrt f return journey
Rückflug (pl **Rückflüge**) m return flight
Rückgabe f return
Rückgrat (pl **Rückgrate**) nt spine
Rückkehr f return ▷ *bei unserer Rückkehr* on our return
Rücklicht (pl **Rücklichter**) nt rear light
Rückreise f return journey
Rücksicht f consideration; **auf jemanden Rücksicht nehmen** to show consideration for somebody
rücksichtslos adj inconsiderate; **ein rücksichtsloser Fahrer** a reckless driver
rücksichtsvoll adj considerate
Rücksitz (pl **Rücksitze**) m back seat ▷ *Dieser Sportwagen hat keine Rücksitze.* This sports car has no back seats.; **auf dem Rücksitz** in the back
Rückspiegel (pl **Rückspiegel**) m rear-view mirror
Rückspiel (pl **Rückspiele**) nt return match

Rücktritt (pl **Rücktritte**) m resignation

rückwärts adv backwards ▷ rückwärts zählen to count backwards

Rückwärtsgang (pl **Rückwärtsgänge**) m reverse gear

Rückweg (pl **Rückwege**) m way back

Ruder (pl **Ruder**) nt ❶ oar ▷ ein Boot mit zwei Rudern a boat with two oars ❷ rudder ▷ Der Steuermann steht am Ruder. The helmsman stands at the rudder.

Ruderboot (pl **Ruderboote**) nt rowing boat

rudern (perf **hat/ist gerudert**) vb [88]
Use **haben** for the perfect tense when you describe the activity and **sein** when you describe the motion.
to row ▷ Zuerst ist er gerudert, dann sie. First he rowed, then she did. ▷ Wir sind über den See gerudert. We rowed across the lake.

Ruf (pl **Rufe**) m ❶ shout ▷ Wir hörten seine Rufe. We heard his shouts. ❷ reputation ▷ Das schadet seinem Ruf. This will damage his reputation.

rufen (imperf **rief**, perf **hat gerufen**) vb [56] ❶ to call out ▷ Ich habe gerufen, es hat mich aber niemand gehört. I called out, but nobody heard me.; **Der Patient rief nach der Schwester.** The patient called for the nurse. ❷ to call ▷ Wir sollten den Arzt rufen. We ought to call the doctor. ▷ Sie hat mir ein Taxi gerufen. She called me a taxi. ❸ to shout ▷ Sie rief um Hilfe. She shouted for help.

Rufnummer f telephone number

Ruhe f ❶ rest ▷ Nach den anstrengenden Tagen brauche ich etwas Ruhe. After the strain of the last few days I need a rest. ❷ peace ▷ Jetzt kann ich in Ruhe arbeiten. Now I can work in peace. ❸ peace and quiet ▷ Die Kinder sind weg, ich genieße die Ruhe. The children are out and I'm enjoying the peace and quiet.; **in aller Ruhe** calmly; **jemanden aus der Ruhe bringen** to unsettle somebody ❹ silence ▷ Ich bitte um etwas mehr Ruhe. I would ask you for a bit more silence.; **Ruhe!** Silence!; **jemanden in Ruhe lassen** to leave somebody alone; **sich zur Ruhe setzen** to retire

ruhig adj, adv ❶ quiet ▷ Im Haus war alles ruhig. The house was completely quiet. ▷ Die Kinder haben ruhig gespielt. The children played quietly. ▷ Seid endlich ruhig! Will you be quiet! ❷ still ▷ Bleib ruhig stehen, dann tut dir der Hund nichts. If you keep still the dog won't hurt you.; **eine ruhige Hand** a steady hand ❸ calm ▷ Wie kannst du so ruhig bleiben? How can you stay so calm? ▷ Ich bin ganz ruhig in die Prüfung gegangen. I went quite calmly into the exam.; **ein ruhiges Gewissen** a clear conscience; **Kommen Sie ruhig herein!** Come on in.

Ruhm m fame

Rührei (pl **Rühreier**) nt scrambled eggs pl

rühren vb [38] ❶ to stir ▷ Sie rührte mit dem Löffel in der Soße. She stirred the sauce with the spoon. ❷ to move ▷ Ich kann meine Beine nicht rühren. I can't move my legs.; **sich rühren** to move; **jemanden rühren** to move somebody

rührend adj touching ▷ eine rührende Geschichte a touching story ▷ Er ist rührend naiv. He's touchingly naive.

Ruine f ruin

ruinieren (perf **hat ruiniert**) vb [76] to ruin

Rumäne (gen **Rumänen**, pl **Rumänen**) m Romanian

Rumänien nt Romania

Rumänin f Romanian

rumänisch adj Romanian

Rummelplatz (gen **Rummelplatzes**, pl **Rummelplätze**) m fairground

rund adj, adv ❶ round ▷ Sie hat ein rundes Gesicht. She's got a round face. ❷ about ▷ Das kostet rund hundert Euro. It costs

Runde f ❶ lap ▷ *Das Auto fuhr ein paar Runden.* The car drove a few laps. ❷ round ▷ *Diese Runde zahle ich.* I'll get this round.

* It isn't usual to buy rounds in
* Germany. Normally people just order
* what they want from the waiter,
* and pay when they leave. You can,
* however, buy a round (**eine Runde**
* **schmeißen**) if you're feeling generous.

❸ lap ▷ *Er liegt in der letzten Runde in Führung.* He's in the lead on the last lap. ❹ party ▷ *Wir waren eine fröhliche Runde.* We were a merry party.

Rundfahrt f round trip
Rundfunk m broadcasting; **im Rundfunk** on the radio
runter adv ❶ off ▷ *Runter vom Tisch!* Get off the table! ❷ down ▷ *Dann ging's den Berg runter.* Then off we went down the mountain.
runterladen (*pres* **lädt runter**, *imperf* **lud runter**, *perf* **hat runtergeladen**) vb (computer) to download ▷ *eine Datei runterladen* to download a file
Ruß (*gen* **Rußes**) m soot
Russe (*gen* **Russen**, *pl* **Russen**) m Russian
Rüssel (*pl* **Rüssel**) m ❶ snout ▷ *der Rüssel eines Schweins* a pig's snout ❷ trunk ▷ *der Rüssel eines Elefanten* an elephant's trunk
rußig adj sooty
Russin f Russian
russisch adj Russian
Russland nt Russia
Rüstung f ❶ suit of armour ▷ *In der Burg standen ein paar rostige Rüstungen.* There were a couple of rusty suits of armour in the castle. ❷ armaments pl ▷ *Es wird viel Geld für Rüstung ausgegeben.* A lot of money is spent on armaments.
Rutschbahn f slide

rutschen (*perf* **ist gerutscht**) vb [48]
❶ to slip ▷ *Sie ist auf dem Eis gerutscht und hingefallen.* She slipped and fell on the ice. ▷ *Der Teller ist mir aus der Hand gerutscht.* The plate slipped out of my hand. ❷ to move over ▷ *Rutsch mal ein bisschen!* Move over a bit.

S

Saal (pl **Säle**) m hall
Saarland nt Saarland
- The **Saarland** is one of the 16 **Länder**.
- Its capital is Saarbrücken. While its
- coal and steel industries have been in
- crisis, it still has flourishing ceramics
- and glass industries.

Sache f ① thing ▷ *Räum bitte deine Sachen weg.* Please put your things away. ▷ *Pack warme Sachen ein.* Pack warm things. ▷ *Was machst du denn für Sachen?* The things you do! ② matter ▷ *Wir sollten diese Sache ausdiskutieren.* We should discuss this matter fully. ▷ *Die Polizei wird dieser Sache nachgehen.* The police will investigate this affair. ③ job ▷ *Es ist deine Sache, dich darum zu kümmern.* It's your job to see to it.; **Mach keine Sachen!** Don't be silly!; **zur Sache** to the point
sachlich adj ① objective ▷ *ein sehr sachlicher Bericht* a very objective report ▷ *Du solltest sachlich bleiben.* You should remain objective. ② factual ▷ *Was er sagt, ist sachlich falsch.* What he says is factually inaccurate.
sächlich adj neuter
Sachsen nt Saxony
- **Sachsen** is one of the 16 **Länder**. Its
- capital is Dresden. Its largest city,
- Leipzig, is famous for its industrial
- fair and was one of the main centres
- of the peaceful revolt against the
- DDR regime.

Sachsen-Anhalt nt Saxony-Anhalt
- **Sachsen-Anhalt** is one of the 16
- **Länder**. Its capital is Magdeburg. It
- has a rich cultural past: Martin
- Luther and Georg Friedrich Händel
- were born here, and the Bauhaus
- school of architecture was situated
- in Dessau.

sächsisch adj Saxon
sachte adv softly
Sack (pl **Säcke**) m sack
Sackgasse f cul-de-sac
Saft (pl **Säfte**) m juice
saftig adj juicy
Säge f saw
sagen vb [38] ① to say ▷ *Ich kann noch nicht sagen, ob ich komme.* I can't say yet if I'll come. ▷ *Habe ich etwas Falsches gesagt?* Have I said something wrong? ▷ *Wie sagt man 'danke' auf Japanisch?* How do you say 'thank you' in Japanese? ▷ *Was sagst du zu meinem Vorschlag?* What do you say to my suggestion?; **Man sagt, dass ...** It's said that ... ② to tell ▷ *Kannst du ihm bitte sagen, er soll seine Eltern anrufen.* Can you tell him to call his parents. ▷ *Ich werde es ihr sagen.* I'll tell her. ▷ *Sag ihm, er solle das nicht tun.* Tell him he shouldn't do it.; **etwas zu jemandem sagen** to call somebody something; **zu sagen haben** to have a say; **Das hat nichts zu sagen.** It doesn't mean anything.
sägen vb [38] to saw
sah vb see **sehen**

Sahne f cream
Saison (pl **Saisons**) f season
Saite f string
Saiteninstrument (pl **Saiteninstrumente**) nt stringed instrument
Salat (pl **Salate**) m ❶ salad ▷ *Es gab verschiedene Salate.* There were various salads. ❷ lettuce ▷ *Am liebsten mag ich grünen Salat.* I like lettuce best.
Salbe f ointment
Salz (gen **Salzes**) nt salt
salzen (perf **hat gesalzen**) vb to salt
salzig adj salty
Salzkartoffeln fpl boiled potatoes pl
Salzstange f pretzel stick
Samen (pl **Samen**) m seed ▷ *Hast du die Blumensamen schon ausgesät?* Have you sown the flower seeds yet?
sammeln vb [34] ❶ to collect ▷ *Er sammelt Briefmarken.* He collects stamps. ▷ *Sie sammeln für ein Waisenhaus.* They're collecting for an orphanage. ▷ *Altpapier wird gesammelt und wiederverwertet.* Waste paper is collected and recycled. ❷ to gather ▷ *Wir haben Pilze gesammelt.* We gathered mushrooms.
Sammlung f collection
Samstag (pl **Samstage**) m Saturday ▷ *am Samstag* on Saturday
samstags adv on Saturdays
samt prep

The preposition **samt** takes the dative.

with ▷ *Sie kamen samt Kindern und Hund.* They came with their children and dog.
Samt (pl **Samte**) m velvet
Sand m sand
Sandale f sandal
Sandkasten (pl **Sandkästen**) m sandpit
Sandstrand (pl **Sandstrände**) m sandy beach
sandte vb see **senden**

sanft adj gentle ▷ *etwas sanft berühren* to touch something gently
sang vb see **singen**
Sänger (pl **Sänger**) m singer
Sängerin f singer
Sarg (pl **Särge**) m coffin
saß vb see **sitzen**
Satellit (gen **Satelliten**, pl **Satelliten**) m satellite
Satellitenfernsehen nt satellite television
satt adj ❶ full ▷ *Ich bin satt.* I'm full.; **Wir sind nicht satt geworden.** We didn't get enough to eat.; **sich satt essen** to eat one's fill; **satt machen** to be filling; **jemanden satt sein** to be fed up with somebody ❷ rich ▷ *satte Farben* rich colours ▷ *ein sattes Rot* a rich red
Sattel (pl **Sättel**) m saddle
Satz (gen **Satzes**, pl **Sätze**) m ❶ sentence ▷ *Bitte antworte mit einem ganzen Satz.* Please answer in a complete sentence.; **ein Nebensatz** a subordinate clause; **ein Adverbialsatz** an adverbial clause ❷ theorem ▷ *der Satz des Pythagoras* Pythagoras' theorem ❸ set ▷ *Jabeur hat den ersten Satz verloren.* Jabeur lost the first set. ▷ *ein Satz Schraubenschlüssel* a set of screwdrivers ❹ rate ▷ *Die Krankenversicherung hat ihre Sätze erhöht.* The health insurance has increased its rates.
Satzzeichen (pl **Satzzeichen**) nt punctuation mark
sauber adj ❶ clean ▷ *Die Wäsche ist nicht sauber geworden.* The washing hasn't come up clean. ❷ fine ▷ *Du bist mir ein sauberer Freund!* You're a fine friend!; **sauber machen** to clean
Sauberkeit f cleanness
saubermachen vb [48] see **sauber**
Sauce f sauce
sauer adj ❶ sour ▷ *Der Apfel ist sauer.* The apple is sour. ▷ *Die Milch ist sauer geworden.* The milk has turned sour.

GERMAN > ENGLISH

❷ acid ▷ *saurer Regen* acid rain ❸ cross ▷ *Ich bin sauer auf meine Freundin.* I'm cross with my girlfriend.

Sauerkraut *nt* sauerkraut *(pickled cabbage)*

Sauerstoff *m* oxygen

saufen (*pres* **säuft**, *imperf* **soff**, *perf* **hat gesoffen**) *vb* (*informal*) to booze

saugen (*imperf* **saugte** *or* **sog**, *perf* **hat gesaugt** *or* **gesogen**) *vb* to suck

Säugetier (*pl* **Säugetiere**) *nt* mammal

Säugling (*pl* **Säuglinge**) *m* infant

Säule *f* column

Sauna (*pl* **Saunas**) *f* sauna

Säure *f* acid ▷ *Die Säure hat den Stein zerfressen.* The acid has eaten away at the stone.

Saxofon (*pl* **Saxofone**) *nt* saxophone ▷ *Er spielt Saxofon.* He plays the saxophone.

Schach *nt* chess ▷ *Ich kann nicht Schach spielen.* I can't play chess.

Schachbrett (*pl* **Schachbretter**) *nt* chessboard

Schachfigur *f* chessman

Schachtel *f* box

schade *adj, excl* a pity ▷ *Es ist schade um das gute Essen.* It's a pity to waste good food. ▷ *Das ist aber schade.* That's a pity.; **Wie schade!** What a pity!; **für etwas zu schade sein** to be too good for something; **sich für etwas zu schade sein** to consider oneself too good for something

Schädel (*pl* **Schädel**) *m* skull

schaden *vb* [54] *jemandem schaden* to harm somebody; **einer Sache schaden** to damage something; **es kann nicht schaden ...** it can't do any harm ...

Schaden (*pl* **Schäden**) *m* ❶ damage ▷ *Der Schaden an seinem Auto war nicht so groß.* The damage to his car wasn't too bad. ❷ injury ▷ *Sie hat den Unfall ohne Schaden überstanden.* She came out of

187 | **schälen**

the accident without injury. ❸ disadvantage ▷ *Es soll dein Schaden nicht sein.* It won't be to your disadvantage.

schädigen (*perf* **hat geschädigt**) *vb* [38] to damage

schädlich *adj* harmful ▷ *Rauchen ist schädlich.* Smoking is harmful. ▷ *Alkohol ist für die Leber schädlich.* Alcohol is harmful to your liver.

Schadstoff (*pl* **Schadstoffe**) *m* harmful substance

Schaf (*pl* **Schafe**) *nt* sheep ▷ *zehn Schafe* ten sheep

Schäferhund (*pl* **Schäferhunde**) *m* Alsatian

schaffen (1) (*imperf* **schuf**, *perf* **hat geschaffen**) *vb* to create ▷ *Die Regierung will neue Arbeitsplätze schaffen.* The government wants to create new jobs.

schaffen (2) (*imperf* **schaffte**, *perf* **hat geschafft**) *vb* [48] ❶ to manage ▷ *Die Übersetzung schaffe ich heute noch.* I'll manage that translation today. ▷ *Er schafft das nicht allein.* He won't manage to do that on his own. ▷ *Wir haben den Zug gerade noch geschafft.* We just managed to catch the train.; **eine Prüfung schaffen** to pass an exam; **Ich bin geschafft!** I'm shattered!

Schal (*pl* **Schale** *or* **Schals**) *m* scarf

Schale *f* ❶ skin ▷ *eine Bananenschale* a banana skin ❷ peel ▷ *die Kartoffelschalen* the potato peel ▷ *eine Zitronenschale* lemon peel ❸ shell ▷ *Die Nussschalen nicht in den Kompost werfen.* Don't throw the nutshells onto the compost heap. ▷ *Diese Eier haben sehr dünne Schalen.* These eggs have very thin shells. ❹ bowl ▷ *Auf dem Tisch stand eine Schale mit Obst.* There was a bowl of fruit on the table.

schälen *vb* [38] ❶ to peel ▷ *einen Apfel schälen* to peel an apple ❷ to shell

▷ **Nüsse schälen** to shell nuts; **sich schälen** to peel

Schall m sound

Schallplatte f record

schalten vb [2] ❶ to switch ▷ **den Herd auf 'aus' schalten** to switch the oven to 'off' ❷ to change gear ▷ **Du solltest schalten.** You should change gear.; **in den vierten Gang schalten** to change into fourth ❸ (informal) to catch on ▷ **Ich habe zu spät geschaltet.** I caught on too late.

Schalter (pl **Schalter**) m ❶ counter ▷ **Zahlen Sie bitte am Schalter dort drüben.** Please pay at the counter over there. ❷ switch ▷ **Wo ist der Lichtschalter?** Where is the light switch?

Schaltjahr (pl **Schaltjahre**) nt leap year

sich **schämen** vb [38] to be ashamed ▷ **sich einer Sache schämen** to be ashamed of something

Schande f disgrace

scharf adj ❶ sharp ▷ **ein scharfes Messer** a sharp knife ▷ **eine scharfe Kurve** a sharp corner; **ein scharfer Wind** a biting wind ❷ hot ▷ **Indisches Essen ist schärfer als deutsches.** Indian food is hotter than German food.; **scharfe Munition** live ammunition; **scharf schießen** to shoot with live ammunition; **scharf nachdenken** to think hard; **auf etwas scharf sein** (informal) to be mad about something; **auf jemanden scharf sein** to fancy somebody

Schatten (pl **Schatten**) m ❶ shadow ❷ shade ▷ **Wir saßen im Schatten.** We sat in the shade.

schattig adj shady

Schatz (gen **Schatzes**, pl **Schätze**) m ❶ treasure ▷ **der Schatz der Piraten** the pirates' treasure ❷ darling ▷ **Du bist ein Schatz!** You're a darling! ▷ **Mein Schatz.** My darling.

schätzen vb [36] ❶ to guess ▷ **Schätz mal, wie viel das gekostet hat.** Guess how much that cost.; **Man kann sein Alter schlecht schätzen.** It's difficult to tell how old he is. ❷ to value ▷ **Ich werde die alte Uhr schätzen lassen.** I'm going to have the old clock valued. ❸ to appreciate ▷ **Ich schätze deine Hilfe sehr.** I really appreciate your help.

Schaubild (pl **Schaubilder**) nt diagram

schauen vb [38] to look ▷ **Schau mal an die Tafel.** Look at the board.

Schauer (pl **Schauer**) m ❶ shower ▷ **Für morgen sind Schauer angesagt.** Showers are forecast for tomorrow. ❷ shudder ▷ **Ein Schauer überlief sie.** A shudder ran through her body.

Schaufel f shovel

Schaufenster (pl **Schaufenster**) nt shop window

Schaufensterbummel (pl **Schaufensterbummel**) m window shopping

Schaukel f swing

schaukeln vb [34] to swing

Schaumgummi m foam rubber

Schauspiel nt play (theatre)

Schauspieler (pl **Schauspieler**) m actor

Schauspielerin f actress

Scheck (pl **Schecks**) m cheque

Scheckkarte f cheque card

Scheibe f slice ▷ **Sie belegte das Brot mit mehreren Scheiben Wurst.** She put several slices of cold meat on the bread.

Scheibenwischer (pl **Scheibenwischer**) m windscreen wiper

scheiden (imperf **schied**, perf **hat geschieden**) vb **sich scheiden lassen** to get a divorce; **geschieden sein** to be divorced

Scheidung f divorce

Schein (pl **Scheine**) m ❶ light ▷ **beim Schein einer Kerze** by the light of a candle ❷ appearance ▷ **Der Schein trügt.** Appearances are deceptive. ❸ note ▷ **Er**

hat in großen Scheinen bezahlt. He paid in large notes. ❸ certificate ▷ *Am Ende des Semesters bekommt man einen Schein.* You get a certificate at the end of the semester.; **etwas zum Schein tun** to pretend to do something

scheinbar *adv* apparently

scheinen (*imperf* **schien**, *perf* **hat geschienen**) *vb* [57] ❶ to shine ▷ *Die Sonne scheint.* The sun is shining. ❷ to seem ▷ *Sie scheint glücklich zu sein.* She seems to be happy.

Scheinwerfer (*pl* **Scheinwerfer**) *m* ❶ headlamp ▷ *Die Scheinwerfer des entgegenkommenden Autos haben mich geblendet.* The headlamps of the approaching car blinded me. ❷ floodlight ▷ *Die Scheinwerfer beleuchteten das Stadion.* The floodlights lit the stadium. ❸ spotlight ▷ *Das Gemälde wird von einem Scheinwerfer angestrahlt.* The painting is lit up by a spotlight.

scheitern (*perf* **ist gescheitert**) *vb* [88] to fail

Schenkel (*pl* **Schenkel**) *m* thigh

schenken *vb* [38] ❶ to give ▷ *Was haben dir deine Eltern zum Geburtstag geschenkt?* What did your parents give you for your birthday? ▷ *Das habe ich geschenkt bekommen.* I was given it as a present. ❷ to pour ▷ *Sie schenkte ihm noch etwas Rotwein ins Glas.* She poured some more red wine into his glass.; **sich schenken** to skip something ▷ *Die Geigenstunde werde ich mir heute schenken.* I'm going to skip my violin lesson today.; **Das ist geschenkt!** (1) That's a giveaway! (2) That's worthless!

Schere *f* ❶ scissors *pl* ▷ *eine Schere* a pair of scissors ❷ shears *pl* ▷ *Wo ist die Schere, um die Hecke zu schneiden?* Where are the shears for cutting the hedge?

Scherz (*gen* **Scherzes**, *pl* **Scherze**) *m* joke ▷ *Das war doch nur ein Scherz!* It was only a joke.; **zum Scherz** for fun

scheußlich *adj* dreadful ▷ *Das Wetter war scheußlich.* The weather was dreadful.; **Das tut scheußlich weh.** It hurts dreadfully.

Schi (*pl* **Schi** *or* **Schier**) *m* see **Ski**

Schicht *f* ❶ layer ▷ *Auf dem Weg lag eine Schicht Sand.* There was a layer of sand on the path. ❷ class ▷ *soziale Schichten* social classes ❸ shift ▷ *Mein Vater arbeitet Schicht.* My father works shifts.

schick *adj* stylish ▷ *ein schicker Hosenanzug* a stylish trouser suit; **schick angezogen** stylishly dressed

schicken *vb* [48] to send ▷ *Ich habe ihr ein Päckchen geschickt.* I've sent her a parcel. ▷ *Sie hat ihren Sohn zum Bäcker geschickt.* She sent her son to the baker's.

Schicksal *nt* fate

schieben (*imperf* **schob**, *perf* **hat geschoben**) *vb* to push ▷ *Wir mussten das Auto schieben.* We had to push the car. ▷ *Könnt ihr mal schieben?* Could you lot push?; **die Schuld auf jemanden schieben** to put the blame on somebody

Schiedsrichter (*pl* **Schiedsrichter**) *m* ❶ referee ▷ *Der Schiedsrichter pfiff das Spiel an.* The referee blew the whistle to start the game. ❷ umpire ▷ *Bei einem Tennisspiel sagt der Schiedsrichter den Spielstand an.* In a tennis match the umpire gives the score.

Schiedsrichterin *f* ❶ referee ❷ umpire

schief *adj*, *adv* crooked ▷ *Die Wände des Hauses sind schief.* The walls of the house are crooked.; **Das Bild hängt schief.** The picture isn't hanging straight.; **der Schiefe Turm von Pisa** the Leaning Tower of Pisa; **ein schiefer Blick** a funny look; **Er hatte seinen Hut schief aufgesetzt.** He was wearing his hat at an angle.

schiefgehen (*imperf* **ging schief**, *perf* **ist schiefgegangen**) *vb* [29] to go wrong

schielen vb [38] to squint
schien vb see **scheinen**
Schiene f ❶ rail ▷ *Die Schienen sind verrostet.* The rails have rusted. ❷ splint ▷ *Sie hatte den Arm in einer Schiene.* She had her arm in a splint.
schießen (*imperf* **schoss**, *perf* **hat geschossen**) vb ❶ to shoot ▷ *Nicht schießen!* Don't shoot! ▷ *Er hat ein Kaninchen geschossen.* He shot a rabbit. ▷ *Er hat auf einen Polizisten geschossen.* He shot at a police officer. ❷ to kick ▷ *Sie schoss den Ball ins Tor.* She kicked the ball into the goal.
Schiff (*pl* **Schiffe**) *nt* ship
Schifffahrt f shipping
Schild (*pl* **Schilder**) *nt* sign ▷ *Das ist eine Einbahnstraße, hast du das Schild nicht gesehen?* This is a one-way street, didn't you see the sign?; **ein Namensschild** a nameplate
Schildkröte f ❶ tortoise ❷ turtle
Schimmel (*pl* **Schimmel**) *m* ❶ mould ▷ *Auf dem Käse ist Schimmel.* There's mould on the cheese. ❷ white horse ▷ *Sie ritt auf einem Schimmel.* She rode a white horse.
schimmelig *adj* mouldy
Schimpanse (*gen* **Schimpansen**, *pl* **Schimpansen**) *m* chimpanzee
schimpfen vb [38] to scold ▷ *Hat deine Mutter geschimpft?* Did your mother scold you?; **auf jemanden schimpfen** to curse somebody; **über etwas schimpfen** to complain about something
Schimpfwort (*pl* **Schimpfwörter**) *nt* term of abuse
Schinken (*pl* **Schinken**) *m* ham
Schirm (*pl* **Schirme**) *m* umbrella ▷ *Nimm einen Schirm mit!* Take an umbrella!; **der Sonnenschirm** the sunshade; **eine Mütze mit Schirm** a peaked cap
Schlacht f battle
schlachten vb [2] to slaughter
Schlachthof (*pl* **Schlachthöfe**) *m* slaughterhouse
Schlaf *m* sleep
Schlafanzug (*pl* **Schlafanzüge**) *m* pyjamas *pl* ▷ *ein Schlafanzug* a pair of pyjamas
schlafen (*pres* **schläft**, *imperf* **schlief**, *perf* **hat geschlafen**) vb [58] to sleep ▷ *Hast du gut geschlafen?* Did you sleep well? ▷ *Schlaf gut!* Sleep well.; **schlafen gehen** to go to bed
schlaff *adj* ❶ exhausted ▷ *Nach der Gartenarbeit war ich total schlaff.* I was completely exhausted after working in the garden. ❷ slack ▷ *Das Seil ist zu schlaff.* The rope is too slack.
schlaflos *adj* sleepless
Schlafsaal (*pl* **Schlafsäle**) *m* dormitory
Schlafsack (*pl* **Schlafsäcke**) *m* sleeping bag
Schlaftablette f sleeping pill
Schlafzimmer (*pl* **Schlafzimmer**) *nt* bedroom
Schlag (*pl* **Schläge**) *m* ❶ blow ▷ *ein Schlag auf den Kopf* a blow to the head ▷ *Ich bin durchgefallen, das ist ein Schlag.* I've failed, that's a blow. ❷ stroke ▷ *Mein Opa hat einen Schlag gehabt und ist gelähmt.* My granddad's had a stroke and he's now paralysed. ❸ shock ▷ *Fass nicht an den Draht, sonst bekommst du einen Schlag.* Don't touch that wire, otherwise you'll get a shock.; **Er hat von seinem Vater Schläge bekommen.** (*informal*) His father gave him a hiding.; **mit einem Schlag** all at once
schlagen (*pres* **schlägt**, *imperf* **schlug**, *perf* **hat geschlagen**) vb [59] ❶ to beat ▷ *Meine Eltern haben mich noch nie geschlagen.* My parents have never beaten me. ▷ *England hat Holland vier zu eins geschlagen.* England beat Holland four one. ▷ *Ihr Herz schlug schneller.* Her heart beat faster.; **Sahne schlagen** to

whip cream ❷ to hit ▷ *Er schlug mit dem Hammer auf den Nagel.* He hit the nail with the hammer. ▷ *Sie schlug mit der Faust auf den Tisch.* She hit the table with her fist.; **Er schlägt den Nagel in die Wand.** He hammers the nail into the wall. ❸ to strike ▷ *Die Uhr schlägt zehn.* The clock strikes ten. ▷ *Es hat eben zehn geschlagen.* It's just struck ten.; **nach jemandem schlagen** to take after somebody; **sich gut schlagen** to do well

Schlager (pl **Schlager**) m hit

Schläger (pl **Schläger**) m ❶ thug ▷ *Franz ist ein Schläger.* Franz is a thug. ❷ bat ▷ *Baseball und Tischtennis spielt man mit einem Schläger.* You play baseball and table tennis with a bat. ❸ racket ▷ *Für Tennis, Federball und Squash braucht man einen Schläger.* You need a racket for tennis, badminton and squash.; **ein Golfschläger** a golf club; **ein Hockeyschläger** a hockey stick

Schlägerei f fight
schlagfertig adj quick-witted
Schlagsahne f whipped cream
Schlagzeile f headline
Schlagzeug (pl **Schlagzeuge**) nt drums pl ▷ *Er spielt Schlagzeug.* He plays the drums. ▷ *Am Schlagzeug: Freddy Braun.* On drums: Freddy Braun.
Schlamm m mud
Schlange f ❶ snake ▷ *eine giftige Schlange* a poisonous snake ❷ queue ▷ *Vor dem Kino stand eine lange Schlange.* There was a long queue outside the cinema.; **Schlange stehen** to queue
schlank adj slim ▷ *Sie ist sehr schlank.* She's very slim.
Schlankheitskur f diet ▷ *eine Schlankheitskur machen* to be on a diet
schlapp adj worn out ▷ *Ich fühle mich schlapp.* I feel worn out.
schlau adj cunning

Schlauch (pl **Schläuche**) m ❶ hose ▷ *Er hat den Garten mit dem Schlauch gespritzt.* He watered the garden with the hose. ❷ inner tube ▷ *Ich brauche einen neuen Schlauch für mein Fahrrad.* I need a new inner tube for my bike.

Schlauchboot (pl **Schlauchboote**) nt rubber dinghy

schlecht adj, adv ❶ bad ▷ *Er ist in Mathe schlecht.* He is bad at maths. ▷ *Meine Augen werden immer schlechter.* My eyes are getting worse.; **ein schlechtes Gewissen** a guilty conscience ❷ badly ▷ *Ich habe schlecht geschlafen.* I slept badly.; **schlecht gelaunt** in a bad mood; **Mir ist schlecht.** I feel sick.; **ein schlecht bezahlter Job** a poorly paid job; **Ihm geht es schlecht.** He's in a bad way.

schlechtmachen vb [48] **jemanden schlechtmachen** to run somebody down

schleichen (imperf **schlich**, perf **ist geschlichen**) vb to creep

Schleife f ❶ loop ▷ *Der Fluss macht eine Schleife.* The river makes a loop. ❷ bow ▷ *Sie hatte eine Schleife im Haar.* She had a bow in her hair.

Schleswig-Holstein nt Schleswig-Holstein
- Schleswig-Holstein is one of the
- 16 **Länder**. Its capital is Kiel. It is
- Germany's northernmost state,
- bordered by the North Sea and the
- Baltic, and by Denmark in the north.

schleudern (perf **hat/ist geschleudert**) vb [88]

For the perfect tense use **haben** when the verb has an object and **sein** when it has no object.

❶ to hurl ▷ *Sie hat das Buch in die Ecke geschleudert.* She hurled the book into the corner. ❷ to spin ▷ *Du solltest die nasse Wäsche schleudern.* You should spin the wet washing. ❸ to skid ▷ *Das Auto ist geschleudert.* The car skidded.

schlief vb see **schlafen**

schließen (imperf **schloss**, perf **hat geschlossen**) vb to shut ▷ *Schließ bitte das Fenster.* Please shut the window. ▷ *Wann schließen die Geschäfte?* When do the shops shut? ▷ *Die Läden sind geschlossen.* She had her eyes shut. ▷ *Der Betrieb wurde geschlossen.* The company was shut down.; **mit jemandem Freundschaft schließen** to make friends with somebody; **etwas aus etwas schließen** to gather something from something

schließlich adv finally; **schließlich doch** after all

schlimm adj bad

schlimmer adj worse

schlimmste adj worst ▷ *mein schlimmster Feind* my worst enemy

Schlips m tie (necktie)

Schlitten (pl **Schlitten**) m sledge ▷ *Im Winter sind wir viel Schlitten gefahren.* We went sledging a lot in the winter.

Schlittschuh (pl **Schlittschuhe**) m skate; **Schlittschuh laufen** to skate

Schlitz (gen **Schlitzes**, pl **Schlitze**) m ❶ slit ▷ *Der Rock hat hinten einen Schlitz.* The skirt has a slit at the back. ❷ slot ▷ *Du musst das Zwei-Euro-Stück in den Schlitz werfen.* You have to put the two-euro coin in the slot. ❸ flies pl ▷ *Der Schlitz an deiner Hose ist auf.* Your flies are open.

schloss vb see **schließen**

Schloss (gen **Schlosses**, pl **Schlösser**) nt ❶ lock ▷ *Sie steckte den Schlüssel ins Schloss.* She put the key in the lock. ❷ clasp ▷ *Kannst du mir bitte das Schloss an meiner Kette aufmachen?* Can you please open the clasp of my necklace? ❸ chateau ▷ *das Schloss in Versailles* the chateau of Versailles

Schluckauf m hiccups pl ▷ *Er hatte einen Schluckauf.* He had hiccups.

schlucken vb [48] to swallow

schlug vb see **schlagen**

Schluss (gen **Schlusses**, pl **Schlüsse**) m ❶ end ▷ *am Schluss des Jahres* at the end of the year ❷ ending ▷ *Das Buch hat einen traurigen Schluss.* The book has a sad ending. ❸ conclusion ▷ *Ich habe meine Schlüsse gezogen.* I've drawn my conclusions.; **zum Schluss** finally; **Schluss machen** to finish; **mit jemandem Schluss machen** to finish with somebody

Schlüssel (pl **Schlüssel**) m key ▷ *Wo ist mein Fahrradschlüssel?* Where's the key for my bike? ▷ *der Schlüssel zum Erfolg* the key to success

Schlüsselbund (pl **Schlüsselbunde**) m bunch of keys

Schlüsselring (pl **Schlüsselringe**) m keyring

Schlussverkauf m sales pl ▷ *Dieses Kleid habe ich im Schlussverkauf bekommen.* I got this dress in the sales.

schmal adj ❶ narrow ▷ *ein schmaler Durchgang* a narrow passageway ❷ thin ▷ *Sie hat ein schmales Gesicht.* She has a thin face.

> Be careful! **schmal** does not mean **small**.

schmecken vb [48] to taste ▷ *Wie schmeckt eine Mango?* What does a mango taste like? ▷ *Das schmeckt gut.* That tastes good.; **Es schmeckt ihm.** He likes it.

schmeicheln vb [38] jemandem schmeicheln to flatter somebody

schmeißen (imperf **schmiss**, perf **hat geschmissen**) vb to throw

schmelzen (pres **schmilzt**, imperf **schmolz**, perf **ist geschmolzen**) vb to melt ▷ *Das Eis ist geschmolzen.* The ice has melted.

Schmerz (gen **Schmerzes**, pl **Schmerzen**) m ❶ pain ▷ *ein stechender Schmerz in der Seite* a stabbing pain in the side ❷ grief ▷ *Sie verbarg ihren*

Schmerz über diesen Verlust. She hid her grief over her loss.

schmerzen (*perf* **hat geschmerzt**) *vb* [**36**] to hurt

Schmerzmittel (*pl* **Schmerzmittel**) *nt* painkiller

Schmerztablette *f* painkiller

Schmetterling (*pl* **Schmetterlinge**) *m* butterfly

Schminke *f* make-up

schminken *vb* [**38**] to make up ▷ *Hast du dir die Augen geschminkt?* Have you made up your eyes?; **Ich schminke mich selten.** I seldom use make-up.

Schmuck *m* ❶ jewellery ▷ *Sie trägt selten Schmuck.* She seldom wears jewellery. ❷ decoration ▷ *bunte Kugeln als Schmuck für den Weihnachtsbaum* bright baubles as Christmas tree decorations

schmücken *vb* [**38**] to decorate

schmuggeln *vb* [**34**] to smuggle

schmusen *vb* [**38**] to cuddle ▷ *Sie hat mit Felix geschmust.* She cuddled Felix.

Schmutz (*gen* **Schmutzes**) *m* dirt

schmutzig *adj* dirty

Schnabel (*pl* **Schnäbel**) *m* beak ▷ *Der Schnabel der Amsel ist gelb.* The blackbird's beak is yellow.

Schnalle *f* buckle

Schnaps (*gen* **Schnapses**, *pl* **Schnäpse**) *m* schnapps

schnarchen *vb* [**48**] to snore

schnaufen *vb* [**38**] to puff

Schnauze *f* ❶ nose ▷ *Der Hund hat eine kalte Schnauze.* The dog has a cold nose. ❷ (*informal*) gob ▷ *Halt die Schnauze!* Shut your gob!; **die Schnauze von etwas voll haben** to be fed up to the back teeth of something

> Word for word, **die Schnauze von etwas voll haben** means 'to have one's gob full of something'.

sich **schnäuzen** *vb* [**36**] to blow one's nose

Schnecke *f* snail; **eine Nacktschnecke** a slug

> Word for word, **eine Nacktschnecke** means 'a naked snail'.

Schnee *m* snow ▷ *Heute Nacht ist viel Schnee gefallen.* A lot of snow fell last night.

Schneeball (*pl* **Schneebälle**) *m* snowball

Schneemann (*pl* **Schneemänner**) *m* snowman

schneiden (*imperf* **schnitt**, *perf* **hat geschnitten**) *vb* [**60**] to cut ▷ *Kannst du bitte Brot schneiden?* Can you cut some bread, please? ▷ *jemandem die Haare schneiden* to cut somebody's hair ▷ *Du solltest dir die Haare schneiden lassen.* You should have your hair cut.; **sich schneiden** (1) to cut oneself ▷ *Ich habe mich geschnitten.* I've cut myself. ▷ *Ich habe mir in den Finger geschnitten.* I've cut my finger. (2) to intersect ▷ *Die beiden Geraden schneiden sich.* The two straight lines intersect.

schneien *vb* [**38**] **Es schneit.** It's snowing.

schnell *adj*, *adv* ❶ fast ▷ *Sie hat ein schnelles Auto.* She has a fast car. ▷ *Sie ist schnell gefahren.* She drove fast. ❷ quickly ▷ *Ich rief schnell einen Krankenwagen.* I quickly phoned for an ambulance.

Schnelligkeit *f* speed

Schnellimbiss (*gen* **Schnellimbisses**, *pl* **Schnellimbisse**) *m* snack bar

schnellstens *adv* as quickly as possible

Schnellzug (*pl* **Schnellzüge**) *m* express train

sich **schneuzen** *vb* [**36**] *see* **schnäuzen**

schnitt *vb see* **schneiden**

Schnitt (*pl* **Schnitte**) *m* ❶ cut ▷ *Der Schnitt blutet.* The cut's bleeding. ▷ *Das Kleid hat einen eleganten Schnitt.* The dress has an elegant cut. ❷ average ▷ *Ich habe im Zeugnis einen Schnitt von* drei. I've got an average of C in my report. ❸ pattern ▷ *Hast du zu dem Rock einen Schnitt?* Have you got a pattern for this skirt?

Schnitzel (pl **Schnitzel**) nt escalope ▷ *Ich bestelle mir ein Schnitzel.* I'm going to order an escalope.

schnitzen vb [48] to carve

Schnuller (pl **Schnuller**) m dummy ▷ *Das Baby saugte am Schnuller.* The baby sucked the dummy.

Schnupfen (pl **Schnupfen**) m cold ▷ *Meine Schwester hat Schnupfen.* My sister has a cold.

Schnur (pl **Schnüre**) f ❶ string ▷ *Du solltest eine Schnur um das Päckchen machen.* You should put string round the parcel. ❷ flex ▷ *Die Schnur von der Lampe ist zu kurz.* The flex of the lamp is too short.

Schnurrbart (pl **Schnurrbärte**) m moustache

Schnürsenkel (pl **Schnürsenkel**) m shoelace

Schock (pl **Schocks**) m shock

Schokolade f chocolate ▷ *eine heiße Schokolade* a hot chocolate

schon adv ❶ already ▷ *Ich bin schon fertig.* I've already finished. ❷ yet ▷ *Ist er schon da?* Is he there yet?; **Warst du schon einmal da?** Have you ever been there?; **Ich war schon einmal da.** I've been there before.; **Das war schon immer so.** That's always been the case.; **Hast du schon gehört?** Have you heard?; **schon oft** often; **schon der Gedanke** the very thought; **Du wirst schon sehen.** You'll see.; **Das wird schon noch gut.** That'll be OK.; **ja schon, aber ...** yes, but ...; **schon möglich** possible; **Schon gut!** OK!; **Du weißt schon.** You know.; **Komm schon!** Come on!

schön adj ❶ beautiful ▷ *Sie haben ein schönes Haus.* They have a beautiful house. ❷ nice ▷ *Es waren schöne Ferien.* The holidays were nice. ▷ *Schönes Wochenende!* Have a nice weekend.; **sich schön machen** to make oneself look nice; **Schöne Grüße an deine Eltern!** Regards to your parents.; **ganz schön frech** (informal) pretty damn cheeky; **na schön** very well

schonend adj, adv gentle ▷ *jemandem etwas schonend beibringen* to break something gently to somebody

Schönheit f beauty

schöpfen vb [38] to ladle ▷ *Sie schöpfte Suppe in die Teller.* She ladled soup into the plates.; **Luft schöpfen** to get some air

Schornstein (pl **Schornsteine**) m chimney

schoss vb see **schießen**

Schotte (gen **Schotten**, pl **Schotten**) m Scot; **Er ist Schotte.** He's Scottish.

Schottin f Scot; **Sie ist Schottin.** She's Scottish.

schottisch adj Scottish

Schottland nt Scotland

schräg adj sloping ▷ *Das Haus hat ein schräges Dach.* The house has a sloping roof.; **schräg gegenüber** diagonally opposite

Schrägstrich (pl **Schrägstriche**) m slash

Schrank (pl **Schränke**) m ❶ cupboard ▷ *Der Besen ist im Schrank in der Küche.* The broom's in the cupboard in the kitchen. ❷ wardrobe ▷ *Ich räume meine Kleider in den Schrank.* I'll put my clothes away in the wardrobe.

Schranke f barrier

Schraube f ❶ screw ❷ bolt

Schraubenschlüssel (pl **Schraubenschlüssel**) m spanner

> Word for word, **Schraubenschlüssel** means 'screw key'.

Schraubenzieher (pl **Schraubenzieher**) m screwdriver

GERMAN > ENGLISH

Schreck m fright ▷ *Ich habe einen furchtbaren Schreck bekommen.* I got a terrible fright.

schreckhaft adj jumpy

schrecklich adj, adv ❶ terrible ▷ *Das Wetter war schrecklich schlecht.* The weather was terrible. ❷ terribly ▷ *Das tut schrecklich weh.* It hurts terribly. ▷ *Es tut mir schrecklich leid.* I'm terribly sorry.

Schrei (pl **Schreie**) m ❶ scream ▷ *Als sie die Spinne sah, stieß sie einen Schrei aus.* When she saw the spider she let out a scream. ❷ shout ▷ *Wir hörten einen Schrei um Hilfe.* We heard a shout for help.

schreiben (imperf **schrieb**, perf **hat geschrieben**) vb [61] ❶ to write ▷ *Ich habe ihr einen Brief geschrieben.* I've written her a letter. ▷ *Wir sollten uns schreiben.* We should write to each other. ❷ to spell ▷ *Wie schreibt man seinen Namen?* How do you spell his name?

Schreibmaschine f typewriter

Schreibtisch (pl **Schreibtische**) m desk

Schreibwaren fpl stationery sg

schreien (imperf **schrie**, perf **hat geschrien**) vb [62] ❶ to scream ▷ *Sie schrie vor Schmerzen.* She screamed with pain. ❷ to shout ▷ *Wir haben geschrien, du hast uns aber nicht gehört.* We shouted but you didn't hear us.

Schreiner (pl **Schreiner**) m joiner

schrieb vb see **schreiben**

Schrift f ❶ writing ▷ *Sie hat eine schöne Schrift.* She has lovely writing. ❷ font ▷ *Welche Schrift soll ich für das Dokument nehmen?* Which font should I use for the document?

schriftlich adj, adv written ▷ *eine schriftliche Entschuldigung* a written apology; **etwas schriftlich festhalten** to put something in writing

Schriftsteller (pl **Schriftsteller**) m writer

Schriftstellerin f writer

schrill adj shrill

Schritt (pl **Schritte**) m ❶ step ▷ *Er machte einen vorsichtigen Schritt nach vorn.* He took a careful step forward. ❷ walk ▷ *Ich habe dich an deinem Schritt erkannt.* I recognized you by your walk. ❸ pace ▷ *Sie ging mit schnellen Schritten nach Hause.* She walked home at a brisk pace.; **Schritt fahren** to drive at walking pace

Schrott m scrap metal

Schublade f drawer

schüchtern adj shy

Schuh (pl **Schuhe**) m shoe

Schuhcreme (pl **Schuhcremes**) f shoe polish

Schuhgröße f shoe size ▷ *Welche Schuhgröße hast du?* What shoe size are you?

Schulaufgaben fpl homework sg ▷ *Heute haben wir keine Schulaufgaben bekommen.* We didn't get any homework today.

Schulbuch (pl **Schulbücher**) nt school book

schuld adj **an etwas schuld sein** to be to blame for something; **Er ist schuld.** It's his fault.

Schuld f ❶ guilt ▷ *Seine Schuld konnte nicht bewiesen werden.* His guilt couldn't be proved. ❷ fault ▷ *Es war deine Schuld, dass wir zu spät kamen.* It was your fault that we arrived late.; **jemandem Schuld geben** to blame somebody

schulden vb [54] to owe ▷ *Was schulde ich dir?* How much do I owe you?

Schulden fpl debt sg ▷ *Ich muss noch meine Schulden bei dir bezahlen.* I still have to pay off my debts to you. ▷ *Staatsschulden* national debt

schuldig adj guilty ▷ *Meinst du, dass die Angeklagte schuldig ist?* Do you think

Schuldirektor (pl **Schuldirektoren**) m head teacher

Schuldirektorin f head teacher

Schule f school ▷ *in der Schule* at school

Schüler (pl **Schüler**) m pupil

Schülerin f pupil

Schulferien pl school holidays pl

schulfrei adj *ein schulfreier Tag* a holiday; *Sonntag ist schulfrei.* Sunday isn't a school day.

Schulhof (pl **Schulhöfe**) m playground

Schuljahr (pl **Schuljahre**) nt school year

schulpflichtig adj of school age

Schulstunde f period

Schultag (pl **Schultage**) m *mein erster Schultag* my first day at school

Schultasche f school bag

Schulter f shoulder

Schulzeugnis (gen **Schulzeugnisses**, pl **Schulzeugnisse**) nt school report

Schürze f apron

Schuss (gen **Schusses**, pl **Schüsse**) m shot ▷ *Wir hörten einen Schuss.* We heard a shot.

Schüssel f bowl

Schusswaffe f firearm

Schuster (pl **Schuster**) m cobbler

Schutt m rubble ▷ *Der Schutt von der Baustelle wird morgen weggebracht.* The rubble from the building site will be removed tomorrow.; *Schutt abladen verboten!* No dumping!

schütteln vb [34] to shake; *sich schütteln* to shake oneself

schütten vb [2] ❶ to pour ▷ *Soll ich dir Saft ins Glas schütten?* Shall I pour you some juice? ❷ to spill ▷ *Pass auf, dass du den Kaffee nicht auf die Tischdecke schüttest.* Be careful that you don't spill coffee on the tablecloth.; *Es schüttet.* It's pouring down.

Schutz (gen **Schutzes**) m ❶ protection ▷ *Zum Schutz gegen die Sonne solltest du dich eincremen.* You should put some cream on to protect against the sun. ❷ shelter ▷ *Sie suchten Schutz in der Berghütte.* They took shelter in a mountain hut.; *jemanden in Schutz nehmen* to stand up for somebody

Schütze (gen **Schützen**, pl **Schützen**) m ❶ marksman ▷ *Er ist ein guter Schütze.* He's a good marksman. ❷ Sagittarius ▷ *Martin ist Schütze.* Martin's Sagittarius.

schützen vb [36] to protect ▷ *Die Pflanzen sollten vor zu großer Hitze geschützt werden.* The plants should be protected from too much heat. ▷ *Diese Creme schützt die Haut gegen Sonnenbrand.* This cream protects the skin from sunburn.; *sich gegen etwas schützen* to protect oneself from something

schwach adj weak ▷ *Ihre Stimme wurde immer schwächer.* Her voice became weaker and weaker.; *Das war eine schwache Leistung!* That wasn't very good.

Schwäche f weakness

Schwachsinn m balderdash

Schwager (pl **Schwäger**) m brother-in-law

Schwägerin f sister-in-law

schwamm vb see **schwimmen**

Schwamm (pl **Schwämme**) m sponge

schwanger adj pregnant ▷ *Sie ist im dritten Monat schwanger.* She's three months pregnant.

schwanken vb [38] ❶ to sway ▷ *Das Schiff schwankte.* The ship swayed. ❷ to stagger ▷ *Er schwankte und fiel dann um.* He staggered and fell down. ❸ to fluctuate ▷ *Die Temperaturen schwanken.* Temperatures are fluctuating. ▷ *Der Kurs des Pfunds schwankt.* The exchange rate of the pound is fluctuating.

Schwanz (gen **Schwanzes**, pl **Schwänze**) m tail

schwänzen vb [36] (informal) to skive off ▷ *Ich habe heute die Turnstunde geschwänzt.* I skived off PE today.

Schwarm (pl **Schwärme**) m swarm ▷ *ein Schwarm Fliegen* a swarm of flies; *Er ist mein Schwarm.* (informal) I have a crush on him.

schwärmen (perf **ist/hat geschwärmt**) vb [38]

> Use **sein** to form the perfect tense for 'to swarm'.

to swarm ▷ *Die Bienen sind aus dem Bienenstock geschwärmt.* The bees swarmed out of the hive.; **schwärmen für** (informal) to have a crush on; **schwärmen von** to rave about

schwarz adj ❶ black ▷ *Der Himmel wurde immer schwärzer.* The sky turned blacker and blacker.; **Schwarzes Brett** notice board

> Word for word, **Schwarzes Brett** means 'black board'.

ins Schwarze treffen to hit the bull's eye ❷ (person) Black

Schwarzbrot (pl **Schwarzbrote**) nt brown rye bread

Schwarze (gen **Schwarzen**, pl **Schwarzen**) mf Black person

schwarzfahren (pres **fährt schwarz**, imperf **fuhr schwarz**, perf **ist schwarzgefahren**) vb [21] *Sie fährt in der Straßenbahn immer schwarz.* She never pays her tram fare.

schwarzsehen (pres **sieht schwarz**, imperf **sah schwarz**, perf **hat schwarzgesehen**) vb [64] to look on the black side of things ▷ *Sieh doch nicht immer so schwarz.* Don't always look on the black side of things.

Schwarzwald m Black Forest

schwarz-weiß adj black and white

schwätzen vb [48] to chatter

Schwätzer (pl **Schwätzer**) m (informal) windbag

Schwede (gen **Schweden**, pl **Schweden**) m Swede; **Er ist Schwede.** He's Swedish.

Schweden nt Sweden

Schwedin f Swede

schwedisch adj Swedish

schweigen (imperf **schwieg**, perf **hat geschwiegen**) vb ❶ to be silent ▷ *Die Kinder finden es schwierig, mehr als fünf Minuten lang zu schweigen.* The children find it difficult to be silent for more than five minutes. ❷ to stop talking ▷ *Sag ihm, er soll schweigen.* Tell him to stop talking.

Schwein (pl **Schweine**) nt ❶ pig; **Schwein haben** to be really lucky

Schweinebraten (pl **Schweinebraten**) m roast pork

Schweinefleisch nt pork

Schweiß (gen **Schweißes**) m sweat

Schweiz f Switzerland

Schweizer (pl **Schweizer**) m Swiss ▷ *die Schweizer* the Swiss

Schweizerin f Swiss

schweizerisch adj Swiss

schwer adj, adv ❶ heavy ▷ *Ich habe einen schweren Koffer.* I have a heavy suitcase. ▷ *Er hat eine schwere Erkältung.* He has a heavy cold.; **Ich habe einen schweren Kopf.** I've got a headache.

> Word for word, **Ich habe einen schweren Kopf** means 'I have a heavy head'.

❷ difficult ▷ *Die Mathearbeit war schwer.* The maths test was difficult.; **Er ist schwer verletzt.** He's badly injured.

schwerfallen (pres **fällt schwer**, imperf **fiel schwer**, perf **ist schwergefallen**) vb [22] **jemandem schwerfallen** to be difficult for somebody

Schwert (pl **Schwerter**) nt sword

Schwester f ❶ sister ▷ *Meine Schwester ist jünger als ich.* My sister's younger

Schwiegereltern pl parents-in-law pl

Schwiegermutter (pl **Schwiegermütter**) f mother-in-law

Schwiegersohn (pl **Schwiegersöhne**) m son-in-law

Schwiegertochter (pl **Schwiegertöchter**) f daughter-in-law

Schwiegervater (pl **Schwiegerväter**) m father-in-law

schwierig adj difficult

Schwierigkeit f difficulty

Schwimmbad (pl **Schwimmbäder**) nt swimming pool

Schwimmbecken (pl **Schwimmbecken**) nt swimming pool

schwimmen (imperf **schwamm**, perf **ist geschwommen**) vb [63] ❶ to swim ▷ *Er kann nicht schwimmen.* He can't swim. ❷ to float ▷ *Auf dem Fluss schwammen Äste.* Branches were floating on the river.

Schwindel m ❶ dizzy spell ▷ *Bei hohem Fieber muss man auch mit Schwindel rechnen.* If you have high temperature, you can also expect to have dizzy spells. ❷ fraud ▷ *Der Schwindel wurde entdeckt.* The fraud was discovered.

schwindelfrei adj **schwindelfrei sein** to have a good head for heights

schwindeln vb [34] (*informal*) to fib

schwindlig adj dizzy; **Mir ist schwindlig.** I feel dizzy.

schwitzen vb [36] to sweat

schwören (imperf **schwor**, perf **hat geschworen**) vb to swear

schwul adj gay

schwül adj close

Schwule (gen **Schwulen**, pl **Schwulen**) mf gay person

Schwung (pl **Schwünge**) m swing ▷ *Sie setzte das Pendel in Schwung.* She started the pendulum swinging.; **jemanden in Schwung bringen** to get somebody going

sechs num six

Sechs f ❶ six ❷ unsatisfactory
 • German marks range from one (**sehr gut**) to six (**ungenügend**).

sechste adj sixth ▷ *Er kam als Sechster.* He was the sixth to arrive.

Sechstel (pl **Sechstel**) nt sixth

sechzehn num sixteen

sechzig num sixty

See f sea ▷ *auf See* at sea; **an die See fahren** to go to the seaside
▶ m lake ▷ *der Genfer See* Lake Geneva

Seehund (pl **Seehunde**) m seal

seekrank adj seasick

Seele f soul

Segel (pl **Segel**) nt sail

Segelboot (pl **Segelboote**) nt yacht

Segelflugzeug (pl **Segelflugzeuge**) nt glider

segeln (perf **ist gesegelt**) vb [34] to sail

Segelschiff (pl **Segelschiffe**) nt sailing ship

Segen (pl **Segen**) m blessing

sehen (pres **sieht**, imperf **sah**, perf **hat gesehen**) vb [64] ❶ to see ▷ *Hast du den Film schon gesehen?* Have you seen the film yet?; **siehe Seite fünf** see page five ❷ to look ▷ *Sieh mal an die Tafel.* Look at the board.; **schlecht sehen** to have bad eyesight; **mal sehen, ob ...** let's see if ...; **Kommst du mit? — Mal sehen.** Are you coming? — We'll see.

sehenswert adj worth seeing

Sehenswürdigkeiten fpl sights pl

sich sehnen vb [38] **sich sehnen nach** to long for

Sehnsucht (pl **Sehnsüchte**) f longing

sehnsüchtig adj longing

sehr adv ❶ very ▷ *Das ist sehr schön.* That's very nice.; **sehr gut** very good
 • German marks range from one (**sehr gut**) to six (**ungenügend**).
❷ a lot ▷ *Sie hat sehr geweint.* She cried

a lot.; **zu sehr** too much; **Sehr geehrter Herr Ahlers** Dear Mr Ahlers

Seide f silk

Seife f soap

Seifenoper f soap opera

Seil (pl **Seile**) nt ❶ rope ▷ *Sie hatten ihn mit einem Seil gefesselt.* They had tied him up with a rope. ❷ cable ▷ *das Seil des Skilifts* the cable of the ski lift

Seilbahn f cable car

sein (pres **ist**, imperf **war**, perf **ist gewesen**) vb [65] to be ▷ *Ich bin müde.* I'm tired. ▷ *Du bist doof.* You're stupid. ▷ *Er ist reich.* He's rich. ▷ *Sie ist Lehrerin.* She's a teacher. ▷ *Es ist kalt.* It's cold. ▷ *Wir sind Schüler am Gymnasium.* We're pupils at the grammar school. ▷ *Wir waren dort. We were there.* ▷ *Wir sind im Schwimmbad gewesen.* We've been to the swimming pool. ▷ *Seien Sie nicht böse.* Don't be angry. ▷ *Morgen bin ich in Rom.* Tomorrow I'll be in Rome.; **Das wäre gut.** That would be a good thing.; **Wenn ich Sie wäre ...** If I were you ...; **Das wär's.** That's it.; **Mir ist kalt.** I'm cold.; **Was ist?** What's the matter?; **Ist was?** Is something the matter?; **es sei denn, dass ...** unless ...; **wie dem auch sei** be that as it may; **Wie wäre es mit ...?** How about ...?; **Lass das sein!** Stop that!; **sich etwas bewusst sein** to be aware of something ▷ *Sie war sich der Frist bewusst.* She was aware of the deadline.

▶ adj ❶ his ▷ *Sein Deutschlehrer ist nett.* His German teacher's nice. ▷ *Seine Mutter erlaubt das nicht.* His mother doesn't allow it. ▷ *Das ist sein Buch.* That's his book. ▷ *Seine Eltern sind klasse.* His parents are great. ▷ *Das ist nicht mein Füller, das ist seiner.* That's not my pen, it's his. ▷ *Meine Mutter heißt Anne, seine auch.* My mother's called Anne, so is his. ❷ its ▷ *Der Fuchs kam aus seiner Höhle.* The fox came out of its lair. ▷ *Jedes Buch hat seinen Platz.* Each book has its place.

seiner pron

seiner is the genitive of **er**.

of him ▷ *Wir gedenken seiner.* We're thinking of him.

seinetwegen adv ❶ for his sake ▷ *Ihr müsst seinetwegen nicht auf euren Urlaub verzichten.* You don't have to do without your holiday for his sake. ❷ on his account ▷ *Hat sie sich seinetwegen so aufgeregt?* Did she get so upset on his account? ❸ as far as he's concerned ▷ *Er sagt, dass du seinetwegen gehen kannst.* He says that as far as he's concerned you can go.

seit prep, conj

The preposition **seit** takes the dative.

❶ since ▷ *Seit er verheiratet ist, spielt er nicht mehr Fußball.* He's stopped playing football since he got married. ▷ *Seit letztem Jahr habe ich nichts mehr von ihm gehört.* I haven't heard anything from him since last year. ❷ for ▷ *Er ist seit einer Woche hier.* He's been here for a week. ▷ *seit Langem* for a long time

seitdem adv, conj since ▷ *Seitdem sie im Gymnasium ist, hat sie kaum mehr Zeit.* Since she's been going to grammar school, she's hardly had any time.; **Ich habe seitdem nichts mehr von ihr gehört.** I haven't heard from her since then.

Seite f ❶ side ▷ *Die rechte Seite des Autos war beschädigt.* The right side of the car was damaged. ❷ page ▷ *Das steht auf Seite fünfzig.* It's on page fifty.

Sekretär m secretary

Sekretariat (pl **Sekretariate**) nt secretary's office

Sekretärin f secretary

Sekt (pl **Sekte**) m sparkling wine

Sekunde f second ▷ *zehn Sekunden* ten seconds

selber pron = selbst
selbst pron, adv ❶ on one's own ▷ *Das Kind kann sich selbst anziehen.* The child can get dressed on her own. ▷ *Ich werde schon selbst eine Lösung finden.* I'll find a solution on my own.; **ich selbst** I myself; **er selbst** he himself; **wir selbst** we ourselves; **Sie ist die Liebenswürdigkeit selbst.** She's kindness itself.; **Er braut sein Bier selbst.** He brews his own beer.; **von selbst** by itself ❷ even ▷ *Selbst meine Mutter findet Oasis gut.* Even my mother likes Oasis.; **selbst wenn** even if
selbstständig adj see **selbstständig**
Selbstbedienung f self-service
selbstbewusst adj self-confident
Selbstmord (pl **Selbstmorde**) m suicide ▷ *Selbstmord begehen* to commit suicide
Selbstmordanschlag (pl **Selbstmordanschläge**) m suicide attack
selbstsicher adj self-assured
selbstständig adj ❶ independent ▷ *Du solltest langsam selbstständiger werden.* It's about time you started to become more independent. ▷ *ein selbstständiger Staat* an independent country ❷ on one's own ▷ *Kannst du das nicht selbstständig entscheiden?* Can't you decide on your own?; **sich selbstständig machen** to become self-employed
selbstverständlich adj, adv ❶ obvious ▷ *Das ist für mich durchaus nicht selbstverständlich.* It's not at all obvious to me.; **Es ist doch selbstverständlich, dass man da hilft.** It goes without saying that you should help.; **Ich halte das für selbstverständlich.** I take that for granted. ❷ of course ▷ *Ich habe mich selbstverständlich sofort bedankt.* Of course I said thank you immediately. ▷ *Kommt er mit? — Selbstverständlich.* Is he coming? — Of course. ▷ *Ich habe selbstverständlich nicht unterschrieben.* Of course I didn't sign.
Selbstvertrauen nt self-confidence
Sellerie m celeriac
selten adj, adv ❶ rare ▷ *eine seltene Pflanze* a rare plant ❷ rarely ▷ *Wir gehen selten ins Kino.* We rarely go to the cinema.
seltsam adj curious
Semester (pl **Semester**) nt semester
senden (imperf **sendete** or **sandte**, perf **hat gesendet** or **gesandt**) vb ❶ to send ▷ *Bitte senden Sie mir Ihren neuesten Katalog.* Please send me your latest catalogue. ❷ to broadcast ▷ *Der Spielfilm wird im dritten Programm gesendet.* The film will be broadcast on Channel three. ▷ *Wir senden bis Mitternacht.* We broadcast until midnight.
Sendung f ❶ transmission ▷ *Während der Sendung darf das Studio nicht betreten werden.* Nobody's allowed to enter the studio during transmission. ❷ programme ▷ *Kennst du die Sendung 'Tiere im Zoo'?* Do you know the programme 'Animals in the Zoo'? ❸ consignment ▷ *Für Sie ist eine Sendung mit Mustern angekommen.* A consignment of samples has arrived for you.
Senf (pl **Senfe**) m mustard
Sensation f sensation
sensibel adj sensitive ▷ *Sie ist ein sehr sensibler Mensch.* She's a very sensitive person.

> Be careful! **sensibel** does not mean sensible.

sentimental adj sentimental ▷ *Nun werd nicht sentimental!* Now don't get sentimental.
September m September ▷ *im September* in September ▷ *am elften September* on the eleventh of September ▷ *Ulm, den 10. September 2025* Ulm,

10 September 2025 ▷ *Heute ist der elfte September.* Today is the eleventh of September.
Serie f series sg
seriös adj respectable

> Be careful! **seriös** does not mean **serious**.

Server (pl **Server**) m server
Service (gen **Service** or **Services**, pl **Service**) nt set ▷ *Sie hat ein hübsches Teeservice aus Porzellan.* She has a lovely china tea set.
▶ m service ▷ *In dem Hotel ist der Service ausgezeichnet.* The service in the hotel is excellent.
Serviette f serviette
servus excl ❶ hello! ❷ goodbye!
Sessel (pl **Sessel**) m armchair
setzen vb [36] to put ▷ *Sie setzte das Kind auf den Stuhl.* She put the child on the chair. ▷ *Er setzte das Glas an den Mund.* He put the glass to his lips. ▷ *Hast du meinen Namen auf die Liste gesetzt?* Have you put my name on the list? ▷ *ein Komma setzen* to put a comma; **jemandem eine Frist setzen** to set somebody a deadline; **sich setzen (1)** to settle ▷ *Der Kaffeesatz hat sich gesetzt.* The coffee grounds have settled. **(2)** to sit down ▷ *Setz dich doch!* Do sit down! ▷ *Er setzte sich aufs Sofa.* He sat down on the sofa.; **auf etwas setzen** to bet on something ▷ *Er hat hundert Euro auf die Nummer zwei gesetzt.* He bet a hundred euros on number two.
Seuche f epidemic
seufzen vb [36] to sigh
Sexismus m sexism
sexuell adj sexual
Shampoo (pl **Shampoos**) nt shampoo
Sibirien nt Siberia
sich pron ❶ himself ▷ *Er redet mit sich selbst.* He's talking to himself. herself ▷ *Sie spricht nicht gern über sich selbst.* She doesn't like to talk about herself. ▷ *Sie wäscht sich.* She's washing herself. ▷ *Sie hat sich einen Pullover gekauft.* She bought herself a jumper. itself ▷ *Das Boot hat sich wieder aufgerichtet.* The boat righted itself. ❷ themselves ▷ *Meine Eltern haben sich ein neues Auto gekauft.* My parents have bought themselves a new car. ▷ *Sie bleiben gern unter sich.* They keep themselves to themselves. ❸ each other ▷ *Sie lieben sich.* They love each other.; **Sie wäscht sich die Haare.** She's washing her hair.; **Er schneidet sich die Nägel.** He's cutting his nails.; **Man fragt sich, ob ...** One wonders whether ...; **Sie wiederholen sich.** You're repeating yourself.; **Haben Sie Ihren Ausweis bei sich?** Do you have your pass on you?; **Dieser Artikel verkauft sich gut.** This article sells well.
sicher adj, adv ❶ safe ▷ *Das ist ein sehr sicheres Auto.* It's a very safe car. ❷ certain ▷ *Der Termin ist noch nicht sicher.* The date isn't certain yet.; **Ich bin nicht sicher.** I'm not sure. ❸ reliable ▷ *eine sichere Methode* a reliable method; **vor jemandem sicher sein** to be safe from somebody; **vor etwas sicher sein** to be safe from something ❹ definitely ▷ *Sie kommt sicher nicht mehr.* She's definitely not coming anymore.; **Er weiß das sicher schon.** I'm sure he knows that already.; **sicher nicht** surely not; **Aber sicher!** Of course!
Sicherheit f safety ▷ *Tragen Sie einen Helm zu Ihrer eigenen Sicherheit.* Wear a helmet for your own safety. ▷ *Diese Maßnahmen dienen der Sicherheit der Fluggäste.* These measures are for passenger safety.; **Hier sind wir in Sicherheit.** We're safe here.; **Ich kann nicht mit Sicherheit sagen, ob ich komme.** I can't say for sure if I'll come.

Sicherheitsgurt (pl **Sicherheitsgurte**) m seat belt

sicherlich adv certainly

sichern vb [88] to secure ▷ Maßnahmen, die Arbeitsplätze sichern measures to secure jobs; **Daten sichern** to back up data; **jemandem etwas sichern** to secure something for somebody

Sicherung f ❶ securing ▷ Maßnahmen zur Sicherung der Arbeitsplätze measures for securing jobs ❷ fuse ▷ Die Sicherung ist durchgebrannt. The fuse has blown.

Sicht f view ▷ Wir hatten eine gute Sicht auf die Berge. We had a good view of the mountains. ▷ Du versperrst mir die Sicht. You're blocking my view.; **auf lange Sicht** on a long-term basis; **aus jemandes Sicht** as somebody sees it

sichtbar adj visible

sie pron ❶ she ▷ Sie ist sehr hübsch. She's very pretty. ❷ it ▷ Schöne Tasche, ist sie neu? Lovely bag, is it new? ▷ Kann ich deine Tasche haben, oder brauchst du sie noch? Can I have your bag or do you need it? ❸ her ▷ Ich kenne sie nicht. I don't know her. ❹ they ▷ Sie sind alle gekommen. They all came. ❺ them ▷ Ich habe sie alle eingeladen. I've invited all of them.

Sie pron you ▷ Möchten Sie mitkommen? Would you like to come? ▷ Ich kenne Sie. I know you.

- The formal form of address **Sie**
- (singular and plural) is used when
- addressing people you don't know or
- your superiors. Teachers generally
- say **Sie** to pupils over the age of 16.

Sieb (pl **Siebe**) nt ❶ sieve ▷ Wir sollten da Mehl durch ein Sieb schütten. We should rub the flour through a sieve. ❷ strainer ▷ Hast du ein Teesieb? Have you got a tea strainer?

sieben num seven

siebte adj seventh ▷ Er kam als Siebter. He was the seventh to arrive.

siebzehn num seventeen

siebzig num seventy

Siedlung f ❶ settlement (of people, houses) ❷ estate ▷ Sie wohnt in unserer Siedlung. She lives on our estate.

Sieg (pl **Siege**) m victory

siegen vb [38] to win ▷ Welche Mannschaft hat gesiegt? Which team won?

Sieger (pl **Sieger**) m winner ▷ Brasilien war 1994 Sieger der Fußballweltmeisterschaft. Brazil was the winner of the 1994 World Cup.

siehe vb see **sehen**

siezen vb [36] to address as 'Sie'

- The formal form of address **Sie**
- (singular and plural) is used when
- addressing people you don't know or
- your superiors. Teachers generally
- say **Sie** to pupils over the age of 16.

Silbe f syllable

Silber nt silver

Silvester (pl **Silvester**) nt New Year's Eve

simsen vb [36] (informal) to text

singen (imperf **sang**, perf **hat gesungen**) vb [66] to sing

Singular (pl **Singulare**) m singular

sinken (imperf **sank**, perf **ist gesunken**) vb [67] ❶ to sink ▷ Das Schiff ist gesunken. The ship has sunk. ❷ to fall ▷ Die Preise für Computer sind gesunken. The prices of computers have fallen.

Sinn (pl **Sinne**) m ❶ sense ▷ die fünf Sinne the five senses ❷ meaning ▷ Ich verstehe den Sinn dieses Satzes nicht. I don't understand the meaning of this sentence. ▷ Was ist der Sinn des Lebens? What's the meaning of life?; **Sinn für etwas haben** to have a sense of something; **jemandem in den Sinn kommen** to come to somebody; **Es hat keinen Sinn.** There's no point.

sinnlos adj ❶ pointless ▷ Es ist sinnlos, das zu tun. It's pointless doing that.

❷ meaningless ▷ *Er hat sinnloses Zeug geredet.* He talked meaningless rubbish.

sinnvoll *adj* sensible ▷ *Das wäre eine sinnvolle Änderung.* That would be a sensible change.

Situation *f* situation

Sitz (*gen* Sitzes, *pl* Sitze) *m* seat

sitzen *vb* [68] ❶ to sit ▷ *Er saß auf dem Stuhl.* He was sitting on the chair.; **sitzen bleiben (1)** to remain seated ▷ *Bitte bleiben Sie sitzen.* Please remain seated. **(2)** to have to repeat a year
- In Germany, pupils do not
- automatically move up (**versetzt**
- **werden**) to the next class at the
- end of the school year. If their
- performance is not good enough,
- they have to repeat the school year.
- This is known as **sitzen bleiben**.

▷ *Ich habe Angst, dass ich dieses Jahr sitzen bleibe.* I'm worried that I'll have to repeat this year. ❷ to fit ▷ *Diese Hose sitzt.* These trousers fit well.

Sitzplatz (*gen* Sitzplatzes, *pl* Sitzplätze) *m* seat

Sitzung *f* meeting

Skandal (*pl* Skandale) *m* scandal

Skandinavien *nt* Scandinavia

skandinavisch *adj* Scandinavian

Skelett (*pl* Skelette) *nt* skeleton

Ski (*pl* Ski *or* Skier) *m* ski; **Ski fahren** to ski

Skifahrer (*pl* Skifahrer) *m* skier

Skilaufen *nt* skiing

Skilehrer (*pl* Skilehrer) *m* ski instructor

Skilift (*pl* Skilifte *or* Skilifts) *m* ski lift

Skorpion (*pl* Skorpione) *m* ❶ scorpion ❷ Scorpio ▷ *Sie ist Skorpion.* She's Scorpio.

Slip (*pl* Slips) *m* pants *pl* ▷ *ein Slip* a pair of pants

Slowakei *f* Slovakia

Smartphone (*pl* Smartphones) *nt* smartphone

SMS (*pl* SMS) *f* text message; *Er hat mir eine SMS geschickt.* He texted me.

so *adv*, *conj*, *excl* ❶ so ▷ *Ich hatte mich so darauf gefreut.* I was so looking forward to it. ▷ *So schön* so nice ▷ *zwanzig oder so* twenty or so; **und so weiter** and so on; **so ... wie ... as ... as ...** ▷ *Sie ist so groß wie ich.* She's as tall as me. ❷ so much ▷ *Das hat ihn so geärgert, dass ...* That annoyed him so much that ... ❸ like that ▷ *Mach es nicht so.* Don't do it like that.; **... oder so was ...** or something like that; **so einer wie ich** somebody like me; **Na so was!** Well, well!; **so dass** so that; **So?** Really?

sobald *conj* as soon as

Söckchen (*pl* Söckchen) *nt* ankle sock

Socke *f* sock

sodass *conj* so that

Sofa (*pl* Sofas) *nt* sofa

sofort *adv* immediately

sogar *adv* even

sogenannt *adj* so-called ▷ *unsere sogenannte Demokratie* our so-called democracy

sogleich *adv* straight away

Sohle *f* sole

Sohn (*pl* Söhne) *m* son

solange *conj* as long as ▷ *Ich will arbeiten, solange ich kann.* I want to work for as long as I can.

solch *pron* such ▷ *Sie ist solch eine nette Frau.* She's such a nice lady. ▷ *eine solche Frechheit* such a cheek; **ein solcher** a ... like that

Soldat (*gen* Soldaten, *pl* Soldaten) *m* soldier

solide *adj* ❶ solid ▷ *Dieser Tisch ist aus solidem Holz.* This table is made of solid wood. ❷ sound ▷ *Sie hat solide Grammatikkenntnisse.* She has a sound grasp of grammar. ❸ respectable ▷ *Wir führen ein solides Leben.* We lead a respectable life. ▷ *Er ist solide geworden.* He's become respectable.

sollen (*imperf* sollte, *perf* hat gesollt *or* sollen) *vb* [69]

sollen The past participle **sollen** is used when **sollen** is a modal auxiliary. ❶ to be supposed to ▷ *Ich soll um fünf Uhr dort sein.* I'm supposed to be there at five o'clock. ▷ *Was soll das heißen?* What's that supposed to mean? ▷ *Morgen soll es schön werden.* It's supposed to be nice tomorrow. ❷ to have to ▷ *Du sollst sofort nach Hause.* You have to go home immediately. ▷ *Sie sagt, du sollst nach Hause kommen.* She says that you have to come home.; **Sag ihm, er soll warten.** Tell him he's to wait. ❸ should ▷ *Ich sollte meine Hausaufgaben machen.* I should do my homework. ▷ *Du hättest nicht gehen sollen.* You shouldn't have gone. ▷ *Was soll ich machen?* What should I do? ▷ *Ich hätte eigentlich nicht gesollt.* I really shouldn't have. ▷ *Das sollst du nicht.* You shouldn't do that.; **Sie soll verheiratet sein.** She's said to be married.; **Man sollte glauben, dass ...** You would think that ...; **Soll ich dir helfen?** Shall I help you?; **Soll ich?** Shall I?; **Was soll das?** What's all this?; **Was soll's?** (informal) What the hell!

Sommer (pl **Sommer**) m summer ▷ *im Sommer* in summer

Sommerferien pl summer holidays pl

sommerlich adj ❶ summery ▷ *ein sommerliches Kleid* a summery dress ❷ summer ▷ *sommerliche Kleidung* summer clothes ▷ *sommerliches Wetter* summer weather

Sommerschlussverkauf (pl **Sommerschlussverkäufe**) m summer sale

Sommersprossen fpl freckles pl

Sonderangebot (pl **Sonderangebote**) nt special offer

sonderbar adj strange

sondern conj but; **nicht nur ..., sondern auch** not only ..., but also

Sonderpreis m special price

Sonnabend (pl **Sonnabende**) m Saturday ▷ *am Sonnabend* on Saturday

sonnabends adv on Saturdays

Sonne f sun

sich **sonnen** vb [38] to sun oneself

Sonnenbrand (pl **Sonnenbrände**) m sunburn

Sonnenbrille f sunglasses pl ▷ *Sie trug eine Sonnenbrille.* She was wearing sunglasses.

Sonnenenergie f solar power

Sonnenmilch f suntan lotion

Sonnenschein m sunshine

Sonnenschirm (pl **Sonnenschirme**) m sunshade

Sonnenstich m sunstroke

sonnig adj sunny

Sonntag (pl **Sonntage**) m Sunday ▷ *am Sonntag* on Sunday

sonntags adv on Sundays

sonst adv, conj ❶ normally ▷ *Was ist mit dir? Du bist doch sonst nicht so still.* What's wrong with you? You're not normally so quiet. ▷ *Die Kinder sind sonst eigentlich artiger.* The children normally behave better. ❷ else ▷ *Wer sonst?* Who else? ▷ *Was sonst?* What else? ▷ *Sonst war niemand da.* Nobody else was there. ▷ *sonst nichts* nothing else; **sonst noch etwas;** Haben Sie sonst noch einen Wunsch? Would you like anything else?; **Sonst noch etwas?** Anything else?; **sonst wo** somewhere else ❸ otherwise ▷ *Ich habe etwas Kopfschmerzen, aber sonst geht's mir gut.* I've got a headache, otherwise I feel fine.

sonstig adj other

Sorge f worry; **Ich mache mir Sorgen.** I'm worried.

sorgen vb [38] **für jemanden sorgen** to look after somebody; **für etwas sorgen** to see to something; **sich um jemanden sorgen** to worry about somebody

sorgfältig adj careful
Sorte f ❶ sort ▷ *Welche Sorte Äpfel ist das?* What sort of apple is that? ❷ brand ▷ *Welche Sorte Waschmittel verwenden Sie?* What brand of detergent do you use?
sortieren (perf **hat sortiert**) vb [76] to sort out
Soße f ❶ sauce ▷ *Eis mit Himbeersoße* ice cream with raspberry sauce ❷ gravy ▷ *Schweinebraten mit Soße* roast pork with gravy ❸ dressing ▷ *Salat mit einer Joghurtsoße* salad with a yoghurt dressing
Souvenir (pl **Souvenirs**) nt souvenir
soviel adv see **viel**
▶ *conj* as far as ▷ *soviel ich weiß* as far as I know
soweit adv see **weit**
▶ *conj* as far as ▷ *Soweit ich weiß, kann er nicht kommen.* As far as I know, he can't come.
sowenig adv see **wenig**
sowie conj as soon as ▷ *Ich rufe an, sowie ich Bescheid weiß.* I'll phone as soon as I know.
sowieso adv anyway
sowohl conj **sowohl ... als auch** both ... and
sozial adj social; **soziale Medien** social media
Sozialhilfe f social security ▷ *Sozialhilfe bekommen* to be on social security
Sozialkunde f social studies sg
Spalte f ❶ crack ▷ *Durch die Trockenheit hatten sich tiefe Spalten gebildet.* Deep cracks had formed as a result of the dry spell. ❷ column ▷ *Der Text ist in zwei Spalten gedruckt.* The text is printed in two columns.
spalten vb [2] to split
Spanien nt Spain
Spanier (pl **Spanier**) m Spaniard; **Er ist Spanier.** He's Spanish.; **die Spanier** the Spanish

Spanierin f Spaniard; **Sie ist Spanierin.** She's Spanish.
spanisch adj Spanish
Spanisch (gen **Spanischen**) nt Spanish ▷ *Er lernt Spanisch in der Schule.* He's learning Spanish at school.
spannend adj exciting
Spannung f ❶ suspense ▷ *ein Film voller Spannung* a film full of suspense ❷ tension ▷ *Das führte zu Spannungen zwischen den beiden Ländern.* That caused tension between the two countries.
Sparbuch (pl **Sparbücher**) nt savings book
sparen vb [38] to save ▷ *Wir müssen sparen.* We have to save. ▷ *Sie hat zweihundert Euro gespart.* She's saved two hundred euros. ▷ *Energie sparen* to save energy ▷ *Er spart für ein Mountainbike.* He's saving for a mountain bike.; **sich etwas sparen** (1) not to bother with something ▷ *Den Film kannst du dir sparen.* Don't bother with that film. (2) to keep something to oneself ▷ *Spar dir deine Bemerkungen.* You can keep your remarks to yourself.; **mit etwas sparen** to be sparing with something; **an etwas sparen** to economize on something ▷ *Sie spart in letzter Zeit am Essen.* She's been economizing on food recently.

▌ Be careful! **sparen** does not mean **to spare**.

Spargel m asparagus
Sparkasse f savings bank
sparsam adj ❶ economical ▷ *ein sparsames Auto* an economical car ▷ *Wir sollten mit den Rohstoffen sparsam umgehen.* We should be economical with raw materials. ❷ thrifty ▷ *Sie ist sehr sparsam.* She's very thrifty.
Sparschwein (pl **Sparschweine**) nt piggy bank
Spaß (gen **Spaßes**, pl **Späße**) m fun ▷ *Wir hatten in den Ferien viel Spaß.* We

had great fun in the holidays.; **Sie versteht keinen Spaß.** She has no sense of humour.

> Word for word, **Sie versteht keinen Spaß** means 'She doesn't understand fun'.

Skifahren macht mir Spaß. I like skiing.; **zum Spaß** for fun; **Viel Spaß!** Have fun!

spät adj, adv late ▷ *Es wird spät.* It's getting late. ▷ *Wir kamen zu spät.* We were late.; **Wie spät ist es?** What's the time?

später adj, adv later ▷ **Bis später!** See you later!

spätestens adv at the latest

Spatz (gen **Spatzen**, pl **Spatzen**) m sparrow

spazieren vb [76] **spazieren fahren** to go for a drive; **spazieren gehen** to go for a walk

Spaziergang (pl **Spaziergänge**) m walk ▷ *einen Spaziergang machen* to go for a walk

Speck m bacon

Speerwerfen nt throwing the javelin

Speicher (pl **Speicher**) m ❶ loft ▷ *Die alten Möbel sind auf dem Speicher.* The old furniture's in the loft. ❷ storehouse ▷ *Die alten Speicher am Hafen wurden zu Wohnungen umgebaut.* The old storehouses at the harbour were converted into flats. ❸ memory ▷ *Ich will den Speicher meines Computers erweitern.* I want to expand the memory of my computer.

speichern (perf **hat gespeichert**) vb [88] ❶ to store ▷ *Energie speichern* to store energy ❷ to save ▷ *eine Datei speichern* to save a file

Speiseeis nt ice cream

Speisekarte f menu ▷ *Könnte ich bitte die Speisekarte haben?* Could I have the menu please?

Speisesaal m dining room

Speisewagen (pl **Speisewagen**) m dining car

Spende f donation

spenden vb [54] to donate ▷ *Ich habe zwanzig Euro gespendet.* I've donated twenty euros.; **Blut spenden** to give blood

> Be careful! **spenden** does not mean **to spend**.

Spender (pl **Spender**) m donor

spendieren (perf **hat spendiert**) vb [76] **jemandem etwas spendieren** (informal) to stand somebody something

Sperre f ❶ barrier ▷ *Vor dem Eingang befand sich eine Sperre.* There was a barrier in front of the entrance. ❷ ban ▷ *Er erhielt eine Sperre von drei Monaten.* He got a three-month ban.

sperren (perf **hat gesperrt**) vb [38] ❶ to close ▷ *Die Polizei hat die Straße gesperrt.* The police closed the road. ❷ to obstruct ▷ *Es ist verboten, gegnerische Spieler zu sperren.* Obstructing the opposition is not allowed. ❸ to lock ▷ *Diese Dateien sind gesperrt.* These files are locked.

Spezialität f speciality

speziell adj, adv ❶ special ▷ *Haben Sie spezielle Wünsche?* Do you have any special requests? ❷ especially ▷ *Das ist speziell für dich gemacht worden.* It was made especially for you.

Spiegel (pl **Spiegel**) m mirror ▷ *Er sah in den Spiegel.* He looked in the mirror.

Spiegelbild (pl **Spiegelbilder**) nt reflection

Spiegelei (pl **Spiegeleier**) nt fried egg

Spiel (pl **Spiele**) nt ❶ game ▷ *Sollen wir ein Spiel spielen?* Shall we play a game? ▷ *Hast du das Spiel England gegen Deutschland gesehen?* Did you see the England-Germany game? ❷ pack ▷ *Hast du ein Spiel Karten?* Do you have a pack of cards?; **ein Theaterspiel** a play

spielen vb [38] to play ▷ *Die Kinder spielen im Garten.* The children are playing in the garden. ▷ *Wollen wir Tennis spielen?* Shall we play tennis? ▷ *Wer spielt den Hamlet?* Who's playing Hamlet? ▷ *Wir haben um Geld gespielt.* We played for money.

Spieler (pl **Spieler**) m ❶ player ▷ *Wir brauchen noch einen dritten Spieler.* We still need a third player. ❷ gambler ▷ *Er ist ein leidenschaftlicher Spieler.* He's a passionate gambler.

Spielerin f ❶ player ❷ gambler

Spielfeld (pl **Spielfelder**) nt pitch

Spielfilm (pl **Spielfilme**) m feature film

Spielkonsole f games console

Spielplatz (gen **Spielplatzes**, pl **Spielplätze**) m playground

Spielzeug (pl **Spielzeuge**) nt toy

Spinat m spinach

Spinne f spider

spinnen (imperf **spann**, perf **hat gesponnen**) vb ❶ to spin ▷ *Wolle spinnen* to spin wool ❷ to be crazy ▷ *Du spinnst wohl!* You're crazy!

Spionage f espionage

spionieren (perf **hat spioniert**) vb [76] to spy

spitz adj pointed; **ein spitzer Winkel** an acute angle; **eine spitze Zunge** a sharp tongue; **eine spitze Bemerkung** a caustic remark

spitze adj (informal) great; *Das war spitze!* That was great!

Spitze f ❶ point ▷ *Die Spitze des Bleistifts ist abgebrochen.* The point of the pencil has broken off. ❷ peak ▷ *Die Spitzen der Berge waren schneebedeckt.* The peaks of the mountains were covered with snow. ❸ top ▷ *Welche Mannschaft liegt an der Spitze?* Which team is top? ❹ lace ▷ *An ihrem Kleid war ein Kragen aus Spitze.* Her dress had a lace collar.

Spitzer (pl **Spitzer**) m pencil sharpener

Spitzname (gen **Spitznamens**, pl **Spitznamen**) m nickname

Splitter (pl **Splitter**) m splinter

sponsern vb [88] to sponsor

Sport m sport

Sportart f sport ▷ *verschiedene Sportarten* various sports

Sportler (pl **Sportler**) m sportsman

Sportlerin f sportswoman

sportlich adj sporty ▷ *Bettina ist sehr sportlich.* Bettina is very sporty.

Sportplatz (gen **Sportplatzes**, pl **Sportplätze**) m sports field

Sportverein (pl **Sportvereine**) m sports club

Sportzentrum (pl **Sportzentren**) nt sports centre

sprach vb see **sprechen**

Sprache f language

Sprachführer (pl **Sprachführer**) m phrase book

> Word for word, **Sprachführer** means 'language guide'.

Sprachlabor (pl **Sprachlabors** or **Sprachlabore**) nt language laboratory

sprachlich adj linguistic

sprachlos adj speechless

Sprachsteuerung f voice control

sprang vb see **springen**

sprechen (pres **spricht**, imperf **sprach**, perf **hat gesprochen**) vb [70] ❶ to talk ▷ *Seid bitte ruhig, wenn ich spreche.* Please be quiet, I'm talking. ▷ *Du sprichst so leise.* You talk so quietly. ▷ *Wir haben von dir gesprochen.* We were talking about you. ❷ to say ▷ *Sie hat kein Wort gesprochen.* She didn't say a word. ❸ to speak ▷ *Ich spreche Italienisch ziemlich schlecht.* I speak Italian pretty badly.; **jemanden sprechen** to speak to somebody; **mit jemandem über etwas sprechen** to speak to somebody about something; *Das spricht für ihn.* That's a point in his favour.

Sprecher m speaker

Sprecherin f speaker

Sprechstunde f surgery (doctor's)

spricht vb see **sprechen**

Sprichwort (pl **Sprichwörter**) nt proverb

springen (imperf **sprang**, perf **ist gesprungen**) vb [71] ❶ to jump ▷ *Er sprang über den Zaun.* He jumped over the fence. ❷ to crack ▷ *Das Glas ist gesprungen.* The glass has cracked.

Spritze f ❶ syringe ▷ *Die Spritze muss steril sein.* The syringe has to be sterile. ❷ injection ▷ *Der Arzt hat mir eine Spritze gegeben.* The doctor gave me an injection. ❸ nozzle ▷ *Die Spritze am Gartenschlauch ist nicht dicht.* The nozzle on the garden hose leaks.

spritzen (perf **hat/ist gespritzt**) vb [36]

Use **haben** to form the perfect tense. Use **sein** to form the perfect tense for 'to spurt out'.

❶ to spray ▷ *Er hat sein Fahrrad grün gespritzt.* He's sprayed his bike green.; **den Garten spritzen** to water the garden; **jemanden nass spritzen** to splash somebody ❷ to spurt out ▷ *Das Blut spritzte aus der Wunde.* The blood spurted out of the wound.

Sprudel (pl **Sprudel**) m mineral water; **süßer Sprudel** lemonade

sprühen (perf **hat/ist gesprüht**) vb [38]

For the perfect tense use **haben** when the verb has an object and **sein** when there is no object. Use **haben** to form the perfect tense for 'to sparkle'.

❶ to spray ▷ *Sie hat Haarspray auf ihre Haare gesprüht.* She sprayed her hair with hairspray. ❷ to fly ▷ *In alle Richtungen sind Funken gesprüht.* Sparks flew in all directions. ❸ to sparkle ▷ *Er hat gestern Abend vor Witz gesprüht.* He was sparkling with humour yesterday evening.

Sprung (pl **Sprünge**) m ❶ jump ▷ *Das war ein weiter Sprung.* That was a long jump. ❷ crack ▷ *Die Tasse hat einen Sprung.* There is a crack in the cup.

Sprungbrett (pl **Sprungbretter**) nt springboard

spucken vb [38] to spit

Spüle f kitchen sink

spülen vb [38] ❶ to rinse ▷ *Wollsachen muss man gut spülen.* Woollens have to be rinsed well. ❷ to wash up ▷ *Wenn du spülst, dann trockne ich ab.* If you wash up I'll dry.

Spülmaschine f dishwasher

Spülmittel (pl **Spülmittel**) nt washing-up liquid

Spur f ❶ track ▷ *Wir sahen Spuren im Sand.* We saw tracks in the sand. ❷ lane ▷ *Der Fahrer vor mir hat plötzlich die Spur gewechselt.* The driver in front of me suddenly changed lane. ❸ trace ▷ *Auf ihrem Gesicht sah man die Spuren der Anstrengung.* You could see the traces of strain on her face.; **eine Bremsspur** skidmarks pl ❹ trail ▷ *Die Polizei verfolgte seine Spur.* The police followed his trail.; **Das Essen war eine Spur zu scharf.** The meal was a touch too spicy.

spüren vb [38] to feel

Staat (pl **Staaten**) m state; **die Vereinigten Staaten von Amerika** the United States of America

staatlich adj ❶ state ▷ *staatliche Fördermittel* state subsidies ▷ *eine staatliche Schule* a state school ❷ state-run ▷ *eine staatliche Einrichtung* a state-run organization

stabil adj ❶ stable ▷ *Die Lage ist stabil.* The situation is stable. ▷ *Sie ist psychisch stabil.* She's mentally stable. ❷ sturdy ▷ *stabile Möbel* sturdy furniture

Stachel (pl **Stacheln**) m ❶ spike ▷ *Ich habe mir die Hose an einem Stachel aufgerissen.* I've torn my trousers on a spike. ❷ spine ▷ *Ein Igel hat Stacheln.* A hedgehog has spines. ▷ *Dieser Kaktus hat lange Stacheln.* This cactus has long spines. ❸ sting ▷ *Ich habe versucht, den Stachel der Biene herauszuziehen.* I tried to take the bee sting out.

Stachelbeere f gooseberry

Stacheldraht (pl **Stacheldrähte**) m barbed wire

Stadion (pl **Stadien**) nt stadium

Stadt (pl **Städte**) f town

Stadtkreis (pl **Stadtkreise**) m town borough

Stadtmitte f town centre

Stadtplan (pl **Stadtpläne**) m street map

Stadtrand (pl **Stadtränder**) m outskirts pl

Stadtrundfahrt f tour of the city

Stadtteil (pl **Stadtteile**) m part of town

Stadtzentrum (pl **Stadtzentren**) nt city centre

stahl vb see **stehlen**

Stahl m steel

Stall (pl **Ställe**) m stable ▷ *Die Pferde sind im Stall.* The horses are in the stable.; **ein Hühnerstall** a henhouse

Stamm (pl **Stämme**) m ❶ trunk ▷ *Der Baum hat einen dicken Stamm.* The tree has a thick trunk. ❷ tribe ▷ *Er gehört zum Stamm der Bantus.* He belongs to the Bantu tribe. ❸ stem ▷ *Die Endung wird an den Stamm des Verbs angehängt.* The ending's added to the stem of the verb.

stammen vb [38] **stammen aus** to come from

Stammgast (pl **Stammgäste**) m regular customer

Stammtisch (pl **Stammtische**) m table for the regulars

* In Germany it is usual for a group of
* friends to reserve a table in the same
* pub or restaurant for the same time
* each week.

stand vb see **stehen**

Stand (pl **Stände**) m ❶ state ▷ *Was ist der Stand der Dinge?* What's the state of affairs? ❷ score ▷ *Sie sind beim Stand von eins zu eins in die Pause.* The score was one all at half-time. ❸ stand ▷ *An welchen Stand hast du den Luftballon gekauft?* Which stand did you buy the balloon at? ❹ level ▷ *Prüf mal den Ölstand.* Check the oil level.; **zu Stande** see **zustande**

ständig adj constant ▷ *Musst du ständig stören?* Do you constantly have to interrupt?

Standort (pl **Standorte**) m location

Stapel (pl **Stapel**) m pile

Star m ❶ celebrity ❷ star ▷ *Sie war der Star des Filmfestivals.* She was the star of the film festival.

starb vb see **sterben**

stark adj ❶ strong ▷ *Mein Bruder ist stärker als du.* My brother's stronger than you. ❷ heavy ▷ *starke Regenfälle* heavy rain; **starke Kopfschmerzen** a splitting headache ❸ (*informal*) great ▷ *Das war stark!* That was great!

Start (pl **Starts**) m ❶ start ▷ *Es waren über hundert Läufer am Start.* There were over a hundred runners at the start. ❷ takeoff ▷ *Die Maschine war bereit zum Start.* The machine was ready for takeoff.

starten vb [2] ❶ to start ▷ *Wann startet das Rennen?* When does the race start? ❷ to take off ▷ *Das Flugzeug startet gleich.* The plane is about to take off.

statt conj, prep

The preposition **statt** takes the genitive or the dative.

instead of ▷ *Statt nach Hause zu gehen, sind wir noch in die Disco.* Instead of going home, we went to the disco. ▷ *Sie kam statt ihres Bruders.* She came instead of her brother.

stattdessen adv instead ▷ *Das Schwimmbad war zu, also spielten wir stattdessen Tennis.* The pool was closed, so we played tennis instead.

stattfinden (*imperf* **fand statt**, *perf* **hat stattgefunden**) *vb* [24] to take place

Stau (*pl* **Staus**) *m* traffic jam ▷ *Wir sind im Stau stecken geblieben.* We were stuck in a traffic jam.

Staub *m* dust; **Staub wischen** to dust

staubig *adj* dusty

staubsaugen (*perf* **hat staubgesaugt**) *vb* [38] to hoover

Staubsauger (*pl* **Staubsauger**) *m* vacuum cleaner

staunen *vb* [38] to be astonished

stechen (*pres* **sticht**, *imperf* **stach**, *perf* **hat gestochen**) *vb* [4] ❶ to prick ▷ *Ich habe mich mit der Nadel gestochen.* I've pricked myself with the needle. ❷ to sting ▷ *Mich hat eine Biene gestochen.* A bee stung me. ❸ to bite ▷ *Reibe dich ein, damit du nicht gestochen wirst.* Rub something on so that you won't be bitten. ❹ to trump ▷ *Sie hat meine Dame gestochen.* She trumped my queen.

Steckdose *f* socket

stecken *vb* [48] ❶ to put ▷ *Sie steckte ihren Geldbeutel in die Tasche.* She put her purse in her bag. ❷ to insert ▷ *Stecken Sie die Münze in den Schlitz.* Insert the coin into the slot. ❸ to stick ▷ *Steck deinen Finger nicht in das Loch!* Don't stick your finger in the hole. ❹ to pin ▷ *Ich steckte das Abzeichen an meine Jacke.* I pinned the badge onto my jacket. ❺ to be stuck ▷ *Wir stecken im Stau.* We are stuck in a traffic jam.; **Wo steckt sie nur?** Where on earth is she?

Stecker (*pl* **Stecker**) *m* plug

stehen (*imperf* **stand**, *perf* **hat gestanden**) *vb* [72] ❶ to stand ▷ *Es war so voll, dass wir stehen mussten.* It was so full that we had to stand. ❷ to be ▷ *Vor unserem Haus steht eine Kastanie.* There's a chestnut tree in front of our house. ❸ to say ▷ *In der Zeitung steht, dass das Wetter besser wird.* It says in the newspaper that the weather will improve.; **zum Stehen kommen** to come to a halt; **Es steht schlecht um ihn.** Things are bad for him.; **jemandem stehen** to suit somebody; **Wie steht's?** (1) How are things? (2) What's the score?; **stehen bleiben** to stop

Stehlampe *f* standard lamp

stehlen (*pres* **stiehlt**, *imperf* **stahl**, *perf* **hat gestohlen**) *vb* [73] to steal

steif *adj* stiff

steigen (*imperf* **stieg**, *perf* **ist gestiegen**) *vb* [74] ❶ to rise ▷ *Der Ballon stieg zum Himmel.* The balloon rose into the sky. ❷ to climb ▷ *Sie ist auf die Leiter gestiegen.* She climbed up the ladder.; **in etwas steigen** to get into something; **Sie stieg in den Zug.** She got on the train.; **auf etwas steigen** to get on something

steil *adj* steep

Stein (*pl* **Steine**) *m* stone

Steinbock (*pl* **Steinböcke**) *m* Capricorn ▷ *Er ist Steinbock.* He's Capricorn.

steinig *adj* stony

Stelle *f* ❶ place ▷ *Ich habe mir die Stelle im Buch angestrichen.* I've marked the place in the book.; **an dieser Stelle** at this point ❷ job ▷ *Ich suche eine neue Stelle.* I'm looking for a new job. ❸ office ▷ *Bei welcher Stelle kann man einen Pass bekommen?* In which office can you get a passport?; **An deiner Stelle würde ich das nicht tun.** I wouldn't do it if I were you.

stellen *vb* [38] ❶ to put ▷ *Ich habe die Vase auf den Tisch gestellt.* I put the vase on the table. ❷ to set ▷ *Stell deine Uhr nach meiner.* Set your watch by mine. ❸ to supply ▷ *Die Lehrbücher werden gestellt.* The course books will be supplied.; **sich irgendwohin stellen** to stand somewhere; **sich stellen** to give oneself up; **sich dumm stellen** to pretend to be stupid

Stellenanzeige f job advertisement

Stellung f position ▷ *In welcher Stellung schläfst du?* Which position do you sleep in? ▷ *Er hat eine gute Stellung.* He has a good position.; **zu etwas Stellung nehmen** to comment on something

Stellvertreter (pl **Stellvertreter**) m deputy

Stempel (pl **Stempel**) m stamp

stempeln vb [34] to stamp; **jemanden zum Sündenbock stempeln** to make somebody a scapegoat

sterben (pres **stirbt**, imperf **starb**, perf **ist gestorben**) vb [75] to die

Stereoanlage f stereo

Stern (pl **Sterne**) m star ▷ *die Sterne am Himmel* the stars in the sky

Sternzeichen (pl **Sternzeichen**) nt star sign ▷ *Was ist dein Sternzeichen?* What star sign are you?

Steuer (pl **Steuer**) nt wheel ▷ *Wer saß am Steuer?* Who was at the wheel? ▶ f tax ▷ *Wir müssen viel Steuern bezahlen.* We have to pay a lot of tax.

Steuerrad (pl **Steuerräder**) nt steering wheel

Stich (pl **Stiche**) m ❶ bite ▷ *Das Mittel schützt vor Stichen.* This gives protection from bites. ▷ *ein Mückenstich* a midge bite; **ein Bienenstich** a bee sting ❷ stab ▷ *Er tötete sie mit zwölf Stichen.* He killed her by stabbing her twelve times. ❸ stitch ▷ *Sie hat den Aufhänger mit ein paar Stichen angenäht.* She sewed on the loop with a couple of stitches. ▷ *Die Wunde wurde mit drei Stichen genäht.* Three stitches were put in the wound. ❹ trick ▷ *Ich habe beim letzten Spiel keinen Stich gemacht.* I didn't win any tricks in the last game. ❺ engraving ▷ *ein Kupferstich* a copper engraving; **jemanden im Stich lassen** to leave somebody in the lurch

sticken vb [38] to embroider

Stickstoff m nitrogen

Stiefel (pl **Stiefel**) m boot

Stiefkind (pl **Stiefkinder**) nt stepchild

Stiefmutter (pl **Stiefmütter**) f stepmother

Stiefvater (pl **Stiefväter**) m stepfather

stiehlt vb see **stehlen**

Stiel (pl **Stiele**) m ❶ handle ▷ *der Stiel des Besens* the broom handle ❷ stem ▷ *Er hat den Stiel der Tulpe abgeknickt.* He snapped the stem off the tulip.

Stier (pl **Stiere**) m ❶ bull ▷ *Der Stier wurde getötet.* The bull was killed. ❷ Taurus ▷ *Brigitte ist Stier.* Brigitte's Taurus.

Stift (pl **Stifte**) m ❶ peg ▷ *Das Brett wird mit Stiften an der Wand befestigt.* The board is fixed to the wall with pegs. ❷ crayon ▷ *Sebastian hat lauter bunte Stifte bekommen.* Sebastian got lots of coloured crayons. ❸ pencil ▷ *Schreib lieber mit Kuli als mit einem Stift.* I'd rather you wrote with a Biro than a pencil.

stiften vb [2] ▷ *Sie hat eine Runde Eis gestiftet.* She bought us all an ice cream.; **Unruhe stiften** to cause trouble

Stil (pl **Stile**) m style

still adj quiet ▷ *Seid mal still.* Be quiet.; **Sie stand ganz still.** She stood quite still.

Stille f quietness; **in aller Stille** quietly

stillhalten (pres **hält still**, imperf **hielt still**, perf **hat stillgehalten**) vb [33] to keep still

stillschweigend adv tacitly

Stimme f ❶ voice ▷ *Er hat eine laute Stimme.* He has a loud voice. ❷ vote ▷ *Er bekam nur zwanzig Stimmen.* He only got twenty votes.; **Wem hast du deine Stimme gegeben?** Who did you vote for?

stimmen vb [38] ❶ to be right ▷ *Die Übersetzung stimmt nicht.* The translation isn't right. ▷ *Das stimmt nicht!* That's not right! ❷ to tune ▷ *ein Instrument stimmen* to tune an instrument ❸ to vote ▷ *stimmen für* to vote for ▷ *stimmen gegen* to vote against; **Stimmt so!** Keep the change.

Stimmung f mood

stinken (*imperf* **stank**, *perf* **hat gestunken**) vb to stink

stirbt vb see **sterben**

Stirn f forehead

Stock (1) (pl **Stöcke**) m stick ▷ *Er hat ihn mit einem Stock geschlagen.* He hit him with a stick.

Stock (2) (pl **Stock** or **Stockwerke**) m floor ▷ *Wir wohnen im dritten Stock.* We live on the third floor.

Stoff (pl **Stoffe**) m ❶ fabric ▷ *Das ist ein hübscher Stoff.* That's a pretty fabric. ❷ material ▷ *Ich sammle Stoff für mein Referat.* I'm collecting material for my assignment.

stöhnen vb [38] to groan

stolpern (*perf* **ist gestolpert**) vb [88] ❶ to stumble ▷ *Er ist gestolpert und gefallen.* He stumbled and fell. ❷ to trip ▷ *Er ist über einen Stein gestolpert.* He tripped over a stone.

stolz adj proud ▷ *Ich bin stolz auf dich.* I'm proud of you.

stören vb [38] to disturb ▷ *Störe ich? Am I disturbing you?* ▷ *Ich will nicht länger stören.* I won't disturb you any longer.; **Stört es dich, wenn ich rauche?** Do you mind if I smoke?; **Die Leitung war gestört.** It was a bad line.; **sich an etwas stören** to worry about something

Störung f ❶ interruption ▷ *Diese dauernden Störungen regen mich auf.* These constant interruptions are getting on my nerves. ❷ interference ▷ *Es war eine Störung beim Bild.* There was interference in the picture.

stoßen (*pres* **stößt**, *imperf* **stieß**, *perf* **hat gestoßen**) vb **den Kopf an etwas stoßen** to bump one's head on something; **sich stoßen** to bump oneself; **sich an etwas stoßen** to take exception to something; **an etwas stoßen** to bump into something; **auf etwas stoßen** to come across

stottern vb [88] to stutter

Strafarbeit f lines pl ▷ *Ich habe eine Strafarbeit bekommen.* I got lines.

Strafe f ❶ punishment ▷ *Zur Strafe müsst ihr länger bleiben.* You'll be kept in after school as a punishment.; **eine Gefängnisstrafe** a prison sentence ❷ fine ▷ *Er musste eine Strafe von fünfzig Euro bezahlen.* He had to pay a fifty euro fine.

Strahl (pl **Strahlen**) m ❶ ray ▷ *radioaktive Strahlen* radioactive rays ▷ *ein Sonnenstrahl* a ray of sunlight; **ein Lichtstrahl** a beam of light ❷ jet ▷ *ein Wasserstrahl* a jet of water

strahlen vb [38] ❶ to shine ▷ *Die Sterne strahlten hell.* The stars shone brightly. ❷ to beam ▷ *Sie strahlte, als sie das hörte.* She beamed when she heard that.

Strahlung f radiation

Strand (pl **Strände**) m ❶ beach ▷ *Wir haben den ganzen Tag am Strand gelegen.* We lay on the beach all day. ❷ shore ▷ *Das wurde an den Strand gespült.* That was washed up on the shore.

strapazieren (*perf* **hat strapaziert**) vb [76] ❶ to be hard on ▷ *Du hast heute deinen Computer ganz schön strapaziert.* You've been really hard on your computer today. ❷ to wear out ▷ *Die Wanderung hat uns ziemlich strapaziert.* The walk has really worn us out.

Straße f ❶ street ▷ *In welcher Straße wohnt Thomas?* Which street does Thomas live in? ❷ road ▷ *Wir sind die Straße entlang der Küste gefahren.* We drove along the coast road.

Straßenbahn f tram

Strauß (gen **Straußes**, pl **Sträuße**) m bunch of flowers ▷ *Wir haben unserer Gastgeberin einen Strauß mitgebracht.* We brought our hostess a bunch of flowers.

streamen vb [48] to stream (online content)

Streaming nt streaming (online content)

Strecke f ❶ distance ▷ *Wir haben diese Strecke an einem Tag zurückgelegt.* We covered this distance in one day. ▷ *Bis zu ihm ist es noch eine ziemliche Strecke.* It's still quite a distance to his place. ❷ line ▷ *Auf der Strecke zwischen Stuttgart und Ulm gab es ein Zugunglück.* There's been a train accident on the Stuttgart to Ulm line.

streicheln vb [88] to stroke

streichen (imperf **strich**, perf **hat gestrichen**) vb ❶ to stroke ▷ *Sie strich über seine Haare.* She stroked his hair. ❷ to spread ▷ *Sie strich Honig aufs Brot.* She spread honey on the bread. ❸ to paint ▷ *Ich muss dringend mein Zimmer streichen.* I really must paint my room. ❹ to delete ▷ *Den zweiten Satz kannst du streichen.* You can delete the second sentence. ❺ to cancel ▷ *Der Direktor hat den Schulausflug gestrichen.* The head teacher has cancelled the school trip.

Streichholz (gen **Streichholzes**, pl **Streichhölzer**) nt match

Streifen (pl **Streifen**) m strip

Streik (pl **Streiks**) m strike

streiken vb [38] to go on strike; *Sie streiken.* They're on strike.

Streit (pl **Streite**) m argument

sich streiten (imperf **stritt**, perf **hat gestritten**) vb to argue ▷ *Sie streiten sich ständig.* They argue constantly.; *Darüber lässt sich streiten.* That's debatable.

streng adj ❶ strict ▷ *Meine Eltern sind furchtbar streng.* My parents are terribly strict. ❷ severe ▷ *Es war ein strenger Winter.* It was a severe winter. ▷ *Das wird streng bestraft.* That will be severely punished. ❸ sharp ▷ *Wo kommt der strenge Geruch her?* Where's that sharp smell coming from?

Stress (gen **Stresses**) m stress; *Ich bin im Stress!* (informal) I'm stressed out.

stressen (pres **stresst**, imperf **stresste**, perf **hat gestresst**) vb [48] to put under stress

stressig adj stressful

Strich (pl **Striche**) m ❶ line ▷ *Mach einen Strich unter die Spalte.* Draw a line under the column. ❷ stroke ▷ *Mit ein paar Strichen zeichnete er ein Haus.* He drew a house with a couple of strokes

Strichkode (pl **Strichkodes**) m bar code

Strick (pl **Stricke**) m rope

stricken vb [48] to knit

Stroh nt straw

Strohhalm (pl **Strohhalme**) m drinking straw

Strom (pl **Ströme**) m ❶ current ▷ *der Wechselstrom* alternating current; *Vorsicht, auf dem Draht ist Strom.* Be careful, the wire is live. ❷ electricity ▷ *Sie haben den Strom abgeschaltet.* They've cut off the electricity. ❸ stream ▷ *Ein Strom von Zuschauern kam aus dem Stadion.* A stream of spectators was coming out of the stadium.

Strömung f current

Strumpf (pl **Strümpfe**) m stocking

Strumpfhose f tights pl ▷ *eine Strumpfhose* a pair of tights

> Word for word, **eine Strumpfhose** means 'a pair of stocking trousers'.

Stück (pl **Stücke**) nt ❶ piece ▷ *Sie schnitt ein Stück Käse ab.* She cut off a piece of cheese. ❷ play ▷ *Wir haben ein Stück von Brecht angesehen.* We saw a play by Brecht.

Student (gen **Studenten**, pl **Studenten**) m student

Studentin f student
Studie (pl **Studien**) f ① study ▷ *eine Studie über das Schulwesen* a study of the school system ② sketch ▷ *Die Künstlerin machte zuerst mehrere Studien.* The artist did several sketches first.
studieren (perf **hat studiert**) vb [76] to study ▷ *Mein Bruder studiert Physik.* My brother's studying physics.
Studium (pl **Studien**) nt studies pl
Stufe f ① step ▷ *Vorsicht, Stufe!* Mind the step! ② stage ▷ *Er hat bereits eine fortgeschrittene Stufe erreicht.* He's already reached an advanced stage. ▷ *eine Entwicklungsstufe* a stage of development
Stuhl (pl **Stühle**) m chair
stumm adj silent ▷ *Sie blieb stumm.* She remained silent.
stumpf adj blunt ▷ *Er wurde mit einem stumpfen Gegenstand am Kopf getroffen.* He was hit on the head with a blunt object.; **ein stumpfer Winkel** an obtuse angle
Stunde f ① hour ▷ *Ich komme in einer Stunde.* I'll come in an hour. ② lesson ▷ *Was haben wir in der letzten Stunde behandelt?* What did we do in the last lesson?
Stundenplan (pl **Stundenpläne**) m timetable
stündlich adj hourly ▷ *stündlich verkehren* to run hourly
stur adj obstinate
Sturm (pl **Stürme**) m storm
stürmen (perf **ist/hat gestürmt**) vb [38]

Use **sein** to form the perfect tense for 'to storm (out)'. Use **haben** to form the perfect tense for all other meanings.

to storm ▷ *Er ist aus dem Zimmer gestürmt.* He stormed out of the room. ▷ *Die Polizei hat das Gebäude gestürmt.* The police stormed the building.; *Es stürmt.* There's a gale blowing.
stürmisch adj stormy
Sturz (gen **Sturzes**, pl **Stürze**) m ① fall ▷ *Bei dem Sturz hat sie sich das Bein gebrochen.* She broke her leg in the fall. ② overthrow ▷ *Alle freuten sich über den Sturz des Diktators.* Everybody was pleased about the overthrow of the dictator.
stürzen (perf **hat/ist gestürzt**) vb [36]

Use **sein** to form the perfect tense. Use **haben** to form the perfect tense for 'to overthrow' and for **sich stürzen**.

① to fall ▷ *Sie ist vom Pferd gestürzt.* She fell off a horse. ② to rush ▷ *Er kam ins Zimmer gestürzt.* He rushed into the room. ③ to overthrow ▷ *Die Regierung wurde gestürzt.* The government has been overthrown.; **sich stürzen** to plunge
Sturzhelm (pl **Sturzhelme**) m crash helmet
Stütze f support
Subjekt (pl **Subjekte**) nt subject
Substantiv (pl **Substantive**) nt noun
Suche f search
suchen vb [48] to look for ▷ *Ich suche meinen Radiergummi.* I'm looking for my rubber. ▷ *Wir haben gesucht, es aber nicht gefunden.* We looked for it but couldn't find it. ▷ *Er wird von der Polizei gesucht.* The police are looking for him.; **nach etwas suchen** to look for something
Suchmaschine f (internet) search engine
süchtig adj addicted ▷ *kaffeesüchtig* addicted to coffee
Südafrika nt South Africa
Südamerika nt South America
Süden m south
südlich adj, prep, adv southerly ▷ *in südlicher Richtung* in a southerly direction; **südlich einer Sache** to the south of something; **südlich von** south of

Südpol m South Pole ▷ *am Südpol* at the South Pole
Summe f total
summen vb [**38**] ❶ to buzz ▷ *Die Bienen summten.* The bees were buzzing. ❷ to hum ▷ *Sie summte vor sich hin.* She was humming. ▷ *Er hat ein Lied gesummt.* He hummed a song.
Sünde f sin
super adj (informal) super
Superlativ (pl **Superlative**) m superlative
Supermarkt (pl **Supermärkte**) m supermarket
Suppe f soup
Surfbrett (pl **Surfbretter**) nt surfboard
surfen (perf **hat gesurft**) vb [**38**] to surf; **im Internet surfen** to surf the Net
süß adj sweet
Süßigkeit f sweet ▷ *Sie isst gern Süßigkeiten.* She likes eating sweets.
Süßstoff (pl **Süßstoffe**) m sweetener
Süßwaren pl confectionery sg
Symbol (pl **Symbole**) nt symbol
sympathisch adj likeable ▷ *Er ist ein sympathischer Mensch.* He's a likeable person.; **Er ist mir sympathisch.** I like him.

> Be careful! **sympathisch** does not mean **sympathetic**.

Synagoge f synagogue
synchronisieren (perf **hat synchronisiert**) vb [**76**] to dub ▷ *ein synchronisierter Film* a dubbed film
synthetisch adj synthetic
System (pl **Systeme**) nt system
systematisch adj systematic
Szene f scene

Tabak (pl **Tabake**) m tobacco
Tabelle f table
Tablet (pl **Tablets**) nt tablet (computer)
Tablett (pl **Tablette**) nt tray
Tablette f tablet
Tachometer (pl **Tachometer**) m speedometer
tadellos adj faultless
Tafel f blackboard ▷ *Der Lehrer schrieb das Wort an die Tafel.* The teacher wrote the word on the blackboard.; **eine Tafel Schokolade** a bar of chocolate
Tag (pl **Tage**) m ❶ day ▷ *Ich war den ganzen Tag weg.* I was away all day. ❷ daylight ▷ *Wir möchten noch bei Tag ankommen.* We want to arrive in daylight.; **an den Tag kommen** to come to light; **Guten Tag!** Hello!
Tageblatt (pl **Tageblätter**) nt daily newspaper
Tagebuch (pl **Tagebücher**) nt diary ▷ *ein Tagebuch führen* to keep a diary
tagelang adv for days

Tagesanbruch m dawn ▷ *bei Tagesanbruch* at dawn
Tagesgericht (pl **Tagesgerichte**) nt dish of the day
Tageskarte f ❶ menu of the day ❷ day ticket
Tageslicht nt daylight
Tageszeitung f daily paper
täglich adj, adv daily
tagsüber adv during the day
Taille f waist
Takt (pl **Takte**) m tact ▷ *Sie behandelte die Sache mit viel Takt.* She showed great tact in dealing with the matter.; **keinen Takt haben** to be tactless; **den Takt angeben** to keep time; **im Stundentakt** at hourly intervals
Taktik f tactics pl ▷ *Das ist die falsche Taktik.* Those are the wrong tactics.
taktisch adj tactical ▷ *Das war taktisch unklug.* That was a tactical mistake.
taktlos adj tactless
taktvoll adj tactful
Tal (pl **Täler**) nt valley
Talent (pl **Talente**) nt talent
talentiert adj talented
Tank (pl **Tanks**) m tank
tanken vb [38] to get petrol ▷ *Wir müssen noch tanken.* We still have to get petrol.
Tankstelle f petrol station
Tanne f fir
Tante f aunt
Tanz (gen **Tanzes**, pl **Tänze**) m dance
tanzen vb [36] to dance
Tanzschule f dancing school
* It is very common for German boys
* and girls to go to a **Tanzschule** when
* they are about 14.
Tapete f wallpaper
tapezieren (perf **hat tapeziert**) vb [76] to wallpaper
tapfer adj brave
Tapferkeit f bravery
Tasche f ❶ pocket ▷ *Er hatte die Hände in der Hosentasche.* He had his hands in his trouser pockets. ❷ bag ▷ *Sie kann ihre Tasche nicht finden.* She can't find her bag.
Taschenbuch (pl **Taschenbücher**) nt paperback
Taschendieb m pickpocket
Taschengeld (pl **Taschengelder**) nt pocket money
Taschenlampe f torch
Taschenmesser (pl **Taschenmesser**) nt penknife
Taschenrechner (pl **Taschenrechner**) m pocket calculator
Taschentuch (pl **Taschentücher**) nt handkerchief
Tasse f cup ▷ *eine Tasse Tee* a cup of tea
Tastatur f keyboard
Taste f ❶ button ▷ *Welche Taste muss ich drücken, um die Waschmaschine anzustellen?* What button do I have to press to start the washing machine? ❷ key ▷ *Bei der Schreibmaschine und der Computertastatur gibt es eine Hochstelltaste.* There's a shift key on the typewriter and the computer keyboard.
tat vb see **tun**
Tat (pl **Taten**) f ❶ deed ▷ *Das war eine tapfere Tat.* That was a brave deed. ▷ *eine gute Tat* a good deed ❷ crime ▷ *Der Beschuldigte hat die Tat gestanden.* The accused confessed to the crime.; **in der Tat** indeed
Täter (pl **Täter**) m culprit
tätig adj **tätig sein** to work ▷ *Sie als Journalistin tätig.* She works as a journalist.
Tätigkeit f ❶ activity ❷ occupation
tätowieren (perf **hat tätowiert**) vb [76] to tattoo
Tätowierung f tattoo
Tatsache f fact
tatsächlich adj, adv actual ▷ *Der tatsächliche Grund war ein anderer als der, den sie angegeben hatte.* The actual reason was different from the one she

gave. ❷ really ▷ *Das hat sie tatsächlich gesagt.* She really did say that. ▷ *Er ist tatsächlich rechtzeitig gekommen.* He really has come in time.

taub adj deaf ▷ *Sie ist auf dem rechten Ohr taub.* She's deaf in her right ear.

Taube f ❶ pigeon ▷ *die Tauben auf dem Marktplatz* the pigeons in the market square ❷ dove ▷ *die Friedenstaube* the dove of peace

tauchen (*perf* **hat/ist getaucht**) vb [48]

Use **haben** for the perfect tense when you describe the activity and **sein** when you describe the motion.

❶ to dip ▷ *Sie hat ihren Zeh ins Wasser getaucht.* She dipped her toe into the water. ❷ to dive ▷ *Als Kind habe ich viel getaucht.* I used to dive a lot as a child. ▷ *Er ist nach dem versunkenen Schatz getaucht.* He dived in search of the sunken treasure.

tauen vb [38] *Es taut.* It's thawing.

Taufe f christening

taufen vb [38] to christen

taugen vb [38] **nichts taugen** to be no good

tauschen vb [48] to exchange

täuschen vb [48] ❶ to deceive ▷ *Du hast mich bewusst getäuscht.* You deliberately deceived me. ❷ to be deceptive ▷ *Der äußere Anschein täuscht oft.* Appearances are often deceptive.; **sich täuschen** to be wrong

tausend num thousand

Taxi (gen **Taxis**, pl **Taxis**) nt taxi

Taxifahrer (pl **Taxifahrer**) m taxi driver

Taxistand (pl **Taxistände**) m taxi rank

Team nt team

Technik f ❶ technology ▷ *hoch entwickelte Technik* advanced technology; **die Gentechnik** genetic engineering ❷ technique ▷ *Sie beherrscht diese Technik des Hochsprungs noch nicht.* She hasn't mastered this high-jump technique yet.

Techniker (pl **Techniker**) m technician

technisch adj technical

Technologie f technology

Tee (pl **Tees**) m tea ▷ *Tee mit Milch und Zucker* tea with milk and sugar ▷ *Tee mit Zitrone* lemon tea ▷ *Kamillentee* camomile tea

Teebeutel (pl **Teebeutel**) m tea bag

Teekanne f teapot

Teelöffel (pl **Teelöffel**) m teaspoon; **ein Teelöffel Zucker** a teaspoonful of sugar

Teer m tar

Teich (pl **Teiche**) m pond

Teig (pl **Teige**) m dough

Teil (pl **Teile**) m

You can also say **das Teil**.

❶ part ▷ *der erste Teil des Buches* the first part of the book; **das Ersatzteil** the spare part ❷ share ▷ *Ich möchte meinen Teil am Gewinn.* I would like my share of the profit. ❸ component part ▷ *Er hat das Fahrrad in seine Teile zerlegt.* He dismantled the bike into its component parts.; **zum Teil** partly

teilen vb [38] to divide; **mit jemandem teilen** to share with somebody

teilnehmen (*pres* **nimmt teil**, *imperf* **nahm teil**, *perf* **hat teilgenommen**) vb [52] **an etwas teilnehmen** to take part in something

Teilnehmer (pl **Teilnehmer**) m participant

Teilnehmerin f participant

teils adv partly

teilweise adv in parts ▷ *Das Buch war teilweise sehr spannend.* The book was thrilling in parts.; **Sie waren teilweise beschädigt.** Some of them were damaged.

Teilzeitarbeit f part-time work

Telefon (pl **Telefone**) nt telephone; **am Telefon** on the phone

Telefonanruf (pl **Telefonanrufe**) m telephone call

Telefonat (pl **Telefonate**) nt phone call

Telefonbuch (pl **Telefonbücher**) nt phone book

Telefonhörer (pl **Telefonhörer**) m receiver ▷ *Er nahm den Telefonhörer ab.* He picked up the receiver.

telefonieren (perf **hat telefoniert**) vb [76] to telephone; *Ich habe gestern mit ihr telefoniert.* I talked to her on the phone yesterday.

telefonisch adj telephone ▷ *eine telefonische Nachricht* a telephone message; *Sie können mich telefonisch erreichen.* You can contact me by phone.

Telefonkarte f phonecard

Telefonnummer f telephone number

Telefonzelle f telephone box

Telegramm (pl **Telegramme**) nt telegram

Teleskop (pl **Teleskope**) nt telescope

Teller (pl **Teller**) m plate

Tempel m temple (religious)

Temperament (pl **Temperamente**) nt *Sie hat ein ziemlich lebhaftes Temperament.* She's quite a vivacious person.

temperamentvoll adj vivacious

Temperatur f temperature

Tempo (pl **Tempos**) nt ❶ speed ▷ *Er ist mit einem irren Tempo gefahren.* He drove at breakneck speed. ❷ rate ▷ *Wir müssen unser Arbeitstempo steigern.* We must increase our work rate.

tendieren (perf **hat tendiert**) vb [76] **zu etwas tendieren** to tend towards something

Tennis (gen **Tennis**) nt tennis

Tennisplatz (gen **Tennisplatzes**, pl **Tennisplätze**) m tennis court

Tennisschläger (pl **Tennisschläger**) m tennis racket

Tennisspieler (pl **Tennisspieler**) m tennis player

Teppich (pl **Teppiche**) m carpet

Teppichboden (pl **Teppichböden**) m wall-to-wall carpet

Termin (pl **Termine**) m ❶ date ▷ *Habt ihr schon einen Termin ausgemacht?* Have you already arranged a date? ❷ deadline ▷ *Ich muss den Aufsatz bis zu dem Termin fertig haben.* I must have the essay finished by that deadline. ❸ appointment ▷ *Ich habe einen Termin beim Zahnarzt.* I've got an appointment with the dentist.

Terminkalender (pl **Terminkalender**) m appointments diary

Terrasse f terrace

Terror m terror

Terrorismus (gen **Terrorismus**) m terrorism

Terrorist (gen **Terroristen**, pl **Terroristen**) m terrorist

Tesafilm® m Sellotape®

Test (pl **Tests**) m test

Testament (pl **Testamente**) nt will ▷ *sein Testament machen* to make one's will

testen vb [2] to test

teuer adj expensive

Teufel (pl **Teufel**) m devil

Text (pl **Texte**) m ❶ text ▷ *Lest den Text auf Seite zehn.* Read the text on page ten. ❷ lyrics pl ▷ *Kannst du mir den Text von dem Song übersetzen?* Can you translate the lyrics of the song for me?

Textilien pl textiles pl

Textverarbeitung f word processing

Theater (pl **Theater**) nt ❶ theatre ▷ *Wir gehen ins Theater.* We're going to the theatre.; **Theater spielen** to act ❷ (informal) fuss ▷ *Mach nicht so ein Theater!* Don't make such a fuss.

Theaterstück (pl **Theaterstücke**) nt play

Theke f ❶ bar ▷ *Er stand an der Theke und trank ein Bier.* He stood at the bar drinking a beer. ❷ counter ▷ *Das* bekommen Sie an der Käsetheke. You'll get that at the cheese counter.

Thema (pl **Themen**) nt subject

theoretisch adj theoretical ▷ *Rein theoretisch betrachtet ist das richtig.* From a purely theoretical point of view, that's correct.

Theorie f theory

Therapie f therapy

Thermometer (pl **Thermometer**) nt thermometer

Thermosflasche f Thermos®

These f thesis

Thron (pl **Throne**) m throne

Thunfisch (pl **Thunfische**) m tuna

Thüringen nt Thuringia
- Thüringen is one of the 16 Länder.
- Its capital is Erfurt. With its extensive forests, it is sometimes called 'Germany's green heartland'. It is not only rural, however: the Zeiss precision engineering company is based in Jena.

ticken vb [48] to tick ▷ *Die Uhr tickte.* The clock was ticking.; *Du tickst ja nicht richtig!* (informal) You're off your rocker!

> Word for word, **Du tickst ja nicht richtig** means 'You're not ticking right'.

Ticket (pl **Tickets**) nt ticket ▷ *Ich habe zwei Tickets online gebucht.* I booked two tickets online.

tief adj ① deep ▷ *Wie tief ist das Wasser?* How deep is the water? ② (neckline, price, note) low ▷ *ein tief ausgeschnittenes Kleid* a low-cut dress

Tief (pl **Tiefs**) nt depression ▷ *ein Tief über Norddeutschland* a depression over North Germany

Tiefdruck m low pressure

Tiefe f depth

tiefgekühlt adj frozen

Tiefkühltruhe f freezer

Tier (pl **Tiere**) nt animal

Tierarzt (gen **Tierarztes**, pl **Tierärzte**) m vet

Tierärztin f vet

Tiergarten (pl **Tiergärten**) m zoo

tierisch adj ① animal ▷ *tierische Fette* animal fats ② terrible ▷ *Du hast dich tierisch benommen.* You behaved terribly.

Tierkreis (gen **Tierkreises**, pl **Tierkreise**) m zodiac

> Word for word, **Tierkreis** means 'animal circle'.

Tierquälerei f cruelty to animals

Tiger (pl **Tiger**) m tiger

Tinte f ink

Tintenfisch (pl **Tintenfische**) m squid

Tipp (pl **Tipps**) m tip

tippen vb [48] ① to tap ▷ *Sie tippte leicht an die Statue.* She lightly tapped the statue. ② to type ▷ *Tippst du dein Referat?* Are you typing your assignment?; **im Lotto tippen** to play the lottery; **Auf wen tippst du bei den Wahlen?** Who're you tipping to win the elections?

Tippfehler (pl **Tippfehler**) m typing error

Tirol nt Tyrol

Tisch (pl **Tische**) m table ▷ *bei Tisch* at table

Tischdecke f tablecloth

Tischtennis nt table tennis

Tischtuch (pl **Tischtücher**) nt tablecloth

Titel (pl **Titel**) m title

Toast (pl **Toasts**) m toast

Toastbrot (pl **Toastbrote**) nt bread for toasting

Toaster (pl **Toaster**) m toaster

toben vb [38] ① to rage ▷ *Der Sturm tobte die ganze Nacht.* The storm raged all night long. ② to go mad ▷ *Wenn er das erfährt, wird er toben.* If he finds out he'll go mad. ③ to romp about ▷ *Die Kinder toben im Garten.* The children are romping about in the garden.

Tochter (pl **Töchter**) f daughter

Tod (pl **Tode**) m death

todernst adj, adv ① grave ▷ *ein todernstes Gesicht* a grave face ② in deadly earnest ▷ *Er hat das todernst gesagt.* He said it in deadly earnest.
Todesstrafe f death penalty
todkrank adj critically ill
tödlich adj deadly ▷ *eine tödliche Waffe* a deadly weapon; **ein tödlicher Unfall** a fatal accident
todmüde adj exhausted
Toilette f toilet
Toilettenpapier nt toilet paper
tolerant adj tolerant
toll adj (informal) terrific
Tollwut f rabies sg
Tomate f tomato
Ton (pl **Töne**) m ① sound ▷ *Es war kein Ton zu hören.* Not a sound could be heard. ② note ▷ *Mit welchem Ton fängt das Lied an?* What note does the song start on? ③ tone of voice ▷ *Sein Ton gefiel mir nicht.* I didn't like his tone of voice. ④ shade ▷ *Pastelltöne sind in.* Pastel shades are in. ⑤ stress ▷ *Bei Substantiven liegt der Ton meist auf der ersten Silbe.* Nouns are usually stressed on the first syllable.
Tonne f ton ▷ *Es wiegt drei Tonnen.* It weighs three tons.
Topf (pl **Töpfe**) m pot
toppen vb to do better than; **einen Rekord toppen** to break a record
Tor (pl **Tore**) nt ① gate ▷ *Das Tor war offen.* The gate was open. ② goal ▷ *Wer hat das zweite Tor geschossen?* Who scored the second goal?
Torf m peat
Torte f ① gateau ② flan
Torwart (pl **Torwarte**) m goalkeeper
tot adj dead; **Er war sofort tot.** He was killed instantly.
total adj, adv ① complete ▷ *Das ist doch der totale Wahnsinn.* But that's complete madness. ② completely ▷ *Das ist total verrückt.* That's completely mad.

totalitär adj totalitarian
Tote (gen **Toten**, pl **Toten**) mf dead body ▷ *Auf der Straße lag ein Toter.* There was a dead body lying in the road.; **die Toten begraben** to bury the dead
töten vb [2] to kill
Tour (pl **Touren**) f trip ▷ *auf Tour gehen* to go on a trip; **auf vollen Touren** at full speed
Tourismus (gen **Tourismus**) m tourism
Tourist (gen **Touristen**, pl **Touristen**) m tourist
Touristeninformation f tourist information (office)
Tournee f tour ▷ *Beyoncé auf Tournee* Beyoncé on tour ▷ *auf Tournee gehen* to go on tour
Tracht f traditional costume ▷ *Im Schwarzwald tragen die Frauen noch Tracht.* Women still wear traditional costume in the Black Forest.; **eine Tracht Prügel** a sound beating
Tradition f tradition
traditionell adj traditional
traf vb see **treffen**
tragbar adj portable ▷ *ein tragbarer Fernseher* a portable TV
träge adj sluggish
tragen (pres **trägt**, imperf **trug**, perf **hat getragen**) vb [77] ① to carry ▷ *Kannst du meinen Koffer tragen?* Can you carry my case? ② to bear ▷ *die Verantwortung tragen* to bear responsibility ③ (clothes, glasses) to wear ▷ *Sie trug ein weißes Kleid und eine Sonnenbrille.* She was wearing a white dress and sunglasses.
Tragetasche f carrier bag
tragisch adj tragic
Tragödie f tragedy
Trainer (pl **Trainer**) m coach
Trainerin f coach
trainieren (perf **hat trainiert**) vb [76] ① to train ▷ *Sie trainiert täglich für den Wettkampf.* She trains for the competition every day. ② to coach

▷ *Wer trainiert diese Tennisspielerin?* Who coaches this tennis player? ❸ **to practise** ▷ *Diese Übung muss ich noch mehr trainieren.* I need to practise this exercise more.

Training (pl **Trainings**) nt training

Trainingsanzug (pl **Trainingsanzüge**) m track suit

trampen vb [38] to hitchhike

Tramper (pl **Tramper**) m hitchhiker

Tramperin f hitchhiker

Träne f tear ▷ *in Tränen ausbrechen* to burst into tears

trank vb see **trinken**

trans adj trans(gender)

Transport (pl **Transporte**) m transport

transportieren (perf hat **transportiert**) vb [76] to transport

Transportmittel (pl **Transportmittel**) nt means of transport sg

Traube f grape

trauen vb [38] jemandem trauen to trust somebody; **sich trauen** to dare

Traum (pl **Träume**) m dream

träumen vb [38] to dream ▷ *Ich habe von dir geträumt.* I dreamt about you.

traumhaft adj wonderful ▷ *Es waren traumhafte Ferien.* It was a wonderful holiday.

traurig adj sad

Traurigkeit f sadness

treffen (pres **trifft**, imperf **traf**, perf **hat getroffen**) vb [78] ❶ to hit ▷ *Er hat die Zielscheibe getroffen.* He hit the target. ▷ *Sie wurde am Kopf getroffen.* She was hit on the head.; **Du hast nicht getroffen.** You missed. ❷ to meet ▷ *Ich habe ihn gestern im Supermarkt getroffen.* I met him yesterday in the supermarket. ▷ *Wir sind in London auf ihn getroffen.* We met him in London.; **sich treffen** to meet ❸ to affect ▷ *Die Bemerkung hat sie sehr getroffen.* The remark affected her deeply.; **eine Entscheidung treffen** to make a decision; **Maßnahmen treffen** to take steps; **Es traf sich, dass ...** It so happened that ...; **Das trifft sich gut!** How very convenient!

Treffen (pl **Treffen**) nt meeting

Treffer (pl **Treffer**) m ❶ hit ▷ *Das Schiff musste einen Volltreffer hinnehmen.* The ship took a direct hit. ❷ goal ▷ *Klinsmann hat einen Treffer erzielt.* Klinsmann scored a goal. ▷ *Ich hatte vier Treffer im Lotto.* I got four numbers in the lottery.

Treffpunkt (pl **Treffpunkte**) m meeting place

treiben (imperf **trieb**, perf **hat/ist getrieben**) vb

Use **haben** to form the perfect tense. Use **sein** to form the perfect tense for 'to drift'.

❶ to drive ▷ *Sie trieben die Kühe auf das Feld.* They drove the cows into the field.; **Sport treiben** to do sport; **Unsinn treiben** to fool around; **jemanden zu etwas treiben** to drive somebody to something; **Sie hat uns zur Eile getrieben.** She made us hurry up. ❷ to drift ▷ *Das Schiff trieb aufs Meer getrieben.* The ship drifted out to sea.

Treibhaus (gen **Treibhauses**, pl **Treibhäuser**) nt greenhouse

Treibhauseffekt m greenhouse effect

Treibstoff (pl **Treibstoffe**) m fuel

trennen vb [38] ❶ to separate ▷ *Er hat die beiden Raufbolde getrennt.* He separated the two ruffians. ❷ to make a distinction between ▷ *Diese beiden Begriffe muss man sauber trennen.* You have to make a clear distinction between these two concepts. ❸ to hyphenate ▷ *Wie wird dieses Wort getrennt?* Where do you hyphenate this word?; **sich trennen** to separate; **Du solltest dich von ihm trennen.** You ought to leave him.; **sich von etwas trennen** to part with something

Trennung f separation

Treppe f stairs pl

Treppenhaus (gen **Treppenhauses**, pl **Treppenhäuser**) nt staircase

treten (pres **tritt**, imperf **trat**, perf **hat/ist getreten**) vb [79]

> For the perfect tense use **haben** when the verb has an object and **sein** when there is no object.

① to step ▷ *Sie ist in die Pfütze getreten.* She stepped in the puddle. ▷ *Er trat auf die Bremse.* He stepped on the brakes. ▷ *Er trat ans Mikrofon.* He stepped up to the microphone.; **mit jemandem in Verbindung treten** to get in touch with somebody; **in Erscheinung treten** to appear ② to kick ▷ *Sie hat mich getreten.* She kicked me. ▷ *Sie trat nach dem Hund.* She kicked the dog. ③ to tread ▷ *Er ist mir auf den Fuß getreten.* He trod on my foot.

treu adj faithful ▷ *Bist du mir auch treu gewesen?* Have you been faithful to me?

Treue f faithfulness

Tribüne f ① grandstand ▷ *Die Fans auf der Tribüne pfiffen.* The fans on the grandstand whistled. ② platform ▷ *Der Redner stand auf einer Tribüne.* The speaker stood on a platform.

Trichter (pl **Trichter**) m ① funnel ▷ *Sie hat das Öl mit einem Trichter in die Flasche gefüllt.* She used a funnel to fill the bottle with oil. ② crater ▷ *Das Gelände war von Bombentrichtern übersät.* The area was pitted with bomb craters.

Trick (pl **Tricks**) m trick ▷ *Das war ein fauler Trick.* That was a dirty trick.

Trickfilm (pl **Trickfilme**) m cartoon

trieb vb see **treiben**

trifft vb see **treffen**

Trimester (pl **Trimester**) nt term (university)

trinkbar adj drinkable

trinken (imperf **trank**, perf **hat getrunken**) vb [80] to drink; *Ich habe zu viel getrunken.* I've had too much to drink.

Trinkgeld (pl **Trinkgelder**) nt tip ▷ *Er gab dem Taxifahrer ein großzügiges Trinkgeld.* He gave the taxi driver a generous tip.

Trinkwasser (pl **Trinkwässer**) nt drinking water

trocken adj dry

trocknen vb [53] to dry

Trödel m (informal) junk

Trödelmarkt (pl **Trödelmärkte**) m flea market

trödeln vb [88] to dawdle

Trommel f drum ▷ *Er spielt Trommel.* He plays the drums.

Trommelfell (pl **Trommelfelle**) nt eardrum

trommeln vb [34] to drum

Trompete f trumpet ▷ *Sie spielt Trompete.* She plays the trumpet.

Tropen pl tropics pl

Tropfen (pl **Tropfen**) m drop

tropisch adj tropical

Trost m consolation

trösten vb [2] to console

trostlos adj bleak ▷ *eine trostlose Landschaft* a bleak landscape

Trostpreis (gen **Trostpreises**, pl **Trostpreise**) m consolation prize

Trottel (pl **Trottel**) m (informal) prat

trotz prep

> The preposition **trotz** takes the dative or genitive.

in spite of

Trotz (gen **Trotzes**) m defiance ▷ *ihm zum Trotz* in defiance of him; **etwas aus Trotz tun** to do something defiantly

trotzdem adv all the same ▷ *Ich gehe trotzdem.* I'm going all the same.

trotzig adj defiant

trüb adj ① dull ▷ *Es war ein trüber Tag.* It was a dull day. ② cloudy ▷ *Das Wasser war trüb.* The water was cloudy. ③ gloomy ▷ *Die Zukunftsaussichten sind*

Trubel m hurly-burly

trübsinnig adj gloomy

trug vb see **tragen**

trügen (imperf **trog**, perf **hat getrogen**) vb to be deceptive ▷ *Der Schein trügt.* Appearances are deceptive.

Trümmer pl ❶ wreckage sg ▷ *die Trümmer des Flugzeugs* the wreckage of the aeroplane ❷ ruins pl ▷ *Nach dem Bombenangriff war die Stadt voller Trümmer.* After the air raid the town was in ruins.

Trumpf (pl **Trümpfe**) m trump ▷ *Herz ist Trumpf.* Hearts is trumps.

Trunkenheit f drunkenness; **Trunkenheit am Steuer** drink-driving

> Word for word, **Trunkenheit am Steuer** means 'drunkenness at the steering wheel'.

Truppen fpl troops pl

Truthahn (pl **Truthähne**) m turkey

Tscheche (gen **Tschechen**, pl **Tschechen**) m Czech

Tschechien nt Czechia

Tschechin f Czech

tschechisch adj Czech ▷ *die tschechische Rebublik* the Czech Republic

tschüs excl cheerio!

T-Shirt (pl **T-Shirts**) nt T-shirt

Tube f tube ▷ *eine Tube Zahnpasta* a tube of toothpaste

Tuch (pl **Tücher**) nt ❶ cloth ▷ *Mit welchem Tuch soll ich abstauben?* Which cloth should I use for dusting? ❷ towel ▷ *Nimm dir ein großes Tuch ins Schwimmbad mit.* Take a large towel with you to the swimming baths. ❸ scarf ▷ *Sie hatte ein seidenes Tuch um den Hals.* She wore a silk scarf around her neck.

tüchtig adj competent ▷ *Er ist ein sehr tüchtiger Mensch.* He's a very competent person.; **Er nahm einen tüchtigen Schluck aus der Flasche.** (informal) He took a hefty swig from the bottle.

Tulpe f tulip

tun (imperf **tat**, perf **hat getan**) vb [81] ❶ to do ▷ *Was sollen wir jetzt tun?* What shall we do now? ▷ *Er hat den ganzen Tag nichts getan.* He hasn't done anything all day. ▷ *Was kann ich für Sie tun?* What can I do for you? ❷ to put ▷ *Sie tat die Teller in den Schrank.* She put the plates in the cupboard. ❸ to act ▷ *Tu nicht so unschuldig!* Don't act so innocent. ❹ to pretend ▷ *Sie tat, als ob sie schliefe.* She pretended to be sleeping. ▷ *Er ist nicht krank, er tut nur so.* He isn't ill, he's only pretending.; **Der Hund tut dir bestimmt nichts.** The dog won't hurt you.; **Hoffentlich hast du dir bei dem Sturz nichts getan.** I hope you didn't hurt yourself when you fell.; **Es tut sich viel.** A lot's happening.; **mit etwas zu tun haben** to have something to do with something; **Das tut nichts zur Sache.** That's neither here nor there.

Tunfisch (pl **Tunfische**) m tuna

Tunnel (pl **Tunnel**) m tunnel

Tür f door

Türke (gen **Türken**, pl **Türken**) m Turk

Türkei f Turkey

Türkis f Turk

türkis adj turquoise

türkisch adj Turkish

Turm (pl **Türme**) m ❶ tower ▷ *die Türme der Burg* the castle towers ❷ steeple ▷ *Das Ulmer Münster hat den höchsten Kirchturm der Welt.* Ulm Cathedral has the world's highest steeple. ❸ rook ▷ *Er machte einen Zug mit dem Turm.* He moved his rook.

turnen vb [38] ❶ to do gymnastics ▷ *Sie turnt nicht gern.* She doesn't like doing gymnastics. ❷ to perform ▷ *Sie hat die Kür hervorragend geturnt.* She performed the free programme brilliantly.

Turnen nt ❶ gymnastics sg ▷ *Die Russinnen sind im Turnen gut.* The Russian women are good at gymnastics. ❷ physical education ▷ *Wir haben in der vierten Stunde Turnen.* We have PE in the fourth period.
Turnhalle f gym
Turnhose f gym shorts pl ▷ *eine Turnhose* a pair of gym shorts
Turnier (pl **Turniere**) nt tournament
Turnschuh (pl **Turnschuhe**) m trainer ▷ *ein Paar Turnschuhe* a pair of trainers
Turnzeug nt gym things pl ▷ *Wo ist mein Turnzeug?* Where are my gym things?
Tüte f bag
Typ (pl **Typen**) m ❶ type ▷ *Er ist ein athletischer Typ.* He's an athletic type. ❷ (informal) bloke ▷ *der Typ da drüben* the bloke over there
typisch adj typical ▷ *typisch für* typical of

U-Bahn f underground ▷ *mit der U-Bahn fahren* to travel by underground
U-Bahn-Station f underground station
übel adj bad ▷ *ein übler Geruch* a bad smell ▷ *eine üble Lage* a bad situation ▷ *Nicht übel!* Not bad.; **jemandem ist übel** somebody feels sick; **Sie hat dir die Bemerkung übel genommen.** She was offended by your remark.
Übelkeit f nausea
übelnehmen vb [52] see **übel**
üben vb [38] to practise
über prep, adv

Use the accusative to express movement or a change of place. Use the dative when there is no change of place.

❶ over ▷ *Über dem Tisch hängt eine Lampe.* There's a lamp hanging over the table. ▷ *Sie legten ein Brett über das Loch.* They put a board over the hole. ▷ *Flugzeuge dürfen nicht über dieses Gebiet fliegen.* Planes are not allowed to fly over this area. ▷ **Über Weihnachten bin ich zu Hause.** I'm at home over Christmas. ▷ **Kinder über zwölf Jahren** children over twelve years of age ▷ **Das hat über hundert Euro gekostet.** It cost over a hundred euros. ❷ above ▷ **Das Flugzeug flog hoch über der Stadt.** The plane flew high above the town.; **den ganzen Tag über** all day long; **zwei Grad über null** two degrees above zero; **ein Scheck über zweihundert Euro** a cheque for two hundred euros ❸ across ▷ **Er ging quer über das Feld.** He went across the field. ❹ via ▷ **nach Köln über Aachen** to Cologne via Aachen ▷ **über Satellit** via satellite ❺ about ▷ **Wir haben über das Wetter geredet.** We talked about the weather. ▷ **ein Buch über …** a book about … ❻ through ▷ **Ich habe den Job über einen Freund bekommen.** I got the job through a friend.; **über jemanden lachen** to laugh at somebody; **Sie liebt ihn über alles.** She loves him more than anything.; **über und über** over and over; **über kurz oder lang** sooner or later; **etwas über haben** (*informal*) to be fed up with something

überall *adv* everywhere

überbieten (*imperf* **überbot**, *perf* **hat überboten**) *vb* [8] ❶ to outbid ▷ **Er bot zweitausend Euro, aber wir haben ihn überboten.** He bid two thousand euros but we outbid him.; **einen Rekord überbieten** to break a record; **sich überbieten** to excel oneself

Überblick (*pl* **Überblicke**) *m* ❶ view ▷ **Von hier aus hat man einen guten Überblick über das Gelände.** You can get a good view of the area from here. ❷ overview ▷ **ein Überblick über die unregelmäßigen Verben** an overview of irregular verbs ❸ overall impression ▷ **Ich muss mir erst mal einen Überblick verschaffen.** I have to get an overall impression first.; **den Überblick verlieren** to lose track of things; **Sie hat den Überblick über ihre Arbeit verloren.** She has no idea where she is with her work.

überdenken (*imperf* **überdachte**, *perf* **hat überdacht**) *vb* [14] to think over

übereinander *adv* one on top of the other ▷ **Sie legte die Bücher übereinander.** She put one book on top of the other.; **übereinander sprechen** to talk about each other

überfahren (*pres* **überfährt**, *imperf* **überfuhr**, *perf* **hat überfahren**) *vb* [21] to run over ▷ **Die Katze wurde von einem Auto überfahren.** The cat was run over by a car.

Überfahrt *f* crossing

Überfall (*pl* **Überfälle**) *m* ❶ raid ▷ **ein Banküberfall** a bank raid ▷ **ein Überfall auf ein fremdes Land** a raid on a foreign country ❷ assault ▷ **Er wurde das Opfer eines Überfalls.** He was the victim of an assault.

überfallen (*pres* **überfällt**, *imperf* **überfiel**, *perf* **hat überfallen**) *vb* [22] ❶ to attack ▷ **Sie ist im Park überfallen worden.** She was attacked in the park.; **eine Bank überfallen** to raid a bank ❷ to descend on ▷ **Am Wochenende hat mich meine Freundin mit ihren Eltern überfallen.** My girlfriend and her parents descended on me at the weekend.

überfällig *adj* overdue

überflüssig *adj* superfluous

überfordern (*perf* **hat überfordert**) *vb* [88] to ask too much of ▷ **Unser Mathelehrer überfordert uns.** Our maths teacher asks too much of us.

überfüllt *adj* ❶ overcrowded ▷ **Die Gefängnisse sind völlig überfüllt.** The prisons are completely overcrowded. ❷ oversubscribed ▷ **Der Computerkurs ist überfüllt.** The computer course is oversubscribed.

Übergang (pl **Übergänge**) m
① crossing ▷ *ein Fußgängerübergang* a pedestrian crossing ② transition ▷ *der Übergang vom Sommer zum Herbst* the transition from summer to autumn

übergeben (pres **übergibt**, imperf **übergab**, perf **hat übergeben**) vb [28] to hand over ▷ *Sie hat uns die Schlüssel übergeben.* She handed the keys over to us.; **sich übergeben** to be sick

übergewichtig adj overweight

überhaupt adv ① at all ▷ *Kannst du überhaupt Auto fahren?* Can you drive a car at all? ▷ *Hast du überhaupt zugehört?* Have you been listening at all? ▷ *Ich habe überhaupt keine Lust.* I don't feel like it at all. ② in general ▷ *Die Engländer sind überhaupt sehr höflich.* In general the English are very polite.; **überhaupt nicht** not at all; **überhaupt nichts** nothing at all

überheblich adj arrogant

überholen (perf **hat überholt**) vb [18]
① to overtake ▷ *Er hat rechts überholt.* He overtook on the right. ② to check over ▷ *Ich muss mein Fahrrad überholen.* I have to check my bike over.

überholt adj out-of-date

Überholverbot (pl **Überholverbote**) nt restriction on overtaking

überlassen (pres **überlässt**, imperf **überließ**, perf **hat überlassen**) vb [42] **jemandem etwas überlassen** to leave something up to somebody

überlasten (perf **hat überlastet**) vb [2] to overload ▷ *Der Aufzug war überlastet.* The lift was overloaded.; **Ich fühle mich überlastet.** I feel overworked.

überleben (perf **hat überlebt**) vb [18] to survive

überlegen (perf **hat überlegt**) vb [82] to think about ▷ *Ich muss mir deinen Vorschlag überlegen.* I'll have to think about your suggestion. ▷ *Überleg doch mal.* Think about it.

▶ adj ① better ▷ *Er ist ihr in Englisch überlegen.* He's better at English than she is. ② convincingly ▷ *Unsere Mannschaft hat überlegen gewonnen.* Our team won convincingly.

überlisten (perf **hat überlistet**) vb [2] to outwit

überm = **über dem**

übermäßig adj excessive

übermorgen adv the day after tomorrow

übernächste adj next but one ▷ *An der übernächsten Haltestelle muss ich aussteigen.* I need to get off at the next stop but one.

übernachten (perf **hat übernachtet**) vb [2] **bei jemandem übernachten** to spend the night at somebody's house

Übernachtung f overnight stay; **Übernachtung mit Frühstück** bed and breakfast

übernehmen (pres **übernimmt**, imperf **übernahm**, perf **hat übernommen**) vb [52] to take over ▷ *Er hat das Geschäft seines Vaters übernommen.* He's taken over his father's business. ▷ *Er hat das Amt des Klassensprechers übernehmen.* He took over as class representative.; **sich übernehmen** to take on too much

überprüfen (perf **hat überprüft**) vb [18] to check

überqueren (perf **hat überquert**) vb [7] to cross

überraschen (perf **hat überrascht**) vb [18] to surprise

überrascht adj surprised

Überraschung f surprise

überreden (perf **hat überredet**) vb [54] to persuade ▷ *Kannst du sie nicht überreden mitzukommen?* Can't you persuade her to come?

übers = **über das**

überschätzen (perf **hat überschätzt**) vb [36] to overestimate

überschlagen (pres **überschlägt**, imperf **überschlug**, perf **hat überschlagen**) vb [59] to estimate ▷ *Wir sollten die Kosten für das Fest überschlagen.* We should estimate how much the party will cost.; **eine Seite überschlagen** to miss a page; **Das Auto hat sich überschlagen.** The car rolled over.

Überschrift f heading

Überschuss (gen **Überschusses**, pl **Überschüsse**) m surplus ▷ *ein Überschuss an* a surplus of

Überschwemmung f flood

übersehen (pres **übersieht**, imperf **übersah**, perf **hat übersehen**) vb [64] ❶ to overlook ▷ *Sie hat ein paar Fehler übersehen.* She overlooked a couple of mistakes. ❷ to see ▷ *Wir können die Folgen noch nicht übersehen.* We can't see the consequences yet.

übersetzen (perf **hat übersetzt**) vb [36] to translate ▷ *Übersetzt den Text ins Englische.* Translate the text into English.

Übersetzer (pl **Übersetzer**) m translator

Übersetzerin f translator

Übersetzung f translation ▷ *Das war eine schwierige Übersetzung.* That was a difficult translation.

Übersicht f ❶ view ▷ *Von hier aus hat man eine gute Übersicht.* You get a good view from here. ❷ overview ▷ *eine Übersicht über die unregelmäßigen Verben* an overview of irregular verbs

übersichtlich adj clear ▷ *Die Tabelle ist nicht besonders übersichtlich.* The table isn't particularly clear. ▷ *etwas übersichtlich gestalten* to arrange something clearly; **ein übersichtliches Gelände** open country

überspringen (imperf **übersprang**, perf **hat übersprungen**) vb [71] ❶ to jump over ▷ *Er hat die Hürde übersprungen.* He jumped over the hurdle. ❷ to skip ▷ *Das nächste Kapitel können wir überspringen.* We can skip the next chapter.

überstehen (imperf **überstand**, perf **hat überstanden**) vb [72] ❶ to get over ▷ *Wir haben das Schlimmste überstanden.* We've got over the worst. ❷ to survive ▷ *Die Pflanze hat den Winter nicht überstanden.* The plant didn't survive the winter.

übersteigen (imperf **überstieg**, perf **hat überstiegen**) vb [74] to exceed ▷ *Das übersteigt unsere Erwartungen.* That exceeds our expectations.

überstimmen (perf **hat überstimmt**) vb [7] to outvote

Überstunden fpl overtime sg ▷ *Er macht viele Überstunden.* He does a lot of overtime.

überstürzen (perf **hat überstürzt**) vb [36] ❶ to rush ▷ *Du solltest nichts überstürzen.* You shouldn't rush into things.; **sich überstürzen** to follow one another in rapid succession

überstürzt adj ❶ rash ▷ *eine überstürzte Entscheidung* a rash decision ❷ in a rush ▷ *Sie sind überstürzt abgereist.* They left in a rush.

übertragen (pres **überträgt**, imperf **übertrug**, perf **hat übertragen**) vb [77] ❶ to broadcast ▷ *Wir übertragen das Spiel live.* We're broadcasting the game live. ❷ to copy ▷ *Sie hat den Text in ihr Heft übertragen.* She copied the text into her exercise book. ❸ to transmit ▷ *eine Krankheit übertragen* to transmit an illness; **Sie hat mir diese Aufgabe übertragen.** She has assigned this task to me.; **sich übertragen auf** to spread to
▶ adj figurative ▷ *die übertragene Bedeutung eines Wortes* the figurative meaning of a word

übertreffen (pres **übertrifft**, imperf **übertraf**, perf **hat übertroffen**) vb [78] to surpass

übertreiben (*imperf* **übertrieb**, *perf* **hat übertrieben**) *vb* to exaggerate

Übertreibung *f* exaggeration

übertrieben *adj* excessive

überwachen (*perf* **hat überwacht**) *vb* [18] ❶ to supervise ▷ *Wer soll die Kinder überwachen?* Who will supervise the children? ❷ to keep under surveillance ▷ *Die Polizei überwacht ihn.* The police are keeping him under surveillance.

überweisen (*imperf* **überwies**, *perf* **hat überwiesen**) *vb* to transfer

überwinden (*imperf* **überwand**, *perf* **hat überwunden**) *vb* to overcome ▷ *Jetzt haben wir alle Schwierigkeiten überwunden.* Now we've overcome all difficulties.; **sich überwinden** to force oneself

überzeugen (*perf* **hat überzeugt**) *vb* [18] to convince

überzeugend *adj* convincing

Überzeugung *f* conviction ▷ *Er sagte es ohne große Überzeugung.* He said it without much conviction.

üblich *adj* usual

U-Boot (*pl* **U-Boote**) *nt* submarine

übrig *adj* remaining ▷ *Die übrigen Gäste sind auch bald gegangen.* The remaining guests left soon afterwards.; **Ist noch Kuchen übrig?** Is there any cake left?; **die Übrigen** the others; **das Übrige** the rest; **im Übrigen** besides; **übrig bleiben** to be left; **übrig lassen** to leave

übrigens *adv* by the way ▷ *Übrigens, du schuldest mir noch zehn Euro.* By the way, you still owe me ten euros.

übrighaben (*pres* **hat übrig**, *imperf* **hatte übrig**, *perf* **hat übriggehabt**) *vb* [32] **für jemanden etwas übrighaben** to be fond of somebody

übriglassen *vb* [42] see **übrig**

Übung *f* ❶ practice ▷ *Mir fehlt die Übung.* I need more practice. ▷ *Übung macht den Meister.* Practice makes perfect. ❷ exercise ▷ *Bitte macht jetzt Übung dreizehn.* Please do exercise thirteen now. ▷ *eine Turnübung* a gym exercise

Ufer (*pl* **Ufer**) *nt* ❶ bank ▷ *Wir saßen am Ufer des Rheins.* We sat on the bank of the Rhine. ❷ shore ▷ *Treibholz, das ans Ufer gespült wurde* driftwood which was washed up onto the shore

Uhr *f* ❶ clock ▷ *Die Uhr am Bahnhof sollte richtig gehen.* The station clock should be right. ❷ watch ▷ *Er sah auf seine Uhr.* He looked at his watch.; **Wie viel Uhr ist es?** What time is it?; **ein Uhr** one o'clock; **zwanzig Uhr** eight o'clock in the evening; **um fünf Uhr** at five o'clock

Uhrzeigersinn *m* **im Uhrzeigersinn** clockwise; **entgegen dem Uhrzeigersinn** anticlockwise

Uhrzeit *f* time

Ultraschall *m* ultrasound

um *prep, conj, adv*

▎ The preposition **um** takes the accusative.

❶ round ▷ *Sie legte sich einen Schal um den Hals.* She wrapped a scarf round her neck. ▷ *Wir sind um die Stadt herumgefahren.* We drove round the town.; **um Weihnachten** around Christmas ❷ at ▷ *um acht Uhr* at eight o'clock ❸ by ▷ *etwas um vier Zentimeter kürzen* to shorten something by four centimetres; **um zehn Prozent teurer** ten per cent more expensive; **um vieles besser** better by far ❹ for ▷ *der Kampf um den Titel* the battle for the title ▷ *um Geld spielen* to play for money; **um ... willen** for the sake of ...

▎ **um ... willen** takes the genitive.
▷ *um meiner Mutter willen* for my mother's sake; **um ... zu** in order to ...

▎ **um ... zu** is used with the infinitive.
▷ *Ich gehe in die Schule, um etwas zu lernen.* I go to school in order to learn something.; **zu klug, um zu ...** too

umarmen (perf **hat umarmt**) vb [7] to hug ▷ *Sie umarmten sich.* They hugged.

umbringen (imperf **brachte um**, perf **hat umgebracht**) vb [13] to kill

umdrehen (perf **hat umgedreht**) vb [4] to turn round ▷ *Dreh das Bild mal um.* Turn the picture round.; **sich umdrehen** to turn round

umfallen (pres **fällt um**, imperf **fiel um**, perf **ist umgefallen**) vb [22] to fall down

Umfang m ❶ extent ▷ *Der Umfang der Arbeiten war am Anfang nicht absehbar.* The extent of the work couldn't be seen at the beginning. ❷ circumference ▷ *Berechnet den Umfang des Kreises.* Calculate the circumference of the circle.

Umfrage f poll

Umgang m erfahren im Umgang mit Kindern experienced in dealing with children; **der Umgang mit dem Computer** working with computers

Umgangssprache f colloquial language

umgeben (pres **umgibt**, imperf **umgab**, perf **hat umgeben**) vb [28] to surround

Umgebung f ❶ surroundings pl ▷ *ein Haus in schöner Umgebung* a house in beautiful surroundings ❷ environment ▷ *Diese Pflanze wächst am besten in sonniger Umgebung.* This plant grows best in a sunny environment.

umgehen (1) (imperf **ging um**, perf **ist umgegangen**) vb [29]

> Note that here the stress is on **um**.

mit jemandem grob umgehen to treat somebody roughly; **mit Geld sparsam umgehen** to be careful with one's money; **Sie kann nicht gut mit Geld umgehen.** She's not very good with money.

umgehen (2) (imperf **umging**, perf **hat umgangen**) vb [29]

> Note that here the stress is on **gehen**.

to avoid ▷ *Dieses Problem sollten wir besser umgehen.* It would be better if we could avoid this problem.

umgehend adj immediate

Umgehungsstraße f bypass

umgekehrt adj, adv ❶ reverse ▷ *in umgekehrter Reihenfolge* in reverse order; **genau umgekehrt** exactly the opposite ❷ the other way around ▷ *Du musst das Bild umgekehrt hängen.* You'll have to hang the picture the other way round. ▷ *Mach das doch umgekehrt, und fang hiermit an.* Do it the other way round and start here.; **... und umgekehrt** ... and vice versa

umhauen (perf **hat umgehauen**) vb [4] ❶ to bowl over ▷ *Die Neuigkeit wird dich umhauen.* The news will bowl you over. ❷ to fell ▷ *Sie haben die alte Eiche umgehauen.* They've felled the old oak tree.

umkehren (perf **hat/ist umgekehrt**) vb [4]

> For the perfect tense use **haben** when the verb has an object and **sein** when there is no object.

❶ to turn back ▷ *Wir sind auf halbem Weg umgekehrt.* We turned back halfway. ❷ to turn round ▷ *Warum hast du das Bild umgekehrt?* Why did you turn the picture round? ❸ to turn inside out ▷ *Sie hat ihre Tasche umgekehrt, den Schlüssel aber nicht gefunden.* She turned her bag inside out but couldn't find the key. ❹ to turn upside down ▷ *Kehr mal den Eimer um, dann kann ich mich draufstellen.* Turn the bucket upside down so that I can stand on it.

umkippen (perf **hat/ist umgekippt**) vb [4]

> For the perfect tense use **haben** when the verb has an object and **sein** when there is no object.

Umkleidekabine | 230   **GERMAN > ENGLISH**

❶ to tip over ▷ *Der Stuhl ist umgekippt.* The chair tipped over. ❷ to overturn ▷ *Sie haben das Boot umgekippt.* They overturned the boat. ❸ *(informal)* to keel over ▷ *Wenn ich Blut sehe, kippe ich immer um.* I keel over whenever I see blood.

Umkleidekabine f changing cubicle

Umkleideraum (pl **Umkleideräume**) m changing room

umkommen (*imperf* **kam um**, *perf* **ist umgekommen**) *vb* [**40**] to be killed ▷ *Alle Passagiere sind umgekommen.* All the passengers were killed.

Umkreis (*gen* **Umkreises**, *pl* **Umkreise**) m neighbourhood; **im Umkreis von** within a radius of

Umlaut (*pl* **Umlaute**) m umlaut

umlegen (*perf* **hat umgelegt**) *vb* [**4**] ❶ to put on ▷ *Du solltest dir eine Jacke umlegen.* You should put on a jacket.; **die Kosten für etwas umlegen** to divide the cost of something ❷ *(informal)* to bump off ▷ *Er ist von der Mafia umgelegt worden.* He was bumped off by the Mafia.

umleiten (*perf* **hat umgeleitet**) *vb* [**4**] to divert

Umleitung f diversion

umrechnen (*perf* **hat umgerechnet**) *vb* [**4**] to convert

Umrechnung f conversion

umrühren (*perf* **hat umgerührt**) *vb* [**4**] to stir

ums = **um das**

Umsatz (*gen* **Umsatzes**, *pl* **Umsätze**) m turnover

umschalten (*perf* **hat umgeschaltet**) *vb* [**4**] to switch ▷ *Schalt bitte ins zweite Programm um.* Please switch over to Channel two.; **Die Ampel hat auf Gelb umgeschaltet.** The traffic lights changed to amber.; **Wir schalten um ins Studio.** We'll now go back to the studio.

Umschlag (*pl* **Umschläge**) m
❶ cover ▷ *Alle meine Mathehefte haben einen schwarzen Umschlag.* All my maths exercise books have a black cover. ❷ jacket ▷ *Ich habe den Umschlag von dem Wörterbuch abgemacht.* I took the jacket off the dictionary. ❸ envelope ▷ *Sie steckte den Brief in den Umschlag.* She put the letter in the envelope.

sich umsehen (*pres* **sieht sich um**, *imperf* **sah sich um**, *perf* **hat sich umgesehen**) *vb* [**64**] to look around ▷ *Als sie Schritte hörte, sah sie sich um.* When she heard steps, she looked around.; **sich nach etwas umsehen** to look for something

umso *conj* so much ▷ *umso besser* so much the better ▷ *umso schlimmer* so much the worse; **Je mehr ich höre, umso weniger verstehe ich.** The more I hear the less I understand.

umsonst *adv* ❶ in vain ▷ *Wir haben umsonst gewartet.* We waited in vain. ❷ for nothing ▷ *Wir sind umsonst ins Museum gekommen.* We got into the museum for nothing. ❸ free of charge ▷ *Diese Broschüre gibt es umsonst.* This brochure is free of charge.

Umstand (*pl* **Umstände**) m circumstance ▷ *unter keinen Umständen* under no circumstances; **Wenn es keine Umstände macht.** If it's no trouble.; **unter Umständen** possibly; **in anderen Umständen sein** to be pregnant

> Word for word, **in anderen Umständen sein** means 'to be in different circumstances'.

umständlich *adj* ❶ complicated ▷ *Das ist aber umständlich, wie du das machst.* The way you do it is complicated. ❷ long-winded ▷ *eine umständliche Erklärung* a long-winded explanation

umsteigen (*imperf* **stieg um**, *perf* **ist umgestiegen**) *vb* [74] to change ▷ *Wir müssen in München umsteigen.* We have to change in Munich.

umstellen (1) (*perf* **hat umgestellt**) *vb* [4]
▌ Note that here the stress is on **um**.
to move ▷ *Ich werde meinen Schreibtisch umstellen.* I'm going to move my desk.; **auf metrische Maße umstellen** to go over to the metric system; **sich umstellen** to adapt

umstellen (2) (*perf* **hat umstellt**) *vb* [7]
▌ Note that here the stress is on **stellen**.
to surround ▷ *Die Polizei hat das Haus umstellt.* The police have surrounded the house.

umstritten *adj* controversial ▷ *ein umstrittenes Thema* a controversial subject

Umtausch *m* exchange

umtauschen (*perf* **hat umgetauscht**) *vb* [4] to exchange

Umweg (*pl* **Umwege**) *m* detour ▷ *Wir haben einen Umweg gemacht.* We made a detour.

Umwelt *f* environment

umweltfreundlich *adj* environmentally-friendly

Umweltschützer (*pl* **Umweltschützer**) *m* environmentalist

Umweltverschmutzung *f* environmental pollution

umziehen (*imperf* **zog um**, *perf* **hat/ist umgezogen**) *vb* [96]
▌ Use **haben** to form the perfect tense. Use **sein** to form the perfect tense for 'to move'.
① to change ▷ *Ich habe Carolin heute schon zweimal umgezogen.* I've already changed Carolin's clothes twice today.; **sich umziehen** to get changed
② to move ▷ *Mein Freund ist nach Bremen umgezogen.* My friend's moved to Bremen.

Umzug (*pl* **Umzüge**) *m* ① move ▷ *Alle meine Freunde haben beim Umzug geholfen.* All my friends helped with the move. ② procession ▷ *Zu Karneval finden überall Umzüge statt.* There are processions everywhere during the Carnival.

unabhängig *adj* independent

Unabhängigkeit *f* independence

unangebracht *adj* uncalled-for

unangenehm *adj* unpleasant

Unannehmlichkeiten *fpl* trouble *sg* ▷ *Das gibt Unannehmlichkeiten mit dem Klassenlehrer.* That'll cause trouble with the class teacher.

unanständig *adj* improper

unartig *adj* naughty

unaufmerksam *adj* inattentive

unausstehlich *adj* intolerable

unbeabsichtigt *adj* unintentional

unbedeutend *adj* unimportant

unbedingt *adj*, *adv* ① unconditional ▷ *Ich verlange unbedingten Gehorsam.* I demand unconditional obedience. ② really ▷ *Er wollte unbedingt nach Hause.* He really wanted to go home. ▷ *Den Film musst du dir unbedingt ansehen.* You really have to see that film.

unbegreiflich *adj* inconceivable

unbekannt *adj* unknown

unbeliebt *adj* unpopular

unbequem *adj* uncomfortable ▷ *Das Bett ist unbequem.* The bed's uncomfortable.

unbestimmt *adj* ① indefinite ▷ *der unbestimmte Artikel* the indefinite article ② uncertain ▷ *Es ist noch unbestimmt, wann wir Ferien machen.* It's still uncertain when we're going on holiday.

unbewusst *adj* unconscious

und *conj* and ▷ *und so weiter* and so on; **Na und?** So what?

undankbar *adj* ungrateful

undeutlich adj indistinct
unehrlich adj dishonest
unempfindlich adj practical ▷ *Wir brauchen für das Sofa einen unempfindlichen Bezug.* We need a practical cover for the sofa.; **Ich bin gegen Kälte unempfindlich.** I don't feel the cold.
unendlich adj infinite
unentschieden adj undecided; **unentschieden enden** to end in a draw
unerfahren adj inexperienced
unerfreulich adj unpleasant
unerträglich adj unbearable ▷ *Die Schmerzen sind unerträglich.* The pain's unbearable.
unerwünscht adj undesirable
unfähig adj incapable ▷ *zu etwas unfähig sein* to be incapable of something
unfair adj unfair
Unfall (gen **Unfalls**, pl **Unfälle**) m accident
unfreundlich adj unfriendly
Unfreundlichkeit f unfriendliness
Unfug m ❶ mischief ▷ *Die Kinder machen dauernd Unfug.* The children are always getting up to mischief. ❷ nonsense ▷ *Red nicht so einen Unfug.* Don't talk such nonsense.
Ungar (gen **Ungarn**, pl **Ungarn**) m Hungarian
Ungarin f Hungarian
ungarisch adj Hungarian
Ungarn nt Hungary
Ungeduld f impatience
ungeduldig adj impatient
ungeeignet adj unsuitable
ungefähr adj approximate ▷ *Kannst du mir eine ungefähre Zeit nennen?* Can you give me an approximate time? ▷ *um ungefähr zwei Uhr* at approximately two o'clock
ungefährlich adj harmless
Ungeheuer (pl **Ungeheuer**) nt monster ▷ *das Ungeheuer von Loch Ness* the Loch Ness monster

ungehörig adj impertinent
ungehorsam adj disobedient
ungeklärt adj unsolved ▷ *ein ungeklärtes Rätsel* an unsolved puzzle
ungelegen adj inconvenient ▷ *Ich hoffe, ich komme nicht ungelegen.* I hope I haven't come at an inconvenient time.
ungelernt adj unskilled ▷ *ein ungelernter Arbeiter* an unskilled worker
ungemütlich adj ❶ uncomfortable ▷ *ein ungemütlicher Stuhl* an uncomfortable chair ❷ disagreeable ▷ *Jetzt wird er ungemütlich.* Now he's going to get disagreeable.
ungenau adj inaccurate
ungenießbar adj ❶ inedible ▷ *Das Essen war ungenießbar.* The food was inedible. ❷ undrinkable ▷ *Diese Limonade ist ungenießbar.* This lemonade's undrinkable. ❸ unbearable ▷ *Du bist heute aber ungenießbar.* You're really unbearable today.
ungenügend adj ❶ insufficient ▷ *eine ungenügende Menge* an insufficient amount ❷ unsatisfactory
* German marks range from one (**sehr gut**) to six (**ungenügend**).
ungepflegt adj *ein ungepflegter Garten* a neglected garden; *ungepflegte Hände* uncared-for hands
ungerade adj *eine ungerade Zahl* an odd number
ungerecht adj unjust
Ungerechtigkeit f injustice
ungern adv reluctantly
ungeschickt adj clumsy
ungestört adj undisturbed
ungesund adj unhealthy
ungewiss adj uncertain
Ungewissheit f uncertainty
ungewöhnlich adj unusual
ungewohnt adj unaccustomed
Ungeziefer nt vermin
ungezogen adj rude
unglaublich adj incredible

Unglück (pl **Unglücke**) nt ❶ accident ▷ *Er ist bei einem Unglück ums Leben gekommen.* He lost his life in an accident. ❷ misfortune ▷ *Lass sie in ihrem Unglück nicht allein.* Don't leave her alone in her misfortune. ❸ bad luck ▷ *Eine schwarze Katze bringt Unglück.* A black cat means bad luck.

unglücklich adj ❶ unhappy ▷ *Sie ist furchtbar unglücklich.* She's terribly unhappy. ❷ unfortunate ▷ *ein unglücklicher Zufall* an unfortunate coincidence ▷ *eine unglückliche Formulierung* an unfortunate choice of words; **Sie ist unglücklich gefallen.** She fell awkwardly.

ungültig adj invalid

ungünstig adj unfavourable

unheilbar adj incurable

unheimlich adj, adv ❶ weird ▷ *Das war ein unheimliches Geräusch.* That was a weird noise.; **Mir wird's etwas unheimlich.** I'm getting a bit scared. ❷ incredibly ▷ *Das hat mich unheimlich gefreut.* I was incredibly pleased about it.

unhöflich adj impolite

Uni (pl **Unis**) f (informal) uni

Uniform f uniform

uninteressant adj uninteresting

Universität f university

unklar adj unclear; **über etwas im Unklaren sein** to be unclear about something; **jemanden über etwas im Unklaren lassen** to leave somebody in the dark about something

unklug adj unwise

Unkosten pl expenses pl

unlogisch adj illogical

unlösbar adj insoluble ▷ *ein unlösbares Problem* an insoluble problem

unmissverständlich adj unmistakeable

unmittelbar adj immediate

unmöglich adj impossible

unmoralisch adj immoral

unnötig adj unnecessary

unordentlich adj untidy

Unordnung f disorder

unparteiisch adj impartial

unpassend adj ❶ inappropriate ▷ *unpassende Kleidung* inappropriate clothes ❷ inopportune ▷ *zu einer unpassenden Zeit* at an inopportune time

unpersönlich adj impersonal ▷ *das unpersönliche Fürwort* the impersonal pronoun

unpraktisch adj unpractical

unpünktlich adj **Sie ist immer unpünktlich.** She's always late.

unrecht adj wrong ▷ *Du tust ihr unrecht.* You are wronging her.; **unrecht haben** to be wrong

Unrecht nt wrong ▷ *ein großes Unrecht* a great wrong; **zu Unrecht** wrongly

unregelmäßig adj irregular ▷ *ein unregelmäßiges Verb* an irregular verb

unreif adj ❶ not ripe ▷ *Der Apfel ist noch unreif.* The apple's not ripe yet. ❷ immature ▷ *Elisabeth ist noch furchtbar unreif.* Elisabeth's still terribly immature.

unrichtig adj incorrect

Unruhe f unrest

unruhig adj restless

uns pron
uns is the accusative and dative of **wir**.
❶ us ▷ *Sie haben uns eingeladen.* They've invited us. ❷ to us ▷ *Sie haben es uns gegeben.* They gave it to us. ❸ ourselves ▷ *Wir fragen uns, ob das sein muss.* We're asking ourselves whether that is necessary. ❹ each other ▷ *Wir lieben uns.* We love each other.

unschlagbar adj invincible

Unschuld f innocence

unschuldig adj innocent

unser adj ❶ not our ▷ *Unser Deutschlehrer ist nett.* Our German teacher's nice.

▷ Unser Haus ist ganz in der Nähe der Schule. Our house is very near the school. ▷ Unsere Lehrer sind prima. Our teachers are great. ❷ ours ▷ Das ist nicht euer Lehrer, das ist unserer. He's not your teacher, he's ours. ▷ Seine Note war besser als unsere. His mark was better than ours. ▷ Deine Eltern sind netter als unsere. Your parents are nicer than ours.

unseretwegen adv ❶ for our sake ▷ Ihr braucht unseretwegen nicht zu warten. You needn't wait for our sake. ❷ on our account ▷ Hat sie sich unseretwegen so aufgeregt? Did she get so upset on our account? ❸ as far as we're concerned ▷ Unseretwegen kann man das gern anders machen. As far as we're concerned you're welcome to do it differently.

unsicher adj ❶ uncertain ▷ Es ist unsicher, ob wir kommen können. It's uncertain whether we can come. ❷ insecure ▷ Elisabeth ist sehr unsicher. Elisabeth's very insecure.

unsichtbar adj invisible

Unsinn m nonsense ▷ Unsinn erzählen to talk nonsense; **Unsinn machen** to do silly things

unsympathisch adj unpleasant ▷ ein unsympathischer Mensch an unpleasant person; **Er ist mir unsympathisch.** I don't like him.

unten adv ❶ at the bottom ▷ Das beste Buch lag unten auf dem Stapel. The best book was at the bottom of the pile. ▷ Er stand unten an der Treppe. He was standing at the bottom of the stairs. ▷ unten am Berg at the bottom of the mountain ❷ downstairs ▷ Mutter ist unten in der Küche. Mother's downstairs in the kitchen.; **nach unten** down

unter prep ❶ under
> Use the accusative to express movement or a change of place. Use the dative when there is no change of place.

▷ Die Katze lag unter dem Tisch. The cat lay under the table. ▷ Der Ball rollte unter den Tisch. The ball rolled under the table. ▷ unter achtzehn Jahren under eighteen years of age ❷ below ▷ Temperaturen unter null below-zero temperatures ❸ among ▷ Unter den Büchern war auch ein Atlas. There was also an atlas among the books.; **Sie waren unter sich.** They were by themselves.; **einer unter ihnen** one of them; **unter anderem** among other things

unterbrechen (pres **unterbricht**, imperf **unterbrach**, perf **hat unterbrochen**) vb [11] to interrupt

Unterbrechung f interruption

unterdrücken (perf **hat unterdrückt**) vb [7] ❶ to suppress ▷ Sie unterdrückte ein Lächeln. She suppressed a smile. ❷ to oppress ▷ Menschen unterdrücken to oppress people

untere adj lower ▷ die unteren Stockwerke the lower floors

untergehen (imperf **ging unter**, perf **ist untergegangen**) vb [29] ❶ to sink ❷ to set ▷ sobald die Sonne untergegangen ist ... as soon as the sun has set ...; **Die Welt geht unter.** The world's coming to an end.; **Seine Rede ging im Lärm unter.** His speech was drowned out by the noise.

Untergeschoss nt basement

unterhalb prep
> The preposition **unterhalb** takes the genitive.

below ▷ Ihr Haus befindet sich unterhalb der Kirche. Her house is below the church.

unterhalten (pres **unterhält**, imperf **unterhielt**, perf **hat unterhalten**) vb [33] ❶ to entertain ▷ Sie hat uns den ganzen Abend mit lustigen Geschichten unterhalten. She entertained us with funny stories all evening. ❷ to run ▷ Das

GERMAN > ENGLISH

Schwimmbad wird von der Stadt unterhalten. The swimming pool is run by the town council.; **sich unterhalten** to talk

unterhaltsam adj entertaining

Unterhaltung f ❶ talk ▷ *Es war eine sehr aufschlussreiche Unterhaltung.* It was a very informative talk. ❷ entertainment ▷ *Zur Unterhaltung der Gäste spielt die örtliche Musikkapelle.* Entertainment will be provided by the local brass band.

Unterhemd (pl **Unterhemden**) nt vest

Unterhose f underpants pl ▷ *eine Unterhose* a pair of underpants

Unterkunft (pl **Unterkünfte**) f accommodation

Untermieter (pl **Untermieter**) m lodger

unternehmen (pres **unternimmt**, imperf **unternahm**, perf **hat unternommen**) vb [52] **Was sollen wir heute unternehmen?** What shall we do today?

Unternehmen (pl **Unternehmen**) nt enterprise

Unternehmer (pl **Unternehmer**) m entrepreneur

Unterricht m lessons pl ▷ *Nachmittags haben wir selten Unterricht.* We seldom have lessons in the afternoon.

unterrichten (perf **hat unterrichtet**) vb [2] ❶ to teach ▷ *Sie unterrichtet Englisch und Französisch.* She teaches English and French.; **Wer unterrichtet euch in Sport?** Who do you have for sport? ❷ to inform ▷ *Wir müssen deine Eltern davon unterrichten.* We'll have to inform your parents.

Unterrock (pl **Unterröcke**) m underskirt

untersagt adj forbidden

unterschätzen (perf **hat unterschätzt**) vb [36] to underestimate

unterscheiden (imperf **unterschied**, perf **hat unterschieden**) vb [60] to distinguish ▷ *Man muss zwischen Sachlichkeit und Unfreundlichkeit unterscheiden.* You have to distinguish between objectivity and unfriendliness.; **sich unterscheiden** to differ

Unterschied (pl **Unterschiede**) m difference; **im Unterschied zu** as distinct from

unterschiedlich adj different ▷ *Sie haben sehr unterschiedliche Begabungen.* They have very different talents. ▷ *Sie sind unterschiedlich groß.* They're different sizes.; **Das Wetter war sehr unterschiedlich.** The weather was mixed.

unterschreiben (imperf **unterschrieb**, perf **hat unterschrieben**) vb [61] to sign ▷ *Du musst das Zeugnis unterschreiben lassen.* You have to have the report signed.

Unterschrift f signature

unterste adj bottom ▷ *Es ist im untersten Fach.* It's on the bottom shelf.; **Sie ist in der untersten Klasse.** She's in the first form.

unterstreichen (imperf **unterstrich**, perf **hat unterstrichen**) vb to underline

unterstützen (perf **hat unterstützt**) vb [36] to support

Unterstützung f support

untersuchen (perf **hat untersucht**) vb [36] to examine

Untersuchung f examination

Untertasse f saucer ▷ *eine fliegende Untertasse* a flying saucer

unterteilen (perf **hat unterteilt**) vb [7] to divide up

Untertitel (pl **Untertitel**) m subtitle

Unterwäsche f underwear

unterwegs adv on the way

untreu adj unfaithful ▷ *Ich hoffe, du warst mir nicht untreu.* I hope you weren't unfaithful to me.

untröstlich adj inconsolable
unübersichtlich adj unclear ▷ *eine unübersichtliche Darstellung* an unclear presentation; **eine unübersichtliche Kurve** a blind corner
ununterbrochen adj uninterrupted
unveränderlich adj unchangeable
unverantwortlich adj irresponsible
unverbesserlich adj incorrigible
unverbleit adj unleaded ▷ *Ich fahre unverbleit.* I use unleaded.
unvergesslich adj unforgettable
unverkrampft adj relaxed
unvermeidlich adj unavoidable
unvernünftig adj foolish
unverschämt adj impudent
Unverschämtheit f impudence
unverzeihlich adj unpardonable
unvollständig adj incomplete
unvorsichtig adj careless
unvorstellbar adj inconceivable
unwahr adj untrue
unwahrscheinlich adj, adv ❶ unlikely ▷ *eine unwahrscheinliche Geschichte* an unlikely story ❷ incredibly ▷ *Ich habe mich unwahrscheinlich gefreut.* I was incredibly pleased.
unwichtig adj unimportant
unwirksam adj ineffective
unzählig adj countless
unzufrieden adj dissatisfied
unzutreffend adj incorrect
updaten vb [38] to update
uralt adj ancient
Ureinwohner (pl **Ureinwohner**) m original inhabitant
Urin (pl **Urine**) m urine
Urkunde f certificate
Urlaub (pl **Urlaube**) m holiday ▷ *Wir fahren morgen in Urlaub.* We're going on holiday tomorrow. ▷ *Wo warst du im Urlaub?* Where did you go on holiday?
Ursache f cause; **Keine Ursache!** That's all right.

ursprünglich adj, adv ❶ original ▷ *Wir mussten unsere ursprünglichen Pläne aufgeben.* We had to abandon our original plans. ❷ originally ▷ *Ursprünglich wollten wir nach Griechenland fahren.* We originally wanted to go to Greece.
Urteil (pl **Urteile**) nt ❶ opinion ▷ *Wie lautet dein Urteil?* What's your opinion? ❷ sentence ▷ *Die Richter haben das Urteil noch nicht verkündet.* The judges haven't passed sentence yet.
urteilen vb [38] to judge
Urwald (pl **Urwälder**) m jungle
USA pl USA sg; **aus den USA** from the USA; **in den USA** in the USA; **nach den USA** to the USA
usw. abbr (= *und so weiter*) etc

V

vage adj vague
Vanille f vanilla
Vase f vase
Vater (pl **Väter**) m father
Vati (pl **Vatis**) m (informal) daddy
Veganer (pl **Veganer**) m vegan
Veganerin f vegan
veganisch adj vegan
Vegetarier (pl **Vegetarier**) m vegetarian
Vegetarierin f vegetarian
vegetarisch adj vegetarian
Veilchen (pl **Veilchen**) nt violet
Vene f vein
Ventil (pl **Ventile**) nt valve
verabreden (perf **hat verabredet**) vb [54] to arrange ▷ Wir sollten Zeit und Ort des Treffens verabreden. We ought to arrange when and where to meet.; **sich mit jemandem verabreden** to arrange to meet somebody; **mit jemandem verabredet sein** to have arranged to meet somebody
Verabredung f date
verabschieden (perf **hat verabschiedet**) vb [54] to say goodbye to ▷ Wir verabschiedeten unsere Gäste. We said goodbye to our guests.; **sich verabschieden** to take one's leave
veralten (perf **ist veraltet**) vb [2] to become obsolete
veränderlich adj changeable
verändern (perf **hat verändert**) vb [88] to change; **sich verändern** to change
Veränderung f change
Veranlagung f disposition ▷ eine nervöse Veranlagung a nervous disposition
veranlassen (perf **hat veranlasst**) vb [84] etwas veranlassen to have something done; **sich veranlasst sehen, etwas zu tun** to be prompted to do something
veranstalten (perf **hat veranstaltet**) vb [2] to organize
Veranstalter (pl **Veranstalter**) m organizer
Veranstaltung f event
verantworten (perf **hat verantwortet**) vb [2] to take responsibility for ▷ Wenn das nicht klappt, hast du das zu verantworten. If it doesn't work, you'll have to take responsibility for it.; **Das kann ich nicht verantworten.** I couldn't possibly allow that.
verantwortlich adj responsible
Verantwortung f responsibility
verarbeiten (perf **hat verarbeitet**) vb [2] ❶ to process ▷ In diesem Werk wird Metall verarbeitet. Metal is processed in this factory.; **etwas zu etwas verarbeiten** to make something into something ❷ to digest ▷ Ich muss die Reiseeindrücke erst noch verarbeiten. I still have to digest my impressions from the journey.

verärgern (perf **hat verärgert**) vb [88] to annoy

Verb (pl **Verben**) nt verb

Verband (pl **Verbände**) m ❶ dressing; **Die Schwester hat ihm einen Verband angelegt.** The nurse dressed his wound. ❷ association ▷ *Die Bauern haben sich zu einem Verband zusammengeschlossen.* The farmers have formed an association.

Verbandskasten (pl **Verbandskästen**) m first-aid box

verbergen (pres **verbirgt**, imperf **verbarg**, perf **hat verborgen**) vb to hide; **sich vor jemandem verbergen** to hide from somebody

verbessern (perf **hat verbessert**) vb [88] ❶ to improve ▷ *Ich konnte meine Noten verbessern.* I was able to improve my marks. ❷ to correct ▷ *Meine Mutter hat meine Hausaufgaben verbessert.* My mother corrected my homework.; **sich verbessern** to improve

Verbesserung f ❶ improvement ▷ *eine Verbesserung seiner Leistungen* an improvement in his work ❷ correction ▷ *Schreibt bitte die Verbesserung ins Heft.* Please write the correction in your exercise book.

verbieten (imperf **verbot**, perf **hat verboten**) vb [8] to forbid ▷ *Meine Mutter hat mir verboten, mit Frank auszugehen.* My mother forbade me to go out with Frank.

verbinden (imperf **verband**, perf **hat verbunden**) vb ❶ to combine ▷ *Ich habe das Nützliche mit dem Angenehmen verbunden.* I was able to combine business with pleasure. ❷ to bandage ▷ *Die Wunde muss verbunden werden.* The wound has to be bandaged.; **jemandem die Augen verbinden** to blindfold somebody ❸ to connect ▷ *Ein Kanal verbindet die beiden Flüsse.* A canal connects the two rivers. ❹ sich verbinden to put through ▷ *Können Sie mich bitte mit Frau Karl verbinden?* Can you put me through to Mrs Karl, please?; **Sie sind falsch verbunden.** You've got the wrong number.

Verbindung (pl **Verbindungen**) f ❶ connection ▷ *Es gibt eine direkte Verbindungen nach München.* There is a direct connection to Munich. ❷ communication **Unsere Verbindung wurde unterbrochen.** We were cut off.; **Die Verbindung mit Nepal war sehr schlecht.** The line to Nepal was really bad.

verbleit adj leaded

verblüffen (perf **hat verblüfft**) vb [84] to amaze

verbluten (perf **ist verblutet**) vb [2] to bleed to death

verborgen adj hidden

Verbot (pl **Verbote**) nt ban ▷ *Die Regierung verhängte ein Verbot für Rindfleischimporte aus England.* The government imposed a ban on beef imports from England.

verboten adj forbidden; **Rauchen verboten!** No smoking

Verbrauch m consumption

verbrauchen (perf **hat verbraucht**) vb [84] to use up ▷ *Das Gerät verbraucht viel Strom.* The machine uses up a lot of electricity.

Verbraucher (pl **Verbraucher**) m consumer

Verbrauchermarkt (pl **Verbrauchermärkte**) m hypermarket

Verbrechen (pl **Verbrechen**) nt crime

Verbrecher (pl **Verbrecher**) m criminal

verbreiten (perf **hat verbreitet**) vb [2] ❶ to spread ▷ *eine Krankheit verbreiten* to spread a disease ❷ to broadcast ▷ *eine Nachricht verbreiten* to broadcast a message; **sich verbreiten** to spread

verbrennen (imperf **verbrannte**, perf **hat verbrannt**) vb [12] ❶ to burn ▷ *In* dieser Anlage wird Müll verbrannt. Waste is burnt in this plant. ❷ to cremate ▷ Sie möchte nach ihrem Tod verbrannt werden. She'd like to be cremated when she dies.

verbringen (imperf **verbrachte**, perf **hat verbracht**) vb [13] to spend ▷ Wir haben das Wochenende im Schwarzwald verbracht. We spent the weekend in the Black Forest.

Verdacht (pl **Verdachte**) m suspicion

verdächtig adj suspicious

verdächtigen (perf **hat verdächtigt**) vb [84] to suspect

verdammt adj, adv (informal) damned ▷ Diese verdammten Fliegen! These damned flies!; **Verdammt noch mal!** Damn it all!; **Verdammt!** Damn!

verdampfen (perf **ist verdampft**) vb [7] to evaporate

verdanken (perf **hat verdankt**) vb [84] **jemandem sein Leben verdanken** to owe one's life to somebody

verdauen (perf **hat verdaut**) vb [84] to digest

verdaulich adj Das ist schwer verdaulich. That's hard to digest.

Verdauung f digestion

verderben (pres **verdirbt**, imperf **verdarb**, perf **hat/ist verdorben**) vb

Use **haben** to form the perfect tense. Use **sein** to form the perfect tense for 'to go bad'.

❶ to ruin ▷ Du verdirbst dir bei dem schlechten Licht die Augen. You'll ruin your eyes in this bad light. ▷ Er hat mir den Urlaub verdorben. He ruined my holiday. ❷ to corrupt ▷ Geld verdirbt die Menschen. Money corrupts people.; **es mit jemandem verderben** to get into somebody's bad books ❸ to go bad ▷ Die Wurst ist verdorben. The sausage has gone bad.

verdienen (perf **hat verdient**) vb [84] ❶ to earn ▷ Wie viel verdient dein Vater? How much does your father earn? ❷ to deserve ▷ Du hast die Strafe verdient. You deserved the punishment.

verdreifachen (perf **hat verdreifacht**) vb [7] to treble

verdünnen (perf **hat verdünnt**) vb [7] to dilute

verdunsten (perf **ist verdunstet**) vb [2] to evaporate

verdursten (perf **ist verdurstet**) vb [2] to die of thirst

Verein (pl **Vereine**) m club ▷ ein Sportverein a sports club

vereinbar adj compatible ▷ mit etwas vereinbar compatible with something

vereinbaren (perf **hat vereinbart**) vb [84] to agree on

Vereinbarung f agreement

vereinen (perf **hat vereint**) vb [84] ❶ to unite ▷ Das geteilte Land wurde wieder vereint. The divided country was reunited. ❷ to reconcile ▷ Ich kann das nicht mit meinem Gewissen vereinen. I can't reconcile that with my conscience.; **Mit vereinten Kräften schaffen wir das.** If we all pull together, we'll manage to do it.; **die Vereinten Nationen** the United Nations

vereinfachen (perf **hat vereinfacht**) vb [84] to simplify

vereinigen (perf **hat vereinigt**) vb [84] to unite

vereinzelt adj isolated ▷ vereinzelte Schauer isolated showers

vererben (perf **hat vererbt**) vb [18] to leave ▷ Meine Oma hat mir all ihre Bücher vererbt. My granny left me all her books.; **sich vererben** to be hereditary

verfahren (pres **verfährt**, imperf **verfuhr**, perf **hat/ist verfahren**) vb [21] ❶ to proceed ▷ Wie sollen wir verfahren? How shall we proceed? ❷ to use up ▷ Wir haben 50 Liter Benzin verfahren. We have used up 50 litres of petrol.; **Wir haben uns verfahren.** We have lost our way.

Verfahren (pl **Verfahren**) nt ❶ process ▷ *Das ist ein neuartiges Verfahren zum Recyceln von Plastik.* This is a new recycling process for plastic. ❷ proceedings pl ▷ *ein Verfahren gegen jemanden einleiten* to bring proceedings against somebody

Verfassung f ❶ constitution ▷ *Die Opposition hat eine Änderung der Verfassung beantragt.* The opposition's called for an amendment to the constitution. ❷ state ▷ *Ich bin nicht in der Verfassung, da mitzumachen.* I'm in no state to join in.

verfolgen (perf **hat verfolgt**) vb [84] ❶ to pursue ▷ *Die Polizei verfolgte die Täter.* The police pursued the culprits.; **Die Hunde verfolgten ihre Fährte.** The dogs tracked them. ❷ to persecute ▷ *In vielen Ländern werden Minderheiten verfolgt.* Minorities are persecuted in many countries.

Verfolgung f ❶ hunt ▷ *Die Verfolgung der Täter war erfolgreich.* The hunt for the culprits had a successful outcome. ❷ persecution ▷ *die Verfolgung von Minderheiten* the persecution of minorities

verfügbar adj available

verführen (perf **hat verführt**) vb [84] ❶ to tempt ▷ *Verführ mich nicht, ich habe schon zwei Stück Kuchen gegessen.* Don't tempt me, I've already had two pieces of cake. ❷ to seduce

Vergangenheit f past ▷ *in der Vergangenheit* in the past

vergaß vb see **vergessen**

vergeben (pres **vergibt**, imperf **vergab**, perf **hat vergeben**) vb [28] to forgive ▷ *Kannst du mir noch einmal vergeben?* Can you forgive me one more time? ▷ *Diese Lüge werde ich dir nie vergeben.* I'll never forgive you for that lie.;

vergeben sein to be taken; **Er ist schon vergeben.** He's already spoken for.

> Word for word, **Er ist schon vergeben** means 'He is already given away'.

vergeblich adv, adj in vain ▷ *Wir haben uns vergeblich bemüht.* We tried, but in vain. ▷ *All mein Reden war vergeblich.* All my words were in vain.

vergehen (imperf **verging**, perf **ist vergangen**) vb [29] to pass; **Wie schnell doch die Zeit vergeht!** How time flies!; **Mir ist der Appetit vergangen.** I've lost my appetite.; **sich an jemandem vergehen** to indecently assault somebody

vergessen (pres **vergisst**, imperf **vergaß**, perf **hat vergessen**) vb [83] to forget ▷ *Ich habe seinen Namen vergessen.* I've forgotten his name.; **Vergiss nicht, die Blumen zu gießen.** Remember to water the flowers.

vergesslich adj forgetful

vergeuden (perf **hat vergeudet**) vb [7] to squander

vergewaltigen (perf **hat vergewaltigt**) vb [7] to rape ▷ *Er hat eine Frau vergewaltigt.* He raped a woman.

Vergewaltigung f rape

sich **vergewissern** (perf **hat sich vergewissert**) vb [88] to make sure

vergiften (perf **hat vergiftet**) vb [2] to poison

Vergiftung f poisoning

vergisst vb see **vergessen**

Vergleich (pl **Vergleiche**) m comparison; **im Vergleich zu** compared with

vergleichen (imperf **verglich**, perf **hat verglichen**) vb to compare ▷ *Er hat mein Wörterbuch mit seinem verglichen.* He compared my dictionary with his. ▷ *Man kann doch Äpfel und Birnen nicht* *vergleichen.* You can't compare apples and pears.

Vergnügen (pl **Vergnügen**) nt pleasure; *Viel Vergnügen!* Have fun!

vergnügt adj cheerful

vergraben (pres **vergräbt**, imperf **vergrub**, perf **hat vergraben**) vb to bury

vergrößern (perf **hat vergrößert**) vb [88] ❶ to enlarge ▷ *Ich habe das Foto vergrößern lassen.* I had the photo enlarged. ❷ to extend ▷ *Wir wollen das Haus vergrößern.* We want to extend the house.; **sich vergrößern** to grow larger

verhaften (perf **hat verhaftet**) vb [2] to arrest

sich **verhalten** (pres **verhält sich**, imperf **verhielt sich**, perf **hat sich verhalten**) vb [33] to behave ▷ *Er hat sich uns gegenüber sehr fair verhalten.* He behaved very fairly towards us.

Verhalten nt behaviour

Verhältnis (gen **Verhältnisses**, pl **Verhältnisse**) nt ❶ affair ▷ *Er hat ein Verhältnis mit einer verheirateten Frau.* He's having an affair with a married woman. ❷ proportion ▷ *Unser Gehalt steht in keinem Verhältnis zu unserer Leistung.* Our salary is not in proportion to our efforts.; **Verhältnisse** (1) conditions ▷ *Wenn die Verhältnisse anders wären, könnten wir die Arbeit schneller beenden.* If conditions were different we could get the work finished sooner. (2) background sg ▷ *Er kommt aus bescheidenen Verhältnissen.* He comes from a modest background.; **über seine Verhältnisse leben** to live beyond one's means

verhältnismäßig adv relatively

verhandeln (perf **hat verhandelt**) vb [34] to negotiate ▷ *Sie verhandeln einen Waffenstillstand.* They're negotiating a ceasefire.; *Mein Fall wird nächste Woche vor dem Arbeitsgericht verhandelt.* My case is being heard by the industrial tribunal next week.

Verhandlung f ❶ negotiation ▷ *die Friedensverhandlungen* peace negotiations ▷ *Wir sind mit der Firma noch in Verhandlung.* We're still involved in negotiations with the company. ❷ trial ▷ *Die Verhandlung gegen Klung ist morgen.* Klung's trial is tomorrow. ❸ hearing ▷ *die Verhandlung vor dem Arbeitsgericht* the hearing before the industrial tribunal

verharmlosen (perf **hat verharmlost**) vb [7] to play down

verhauen (perf **hat verhauen**) vb [7] to beat up

verheerend adj devastating

verheimlichen (perf **hat verheimlicht**) vb [7] **jemandem etwas verheimlichen** to keep something secret from somebody

verheiratet adj married

verhindern (perf **hat verhindert**) vb [88] to prevent; **verhindert sein** to be unable to make it

verhungern (perf **ist verhungert**) vb [88] to starve to death

Verhütungsmittel (pl **Verhütungsmittel**) nt contraceptive

sich **verirren** (perf **hat sich verirrt**) vb [84] to get lost ▷ *Wir hatten uns im Nebel verirrt.* We lost our way in the fog.

Verkauf (pl **Verkäufe**) m sale

verkaufen (perf **hat verkauft**) vb [84] to sell

Verkäufer (pl **Verkäufer**) m shop assistant ▷ *Der Verkäufer hat uns sehr gut beraten.* The shop assistant was extremely helpful.

Verkäuferin f shop assistant ▷ *Sie ist Verkäuferin in einer Modeboutique.* She's a shop assistant in a fashion boutique.

Verkehr m traffic ▷ *Heute war viel Verkehr auf den Straßen.* There was heavy traffic on the roads today.

Verkehrsampel f traffic lights pl

Verkehrsmeldung f traffic announcement

Verkehrsmittel (pl **Verkehrsmittel**) nt means of transport sg

Verkehrsschild (pl **Verkehrsschilder**) nt road sign

Verkehrsunfall (pl **Verkehrsunfälle**) m traffic accident

Verkehrszeichen (pl **Verkehrszeichen**) nt traffic sign

verkehrt adj wrong ▷ *Das war die verkehrte Antwort.* That was the wrong answer.; **verkehrt herum** back to front

sich **verkleiden** (perf **hat sich verkleidet**) vb [54] to dress up ▷ *Sie verkleidete sich als Hexe.* She dressed up as a witch.

verkleinern (perf **hat verkleinert**) vb [88] to reduce ▷ *Wir sollten den Zeilenabstand verkleinern.* We should reduce the line spacing.; **sich verkleinern** to grow smaller

Verlag (pl **Verlage**) m publisher

verlangen (perf **hat verlangt**) vb [84] to ask for ▷ *Ich verlange etwas mehr Verständnis.* I'm asking for a bit more understanding. ▷ *Wie viel hat er dafür verlangt?* How much did he ask for it?; **etwas von jemandem verlangen** to expect something of somebody

verlängern (perf **hat verlängert**) vb [88] ❶ to extend ▷ *Wir haben die Ferien um eine Woche verlängert.* We've extended our holiday by a week. ❷ to lengthen ▷ *Wir müssen das Seil verlängern.* We'll have to lengthen the rope.

verlassen (pres **verlässt**, imperf **verließ**, perf **hat verlassen**) vb [42] to leave ▷ *Er hat seine Frau und Kinder verlassen.* He's left his wife and children.; **Verlassen Sie sofort das Gebäude!** Get out of the building immediately.; **sich verlassen auf** to depend on

▶ adj ❶ deserted ▷ *eine verlassene Gegend* a deserted area ▷ *die verlassene Ehefrau* the deserted wife ❷ empty ▷ *ein verlassenes Haus* an empty house

sich **verlaufen** (pres **verläuft sich**, imperf **verlief sich**, perf **hat sich verlaufen**) vb [43] ❶ to get lost ▷ *Wir haben uns im Wald verlaufen.* We got lost in the forest. ❷ to disperse ▷ *Nach Ende der Veranstaltung verlief sich die Menge.* After the event the crowd dispersed.

verlegen adj embarrassed; **nicht verlegen um** never at a loss for

verleihen (imperf **verlieh**, perf **hat verliehen**) vb ❶ to lend ▷ *Ich habe mein Wörterbuch an sie verliehen.* I've lent her my dictionary. ❷ to hire out ▷ *Ich suche jemanden, der Fahrräder verleiht.* I'm looking for somebody who hires out bikes. ❸ to award ▷ *Sie hat einen Preis verliehen bekommen.* She was awarded a prize.

verleiten (perf **hat verleitet**) vb [2] **jemanden dazu verleiten, etwas zu tun** to tempt somebody into doing something

verlernen (perf **hat verlernt**) vb [84] to forget

verletzen (perf **hat verletzt**) vb [36] ❶ to hurt ▷ *Deine Bemerkung hat mich verletzt.* Your remark hurt me. ❷ to injure ▷ *Sie ist schwer verletzt.* She's seriously injured.; **ein Gesetz verletzen** to violate a law

Verletzte (gen **Verletzten**, pl **Verletzten**) mf injured person ▷ *Auf der Straße lag ein Verletzter.* An injured person was lying in the street.

Verletzung f injury; **Er hatte schwere Verletzungen.** He was seriously injured.; **Das ist eine Verletzung der Spielregeln.** That's against the rules of the game.

sich verlieben (perf **hat sich verliebt**) vb [84] **sich in jemanden verlieben** to fall in love with somebody

verliebt adj in love ▷ *Ich bin in Anke verliebt.* I'm in love with Anke.

verlieren (imperf **verlor**, perf **hat verloren**) vb [85] to lose

Verlierer (pl **Verlierer**) m loser

sich verloben (perf **hat sich verlobt**) vb [84] **sich mit jemandem verloben** to get engaged to somebody

Verlobte (gen **Verlobten**, pl **Verlobten**) m fiancé ▷ *Mathias ist mein Verlobter.* Mathias is my fiancé.

Verlobte (gen **Verlobten**, pl **Verlobten**) f fiancée ▷ *Ingrid ist seine Verlobte.* Ingrid's his fiancée.

Verlobung f engagement

verloren adj lost ▷ *die verlorene Zeit wieder einholen* to make up for lost time; **verlorene Eier** poached eggs; **verloren gehen** to get lost

Verlosung f raffle

Verlust (pl **Verluste**) m loss

vermehren (perf **hat vermehrt**) vb [7] increase ▷ *Die Firma hat ihren Umsatz vermehrt.* The company has increased its turnover.; **sich vermehren** to reproduce

vermeiden (imperf **vermied**, perf **hat vermieden**) vb to avoid

vermieten (perf **hat vermietet**) vb [2] ❶ to let ▷ *"Zimmer zu vermieten"* "Rooms to let" ❷ to rent ▷ *Sie vermietet Zimmer.* She rents rooms. ❸ to hire out ▷ *Wir vermieten Boote und Fahrräder.* We hire out boats and bikes.

Vermieter (pl **Vermieter**) m landlord

Vermieterin f landlady

vermissen (perf **hat vermisst**) vb [7] to miss ▷ *Ich habe dich vermisst.* I missed you.; **Ich vermisse eines meiner Bücher.** One of my books is missing.

Vermögen (pl **Vermögen**) nt wealth; **ein Vermögen kosten** to cost a fortune

vermuten (perf **hat vermutet**) vb [2] ❶ to guess ▷ *Ich kann nur vermuten, was er damit gemeint hat.* I can only guess what he meant by that.; **Man vermutet, dass er im Ausland ist.** He is thought to be abroad. ❷ to suspect ▷ *Die Polizei vermutet, dass er der Täter ist.* The police suspect that he's the culprit. ❸ to suppose ▷ *Ich vermute, dass er das noch nicht weiß.* I don't suppose that he knows that yet.

vermutlich adj, adv ❶ probable ▷ *die vermutliche Ursache* the probable cause ❷ probably ▷ *Sie ist vermutlich schon gegangen.* She has probably already left.

Vermutung f ❶ supposition ▷ *Das legt die Vermutung nahe, dass sie schon gegangen ist.* It seems a likely supposition that she's already gone. ❷ suspicion ▷ *Die Polizei hat eine Vermutung, wer der Täter gewesen sein könnte.* The police have a suspicion as to who the culprit could have been.

vernachlässigen (perf **hat vernachlässigt**) vb [84] to neglect

vernichten (perf **hat vernichtet**) vb [2] to destroy; **Insekten vernichten** to exterminate insects; **Unkraut vernichten** to eradicate weeds

Vernunft f reason

vernünftig adj reasonable ▷ *Sei doch vernünftig!* Be reasonable! ▷ *ein vernünftiger Preis* a reasonable price; **etwas Vernünftiges essen** to eat something decent

veröffentlichen (perf **hat veröffentlicht**) vb [84] to publish

Verpackung f packing

verpassen (perf **hat verpasst**) vb [7] to miss; **jemandem eine Ohrfeige verpassen** to give somebody a clip round the ear

verpflegen (perf **hat verpflegt**) vb [7] to cater for ▷ *Die Flüchtlinge wurden vom*

Roten Kreuz verpflegt. The Red Cross catered for the refugees.

Verpflegung f food ▷ *Für Ihre Verpflegung wird gesorgt.* Food will be laid on. ▷ *Die Verpflegung im Schullandheim war gut.* The food at the school camp was good.

verpflichten (*perf* **hat verpflichtet**) *vb* [2] to sign ▷ *Der VfB will Köpke verpflichten.* VfB want to sign Köpke.; **sich verpflichten, etwas zu tun** to promise to do something; **Sie haben sich verpflichtet, für Ersatz zu sorgen.** You undertook to find a replacement.; **verpflichtet sein, etwas zu tun** to be obliged to do something; **Er ist zum Stillschweigen verpflichtet.** He's sworn to silence.; **Das verpflichtet Sie zu nichts.** This doesn't commit you to anything.; **jemandem zu Dank verpflichtet sein** to be obliged to somebody

verprügeln (*perf* **hat verprügelt**) *vb* [7] to beat up

verraten (*pres* **verrät**, *imperf* **verriet**, *perf* **hat verraten**) *vb* ❶ to betray ▷ *Er hat seine Mittäter verraten.* He betrayed his accomplices. ❷ to report ▷ *Fritz hat uns beim Lehrer verraten.* Fritz reported us to the teacher. ❸ to tell ▷ *Verrate mir doch, wer es war.* Tell me who it was. ▷ *Ich habe dieses Geheimnis niemandem verraten.* I haven't told anyone the secret.; **sich verraten** to give oneself away

verreisen (*perf* **ist verreist**) *vb* [84] to go away ▷ *Ich möchte diesen Sommer verreisen.* I'd like to go away this summer.; **Wir wollen nach Israel verreisen.** We intend to go to Israel.

verrenken (*perf* **hat verrenkt**) *vb* [7] to sprain ▷ *Er hat sich den Knöchel verrenkt.* He sprained his ankle.

verrosten (*perf* **ist verrostet**) *vb* [2] to rust

verrückt *adj* crazy

Vers (*gen* **Verses**, *pl* **Verse**) *m* verse

Versager (*pl* **Versager**) *m* failure

versalzen (*perf* **hat versalzen**) *vb* to put too much salt in ▷ *Sie hat die Suppe versalzen.* She put too much salt in the soup.; **Die Suppe ist versalzen.** There's too much salt in the soup.

versammeln (*perf* **hat versammelt**) *vb* [34] to assemble

Versammlung f meeting

Versandhaus (*gen* **Versandhauses**, *pl* **Versandhäuser**) *nt* mail-order firm

versäumen (*perf* **hat versäumt**) *vb* [84] to miss ▷ *Ich habe wegen Krankheit drei Stunden versäumt.* I missed three lessons due to illness. ▷ *Sie sollten nicht versäumen, sich die Kathedrale anzusehen.* Don't miss a visit to the cathedral.; **es versäumen, etwas zu tun** to fail to do something

verschenken (*perf* **hat verschenkt**) *vb* [7] to give away

verschicken (*perf* **hat verschickt**) *vb* [7] to send away

verschieben (*imperf* **verschob**, *perf* **hat verschoben**) *vb* to postpone ▷ *Wir müssen das Fest verschieben.* We'll have to postpone the party.

verschieden *adj* different ▷ *Die zwei Brüder sind sehr verschieden.* The two brothers are very different. ▷ *Sie sind verschieden groß.* They are different sizes.; **verschiedene** various

verschlafen (*pres* **verschläft**, *imperf* **verschlief**, *perf* **hat verschlafen**) *vb* [58] ❶ to sleep in ▷ *Tut mir leid, ich habe verschlafen.* Sorry, I slept in. ❷ to sleep through ▷ *Er hat den ganzen Vormittag verschlafen.* He slept through the whole morning. ❸ to forget ▷ *Ich habe deinen Geburtstag total verschlafen.* I completely forgot your birthday.

▶ *adj* sleepy ▷ *Sie sah mich mit einem verschlafenen Blick an.* She gave me a sleepy look. ▷ *ein verschlafenes kleines Dorf* a sleepy little village

verschlechtern (*perf* **hat verschlechtert**) *vb* [88] **to make worse** ▷ *Das verschlechtert die Lage.* That makes the situation worse.; **sich verschlechtern** (1) to get worse ▷ *Die Lage hat sich verschlechtert.* The situation's got worse. ▷ *In Englisch habe ich mich verschlechtert.* My marks in English have got worse. (2) to deteriorate ▷ *Sein Gesundheitszustand hat sich noch weiter verschlechtert.* His condition has deteriorated even further.

verschlimmern (*perf* **hat verschlimmert**) *vb* [88] **to make worse** ▷ *Du verschlimmerst alles, wenn du weiter lügst.* You'll make everything worse if you go on lying.; **sich verschlimmern** to get worse

Verschluss (*gen* **Verschlusses**, *pl* **Verschlüsse**) *m* ❶ cap ▷ *Die Flasche hat einen kindersicheren Verschluss.* The bottle has a childproof cap. ❷ fastening ▷ *Kannst du mir den Verschluss an meinem Kleid aufmachen?* Can you undo the fastening of my dress? ❸ catch ▷ *der Verschluss der Tasche* the catch of the bag ▷ *der Verschluss an einer Halskette* the catch of a necklace

verschmutzen (*perf* **hat verschmutzt**) *vb* [7] ❶ to soil; **stark verschmutzt** very dirty ❷ to pollute ▷ *die Umwelt verschmutzen* to pollute the environment

Verschmutzung *f* pollution

verschneit *adj* snow-covered ▷ *eine verschneite Straße* a snow-covered road

verschonen (*perf* **hat verschont**) *vb* [84] **jemanden mit etwas verschonen** to spare somebody something

verschreiben (*imperf* **verschrieb**, *perf* **hat verschrieben**) *vb* [61] to prescribe ▷ *Der Arzt hat mir Antibiotika verschrieben.* The doctor prescribed me antibiotics.; **sich verschreiben** to make a spelling mistake

verschütten (*perf* **hat verschüttet**) *vb* [7] to spill ▷ *Sie hat den Kaffee verschüttet.* She spilt the coffee.; **verschüttet werden** to be buried

verschweigen (*imperf* **verschwieg**, *perf* **hat verschwiegen**) *vb* **jemandem etwas verschweigen** to keep something from somebody

verschwenden (*perf* **hat verschwendet**) *vb* [7] to waste ▷ *Zeit verschwenden* to waste time

Verschwendung *f* waste

verschwinden (*imperf* **verschwand**, *perf* **ist verschwunden**) *vb* [86] to disappear

verschwommen *adj* blurred

Versehen (*pl* **Versehen**) *nt* oversight ▷ *Das war ein Versehen.* It was an oversight.; **aus Versehen** by mistake

versehentlich *adv* by mistake

versenden (*imperf* **versendete** or **versandte**, *perf* **hat versendet** or **versandt**) *vb* to dispatch

versetzen (*perf* **hat versetzt**) *vb* [7] to transfer ▷ *Mein Vater wird nach Berlin versetzt.* My father's being transferred to Berlin.; **jemanden in die nächste Klasse versetzen** to move somebody up into the next class

- In Germany, pupils do not
- automatically move up (**versetzt**
- **werden**) to the next class at the
- end of the school year. If their
- performance is not good enough,
- they have to repeat the school year.
- This is known as **sitzen bleiben**.

jemanden versetzen (*informal*) to stand somebody up; **sich in jemandes Lage versetzen** to put oneself in somebody's shoes; **jemandem einen Schlag versetzen** to hit somebody; **jemandem einen Tritt versetzen** to kick somebody; **jemanden in gute Laune versetzen** to put somebody in a good mood

verseuchen (*perf* **hat verseucht**) *vb* [7] to contaminate

versichern (*perf* **hat versichert**) *vb* [88] ❶ to assure ▷ *Er hat mir versichert, dass das stimmt.* He assured me that this is correct. ❷ to insure ▷ *Wir sind nicht gegen Diebstahl versichert.* We are not insured against theft.

Versicherung *f* insurance

sich **versöhnen** (*perf* **hat sich versöhnt**) *vb* [84] to make up ▷ *Na, habt ihr euch wieder versöhnt?* Well, have you two made up again?; **sich mit jemandem versöhnen** to make it up with somebody

versorgen (*perf* **hat versorgt**) *vb* [7] to supply ▷ *Von hier aus wird die Stadt mit Elektrizität versorgt.* The town is supplied with electricity from here.; **einen Kranken versorgen** to look after a patient; **eine Familie versorgen** to support a family

sich **verspäten** (*perf* **hat sich verspätet**) *vb* [2] to be late

verspätet *adj* late ▷ *die verspätete Ankunft* the late arrival; **der verspätete Flug** the delayed flight; **verspätete Glückwünsche** belated best wishes

Verspätung *f* delay; **Verspätung haben** to be late

versprechen (*pres* **verspricht**, *imperf* **versprach**, *perf* **hat versprochen**) *vb* [70] to promise ▷ *Du hast es versprochen.* You promised.; **Ich habe mir von dem Kurs mehr versprochen.** I expected more from this course.

Versprechen (*pl* **Versprechen**) *nt* promise ▷ *Sie hat ihr Versprechen gehalten.* She kept her promise.

Verstand *m* mind ▷ *den Verstand verlieren* to go out of one's mind; **über jemandes Verstand gehen** to be beyond somebody

verständigen (*perf* **hat verständigt**) *vb* [7] to inform ▷ *Wir müssen ihre Eltern verständigen.* We must inform her parents.; **sich verständigen** to communicate; **sich auf etwas verständigen** to agree on something

verständlich *adj* understandable; **sich verständlich ausdrücken** to express oneself clearly

Verständnis (*pl* **Verständnisse**) *nt* understanding

verstärken (*perf* **hat verstärkt**) *vb* [7] ❶ to strengthen ▷ *Wir müssen den Karton verstärken.* We'll have to strengthen the box. ▷ *ein Team verstärken* to strengthen a team ❷ to amplify ▷ *den Ton verstärken* to amplify the sound; **Das verstärkt die Schmerzen.** That makes the pain worse.

Verstärker (*pl* **Verstärker**) *m* amplifier

Verstärkung *f* reinforcements *pl* ▷ *Wir brauchen Verstärkung.* We need reinforcements.

verstauchen (*perf* **hat verstaucht**) *vb* [7] to sprain ▷ *Ich habe mir den Knöchel verstaucht.* I've sprained my ankle.

Versteck (*pl* **Verstecke**) *nt* hiding place

verstecken (*perf* **hat versteckt**) *vb* [7] to hide

verstehen (*imperf* **verstand**, *perf* **hat verstanden**) *vb* [72] to understand ▷ *Ich habe die Frage nicht verstanden.* I didn't understand the question. ▷ *Ich verstehe nicht.* I don't understand.; **sich verstehen mit** to get on with ▷ *Wie verstehst du dich mit deiner Schwester?* How do you get on with your sister?; **Das versteht sich von selbst.** That goes without saying.

verstopft *adj* ❶ blocked ▷ *ein verstopfter Abfluss* a blocked drain ❷ constipated

▷ *Ich bin seit gestern verstopft.* I've been constipated since yesterday.

verstreuen (*perf* **hat verstreut**) *vb* [7] to scatter

Versuch (*pl* **Versuche**) *m* ❶ attempt ▷ *Ich habe den Versuch gemacht, Spanisch zu lernen.* I made an attempt to learn Spanish. ▷ *Sie ist schon beim ersten Versuch gescheitert.* She failed at the very first attempt. ❷ experiment ▷ *Versuche mit Tieren lehnen wir ab.* We disapprove of experiments with animals.

versuchen (*perf* **hat versucht**) *vb* [84] ❶ to try ▷ *Ich versuche zu kommen.* I'll try to come. ▷ *Willst du mal die Soße versuchen?* Would you like to try the sauce?; **sich an etwas versuchen** to try one's hand at something

vertagen (*perf* **hat vertagt**) *vb* [7] to adjourn

vertauschen (*perf* **hat vertauscht**) *vb* [7] ❶ to mix up ▷ *Die Babys wurden im Krankenhaus vertauscht.* They mixed the babies up at the hospital. ▷ *Er hat offensichtlich seinen Mantel mit meinem vertauscht.* He must have got his coat and mine mixed up. ❷ to exchange ▷ *Er hat seinen Sportwagen mit einem Familienwagen vertauscht.* He exchanged his sports car for a family car.

verteidigen (*perf* **hat verteidigt**) *vb* [84] to defend

Verteidiger (*pl* **Verteidiger**) *m* ❶ defender ▷ *Der Verteidiger wurde gefoult.* The defender was fouled. ❷ defence counsel ▷ *Wer ist der Verteidiger des Angeklagten?* Who's counsel for the defence?

verteilen (*perf* **hat verteilt**) *vb* [84] ❶ to hand out ▷ *Sie verteilte die Hefte an die Schüler.* She handed the exercise books out to the pupils. ❷ to spread ▷ *Die Salbe sollte gleichmäßig auf der Haut verteilt werden.* The ointment should be spread evenly over the skin.

Vertrag (*pl* **Verträge**) *m* ❶ contract ▷ *ein Arbeitsvertrag* a contract of employment ❷ treaty ▷ *ein Friedensvertrag* a peace treaty

vertragen (*pres* **verträgt**, *imperf* **vertrug**, *perf* **hat vertragen**) *vb* [77] ❶ to be able to stand ▷ *Ich vertrage die Hitze nicht.* I can't stand the heat. ❷ to tolerate ▷ *Ich kann eine solche Behandlung nicht vertragen.* I can't tolerate such treatment.; **sich vertragen** to get along; **sich wieder vertragen** to patch things up

verträglich *adj* ❶ good-natured ▷ *ein verträglicher Mensch* a good-natured person ❷ easily digestible ▷ *Im Sommer sollte man nur leicht verträgliche Speisen zu sich nehmen.* In summer, you should only eat easily digestible food.; **Das Medikament ist gut verträglich.** The drug has no side effects.

vertrauen (*perf* **hat vertraut**) *vb* [84] **jemandem vertrauen** to trust somebody; **vertrauen auf** to rely on; **Ich vertraue auf mein Glück.** I'm trusting my luck.

Vertrauen *nt* trust ▷ *Vertrauen zu jemandem haben* to have trust in somebody

vertraulich *adj* ❶ confidential ▷ *ein vertrauliches Gespräch* a confidential talk ❷ familiar ▷ *Ich verbitte mir diesen vertraulichen Ton.* I'll not have you talking to me in such familiar way.

vertraut *adj* familiar ▷ *vertraute Gesichter* familiar faces

vertreiben (*imperf* **vertrieb**, *perf* **hat vertrieben**) *vb* ❶ to drive ▷ *Er hat uns von seinem Grundstück vertrieben.* He drove us off his land. ❷ to sell ▷ *Wir vertreiben Hardware und Software.* We sell hardware and software.; **sich die Zeit vertreiben** to pass the time

vertreten (pres **vertritt**, imperf **vertrat**, perf **hat vertreten**) vb [79] ❶ to stand in for ▷ *Während ich in Urlaub bin, vertritt mich Frau Wengel.* While I'm on holiday, Mrs Wengel's standing in for me. ❷ to represent ▷ *Die Lobby vertritt die Interessen der Wirtschaft.* The lobby represents business interests.; **eine Meinung vertreten** to hold an opinion; **sich den Fuß vertreten** to twist one's ankle; **sich die Beine vertreten** to stretch one's legs

Vertreter (pl **Vertreter**) m sales representative ▷ *Er ist Vertreter für Collins.* He's a sales representative for Collins.

Vertrieb (pl **Vertriebe**) m ❶ sale ▷ *Der Vertrieb von Raubkopien steht unter Strafe.* The sale of pirate copies is punishable by law. ❷ marketing department ▷ *Sie arbeitet im Vertrieb.* She works in the marketing department.

sich **vertun** (imperf **vertat sich**, perf **hat sich vertan**) vb [81] to make a mistake

verunglücken (perf **ist verunglückt**) vb [84] to have an accident ▷ *Sie sind mit dem Auto verunglückt.* They've had a car accident.

verursachen (perf **hat verursacht**) vb [84] to cause

verurteilen (perf **hat verurteilt**) vb [84] to condemn

Verwaltung f administration ▷ *Er arbeitet in der Verwaltung.* He works in administration.

verwandt adj **mit jemandem verwandt sein** to be related to somebody

Verwandte (gen **Verwandten**, pl **Verwandten**) mf relative ▷ *Ein Verwandter von mir ist gestern gestorben.* A relative of mine died yesterday.

Verwandtschaft f relations pl ▷ *Die ganze Verwandtschaft war eingeladen.* All my relations were invited.

verwechseln (perf **hat verwechselt**) vb [34] ❶ to confuse ▷ *Du darfst die beiden Begriffe nicht verwechseln.* You mustn't confuse the two ideas. ❷ to mix up ▷ *Sie haben offensichtlich die Mäntel verwechselt.* They must have got their coats mixed up.; **verwechseln mit (1)** to confuse with ▷ *Ich verwechsle 'akut' immer mit 'aktuell'.* I always confuse 'akut' with 'aktuell'. **(2)** to mistake for ▷ *Ich habe dich mit deiner Schwester verwechselt.* I mistook you for your sister.; **Sie sind zum Verwechseln ähnlich.** They're the spitting image of each other.

Verwechslung f mix-up

verweigern (perf **hat verweigert**) vb [88] **jemandem etwas verweigern** to refuse somebody something; **den Gehorsam verweigern** to refuse to obey; **die Aussage verweigern** to refuse to testify

Verweis (gen **Verweises**, pl **Verweise**) m reprimand ▷ *Er hat für sein Zuspätkommen einen schweren Verweis bekommen.* He was given a severe reprimand for being late.

verwelken (perf **ist verwelkt**) vb [7] to fade

verwenden (imperf **verwendete** or **verwandte**, perf **hat verwendet** or **verwandt**) vb ❶ to use ▷ *Verwenden Sie einen Computer?* Do you use a computer? ❷ (effort, time, work) to spend ▷ *Ich habe auf diesen Aufsatz viel Zeit verwendet.* I spent a lot of time on this essay.

verwerten (perf **hat verwertet**) vb [2] to utilize

verwirren (perf **hat verwirrt**) vb [84] ❶ to confuse ▷ *Jetzt hast du mich total verwirrt.* Now you've completely confused me. ❷ (thread) to tangle up

▷ *Die Katze hat die Wolle verwirrt.* The cat's tangled the wool up.

verwöhnen (*perf* **hat verwöhnt**) *vb* [84] to spoil

verwunden (*perf* **hat verwundet**) *vb* [7] to wound

Verwundete (*gen* **Verwundeten**, *pl* **Verwundeten**) *mf* injured person ▷ *Der Arzt versorgt gerade einen Verwundeten.* The doctor is just attending to an injured person.

Verwundung *f* injury

Verzeichnis (*gen* **Verzeichnisses**, *pl* **Verzeichnisse**) *nt* list ▷ *Am Ende des Buches ist ein Verzeichnis aller Fachbegriffe.* At the end of the book there's a list of all the technical terms.; **das Inhaltsverzeichnis** the table of contents

verzeihen (*imperf* **verzieh**, *perf* **hat verziehen**) *vb* to forgive ▷ *jemandem etwas verzeihen* to forgive somebody for something

Verzeihung *f* forgiveness; **Verzeihung!** (1) sorry ▷ *Verzeihung, ich wollte dich nicht treten.* Sorry, I didn't mean to kick you. (2) excuse me ▷ *Verzeihung, aber können Sie mir sagen, wie spät es ist?* Excuse me, could you tell me what time it is?

verzichten (*perf* **hat verzichtet**) *vb* [2] **auf etwas verzichten** (1) to do without something ▷ *Ich werde heute wohl auf meinen Mittagsschlaf verzichten müssen.* It looks like I'll have to do without my afternoon nap today. ▷ *Ich verzichte auf deine Hilfe.* I can do without your help. (2) to forego something ▷ *Er hat auf die Bezahlung verzichtet.* He forewent payment. ▷ *Ich verzichte nicht auf meine Rechte.* I won't forego my rights.

Verzierung *f* decoration

verzögern (*perf* **hat verzögert**) *vb* [88] to delay

Verzögerung *f* delay

verzweifeln (*perf* **ist verzweifelt**) *vb* [7] to despair

verzweifelt *adj* desperate

Verzweiflung *f* despair

Vetter (*pl* **Vettern**) *m* cousin

Video (*pl* **Videos**) *nt* video

Videocall (*pl* **Videocalls**) *m* video call

Vieh *nt* cattle *pl* ▷ *Das Vieh ist auf der Weide.* The cattle are out in the meadow.

viel *adj*, *adv* **❶** a lot of ▷ *Sie haben viel Arbeit.* They've got a lot of work. **❷** much ▷ *Wir haben nicht viel Geld.* We haven't got much money. ▷ *Wir haben nicht viel gelernt.* We didn't learn much.; **Vielen Dank!** Thank you very much. **❸** a lot ▷ *Wir haben viel gesehen.* We saw a lot.; **viel zu wenig** far too little; **Viel Glück!** Good luck.; **so viel** so much; **so viel wie** as much as; **wie viel?** how much?; **zu viel** too much

viele *pron pl* **❶** a lot of ▷ *Sie hat viele Bücher.* She's got a lot of books. **❷** many ▷ *Er hat nicht viele Fehler gemacht.* He didn't make many mistakes. ▷ *Viele Schüler mögen Chemie nicht.* Many pupils don't like chemistry.; **Viele wissen das nicht.** A lot of people don't know that.

vieles *pron* many things *pl* ▷ *Vieles war neu für mich.* Many things were new to me.

vielleicht *adv* perhaps

vielmals *adv* **Danke vielmals!** Many thanks!

vielseitig *adj* many-sided

vielversprechend *adj* promising

vier *num* four

Vier *f* **❶** four **❷** adequate
⁞ German marks range from one (**sehr**
⁞ **gut**) to six (**ungenügend**).

Viereck (*pl* **Vierecke**) *nt* **❶** rectangle **❷** square

viereckig *adj* **❶** rectangular **❷** square

vierte *adj* fourth ▷ *Sie hat erst beim vierten Klingeln abgenommen.* She didn't answer until the fourth ring. ▷ *Er kam als Vierter.* He was the fourth to arrive.

Viertel (pl **Viertel**) nt quarter ▷ *Viertel vor zwei* quarter to two

Vierteljahr (pl **Vierteljahre**) nt quarter

vierteln vb [88] ❶ to divide by four ▷ *wenn man den Betrag viertelt ...* if you divide the amount by four ... ❷ to cut into quarters ▷ *Sie hat den Kuchen geviertelt.* She cut the cake into quarters.

Viertelstunde f quarter of an hour

vierzehn num fourteen; **in vierzehn Tagen** in a fortnight

vierzig num forty

Villa (pl **Villen**) f villa

virtuell adj virtual ▷ *die virtuelle Realität* virtual reality

Virus nt virus

Visitenkarte f business card

Visum (pl **Visa**) nt visa

Vitamin (pl **Vitamine**) nt vitamin

Vogel (pl **Vögel**) m bird; **einen Vogel haben** (*informal*) to have a screw loose; **jemandem den Vogel zeigen** to make a rude sign

> Word for word, **jemandem den Vogel zeigen** means 'to show somebody the bird'.
>
> • In Germany you make a rude sign at
> • somebody by tapping your forehead
> • to show that you think they are
> • stupid.

Vokabel f word

Vokabular (pl **Vokabulare**) nt vocabulary

Vokal (pl **Vokale**) m vowel

Volk (pl **Völker**) nt ❶ people ▷ *das einfache Volk* the simple people ❷ nation ▷ *das deutsche Volk* the German nation

Volksfest (pl **Volksfeste**) nt fair

Volkshochschule f adult education classes pl

Volkswirtschaft f economics sg

voll adj full; **voll und ganz** completely; **jemanden für voll nehmen** to take somebody seriously

völlig adj, adv ❶ complete ▷ *bis zur völligen Erschöpfung* to the point of complete exhaustion ❷ completely ▷ *Das ist völlig unmöglich.* That's completely impossible. ▷ *Ich bin völlig deiner Meinung.* I completely agree with you.

volljährig adj of age ▷ *volljährig werden* to come of age

vollkommen adj perfect ▷ *vollkommen richtig* perfectly right; **vollkommen unmöglich** completely impossible

Vollkornbrot (pl **Vollkornbrote**) nt wholemeal bread

vollmachen vb [48] to fill up

Vollmacht f power of attorney

Vollmond m full moon ▷ *bei Vollmond* at full moon

Vollpension f full board

vollständig adj complete

volltanken vb [4] to fill up (*car*)

vom = **von dem**

von prep

> **von** takes the dative.

❶ from ▷ *von Hamburg nach Kiel* from Hamburg to Kiel; **von ... bis** from ... to; **von ... an** from ...; **von ... aus** from ...; **etwas von sich aus tun** to do something of one's own accord; **von mir aus** I don't mind; **Von wo bist du?** Where are you from?; **Von wann ist der Brief?** When's the letter from? ❷ by ▷ *Ich bin von einem Hund gebissen worden.* I was bitten by a dog. ▷ *ein Gedicht von Schiller* a poem by Schiller; **von etwas kommen** to be caused by something ❸ of ▷ *ein Freund von mir* a friend of mine ▷ *Wie nett von dir!* How nice of you!; **jeweils zwei von zehn** two out of every ten ❹ about ▷ *Er erzählte vom Urlaub.* He talked about his holiday.; **Von wegen!** (*informal*) No way!

voneinander adv from each other

vor prep, adv

> Use the accusative to express movement or a change of place. Use the dative when there is no change of place.

① in front of ▷ *Er stand vor dem Spiegel.* He stood in front of the mirror. ▷ *Stell den Stuhl vor das Fenster.* Put the chair in front of the window. ② before ▷ *Der Artikel steht vor dem Substantiv.* The article goes before the noun. ▷ *Vor der Kirche links abbiegen.* Turn left just before you get to the church. ▷ *Ich war vor ihm da.* I was there before him. ③ ago ▷ *vor zwei Tagen* two days ago ▷ *vor einem Jahr* a year ago; **Es ist fünf vor vier.** It's five to four.; **vor Kurzem** a little while ago ④ with ▷ *vor Wut* with rage ▷ *vor Liebe* with love; **vor Hunger sterben** to die of hunger; **vor lauter Arbeit** because of work; **vor allem** above all; **vor und zurück** backwards and forwards

vorankommen (*imperf* **kam voran**, *perf* **ist vorangekommen**) *vb* [40] to make progress

voraus adv ahead ▷ *Fahr du schon mal voraus.* You go on ahead. ▷ *Er war seiner Zeit voraus.* He was ahead of his time.; **im Voraus** in advance

vorausgehen (*imperf* **ging voraus**, *perf* **ist vorausgegangen**) *vb* [29] ① to go on ahead ▷ *Geht ihr voraus, ich komme nach.* Go on ahead, I'll catch up with you. ② to precede ▷ *Der Schlägerei ging ein Streit voraus.* The fight was preceded by an argument.

voraussetzen (*perf* **hat vorausgesetzt**) *vb* [15] to assume ▷ *Ich setze voraus, dass du auch kommst.* I assume that you're coming too.; **vorausgesetzt, dass ...** provided that ...

Voraussetzung *f* prerequisite; **unter der Voraussetzung, dass ...** provided that ...

voraussichtlich adv probably

vorbei adv past ▷ *Fahren Sie am Rathaus vorbei.* Drive past the town hall.; **Ich sehe noch kurz bei ihr vorbei.** I'll just pop round to her place.; **vorbei sein** to be over

vorbeigehen (*imperf* **ging vorbei**, *perf* **ist vorbeigegangen**) *vb* [29] to go past ▷ *Er ging vorbei, ohne zu grüßen.* He went past without saying hello.; **an etwas vorbeigehen** to go past something; **bei jemandem vorbeigehen** to call in at somebody's

vorbeikommen (*imperf* **kam vorbei**, *perf* **ist vorbeigekommen**) *vb* [40] **bei jemandem vorbeikommen** to drop in on somebody

vorbereiten (*perf* **hat vorbereitet**) *vb* [2] to prepare

Vorbereitung *f* preparation

vorbeugen (*perf* **hat vorgebeugt**) *vb* [4] **sich vorbeugen** to lean forward; **einer Sache vorbeugen** to prevent something

Vorbild (*pl* **Vorbilder**) *nt* role model ▷ *Er ist mein Vorbild.* He's my role model.; **sich jemanden zum Vorbild nehmen** to follow somebody's example

vordere adj front ▷ *Das Haus hat einen vorderen und einen hinteren Eingang.* The house has a front door and a back door.

Vordergrund *m* foreground

Vorderseite *f* front

vorderste adj front ▷ *die vorderste Reihe* the front row

voreilig adj hasty ▷ *Du solltest nicht voreilig urteilen.* You shouldn't make hasty judgements.

vorerst adv for the moment

Vorfahrt *f* right of way; **Vorfahrt achten!** Give way!

Vorfall (*pl* **Vorfälle**) *m* incident

vorführen (*perf* **hat vorgeführt**) *vb* [4] to show

vorgehen (*imperf* **ging vor**, *perf* **ist vorgegangen**) *vb* [29] ❶ to go on ahead ▷ *Geht ihr vor, ich komme nach.* Go on ahead, I'll catch up. ❷ to go up to ▷ *Sie ging ans Rednerpult vor.* She went up to the lectern. ❸ to proceed ▷ *Ich weiß nicht, wie wir vorgehen sollen.* I don't know how we should proceed.; **Die Uhr geht vor.** The clock is fast.; **Was geht hier vor?** What's going on here?

vorgestern *adv* the day before yesterday

vorhaben (*pres* **hat vor**, *imperf* **hatte vor**, *perf* **hat vorgehabt**) *vb* [32] to intend ▷ *Wir haben vor, nach Italien zu fahren.* We intend to go to Italy. ▷ *Was hast du vor?* What do you intend to do?; **Ich habe heute viel vor.** I've got a lot planned for today.; **Hast du schon was vor?** Have you got anything on?; **Was hast du heute Abend vor?** What are you doing this evening?

Vorhang (*pl* **Vorhänge**) *m* curtain

vorher *adv* beforehand

Vorhersage *f* forecast

vorhersehbar *adj* predictable

vorhersehen (*pres* **sieht vorher**, *imperf* **sah vorher**, *perf* **hat vorhergesehen**) *vb* [64] to foresee

vorhin *adv* just now

vorig *adj* previous

vorkommen (*imperf* **kam vor**, *perf* **ist vorgekommen**) *vb* [40] ❶ to happen ▷ *So ein Fehler sollte nicht vorkommen.* A mistake like that shouldn't happen.; **Es kommt vor, dass ich früh ins Bett gehe.** I sometimes go to bed early.; **jemandem vorkommen** to seem to somebody; **sich dumm vorkommen** to feel stupid ❷ to come out ▷ *Komm endlich hinter dem Schrank vor.* Come out from behind that cupboard, will you?

vorläufig *adj* provisional

vorlaut *adj* impertinent

vorlesen (*pres* **liest vor**, *imperf* **las vor**, *perf* **hat vorgelesen**) *vb* [45] to read out

vorletzte *adj* last but one ▷ *Ich wohne im vorletzten Haus.* My house is the last but one.

Vorliebe *f* partiality; **eine Vorliebe für etwas haben** to be partial to something

Vormittag (*pl* **Vormittage**) *m* morning ▷ *am Vormittag* in the morning

vormittags *adv* in the morning

vorn *adv* in front ▷ *Der deutsche Schwimmer liegt vorn.* The German swimmer is in front.; **Er stand ganz vorn in der Schlange.** He was right at the front of the queue.; **nach vorn** to the front; **von vorn anfangen** to start at the beginning; **wieder von vorn anfangen** to start again from the beginning

Vorname (*gen* **Vornamens**, *pl* **Vornamen**) *m* first name

vornehm *adj* ❶ distinguished ▷ *eine vornehme Familie* a distinguished family ❷ sich vornehm ausdrücken to use refined language ▷ *vornehme Manieren* refined manners ❸ posh ▷ *ein vornehmes Hotel* a posh hotel ❹ elegant ▷ *eine vornehme Dame* an elegant lady

vornehmen (*pres* **nimmt vor**, *imperf* **nahm vor**, *perf* **hat vorgenommen**) *vb* [52] **sich etwas vornehmen** to resolve to do something

vornherein *adv* **von vornherein** from the start

Vorort (*pl* **Vororte**) *m* suburb

Vorrat (*pl* **Vorräte**) *m* stock ▷ *solange der Vorrat reicht* while stocks last

vorrätig *adj* in stock

Vorschlag (*pl* **Vorschläge**) *m* suggestion

vorschlagen (*pres* **schlägt vor**, *imperf* **schlug vor**, *perf* **hat vorgeschlagen**) *vb* [59] to suggest

Vorschrift f rule ▷ *Das ist gegen die Vorschriften.* It's against the rules.
Vorsicht f caution; **Vorsicht!** (1) Look out! (2) Caution!; **Vorsicht, Stufe!** Mind the step.
vorsichtig adj careful
Vorspeise f starter
Vorsprung (pl **Vorsprünge**) m lead ▷ *Wir haben einen Vorsprung vor unseren Konkurrenten gewonnen.* We have gained a lead over our competitors.
Vorstadt (pl **Vorstädte**) f suburbs pl
vorstellbar adj conceivable
vorstellen (perf **hat vorgestellt**) vb [4] **sich etwas vorstellen** to imagine something; **jemandem jemanden vorstellen** to introduce somebody to somebody
Vorstellung f ❶ performance ▷ *Die Vorstellung endet gegen zehn Uhr.* The performance ends at about ten. ❷ idea ▷ *Hast du eine Vorstellung, wie wir das machen sollen?* Have you got any idea how we should do that? ▷ *Du hast ja keine Vorstellung, wie weh das tut.* You've no idea how much it hurts.
Vorstellungsgespräch (pl **Vorstellungsgespräche**) nt interview (for job)
Vorteil (pl **Vorteile**) m advantage; **im Vorteil sein** to have the advantage
Vortrag (pl **Vorträge**) m talk ▷ *einen Vortrag halten* to give a talk
vorüber adv over
vorübergehend adj ❶ passing ▷ *eine vorübergehende Phase* a passing phase ❷ temporarily ▷ *Das Geschäft ist vorübergehend geschlossen.* The shop's temporarily closed.
Vorurteil (pl **Vorurteile**) nt prejudice
Vorwahl f dialling code ▷ *Was ist die Vorwahl von Liverpool?* What's the dialling code for Liverpool?
Vorwand (pl **Vorwände**) m pretext
vorwärts adv forward

vorwerfen (pres **wirft vor**, imperf **warf vor**, perf **hat vorgeworfen**) vb [92] **jemandem etwas vorwerfen** to accuse somebody of something; **sich nichts vorzuwerfen haben** to have nothing to reproach oneself for
vorwiegend adv predominantly
Vorwort (pl **Vorworte**) nt preface
Vorwurf (pl **Vorwürfe**) m reproach; **jemandem Vorwürfe machen** to reproach somebody; **sich Vorwürfe machen** to reproach oneself
vorziehen (imperf **zog vor**, perf **hat vorgezogen**) vb [96] ❶ to prefer ▷ *Was ziehst du vor: Kaffee oder Tee?* Do you prefer coffee or tea? ❷ to pull forward ▷ *Du solltest den Stuhl etwas vorziehen.* You should pull your chair forward a bit.
vulgär adj vulgar ▷ *sich vulgär ausdrücken* to use vulgar language
Vulkan (pl **Vulkane**) m volcano

W

Waage f ① scales pl ▷ *Die Waage stimmt nicht genau.* The scales aren't accurate. ② Libra ▷ *Ulla ist Waage.* Ulla's Libra.
waagerecht adj horizontal
wach adj wach sein to be awake
Wache f guard ▷ Wache stehen to stand guard
Wachs (gen **Wachses**, pl **Wachse**) nt wax
wachsen (pres **wächst**, imperf **wuchs**, perf **ist gewachsen**) vb [87] to grow
Wachstum nt growth
wackelig adj wobbly
Wade f calf ▷ *Ich habe mich an der Wade verletzt.* I've hurt my calf.
Waffe f weapon
Waffel f ① waffle ▷ *Heute gab's zum Mittagessen Waffeln.* We had waffles for lunch today. ② wafer ▷ *Willst du eine Waffel zu deinem Eis?* Would you like a wafer with your ice?
wagen vb [38] es wagen, etwas zu tun to dare to do something; sich irgendwohin wagen to dare to go somewhere
Wagen (pl **Wagen**) m ① car ▷ *Seid ihr mit dem Wagen da?* Did you come by car? ② carriage ▷ *ein Eisenbahnwagen* a railway carriage; **ein Pferdewagen** a cart
Wagenheber (pl **Wagenheber**) m jack (for car)
Wahl (pl **Wahlen**) f ① choice ▷ *Du hast die Wahl.* It's your choice. ② election ▷ *Wann sind die nächsten Wahlen?* When are the next elections?
wählen vb [38] ① to choose ▷ *Du kannst wählen, entweder das rote oder das grüne.* You can choose, either the red one or the green one. ② to vote ▷ *Wer wurde zum Klassensprecher gewählt?* Who was voted class representative?; **Wählt Kowalski!** Vote for Kowalski.; **Nächsten Sonntag wird gewählt.** There are elections next Sunday. ③ to dial ▷ *Sie wählte die Nummer ihrer Freundin.* She dialled her friend's number.
wählerisch adj particular
Wahlfach (pl **Wahlfächer**) nt optional subject
Wahnsinn m madness
wahnsinnig adj, adv ① mad ▷ *Wer hatte denn diese wahnsinnige Idee?* Whose mad idea was it? ② incredibly ▷ *Das Kleid war wahnsinnig schön.* The dress was incredibly pretty. ▷ *Das tut wahnsinnig weh.* It's incredibly sore.
wahr adj true ▷ *eine wahre Geschichte* a true story; **Sie ist verheiratet, nicht wahr?** She's married, isn't she?
während prep, conj

> The preposition **während** takes the genitive.

① during ▷ *Was hast du während der Ferien gemacht?* What did you do during the holidays? ② while ▷ *Sie sah fern, während sie ihre Hausaufgaben machte.*

She was watching TV while she was doing her homework. ❸ **whereas** ▷ *Er ist ganz nett, während seine Frau unhöflich ist.* He's quite nice, whereas his wife's impolite.

Wahrheit f truth

wahrnehmen (*pres* **nimmt wahr**, *imperf* **nahm wahr**, *perf* **hat wahrgenommen**) *vb* [52] to perceive

Wahrsager (*pl* **Wahrsager**) *m* fortune teller

Wahrsagerin f fortune teller

wahrscheinlich *adj, adv* ❶ likely ▷ *Das ist nicht sehr wahrscheinlich.* That's not very likely. ❷ probably ▷ *Er kommt wahrscheinlich nicht.* He's probably not coming.

Währung f currency

Wal (*pl* **Wale**) *m* whale

Wald (*pl* **Wälder**) *m* ❶ wood ▷ *Hinter unserem Haus ist ein Wald.* There's a wood behind our house. ❷ forest ▷ *die Wälder Kanadas* the forests of Canada

Wales *nt* Wales

Walfisch (*pl* **Walfische**) *m* whale

Waliser (*pl* **Waliser**) *m* Welshman; *Er ist Waliser.* He's Welsh.; **die Waliser** the Welsh

Waliserin f Welshwoman; *Sie ist Waliserin.* She's Welsh.

walisisch *adj* Welsh

Walnuss (*pl* **Walnüsse**) f walnut

Wand (*pl* **Wände**) f wall

Wanderer (*pl* **Wanderer**) *m* rambler

Wanderin f rambler

wandern (*perf* **ist gewandert**) *vb* [88] to hike ▷ *Wir sind am Wochenende gewandert.* We went hiking at the weekend.

Wanderung f hike

Wandschrank (*pl* **Wandschränke**) *m* wall cupboard

wann *adv* when

war *vb see* **sein**

Ware f goods *pl*

Warenhaus (*gen* **Warenhauses**, *pl* **Warenhäuser**) *nt* department store

warf *vb see* **werfen**

warm *adj* warm ▷ *Heute ist es wärmer als gestern.* It's warmer today than yesterday.; **ein warmes Essen** a hot meal; **Mir ist warm.** I'm warm.

Wärme f warmth

Wärmflasche f hot-water bottle

warnen *vb* [38] to warn ▷ *jemanden vor etwas warnen* to warn somebody of something

Warnung f warning

warten *vb* [2] to wait ▷ *Ich habe eine Stunde gewartet.* I waited an hour.; **warten auf** to wait for; **auf sich warten lassen** to take a long time

Wartesaal (*pl* **Wartesäle**) *m* waiting room (in station)

Wartezimmer (*pl* **Wartezimmer**) *nt* waiting room

warum *adv* why

was *pron* ❶ what ▷ *Was hast du gesagt?* What did you say? ▷ *Was für eine Enttäuschung!* What a disappointment!; **Was für ein ...** What kind of ... ❷ something ▷ *Heute gibt's was Leckeres zum Mittagessen.* We're having something delicious for lunch today.

Waschbecken (*pl* **Waschbecken**) *nt* washbasin

Wäsche f washing ▷ *Wäsche waschen* to do the washing; **die Bettwäsche** bed linen; **die Unterwäsche** underwear

Wäscheklammer f clothes peg

waschen (*pres* **wäscht**, *imperf* **wusch**, *perf* **hat gewaschen**) *vb* [89] to wash; **sich waschen** to have a wash; **sich die Hände waschen** to wash one's hands

Waschmaschine f washing machine

Waschmittel (*pl* **Waschmittel**) *nt* detergent

Waschpulver (*pl* **Waschpulver**) *nt* washing powder

Waschsalon (pl **Waschsalons**) m launderette
Wasser (pl **Wasser** or **Wässer**) nt water
wasserdicht adj waterproof
Wasserfall (pl **Wasserfälle**) m waterfall
Wasserhahn (pl **Wasserhähne**) m tap
Wassermann m Aquarius ▷ *Gerda ist Wassermann.* Gerda's Aquarius.
Wassermelone f water melon
Wasserstoff m hydrogen
Watte f cotton wool
Webseite f web page
Wechsel (pl **Wechsel**) m change
Wechselkurs (gen **Wechselkurses**, pl **Wechselkurse**) m rate of exchange
wechseln vb [34] ❶ to change ▷ *Wir mussten einen Reifen wechseln.* We had to change a tyre. ▷ *Wie viel Geld wechselst du?* How much money are you changing?; **Blicke wechseln** to exchange glances ❷ to have change ▷ *Können Sie wechseln?* Do you have any change? ▷ *Kannst du mir zwanzig Euro in Münzen wechseln?* Have you got change for twenty euros?
Wechselstube f bureau de change
wecken vb [38] to wake up
Wecker (pl **Wecker**) m alarm clock
weder conj neither; **weder ... noch ...** neither ... nor ...
weg adv away ▷ *Geh weg!* Go away!; **Weg da!** Out of the way!; **Finger weg!** Hands off!; **Er war schon weg.** He'd already left.
Weg (pl **Wege**) m ❶ way ▷ *Es gibt sicher einen Weg, das zu reparieren.* There must be a way to repair it. ❷ path ▷ *Ein Weg führte zur Kapelle hinauf.* A path led up to the chapel. ❸ route ▷ *Welchen Weg habt ihr genommen?* Which route did you take?; **sich auf den Weg machen** to be on one's way; **jemandem aus dem Weg gehen** to keep out of somebody's way

GERMAN > ENGLISH

wegen prep
 The preposition **wegen** takes the dative or sometimes the genitive.
 because of ▷ *Wegen dir bin ich zu spät gekommen.* Because of you I arrived late. ▷ *Wegen des schlechten Wetters wurde die Veranstaltung abgesagt.* The event was cancelled because of the bad weather.
weggehen (imperf **ging weg**, perf **ist weggegangen**) vb [29] to go away
weglassen (pres **lässt weg**, imperf **ließ weg**, perf **hat weggelassen**) vb [42] to leave out
weglaufen (pres **läuft weg**, imperf **lief weg**, perf **ist weggelaufen**) vb [43] to run away
wegmachen (perf **hat weggemacht**) vb [48] to get rid of ▷ *einen Fleck wegmachen* to get rid of a stain
wegnehmen (pres **nimmt weg**, imperf **nahm weg**, perf **hat weggenommen**) vb [52] to take away
wegtun (imperf **tat weg**, perf **hat weggetan**) vb [81] to put away
Wegweiser (pl **Wegweiser**) m signpost
wegwerfen (pres **wirft weg**, imperf **warf weg**, perf **hat weggeworfen**) vb [92] to throw away
weh adj see **wehtun**
sich **wehren** vb [38] to defend oneself
wehtun (imperf **tat weh**, perf **hat wehgetan**) vb [81] ❶ to hurt ▷ *Mein Bein tut weh.* My leg hurts. ❷ to be sore ▷ *Mein Hals tut weh.* My throat's sore.; **Es tut weh** It's sore; **sich wehtun** to hurt oneself; **jemandem wehtun** to hurt somebody
weiblich adj feminine ▷ *ein weibliches Substantiv* a feminine noun
weich adj soft ▷ *ein weiches Bett* a soft bed
sich **weigern** vb [88] to refuse
Weihnachten (gen **Weihnachten**) nt Christmas ▷ *an Weihnachten* at

Christmas; **Frohe Weihnachten!** Merry Christmas.
Weihnachtsferien pl Christmas holidays pl
Weihnachtslied (pl **Weihnachtslieder**) nt Christmas carol
Weihnachtsmann (pl **Weihnachtsmänner**) m Father Christmas
Weihnachtsmarkt (pl **Weihnachtsmärkte**) m Christmas fair
Weihnachtstag (pl **Weihnachtstage**) m **der erste Weihnachtstag** Christmas Day

> Word for word, **der erste Weihnachtstag** means 'the first day of Christmas'.

der zweite Weihnachtstag Boxing Day

> Word for word, **der zweite Weihnachtstag** means 'the second day of Christmas'.

weil conj because
Weile f while ▷ *Es wird eine Weile dauern.* It'll take a while.
Wein (pl **Weine**) m wine
Weinberg (pl **Weinberge**) m vineyard

> Word for word, **Weinberg** means 'wine mountain'.

Weinbrand (pl **Weinbrände**) m brandy
weinen vb [38] to cry; **Das ist zum Weinen.** It's enough to make you cry.
Weinglas (gen **Weinglases**, pl **Weingläser**) nt wine glass
Weinkarte f wine list
Weinkeller (pl **Weinkeller**) m ❶ wine cellar ❷ wine bar
Weinstube f wine bar
Weintraube f grape
Weise f way ▷ *Die Art und Weise, wie er uns behandelt hat.* The way he treated us.; **auf diese Weise** in this way
Weisheit f wisdom
weiß vb see **wissen**
▶ adj ❶ white ❷ (person) White
Weißbrot (pl **Weißbrote**) nt white bread
Weißwein (pl **Weißweine**) m white wine
weit adj, adv ❶ long ▷ *Das ist eine weite Reise.* That's a long journey. ▷ *Das war sein weitester Wurf.* That was his longest throw. ❷ far ▷ *Wie weit ist es ...?* How far is it ...? ▷ *Nach Berlin ist es weiter als nach München.* It's further to Berlin than to Munich. ▷ *so weit wie möglich* as far as possible ▷ *Das geht zu weit.* That's going too far. ❸ baggy ▷ *Sie hatte einen weiten Pulli an.* She was wearing a baggy pullover.; **ein weiter Begriff** a broad idea; **so weit sein** to be ready; **Ich bin so weit zufrieden.** By and large I'm quite satisfied.
weitaus adv by far
weiter adj, adv ❶ further ▷ *Wenn du noch weitere Fragen hast ...* If you have any further questions ... ▷ *Alles Weitere besprechen wir morgen.* We can discuss any further details tomorrow.; **ohne weiteres** just like that; **weiter nichts** nothing else; **weiter niemand** nobody else
Weiterbildung f further education
weitere adj, adv see **weiter**
weitergehen (imperf **ging weiter**, perf **ist weitergegangen**) vb [29] to go on
weiterhin adv **etwas weiterhin tun** to go on doing something
weiterleiten (perf **hat weitergeleitet**) vb [4] to pass on
weitermachen (perf **hat weitergemacht**) vb [48] to continue
Weitsprung m long jump
Weizen m wheat
welche pron ❶ which ▷ *Welcher Mann?* Which man? ▷ *Welche Frau?* Which woman? ▷ *Welches Mädchen?* Which girl? ▷ *Welcher von beiden?* Which of the two? ▷ *Welchen hast du genommen?* Which one did you take? ❷ what ▷ *Welch eine Überraschung!* What a surprise!; **Welche Freude!** What joy!

③ some ▷ *Ich habe Kirschen, willst du welche?* I have some cherries, would you like some? ▷ *Ich habe welche.* I have some. ④ any ▷ *Ich brauche Briefmarken, hast du welche?* I need stamps, have you got any? ▷ *Ich brauche Kleingeld, hast du welches?* I need change, have you got any?

Welle f wave
Wellenlänge f wavelength
Wellensittich (pl **Wellensittiche**) m budgie
Welt f world
Weltall nt universe
weltberühmt adj world-famous
Weltkrieg (pl **Weltkriege**) m world war
Weltmeister (pl **Weltmeister**) m world champion
Weltraum m space
weltweit adj, adv worldwide
wem pron
> wem is the dative of wer.

to whom; **Mit wem bist du gekommen?** Who did you come with?
wen pron
> wen is the accusative of wer.

whom; **Wen hast du gesehen?** Who did you see?
wenig adj, adv little; **so wenig wie** as little as; **zu wenig** too little
wenige pron pl few pl ▷ *Das wissen nur wenige.* Only a few people know that.
weniger adj, adv ❶ less ▷ *Ich habe weniger Geld als du.* I have less money than you. ❷ fewer ▷ *Ich habe weniger Fehler gemacht.* I've made fewer mistakes. ❸ minus ▷ *Zehn weniger drei ist sieben.* Ten minus three is seven.
wenigste adj least ▷ *Das ist das wenigste, was ich tun kann.* That's the least I can do.; **am wenigsten** the least
wenigstens adv at least
wenn conj ❶ if ▷ *Wenn er anruft, sag mir Bescheid.* If he calls, tell me.; **selbst wenn ...** even if ...; **wenn ich doch ...** if only I ... ❷ when ▷ *Wenn ich nach Hause komme, dusche ich erst mal.* When I get home, the first thing I'm going to do is have a shower.; **immer wenn** whenever

wer pron who
> Be careful! wer does not mean where.

werben (pres **wirbt**, imperf **warb**, perf **hat geworben**) vb [**90**] to advertise ▷ *Im Fernsehen wird zu viel geworben.* There's too much advertising on TV.; **Mitglieder werben** to recruit members
Werbespot (pl **Werbespots**) m commercial
Werbung f ❶ advert ▷ *Hast du die Werbung für den neuen Schokoriegel gesehen?* Have you seen the advert for the new chocolate bar? ▷ *Wenn Werbung kommt, schalte ich um.* I switch over when the adverts come on. ❷ advertising ▷ *Er arbeitet in der Werbung.* He works in advertising.; **für etwas Werbung machen** to advertise something
werden vb [**91**] ❶ to become ▷ *Sie ist Lehrerin geworden.* She became a teacher. ▷ *Er ist reich geworden.* He became rich. ▷ *Was ist aus ihm geworden?* What became of him?; **Erster werden** to come first; **Was willst du einmal werden?** What do you want to be?; **rot werden** to turn red; **Es ist gut geworden.** It turned out well.; **Die Fotos sind gut geworden.** The photos have come out well.; **Es ist nichts geworden.** It came to nothing.; **Es wird Tag.** It's getting light.; **Es wird Nacht.** It's getting dark.; **Mir wird kalt.** I'm getting cold.; **Mir wird schlecht.** I feel sick. ❷ will
> werden is used to form the future tense.

Das muss anders werden. That'll have to change. ▷ *Er wird es tun.* He'll do it. ▷ *Er wird das nicht tun.* He won't do it. ▷ *Sie wird in der Küche sein.* She'll be in the kitchen.; **Es wird gleich regnen.** It's going to rain. ❸ to be

■ **werden** is used to form the passive. ▷ *gebraucht werden* to be needed ▷ *Er ist erschossen worden.* He's been shot. ▷ *Mir wurde gesagt, dass ...* I was told that ...

■ **werden** is used to form the conditional tense.

Ich würde ... I would ...; **Er würde gern ...** He'd like to ...; **Ich würde lieber ...** I'd rather ...

werfen (*pres* **wirft**, *imperf* **warf**, *perf* **hat geworfen**) *vb* [92] to throw

Werkstatt (*pl* **Werkstätten**) *f*
❶ workshop ▷ *eine Werkstatt für Behinderte* a workshop for people with disabilities ❷ garage ▷ *Das Auto ist in der Werkstatt.* The car's in the garage.

Werktag (*pl* **Werktage**) *m* working day
werktags *adv* on working days
Werkzeug (*pl* **Werkzeuge**) *nt* tool
wert *adj* worth ▷ *Wie viel ist das Bild wert?* How much is that picture worth? ▷ *Das ist nichts wert.* It's not worth anything. ▷ *Das ist viel wert.* It's worth a lot.

Wert (*pl* **Werte**) *m* value; **Wert legen auf** to attach importance to; **Es hat doch keinen Wert.** There's no point.

wertlos *adj* worthless
wertvoll *adj* valuable
Wesen (*pl* **Wesen**) *nt* manner ▷ *Er hat ein freundliches Wesen.* He has a friendly manner.

wesentlich *adj* significant
weshalb *adv* why
Wespe *f* wasp
wessen *pron*
■ **wessen** is the genitive of **wer**. whose
Weste *f* waistcoat
Westen *m* west

westlich *adj*, *prep*, *adv* westerly ▷ *in westlicher Richtung* in a westerly direction; **westlich einer Sache** to the west of something; **westlich von** west of

weswegen *adv* why
Wettbewerb (*pl* **Wettbewerbe**) *m* competition
Wette *f* bet
wetten *vb* [2] to bet ▷ *Ich wette, du fällst durchs Examen.* I bet you fail the exam.
Wetter *nt* weather
Wetterbericht (*pl* **Wetterberichte**) *m* weather report
Wetterlage (*pl* **Wetterlagen**) *f* weather situation
Wettervorhersage *f* weather forecast
Wettkampf (*pl* **Wettkämpfe**) *m* contest
Wettlauf (*pl* **Wettläufe**) *m* race
wichtig *adj* important
Widder (*pl* **Widder**) *m* ❶ ram ❷ Aries ▷ *Horst ist Widder.* Horst's Aries.
widerlich *adj* disgusting
widersprechen (*pres* **widerspricht**, *imperf* **widersprach**, *perf* **hat widersprochen**) *vb* [70] jemandem widersprechen to contradict somebody
Widerspruch (*pl* **Widersprüche**) *m* contradiction
Widerstand (*pl* **Widerstände**) *m* resistance
widerwillig *adj* unwilling
wie *adv* ❶ how ▷ *Wie groß?* How big? ▷ *Wie schnell?* How fast? ▷ *Wie schön!* How lovely! ▷ *Und wie!* And how! ▷ *Wie wär's?* How about it? ▷ *Wie geht's dir?* How are you?; **Wie bitte? (1)** Pardon? ▷ *Wie bitte, was haben Sie gesagt?* Pardon, what did you say? **(2)** What? ▷ *Wie bitte, du willst zweitausend Euro von mir haben?* What? You want me to give you two thousand euros?; **so schön wie ...**

as beautiful as ...; **wie ich schon sagte** as I said ❷ like ▷ *wie du* like you ▷ *singen wie ein ...* to sing like a ...; **wie zum Beispiel** such as

wieder *adv* again ▷ *wieder da sein* to be back again ▷ *Gehst du schon wieder?* Are you off again?; **wieder ein ...** another ...

wiederaufbereiten (*perf* **hat wiederaufbereitet**) *vb* [2] to recycle

wiederbekommen (*imperf* **bekam wieder**, *perf* **hat wiederbekommen**) *vb* [40] to get back

wiedererkennen (*imperf* **erkannte wieder**, *perf* **hat wiedererkannt**) *vb* [39] to recognize

wiederholen (*perf* **hat wiederholt**) *vb* [4] to repeat

Wiederholung *f* ❶ repetition ▷ *Es darf keine Wiederholung dieses Vorfalls geben.* There must be no repetition of this incident. ❷ repeat ▷ *Im Fernsehen kommen zu viele Wiederholungen.* There are too many repeats on TV.

Wiederhören *nt* **Auf Wiederhören!** Goodbye! (on telephone, radio)

wiedersehen (*pres* **sieht wieder**, *imperf* **sah wieder**, *perf* **hat wiedergesehen**) *vb* [4] to see again; **Auf Wiedersehen!** Goodbye.

wiederverwerten (*perf* **hat wiederverwertet**) *vb* [7] to recycle

Wiege *f* cradle

wiegen (*imperf* **wog**, *perf* **hat gewogen**) *vb* to weigh ▷ *Ich habe mich heute früh gewogen.* I weighed myself this morning.

Wien *nt* Vienna

Wiese *f* meadow

wieso *adv* why

wie viel *adj* how much ▷ *Wie viel hat das gekostet?* How much did it cost?; **wie viel Menschen** how many people

wievielte *adj* **Zum wievielten Mal?** How many times?; **Den Wievielten haben wir?** What's the date?

Wi-Fi *nt* Wi-Fi

wild *adj* wild

will *vb* see **wollen**

Wille (*gen* **Willens**, *pl* **Willen**) *m* will ▷ *Ich habe es aus freiem Willen getan.* I did it of my own free will.

willkommen *adj* welcome ▷ *Herzlich willkommen!* Welcome!; **jemanden willkommen heißen** to welcome somebody

wimmeln *vb* [88] **Es wimmelt von ...** It's teeming with ...

Wimper *f* eyelash

Wimperntusche *f* mascara

Wind (*pl* **Winde**) *m* wind

Windel *f* nappy ▷ *Kannst du dem Baby die Windeln wechseln?* Can you change the baby's nappy?

Windenergie *f* wind energy

windig *adj* windy ▷ *Es ist windig.* It's windy.

Windmühle *f* windmill

Windpark *m* wind farm

Windpocken *pl* chickenpox *sg* ▷ *Windpocken sind ansteckend.* Chickenpox is catching.

Windschutzscheibe *f* windscreen

Windsurfen *nt* windsurfing

Winkel (*pl* **Winkel**) *m* ❶ angle ▷ *ein spitzer Winkel* an acute angle ❷ corner ▷ *Ich habe jeden Winkel des Zimmers durchsucht.* I've searched every corner of the room.

winken *vb* [38] to wave ▷ *jemandem winken* to wave to somebody

Winter (*pl* **Winter**) *m* winter ▷ *im Winter* in winter

winzig *adj* tiny

wir *pron* we ▷ *Wir kommen.* We're coming.; **wir alle** all of us; **Wir sind's.** It's us.

Wirbelsäule *f* spine

wird *vb* see **werden**

wirft *vb* see **werfen**

wirken *vb* [38] ❶ to have an effect ▷ *Die Tablette wirkt schon.* The pill's already having an effect. ❷ to seem ▷ *Er wirkte traurig.* He seemed sad.

wirklich *adj, adv* ❶ real ▷ *Er ist ein wirklicher Freund.* He's a real friend. ❷ really ▷ *Das ist wirklich passiert.* That really happened. ▷ *Ich weiß es wirklich nicht.* I really don't know.

Wirklichkeit *f* reality

wirksam *adj* effective

Wirkung *f* effect ▷ *Wirkung auf etwas haben* to have an effect on something

wirr *adj* confused

Wirsing *m* savoy cabbage

wirst *vb see* **werden**

Wirt (*pl* **Wirte**) *m* landlord

Wirtin *f* landlady

Wirtschaft *f* ❶ pub ▷ *Wir sind in einer Wirtschaft eingekehrt.* We stopped at a pub. ❷ economy ▷ *Die Wirtschaft leidet unter der Rezession.* The economy's suffering because of the recession.

wirtschaftlich *adj* ❶ economical ▷ *Die große Packung ist wirtschaftlicher.* The large packet's more economical. ❷ economic ▷ *ein wirtschaftlicher Aufschwung* an economic upswing

Wirtschaftslehre *f* economics *sg*

Wirtshaus (*gen* **Wirtshauses**, *pl* **Wirtshäuser**) *nt* inn

wischen *vb* [48] ❶ to wipe ❷ to swipe (phone screen) ▷ *Zum Entsperren über den Screen wischen.* Swipe the screen to unlock.

wissen (*pres* **weiß**, *imperf* **wusste**, *perf* **hat gewusst**) *vb* [93] to know ▷ *Sie weiß sehr viel.* She knows a lot. ▷ *Weißt du, wie die Hauptstadt von Deutschland heißt?* Do you know what the capital of Germany is called? ▷ *Ich weiß es nicht.* I don't know.; **Was weiß ich!** How should I know?

Wissen *nt* knowledge

Wissenschaft *f* science

Wissenschaftler (*pl* **Wissenschaftler**) *m* scientist

Wissenschaftlerin *f* scientist

wissenschaftlich *adj* scientific

Witwe *f* widow ▷ *Sie ist Witwe.* She's a widow.

Witwer (*pl* **Witwer**) *m* widower ▷ *Er ist Witwer.* He's a widower.

Witz (*gen* **Witzes**, *pl* **Witze**) *m* joke ▷ *einen Witz erzählen* to tell a joke

witzig *adj* funny

wo *adv* where ▷ *Wo warst du?* Where were you?

> Be careful! **wo** does not mean **who**.

woanders *adv* elsewhere

wobei *adv* ❶ with/during which ❷ in the process of which; **wobei mir gerade einfällt** ... which reminds me ...

Woche *f* week ▷ *nächste Woche* next week

Wochenende (*pl* **Wochenenden**) *nt* weekend ▷ *am Wochenende* at the weekend

wochenlang *adj, adv* for weeks

Wochentag (*pl* **Wochentage**) *m* weekday

wöchentlich *adj, adv* weekly

wodurch *adv* ❶ how ❷ through which; *alles, wodurch sie glücklich geworden war* everything which had made her happy

wofür *adv* what ... for ▷ *Wofür brauchst du das Geld?* What do you need the money for?

wog *vb see* **wiegen**

woher *adv* where ... from ▷ *Woher sind Sie?* Where do you come from?

wohin *adv* where ... to ▷ *Wohin zieht ihr um?* Where are you moving to? ❷ where ▷ *Wohin gehst du?* Where are you going?

wohl *adv* probably ▷ *Das hat er wohl vergessen.* He's probably forgotten.; **Es ist wohl gestohlen worden.** It must have been stolen.; **Das ist doch wohl nicht dein Ernst!** Surely you're not being serious!; **Das mag wohl sein.**

That may well be.; **Ob das wohl stimmt?** I wonder if that's true.; **Er weiß das sehr wohl.** He knows that perfectly well.; **Ich muss wohl oder übel hingehen.** I have to go whether I like it or not.

Wohl nt benefit ▷ *zu eurem Wohl* for your benefit; **Zum Wohl!** Cheers!

sich **wohlfühlen** vb [4] ❶ to be happy ▷ *Ich fühle mich in diesem Haus sehr wohl.* I'm very happy in this house. ❷ to feel well ▷ *Sie fühlte sich nicht wohl.* She didn't feel well.

Wohnblock (pl **Wohnblocks**) m block of flats

wohnen vb [38] to live ▷ *Ich wohne in Bremen.* I live in Bremen.

Wohngemeinschaft f ▷ *Ich wohne in einer Wohngemeinschaft.* I share a flat.

Wohnheim (pl **Wohnheime**) nt ❶ home ▷ *ein Wohnheim für ältere Menschen* a home for senior citizens; **ein Studentenwohnheim** a hall of residence ❷ hostel

Wohnort (pl **Wohnorte**) m place of residence

Wohnsitz (gen **Wohnsitzes**, pl **Wohnsitze**) m place of residence

Wohnung f flat

Wohnwagen (pl **Wohnwagen**) m caravan

Wohnzimmer (pl **Wohnzimmer**) nt living room

Wolf (pl **Wölfe**) m wolf

Wolke f cloud

Wolkenkratzer (pl **Wolkenkratzer**) m skyscraper

wolkig adj cloudy

Wolle f wool

wollen (pres **will**, imperf **wollte**, perf **hat gewollt** or **wollen**) vb [94]

The past participle **wollen** is used when **wollen** has a modal auxiliary.

to want ▷ *Er hat nicht gewollt.* He didn't want to. ▷ *Er wollte das nicht.* He didn't want it. ▷ *Ich will nach Hause.* I want to go home. ▷ *Ich will, dass du mir zuhörst.* I want you to listen to me.; **Wenn du willst.** If you like.; **etwas tun wollen** to want to do something; **etwas gerade tun wollen** to be on the point of doing something; **Ich wollte, ich wäre ...** I wish I were ...

womit adv ❶ with which ▷ *Das ist der Gegenstand, womit er erschlagen wurde.* This is the instrument with which he was killed. ❷ what ... with ▷ *Womit hast du das repariert?* What did you repair it with?

wonach adv ❶ what ... for ▷ *Das war genau, wonach er gesucht hatte.* That was just what he had been looking for. ❷ what ... by ▷ *Wonach sollen wir die Uhr stellen?* What shall we set the clock by?; **der Tag, wonach er verunglückte** the day before his accident

woran adv ▷ *das Paket, woran dieser Zettel hing* the parcel the note was attached to; **Woran war dieser Zettel befestigt?** What was this note attached to?; **Woran ist er gestorben?** What did he die of?

worauf adv what ... on ▷ *Worauf soll ich den Computer stellen?* What shall I put the computer on?; **der Tisch, worauf der Computer steht** the table the computer is on

woraus adv ▷ *das Material, woraus es hergestellt ist* the material it is made of; **das Leck, woraus Gas strömte** the hole gas was pouring out of

worin adv what ... in ▷ *Worin war das versteckt?* What was it hidden in?; **die Schublade, worin der Schlüssel ist** the drawer the key is in; **Worin besteht der Unterschied?** What's the difference?

Wort (pl **Wörter** or **Worte**) nt word ▷ *Sie sprach ein paar bewegende Worte.* She said a few moving words. ▷ *Manche Wörter werden wie im Französischen ausgesprochen.* Some words are pronounced as in French.; **jemanden beim Wort nehmen** to take somebody at his word; **mit anderen Worten** in other words

Wörterbuch (pl **Wörterbücher**) nt dictionary

> Word for word, **Wörterbuch** means 'word book'.

wörtlich adj literal

Wortschatz (gen **Wortschatzes**) m vocabulary

Wortspiel (pl **Wortspiele**) nt pun

worüber adv *das Thema, worüber wir reden* the subject we're talking about; *der Tisch, worüber eine Lampe hing* the table a lamp was hanging over; *Worüber kann ich meinen Mantel legen?* Where can I put my coat?

worum adv about what ▷ *Worum ging es?* What was it about?

worunter adv what ... under ▷ *Worunter hat sich die Katze verkrochen?* What did the cat crawl under?; *der Tisch, worunter die Katze lag* the table the cat was lying under

wovon adv *Das war es, wovon wir sprachen.* That was what we were talking about.; *das Essen, wovon ihm schlecht wurde* the food which made him ill

wovor adv *das Haus, wovor du stehst* the house you're standing in front of; *die Arbeit, wovor sie am meisten Angst hat* the test which she's most afraid of

wozu adv ❶ why ▷ *Wozu willst du das wissen?* Why do you want to know that? ❷ what ... for ▷ *Wozu dient dieser Schalter?* What's this switch for? ▷ *Wozu brauchst du einen Computer?* What do you need a computer for?

Wrack (pl **Wracks**) nt wreck

Wucher m *Das ist Wucher!* (informal) That's daylight robbery!

wund adj sore ▷ *Ich habe mir die Füße beim Einkaufen wund gelaufen.* My feet are sore from going round the shops.

Wunde f wound

Wunder (pl **Wunder**) nt miracle; **es ist kein Wunder** it's no wonder

wunderbar adj wonderful

wundern vb [88] to surprise ▷ *Diese Frage hat mich sehr gewundert.* This question really surprised me.; **sich wundern über** to be surprised at; *Ich muss mich schon über dich wundern.* I must say you surprise me.; *Es wundert mich, dass du das fragst.* I'm surprised you ask.; *Er wird sich noch wundern!* He's in for a surprise!

wunderschön adj beautiful

wundervoll adj wonderful

Wunsch (pl **Wünsche**) m wish

wünschen vb [48] to wish ▷ *Ich wünsche dir viel Erfolg!* I wish you every success.; **sich etwas wünschen** to want something

wurde vb see **werden**

Wurf (pl **Würfe**) m throw

Würfel (pl **Würfel**) m ❶ dice ▷ *zwei Würfel* two dice ▷ *Wir haben Würfel gespielt.* We played dice. ❷ cube ▷ *Ein Würfel hat sechs gleich große Flächen.* A cube has six equal surfaces.

würfeln vb [34] ❶ to throw a dice ▷ *Ich bin dran mit Würfeln.* It's my turn to throw the dice. ▷ *Wir haben darum gewürfelt, wer abwaschen muss.* We threw a dice to see who was going to wash up. ❷ to dice ▷ *den Speck würfeln* to dice the bacon

Wurm (pl **Würmer**) m worm

Wurst (pl **Würste**) f ❶ sausage ▷ *Leberwurst* liver sausage ❷ cold meat; **eine Wurstplatte** a platter of cold meat; **Das ist mir Wurst.** (informal) I don't give a toss.

Würstchen (pl **Würstchen**) nt sausage
Würze f seasoning
Wurzel f root
wusch vb see **waschen**
wusste vb see **wissen**
Wüste f desert
Wut f rage; **eine Wut haben** to be furious
wütend adj furious ▷ *Ich bin wütend auf ihn.* I'm furious with him.

x-beliebig adj any ... whatever ▷ *Wähle eine x-beliebige Zahl.* Choose any number whatever.
x-mal adv any number of times ▷ *Ich habe es ihm x-mal gesagt.* I've told him any number of times.
Xylofon (pl **Xylofone**) nt xylophone

Y Z

Yoga (*gen* **Yoga** *or* **Yogas**) *nt* yoga
Ypsilon (*gen* **Ypsilon** *or* **Ypsilons**, *pl* **Ypsilons**) *nt* the letter Y

zäh *adj* ❶ tough ▷ *Das Steak ist zäh.* The steak's tough. ▷ *Ich bin zäh, ich halte es noch eine Weile aus.* I'm tough, I can stand it for a bit yet. ❷ slow-moving ▷ *Der Verkehr war zäh.* Traffic was slow-moving.
Zahl *f* number
zahlen *vb* [**38**] to pay ▷ *Wie viel hast du dafür gezahlt?* How much did you pay for it?; **Zahlen bitte!** The bill, please!
zählen *vb* [**38**] to count ▷ *Ich zähle bis drei.* I'll count to three. ▷ *Ich habe die Hefte gezählt.* I've counted the exercise books.; **zählen auf** to count on; **zählen zu** to be one of
zahlreich *adj* numerous
Zahlung *f* payment
Zahlwort (*pl* **Zahlwörter**) *nt* numeral
zahm *adj* tame
Zahn (*pl* **Zähne**) *m* tooth
Zahnarzt (*gen* **Zahnarztes**, *pl* **Zahnärzte**) *m* dentist
Zahnbürste *f* toothbrush

Zahncreme (pl **Zahncremes**) f toothpaste

Zahnpasta (pl **Zahnpasten**) f toothpaste

Zahnschmerzen pl toothache sg ▷ Zahnschmerzen sind sehr unangenehm. Toothache is very unpleasant.

Zange f ❶ pliers pl ▷ Ich brauche eine isolierte Zange. I need a pair of insulated pliers. ❷ pincers pl ▷ die Zangen eines Hummers a lobster's pincers

zappeln vb [34] ❶ to wriggle ▷ Der Fisch zappelt noch. The fish is still wriggling. ❷ to fidget ▷ Hör auf zu zappeln. Stop fidgeting.

zart adj ❶ soft ▷ zarte Haut soft skin ❷ gentle ▷ eine zarte Berührung a gentle touch ❸ delicate ▷ zarte Farben delicate colours ▷ Sie ist ein sehr zartes Kind. She's a very delicate child.; **zartes Fleisch** tender meat

zärtlich adj loving ▷ Mein Freund ist sehr zärtlich. My boyfriend's very loving. ▷ ein zärtlicher Kuss a loving kiss ▷ eine zärtliche Berührung a loving touch

Zauberei f magic

Zaun (pl **Zäune**) m fence

z. B. abbr (= zum Beispiel) e.g.

Zebrastreifen (pl **Zebrastreifen**) m zebra crossing

Zehe f toe ▷ die große Zehe the big toe; **eine Knoblauchzehe** a clove of garlic

zehn num ten

zehnte adj tenth

Zeichen (pl **Zeichen**) nt sign

Zeichentrickfilm (pl **Zeichentrickfilme**) m animated cartoon

zeichnen vb [53] to draw ▷ Marek kann gut zeichnen. Marek's good at drawing. ▷ Sie hat eine Maus gezeichnet. She's drawn a mouse.

Zeichnung f drawing

Zeigefinger (pl **Zeigefinger**) m index finger

zeigen vb [38] ❶ to show ▷ Sie hat mir ihre Fotos gezeigt. She showed me her photos. ▷ Zeig mal, was du da hast. Show us what you've got there. ❷ to point ▷ Sie zeigte an die Tafel. She pointed to the blackboard.; **zeigen auf** to point at; **es wird sich zeigen** time will tell; **Es zeigte sich, dass ...** It turned out that ...

Zeiger (pl **Zeiger**) m ❶ hand ▷ der große und der kleine Zeiger der Uhr the big hand and the little hand of the clock ❷ pointer ▷ der Zeiger der Waage the pointer of the scales

Zeile f line ▷ Ich schreibe ihr ein paar Zeilen. I'm going to write her a few lines.

Zeit f ❶ time ▷ Wir haben keine Zeit mehr. We haven't got any more time. ▷ Um welche Zeit seid ihr nach Hause gekommen? What time did you get home? ❷ tense ▷ die Zeiten der Vergangenheit the past tenses; **sich Zeit lassen** to take one's time; **in letzter Zeit** recently; **von Zeit zu Zeit** from time to time; **Zeit raubend** see **zeitraubend**

zeitlich adj chronological

zeitnah adj, adv ❶ prompt ▷ eine zeitnahe Antwort a prompt reply ❷ promptly ▷ Der Aufzug wurde zeitnah repariert. The lift was repaired promptly.

Zeitlupe f slow motion ▷ in Zeitlupe in slow motion

Zeitpunkt (pl **Zeitpunkte**) m ❶ moment ▷ Das ist nicht der richtige Zeitpunkt. This isn't the right moment. ❷ point in time ▷ Zu diesem Zeitpunkt war ich immer noch in Wien. At that point in time, I was still in Vienna.

zeitraubend adj time-consuming

Zeitraum (pl **Zeiträume**) m period ▷ innerhalb dieses Zeitraums within this period

Zeitschrift f magazine

Zeitung f newspaper

Zelle f ❶ cell ▷ *Im Alter sterben die Zellen ab.* Cells die off in old age. ❷ call box ▷ *Ich rufe aus einer Zelle an.* I'm phoning from a call box.

Zelt (pl **Zelte**) nt tent

zelten vb [2] to camp

Zeltplatz (gen **Zeltplatzes**, pl **Zeltplätze**) m camp site

Zement (pl **Zemente**) m cement

zensieren (perf **hat zensiert**) vb [76] ❶ to censor ▷ *Der Film wurde zensiert.* The film was censored. ❷ to give a mark ▷ *Wie hat deine Deutschlehrerin den Aufsatz zensiert?* What mark did your German teacher give you for your essay?

Zensur f mark ▷ *Ich habe durchweg gute Zensuren.* I've got good marks in everything.

Zentimeter (pl **Zentimeter**) m centimetre

Zentner (pl **Zentner**) m hundredweight ▷ *drei Zentner* three hundredweight

zentral adj central

Zentrale f ❶ head office ▷ *Das Gerät müssen wir in der Zentrale anfordern.* We'll have to order the appliance from the head office. ❷ switchboard ▷ *Du musst dich über die Zentrale verbinden lassen.* You have to go through the switchboard.

Zentralheizung f central heating

Zentrum (pl **Zentren**) nt centre

zerbrechen (pres **zerbricht**, imperf **zerbrach**, perf **hat/ist zerbrochen**) vb [11]

For the perfect tense use **haben** when the verb has an object and **sein** when there is no object.

to break ▷ *Sie hat den Teller zerbrochen.* She's broken the plate. ▷ *Der Teller ist zerbrochen.* The plate broke.

zerbrechlich adj fragile

zerreißen (imperf **zerriss**, perf **hat/ist zerrissen**) vb

For the perfect tense use **haben** when the verb has an object and **sein** when there is no object.

❶ to tear to pieces ▷ *Sie hat seinen Brief zerrissen.* She tore his letter to pieces. ❷ to tear ▷ *Der Umschlag ist unterwegs zerrissen.* The envelope got torn in the post.

zerren vb [38] to drag ▷ *Er zerrte sie in die Büsche.* He dragged her into the bushes.; **zerren an** to tug at

zerrissen vb see **zerreißen**

zerschlagen (pres **zerschlägt**, imperf **zerschlug**, perf **hat zerschlagen**) vb [59] to smash ▷ *Sie haben alles Porzellan zerschlagen.* They smashed all the china.; **sich zerschlagen** to fall through

zerstören (pres **hat zerstört**) vb [95] to destroy

Zerstörung f destruction

zerstreut adj ❶ absent-minded ▷ *Er ist furchtbar zerstreut.* He's terribly absent-minded. ❷ scattered ▷ *Sie sammelte die zerstreuten Seiten auf.* She picked up the scattered pages.

Zettel (pl **Zettel**) m ❶ note ▷ *Auf dem Küchentisch liegt ein Zettel für dich.* There's a note on the kitchen table for you. ❷ piece of paper ▷ *Sie schrieb seine Telefonnummer auf einen Zettel.* She wrote his telephone number on a piece of paper. ❸ form ▷ *Wenn du dem Klub beitreten willst, musst du diesen Zettel ausfüllen.* If you want to join the club you'll have to fill in this form.

Zeug nt ❶ (informal) stuff ▷ *Was ist das für ein Zeug?* What's this stuff? ▷ *mein Sportzeug* my sports stuff ❷ gear ▷ *mein Angelzeug* my fishing gear; **dummes Zeug** nonsense; **das Zeug haben zu** to have the makings of

Zeuge (gen **Zeugen**, pl **Zeugen**) m witness

Zeugin f witness

Zeugnis (gen **Zeugnisses**, pl **Zeugnisse**) nt report ▷ *Oliver hat ein sehr gutes Zeugnis.* Oliver's got a very good report.

Ziege f goat

Ziegel (pl **Ziegel**) m ❶ brick ▷ *eine Mauer aus Ziegeln* a brick wall ❷ tile ▷ *Deutsche Dächer sind meist mit roten Ziegeln gedeckt.* German roofs are usually covered with red tiles.

ziehen (imperf **zog**, perf **hat/ist gezogen**) vb [96]

> Use **sein** to form the perfect tense for 'to move' (house) and 'to roam'. Use **haben** for 'to move' (in chess), 'to draw' and 'to pull'.

❶ to draw ▷ *Er hat eine Niete gezogen.* He drew a blank. ❷ to pull ▷ *Sie zog mich am Ärmel.* She pulled at my sleeve. ❸ to move ▷ *Sie sind nach Wuppertal gezogen.* They've moved to Wuppertal. ▷ *Er zog mit seinem Turm.* He moved his rook. ❹ to roam ▷ *Wildtiere ziehen frei durch den Nationalpark.* Wild animals roam throughout the national park.; **Es zieht.** There's a draught.; **sich in die Länge ziehen** to be drawn out

Ziel (pl **Ziele**) nt ❶ destination ▷ *Unser heutiges Ziel ist Bonn.* Our destination today is Bonn. ❷ finishing line ▷ *Er ging als Erster durchs Ziel.* He was the first to cross the finishing line. ❸ target ▷ *Ulm war das Ziel eines Bombenangriffs.* Ulm was the target of an air raid. ❹ goal ▷ *Es ist nicht mein Ziel im Leben, reich zu werden.* Getting rich is not my goal in life.

zielen vb [38] to aim ▷ *Er hat auf seine Beine gezielt.* He aimed at his legs.

ziemlich adj, adv ❶ quite ▷ *Das war eine ziemliche Katastrophe.* That was quite a disaster. ❷ fair ▷ *eine ziemliche Menge Fehler* a fair number of mistakes ❸ rather ▷ *Er war ziemlich sauer.* He was rather cross.; **ziemlich viel** quite a bit

zierlich adj dainty

Ziffer f figure

zig adj (informal) umpteen

Zigarette f cigarette

Zigarettenschachtel f cigarette packet

Zigarre f cigar

Zimmer (pl **Zimmer**) nt room; **'Zimmer frei'** 'Vacancies'

Zimmermädchen (pl **Zimmermädchen**) nt chambermaid

Zimt m cinnamon

Zinn nt ❶ tin ▷ *In Cornwall wurde früher Zinn abgebaut.* They used to mine tin in Cornwall. ❷ pewter ▷ *Mein Bruder sammelt Zinn.* My brother collects pewter.

Zins (gen **Zinses**, pl **Zinsen**) m interest ▷ *acht Prozent Zinsen* eight per cent interest

zirka adv approximately

Zirkus (gen **Zirkus**, pl **Zirkusse**) m circus

Zitat (pl **Zitate**) nt quotation

zitieren (perf **hat zitiert**) vb [76] to quote

Zitrone f lemon

Zitronensaft (pl **Zitronensäfte**) m lemon juice

zittern vb [88] to tremble ▷ *vor Angst zittern* to tremble with fear; **Sie zitterte vor Kälte.** She was shivering.

zivil adj civil; **zivile Partnerschaft** civil partnership

Zivildienst m community service

> Until the abolition of compulsory military service in 2011, those young men who opted out of this could choose to do **Zivildienst** or community service instead, for example with the Red Cross.

zögern vb [88] to hesitate

Zoll (pl **Zölle**) m ❶ customs pl ▷ *Wir mussten am Zoll lange warten.* We had to wait a long time at customs. ❷ duty

▷ *Darauf musst du Zoll bezahlen.* You have to pay duty on that.

Zollbeamte (gen **Zollbeamten**, pl **Zollbeamten**) m customs official ▷ *Ein Zollbeamter hat unser Auto durchsucht.* A customs official searched our car.

Zollkontrolle f customs check

Zone f zone

Zoo (pl **Zoos**) m zoo

Zopf (pl **Zöpfe**) m ❶ plait ▷ *zwei blonde Zöpfe* two blonde plaits ❷ pigtail ▷ *Sie hatte ihre Haare zu einem Zopf zusammengebunden.* She had put her hair into a pigtail.

Zorn m anger

zornig adj angry

zu prep, conj, adv

▪ The preposition zu takes the dative.

❶ to ▷ *zum Bahnhof gehen* to go to the station ▷ *zum Arzt gehen* to go to the doctor ▷ *zur Schule gehen* to go to school ▷ *zur Kirche gehen* to go to church ▷ *Sollen wir zu euch gehen?* Shall we go to your place?; *Sie sah zu ihm hin.* She looked towards him.; **zum Fenster herein** through the window; **zu meiner Linken** on my left

▪ zu is used with the infinitive.

▷ *etwas zu essen* something to eat ▷ *ohne es zu wissen* without knowing it ❷ at ▷ *zu Ostern* at Easter; **zu Hause** at home; **bis zum ersten Mai (1)** until the first of May ▷ *Das Sonderangebot gilt bis zum ersten Mai.* The special offer is valid until the first of May. **(2)** by the first of May ▷ *Bis zum ersten Mai muss mein Referat fertig sein.* My assignment has to be finished by the first of May.; **zu meinem Geburtstag** for my birthday; **zu meiner Zeit** in my time ❸ with ▷ *Wein zum Essen trinken* to drink wine with one's meal; **sich zu jemandem setzen** to sit down beside somebody ❹ on ▷ *Anmerkungen zu etwas* notes on something ❺ for ▷ *Wasser zum Waschen* water for washing; **Papier zum Schreiben** paper to write on; **zu etwas werden** to develop into something; **jemanden zu etwas machen** to make somebody something; **drei zu zwei** three two; **das Stück zu drei Euro** at three euros each; **zum ersten Mal** for the first time; **zum meiner Freude** to my delight; **zum Scherz** as a joke; **zu Fuß** on foot; *Es ist zum Weinen.* It's enough to make you cry. ❻ too ▷ *zu schnell* too fast ▷ *zu sehr* too much ❼ closed ▷ *Die Geschäfte haben zu.* The shops are closed.; **zu sein** to be shut

Zubehör (pl **Zubehöre**) nt accessories pl ▷ *Das Zubehör kostet extra.* You pay extra for the accessories.

zubereiten (perf **hat zubereitet**) vb [2] to prepare

Zucchini pl courgette sg

züchten vb [2] ❶ to breed ▷ *Er züchtet Tauben.* He breeds pigeons. ❷ to grow ▷ *Mein Vater züchtet Rosen.* My father grows roses.

zucken vb [38] ❶ to twitch ▷ *Seine Mundwinkel zuckten.* The corners of his mouth twitched. ❷ to flash ▷ *Ein Blitz zuckte durch die Nacht.* Lightning flashed across the night sky.; **mit den Schultern zucken** to shrug one's shoulders

Zucker m ❶ sugar ▷ *Ich nehme keinen Zucker in den Tee.* I don't take sugar in my tea. ❷ diabetes ▷ *Meine Tante hat Zucker.* My aunt's got diabetes.

Zuckerfest nt Eid (al-Fitr)

zudecken (perf **hat zugedeckt**) vb [4] ❶ to cover up ▷ *Man sollte das Loch zudecken.* They ought to cover up the hole. ❷ to tuck up ▷ *Sie deckte die Kinder zu.* She tucked the children up.

zueinander adv ❶ to one another ▷ *Seid nett zueinander.* Be nice to one another.; *Wir haben viel Vertrauen zueinander.* We trust each other.

❷ together ▷ *Wir halten zueinander, egal, was kommt.* Whatever happens, we'll stick together.

zuerst adv ❶ first ▷ *Was soll ich zuerst machen?* What shall I do first? ▷ *Er ist zuerst gekommen, dann kam seine Schwester.* He arrived first, then his sister. ❷ at first ▷ *Zuerst war sie noch etwas schüchtern.* At first, she was still a bit shy.; **zuerst einmal** first of all

Zufahrt f approach road; **'keine Zufahrt'** 'no access'

Zufall (pl **Zufälle**) m ❶ chance ▷ *Wie es der Zufall so wollte ...* As chance would have it...; **durch Zufall** by chance ❷ coincidence ▷ *Es war schon ein Zufall, dass ich ihn in London begegnet bin.* It was quite a coincidence that I met him in London. ▷ *Was für ein glücklicher Zufall!* What a happy coincidence! ▷ *So ein Zufall!* What a coincidence!

zufällig adj, adv ❶ chance ▷ *eine zufällige Begegnung* a chance meeting ❷ by chance ▷ *Ich habe das Restaurant ganz zufällig gefunden.* I found the restaurant quite by chance.; *Ich habe zufällig Zeit.* I happen to have time. ❸ by any chance ▷ *Hast du zufällig mein Heft gesehen?* Have you seen my exercise book by any chance?

zufrieden adj satisfied ▷ *Ich bin mit deinen Leistungen nicht zufrieden.* I'm not satisfied with your work. ▷ *Bist du jetzt zufrieden?* Are you satisfied now? ▷ *ein zufriedener Gesichtsausdruck* a satisfied expression

zufrieren (imperf **fror zu**, perf **ist zugefroren**) vb to freeze over ▷ *Der See ist zugefroren.* The lake's frozen over.

Zug (pl **Züge**) m ❶ train ▷ *Wir sind mit dem Zug gefahren.* We went by train. ❷ draught ▷ *Hier ist ein furchtbarer Zug.* There's a terrible draught in here. ❸ move ▷ *Du bist am Zug.* It's your move. ❹ gulp ▷ *Er trank das Glas auf einen Zug leer.* He emptied the glass in one gulp. ❺ trait ▷ *Sein Geiz ist ein unangenehmer Zug an ihm.* His meanness is an unpleasant trait.; **etwas in vollen Zügen genießen** to enjoy something to the full

Zugabe f ❶ free gift ▷ *ein Handy als Zugabe.* a mobile as a free gift ❷ encore ▷ *Die Zuhörer brüllten: 'Zugabe, Zugabe'.* The audience roared: 'encore, encore'.

zugeben (pres **gibt zu**, imperf **gab zu**, perf **hat zugegeben**) vb [**28**] to admit ▷ *Gib doch zu, dass du dich getäuscht hast.* Admit you were wrong. ▷ *Sie wollte ihren Irrtum nicht zugeben.* She didn't want to admit her mistake.

zugehen (imperf **ging zu**, perf **ist zugegangen**) vb [**29**] to shut ▷ *Die Tür geht nicht zu.* The door won't shut.; **auf jemanden zugehen** to walk up to somebody; **auf etwas zugehen** to walk towards something; **Es geht dort seltsam zu.** There are strange goings-on there.; **dem Ende zugehen** to be nearing the end

Zugführer (pl **Zugführer**) m chief guard (on train)

zügig adj swift ▷ *eine zügige Entscheidung* a swift decision

zugreifen (imperf **griff zu**, perf **hat zugegriffen**) vb ❶ to help oneself ▷ *Greift ungeniert zu, es ist genügend Kuchen da!* Feel free to help yourselves, there's plenty of cake. ❷ to seize ▷ *Er sah das Seil und griff zu.* He saw the rope and seized it. ❸ to lend a hand ▷ *Du könntest ruhig ein bisschen zugreifen und mich nicht alles allein machen lassen.* You could at least lend a hand a bit instead of letting me do everything.

zugrunde adv **elend zugrunde gehen** to come to a wretched end; **zugrunde richten** to destroy; **einer Sache etwas zugrunde legen** to base something on something

GERMAN > ENGLISH

zugunsten prep

> The preposition **zugunsten** takes the dative or the genitive.

in favour of ▷ *Das Gericht entschied zugunsten des Angeklagten.* The court decided in favour of the accused.

Zuhause (gen **Zuhause**) nt home

zuhören (perf **hat zugehört**) vb [4] **to listen** ▷ *Du hörst mir ja gar nicht zu.* You're not listening to me at all.

Zuhörer (pl **Zuhörer**) m listener

zukommen (imperf **kam zu**, perf **ist zugekommen**) vb [40] ① **auf jemanden zukommen** to come up to somebody; **jemandem etwas zukommen lassen** to give somebody something; **etwas auf sich zukommen lassen** to take something as it comes

Zukunft f future ▷ *in Zukunft* in the future

zulassen (pres **lässt zu**, imperf **ließ zu**, perf **hat zugelassen**) vb [42] ① **to allow** ▷ *Ich kann es nicht zulassen, dass du so spät noch fernsiehst.* I can't allow you to watch TV so late. ② **to register** ▷ *Hast du dein Moped schon zugelassen?* Have you registered your moped yet? ③ **to leave closed** ▷ *Bitte lass das Fenster zu.* Please leave the window closed.

zulässig adj permissible

zuletzt adv ① **last** ▷ *Er wurde zuletzt in Begleitung einer Dame gesehen.* He was last seen in the company of a lady. ▷ *Wir sollten das zuletzt machen.* We should do that last. ② **in the end** ▷ *Zuletzt hat sie es dann doch verstanden.* In the end she understood.

zuliebe adv **jemandem zuliebe** to please somebody

zum = **zu dem**

zumachen (perf **hat zugemacht**) vb [4] ① **to shut** ▷ *Mach bitte die Tür zu.* Please shut the door. ▷ *Wann machen die Geschäfte zu?* When do the shops shut? ② **to fasten** ▷ *Kannst du mal bitte mein Kleid zumachen?* Can you fasten my dress, please?

zumindest adv at least

zumute adv **Wie ist ihm zumute?** How does he feel?

zumuten (perf **hat zugemutet**) vb [2] **jemandem etwas zumuten** to ask something of somebody

zunächst adv **first of all** ▷ *Wir sollten zunächst diese Frage klären.* We ought to clear this issue up first of all.; **zunächst einmal** to start with

zunehmen (pres **nimmt zu**, imperf **nahm zu**, perf **hat zugenommen**) vb [52] ① **to increase** ▷ *Der Lärm nahm zu.* The noise increased. ② **to put on weight** ▷ *Ich habe schon wieder zugenommen.* I've put on weight yet again.; **Er hat fünf Kilo zugenommen.** He's put on five kilos.

Zuneigung f affection

Zunge f tongue

zur = **zu der**

zurechtkommen (imperf **kam zurecht**, perf **ist zurechtgekommen**) vb [40] **to manage**

zurechtlegen (perf **hat zurechtgelegt**) vb [4] **to sort out** ▷ *Ich habe die Sachen für die Ferien schon zurechtgelegt.* I've already sorted out my things for my holiday.; **sich eine Ausrede zurechtlegen** to think up an excuse

zurück adv back

zurückbekommen (imperf **bekam zurück**, perf **hat zurückbekommen**) vb [40] **to get back**

zurückbringen (imperf **brachte zurück**, perf **hat zurückgebracht**) vb [13] **to bring back**

zurückfahren (pres **fährt zurück**, imperf **fuhr zurück**, perf **ist/hat zurückgefahren**) vb [21]

> For the perfect tense use **haben** when the verb has an object and **sein** when there is no object.

to return ▷ *Wann fahrt ihr zurück?* When do you return?; **jemanden zurückfahren** to drive somebody back

zurückgeben (*pres* **gibt zurück**, *imperf* **gab zurück**, *perf* **hat zurückgegeben**) *vb* [**28**] to give back ▷ *Gib mir bitte mein Buch zurück.* Please give me my book back.

zurückgehen (*imperf* **ging zurück**, *perf* **ist zurückgegangen**) *vb* [**29**] ❶ to go back ▷ *Wir sollten zurückgehen, bevor es zu spät wird.* We should go back before it gets too late. ❷ to recede ▷ *Das Hochwasser ist zurückgegangen.* The floodwater receded. ❸ to fall ▷ *Die Nachfrage geht zurück.* Demand is falling.; **zurückgehen auf** to date back to

zurückhaltend *adj* reserved ▷ *Er ist sehr zurückhaltend.* He is very reserved.

zurückkehren (*perf* **ist zurückgekehrt**) *vb* [**15**] to return

zurückkommen (*imperf* **kam zurück**, *perf* **ist zurückgekommen**) *vb* [**40**] to come back ▷ *Er kam nach dem Film zurück.* He came back after the film. ▷ *Darf ich auf das zurückkommen, was Sie vorhin gesagt haben?* May I come back to what you were saying earlier?; **Komm nicht zu spät zurück.** Don't be too late back.

zurücklegen (*perf* **hat zurückgelegt**) *vb* [**15**] ❶ to put back ▷ *Leg das Buch bitte an seinen Platz zurück.* Please put the book back in its place. ❷ to put by ▷ *Wir haben für die Ferien etwas Geld zurückgelegt.* We've put some money by for the holidays. ❸ to put aside ▷ *Können Sie mir diesen Pulli bitte zurücklegen?* Could you put this pullover aside for me, please? ❹ to cover ▷ *Wir haben heute zweihundert Kilometer zurückgelegt.* We've covered two hundred kilometres today.

zurücknehmen (*pres* **nimmt zurück**, *imperf* **nahm zurück**, *perf* **hat zurückgenommen**) *vb* [**52**] to take back

zurücktreten (*pres* **tritt zurück**, *imperf* **trat zurück**, *perf* **ist zurückgetreten**) *vb* [**79**] ❶ to step back ▷ *Treten Sie etwas zurück bitte!* Step back a bit, please. ❷ to resign ▷ *Warum ist er zurückgetreten?* Why did he resign?

zurückzahlen (*perf* **hat zurückgezahlt**) *vb* [**15**] to repay ▷ *Du solltest endlich das geliehene Geld zurückzahlen.* It's high time you repaid the money you borrowed.

zurzeit *adv* at the moment

zusagen (*perf* **hat zugesagt**) *vb* [**4**] ❶ to promise ▷ *Er hat mir seine Hilfe zugesagt.* He promised to help me. ❷ to accept an invitation ▷ *Die meisten Gäste haben zugesagt.* Most of the guests have accepted the invitation.; **jemandem zusagen** to appeal to somebody

zusammen *adv* together

Zusammenarbeit *f* cooperation

zusammenbleiben (*imperf* **blieb zusammen**, *perf* **sind zusammengeblieben**) *vb* [**10**] to stay together

zusammenbrechen (*pres* **bricht zusammen**, *imperf* **brach zusammen**, *perf* **ist zusammengebrochen**) *vb* [**11**] ❶ to collapse ▷ *Das Gebäude ist zusammengebrochen.* The building collapsed. ❷ to break down ▷ *Als sie von seinem Tod erfuhr, ist sie zusammengebrochen.* When she heard of his death she broke down.

zusammenfassen (*perf* **hat zusammengefasst**) *vb* [**15**] to summarize ▷ *Sie fasste das Gesagte noch einmal kurz zusammen.* She briefly summarized once again what had been said.

Zusammenfassung *f* summary

Zusammenhang (*pl* **Zusammenhänge**) *m* connection

▷ **Gibt es einen Zusammenhang zwischen diesen Ereignissen?** Is there a connection between these events?; **im Zusammenhang mit** in connection with; **aus dem Zusammenhang** out of context

zusammenhängen (*imperf* **hing zusammen**, *perf* **hat zusammengehangen**) *vb* [69] to be connected ▷ *Die beiden Ereignisse hängen miteinander zusammen.* The two events are connected.

zusammenkommen (*imperf* **kam zusammen**, *perf* **ist zusammengekommen**) *vb* [40] ❶ to meet up ▷ *Früher sind wir öfter zusammengekommen.* We used to meet up more often. ❷ to come together ▷ *Es ist alles zusammengekommen.* Everything came together.

zusammennehmen (*pres* **nimmt zusammen**, *imperf* **nahm zusammen**, *perf* **hat zusammengenommen**) *vb* [52] to summon up ▷ *Ich musste meinen ganzen Mut zusammennehmen.* I had to summon up all my courage.; **alles zusammengenommen** all in all; **sich zusammennehmen** to pull oneself together

zusammenpassen (*perf* **hat zusammengepasst**) *vb* [4] ❶ to be well suited ▷ *Die beiden passen gut zusammen.* The two are well suited. ❷ to go together ▷ *Der Pulli und die Hose passen nicht zusammen.* The pullover and the trousers don't go together.

Zusammensein *nt* get-together ▷ *ein gemütliches Zusammensein* a cosy get-together

zusammenstellen (*perf* **hat zusammengestellt**) *vb* [15] ❶ to put together ▷ *Stellt alle Stühle zusammen.* Put all the chairs together. ❷ to compile ▷ *Ich habe eine Wunschliste zusammengestellt.* I've compiled a list of presents I'd like.

Zusammenstoß (*gen* **Zusammenstoßes**, *pl* **Zusammenstöße**) *m* collision

zusammenstoßen (*pres* **stößt zusammen**, *imperf* **stieß zusammen**, *perf* **sind zusammengestoßen**) *vb* to collide

zusammenzählen (*perf* **hat zusammengezählt**) *vb* [4] to add up

zusätzlich *adj, adv* ❶ additional ▷ *Wir sollen eine zusätzliche Englischstunde bekommen.* We're to get an additional English lesson. ❷ in addition ▷ *Zusätzlich zu den Matheaufgaben muss ich noch Physik machen.* I still have some physics to do in addition to my maths homework.

zuschauen (*perf* **hat zugeschaut**) *vb* [4] to watch ▷ *Habt ihr beim Match zugeschaut?* Did you watch the match?

Zuschauer *pl* audience *sg* ▷ *Die Zuschauer haben geklatscht.* The audience clapped.

Zuschlag (*pl* **Zuschläge**) *m* surcharge ▷ *Für den ICE brauchst du einen Zuschlag.* You have to pay a surcharge if you go by Intercity Express.

zusehen (*pres* **sieht zu**, *imperf* **sah zu**, *perf* **hat zugesehen**) *vb* [64] to watch ▷ *Wir haben beim Match zugesehen.* We watched the match. ▷ *Er stand nur dabei und sah zu.* He just stood there watching.; **jemandem zusehen** to watch somebody; **zusehen, dass etwas gemacht wird** to make sure something is done

zusenden (*imperf* **sendete** or **sandte zu**, *perf* **hat zugesendet** or **zugesandt**) *vb* to send ▷ *Wir werden Ihnen unseren Prospekt zusenden.* We'll send you our brochure.

Zustand (*pl* **Zustände**) *m* ❶ state ▷ *Das Haus war in einem furchtbaren Zustand.*

The house was in an awful state. ▷ *Das sind hier ja schreckliche Zustände.* This is a terrible state of affairs. ❷ condition ▷ *Das Auto ist noch in gutem Zustand.* The car's still in good condition.

zustande *adv* **zustande bringen** to bring about; **zustande kommen** to come about

zuständig *adj* *Dafür bin ich nicht zuständig.* That's not my responsibility.; **der zuständige Beamte** the official in charge

zustimmen (*perf* **hat zugestimmt**) *vb* [4] to agree ▷ *Ich stimme dir zu.* I agree with you.

Zustimmung *f* ❶ consent ▷ *Du brauchst die Zustimmung deiner Eltern.* You need your parents' consent. ❷ approval ▷ *wenn das deine Zustimmung findet* if that meets with your approval

zustoßen (*pres* **stößt zu**, *imperf* **stieß zu**, *perf* **ist zugestoßen**) *vb* to happen ▷ *Ihm ist doch hoffentlich nichts zugestoßen.* Let's hope nothing's happened to him.

Zutaten *fpl* ingredients *pl*

zutreffen (*pres* **trifft zu**, *imperf* **traf zu**, *perf* **hat zugetroffen**) *vb* [78] ❶ to be true ▷ *Es trifft nicht zu, dass ich das Buch mitgenommen habe.* It's not true that I took the book with me. ❷ to apply ▷ *Diese Beschreibung trifft nicht auf sie zu.* This description doesn't apply to her.

zutreffend *adj* **Zutreffendes bitte unterstreichen.** Please underline where applicable.

zuverlässig *adj* reliable

zuversichtlich *adj* confident

zuviel *adv see* **viel**

zuvor *adv* before ▷ *der Tag zuvor* the day before

zuwenig *adv see* **wenig**

zuziehen (*imperf* **zog zu**, *perf* **hat zugezogen**) *vb* [96] ❶ to draw ▷ *Es wird dunkel, zieh bitte die Vorhänge zu.* It's getting dark, please draw the curtains. ❷ to call in ▷ *Wir sollten einen Fachmann zuziehen.* We should call in an expert.; **sich etwas zuziehen** to catch something

Zwang (*pl* **Zwänge**) *m* compulsion

zwängen *vb* [38] to squeeze

zwanglos *adj* informal ▷ *ein zwangloses Gespräch* an informal talk

zwanzig *num* twenty

zwar *adv* although ▷ *Ich habe das zwar gesagt, aber es war nicht so gemeint.* Although I said it, it wasn't meant like that.; **das ist zwar ..., aber ...** that may be ... but ... ▷ *Das ist zwar viel, aber mir reicht es nicht.* That may be a lot, but it's not enough for me.; **und zwar (1)** to be precise ▷ *und zwar am Sonntag* on Sunday to be precise **(2)** in fact ▷ *und zwar so schnell, dass ...* in fact, so quickly that ...

Zweck (*pl* **Zwecke**) *m* ❶ purpose ▷ *Was ist der Zweck Ihres Besuchs?* What's the purpose of your visit? ❷ point ▷ *Was ist der Zweck dieser Übung?* What's the point of this exercise? ▷ *Es hat keinen Zweck.* There's no point.

zwecklos *adj* pointless

zwei *num* two

Zwei *f* ❶ two ❷ good
: German marks range from one (**sehr gut**) to six (**ungenügend**).

zweideutig *adj* ❶ ambiguous ▷ *Sie hat sich zweideutig ausgedrückt.* She expressed herself very ambiguously. ❷ suggestive ▷ *Er macht immer so zweideutige Witze.* He's always making such suggestive jokes.

zweierlei *adj* two different ▷ *zweierlei Stoff* two different kinds of material ▷ *Das sind doch zweierlei Dinge.* They're two different things.; **zweierlei Meinung** of differing opinions

zweifach *adj, adv* ❶ double ▷ *die zweifache Menge* double the quantity ❷ twice ▷ *Der Brief war zweifach gefaltet.* The letter had been folded twice.

Zweifel (pl **Zweifel**) m doubt ▷ ohne Zweifel without doubt

zweifelhaft adj ❶ doubtful ▷ Es ist noch zweifelhaft, ob wir kommen. It's still doubtful whether we're coming. ❷ dubious ▷ eine zweifelhafte Lösung a dubious solution; **ein zweifelhaftes Kompliment** a backhanded compliment

zweifellos adv doubtless; **Sie hat sich zweifellos bemüht.** There's no doubt that she tried.

zweifeln vb [34] **an etwas zweifeln** to doubt something; **zweifeln, ob** to doubt whether

Zweig (pl **Zweige**) m branch

Zweigstelle f branch ▷ Die nächste Zweigstelle ist in Villach. The nearest branch is in Villach.

zweihundert num two hundred

zweimal adv twice

zweit adv **zu zweit** (1) together ▷ Wir fahren zu zweit in die Ferien. We're going on holiday together. (2) in twos ▷ Stellt euch zu zweit auf. Line up in twos.

zweitbeste adj second best

zweite adj second ▷ Er kam als Zweiter. He was the second to arrive.

zweitens adv secondly

Zwetschge f damson

Zwieback (pl **Zwiebacke**) m rusk

Zwiebel f onion ▷ Sebastian mag keine Zwiebeln. Sebastian doesn't like onions.

Zwilling (pl **Zwillinge**) m twin ▷ Diese Zwillinge sehen sich zum Verwechseln ähnlich. The twins are the spitting image of each other.; **Zwillinge** Gemini

zwingen (imperf **zwang**, perf **hat gezwungen**) vb [97] to force

zwischen prep

> Use the accusative to express movement or a change of place. Use the dative when there is no change of place.

between ▷ Er stand zwischen den beiden Mädchen. He was standing between the two girls. ▷ Stell deinen Stuhl zwischen unsere. Put your chair between ours.

Zwischending nt cross ▷ Das ist ein Zwischending zwischen einem Hotel und einer Jugendherberge. It's a cross between a hotel and a youth hostel.

zwischendurch adv in between ▷ Wir haben zwischendurch eine Pause gemacht. We had a break in between.

Zwischenfall (pl **Zwischenfälle**) m incident

Zwischenfrage f question

zwölf num twelve

Zypern nt Cyprus

A n (school mark) Eins f (pl Einsen) ▷ I got an A for my essay. Ich habe für meinen Aufsatz eine Eins bekommen.

a art

In the nominative use **ein** for masculine and neuter nouns, **eine** for feminine nouns.

① ein ▷ a man ein Mann ▷ I saw a man. Ich habe einen Mann gesehen. ▷ a child ein Kind ▷ an apple ein Apfel **②** eine ▷ a woman eine Frau ▷ He gave it to a woman. Er hat es einer Frau gegeben.

Do not translate 'a' when you want to describe what somebody does for a living.

▷ He's a butcher. Er ist Metzger. ▷ She's a doctor. Sie ist Ärztin.; **once a week** einmal pro Woche; **thirty kilometres an hour** dreißig Kilometer in der Stunde; **thirty pence a kilo** dreißig Pence das Kilo; **a hundred pounds** einhundert Pfund

abandon vb **①** (place) verlassen [42] **②** (plan, idea) aufgeben [28]

abbey n Kloster nt (pl Klöster)

abbreviation n Abkürzung f

ability n Fähigkeit f; **to have the ability to do something** fähig sein [65], etwas zu tun

able adj **to be able to do something** etwas tun können [41]

abolish vb abschaffen [4]

abortion n Abtreibung f; **She had an abortion.** Sie hat abgetrieben.

about prep, adv **①** (concerning) wegen ▷ I'm phoning about tomorrow's meeting. Ich rufe wegen des morgigen Treffens an. **②** (approximately) etwa ▷ It takes about ten hours. Es dauert etwa zehn Stunden. ▷ about a hundred pounds etwa hundert Pfund ▷ at about eleven o'clock um etwa elf Uhr **③** (around) in ... herum ▷ to walk about the town in der Stadt herumlaufen **④** über ▷ a book about London ein Buch über London; **to be about to do something** gerade etwas tun wollen [94]; **to talk about something** über etwas reden [54]; **What's the film about?** Wovon handelt der Film?; **How about going to the cinema?** Wie wär's, wenn wir ins Kino gingen?

above prep, adv über ▷ above forty degrees über vierzig Grad

Use the accusative to express movement or a change of place. Use the dative when there is no change of place.

▷ He put his hands above his head. Er hielt die Hände über den Kopf. ▷ It's in the cupboard above the sink. Es ist im Schrank über der Spüle.; **the flat above** die Wohnung darüber; **mentioned above** oben erwähnt; **above all** vor allem

abroad adv **①** im Ausland ▷ She lives abroad. Sie lebt im Ausland. **②** ins Ausland ▷ to go abroad ins Ausland gehen

absence n Abwesenheit f

absent adj abwesend

absent-minded adj zerstreut ▷ *She's a bit absent-minded.* Sie ist etwas zerstreut.

absolutely adv ❶ (*completely*) völlig ▷ *Beate's absolutely right.* Beate hat völlig recht. ❷ ganz sicher ▷ *Do you think it's a good idea? — Absolutely!* Meinst du, das ist eine gute Idee? — Ganz sicher!

abuse n (*of power, drugs*) Missbrauch m; **abuse of prisoners** die Gefangenenmisshandlung; **to shout abuse at somebody** jemanden beschimpfen [18]
▶vb missbrauchen [49]; **to abuse drugs** Drogen missbrauchen [49]; **abused children** misshandelte Kinder

academic adj **the academic year** das Studienjahr

academy n Akademie f ▷ *a military academy* eine Militärakademie

accelerate vb beschleunigen [7]

accelerator n Gaspedal nt (pl Gaspedale)

accent n Akzent m (pl Akzente) ▷ *He's got a German accent.* Er hat einen deutschen Akzent.

accept vb annehmen [1]

acceptable adj annehmbar

access n ❶ Zugang m ▷ *He has access to confidential information.* Er hat Zugang zu vertraulichen Informationen. ❷ Besuchsrecht nt ▷ *The father has access to the children.* Der Vater hat ein Besuchsrecht.

accessory n **fashion accessories** die Modeartikel mpl

accident n Unfall m (pl Unfälle) ▷ *to have an accident* einen Unfall haben; **by accident** (1) (*by mistake*) versehentlich ▷ *The burglar killed him by accident.* Der Einbrecher hat ihn versehentlich getötet. (2) (*by chance*) zufällig ▷ *She met him by accident.* Sie ist ihm zufällig begegnet.

accidental adj zufällig

accommodation n Unterkunft f (pl Unterkünfte)

accompany vb begleiten [2]

according to prep laut ▷ *According to him, everyone had gone.* Laut ihm waren alle weggegangen.

account n ❶ Konto nt (pl Konten) ▷ *a bank account* ein Bankkonto; **to do the accounts** die Buchführung machen [48] ❷ (*report*) Bericht m (pl Berichte); **He gave a detailed account of what happened.** Er berichtete genau, was passiert war.; **to take something into account** etwas berücksichtigen [7]; **on account of** wegen; **to account for** erklären [19]

accountant n ❶ (*bookkeeper*) Buchhalter m (pl Buchhalter), Buchhalterin f ▷ *She's an accountant.* Sie ist Buchhalterin. ❷ (*tax consultant*) Steuerberater m (pl Steuerberater), Steuerberaterin f

accuracy n Genauigkeit f

accurate adj genau ▷ *accurate information* genaue Information

accurately adv genau

accuse vb **to accuse somebody** (1) jemanden beschuldigen [84] ▷ *She accused me of lying.* Sie beschuldigte mich, ich würde lügen. (2) (*police*) jemanden anklagen [4] ▷ *The police are accusing her of murder.* Die Polizei klagt sie wegen Mordes an.

ace n Ass nt (gen Asses, pl Asse) ▷ *the ace of hearts* das Herzass

ache n Schmerz m (gen Schmerzes, pl Schmerzen) ▷ *I have an ache in my side.* Ich habe Schmerzen in der Seite.
▶vb wehtun [81] ▷ *My leg's aching.* Mein Bein tut weh.

achieve vb ❶ (*an aim*) erreichen [19] ❷ (*victory*) erringen (imperf errang, perf hat errungen)

achievement n Leistung f ▷ *That was quite an achievement.* Das war eine Leistung.

acid n Säure f; **acid rain** saurer Regen m
acne n Akne f ▷ *She's got acne.* Sie hat Akne.
acquit vb **to be acquitted** freigesprochen werden [**91**]
acrobat n Akrobat m (gen Akrobaten, pl Akrobaten), Akrobatin f ▷ *He's an acrobat.* Er ist Akrobat.
across prep, adv über

Use the accusative to express movement or a change of place.
Use the dative when there is no change of place.

▷ *the shop across the road* der Laden über der Straße ▷ *to walk across the road* über die Straße gehen; **across from** (*opposite*) gegenüber
act vb ❶ (*in play, film*) spielen [**38**] ▷ *He acts well.* Er spielt gut. ▷ *She's playing the part of Juliet.* Sie spielt die Rolle der Julia. ❷ (*take action*) handeln [**34**] ▷ *The police acted quickly.* Die Polizei hat schnell gehandelt.; **She acts as his interpreter.** Sie übersetzt für ihn.
▶ n (*in play*) Akt m (pl Akte) ▷ *in the first act* im ersten Akt
action n Handlung f; **The film was full of action.** In dem Film gab es viel Action.; **to take firm action against somebody** hart gegen jemanden vorgehen [**29**]
active adj aktiv ▷ *He's a very active person.* Er ist ein sehr aktiver Mensch. ▷ *an active volcano* ein aktiver Vulkan
activity n Tätigkeit f; **outdoor activities** die Aktivitäten im Freien
actor n Schauspieler m (pl Schauspieler) ▷ *His father is a well-known actor.* Sein Vater ist ein bekannter Schauspieler.
actress n Schauspielerin f ▷ *Her sister is a well-known actress.* Ihre Schwester ist eine bekannte Schauspielerin.
actual adj wirklich ▷ *The film is based on actual events.* Der Film basiert auf wirklichen Begebenheiten.

Be careful not to translate *actual* by **aktuell**.

actually adv ❶ (*really*) wirklich ▷ *Did it actually happen?* Ist das wirklich passiert? ❷ (*in fact*) eigentlich ▷ *Actually, I don't know him at all.* Eigentlich kenne ich ihn überhaupt nicht.
AD abbr n. Chr. (= nach Christus) ▷ *in 800 AD* im Jahre 800 n. Chr.
ad n ❶ (*in paper*) Anzeige f ❷ (*on TV, radio*) Werbung f
adapt vb bearbeiten [**2**] ▷ *His novel was adapted for television.* Sein Roman wurde fürs Fernsehen bearbeitet.; **to adapt to something** (*get used to*) sich in etwas eingewöhnen [**7**]
adaptor n Adapter m (pl Adapter)
add vb hinzufügen [**15**] ▷ *Add two eggs to the mixture.* Fügen Sie dem Teig zwei Eier hinzu.; **to add up** zusammenzählen [**4**]
addict n (*drug addict*) Süchtige m (gen Süchtigen, pl Süchtigen), Süchtige f (gen Süchtigen) ▷ *an addict* (*man*) ein Süchtiger; **Martin's a football addict.** Martin ist ein Fußballnarr.
addicted adj süchtig ▷ *She's addicted to coffee.* Sie ist kaffeesüchtig. ▷ *He's addicted to YouTube.* Er ist süchtig nach YouTube.
addition n **in addition** außerdem; **in addition to** zusätzlich zu
address n Adresse f ▷ *What's your address?* Wie ist Ihre Adresse?
▶ vb ❶ (*envelope, letter*) adressieren [**76**] ❷ (*speak to*) sprechen [**70**] zu ▷ *She addressed the audience.* Sie sprach zum Publikum.
ADHD abbr (= Attention Deficit Hyperactivity Disorder) ADHS (= Aufmerksamkeitsdefizit-Hyperaktivitätsstörung)
adjective n Adjektiv nt (pl Adjektive)
adjust vb einstellen [**4**] ▷ *He adjusted the seat to the right height.* Er stellte den Stuhl auf die richtige Höhe ein.; **to adjust to something** (*get used to*) sich in etwas eingewöhnen [**7**]

adjustable adj verstellbar
administration n Verwaltung f
admiral n Admiral m (pl Admirale)
admire vb bewundern [88]
admission n Eintritt m ▷ 'admission free' 'Eintritt frei'
admit vb zugeben [28] ▷ I must admit that ... Ich muss zugeben, dass ... ▷ He admitted that he'd done it. Er gab zu, dass er es getan hat.
adolescent n Jugendliche m (gen Jugendlichen, pl Jugendlichen), Jugendliche f (gen Jugendlichen) ▷ an adolescent (male) ein Jugendlicher
adopt vb ❶ (child) adoptieren [76] ▷ Phil was adopted. Phil wurde adoptiert. ❷ (idea) annehmen [1] ▷ Her suggestion was adopted. Ihr Vorschlag wurde angenommen.
adopted adj adoptiert; **an adopted son** ein Adoptivsohn
adoption n Adoption f
adore vb bewundern [88]
Adriatic Sea n Adria f
adult n Erwachsene m (gen Erwachsenen, pl Erwachsenen), Erwachsene f (gen Erwachsenen) ▷ an adult (man) ein Erwachsener; **adult education** die Erwachsenenbildung
advance vb ❶ (move forward) vorrücken [4] (perf ist vorgerückt) ▷ The troops are advancing. Die Truppen rücken vor. ❷ (progress) Fortschritte machen [48] ▷ Technology has advanced a lot. Die Technik hat große Fortschritte gemacht.
▶ n **in advance** vorher
advanced adj fortgeschritten
advantage n Vorteil m (pl Vorteile) ▷ Going to university has many advantages. Das Studium hat viele Vorteile.; **to take advantage of something** etwas ausnutzen [4]; **to take advantage of somebody** jemanden ausnutzen [4]

adventure n Abenteuer nt (pl Abenteuer)
adverb n Adverb nt (pl Adverbien)
advert n see advertisement
advertise vb annoncieren [76] ▷ Jobs are advertised in the paper. Stellenangebote werden in der Zeitung annonciert.
advertisement n ❶ (in paper) Anzeige f ❷ (on TV, radio) Werbung f
advertising n Werbung f ▷ She works in advertising. Sie ist in der Werbung tätig. ▷ They've increased spending on advertising. Sie geben mehr Geld für Werbung aus.
advice n Rat m ▷ **to give somebody advice** jemandem einen Rat geben; **a piece of advice** ein Rat
advise vb raten (pres rät, imperf riet, perf hat geraten) ▷ He advised me to wait. Er riet mir zu warten. ▷ He advised me not to go. Er hat mir geraten, nicht zu gehen.
aerial n Antenne f
aerobics npl Aerobic nt ▷ I'm going to aerobics tonight. Ich mache heute Abend Aerobic.
aeroplane n Flugzeug nt (pl Flugzeuge)
aerosol n Spray m (pl Sprays)
affair n ❶ (romantic) Verhältnis nt (gen Verhältnisses, pl Verhältnisse) ▷ **to have an affair with somebody** mit jemandem ein Verhältnis haben ❷ (event) Angelegenheit f
affect vb ❶ (influence) beeinflussen [7] ▷ Does junk food affect children's behaviour? Beeinflusst Junkfood das Verhalten von Kindern? ❷ (have effect on) beeinträchtigen [84] ▷ The weather has affected sales. Das Wetter hat den Absatz beeinträchtigt.
affectionate adj liebevoll
afford vb sich leisten [2] ▷ I can't afford a new pair of jeans. Ich kann mir keine neue Jeans leisten. ▷ We can't afford to

afraid adj to be afraid of something vor etwas Angst haben [32]; **I'm afraid I can't come.** Ich kann leider nicht kommen.; **I'm afraid so.** Ja, leider..; **I'm afraid not.** Leider nicht.

Africa n Afrika nt; **from Africa** aus Afrika; **to Africa** nach Afrika

African adj afrikanisch
▶ n Afrikaner m (pl Afrikaner), Afrikanerin f

after prep, adv, conj nach ▷ after dinner nach dem Abendessen ▷ He ran after me. Er rannte mir nach.; **soon after** kurz danach; **After I'd had a rest** nachdem ich mich ausgeruht hatte; **After eating I left.** Nachdem ich gegessen hatte, ging ich.; **after all** schließlich

afternoon n Nachmittag m (pl Nachmittage) ▷ three o'clock in the afternoon drei Uhr nachmittags ▷ this afternoon heute Nachmittag ▷ on Saturday afternoon Samstag Nachmittag

afters npl Nachtisch msg (pl Nachtische)

aftershave n Aftershave nt (pl Aftershaves)

afterwards adv danach ▷ She left not long afterwards. Sie ging kurz danach.

again adv ❶ (once more) wieder ▷ They're friends again. Sie sind wieder Freunde. ❷ (one more time) noch einmal ▷ Can you tell me again? Kannst du mir das noch einmal sagen?; **not ... again** nie mehr; **Do it again!** Mach's noch mal!; **again and again** immer wieder

against prep gegen ▷ He leant against the wall. Er lehnte gegen die Wand. ▷ I'm against animal testing. Ich bin gegen Tierversuche.

age n Alter nt (pl Alter) ▷ an age limit eine Altersgrenze; **at the age of sixteen** mit sechzehn; **I haven't seen her for ages.** Ich habe sie schon ewig nicht mehr gesehen.

agenda n Tagesordnung f

agent n Agent m (gen Agenten, pl Agenten), Agentin f; **an estate agent** ein Immobilienmakler; **a travel agent** ein Reisebüro

aggressive adj aggressiv

ago adv **two days ago** vor zwei Tagen; **two years ago** vor zwei Jahren; **not long ago** vor Kurzem; **How long ago did it happen?** Wie lange ist das her?

agony n **He was in agony.** Er hatte furchtbare Schmerzen.

agree vb **to agree with somebody** jemandem zustimmen [4]; **to agree to do something** bereit sein [65], etwas zu tun; **to agree that ...** (admit) zugeben [28], dass ...; **Garlic doesn't agree with me.** Ich vertrage Knoblauch nicht.

agreement n Abmachung f; **to be in agreement** übereinstimmen [4]

agricultural adj landwirtschaftlich

agriculture n Landwirtschaft f

ahead adv voraus ▷ We sent him on ahead. Wir schickten ihn voraus.; **The Germans are five points ahead.** Die Deutschen führen mit fünf Punkten.; **She looked straight ahead.** Sie sah geradeaus.; **ahead of time** vorzeitig; **to plan ahead** vorausplanen [15]; **Go ahead!** Ja bitte!

AI abbr (= artificial intelligence) KI f (= künstliche Intelligenz)

aid n **in aid of charity** für wohltätige Zwecke

AIDS n Aids nt (gen Aids) ▷ He died of AIDS. Er starb an Aids.

aim vb **to aim at** zielen [38] auf; **The film is aimed at children.** Der Film ist für Kinder gedacht.; **to aim to do something** beabsichtigen [84], etwas zu tun
▶ n Ziel nt (pl Ziele) ▷ The aim of the festival

air n Luft f (pl Lüfte); **to get some fresh air** frische Luft schnappen [**48**]; **by air** mit dem Flugzeug
air-conditioned adj mit Klimaanlage
air conditioning n Klimaanlage f
Air Force n Luftwaffe f
air hostess n Stewardess f (pl Stewardessen) ▷ *She's an air hostess.* Sie ist Stewardess.
airline n Fluggesellschaft f
airmail n **by airmail** mit Luftpost
airplane n (US) Flugzeug nt (pl Flugzeuge)
airport n Flughafen m (pl Flughäfen)
aisle n ❶ (in church) Mittelgang m (pl Mittelgänge) ❷ (in plane) Gang m (pl Gänge) ▷ *an aisle seat* ein Platz am Gang
alarm n (warning) Alarm m (pl Alarme); **a fire alarm** ein Feueralarm
alarm clock n Wecker m (pl Wecker)
album n Album nt (pl Alben)
alcohol n Alkohol m
alcoholic n Alkoholiker m (pl Alkoholiker), Alkoholikerin f ▷ *He's an alcoholic.* Er ist Alkoholiker.
▶ adj alkoholisch ▷ *alcoholic drinks* alkoholische Getränke
alert adj ❶ (bright) aufgeweckt ▷ *He's a very alert baby.* Er ist ein sehr aufgewecktes Baby. ❷ (paying attention) wachsam ▷ *We must stay alert.* Wir müssen wachsam bleiben.
A levels npl Abitur nt sg
* Germans take their **Abitur** at the age
* of 19. The students sit examinations in
* a variety of subjects to attain an
* overall grade. If you pass, you have the
* right to apply for a place at university.
alike adv **to look alike** sich ähnlich sehen [**64**]
alive adj am Leben
all adj, pron, adv ❶ alle ▷ *all the books* alle Bücher; **all the time** die ganze Zeit; **all day** den ganzen Tag ❷ alles ▷ *He ate it all.* Er hat alles gegessen. ▷ *I ate all of it.* Ich habe alles gegessen.; **All of us went.** Wir sind alle hingegangen.; **after all** schließlich; **all alone** ganz allein; **not at all** überhaupt nicht; **The score is five all.** Es steht fünf zu fünf.
allergic adj allergisch; **to be allergic to something** allergisch gegen etwas sein [**65**]
allergy n Allergie f (pl Allergien) ▷ *Have you got any allergies?* Hast du Allergien?
allow vb **to be allowed to do something** etwas tun dürfen [**16**]; **to allow somebody to do something** jemandem erlauben [**19**], etwas zu tun
all right adv ❶ (okay) gut ▷ *Everything turned out all right.* Alles ist gut gegangen.; **Are you all right?** Bist du in Ordnung? ❷ (not bad) okay ▷ *The film was all right.* Der Film war okay. ❸ (when agreeing) einverstanden ▷ *We'll talk about it later. — All right.* Wir reden später darüber. — Einverstanden.; **Is that all right with you?** Ist das okay?
almond n Mandel f (pl Mandeln)
almost adv fast ▷ *I've almost finished.* Ich bin fast fertig.
alone adj, adv allein ▷ *She lives alone.* Sie lebt allein.; **to leave somebody alone** jemanden in Ruhe lassen [**42**]; **to leave something alone** etwas nicht anfassen [**31**]
along prep, adv entlang ▷ *Chris was walking along the beach.* Chris ging am Strand entlang.; **all along** die ganze Zeit
aloud adv laut ▷ *He read the poem aloud.* Er las das Gedicht vor.
alphabet n Alphabet nt (pl Alphabete)
Alps npl Alpen fpl
already adv schon ▷ *Liz had already gone.* Liz war schon weg.
also adv auch
▌ Be careful not to translate **also** by the German word **also**.

ENGLISH > GERMAN

alter vb verändern [88]

alternate adj **on alternate days** abwechselnd jeden zweiten Tag

alternative n Alternative f ▷ *Fruit is a healthy alternative to chocolate.* Obst ist eine gesunde Alternative zu Schokolade.; **You have no alternative.** Du hast keine andere Wahl.; **There are several alternatives.** Es gibt mehrere Möglichkeiten.
▶ adj andere ▷ *an alternative solution* eine andere Lösung ▷ *an alternative suggestion* ein anderer Vorschlag; **alternative medicine** die alternative Medizin

alternatively adv **Alternatively, we could just stay at home.** Wir könnten auch zu Hause bleiben.

although conj obwohl ▷ *Although she was tired, she stayed up late.* Obwohl sie müde war, blieb sie lange auf.

altogether adv ❶ (in total) insgesamt ▷ *You owe me twenty pounds altogether.* Du schuldest mir insgesamt zwanzig Pfund. ❷ (completely) ganz ▷ *I'm not altogether happy with your work.* Ich bin mit Ihrer Arbeit nicht ganz zufrieden.

aluminium (US **aluminum**) n Aluminium nt

always adv immer ▷ *He's always moaning.* Er beklagt sich immer.

am vb see **be**

a.m. abbr morgens ▷ *at four a.m.* um vier Uhr morgens

amateur n Amateur m (pl Amateure), Amateurin f ▷ *He's an amateur.* Er ist Amateur.

amaze vb **to be amazed** erstaunt sein [65]

amazing adj ❶ (surprising) erstaunlich ▷ *That's amazing news!* Das sind erstaunliche Neuigkeiten! ❷ (excellent) ausgezeichnet ▷ *Vivian's an amazing cook.* Vivian ist eine ausgezeichnete Köchin.

ambassador n Botschafter m (pl Botschafter), Botschafterin f

ambition n Ehrgeiz m (gen Ehrgeizes)

ambitious adj ehrgeizig ▷ *She's very ambitious.* Sie ist sehr ehrgeizig.

ambulance n Krankenwagen m (pl Krankenwagen)

amenities npl **The hotel has very good amenities.** Das Hotel hat viel zu bieten.

America n Amerika nt; **from America** aus Amerika; **in America** in Amerika; **to America** nach Amerika

American adj amerikanisch ▷ *He's American.* Er ist Amerikaner. ▷ *She's American.* Sie ist Amerikanerin.
▶ n Amerikaner m (pl Amerikaner), Amerikanerin f; **the Americans** die Amerikaner

among prep unter ▷ *I was among friends.* Ich war unter Freunden.; **among other things** unter anderem

amount n ❶ Betrag m (pl Beträge) ▷ *a large amount of money* ein großer Geldbetrag ❷ Menge f ▷ *a huge amount of rice* eine enorme Menge Reis

amp n ❶ (of electricity) Ampere nt (gen Ampere, pl Ampere) ❷ (for hi-fi) Verstärker m (pl Verstärker)

amplifier n (for hi-fi) Verstärker m (pl Verstärker)

amuse vb belustigen [7]; **He was most amused by the story.** Er fand die Geschichte sehr lustig.

amusement n (enjoyment) Vergnügen nt (pl Vergnügen); **amusement arcade** die Spielhalle

an art see **a**

analyse vb analysieren [76]

analysis n Analyse f

ancestor n Vorfahr m (gen Vorfahren, pl Vorfahren), Vorfahrin f

anchor n Anker m (pl Anker)

ancient adj alt ▷ *This is an ancient custom.* Das ist ein alter Brauch.;

ancient Greece das antike Griechenland; **an ancient monument** ein historisches Denkmal

and *conj* und ▷ *you and me* du und ich ▷ *Two and two are four.* Zwei und zwei gibt vier. ▷ *He talked and talked.* Er redete und redete.; **Please try and come!** Versuche bitte zu kommen!; **better and better** immer besser

angel *n* Engel *m* (*pl* Engel)
▍ Be careful not to translate **angel** by the German word **Angel**.

anger *n* Wut *f*

angle *n* Winkel *m* (*pl* Winkel)

angry *adj* böse ▷ *Dad looks very angry.* Papa sieht sehr böse aus.; **to be angry with somebody** mit jemandem böse sein [65]; **to get angry** wütend werden [91]

animal *n* Tier *nt* (*pl* Tiere)

ankle *n* Fußknöchel *m* (*pl* Fußknöchel)

anniversary *n* Jahrestag *m* (*pl* Jahrestage); **wedding anniversary** der Hochzeitstag

announce *vb* ankündigen [4]

announcement *n* Ankündigung *f*

annoy *vb* ärgern [88] ▷ *He's really annoying me.* Er ärgert mich echt.; **to get annoyed** wütend werden [91]

annoying *adj* ärgerlich ▷ *It's really annoying.* Es ist wirklich ärgerlich.

annual *adj* jährlich ▷ *an annual meeting* ein jährliches Treffen

anonymous *adj* anonym

anorak *n* Anorak *m* (*pl* Anoraks)

another *adj*
▍ Use **noch ein** for masculine and neuter nouns, **noch eine** for feminine nouns.

❶ noch ein ▷ *I bought another hat.* Ich habe noch einen Hut gekauft. ▷ *Would you like another piece of cake?* Möchtest du noch ein Stück Kuchen?
noch eine ▷ *Would you like another cup of tea?* Möchten Sie noch eine Tasse Tee?
▍ Use **ein anderer** for masculine, **eine andere** for feminine and **ein anderes** for neuter nouns.

❷ (*different*) ein anderer ▷ *Could you show me another hat?* Könnten Sie mir einen anderen Hut zeigen? eine andere ▷ *My girlfriend goes to another school.* Meine Freundin besucht eine andere Schule.
ein anderes ▷ *Have you got another shirt?* Haben Sie noch ein anderes Hemd?; **another time** ein andermal

answer *vb* beantworten [2] ▷ *Can you answer my question?* Kannst du meine Frage beantworten?; **to answer the phone** ans Telefon gehen [29]; **to answer the door** aufmachen [4]
▶ *n* ❶ (*to question*) Antwort *f* ❷ (*to problem*) Lösung *f*

answering machine *n* Anrufbeantworter *m* (*pl* Anrufbeantworter)

ant *n* Ameise *f*

Antarctic *n* Antarktis *f*

anthem *n* **the national anthem** die Nationalhymne

antibiotic *n* Antibiotikum *nt* (*pl* Antibiotika)

antique *n* (*furniture*) Antiquität *f*

antique shop *n* Antiquitätenladen *m* (*pl* Antiquitätenläden)

antiseptic *n* Antiseptikum *nt* (*pl* Antiseptika)

any *adj, pron, adv*
▍ In most cases 'any' is not translated.
▷ *Would you like any bread?* Möchten Sie Brot? ▷ *Have you got any mineral water?* Haben Sie Mineralwasser?
▍ Use **kein** for 'not any'.
▷ *We haven't got any milk left.* Wir haben keine Milch mehr. ▷ *I haven't got any money.* Ich habe kein Geld. ▷ *I haven't got any books.* Ich habe keine Bücher.
▷ *Sorry, we haven't got any.* Tut mir leid, wir haben keine.; **any more (1)** (*additional*) noch etwas ▷ *Would you*

like any more coffee? Möchten Sie noch etwas Kaffee? **(2)** (no longer) nicht mehr ▷ I don't love him any more. Ich liebe ihn nicht mehr.

anybody pron ❶ (in question) jemand ▷ Has anybody got a pen? Hat jemand etwas zum Schreiben? ❷ (no matter who) jeder ▷ Anybody can learn to swim. Jeder kann schwimmen lernen.

■ Use **niemand** for 'not ... anybody'. ▷ I can't see anybody. Ich kann niemanden sehen.

anyhow adv sowieso

anyone pron ❶ (in question) jemand ❷ (no matter who) jeder

anything pron ❶ (in question) etwas ▷ Would you like anything to eat? Möchtest du etwas zu essen? ❷ (no matter what) alles ▷ Anything could happen. Alles könnte passieren.

■ Use **nichts** for 'not ... anything'. ▷ I can't hear anything. Ich kann nichts hören.

anyway adv sowieso ▷ He doesn't want to go out and anyway he's not allowed. Er will nicht ausgehen, und er darf es sowieso auch nicht.

anywhere adv ❶ (in question) irgendwo ▷ Have you seen my coat anywhere? Hast du irgendwo meinen Mantel gesehen? ❷ überall ▷ You can buy stamps almost anywhere. Man kann fast überall Briefmarken kaufen.

■ Use **nirgends** for 'not ... anywhere'. ❸ nirgends ▷ I can't find it anywhere. Ich kann es nirgends finden.

apart adv The two towns are ten kilometres apart. Die zwei Städte liegen zehn Kilometer voneinander entfernt.; **apart from** abgesehen von

apartment n Wohnung f

apologize vb sich entschuldigen [18] ▷ He apologized for being late. Er entschuldigte sich für sein Zuspätkommen.; **I apologize!** Ich bitte um Entschuldigung!

apology n Entschuldigung f

apostrophe n Apostroph m (pl Apostrophe)

app n (= application) App f (pl Apps)

apparent adj offensichtlich

apparently adv offensichtlich

appeal vb bitten [9] ▷ They appealed for help. Sie baten um Hilfe.; **to appeal to somebody** (attract) jemanden reizen [36] ▶ n Aufruf m (pl Aufrufe)

appear vb ❶ (come into view) kommen [40] ▷ The bus appeared around the corner. Der Bus kam um die Ecke.; **to appear on TV** im Fernsehen auftreten [79] ❷ (seem) scheinen [57] ▷ She appeared to be asleep. Sie schien zu schlafen.

appendicitis n Blinddarmentzündung f

appetite n Appetit m

applaud vb klatschen [48]

applause n Beifall m

apple n Apfel m (pl Äpfel); **an apple tree** ein Apfelbaum m

applicant n Bewerber m (pl Bewerber), Bewerberin f ▷ There were a hundred applicants for the job. Es gab hundert Bewerber für die Stelle.

application n a job application eine Bewerbung

application form n ❶ (for job) Bewerbungsformular nt (pl Bewerbungsformulare) ❷ (for university) Anmeldeformular nt (pl Anmeldeformulare)

apply vb to apply for a job sich für eine Stelle bewerben [90]; **to apply to** (be relevant) zutreffen [78] auf

appointment n Termin m (pl Termine) ▷ I've got a dental appointment. Ich habe einen Zahnarzttermin.

appreciate vb zu schätzen wissen [93] ▷ I really appreciate your help. Ich weiß deine Hilfe wirklich zu schätzen.

apprentice n ❶ Lehrling m (pl Lehrlinge) (old)

■ **der Lehrling** is also used for women.

▷ She is an apprentice. Sie ist Lehrling. ❷ **Auszubildende** m (gen Auszubildenden, pl Auszubildenden), **Auszubildende** f (gen Auszubildenden) ▷ He is an apprentice. Er is Auszubildender.

approach vb ❶ (get nearer to) sich nähern [88] ▷ He approached the house. Er näherte sich dem Haus. ❷ (tackle) angehen [29] ▷ to approach a problem ein Problem angehen

appropriate adj passend ▷ That dress isn't very appropriate for an interview. Dieses Kleid ist für ein Vorstellungsgespräch nicht sehr passend.

approval n Zustimmung f

approve vb to approve of gutheißen; **They didn't approve of his girlfriend.** Sie hatten etwas gegen seine Freundin.

approximate adj ungefähr

apricot n Aprikose f

April n April m ▷ in April im April; **April Fool's Day** der erste April; **April Fool!** April, April!

apron n Schürze f

Aquarius n Wassermann m ▷ I'm Aquarius. Ich bin Wassermann.

Arab adj arabisch ▷ the Arab countries die arabischen Länder
▶ n Araber m (pl Araber), Araberin f

Arabic adj arabisch

arch n Bogen m (pl Bögen)

archaeologist (US **archeologist**) n Archäologe m (gen Archäologen, pl Archäologen), Archäologin f ▷ She's an archaeologist. Sie ist Archäologin.

archaeology (US **archeology**) n Archäologie f

archbishop n Erzbischof m (pl Erzbischöfe)

archeologist n (US) Archäologe m (gen Archäologen, pl Archäologen), Archäologin f

archeology n (US) Archäologie f

architect n Architekt m (gen Architekten, pl Architekten), Architektin f ▷ She's an architect. Sie ist Architektin.

architecture n Architektur f

Arctic n Arktis f

are vb see **be**

area n ❶ Gegend f ▷ She lives in the London area. Sie lebt in der Gegend von London. ❷ Viertel nt (pl Viertel) ▷ my favourite area of London mein Lieblingsviertel von London ❸ Fläche f ▷ an area of one thousand square metres eine Fläche von eintausend Quadratmetern

Argentina n Argentinien nt; **from Argentina** aus Argentinien

Argentinian adj argentinisch

argue vb streiten (imperf stritt, perf hat gestritten) ▷ They never stop arguing. Sie streiten dauernd.

argument n Streit m (pl Streite); **to have an argument** Streit haben [32]

Aries n Widder m ▷ I'm Aries. Ich bin Widder.

arm n Arm m (pl Arme)

armchair n Sessel m (pl Sessel)

army n Armee f (pl Armeen)

around prep, adv ❶ um ▷ around the corner um die Ecke ❷ (approximately) etwa ▷ around a hundred pounds etwa einhundert Pfund ❸ (date, time) gegen ▷ around eight p.m. gegen acht Uhr abends; **around here (1)** (nearby) hier in der Nähe ▷ Is there a chemist's around here? Gibt es hier in der Nähe eine Apotheke? **(2)** (in this area) hier in der Gegend ▷ He lives around here. Er wohnt hier in der Gegend.

arrange vb **to arrange to do something** verabreden [84], etwas zu tun; **to arrange a meeting** ein Treffen ausmachen [48]; **to arrange a party** eine Party vorbereiten [2]

ENGLISH > GERMAN

arrangement n (plan) Plan m (pl Pläne); **They made arrangements to go out on Friday night.** Sie haben verabredet, am Freitagabend auszugehen.

arrest vb verhaften [2] ▷ *The police have arrested five people.* Die Polizei hat fünf Leute verhaftet.
▶ n Verhaftung f; **You're under arrest!** Sie sind verhaftet!

arrival n Ankunft f (pl Ankünfte)

arrive vb ankommen [40] ▷ *I arrived at five o'clock.* Ich bin um fünf Uhr angekommen.

arrogant adj arrogant

arrow n Pfeil m (pl Pfeile)

art n Kunst f (pl Künste)

artery n Arterie f

art gallery n Kunstgalerie f

article n Artikel m (pl Artikel)
▷ *a newspaper article* ein Zeitungsartikel

artificial adj künstlich

artist n Künstler m (pl Künstler), Künstlerin f ▷ *She's an artist.* Sie ist Künstlerin.

artistic adj künstlerisch

as conj, adv ❶ (while) als ▷ *He came in as I was leaving.* Er kam herein, als ich gehen wollte.; **He works as a waiter in the holidays.** In den Ferien jobbt er als Kellner. ❷ (since) da ▷ *As it's Sunday, you can have a lie-in.* Da es Sonntag ist, kannst du ausschlafen.; **as ... as** so ... wie; **as much ... as** so viel ... wie; **as soon as possible** sobald wie möglich; **as from tomorrow** ab morgen; **as if** ob; **as though** als ob

Note that **als ob** is followed by the subjunctive.

▷ *She acted as though she hadn't seen me.* Sie tat so, als ob sie mich nicht sähe.

ash n Asche f

ashamed adj **to be ashamed** sich schämen [38]

ashtray n Aschenbecher m (pl Aschenbecher)

287 | **assure**

Asia n Asien nt; **from Asia** aus Asien

Asian adj asiatisch ▷ *He's Asian.* Er ist Asiate. ▷ *She's Asian.* Sie ist Asiatin.
▶ n Asiate m (gen Asiaten, pl Asiaten), Asiatin f

ask vb ❶ (inquire, request) fragen [38]
▷ *'Have you finished?' she asked.* 'Bist du fertig?' fragte sie.; **to ask somebody something** jemanden etwas fragen [38]; **to ask for something** um etwas bitten [9]; **to ask somebody to do something** jemanden bitten [9], etwas zu tun; **to ask about something** sich nach etwas erkundigen [19]; **to ask somebody a question** jemanden etwas fragen [38] ❷ (invite) einladen (pres lädt ein, imperf lud ein, perf hat eingeladen) ▷ *Have you asked Matthew to the party?* Hast du Matthew zur Party eingeladen?; **He asked her out.** (on a date) Er hat sie um ein Rendezvous gebeten.

asleep adj **to be asleep** schlafen [58]; **to fall asleep** einschlafen [58]

asparagus n Spargel m (pl Spargel)

aspirin n Schmerztablette f

assembly n (in school) Versammlung f

assignment n (in school) Referat nt (pl Referate)

assistance n Hilfe f

assistant n ❶ (in shop) Verkäufer m (pl Verkäufer), Verkäuferin f ❷ (helper) Assistent m (gen Assistenten, pl Assistenten), Assistentin f

association n Verband m (pl Verbände)

assortment n ❶ (choice) Auswahl f
▷ *an assortment of cheeses* eine Auswahl an Käse ❷ (mixture) Mischung f ▷ *an assortment of biscuits* eine Keksmischung

assume vb annehmen [1] ▷ *I assume she won't be coming.* Ich nehme an, dass sie nicht kommt.

assure vb versichern [88] ▷ *He assured me he was coming.* Er versicherte mir, dass er kommt.

asthma n Asthma nt ▷ *I've got asthma.* Ich habe Asthma.
astonishing adj erstaunlich
astrology n Astrologie f
astronaut n Astronaut m (gen Astronauten, pl Astronauten), Astronautin f
astronomy n Astronomie f
asylum n Asyl nt ▷ *to ask for asylum* um Asyl bitten
asylum seeker n Asylbewerber m (pl Asylbewerber), Asylbewerberin f
at prep ❶ um ▷ *at four o'clock* um vier Uhr ❷ an ▷ *at Christmas* an Weihnachten ▷ *What are you doing at the weekend?* Was machst du am Wochenende?; **at night** nachts ❸ mit ▷ *at fifty kilometres per hour* mit fünfzig Stundenkilometern ❹ in ▷ *at school* in der Schule ▷ *at the office* im Büro; **at home** zu Hause; **two at a time** jeweils zwei; **at the races** beim Pferderennen
▶ n (@ symbol) At-Zeichen nt (pl At-Zeichen)
ate vb see **eat**
Athens n Athen nt
athlete n Athlet m (gen Athleten, pl Athleten), Athletin f
athletic adj athletisch
athletics n Leichtathletik f ▷ *I like watching the athletics on TV.* Ich sehe mir im Fernsehen gern Leichtathletik an.
Atlantic n Atlantik m
atlas n Atlas m (gen Atlasses, pl Atlanten)
atmosphere n Atmosphäre f
atom n Atom nt (pl Atome)
attach vb festbinden (imperf band fest, perf hat festgebunden) ▷ *They attached a rope to the car.* Sie banden ein Seil am Auto fest.; **Please find attached ...** Anbei erhalten Sie ...
attached adj **to be attached to somebody** an jemandem hängen [35]
attack vb angreifen (imperf griff an, perf hat angegriffen) ▷ *The dog attacked me.*

Der Hund hat mich angegriffen.
▶ n Angriff m (pl Angriffe)
attempt n Versuch m (pl Versuche) ▷ *She gave up after several attempts.* Sie gab nach mehreren Versuchen auf.
▶ vb versuchen [**84**]; **to attempt to do something** versuchen [**84**], etwas zu tun
attend vb teilnehmen [**52**] ▷ *to attend a meeting* an einem Treffen teilnehmen
attention n Aufmerksamkeit f; **to pay attention to something** auf etwas achten [**2**]
attic n Speicher m (pl Speicher)
attitude n Einstellung f ▷ *I really don't like your attitude!* Mir gefällt deine Einstellung nicht!
attorney n (US) Rechtsanwalt m (pl Rechtsanwälte), Rechtsanwältin f ▷ *My mother's an attorney.* Meine Mutter ist Rechtsanwältin.
attract vb anziehen [**96**] ▷ *The Lake District attracts lots of tourists.* Der Lake District zieht viele Touristen an.
attraction n Attraktion f ▷ *a tourist attraction* eine Touristenattraktion
attractive adj attraktiv ▷ *She's very attractive.* Sie ist sehr attraktiv.
aubergine n Aubergine f
auction n Auktion f
audience n (in theatre) Zuschauer mpl ▷ *The audience clapped.* Die Zuschauer klatschten.
August n August m ▷ *in August* im August
aunt n Tante f ▷ *my aunt* meine Tante
aunty n Tante f ▷ *my aunty* meine Tante
au pair n Au-pair-Mädchen nt (pl Au-pair-Mädchen) ▷ *She's an au pair.* Sie ist Au-pair-Mädchen.
Australia n Australien nt
Australian adj australisch ▷ *He's Australian.* Er ist Australier. ▷ *She's Australian.* Sie ist Australierin.

ENGLISH > GERMAN

▶ *n* Australier *m* (*pl* Australier), Australierin *f*

Austria *n* Österreich *nt*; **from Austria** aus Österreich; **in Austria** in Österreich; **to Austria** nach Österreich

Austrian *adj* österreichisch ▷ *He's Austrian.* Er ist Österreicher. ▷ *She's Austrian.* Sie ist Österreicherin.
▶ *n* Österreicher *m* (*pl* Österreicher), Österreicherin *f*; **the Austrians** die Österreicher

author *n* Autor *m* (*pl* Autoren), Autorin *f* ▷ *She's a famous author.* Sie ist eine berühmte Autorin.

autistic *adj* autistisch

autobiography *n* Autobiografie *f*

autograph *n* Autogramm *nt* (*pl* Autogramme) ▷ *May I have your autograph?* Kann ich Ihr Autogramm haben?

automatic *adj* automatisch ▷ *an automatic door* eine automatische Tür

automatically *adv* automatisch

autumn *n* Herbst *m* (*pl* Herbste) ▷ *in autumn* im Herbst

availability *n* (*of goods*) Erhältlichkeit *f*; **subject to availability** falls vorrätig

available *adj* erhältlich ▷ *Brochures are available on request.* Prospekte sind auf Anfrage erhältlich.; **Is Mr Cooke available today?** Ist Herr Cooke heute zu sprechen?

avalanche *n* Lawine *f*

avatar *n* Avatar *m* (*pl* Avatars)

avenue *n* Allee *f*

average *n* Durchschnitt *m* (*pl* Durchschnitte) ▷ *on average* im Durchschnitt
▶ *adj* durchschnittlich ▷ *the average price* der durchschnittliche Preis

avocado *n* Avocado *f* (*pl* Avocados)

avoid *vb* ❶ meiden (*imperf* mied, *perf* hat gemieden) ▷ *He avoids her when she's in a bad mood.* Er meidet sie, wenn sie schlechte Laune hat. ❷ vermeiden ▷ *You should avoid going out on your own at night.* Du solltest vermeiden, nachts allein auszugehen.

awake *adj* **to be awake** wach sein [65]

award *n* Preis *m* (*pl* Preise) ▷ *He's won an award.* Er hat einen Preis bekommen. ▷ *the award for the best actor* der Preis für den besten Schauspieler

aware *adj* **to be aware that ...** sich bewusst sein [65], dass ... [37]; **to be aware of something** etwas merken [38]; **not that I am aware of** nicht dass ich wüsste

away *adj*, *adv* (*not here*) weg ▷ *Felix is away today.* Felix ist heute weg. ▷ *He's away for a week.* Er ist eine Woche lang weg.; **The town's two kilometres away.** Die Stadt ist zwei Kilometer entfernt.; **The coast is two hours away by car.** Zur Küste sind es mit dem Auto zwei Stunden.; **Go away!** Geh weg!

away match *n* Auswärtsspiel *nt* (*pl* Auswärtsspiele) ▷ *Our team has an away match this week.* Unsere Mannschaft hat diese Woche ein Auswärtsspiel.

awful *adj* schrecklich ▷ *That's awful!* Das ist schrecklich!; **an awful lot of ...** furchtbar viel ...

awkward *adj* ❶ (*difficult*) schwierig ▷ *an awkward situation* eine schwierige Situation ▷ *It's a bit awkward for me to come and see you.* Es ist für mich etwas schwierig, dich zu besuchen.
❷ (*embarrassing*) unangenehm ▷ *an awkward question* eine unangenehme Frage

axe *n* Axt *f* (*pl* Äxte)

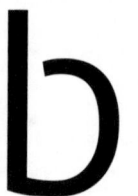

baby n Baby nt (pl Babys)
babysit vb babysitten [2] ▷ Veronika is babysitting for her friend. Veronika babysittet bei ihrer Freundin.
babysitter n Babysitter m (pl Babysitter), Babysitterin f
babysitting n Babysitten nt
back n ❶ (of person, horse, book) Rücken m (pl Rücken) ❷ (of page, house) Rückseite f ▷ Write your name on the back. Schreiben Sie Ihren Namen auf die Rückseite.; **in the back of the car** hinten im Auto; **at the back** hinten
▶ adj, adv hintere ▷ the back wheel of my bike das hintere Rad meines Fahrrads; **the back seat** der Rücksitz; **the back door** die Hintertür; **to get back** zurückkommen [40]; **We went there by bus and walked back.** Wir sind mit dem Bus hingefahren und zu Fuß zurückgegangen.; **He's not back yet.** Er ist noch nicht zurück.; **to call somebody back** jemanden zurückrufen [56]
▶ vb **to back somebody** für jemanden sein [65]; **to back a horse** auf ein Pferd setzen [36]; **to back out** einen Rückzieher machen [48]; **to back somebody up** jemanden unterstützen [36]
backache n Rückenschmerzen mpl ▷ to have backache Rückenschmerzen haben
backbone n Rückgrat nt (pl Rückgrate)
backfire vb (go wrong) schiefgehen [29] (imperf ging schief, perf ist schiefgegangen)
background n Hintergrund m (pl Hintergründe) ▷ a house in the background ein Haus im Hintergrund ▷ his family background sein familiärer Hintergrund; **background noise** die Hintergrundgeräusche ntpl
backhand n Rückhand f (pl Rückhände)
backing n (support) Unterstützung f
backpack n Rucksack m (pl Rucksäcke)
backpacker n Wanderer m (pl Wanderer), Wanderin f
back pain n Rückenschmerzen mpl ▷ to have back pain Rückenschmerzen haben
backside n Hintern m (pl Hintern)
backstroke n Rückenschwimmen nt
backup n (support) Unterstützung f; **a backup file** eine Sicherungsdatei
backwards adv zurück ▷ to take a step backwards einen Schritt zurück machen; **to fall backwards** nach hinten fallen [22]
bacon n Speck m ▷ bacon and eggs Eier mit Speck
bad adj ❶ schlecht ▷ a bad film ein schlechter Film ▷ the bad weather das schlechte Wetter ▷ to be in a bad mood schlechte Laune haben ▷ not bad nicht schlecht ▷ That's not bad at all. Das ist gar nicht schlecht.; **to be bad at something** in etwas schlecht sein [65] ❷ (serious) schlimm ▷ a bad accident ein schlimmer Unfall ❸ (naughty) böse

ENGLISH > GERMAN

▷ *You bad boy!* Du böser Junge!; **to go bad** (food) schlecht werden [**91**]; **I feel bad about it.** Das tut mir echt leid.
badge n ❶ (metal) Button m (pl Buttons) ❷ (sticker) Aufkleber m (pl Aufkleber)
badly adv schlecht ▷ *badly paid* schlecht bezahlt; **badly wounded** schwer verletzt; **He's badly in need of some money.** Er braucht dringend Geld.
badminton n Badminton nt ▷ *to play badminton* Badminton spielen
bad-tempered adj **to be bad-tempered (1)** (by nature) griesgrämig sein [**65**] ▷ *He's a really bad-tempered person.* Er ist wirklich ein griesgrämiger Mensch. **(2)** (temporarily) schlechte Laune haben [**32**] ▷ *He was really bad-tempered today.* Er hatte gestern wirklich schlechte Laune.
baffle vb verblüffen [**84**] ▷ *She was baffled.* Sie war verblüfft.
bag n Tasche f; **an old bag** (person) eine alte Schachtel
baggage n Gepäck nt
baggage reclaim n Gepäckausgabe f
bagpipes npl Dudelsack m (pl Dudelsäcke) ▷ *Ed plays the bagpipes.* Ed spielt Dudelsack.
baguette n Baguette nt/f
bake vb backen (pres bäckt, imperf backte, perf hat gebacken) ▷ *to bake a cake* einen Kuchen backen
baker n Bäcker m (pl Bäcker), Bäckerin f ▷ *He's a baker.* Er ist Bäcker.
bakery n Bäckerei f
balance n Gleichgewicht nt ▷ *to lose one's balance* das Gleichgewicht verlieren
▶ vb balancieren [**76**] (perf ist balanciert) ▷ *I balanced on the window ledge.* Ich balancierte auf dem Fensterbrett.; **The boxes were carefully balanced.** Die Kartons befanden sich genau im Gleichgewicht.

balanced adj ausgewogen ▷ *a balanced diet* eine ausgewogene Ernährung
balcony n Balkon m (pl Balkone)
bald adj glatzköpfig; **to be bald** eine Glatze haben [**32**]
ball n Ball m (pl Bälle)
ballet n Ballett nt (pl Ballette)

> Note that you pronounce the 'tt' in German.

▷ *We went to a ballet.* Wir sind ins Ballett gegangen.; **ballet lessons** Ballettstunden
ballet dancer n Balletttänzer m (pl Balletttänzer), Balletttänzerin f
ballet shoes npl Ballettschuhe mpl
balloon n (at parties) Luftballon m (pl Luftballone); **a hot-air balloon** ein Heißluftballon
ballpoint pen n Kugelschreiber m (pl Kugelschreiber)
ban n Verbot nt (pl Verbote)
▶ vb verbieten [**8**] (imperf verbot, perf hat verboten) ▷ *to ban somebody from doing something* jemandem verbieten, etwas zu tun; **She was banned from driving.** Sie bekam Fahrverbot.
banana n Banane f ▷ *a banana skin* eine Bananenschale
band n ❶ (rock band) Band f (pl Bands) ❷ (brass band) Kapelle f
bandage n Verband m (pl Verbände)
▶ vb verbinden (imperf verband, perf hat verbunden) ▷ *She bandaged his arm.* Sie verband ihm den Arm.
Band-Aid® n (US) Heftpflaster nt (pl Heftpflaster)
bang n ❶ Knall m (pl Knalle) ▷ *I heard a loud bang.* Ich habe einen lauten Knall gehört. ❷ Schlag m (pl Schläge) ▷ *a bang on the head* ein Schlag auf den Kopf; **Bang!** Peng!
▶ vb (part of body) anschlagen [**59**] (pres schlägt an, imperf schlug an, perf hat angeschlagen) ▷ *I banged my head.* Ich habe mir den Kopf angeschlagen.; **to**

bang the door die Tür zuknallen [**4**]; **to bang on the door** gegen die Tür hämmern [**34**]

bank n ❶ (financial) Bank f (pl Banken) ❷ (of river, lake) Ufer nt (pl Ufer)

bank on vb sich verlassen [**42**] auf (pres verlässt, imperf verließ, perf hat verlassen)

bank account n Bankkonto nt (pl Bankkonten)

banker n Banker m (pl Banker), Bankerin f

bank holiday n Feiertag m (pl Feiertage)

banknote n Banknote f

bankrupt adj bankrott

bar n ❶ (pub) Bar f (pl Bars) ❷ (counter) Theke f; **a bar of chocolate** eine Tafel Schokolade; **a bar of soap** ein Stück Seife

barbecue n Barbecue nt (pl Barbecues); **We could have a barbecue this evening.** Wir könnten heute Abend grillen.

bare adj nackt

barefoot adj, adv barfuß ▷ They go around barefoot. Sie laufen barfuß herum.

barely adv kaum ▷ I could barely hear her. Ich konnte sie kaum hören.

bargain n Schnäppchen nt (pl Schnäppchen) ▷ It was a bargain! Das war ein Schnäppchen!

barge n Kahn m (pl Kähne)

bark vb bellen [**38**]

barmaid n Bardame f ▷ She's a barmaid. Sie ist Bardame.

barman n Barkeeper m (pl Barkeeper) ▷ He's a barman. Er ist Barkeeper.

barn n Scheune f

barrel n Fass nt (gen Fasses, pl Fässer)

barrier n Schranke f

base n (basis) Basis f (pl Basen) ▷ a good base for a successful career eine gute Basis für eine erfolgreiche Karriere ❷ (of lamp, mountain) Fuß m (gen Fußes, pl Füße) ❸ (of container) Boden m (pl Böden) ❹ (for paint, make-up) Grundlage f ❺ (military) Stützpunkt m (pl Stützpunkte)

baseball n Baseball m ▷ a baseball cap eine Baseballmütze

based adj **based on** basierend auf

basement n Untergeschoss nt (gen Untergeschosses, pl Untergeschosse)

bash vb **to bash something in** etwas einschlagen [**59**]
▶ n **I'll have a bash.** Ich versuch's mal.

basic adj ❶ (knowledge, education) elementar; **basic vocabulary** der Grundwortschatz; **It's a basic model.** Es ist ein Grundmodell. ❷ einfach ▷ The accommodation is pretty basic. Die Unterkunft ist sehr einfach.

basically adv eigentlich ▷ Basically, I just don't like him. Eigentlich mag ich ihn nicht.

basics npl Grundlagen fpl

basin n (washbasin) Waschbecken nt (pl Waschbecken)

basis n **on a daily basis** täglich; **on a regular basis** regelmäßig

basket n Korb m (pl Körbe)

basketball n Basketball m

bass n Bass m (pl Basses, pl Bässe) ▷ He plays bass. Er spielt Bass. ▷ He's a bass. Er singt Bass.; **a bass drum** eine Basstrommel; **a bass guitar** eine Bassgitarre

bassoon n Fagott nt (pl Fagotte) ▷ I play the bassoon. Ich spiele Fagott.

bat n ❶ (for cricket, rounders, table tennis) Schläger m (pl Schläger) ❷ (animal) Fledermaus f (pl Fledermäuse)

bath n ❶ Bad nt (pl Bäder) ▷ a hot bath ein heißes Bad; **to have a bath** baden [**54**] ❷ (bathtub) Badewanne f ▷ There's a spider in the bath. In der Badewanne ist eine Spinne.

bathe vb baden [**54**]

bathroom n Badezimmer nt (pl Badezimmer)
bath towel n Badetuch nt (pl Badetücher)
batter n Pfannkuchenteig m
battery n Batterie f
battle n Schlacht f ▷ *the Battle of Hastings* die Schlacht von Hastings; **It was a battle, but we managed in the end.** Es war ein Kampf, aber wir haben es schließlich geschafft.
bay n Bucht f
BC abbr (= before Christ) v. Chr. (= vor Christus) ▷ *in 200 BC* im Jahre 200 v. Chr.
be vb sein [65] (pres ist, imperf war, perf ist gewesen) ▷ *I'm tired.* Ich bin müde. ▷ *You're late.* Du bist spät dran. ▷ *She's English.* Sie ist Engländerin. ▷ *It's cold.* Es ist kalt. ▷ *It's a nice day.* Es ist ein schöner Tag. ▷ *It's four o'clock.* Es ist vier Uhr. ▷ *I'm fourteen.* Ich bin vierzehn. ▷ *We are all happy.* Wir sind alle glücklich. ▷ *I've been ill.* Ich war krank. ▷ *I've never been to Dresden.* Ich war noch nie in Dresden.; **to be beaten** geschlagen werden [91]

> Questions like 'isn't it?' don't exist in German.
> ▷ *The film was good, wasn't it?* Der Film war gut, nicht wahr?

> You do not translate 'a' when you want to describe somebody's occupation.
> ▷ *She's a doctor.* Sie ist Ärztin.; **I'm cold.** Mir ist kalt.; **I'm hungry.** Ich habe Hunger.

beach n Strand m (pl Strände)
bead n Perle f
beak n Schnabel m (pl Schnäbel)
beam n Strahl m (pl Strahlen)
beans npl Bohnen fpl; **baked beans** gebackene Bohnen
- Few Germans eat baked beans and
- not many shops sell them.
broad beans dicke Bohnen; **green beans** grüne Bohnen; **kidney beans** Kidneybohnen
bean sprouts npl Sojasprossen mpl
bear n Bär m (gen Bären, pl Bären)
▶ vb (endure) ertragen [77] (pres erträgt, imperf ertrug, perf hat ertragen) ▷ *I can't bear it.* Ich kann es nicht ertragen.; **to bear up** sich halten [33]; **Bear up!** Kopf hoch!; **If you would bear with me for a moment ...** Wenn Sie sich bitte einen Moment gedulden könnten ...
beard n Bart m (pl Bärte) ▷ *He's got a beard.* Er hat einen Bart.; **a man with a beard** ein bärtiger Mann
bearded adj bärtig
beat n Rhythmus m (gen Rhythmus, pl Rhythmen)
▶ vb schlagen [59] (pres schlägt, imperf schlug, perf hat geschlagen) ▷ *We beat them three nil.* Wir haben sie drei zu null geschlagen.; **Beat it!** (informal) Hau ab!; **to beat somebody up** jemanden zusammenschlagen [59]
beautiful adj schön
beautifully adv schön
beauty n Schönheit f
became vb see **become**
because conj weil ▷ *I did it because ...* Ich habe es getan, weil ...; **because of** wegen
become vb werden [91] (pres wird, imperf wurde, perf ist geworden) ▷ *He became famous.* Er wurde berühmt.

> Be careful not to translate **to become** by bekommen.

bed n Bett nt (pl Betten) ▷ *in bed* im Bett; **to go to bed** ins Bett gehen [29]; **bed and breakfast** Zimmer nt mit Frühstück nt ▷ *How much is it for bed and breakfast?* Wie viel kostet das Zimmer mit Frühstück?; **We stayed in a bed and breakfast.** Wir waren in einer Frühstückspension.
bedclothes npl Bettwäsche fsg
bedding n Bettzeug nt

bedroom n Schlafzimmer nt (pl Schlafzimmer)

bedsit n **She lives in a bedsit.** Sie wohnt in einem möblierten Zimmer nt.

bedspread n Tagesdecke f

bedtime n **Ten o'clock is my usual bedtime.** Ich gehe normalerweise um zehn Uhr ins Bett.; **Bedtime!** Ab ins Bett!

bee n Biene f

beef n Rindfleisch nt; **roast beef** das Roastbeef

beefburger n Frikadelle f

been vb see **be**

beer n Bier nt (pl Biere or Bier)

When ordering more than one beer use the plural form **Bier**.
▷ *Two beers, please!* Zwei Bier bitte!

beetle n Käfer m (pl Käfer)

beetroot n Rote Bete f

before prep, conj, adv ❶ vor ▷ *before Tuesday* vor Dienstag ❷ bevor ▷ *Wash your hands before eating.* Wasch die Hände bevor du isst. ▷ *I'll phone before I leave.* Ich rufe an, bevor ich gehe. ❸ (*already*) schon ▷ *I've seen this film before.* Ich habe diesen Film schon gesehen. ▷ *Have you been to Scotland before?* Warst du schon einmal in Schottland?; **the day before** am Tag davor; **the week before** die Woche davor

beforehand adv vorher

beg vb ❶ (*for money*) betteln [34] ❷ anflehen [4] (perf hat angefleht) ▷ *He begged me to stop.* Er flehte mich an aufzuhören.

began vb see **begin**

beggar n Bettler m (pl Bettler), Bettlerin f

begin vb anfangen [23] (pres fängt an, imperf fing an, perf hat angefangen); **to begin doing something** anfangen [23], etwas zu tun

beginner n Anfänger m (pl Anfänger), Anfängerin f ▷ *I'm just a beginner.* Ich bin noch Anfänger.

beginning n Anfang m (pl Anfänge) ▷ *in the beginning* am Anfang

begun vb see **begin**

behalf n **on behalf of somebody** für jemanden

behave vb sich benehmen [52] (pres benimmt sich, imperf benahm sich, perf hat sich benommen) ▷ *He behaved like an idiot.* Er hat sich wie ein Idiot benommen. ▷ *She behaved very badly.* Sie hat sich sehr schlecht benommen.; **to behave oneself** sich anständig benehmen [52]; **Behave!** Sei brav!

behaviour (US **behavior**) n Benehmen nt

behind prep, adv hinter

Use the accusative to express movement or a change of place. Use the dative where there is no change of place.

▷ *the wall behind the television* die Wand hinter dem Fernseher ▷ *The book fell behind the television.* Das Buch fiel hinter den Fernseher.; **to be behind** (*late*) im Rückstand sein [65]
▶ n Hintern m (gen Hinterns, pl Hintern)

beige adj beige

Belgian adj belgisch; **He's Belgian.** Er ist Belgier.; **She's Belgian.** Sie ist Belgierin.
▶ n Belgier m (pl Belgier), Belgierin f; **the Belgians** die Belgier

Belgium n Belgien nt; **from Belgium** aus Belgien; **in Belgium** in Belgien

believe vb glauben [38] ▷ *I don't believe you.* Ich glaube dir nicht.; **to believe in something** an etwas glauben [38]

bell n ❶ (*doorbell, in school*) Klingel f; **to ring the bell** klingeln [34]; **When the bell rings the children go out into the playground.** Wenn es klingelt, gehen die Kinder auf den Schulhof. ❷ (*in church*) Glocke f ❸ Glöckchen nt (pl Glöckchen) ▷ *Our cat has a bell on its neck.* Unsere Katze hat ein Glöckchen um den Hals.

belong vb gehören [**38**] (perf hat gehört); **to belong to somebody** jemandem gehören [**38**]; **Do you belong to the club?** Bist du Mitglied im Klub?; **Where does this belong?** Wo gehört das hin?

belongings npl Sachen fpl

below prep, adv ❶ unterhalb ▷ *below the castle* unterhalb der Burg ❷ unter

> Use the accusative to express movement or a change of place. Use the dative when there is no change of place.

▷ *The sun sank below the horizon.* Die Sonne sank unter den Horizont. ▷ *We were below the clouds.* Wir waren unter den Wolken. ❸ darunter ▷ *on the floor below* im Stock darunter; **ten degrees below freezing** zehn Grad unter null

belt n Gürtel m (pl Gürtel)

bench n ❶ (seat) Bank f (pl Bänke) ❷ (for woodwork) Werkbank f (pl Werkbänke)

benchmark n Maßstab m (pl Maßstäbe)

bend n ❶ (in road) Kurve f ❷ (in river) Biegung f

▶ vb ❶ (leg, arm) beugen [**38**] ▷ *I can't bend my arm.* Ich kann den Arm nicht beugen.; **to bend down** sich bücken [**48**]; **to bend over** sich nach vorne beugen [**38**] ❷ (object) verbiegen [**38**] (imperf verbog, perf hat verbogen) ▷ *You've bent it.* Du hast es verbogen.; **It bends easily.** Das lässt sich leicht biegen.; **'do not bend'** 'nicht knicken'

beneath prep unter

> Use the accusative to express movement or a change of place. Use the dative when there is no change of place.

▷ *He placed his boots beneath the chair.* Er stellte seine Stiefel unter den Stuhl. ▷ *She found his jumper beneath the bed.* Sie fand seinen Pullover unter dem Bett.

benefit n (advantage) Vorteil m (pl Vorteile); **unemployment benefit** die Arbeitslosenunterstützung

▶ vb profitieren [**76**] ▷ *You'll benefit from that experience.* Du wirst von dieser Erfahrung profitieren.; **He benefited from the change.** Die Veränderung hat ihm gutgetan.

bent vb see **bend**

▶ adj verbogen ▷ *a bent fork* eine verbogene Gabel

berth n ❶ (on ship) Koje f ❷ (on train) Schlafwagenplatz m (pl Schlafwagenplätze)

beside prep neben

> Use the accusative to express movement or a change of place. Use the dative when there is no change of place.

▷ *the lamp beside the television* die Lampe neben dem Fernseher ▷ *Put that chair beside the television.* Stell den Stuhl neben den Fernseher.; **I was beside myself.** Ich war außer mir.; **That's beside the point.** Das tut hier nichts zur Sache.

best adj, adv ❶ beste ▷ *He's the best player in the team.* Er ist der beste Spieler der Mannschaft. ▷ *Janet's the best at maths.* Janet ist in Mathe die Beste. ❷ am besten ▷ *Emma sings best.* Emma singt am besten.; **to do one's best** sein Bestes tun [**81**]; **to make the best of it** das Beste daraus machen [**48**]

best man n Trauzeuge m (gen Trauzeugen, pl Trauzeugen)

- There is no real equivalent in
- Germany to 'best man'. A **Trauzeuge**
- is merely an official witness to the
- wedding ceremony.

bet n Wette f ▷ *to make a bet* eine Wette machen

▶ vb wetten [**2**]; **I bet you he won't come.** Wetten, dass er nicht kommt.; **I bet he forgot.** Wetten, dass er es vergessen hat.

better adj, adv besser ▷ This one's better than that one. Dieses hier ist besser als das da. ▷ a better way to do it eine bessere Methode ▷ You'd better do it straight away. Das machst du besser sofort. ▷ I'd better go home. Ich gehe besser nach Hause. ▷ That's better! Das ist schon besser!; **better still** noch besser; **to get better (1)** (improve) besser werden [91] ▷ I hope the weather gets better soon. Ich hoffe, das Wetter wird bald besser. ▷ My German is getting better. Mein Deutsch wird besser. **(2)** (from illness) sich erholen [19]; **I hope you get better soon.** Gute Besserung!; **to feel better** sich besser fühlen [38]

between prep zwischen

Use the accusative to express movement or a change of place. Use the dative when there is no change of place.

▷ The cathedral is between the town hall and the river. Der Dom liegt zwischen dem Rathaus und dem Fluss. ▷ He sat down between the two girls. Er setzte sich zwischen die beiden Mädchen. ▷ between fifteen and twenty minutes zwischen fünfzehn und zwanzig Minuten

beware vb zwischen 'Beware of the dog!' 'Vorsicht bissiger Hund!'

bewilder vb verwirren [84] ▷ She was bewildered. Sie war verwirrt.

beyond prep hinter ▷ There was a lake beyond the mountain. Hinter dem Berg war ein See.; **beyond belief** nicht zu glauben; **beyond repair** nicht mehr zu reparieren

bi adj (= bisexual) bi (= bisexuell)

Bible n Bibel f

bicycle n Fahrrad nt (pl Fahrräder)

big adj groß ▷ a big house ein großes Haus ▷ a bigger house ein größeres Haus ▷ my big brother mein großer Bruder ▷ her big sister ihre große Schwester; **He's a big guy.** Er ist kräftig gebaut.

bigheaded adj eingebildet

bike n Fahrrad nt (pl Fahrräder) ▷ by bike mit dem Fahrrad

bikini n Bikini m (pl Bikinis)

bilingual adj zweisprachig

bill n ❶ Rechnung f ▷ the gas bill die Gasrechnung; **Can we have the bill, please?** Können wir bitte zahlen? ❷ (banknote) Geldschein m (pl Geldscheine) ▷ a dollar bill ein Dollarschein

billion n Milliarde f

bin n ❶ (indoors) Abfalleimer m (pl Abfalleimer) ❷ (outside) Mülleimer m (pl Mülleimer)

binoculars npl Fernglas nt (pl Ferngläser) ▷ a pair of binoculars ein Fernglas

biochemistry n Biochemie f

biography n Biografie f

biology n Biologie f

bird n Vogel m (pl Vögel)

bird-watching n My hobby's bird-watching. Mein Hobby ist das Beobachten von Vögeln.

Biro® n Kuli m (pl Kulis)

birth n Geburt f ▷ date of birth das Geburtsdatum

birth certificate n Geburtsurkunde f

birth control n Empfängnisverhütung f

birthday n Geburtstag m (pl Geburtstage) ▷ When's your birthday? Wann hast du Geburtstag? ▷ a birthday cake ein Geburtstagskuchen ▷ I'm going to have a birthday party. Ich gebe eine Geburtstagsparty.

biscuit n Keks m (pl Kekse)

bishop n Bischof m (pl Bischöfe)

bit vb see **bite**
▶ n (piece) Stück nt (pl Stücke) ▷ Would you like another bit? Möchtest du noch ein Stück? ▷ a bit of cake ein Stück Kuchen; **a bit (1)** etwas ▷ He's a bit mad.

Er ist etwas verrückt. ▷ *a bit too hot* etwas zu heiß **(2)** ein bisschen ▷ *Wait a bit!* Warte ein bisschen! ▷ *Do you play football? — A bit.* Spielst du Fußball? — Ein bisschen.; **a bit of** *(a little)* etwas ▷ *a bit of music* etwas Musik ▷ *It's a bit of a nuisance.* Das ist schon etwas ärgerlich.; **to fall to bits** kaputtgehen **[29]**; **to take something to bits** etwas auseinandernehmen **[52]**; **bit by bit** nach und nach

bite *vb* ❶ *(person, dog)* beißen **[6]** *(imperf* biss, *perf* hat gebissen) ❷ *(insect)* stechen *(pres* sticht, *imperf* stach, *perf* hat gestochen) ▷ *I got bitten by mosquitoes.* Ich bin von Mücken gestochen worden.; **to bite one's nails** an den Nägeln kauen **[38]**
▶ *n* ❶ *(insect bite)* Stich *m* (*pl* Stiche) ❷ *(animal bite)* Biss *m* (*gen* Bisses, *pl* Bisse); **to have a bite to eat** eine Kleinigkeit essen **[20]**

bitter *adj* ❶ bitter ❷ *(weather, wind)* bitterkalt ▷ *It's bitter today.* Heute ist es bitterkalt.

Black *n (person)* Schwarze; **a Black woman** eine Schwarze

black *adj* schwarz ▷ *a black jacket* eine schwarze Jacke

blackberry *n* Brombeere *f*

blackbird *n* Amsel *f*

blackboard *n* Tafel *f*

blackcurrant *n* Schwarze Johannisbeere *f*

blackmail *n* Erpressung *f* ▷ *That's blackmail!* Das ist Erpressung!
▶ *vb* erpressen **[7]** *(perf* hat erpresst) ▷ *He blackmailed her.* Er erpresste sie.

black pudding *n* Blutwurst *f* (*pl* Blutwürste)

blacksmith *n* Schmied *m* ▷ *He's a blacksmith.* Er ist Schmied.

blade *n* Klinge *f*

blame *vb* Don't blame me! Ich bin nicht schuld!; **I blame him.** Ich gebe ihm die Schuld.; **He blamed it on my sister.** Er gab meiner Schwester die Schuld.

blank *adj* leer; **My mind went blank.** Ich hatte ein Brett vor dem Kopf.
▶ *n* Lücke *f* ▷ *Fill in the blanks.* Füllt die Lücken aus.

blanket *n* Decke *f*

blast *n* **a bomb blast** eine Bombenexplosion

blaze *n* Feuer *nt* (*pl* Feuer)

blazer *n* Blazer *m* (*pl* Blazer)

bleach *n* Bleichmittel *nt* (*pl* Bleichmittel)

bleed *vb* bluten **[2]** ▷ *My nose is bleeding.* Ich blute aus der Nase.

blender *n* Mixer *m* (*pl* Mixer)

bless *vb* *(religiously)* segnen **[53]**; **Bless you!** *(after sneezing)* Gesundheit!

blew *vb* see **blow**

blind *adj* blind
▶ *n (fabric)* Rollo *nt* (*pl* Rollos)

blink *vb* zwinkern **[88]**

blister *n* Blase *f*

blizzard *n* Schneesturm *m* (*pl* Schneestürme)

block *n* Block *m* (*pl* Blöcke) ▷ *He lives in our block.* Er lebt in unserem Block.; **a block of flats** ein Wohnblock *m*
▶ *vb* blockieren **[76]** *(perf* hat blockiert)

blog *n (internet)* Blog *m/nt*
▶ *vb* bloggen **[48]**

blogger *n* Blogger *m* (*pl* Blogger), Bloggerin *f*

blogpost *n* Blogpost *m* (*pl* Blogposts)

blonde *adj* blond ▷ *She's got blonde hair.* Sie hat blondes Haar.

blood *n* Blut *nt*

blood pressure *n* Blutdruck *m* ▷ *to have high blood pressure* hohen Blutdruck haben

blood test *n* Blutuntersuchung *f*

blouse *n* Bluse *f*

blow *n* Schlag *m* (*pl* Schläge)
▶ *vb* ❶ *(person)* blasen *(pres* bläst, *imperf* blies, *perf* hat geblasen) ❷ *(wind)* wehen

blow-dry | 298   **ENGLISH > GERMAN**

[38]; **to blow one's nose** sich die Nase putzen [36] ▷ *Blow your nose!* Putz dir die Nase!; **to blow a whistle** pfeifen; **to blow out a candle** eine Kerze ausblasen; **to blow up (1)** in die Luft jagen [38] ▷ *The terrorists blew up a police station.* Die Terroristen haben ein Polizeirevier in die Luft gejagt. **(2)** aufblasen ▷ *to blow up a balloon* einen Luftballon aufblasen; **The house blew up.** Das Haus flog in die Luft.

blow-dry n Föhnen nt ▷ *A cut and blow-dry, please.* Schneiden und Föhnen bitte.

blown vb see **blow**

blue adj blau ▷ *a blue dress* ein blaues Kleid; **It came out of the blue.** Das kam aus heiterem Himmel.

blues npl (music) Blues msg (gen Blues)

blunder n Schnitzer m (pl Schnitzer)

blunt adj ❶ (person) unverblümt ❷ (knife) stumpf

blush vb rot werden [91] (pres wird rot, imperf wurde rot, perf ist rot geworden)

board n ❶ Brett nt (pl Bretter) ❷ (blackboard) Tafel f ▷ *Write it on the board.* Schreib es an die Tafel.; **It's on the board in the office.** (noticeboard) Es hängt am schwarzen Brett im Büro.; **on board** an Bord; **full board** die Vollpension

boarder n Internatsschüler m (pl Internatsschüler), Internatsschülerin f

board game n Brettspiel nt (pl Brettspiele)

boarding card n Bordkarte f

boarding school n Internat nt (pl Internate) ▷ *I go to boarding school.* Ich gehe in ein Internat.

boast vb prahlen [38] ▷ *to boast about something* mit etwas prahlen

boat n Boot nt (pl Boote)

body n Körper m (pl Körper)

bodybuilding n Bodybuilding nt ▷ *He does bodybuilding.* Er macht Bodybuilding.

bodyguard n Leibwächter m (pl Leibwächter)

boil n Furunkel m (pl Furunkel)
▷ vb kochen [48] ▷ *to boil some water* Wasser kochen ▷ *to boil an egg* ein Ei kochen ▷ *The water's boiling.* Das Wasser kocht.; **to boil over** überkochen [4]

boiled adj **a soft-boiled egg** ein weich gekochtes Ei nt; **boiled potatoes** Salzkartoffeln fpl

boiling adj **It's boiling in here!** Hier ist eine Bruthitze!; **boiling hot** brütend heiß

bolt n ❶ (on door) Riegel m (pl Riegel) ❷ (with nut) Bolzen m (pl Bolzen)

bomb n Bombe f

▌ Note that you pronounce the second 'b' in German.

▷ vb bombardieren [76] (perf hat bombardiert)

bomber n Bomber m (pl Bomber)

▌ Note that you pronounce the second 'b' in German.

bombing n Bombenangriff m (pl Bombenangriffe)

bone n ❶ (of human, animal) Knochen m (pl Knochen) ❷ (of fish) Gräte f

bonfire n Feuer nt (pl Feuer)

bonnet n (of car) Motorhaube f

bonus n ❶ (extra payment) Bonus m (pl Bonusse) ❷ (added advantage) Vorteil m

book n Buch nt (pl Bücher)
▷ vb buchen [48] ▷ *We haven't booked.* Wir haben nicht gebucht.

bookcase n ❶ (open) Bücherregal nt (pl Bücherregale) ❷ (with doors) Bücherschrank m (pl Bücherschränke)

booklet n Broschüre f

bookshelf n Bücherbrett nt (pl Bücherbretter); **bookshelves** das Bücherregal sg

bookshop n Buchhandlung f

boot n ❶ (of car) Kofferraum m (pl Kofferräume) ❷ (footwear) Stiefel m (pl Stiefel); **football boots** die Fußballschuhe mpl

ENGLISH > GERMAN

border n Grenze f
bore vb see **bear**
bored adj to be bored sich langweilen [38]; **She gets bored easily.** Ihr wird schnell langweilig.
boring adj langweilig
born adj to be born geboren werden [91]
borne vb see **bear**
borrow vb ausleihen (imperf lieh aus, perf hat ausgeliehen) ▷ Can I borrow your pen? Kann ich deinen Schreiber ausleihen?; **to borrow something from somebody** sich etwas von jemandem leihen
Bosnia n Bosnien nt; **from Bosnia** aus Bosnien; **to Bosnia** nach Bosnien
Bosnian adj bosnisch
boss n Chef m (pl Chefs), Chefin f
boss around vb to boss somebody around jemanden herumkommandieren [76]
bossy adj herrisch
both adj, pron beide ▷ We both went. Wir sind beide gegangen. ▷ Emma and Jane both went. Emma und Jane sind beide gegangen. ▷ Both of your answers are wrong. Beide Antworten sind falsch. ▷ Both of them have left. Beide sind gegangen. ▷ Both of us went. Wir sind beide gegangen.; **both ... and** sowohl ... als auch
bother n Ärger m ▷ We had a spot of bother with the car. Wir hatten Ärger mit dem Auto.; **No bother!** Kein Problem!
▶ vb ❶ (worry) beunruhigen [7] (perf hat beunruhigt) ▷ Is something bothering you? Beunruhigt dich etwas? ❷ (disturb) stören [38] ▷ I'm sorry to bother you. Es tut mir leid, dass ich dich störe.; **Don't bother!** Nicht nötig!; **to bother to do something** es für nötig halten [24], etwas zu tun ▷ He didn't bother to tell me about it. Er hat es nicht für nötig gehalten, es mir zu sagen.
bottle n Flasche f

299 | **boyfriend**

bottle bank n Altglascontainer m (pl Altglascontainer)
bottle-opener n Flaschenöffner m (pl Flaschenöffner)
bottom n ❶ (of container, bag, sea) Boden m (pl Böden) ❷ (buttocks) Hintern m (gen Hintern, pl Hintern) ❸ (of list) Ende nt (pl Enden); **at the bottom of page two** unten auf Seite zwei
▶ adj unterste ▷ the bottom shelf das unterste Regalbrett; **the bottom sheet** das Bettlaken
bought vb see **buy**
bounce vb hüpfen [38] (perf ist gehüpft)
bouncer n Rausschmeißer m (pl Rausschmeißer)
bound adj **He's bound to say that.** Er muss das ja sagen.; **She's bound to come.** Sie kommt sicher.
boundary n Grenze f
bow n (knot) Schleife f ▷ to tie a bow eine Schleife machen ❷ Bogen m (pl Bogen) ▷ a bow and arrow ein Pfeil und Bogen
▶ vb sich verneigen [84] (perf hat sich verneigt)
bowl n (for soup, cereal) Schale f
▶ vb (in cricket) werfen [92] (pres wirft, imperf warf, perf hat geworfen)
bowling n Bowling nt; **to go bowling** Bowling spielen [38]; **a bowling alley** eine Bowlingbahn
bow tie n Fliege f
box n Schachtel f ▷ a box of matches eine Schachtel Streichhölzer; **a cardboard box** ein Karton m
boxer n Boxer m (pl Boxer)
boxer shorts npl Boxershorts pl ▷ He was wearing a pair of boxer shorts. Er trug Boxershorts.
boxing n Boxen nt
Boxing Day n **It was Boxing Day.** Es war der zweite Weihnachtstag.
boy n Junge m (gen Jungen, pl Jungen)
boyfriend n Freund m (pl Freunde)

▷ Have you got a boyfriend? Hast du einen Freund?
bra n BH m (pl BHs)
brace n (on teeth) Zahnspange f ▷ She wears a brace. Sie hat eine Zahnspange.
bracelet n Armband nt (pl Armbänder)
brackets npl Klammern fpl ▷ in brackets in Klammern
brain n Gehirn nt (pl Gehirne)
brainy adj gescheit
brake n Bremse f
▶ vb bremsen [36]
branch n ❶ (of tree) Zweig m (pl Zweige) ❷ (of bank) Filiale f
brand n Marke f ▷ a well-known brand of coffee eine bekannte Kaffeemarke
brand-new adj brandneu
brandy n Weinbrand m (pl Weinbrände)
brass n (metal) Messing nt; **the brass section** die Blechbläser mpl
brass band n Blaskapelle f
brave adj mutig

> Be careful not to translate **brave** by **brav**.

Brazil n Brasilien nt; **from Brazil** aus Brasilien; **to Brazil** nach Brasilien
bread n Brot nt (pl Brote); **brown bread** das Graubrot; **white bread** das Weißbrot
* There is a huge variety of types of
* bread in Germany which can't simply
* be divided into brown and white.

break n (rest) Pause f ▷ to take a break eine Pause machen ▷ during morning break während der Vormittagspause; **the Christmas break** die Weihnachtsferien mpl; **Give me a break!** Mach mal halblang!
▶ vb ❶ kaputt machen [48] (perf hat kaputt gemacht) ▷ Careful, you'll break something! Vorsicht, du machst sonst was kaputt! ❷ (record, law) brechen [11] (pres bricht, imperf brach, perf hat gebrochen) ▷ to break a promise sein Versprechen brechen; **to break one's leg** sich das Bein brechen [11]; **He broke his arm.** Er hat sich den Arm gebrochen. ❸ (get broken) brechen [11] ▷ Careful, it'll break! Vorsicht, es bricht!
break down vb eine Panne haben [32] (pres hat eine Panne, imperf hatte eine Panne, perf hat eine Panne gehabt)
break in vb einbrechen [11] (pres bricht ein, imperf brach ein, perf hat eingebrochen)
break into vb einbrechen [11] in (pres bricht ein, imperf brach ein, perf ist eingebrochen)
break off vb abbrechen [11] (pres bricht ab, imperf brach ab, perf hat abgebrochen)
break open vb (door, cupboard) aufbrechen [11] (pres bricht auf, imperf brach auf, perf hat aufgebrochen)
break out vb ausbrechen [11] (pres bricht aus, imperf brach aus, perf ist ausgebrochen)
break up vb ❶ (crowd) sich auflösen [4] (perf hat sich aufgelöst) ❷ (meeting, party) zu Ende gehen [29] (imperf ging zu Ende, perf ist zu Ende gegangen) ❸ (couple) sich trennen [38]
breakdown n ❶ (in vehicle) Panne f ▷ to have a breakdown eine Panne haben ❷ (mental) Nervenzusammenbruch m (pl Nervenzusammenbrüche) ▷ to have a breakdown einen Nervenzusammenbruch haben
breakfast n Frühstück nt (pl Frühstücke) ▷ What would you like for breakfast? Was möchtest du zum Frühstück?; **to have breakfast** frühstücken [38]
break-in n Einbruch m (pl Einbrüche)
break time n (in school) Pause f
breast n Brust f (pl Brüste); **chicken breast** die Hähnchenbrust
breaststroke n Brustschwimmen nt
breath n Atem m ▷ to be out of breath außer Atem sein; **to have bad breath**

Mundgeruch haben [32]; **to get one's breath back** verschnaufen [84]

breathe vb atmen [3]; **to breathe in** einatmen [4]; **to breathe out** ausatmen [4]

breed vb züchten [2] ▷ *to breed dogs* Hunde züchten
▶ n Rasse *f*

breeze n Brise *f*

brewery n Brauerei *f*

bribe n Bestechung *f*
▶ vb bestechen (*pres* besticht, *imperf* bestach, *perf* hat bestochen)

brick n Backstein m (*pl* Backsteine) ▷ *a brick wall* eine Backsteinmauer

bride n Braut *f* (*pl* Bräute)

bridegroom n Bräutigam m (*pl* Bräutigame)

bridesmaid n Brautjungfer *f*

bridge n ❶ Brücke *f* ▷ *a suspension bridge* eine Hängebrücke ❷ Bridge nt (*gen* Bridge) ▷ *to play bridge* Bridge spielen

brief adj kurz

briefcase n Aktentasche *f*

briefly adv kurz

briefs npl Unterhose *f* ▷ *a pair of briefs* eine Unterhose

bright adj ❶ (*light*) hell ❷ (*colour*) leuchtend ▷ *a brighter colour* eine leuchtendere Farbe; **bright blue** hellblau ❸ intelligent ▷ *He's not very bright.* Er ist nicht besonders intelligent.

brilliant adj ❶ (*wonderful*) prima ▷ *Brilliant!* Prima! ❷ (*clever*) glänzend ▷ *a brilliant scientist* ein glänzender Wissenschaftler

bring vb ❶ bringen [13] (*imperf* brachte, *perf* hat gebracht) ▷ *Could you bring me my trainers?* Könntest du mir meine Sportschuhe bringen? ❷ (*bring along*) mitbringen [13] ▷ *Bring warm clothes.* Bringt warme Kleidung mit! ▷ *Can I bring a friend?* Darf ich einen Freund mitbringen?; **to bring about** herbeiführen [4]; **to bring back** zurückbringen [13]; **to bring forward** vorverlegen [84]; **to bring up** aufziehen [96]

Britain n Großbritannien nt; **from Britain** aus Großbritannien; **in Britain** in Großbritannien; **to Britain** nach Großbritannien; **Great Britain** Großbritannien

British adj britisch; *He's British.* Er ist Brite.; *She's British.* Sie ist Britin.; **the British** die Briten mpl; **the British Isles** die Britischen Inseln

Brittany n Bretagne *f*; **in Brittany** in der Bretagne

broad adj (*wide*) breit; **in broad daylight** am helllichten Tag

broadband n Breitband nt

broadcast n Sendung *f*
▶ vb senden ▷ *The interview was broadcast all over the world.* Das Interview wurde in der ganzen Welt gesendet.

broccoli nsg Brokkoli mpl ▷ *Broccoli is her favourite vegetable.* Ihr Lieblingsgemüse ist Brokkoli.

brochure n Broschüre *f*

broke vb *see* **break**
▶ adj **to be broke** (*without money*) pleite sein [65]

broken vb *see* **break**
▶ adj ❶ kaputt ▷ *It's broken.* Es ist kaputt. ❷ (*limb*) gebrochen ▷ *He's got a broken arm.* Er hat einen gebrochenen Arm.

bronchitis n Bronchitis *f*

bronze n Bronze *f* ▷ *the bronze medal* die Bronzemedaille

brooch n Brosche *f*

broom n Besen m (*pl* Besen)

brother n Bruder m (*pl* Brüder) ▷ *my brother* mein Bruder ▷ *my big brother* mein großer Bruder

brother-in-law n Schwager m (*pl* Schwäger)

brought vb see **bring**
brown adj braun; **brown bread** das Graubrot
browse vb (computer) browsen [**38**] (perf hat gebrowst); **to browse in a shop** sich in einem Geschäft umsehen [**64**]
brush n ❶ Bürste f ❷ (paintbrush) Pinsel m (pl Pinsel)
▶ vb bürsten [**2**]; **to brush one's hair** sich die Haare bürsten [**2**]; **to brush one's teeth** die Zähne putzen [**36**]
Brussels n Brüssel nt; **to Brussels** nach Brüssel
Brussels sprouts npl Rosenkohl msg
▷ *Do you like Brussels sprouts?* Magst du Rosenkohl?
bubble n Blase f
bubble bath n Schaumbad nt (pl Schaumbäder)
bubble gum n Bubblegum m (pl Bubblegums)
bucket n Eimer m (pl Eimer)
buckle n (on belt, watch, shoe) Schnalle f
Buddhism n Buddhismus m (gen Buddhismus)
Buddhist adj buddhistisch
budgie n Wellensittich m (pl Wellensittiche)
buffet n Büfett nt (pl Büfetts)
buffet car n Speisewagen m (pl Speisewagen)
bug n ❶ (insect) Wanze f; **There are many bugs there.** Dort gibt es viel Ungeziefer.; **a stomach bug** eine Magen-Darm-Infektion; **There's a bug going round.** Da geht etwas herum. ❷ (in computer) Programmfehler m (pl Programmfehler)
buggy n Kinderwagen m (pl Kinderwagen)
build vb bauen [**38**] ▷ *They're going to build houses here.* Hier werden Häuser gebaut.; **to build up** (increase) zunehmen [**52**]
builder n ❶ (owner of firm) Bauunternehmer m (pl Bauunternehmer), Bauunternehmerin f ❷ (worker) Bauarbeiter m (pl Bauarbeiter), Bauarbeiterin f
building n Gebäude nt (pl Gebäude)
built vb see **build**
bulb n (electric) Glühbirne f
Bulgaria n Bulgarien nt; **from Bulgaria** aus Bulgarien; **to Bulgaria** nach Bulgarien
bull n Stier m (pl Stiere)
bullet n Kugel f
bullfighting n Stierkampf m (pl Stierkämpfe)
bully n **He's a big bully.** Er tyrannisiert andere gern.
▶ vb tyrannisieren [**76**] (perf hat tyrannisiert)
bum n (informal: bottom) Po m (pl Pos)
bum bag n Gürteltasche f
bump n ❶ (lump) Beule f ❷ (minor accident) Zusammenstoß m (gen Zusammenstoßes, pl Zusammenstöße); **We had a bump.** Es hat gebumst.
▶ vb **to bump into something** gegen etwas laufen [**43**]; **We bumped into his car.** Wir sind in sein Auto gefahren.; **I bumped into an old friend.** Ich bin zufällig einem alten Freund begegnet.
bumper n Stoßstange f
bumpy adj holperig
bun n Brötchen nt (pl Brötchen)
bunch n **a bunch of flowers** ein Blumenstrauß m; **a bunch of grapes** eine Traube; **a bunch of keys** ein Schlüsselbund m
bunches npl Rattenschwänze mpl
▷ *She has her hair in bunches.* Sie hat Rattenschwänze.
bungalow n Bungalow m (pl Bungalows)
bunk n ❶ Bett nt (pl Betten) ❷ (on ship) Koje f
burger n Hamburger m (pl Hamburger)

burglar n Einbrecher m (pl Einbrecher), Einbrecherin f

burglary n Einbruch m (pl Einbrüche)

burgle vb einbrechen [11] in (pres bricht ein, imperf brach ein, perf ist eingebrochen) ▷ *Her house was burgled.* Bei ihr wurde eingebrochen.

burn n Verbrennung f
▶ vb ❶ (rubbish, documents) verbrennen [12] ❷ (food) anbrennen lassen [42] ▷ *I burned the cake.* Ich habe den Kuchen anbrennen lassen. ❸ (CD, DVD) brennen [12]; **to burn oneself** sich verbrennen [12]; **I've burned my hand.** Ich habe mir die Hand verbrannt.; **to burn down** abbrennen [12]

burst vb platzen [36] (perf ist geplatzt) ▷ *The balloon burst.* Der Luftballon ist geplatzt.; **to burst a balloon** einen Luftballon platzen lassen [42]; **to burst out laughing** laut loslachen [4]; **to burst into flames** in Flammen aufgehen [29]; **to burst into tears** in Tränen ausbrechen [11]

bury vb ❶ (dead people, animals) begraben (pres begräbt, imperf begrub, perf hat begraben) ▷ *We buried my guinea pig in the garden.* Wir haben mein Meerschweinchen im Garten begraben. ❷ (things) vergraben ▷ *My dog buries his bones.* Mein Hund vergräbt seine Knochen.

bus n Bus m (gen Busses, pl Busse) ▷ *the bus driver* der Busfahrer ▷ *the school bus* der Schulbus; **a bus pass** (monthly) eine Monatskarte für den Bus
- Almost all German cities operate
- an integrated public transport
- system; you can buy a weekly
- (**Wochenkarte**), monthly
- (**Monatskarte**) or yearly
- (**Jahreskarte**) pass which is valid
- for that period on all buses, trams
- and light railway vehicles in a
- particular zone.

a bus station ein Busbahnhof m; **a bus ticket** eine Busfahrkarte

bush n Busch m (pl Büsche)

business n ❶ (firm) Firma f (pl Firmen) ▷ *He's got his own business.* Er hat seine eigene Firma. ❷ (commerce) Geschäft nt (pl Geschäfte) ▷ *a business trip* eine Geschäftsreise ▷ *He's away on business.* Er ist geschäftlich unterwegs.; **It's none of my business.** Das geht mich nichts an.

businessman n Geschäftsmann m (pl Geschäftsleute)

businesswoman n Geschäftsfrau f

bus stop n Bushaltestelle f

bust n (chest) Busen m (pl Busen); **bust measurement** die Oberweite

busy adj ❶ (person) beschäftigt ❷ (shop, street) belebt ❸ (phone line) besetzt; **It's been a busy day.** Es war viel los heute.

but conj aber ▷ *I'd like to come, but I'm busy.* Ich würde gerne kommen, aber ich habe zu tun.

butcher n Metzger m (pl Metzger), Metzgerin f ▷ *He's a butcher.* Er ist Metzger.

butcher's n Metzgerei f

butter n Butter f

butterfly n Schmetterling m (pl Schmetterlinge)

button n Knopf m (pl Knöpfe)

buy vb kaufen [38] ▷ *He bought me an ice cream.* Er hat mir ein Eis gekauft.; **to buy something from somebody** etwas von jemandem kaufen [38]
▶ n Kauf m (pl Käufe) ▷ *It was a good buy.* Es war ein guter Kauf.

by prep ❶ von ▷ *They were caught by the police.* Sie wurden von der Polizei erwischt. ▷ *a painting by Picasso* ein Gemälde von Picasso ❷ mit ▷ *by car* mit dem Auto ▷ *by train* mit dem Zug ▷ *by bus* mit dem Bus ❸ (close to) bei ▷ *Where's the bank? — It's by the post office.* Wo ist die Bank? — Sie ist bei der

Post.; **by day** bei Tag; **by night** bei Nacht ❹ *(not later than)* bis ▷ *We have to be there by four o'clock.* Wir müssen bis vier Uhr dort sein.; **by the time ...** bis ... ▷ *By the time I got there it was too late.* Bis ich dort war, war es zu spät.; **That's fine by me.** Ist in Ordnung!; **all by himself** ganz allein; **all by herself** ganz allein; **I did it all by myself.** Ich habe es ganz allein gemacht.; **by the way** übrigens
bye *excl* tschüss!
bypass *n (road)* Umgehungsstraße *f*

C

cab *n* Taxi *nt (pl* Taxis)
cabbage *n* Kohl *m*
cabin *n (on ship)* Kabine *f*
cable *n* Kabel *nt (pl* Kabel)
cable car *n* Drahtseilbahn *f*
cable television *n* Kabelfernsehen *nt*
cactus *n* Kaktus *m (gen* Kaktus, *pl* Kakteen)
café *n* Imbissstube *f*
cage *n* Käfig *m (pl* Käfige)
cagoule *n* Windjacke *f*
cake *n* Kuchen *m (pl* Kuchen)
calculate *vb* rechnen **[53]**
calculation *n* Rechnung *f*
calculator *n* Taschenrechner *m (pl* Taschenrechner)
calendar *n* Kalender *m (pl* Kalender)
calf *n* ❶ *(of cow)* Kalb *nt (pl* Kälber) ❷ *(of leg)* Wade *f*
call *n (by phone)* Anruf *m (pl* Anrufe) ▷ *Thanks for your call.* Danke für Ihren Anruf.; **a phone call** ein Telefongespräch *nt*; **to be on call** *(doctor)* Bereitschaftsdienst haben **[32]**

ENGLISH > GERMAN   305 | **candidate**

▶ vb ❶ (by phone) anrufen [56] (imperf rief an, perf hat angerufen) ▷ I'll tell him you called. Ich sage ihm, dass du angerufen hast. ▷ This is the number to call. Das ist die Nummer, die du anrufen musst.; **to call back** (phone again) zurückrufen [56] ❷ (fetch) rufen [56] ▷ We called the police. Wir haben die Polizei gerufen. ❸ (by name) nennen (imperf nannte, perf hat genannt) ▷ Everyone calls him Jimmy. Alle nennen ihn Jimmy.; **to be called** heißen; **to call somebody names** jemanden beschimpfen [18]; **to call for** abholen [4]; **to call off** absagen [4]

call box n Telefonzelle f

call centre n Callcenter nt (pl Callcenters)

calm adj ruhig

calm down vb sich beruhigen [18] (perf hat sich beruhigt)

Calor gas® n Butangas nt

calorie n Kalorie f

calves npl see **calf**

camcorder n Camcorder m (pl Camcorder)

came vb see **come**

camel n Kamel nt (pl Kamele)

camera n ❶ (for photos) Fotoapparat m (pl Fotoapparate) ❷ (for filming, TV) Kamera f (pl Kameras)

cameraman n Kameramann m (pl Kameramänner)

cameraphone n Fotohandy nt (pl Fotohandys)

camp vb zelten [2]
▶ n Lager nt (pl Lager); **a camp bed** eine Campingliege

campaign n Kampagne f
▶ vb sich einsetzen [36] (perf hat sich eingesetzt) ▷ They are campaigning for a change in the law. Sie setzen sich für eine Gesetzesänderung ein.

camper n ❶ (person) Camper m (pl Camper), Camperin f ❷ (van) Wohnmobil nt (pl Wohnmobile)

camping n Camping nt; **to go camping** zelten [2]

camping gas n Campinggas nt

campsite n Zeltplatz m (pl Zeltplätze)

can vb können [41] (pres kann, imperf konnte, perf hat können) ▷ I can't come. Ich kann nicht kommen. ▷ Can I help you? Kann ich dir helfen? ▷ You could hire a bike. Du könntest dir ein Fahrrad mieten. ▷ I couldn't sleep. Ich konnte nicht schlafen. ▷ I can swim. Ich kann schwimmen. ▷ He can't drive. Er kann nicht Auto fahren. ▷ Can you speak German? Können Sie Deutsch?; **That can't be true!** Das darf nicht wahr sein!; **You could be right.** Da könntest du recht haben.
▶ n ❶ (tin) Dose f ▷ a can of sweetcorn eine Dose Mais ▷ a can of beer eine Dose Bier ❷ (jerry can) Kanister m (pl Kanister) ▷ a can of petrol ein Benzinkanister

Canada n Kanada nt; **from Canada** aus Kanada; **in Canada** in Kanada; **to Canada** nach Kanada

Canadian adj kanadisch ▷ He's Canadian. Er ist Kanadier. ▷ She's Canadian. Sie ist Kanadierin.
▶ n Kanadier m (pl Kanadier), Kanadierin f

canal n Kanal m (pl Kanäle)

Canaries n **the Canaries** die Kanarischen Inseln fpl

canary n Kanarienvogel m (pl Kanarienvögel)

cancel vb ❶ absagen [4] (perf hat abgesagt) ▷ The match was cancelled. Das Spiel wurde abgesagt. ❷ (booking) stornieren [76] (perf hat storniert) ▷ He cancelled his hotel booking. Er hat seine Hotelreservierung storniert.

cancer n Krebs m (gen Krebses) ▷ He's got cancer. Er hat Krebs.; **I'm Cancer.** Ich bin Krebs.

candidate n Kandidat m (gen Kandidaten, pl Kandidaten), Kandidatin f

candle n Kerze f
candy n (US) ❶ (sweet) Bonbon nt (pl Bonbons), ❷ (sweets) Süßigkeit f
candyfloss n Zuckerwatte f
canned adj (food) in Dosen ▷ canned soup Suppe in Dosen
cannot vb see can
canoe n Kanu nt (pl Kanus)
canoeing n to go canoeing Kanu fahren [21]
can-opener n Dosenöffner m (pl Dosenöffner)
can't vb see can
canteen n Kantine f
canvas n Leinwand f (pl Leinwände)
cap n ❶ (hat) Mütze f ❷ (of bottle, tube) Verschluss m (gen Verschlusses, pl Verschlüsse)
capable adj fähig; **to be capable of doing something** etwas tun können [41]
capacity n ❶ Fähigkeit f ▷ He has the capacity to succeed. Er hat die Fähigkeit, Erfolg zu haben. ❷ (quantity) Fassungsvermögen nt ▷ a capacity of fifty litres ein Fassungsvermögen von fünfzig Litern
cape n Kap nt (pl Kaps) ▷ Cape Horn Kap Hoorn
capital n ❶ Hauptstadt f (pl Hauptstädte) ▷ Cardiff is the capital of Wales. Cardiff ist die Hauptstadt von Wales. ❷ (letter) Großbuchstabe m (gen Großbuchstaben, pl Großbuchstaben) ▷ Write your address in capitals. Schreib deine Adresse in Großbuchstaben.
capitalism n Kapitalismus m (gen Kapitalismus)
Capricorn n Steinbock m ▷ I'm Capricorn. Ich bin Steinbock.
captain n Kapitän m (pl Kapitäne), Kapitänin f ▷ She's captain of the hockey team. Sie ist die Kapitänin der Hockeymannschaft.
capture vb ❶ (person) gefangen nehmen [52] (pres nimmt gefangen, imperf nahm gefangen, perf hat gefangen genommen) ▷ He was captured by the enemy. Er wurde vom Feind gefangen genommen. ❷ (animal) fangen [23] (pres fängt, imperf fing, perf hat gefangen) ▷ They managed to capture the lion. Sie konnten den Löwen fangen.
car n Auto nt (pl Autos); **to go by car** mit dem Auto fahren [21]; **a car crash** ein Autounfall m
caramel n (sweet) Karamellbonbon nt (pl Karamellbonbons)
caravan n Wohnwagen m (pl Wohnwagen) ▷ a caravan site ein Campingplatz für Wohnwagen
car boot sale n Flohmarkt m (pl Flohmärkte)
card n Karte f; **a card game** ein Kartenspiel nt
cardboard n Karton m (pl Kartons)
cardigan n Strickjacke f
card phone n Kartentelefon nt (pl Kartentelefone)
care n Vorsicht f; **with care** vorsichtig; **to take care of** aufpassen [4] auf; **Take care!** (1) (Be careful!) Sei vorsichtig! (2) (Look after yourself!) Pass auf dich auf! ▶ vb to care about achten [2] auf; **I don't care!** Das ist mir egal!; **to care for somebody** (patients, old people) jemanden pflegen [38]
career n Karriere f
careful adj vorsichtig ▷ Be careful! Sei vorsichtig!
carefully adv ❶ sorgsam ▷ She carefully avoided the subject. Sie vermied das Thema sorgsam. ❷ (safely) vorsichtig ▷ Drive carefully! Fahr vorsichtig!; **Think carefully!** Denk gut nach!
careless adj ❶ (work) schluderig; **a careless mistake** ein Flüchtigkeitsfehler m ❷ (person) nachlässig ▷ She's very careless. Sie ist

ENGLISH > GERMAN

sehr nachlässig. ❸ **unvorsichtig** ▷ *a careless driver* ein unvorsichtiger Fahrer

caretaker n Hausmeister m (pl Hausmeister), Hausmeisterin f

car ferry n Autofähre f

cargo n Fracht f

car hire n Autoverleih m (pl Autoverleihe)

Caribbean adj karibisch
▶ n (islands) Karibik f ▷ *We're going to the Caribbean.* Wir fahren in die Karibik. ▷ *He's from the Caribbean.* Er kommt aus der Karibik.

carnation n Nelke f

carnival n Karneval m (pl Karnevale)

carol n *a Christmas carol* ein Weihnachtslied nt

car park n Parkplatz m (pl Parkplätze)

carpenter n Schreiner m (pl Schreiner), Schreinerin f ▷ *He's a carpenter.* Er ist Schreiner.

carpentry n Schreinerei f

carpet n Teppich m (pl Teppiche) ▷ *a Persian carpet* ein Perserteppich

carriage n Eisenbahnwagen m (pl Eisenbahnwagen)

carrier bag n Tragetasche f

carrot n Karotte f

carry vb tragen [77] (pres trägt, imperf trug, perf hat getragen) ▷ *He carried her bag.* Er trug ihre Tasche.; **a plane carrying a hundred passengers** ein Flugzeug mit hundert Passagieren an Bord; **to carry on** weitermachen [48]; **She carried on talking.** Sie redete weiter.; **to carry out** (orders) ausführen [4]

carrycot n Babytragetasche f

cart n Karren m (pl Karren)

carton n (of milk, juice) Tüte f

cartoon n ❶ (film) Zeichentrickfilm m (pl Zeichentrickfilme) ❷ (in newspaper) Cartoon m (pl Cartoons); **a strip cartoon** ein Comic m

307 | catastrophe

cartridge n Patrone f

carve vb (meat) aufschneiden [60] (imperf schnitt auf, perf hat aufgeschnitten)

case n ❶ Koffer m (pl Koffer) ▷ *I've packed my case.* Ich habe meinen Koffer gepackt. ❷ Fall m (pl Fälle) ▷ *in some cases* in manchen Fällen ▷ *Which case does 'außer' take?* Welcher Fall steht nach 'außer'?; **in that case** in dem Fall; **in case** für den Fall; **just in case** für alle Fälle

cash n Bargeld nt ▷ *I desperately need some cash.* Ich brauche dringend Bargeld.; **in cash** in bar ▷ *two thousand pounds in cash* zweitausend Pfund in bar; **to pay cash** bar bezahlen [7]; **I'm a bit short of cash.** Ich bin etwas knapp bei Kasse.; **a cash card** eine Geldautomatenkarte; **the cash desk** die Kasse; **a cash machine** ein Geldautomat m; **a cash register** eine Registrierkasse

cashew nut n Cashewnuss f (pl Cashewnüsse)

cashier n Kassierer m (pl Kassierer), Kassiererin f

cashmere n Kaschmir m ▷ *a cashmere sweater* ein Kaschmirpullover

casino n Kasino nt (pl Kasinos)

cast n Besetzung f ▷ *After the play, we met the cast.* Nach dem Stück haben wir die Besetzung kennengelernt.

castle n Burg f

casual adj ❶ leger ▷ *casual clothes* legere Kleidung ❷ lässig ▷ *a casual attitude* eine lässige Haltung ❸ beiläufig ▷ *It was just a casual remark.* Es war nur eine beiläufige Bemerkung.

casualty n (hospital department) Unfallstation f

cat n Katze f ▷ *Have you got a cat?* Hast du eine Katze?

catalogue n Katalog m (pl Kataloge)

catastrophe n Katastrophe f

catch vb ❶ fangen [23] (pres fängt, imperf fing, perf hat gefangen) ▷ My cat catches birds. Meine Katze fängt Vögel.; **to catch a thief** einen Dieb fassen [31]; **to catch somebody doing something** jemanden dabei erwischen [48], wie er etwas tut ❷ (bus, train) nehmen [52] (pres nimmt, imperf nahm, perf hat genommen) ▷ We caught the last bus. Wir haben den letzten Bus genommen. ❸ (hear) mitbekommen [40] (imperf bekam mit, perf hat mitbekommen) ▷ I didn't catch his name. Ich habe seinen Namen nicht mitbekommen.; **to catch up** aufholen [38]; **to catch a cold** einen Schnupfen bekommen [40]

catering n Who did the catering? Wer hat das Essen und die Getränke geliefert?

cathedral n Kathedrale f

Catholic adj katholisch
▶ n Katholik m (gen Katholiken, pl Katholiken), Katholikin f; **I'm a Catholic.** Ich bin katholisch.

cattle npl Vieh nt sg

caught vb see **catch**

cauliflower n Blumenkohl m (pl Blumenkohle)

cause n Ursache f ▷ the cause of the fire die Ursache des Feuers
▶ vb verursachen [84] (perf hat verursacht) ▷ to cause an accident einen Unfall verursachen

cautious adj vorsichtig

cave n Höhle f

caviar n Kaviar m

CD n (= compact disc) CD f (pl CDs)

CD player n CD-Spieler m (pl CD-Spieler)

CDT n (= Craft, Design and Technology) Arbeitslehre f

ceiling n Decke f

celebrate vb (birthday) feiern [88]

celebration n Feier f

celebrity n Berühmtheit f

celery n Stangensellerie m (gen Stangensellerie, pl Stangenselleries)

cell n Zelle f

cellar n Keller m (pl Keller) ▷ a wine cellar ein Weinkeller

cello n Cello nt (pl Celli) ▷ I play the cello. Ich spiele Cello.

cell phone n (US) Handy nt (pl Handys)

cement n Zement m

cemetery n Friedhof m (pl Friedhöfe)

cent n Cent m (pl Cents or Cent)

When talking about amounts of money use the plural form **Cent**.
▷ twenty cents zwanzig Cent

center n (US) Zentrum nt (pl Zentren)

centigrade adj twenty degrees centigrade zwanzig Grad Celsius

centimetre (US **centimeter**) n Zentimeter m (pl Zentimeter) ▷ twenty centimetres zwanzig Zentimeter

central adj zentral

central heating n Zentralheizung f

centre (US **center**) n Zentrum nt (pl Zentren) ▷ a sports centre ein Sportzentrum

century n Jahrhundert nt (pl Jahrhunderte) ▷ the twentieth century das zwanzigste Jahrhundert ▷ the twenty-first century das einundzwanzigste Jahrhundert

cereal n Getreideflocken fpl ▷ I have cereal for breakfast. Zum Frühstück esse ich Getreideflocken.

ceremony n Zeremonie f

certain adj ❶ sicher ▷ I'm absolutely certain it was him. Ich bin ganz sicher, dass er es war.; **I don't know for certain.** Ich bin mir nicht sicher.; **to make certain** sich vergewissern [88] ❷ bestimmt ▷ a certain person eine bestimmte Person

certainly adv natürlich ▷ I certainly expected something better. Ich habe natürlich etwas Besseres erwartet.; **Certainly not!** Sicher nicht!; **So it was**

a surprise? — It certainly was! Also war's eine Überraschung? — Und ob!
certificate n Urkunde f
CFC n (= chlorofluorocarbon) FCKW m (= Fluorchlorkohlenwasserstoff)
chain n Kette f
chair n ❶ Stuhl m (pl Stühle) ▷ a table and four chairs ein Tisch und vier Stühle ❷ (armchair) Sessel m (pl Sessel)
chairlift n Sessellift m (pl Sessellifte)
chairman n Vorsitzende m (gen Vorsitzenden, pl Vorsitzenden) ▷ a chairman ein Vorsitzender
chairperson n Vorsitzende m (gen Vorsitzenden, pl Vorsitzenden), Vorsitzende f (gen Vorsitzenden)
chairwoman n Vorsitzende f (gen Vorsitzenden, pl Vorsitzenden) ▷ a chairwoman eine Vorsitzende
chalk n Kreide f
challenge n Herausforderung f
▶ vb **She challenged me to a race.** Sie wollte mit mir um die Wette laufen.
champion n Meister m (pl Meister), Meisterin f
championship n Meisterschaft f
chance n ❶ Chance f ▷ Do you think I've got any chance? Meinst du, ich habe eine Chance? ▷ Their chances of winning are very good. Ihre Gewinnchancen sind sehr gut. ❷ Möglichkeit f ▷ a chance to travel eine Möglichkeit, auf Reisen zu gehen; **I'll write when I get the chance.** Ich schreibe, sobald ich dazu komme.; **by chance** zufällig; **to take a chance** ein Risiko eingehen [29]
change vb ❶ sich verändern [88] (perf hat sich verändert) ▷ The town has changed a lot. Die Stadt hat sich sehr verändert. ❷ (money, job) wechseln [34] ▷ I'd like to change fifty pounds. Ich würde gern fünfzig Pfund wechseln. ▷ He wants to change his job. Er möchte den Job wechseln.; **You have to change trains in Stuttgart.** Sie müssen in Stuttgart umsteigen.; **I'm going to change my shoes.** Ich ziehe andere Schuhe an.; **to change one's mind** es sich anders überlegen [82]; **to change gear** schalten [2] ❸ sich umziehen [96] (imperf zog sich um, perf hat sich umgezogen) ▷ She's changing to go out. Sie zieht sich zum Ausgehen um.; **to get changed** sich umziehen [96] ❹ (swap) umtauschen [4] (perf hat umgetauscht) ▷ Can I change this sweater? It's too small. Kann ich diesen Pullover umtauschen? Er ist zu klein.
▶ n ❶ Änderung f; **There's been a change of plan.** Die Pläne haben sich geändert.; **a change of clothes** Kleidung zum Wechseln; **for a change** zur Abwechslung ❷ (money) Kleingeld nt ▷ I haven't got any change. Ich habe kein Kleingeld.
changing room n Umkleideraum m (pl Umkleideräume)
channel n (TV) Programm nt (pl Programme) ▷ There's football on the other channel. Im anderen Programm gibt es Fußball.; **the English Channel** der Ärmelkanal; **the Channel Islands** die Kanalinseln; **the Channel Tunnel** der Kanaltunnel
chaos n Chaos nt (gen Chaos)
chapel n (part of church) Kapelle f
chapter n Kapitel nt (pl Kapitel)
character n ❶ Charakter m (pl Charaktere) ▷ Give me some idea of his character. Beschreiben Sie mir seinen Charakter.; **She's quite a character.** Sie ist ein Unikum. ❷ (in play, film) Figur f ▷ the character played by Tom Cruise die Figur, die Tom Cruise spielt
characteristic n Merkmal nt (pl Merkmale)
charcoal n Holzkohle f
charge n Gebühr f ▷ Is there a charge for delivery? Wird für die Zustellung eine Gebühr erhoben? ▷ an extra charge eine

Extragebühr; **free of charge** kostenlos; **to be in charge** die Verantwortung haben [**32**]
▶ vb ① (money) verlangen [**84**] (perf hat verlangt) ▷ How much did he charge you? Wie viel hat er verlangt? ▷ They charge ten pounds an hour. Sie verlangen zehn Pfund die Stunde. ② (with crime) anklagen [**4**] (perf hat angeklagt) ▷ The police have charged him with murder. Die Polizei hat ihn des Mordes angeklagt. ③ (phone, EV) aufladen (perf hat aufgeladen) ▷ Where can I charge my phone? Wo kann ich mein Handy aufladen?

charity n Wohlfahrt f ▷ She does a lot of work for charity. Sie arbeitet viel für die Wohlfahrt.; **He gave the money to charity.** Er hat das Geld für wohltätige Zwecke gespendet.

charm n Charme m
▌ Note that the 'e' in **Charme** is silent.
▷ He's got a lot of charm. Er hat viel Charme.

charming adj bezaubernd

chart n Grafik f ▷ The chart shows the rise of unemployment. Die Grafik stellt den Anstieg der Arbeitslosigkeit dar.; **the charts** die Hitparade sg

charter flight n Charterflug m (pl Charterflüge)

chase vb verfolgen [**84**] (perf hat verfolgt)
▶ n Verfolgung f; **a car chase** eine Verfolgungsjagd im Auto

chat n Schwätzchen nt (pl Schwätzchen); **to have a chat** ein Schwätzchen halten

chat room n Chatroom m (pl Chatrooms)

chat show n Talkshow f (pl Talkshows)

chauvinist n **male chauvinist** der Chauvi

cheap adj billig ▷ a cheap T-shirt ein billiges T-Shirt ▷ It's cheaper by bus. Mit dem Bus ist es billiger.

cheat vb betrügen (imperf betrog, perf hat betrogen) ▷ He cheated me. Er hat mich betrogen.; **You're cheating!** (in games, at school) Du schummelst!
▶ n Betrüger m (pl Betrüger), Betrügerin f

check n ① Kontrolle f ▷ a security check eine Sicherheitskontrolle ② (US: bill) Rechnung f ▷ The waiter brought us the check. Der Kellner brachte uns die Rechnung. ③ (US) Scheck m (pl Schecks) ▷ to write a check einen Scheck ausstellen
▶ vb nachsehen [**84**] (pres sieht nach, imperf sah nach, perf hat nachgesehen) ▷ I'll check the time of the train. Ich sehe die Abfahrtszeiten des Zuges nach.
▷ Could you check the oil, please? Könnten Sie bitte das Öl nachsehen?; **to check in** einchecken [**4**]; **to check out** (from hotel) sich auschecken

checked adj kariert ▷ a checked shirt ein kariertes Hemd

checkers nsg (US) Dame f ▷ Checkers is her favourite game. Dame ist ihr Lieblingsspiel.

check-in n Check-in m (pl Check-ins)

checkout n Kasse f

check-up n Check-up m (pl Check-ups)

cheddar n Cheddar m (pl Cheddars)

cheek n ① Wange f ▷ He kissed her on the cheek. Er küsste sie auf die Wange. ② Frechheit f ▷ What a cheek! So eine Frechheit!

cheeky adj frech ▷ Don't be cheeky! Sei nicht so frech! ▷ a cheeky smile ein freches Lächeln

cheer n Hurraruf m; **to give a cheer** Hurra rufen [**56**]; **Cheers!** (1) (good health) Prost! (2) (thanks) Danke schön!
▶ vb ① (team) anfeuern [**4**] (perf hat angefeuert) ② (speaker) zujubeln [**4**] (perf hat zugejubelt) ▷ The speaker was cheered. Dem Redner wurde zugejubelt.; **to cheer somebody up** jemanden aufheitern [**88**] ▷ I was trying

ENGLISH > GERMAN

to cheer him up. Ich habe versucht, ihn aufzuheitern.; **Cheer up!** Kopf hoch!

cheerful adj fröhlich
cheerio excl tschüss
cheese n Käse m (pl Käse)
chef n Küchenchef m (pl Küchenchefs)
chemical n Chemikalie f
chemist n ❶ (pharmacist) Apotheker m (pl Apotheker), Apothekerin f ❷ (pharmacy) Apotheke f ▷ You get it from the chemist. Du bekommst das in der Apotheke. ❸ (shop selling toiletries) Drogerie f ❹ (scientist) Chemiker m (pl Chemiker), Chemikerin f
chemistry n Chemie f ▷ the chemistry lab das Chemielabor
cheque n Scheck m (pl Schecks) (old) ▷ to write a cheque einen Scheck ausstellen ▷ to pay by cheque mit Scheck bezahlen
chequebook n Scheckheft nt (pl Scheckhefte) (old)
cherry n Kirsche f
chess n Schach nt ▷ to play chess Schach spielen
chessboard n Schachbrett nt (pl Schachbretter)
chest n (of person) Brust f (pl Brüste); **his chest measurement** seine Oberweite; **a chest of drawers** ein Kommode
chestnut n Kastanie f
chew vb kauen [38]
chewing gum n Kaugummi m (pl Kaugummis)
chick n Küken nt (pl Küken) ▷ a hen and her chicks eine Henne mit ihren Küken
chicken n ❶ (food) Hähnchen nt (pl Hähnchen) ▷ I bought a chicken in the supermarket. Ich habe im Supermarkt ein Hähnchen gekauft. ❷ (live) Huhn nt (pl Hühner) ▷ They keep chickens. Sie halten Hühner.
chickenpox nsg Windpocken pl ▷ My sister has chickenpox. Meine Schwester hat Windpocken.
chickpeas npl Kichererbsen fpl

311 | **choice**

chief n Chef m (pl Chefs) ▷ the chief of security der Sicherheitschef
▶ adj hauptsächlich ▷ the chief reason der hauptsächliche Grund
child n Kind nt (pl Kinder) ▷ all the children alle Kinder
childish adj kindisch
child minder n Tagesmutter f (pl Tagesmütter)
children npl see **child**
Chile n Chile nt; **from Chile** aus Chile; **to Chile** nach Chile
chill vb kalt stellen [38] ▷ Put the wine in the fridge to chill. Stell den Wein kalt.
chilli n Chili m (pl Chilis); **chilli peppers** die Peperoni pl
chilly adj kühl
chimney n Schornstein m (pl Schornsteine)
chin n Kinn nt (pl Kinne)
China n China nt
china n Porzellan nt ▷ a china plate ein Porzellanteller m
Chinese adj chinesisch ▷ a Chinese restaurant ein chinesisches Restaurant; **a Chinese man** ein Chinese; **a Chinese woman** eine Chinesin
▶ n (language) Chinesisch nt (gen Chinesischen); **the Chinese** (people) die Chinesen
chip n (in computer) Chip m (pl Chips)
chips npl ❶ (fried potatoes) Pommes frites fpl ▷ We bought some chips. Wir haben Pommes frites gekauft. ❷ (crisps) die Kartoffelchips mpl

> Be careful not to translate **chips** by the German word **Chips**.

chiropodist n Fußpfleger m (pl Fußpfleger), Fußpflegerin f ▷ He's a chiropodist. Er ist Fußpfleger.
chives npl Schnittlauch m
chocolate n Schokolade f ▷ a chocolate cake ein Schokoladenkuchen ▷ hot chocolate heiße Schokolade
choice n Wahl f ▷ I had no choice. Ich hatte keine andere Wahl.

choir n Chor m (pl Chöre) ▷ *I sing in the school choir.* Ich singe im Schulchor.

choke vb ersticken (perf ist erstickt) ▷ *He's choking!* Er erstickt!

choose vb auswählen [4] (perf hat ausgewählt) ▷ *She chose the red shirt.* Sie hat das rote Hemd ausgewählt.

chop vb klein hacken [48] (perf hat gehackt) ▷ *She chopped the onions.* Sie hackte die Zwiebeln klein.
▶ n Kotelett nt (pl Koteletts) ▷ *a pork chop* ein Schweinekotelett

chopsticks npl Stäbchen ntpl

chose vb see **choose**

chosen vb see **choose**

Christ n Christus (gen Christi) ▷ *the birth of Christ* die Geburt Christi

christening n Taufe f

Christian n Christ m (gen Christen, pl Christen), Christin f
▶ adj christlich

Christian name n Vorname m (gen Vornamens, pl Vornamen)

Christmas n Weihnachten nt ▷ *Happy Christmas!* Fröhliche Weihnachten!; **Christmas Day** der erste Weihnachtsfeiertag; **Christmas Eve** Heiligabend
- Traditionally, in Germany gifts are
- exchanged on Christmas Eve.

a Christmas tree ein Weihnachtsbaum m; **a Christmas card** eine Weihnachtskarte
- Most Germans send very few
- Christmas cards.

Christmas dinner das Weihnachtsessen
- Germans traditionally eat goose at
- Christmas rather than turkey.

Christmas pudding
- Germans don't have any traditional
- dessert at Christmas. Most know
- what Christmas pudding is, but
- almost always refer to it as
- **Plumpudding**.

chuck out vb rauswerfen [92] (pres wirft raus, imperf warf raus, perf hat rausgeworfen) ▷ *Chuck out those old magazines.* Wirf diese alten Zeitschriften raus.

chunk n Stück nt (pl Stücke) ▷ *Cut the meat into chunks.* Schneiden Sie das Fleisch in Stücke.

church n Kirche f ▷ *I don't go to church.* Ich gehe nicht in die Kirche.; **the Church of England** die anglikanische Kirche

cider n Apfelwein m

cigar n Zigarre f

cigarette n Zigarette f

cigarette lighter n Zigarettenanzünder m (pl Zigarettenanzünder)

cinema n Kino nt (pl Kinos) ▷ *I'm going to the cinema this evening.* Ich gehe heute Abend ins Kino.

cinnamon n Zimt m

circle n Kreis m (pl Kreise)

circular adj rund

circumstances npl Umstände mpl

circus n Zirkus m (gen Zirkus, pl Zirkusse)

citizen n Bürger m (pl Bürger), Bürgerin f; **a German citizen** ein deutscher Staatsbürger

city n Stadt f (pl Städte); **the city centre** die Innenstadt; **the City** die Londoner City

civilization n Zivilisation f

civil servant n Beamte m (gen Beamten, pl Beamten), Beamtin f
- In Germany most teachers are
- **Beamte**.

▷ *He's a civil servant.* Er ist Beamter.

civil war n Bürgerkrieg m (pl Bürgerkriege)

claim vb ❶ behaupten [2] (perf hat behauptet) ▷ *He claims to have found the money.* Er behauptet, er habe das Geld gefunden.
■ Note the use of the subjunctive.

ENGLISH > GERMAN

❷ (receive) bekommen [**40**] (imperf bekam, perf hat bekommen) ▷ She's claiming unemployment benefit. Sie bekommt Arbeitslosenunterstützung.; **to claim on one's insurance** seine Versicherung in Anspruch nehmen [**52**]
▶ n (on insurance policy) Anspruch m (pl Ansprüche); **to make a claim for damages** Schadensersatz beanspruchen [**7**]

clap vb (applaud) klatschen [**48**] ▷ The audience clapped. Das Publikum klatschte.; **to clap one's hands** klatschen [**48**]

clarinet n Klarinette f ▷ I play the clarinet. Ich spiele Klarinette.

clash vb ❶ (colours) sich beißen [**6**] (imperf bissen sich, perf haben sich gebissen) ▷ These colours clash. Diese Farben beißen sich. ❷ (events) sich überschneiden [**60**] (imperf überschnitt sich, perf hat sich überschnitten) ▷ The concert clashes with Ann's party. Das Konzert überschneidet sich mit Anns Party.

clasp n (of necklace) Verschluss m (gen Verschlusses, pl Verschlüsse)

class n ❶ (group) Klasse f ▷ We're in the same class. Wir sind in derselben Klasse. ❷ (lesson) Stunde f ▷ I go to dancing classes. Ich nehme Tanzstunden.

classic adj klassisch ▷ a classic example ein klassisches Beispiel
▶ n (book, film) Klassiker m (pl Klassiker)

classical adj klassisch ▷ I like classical music. Ich mag klassische Musik.

classmate n Klassenkamerad m (gen Klassenkameraden, pl Klassenkameraden), Klassenkameradin f

classroom n Klassenzimmer f (pl Klassenzimmer)

classroom assistant n Assistenzlehrkraft f (pl Assistenzlehrkräfte)

clause n ❶ (in legal document) Klausel f ❷ (in grammar) Satz m (gen Satzes, pl Sätze)

claw n ❶ (of cat, dog) Kralle f ❷ (of bird) Klaue f ❸ (of crab, lobster) Schere f

clean adj sauber ▷ a clean shirt ein sauberes Hemd
▶ vb sauber machen [**48**] (perf hat sauber gemacht)

cleaner n Putzmann m (pl Putzmänner), Putzfrau f ▷ She's a cleaner. Sie ist Putzfrau.

cleaner's n Reinigung f

cleansing lotion n Reinigungslotion f

clear adj ❶ klar ▷ It's clear you don't believe me. Es ist klar, dass du mir nicht glaubst. ❷ (road, way) frei ▷ The road's clear now. Die Straße ist jetzt frei.
▶ vb ❶ räumen [**38**] ▷ The police are clearing the road after the accident. Die Polizei räumt die Straße nach dem Unfall. ❷ (fog, mist) sich auflösen [**4**] (perf hat sich aufgelöst) ▷ The mist soon cleared. Der Nebel löste sich bald auf.;
to be cleared of a crime von einem Verbrechen freigesprochen werden [**91**]; **to clear the table** den Tisch abräumen [**4**]; **to clear up** aufräumen [**4**]; **I think it's going to clear up.** (weather) Ich glaube, es hellt sich auf.

clearly adv klar ▷ She explained it very clearly. Sie hat es sehr klar erklärt. ▷ The English coast was clearly visible. Die englische Küste war klar zu sehen.; **to speak clearly** deutlich sprechen [**70**]

clementine n Klementine f

clench vb She clenched her fists. Sie ballte die Fäuste.

clerk n Büroangestellte m (gen Büroangestellten, pl Büroangestellten), Büroangestellte f (gen Büroangestellten) ▷ She's a clerk. Sie ist Büroangestellte.

clever adj ❶ klug ▷ She's very clever. Sie ist sehr klug. ❷ (ingenious) genial ▷ a

click on | 314   **ENGLISH > GERMAN**

clever system ein geniales System ▷ *What a clever idea!* Das ist eine geniale Idee!

click on vb (computer) anklicken [4] (perf hat angeklickt) ▷ *to click on an icon* ein Icon anklicken; **to click on the mouse** mit der Maus klicken [48]

client n Klient m (gen Klienten, pl Klienten), Klientin f

cliff n Klippe f

climate n Klima nt (pl Klimas)

climate change n Klimawandel m

climate crisis n Klimakrise f

climate emergency n Klimanotstand m

climb vb ❶ steigen [74] auf (imperf stieg, perf ist gestiegen) ▷ *We're going to climb Snowdon.* Wir steigen auf den Snowdon. ❷ (stairs) hinaufgehen [29] (imperf ging hinauf, perf ist hinaufgegangen) ▷ *I watched him climb the stairs.* Ich sah ihn die Treppe hinaufgehen.; **She finds it difficult to climb the stairs.** Das Treppensteigen fällt ihr schwer.

climber n Kletterer m (pl Kletterer), Kletterin f

climbing n Klettern nt; **to go climbing** klettern gehen [29]

clingfilm n Frischhaltefolie f

clinic n Klinik f

cloakroom n ❶ (for coats) Garderobe f ❷ (toilet) Toilette f

clock n Uhr f; **a grandfather clock** eine Standuhr; **an alarm clock** ein Wecker m; **a clock radio** ein Radiowecker m

close adj, adv ❶ (near) nahe ▷ *close relations* nahe Verwandte ▷ *I'm very close to my sister.* Ich stehe meiner Schwester sehr nahe.; **The shops are very close.** Die Geschäfte sind ganz in der Nähe.; **She's a close friend of mine.** Sie ist eine gute Freundin von mir.; **Come closer!** Komm näher!; **close to** in der Nähe ❷ (contest) knapp ▷ *It's going to be very close.* Das wird sehr knapp. ❸ (weather) schwül ▷ *It's close today.* Es ist schwül heute.

▶ vb schließen (imperf schloss, perf hat geschlossen) ▷ *What time does the pool close?* Wann schließt das Schwimmbad? ▷ *The doors close automatically.* Die Türen schließen automatisch.; **Please close the door.** Bitte mach die Tür zu.

closed adj geschlossen ▷ *The bank's closed.* Die Bank ist geschlossen.

closely adv (look, examine) genau

cloth n (material) Stoff m (pl Stoffe); **a cloth** ein Lappen m

clothes npl Kleider ntpl ▷ *new clothes* neue Kleider; **a clothes line** eine Wäscheleine; **a clothes peg** eine Wäscheklammer

cloud n ❶ (in sky, of dust) Wolke f ❷ (internet) Cloud f

cloudy adj bewölkt

clove n a clove of garlic eine Knoblauchzehe

clown n Clown m (pl Clowns)

club n Klub m (pl Klubs) ▷ *a tennis club* ein Tennisklub ▷ *the youth club* der Jugendklub; **clubs** (in cards) Kreuz nt

club together vb zusammenlegen [15] (perf hat zusammengelegt)

clubbing n **to go clubbing** in Klubs gehen [29]

clue n Hinweis m (pl Hinweise) ▷ *an important clue* ein wichtiger Hinweis; **I haven't a clue.** Ich habe keine Ahnung.

clumsy adj tollpatschig ▷ *Toby is even clumsier than his sister.* Toby ist noch tollpatschiger als seine Schwester.

clutch n (of car) Kupplung f
▶ vb umklammern [34] (perf hat umklammert) ▷ *She clutched my arm.* Sie umklammerte meinen Arm.

clutter n Kram m ▷ *There's so much clutter in here.* Hier liegt so viel Kram herum.

coach n ❶ Reisebus m (gen Reisebusses, pl Reisebusse); **by coach** mit dem Bus; **the coach station** der Busbahnhof;

ENGLISH > GERMAN

a coach trip eine Busreise ❷ *(trainer)* Trainer *m (pl* Trainer), Trainerin *f* ▷ *the German coach* der deutsche Trainer
coal *n* Kohle *f* ▷ *a coal mine* eine Kohlezeche; **a coal miner** ein Bergarbeiter *m*
coarse *adj* ❶ grob ▷ *coarse black cloth* grober schwarzer Stoff ❷ grobkörnig ▷ *The sand is very coarse on that beach.* Der Sand an diesem Strand ist sehr grobkörnig.
coast *n* Küste *f* ▷ *It's on the west coast of Scotland.* Es liegt an der Westküste Schottlands.
coastguard *n* Küstenwache *f*
coat *n* Mantel *m (pl* Mäntel) ▷ *a warm coat* ein warmer Mantel; **a coat of paint** ein Anstrich *m*
coat hanger *n* Kleiderbügel *m (pl* Kleiderbügel)
cobweb *n* Spinnennetz *nt*
cockerel *n* Hahn *m (pl* Hähne)
cocoa *n* Kakao *m (pl* Kakaos *or* Kakao) ▷ *a cup of cocoa* eine Tasse Kakao

> When ordering more than one cup of cocoa use the plural form **Kakao.**
> ▷ *Two cocoas, please.* Zwei Kakao bitte.

coconut *n* Kokosnuss *f (pl* Kokosnüsse)
code *n* Code *m (pl* Codes)
▶ *vb* codieren [76]
coffee *n* Kaffee *m (pl* Kaffees *or* Kaffee) ▷ *A cup of coffee, please.* Eine Tasse Kaffee, bitte.

> When ordering more than one coffee use the plural form **Kaffee.**
> ▷ *Two coffees, please.* Zwei Kaffee bitte.

coffee table *n* Couchtisch *m (pl* Couchtische)
coffin *n* Sarg *m (pl* Särge)
coin *n* Münze *f*; **a two-euro coin** ein Zweieurostück *nt*
coincidence *n* Zufall *m (pl* Zufälle)
Coke® *n* Cola *f (pl* Colas) ▷ *a can of Coke®* eine Dose Cola
colander *n* Seiher *m (pl* Seiher)

315 | collect

cold *adj* kalt ▷ *The water's cold.* Das Wasser ist kalt. ▷ *It's cold today.* Heute ist es kalt.

> When you talk about a person being 'cold', you use the impersonal construction.
> ▷ *I'm cold.* Mir ist kalt. ▷ *Are you cold?* Ist dir kalt?

▶ *n* ❶ Kälte *f* ▷ *I can't stand the cold.* Ich kann Kälte nicht aussstehen. ❷ Schnupfen *m (pl* Schnupfen) ▷ *to catch a cold* einen Schnupfen bekommen ▷ *to have a cold* einen Schnupfen haben ▷ *I've got a bad cold.* Ich habe einen üblen Schnupfen.; **a cold sore** ein Fieberbläschen *nt*
coleslaw *n* Krautsalat *m (pl* Krautsalate)
collapse *vb* zusammenbrechen [11] *(pres* bricht zusammen, *imperf* brach zusammen, *perf* ist zusammengebrochen) ▷ *He collapsed.* Er brach zusammen.
collar *n* ❶ *(of coat, shirt)* Kragen *m (pl* Kragen) ❷ *(for animal)* Halsband *nt (pl* Halsbänder)
collarbone *n* Schlüsselbein *nt (pl* Schlüsselbeine) ▷ *I broke my collarbone.* Ich habe mir das Schlüsselbein gebrochen.
colleague *n* Kollege *m (gen* Kollegen, *pl* Kollegen), Kollegin *f*
collect *vb* ❶ einsammeln [4] *(perf* hat eingesammelt) ▷ *The teacher collected the exercise books.* Der Lehrer hat die Hefte eingesammelt. ❷ sammeln [34] ▷ *I collect stamps.* Ich sammle Briefmarken. ▷ *They're collecting for charity.* Sie sammeln für wohltätige Zwecke. ❸ *(come to fetch)* abholen [4] *(perf* hat abgeholt) ▷ *Their mother collects them from school.* Ihre Mutter holt sie von der Schule ab. ▷ *They collect the rubbish twice a week.* Der Müll wird zweimal pro Woche abgeholt.

collection n Sammlung f ▷ my CD collection meine CD-Sammlung ▷ a collection for charity eine Spendensammlung

collector n Sammler m (pl Sammler), Sammlerin f

college n Fachhochschule f
* A **Fachhochschule** is an institute of higher education for pupils aged over 18, which combines academic studies with work experience. It is oriented towards the needs of industry and commerce.

collide vb zusammenstoßen (pres stößt zusammen, imperf stieß zusammen, perf ist zusammengestoßen)

collie n Collie m (pl Collies)

collision n Zusammenstoß m (gen Zusammenstoßes, pl Zusammenstöße)

colon n (punctuation mark) Doppelpunkt m

colonel n Oberst m (gen Obersten, pl Obersten)

colour (US **color**) n Farbe f ▷ What colour is it? Welche Farbe hat es?

colourful (US **colorful**) adj farbig

comb n Kamm m (pl Kämme)
▶ vb to comb one's hair sich kämmen [38]

combination n Kombination f

combine vb vereinen [84] (perf hat vereint) ▷ The film combines humour with suspense. Der Film vereint Humor und Spannung.

come vb kommen [40] (imperf kam, perf ist gekommen) ▷ I'm coming! Ich komme! ▷ The letter came this morning. Der Brief kam heute früh. ▷ Can I come too? Kann ich mitkommen? ▷ Some friends came to see us. Einige Freunde sind zu Besuch gekommen. ▷ I'll come with you. Ich komme mit dir.; **to come across** zufällig finden [24]; **She comes across as a nice girl.** Sie scheint ein nettes Mädchen zu sein.; **to come back** zurückkommen [40]; **to come down** (1) (person, lift) herunterkommen [40] (2) (prices) fallen [22]; **to come from** kommen [40] aus; **to come in** hereinkommen [40]; **Come on!** Na komm!; **to come out** herauskommen [40]; **to come round** (after faint, operation) wieder zu sich kommen [40]; **to come up** heraufkommen [40]; **to come up to somebody** auf jemanden zukommen [40]

comedian n Komiker m (pl Komiker), Komikerin f

comedy n Komödie f

comfortable adj bequem; **I'm very comfortable, thanks.** Danke, ich fühle mich sehr wohl.

comic n (magazine) Comicheft nt (pl Comichefte)

comic strip n Comicstrip m (pl Comicstrips)

comma n Komma nt (pl Kommas)

command n Befehl m (pl Befehle)

comment n Kommentar m (pl Kommentare) ▷ He made no comment. Er gab keinen Kommentar ab. ▷ No comment! Kein Kommentar!
▶ vb to comment on something eine Bemerkung zu etwas machen [48]

commentary n (on TV, radio) Kommentar m (pl Kommentare)

commentator n (sports) Sportreporter m (pl Sportreporter), Sportreporterin f

commercial n Werbespot m (pl Werbespots)

commit vb to commit a crime ein Verbrechen begehen [29]; **to commit oneself** sich festlegen [4]; **to commit suicide** Selbstmord begehen [29]

committee n Ausschuss m (gen Ausschusses, pl Ausschüsse)

common adj gebräuchlich ▷ 'Smith' is a very common surname. 'Smith' ist ein sehr gebräuchlicher Nachname.; **in common** gemein

ENGLISH > GERMAN

▶ n Gemeindewiese f ▷ We went for a walk on the common. Wir sind auf der Gemeindewiese spazieren gegangen.

Commons npl **the House of Commons** das britische Unterhaus

communicate vb kommunizieren [**76**] (perf hat kommuniziert)

communication n Kommunikation f

communion n Kommunion f ▷ my First Communion meine Erstkommunion

communism n Kommunismus m (gen Kommunismus)

community n Gemeinschaft f; **the local community** die Gemeinde

commute vb pendeln [**34**] (perf ist gependelt) ▷ She commutes between Liss and London. Sie pendelt zwischen Liss und London.

compact disc n Compact Disc f (pl Compact Discs); **compact disc player** der CD-Spieler

company n ❶ Unternehmen nt (pl Unternehmen) ▷ He works for a big company. Er arbeitet für ein großes Unternehmen. ❷ Gesellschaft f ▷ an insurance company eine Versicherungsgesellschaft; **a theatre company** ein Theaterensemble nt; **to keep somebody company** jemandem Gesellschaft leisten [**2**]

comparatively adv relativ

compare vb vergleichen (imperf verglich, perf hat verglichen) ▷ People always compare him with his brother. Die Leute vergleichen ihn immer mit seinem Bruder.; **compared with** im Vergleich zu

comparison n Vergleich m (pl Vergleiche)

compartment n Abteil nt (pl Abteile)

compass n Kompass m (gen Kompasses, pl Kompasse)

compensation n Schadenersatz m ▷ I got a thousand pounds compensation. Ich bekam tausend Pfund Schadenersatz.

compete vb teilnehmen [**52**] (pres nimmt teil, imperf nahm teil, perf hat teilgenommen) ▷ I'm competing in the marathon. Ich nehme am Marathon teil.; **to compete for something** um etwas kämpfen [**38**]; **There are fifty students competing for six places.** Fünfzig Studenten bewerben sich auf sechs Studienplätze.

competent adj kompetent

competition n (organized event) Wettbewerb m (pl Wettbewerbe) ▷ a singing competition ein Gesangswettbewerb

competitive adj **I'm a very competitive person.** Ich bin ein sehr ehrgeiziger Mensch.

competitor n (participant) Teilnehmer m (pl Teilnehmer), Teilnehmerin f

complain vb sich beschweren [**18**] (perf hat sich beschwert) ▷ I'm going to complain to the manager. Ich werde mich beim Geschäftsführer beschweren. ▷ We complained about the noise. Wir haben uns über den Lärm beschwert.

complaint n Beschwerde f ▷ There were lots of complaints about the food. Es gab viele Beschwerden über das Essen.

complete adj vollständig

completely adv völlig

complexion n Teint m (pl Teints)

complicated adj kompliziert

compliment n Kompliment nt (pl Komplimente)

▶ vb **They complimented me on my German.** Sie haben mir Komplimente zu meinem Deutsch gemacht.

compose vb (music) komponieren [**76**] (perf hat komponiert); **to be composed of something** aus etwas bestehen [**72**]

composer n Komponist m (gen Komponisten, pl Komponisten), Komponistin f

comprehension n (school exercise) Verständnis nt

comprehensive adj umfassend
▷ a comprehensive guide ein umfassender Reiseführer

comprehensive school n Gesamtschule f
* **Gesamtschulen** are the exception
* rather than the rule in Germany.

compulsory adj obligatorisch
computer n Computer m (pl Computer)
computer game n Computerspiel nt (pl Computerspiele)
computer programmer n Programmierer m (pl Programmierer), Programmiererin f ▷ She's a computer programmer. Sie ist Programmiererin.
computer science n Informatik f
computing n Informatik f
concentrate vb sich konzentrieren [76] (perf hat sich konzentriert) ▷ I couldn't concentrate. Ich konnte mich nicht konzentrieren.
concentration n Konzentration f
concern n Sorge f ▷ to express concern about something Sorge über etwas ausdrücken
▶ vb betreffen [78] (pres betrifft, imperf betraf, perf hat betroffen) ▷ It concerns all of us. Es betrifft uns alle.
concerned adj to be concerned sich Sorgen machen [48]; **as far as I'm concerned** was mich betrifft
concerning prep bezüglich ▷ For further information concerning the job, contact Mr Ross. Für weitere Informationen bezüglich der Stelle wenden Sie sich an Herrn Ross.
concert n Konzert nt (pl Konzerte)
concrete n Beton m (pl Betons)
condemn vb verurteilen [84] (perf hat verurteilt)
condition n ❶ Bedingung f ▷ I'll do it, on one condition ... Ich mache es unter einer Bedingung ... ❷ Zustand m (pl Zustände) ▷ in good condition in gutem Zustand

conditional n Konditional m
conditioner n (for hair) Spülung f
condom n Kondom nt (pl Kondome)
conduct vb (orchestra) dirigieren [76] (perf hat dirigiert)
conductor n Dirigent m (gen Dirigenten, pl Dirigenten), Dirigentin f
cone n ❶ Eistüte f ▷ an ice-cream cone eine Eistüte ❷ (geometric shape) Kegel m (pl Kegel); **a traffic cone** ein Pylon m
conference n Konferenz f
confess vb gestehen [72] (imperf gestand, perf hat gestanden) ▷ He finally confessed. Er hat schließlich gestanden. ▷ He confessed to the murder. Er hat den Mord gestanden.
confession n ❶ Geständnis nt (gen Geständnisses, pl Geständnisse) ▷ He signed a confession. Er unterschrieb ein Geständnis. ❷ (in church) Beichte f ▷ to go to confession zur Beichte gehen
confidence n ❶ Vertrauen nt ▷ I've got confidence in you. Ich habe Vertrauen in dich. ❷ Selbstvertrauen nt ▷ She lacks confidence. Sie hat zu wenig Selbstvertrauen.
confident adj ❶ (sure of something) zuversichtlich ▷ I'm confident everything will be okay. Ich bin zuversichtlich, dass alles gut gehen wird. ❷ (self-assured) selbstbewusst ▷ She seems to be a confident person. Sie scheint eine selbstbewusste Frau zu sein.
confidential adj vertraulich
confirm vb (booking) bestätigen [18] (perf hat bestätigt)
confuse vb durcheinanderbringen [13] (imperf brachte durcheinander, perf hat durcheinandergebracht) ▷ Don't confuse me! Bring mich nicht durcheinander!
confused adj durcheinander
confusing adj verwirrend
confusion n Durcheinander nt

congratulate vb beglückwünschen [**7**] (perf hat beglückwünscht) ▷ *All my friends congratulated me.* Alle meine Freunde haben mich beglückwünscht.

congratulations npl Glückwunsch m (pl Glückwünsche) ▷ *Congratulations on your new job!* Herzlichen Glückwunsch zum neuen Job!

conjunction n Konjunktion f

conjurer n Zauberkünstler m (pl Zauberkünstler), Zauberkünstlerin f

connection n ❶ Zusammenhang m (pl Zusammenhänge) ▷ *There's no connection between the two events.* Es besteht kein Zusammenhang zwischen den beiden Ereignissen. ❷ (electrical) Kontakt m (pl Kontakte) ▷ *There's a loose connection.* Da ist ein Wackelkontakt. ❸ (of trains, planes) Anschluss m (gen Anschlusses, pl Anschlüsse) ▷ *We missed our connection.* Wir haben unseren Anschluss verpasst.

conscience n Gewissen nt ▷ *I have a guilty conscience.* Ich habe ein schlechtes Gewissen.

conscious adj bewusst ▷ *politically conscious* politisch bewusst ▷ *a conscious effort* eine bewusste Anstrengung; **to be conscious of something (1)** (know) sich einer Sache bewusst sein [**65**] ▷ *I was conscious of his disapproval.* Ich war mir seiner Missbilligung bewusst. **(2)** (notice) etwas bemerken [**7**] ▷ *She was conscious of Max looking at her.* Sie hatte bemerkt, dass Max sie ansah.

consciousness n Bewusstsein nt; **to lose consciousness** bewusstlos werden [**91**]

consequence n Folge f

consequently adv folglich

conservation n Schutz m ▷ *nature conservation* der Naturschutz

conservative adj konservativ; **the Conservative Party** die Konservative Partei

conservatory n Wintergarten m (pl Wintergärten)

consider vb in Erwägung ziehen [**96**] (imperf zog in Erwägung, perf hat in Erwägung gezogen) ▷ *We considered cancelling our holiday.* Wir zogen in Erwägung, den Urlaub abzusagen.; **I'm considering the idea.** Ich denke darüber nach.; **He considered it a waste of time.** Er hielt es für Zeitverschwendung.

considerate adj aufmerksam ▷ *That was very considerate of you.* Das war sehr aufmerksam von dir.; **not very considerate** nicht sehr rücksichtsvoll

considering prep ❶ dafür, dass ▷ *Considering we were there for a month ...* Dafür, dass wir einen Monat waren ... ❷ unter den Umständen ▷ *I got a good mark, considering.* Unter den Umständen bekam ich eine gute Note.

consist vb to consist of bestehen [**72**] aus

consistent adj beständig ▷ *He's our most consistent player.* Er ist unser beständigster Spieler.

consonant n Konsonant m (gen Konsonanten, pl Konsonanten)

constant adj beständig

constantly adv dauernd

constipated adj verstopft

construct vb bauen [**38**]

construction n Bau m

consult vb ❶ (solicitor, doctor) um Rat fragen [**38**] ❷ (book) nachsehen [**64**] in (pres sieht nach, imperf sah nach, perf hat nachgesehen) ▷ *Consult the dictionary!* Sieh im Wörterbuch nach!

consumer n Verbraucher m (pl Verbraucher), Verbraucherin f

contact n Kontakt m (pl Kontakte) ▷ *I'm in contact with her.* Ich bin in Kontakt mit ihr.
▶ vb sich in Verbindung setzen [**36**] mit ▷ *Please contact us immediately.* Bitte

setzen Sie sich sofort mit uns in Verbindung.; **Where can we contact you?** Wo können wir Sie erreichen?
contact lenses npl Kontaktlinsen fpl
contactless adj (payment) kontaktlos
contain vb enthalten [33] (pres enthält, imperf enthielt, perf hat enthalten)
container n Behälter m (pl Behälter)
contents npl Inhalt m; **table of contents** das Inhaltsverzeichnis
contest n Wettbewerb m (pl Wettbewerbe)
contestant n Teilnehmer m (pl Teilnehmer), Teilnehmerin f
context n Zusammenhang m (pl Zusammenhänge)
continent n Kontinent m (pl Kontinente) ▷ *How many continents are there?* Wie viele Kontinente gibt es?; **the Continent** Kontinentaleuropa nt; **I've never been to the Continent.** Ich war noch nie auf dem Kontinent.
continental quilt n Steppdecke f
continue vb weitermachen [48] (perf hat weitergemacht) ▷ *We'll continue tomorrow.* Wir machen morgen weiter.; **Please continue!** Bitte fahren Sie fort!; **She continued talking to her friend.** Sie redete weiter mit ihrer Freundin.
continuous adj laufend; **continuous assessment** laufende Leistungskontrolle
contraceptive n Verhütungsmittel nt (pl Verhütungsmittel)
contract n Vertrag m (pl Verträge)
contradict vb widersprechen [70] (pres widerspricht, imperf widersprach, perf hat widersprochen) ▷ *Don't contradict me!* Widersprich mir nicht!
contrary n Gegenteil nt; **on the contrary** im Gegenteil
contrast n Kontrast m (pl Kontraste)
contribute vb beitragen [77] (pres trägt bei, imperf trug bei, perf hat beigetragen) ▷ *The treaty will contribute to world peace.* Der Vertrag wird zum Weltfrieden beitragen. ❷ (donate) spenden [54] ▷ *She contributed ten pounds.* Sie hat zehn Pfund gespendet.
contribution n Beitrag m (pl Beiträge)
control n Kontrolle f; **to lose control** (of vehicle) die Kontrolle verlieren [85]; **the controls** (of machine) die Bedienelemente ntpl; **to be in control** das Sagen haben [32]; **to keep control** (of people) Disziplin halten [33]; **out of control** (child, class) außer Rand und Band
▶ vb ❶ (country, organization) unter Kontrolle haben [32] (pres hat unter Kontrolle, imperf hatte unter Kontrolle, perf hat unter Kontrolle gehabt) ❷ Disziplin halten [33] in (pres hält Disziplin in, imperf hielt Disziplin in, perf hat Disziplin gehalten in) ▷ *He can't control the class.* Er kann in der Klasse keine Disziplin halten. ❸ unter Kontrolle halten [33] ▷ *I couldn't control the horse.* Ich konnte das Pferd nicht mehr unter Kontrolle halten. ❹ (regulate) regeln [34] ▷ *You can control the volume.* Sie können die Lautstärke regeln.; **to control oneself** sich beherrschen [7]
controversial adj umstritten ▷ *a controversial book* ein umstrittenes Buch
convenient adj (place) günstig ▷ *The hotel's convenient for the airport.* Das Hotel ist in günstiger Lage zum Flughafen. ▷ *It's not convenient for me right now.* Es ist gerade ungünstig.; **Would Monday be convenient for you?** Würde dir Montag passen?
conventional adj konventionell
conversation n Unterhaltung f; **a German conversation class** deutsche Konversation
convert vb umbauen [4] (perf hat umgebaut) ▷ *We've converted the loft into a spare room.* Wir haben den Speicher zu einem Gästezimmer umgebaut.

ENGLISH > GERMAN

conviction n Überzeugung f ▷ *She spoke with great conviction.* Sie sprach mit großer Überzeugung.; **He has three previous convictions for robbery.** Er ist bereits dreimal wegen Raubes vorbestraft.

convince vb überzeugen [18] (*perf* hat überzeugt) ▷ *I'm not convinced.* Ich bin nicht überzeugt.

cook vb kochen [48] ▷ *I can't cook.* Ich kann nicht kochen. ▷ *She's cooking lunch.* Sie kocht das Mittagessen.; **to be cooked** fertig sein [65]
▶ n Koch m (pl Köche), Köchin f ▷ *Werner's an excellent cook.* Werner ist ein ausgezeichneter Koch.

cooker n Herd m (pl Herde) ▷ *a gas cooker* ein Gasherd

cookery n Kochen nt; **a cookery class** ein Kochkurs m

cookie n (US) Keks m (gen Kekses, pl Kekse)

cooking n Kochen nt; **I like cooking.** Ich koche gern.

cool adj ❶ (of bottle) kühl ▷ *a cooler place* ein kühlerer Ort ❷ (great) cool ▷ *That's really cool!* Das ist echt cool!; **to stay cool** (keep calm) ruhig bleiben [10]
▶ vb kühlen [38]; **Just cool it!** (*informal*) Immer mit der Ruhe!

cooperation n Zusammenarbeit f

cop n Polizist m (gen Polizisten, pl Polizisten), Polizistin f

co-parent vb eine gemeinsame Elternschaft eingehen [29]

cope vb es schaffen [48] ▷ *It was hard, but we coped.* Es war schwer, aber wir haben es geschafft.; **to cope with** bewältigen [84]

copper n ❶ Kupfer nt ▷ *a copper bracelet* ein Kupferarmband ❷ (police officer) Polizist m (gen Polizisten, pl Polizisten), Polizistin f

copy n ❶ (of letter, document) Kopie f ❷ (of book) Exemplar nt (pl Exemplare)
▶ vb ❶ (write down) abschreiben [61] (*imperf* schrieb ab, *perf* hat abgeschrieben) ▷ *She copied the sentence.* Sie schrieb den Satz ab. ▷ *The teacher accused him of copying.* Der Lehrer warf ihm vor, abgeschrieben zu haben. ❷ (person) nachmachen [4] (*perf* hat nachgemacht) ▷ *She always copies her sister.* Sie macht ihrer Schwester alles nach. ❸ (computer) kopieren [76] (*perf* hat kopiert) ▷ *to copy and paste* kopieren und einfügen

core n (of fruit) Stein m

cork n ❶ (of bottle) Korken m (pl Korken) ❷ (material) Kork m ▷ *a cork table mat* ein Korkuntersetzer m

corkscrew n Korkenzieher m (pl Korkenzieher)

corn n ❶ (wheat) Getreide nt (pl Getreide) ❷ (sweetcorn) Mais m; **corn on the cob** der Maiskolben

corner n ❶ Ecke f ▷ *in a corner of the room* in einer Ecke des Zimmers ▷ *the shop on the corner* das Geschäft an der Ecke ▷ *He lives just round the corner.* Er wohnt gleich um die Ecke. ❷ (in football) Eckball m (pl Eckbälle)

cornflakes npl Cornflakes pl

Cornwall n Cornwall nt; **in Cornwall** in Cornwall

corpse n Leiche f

correct adj richtig ▷ *That's correct.* Das ist richtig. ▷ *the correct answer* die richtige Antwort
▶ vb korrigieren [76] (*perf* hat korrigiert)

correction n Verbesserung f

correctly adv richtig

corridor n Korridor m (pl Korridore)

corruption n Korruption f

Corsica n Korsika nt; **from Corsica** aus Korsika; **to Corsica** nach Korsika

cosmetics npl Kosmetika ntpl

cosmetic surgery n Schönheitschirurgie f

cost vb kosten [2] ▷ *The meal cost seventy euros.* Das Essen hat siebzig Euro

gekostet. ▷ *How much does it cost?* Wie viel kostet das? ▷ *It costs too much.* Das kostet zu viel.
▶ n Kosten pl ▷ *the cost of living* die Lebenshaltungskosten; **at all costs** um jeden Preis

costume n Kostüm nt (pl Kostüme)

cosy adj gemütlich

cot n ❶ (*for children*) Kinderbett nt (pl Kinderbetten) ❷ (*camp bed*) Campingliege f

cotton n Baumwolle f ▷ *a cotton shirt* ein Baumwollhemd nt; **cotton candy** die Zuckerwatte; **cotton wool** die Watte

couch n Couch f (pl Couchs)

cough vb husten [2]
▶ n Husten m ▷ *a bad cough* ein schlimmer Husten ▷ *I've got a cough.* Ich habe Husten.

could vb see **can**

council n Gemeinderat m (pl Gemeinderäte) ▷ *He's on the council.* Er ist im Gemeinderat.; **a council estate** eine Siedlung des sozialen Wohnungsbaus; **a council house** eine Sozialwohnung

- In Germany the council provides flats
- rather than houses.

councillor n Gemeinderat m (pl Gemeinderäte), Gemeinderätin f ▷ *She's a local councillor.* Sie ist Gemeinderätin.

count vb zählen [38]; **to count on** zählen [38] auf

counter n ❶ (*in shop*) Ladentisch m (pl Ladentische) ❷ (*in post office, bank*) Schalter m (pl Schalter) ❸ (*in game*) Spielmarke f

country n Land nt (pl Länder) ▷ *the border between the two countries* die Grenze zwischen den beiden Ländern; **in the country** auf dem Land; **country dancing** der Volkstanz

countryside n Landschaft f

county n Grafschaft f

- The nearest German equivalent of a
- county would be a **Bundesland**.

the county council der Grafschaftsrat

- The nearest German equivalent of a
- county council would be the
- **Landtag**.

couple n Paar nt (pl Paare) ▷ *the couple who live next door* das Paar von nebenan; **a couple** ein paar

Note that in this sense **paar** is spelt with a small 'p'.

▷ *a couple of hours* ein paar Stunden

courage n Mut m

courgette n Zucchini f (pl Zucchini)

courier n ❶ (*for tourists*) Reiseleiter m (pl Reiseleiter), Reiseleiterin f ❷ (*delivery service*) Kurier m (pl Kuriere) ▷ *They sent it by courier.* Sie haben es mit Kurier geschickt.

course n ❶ Kurs m (pl Kurse) ▷ *a German course* ein Deutschkurs ▷ *to go on a course* einen Kurs machen ❷ Gang m (pl Gänge) ▷ *the first course* der erste Gang; **the main course** das Hauptgericht ❸ Platz m (pl Plätze) ▷ *a golf course* ein Golfplatz; **of course** natürlich

court n ❶ (*of law*) Gericht nt (pl Gerichte) ▷ *He was in court last week.* Er war letzte Woche vor Gericht. ❷ (*tennis*) Platz m (pl Plätze) ▷ *There are tennis and squash courts.* Es gibt Tennis- und Squashplätze.

courtyard n Hof m (pl Höfe)

cousin n ❶ (*man*) Vetter m (pl Vettern) ❷ (*woman*) Cousine f

cover n ❶ (*of book*) Umschlag m (pl Umschläge) ❷ (*of duvet*) Bezug m (pl Bezüge)
▶ vb ❶ bedecken [18] (*perf* hat bedeckt) ▷ *Cover the dough with a cloth.* Bedecke den Teig mit einem Tuch.; **My face was covered with mosquito bites.** Mein Gesicht war voller Mückenstiche.
❷ decken [38] ▷ *Our insurance didn't cover it.* Unsere Versicherung hat das nicht gedeckt.; **to cover up a scandal** einen Skandal vertuschen [7]

ENGLISH > GERMAN

Covid n Covid-19 nt
cow n Kuh f (pl Kühe)
coward n Feigling m (pl Feiglinge)
▪ **der Feigling** is also used for women.
▷ *She's a coward.* Sie ist ein Feigling.
cowboy n Cowboy m (pl Cowboys)
crab n Krabbe f
crack n ① (in wall) Riss m (gen Risses, pl Risse) ② (in cup, window) Sprung m (pl Sprünge) ③ (drug) Crack nt; **I'll have a crack at it.** Ich werd's mal versuchen.
▶ vb ① (nut) knacken **[48]** ② (egg) aufschlagen **[59]** (pres schlägt auf, imperf schlug auf, perf hat aufgeschlagen); **to crack a joke** einen Witz reißen; **to crack down on** hart durchgreifen gegen
cracked adj (cup, window) kaputt
cracker n ① (biscuit) Cracker m (pl Cracker) ② (Christmas cracker) Knallbonbon m (pl Knallbonbons)
craft n Werken nt ▷ *We do craft at school.* Wir haben Werken in der Schule.; **a craft centre** ein Kunstgewerbezentrum nt
crane n (machine) Kran m
crash vb kaputt fahren **[21]** (pres fährt kaputt, imperf fuhr kaputt, perf hat kaputt gefahren) ▷ *He's crashed his car.* Er hat sein Auto kaputt gefahren.; **The plane crashed.** Das Flugzeug stürzte ab.; **to crash into something** auf etwas fahren **[21]**
▶ n ① (of car) Unfall m (pl Unfälle) ② (of plane) Unglück nt (pl Unglücke); **a crash helmet** ein Sturzhelm m; **a crash course** ein Crashkurs m
crawl vb (baby) krabbeln **[88]** (perf ist gekrabbelt)
▶ n Kraulen nt; **to do the crawl** kraulen **[38]**
crazy adj verrückt
cream adj (colour) cremefarben
▶ n Sahne f ▷ *strawberries and cream* Erdbeeren mit Sahne ▷ *a cream cake* eine Sahnetorte; **cream cheese** der Frischkäse; **sun cream** die Sonnencreme
crease n Falte f
creased adj zerknittert
create vb schaffen (imperf schuf, perf hat geschaffen)
creative adj kreativ
creature n Lebewesen nt (pl Lebewesen)
crèche n Kinderkrippe f
credit n Kredit m (pl Kredite) ▷ *on credit* auf Kredit
credit card n Kreditkarte f
creep n **It gives me the creeps.** Es ist mir nicht geheuer.
▶ vb kriechen (imperf kroch, perf ist gekrochen)
crew n Mannschaft f
crew cut n Bürstenhaarschnitt m (pl Bürstenhaarschnitte)
cricket n ① Cricket nt
▪ Cricket is practically never played in Germany.
▷ *I play cricket.* Ich spiele Cricket.; **a cricket bat** ein Cricketschläger m
② (insect) Grille f
crime n ① Verbrechen nt (pl Verbrechen) ▷ *Murder is a crime.* Mord ist ein Verbrechen. ② (lawlessness) Kriminalität f ▷ *Crime is rising.* Die Kriminalität nimmt zu.
criminal n Verbrecher m (pl Verbrecher), Verbrecherin f
▶ adj kriminell ▷ *It's criminal!* Das ist kriminell!; **It's a criminal offence.** Das ist eine strafbare Handlung.; **to have a criminal record** vorbestraft sein **[65]**
crisis n Krise f
crisp adj (food) knusprig
crisps npl Chips mpl ▷ *a bag of crisps* eine Tüte Chips
critical adj kritisch
criticism n Kritik f

criticize vb kritisieren [76] (perf hat kritisiert)
Croatia n Kroatien nt; **from Croatia** aus Kroatien; **to Croatia** nach Kroatien
crochet vb häkeln [34]
crocodile n Krokodil nt (pl Krokodile)
crook n (criminal) Verbrecher m (pl Verbrecher)
crop n Ernte f ▷ a good crop of apples eine gute Apfelernte
cross n Kreuz nt (pl Kreuze)
▶ adj böse ▷ to be cross about something wegen etwas böse sein
▶ vb (street, bridge) überqueren [7] (perf hat überquert); **to cross out** durchstreichen; **to cross over** hinübergehen [29]
cross-country n (race) Querfeldeinrennen nt (pl Querfeldeinrennen); **cross-country skiing** der Langlauf
crossing n ❶ (by boat) Überfahrt f ▷ the crossing from Dover to Calais die Überfahrt von Dover nach Calais ❷ (for pedestrians) Fußgängerüberweg m (pl Fußgängerüberwege)
crossroads nsg Kreuzung f
crossword n Kreuzworträtsel nt (pl Kreuzworträtsel) ▷ I like doing crosswords. Ich mache gern Kreuzworträtsel.
crouch down vb sich niederkauern [15] (perf hat sich niedergekauert)
crow n Krähe f
crowd n Menge f; **the crowd** (at sports match) die Zuschauer mpl
▶ vb sich drängen [38] ▷ The children crowded round the model. Die Kinder drängten sich um das Modell.
crowded adj voll
crown n Krone f
crude adj (vulgar) ordinär
cruel adj grausam
cruise n Kreuzfahrt f ▷ to go on a cruise eine Kreuzfahrt machen

crumb n Krümel m (pl Krümel)
crush vb ❶ zerquetschen [95] (perf hat zerquetscht) ▷ The tomatoes got crushed. Die Tomaten wurden zerquetscht. ❷ (finger) quetschen [48] ▷ I crushed my finger in the car door. Ich habe mir den Finger in der Autotür gequetscht.
▶ n **to have a crush on somebody** für jemanden schwärmen [38]
crutch n Krücke f
cry n Schrei m ▷ a cry of fear ein Angstschrei; **to have a good cry** sich ausweinen [4]
▶ vb weinen [38] ▷ The baby's crying. Das Baby weint.
crystal n Kristall m (pl Kristalle)
cub n ❶ Junge nt (gen Jungen, pl Jungen) ▷ the lioness and her cub die Löwin und ihr Junges ❷ (scout) Wölfling m (pl Wölflinge)
cube n Würfel m (pl Würfel)
cubic adj **a cubic metre** ein Kubikmeter m
cucumber n Gurke f
cuddle n **Come and give me a cuddle.** Komm und nimm mich in den Arm.
▶ vb **to cuddle somebody** jemanden in den Arm nehmen [52]
cue n (for snooker, pool) Queue nt (pl Queues)

  Queue is pronounced as if spelt 'Kö'.

cultural adj kulturell
culture n Kultur f
cunning adj schlau
cup n ❶ Tasse f ▷ a china cup eine Porzellantasse ▷ a cup of coffee eine Tasse Kaffee ❷ (trophy) Pokal m (pl Pokale)
cupboard n Schrank m (pl Schränke)
cure vb heilen [38]
▶ n Mittel nt (pl Mittel) ▷ a cure for a cold ein Mittel gegen Schnupfen
curious adj neugierig
curl n Locke f
▶ vb (hair) in Locken legen [38]
curly adj lockig ▷ When I was young my hair was curlier. Als ich jung war, waren meine Haare lockiger.

currant n (dried fruit) Korinthe f
currency n Währung f ▷ foreign currency ausländische Währung
current n Strömung f ▷ The current is very strong. Die Strömung ist sehr stark.
▶ adj aktuell ▷ the current situation the aktuelle Lage
current affairs npl Tagespolitik fsg
curriculum n Lehrplan m (pl Lehrpläne)
curriculum vitae n Lebenslauf m (pl Lebensläufe)
curry n Curry nt (pl Currys)
curtain n Vorhang m (pl Vorhänge)
cushion n Kissen nt (pl Kissen)
custard n (for pouring) Vanillesoße f
custody n (of child) Sorgerecht nt ▷ He got custody of his son. Er bekam das Sorgerecht für seinen Sohn.; **to be remanded in custody** inhaftiert werden [91]
custom n Brauch m (pl Bräuche) ▷ It's an old custom. Es ist ein alter Brauch.
customer n Kunde m (gen Kunden, pl Kunden), Kundin f
customs npl Zoll m (pl Zölle)
customs officer n Zollbeamte m (gen Zollbeamten, pl Zollbeamten), Zollbeamtin f ▷ a customs officer (man) ein Zollbeamter
cut n ❶ Schnittwunde f ▷ He's got a cut on his forehead. Er hat eine Schnittwunde an der Stirn. ❷ (in price) Senkung f ❸ (in spending) Kürzung f; **a cut and blow-dry** Schneiden und Föhnen
▶ vb ❶ schneiden [60] (imperf schnitt, perf hat geschnitten) ▷ I'll cut some bread. Ich schneide Brot.; **I cut my foot on a piece of glass.** Ich habe mir den Fuß an einer Glasscherbe verletzt.; **to cut oneself** sich schneiden [60] ▷ Watch you don't cut yourself! Pass auf, dass du dich nicht schneidest! ❷ (price) senken [38] ❸ (spending) kürzen [36]; **to cut down (1)** (tree) fällen [38] **(2)** einschränken [4] ▷ I'm cutting down

on chocolate. Ich bin dabei, meinen Schokoladenkonsum einzuschränken.; **The electricity was cut off.** Der Strom wurde abgestellt.; **to cut up** (vegetables, meat) klein schneiden [60]
cute adj niedlich
cutlery n Besteck nt (pl Bestecke)
CV n (= curriculum vitae) Lebenslauf m (pl Lebensläufe)
cyberbully n Cybermobber m (pl Cybermobber), Cybermobberin f (pl Cybermobberinnen)
cyberbullying n Cybermobbing nt
cybercrime n Cyberkriminalität f
cycle vb Rad fahren [21] (pres fährt Rad, imperf fuhr Rad, perf ist Rad gefahren) ▷ I like cycling. Ich fahre gern Rad.; **I cycle to school.** Ich fahre mit dem Rad zur Schule.
▶ n Fahrrad nt (pl Fahrräder) ▷ a cycle ride eine Fahrradtour
cycling n Radfahren nt ▷ My hobby is cycling. Radfahren ist mein Hobby.
cyclist n Radfahrer m (pl Radfahrer), Radfahrerin f
cylinder n Zylinder m (pl Zylinder)
Cyprus n Zypern nt; **from Cyprus** aus Zypern; **in Cyprus** auf Zypern; **to Cyprus** nach Zypern
Czech adj tschechisch; **the Czech Republic** die Tschechische Republik
▶ n ❶ (person) Tscheche m (gen Tschechen, pl Tschechen), Tschechin f ❷ (language) Tschechisch nt (gen Tschechischen)
Czechia n Tschechien nt

d

dad n Papa m (pl Papas) ▷ *his dad* sein Papa ▷ *I'll ask Dad.* Ich werde Papa fragen.
daffodil n Osterglocke f
daft adj verrückt
daily adj, adv täglich ▷ *It's part of my daily routine.* Es gehört zu meiner täglichen Routine. ▷ *The pool is open daily from nine a.m. to six p.m.* Das Schwimmbad ist täglich von neun bis achtzehn Uhr geöffnet.
dairy products npl Milchprodukte ntpl
daisy n Gänseblümchen nt (pl Gänseblümchen)
dam n Damm m (pl Dämme)
damage n Schaden m (pl Schäden) ▷ *The storm did a lot of damage.* Der Sturm hat viel Schaden angerichtet.
▶ vb beschädigen [**7**] (perf hat beschädigt)
damp adj feucht
dance n Tanz m (pl Tänze) ▷ *The last dance was a waltz.* Der letzte Tanz war ein Walzer. ▷ *Are you going to the dance tonight?* Gehst du heute Abend zum Tanz?
▶ vb tanzen [**36**]
dancer n Tänzer m (pl Tänzer), Tänzerin f
dancing n Tanzen nt; **to go dancing** tanzen gehen [**29**]
dandruff n Schuppen fpl
Dane n Däne m (gen Dänen, pl Dänen), Dänin f
danger n Gefahr f; **in danger** in Gefahr; **I'm in danger of failing maths.** Es könnte durchaus sein, dass ich in Mathe durchfalle.
dangerous adj gefährlich
Danish adj dänisch
▶ n (language) Dänisch nt (gen Dänischen)
Danube n Donau f
dare vb sich trauen [**38**]; **to dare to do something** sich trauen [**38**], etwas zu tun; **I dare say it'll be okay.** Ich denke, dass das in Ordnung ist.
daring adj mutig
dark adj dunkel ▷ *It's dark.* Es ist dunkel. ▷ *It's getting dark.* Es wird dunkel. ▷ *She's got dark hair.* Sie hat dunkle Haare. ▷ *a dark green sweater* ein dunkelgrüner Pullover
▶ n Dunkelheit f ▷ *after dark* nach Einbruch der Dunkelheit; **in the dark** im Dunkeln; **I'm afraid of the dark.** Ich habe Angst im Dunkeln.
darkness n Dunkelheit f; **The room was in darkness.** Das Zimmer war dunkel.
darling n Liebling m (pl Lieblinge)
■ **der Liebling** is also used for women.
▷ *Thank you, darling!* Danke, Liebling!
dart n Pfeil m (pl Pfeile); **to play darts** Darts spielen [**38**]
dashboard n Armaturenbrett nt (pl Armaturenbretter)
data npl Daten pl
database n (on computer) Datenbank f (pl Datenbanken)

date n ❶ Datum nt (pl Daten) ▷ my date of birth mein Geburtsdatum; **What's the date today?** Der Wievielte ist heute?; **to have a date with somebody** mit jemandem eine Verabredung haben [32] ▷ She's got a date with Ian tonight. Sie hat heute Abend eine Verabredung mit Ian.; **out of date** (1) (passport) abgelaufen (2) (technology) veraltet (3) (clothes) altmodisch ❷ (fruit) Dattel f

daughter n Tochter f (pl Töchter)

daughter-in-law n Schwiegertochter f (pl Schwiegertöchter)

dawn n Morgengrauen nt ▷ at dawn im Morgengrauen

day n Tag m (pl Tage) ▷ We stayed in Vienna for three days. Wir sind drei Tage in Wien geblieben. ▷ I stayed at home all day. Ich war den ganzen Tag zu Hause.; **every day** jeden Tag; **during the day** tagsüber; **the day before** der Tag davor; **the day before my birthday** der Tag vor meinem Geburtstag; **the day after** der Tag danach; **the day after my birthday** der Tag nach meinem Geburtstag; **the day before yesterday** vorgestern; **the day after tomorrow** übermorgen

dead adj, adv ❶ tot ▷ He was already dead. Er war schon tot.; **He was shot dead.** Er wurde erschossen. ❷ (totally) völlig ▷ You're dead right! Du hast völlig recht!; **dead on time** ganz pünktlich

dead end n Sackgasse f

deadline n Termin m (pl Termine) ▷ We'll never meet the deadline. Den Termin schaffen wir nie.

dead spot n (mobile) Funkloch nt (pl Funklöcher)

deaf adj taub

deafening adj ohrenbetäubend

deal n Geschäft nt (pl Geschäfte); **It's a deal!** Abgemacht!; **a great deal** viel
▶ vb (cards) geben [28] (pres gibt, imperf gab, perf hat gegeben) ▷ It's your turn to deal. Du gibst!; **to deal with something** sich um etwas kümmern [38]

dealer n Händler m (pl Händler), Händlerin f ▷ a drug dealer ein Drogenhändler ▷ an antique dealer ein Antiquitätenhändler

dear adj ❶ lieb; **Dear Mrs Sinclair** (1) Liebe Frau Sinclair (2) (more formal) Sehr geehrte Frau Sinclair; **Dear Sir/Madam** (in a circular) Sehr geehrte Damen und Herren ❷ (expensive) teuer

death n Tod m (pl Tode) ▷ after her death nach ihrem Tod ▷ I was bored to death. Ich habe mich zu Tode gelangweilt.

debate n Debatte f
▶ vb debattieren [76] (perf hat debattiert) ▷ We debated the issue. Wir haben die Frage debattiert.

debt n Schulden fpl ▷ He's got a lot of debts. Er hat viele Schulden.; **to be in debt** verschuldet sein [65]

decade n Jahrzehnt nt (pl Jahrzehnte)

decaffeinated adj entkoffeiniert

deceive vb täuschen [48]

December n Dezember m ▷ in December im Dezember

decent adj ordentlich ▷ a decent education eine ordentliche Ausbildung

decide vb ❶ beschließen (imperf beschloss, perf hat beschlossen) ▷ I decided to write to her. Ich habe beschlossen, ihr zu schreiben. ▷ I decided not to go. Ich habe beschlossen, nicht hinzugehen. ❷ sich entscheiden (imperf entschied sich, perf hat sich entschieden) ▷ I can't decide. Ich kann mich nicht entscheiden. ▷ Haven't you decided yet? Hast du dich noch nicht entschieden?; **to decide on something** über etwas entscheiden

decimal adj dezimal ▷ the decimal system das Dezimalsystem

decision n Entscheidung f ▷ to make a decision eine Entscheidung treffen

deck n ❶ (of ship) Deck nt (pl Decks) ▷ on deck an Deck ❷ (of cards) Spiel nt (pl Spiele)

deckchair n Liegestuhl m (pl Liegestühle)

declare vb erklären [19] (perf hat erklärt)

decline vb ❶ ablehnen [4] (perf hat abgelehnt) ▷ He declined to comment. Er lehnte einen Kommentar ab. ❷ zurückgehen [29] (imperf ging zurück, perf ist zurückgegangen) ▷ The birth rate is declining. Die Geburtenrate geht zurück.

decorate vb ❶ dekorieren [76] (perf hat dekoriert) ▷ I decorated the cake with glacé cherries. Ich habe den Kuchen mit glasierten Kirschen dekoriert. ❷ (paint) streichen (imperf strich, perf hat gestrichen) ❸ (wallpaper) tapezieren [76] (perf hat tapeziert)

decorations npl Schmuck m ▷ Christmas decorations der Weihnachtsschmuck

decrease n Abnahme f ▷ a decrease in the number of unemployed people eine Abnahme der Arbeitslosenzahl ▶ vb abnehmen [52] (pres nimmt ab, imperf nahm ab, perf hat abgenommen)

deduct vb abziehen [96] (imperf zog ab, perf hat abgezogen)

deep adj (water, hole, cut) tief ▷ How deep is the lake? Wie tief ist der See? ▷ a hole four metres deep ein vier Meter tiefes Loch ▷ He's got a deep voice. Er hat eine tiefe Stimme.; **to take a deep breath** tief einatmen [3]; **The snow was really deep.** Es lag sehr viel Schnee.

deeply adv (depressed) zutiefst

deer n Reh nt (pl Rehe)

defeat n Niederlage f ▶ vb besiegen [7] (perf hat besiegt)

defect n Defekt m (pl Defekte)

defence (US **defense**) n Verteidigung f

defend vb verteidigen [84] (perf hat verteidigt)

defender n Verteidiger m (pl Verteidiger), Verteidigerin f

defense n (US) Verteidigung f

define vb definieren [76] (perf hat definiert)

definite adj ❶ genau ▷ I haven't got any definite plans. Ich habe noch keine genauen Pläne. ❷ eindeutig ▷ It's a definite improvement. Es ist eine eindeutige Verbesserung. ❸ sicher ▷ Perhaps we'll go to Spain, but it's not definite. Vielleicht fahren wir nach Spanien, aber es ist noch nicht sicher.; **He was definite about it.** Er war sich sehr sicher.

definitely adv eindeutig ▷ He's definitely the best. Er ist eindeutig der Beste.; **He's the best player. — Definitely!** Er ist der beste Spieler. — Absolut!; **I definitely think he'll come.** Ich bin sicher, dass er kommt.

definition n Definition f

degree n ❶ Grad m (pl Grade) ▷ a temperature of thirty degrees eine Temperatur von dreißig Grad ❷ Universitätsabschluss m (gen Universitätsabschlusses, pl Universitätsabschlüsse) ▷ a degree in English ein Universitätsabschluss in Englisch

delay vb verschieben (imperf verschob, perf hat verschoben) ▷ We delayed our departure. Wir haben unsere Abreise verschoben.; **to be delayed** Verspätung haben [32] ▶ n Verzögerung f; **without delay** unverzüglich

delete vb (on computer, tape) löschen [48]

deliberate adj absichtlich

deliberately adv absichtlich ▷ She did it deliberately. Sie hat es absichtlich getan.

delicate adj ❶ zierlich ▷ She has very delicate hands. Sie hat sehr zierliche Hände. ❷ (object) zerbrechlich ▷ That

delicatessen nsg Feinkostgeschäft nt (pl Feinkostgeschäfte)

delicious adj köstlich

delight n Freude f

delighted adj hocherfreut ▷ He'll be delighted. Er wird hocherfreut sein.

deliver vb ❶ (press trägt aus, imperf trug aus, perf hat ausgetragen) austragen [77] ▷ I deliver newspapers. Ich trage Zeitungen aus. ❷ (mail) ausliefern [4] (perf hat ausgeliefert)

delivery n Lieferung f

demand vb fordern [88]
▶ n (for product) Nachfrage f

democracy n Demokratie f

democratic adj demokratisch

demolish vb (building) abreißen (imperf riss ab, perf hat abgerissen)

demonstrate vb ❶ (show) vorführen [4] (perf hat vorgeführt) ▷ She demonstrated the technique. Sie hat die Methode vorgeführt. ❷ (protest) demonstrieren [76] (perf hat demonstriert) ▷ to demonstrate against something gegen etwas demonstrieren

demonstration n ❶ (of method, technique) Vorführung f ❷ (protest) Demonstration f

demonstrator n (protester) Demonstrant m (gen Demonstranten, pl Demonstranten), Demonstrantin f

denim n Jeansstoff m; **a denim jacket** eine Jeansjacke

Denmark n Dänemark nt; **from Denmark** aus Dänemark; **to Denmark** nach Dänemark

dense adj ❶ (crowd, fog) dicht ❷ (smoke) dick; **He's so dense!** (informal) Er ist furchtbar blöd!

dent n Delle f
▶ vb eindellen [4] (perf hat eingedellt)

dental adj **dental treatment** die Zahnbehandlung; **dental floss** die Zahnseide; **dental surgeon** der Zahnarzt

dentist n Zahnarzt m (pl Zahnärzte), Zahnärztin f ▷ Catherine is a dentist. Catherine ist Zahnärztin.

deny vb leugnen [53] ▷ She denied everything. Sie hat alles geleugnet.

deodorant n Deo nt (pl Deos)

depart vb ❶ (person) abreisen [4] (perf ist abgereist) ❷ (train) abfahren [21] (pres fährt ab, imperf fuhr ab, perf ist abgefahren)

department n ❶ (in shop) Abteilung f ▷ the shoe department die Schuhabteilung ❷ (university, school) Fachbereich m (pl Fachbereiche) ▷ the English department der Fachbereich Englisch

department store n Kaufhaus nt (gen Kaufhauses, pl Kaufhäuser)

departure n Abfahrt f

departure lounge n Abflughalle f

depend vb **to depend on** abhängen [35] von; **depending on the weather** je nach Wetterlage; **It depends.** Das kommt drauf an.

deposit n ❶ (part payment) Anzahlung f ▷ You have to pay a deposit when you book. Sie müssen eine Anzahlung leisten, wenn Sie buchen. ❷ (when hiring something) Kaution f ▷ You get the deposit back when you return the bike. Sie bekommen die Kaution zurück, wenn Sie das Fahrrad zurückbringen. ❸ (on bottle) Pfand nt (pl Pfänder)

depressed adj deprimiert ▷ I'm feeling depressed. Ich bin deprimiert.

depressing adj deprimierend

depth n Tiefe f

deputy head n Konrektor m (pl Konrektoren), Konrektorin f

descend vb hintersteigen [74] (imperf stieg hinunter, perf ist hinuntergestiegen)

describe vb beschreiben [61] (imperf beschrieb, perf hat beschrieben)

description n Beschreibung f

desert n Wüste f

desert island n einsame Insel f

deserve vb verdienen [84] (perf hat verdient) ▷ He deserves a holiday. Er hat einen Urlaub verdient.; **She deserves to be punished.** Sie gehört bestraft.

design n ❶ Design nt (pl Designs) ▷ fashion design das Modedesign; **It's a completely new design.** Es ist eine völlig neue Konstruktion. ❷ (pattern) Muster nt (pl Muster) ▷ a geometric design ein geometrisches Muster
▶ vb (clothes, furniture) entwerfen [92] (pres entwirft, imperf entwarf, perf hat entworfen)

designer n (of clothes) Modeschöpfer m (pl Modeschöpfer), Modeschöpferin f; **designer clothes** die Designerkleidung sg

desire n Verlangen nt (pl Verlangen)
▶ vb wünschen [48] ▷ if desired falls gewünscht

desk n ❶ (in office) Schreibtisch m (pl Schreibtische) ❷ (in school) Bank f (pl Bänke) ❸ (in hotel) Rezeption f ❹ (at airport) Schalter m (pl Schalter)

desktop n Desktop m (pl Desktops)

despair n Verzweiflung f; **I was in despair.** Ich war verzweifelt.

desperate adj verzweifelt ▷ a desperate situation eine verzweifelte Lage; **to get desperate** fast verzweifeln [7]; **I'm desperate for a drink.** Ich brauche dringend etwas zu trinken.

desperately adv ❶ äußerst ▷ We're desperately worried. Wir sind äußerst besorgt. ❷ verzweifelt ▷ He was desperately trying to persuade her. Er versuchte verzweifelt, sie zu überzeugen.

despise vb verachten [18] (perf hat verachtet)

despite prep trotz ▷ despite the bad weather trotz des schlechten Wetters

dessert n Nachtisch m ▷ for dessert zum Nachtisch

destination n Ziel nt (pl Ziele)

destroy vb zerstören [95] (perf hat zerstört)

destruction n Zerstörung f

detached house n Einzelhaus nt (gen Einzelhauses, pl Einzelhäuser)

detail n Detail nt (pl Details); **in detail** ganz genau

detailed adj ausführlich

detective n Detektiv m (pl Detektive), Detektivin f; **a private detective** ein Privatdetektiv; **a detective story** eine Detektivgeschichte

detention n to get a detention nachsitzen müssen [51]

detergent n Waschmittel nt (pl Waschmittel)

determined adj entschlossen; **to be determined to do something** entschlossen sein [65], etwas zu tun

detour n Umweg m (pl Umwege)

devastated adj am Boden zerstört ▷ I was devastated. Ich war am Boden zerstört.

develop vb ❶ entwickeln [34] (perf hat entwickelt) ▷ to get a film developed einen Film entwickeln lassen [42] ❷ sich entwickeln [34] (perf hat sich entwickelt) ▷ Girls develop faster. Mädchen entwickeln sich schneller. ▷ The argument developed into a fight. Der Streit entwickelte sich zu einer Schlägerei.; **a developing country** ein Entwicklungsland nt

development n Entwicklung f ▷ the latest developments die neuesten Entwicklungen

devil n Teufel m (pl Teufel) ▷ Poor devil! Armer Teufel!

ENGLISH > GERMAN

devoted adj He's completely devoted to her. Er liebt sie über alles.

diabetes n Zucker m ▷ She's got diabetes. Sie hat Zucker.

diabetic n Zuckerkranke(r) m (gen Zuckerkranken, pl Zuckerkranken), Zuckerkranke f (gen Zuckerkranken); **I'm a diabetic.** Ich habe Zucker.

diagonal adj diagonal

diagram n Diagramm nt (pl Diagramme)

dial vb (number) wählen [38]; **He dialled the wrong number.** Er hat sich verwählt.

dialling tone n Amtszeichen nt (pl Amtszeichen)

dialogue n Dialog m (pl Dialoge)

diamond n Diamant m (gen Diamanten, pl Diamanten) ▷ a diamond ring ein Diamantring m; **diamonds** (in cards) das Karo

diaper n (US) Windel f

diarrhoea n Durchfall m (pl Durchfälle) ▷ I've got diarrhoea. Ich habe Durchfall.

diary n ❶ Kalender m (pl Kalender) ▷ I've got her address in my diary. Ich habe ihre Adresse in meinem Kalender. ❷ Tagebuch nt (pl Tagebücher) ▷ I keep a diary. Ich führe ein Tagebuch.

dice n Würfel m (pl Würfel)

dictation n Diktat nt (pl Diktate)

dictator n Diktator m (pl Diktatoren)

dictionary n Wörterbuch nt (pl Wörterbücher)

did vb see **do**

die vb sterben [75] (pres stirbt, imperf starb, perf ist gestorben) ▷ She's dying. Sie stirbt. ▷ He died last year. Er ist letztes Jahr gestorben.; **to be dying to do something** es kaum erwarten können [41], etwas zu tun

die down vb nachlassen [42] (pres lässt nach, imperf ließ nach, perf hat nachgelassen)

diesel n ❶ (fuel) Diesel m ▷ Thirty litres of diesel, please. Dreißig Liter Diesel, bitte. ❷ (car) Diesel m (pl Diesel) ▷ Our car's a diesel. Unser Auto ist ein Diesel.

diet n ❶ Nahrung f ▷ a healthy diet gesunde Nahrung ❷ (for slimming) Diät f; **I'm on a diet.** Ich mache eine Diät.
▶ vb eine Diät machen [48] ▷ I've been dieting for two months. Ich mache seit zwei Monaten eine Diät.

difference n Unterschied m (pl Unterschiede) ▷ There's not much difference in age between us. Es besteht kein großer Altersunterschied zwischen uns.; **It makes no difference.** Das ist egal.

different adj verschieden ▷ We are very different. Wir sind sehr verschieden.; **Berlin is different from London.** Berlin ist anders als London.

difficult adj schwierig ▷ It's difficult to choose. Es ist schwierig, sich zu entscheiden.

difficulty n Schwierigkeit f ▷ to have difficulty doing something Schwierigkeiten haben, etwas zu tun; **without difficulty** problemlos

dig vb ❶ (hole) graben (pres gräbt, imperf grub, perf hat gegraben) ❷ (garden) umgraben (perf hat umgegraben); **to dig something up** etwas ausgraben

digestion n Verdauung f

digital adj digital ▷ the digital revolution die digitale Revolution; **a digital camera** eine Digitalkamera; **a digital radio** ein DAB-Radio m; **a digital watch** eine Digitaluhr; **digital TV** das Digitalfernsehen

dim adj ❶ (light) schwach ❷ (stupid) beschränkt

dimension n (measurement) Maß nt (gen Maßes, pl Maße)

din n Krach m (pl Kräche)

diner n (US) Gaststätte f

dinghy n **a rubber dinghy** ein Gummiboot nt; **a sailing dinghy** ein Segelboot nt

dining room n Esszimmer nt (pl Esszimmer)

dinner n ❶ (at midday) Mittagessen nt (pl Mittagessen) ❷ (in the evening) Abendessen nt (pl Abendessen)

dinner party n Abendgesellschaft f; **We're having a dinner party on Saturday.** Wir haben am Samstag Leute zum Essen eingeladen.

dinner time n Essenszeit f

dinosaur n Dinosaurier m (pl Dinosaurier)

diploma n Diplom nt (pl Diplome); **She has a diploma in social work.** Sie hat Sozialarbeiterin gelernt.

direct adj, adv direkt ▷ *the most direct route* der direkteste Weg ▷ *You can't fly to Stuttgart direct from Glasgow.* Sie können von Glasgow nicht direkt nach Stuttgart fliegen.
▶ vb (film, play) Regie führen [38] bei ▷ *Who directed the film?* Wer hat bei dem Film Regie geführt?

direction n Richtung f ▷ *We're going in the wrong direction.* Wir fahren in die falsche Richtung.; **to ask somebody for directions** jemanden nach dem Weg fragen [38]

director n ❶ (of company) Direktor m (pl Direktoren), Direktorin f ❷ (of play, film) Regisseur m (pl Regisseure), Regisseurin f ❸ (of programme) Leiter m (pl Leiter), Leiterin f

directory n ❶ Verzeichnis nt (gen Verzeichnisses, pl Verzeichnisse) ▷ *file directory* das Dateiverzeichnis ❷ (telephone book) Telefonbuch nt (pl Telefonbücher)

dirt n Schmutz m

dirty adj schmutzig ▷ *to get dirty* sich schmutzig machen ▷ *to get something dirty* etwas schmutzig machen ▷ *a dirty joke* ein schmutziger Witz

disabled adj behindert

disadvantage n Nachteil m (pl Nachteile)

disagree vb **We always disagree.** Wir sind nie einer Meinung.; **I disagree!** Ich bin anderer Meinung.; **He disagreed with me.** Er war anderer Meinung als ich.

disagreement n Meinungsverschiedenheit f

disappear vb verschwinden [86] (imperf verschwand, perf ist verschwunden)

disappearance n Verschwinden nt

disappointed adj enttäuscht

disappointment n Enttäuschung f

disaster n Katastrophe f

disastrous adj katastrophal

disc n Platte f

discipline n Disziplin f

disc jockey n Diskjockey m (pl Diskjockeys)

disco n Disco f (pl Discos) ▷ *There's a disco at the school tonight.* Heute Abend gibt es in der Schule eine Disco.

disconnect vb ❶ (electrical equipment) ausstecken [4] (perf hat ausgesteckt) ❷ (telephone, water supply) abstellen [4] (perf hat abgestellt)

discount n Rabatt m (pl Rabatte) ▷ *a discount of twenty per cent* zwanzig Prozent Rabatt; **a discount for students** eine Studentenermäßigung

discourage vb entmutigen [18] (perf hat entmutigt); **to get discouraged** sich entmutigen lassen [42]

discover vb entdecken [18] (perf hat entdeckt)

discovery n Entdeckung f

discrimination n Diskriminierung f ▷ *racial discrimination* die Rassendiskriminierung

discuss vb ❶ besprechen [70] (pres bespricht, imperf besprach, perf hat besprochen) ▷ *I'll discuss it with my parents.* Ich werde es mit meinen Eltern besprechen. ❷ (topic) diskutieren [76] über (perf hat diskutiert) ▷ *We discussed*

ENGLISH > GERMAN

the problem. Wir haben über das Problem diskutiert.
discussion n Diskussion f
disease n Krankheit f
disgraceful adj schändlich
disguise vb verkleiden [54] (perf hat verkleidet) ▷ He was disguised as a police officer. Er war als Polizist verkleidet.
disgusted adj angewidert ▷ I was absolutely disgusted. Ich war total angewidert.
disgusting adj ❶ (food, smell) widerlich ▷ It looks disgusting. Es sieht widerlich aus. ❷ (disgraceful) abscheulich ▷ That's disgusting! Das ist abscheulich!
dish n ❶ Schüssel f ▷ a china dish eine Porzellanschüssel; **the dishes** das Geschirr sg; **to do the dishes** abwaschen [89] ❷ (food) Gericht nt (pl Gerichte) ▷ a vegetarian dish ein vegetarisches Gericht
dishonest adj unehrlich
dishwasher n Geschirrspülmaschine f
disinfectant n Desinfektionsmittel nt (pl Desinfektionsmittel)
disk n Platte f; **the hard disk** die Festplatte
dismal adj kläglich ▷ a dismal failure ein kläglicher Fehlschlag
dismiss vb (employee) entlassen [42] (pres entlässt, imperf entließ, perf hat entlassen)
disobedient adj ungehorsam
display n (of goods) Auslage f; **to be on display** ausgestellt sein [65]; **a firework display** ein Feuerwerk nt
▶ vb ❶ zeigen [38] ▷ She proudly displayed her medal. Sie zeigte stolz ihre Medaille. ❷ (in shop window) ausstellen [4] (perf hat ausgestellt) ▷ the fruit displayed in the shop window ... das Obst, das im Schaufenster ausgestellt war ...
disposable adj zum Wegwerfen; **disposable nappies** die Wegwerfwindeln fpl

333 | diver

disqualify vb disqualifizieren [76] (perf hat disqualifiziert); **to be disqualified** disqualifiziert werden [91]
disrupt vb ❶ stören [38] ▷ Protesters disrupted the meeting. Protestierende haben die Versammlung gestört. ❷ (service) unterbrechen [11] (pres unterbricht, imperf unterbrach, perf hat unterbrochen) ▷ Train services were disrupted. Der Zugverkehr wurde unterbrochen.
dissolve vb ❶ auflösen [4] (perf hat aufgelöst) ▷ Dissolve the crystals in water. Löse die Kristalle in Wasser auf. ❷ sich auflösen [4] ▷ Sugar dissolves quickly in hot tea. Zucker löst sich in heißem Tee schnell auf.
distance n Entfernung f ▷ a distance of forty kilometres eine Entfernung von vierzig Kilometern; **It's within walking distance.** Man kann zu Fuß hingehen.; **in the distance** in der Ferne
distant adj weit ▷ in the distant future in weiter Zukunft
distract vb ablenken [4] (perf hat abgelenkt)
distribute vb verteilen [84] (perf hat verteilt)
district n ❶ (of town) Viertel nt (pl Viertel) ❷ (of country) Gegend f
disturb vb stören [38]; **I'm sorry to disturb you.** Verzeihen Sie die Störung.
ditch n Graben m (pl Gräben)
▶ vb (informal) Schluss machen [48] mit ▷ She's just ditched her boyfriend. Sie hat gerade mit ihrem Freund Schluss gemacht.
dive n Kopfsprung m (pl Kopfsprünge)
▶ vb ❶ (under water) tauchen [48] ▷ They are diving for pearls. Sie tauchen nach Perlen. ❷ (into water) einen Kopfsprung machen [48] ▷ She dived into the water. Sie machte einen Kopfsprung ins Wasser.
diver n (with breathing apparatus) Taucher m (pl Taucher), Taucherin f

diversion n (for traffic) Umleitung f
diversity n Diversität f
divide vb ❶ teilen [38] ▷ Divide the pastry in half. Teilen Sie den Teig in zwei Teile. ▷ Twelve divided by three is four. Zwölf geteilt durch drei macht vier. ❷ sich aufteilen [4] (perf hat sich aufgeteilt) ▷ We divided into two groups. Wir haben uns in zwei Gruppen aufgeteilt.
diving n ❶ (under water) Tauchen nt ❷ (into water) Springen nt; **diving board** das Sprungbrett
division n ❶ Division f ▷ division and multiplication Division und Multiplikation; **the division of labour** die Arbeitsteilung ❷ (in football) Liga f (pl Ligen)
divorce n Scheidung f
divorced adj geschieden ▷ My parents are divorced. Meine Eltern sind geschieden.
Diwali n Diwali nt
DIY n (= do-it-yourself) Heimwerken nt; **to do DIY** Heimwerker sein [65]; **a DIY shop** ein Geschäft für Heimwerker; **DIY superstore** der Baumarkt
dizzy adj **I feel dizzy.** Mir ist schwindlig.
DJ n (= disc jockey) Diskjockey m (pl Diskjockeys)
do vb ❶ machen [48] ▷ What are you doing this evening? Was macht ihr heute Abend? ▷ I haven't done my homework. Ich habe meine Hausaufgaben noch nicht gemacht. ▷ She did it by herself. Sie hat es allein gemacht. ❷ tun [81] ▷ What shall I do? Was soll ich tun? ▷ I'll do my best. Ich werde mein Bestes tun. ▷ I'll tell you what to do. Ich sage dir, was du tun sollst.

> In combination with certain nouns and verbs 'do' is not translated.

▷ I do a lot of cycling. Ich fahre viel Rad. ▷ She was doing her knitting. Sie strickte. ▷ to do the ironing bügeln; **to do well** erfolgreich sein [65] ▷ The firm is doing well. Die Firma ist sehr erfolgreich.; **She's doing well at school.** Sie ist gut in der Schule. ❸ (be enough) reichen [48] ▷ It's not very good, but it'll do. Es ist nicht besonders gut, aber es wird reichen. ▷ That'll do, thanks. Danke, das reicht.

> In English 'do' is used to make questions. In German, questions are expressed by reversing the order of verb and subject.

▷ Do you like German food? Magst du deutsches Essen? ▷ Where does he live? Wo wohnt er? ▷ Do you speak English? Sprechen Sie Englisch? ▷ What do you do in your spare time? Was machen Sie in Ihrer Freizeit? ▷ Where did you go for your holidays? Wohin seid ihr in den Ferien gefahren?

> Use **nicht** in negative sentences for 'don't'.

▷ I don't understand. Ich verstehe nicht. ▷ Why didn't you come? Warum bist du nicht gekommen?

> 'do' is not translated when it is used in place of another verb.

▷ I hate maths. — So do I. Ich hasse Mathe. — Ich auch. ▷ I didn't like the film. — Neither did I. Ich mochte den Film nicht. — Ich auch nicht. ▷ Do you like horses? — No, I don't. Magst du Pferde? — Nein.

> Questions like 'doesn't it?' don't exist in German.

▷ The bus stops at the youth hostel, doesn't it? Der Bus hält an der Jugendherberge, nicht wahr? ▷ You go swimming on Fridays, don't you? Du gehst freitags schwimmen, nicht wahr?; **How do you do?** Guten Tag!; **I could do with a holiday.** Ich könnte einen Urlaub gebrauchen.
do up vb ❶ (shoes, shirt, cardigan) zumachen [4] ▷ Do up your shoes! Mach deine Schuhe zu! ❷ (renovate)

ENGLISH > GERMAN

renovieren [**76**] ▷ *They're doing up an old cottage.* Sie renovieren ein altes Haus.

do without *vb* ohne etwas auskommen [**40**] ▷ *I couldn't do without my computer.* Ich käme nicht ohne meinen Computer aus.

doctor *n* Arzt *m* (*pl* Ärzte), Ärztin *f* ▷ *She's a doctor.* Sie ist Ärztin. ▷ *She'd like to be a doctor.* Sie möchte gerne Ärztin werden.

document *n* Dokument *nt* (*pl* Dokumente)

documentary *n* Dokumentarfilm *m* (*pl* Dokumentarfilme)

dodge *vb* (*attacker*) ausweichen (*imperf* wich aus, *perf* ist ausgewichen) ▷ *to dodge something* einer Sache ausweichen

Dodgems® *npl* Autoskooter *msg* (*pl* Autoskooter) ▷ *to go on the Dodgems* Autoskooter fahren

does *vb see* do

doesn't = **does not**

dog *n* Hund *m* (*pl* Hunde) ▷ *Have you got a dog?* Hast du einen Hund?

do-it-yourself *n* Heimwerken *nt*

dole *n* Arbeitslosenunterstützung *f*; **to be on the dole** stempeln gehen [**29**]; **to go on the dole** sich arbeitslos melden [**54**]

doll *n* Puppe *f*

dollar *n* Dollar *m* (*pl* Dollars *or* Dollar)
  When talking about amounts of money use the plural form **Dollar**.
  ▷ *That costs fifty dollars.* Das kostet fünfzig Dollar.

dolphin *n* Delfin *m* (*pl* Delfine)

dominoes *nsg* **to have a game of dominoes** Domino spielen [**38**]

donate *vb* spenden [**54**]

done *vb see* do

donkey *n* Esel *m* (*pl* Esel)

don't = **do not**

door *n* Tür *f*

doorbell *n* Klingel *f*; **to ring the doorbell** klingeln [**34**]; **Suddenly the doorbell rang.** Es klingelte plötzlich.

335 | **down**

doorstep *n* Eingangsstufe *f*

dormitory *n* Schlafsaal *m* (*pl* Schlafsäle)

dot *n* (*on letter 'i', in email address*) Punkt *m* (*pl* Punkte); **on the dot** genau

double *vb* sich verdoppeln [**34**] (*perf* hat sich verdoppelt) ▷ *The number of attacks has doubled.* Die Zahl der Überfälle hat sich verdoppelt.
  ▷ *adj, adv* doppelt ▷ *a double helping* eine doppelte Portion; **to cost double** doppelt so viel kosten [**2**]; **a double bed** ein Doppelbett *nt*; **a double room** ein Doppelzimmer *nt*; **a double-decker bus** ein Doppeldeckerbus *m*

double bass *n* Kontrabass *m* (*gen* Kontrabasses, *pl* Kontrabässe) ▷ *I play the double bass.* Ich spiele Kontrabass.

double-click *vb* (*computer*) doppelklicken [**15**] (*perf* hat doppelgeklickt)

double glazing *n* Doppelfenster *nt* (*pl* Doppelfenster)

doubles *npl* (*in tennis*) Doppel *nt* (*pl* Doppel) ▷ *to play mixed doubles* gemischtes Doppel spielen

doubt *n* Zweifel *m* (*pl* Zweifel) ▷ *I have my doubts.* Ich habe meine Zweifel.
  ▷ *vb* bezweifeln [**34**] (*perf* hat bezweifelt) ▷ *I doubt it.* Das bezweifle ich.; **to doubt that** bezweifeln [**34**], dass

doubtful *adj* **to be doubtful about doing something** nicht wissen [**93**], ob man etwas tun soll; **It's doubtful.** Es ist fraglich.; **You sound doubtful.** Du scheinst nicht sicher zu sein.

dough *n* Teig *m* (*pl* Teige)

doughnut *n* Berliner *m* (*pl* Berliner) ▷ *a jam doughnut* ein gefüllter Berliner

Dover *n* Dover *nt* ▷ *We went from Dover to Boulogne.* Wir sind von Dover nach Boulogne gefahren.

down *adv, adj, prep* ❶ (*below*) unten ▷ *down on the first floor* unten im ersten

Stock ▷ *It's down there.* Es ist da unten. ❷ *(to the ground)* auf den Boden ▷ *He threw down his racket.* Er warf seinen Schläger auf den Boden.; **They live just down the road.** Sie wohnen etwas weiter unten.; **to come down** herunterkommen **[40]**; **to go down** hinuntergehen **[29]**; **to sit down** sich hinsetzen **[15]**; **to feel down** niedergeschlagen sein **[65]**; **The computer's down.** Der Computer ist abgestürzt.

download *vb (computer)* runterladen *(pres* lädt runter, *imperf* lud runter, *perf* hat runtergeladen) ▷ *to download a file* eine Datei runterladen
▶ *n* Download *m (pl* Downloads) ▷ *a free download* ein Gratis-Download

downstairs *adv, adj* ❶ unten ▷ *The bathroom's downstairs.* Das Badezimmer ist unten.; **the people downstairs** die Leute von unten; **to go downstairs** nach unten gehen **[29]** ❷ untere ▷ *the downstairs bathroom* das untere Badezimmer

downtown *adv (US)* im Stadtzentrum

doze *vb* dösen **[38]**; **to doze off** einnicken **[4]**

dozen *n* Dutzend *nt (pl* Dutzende *or* Dutzend)

> When talking about more than one dozen use the plural form **Dutzend**.

▷ *two dozen eggs* zwei Dutzend Eier; **I've told you that dozens of times.** Ich habe dir das schon x-mal gesagt.

draft *n (US)* Luftzug *m (pl* Luftzüge)

drag *vb (thing, person)* schleppen **[48]**
▶ *n* **It's a real drag!** *(informal)* Das ist echt öde!; **in drag** in Frauenkleidern

dragon *n* Drache *m (gen* Drachen, *pl* Drachen)

drain *n* Abfluss *m (gen* Abflusses, *pl* Abflüsse) ▷ *The drains are blocked.* Der Abfluss ist verstopft.

▶ *vb (vegetables, pasta)* abtropfen lassen **[42]** *(pres* lässt abtropfen, *imperf* ließ abtropfen, *perf* hat abtropfen lassen)

drama *n* Drama *nt (pl* Dramen) ▷ *Drama is my favourite subject.* Darstellendes Spiel ist mein Lieblingsfach.; **drama school** die Schauspielschule

dramatic *adj* dramatisch ▷ *It was really dramatic!* Es war wirklich dramatisch! ▷ *a dramatic improvement* eine dramatische Besserung

drank *vb see* **drink**

drapes *npl (US)* Vorhänge *mpl*

draught *n* Luftzug *m (pl* Luftzüge); **There's a draught!** Es zieht!

draughts *nsg* Dame *f* ▷ *to play draughts* Dame spielen

draw *n* ❶ *(sport)* Unentschieden *nt (pl* Unentschieden) ▷ *The game ended in a draw.* Das Spiel endete mit einem Unentschieden. ❷ *(in lottery)* Ziehung *f* ▷ *The draw takes place on Saturday.* Die Ziehung findet am Samstag statt.
▶ *vb* ❶ malen **[38]** ▷ *He's good at drawing.* Er kann gut malen. ▷ *to draw a picture* ein Bild malen; **to draw a line** einen Strich machen **[48]** ❷ *(sport)* unentschieden spielen ▷ *We drew two all.* Wir haben zwei zu zwei gespielt.; **to draw the curtains** die Vorhänge zuziehen **[96]**; **to draw lots** losen **[38]**

draw on *vb* zurückgreifen auf *(imperf* griff zurück, *perf* hat zurückgegriffen)

draw up *vb* halten **[33]** *(pres* hält, *imperf* hielt, *perf* hat gehalten)

drawback *n* Nachteil *m (pl* Nachteile)

drawer *n* Schublade *f*

drawing *n* Zeichnung *f*

drawing pin *n* Reißzwecke *f*

drawn *vb see* **draw**

dreadful *adj* ❶ furchtbar ▷ *a dreadful mistake* ein furchtbarer Fehler ▷ *You look dreadful. (ill)* Du siehst furchtbar aus. ▷ *I feel dreadful.* Ich fühle mich

dream furchtbar. ❷ schrecklich ▷ *The weather was dreadful.* Das Wetter war schrecklich.
dream vb träumen [38] ▷ *I dreamt I was in Belgium.* Ich habe geträumt, ich sei in Belgien.

▪ Note the use of the subjunctive.

▶ n Traum m (pl Träume) ▷ *It was just a dream.* Es war nur ein Traum. ▷ *A bad dream* ein böser Traum
drench vb **to get drenched** klatschnass werden [91]
dress n Kleid nt (pl Kleider)
▶ vb **sich anziehen** [96] (imperf zog sich an, perf hat sich angezogen) ▷ *I got up, dressed, and went downstairs.* Ich stand auf, zog mich an und ging hinunter.; **to dress somebody** jemanden anziehen [96]; **to get dressed** sich anziehen [96]; **to dress up** sich verkleiden [54]
dressed adj angezogen ▷ *I'm not dressed yet.* Ich bin noch nicht angezogen. ▷ *How was she dressed?* Wie war sie angezogen?; **She was dressed in a green sweater and jeans.** Sie hatte einen grünen Pullover und Jeans an.
dresser n (furniture) Kommode f
dressing n (for salad) Dressing nt (pl Dressings)
dressing gown n Morgenmantel m (pl Morgenmäntel)
dressing table n Frisiertisch m (pl Frisiertische)
drew vb see **draw**
drier n ❶ (for washing) Wäschetrockner m (pl Wäschetrockner) ❷ (for hair) Haartrockner m (pl Haartrockner)
drift n **a snow drift** eine Schneeverwehung
▶ vb (boat, snow) treiben (imperf trieb, perf ist getrieben)
drill n Bohrer m (pl Bohrer)
▶ vb bohren [38]
drink vb trinken [80] (imperf trank, perf hat getrunken) ▷ *What would you like to drink?* Was möchtest du trinken? ▷ *She drank three cups of tea.* Sie trank drei Tassen Tee. ▷ *He'd been drinking.* Er hatte getrunken. ▷ *I don't drink.* Ich trinke nicht.
▶ n ❶ Getränk nt (pl Getränke) ▷ *a cold drink* ein kaltes Getränk ▷ *a hot drink* ein heißes Getränk ❷ (alcoholic) Drink m (pl Drinks); **They've gone out for a drink.** Sie sind etwas trinken gegangen.; **to have a drink** etwas trinken [80]
drive n ❶ Fahrt f ▷ *It's a long drive.* Es ist eine lange Fahrt.; **to go for a drive** fahren [21] ▷ *We went for a drive in the country.* Wir sind aufs Land gefahren. ❷ (of house) Auffahrt f ▷ *He parked his car in the drive.* Er parkte sein Auto in der Auffahrt.
▶ vb ❶ fahren [21] (pres fährt, imperf fuhr, perf ist/hat gefahren) ▷ *My mother drives me to school.* Meine Mutter fährt mich in die Schule. ▷ *I drove down to London.* Ich bin nach London gefahren.

▪ When **fahren** is used with an object it takes **haben** not **sein**.

▷ *He drove me home.* Er hat mich nach Hause gefahren. ❷ (operate a car) Auto fahren [21] (pres fährt Auto, imperf fuhr Auto, perf ist Auto gefahren) ▷ *Can you drive?* Kannst du Auto fahren?; **She's learning to drive.** Sie macht den Führerschein. ❸ (go by car) mit dem Auto fahren [21] ▷ *Did you go by train? — No, we drove.* Seid ihr mit dem Zug gefahren? — Nein, wir sind mit dem Auto gefahren.; **to drive somebody mad** jemanden wahnsinnig machen [48] ▷ *He drives her mad.* Er macht sie wahnsinnig.
driver n Fahrer m (pl Fahrer), Fahrerin f ▷ *She's an excellent driver.* Sie ist eine ausgezeichnete Fahrerin. ▷ *He's a bus driver.* Er ist Busfahrer.
driver's license n (US) Führerschein m (pl Führerscheine)
driving instructor n Fahrlehrer m (pl Fahrlehrer), Fahrlehrerin f ▷ *He's a driving instructor.* Er ist Fahrlehrer.

driving lesson n Fahrstunde f
driving licence n Führerschein m (pl Führerscheine)
driving test n Fahrprüfung f; **to take one's driving test** die Fahrprüfung machen [48]; **She's just passed her driving test.** Sie hat gerade ihren Führerschein gemacht.
drop n Tropfen m (pl Tropfen) ▷ *a drop of water* ein Wassertropfen
▶ vb ❶ fallen lassen [42] (pres lässt fallen, imperf ließ fallen, perf hat fallen lassen) ▷ *I dropped the glass.* Ich habe das Glas fallen lassen. ❷ (abandon) aufgeben [28] (pres gibt auf, imperf gab auf, perf hat aufgegeben) ▷ *I'm going to drop chemistry.* Ich gebe Chemie auf. ❸ absetzen [36] (perf hat abgesetzt) ▷ *Could you drop me at the station?* Könntest du mich am Bahnhof absetzen?
drought n Dürre f
drove vb see **drive**
drown vb ertrinken [80] (imperf ertrank, perf ist ertrunken) ▷ *A boy drowned here yesterday.* Hier ist gestern ein Junge ertrunken.
drug n ❶ (medicine) Medikament nt (pl Medikamente) ▷ *They need food and drugs.* Sie brauchen Nahrung und Medikamente. ❷ (illegal) Droge f ▷ *hard drugs* harte Drogen ▷ *soft drugs* weiche Drogen ▷ *to take drugs* Drogen nehmen; **a drug addict** (man) ein Drogensüchtiger; **She's a drug addict.** Sie ist drogensüchtig.
drugstore n (US) Drugstore m (pl Drugstores)
drum n Trommel f ▷ *an African drum* eine afrikanische Trommel; **a drum kit** ein Schlagzeug nt; **drums** das Schlagzeug sg
drummer n (in rock group) Schlagzeuger m (pl Schlagzeuger), Schlagzeugerin f
drunk vb see **drink**
▶ adj betrunken ▷ *He was drunk.* Er war betrunken.
▶ n Betrunkene m (gen Betrunkenen, pl Betrunkenen), Betrunkene f (gen Betrunkenen) ▷ *a drunk* (man) ein Betrunkener ▷ *The streets were full of drunks.* Die Straßen waren voll von Betrunkenen.
dry adj trocken ▷ *The paint isn't dry yet.* Die Farbe ist noch nicht trocken.; **a long dry period** eine lange Trockenzeit
▶ vb ❶ trocknen [53] ▷ *The washing will dry quickly in the sun.* Die Wäsche wird in der Sonne schnell trocknen. ▷ *some dried flowers* getrocknete Blumen; **to dry one's hair** sich die Haare föhnen [38] ❷ (clothes) trocknen lassen [42] (pres lässt trocknen, imperf ließ trocknen, perf hat trocknen lassen) ▷ *There's nowhere to dry clothes here.* Hier kann man nirgends Kleider trocknen lassen.; **to dry the dishes** das Geschirr abtrocknen [53]
dry-cleaner's n Reinigung f
dryer n (for clothes) Wäschetrockner m (pl Wäschetrockner); **a tumble dryer** ein Wäschetrockner; **a hair dryer** ein Föhn m
dubbed adj synchronisiert ▷ *The film was dubbed into German.* Der Film war deutsch synchronisiert.
dubious adj (situation, character) dubios; **My parents were a bit dubious about it.** Meine Eltern hatten ihre Zweifel.
duck n Ente f
due adj, adv **to be due to do something** etwas tun sollen [69]; **The plane's due in half an hour.** Das Flugzeug sollte in einer halben Stunde ankommen.; **When's the baby due?** Wann kommt das Baby?; **due to** wegen
dug vb see **dig**
dull adj ❶ langweilig ▷ *He's nice, but a bit dull.* Er ist nett, aber ein bisschen langweilig. ❷ (weather, day) trüb
dumb adj (stupid) blöd ▷ *That was a really dumb thing I did!* Da habe ich etwas echt Blödes gemacht!

ENGLISH > GERMAN

dummy n (for baby) Schnuller m (pl Schnuller)

dump n It's a real dump! (informal) Das ist ein Drecksloch!; **a rubbish dump** eine Müllkippe
▶ vb ❶ (waste) abladen (pres lädt ab, imperf lud ab, perf hat abgeladen); 'no dumping' 'Schutt abladen verboten'
❷ (informal: get rid of) Schluss machen [48] mit ▷ He's just dumped his girlfriend. Er hat gerade mit seiner Freundin Schluss gemacht.

dungarees npl Latzhose f ▷ a pair of dungarees eine Latzhose

dungeon n Verlies nt (pl Verliese)

during prep während ▷ during the holidays während der Ferien; **during the day** tagsüber

dusk n Dämmerung f ▷ at dusk bei Dämmerung

dust n Staub m
▶ vb abstauben [4] (perf hat abgestaubt) ▷ I dusted the shelves. Ich habe das Regal abgestaubt.; **I hate dusting!** Ich hasse Staubwischen!

dustbin n Mülleimer m (pl Mülleimer)

dustman n Müllmann m (pl Müllmänner); **He's a dustman.** Er arbeitet bei der Müllabfuhr.

dusty adj staubig

Dutch adj holländisch ▷ She's Dutch. Sie ist Holländerin.
▶ n (language) Holländisch nt (gen Holländischen); **the Dutch** die Holländer mpl

Dutchman n Holländer m (pl Holländer)

Dutchwoman n Holländerin f

duty n Pflicht f ▷ It was his duty to tell the police. Es war seine Pflicht, die Polizei zu informieren.; **to be on duty** Dienst haben [32]

duty-free adj zollfrei; **the duty-free shop** der Duty-free-Laden

duvet n Steppdecke f (pl Steppdecken)

DVD n (= digital video disc) DVD f (pl DVDs)

339 | dyspraxia

DVD player n DVD-Player m (pl DVD-Player)

dye n Farbstoff m; **hair dye** das Haarfärbemittel
▶ vb färben [38] ▷ to dye something red etwas rot färben ▷ She has dyed her hair blonde. Sie hat blond gefärbte Haare.

dynamic adj dynamisch

dyslexia n Legasthenie f; **She has dyslexia.** Sie ist Legasthenikerin.

dyslexic adj legasthenisch; **She is dyslexic.** Sie ist Legasthenikerin.

dyspraxia n Dyspraxie f; **She has dyspraxia.** Sie leidet an Dyspraxie.

e

each adj, pron jeder ▷ *Each person has their own desk.* Jeder hat seinen eigenen Schreibtisch. ▷ *They have ten points each.* Jeder hat zehn Punkte. ▷ *He gave each of us ten pounds.* Er gab jedem von uns zehn Pfund. ▷ *each day* jeder Tag jede ▷ *Each dancer wore a different costume.* Jede Tänzerin trug ein anderes Kostüm. ▷ *He gave each of the dancers a red rose.* Er gab jeder Tänzerin eine rote Rose. jedes ▷ *Each house has a garden.* Jedes Haus hat einen Garten. ▷ *The girls each have their own bedroom.* Jedes der Mädchen hat sein eigenes Zimmer.; **each other** einander; **They don't know each other.** Sie kennen sich nicht.

eagle n Adler m (pl Adler)

ear n Ohr nt (pl Ohren)

earache n Ohrenschmerzen mpl ▷ *to have earache* Ohrenschmerzen haben

earlier adv ❶ vorher ▷ *I saw him earlier.* Ich habe ihn vorher gesehen. ❷ (*in the morning*) früher ▷ *I ought to get up earlier.* Ich sollte früher aufstehen.

early adv, adj früh ▷ *I have to get up early.* Ich muss früh aufstehen. ▷ *I came early to get a good seat.* Ich bin früh gekommen, um einen guten Platz zu bekommen.; **to have an early night** früh ins Bett gehen [**29**]

earn vb verdienen [**84**] (*perf* hat verdient) ▷ *She earns five pounds an hour.* Sie verdient fünf Pfund in der Stunde.

earnings npl Verdienst m (pl Verdienste)

earphones npl Kopfhörer mpl

earring n Ohrring m (pl Ohrringe)

earth n Erde f

earthquake n Erdbeben nt (pl Erdbeben)

easily adv leicht

east adj, adv nach Osten ▷ *We were travelling east.* Wir sind nach Osten gefahren.; **the east coast** die Ostküste; **east of** östlich von
▶ n Osten m ▷ *in the east* im Osten

Easter n Ostern nt ▷ *at Easter* an Ostern ▷ *We went to Spain for Easter.* Wir waren über Ostern in Spanien.

Easter egg n Osterei nt (pl Ostereier)

eastern adj östlich ▷ *the eastern part of the island* der östliche Teil der Insel; **Eastern Europe** Osteuropa nt

easy adj einfach

eat vb essen [**20**] (pres isst, imperf aß, perf hat gegessen) ▷ *Would you like something to eat?* Möchtest du etwas essen?

e-book n E-Book nt (pl E-Books)

echo n Echo nt (pl Echos)

ecology n Ökologie f

economic adj (profitable) rentabel

economical adj sparsam

economics nsg Volkswirtschaft f ▷ *He's studying economics.* Er studiert Volkswirtschaft.

economy n Wirtschaft f ▷ *the German economy* die deutsche Wirtschaft

ecstasy n (drug) Ecstasy nt (gen Ecstasy); **to be in ecstasy** entzückt sein [**65**]

eczema n Hautausschlag m (pl Hautausschläge)

edge n ❶ Rand m (pl Ränder) ▷ They live on the edge of the moors. Sie leben am Rand des Moors. ❷ (of table) Kante f ❸ (of lake) Ufer nt (pl Ufer)

Edinburgh n Edinburgh nt

editor n (of newspaper) Redakteur m (pl Redakteure), Redakteurin f

education n ❶ Bildungswesen nt ▷ There should be more investment in education. Es sollte mehr Geld ins Bildungswesen investiert werden. ❷ (teaching) Lehramt nt ▷ She works in education. Sie ist im Lehramt tätig.

educational adj (experience) lehrreich ▷ It was very educational. Das war sehr lehrreich.

effect n Effekt m (pl Effekte) ▷ special effects Spezialeffekte

effective adj effektiv

efficient adj effizient

effort n Bemühung f; **to make an effort to do something** sich bemühen [7], etwas zu tun

e.g. abbr z. B. (= zum Beispiel)

egg n Ei nt (pl Eier) ▷ a hard-boiled egg ein hart gekochtes Ei ▷ a soft-boiled egg ein weich gekochtes Ei; **a fried egg** ein Spiegelei; **scrambled eggs** die Rühreier ntpl

egg cup n Eierbecher m (pl Eierbecher)

eggplant n (US) Aubergine f

Egypt n Ägypten nt ▷ to Egypt nach Ägypten

Eid n Eid al-Fitr nt

eight num acht ▷ She's eight. Sie ist acht.

eighteen num achtzehn ▷ She's eighteen. Sie ist achtzehn.

eighteenth adj achtzehnte ▷ the eighteenth of August der achtzehnte August

eighth adj achte ▷ the eighth floor der achte Stock ▷ the eighth of August der achte August

eighty num achtzig ▷ She's eighty. Sie ist achtzig.

either adv, conj, pron ❶ auch kein ▷ I don't like milk, and I don't like eggs either. Ich mag keine Milch und ich mag auch keine Eier. ❷ auch nicht ▷ I've never been to Spain. — I haven't either. Ich war noch nie in Spanien. — Ich auch nicht.; **either ... or ...** entweder ... oder ... ▷ You can have either ice cream or yoghurt. Du kannst entweder Eis oder Joghurt haben.; **either of them** einer von beiden ▷ Take either of them. Nimm einen von beiden.; **I don't like either of them.** Ich mag keinen von beiden.

elastic n Gummiband nt (pl Gummibänder)

elastic band n Gummiband nt (pl Gummibänder)

elbow n Ellbogen m (pl Ellbogen)

elder adj älter ▷ my elder sister meine ältere Schwester

elderly adj älter ▷ an elderly lady eine ältere Dame

eldest adj älteste ▷ my eldest brother mein ältester Bruder ▷ my eldest sister meine älteste Schwester ▷ He's the eldest. Er ist der Älteste.

elect vb wählen [38]

election n Wahl f ▷ The general election takes place tomorrow. Morgen finden die allgemeinen Wahlen statt.

electric adj elektrisch ▷ an electric fire ein elektrischer Ofen ▷ an electric guitar eine elektrische Gitarre; **an electric blanket** eine Heizdecke

electrical adj elektrisch; **an electrical engineer** ein Elektrotechniker

electrician n Elektriker m (pl Elektriker), Elektrikerin f ▷ He's an electrician. Er ist Elektriker.

electricity n Strom m ▷ They cut off our electricity. Sie haben den Strom abgestellt.

electronic adj elektronisch

electronics nsg Elektronik f ▷ *My hobby is electronics.* Elektronik ist mein Hobby.
elegant adj elegant
elementary school n (US) Grundschule f
elephant n Elefant m (gen Elefanten, pl Elefanten)
elevator n (US) Aufzug m (pl Aufzüge)
eleven num elf ▷ *She's eleven.* Sie ist elf.
eleventh adj elfte ▷ *the eleventh floor* der elfte Stock ▷ *the eleventh of August* der elfte August
else adv ❶ anders ▷ *somebody else* jemand anders ▷ *nobody else* niemand anders ▷ *somewhere else* irgendwo anders ▷ *anywhere else* irgendwo anders ❷ anderes ▷ *nothing else* nichts anderes ▷ *something else* etwas anderes ▷ *anything else* etwas anderes; **Would you like anything else?** Möchtest du noch etwas?; **I don't want anything else.** Ich will nichts anderes.; **Give me the money, or else!** Gib mir das Geld, sonst gibt's was!
email n E-Mail f (pl E-Mails) ▷ *My email address is ...* Meine E-Mail-Adresse ist ... ▶ vb mailen [38] (perf hat gemailt) ▷ *Did you email me?* Hast du es gemailt?; **to email somebody** jemandem eine E-Mail senden
embankment n Böschung f
embarrassed adj verlegen ▷ *He seemed to be pretty embarrassed.* Er schien sehr verlegen.; **I was really embarrassed.** Es war mir wirklich peinlich.
embarrassing adj peinlich ▷ *It was so embarrassing.* Es war so peinlich.
embassy n Botschaft f
embroider vb besticken [7] (perf hat bestickt)
embroidery n Stickerei f; **I do embroidery.** Ich sticke.
emergency n Notfall m (pl Notfälle) ▷ *This is an emergency!* Dies ist ein Notfall! ▷ *in an emergency* in einem Notfall; **an emergency exit** ein Notausgang m; **an emergency landing** eine Notlandung; **the emergency services** die Rettungsdienste mpl
emigrate vb auswandern [88] (perf ist ausgewandert)
emoji n Emoji nt (pl Emojis)
emotion n Gefühl nt (pl Gefühle)
emotional adj (person) emotional
emperor n Kaiser m (pl Kaiser)
emphasize vb betonen [7] (perf hat betont)
empire n Reich nt (pl Reiche)
employ vb beschäftigen [18] (perf hat beschäftigt) ▷ *The factory employs six hundred people.* Die Fabrik beschäftigt sechshundert Leute.
employee n Angestellte m (gen Angestellten, pl Angestellten), Angestellte f (pl Angestellten) ▷ *He's an employee.* Er ist Angestellter.
employer n Arbeitgeber m (pl Arbeitgeber), Arbeitgeberin f
employment n Beschäftigung f
empty adj leer
▶ vb leeren [38]; **to empty something out** etwas ausleeren [4]
encourage vb ermutigen [7] (perf hat ermutigt); **to encourage somebody to do something** jemanden ermutigen [7], etwas zu tun
encouragement n Ermutigung f
encyclopedia n Lexikon nt (pl Lexika)
end n Ende nt (pl Enden) ▷ *the end of the holidays* das Ende der Ferien ▷ *at the end of the street* am Ende der Straße ▷ *at the other end of the table* am anderen Ende des Tisches; **the end of the film** der Schluss des Films; **in the end** schließlich; **for hours on end** stundenlang
▶ vb zu Ende sein [65] (pres ist zu Ende, imperf war zu Ende, perf ist zu Ende gewesen) ▷ *What time does the film end?*

Wann ist der Film zu Ende?; **to end up doing something** schließlich etwas tun [**81**]

ending n Schluss m (gen Schlusses, pl Schlüsse) ▷ *It was an exciting film, especially the ending.* Es war ein spannender Film, besonders am Schluss.

endless adj endlos ▷ *The journey seemed endless.* Die Reise erschien endlos.

enemy n Feind m (pl Feinde), Feindin f

energetic adj (person) voller Energie

energy n Energie f

engaged adj ❶ (busy, in use) besetzt ▷ *I phoned, but it was engaged.* Ich habe angerufen, aber es war besetzt. ❷ (to be married) verlobt ▷ *She's engaged to Brian.* Sie ist mit Brian verlobt.; **to get engaged** sich verloben [**84**]

engagement n Verlobung f ▷ *an engagement ring* ein Verlobungsring m

engine n Motor m (pl Motoren)

engineer n ❶ Ingenieur m (pl Ingenieure), Ingenieurin f ▷ *He's an engineer.* Er ist Ingenieur. ❷ (train driver) Lokomotivführer m (pl Lokomotivführer)

engineering n Technik f ▷ *genetic engineering* die Gentechnik; **mechanical engineering** der Maschinenbau

England n England nt; **from England** aus England; **in England** in England; **to England** nach England
* Germans frequently use **England** to mean Great Britain or the United Kingdom.

English adj englisch; **He's English.** Er ist Engländer.; **She's English.** Sie ist Engländerin.; **English people** die Engländer mpl
▶ n (language) Englisch nt (gen Englischen) ▷ *Do you speak English?* Sprechen Sie Englisch?; **the English** (people) die Engländer mpl

Englishman n Engländer m (pl Engländer)

Englishwoman n Engländerin f

enjoy vb genießen (imperf genoss, perf hat genossen) ▷ *I enjoyed my holiday.* Ich habe meinen Urlaub genossen.; **Did you enjoy the film?** Hat dir der Film gefallen?; **Did you enjoy your meal?** Hat es Ihnen geschmeckt?; **to enjoy oneself** sich amüsieren [**76**]

enjoyable adj nett

enlargement n (of photo) Vergrößerung f

enormous adj riesig

enough pron, adj genug ▷ *enough time* genug Zeit ▷ *I didn't have enough money.* Ich hatte nicht genug Geld. ▷ *big enough* groß genug ▷ *warm enough* warm genug; **Have you got enough?** Reicht dir das?; **I've had enough!** Mir reicht's!; **That's enough.** Das reicht.

enquire vb sich erkundigen [**19**] (perf hat sich erkundigt); **to enquire about something** sich nach etwas erkundigen [**19**]

enquiry n (official investigation) Untersuchung f; **to make an enquiry** sich erkundigen [**19**]

enter vb (room) betreten [**79**] (pres betritt, imperf betrat, perf hat betreten); **to enter a competition** an einem Wettbewerb teilnehmen [**52**]

entertain vb (guests) unterhalten [**33**] (pres unterhält, imperf unterhielt, perf hat unterhalten)

entertaining adj unterhaltsam

enthusiasm n Begeisterung f

enthusiast n *a railway enthusiast* ein Eisenbahnfan m; **She's a DIY enthusiast.** Sie ist begeisterte Heimwerkerin.

enthusiastic adj begeistert

entire adj ganz ▷ *the entire world* die ganze Welt

entirely adv ganz

entrance n Eingang m (pl Eingänge); **an entrance exam** eine Aufnahmeprüfung; **entrance fee** der Eintritt

entry n (way in) Eingang m (pl Eingänge); **'no entry'** (1) (on door) 'kein Zutritt' (2) (on road sign) 'Einfahrt verboten'; **an entry form** ein Teilnahmeformular nt

entry phone n Gegensprechanlage f

envelope n Umschlag m (pl Umschläge)

envious adj neidisch

environment n Umwelt f

environmental adj **environmental pollution** die Umweltverschmutzung; **environmental protection** der Umweltschutz

environmentally-friendly adj umweltfreundlich

envy n Neid m
▶ vb beneiden [54] (perf hat beneidet)
▷ I don't envy you! Ich beneide dich nicht!

epileptic adj epileptisch

episode n (of TV programme, story) Folge f

equal adj gleich
▶ vb Ten times two equals twenty. Zehn mal zwei ist gleich zwanzig.

equality n Gleichheit f

equalize vb (in sport) ausgleichen (imperf glich aus, perf hat ausgeglichen)

equator n Äquator m

equipment n Ausrüstung f ▷ fishing equipment die Anglerausrüstung ▷ skiing equipment die Skiausrüstung

equipped adj **equipped with** ausgerüstet mit; **to be well equipped** gut ausgestattet sein [65]

error n Fehler m (pl Fehler)

escalator n Rolltreppe f

escape n (from prison) Ausbruch m (pl Ausbrüche)
▶ vb ausbrechen [11] (pres bricht aus, imperf brach aus, perf ist ausgebrochen) ▷ A lion has escaped. Ein Löwe ist ausgebrochen. ▷ to escape from prison aus dem Gefängnis ausbrechen

escort n Eskorte f ▷ a police escort eine Polizeieskorte

especially adv besonders ▷ It's very hot there, especially in the summer. Dort ist es sehr heiß, besonders im Sommer.

essay n Aufsatz m (pl Aufsätze) ▷ a history essay ein Aufsatz in Geschichte

essential adj wichtig ▷ It's essential to bring warm clothes. Es ist ganz wichtig, warme Kleidung mitzubringen.

estate n (housing estate) Siedlung f ▷ I live on an estate. Ich wohne in einer Siedlung.

estate agent n Immobilienmakler m (pl Immobilienmakler), Immobilienmaklerin f

estate car n Kombiwagen m (pl Kombiwagen)

estimate vb schätzen [36] ▷ They estimated it would take three weeks. Sie schätzten, dass es drei Wochen dauern würde.

etc abbr (= et cetera) usw. (= und so weiter)

Ethiopia n Äthiopien nt; **in Ethiopia** in Äthiopien

ethnic adj **①** (identity) ethnisch ▷ an ethnic minority eine ethnische Minderheit **②** (clothes, music) folkloristisch

e-ticket n E-Ticket nt (pl E-Tickets)

EU n (= European Union) EU f (= Europäische Union)

euro n Euro m (pl Euros or Euro)
When talking about amounts of money use the plural form **Euro**.
▷ fifty euros fünfzig Euro

Europe n Europa nt; **from Europe** aus Europa; **in Europe** in Europa; **to Europe** nach Europa

European adj europäisch; **He's European.** Er ist Europäer.
▶ n (person) Europäer m (pl Europäer), Europäerin f

ENGLISH > GERMAN

EV abbr (= electric vehicle) E-Auto nt (= Elektroauto)

eve n **Christmas Eve** der Heilige Abend; **New Year's Eve** Silvester nt

even adv ① sogar ▷ *I like all animals, even snakes.* Ich mag alle Tiere, sogar Schlangen.; **even if** selbst wenn; **not even** nicht einmal; **even though** obwohl; **I liked Hamburg even more than Munich.** Hamburg hat mir noch besser gefallen als München.
▶ adj gleichmäßig ▷ *an even layer of snow* eine gleichmäßige Schneeschicht; **an even number** eine gerade Zahl; **to get even with somebody** es jemandem heimzahlen [4]

evening n Abend m (pl Abende) ▷ *in the evening* am Abend ▷ *all evening* den ganzen Abend ▷ *yesterday evening* gestern Abend ▷ *tomorrow evening* morgen Abend; **Good evening!** Guten Abend!

evening class n Abendkurs m (pl Abendkurse)

event n Ereignis nt (gen Ereignisses, pl Ereignisse); **a sporting event** eine Sportveranstaltung

eventful adj ereignisreich

eventual adj schließlich; **the eventual outcome** das Endergebnis

> Be careful not to translate **eventual** by **eventuell**.

eventually adv schließlich

ever adv ① schon einmal ▷ *Have you ever been to America?* Warst du schon einmal in Amerika? ▷ *Have you ever seen her?* Hast du sie schon einmal gesehen? ② je ▷ *the best I've ever seen* das Beste, was ich je gesehen habe; **for the first time ever** das allererste Mal; **ever since** seit; **ever since then** seither

every adj jeder ▷ *every student* jeder Student ▷ *every day* jeden Tag
jede ▷ *every mother* jede Mutter ▷ *every week* jede Woche

345 | **except**

jedes ▷ *every child* jedes Kind ▷ *every year* jedes Jahr; **every time** jedes Mal; **every now and then** ab und zu

everybody pron ① alle ▷ *Everybody had a good time.* Alle hatten ihren Spaß.
② jeder ▷ *Everybody makes mistakes.* Jeder macht mal Fehler.

everyone pron ① alle ② jeder

everything pron alles ▷ *You've thought of everything?* Du hast an alles gedacht? ▷ *Money isn't everything.* Geld ist nicht alles.

everywhere adv überall ▷ *I've looked everywhere.* Ich habe überall gesucht. ▷ *There were police officers everywhere.* Überall waren Polizisten.

evil adj böse

exact adj genau

exactly adv genau ▷ *exactly the same* genau das gleiche ▷ *It's exactly ten o'clock.* Es ist genau zehn Uhr.

exaggerate vb übertreiben (imperf übertrieb, perf hat übertrieben)

exaggeration n Übertreibung f

exam n Prüfung f ▷ *a German exam* eine Deutschprüfung ▷ *the exam results* die Prüfungsergebnisse

examination n Prüfung f; **a medical examination** eine ärztliche Untersuchung

examine vb untersuchen [18] (perf hat untersucht) ▷ *The doctor examined him.* Der Arzt untersuchte ihn.; **He examined her passport.** Er prüfte ihren Pass.

examiner n Prüfer m (pl Prüfer), Prüferin f

example n Beispiel nt (pl Beispiele); **for example** zum Beispiel

excellent adj ausgezeichnet ▷ *Her results were excellent.* Ihre Noten waren ausgezeichnet.

except prep außer ▷ *everyone except me* alle außer mir; **except for** abgesehen von; **except that** außer, dass

exception n Ausnahme f ▷ *to make an exception* eine Ausnahme machen

exchange vb tauschen [48] ▷ *I exchanged the book for a DVD.* Ich habe das Buch gegen eine DVD getauscht.

exchange rate n Wechselkurs m (pl Wechselkurse)

excited adj aufgeregt

exciting adj aufregend

exclamation mark n Ausrufezeichen nt (pl Ausrufezeichen)

excuse n Entschuldigung f
▷ vb Excuse me! Entschuldigung!

exercise n ❶ Übung f ▷ *an exercise book* ein Übungsheft ❷ Bewegung f ▷ *You need more exercise.* Sie brauchen mehr Bewegung.; **an exercise bike** ein Heimtrainer m; **She does her exercises every morning.** Sie macht jeden Morgen ihre Gymnastik.

exhaust n Auspuff m; **exhaust fumes** die Abgase ntpl

exhausted adj erschöpft

exhaust pipe n Auspuffrohr nt (pl Auspuffrohre)

exhibition n Ausstellung f

exist vb existieren [76] (perf hat existiert); **It doesn't exist.** Das gibt es nicht.

exit n (way out) Ausgang m (pl Ausgänge)

expect vb ❶ erwarten [2] (perf hat erwartet) ▷ *I'm expecting him for dinner.* Ich erwarte ihn zum Abendessen. ▷ *She's expecting a baby.* Sie erwartet ein Kind. ▷ *I didn't expect that from him.* Das habe ich von ihm nicht erwartet. ❷ annehmen [1] (pres nimmt an, imperf nahm an, perf hat angenommen) ▷ *I expect he'll be late.* Ich nehme an, dass er sich verspäten wird. ▷ *I expect so.* Das nehme ich mal an.

expedition n Expedition f

expel vb **to get expelled** (from school) von der Schule verwiesen werden [91]

expenses npl Kosten pl

expensive adj teuer

experience n Erfahrung f
▷ vb ❶ haben [32] (pres hat, imperf hatte, perf hat gehabt) ▷ *They're experiencing some problems.* Sie haben einige Probleme. ❷ (feel) empfinden [24] (imperf empfand, perf hat empfunden) ▷ *He experienced fear and excitement.* Er empfand Angst und Aufregung.

experienced adj erfahren

experiment n Experiment nt (pl Experimente)

expert n Fachmann m (pl Fachleute), Fachfrau f ▷ *He's a computer expert.* Er ist Computerfachmann.; **He's an expert cook.** Er kocht ausgezeichnet.

expire vb (passport) ablaufen [43] (pres läuft ab, imperf lief ab, perf ist abgelaufen)

explain vb erklären [19] (perf hat erklärt)

explanation n Erklärung f

explode vb explodieren [76] (perf ist explodiert)

explore vb (place) erkunden [18] (perf hat erkundet)

explosion n Explosion f

export vb exportieren [76] (perf hat exportiert)

express vb ausdrücken [4] (perf hat ausgedrückt); **to express oneself** sich ausdrücken [4]

expression n Ausdruck m (pl Ausdrücke); **It's an English expression.** Das ist eine englische Redewendung.

expressway n (US) Schnellstraße f

extension n ❶ (of building) Anbau m (pl Anbauten) ❷ (telephone) Apparat m (pl Apparate) ▷ *Extension 3137, please.* Apparat 3137, bitte.

extent n **to some extent** in gewisser Weise

exterior adj äußere ▷ *the exterior walls* die äußeren Wände

extinct *adj* to become extinct aussterben [75]; **to be extinct** ausgestorben sein [65]
extinguisher *n* (fire extinguisher) Feuerlöscher *m* (pl Feuerlöscher)
extra *adj, adv* zusätzlich ▷ *an extra blanket* eine zusätzliche Decke; **to pay extra** extra bezahlen [7]; **Breakfast is extra.** Frühstück wird extra berechnet.; **It costs extra.** Das kostet extra.
extraordinary *adj* außergewöhnlich
extravagant *adj* (person) verschwenderisch
extreme *adj* extrem
extremely *adv* äußerst
extremist *n* Extremist *m* (gen Extremisten, pl Extremisten), Extremistin *f*
eye *n* Auge *nt* (pl Augen) ▷ *I've got green eyes.* Ich habe grüne Augen.; **to keep an eye on something** auf etwas aufpassen [31]
eyebrow *n* Augenbraue *f*
eyelash *n* Wimper *f*
eyelid *n* Augenlid *nt* (pl Augenlider)
eyeliner *n* Eyeliner *m* (pl Eyeliner)
eye shadow *n* Lidschatten *m* (pl Lidschatten)
eyesight *n* Sehvermögen *nt* ▷ *Her eyesight is deteriorating.* Ihr Sehvermögen lässt nach.; **to have good eyesight** gute Augen haben [32]

f

fabric *n* Stoff *m* (pl Stoffe)
fabulous *adj* traumhaft ▷ *The show was fabulous.* Die Show war traumhaft.
face *n* ❶ (of person) Gesicht *nt* (pl Gesichter) ❷ (of clock) Zifferblatt *nt* (pl Zifferblätter) ❸ (of cliff) Wand *f* (pl Wände); **on the face of it** auf den ersten Blick; **in the face of these difficulties** angesichts dieser Schwierigkeiten; **face to face** Auge in Auge; **a face cloth** ein Waschlappen *m*
▶ *vb* (place, problem) konfrontiert sein [65] mit (*pres ist* konfrontiert mit, *imperf* war konfrontiert mit, *perf ist* konfrontiert gewesen mit); **to face up to something** sich einer Sache stellen [38]
Facebook® *n* Facebook®
facilities *npl* Einrichtungen *fpl*; **This school has excellent facilities.** Diese Schule ist ausgezeichnet ausgestattet.; **toilet facilities** Toiletten *fpl*; **cooking facilities** die Kochgelegenheit *sg*
fact *n* Tatsache *f*; **in fact** tatsächlich
factory *n* Fabrik *f*

fail vb ❶ durchfallen [22] in (pres fällt durch, imperf fiel durch, perf durchgefallen) ▷ *I failed the history exam.* Ich bin in der Geschichtsprüfung durchgefallen. ❷ durchfallen [22] ▷ *In our class, no one failed.* In unserer Klasse ist niemand durchgefallen. ❸ versagen [84] (perf hat versagt) ▷ *My brakes failed.* Meine Bremsen haben versagt.; **to fail to do something** etwas nicht tun [81]
▶ n **without fail** ganz bestimmt

failure n ❶ Versagen nt ▷ *a mechanical failure* ein mechanisches Versagen; **feelings of failure** das Gefühl zu versagen ❷ Versager m (pl Versager), Versagerin f ▷ *He's a failure.* Er ist ein Versager.

faint adj schwach ▷ *His voice was very faint.* Seine Stimme war sehr schwach.; **I feel faint.** Mir ist schwindlig.
▶ vb ❶ ohnmächtig werden [91] (pres wird ohnmächtig, imperf wurde ohnmächtig, perf ist ohnmächtig geworden) ▷ *All of a sudden she fainted.* Plötzlich wurde sie ohnmächtig.

fair adj ❶ fair ▷ *That's not fair.* Das ist nicht fair. ❷ (hair) blond ▷ *He's got fair hair.* Er hat blonde Haare. ❸ (skin) hell ▷ *people with fair skin* Menschen mit heller Haut ❹ (weather) schön ▷ *The weather was fair.* Das Wetter war schön. ❺ (good enough) gut ▷ *I have a fair chance of winning.* Ich habe gute Gewinnchancen. ❻ (sizeable) ordentlich ▷ *That's a fair distance.* Das ist eine ordentliche Entfernung.
▶ n Volksfest nt (pl Volksfeste) ▷ *They went to the fair.* Sie sind aufs Volksfest gegangen.; **a trade fair** eine Handelsmesse

fairground n Rummelplatz m (pl Rummelplätze)

fairly adv ❶ gerecht ▷ *The cake was divided fairly.* Der Kuchen wurde gerecht verteilt. ❷ (quite) ziemlich ▷ *That's fairly good.* Das ist ziemlich gut.

fairy n Fee f
fairy tale n Märchen nt (pl Märchen)
faith n ❶ Glaube m (gen Glaubens) ▷ *the Catholic faith* der katholische Glaube ❷ Vertrauen nt ▷ *People have lost faith in the government.* Die Menschen haben das Vertrauen in die Regierung verloren.
faithful adj treu
faithfully adv **Yours faithfully ...** (in letter) Hochachtungsvoll ...
fake n Fälschung f ▷ *The painting was a fake.* Das Gemälde war eine Fälschung.
▶ adj gefälscht ▷ *a fake certificate* eine gefälschte Urkunde; **She wore fake fur.** Sie trug eine Pelzimitation.
fall n ❶ Sturz m (gen Sturzes, pl Stürze) ▷ *She had a nasty fall.* Sie ist übel gestürzt.; **a fall of snow** ein Schneefall m; **Niagara Falls** die Niagarafälle ❷ (US: autumn) Herbst m (pl Herbste) ▷ *in fall* im Herbst
▶ vb ❶ hinfallen [22] (perf ist hingefallen) ▷ *He tripped and fell.* Er ist gestolpert und hingefallen. ❷ fallen [22] ▷ *Prices are falling.* Die Preise fallen.; **to fall apart** auseinanderfallen [22]; **to fall down** (1) (person) hinfallen [22] ▷ *She's fallen down.* Sie ist hingefallen. (2) (building) einfallen [22] ▷ *The wall fell down.* Die Mauer ist eingefallen.; **to fall for** (1) hereinfallen [22] auf ▷ *They fell for it.* Sie sind darauf hereingefallen. (2) sich verlieben [84] in ▷ *She's falling for him.* Sie ist dabei, sich in ihn zu verlieben.; **to fall off** herunterfallen [22] von; **to fall out** sich zerstreiten; **to fall through** ins Wasser fallen [22]
false adj falsch; **a false alarm** ein falscher Alarm; **false teeth** das Gebiss
fame n Ruhm m
familiar adj vertraut ▷ *a familiar face* ein vertrautes Gesicht; **to be familiar with something** mit etwas vertraut sein [65]
family n Familie f ▷ *the Airlie family* die Familie Airlie

ENGLISH > GERMAN   349 | **favourite**

famine n Hungersnot f (pl Hungersnöte)
famous adj berühmt
fan n ① (hand-held) Fächer m (pl Fächer) ❷ (electric) Ventilator m (pl Ventilatoren) ❸ (of person, band, sport) Fan m (pl Fans)
▪ **der Fan** is also used for women.
▷ I'm a fan of theirs. Ich bin ein Fan von ihnen.; football fans Fußballfans
fanatic n Fanatiker m (pl Fanatiker), Fanatikerin f
fancy vb to fancy something Lust auf etwas haben [32]; to fancy doing something Lust haben [32], etwas zu tun; He fancies her. Er steht auf sie.
fancy dress n Kostüm nt (pl Kostüme); He was wearing fancy dress. Er war kostümiert.; a fancy-dress ball ein Kostümball m
fantastic adj fantastisch
far adj, adv weit ▷ Is it far? Ist es weit? ▷ How far is it? Wie weit ist es? ▷ How far is it to Geneva? Wie weit ist es nach Genf?; far from (1) weit entfernt von ▷ It's not far from London. Es ist nicht weit von London entfernt. (2) überhaupt nicht ▷ It's far from easy. Es ist überhaupt nicht einfach.; **How far have you got?** (with a task) Wie weit bist du gekommen?; **at the far end** am anderen Ende ▷ at the far end of the room am anderen Ende des Zimmers; **far better** viel besser; **as far as I know** soviel ich weiß; **the Far East** der Ferne Osten
fare n Fahrpreis m (pl Fahrpreise); half fare halber Preis; full fare voller Preis
farm n Bauernhof m (pl Bauernhöfe)
farmer n Bauer m (gen Bauern, pl Bauern), Bäuerin f ▷ He's a farmer. Er ist Bauer.; a farmers' market ein Bauernmarkt m
farmhouse n Bauernhaus nt (gen Bauernhauses, pl Bauernhäuser)
farming n Landwirtschaft f; **dairy farming** die Milchwirtschaft

fascinating adj faszinierend
fashion n Mode f; **in fashion** in Mode
fashionable adj modisch ▷ Jane wears very fashionable clothes. Jane trägt sehr modische Kleidung.; **a fashionable restaurant** ein Restaurant, das in Mode ist
fast adj, adv schnell ▷ He can run fast. Er kann schnell laufen. ▷ a fast car ein schnelles Auto; **That clock's fast.** Die Uhr geht vor.; **He's fast asleep.** Er schläft fest.

▪ Be careful not to translate **fast** by the German word **fast**.

fast food n Fast Food nt
fat adj (person) dick
▶ n ① Fett nt (pl Fette); **It's very high in fat.** Es ist sehr fett.
fatal adj ① (causing death) tödlich ▷ a fatal accident ein tödlicher Unfall ❷ (disastrous) fatal ▷ He made a fatal mistake. Er machte einen fatalen Fehler.
father n Vater m (pl Väter) ▷ my father mein Vater; **Father Christmas** der Weihnachtsmann
father-in-law n Schwiegervater m (pl Schwiegerväter)
faucet n (US) Wasserhahn m (pl Wasserhähne)
fault n ① (mistake) Schuld f ▷ It's my fault. Es ist meine Schuld. ❷ (defect) Fehler m (pl Fehler) ▷ a mechanical fault ein mechanischer Fehler
favour (US **favor**) n Gefallen m (pl Gefallen); **to do somebody a favour** jemandem einen Gefallen tun [81]; **to be in favour of something** für etwas sein [65]
favourite (US **favorite**) adj Blue's my favourite colour. Blau ist meine Lieblingsfarbe.
▶ n ① Liebling m (pl Lieblinge)
▪ **der Liebling** is also used for women.
▷ She's his favourite. Sie ist sein Liebling.
❷ Favorit m (pl Favoriten), Favoritin f

fax n Fax nt (gen Fax, pl Faxe)
▶ vb faxen [**36**]
fear n Furcht f
▶ vb befürchten [**2**] (perf hat befürchtet)
▷ *You have nothing to fear.* Sie haben nichts zu befürchten.
feather n Feder f
feature n (of person, object) Eigenschaft f
▷ *an important feature* eine wichtige Eigenschaft
February n Februar m ▷ *in February* im Februar
fed vb see **feed**
fed up adj *to be fed up with something* etwas satthaben [**32**]
feed vb füttern [**88**] ▷ *Have you fed the cat?* Hast du die Katze gefüttert?; **He worked hard to feed his family.** Er arbeitete hart, um seine Familie zu ernähren.
feel vb ❶ sich fühlen [**38**] ▷ *I don't feel well.* Ich fühle mich nicht wohl. ▷ *I feel a bit lonely.* Ich fühle mich einsam. ❷ spüren [**38**] ▷ *I didn't feel much pain.* Ich habe keine großen Schmerzen gespürt. ❸ befühlen [**7**] (perf hat befühlt) ▷ *The doctor felt his forehead.* Der Arzt hat ihm die Stirn befühlt.; **I was feeling hungry.** Ich hatte Hunger.; **I felt very cold.** Mir war sehr kalt.; **I feel like ...** (want) Ich habe Lust auf ...
feeling n Gefühl nt (pl Gefühle) ▷ *a feeling of satisfaction* ein Gefühl der Befriedigung; **an itchy feeling** ein Jucken nt
feet npl see **foot**
fell vb see **fall**
felt vb see **feel**
felt-tip pen n Filzschreiber m (pl Filzschreiber)
female adj weiblich ▷ *a female animal* ein weibliches Tier ▷ *the female sex* das weibliche Geschlecht

In many cases, the ending indicates clearly whether the noun refers to a man or a woman and there is therefore no need for the word 'female'.

▷ *male and female students* Studenten und Studentinnen
▶ n (animal) Weibchen nt (pl Weibchen)
feminine adj feminin
feminist n Feminist m (gen Feministen, pl Feministen), Feministin f
fence n Zaun m (pl Zäune)
fern n Farn m (pl Farne)
ferocious adj wild
ferry n Fähre f
festival n Festival nt (pl Festivals) ▷ *a jazz festival* ein Jazzfestival
fetch vb ❶ holen [**38**] ▷ *Fetch the bucket.* Hol den Eimer. ❷ (sell for) einbringen [**13**] (imperf brachte ein, perf hat eingebracht) ▷ *His painting fetched five thousand pounds.* Sein Bild hat fünftausend Pfund eingebracht.
fever n (temperature) Fieber nt
few adj, pron (not many) wenige ▷ *few books* wenige Bücher; **a few** ein paar; **quite a few people** einige Leute
fewer adj weniger ▷ *There are fewer people than there were yesterday.* Es sind weniger Leute da als gestern. ▷ *There are fewer students in this class.* In dieser Klasse sind weniger Schüler.
fiancé n Verlobte m (gen Verlobten, pl Verlobten) ▷ *He's my fiancé.* Er ist mein Verlobter.
fiancée n Verlobte f (gen Verlobten, pl Verlobten) ▷ *She's my fiancée.* Sie ist meine Verlobte.
fiction n (novels) Romane mpl
field n ❶ (in countryside) Feld nt (pl Felder) ▷ *a field of wheat* ein Weizenfeld ❷ (for sport) Platz m (gen Platzes, pl Plätze) ▷ *a football field* ein Fußballplatz ❸ (subject) Gebiet nt (pl Gebiete) ▷ *He's*

ENGLISH > GERMAN

an expert in his field. Er ist Fachmann auf seinem Gebiet.
fierce *adj* ❶ gefährlich ▷ *The dog looked very fierce.* Der Hund sah sehr gefährlich aus. ❷ heftig ▷ *a fierce attack on* ein heftiger Angriff; **The wind was very fierce.** Es wehte ein sehr scharfer Wind.
fifteen *num* fünfzehn ▷ *I'm fifteen.* Ich bin fünfzehn.
fifteenth *adj* fünfzehnte ▷ *the fifteenth of August* der fünfzehnte August
fifth *adj* fünfte ▷ *the fifth floor* der fünfte Stock ▷ *the fifth of August* der fünfte August
fifty *num* fünfzig ▷ *He's fifty.* Er ist fünfzig.
fight *n* ❶ Schlägerei f ▷ *There was a fight in the pub.* In der Kneipe gab es eine Schlägerei. ❷ Kampf *m* (*pl* Kämpfe) ▷ *the fight against cancer* der Kampf gegen Krebs
▶ *vb* ❶ (*physically*) sich prügeln [34] ▷ *They were fighting.* Sie haben sich geprügelt. ❷ (*quarrel*) streiten (*imperf* stritt, *perf* hat gestritten) ▷ *He's always fighting with his wife.* Er streitet dauernd mit seiner Frau. ❸ (*combat*) bekämpfen [7] (*perf* hat bekämpft) ▷ *Doctors fought the disease.* Die Ärzte bekämpften die Krankheit.
fight back *vb* sich wehren [38]
figure *n* ❶ (*number*) Zahl f ▷ *Can you give me the exact figures?* Können Sie mir genaue Zahlen nennen? ❷ (*outline of person*) Gestalt f ▷ *Mary saw the figure of a man on the bridge.* Mary sah die Gestalt eines Mannes auf der Brücke. ❸ (*shape*) Figur f ▷ *She's got a good figure.* Sie hat eine gute Figur. ▷ *I have to watch my figure.* Ich muss auf meine Figur achten. ❹ (*personality*) Persönlichkeit f ▷ *She's an important political figure.* Sie ist eine wichtige politische Persönlichkeit.
figure out *vb* ❶ ausrechnen [4] (*perf* hat ausgerechnet) ❷ herausfinden [24]

351 | **finally**

(*imperf* fand heraus, *perf* hat herausgefunden) ❸ schlau werden [91] aus (*pres* wird schlau, *imperf* wurde schlau, *perf* ist schlau geworden)
file *n* ❶ (*document*) Akte f ▷ *Have we got a file on the suspect?* Haben wir eine Akte über den Verdächtigen? ❷ (*folder*) Aktenmappe f ▷ *She keeps all her letters in a cardboard file.* Sie bewahrt all ihre Briefe in einer Aktenmappe auf. ❸ (*ring binder*) Aktenordner *m* (*pl* Aktenordner) ❹ (*on computer*) Datei f ❺ (*for nails, metal*) Feile f
▶ *vb* ❶ (*papers*) abheften [2] (*perf* hat abgeheftet) ❷ (*nails, metal*) feilen [38] ▷ *I'll have to file my nails.* Ich muss mir die Nägel feilen.
fill *vb* füllen [38] ▷ *She filled the glass with water.* Sie füllte das Glas mit Wasser.; **to fill in** (1) ausfüllen [4] ▷ *Can you fill this form in, please?* Können Sie bitte dieses Formular ausfüllen? **(2)** auffüllen [4] ▷ *He filled the hole in with soil.* Er füllte das Loch mit Erde auf.; **to fill up** vollmachen [48] ▷ *He filled the cup up to the brim.* Er machte die Tasse bis zum Rand voll.; **Fill it up, please.** (*at petrol station*) Volltanken, bitte.
film *n* Film *m* (*pl* Filme)
film star *n* Filmstar *m* (*pl* Filmstars)

der Filmstar is also used for women.

▷ *She's a film star.* Sie ist ein Filmstar.
filthy *adj* schmutzig
final *adj* ❶ (*last*) letzte ▷ *our final match of the season* unser letztes Spiel der Saison ❷ (*definite*) endgültig ▷ *a final decision* eine endgültige Entscheidung.; **I'm not going and that's final.** Ich gehe nicht, und damit basta.
▶ *n* Finale *nt* (*pl* Finale) ▷ *Jabeur is in the final.* Jabeur ist im Finale.
finally *adv* ❶ (*lastly*) schließlich ▷ *Finally, I would like to say ...* Und schließlich möchte ich sagen ... ❷ (*eventually*)

financial *adj* finanziell

find *vb* finden [24] (*imperf* fand, *perf* hat gefunden) ▷ *I can't find the exit.* Ich kann den Ausgang nicht finden. ▷ *Did you find your pen?* Hast du deinen Schreiber gefunden?; **to find something out** etwas herausfinden [24] ▷ *I'm determined to find out the truth.* Ich bin entschlossen, die Wahrheit herauszufinden.; **to find out about (1)** *(make enquiries)* sich erkundigen [19] nach ▷ *Try to find out about the cost of a hotel.* Versuche, dich nach dem Preis für ein Hotel zu erkundigen. **(2)** *(by chance)* erfahren [21] ▷ *I found out about their affair.* Ich habe von ihrem Verhältnis erfahren.

fine *adj, adv* ❶ *(very good)* ausgezeichnet ▷ *He's a fine musician.* Er ist ein ausgezeichneter Musiker.; **How are you? — I'm fine.** Wie geht's? — Gut!; **I feel fine.** Mir geht's gut.; **The weather is fine today.** Das Wetter ist heute schön. ❷ *(not coarse) fein* ▷ *She's got very fine hair.* Sie hat sehr feine Haare.
▶ *n* ❶ Geldbuße *f* ▷ *She got a fine.* Sie hat eine Geldbuße bekommen. ❷ *(for traffic offence)* Strafzettel *m* (*pl* Strafzettel) ▷ *I got a fine for speeding.* Ich habe einen Strafzettel bekommen, weil ich zu schnell gefahren bin.

finger *n* Finger *m* (*pl* Finger) ▷ *my little finger* mein kleiner Finger

fingernail *n* Fingernagel *m* (*pl* Fingernägel)

finish *n* *(of race)* Finish *nt* (*pl* Finishs) ▷ *We saw the finish of the London Marathon.* Wir sahen das Finish des Londoner Marathonlaufs.
▶ *vb* ❶ fertig sein [65] (*pres* ist fertig, *imperf* war fertig, *perf* ist fertig gewesen) ▷ *I've finished!* Ich bin fertig! ❷ zu Ende sein [65] (*pres* ist zu Ende, *imperf* war zu Ende, *perf* ist zu Ende gewesen) ▷ *The film has finished.* Der Film ist zu Ende.; **I've finished the book.** Ich habe das Buch zu Ende gelesen.; **to finish doing something** etwas zu Ende machen [48]

Finland *n* Finnland *nt*; **from Finland** aus Finnland; **to Finland** nach Finnland

Finn *n* Finne *m* (*gen* Finnen, *pl* Finnen), Finnin *f*

Finnish *adj* finnisch; **She's Finnish.** Sie ist Finnin.
▶ *n (language)* Finnisch *nt* (*gen* Finnischen)

fir *n* Tanne *f*; **fir cone** der Tannenzapfen; **fir tree** der Tannenbaum

fire *n* ❶ Feuer *nt* (*pl* Feuer) ▷ *He made a fire to warm himself up.* Er machte ein Feuer, um sich aufzuwärmen.; **to be on fire** brennen [12] ❷ *(accidental)* Brand *m* (*pl* Brände); **The house was destroyed by fire.** Das Haus ist abgebrannt. ❸ *(heater)* Heizung *f* ▷ *Turn the fire on.* Mach die Heizung an.; **the fire brigade** die Feuerwehr; **a fire alarm** ein Feueralarm *m*; **a fire engine** ein Feuerwehrauto *nt*; **a fire escape** *(stairs)* eine Feuertreppe; **a fire extinguisher** ein Feuerlöscher *m*; **a fire station** eine Feuerwehrstation
▶ *vb (shoot)* schießen (*imperf* schoss, *perf* hat geschossen) ▷ *She fired twice.* Sie hat zweimal geschossen.; **to fire at somebody** auf jemanden schießen; **to fire a gun** einen Schuss abgeben [28]; **to fire somebody** jemanden feuern [34]

firefighter *n* Feuerwehrmann *m* (*pl* Feuerwehrleute), Feuerwehrfrau *f* ▷ *She's a firefighter.* Sie ist Feuerwehrfrau.

fireworks *npl* Feuerwerk *nt* (*pl* Feuerwerke) ▷ *Are you going to see the fireworks?* Seht ihr euch das Feuerwerk an?

ENGLISH > GERMAN

firm adj streng ▷ *to be firm with somebody* streng mit jemandem sein
▶ n Firma f (pl Firmen) ▷ *He works for a large firm in London.* Er arbeitet für eine große Firma in London.

first adj, adv ❶ erste ▷ *my first boyfriend* mein erster Freund ▷ *the first time* das erste Mal ▷ *the first of August* der erste August; **Rachel came first.** *(in exam, race)* Rachel war Erste.; **John came first.** *(in exam, race)* John war Erster. ❷ zuerst ▷ *I want to get a job, but first I have to pass my exams.* Ich will mir einen Job suchen, aber zuerst muss ich meine Prüfung bestehen.; **first of all** zuallererst
▶ n Erste m (gen Ersten, pl Ersten), Erste f (gen Ersten) ▷ *She was the first to arrive.* Sie ist als Erste angekommen.; **at first** zuerst

first aid n Erste Hilfe f; **a first aid kit** ein Verbandzeug nt

first-class adj ❶ erster Klasse ▷ *a first-class ticket* ein Ticket erster Klasse ❷ erstklassig ▷ *a first-class meal* ein erstklassiges Essen

* In Germany there is no first-class or
* second-class post. However, letters
* cost more to send than postcards,
* so you have to remember to say
* what you are sending when buying
* stamps. There is also an express
* service.

firstly adv ❶ zuerst ▷ *Firstly, let's see what the book is about.* Wir wollen erst mal sehen, wovon das Buch handelt. ❷ erstens ▷ *firstly ... secondly ...* erstens ... zweitens ...

fish n Fisch m (pl Fische) ▷ *I caught three fish.* Ich habe drei Fische gefangen. ▷ *I don't like fish.* Ich mag Fisch nicht.
▶ vb fischen [48]; **to go fishing** fischen gehen [29]

fisherman n Fischer m (pl Fischer) ▷ *He's a fisherman.* Er ist Fischer.

fish finger n Fischstäbchen nt (pl Fischstäbchen)

fishing n Angeln nt ▷ *My hobby is fishing.* Angeln ist mein Hobby.

fishing boat n Fischerboot nt (pl Fischerboote)

fishing rod n Angel f

fishing tackle n Angelzeug nt

fishmonger's n Fischladen m (pl Fischläden)

fist n Faust f (pl Fäuste)

fit vb ❶ *(be the right size)* passen [31] (perf hat gepasst) ▷ *Does it fit?* Passt es? ▷ *These trousers don't fit me.* *(wrong size)* Diese Hose passt mir nicht. ❷ *(fix up)* einbauen [4] (perf hat eingebaut) ▷ *He fitted an alarm in his car.* Er hat eine Alarmanlage in sein Auto eingebaut. ❸ *(attach)* anbringen [13] (imperf brachte an, perf hat angebracht) ▷ *She fitted a plug to the hair dryer.* Sie brachte am Föhn einen Stecker an.; **to fit in (1)** *(match up)* passen [31] zu ▷ *That story doesn't fit in with what he told us.* Diese Geschichte passt nicht zu dem, was er uns gesagt hat. **(2)** *(person)* sich einpassen [4] ▷ *She fitted in well at her new school.* Sie hat sich in ihrer neuen Schule gut eingepasst.
▶ adj *(healthy)* fit ▷ *He felt relaxed and fit after his holiday.* Nach seinem Urlaub fühlte er sich entspannt und fit.
▶ n **to have a fit (1)** *(medical)* einen Anfall haben [32] **(2)** *(be angry)* Zustände bekommen [40]

fitness f Fitness f; **a fitness centre** ein Fitnesscenter nt

five num fünf ▷ *He's five.* Er ist fünf.

fix vb ❶ *(mend)* reparieren [76] (perf hat repariert) ▷ *Can you fix my bike?* Kannst du mein Fahrrad reparieren? ❷ *(decide)* festlegen [82] (perf hat festgelegt) ▷ *Let's fix a date for the party.* Lass uns einen Tag für die Party festlegen. ▷ *They fixed a price for the car.* Sie haben einen Preis

fizzy | 354

für das Auto festgelegt. ❸ machen [48] ▷ Janice fixed some food for us. Janice hat uns etwas zum Essen gemacht.

fizzy adj mit Kohlensäure ▷ I don't like fizzy drinks. Ich mag keine Getränke mit Kohlensäure.

flag n Fahne f

flame n Flamme f

flan n ❶ (sweet) Kuchen m (pl Kuchen) ▷ a raspberry flan ein Himbeerkuchen ❷ (savoury) Quiche f (pl Quiches) ▷ a cheese and onion flan eine Käse-Zwiebel-Quiche

flap vb flattern [34] mit ▷ The bird flapped its wings. Der Vogel flatterte mit den Flügeln.

flash n Blitzlicht nt (pl Blitzlichter) ▷ Has your camera got a flash? Hat dein Fotoapparat ein Blitzlicht?; **a flash of lightning** ein Blitz m; **in a flash** blitzschnell
▶ vb ❶ blinken [38] ▷ The police car's blue light was flashing. Das Blaulicht des Polizeiautos blinkte. ❷ leuchten [2] mit ▷ They flashed a torch in his face. Sie leuchteten ihm mit einer Taschenlampe ins Gesicht.; **She flashed her headlights.** Sie betätigte die Lichthupe.

flask n Thermosflasche® f

flat adj ❶ flach ▷ flat shoes flache Schuhe; **a flat roof** ein Flachdach nt ❷ (tyre) platt ▷ I've got a flat tyre. Ich habe einen platten Reifen.
▶ n Wohnung f ▷ She lives in a flat. Sie wohnt in einer Wohnung.

flatscreen n Flachbildschirm m (pl Flachbildschirme) ▷ a flatscreen TV ein Flachbildschirm-Fernseher m

flatter vb schmeicheln [38] ▷ Are you trying to flatter me? Willst du mir schmeicheln? ▷ I feel flattered. Ich fühle mich geschmeichelt.

flavour (US **flavor**) n Geschmack m (pl Geschmäcke) ▷ This cheese has a very strong flavour. Dieser Käse hat einen sehr pikanten Geschmack.; **Which flavour of ice cream would you like?** Was für ein Eis möchtest du?

flea n Floh m (pl Flöhe)

flew vb see **fly**

flexible adj flexibel; **flexible working hours** gleitende Arbeitszeit

flick vb schnipsen [48] ▷ She flicked the ash off her jumper. Sie schnipste die Asche von ihrem Pullover.; **to flick through a book** ein Buch durchblättern [15]

flight n Flug m (pl Flüge) ▷ What time is the flight to Munich? Um wie viel Uhr geht der Flug nach München?; **a flight of stairs** eine Treppe

flight attendant n Flugbegleiter m (pl Flugbegleiter), Flugbegleiterin f

fling vb schmeißen (imperf schmiss, perf hat geschmissen) ▷ He flung the dictionary onto the floor. Er schmiss das Wörterbuch auf den Boden.

float vb schwimmen [63] (imperf schwamm, perf ist geschwommen) ▷ A leaf was floating on the water. Auf dem Wasser schwamm ein Blatt.

flood n ❶ Überschwemmung f ▷ The rain has caused many floods. Der Regen hat zu vielen Überschwemmungen geführt. ❷ Flut f ▷ He received a flood of letters. Er erhielt eine Flut von Briefen.
▶ vb überschwemmen [18] (perf hat überschwemmt) ▷ The river has flooded the village. Der Fluss hat das Dorf überschwemmt.

floor n ❶ Fußboden m (pl Fußböden); **a tiled floor** ein Fliesenboden m; **on the floor** auf dem Boden ❷ (storey) Stock m (pl Stock); **the first floor** der erste Stock; **the ground floor** das Erdgeschoss
▌ Be careful not to translate **floor** by Flur.

florist n Florist m (gen Floristen, pl Floristen), Floristin f

flour n Mehl nt (pl Mehle)

flow vb fließen [27] (imperf floss, perf ist geflossen) ▷ *Water was flowing from the pipe.* Aus dem Rohr floss Wasser.

flower n Blume f
▶ vb blühen [38]

flown vb see **fly**

flu n Grippe f ▷ *She's got flu.* Sie hat Grippe.

fluent adj *He speaks fluent German.* Er spricht fließend Deutsch.

flung vb see **fling**

flush n (of toilet) Spülung f
▶ vb to flush the toilet spülen [38]

flute n Querflöte f ▷ *I play the flute.* Ich spiele Querflöte.

fly n (insect) Fliege f
▶ vb fliegen [25] (imperf flog, perf ist geflogen) ▷ *He flew from Berlin to New York.* Er flog von Berlin nach New York.; **to fly away** wegfliegen [25]

focus n **to be out of focus** unscharf sein [65] ▷ *The house is out of focus in this photo.* Das Haus ist auf diesem Foto unscharf.
▶ vb scharf einstellen [4] (perf hat scharf eingestellt) ▷ *Try to focus the binoculars.* Versuch, das Fernglas scharf einzustellen.; **to focus on something** (1) (with camera) die Kamera auf etwas einstellen [4] ▷ *The cameraman focused on the bird.* Der Kameramann stellte die Kamera auf den Vogel ein. (2) (concentrate) sich auf etwas konzentrieren [76] ▷ *Let's focus on the plot.* Wir wollen uns auf die Handlung konzentrieren.

fog n Nebel m (pl Nebel)

foggy adj neblig ▷ *a foggy day* ein nebliger Tag

foil n (kitchen foil) Alufolie f ▷ *She wrapped the meat in foil.* Sie wickelte das Fleisch in Alufolie.

fold n Falte f
▶ vb falten [2] ▷ *He folded the newspaper in half.* Er faltete die Zeitung in der Mitte zusammen.; **to fold up** (1) (paper) zusammenfalten [2] (chair) zusammenklappen [4]; **to fold one's arms** die Arme verschränken [7] ▷ *She folded her arms.* Sie verschränkte die Arme.

folder n ❶ Mappe f ▷ *She kept all her letters in a folder.* Sie bewahrte all ihre Briefe in einer Mappe auf. ❷ (ring binder) Ordner m (pl Ordner)

follow vb ❶ folgen [38] (perf ist gefolgt) ▷ *She followed him.* Sie folgte ihm.; **You go first and I'll follow.** Geh du vor, ich komme nach. ❷ followen [38] (on social media)

following adj folgend ▷ *the following day* am folgenden Tag

fond adj **to be fond of somebody** jemanden gernhaben [32]

food n Nahrung f; **We need to buy some food.** Wir müssen etwas zum Essen kaufen.; **cat food** das Katzenfutter; **dog food** das Hundefutter

fool n Idiot m (gen Idioten, pl Idioten), Idiotin f

foot n ❶ (of person) Fuß m (gen Fußes, pl Füße) ▷ *My feet are aching.* Mir tun die Füße weh.; **on foot** zu Fuß ❷ (12 inches) Fuß m (pl Fuß)

- In Germany measurements are in
- metres and centimetres rather than
- feet and inches. A foot is about 30
- centimetres.

▷ *Dave is six foot tall.* Dave ist ein Meter achtzig groß. ▷ *That mountain is five thousand feet high.* Dieser Berg ist eintausendsechshundert Meter hoch.

football n Fußball m (pl Fußbälle) ▷ *I like playing football.* Ich spiele gern Fußball. ▷ *Paul threw the football over the fence.* Paul warf den Fußball über den Zaun.

footballer n Fußballer m (pl Fußballer), Fußballerin f

footpath n Fußweg m (pl Fußwege) ▷ the footpath through the forest der Fußweg durch den Wald

for prep

> There are several ways of translating 'for'. Scan the examples to find one that is similar to what you want to say.

❶ für ▷ a present for me ein Geschenk für mich ▷ He works for the government. Er arbeitet für die Regierung. ▷ I'll do it for you. Ich mache es für dich. ▷ Are you for or against the idea? Bist du für oder gegen die Idee? ▷ Oxford is famous for its university. Oxford ist für seine Universität berühmt. ▷ I sold it for five pounds. Ich habe es für fünf Pfund verkauft.; **What for?** Wofür?

> When referring to periods of time, use **lang** for the future and completed action in the past, and **seit** (with the German verb in the present tense) for something that started in the past and is still going on.

❷ lang ▷ He worked in Germany for two years. Er hat zwei Jahre lang in Deutschland gearbeitet. ▷ She will be away for a month. Sie wird einen Monat lang weg sein.; **There are road works for three kilometres.** Es gibt dort über drei Kilometer Bauarbeiten. ❸ seit ▷ He's been learning German for two years. Er lernt seit zwei Jahren Deutsch. ▷ She's been away for a month. Sie ist seit einem Monat weg.; **What's the German for 'lion'?** Wie sagt man 'lion' auf Deutsch?; **It's time for lunch.** Es ist Zeit zum Mittagessen.; **the train for London** der Zug nach London; **for sale** zu verkaufen

forbid vb verbieten [8] (imperf verbot, perf hat verboten); **to forbid somebody to do something** jemandem verbieten, etwas zu tun [81]

forbidden adj verboten ▷ Smoking is strictly forbidden. Rauchen ist streng verboten.

force n Gewalt f ▷ the forces of nature die Naturgewalten; **The force of the explosion blew out all the windows.** Die Explosion war so stark, dass alle Fenster kaputtgingen.; **in force** in Kraft

▶ vb zwingen [97] (imperf zwang, perf hat gezwungen) ▷ They forced him to open the safe. Sie zwangen ihn, den Safe aufzumachen.

forecast n **the weather forecast** die Wettervorhersage

forehead n Stirn f

foreign adj ausländisch

foreigner n Ausländer m (pl Ausländer), Ausländerin f

forest n Wald m (pl Wälder)

forever adv ❶ für immer ▷ He's gone forever. Er ist für immer weg. ❷ (always) dauernd ▷ She's forever complaining. Sie beklagt sich dauernd.

forgave vb see **forgive**

forge vb fälschen [38] ▷ She tried to forge his signature. Sie versuchte, seine Unterschrift zu fälschen.

forged adj gefälscht ▷ forged banknotes gefälschte Banknoten

forget vb vergessen [83] (pres vergisst, imperf vergaß, perf hat vergessen) ▷ I've forgotten his name. Ich habe seinen Namen vergessen. ▷ I'm sorry, I completely forgot! Tut mir leid, das habe ich total vergessen!

forgetful adj vergesslich

forgive vb **to forgive somebody** jemandem verzeihen; **to forgive somebody for doing something** jemandem verzeihen, etwas getan zu haben

fork n ❶ (for eating, gardening) Gabel f ▷ He ate his chips with a fork. Er aß seine Pommes frites mit einer Gabel. ❷ (in

road) Gabelung f; **There was a fork in the road.** Die Straße gabelte sich.

form n ① (paper) Formular nt (pl Formulare) ▷ *to fill in a form* ein Formular ausfüllen ② (type) Form f ▷ *I'm against hunting in any form.* Ich bin gegen die Jagd in jeglicher Form.; **in top form** in Topform

formal adj ① (occasion) formell ▷ *a formal dinner* ein formelles Abendessen ② (person) förmlich ③ (language) gehoben ▷ *a formal word* ein gehobener Ausdruck; **formal clothes** die Gesellschaftskleidung sg; **He's got no formal qualifications.** Er hat keinen offiziellen Abschluss.

former adj früher ▷ *a former pupil* ein früherer Schüler ▷ *the former Prime Minister* der frühere Premierminister

forthcoming adj kommend ▷ *the forthcoming meeting* die kommende Besprechung

fortnight n a fortnight vierzehn Tage

fortunate adj **to be fortunate** Glück haben [32]; **It's fortunate that I remembered the map.** Zum Glück habe ich an die Landkarte gedacht.

fortunately adv zum Glück ▷ *Fortunately, it didn't rain.* Zum Glück hat es nicht geregnet.

fortune n Vermögen nt (pl Vermögen) ▷ *Kate earns a fortune!* Kate verdient ein Vermögen!; **to tell somebody's fortune** jemandem wahrsagen [15]

forty num vierzig ▷ *He's forty.* Er ist vierzig.

forward adv **to move forward** sich vorwärtsbewegen [4]
▶ vb nachsenden (imperf sandte nach, perf hat nachgesandt) ▷ *He forwarded all her letters.* Er sandte alle ihre Briefe nach.

foster child n Pflegekind nt (pl Pflegekinder) ▷ *She's their foster child.* Sie ist ihr Pflegekind.

fought vb see **fight**

foul adj furchtbar ▷ *The weather was foul.* Das Wetter war furchtbar. ▷ *What a foul smell!* Was für ein furchtbarer Gestank!
▶ n Foul nt (pl Fouls) ▷ *Ferguson committed a foul.* Ferguson hat ein Foul begangen.

fountain n Brunnen m (pl Brunnen)

fountain pen n Füllfederhalter m (pl Füllfederhalter)

four num vier ▷ *She's four.* Sie ist vier.

fourteen num vierzehn ▷ *I'm fourteen.* Ich bin vierzehn.

fourteenth adj vierzehnte ▷ *the fourteenth of August* der vierzehnte August

fourth adj vierte ▷ *the fourth floor* der vierte Stock ▷ *the fourth of August* der vierte August

fox n Fuchs m (gen Fuchses, pl Füchse)

fragile adj zerbrechlich

frame n (for picture) Rahmen m (pl Rahmen)

France n Frankreich nt; **from France** aus Frankreich; **in France** in Frankreich; **to France** nach Frankreich

frantic adj **I was going frantic.** Ich bin fast durchgedreht.; **I was frantic with worry.** Ich habe mir furchtbare Sorgen gemacht.

fraud n ① (crime) Betrug m ▷ *He was jailed for fraud.* Er kam wegen Betrugs ins Gefängnis. ② (person) Betrüger m (pl Betrüger), Betrügerin f ▷ *He's not a real doctor, he's a fraud.* Er ist kein echter Arzt, er ist ein Betrüger.

freckles npl Sommersprossen fpl

free adj ① (free of charge) kostenlos ▷ *a free brochure* eine kostenlose Broschüre ② (not busy, not taken) frei ▷ *Is this seat free?* Ist dieser Platz frei?; **'admission free'** 'Eintritt frei'; **Are you free after school?** Hast du nach der Schule Zeit?
▶ vb befreien [7] (perf hat befreit)

freedom n Freiheit f

freeway n (US) Autobahn f
freeze vb ❶ gefrieren (imperf gefror, perf ist gefroren) ▷ The water had frozen. Das Wasser war gefroren. ❷ (food) einfrieren ▷ She froze the rest of the raspberries. Sie hat die restlichen Himbeeren eingefroren.
freezer n Gefrierschrank m (pl Gefrierschränke)
freezing adj It's freezing! (informal) Es ist eiskalt!; I'm freezing! (informal) Mir ist eiskalt!; three degrees below freezing drei Grad minus
French adj französisch ▷ He's French. Er ist Franzose. ▷ She's French. Sie ist Französin.
▶ n (language) Französisch nt (gen Französischen) ▷ Do you speak French? Sprechen Sie Französisch?; **the French** (people) die Franzosen mpl
French fries npl Pommes frites fpl
French kiss n Zungenkuss m (gen Zungenkusses, pl Zungenküsse)
Frenchman n Franzose m (gen Franzosen, pl Franzosen)
French windows npl Verandatür f
Frenchwoman n Französin f
frequent adj häufig ▷ frequent showers häufige Niederschläge; **There are frequent buses to the town centre.** Es gehen häufig Busse ins Stadtzentrum.
fresh adj frisch ▷ I need some fresh air. Ich brauche frische Luft.
Friday n Freitag m (pl Freitage) ▷ **on Friday** am Freitag ▷ **every Friday** jeden Freitag ▷ **last Friday** letzten Freitag ▷ **next Friday** nächsten Freitag; **on Fridays** freitags
fridge n Kühlschrank m (pl Kühlschränke)
fried adj gebraten ▷ fried onions gebratene Zwiebeln; **a fried egg** ein Spiegelei nt
friend n Freund m (pl Freunde), Freundin f
▶ vb sich befreunden [54] mit

friendly adj freundlich ▷ She's really friendly. Sie ist wirklich freundlich. ▷ Liverpool is a very friendly city. Liverpool ist eine sehr freundliche Stadt.
friendship n Freundschaft f
fright n Schrecken m (pl Schrecken) ▷ I got a terrible fright! Ich habe einen furchtbaren Schrecken bekommen!
frighten vb Angst machen [48] ▷ Horror films frighten him. Horrorfilme machen ihm Angst.
frightened adj **to be frightened** Angst haben [32]; **to be frightened of something** vor etwas Angst haben [32]
frightening adj beängstigend
fringe n (of hair) Pony m (pl Ponys) ▷ She's got a fringe. Sie hat einen Pony.
Frisbee® n Frisbee® nt (pl Frisbees) ▷ **to play Frisbee** Frisbee spielen
frog n Frosch m (pl Frösche)
from prep ❶ (from country, town) aus ▷ I'm from Yorkshire. Ich bin aus Yorkshire. ▷ I come from Perth. Ich bin aus Perth.; **Where do you come from?** Woher sind Sie? ❷ (from person) von ▷ a letter from my sister ein Brief von meiner Schwester; **The hotel is one kilometre from the beach.** Das Hotel ist einen Kilometer vom Strand entfernt. ❸ (number) ab ▷ from ten pounds ab zehn Pfund ▷ from the age of fourteen ab vierzehn; **from ... to ...** (1) (distance) von ... nach ... ▷ He flew from London to Paris. Er flog von London nach Paris. (2) (time) von ... bis ... ▷ from one o'clock to two von eins bis zwei; **The price was reduced from ten pounds to five.** Der Preis war von zehn auf fünf Pfund heruntergesetzt.; **from ... onwards** ab ... ▷ We'll be at home from seven o'clock onwards. Wir werden ab sieben Uhr zu Hause sein.
front n Vorderseite f ▷ the front of the house die Vorderseite des Hauses; **in front** davor; **in front of** vor

ENGLISH > GERMAN

Use the accusative to express movement or a change of place. Use the dative when there is no change of place.

▷ He stood in front of the house. Er stand vor dem Haus.; ▷ He ran in front of a bus. Er lief vor einen Bus.; **in the front** (of car) vorn; **at the front of the train** vorn im Zug

▸ adj vordere ▷ the front row die vordere Reihe ▷ the front seats of the car die vorderen Sitze des Autos; **the front door** die Haustür

frontier n Grenze f

frost n Frost m (pl Fröste)

frosty adj frostig ▷ It's frosty today. Heute ist es frostig.

frown vb die Stirn runzeln [34] ▷ He frowned. Er runzelte die Stirn.

frozen adj (food) tiefgefroren ▷ frozen chips tiefgefrorene Pommes frites

fruit n ❶ Frucht f (pl Früchte) ▷ an exotic fruit eine exotische Frucht ❷ Obst nt ▷ Fruit is very healthy. Obst ist sehr gesund.; **fruit juice** der Fruchtsaft; **a fruit salad** ein Obstsalat m

fruit machine n Spielautomat m (gen Spielautomaten, pl Spielautomaten)

frustrated adj frustriert

fry vb braten (pres brät, imperf briet, perf hat gebraten) ▷ Fry the onions for five minutes. Braten Sie die Zwiebeln fünf Minuten lang.

frying pan n Bratpfanne f

fuel n (for car, aeroplane) Benzin nt (pl Benzine) ▷ to run out of fuel kein Benzin mehr haben

full adj, adv ❶ voll ▷ The tank's full. Der Tank ist voll. ❷ ausführlich ▷ He asked for full information on the job. Er bat um ausführliche Informationen über die Stelle.; **your full name** Name und Vornamen; **My full name is Ian John Marr.** Ich heiße Ian John Marr.; **I'm full.** (after meal) Ich bin satt.; **at full speed** mit Höchstgeschwindigkeit; **There was a full moon.** Es war Vollmond.

full stop n Punkt m (pl Punkte)

full-time adj, adv ganztags ▷ She works full-time. Sie arbeitet ganztags.; **She's got a full-time job.** Sie hat einen Ganztagsjob.

fully adv ganz ▷ He hasn't yet fully recovered. Er hat sich noch nicht ganz erholt.

fumes npl Abgase ntpl ▷ dangerous fumes gefährliche Abgase; **exhaust fumes** Autoabgase

fun adj lustig ▷ She's a fun person. Sie ist ein lustiger Mensch.

▸ n to have fun Spaß haben [**32**]; **for fun** zum Spaß; **to make fun of somebody** sich über jemanden lustig machen [**48**]; That's made Spaß!; **Have fun!** Viel Spaß!; **It's fun!** Das macht Spaß!

funds npl **to raise funds** Spenden sammeln [**34**]

funeral n Beerdigung f

funfair n Volksfest nt (pl Volksfeste)

funny adj ❶ (amusing) lustig ▷ It was really funny. Es war wirklich lustig. ❷ (strange) komisch ▷ There's something funny about him. Er hat etwas Komisches an sich.

fur n ❶ Pelz m (gen Pelzes, pl Pelze) ▷ a fur coat ein Pelzmantel m ❷ Fell nt (pl Felle) ▷ the dog's fur das Fell des Hundes

furious adj wütend ▷ Dad was furious with me. Papa war wütend auf mich.

furniture n Möbel ntpl ▷ a piece of furniture ein Möbelstück nt

further adv, adj weiter entfernt ▷ London is further from Manchester than Leeds is. London ist weiter von Manchester entfernt als Leeds.; **How much further is it?** Wie weit ist es noch?

further education n Weiterbildung f

fuse n Sicherung f ▷ The fuse has blown. Die Sicherung ist durchgebrannt.

fuss n Aufregung f ▷ What's all the fuss about? Was soll die ganze Aufregung?; **to make a fuss** Theater machen [**48**]

fussy adj pingelig ▷ *She is very fussy about her food.* Sie ist mit dem Essen sehr pingelig.
future n ❶ Zukunft f; **in future** in Zukunft; **What are your plans for the future?** Was für Zukunftspläne haben Sie? ❷ *(in grammar)* Futur nt ▷ *Put this sentence into the future.* Setzt diesen Satz ins Futur.

gain vb **to gain weight** zunehmen [**52**]; **to gain speed** schneller werden [**91**]
gallery n Galerie f ▷ *an art gallery* eine Kunstgalerie
gamble vb spielen [**38**]
gambling n Glücksspiel nt (pl Glücksspiele); **He likes gambling.** Er spielt gern.
game n Spiel nt (pl Spiele) ▷ *The children were playing a game.* Die Kinder spielten ein Spiel. ▷ *a game of football* ein Fußballspiel
▶ vb gamen [**48**] *(on computer)*
gamer n *(on computer)* Gamer m (pl Gamer), Gamerin f
gaming n *(on computer)* Gaming nt
gang n Gang f (pl Gangs)
gangster n Gangster m (pl Gangster)
gap n ❶ Lücke f ▷ *There's a gap in the hedge.* In der Hecke ist eine Lücke. ❷ Pause f ▷ *a gap of four years* eine Pause von vier Jahren
garage n ❶ *(for parking cars)* Garage f ❷ *(for repairs)* Werkstatt f (pl Werkstätten)

ENGLISH > GERMAN

garbage n Müll m ▷ *the garbage can* die Mülltonne; **That's garbage!** Das ist Blödsinn!
garden n Garten m (pl Gärten)
garden centre n Gartencenter nt (pl Gartencenter)
gardener n Gärtner m (pl Gärtner), Gärtnerin f ▷ *He's a gardener.* Er ist Gärtner.
gardening n Gartenarbeit f ▷ *Margaret loves gardening.* Margaret liebt Gartenarbeit.
garlic n Knoblauch m
garment n Kleidungsstück nt (pl Kleidungsstücke)
gas n ① Gas nt (pl Gase); **a gas cooker** ein Gasherd m; **a gas cylinder** eine Gasflasche; **a gas fire** ein Gasofen m; **a gas leak** eine undichte Stelle in der Gasleitung ② (US) Benzin nt; **a gas station** eine Tankstelle
gasoline n (US) Benzin nt
gate n ① (*of garden*) Tor nt (pl Tore) ② (*of field*) Gatter nt (pl Gatter) ③ (*at airport*) Flugsteig m (pl Flugsteige)
gather vb (*assemble*) sich versammeln [34] (*perf* haben sich versammelt) ▷ *People gathered in front of the church.* Menschen versammelten sich vor der Kirche.; **to gather speed** schneller werden [91]
gave vb *see* **give**
gay adj schwul
GCSE n (= *General Certificate of Secondary Education*) mittlere Reife f
gear n ① (*in car*) Gang m (pl Gänge) ▷ *in first gear* im ersten Gang; **to change gear** schalten [2] ② Ausrüstung f ▷ *camping gear* die Campingausrüstung; **your sports gear** (*clothes*) dein Sportzeug nt
gear lever n Schalthebel m (pl Schalthebel)
gearshift n (US) Schaltknüppel m (pl Schaltknüppel)

geese npl *see* **goose**
gel n Gel nt (pl Gele)
  Note that in German the 'g' in **Gel** is pronounced like the 'g' in *girl*.
▷ *hair gel* das Haargel
Gemini nsg Zwillinge mpl ▷ *I'm Gemini.* Ich bin Zwilling.
gender n Geschlecht nt (pl Geschlechter)
general n General m (pl Generäle) ▶ adj allgemein; **in general** im Allgemeinen
general knowledge n Allgemeinbildung f
generally adv normalerweise ▷ *I generally go shopping on Saturday.* Ich gehe normalerweise samstags einkaufen.
generation n Generation f ▷ *the younger generation* die jüngere Generation
generous adj großzügig ▷ *That's very generous of you.* Das ist sehr großzügig von Ihnen.
genetically adv genetisch; **genetically modified** genmanipuliert
Geneva n Genf nt; **to Geneva** nach Genf; **Lake Geneva** der Genfer See
genius n Genie nt (pl Genies) ▷ *She's a genius!* Sie ist ein Genie!
gentle adj sanft
gentleman n Gentleman m (pl Gentlemen); **Good morning, gentlemen.** Guten Morgen, meine Herren.
gently adv sanft
gents nsg Herrentoilette f; **'gents'** (*on sign*) 'Herren'
genuine adj ① (*real*) echt ▷ *These are genuine diamonds.* Das sind echte Diamanten. ② (*sincere*) geradlinig ▷ *She's a very genuine person.* Sie ist ein sehr geradliniger Mensch.
geography n Geografie f
gerbil n Wüstenrennmaus f (pl Wüstenrennmäuse)

germ n Bazille f

German adj **deutsch** ▷ He is German. Er ist Deutscher. ▷ She is German. Sie ist Deutsche.; **German shepherd** der Schäferhund
▶ n ① (person) Deutsche m (gen Deutschen, pl Deutschen), Deutsche f (gen Deutschen) ▷ a German (man) ein Deutscher; **the Germans** die Deutschen ② (language) Deutsch nt (gen Deutschen) ▷ Do you speak German? Sprechen sie Deutsch?

Germany n Deutschland nt; **from Germany** aus Deutschland; **in Germany** in Deutschland; **to Germany** nach Deutschland

get vb ① (receive) bekommen [40] (imperf bekam, perf hat bekommen) ▷ I got lots of presents. Ich habe viele Geschenke bekommen. ▷ He got first prize. Er hat den ersten Preis bekommen. ▷ Jackie got good exam results. Jackie hat gute Noten bekommen.; **have got** haben ▷ How many have you got? Wie viele hast du? ② (fetch) holen [38] ▷ Get help! Hol Hilfe! ③ (catch) fassen [31] ▷ They've got the thief. Sie haben den Dieb gefasst. ④ (train, bus) nehmen [52] (pres nimmt, imperf nahm, perf hat genommen) ▷ I'm getting the bus into town. Ich nehme den Bus in die Stadt. ⑤ (understand) verstehen [72] (imperf verstand, perf hat verstanden) ▷ I don't get the joke. Ich verstehe den Witz nicht. ⑥ (go) kommen [40] (imperf kam, perf ist gekommen) ▷ How do you get to the castle? Wie kommt man zur Burg? ⑦ (become) werden [91] (pres wird, imperf wurde, perf ist geworden) ▷ to get old alt werden; **to get something done** etwas machen lassen [42]; **to get something for somebody** jemandem etwas holen [38]; **to have got to do something** etwas tun müssen [51]; **to get away** entkommen [40]; **You'll never get away with it.** Das wird man dir niemals durchgehen lassen.; **to get back (1)** zurückkommen [40] ▷ What time did you get back? Wann seid ihr zurückgekommen? **(2)** zurückbekommen [40] ▷ He got his money back. Er hat sein Geld zurückbekommen.; **to get down** herunterkommen [40]; **to get in** nach Hause kommen [40]; **to get into** einsteigen [74] in; **to get off (1)** (vehicle) aussteigen [74] aus ▷ Isobel got off the train. Isobel stieg aus dem Zug aus. **(2)** (bike) absteigen [74] von ▷ He got off his bike. Er stieg vom Fahrrad ab.; **to get on (1)** (vehicle) einsteigen [74] in ▷ Phyllis got on the bus. Phyllis stieg in den Bus ein. **(2)** (bike) steigen [74] auf ▷ Carol got on her bike. Carol stieg auf ihr Fahrrad.; **to get on with somebody** sich mit jemandem verstehen [72]; **to get out** aussteigen [74] aus; **Get out!** Raus!; **to get something out** etwas hervorholen [4]; **to get over something (1)** sich von etwas erholen [19] ▷ It took her a long time to get over the illness. Sie brauchte lange Zeit, um sich von der Krankheit zu erholen. **(2)** etwas überwinden [86] ▷ He managed to get over the problem. Er konnte das Problem überwinden.; **to get round to something** zu etwas kommen [40]; **to get together** sich treffen [78]; **to get up** aufstehen [72]

ghost n Gespenst nt (pl Gespenster)

giant adj riesig ▷ They ate a giant meal. Sie haben ein riesiges Essen vertilgt.
▶ n Riese m (gen Riesen, pl Riesen), Riesin f

gift n ① (present) Geschenk nt (pl Geschenke) ② (talent) Begabung f; **to have a gift for something** für etwas begabt sein [65]

> Be careful not to translate **gift** by the German word **Gift**.

ENGLISH > GERMAN

giggle vb kichern [88]
gin n Gin m (pl Gins or Gin)
> When ordering more than one gin use the plural form **Gin**.
> ▷ *Three gins, please.* Drei Gin bitte.; **a gin and tonic** ein Gin Tonic
ginger n Ingwer m ▷ *Add a teaspoon of ginger.* Fügen Sie einen Teelöffel Ingwer zu.
▶ *adj* rot ▷ *David has ginger hair.* David hat rote Haare.
giraffe n Giraffe f
girl n Mädchen nt (pl Mädchen) ▷ *They've got a girl and two boys.* Sie haben ein Mädchen und zwei Jungen. ▷ *a five-year-old girl* ein fünfjähriges Mädchen; **an English girl** eine junge Engländerin
girlfriend n Freundin f ▷ *Damon's girlfriend is called Justine.* Damons Freundin heißt Justine. ▷ *She often went out with her girlfriends.* Sie ging oft mit ihren Freundinnen aus.
give vb geben [28] (pres gibt, imperf gab, perf hat gegeben); **to give something to somebody** jemandem etwas geben [28]; **to give something back to somebody** jemandem etwas zurückgeben [28]; **to give in** nachgeben [28]; **to give out** austeilen [4]; **to give up** aufgeben [28]; **to give up doing something** etwas aufgeben [28]; **to give oneself up** sich ergeben [28]; **to give way** (in traffic) die Vorfahrt achten [2]
glad adj froh ▷ *She's glad she's done it.* Sie ist froh, dass sie es getan hat.
glamorous adj (person) glamourös
glass n Glas nt (gen Glases, pl Gläser) ▷ *a glass of milk* ein Glas Milch
glasses npl Brille f ▷ *Veronika wears glasses.* Veronika trägt eine Brille.
gleam vb funkeln [88] ▷ *Her eyes gleamed with excitement.* Ihre Augen funkelten vor Aufregung.

glider n Segelflugzeug nt (pl Segelflugzeuge)
glimpse n to catch a glimpse of somebody jemanden kurz zu sehen bekommen [40]
glitter vb glitzern [88]
global adj weltweit; **on a global scale** weltweit
global warming n Erwärmung der Erdatmosphäre f
globe n Globus m (gen Globus, pl Globen)
gloomy adj ❶ düster ▷ *a small gloomy flat* eine kleine, düstere Wohnung ❷ niedergeschlagen ▷ *She's been feeling very gloomy recently.* Sie fühlt sich in letzter Zeit sehr niedergeschlagen.
glorious adj herrlich
glove n Handschuh m (pl Handschuhe)
glow vb leuchten [2] ▷ *Her watch glows in the dark.* Ihre Uhr leuchtet im Dunkeln.
glue n Klebstoff m (pl Klebstoffe)
▶ vb kleben [38] ▷ *to glue something together* etwas zusammenkleben
gluten n Gluten nt
gluten-free adj glutenfrei
GM abbr (= genetically modified) genmanipuliert ▷ *GM food* genmanipulierte Lebensmittel pl
go n to have a go at doing something etwas versuchen [84] ▷ *He had a go at making a cake.* Er hat versucht, einen Kuchen zu backen.; **Whose go is it?** Wer ist dran?
▶ vb ❶ gehen [29] (imperf ging, perf ist gegangen) ▷ *I'm going to the cinema tonight.* Ich gehe heute Abend ins Kino. ▷ *I'm going now.* Ich gehe jetzt. ❷ (leave) weggehen [29] ▷ *Where's Thomas? — He's gone.* Wo ist Thomas? — Er ist weggegangen. ❸ (vehicle) fahren [21] (pres fährt, imperf fuhr, perf ist gefahren) ▷ *My car won't go.* Mein Auto fährt nicht.; **to go home** nach Hause gehen [29] ▷ *I go home at about*

go after vb (follow) nachgehen [29] (imperf ging nach, perf ist nachgegangen) ▷ I went after him. Ich ging ihm nach.; **Quick, go after them!** Schnell, ihnen nach!

go ahead vb vorangehen [29] (imperf ging voran, perf ist vorangegangen); **to go ahead with something** etwas durchführen [4]

go around vb herumgehen [29] (imperf ging herum, perf ist herumgegangen) ▷ There's a rumour going around that they're getting married. Es geht das Gerücht herum, sie würden heiraten.

go away vb weggehen [29] (imperf ging weg, perf ist weggegangen) ▷ Go away! Geh weg!

go back vb zurückgehen [29] (imperf ging zurück, perf ist zurückgegangen) ▷ We went back to the same place. Wir sind an denselben Ort zurückgegangen.; **Is he still here? — No, he's gone back home.** Ist er noch hier? — Nein, er ist nach Hause gegangen.

go by vb vorbeigehen [29] (imperf ging vorbei, perf ist vorbeigegangen) ▷ Two police officers went by. Zwei Polizisten gingen vorbei.

go down vb ❶ (person) hinuntergehen [29] (imperf ging hinunter, perf ist hinuntergegangen) ▷ to go down the stairs die Treppe hinuntergehen ❷ (decrease) sinken [67] (imperf sank, perf ist gesunken) ▷ The price of computers has gone down. Die Preise für Computer sind gesunken. ❸ (deflate) Luft verlieren [85] (imperf verlor Luft, perf hat Luft verloren) ▷ My airbed kept going down. Meine Luftmatratze verlor dauernd Luft.; **My brother's gone down with flu.** Mein Bruder hat die Grippe bekommen.

go for vb (attack) angreifen [imperf griff an, perf hat angegriffen) ▷ The dog went for me. Der Hund griff mich an.; **Go for it!** (go on!) Na los!

go in vb hineingehen [29] (imperf ging hinein, perf ist hineingegangen) ▷ He knocked and went in. Er klopfte und ging hinein.

go off vb ❶ losgehen [29] (imperf ging los, perf ist losgegangen) ▷ The bomb went off. Die Bombe ging los. ▷ The fire alarm went off. Der Feueralarm ging los. ❷ klingeln [34] ▷ My alarm clock goes off at seven every morning. Mein Wecker klingelt jeden Morgen um sieben Uhr. ❸ schlecht werden [91] (pres wird schlecht, imperf wurde schlecht, perf ist schlecht geworden); **The milk's gone off.** Die Milch ist sauer geworden. ❹ (go away) weggehen [29] ▷ He went off in a huff. Er ist beleidigt weggegangen.

go on vb ❶ (happen) los sein [65] (pres ist los, imperf war los, perf ist los gewesen) ▷ What's going on? Was ist los? ❷ (carry on) dauern [88] ▷ The concert went on until eleven o'clock at night. Das Konzert hat bis nach elf Uhr nachts gedauert.; **to go on doing something** etwas weiter tun [81] ▷ He went on reading. Er las weiter.; **to go on at somebody** auf jemandem herumkritisieren [76] ▷ My parents always go on at me. Meine Eltern kritisieren dauernd an mir herum.; **Go on!** Na los! ▷ Go on, tell us! Na los, sag schon!

go out vb ausgehen [29] (imperf ging aus, perf ist ausgegangen) ▷ Are you going out tonight? Gehst du heute Abend aus? ▷ Suddenly the lights went out.

ENGLISH > GERMAN

Plötzlich ging das Licht aus.; **to go out with somebody** mit jemandem ausgehen [29] ▷ *Are you going out with him?* Gehst du mit ihm aus?

go past vb **to go past something** an etwas vorbeigehen [29] ▷ *He went past the shop.* Er ging an dem Geschäft vorbei.

go round vb **to go round a corner** um die Ecke biegen; **to go round to somebody's house** jemanden besuchen [7]; **to go round a museum** sich ein Museum ansehen [64]; **to go round the shops** einen Einkaufsbummel machen [48]

go through vb (by car) fahren [21] durch (pres fährt, imperf fuhr, perf ist gefahren); **We went through London to get to Birmingham.** Wir sind über London nach Birmingham gefahren.

go up vb ① (person) hinaufgehen [29] (imperf ging hinauf, perf ist hinaufgegangen) ▷ *to go up the stairs* die Treppe hinaufgehen ② (increase) steigen [74] (imperf stieg, perf ist gestiegen) ▷ *The price has gone up.* Der Preis ist gestiegen.; **to go up in flames** in Flammen aufgehen [29] ▷ *The factory went up in flames.* Die Fabrik ist in Flammen aufgegangen.

go with vb passen [31] zu ▷ *Does this blouse go with that skirt?* Passt diese Bluse zu dem Rock?

goal n ① (sport) Tor nt (pl Tore) ▷ *to score a goal* ein Tor schießen ② (aim) Ziel nt (pl Ziele) ▷ *His goal is to become the world champion.* Sein Ziel ist es, Weltmeister zu werden.

goalkeeper n Torwart m (pl Torwarte)

goat n Ziege f; **goat's cheese** der Ziegenkäse

god n Gott m (pl Götter) ▷ *I believe in God.* Ich glaube an Gott.

goddaughter n Patentochter f (pl Patentöchter)

godfather n Patenonkel m (pl Patenonkel) ▷ *my godfather* mein Patenonkel

godmother n Patentante f ▷ *my godmother* meine Patentante

godson n Patensohn m (pl Patensöhne)

goes vb see **go**

goggles npl Schutzbrille f

gold n Gold nt ▷ *They found some gold.* Sie haben Gold gefunden.; **a gold necklace** eine goldene Halskette

goldfish n Goldfisch m (pl Goldfische) ▷ *I've got five goldfish.* Ich habe fünf Goldfische.

golf n Golf nt ▷ *My dad plays golf.* Mein Papa spielt Golf.; **a golf club** (1) (stick) ein Golfschläger m (2) (place) ein Golfklub m

golf course n Golfplatz m (gen Golfplatzes, pl Golfplätze)

gone vb see **go**

good adj ① gut ▷ *It's a very good film.* Das ist ein sehr guter Film.; **Vegetables are good for you.** Gemüse ist gesund.; **to be good at something** gut in etwas sein [65] ② (kind) freundlich ▷ *They were very good to me.* Sie waren sehr freundlich zu mir. ▷ *That's very good of you.* Das ist sehr freundlich von Ihnen. ③ (not naughty) artig ▷ *Be good!* Sei artig!; **for good** für immer; **Good morning!** Guten Morgen!; **Good afternoon!** Guten Tag!; **Good evening!** Guten Abend!; **Good night!** Gute Nacht!; **It's no good complaining.** Es hat keinen Wert, sich zu beklagen.

goodbye excl auf Wiedersehen

Good Friday n Karfreitag m (pl Karfreitage)

good-looking adj gut aussehend; **Andrew's very good-looking.** Andrew sieht sehr gut aus.

goods npl (in shop) Ware f; **a goods train** ein Güterzug m

google vb googeln [88]

goose n Gans f (pl Gänse)
gorgeous adj ❶ hinreißend ▷ *She's gorgeous!* Sie sieht hinreißend aus! ❷ herrlich ▷ *The weather was gorgeous.* Das Wetter war herrlich.
gorilla n Gorilla m (pl Gorillas)
gossip n ❶ (*rumours*) Tratsch m ▷ *Tell me the gossip!* Erzähl mir den neuesten Tratsch! ❷ (*woman*) Klatschtante f ▷ *She's such a gossip!* Sie ist eine furchtbare Klatschtante! ❸ (*man*) Klatschweib nt (pl Klatschweiber) ▷ *What a gossip!* So ein Klatschweib!
▶ vb ❶ (*chat*) schwatzen [**48**] ▷ *They were always gossiping.* Sie haben dauernd geschwatzt. ❷ (*about somebody*) tratschen [**48**] ▷ *They gossiped about her.* Sie haben über sie getratscht.
got vb see **get**
gotten vb see **get**
government n Regierung f
GP n **My sister is a GP in Glasgow.** Meine Schwester ist praktische Ärztin in Glasgow.
GPS n (= *global positioning system*) GPS n (pl GPS)
grab vb packen [**38**] ▷ *She grabbed her umbrella and ran out of the door.* Sie packte ihren Schirm und lief zur Tür hinaus.
graceful adj anmutig
grade n ❶ (*mark*) Note f ▷ *He got good grades.* Er hat gute Noten bekommen. ❷ (*class*) Klasse f ▷ *What grade are you in?* In welcher Klasse bist du?
grade school n (*US*) Grundschule f
gradual adj allmählich
gradually adv allmählich ▷ *We gradually got used to it.* Wir haben uns allmählich daran gewöhnt.
graffiti npl Graffiti pl
grain n Korn nt (pl Körner)
gram n Gramm nt (pl Gramme or Gramm)

> When specifying a quantity of something use the plural form **Gramm**.

▷ *five hundred grams of cheese* fünfhundert Gramm Käse
grammar n Grammatik f
grammar school n Gymnasium nt (pl Gymnasien)

* Gymnasium education begins after
* year 4 of the **Grundschule** and lasts
* until year 13. (However, pupils can
* leave after year 10.) It mainly
* prepares children for university
* education.

grammatical adj grammatisch
gramme n Gramm nt (pl Gramme or Gramm)

> When specifying a quantity of something use the plural form **Gramm**.

▷ *five hundred grammes of cheese* fünfhundert Gramm Käse
grand adj prachtvoll ▷ *She lives in a very grand house.* Sie wohnt in einem prachtvollen Haus.
grandchild n Enkel m (pl Enkel)
granddad n Opa m (pl Opas) ▷ *my granddad* mein Opa
granddaughter n Enkelin f
grandfather n Großvater m (pl Großväter) ▷ *my grandfather* mein Großvater
grandma n Oma f (pl Omas) ▷ *my grandma* meine Oma
grandmother n Großmutter f (pl Großmütter) ▷ *my grandmother* meine Großmutter
grandpa n Opa m (pl Opas) ▷ *my grandpa* mein Opa
grandparents npl Großeltern pl ▷ *my grandparents* meine Großeltern
grandson n Enkel m (pl Enkel)
granny n Oma f (pl Omas) ▷ *my granny* meine Oma
grape n Traube f
grapefruit n Grapefruit f (pl Grapefruits)
graph n grafische Darstellung f

graphics npl Grafik fsg

grass n Gras nt (gen Grases) ▷ *The grass is long.* Das Gras ist hoch.; **to cut the grass** den Rasen mähen [48]

grasshopper n Heuschrecke f

grate vb reiben (imperf rieb, perf hat gerieben) ▷ *to grate some cheese* Käse reiben

grateful adj dankbar

grave n Grab nt (pl Gräber)

gravel n Kies m

graveyard n Friedhof m (pl Friedhöfe)

gravy n Bratensoße f

grease n Fett nt (pl Fette)

greasy adj fettig ▷ *He has greasy hair.* Er hat fettige Haare.; **The food was very greasy.** Das Essen war sehr fettig.

great adj ❶ toll ▷ *That's great!* Das ist toll! ❷ (big) groß ▷ *a great mansion* eine große Villa

Great Britain n Großbritannien nt; **from Great Britain** aus Großbritannien; **in Great Britain** in Großbritannien; **to Great Britain** nach Großbritannien

great-grandfather n Urgroßvater m (pl Urgroßväter)

great-grandmother n Urgroßmutter f (pl Urgroßmütter)

Greece n Griechenland nt; **from Greece** aus Griechenland; **to Greece** nach Griechenland

greedy adj gierig ▷ *Don't be so greedy!* Sei nicht so gierig!

Greek adj griechisch ▷ *I love Greek food.* Ich mag griechisches Essen sehr gern. ▷ *Dionysis is Greek.* Dionysis ist Grieche. ▷ *She's Greek.* Sie ist Griechin.
▶ n ❶ (person) Grieche m (gen Griechen, pl Griechen), Griechin f ❷ (language) Griechisch nt (gen Griechischen)

green adj grün ▷ *a green car* ein grünes Auto ▷ *a green salad* ein grüner Salat; **the Green Party** die Grünen mpl
▶ n Grün nt ▷ *a dark green* ein dunkles Grün; **greens** (vegetables) das Grüngemüse sg; **the Greens** (party) die Grünen mpl

greenhouse n Treibhaus nt (gen Treibhauses, pl Treibhäuser); **the greenhouse effect** der Treibhauseffekt

Greenland n Grönland nt

greetings card n Grußkarte f

grew vb see **grow**

grey adj grau ▷ *She's got grey hair.* Sie hat graue Haare. ▷ *He's going grey.* Er wird grau.

grey-haired adj grauhaarig

grid n ❶ (on map) Gitter nt (pl Gitter) ❷ (of electricity) Netz nt (gen Netzes, pl Netze)

grief n Kummer m

grill n (of cooker) Grill m (pl Grills); **a mixed grill** ein Grillteller m
▶ vb grillen [48]

grin vb grinsen [38] ▷ *Dave grinned at me.* Dave grinste mich an.
▶ n Grinsen nt

grip vb packen [38] ▷ *He gripped my arm tightly.* Er packte mich fest am Arm.

grit n Splitt m (pl Splitte)

groan vb stöhnen [38] ▷ *He groaned with pain.* Er stöhnte vor Schmerzen.
▶ n (of pain) Stöhnen nt

grocer n Lebensmittelhändler m (pl Lebensmittelhändler), Lebensmittelhändlerin f ▷ *He's a grocer.* Er ist Lebensmittelhändler.

groceries npl Einkäufe mpl

grocery store n (US) Lebensmittelgeschäft nt (pl Lebensmittelgeschäfte)

groom n (bridegroom) Bräutigam m (pl Bräutigame) ▷ *the groom and his best man* der Bräutigam und sein Trauzeuge

gross adj (revolting) abscheulich ▷ *It was really gross!* Es war wirklich abscheulich!

ground n ❶ (earth) Boden m (pl Böden) ▷ *The ground's wet.* Der Boden ist nass. ❷ (for sport) Platz m (gen Platzes, pl Plätze)

group n Gruppe f

grow vb ❶ (plant, person, animal) wachsen [87] (pres wächst, imperf wuchs, perf ist gewachsen) ▷ Grass grows quickly. Gras wächst schnell. ▷ Haven't you grown! Bist du aber gewachsen!; **to grow a beard** sich einen Bart wachsen lassen [42]; **He's grown out of his jacket.** Er ist aus der Jacke herausgewachsen.
❷ (increase) zunehmen [52] (pres nimmt zu, imperf nahm zu, perf hat zugenommen) ▷ The number of unemployed has grown. Die Zahl der Arbeitslosen hat zugenommen.
❸ (cultivate) anbauen [4] (perf hat angebaut) ▷ My Dad grows potatoes. Mein Papa baut Kartoffeln an.; **to grow up** erwachsen werden [91]

growl vb knurren [38]

grown vb see grow

growth n Wachstum nt ▷ economic growth das Wirtschaftswachstum

grudge n **to bear a grudge against somebody** einen Groll gegen jemanden haben [32]

gruesome adj furchtbar

guarantee n Garantie f ▷ a five-year guarantee eine Garantie von fünf Jahren
▶ vb garantieren [76] (perf hat garantiert) ▷ I can't guarantee he'll come. Ich kann nicht garantieren, dass er kommt.

guard vb bewachen [7] (perf hat bewacht) ▷ They guarded the palace. Sie bewachten den Palast.; **to guard against something** gegen etwas Vorsichtsmaßnahmen ergreifen
▶ n (of train) Zugbegleiter m (pl Zugbegleiter), Zugbegleiterin f;
a security guard ein Wachmann m;
a guard dog ein Wachhund m

guess vb raten (pres rät, imperf riet, perf hat geraten) ▷ Can you guess what it is? Rate mal, was das ist. ▷ **to guess wrong** falsch raten
▶ n Vermutung f ▷ It's just a guess. Es ist nur eine Vermutung.; **Have a guess!** Rate mal!

guest n Gast m (pl Gäste)
■ Gast is also used for women.
▷ She is our guest. Sie ist unser Gast. ▷ We have guests staying with us. Wir haben Gäste.

guesthouse n Pension f ▷ We stayed in a guesthouse. Wir haben in einer Pension gewohnt.

guide n ❶ (book) Führer m (pl Führer) ▷ We bought a guide to Cologne. Wir haben einen Führer von Köln gekauft.
❷ (person) Führer m (pl Führer), Führerin f ▷ The guide showed us round the castle. Unser Führer hat uns die Burg gezeigt. ❸ (Girl Guide) Pfadfinderin f;
the Guides die Pfadfinderinnen

guidebook n Führer m (pl Führer)

guide dog n Blindenhund m (pl Blindenhunde)

guilty adj schuldig ▷ to feel guilty sich schuldig fühlen ▷ She was found guilty. Sie wurde schuldig gesprochen.

guinea pig n Meerschweinchen nt (pl Meerschweinchen)

guitar n Gitarre f ▷ I play the guitar. Ich spiele Gitarre.

gum n (chewing gum) Kaugummi m (pl Kaugummis); **gums** (in mouth) das Zahnfleisch sg

gun n ❶ (small) Pistole f ❷ (rifle) Gewehr nt (pl Gewehre)

gunpoint n **at gunpoint** mit Waffengewalt

guts npl (informal: courage) Mumm m ▷ He's certainly got guts. Er hat wirklich

Mumm.; **I hate his guts.** Ich kann ihn nicht ausstehen.
guy n Typ m (pl Typen) ▷ Who's that guy? Wer ist der Typ?; **He's a nice guy.** Er ist ein netter Kerl.
gym n Turnhalle f; **gym classes** die Turnstunden
gymnast n Turner m (pl Turner), Turnerin f ▷ She's a gymnast. Sie ist Turnerin.
gymnastics n Turnen nt; **to do gymnastics** turnen [**38**]
Gypsy n Sinto m (pl Sinti), Sinteza f

habit n Angewohnheit f ▷ a bad habit eine schlechte Angewohnheit
had vb see **have**
hadn't = had not
hail n Hagel m
▶ vb hageln [**88**] ▷ It's hailing. Es hagelt.
hair n Haare ntpl ▷ She's got long hair. Sie hat lange Haare. ▷ He's got black hair. Er hat schwarze Haare. ▷ He's losing his hair. Ihm gehen die Haare aus.; **to brush one's hair** sich die Haare bürsten [**2**]; **to wash one's hair** sich die Haare waschen [**89**]; **to have one's hair cut** sich die Haare schneiden lassen [**42**]; **a hair** ein Haar nt
hairbrush n Haarbürste f
hair clip n Haarspange f
haircut n Haarschnitt m (pl Haarschnitte); **to have a haircut** sich die Haare schneiden lassen [**42**]
hairdresser n Friseur m (pl Friseure), Friseuse f ▷ He's a hairdresser. Er ist Friseur.
hairdresser's n Friseur m (pl Friseure) ▷ at the hairdresser's beim Friseur

hair dryer n Haartrockner m (pl Haartrockner)

hair gel n Haargel nt (pl Haargele)

> In German the 'g' in **Haargel** is pronounced like the 'g' in girl.

hairgrip n Haarklemme f

hair spray n Haarspray m (pl Haarsprays)

hairstyle n Frisur f

half n ❶ Hälfte f ▷ *half of the cake* die Hälfte des Kuchens ❷ (ticket) Kinderfahrkarte f ▷ *A half to York, please.* Ein Kinderfahrkarte nach York bitte.; **two and a half** zweieinhalb; **half an hour** eine halbe Stunde; **half past ten** halb elf; **half a kilo** ein halbes Kilo; **to cut something in half** etwas in zwei Teile schneiden [60]

▶ adj, adv ❶ halb ▷ *a half chicken* ein halbes Hähnchen ❷ fast ▷ *He was half asleep.* Er schlief fast.

half-hour n halbe Stunde f

half-price adj, adv zum halben Preis

half-time n Halbzeit f

halfway adv ❶ auf halber Strecke ▷ *halfway between Oxford and London* auf halber Strecke zwischen Oxford und London ❷ in der Mitte ▷ *halfway through the chapter* in der Mitte des Kapitels

hall n ❶ (in house) Flur m (pl Flure) ❷ Saal m (pl Säle) ▷ *the village hall* der Gemeindesaal; **hall of residence** das Wohnheim

hallway n Flur m (pl Flure)

ham n Schinken m (pl Schinken) ▷ *a ham sandwich* ein Schinkensandwich nt

hamburger n Hamburger m (pl Hamburger)

hammer n Hammer m (pl Hämmer)

hamster n Hamster m (pl Hamster)

hand n ❶ (of person) Hand f (pl Hände); **to give somebody a hand** jemandem helfen [37]; **on the one hand ..., on the other hand ...** einerseits ..., andererseits ... ❷ (of clock) Zeiger m (pl Zeiger)

▶ vb reichen [48] ▷ *He handed me the book.* Er reichte mir das Buch.; **to hand something in** etwas abgeben [28]; **to hand something out** etwas austeilen [4]; **to hand something over** etwas übergeben [28]

handbag n Handtasche f

handcuffs npl Handschellen fpl

handkerchief n Taschentuch nt (pl Taschentücher)

handle n ❶ (of door) Klinke f ❷ (of cup) Henkel m (pl Henkel) ❸ (of knife) Griff m (pl Griffe) ❹ (of saucepan) Stiel m (pl Stiele)

▶ vb **He handled it well.** Er hat das gut gemacht.; **Kath handled the travel arrangements.** Kath hat sich um die Reisevorbereitungen gekümmert.

handlebars npl Lenkstange fsg

handmade adj handgemacht

handsome adj gut aussehend ▷ *a handsome man* ein gut aussehender Mann; **He's very handsome.** Er sieht sehr gut aus.

handwriting n Handschrift f

handy adj ❶ praktisch ▷ *This knife's very handy.* Dieses Messer ist sehr praktisch. ❷ **zur Hand** ▷ *Have you got a pen handy?* Hast du einen Schreiber zur Hand?

hang vb ❶ aufhängen [35] (perf hat aufgehängt) ▷ *Mike hung the painting on the wall.* Mike hängte das Bild an der Wand auf. ❷ hängen [35] ▷ *They hanged the criminal.* Sie hängten den Verbrecher.; **to hang around** rumhängen [35]; **to hang on** warten [2]; **to hang up** (1) (clothes) aufhängen [35] ▷ *Hang your jacket up on the hook.* Häng deine Jacke am Haken auf. (2) (phone) auflegen [4] ▷ *I tried to phone him but he hung up on me.* Ich habe versucht, mit ihm zu telefonieren, aber er hat einfach aufgelegt.

hanger n (for clothes) Bügel m (pl Bügel)

ENGLISH > GERMAN

hangover n Kater m (pl Kater) ▷ *to have a hangover* einen Kater haben

happen vb passieren [**76**] (perf ist passiert) ▷ *What's happened?* Was ist passiert?; **as it happens** zufälligerweise

happily adv ❶ fröhlich ▷ *'Don't worry!' he said happily.* 'Mach dir keine Sorgen!' sagte er fröhlich. ❷ (fortunately) zum Glück ▷ *Happily, everything went well.* Zum Glück ging alles gut.

happiness n Glück nt

happy adj glücklich ▷ *Janet looks happy.* Janet sieht glücklich aus.; **I'm very happy with your work.** Ich bin sehr zufrieden mit Ihrer Arbeit.; **Happy birthday!** Herzlichen Glückwunsch zum Geburtstag!

harbour (US **harbor**) n Hafen m (pl Häfen)

hard adj, adv ❶ hart ▷ *This cheese is very hard.* Dieser Käse ist sehr hart. ▷ *He's worked very hard.* Er hat sehr hart gearbeitet. ❷ schwierig ▷ *This question's too hard for me.* Diese Frage ist für mich zu schwierig.

hard disk n (of computer) Festplatte f

hardly adv kaum ▷ *I've hardly got any money.* Ich habe kaum Geld. ▷ *I hardly know you.* Ich kenne Sie kaum.; **hardly ever** fast nie

hard up adj pleite

harm vb **to harm somebody** jemandem wehtun [**81**]; **to harm something** einer Sache schaden [**54**]

harmful adj schädlich ▷ *harmful chemicals* schädliche Chemikalien

harmless adj harmlos ▷ *Most spiders are harmless.* Die meisten Spinnen sind harmlos.

harvest n Ernte f

has vb see **have**

hashtag n (on social media) Hashtag m (pl Hashtags)

hasn't = has not

hat n Hut m (pl Hüte)

hate vb hassen [**31**] ▷ *I hate maths.* Ich hasse Mathe.

hatred n Hass m (gen Hasses)

haunted adj verwunschen ▷ *a haunted house* ein verwunschenes Haus

have vb ❶ haben [**32**] (pres hat, imperf hatte, perf hat gehabt) ▷ *Have you got a sister?* Hast du eine Schwester? ▷ *He has blue eyes.* Er hat blaue Augen. ▷ *I've got a cold.* Ich habe eine Erkältung.

> The perfect tense of most verbs is formed with **haben**.

▷ *They have eaten.* Sie haben gegessen. ▷ *Have you done your homework?* Hast du deine Hausaufgaben gemacht?

> Questions like 'hasn't he?' don't exist in German.

▷ *He's done it, hasn't he?* Er hat es getan, nicht wahr?

> 'have' is not translated when it is used in place of another verb.

▷ *Have you got any money? — No, I haven't.* Hast du Geld? — Nein. ▷ *Does she have any pets? — Yes, she has.* Hat sie Haustiere? — Ja. ▷ *He hasn't done his homework. — Yes, he has.* Er hat seine Hausaufgaben nicht gemacht. — Doch. ❷ sein [**65**] (pres ist, imperf war, perf ist gewesen)

> The perfect tense of some verbs is formed with **sein**.

▷ *They have arrived.* Sie sind angekommen. ▷ *Has he gone?* Ist er gegangen?

> 'have' plus noun is sometimes translated by a German verb.

▷ *He had his breakfast.* Er hat gefrühstückt. ▷ *to have a shower* duschen ▷ *to have a bath* baden; **to have got to do something** etwas tun müssen [**51**] ▷ *She's got to do it.* Sie muss es tun.; **to have a party** eine Party machen [**48**]; **I had my hair cut yesterday.** Ich habe mir gestern die Haare schneiden lassen [**42**].

haven't = have not

hay n Heu nt

hay fever n Heuschnupfen m ▷ Do you get hay fever? Hast du manchmal Heuschnupfen?

hazelnut n Haselnuss f (pl Haselnüsse)

he pron er ▷ He loves dogs. Er liebt Hunde.

head n ❶ (of person) Kopf m (pl Köpfe) ▷ The wine went to my head. Der Wein ist mir in den Kopf gestiegen. ❷ (of private or primary school) Rektor m (pl Rektoren), Rektorin f ❸ (of state secondary school) Direktor m (pl Direktoren), Direktorin f ❹ (leader) Oberhaupt nt (pl Oberhäupter) ▷ a head of state ein Staatsoberhaupt; **to have a head for figures** gut mit Zahlen umgehen können [41]; **Heads or tails?** — Heads. Kopf oder Zahl? — Kopf.
▶ vb **to head for something** auf etwas zugehen [29] ▷ He headed straight for the bar. Er ging direkt auf die Theke zu.

headache n Kopfschmerzen mpl ▷ I've got a headache. Ich habe Kopfschmerzen.

headlight n Scheinwerfer m (pl Scheinwerfer)

headline n Schlagzeile f

headmaster n ❶ (of private or primary school) Rektor m (pl Rektoren) ❷ (of state secondary school) Direktor m (pl Direktoren)

headmistress n ❶ (of private or primary school) Rektorin f ❷ (of state secondary school) Direktorin f

headphones npl Kopfhörer mpl (pl Kopfhörer) ▷ a set of headphones ein Kopfhörer

headquarters npl Hauptquartier nt ▷ The bank's headquarters are in London. Das Hauptquartier der Bank ist in London.

head teacher n ❶ (of private or primary school) Rektor m (pl Rektoren), Rektorin f ❷ (of state secondary school) Direktor m (pl Direktoren), Direktorin f

heal vb heilen [38]

health n Gesundheit f

healthy adj gesund ▷ She's a healthy person. Sie ist gesund. ▷ a healthy diet eine gesunde Ernährung

heap n Haufen m (pl Haufen) ▷ a rubbish heap ein Müllhaufen

hear vb hören [38] ▷ He heard the dog bark. Er hörte den Hund bellen. ▷ She can't hear very well. Sie hört nicht gut.
▷ I heard that she was ill. Ich habe gehört, dass sie krank war. ▷ Did you hear the good news? Hast du die gute Nachricht gehört?; **to hear about something** von etwas hören [38]; **to hear from somebody** von jemandem hören [38]

heart n Herz nt (gen Herzens, pl Herzen); **to learn something by heart** etwas auswendig lernen [38]; **the ace of hearts** das Herzass

heart attack n Herzinfarkt m (pl Herzinfarkte)

heartbroken adj zutiefst betrübt

heat n Hitze f
▶ vb erhitzen [7] (perf hat erhitzt) ▷ Heat gently for five minutes. Erhitzen Sie es bei schwacher Hitze fünf Minuten lang.; **to heat up** (1) (cooked food) aufwärmen [4] ▷ He heated the soup up. Er hat die Suppe aufgewärmt. (2) (water, oven) heiß werden [91] ▷ The water is heating up. Das Wasser wird heiß.

heater n Heizofen m (pl Heizöfen) ▷ an electric heater ein elektrischer Heizofen

heather n Heidekraut nt (pl Heidekräuter)

heating n Heizung f

heaven n Himmel m (pl Himmel)

heavy adj ❶ schwer ▷ This bag's very heavy. Diese Tasche ist sehr schwer.; **heavy rain** starker Regen ❷ (busy) anstrengend ▷ I've got a very heavy week ahead. Ich habe eine anstrengende Woche vor mir.; **to be a heavy drinker** viel trinken [80]

he'd = he would; he had

ENGLISH > GERMAN

hedge n Hecke f
hedgehog n Igel m (pl Igel)
heel n Absatz m (gen Absatzes, pl Absätze)
height n ① (of person) Größe f ② (of object, mountain) Höhe f
held vb see **hold**
helicopter n Hubschrauber m (pl Hubschrauber)
hell n Hölle f; **Hell!** (informal) Mist!
he'll = **he will; he shall**
hello excl hallo
helmet n Helm m (pl Helme)
help vb helfen [37] (pres hilft, imperf half, perf hat geholfen); **to help somebody** jemandem helfen [37]; **Help!** Hilfe!; **Help yourself!** Bedienen Sie sich!; **He can't help it.** Er kann nichts dafür.
▸ n Hilfe f ▷ Do you need any help? Brauchst du Hilfe?
helpful adj hilfreich ▷ a helpful suggestion ein hilfreicher Vorschlag; **He was very helpful.** Er war eine große Hilfe.
help menu n Hilfemenü nt (pl Hilfemenüs)
hen n Henne f
her adj ihr ▷ her father ihr Vater ▷ her mother ihre Mutter ▷ her child ihr Kind ▷ her parents ihre Eltern

▪ Do not use **ihr** with parts of the body.

▷ She's going to wash her hair. Sie wäscht sich die Haare. ▷ She's cleaning her teeth. Sie putzt sich die Zähne. ▷ She's hurt her foot. Sie hat sich am Fuß verletzt.
▸ pron ① sie ▷ I can see her. Ich kann sie sehen. ▷ Look at her! Sieh sie an! ▷ It's her again. Sie ist es schon wieder. ▷ I'm older than her. Ich bin älter als sie.

▪ Use **sie** after prepositions which take the accusative.

▷ I was thinking of her. Ich habe an sie gedacht. ② ihr

▪ Use **ihr** after prepositions which take the dative.

373 | hide

▷ I'm going with her. Ich gehe mit ihr mit. ▷ He sat next to her. Er saß neben ihr.

▪ Use **ihr** when 'her' means 'to her'.

▷ I gave her a book. Ich gab ihr ein Buch. ▷ I told her the truth. Ich habe ihr die Wahrheit gesagt.
herb n Kraut nt (pl Kräuter)
here adv hier ▷ I live here. Ich wohne hier. ▷ Here's Helen. Hier ist Helen. ▷ Here are the books. Hier sind die Bücher. ▷ Here he is! Da ist er ja!
hero n Held m (gen Helden, pl Helden) ▷ He's a real hero! Er ist ein echter Held!
heroin n Heroin nt
heroine n Heldin f ▷ the heroine of the novel die Heldin des Romans
hers pron ① ihrer ▷ Is this her coat? — No, hers is black. Ist das ihr Mantel? — Nein, ihrer ist schwarz.
ihre ▷ Is this her cup? — No, hers is red. Ist das ihre Tasse? — Nein, ihre ist rot.
ihres ▷ Is this her car? — No, hers is white. Ist das ihr Auto? — Nein, ihres ist weiß.
② ihre ▷ my parents and hers meine Eltern und ihre ▷ I have my reasons and she has hers. Ich habe meine Gründe und sie hat ihre.; **Is this hers?** Gehört das ihr? ▷ This book is hers. Dieses Buch gehört ihr. ▷ Whose is this? — It's hers. Wem gehört das? — Es gehört ihr.
herself pron ① sich ▷ She's hurt herself. Sie hat sich verletzt. ▷ She talked mainly about herself. Sie redete hauptsächlich über sich selbst. ② selbst ▷ She did it herself. Sie hat es selbst gemacht.; **by herself** allein
he's = **he is; he has**
hesitate vb zögern [88]
heterosexual adj heterosexuell
hi excl hallo
hiccups npl Schluckauf msg ▷ He had the hiccups. Er hatte einen Schluckauf.
hide vb sich verstecken [7] (perf hat sich versteckt) ▷ He hid behind a bush. Er versteckte sich hinter einem Busch.; **to hide something** etwas verstecken [7]

hide-and-seek n **to play hide-and-seek** Versteckenspielen [38]
hi-fi n Hi-Fi-Anlage f
high adj, adv hoch ▷ *It's too high.* Es ist zu hoch. ▷ *How high is the wall?* Wie hoch ist die Mauer? ▷ *The wall's two metres high.* Die Mauer ist zwei Meter hoch.

▪ Before a noun or after an article, use **hohe**.

▷ *She's got a very high voice.* Sie hat eine sehr hohe Stimme. ▷ *a high price* ein hoher Preis ▷ *a high temperature* eine hohe Temperatur ▷ *at high speed* mit hoher Geschwindigkeit; **It's very high in fat.** Es ist sehr fetthaltig.; **to be high** (*informal: on drugs*) high sein [65]; **to get high** (*informal: on drugs*) high werden [91]

higher education n Hochschulbildung f
high-heeled adj **high-heeled shoes** hochhackige Schuhe
high jump n (*sport*) Hochsprung m (*pl* Hochsprünge)
high-rise n Hochhaus nt (*gen* Hochhauses, *pl* Hochhäuser) ▷ *I live in a high-rise.* Ich wohne in einem Hochhaus.
high school n Gymnasium nt (*pl* Gymnasien)
hijack vb entführen [18] (*perf* hat entführt)
hijacker n Entführer m (*pl* Entführer), Entführerin f
hiking n **to go hiking** wandern gehen [29]
hilarious adj urkomisch ▷ *It was hilarious!* Es war urkomisch!
hill n Hügel m (*pl* Hügel) ▷ *She walked up the hill.* Sie ging den Hügel hinauf.
hill-walking n Bergwandern nt; **to go hill-walking** Bergwanderungen machen [48]
him pron ❶ ihn ▷ *I can see him.* Ich kann ihn sehen. ▷ *Look at him!* Sieh ihn an!

▪ Use **ihn** after prepositions which take the accusative.

▷ *I did it for him.* Ich habe es für ihn getan. ❷ ihm

▪ Use **ihm** after prepositions which take the dative.

▷ *I travelled with him.* Ich bin mit ihm gereist. ▷ *I haven't heard from him.* Ich habe nichts von ihm gehört.

▪ Use **ihm** when 'him' means 'to him'.

▷ *I gave him a book.* Ich gab ihm ein Buch. ▷ *I told him the truth.* Ich habe ihm die Wahrheit gesagt. ❸ er ▷ *It's him again.* Er ist es schon wieder. ▷ *I'm older than him.* Ich bin älter als er.
himself pron ❶ sich ▷ *He's hurt himself.* Er hat sich verletzt. ▷ *He talked mainly about himself.* Er redete hauptsächlich über sich selbst. ❷ selbst ▷ *He did it himself.* Er hat es selbst gemacht.; **by himself** allein
Hindu adj hinduistisch; **a Hindu temple** ein Hindutempel m
hip n Hüfte f
hippie n Hippie m (*pl* Hippies)

▪ **der Hippie** is also used for women.

▷ *She was a hippie.* Sie war ein Hippie.
hippo n Nilpferd nt (*pl* Nilpferde)
hipster n Hipster m (*pl* Hipsters)
hire vb ❶ mieten [2] ▷ *to hire a car* ein Auto mieten ❷ (*person*) anstellen [4] (*perf* hat angestellt) ▷ *They hired a cleaner.* Sie haben eine Putzfrau angestellt.

▶ n Verleih m (*pl* Verleihe); **car hire** der Autoverleih; **for hire** zu vermieten
his adj sein ▷ *his father* sein Vater ▷ *his mother* seine Mutter ▷ *his child* sein Kind ▷ *his parents* seine Eltern

▪ Do not use **sein** with parts of the body.

▷ *He's going to wash his hair.* Er wäscht sich die Haare. ▷ *He's cleaning his teeth.* Er putzt sich die Zähne. ▷ *He's hurt his foot.* Er hat sich am Fuß verletzt.

ENGLISH > GERMAN

▶ pron ❶ seiner ▷ Is this his coat? — No, his is black. Ist das sein Mantel? — Nein, seiner ist schwarz.; **Is this his cup?** — No, his is red. Ist das seine Tasse? — Nein, seine ist rot.; **Is this his car?** — No, his is white. Ist das sein Auto? — Nein, seines ist weiß. ❷ seine ▷ my parents and his meine Eltern und seine ▷ I have my reasons and he has his. Ich habe meine Gründe und er hat seine.; **Is this his?** Gehört das ihm? ▷ This book is his. Dieses Buch gehört ihm. ▷ Whose is this? — It's his. Wem gehört das? — Das gehört ihm.

history n Geschichte f

hit vb ❶ schlagen [59] (pres schlägt, imperf schlug, perf hat geschlagen) ▷ Andrew hit him. Andrew hat ihn geschlagen. ❷ anfahren [21] (pres fährt an, imperf fuhr an, perf hat angefahren) ▷ He was hit by a car. Er wurde von einem Auto angefahren. ❸ treffen [78] (pres trifft, imperf traf, perf hat getroffen) ▷ The arrow hit the target. Der Pfeil traf sein Ziel.; **to hit it off with somebody** sich gut mit jemandem verstehen [72]
▶ n ❶ (song) Hit m (pl Hits) ❷ (success) Erfolg m (pl Erfolge) ▷ The film was a massive hit. Der Film war ein enormer Erfolg.

hitch n Problem nt (pl Probleme) ▷ a slight hitch ein kleines Problem

hitchhike vb per Anhalter fahren [21] (pres fährt, imperf fuhr, perf ist gefahren)

hitchhiker n Anhalter m (pl Anhalter), Anhalterin f

hitchhiking n Trampen nt ▷ Hitchhiking is dangerous. Trampen ist gefährlich.

HIV-negative adj HIV-negativ

HIV-positive adj HIV-positiv

hobby n Hobby nt (pl Hobbys) ▷ What are your hobbies? Welche Hobbys haben Sie?

hockey n Hockey nt ▷ I play hockey. Ich spiele Hockey.

hold vb ❶ (hold on to) halten [33] (pres hält, imperf hielt, perf hat gehalten) ▷ Hold this end of the rope, please. Halt bitte dieses Ende des Seils.; **She held a bottle in her hand.** Sie hatte eine Flasche in der Hand. ❷ (contain) fassen [31] ▷ This bottle holds two litres. Diese Flasche fasst zwei Liter.; **to hold a meeting** eine Versammlung abhalten [33]; **Hold the line!** (on telephone) Bleiben Sie am Apparat!; **Hold it!** (wait) Sekunde!; **to get hold of something** (obtain) etwas bekommen [40]

hold on vb ❶ (keep hold) sich festhalten [33] (pres hält sich fest, imperf hielt sich fest, perf hat sich festgehalten) ❷ (wait) warten [2]

hold up vb to hold up one's hand die Hand heben ▷ I held up my hand. Ich hob die Hand.; **to hold somebody up** (delay) jemanden aufhalten [33]; **to hold up a bank** (rob) eine Bank überfallen [22]

hold-up n ❶ (at bank) Überfall m (pl Überfälle) ❷ (delay) Verzögerung f ❸ (traffic jam) Stau m (pl Staus)

hole n Loch nt (pl Löcher)

holiday n ❶ (from school) Ferien pl ▷ Did you have a good holiday? Hattet ihr schöne Ferien?; **on holiday** in den Ferien; **the school holidays** die Schulferien ❷ (from work) Urlaub m (pl Urlaube) ▷ Did you have a good holiday? Hattet ihr einen schönen Urlaub?; **on holiday** im Urlaub ❸ (public holiday) Feiertag m (pl Feiertage) ▷ Next Wednesday is a holiday. Nächsten Mittwoch ist ein Feiertag. ❹ (day off) He took a day's holiday. Er nahm einen Tag frei.; **a holiday camp** ein Ferienlager nt; **a holiday home** eine Ferienwohnung f

Holland n Holland nt; **from Holland** aus Holland; **in Holland** in Holland; **to Holland** nach Holland

hollow adj hohl

holly n Stechpalme f
holy adj heilig
home n Zuhause nt (gen Zuhause); **at home** zu Hause; **Make yourself at home.** Machen Sie es sich bequem.
▶ adv ❶ zu Hause ▷ *to be at home* zu Hause sein ❷ nach Hause ▷ *to go home* nach Hause gehen; **to get home** nach Hause kommen **[40]**
home address n Addresse f ▷ *What's your home address?* Wie ist Ihre Addresse?
homeland n Heimatland nt (pl Heimatländer)
homeless adj obdachlos; **the homeless** die Obdachlosen mpl
home match n Heimspiel nt (pl Heimspiele)
home page n (internet) Homepage f (pl Homepages)
homesick adj **to be homesick** Heimweh haben **[32]**
homework n Hausaufgaben fpl ▷ *Have you done your homework?* Hast du deine Hausaufgaben gemacht? ▷ *my geography homework* meine Erdkundeaufgaben
homosexual adj homosexuell
honest adj ehrlich ▷ *She's an honest person.* Sie ist ein ehrlicher Mensch. ▷ *He was honest with her.* Er war ehrlich zu ihr.
honestly adv ehrlich ▷ *I honestly don't know.* Ich weiß es ehrlich nicht.
honesty n Ehrlichkeit f
honey n Honig m
honeymoon n Flitterwochen fpl
honour (US **honor**) n Ehre f
hood n ❶ Kapuze f ▷ *a coat with a hood* ein Mantel mit Kapuze ❷ (of car) Motorhaube f
hook n Haken m (pl Haken) ▷ *He hung the painting on the hook.* Er hängte das Bild an den Haken.; **to take the phone off the hook** das Telefon aushängen **[35]**; **a fish-hook** ein Angelhaken
hooligan n Rowdy m (pl Rowdys)
hooray excl hurra

Hoover® n Staubsauger m (pl Staubsauger)
hoover vb staubsaugen **[38]** ▷ *She hoovered the lounge.* Sie hat im Wohnzimmer gestaubsaugt.
hop vb hüpfen **[38]** (perf ist gehüpft)
hope vb hoffen **[38]** ▷ *I hope he comes.* Ich hoffe, er kommt. ▷ *I'm hoping for good results.* Ich hoffe, dass ich gute Noten bekomme.; **I hope so.** Hoffentlich.; **I hope not.** Hoffentlich nicht.
▶ n Hoffnung f; **to give up hope** die Hoffnung aufgeben **[28]**
hopefully adv hoffentlich ▷ *Hopefully he'll make it in time.* Hoffentlich schafft er es noch.
hopeless adj hoffnungslos ▷ *I'm hopeless at maths.* In Mathe bin ich ein hoffnungsloser Fall.
horizon n Horizont m (pl Horizonte)
horizontal adj horizontal
horn n ❶ (of car) Hupe f; **He sounded his horn.** Er hat gehupt. ❷ Horn nt (pl Hörner) ▷ *I play the horn.* Ich spiele Horn.
horoscope n Horoskop nt (pl Horoskope)
horrible adj furchtbar ▷ *What a horrible dress!* Was für ein furchtbares Kleid!
horrify vb entsetzen **[18]** ▷ *I was horrified by the news.* Ich war über die Neuigkeiten entsetzt.
horrifying adj schrecklich ▷ *a horrifying accident* ein schrecklicher Unfall
horror n Horror m
horror film n Horrorfilm m (pl Horrorfilme)
horse n Pferd nt (pl Pferde)
horse-racing n Pferderennen nt (pl Pferderennen)
hose n Schlauch m (pl Schläuche) ▷ *a garden hose* ein Gartenschlauch
 Be careful not to translate **hose** by the German word **Hose**.
hospital n Krankenhaus nt (gen Krankenhauses, pl Krankenhäuser) ▷ *Take me to the hospital!* Bringen Sie

ENGLISH > GERMAN

mich ins Krankenhaus! ▷ *in hospital* im Krankenhaus

hospitality n Gastfreundschaft f

host n ❶ Gastgeber m (pl Gastgeber), Gastgeberin f ❷ (television) Moderator m (pl Moderatoren), Moderatorin f

hostage n Geisel f ▷ *to take somebody hostage* jemanden als Geisel nehmen

hostel n Herberge f

hot adj ❶ (warm) heiß ▷ *a hot bath* ein heißes Bad ▷ *a hot country* ein heißes Land ▷ *It's hot.* Es ist heiß. ▷ *It's very hot today.* Heute ist es sehr heiß.

> When you talk about a person being 'hot', you use the impersonal construction.

▷ *I'm hot.* Mir ist heiß. ▷ *I'm too hot.* Mir ist es zu heiß. ❷ (spicy) scharf ▷ *a very hot curry* ein sehr scharfes Curry

hot dog n Hotdog m (pl Hotdogs)

hotel n Hotel nt (pl Hotels) ▷ *We stayed in a hotel.* Wir haben in einem Hotel übernachtet.

hour n Stunde f ▷ *She always takes hours to get ready.* Sie braucht immer Stunden, bis sie fertig ist.; **a quarter of an hour** eine Viertelstunde; **half an hour** eine halbe Stunde; **two and a half hours** zweieinhalb Stunden

hourly adv, adj stündlich ▷ *There are hourly buses.* Der Bus verkehrt stündlich.; **to be paid hourly** stundenweise bezahlt werden [91]

house n Haus nt (gen Hauses, pl Häuser) ▷ *at his house* bei ihm zu Hause; **We stayed at their house.** Wir haben bei ihnen übernachtet.

housewife n Hausfrau f ▷ *She's a housewife.* Sie ist Hausfrau.

housework n Hausarbeit f ▷ *to do the housework* die Hausarbeit machen

hovercraft n Luftkissenfahrzeug nt (pl Luftkissenfahrzeuge)

how adv wie ▷ *How old are you?* Wie alt bist du? ▷ *How far is it to Edinburgh?* Wie weit ist es nach Edinburgh? ▷ *How long have you been here?* Wie lange sind Sie schon hier? ▷ *How are you?* Wie geht's?; **How much?** Wie viel?; **How many?** Wie viele?

however conj aber ▷ *This, however, isn't true.* Das ist aber nicht wahr.

hug vb umarmen [7] (perf hat umarmt) ▷ *He hugged her.* Er umarmte sie.
▶ n *to give somebody a hug* jemanden umarmen [7]

huge adj riesig

hum vb summen [38] ▷ *She hummed to herself.* Sie summte vor sich hin.

human adj menschlich ▷ *the human body* der menschliche Körper

human being n Mensch m (gen Menschen, pl Menschen)

humour (US **humor**) n Humor m; **to have a sense of humour** Humor haben [32]

hundred num **a hundred** einhundert; **five hundred** fünfhundert; **five hundred and one** fünfhundertundeins; **hundreds of people** Hunderte von Menschen

hung vb see **hang**

Hungarian adj ungarisch

Hungary n Ungarn nt; **from Hungary** aus Ungarn; **to Hungary** nach Ungarn

hunger n Hunger m

hungry adj **to be hungry** Hunger haben [32]

hunt vb jagen [38] ▷ *People used to hunt wild boar.* Menschen haben früher Wildschweine gejagt.; **to go hunting** auf die Jagd gehen [29]; **The police are hunting the killer.** Die Polizei sucht den Mörder.; **to hunt for something** (search) nach etwas suchen [48]

hunting n Jagen nt ▷ *I'm against hunting.* Ich bin gegen Jagen.; **fox-hunting** die Fuchsjagd

hurdle n Hürde f ▷ *the 100 metres hurdles* die 100 Meter Hürden

hurricane n Orkan m (pl Orkane)
hurry vb eilen [**38**] (perf ist geeilt)
▷ Sharon hurried back home. Sharon eilte nach Hause.; **Hurry up!** Beeil dich!
▶ n **to be in a hurry** in Eile sein [**65**]; **to do something in a hurry** etwas auf die Schnelle machen [**48**]; **There's no hurry.** Das eilt nicht.

hurt vb wehtun [**81**] (imperf tat weh, perf hat wehgetan) ▷ That hurts. Das tut weh. ▷ My leg hurts. Mein Bein tut weh. ▷ It hurts to have a tooth out. Es tut weh, wenn einem ein Zahn gezogen wird.; **to hurt somebody (1)** jemandem wehtun [**81**] ▷ You're hurting me! Du tust mir weh! **(2)** (offend) jemanden verletzen [**36**] ▷ His remarks hurt me. Seine Bemerkungen haben mich verletzt.; **to hurt oneself** sich wehtun [**81**] ▷ I fell over and hurt myself. Ich bin hingefallen und habe mir wehgetan.
▶ adj verletzt ▷ Is he badly hurt? Ist er schlimm verletzt? ▷ He was hurt in the leg. Er hatte ein verletztes Bein. ▷ Luckily, nobody got hurt. Zum Glück wurde niemand verletzt. ▷ I was hurt by what he said. Was er sagte hat mich verletzt.

husband n Ehemann m (pl Ehemänner)
hut n Hütte f
hybrid adj hybrid; **hybrid car** das Hybridauto; **hybrid learning** das integrierte Lernen
hymn n Kirchenlied nt (pl Kirchenlieder)
hypermarket n Verbrauchermarkt m (pl Verbrauchermärkte)
hyphen n Bindestrich m (pl Bindestriche)

I pron ich ▷ I speak German. Ich spreche Deutsch. ▷ Ann and I Ann und ich
ice n ❶ Eis nt; **There was ice on the lake.** Der See war gefroren. ❷ (on road) Glatteis nt
iceberg n Eisberg m (pl Eisberge)
ice cream n Eis nt (pl Eis) ▷ vanilla ice cream das Vanilleeis
ice cube n Eiswürfel m (pl Eiswürfel)
ice hockey n Eishockey nt
Iceland n Island nt; **from Iceland** aus Island; **to Iceland** nach Island
ice rink n Eisbahn f
ice-skating n Schlittschuhlaufen nt; **I like ice-skating.** Ich laufe gern Schlittschuh.; **to go ice-skating** Schlittschuh laufen gehen [**29**]
icing n (on cake) Zuckerguss m (gen Zuckergusses); **icing sugar** der Puderzucker
icon n (computer) Icon nt (pl Icons) ▷ to click on an icon ein Icon anklicken
ICT n (= Information and Communications Technology) die IuK (= Informations- und Kommunikationstechnik)

ENGLISH > GERMAN

icy adj eiskalt ▷ *There was an icy wind.* Es wehte ein eiskalter Wind.; **The roads are icy.** Die Straßen sind vereist.

I'd = I had; I would

idea n Idee f ▷ *Good idea!* Gute Idee!

ideal adj ideal

identical adj identisch ▷ *identical to* identisch mit

identification n Identifikation f; **Have you got any identification?** Können Sie sich ausweisen?

identify vb identifizieren [76] (perf hat identifiziert)

identity card n Personalausweis m (pl Personalausweise)

idiom n Redewendung f

idiot n Idiot m (gen Idioten, pl Idioten), Idiotin f

idiotic adj idiotisch

i.e. abbr d. h. (= das heißt)

if conj ❶ wenn ▷ *You can have it if you like.* Wenn du willst, kannst du es haben. ❷ (whether) ob ▷ *Do you know if he's there?* Weißt du, ob er da ist?; **if only** wenn doch nur; **if not** falls nicht

ignore vb ❶ nicht beachten [2] (perf hat nicht beachtet) ▷ *She ignored my advice.* Sie hat meinen Rat nicht beachtet. ❷ ignorieren [76] (perf hat ignoriert) ▷ *She saw me, but she ignored me.* Sie sah mich, hat mich aber ignoriert.; **Just ignore him!** Beachte ihn einfach nicht!

ill adj (sick) krank; **to be taken ill** krank werden [91]

I'll = I will

illegal adj illegal

illness n Krankheit f

illusion n Illusion f

illustration n Illustration f

I'm = I am

image n (public image) Image nt (gen Image, pl Images) ▷ *the company's image* das Image der Firma

imagination n Fantasie f ▷ *You need a lot of imagination to be a writer.* Als

Schriftsteller braucht man viel Fantasie.; **It's just your imagination!** Das bildest du dir nur ein!

imagine vb sich vorstellen [4] (perf hat sich vorgestellt) ▷ *Imagine how I felt!* Stell dir vor, wie mir zumute war!; **Is he angry? — I imagine so.** Ist er böse? — Ich denke schon.

imitate vb nachmachen [4] (perf hat nachgemacht)

imitation n Imitation f

immediate adj sofortig ▷ *We need an immediate answer.* Wir brauchen eine sofortige Antwort.; **in the immediate future** in unmittelbarer Zukunft

immediately adv sofort ▷ *I'll do it immediately.* Ich mache es sofort.

immigrant n Einwanderer m (pl Einwanderer), Einwanderin f

immigration n Einwanderung f

immune adj **to be immune to something** gegen etwas immun sein [65]

impatience n Ungeduld f

impatient adj ungeduldig ▷ *People are getting impatient.* Die Leute werden ungeduldig.

implement vb ausführen [4] (perf hat ausgeführt) ▷ *Chris will implement the plan.* Chris wird den Plan ausführen.

imply vb andeuten [2] (perf hat angedeutet) ▷ *Are you implying I stole it?* Wollen Sie andeuten, ich hätte es gestohlen?

import vb importieren [76] (perf hat importiert)

importance n Wichtigkeit f ▷ *the importance of a good knowledge of German* die Wichtigkeit guter Deutschkenntnisse

important adj wichtig

impose vb auferlegen [4] (perf hat auferlegt) ▷ *to impose a penalty* eine Strafe auferlegen

impossible adj unmöglich

impress vb beeindrucken [7] (perf hat beeindruckt) ▷ *She's trying to impress you.* Sie will dich beeindrucken.

impressed adj beeindruckt ▷ *I'm very impressed!* Ich bin sehr beeindruckt.

impression n Eindruck m (pl Eindrücke) ▷ *I was under the impression that ...* Ich hatte den Eindruck, dass ...

impressive adj beeindruckend

improve vb ① *(make better)* verbessern [88] (perf hat verbessert) ▷ *The hotel has improved its service.* Das Hotel hat den Service verbessert. ② *(get better)* besser werden [91] (pres wird besser, imperf wurde besser, perf ist besser geworden) ▷ *The weather is improving.* Das Wetter wird besser. ▷ *My German has improved.* Mein Deutsch ist besser geworden.

improvement n ① *(of condition)* Verbesserung f ▷ *It's a great improvement.* Das ist eine gewaltige Verbesserung. ② *(of learner)* Fortschritt m (pl Fortschritte) ▷ *There's been an improvement in his German.* Er hat in Deutsch Fortschritte gemacht.

in prep, adv

Use the accusative to express movement or a change of place. Use the dative when there is no change of place.

① in ▷ *It's in my bag.* Es ist in meiner Tasche. ▷ *Put it in my bag.* Tu es in meine Tasche. ▷ *I read it in this book.* Ich habe es in diesem Buch gelesen. ▷ *Write it in your address book.* Schreib es in dein Adressbuch. ▷ *in hospital* im Krankenhaus ▷ *in school* in der Schule ▷ *in London* in London ▷ *in Germany* in Deutschland ▷ *in Switzerland* in der Schweiz ▷ *in May* im Mai ▷ *in spring* im Frühling ▷ *in the rain* im Regen ▷ *I'll see you in three weeks.* Ich sehe dich in drei Wochen.

Sometimes 'in' is not translated.

▷ *It happened in 1996.* Es geschah 1996. ▷ *in the morning* morgens ▷ *in the afternoon* nachmittags ▷ *at six in the evening* um sechs Uhr abends ② mit ▷ *the boy in the blue shirt* der Junge mit dem blauen Hemd ▷ *It was written in pencil.* Es war mit Bleistift geschrieben. ▷ *in a loud voice* mit lauter Stimme ▷ *She paid in dollars.* Sie hat mit Dollar bezahlt. ③ auf ▷ *in German* auf Deutsch ▷ *in English* auf Englisch

'in' is sometimes translated using the genitive.

▷ *the best pupil in the class* der beste Schüler der Klasse ▷ *the tallest person in the family* der Größte der Familie; **in the beginning** am Anfang; **in the country** auf dem Land; **in time** rechtzeitig; **in here** hier drin; **one person in ten** einer von zehn; **to be in** *(at home, work)* da sein [65]; **to ask somebody in** jemanden hereinbitten [9]

inadequate adj unzulänglich

include vb einschließen (imperf schloss ein, perf hat eingeschlossen) ▷ *Service is not included.* Bedienung ist nicht eingeschlossen.

including prep inklusive ▷ *That will be two hundred euros, including VAT.* Das macht zweihundert Euro, inklusive Mehrwertsteuer.

income n Einkommen nt (pl Einkommen)

income tax n Einkommensteuer f

inconsistent adj ① widersprüchlich; **to be inconsistent with ...** im Widerspruch stehen [72] zu ... ② unbeständig ▷ *Your work is very inconsistent.* Die Qualität deiner Arbeit ist sehr unbeständig.

inconvenient adj *That's very inconvenient for me.* Das passt mir gar nicht.

incorrect adj unrichtig

increase n Zunahme f ▷ *an increase in road accidents* eine Zunahme an Verkehrsunfällen

ENGLISH > GERMAN

▶ vb ① (traffic, number) zunehmen [**52**] (pres nimmt zu, imperf nahm zu, perf hat zugenommen) ▷ Traffic on motorways has increased. Der Verkehr auf den Autobahnen hat zugenommen. ② (price, demand) steigen [**74**] (imperf stieg, perf ist gestiegen) ▷ with increasing demand bei steigender Nachfrage ③ (pain, wind) stärker werden [**91**] (pres wird stärker, imperf wurde stärker, perf ist stärker geworden); **to increase in size** größer werden [**91**]; **to increase something** etwas erhöhen [**19**]; **increased cost of living** höhere Lebenshaltungskosten

incredible adj unglaublich

indeed adv wirklich ▷ It's very hard indeed. Es ist wirklich schwer.; **Know what I mean? – Indeed I do.** Weißt du, was ich meine? – Ja, ganz genau.; **Thank you very much indeed!** Ganz herzlichen Dank!

independence n Unabhängigkeit f

independent adj unabhängig; **an independent school** eine Privatschule

index n (in book) Verzeichnis nt (gen Verzeichnisses, pl Verzeichnisse)

India n Indien nt; **from India** aus Indien; **to India** nach Indien

Indian adj ① indisch ② (American Indian) indianisch
▶ n (person) Inder m (pl Inder), Inderin f; **an American Indian** ein Indianer m

indicate vb ① zeigen [**38**] ▷ His reaction indicates how he feels about it. Seine Reaktion zeigt, was er davon hält. ② (make known) andeuten [**2**] (perf hat angedeutet) ▷ He indicated that he may resign. Er hat angedeutet, dass er vielleicht zurücktritt. ③ (technical device) anzeigen [**4**] (perf hat angezeigt) ▷ The gauge indicated a very high temperature. Das Messgerät zeigte eine sehr hohe Temperatur an.; **to indicate left** links blinken [**38**]

indicator n (in car) Blinker m (pl Blinker)

381 | informal

indigestion n Magenverstimmung f; **I've got indigestion.** Ich habe eine Magenverstimmung.

individual n Individuum nt (pl Individuen)
▶ adj individuell

indoor adj **an indoor swimming pool** ein Hallenbad nt

indoors adv im Haus ▷ They're indoors. Sie sind im Haus.; **to go indoors** hineingehen [**29**]

industrial adj industriell

industrial estate n Industriegebiet nt (pl Industriegebiete)

industry n Industrie f ▷ the tourist industry die Tourismusindustrie ▷ the oil industry die Erdölindustrie ▷ I'd like to work in industry. Ich würde gern in der freien Wirtschaft arbeiten.

inevitable adj unvermeidlich

inexperienced adj unerfahren

infant school n Grundschule f
● The **Grundschule** is a primary school
● which children attend from the
● age of 6 to 10. This is the nearest
● equivalent to the infant school,
● which is attended by children from
● the age of 5 to 7. Many children
● attend **Kindergarten** before going
● to the **Grundschule**.

infection n Entzündung f ▷ an ear infection eine Ohrenentzündung ▷ a throat infection eine Halsentzündung

infectious adj ansteckend ▷ It's not infectious. Es ist nicht ansteckend.

infinitive n Infinitiv m (pl Infinitive)

inflation n Inflation f

inform vb informieren [**76**] (perf hat informiert); **to inform somebody of something** jemanden über etwas informieren [**76**]

informal adj ① (person) locker ② (party) zwanglos ▷ 'informal dress' 'zwanglose Kleidung' ③ (colloquial) umgangssprachlich; **informal language** die Umgangssprache;

an informal visit ein inoffizieller Besuch

information n Information f ▷ *important information* wichtige Informationen; **a piece of information** eine Information; **Could you give me some information about Berlin?** Können Sie mir einige Informationen über Berlin geben?

information office n Auskunft f (pl Auskünfte)

information technology n Informationstechnik f

infuriating adj äußerst ärgerlich

ingredient n Zutat f

inhaler n Inhalator m (pl Inhalatoren)

inherit vb erben [**38**]

initials npl Initialen fpl

injection n Spritze f

injure vb verletzen [**36**] (perf hat verletzt)

injured adj verletzt

injury n Verletzung f

ink n Tinte f

in-laws npl Schwiegereltern pl

innocent adj unschuldig

insane adj wahnsinnig

inscription n Inschrift f

insect n Insekt nt (pl Insekten)

insect repellent n Insektenschutzmittel nt (pl Insektenschutzmittel)

insert vb einwerfen [**92**] (pres wirft ein, imperf warf ein, perf hat eingeworfen) ▷ *I inserted a coin.* Ich warf eine Münze ein.

inside n Innere nt (gen Inneren) ▶ adv, prep innen ▷ *inside and outside* innen und außen; **They're inside.** Sie sind drinnen.; **to go inside** hineingehen [**29**]; **Come inside!** Kommt herein!

> Use the accusative to express movement or a change of place. Use the dative when there is no change of place.

inside the house (1) im Haus ▷ *She was inside the house.* Sie war im Haus. (2) ins Haus ▷ *She went inside the house.* Sie ging ins Haus.

insist vb darauf bestehen [**72**] (imperf bestand darauf, perf hat darauf bestanden) ▷ *I didn't want to, but he insisted.* Ich wollte nicht, aber er hat darauf bestanden.; **to insist on doing something** darauf bestehen [**72**], etwas zu tun; **He insisted he was innocent.** Er beteuerte seine Unschuld.

inspect vb kontrollieren [**76**] (perf hat kontrolliert)

inspector n (police) Kommissar m (pl Kommissare), Kommissarin f ▷ *Inspector Jill Brown* Kommissarin Jill Brown

install vb installieren [**76**] (perf hat installiert)

instalment (US **installment**) n ❶ Rate f ▷ *to pay in instalments* in Raten zahlen ❷ (of TV, radio serial) Folge f ❸ (of publication) Teil m

instance n **for instance** zum Beispiel

instant adj sofortig ▷ *It was an instant success.* Es war ein sofortiger Erfolg.; **instant coffee** der Pulverkaffee

instantly adv sofort

instead adv **instead of** (1) (followed by noun) anstelle von ▷ *Use honey instead of sugar.* Nehmen Sie Honig anstelle von Zucker. (2) (followed by verb) statt ▷ *We played tennis instead of going swimming.* Wir spielten Tennis statt schwimmen zu gehen.; **The pool was closed, so we played tennis instead.** Das Schwimmbad war zu, also spielten wir stattdessen Tennis.

instinct n Instinkt m (pl Instinkte)

instruct vb anweisen (imperf wies an, perf hat angewiesen); **to instruct somebody to do something** jemanden anweisen, etwas zu tun

ENGLISH > GERMAN

instructions npl ❶ Anweisungen fpl ▷ Follow the instructions carefully. Befolgen Sie die Anweisungen genau. ❷ (manual) Gebrauchsanweisung f ▷ Where are the instructions? Wo ist die Gebrauchsanweisung?

instructor n Lehrer m (pl Lehrer), Lehrerin f ▷ a skiing instructor ein Skilehrer ▷ a driving instructor ein Fahrlehrer

instrument n Instrument nt (pl Instrumente) ▷ Do you play an instrument? Spielst du ein Instrument?

insulin n Insulin nt

insult n Beleidigung f
▶ vb beleidigen [7] (perf hat beleidigt)

insurance n Versicherung f ▷ his car insurance seine Kraftfahrzeugversicherung; **an insurance policy** eine Versicherungspolice

intelligent adj intelligent

intend vb **to intend to do something** beabsichtigen [7], etwas zu tun

intensive adj intensiv

intention n Absicht f

interest n Interesse nt (pl Interessen) ▷ to show an interest in something Interesse an etwas zeigen ▷ What interests do you have? Welche Interessen hast du?; **My main interest is music.** Ich interessiere mich hauptsächlich für Musik.
▶ vb interessieren [76] (perf hat interessiert) ▷ It doesn't interest me. Das interessiert mich nicht.; **to be interested in something** sich für etwas interessieren [76]

interesting adj interessant

interior n Innere nt (gen Inneren)

interior designer n Innenarchitekt m (gen Innenarchitekten, pl Innenarchitekten), Innenarchitektin f

international adj international

internet n Internet nt ▷ on the internet im Internet

internet user n Internetbenutzer m (pl Internetbenutzer), Internetbenutzerin f

interpreter n Dolmetscher m (pl Dolmetscher), Dolmetscherin f

interrupt vb unterbrechen [11] (pres unterbricht, imperf unterbrach, perf hat unterbrochen)

interruption n Unterbrechung f

interval n (in play, concert) Pause f

interview n ❶ (on TV, radio) Interview nt (pl Interviews) ❷ (for job) Vorstellungsgespräch nt (pl Vorstellungsgespräche)
▶ vb (on TV, radio) interviewen [84] (perf hat interviewt) ▷ I was interviewed on the radio. Ich wurde im Radio interviewt.

interviewer n (on TV, radio) Moderator m (pl Moderatoren), Moderatorin f

into prep in
In this sense **in** is followed by the accusative.
▷ He got into the car. Er stieg ins Auto. ▷ I'm going into town. Ich gehe in die Stadt. ▷ Translate it into German. Übersetzen Sie das ins Deutsche. ▷ Divide into two groups. Teilt euch in zwei Gruppen.

intranet n Intranet nt (pl Intranets)

introduce vb vorstellen [4] (perf hat vorgestellt) ▷ He introduced me to his parents. Er stellte mich seinen Eltern vor.

introduction n (in book) Einleitung f

invade vb eindringen in (imperf drang ein, perf ist eingedrungen) ▷ to invade a country in ein Land eindringen

invalid n Kranke m (gen Kranken, pl Kranken), Kranke f (gen Kranken) ▷ an invalid (man) ein Kranker

invent vb erfinden [24] (imperf erfand, perf hat erfunden)

invention n Erfindung f

invest vb investieren [76] (perf hat investiert)

investigation n (police) Untersuchung f

invisible adj unsichtbar
invitation n Einladung f
invite vb einladen (pres lädt ein, imperf lud ein, perf hat eingeladen) ▷ *He's not invited.* Er ist nicht eingeladen.; **to invite somebody to a party** jemanden zu einer Party einladen
involve vb mit sich bringen [13] (imperf brachte mit sich, perf hat mit sich gebracht) ▷ *This will involve a lot of work.* Das wird viel Arbeit mit sich bringen.; **His job involves a lot of travelling.** Er muss in seinem Job viel reisen.; **to be involved in something** (crime, drugs) in etwas verwickelt sein [65]; **to be involved with somebody** (in relationship) mit jemandem eine Beziehung haben [32]; **I don't want to get involved.** Ich will damit nichts zu tun haben.
iPad® n iPad® nt (pl iPads)
iPhone® n iPhone® nt (pl iPhones)
Iran n Iran m

> Note that the definite article is used in German for countries which are masculine.

from Iran aus dem Iran; **in Iran** im Iran; **to Iran** in den Iran
Iraq n Irak m

> Note that the definite article is used in German for countries which are masculine.

from Iraq aus dem Irak; **in Iraq** im Irak; **to Iraq** in den Irak
Iraqi n Iraker m (pl Iraker), Irakerin f
▶ adj irakisch
Ireland n Irland nt; **from Ireland** aus Irland; **in Ireland** in Irland; **to Ireland** nach Irland
Irish adj irisch ▷ *Irish music* irische Musik; *He's Irish.* Er ist Ire.; *She's Irish.* Sie ist Irin.
▶ n (language) Irisch nt (gen Irischen); **the Irish** (people) die Iren mpl
Irishman n Ire m (gen Iren, pl Iren)
Irishwoman n Irin f
iron n ❶ (metal) Eisen nt ❷ (for clothes) Bügeleisen nt (pl Bügeleisen)
▶ vb bügeln [34]
ironing n Bügeln nt; **to do the ironing** bügeln [34]
ironing board n Bügelbrett nt (pl Bügelbretter)
irresponsible adj (person) verantwortungslos; **That was irresponsible of him.** Das war unverantwortlich von ihm.
irritating adj nervend
is vb see **be**
Islam n Islam m
Islamic adj islamisch; **Islamic law** das Recht des Islams
island n Insel f
isle n **the Isle of Man** die Insel Man; **the Isle of Wight** die Insel Wight
isolated adj (place) abgelegen; **She feels very isolated.** Sie fühlt sich sehr isoliert.; **an isolated case** ein Einzelfall m
Israel n Israel nt; **from Israel** aus Israel; **to Israel** nach Israel
Israeli n Israeli m (gen Israeli, pl Israeli), Israeli f (gen Israeli)
▶ adj israelisch; **He's Israeli.** Er ist Israeli.
issue n ❶ (matter) Frage f ▷ *a controversial issue* eine umstrittene Frage ❷ (of magazine) Ausgabe f
▶ vb (equipment, supplies) ausgeben [28] (pres gibt aus, imperf gab aus, perf hat ausgegeben)
it pron

> Remember to check if 'it' stands for a masculine, feminine or neuter noun, and use the appropriate gender and case.

❶ er ▷ *Your hat?* — *It's on the table.* Dein Hut? — Er ist auf dem Tisch.; sie ▷ *Where's your watch?* — *It's broken.* Wo ist deine Uhr? — Sie ist kaputt.; es ▷ *Have you seen her new dress, it's very* pretty. Hast du ihr neues Kleid gesehen, es ist sehr hübsch. ❷ ihn ▷ *Where's my hat?—I haven't seen it.* Wo ist mein Hut? — Ich habe ihn nicht gesehen.; sie ▷ *Where's your jacket?—I've lost it.* Wo ist deine Jacke? — Ich habe sie verloren. es ▷ *Take my ruler, I don't need it.* Nimm mein Lineal, ich brauche es nicht.; **It's raining.** Es regnet.; **It's six o'clock.** Es ist sechs Uhr.; **It's Friday tomorrow.** Morgen ist Freitag.; **Who is it? — It's me.** Wer ist's? — Ich bin's.; **It's expensive.** Das ist teuer.

Italian *adj* italienisch; **She's Italian.** Sie ist Italienerin.
▶ *n* ❶ (*person*) Italiener *m* (*pl* Italiener), Italienerin *f* ❷ (*language*) Italienisch *nt* (*gen* Italienischen)

italics *npl* Kursivschrift *f*; **in italics** kursiv

Italy *n* Italien *nt*; **from Italy** aus Italien; **in Italy** in Italien; **to Italy** nach Italien

itch *vb* jucken [38] ▷ *It itches.* Es juckt. ▷ *My head's itching.* Mein Kopf juckt.

itchy *adj* **My arm is itchy.** Mein Arm juckt.

it'd = **it had**; **it would**

item *n* (*object*) Artikel *m* (*pl* Artikel)

it'll = **it will**

its *adj*

> Remember to check if 'its' refers back to a masculine, feminine or neuter noun, and use the appropriate gender and case.

sein ▷ *The dog is in its kennel.* Der Hund ist in seiner Hütte.; ihr ▷ *The cup is in its usual place.* Die Tasse ist an ihrem üblichen Platz.; sein ▷ *The baby is in its cot.* Das Baby ist in seinem Bett.

it's = **it is**; **it has**

itself *pron* ❶ sich ▷ *The dog scratched itself.* Der Hund kratzte sich. ❷ selbst ▷ *The heating switches itself off.* Die Heizung schaltet von selbst aus.

I've = **I have**

j

jack *n* ❶ (*for car*) Wagenheber *m* (*pl* Wagenheber) ❷ (*playing card*) Bube *m* (*gen* Buben, *pl* Buben)

jacket *n* Jacke *f*; **jacket potatoes** gebackene Kartoffeln

jail *n* Gefängnis *nt* (*gen* Gefängnisses, *pl* Gefängnisse); **She was sent to jail.** Sie musste ins Gefängnis.
▶ *vb* einsperren [4] (*perf* hat eingesperrt); **He was jailed for ten years.** Er hat zehn Jahre Gefängnis bekommen.

jam *n* Marmelade *f* ▷ *strawberry jam* Erdbeermarmelade; **a traffic jam** ein Verkehrsstau *m*

jammed *adj* **The window's jammed.** Das Fenster klemmt.

janitor *n* Hausmeister *m* (*pl* Hausmeister), Hausmeisterin *f* ▷ *He's a janitor.* Er ist Hausmeister.

January *n* Januar *m* ▷ **in January** im Januar

Japan *n* Japan *nt*

Japanese *adj* japanisch
▶ *n* ❶ (*person*) Japaner *m* (*pl* Japaner),

Japanerin f; **the Japanese** die Japaner mpl ❷ (language) Japanisch nt (gen Japanischen)

jar n Glas nt (gen Glases, pl Gläser) ▷ an empty jar ein leeres Glas ▷ a jar of honey ein Glas Honig

javelin n Speer m (pl Speere)

jaw n Kiefer m (pl Kiefer)

jazz n Jazz m (gen Jazz)

jealous adj eifersüchtig

jeans npl Jeans fpl ▷ a pair of jeans eine Jeans

Jello® n (US) Wackelpudding m

jelly n ❶ (dessert) Wackelpudding m ❷ (jam) Marmelade f

jellyfish n Qualle f

jersey n Pullover m (pl Pullover)

Jesus n Jesus m (gen Jesus)

jet n (plane) Düsenflugzeug nt (pl Düsenflugzeuge)

jetlag n **to be suffering from jetlag** unter der Zeitverschiebung leiden [44]

Jew n Jude m (gen Juden, pl Juden), Jüdin f

jewel n (stone) Edelstein m (pl Edelsteine)

jeweller n Juwelier m (pl Juweliere), Juwelierin f ▷ He's a jeweller. Er ist Juwelier.

jeweller's shop n Juweliergeschäft nt (pl Juweliergeschäfte)

jewellery n Schmuck m

Jewish adj jüdisch

jigsaw n Puzzle nt (pl Puzzles)

job n ❶ Job m (pl Jobs) ▷ He's lost his job. Er hat seinen Job verloren. ▷ I've got a Saturday job. Ich habe einen Samstagsjob. ❷ (chore, task) Arbeit f ▷ That was a difficult job. Das war eine schwierige Arbeit.

jobless adj arbeitslos

jockey n Jockey m (pl Jockeys)

jog vb joggen [48]

jogging n Jogging nt ▷ I like jogging. Ich mag Jogging.; **to go jogging** joggen [48]

join vb ❶ (become member of) beitreten [79] (pres tritt bei, imperf trat bei, perf ist beigetreten) ▷ I'm going to join the tennis club. Ich trete dem Tennisklub bei. ❷ (accompany) sich anschließen (imperf schloss sich an, perf hat sich angeschlossen) ▷ Do you mind if I join you? Macht es dir etwas aus, wenn ich mich dir anschließe?

join in vb ❶ mitmachen [48] (perf hat mitgemacht) ▷ He doesn't join in with what we do. Er macht nicht mit bei den Dingen, die wir tun. ❷ einstimmen [4] (perf hat eingestimmt)

joiner n Schreiner m (pl Schreiner), Schreinerin f ▷ She's a joiner. Sie ist Schreinerin.

joint n ❶ (in body) Gelenk nt (pl Gelenke) ❷ (of meat) Braten m (pl Braten) ❸ (drugs) Joint m (pl Joints)

joke n Witz m (gen Witzes, pl Witze) ▷ to tell a joke einen Witz erzählen
▶ vb Spaß machen [48] ▷ I'm only joking. Ich mache nur Spaß.

Jordan n (country) Jordanien nt

jotter n (pad) Notizblock m (pl Notizblöcke)

journalism n Journalismus m (gen Journalismus)

journalist n Journalist m (gen Journalisten, pl Journalisten), Journalistin f ▷ She's a journalist. Sie ist Journalistin.

journey n ❶ Reise f ▷ I don't like long journeys. Ich mag lange Reisen nicht.; **to go on a journey** eine Reise machen [48] ❷ (to school, work) Fahrt f ▷ the journey to school die Fahrt zur Schule; **a bus journey** eine Busfahrt

joy n Freude f

joystick n (for computer game) Joystick m (pl Joysticks)

judge n Richter m (pl Richter), Richterin f ▷ She's a judge. Sie ist Richterin.
▶ vb (assess) beurteilen [7] (perf hat

beurteilt!) ▷ *You can judge for yourself which is better.* Du kannst das selbst beurteilen, welches besser ist.
judo *n* Judo *nt (gen* Judos)
jug *n* Krug *m (pl* Krüge)
juggler *n* Jongleur *m*, Jongleurin *f*
juice *n* Saft *m (pl* Säfte) ▷ *orange juice* der Orangensaft
July *n* Juli *m* ▷ *in July* im Juli
jumble sale *n* Flohmarkt *m (pl* Flohmärkte)
jump *vb* springen [**71**] (*imperf* sprang, *perf* ist gesprungen) ▷ *to jump out of the window* aus dem Fenster springen ▷ *to jump off the roof* vom Dach springen; **to jump over something** über etwas springen [**71**]
jumper *n* ❶ Pullover *m (pl* Pullover) ❷ *(US: dress)* Trägerkleid *nt (pl* Trägerkleider)
junction *n* ❶ *(of roads)* Kreuzung *f* ❷ *(motorway exit)* Ausfahrt *f*
June *n* Juni *m* ▷ *in June* im Juni
jungle *n* Dschungel *m (pl* Dschungel)
junior *n* **the juniors** die Grundschüler *mpl*
junior school *n* Grundschule *f*
* The **Grundschule** is a primary school
* which children attend from the age
* of 6 to 10.

junk *n (old things)* Krempel *m* ▷ *The attic's full of junk.* Der Speicher ist voller Krempel.; **to eat junk food** Junkfood essen [**20**]; **a junk shop** ein Trödelladen *m*
jury *n (in court)* Geschworenen *mpl*
just *adv* ❶ *(barely)* gerade ▷ *We had just enough money.* Wir hatten gerade genug Geld. ▷ *just in time* gerade noch rechtzeitig ❷ *(shortly)* kurz ▷ *just after Christmas* kurz nach Weihnachten ❸ *(exactly)* genau ▷ *just here* genau hier ❹ *(this minute)* eben ▷ *I did it just now.* Ich habe es eben gemacht. ▷ *He's just arrived.* Er ist eben angekommen.; **I'm rather busy just now.** Ich bin gerade ziemlich beschäftigt.; **I'm just coming!** Ich komme schon! ❺ *(only)* nur ▷ *It's just a suggestion.* Es ist nur ein Vorschlag.
justice *n* Gerechtigkeit *f*

k

kangaroo n Känguru nt (pl Kängurus)
karate n Karate nt (gen Karate) ▷ I like karate. Ich mag Karate.
kebab n Kebab m (pl Kebabs)
keen adj ❶ (enthusiastic) begeistert ▷ He doesn't seem very keen. Er scheint nicht gerade begeistert. ❷ (hardworking) eifrig ▷ She's a keen student. Sie ist eine eifrige Studentin.; **to be keen on something** etwas mögen [50]; **to be keen on somebody** (fancy them) auf jemanden stehen [72]; **to be keen on doing something** Lust haben [32], etwas zu tun
keep vb ❶ (retain) behalten [33] ▷ You can keep it. Das kannst du behalten. ❷ (remain) sein [65] ▷ Keep quiet! Sei still!; **Keep still!** Halt still!; **I keep forgetting my keys.** Ich vergesse dauernd meine Schlüssel.; **to keep on doing something** (1) (continue) etwas weiter tun [81] ▷ He kept on reading. Er las weiter. (2) (repeatedly) etwas dauernd tun [81] ▷ The car keeps on breaking down. Das Auto ist dauernd kaputt.; **'keep out'** 'Kein Zutritt'; **to keep up** mithalten [33] ▷ Matthew walks so fast I can't keep up. Matthew geht so schnell, da kann ich nicht mithalten.
keep-fit n Gymnastik f ▷ I like keep-fit. Ich mache gern Gymnastik.; **I go to keep-fit classes.** Ich gehe zur Gymnastik.
kept vb see keep
kettle n Wasserkessel m (pl Wasserkessel)
key n Schlüssel m (pl Schlüssel)
keyboard n ❶ (of piano, computer) Tastatur f ❷ (of electric organ) Keyboard nt (pl Keyboards) ▷ ... with Mike Moran on keyboards ... mit Mike Moran am Keyboard
kick n Tritt m (pl Tritte)
▶ vb treten [79] (pres tritt, imperf trat, perf hat getreten) ▷ He kicked me. Er hat mich getreten. ▷ He kicked the ball hard. Er trat kräftig gegen den Ball.; **to kick off** (in football) anfangen [23]
kick-off n Anstoß m (gen Anstoßes, pl Anstöße) ▷ Kick-off is at ten o'clock. Um zehn Uhr ist Anstoß.
kid n (child) Kind nt (pl Kinder)
▶ vb Spaß machen [48] ▷ I'm just kidding. Ich mache nur Spaß.
kidnap vb entführen [18] (perf hat entführt)
kidney n Niere f ▷ He's got kidney trouble. Er hat Nierenprobleme. ▷ I don't like kidneys. Ich mag Nieren nicht.
kill vb töten [2]; **to be killed** umkommen [40]; **to kill oneself** sich umbringen [13]
killer n ❶ (murderer) Mörder m (pl Mörder), Mörderin f ▷ The police are searching for the killer. Die Polizei sucht nach dem Mörder. ❷ (hitman) Killer m (pl Killer) ▷ a hired killer ein Auftragskiller; **Meningitis can be a killer.** Hirnhautentzündung kann tödlich sein.

ENGLISH > GERMAN

kilo n Kilo nt (pl Kilos or Kilo) ▷ twenty euros a kilo zwanzig Euro das Kilo
> When specifying a quantity of something use the plural form **Kilo**.
▷ three kilos of tomatoes drei Kilo Tomaten

kilometre n Kilometer m (pl Kilometer) ▷ a hundred kilometres hundert Kilometer

kilt n Kilt m (pl Kilts)

kind adj nett ▷ Thank you for being so kind. Vielen Dank, dass Sie so nett waren.; **to be kind to somebody** zu jemandem nett sein [65]
▶ n Art f ▷ It's a kind of sausage. Es ist eine Art Wurst.; **a new kind of dictionary** ein neuartiges Wörterbuch

kindness n Freundlichkeit f

king n König m (pl Könige)

kingdom n Königreich nt (pl Königreiche)

kiosk n ❶ (phone box) Telefonzelle f ❷ Kiosk m (pl Kioske) ▷ a newspaper kiosk ein Zeitungskiosk

kiss n Kuss m (gen Kusses, pl Küsse) ▷ a passionate kiss ein leidenschaftlicher Kuss
▶ vb ❶ küssen [48] ▷ He kissed me. Er küsste mich. ❷ sich küssen [48] ▷ They kissed. Sie küssten sich.

kit n ❶ (clothes for sport) Zeug nt ▷ I've forgotten my gym kit. Ich habe mein Sportzeug vergessen. ❷ Kasten m (pl Kästen) ▷ a tool kit ein Werkzeugkasten ▷ a first-aid kit ein Erste-Hilfe-Kasten; **puncture repair kit** das Flickzeug; **sewing kit** das Nähzeug

kitchen n Küche f ▷ a fitted kitchen eine Einbauküche; **the kitchen units** die Küchenschränke; **a kitchen knife** ein Küchenmesser nt

kite n Drachen m (pl Drachen)

kitten n Kätzchen nt (pl Kätzchen)

knee n Knie nt (pl Knie) ▷ He was on his knees. Er lag auf den Knien.

knew vb see **know**

389 | **know**

knickers npl Slip m (pl Slips) (women) ▷ a pair of knickers ein Slip

knife n Messer nt (pl Messer); **a sheath knife** ein Fahrtenmesser; **a penknife** ein Taschenmesser

knit vb stricken [48]

knitting n Stricken nt; **I like knitting.** Ich stricke gern.

knives npl see **knife**

knob n ❶ (on door) Griff m ❷ (on radio, TV) Knopf m (pl Knöpfe)

knock vb klopfen [38] ▷ to knock on the door an die Tür klopfen; **Someone's knocking at the door.** Es klopft.; **She was knocked down by a car.** Ein Auto hat sie umgefahren.; **He was knocked out.** (stunned) Er wurde bewusstlos geschlagen.; **to knock somebody out** (defeat) jemanden schlagen [59]; **They were knocked out early in the tournament.** Sie schieden beim Turnier früh aus.; **to knock something over** etwas umstoßen
▶ n There was a knock on the door. Es hat geklopft.

knot n Knoten m (pl Knoten)

know vb
> Use **wissen** for knowing facts, **kennen** for knowing people and places.

❶ wissen [93] (pres weiß, imperf wusste, perf hat gewusst) ▷ It's a long way. — Yes, I know. Es ist weit. — Ja, ich weiß. ▷ I don't know. Ich weiß nicht. ▷ I don't know what to do. Ich weiß nicht, was ich tun soll. ▷ I don't know how to do it. Ich weiß nicht, wie ich es machen soll. ❷ kennen [39] (imperf kannte, perf hat gekannt) ▷ I know her. Ich kenne sie. ▷ I know Berlin well. Ich kenne Berlin gut.; **I don't know any French.** Ich kann kein Französisch.; **to know that …** wissen [93], dass … ▷ I know that you like chocolate. Ich weiß, dass du Schokolade magst. ▷ I didn't know that your dad was a police officer. Ich wusste nicht, dass dein Vater Polizist ist.; **to know about something (1)** *(be aware of)* von etwas wissen [**93**] ▷ *Do you know about the meeting this afternoon?* Weißt du von dem Treffen heute Nachmittag? **(2)** *(be knowledgeable about)* sich mit etwas auskennen [**39**] ▷ *He knows a lot about cars.* Er kennt sich mit Autos aus. ▷ *I don't know much about computers.* Mit Computern kenne ich mich nicht besonders aus.; **to get to know somebody** jemanden kennenlernen [**4**]; **How should I know?** *(I don't know!)* Wie soll ich das wissen?; **You never know!** Man kann nie wissen!

knowledge *n* ❶ *(general knowledge)* Wissen *nt* ▷ *Our knowledge of the universe is limited.* Unser Wissen über das Universum ist begrenzt. ❷ *(things learnt)* Kenntnisse *fpl* ▷ *my knowledge of German* meine Deutschkenntnisse

known *vb see* **know**

Koran *n* Koran *m*

Korea *n* Korea *nt*; **from Korea** aus Korea; **to Korea** nach Korea

kosher *adj* koscher

lab *n* (= *laboratory*) Labor *nt* (*pl* Labors); **a lab technician** ein Laborant *m*

label *n* ❶ *(sticker)* Aufkleber *m* (*pl* Aufkleber) ❷ *(on clothes)* Etikett *nt* (*pl* Etiketts) ❸ *(for luggage)* Anhänger *m* (*pl* Anhänger)

laboratory *n* Labor *nt* (*pl* Labors)

labor union *n* (*US*) Gewerkschaft *f*

lace *n* ❶ *(of shoe)* Schnürsenkel *m* (*pl* Schnürsenkel) ❷ Spitze *f* ▷ *a lace collar* ein Spitzenkragen

lad *n* Junge *m* (*gen* Jungen, *pl* Jungen)

ladder *n* ❶ Leiter *f* ❷ *(in tights)* Laufmasche *f*

lady *n* Dame *f* ▷ *a young lady* eine junge Dame; **Ladies and gentlemen ...** Meine Damen und Herren ...; **the ladies'** die Damentoilette

ladybird *n* Marienkäfer *m* (*pl* Marienkäfer)

laid *vb see* **lay**

laid-back *adj* locker

lain *vb see* **lie**

lake *n* See *m* (*pl* Seen); **Lake Geneva** der Genfer See; **Lake Constance** der Bodensee

ENGLISH > GERMAN | **laugh**

lamb n Lamm nt (pl Lämmer); **a lamb chop** ein Lammkotelett nt

lamp n Lampe f

lamppost n Laternenpfahl m (pl Laternenpfähle)

lampshade n Lampenschirm m

land n Land nt (pl Länder) ▷ *a piece of land* ein Stück Land
▶ vb (plane, passenger) landen [54] (perf ist gelandet)

landing n ❶ (of plane) Landung f ❷ (of staircase) Treppenabsatz m (gen Treppenabsatzes, pl Treppenabsätze)

landlady n Vermieterin f

landlord n Vermieter m (pl Vermieter)

landscape n Landschaft f

lane n ❶ (in country) Sträßchen nt (pl Sträßchen) ❷ (on motorway) Spur f

language n Sprache f ▷ *a difficult language* eine schwierige Sprache; **to use bad language** Kraftausdrücke benutzen [36]

language laboratory n Sprachlabor nt (pl Sprachlabors)

lap n (sport) Runde f ▷ *I ran ten laps.* Ich bin zehn Runden gelaufen.; **on my lap** auf meinem Schoß

laptop n (computer) Laptop m (pl Laptops)

large adj groß ▷ *a large house* ein großes Haus ▷ *a large dog* ein großer Hund

laser n Laser m (pl Laser)

last adj, adv ❶ letzte ▷ *one last time* ein letztes Mal ▷ *the last question* die letzte Frage ▷ *last Friday* letzten Freitag ▷ *last week* letzte Woche ❷ **als Letzte** ▷ *He arrived last.* Er kam als Letzter an. ❸ zuletzt ▷ *I've lost my bag.* — *When did you see it last?* Ich habe meine Tasche verloren. — Wann hast du sie zuletzt gesehen?; **When I last saw him, he was okay.** Als ich ihn das letzte Mal sah, war er in Ordnung.; **the last time I saw her** das letzte Mal als ich sie das letzte Mal sah ▷ *That's the last time I take your advice!* Das ist das letzte Mal, dass ich auf deinen Rat höre!; **last night (1)** (evening) gestern Abend ▷ *I got home at midnight last night.* Ich bin gestern Abend um Mitternacht nach Hause gekommen. **(2)** (sleeping hours) heute Nacht ▷ *I couldn't sleep last night.* Ich konnte heute Nacht nicht schlafen.; **at last** endlich
▶ vb dauern [88] ▷ *The concert lasts two hours.* Das Konzert dauert zwei Stunden.

lastly adv schließlich ▷ *Lastly I'd like to mention that ...* Und schließlich möchte ich erwähnen, dass ...

late adj, adv ❶ zu spät ▷ *Hurry up or you'll be late!* Beeil dich, du kommst sonst zu spät! ▷ *I'm often late for school.* Ich komme oft zu spät zur Schule.; **to arrive late** zu spät kommen [40] ❷ spät ▷ *I went to bed late.* Ich bin spät ins Bett gegangen. ▷ *in the late afternoon* am späten Nachmittag; **in late May** Ende Mai

lately adv in letzter Zeit ▷ *I haven't seen him lately.* Ich habe ihn in letzter Zeit nicht gesehen.

later adv später ▷ *I'll do it later.* Ich mache es später.; **See you later!** Bis später!

latest adj neueste ▷ *the latest news* die neuesten Nachrichten ▷ *their latest album* ihr neuestes Album; **at the latest** spätestens

Latin n Latein nt ▷ *I do Latin.* Ich lerne Latein.

Latin America n Lateinamerika nt; **from Latin America** aus Lateinamerika; **to Latin America** nach Lateinamerika

Latin American adj lateinamerikanisch

laugh n Lachen nt; **It was a good laugh.** (it was fun) Es war lustig.
▶ vb lachen [48]; **to laugh at something** über etwas lachen [48];

to laugh at somebody jemanden auslachen [4]

launch vb ❶ (product) **auf den Markt bringen** [13] (imperf brachte, perf hat gebracht) ❷ (rocket) **abschießen** (imperf schoss ab, perf hat abgeschossen)

Launderette® n Waschsalon m (pl Waschsalons)

Laundromat® n (US) Waschsalon m (pl Waschsalons)

laundry n (clothes) Wäsche f

lavatory n Toilette f

lavender n Lavendel m

law n ❶ Gesetz nt (gen Gesetzes, pl Gesetze) ▷ It's against the law. Das ist gegen das Gesetz. ❷ (subject) Jura ▷ She's studying law. Sie studiert Jura.

lawn n Rasen m (pl Rasen)

lawnmower n Rasenmäher m (pl Rasenmäher)

lawyer n Rechtsanwalt m (pl Rechtsanwälte), Rechtsanwältin f ▷ My mother's a lawyer. Meine Mutter ist Rechtsanwältin.

lay vb

▪ 'lay' is also a form of 'lie (2)' **verb**

legen [38] ▷ She laid the baby in her cot. Sie legte das Baby ins Bettchen.; **to lay the table** den Tisch decken [38]; **to lay something on** (1) (provide) etwas bereitstellen [15] ▷ They laid on extra buses. Sie stellten zusätzliche Busse bereit. (2) (prepare) etwas vorbereiten [2] ▷ They had laid on a special meal. Sie hatten ein besonderes Essen vorbereitet.; **to lay off** entlassen [42] ▷ My father's been laid off. Mein Vater ist entlassen worden.

lay-by n Rastplatz m (gen Rastplatzes, pl Rastplätze)

layer n Schicht f

layout n (of house, garden) Design nt (pl Designs)

lazy adj faul

lb. abbr (= pound) Pfund

lead (1) n ❶ (cable) Kabel nt (pl Kabel) ❷ (for dog) Hundeleine f; **to be in the lead** in Führung sein [65]

lead (2) n (metal) Blei nt

lead vb führen [38] ▷ the street that leads to the station die Straße, die zum Bahnhof führt; **to lead the way** vorangehen [29]; **to lead somebody away** jemanden abführen [4]

leader n ❶ (of expedition, gang) Führer m (pl Führer), Führerin f ❷ (of political party) Anführer m (pl Anführer), Anführerin f

lead singer n Leadsinger m (pl Leadsinger), Leadsingerin f

leaf n Blatt nt (pl Blätter)

leaflet n (advertising) Prospekt m (pl Prospekte) ▷ a leaflet about their products einen Prospekt über ihre Produkte

league n Liga f (gen Liga, pl Ligen) ▷ the Premier League die erste Liga
- 'Premier League' is the direct
- equivalent of the German **Bundesliga**.

They are at the top of the league. Sie sind Tabellenführer.

leak n undichte Stelle f ▷ a gas leak eine undichte Stelle in der Gasleitung
▶ vb ❶ (pipe) undicht sein [65] (pres ist undicht, imperf war undicht, perf ist undicht gewesen) ❷ (water) auslaufen [43] (pres läuft aus, imperf lief aus, perf ist ausgelaufen) ❸ (gas) austreten [79] (pres tritt aus, imperf trat aus, perf ist ausgetreten)

lean vb sich lehnen [38] ▷ Don't lean over too far. Lehn dich nicht zu weit vor. ▷ She leant out of the window. Sie lehnte sich zum Fenster hinaus.; **to lean forward** sich nach vorn beugen [38]; **to lean on something** sich auf etwas stützen [48]; **to be leaning against something** gegen etwas gelehnt sein [65]; **to lean something against a wall** etwas an einer Mauer anlehnen [4]

ENGLISH > GERMAN

leap vb springen [71] (imperf sprang, perf ist gesprungen) ▷ He leapt out of his chair when his team scored. Er sprang vom Stuhl auf, als seine Mannschaft ein Tor schoss.

leap year n Schaltjahr nt (pl Schaltjahre)

learn vb lernen [38] ▷ I'm learning to ski. Ich lerne Ski fahren.

learner n She's a quick learner. Sie lernt schnell.; **German learners** (people learning German) Deutschschüler mpl

learner driver n Fahrschüler m (pl Fahrschüler), Fahrschülerin f

learnt vb see learn

least adv, adj, pron the least n ❶ (followed by noun) wenigste ▷ the least time die wenigste Zeit ▷ She has the least money. Sie hat das wenigste Geld. ❷ (followed by adjective) am wenigsten ... ▷ the least intelligent pupil der am wenigsten intelligente Schüler ▷ the least attractive person die am wenigsten attraktive Person ▷ the least interesting book das am wenigsten interessante Buch **(3)** (after a verb) am wenigsten ▷ Maths is the subject I like the least. Mathe ist das Fach, das ich am wenigsten mag.; **It's the least I can do.** Das ist das wenigste, was ich tun kann.; **at least (1)** mindestens ▷ It'll cost at least two hundred pounds. Das kostet mindestens zweihundert Pfund. **(2)** wenigstens ▷ ... but at least nobody was hurt. ... aber wenigstens wurde niemand verletzt.; **It's totally unfair – at least, that's my opinion.** Das ist total ungerecht – zumindest meiner Meinung nach.

leather n Leder nt (pl Leder) ▷ a black leather jacket eine schwarze Lederjacke

leave vb ❶ (deliberately) lassen [42] (pres lässt, imperf ließ, perf hat gelassen) ▷ He always leaves his camera in the car. Er lässt immer seinen Fotoapparat im Auto. ❷ (by mistake) vergessen [83] (pres vergisst, imperf vergaß, perf hat vergessen) ▷ I've left my book at home. Ich habe mein Buch zu Hause vergessen.; **Don't leave anything behind.** Lassen Sie nichts liegen. ❸ (bus, train) abfahren [21] (pres fährt ab, imperf fuhr ab, perf ist abgefahren) ▷ The bus leaves at eight. Der Bus fährt um acht ab. ❹ (plane) abfliegen [25] (imperf flog ab, perf ist abgeflogen) ▷ The plane leaves at six. Das Flugzeug fliegt um sechs ab. ❺ (person) weggehen [29] (imperf ging weg, perf ist weggegangen) ▷ She's just left. Sie ist eben weggegangen.; **She left home last year.** Sie ist letztes Jahr von zu Hause weggezogen. ❻ (abandon) verlassen [42] (pres verlässt, imperf verließ, perf hat verlassen) ▷ She left her husband. Sie hat ihren Mann verlassen.; **to leave somebody alone** jemanden in Ruhe lassen [42]; **to leave out** auslassen [42]; **I felt really left out.** Ich fühlte mich richtig ausgeschlossen.
▶ n (from job, army) Urlaub m (pl Urlaube) ▷ a week's leave eine Woche Urlaub

leaves npl see leaf

Lebanon n Libanon m

> Note that the definite article is used in German for countries which are masculine.

from Lebanon aus dem Libanon; **in Lebanon** im Libanon; **to Lebanon** in den Libanon

lecture n ❶ (public) Vortrag m (pl Vorträge) ❷ (at university) Vorlesung f

> Be careful not to translate **lecture** by Lektüre.

▶ vb ❶ unterrichten [2] (perf hat unterrichtet) ▷ She lectures at the technical college. Sie unterrichtet an der Fachschule. ❷ (tell off) belehren [7] (perf hat belehrt) ▷ He's always lecturing us. Er belehrt uns andauernd.

lecturer n Dozent m (gen Dozenten, pl Dozenten), Dozentin f ▷ She's a lecturer. Sie ist Dozentin.

led vb see **lead** vb

leek n Lauch m (pl Lauche)

left vb see **leave**
▶ adj, adv ❶ linke ▷ the left foot der linke Fuß ▷ my left arm mein linker Arm ▷ your left hand deine linke Hand ▷ her left eye ihr linkes Auge ❷ links ▷ Turn left at the traffic lights. Biegen Sie an der Ampel links ab.; **Look left!** Sehen Sie nach links!; **I haven't got any money left.** Ich habe kein Geld mehr.
▶ n linke Seite f; **on the left** links

left-hand adj on the left-hand side die linke Seite; **It's on the left-hand side.** Es liegt links.

left-handed adj linkshändig

left-luggage office n Gepäckaufbewahrung f

leg n Bein nt (pl Beine) ▷ I've broken my leg. Ich habe mir das Bein gebrochen.; **a chicken leg** eine Hähnchenkeule; **a leg of lamb** eine Lammkeule

legal adj legal

leggings npl Leggings pl

leisure n Freizeit f ▷ What do you do in your leisure time? Was machen Sie in Ihrer Freizeit?

leisure centre n Freizeitzentrum nt (pl Freizeitzentren)

lemon n Zitrone f

lemonade n Limonade f

lend vb leihen (imperf lieh, perf hat geliehen) ▷ I can lend you some money. Ich kann dir Geld leihen.

length n Länge f; **It's about a metre in length.** Es ist etwa einen Meter lang.

lens n ❶ (contact lens) Kontaktlinse f ❷ (of spectacles) Glas nt (gen Glases, pl Gläser) ❸ (of camera) Objektiv nt (pl Objektive)

Lent n Fastenzeit f ▷ during Lent während der Fastenzeit

lent vb see **lend**

lentil n Linse f

Leo n Löwe m (gen Löwen) ▷ I'm Leo. Ich bin Löwe.

leotard n Gymnastikanzug m (pl Gymnastikanzüge)

lesbian n Lesbe f (informal) **She's a lesbian.** Sie ist lesbisch.

less pron, adv, adj weniger ▷ A bit less, please. Etwas weniger, bitte. ▷ I've got less time for hobbies now. Ich habe jetzt weniger Zeit für Hobbys.; **He's less intelligent than his brother.** Er ist nicht so intelligent wie sein Bruder.; **less than** weniger als

lesson n ❶ Lektion f ▷ 'Lesson Sixteen' (in textbook) 'Lektion sechzehn' ❷ (class) Stunde f ▷ A lesson lasts forty minutes. Eine Stunde dauert vierzig Minuten.

let vb ❶ (allow) lassen [42] (pres lässt, imperf ließ, perf hat gelassen); **to let somebody do something** jemanden etwas tun lassen [42]; **to let somebody down** jemanden enttäuschen [18]; **to let somebody know** jemandem Bescheid sagen [38]; **to let go** (release) loslassen [42]; **to let in** hineinlassen [42]; **Let's go to the cinema!** Lass uns ins Kino gehen!; **Let's go!** Gehen wir! ❷ (hire out) vermieten [2] (perf hat vermietet); **'to let'** 'zu vermieten'

letter n ❶ Brief m (pl Briefe) ▷ She wrote me a long letter. Sie hat mir einen langen Brief geschrieben. ❷ (of alphabet) Buchstabe m (gen Buchstaben, pl Buchstaben) ▷ the letters of the alphabet die Buchstaben des Alphabets

letterbox n Briefkasten m (pl Briefkästen)

lettuce n Kopfsalat m (pl Kopfsalate)

leukaemia n Leukämie f ▷ He suffers from leukaemia. Er leidet an Leukämie.

level adj eben ▷ A snooker table must be perfectly level. Ein Snookertisch muss ganz eben sein.
▶ n ❶ (of river, lake) Wasserstand m (pl Wasserstände) ▷ The level of the river is rising. Der Wasserstand des Flusses

steigt. ❷ (height) Höhe f ▷ at eye level in Augenhöhe; **A levels** das Abitur
● Germans take their **Abitur** at the age of 19. The students sit examinations in a variety of subjects to attain an overall grade. If you pass, you have the right to apply for a place at university.

level crossing n Bahnübergang m (pl Bahnübergänge)

lever n Hebel m (pl Hebel)

liar n Lügner m (pl Lügner), Lügnerin f

liberal adj (opinions) liberal; **the Liberal Democrats** die Liberaldemokraten

Libra n Waage f ▷ I'm Libra. Ich bin Waage.

librarian n Bibliothekar m (pl Bibliothekare), Bibliothekarin f ▷ She's a librarian. Sie ist Bibliothekarin.

library n ❶ (public lending library) Bücherei f ❷ (of school, university) Bibliothek f

licence n Schein m (pl Scheine); **a driving licence** ein Führerschein m

lick vb lecken [48]

lid n Deckel m (pl Deckel)

lie (1) n Lüge f ▷ That's a lie! Das ist eine Lüge!; **to tell a lie** lügen [47]

lie (1) vb (not tell the truth) lügen [47] (imperf log, perf hat gelogen) ▷ I know she's lying. Ich weiß, dass sie lügt.

lie (2) vb liegen [46] (imperf lag, perf hat gelegen) ▷ He was lying on the sofa. Er lag auf dem Sofa. ▷ When I'm on holiday I lie on the beach all day. In den Ferien liege ich den ganzen Tag am Strand.; **to lie down** sich hinlegen [4]; **to be lying down** liegen [46]

lie-in n **to have a lie-in** ausschlafen [58]

lieutenant n Leutnant m (pl Leutnants)

life n Leben nt (pl Leben)

lifebelt n Rettungsring m (pl Rettungsringe)

lifeboat n Rettungsboot nt (pl Rettungsboote)

lifeguard n ❶ (at beach) Rettungsschwimmer m (pl Rettungsschwimmer), Rettungsschwimmerin f ❷ (at swimming pool) Bademeister m (pl Bademeister), Bademeisterin f

life jacket n Schwimmweste f

lifestyle n Lebensstil m (pl Lebensstile)

lift vb hochheben (imperf hob hoch, perf hat hochgehoben) ▷ I can't lift it. Ich kann es nicht hochheben.
▶ n Aufzug m (pl Aufzüge) ▷ The lift isn't working. Der Aufzug geht nicht.; **He gave me a lift to the cinema.** Er hat mich zum Kino gefahren.; **Would you like a lift?** Wollen Sie mitfahren?

light adj ❶ (not heavy) leicht ▷ a light jacket eine leichte Jacke ▷ a light meal ein leichtes Essen ❷ (colour) hell ▷ a light blue sweater ein hellblauer Pullover
▶ n ❶ Licht nt (pl Lichter) ▷ to switch on the light das Licht anmachen ▷ to switch off the light das Licht ausmachen ❷ Lampe f ▷ There's a light by my bed. Ich habe am Bett eine Lampe.; **the traffic lights** die Ampel sg; **Have you got a light?** (for cigarette) Haben Sie Feuer?
▶ vb (candle, cigarette, fire) anzünden [54] (perf hat angezündet)

light bulb n Glühbirne f

lighter n (for cigarettes) Feuerzeug nt (pl Feuerzeuge)

lighthouse n Leuchtturm m (pl Leuchttürme)

lightning n Blitz m (gen Blitzes, pl Blitze); **a flash of lightning** ein Blitz; **There was a flash of lightning.** Es hat geblitzt.

like vb mögen [50] (pres mag, imperf mochte, perf hat gemocht) ▷ I don't like mustard. Ich mag Senf nicht. ▷ I like Paul, but I don't want to go out with him. Ich mag Paul, aber ich will nicht mit ihm ausgehen.; **I like riding.** Ich reite gern.; **Would you like ...?** Möchtest du ...?;

I'd like ... Ich hätte gern ...; **I'd like to ...** Ich würde gern ...; **... if you like** ... wenn du möchtest
▶ prep ❶ (this way) so ▷ *It's fine like that.* So ist es gut. ▷ *Do it like this.* Mach das so. ❷ (similar to) wie ▷ *a city like Munich* eine Stadt wie München ▷ *It's a bit like salmon.* Es ist ein bisschen wie Lachs..; **What's the weather like?** Wie ist das Wetter?; **to look like somebody** jemandem ähnlich sehen [64]

likely adj wahrscheinlich ▷ *That's not very likely.* Das ist nicht sehr wahrscheinlich.; **She's likely to come.** Sie kommt wahrscheinlich.; **She's not likely to come.** Sie kommt wahrscheinlich nicht.

Lilo® n Luftmatratze f

lime n (fruit) Limone f

limit n Grenze f; **the speed limit** die Geschwindigkeitsbegrenzung

limp vb hinken [38]

line n ❶ Linie f ▷ *a straight line* eine gerade Linie ❷ (to divide, cancel) Strich m (pl Striche) ▷ *Draw a line under each answer.* Machen Sie unter jede Antwort einen Strich. ❸ (railway track) Gleis nt (gen Gleises, pl Gleise) ❹ Schlange f ▷ *to stand in line* Schlange stehen; **Hold the line, please.** (on telephone) Bleiben Sie bitte am Apparat.; **It's a very bad line.** (on telephone) Die Verbindung ist sehr schlecht.

linen n Leinen nt ▷ *a linen jacket* eine Leinenjacke

lining n (of clothes) Futter nt (pl Futter)

link n ❶ Zusammenhang m (pl Zusammenhänge) ▷ *the link between smoking and cancer* der Zusammenhang zwischen Rauchen und Krebs ❷ (computer) Link m (pl Links)
▶ vb verbinden (imperf verband, perf hat verbunden)

lion n Löwe m (gen Löwen, pl Löwen)

lip n Lippe f

lip-read vb von den Lippen ablesen [4] (pres liest von den Lippen ab, imperf las von den Lippen ab, perf hat von den Lippen abgelesen); **I'm learning to lip-read.** Ich lerne gerade Lippenlesen.

lipstick n Lippenstift m (pl Lippenstifte)

liquid n Flüssigkeit f

liquidizer n Mixer m (pl Mixer)

list n Liste f
▶ vb aufzählen [4] (perf hat aufgezählt) ▷ *List your hobbies.* Zählen Sie Ihre Hobbys auf.

listen vb zuhören [4] (perf hat zugehört) ▷ *Listen to me!* Hör mir zu!; **Listen to this!** Hör dir das an!

lit vb see **light**

liter n (US) Liter m (pl Liter)

literature n Literatur f ▷ *I'm studying English Literature.* Ich studiere englische Literatur.

litre n Liter m (pl Liter) ▷ *three litres* drei Liter

litter n Abfall m (pl Abfälle)

litter bin n Abfallkorb m (pl Abfallkörbe)

little adj klein ▷ *a little girl* ein kleines Mädchen; **a little** ein bisschen; **very little** sehr wenig; **little by little** nach und nach

live adj ❶ (animal) lebendig ❷ (broadcast) live; **There's live music on Fridays.** Freitags gibt es Livemusik.
▶ vb ❶ leben [38] ▷ *I live with my grandmother.* Ich lebe bei meiner Großmutter. ▷ *They're living together.* Sie leben zusammen.; **to live on something** von etwas leben [38] ❷ (in house, town) wohnen [38] ▷ *Where do you live?* Wo wohnst du? ▷ *I live in Edinburgh.* Ich wohne in Edinburgh.

lively adj lebhaft ▷ *She's got a lively personality.* Sie ist ein lebhafter Typ.

liver n Leber f; **liver sausage** die Leberwurst

livestream n Livestream m (pl Livestreams)
▶ vb livestreamen [76]

ENGLISH > GERMAN

lives npl see **life**

living n **to make a living** sich seinen Lebensunterhalt verdienen [**84**]; **What does she do for a living?** Was macht sie beruflich?

living room n Wohnzimmer nt (pl Wohnzimmer)

lizard n Echse f

load n **loads of** eine Menge; **You're talking a load of rubbish!** Du redest vielleicht einen Unsinn!
▶ vb beladen (pres belädt, imperf belud, perf hat beladen) ▷ He's loading the van right now. Er belädt gerade den Lieferwagen.

loaf n Laib m (pl Laibe); **a loaf of bread** ein Brot nt

loan n (money) Darlehen nt (pl Darlehen)
▶ vb ausleihen (imperf lieh aus, perf hat ausgeliehen)

loaves npl see **loaf**

lobster n Hummer m (pl Hummer)

local adj örtlich ▷ the local police die örtliche Polizei; **the local paper** das Lokalblatt; **a local call** ein Ortsgespräch nt

loch n See m (pl Seen)

lock n Schloss nt (gen Schlosses, pl Schlösser) ▷ The lock is broken. Das Schloss ist kaputt.
▶ vb abschließen (imperf schloss ab, perf hat abgeschlossen) ▷ Make sure you lock your door. Schließen Sie die Tür ab.; **to be locked out** ausgesperrt sein [**65**]

locker n Schließfach nt (pl Schließfächer); **the locker room** der Umkleideraum; **the left-luggage lockers** die Gepäckschließfächer

lodger n Untermieter m (pl Untermieter), Untermieterin f

loft n Speicher m (pl Speicher)

log n (of wood) Scheit nt (pl Scheite)

log in vb (computer) einloggen [**4**] (perf hat eingeloggt)

log off vb (computer) ausloggen [**4**] (perf hat ausgeloggt)

397 | look

log on vb (computer) einloggen [**4**] (perf hat eingeloggt)

log out vb (computer) ausloggen [**4**] (perf hat ausgeloggt)

logical adj logisch

lollipop n Lutscher m (pl Lutscher)

London n London nt; **from London** aus London; **to London** nach London

Londoner n Londoner m (pl Londoner), Londonerin f

loneliness n Einsamkeit f

lonely adj einsam; **to feel lonely** sich einsam fühlen [**38**]

long adj, adv lang ▷ She's got long hair. Sie hat lange Haare. ▷ The room is six metres long. Das Zimmer ist sechs Meter lang.; **how long?** (time) wie lange?

> When you want to say how long you 'have been' doing something, use the present tense in German.

▷ How long have you been here? Wie lange bist du schon da?; **It takes a long time.** Das dauert lange.; **as long as** solange
▶ vb **to long to do something** es kaum erwarten können [**41**], etwas zu tun

longer adv **They're no longer going out together.** Sie gehen nicht mehr miteinander.; **I can't stand it any longer.** Ich halte das nicht länger aus.

long jump n Weitsprung m (pl Weitsprünge)

loo n (informal) Klo nt (pl Klos) ▷ Where's the loo? Wo ist das Klo?; **I need the loo.** (informal) Ich muss mal.

look n **to have a look** ansehen [**64**]; **I don't like the look of it.** Das gefällt mir nicht.
▶ vb sehen ⓘ (pres sieht, imperf sah, perf hat gesehen); **Look!** Sieh mal!; **to look at something** etwas ansehen [**64**] ⓘ (seem) aussehen [**64**] (perf hat ausgesehen) ▷ She looks surprised. Sie sieht überrascht aus. ▷ That cake looks nice. Der Kuchen sieht gut aus. ▷ It looks fine. Es sieht gut aus.; **to look like**

somebody jemandem ähnlich sehen [64]; **What does she look like?** Wie sieht sie aus?; **Look out!** Pass auf!; **to look after** sich kümmern [34] um; **to look for** suchen [48]; **to look forward to something** sich auf etwas freuen [38]; **Looking forward to hearing from you ...** In der Hoffnung, bald etwas von dir zu hören, ...; **to look round** sich umsehen [64]; **to look round a museum** ein Museum ansehen [64]; **to look up** (word, name) nachschlagen [59]

loose adj (clothes) weit; **loose change** das Kleingeld

lord n (feudal) Lord m (pl Lords); **the House of Lords** das Oberhaus; **the Lord** (god) Gott; **Good Lord!** Großer Gott!

lorry n Lastwagen m (pl Lastwagen)

lorry driver n Lastwagenfahrer m (pl Lastwagenfahrer), Lastwagenfahrerin f ▷ He's a lorry driver. Er ist Lastwagenfahrer.

lose vb verlieren [85] (imperf verlor, perf hat verloren) ▷ I've lost my purse. Ich habe meinen Geldbeutel verloren.; **to get lost** sich verlaufen [43]

loss n Verlust m (pl Verluste)

lost vb see **lose**
▶ adj verloren

lost-and-found n (US) Fundbüro nt (pl Fundbüros)

lost property office n Fundbüro nt (pl Fundbüros)

lot n **a lot** viel; **a lot of (1)** viel ▷ He earns a lot of money. Er verdient viel Geld. **(2)** viele ▷ We saw a lot of interesting things. Wir haben viele interessante Dinge gesehen.; **lots of** eine Menge ▷ lots of money eine Menge Geld ▷ lots of friends eine Menge Freunde; **What did you do at the weekend? — Not a lot.** Was hast du am Wochenende gemacht? — Nicht viel.; **Do you like football? —** Not a lot. Magst du Fußball? — Nicht besonders.; **That's the lot.** Das ist alles.

lottery n Lotto nt; **to win the lottery** im Lotto gewinnen [30]

loud adj laut ▷ The television is too loud. Der Fernseher ist zu laut.

loudly adv laut

loudspeaker n Lautsprecher m (pl Lautsprecher)

lounge n Wohnzimmer nt (pl Wohnzimmer)

love n Liebe f; **to be in love** verliebt sein [65]; **to make love** sich lieben [38]; **Give Heike my love.** Grüß Heike von mir.; **Love, Rosemary.** Alles Liebe, Rosemary.
▶ vb ❶ (person, thing) lieben [38] ▷ I love you. Ich liebe dich. ▷ I love chocolate. Ich liebe Schokolade. ❷ (like a lot) mögen [50] (pres mag, imperf mochte, perf hat gemocht) ▷ Everybody loves her. Alle mögen sie.; **I'd love to come.** Ich würde liebend gern kommen.; **I love skiing.** Ich fahre unheimlich gern Ski.

lovely adj wunderbar ▷ What a lovely surprise! Was für eine wunderbare Überraschung! ❷ (pretty) schön ▷ They've got a lovely house. Sie haben ein schönes Haus.; **It's a lovely day.** Es ist ein herrlicher Tag.; **She's a lovely person.** Sie ist ein sehr netter Mensch.; **Is your meal OK? — Yes, it's lovely.** Schmeckt dein Essen? — Ja, prima.; **Have a lovely time!** Viel Spaß!

lover n Liebhaber m (pl Liebhaber), Liebhaberin f

low adj, adv niedrig ▷ low prices niedrige Preise; **That plane is flying very low.** Das Flugzeug fliegt sehr tief.; **the low season** die Nebensaison

lower sixth n zwölfte Klasse f ▷ He's in the lower sixth. Er ist in der zwölften Klasse.

loyalty n Treue f

loyalty card n Kundenkarte f

luck n Glück nt ▷ *She hasn't had much luck.* Sie hat nicht viel Glück gehabt.; **Good luck!** Viel Glück!; **Bad luck!** So ein Pech!

luckily adv zum Glück

lucky adj **to be lucky (1)** *(be fortunate)* Glück haben [**32**] ▷ *He's lucky, he's got a job.* Er hat Glück, er hat Arbeit. **(2)** *(bring luck)* Glück bringen [**13**] ▷ *Black cats are lucky.* Schwarze Katzen bringen Glück.; **He wasn't hurt. — That was lucky!** Er wurde nicht verletzt. — Das war Glück!; **a lucky horseshoe** ein Glückshufeisen nt

luggage n Gepäck nt

lump n ❶ Stück nt (pl Stücke) ▷ *a lump of coal* ein Stück Kohle ❷ *(swelling)* Beule f ▷ *He's got a lump on his forehead.* Er hat eine Beule an der Stirn.

lunch n Mittagessen nt (pl Mittagessen); **to have lunch** zu Mittag essen [**20**]

lung n Lunge f ▷ **lung cancer** der Lungenkrebs

Luxembourg n *(country, city)* Luxemburg nt; **from Luxembourg** aus Luxemburg; **to Luxembourg** nach Luxemburg

luxurious adj luxuriös

luxury n Luxus m *(gen Luxus)* ▷ *It was luxury!* Das war wirklich ein Luxus!; **a luxury hotel** ein Luxushotel nt

lying vb *see* lie

lyrics npl *(of song)* Text msg (pl Texte)

m

macaroni nsg Makkaroni pl

machine n Maschine f

machine gun n Maschinengewehr nt

machinery n Maschinen fpl

mad adj ❶ *(insane)* verrückt ▷ *You're mad!* Du bist verrückt!; **to be mad about** verrückt sein [**65**] nach ❷ *(angry)* wütend ▷ *She'll be mad when she finds out.* Wenn sie das erfährt, wird sie wütend sein.; **to be mad at somebody** wütend auf jemanden sein [**65**]

madam n
> In German no form of address is normally used apart from **Sie**.
▷ *Would you like to order, Madam?* Möchten Sie bestellen?

made vb *see* make

madness n Wahnsinn m ▷ *It's absolute madness.* Das ist totaler Wahnsinn.

magazine n Zeitschrift f

maggot n Made f

magic adj ❶ *(magical)* magisch ▷ *magic powers* magische Kräfte; **a magic trick** ein Zaubertrick m; **a magic wand** ein

Zauberstab m ❷ *(brilliant)* echt toll ▷ *It was magic!* Es war toll!
▶ n Zaubern nt ▷ *My hobby is magic.* Zaubern ist mein Hobby.

magician n *(conjurer)* Zauberkünstler m *(pl* Zauberkünstler*)*, Zauberkünstlerin f

magnet n Magnet m

magnifying glass n Lupe f

maid n *(servant)* Hausangestellte f *(gen* Hausangestellten*)*

maiden name n Mädchenname m *(gen* Mädchennamens, *pl* Mädchennamen*)*

mail n ❶ Post f ▷ *Here's your mail.* Hier ist deine Post.; **by mail** per Post
❷ *(electronic mail)* E-Mail f *(pl* E-Mails*)*

mailbox n *(US)* Briefkasten m *(pl* Briefkästen*)*

mailman n *(US)* Briefträger m *(pl* Briefträger*)*

main adj **the main problem** das Hauptproblem; **the main thing** die Hauptsache

mainly adv hauptsächlich

main road n Hauptstraße f ▷ *I don't like cycling on main roads.* Ich fahre nicht gern auf Hauptstraßen Rad.

majesty n Majestät f; **Your Majesty** Eure Majestät

major adj groß ▷ *a major problem* ein großes Problem; **in C major** C-Dur

Majorca n Mallorca f; **to Majorca** nach Mallorca

majority n Mehrheit f

make n Marke f ▷ *What make is that car?* Welche Marke ist das Auto?
▶ vb ❶ machen [48] ▷ *He made it himself.* Er hat es selbst gemacht. ▷ *I make my bed every morning.* Ich mache jeden Morgen mein Bett. ▷ *Two and two make four.* Zwei und zwei macht vier.; **to make lunch** das Mittagessen machen [48]; **I'm going to make a cake.** Ich werde einen Kuchen backen.
❷ *(manufacture)* herstellen [4] *(perf* hat hergestellt*)* ▷ *made in Germany* in Deutschland hergestellt ❸ *(earn)* verdienen [84] *(perf* hat verdient*)* ▷ *He makes a lot of money.* Er verdient viel Geld.; **to make somebody do something** jemanden zwingen [97], etwas zu tun; **to make a phone call** telefonieren [76]; **to make fun of somebody** sich über jemanden lustig machen [48]; **What time do you make it?** Wie viel Uhr hast du?

make out vb ❶ entziffern [34] *(perf* hat entziffert*)* ❷ verstehen [72] *(imperf* verstand, *perf* hat verstanden*)*
❸ behaupten [2] *(perf* hat behauptet*)*

make up vb ❶ *(invent)* erfinden [24] *(imperf* erfand, *perf* hat erfunden*)*
❷ *(after argument)* sich versöhnen [84] *(perf* hat sich versöhnt*)*

make-up n Make-up nt *(pl* Make-ups*)*

Malaysia n Malaysia nt; **to Malaysia** nach Malaysia

male adj männlich ▷ *a male kitten* ein männliches Katzenjunges ▷ *Sex: male* Geschlecht: männlich

> In many cases, the ending in German indicates clearly whether the noun refers to a man or a woman and there is therefore no need for the word 'male'.

▷ *male and female students* Studenten und Studentinnen; **a male chauvinist** ein Macho m; **a male nurse** ein Krankenpfleger m

mall n Einkaufszentrum nt *(pl* Einkaufszentren*)*

Malta n Malta nt; **from Malta** aus Malta; **to Malta** nach Malta

man n Mann m *(pl* Männer*)* ▷ *an old man* ein alter Mann

manage vb ❶ *(be in charge of)* leiten [2] ▷ *She manages a big store.* Sie leitet ein großes Geschäft. ❷ *(band, football team)* managen [48] ▷ *He manages the team.* Er managt die Mannschaft. ❸ *(get by)* klarkommen [40] *(imperf* kam klar, *perf* ist klargekommen? ▷ *We haven't got much money, but we manage.* Wir haben nicht viel Geld, aber wir kommen klar. ▷ *It's okay, I can manage.* Das ist okay, ich komme klar. ❹ *Can you manage okay?* Schaffst du es? ▷ *I can't manage all that. (food)* Das schaffe ich nicht alles.; **to manage to do something** es schaffen [48], etwas zu tun

management n *(organization)* Leitung f ▷ *the management of the company* die Leitung des Unternehmens ▷ *'under new management'* "unter neuer Leitung"

manager n ❶ *(of company, shop, restaurant)* Geschäftsführer m *(pl* Geschäftsführer), Geschäftsführerin f ❷ *(of performer, football team)* Manager m *(pl* Manager), Managerin f

manageress n Geschäftsführerin f

mandarin n *(fruit)* Mandarine f

mango n Mango f *(pl* Mangos)

mania n Manie f

maniac n Verrückte m *(gen* Verrückten, *pl* Verrückten), Verrückte f *(gen* Verrückten) ▷ *He drives like a maniac.* Er fährt wie ein Verrückter.

mankind n Menschheit f

manner n Art und Weise f ▷ *in this manner* auf diese Art und Weise; **She behaves in an odd manner.** Sie benimmt sich eigenartig.; **He has a confident manner.** Er wirkt selbstsicher.

manners npl Benehmen nt sg ▷ *good manners* gutes Benehmen; **Her manners are appalling.** Sie benimmt sich schrecklich.; **It's bad manners to speak with your mouth full.** Es gehört sich nicht, mit vollem Mund zu sprechen.

mansion n Villa f *(pl* Villen)

mantelpiece n Kaminsims m *(gen* Kaminsimses, *pl* Kaminsimse)

manual n Handbuch nt *(pl* Handbücher)

manufacture vb herstellen [4] *(perf* hat hergestellt)

manufacturer n Hersteller m *(pl* Hersteller)

many adj, pron viele ▷ *The film has many special effects.* In dem Film gibt es viele Spezialeffekte. ▷ *He hasn't got many friends.* Er hat nicht viele Freunde. ▷ *Were there many people at the concert?* Waren viele Leute in dem Konzert?; **very many** sehr viele; **Not many.** Nicht viele.; **How many?** Wie viele?; **How many euros do you get for one pound?** Wie viel Euro bekommt man für ein Pfund?; **too many** zu viele; **so many** so viele

map n ❶ *(of country, area)* Landkarte f ❷ *(of town)* Stadtplan m *(pl* Stadtpläne) ⚠ Be careful not to translate **map** by **Mappe**.

marathon n Marathonlauf m *(pl* Marathonläufe) ▷ *the London marathon* der Londoner Marathonlauf

marble n Marmor m ▷ *a marble statue* eine Marmorstatue; **to play marbles** Murmeln spielen [38]

March n März m ▷ *in March* im März

march n *(demonstration)* Protestmarsch m *(gen* Protestmarsches, *pl* Protestmärsche)
▶ vb ❶ *(soldiers)* marschieren [76] *(perf* ist marschiert) ❷ *(protesters)* aufmarschieren [76] *(perf* ist aufmarschiert)

mare n Stute f

margarine n Margarine f

margin n Rand m *(pl* Ränder) ▷ *I wrote notes in the margin.* Ich schrieb Notizen an den Rand.

marijuana n Marihuana nt

mark n ❶ *(in school)* Note f ▷ *I get good marks for German.* Ich habe in Deutsch gute Noten. ❷ *(stain)* Fleck m *(pl* Flecken) ▷ *You've got a mark on your shirt.* Du hast einen Fleck auf dem Hemd.

market | 402   **ENGLISH > GERMAN**

❸ (old German currency) Mark f (pl Mark)
▶ vb korrigieren [**76**] (perf hat korrigiert)
▷ The teacher hasn't marked my homework yet. Der Lehrer hat meine Hausaufgaben noch nicht korrigiert.

market n Markt m (pl Märkte)

marketing n Marketing nt (gen Marketing)

marmalade n Orangenmarmelade f

marriage n Ehe f

married adj verheiratet ▷ They are not married. Sie sind nicht verheiratet. ▷ They have been married for fifteen years. Sie sind seit fünfzehn Jahren verheiratet.; **a married couple** ein Ehepaar nt

marry vb heiraten [**2**] ▷ He wants to marry her. Er will sie heiraten.; **to get married** heiraten [**2**]

marvellous adj wunderbar ▷ She's a marvellous cook. Sie ist eine wunderbare Köchin. ▷ The weather was marvellous. Das Wetter war wunderbar.

marzipan n Marzipan nt (pl Marzipane)

mascara n Wimperntusche f

masculine adj männlich

mashed potatoes npl Kartoffelbrei m ▷ sausages and mashed potatoes Würstchen mit Kartoffelbrei

mask n Maske f

mass n ❶ Haufen m (pl Haufen) ▷ a mass of books and papers ein Haufen Bücher und Papiere ❷ (in church) Messe f ▷ We go to mass on Sunday. Wir gehen am Sonntag zur Messe.; **the mass media** die Massenmedien

massage n Massage f

massive adj enorm

master vb beherrschen [**7**] (perf hat beherrscht) ▷ to master a language eine Sprache beherrschen

masterpiece n Meisterstück nt (pl Meisterstücke)

mat n (doormat) Vorleger m (pl Vorleger); **a table mat** ein Untersetzer m; **a place mat** ein Set nt

match n ❶ Streichholz nt (gen Streichholzes, pl Streichhölzer) ▷ a box of matches eine Schachtel Streichhölzer ❷ (sport) Spiel nt (pl Spiele) ▷ a football match ein Fußballspiel
▶ vb passen [**31**] zu ▷ The jacket matches the trousers. Die Jacke passt zu der Hose. ▷ These colours don't match. Diese Farben passen nicht zueinander.

mate n (informal) Kumpel m (pl Kumpel)
   der Kumpel is also used for women.
▷ On Friday night I go out with my mates. Freitag Abend gehe ich mit meinen Kumpels aus.

material n ❶ (cloth) Stoff m (pl Stoffe) ❷ (information, ideas) Material nt (pl Materialien) ▷ I'm collecting material for my project. Ich sammle Material für mein Referat.; **raw materials** die Rohstoffe

mathematics nsg Mathematik f

maths nsg Mathe f

matter n Angelegenheit f ▷ It's a serious matter. Das ist eine ernste Angelegenheit.; **It's a matter of life and death.** Es geht um Leben und Tod.; **What's the matter?** Was ist los?; **as a matter of fact** tatsächlich
▶ vb **it doesn't matter (1)** (I don't mind) das macht nichts ▷ I can't give you the money today. — It doesn't matter. Ich kann dir das Geld heute nicht geben. — Das macht nichts. **(2)** (makes no difference) das ist egal ▷ Shall I phone today or tomorrow? — Whenever, it doesn't matter. Soll ich heute oder morgen anrufen? — Wann du willst, das ist egal.; **It matters a lot to me.** Das ist mir sehr wichtig.

mattress n Matratze f

mature adj reif ▷ She's very mature for her age. Sie ist sehr reif für ihr Alter.

maximum n Maximum nt (pl Maxima)
▶ adj **the maximum speed** die Höchstgeschwindigkeit; **the**

maximum amount der Höchstbetrag
May n Mai m ▷ in May im Mai; **May Day** der Erste Mai
may vb **He may come.** Er kommt vielleicht. ▷ **It may rain.** Es regnet vielleicht.; **Are you going to the party? — I don't know, I may.** Gehst du zur Party? – Ich weiß nicht, vielleicht.; **May I smoke?** Darf ich rauchen?
maybe adv vielleicht ▷ maybe not vielleicht nicht ▷ a bit boring, maybe vielleicht etwas langweilig ▷ Maybe she's at home. Vielleicht ist sie zu Hause. ▷ Maybe he'll change his mind. Vielleicht überlegt er es sich anders.
mayonnaise n Mayonnaise f
mayor n Bürgermeister m (pl Bürgermeister), Bürgermeisterin f
me pron mich ▷ Can you hear me? Kannst du mich hören? ▷ Look at me! Sieh mich an!

 Use **mich** after prepositions which take the accusative.

▷ Is this present for me? Ist das Geschenk für mich? ▷ Wait for me! Warte auf mich! ❷ mir

 Use **mir** after prepositions which take the dative.

▷ Will you come with me? Kommst du mit mir mit? ▷ He sat next to me. Er saß neben mir.

 Use **mir** when 'me' means 'to me'.

▷ Give me the book, please! Gib mir bitte das Buch! ▷ She told me the truth. Sie hat mir die Wahrheit erzählt. ❸ ich ▷ It's me! Ich bin's! ▷ Me too! Ich auch! ▷ She's older than me. Sie ist älter als ich.
meal n Essen nt (pl Essen)
mean vb ❶ (signify) bedeuten [2] (perf hat bedeutet) ▷ What does 'besetzt' mean? Was bedeutet 'besetzt'? ▷ I don't know what it means. Ich weiß nicht, was es bedeutet. ❷ (mean to say) meinen [38] ▷ What do you mean? Was meinst du damit? ▷ That's not what I meant. Das

habe ich nicht gemeint. ▷ **Which one do you mean?** Welchen meinst du? ▷ **Do you really mean it?** Meinst du das wirklich?; **to mean to do something** etwas tun wollen **[94]**
▶ adj ❶ (with money) geizig ▷ He's too mean to buy Christmas presents. Er ist zu geizig, um Weihnachtsgeschenke zu kaufen. ❷ (unkind) gemein ▷ You're being mean to me. Du bist gemein zu mir. ▷ That's a really mean thing to say! Das ist gemein, so etwas zu sagen!
meaning n Bedeutung f

 Be careful not to translate **meaning** by Meinung.

meant vb see **mean**
meanwhile adv inzwischen
measles nsg Masern pl ▷ She's got measles. Sie hat Masern.
measure vb ❶ ausmessen (pres misst aus, imperf maß aus, perf hat ausgemessen) ▷ I measured the page. Ich habe die Seite ausgemessen. ❷ messen ▷ The room measures three metres by four. Das Zimmer misst drei auf vier Meter.
measurement n (of object) Maß nt (pl Maße) ▷ What are the measurements of the room? Wie sind die Maße des Zimmers? ▷ What are your measurements? Was sind Ihre Maße?; **my waist measurement** meine Taillenweite; **What's your neck measurement?** Welche Kragenweite haben Sie?
meat n Fleisch nt ▷ I don't eat meat. Ich esse kein Fleisch.
Mecca n Mekka nt
mechanic n Mechaniker m (pl Mechaniker), Mechanikerin f ▷ He's a mechanic. Er ist Mechaniker.
medal n Medaille f; **the gold medal** die Goldmedaille
media npl Medien ntpl
medical adj medizinisch ▷ medical treatment die medizinische Behandlung;

medical insurance die Krankenversicherung; **to have medical problems** gesundheitliche Probleme haben [**32**]; **She's a medical student.** Sie ist Medizinstudentin. ▶ *n* **to have a medical** sich ärztlich untersuchen lassen [**42**]

medicine *n* Medizin *f* ▷ *I want to study medicine.* Ich möchte Medizin studieren. ▷ *I need some medicine.* Ich brauche Medizin.; **alternative medicine** die alternative Medizin

Mediterranean *adj* (person, character, scenery) südländisch

Mediterranean *n* **the Mediterranean** das Mittelmeer

medium *adj* mittlere ▷ *a man of medium height* ein Mann von mittlerer Größe

medium-sized *adj* mittelgroß ▷ *a medium-sized town* eine mittelgroße Stadt

meet *vb* ❶ (by chance) treffen [**78**] (pres trifft, imperf traf, perf hat getroffen) ▷ *I met Paul when I was walking the dog.* Ich habe Paul getroffen, als ich mit dem Hund spazieren war. ❷ (by arrangement) sich treffen [**78**] ▷ *Let's meet in front of the tourist office.* Treffen wir uns doch vor dem Verkehrsbüro. ▷ *I'm going to meet my friends.* Ich treffe mich mit meinen Freunden. ❸ (get to know) kennenlernen [**4**] (perf hat kennengelernt) ▷ *I like meeting new people.* Ich lerne gerne neue Leute kennen.; **Have you met him before?** Kennen Sie ihn? ❹ (pick up) abholen [**4**] (perf hat abgeholt) ▷ *I'll meet you at the station.* Ich hole dich am Bahnhof ab.

meeting *n* ❶ (for work) Besprechung *f* ▷ *a business meeting* eine geschäftliche Besprechung ❷ (socially) Treffen *nt* (pl Treffen) ▷ *their first meeting* ihr erstes Treffen

mega *adj* **He's mega rich.** (*informal*) Er ist superreich.

melon *n* Melone *f*

melt *vb* schmelzen (*pres* schmilzt, *imperf* schmolz, *perf* ist geschmolzen) ▷ *The snow is melting.* Der Schnee schmilzt.

member *n* Mitglied *nt* (pl Mitglieder); **a Member of Parliament (1)** (*man*) ein Abgeordneter **(2)** (*woman*) eine Abgeordnete

meme *n* (internet) Meme *m* (pl Memes)

memorial *n* Denkmal *nt* (pl Denkmäler); **a war memorial** ein Kriegerdenkmal

memorize *vb* auswendig lernen [**38**]

memory *n* ❶ Gedächtnis *nt* (gen Gedächtnisses) ▷ *I haven't got a good memory.* Ich habe kein gutes Gedächtnis. ❷ (recollection) Erinnerung *f* ▷ *to bring back memories* Erinnerungen wachrufen ❸ (computer) Speicher *m* (gen Speicher)

memory stick *n* (for computer) Memorystick® *m* (pl Memorysticks)

men *npl* see **man**

mend *vb* flicken [**48**]

mental *adj* geistig; **mental health** psychische Gesundheit

mention *vb* erwähnen [**19**] (perf hat erwähnt); **Thank you! — Don't mention it!** Danke! — Bitte!

mentor *n* Mentor *m* (pl Mentoren)

menu *n* ❶ Speisekarte *f* ▷ *Could I have the menu please?* Könnte ich bitte die Speisekarte haben? ❷ (on computer) Menü *nt* (pl Menüs)

meringue *n* Meringe *f*

merry *adj* **Merry Christmas!** Fröhliche Weihnachten!

merry-go-round *n* Karussell *nt* (pl Karussells)

mess *n* Unordnung *f* ▷ *His bedroom's always in a mess.* In seinem Schlafzimmer herrscht ständig Unordnung.

mess about *vb* to mess about with something (*interfere with*) an etwas herumfummeln [**4**] ▷ *Stop messing about*

ENGLISH > GERMAN

with my computer! Hör auf, an meinem Computer herumzufummeln!; **Don't mess about with my things!** Lass meine Sachen in Ruhe!

mess up vb **to mess something up** etwas durcheinanderbringen [**13**]

message n Nachricht f
▷ **She messaged me on Facebook.** Sie schickte mir eine Nachricht auf Facebook.

messenger n Bote m (gen Boten, pl Boten), Botin f

messy adj ❶ (dirty) schmutzig ▷ a messy job eine schmutzige Arbeit ❷ (untidy) unordentlich ▷ Your room's really untidy. Dein Zimmer ist wirklich unordentlich. ▷ **She's so messy!** Sie ist so unordentlich!; **My writing is terribly messy.** Ich habe eine schreckliche Schrift.

met vb see **meet**

metal n Metall nt (pl Metalle)

meter n ❶ (for gas, electricity, taxi) Zähler m (pl Zähler) ❷ (parking meter) Parkuhr f

method n Methode f

Methodist n Methodist m (gen Methodisten, pl Methodisten), Methodistin f ▷ **She's a Methodist.** Sie ist Methodistin.

metre n Meter m (pl Meter)

metric adj metrisch

Mexico n Mexiko nt; **from Mexico** aus Mexiko; **to Mexico** nach Mexiko

mice npl see **mouse**

microchip n Mikrochip m (pl Mikrochips)

microphone n Mikrofon nt (pl Mikrofone)

microscope n Mikroskop nt (pl Mikroskope)

microwave n Mikrowelle f

microwave oven n Mikrowellenherd m (pl Mikrowellenherde)

midday n Mittag m (pl Mittage); **at midday** mittags

middle n Mitte f; **in the middle of the road** mitten auf der Straße; **in the middle of the night** mitten in der Nacht; **the middle seat** der mittlere Sitz; **the Middle East** der Nahe Osten

middle-aged adj mittleren Alters
▷ a middle-aged man ein Mann mittleren Alters ▷ **She's middle-aged.** Sie ist mittleren Alters.

middle-class adj **a middle-class family** eine Familie der Mittelschicht

midge n Mücke f

midnight n Mitternacht f; **at midnight** um Mitternacht

midwife n Hebamme f ▷ **She's a midwife.** Sie ist Hebamme.

might vb

▪ Use **vielleicht** to express possibility.
▷ **He might come later.** Er kommt vielleicht später. ▷ **We might go to Spain next year.** Wir fahren nächstes Jahr vielleicht nach Spanien. ▷ **She might not have understood.** Sie hat es vielleicht nicht verstanden.

migraine n Migräne f ▷ **I've got a migraine.** Ich habe Migräne.

mike n Mikro nt (pl Mikros)

mild adj mild ▷ **The winters are quite mild.** Die Winter sind ziemlich mild.

mile n Meile f
▪ In Germany distances and speeds
▪ are expressed in kilometres. A mile is
▪ about 1.6 kilometres.
▷ **It's five miles from here.** Es ist acht Kilometer von hier. ▷ **at fifty miles per hour** mit achtzig Kilometern pro Stunde; **We walked miles!** Wir sind meilenweit gegangen!

military adj militärisch

milk n Milch f ▷ **tea with milk** der Tee mit Milch
▶ vb melken (perf hat gemolken)

milk chocolate n Milchschokolade f

milkman n Milchmann m (pl Milchmänner) ▷ **He's a milkman.** Er ist Milchmann.

milk shake n Milchshake m (pl Milchshakes)

millennium n Jahrtausend nt
millimetre n Millimeter m (pl Millimeter)
million n Million f
millionaire n Millionär m (pl Millionäre), Millionärin f
mince n Hackfleisch nt
mind vb aufpassen [**31**] auf (perf hat aufgepasst) ▷ Could you mind the baby this afternoon? Kannst du heute Nachmittag auf das Baby aufpassen? ▷ Could you mind my bags? Können Sie auf mein Gepäck aufpassen?; **Do you mind if I open the window?** Macht es Ihnen etwas aus, wenn ich das Fenster aufmache?; **I don't mind.** Es macht mir nichts aus.; **Never mind!** Macht nichts!; **Mind that bike!** Pass auf das Fahrrad auf!; **Mind the step!** Vorsicht Stufe!
▸ n to make up one's mind sich entscheiden; **to change one's mind** es sich anders überlegen [**82**]; **Are you out of your mind?** Bist du wahnsinnig?
mindfulness n Achtsamkeit f
mine pron ❶ meiner ▷ Is this your coat? — No, mine's black. Ist das dein Mantel? — Nein, meiner ist schwarz.
meine ▷ Is this your cup? — No, mine's red. Ist das deine Tasse? — Nein, meine ist rot.
meines ▷ Is this your car? — No, mine's green. Ist das dein Auto? — Nein, meines ist grün. ❷ meine ▷ her parents and mine ihre Eltern und meine ▷ Your hands are dirty, mine are clean. Deine Hände sind schmutzig, meine sind sauber.; **It's mine.** Das gehört mir. ▷ This book is mine. Dieses Buch gehört mir. ▷ Whose is this? — It's mine. Wem gehört das? — Es gehört mir.
▸ n Mine f; **a land mine** eine Landmine; **a coal mine** ein Kohlebergwerk nt
miner n Bergarbeiter m (pl Bergarbeiter)
mineral water n Mineralwasser nt (pl Mineralwasser)

miniature adj Miniatur f
minibus n Minibus m (gen Minibusses, pl Minibusse)
minimum n Minimum nt (pl Minima)
▸ adj **minimum age** das Mindestalter; **minimum amount** der Mindestbetrag; **minimum wage** der Mindestlohn
miniskirt n Minirock m (pl Miniröcke)
minister n ❶ (in government) Minister m (pl Minister), Ministerin f ❷ (of church) Pfarrer m (pl Pfarrer), Pfarrerin f
minor adj kleiner ▷ a minor problem ein kleineres Problem ▷ a minor operation eine kleinere Operation; **in D minor** in d-Moll
minority n Minderheit f
mint n ❶ (plant) Pfefferminze f; **mint sauce** die Pfefferminzsoße ❷ (sweet) Pfefferminzbonbon nt (pl Pfefferminzbonbons)
minus prep minus ▷ Sixteen minus three is thirteen. Sechzehn minus drei ist dreizehn. ▷ It's minus two degrees outside. Draußen hat es zwei Grad minus. ▷ I got a B minus. Ich habe eine Zwei minus bekommen.
※ In Germany, grades are given from ● 1 to 6, with 1 being the best.
minute n Minute f; **Wait a minute!** Einen Augenblick!
▸ adj winzig ▷ Her flat is minute. Ihre Wohnung ist winzig.
miracle n Wunder nt (pl Wunder)
mirror n Spiegel m (pl Spiegel)
misbehave vb sich schlecht benehmen [**52**] (pres benimmt sich schlecht, imperf benahm sich schlecht, perf hat sich schlecht benommen)
miscellaneous adj verschieden ▷ miscellaneous items verschiedene Artikel
mischief n Dummheiten fpl ▷ She's always up to mischief. Sie macht dauernd Dummheiten.
mischievous adj verschmitzt

miser n Geizhals m (gen Geizhalses, pl Geizhälse)

miserable adj ❶ (person) unglücklich ▷ You're looking miserable. Du siehst richtig unglücklich aus. ❷ (weather) schrecklich ▷ The weather was miserable. Das Wetter war schrecklich.; **to feel miserable** sich miserabel fühlen [**38**]

misery n ❶ Elend nt ▷ All that money brought nothing but misery. All das Geld hat nichts als Elend gebracht. ❷ (informal) Miesepeter m (pl Miesepeter) ▷ She's a real misery. Sie ist ein richtiger Miesepeter.

mislead vb irreführen [**4**] (perf hat irregeführt)

misprint n Druckfehler m (pl Druckfehler)

Miss n Fräulein nt
- Nowadays it is regarded as old-fashioned to call somebody **Fräulein** and **Frau** is used instead.

▷ Miss Jones Frau Jones

miss vb verpassen [**7**] ▷ Hurry or you'll miss the bus. Beeil dich, sonst verpasst du den Bus! ▷ to miss an opportunity eine Gelegenheit verpassen; **I miss you.** Du fehlst mir.; **He missed the target.** Er hat nicht getroffen.

missing adj fehlend ▷ the missing part das fehlende Teil; **to be missing** fehlen [**38**]

mist n Nebel m (pl Nebel)
- Be careful not to translate **mist** by the German word **Mist**.

mistake n Fehler m (pl Fehler) ▷ It was a mistake to buy those yellow shoes. Es war ein Fehler, diese gelben Schuhe zu kaufen.; **a spelling mistake** ein Rechtschreibfehler; **to make a mistake (1)** (in writing, speaking) einen Fehler machen [**48**] **(2)** (get mixed up) sich vertun [**81**] ▷ I'm sorry, I made a mistake. Tut mir leid, ich habe mich vertan.; **by mistake** aus Versehen ▷ I took his bag by mistake. Ich habe aus Versehen seine Tasche genommen.
▶ vb **He mistook me for my sister.** Er hat mich mit meiner Schwester verwechselt.

mistaken adj **to be mistaken** sich irren [**38**]

mistletoe n Mistel f

mistook vb see **mistake**

misty adj neblig ▷ a misty morning ein nebliger Morgen

misunderstand vb missverstehen [**72**] (imperf missverstand, perf hat missverstanden) ▷ Sorry, I misunderstood you. Entschuldigung, ich habe Sie missverstanden.

misunderstanding n Missverständnis nt (gen Missverständnisses, pl Missverständnisse)

misunderstood vb see **misunderstand**

mix n Mischung f ▷ It's a mix of science fiction and comedy. Es ist eine Mischung aus Sciencefiction und Komödie.; **a cake mix** eine Backmischung
▶ vb ❶ vermischen [**7**] (perf hat vermischt) ▷ Mix the flour with the sugar. Vermischen Sie das Mehl mit dem Zucker. ❷ verbinden (imperf verband, perf hat verbunden) ▷ He's mixing business with pleasure. Er verbindet das Geschäftliche mit dem Vergnügen.; **to mix with somebody** (associate) mit jemandem verkehren [**7**]; **He doesn't mix much.** Er geht nicht viel unter Menschen.; **to mix up** verwechseln [**34**] ▷ I'm getting mixed up. Ich werde ganz konfus.

mixed adj gemischt ▷ a mixed salad ein gemischter Salat ▷ a mixed school eine gemischte Schule; **a mixed grill** ein Grillteller m

mixer n (for food) Mixer m (pl Mixer)

mixture n Mischung f ▷ a mixture of spices eine Gewürzmischung; **cough mixture** der Hustensaft

mix-up n Verwechslung f
MMS n (= multimedia messaging service) MMS® m
moan vb sich beklagen [**7**] (perf hat sich beklagt) ▷ She's always moaning. Sie beklagt sich dauernd.
mobile n (phone) Handy nt (pl Handys)
mobile home n Wohnmobil nt (pl Wohnmobile)
mobile phone n Handy nt (pl Handys)
mock vb sich lustig machen [**48**] über ▷ Stop mocking him! Mach dich nicht über ihn lustig!
▸ adj **a mock exam** eine Übungsprüfung
model n ❶ Modell nt (pl Modelle) ▷ the latest model das neueste Modell ▷ a model of the castle ein Modell der Burg ❷ (fashion) Mannequin nt (pl Mannequins) ▷ She's a famous model. Sie ist ein berühmtes Mannequin.
▸ adj **a model plane** ein Modellflugzeug nt; **a model railway** eine Modelleisenbahn; **He's a model pupil.** Er ist ein vorbildlicher Schüler.
▸ vb als Model arbeiten [**2**] ▷ She was modelling in New York. Sie arbeitete in New York als Model.; **She was modelling a Paul Costello outfit.** Sie führte ein Outfit von Paul Costello vor.
modem n Modem nt (pl Modems)
moderate adj gemäßigt ▷ His views are quite moderate. Er hat sehr gemäßigte Ansichten.; **a moderate amount of alcohol** wenig Alkohol; **a moderate price** ein annehmbarer Preis
modern adj modern
modernize vb modernisieren [**76**] (perf hat modernisiert)
modest adj bescheiden
moisturizer n ❶ (cream) Feuchtigkeitscreme f (pl Feuchtigkeitscremes) ❷ (lotion) Feuchtigkeitslotion f
moldy adj (US) schimmlig

mole n ❶ (animal) Maulwurf m (pl Maulwürfe) ❷ (on skin) Leberfleck m (pl Leberflecke)
moment n Augenblick m (pl Augenblicke) ▷ Could you wait a moment? Können Sie einen Augenblick warten? ▷ in a moment in einem Augenblick ▷ Just a moment! Einen Augenblick!; **at the moment** momentan; **any moment now** jeden Moment
monarchy n Monarchie f
Monday n Montag m (pl Montage) ▷ on Monday am Montag ▷ every Monday jeden Montag ▷ last Monday letzten Montag ▷ next Monday nächsten Montag; **on Mondays** montags
monetize vb monetarisieren [**76**]
money n Geld nt (pl Gelder) ▷ I need to change some money. Ich muss Geld wechseln.; **to make money** Geld verdienen [**84**]
mongrel n Promenadenmischung f ▷ My dog's a mongrel. Mein Hund ist eine Promenadenmischung.
monitor n (of computer) Monitor m (pl Monitore)
monkey n Affe m (gen Affen, pl Affen)
monopoly n Monopol nt; **to play Monopoly**® Monopoly spielen [**38**]
monotonous adj monoton
monster n Monster nt (pl Monster)
month n Monat m (pl Monate) ▷ this month diesen Monat ▷ next month nächsten Monat ▷ last month letzten Monat ▷ every month jeden Monat ▷ at the end of the month Ende des Monats
monthly adj monatlich
monument n Denkmal nt (pl Denkmäler)
mood n Laune f ▷ to be in a bad mood schlechte Laune haben ▷ to be in a good mood gute Laune haben
moody adj ❶ (temperamental) launisch ❷ (in a bad mood) schlecht gelaunt

ENGLISH > GERMAN

moon n Mond m (pl Monde); **There's a full moon tonight.** Heute ist Vollmond.; **to be over the moon** (happy) überglücklich sein [65]
moped n Moped nt (pl Mopeds)
moral adj moralisch
▷ Moral f ▷ *the moral of the story* die Moral der Geschichte; **morals** die Moral sg
more adj, pron, adv mehr ▷ *a bit more* etwas mehr ▷ *There are more girls in the class.* In der Klasse sind mehr Mädchen.; **more than** mehr als

In comparisons you usually add **-er** to the adjective.

▷ *Could you speak more slowly?* Könnten Sie langsamer sprechen?

When referring to an additional amount, over and above what there already is, you usually use **noch**.

▷ *Is there any more?* Gibt es noch mehr?; **There isn't any more.** Es ist nichts mehr da.; **more or less** mehr oder weniger; **more than ever** mehr denn je
morning n Morgen m (pl Morgen) ▷ *every morning* jeden Morgen; **this morning** heute Morgen; **tomorrow morning** morgen früh; **in the morning** morgens; **a morning paper** eine Morgenzeitung
Morocco n Marokko nt; **from Morocco** aus Marokko; **to Morocco** nach Marokko
mortgage n Hypothek f (pl Hypotheken)
Moscow n Moskau nt; **to Moscow** nach Moskau
mosque n Moschee f
mosquito n Stechmücke f; **a mosquito bite** ein Mückenstich m
most adv, adj, pron ❶ die meisten
▷ *most of my friends* die meisten meiner Freunde ▷ *most of them* die meisten von ihnen ▷ *most people* die meisten Menschen ▷ *Most cats are affectionate.*

409 | **mountain**

Die meisten Katzen sind anhänglich. ❷ **am meisten** ▷ *what I hate most* was ich am meisten hasse; **most of the time** meist; **most of the evening** fast den ganzen Abend; **most of the money** fast das ganze Geld; **the most** am meisten; **to make the most of something** das Beste aus etwas machen [48]; **at the most** höchstens

For the superlative you usually add **-ste** to the adjective.

▷ *the most expensive restaurant* das teuerste Restaurant
moth n Motte f
mother n Mutter f (pl Mütter) ▷ *my mother* meine Mutter; **mother tongue** die Muttersprache
mother-in-law n Schwiegermutter f (pl Schwiegermütter)
Mother's Day n Muttertag m (pl Muttertage)

In Germany **Muttertag** is on the second Sunday in May.

motivated adj motiviert ▷ *He is highly motivated.* Er ist höchst motiviert.
motivation n Motivation f
motor n Motor m (pl Motoren) ▷ *The boat has a motor.* Das Boot hat einen Motor.
motorbike n Motorrad nt (pl Motorräder)
motorboat n Motorboot nt (pl Motorboote)
motorcycle n Motorrad nt (pl Motorräder)
motorcyclist n Motorradfahrer m (pl Motorradfahrer), Motorradfahrerin f
motorist n Autofahrer m (pl Autofahrer), Autofahrerin f
motor racing n Autorennen nt (pl Autorennen)
motorway n Autobahn f ▷ *on the motorway* auf der Autobahn
mouldy adj schimmlig
mountain n Berg m (pl Berge); **a mountain bike** ein Mountainbike nt

mountaineer n Bergsteiger m (pl Bergsteiger), Bergsteigerin f

mountaineering n Bergsteigen nt; **I go mountaineering.** Ich gehe bergsteigen.

mountainous adj bergig

mouse n (also for computer) Maus f (pl Mäuse) ▷ white mice weiße Mäuse

mouse mat n (computer) Mousepad nt (pl Mousepads)

mousse n ❶ (food) Creme f (pl Cremes); **chocolate mousse** die Schokoladencreme ❷ (for hair) Schaumfestiger m (pl Schaumfestiger)

moustache n Schnurrbart m (pl Schnurrbärte) ▷ He's got a moustache. Er hat einen Schnurrbart.

mouth n Mund m (pl Münder)

mouthful n Bissen m (pl Bissen)

mouth organ n Mundharmonika f (pl Mundharmonikas) ▷ I play the mouth organ. Ich spiele Mundharmonika.

move n ❶ Zug m (pl Züge) ▷ That was a good move. Das war ein guter Zug.; **It's your move.** Du bist dran. ❷ Umzug m (pl Umzüge) ▷ our move from Oxford to Luton unser Umzug von Oxford nach Luton; **to get a move on** schneller machen [48]; **Get a move on!** Nun mach schon!
▶ vb ❶ bewegen [7] (perf hat bewegt) ▷ I can't move my arm. Ich kann den Arm nicht bewegen. ▷ I was very moved by the film. Der Film hat mich sehr bewegt.; **Could you move your stuff?** Könntest du dein Zeug wegtun?; **Could you move your car?** Könnten Sie Ihr Auto wegfahren? ❷ sich bewegen [7] ▷ Try not to move. Versuche, dich nicht zu bewegen.; **Don't move!** Keine Bewegung! ❸ (vehicle) fahren [21] (pres fährt, imperf fuhr, perf ist gefahren) ▷ The car was moving very slowly. Das Auto fuhr sehr langsam.; **to move house** umziehen [96]; **to move**

forward sich vorwärtsbewegen [15]; **to move in** einziehen [96]; **to move over** rücken [38]

movement n Bewegung f

movie n Film m (pl Filme); **the movies** das Kino sg

moving adj ❶ (not stationary) fahrend ▷ a moving bus ein fahrender Bus ❷ (touching) ergreifend ▷ a moving story eine ergreifende Geschichte

MP n (= Member of Parliament) Abgeordnete m (gen Abgeordneten, pl Abgeordneten), Abgeordnete f (gen Abgeordneten) ▷ an MP (man) ein Abgeordneter ▷ She's an MP. Sie ist Abgeordnete.

MP3 player n MP3-Spieler m (pl MP3-Spieler)

mph abbr (= miles per hour) Meilen pro Stunde

Mr n (= Mister) Herr

Mrs n Frau

MS n (= multiple sclerosis) MS ▷ She's got MS. Sie hat MS.

Ms n Frau

▪ Generally **Frau** is used to address all
▪ women whether married or not.

much adj, adv, pron ❶ viel ▷ I haven't got much money. Ich habe nicht viel Geld. ▷ I haven't got very much money. Ich habe nicht sehr viel Geld. ▷ This is much better. Das ist viel besser. ▷ I feel much better now. Ich fühle mich jetzt viel besser. ❷ sehr

▪ Use **sehr** with most verbs.

▷ I didn't like it much. Es hat mir nicht sehr gefallen. ▷ I enjoyed the film very much. Der Film hat mir sehr gefallen. ❸ viel

▪ Use **viel** with verbs implying
▪ physical activity.

▷ She doesn't travel much. Sie reist nicht viel. ▷ We didn't laugh much. Wir haben nicht viel gelacht.; **Do you go out much?** Gehst du oft aus?; **Thank you very much.** Vielen Dank!; **not much** nicht viel; **How much?** Wie viel?; **too much** zu viel; **so much** so viel

mud n Schlamm m

muddle n Durcheinander nt; **to be in a muddle** durcheinander sein [**65**]

muddle up vb (people) verwechseln [**34**] (perf hat verwechselt)

muddy adj schlammig

muesli n Müsli nt (pl Müsli)

mug n Becher m (pl Becher) ▷ *Do you want a cup or a mug?* Möchtest du eine Tasse oder einen Becher?; **a beer mug** ein Bierkrug m
▶ vb überfallen [**22**] (pres überfällt, imperf überfiel, perf hat überfallen) ▷ *He was mugged in the city centre.* Er wurde in der Innenstadt überfallen.

mugging n Überfall m (pl Überfälle) ▷ *Mugging has increased in recent years.* Die Zahl der Überfälle hat in den letzten Jahren zugenommen.

multiple choice test n Multiple-Choice-Test m (pl Multiple-Choice-Tests)

multiplication n Multiplikation f

multiply vb multiplizieren [**76**] (perf hat multipliziert) ▷ *to multiply six by three* sechs mit drei multiplizieren

mum n Mama f (pl Mamas) ▷ *my mum* meine Mama ▷ *I'll ask Mum.* Ich frage Mama.

mummy n ❶ (mum) Mutti f (pl Muttis) ▷ *Mummy says I can go.* Mutti sagt, ich kann gehen. ❷ (Egyptian) Mumie f

mumps nsg Mumps m ▷ *My brother's got mumps.* Mein Bruder hat Mumps.

Munich n München nt; **to Munich** nach München

murder n Mord m (pl Morde)

⚠ Be careful not to translate **murder** by *Mörder*.

▶ vb ermorden [**53**] (perf hat ermordet) ▷ *He was murdered.* Er wurde ermordet.

murderer n Mörder m (pl Mörder), Mörderin f

muscle n Muskel m (pl Muskeln)

museum n Museum nt (pl Museen)

mushroom n ❶ Pilz m (pl Pilze) ❷ (button mushroom) Champignon m (pl Champignons); **a mushroom omelette** das Champignonomelett

music n Musik f

musical adj musikalisch ▷ *I'm not musical.* Ich bin nicht musikalisch.; **a musical instrument** ein Musikinstrument nt
▶ n Musical nt (pl Musicals)

musician n Musiker m (pl Musiker), Musikerin f

Muslim n Moslem m (pl Moslems), Moslime f ▷ *He's a Muslim.* Er ist Moslem.

mussel n Miesmuschel f

must vb ❶ müssen [**51**] (pres muss, imperf musste, perf hat gemusst) ▷ *I must buy some presents.* Ich muss Geschenke kaufen. ▷ *I really must go now.* Ich muss jetzt wirklich gehen. ▷ *You must be tired.* Du musst müde sein. ▷ *They must have plenty of money.* Sie müssen viel Geld haben. ▷ *You must come and see us.* Sie müssen uns besuchen. ❷ dürfen [**16**] (pres darf, imperf durfte, perf hat gedurft)

⚠ Use **dürfen** in negative sentences.

▷ *You mustn't say things like that.* So was darfst du nicht sagen.; **You mustn't forget to send her a card.** Vergiss nicht, ihr eine Karte zu schicken.

mustard n Senf m (pl Senfe)

mutual adj gegenseitig ▷ *The feeling was mutual.* Das Gefühl war gegenseitig.; **a mutual friend** ein gemeinsamer Freund

my adj mein ▷ *my father* mein Vater ▷ *my aunt* meine Tante ▷ *my car* mein Auto ▷ *my parents* meine Eltern; **my friend (1)** (male) mein Freund **(2)** (female) meine Freundin

⚠ Do not use **mein** with parts of the body.

▷ *I want to wash my hair.* Ich will mir die

Haare waschen. ▷ *I'm going to clean my teeth.* Ich putze mir die Zähne. ▷ *I've hurt my foot.* Ich habe mich am Fuß verletzt.

myself *pron* ❶ mich ▷ *I've hurt myself.* Ich habe mich verletzt. ▷ *When I look at myself in the mirror ...* Wenn ich mich im Spiegel ansehe ... ▷ *I don't like talking about myself.* Ich rede nicht gern über mich selbst. ❷ mir ▷ *I said to myself ...* Ich sagte mir ... ▷ *I am not very pleased with myself.* Ich bin mit mir selbst nicht sehr zufrieden. ❸ selbst ▷ *I made it myself.* Ich habe es selbst gemacht.; **by myself** allein

mysterious *adj* rätselhaft

mystery *n* Rätsel *nt* (*pl* Rätsel); **a murder mystery** (*novel*) ein Krimi *m*

myth *n* ❶ (*legend*) Mythos *m* (*gen* Mythos, *pl* Mythen) ▷ *A Greek myth* ein griechischer Mythos ❷ (*untrue idea*) Märchen *nt* (*pl* Märchen) ▷ *That's a myth.* Das ist ein Märchen.

n

nag *vb* (*scold*) herumnörgeln [15] an (*perf* hat herumgenörgelt) ▷ *She's always nagging me.* Sie nörgelt dauernd an mir herum.

nail *n* Nagel *m* (*pl* Nägel) ▷ *Don't bite your nails!* Kau nicht an den Nägeln!

nailbrush *n* Nagelbürste *f*

nailfile *n* Nagelfeile *f*

nail scissors *npl* Nagelschere *f* ▷ *a pair of nail scissors* eine Nagelschere

nail varnish *n* Nagellack *m* (*pl* Nagellacke); **nail varnish remover** der Nagellackentferner

naked *adj* nackt

name *n* Name *m* (*gen* Namens, *pl* Namen); **What's your name?** Wie heißt du?

nanny *n* Kindermädchen *nt* (*pl* Kindermädchen) ▷ *She's a nanny.* Sie ist Kindermädchen.

napkin *n* Serviette *f*

nappy *n* Windel *f*

narrow *adj* eng

nasty *adj* ❶ (*bad*) übel ▷ *a nasty cold* eine üble Erkältung ▷ *a nasty smell* ein übler

Geruch ❷ *(unfriendly)* böse ▷ *He gave me a nasty look.* Er warf mir einen bösen Blick zu.

nation *n* Nation *f*

national *adj* national; **a national newspaper** eine überregionale Zeitung; **the national elections** die Parlamentswahlen

: In Germany the national elections are called **Bundestagswahlen**.

national anthem *n* Nationalhymne *f*
nationality *n* Staatsangehörigkeit *f*
National Lottery *n* Lotto *nt*
national park *n* Nationalpark *m* (*pl* Nationalparks)
natural *adj* natürlich
naturally *adv* natürlich ▷ *Naturally, we were very disappointed.* Natürlich waren wir sehr enttäuscht.
nature *n* Natur *f*
naughty *adj* böse ▷ *Naughty girl!* Böses Mädchen!; **Don't be naughty!** Sei nicht ungezogen!
navy *n* Marine *f* ▷ *He's in the navy.* Er ist bei der Marine.
navy-blue *adj* marineblau ▷ *a navy-blue shirt* ein marineblaues Hemd
near *adj* nah ▷ *It's fairly near.* Es ist ziemlich nah. ▷ *It's near enough to walk.* Es ist nah genug, um zu Fuß zu gehen.; **nearest** nächste
▶ *prep, adv* in der Nähe von ▷ *I live near Liverpool.* Ich wohne in der Nähe von Liverpool. ▷ *near my house* in der Nähe meines Hauses; **near here** hier in der Nähe; **near to** in der Nähe
nearby *adv, adj* ❶ in der Nähe ▷ *There's a supermarket nearby.* Es gibt einen Supermarkt in der Nähe. ❷ *(close)* nahe gelegen ▷ *a nearby garage* eine nahe gelegene Tankstelle
nearly *adv* fast ▷ *Dinner's nearly ready.* Das Essen ist fast fertig. ▷ *I'm nearly fifteen.* Ich bin fast fünfzehn. ▷ *I nearly missed the train.* Ich habe fast meinen Zug verpasst.

neat *adj* ordentlich ▷ *She has very neat writing.* Sie hat eine sehr ordentliche Schrift.; **a neat whisky** ein Whisky pur
neatly *adv* ordentlich ▷ *neatly folded* ordentlich gefaltet ▷ *neatly dressed* ordentlich gekleidet
necessarily *adv* **not necessarily** nicht unbedingt
necessary *adj* nötig
neck *n* ❶ *(of body)* Hals *m* (*gen* Halses, *pl* Hälse) ❷ *(of garment)* Ausschnitt *m* (*pl* Ausschnitte) ▷ *a V-neck sweater* ein Pullover mit V-Ausschnitt
necklace *n* Halskette *f*
need *vb* brauchen [48] ▷ *I need a bigger size.* Ich brauche eine größere Größe.; **to need to do something** etwas tun müssen [51]
▶ *n* **There's no need to book.** Man braucht nicht zu buchen.
needle *n* Nadel *f*
negative *n* (*photo*) Negativ *nt* (*pl* Negative)
▶ *adj* negativ ▷ *He's got a very negative attitude.* Er hat eine sehr negative Einstellung.
neglected *adj* (*untidy*) ungepflegt ▷ *The garden is neglected.* Der Garten ist ungepflegt.
negotiate *vb* verhandeln [34]
neighbour *n* Nachbar *m* (*gen* Nachbarn, *pl* Nachbarn), Nachbarin *f* ▷ *the neighbours' garden* der Garten der Nachbarn
neighbourhood *n* Nachbarschaft *f*
neither *pron, conj, adv* weder noch ▷ *Carrots or peas? — Neither, thanks.* Karotten oder Erbsen? — Weder noch, danke.; **Neither of them is coming.** Keiner von beiden kommt.; **neither ... nor ...** weder ... noch ... ▷ *Neither Sarah nor Tamsin is coming to the party.* Weder Sarah noch Tamsin kommen zur Party.; **Neither do I.** Ich auch nicht. ▷ *I don't like him. — Neither do I!* Ich mag ihn

nicht. — Ich auch nicht!; **Neither have I.** Ich auch nicht. ▷ *I've never been to Spain. — Neither have I.* Ich war noch nie in Spanien. — Ich auch nicht.

nephew n Neffe m (pl Neffen) ▷ *my nephew* mein Neffe

nerve n Nerv m (pl Nerven) ▷ *She gets on my nerves.* Sie geht mir auf die Nerven.; **He's got a nerve!** Der hat vielleicht Nerven!

nervous adj (tense) nervös ▷ *I bite my nails when I'm nervous.* Wenn ich nervös bin, kaue ich an den Nägeln.; **to be nervous about something** vor etwas Angst haben [**32**]

nest n Nest nt (pl Nester)

Net n **the Net** das Internet

net n Netz nt (gen Netzes, pl Netze) ▷ *a fishing net* ein Fischnetz

netball n Netzball m

Netherlands npl Niederlande pl

> Note that the definite article is used in German for countries which are plural.

from the Netherlands aus den Niederlanden; in the Netherlands in den Niederlanden; to the Netherlands in die Niederlande

network n ❶ Netz nt (gen Netzes, pl Netze) ❷ (for computers) Netzwerk nt (pl Netzwerke)

neurodivergent adj neurodivers

never adv nie ▷ *Have you ever been to Germany? — No, never.* Waren Sie schon mal in Deutschland? — Nein, nie. ▷ *I never write letters.* Ich schreibe nie Briefe. ▷ *Never again!* Nie wieder!; **Never mind.** Macht nichts!

new adj neu ▷ *her new boyfriend* ihr neuer Freund ▷ *I need a new dress.* Ich brauche ein neues Kleid.

news nsg

> **Nachricht** is a piece of news; **Nachrichten** is the news, for example on TV.

❶ Nachrichten fpl ▷ *good news* gute Nachrichten ▷ *I've had some bad news.* Ich habe schlechte Nachrichten bekommen. ▷ *I watch the news every evening.* Ich sehe mir jeden Abend die Nachrichten an. ▷ *I listen to the news every morning.* Ich höre jeden Morgen die Nachrichten. ❷ Nachricht f ▷ *That's wonderful news!* Das ist eine wunderbare Nachricht!

newsagent n Zeitungshändler m (pl Zeitungshändler), Zeitungshändlerin f

news dealer n (US) Zeitungshändler m (pl Zeitungshändler), Zeitungshändlerin f

newspaper n Zeitung f ▷ *I deliver newspapers.* Ich trage Zeitungen aus.

newsreader n Nachrichtensprecher m (pl Nachrichtensprecher), Nachrichtensprecherin f

New Year n Neujahr nt ▷ *to celebrate New Year* Neujahr feiern; **Happy New Year!** Ein gutes neues Jahr!; **New Year's Day** das Neujahr; **New Year's Eve** das Silvester

New Zealand n Neuseeland nt; **from New Zealand** aus Neuseeland; **in New Zealand** in Neuseeland; **to New Zealand** nach Neuseeland

New Zealander n Neuseeländer m (pl Neuseeländer), Neuseeländerin f

next adj, adv, prep ❶ nächste ▷ *next Saturday* nächsten Samstag ▷ *next week* nächste Woche ▷ *next year* nächstes Jahr ▷ *the next train* der nächste Zug; **Next please!** Der Nächste, bitte! ❷ (afterwards) danach ▷ *What happened next?* Was ist danach passiert?; **What shall I do next?** Was soll ich als Nächstes machen?; **next to** neben

> Use the accusative to express movement or a change of place. Use the dative when there is no change of place.

▷ *I sat down next to my sister.* Ich setzte

mich neben meine Schwester. ▷ *The post office is next to the bank.* Die Post ist neben der Bank.; **the next day** am nächsten Tag; **the next time** das nächste Mal; **next door** nebenan; **the next room** das Nebenzimmer

NHS n **The NHS is very important.** Der staatliche Gesundheitsdienst ist sehr wichtig.

- Germany's national health service
- is available to all and is provided
- through a number of public health
- insurers.

nice adj ❶ (kind) nett ▷ *Your parents are nice.* Deine Eltern sind nett. ▷ *It was nice of you to remember my birthday.* Es war nett, dass du an meinen Geburtstag gedacht hast. ▷ **to be nice to somebody** nett zu jemandem sein ❷ (pretty) hübsch ▷ *That's a nice dress!* Das ist ein hübsches Kleid! ▷ *Ulm is a nice town.* Ulm ist eine hübsche Stadt. ❸ schön ▷ *nice weather* schönes Wetter ▷ *It's a nice day.* Es ist ein schöner Tag. ❹ (food) lecker ▷ *This pizza's very nice.* Diese Pizza ist sehr lecker.; **Have a nice time!** Viel Spaß!

nickname n Spitzname m (gen Spitznamens, pl Spitznamen)

niece n Nichte f ▷ *my niece* meine Nichte

Nigeria n Nigeria nt ▷ *in Nigeria* in Nigeria

night n ❶ Nacht f (pl Nächte) ▷ *I want a single room for two nights.* Ich möchte ein Einzelzimmer für zwei Nächte.; **at night** nachts; **Good night!** Gute Nacht!; **a night club** ein Nachtklub m ❷ (evening) Abend m (pl Abende) ▷ *last night* gestern Abend

nightie n Nachthemd nt (pl Nachthemden)

nightmare n Albtraum m (pl Albträume) ▷ *I had a nightmare.* Ich hatte einen Albtraum. ▷ *It was a real nightmare!* Es war ein Albtraum!

nil n null ▷ *We won one nil.* Wir haben eins zu null gewonnen.

nine num neun ▷ *She's nine.* Sie ist neun.

nineteen num neunzehn ▷ *She's nineteen.* Sie ist neunzehn.

nineteenth adj neunzehnte ▷ **the nineteenth of August** der neunzehnte August

ninety num neunzig ▷ *She's ninety.* Sie ist neunzig.

ninth adj neunte ▷ *the ninth floor* der neunte Stock ▷ **the ninth of August** der neunte August

no adv, adj ❶ nein ▷ *Are you coming?* — *No.* Kommst du? — Nein. ▷ *Would you like some more?* — *No thank you.* Möchten Sie noch etwas? — Nein danke. ❷ *(not any)* kein ▷ *There's no hot water.* Es gibt kein heißes Wasser. ▷ *There are no trains on Sundays.* Sonntags verkehren keine Züge. ▷ *No problem.* Kein Problem. ▷ *I've got no idea.* Ich habe keine Ahnung.; **No way!** Auf keinen Fall!; **'no smoking'** 'Rauchen verboten'

nobody pron niemand ▷ *Who's going with you?* — *Nobody.* Wer geht mit dir mit? — Niemand. ▷ *There was nobody in the office.* Es war niemand im Büro.

nod vb nicken [48]

noise n Lärm m ▷ *Please make less noise.* Macht bitte weniger Lärm.

noisy adj laut ▷ *It's too noisy here.* Hier ist es zu laut.

nominate vb nominieren [76] (perf hat nominiert) ▷ *She was nominated for an Oscar.* Sie war für einen Oscar nominiert.

non-binary adj nicht binär

none pron ❶ keiner ▷ *None of my friends wanted to come.* Keiner meiner Freunde wollte kommen. ▷ *How many brothers have you got?* — *None.* Wie viele Brüder hast du? — Keinen.

keine ▷ *Milk? There's none left.* Milch? Es ist keine mehr da.

keines ▷ *Which of the books have you*

read? — None. Welches der Bücher hast du gelesen? — Keines.; **There are none left.** Es sind keine mehr da.

nonsense n Unsinn m ▷ *She talks a lot of nonsense.* Sie redet viel Unsinn. ▷ **Nonsense!** Unsinn!

nonsmoker n Nichtraucher m (pl Nichtraucher), Nichtraucherin f ▷ *She's a nonsmoker.* Sie ist Nichtraucherin.

nonsmoking adj **a nonsmoking area** ein Nichtraucherbereich m

nonstop adj, adv ❶ nonstop ▷ *We flew nonstop.* Wir sind nonstop geflogen.; **a nonstop flight** ein Nonstop-Flug m ❷ ununterbrochen ▷ *Liz talks nonstop.* Liz redet ununterbrochen.

noodles npl Nudeln fpl

noon n Mittag m (pl Mittage); **at noon** um zwölf Uhr mittags

no one pron niemand

nor conj **neither … nor** weder … noch; **Nor do I.** Ich auch nicht.; **Nor have I.** Ich auch nicht.

normal adj normal ▷ *at the normal time* zur normalen Zeit ▷ *a normal car* ein normales Auto

normally adv ❶ (*usually*) normalerweise ▷ *I normally arrive at nine o'clock.* Normalerweise komme ich um neun Uhr. ❷ (*as normal*) normal ▷ *In spite of the strike, the airports are working normally.* Trotz des Streiks arbeiten die Flughäfen normal.

Normandy n Normandie f; **in Normandy** in der Normandie

north adj, adv nach Norden ▷ *We were travelling north.* Wir sind nach Norden gefahren.; **the north coast** die Nordküste f; **a north wind** ein Nordwind m; **north of** nördlich von
▶ n Norden m ▷ *in the north* im Norden

North America n Nordamerika nt; **from North America** aus Nordamerika; **to North America** nach Nordamerika

northeast n Nordosten m ▷ *in the northeast* im Nordosten

northern adj nördlich ▷ *the northern part of the island* der nördliche Teil der Insel; **Northern Europe** Nordeuropa nt

Northern Ireland n Nordirland nt; **from Northern Ireland** aus Nordirland; **in Northern Ireland** in Nordirland; **to Northern Ireland** nach Nordirland

North Pole n Nordpol m

North Sea n Nordsee f

northwest n Nordwesten m ▷ *in the northwest* im Nordwesten

Norway n Norwegen nt; **from Norway** aus Norwegen; **to Norway** nach Norwegen

Norwegian adj norwegisch; **He's Norwegian.** Er ist Norweger.
▶ n ❶ (*person*) Norweger m (pl Norweger), Norwegerin f ❷ (*language*) Norwegisch nt (gen Norwegischen)

nose n Nase f

nosebleed n Nasenbluten nt ▷ *I often get nosebleeds.* Ich habe oft Nasenbluten.

nosey adj neugierig ▷ *She's very nosey.* Sie ist sehr neugierig.

not adv ❶ nicht ▷ *Are you coming or not?* Kommst du oder nicht? ▷ *I'm not sure.* Ich bin nicht sicher. ▷ *It's not raining.* Es regnet nicht.; **not really** eigentlich nicht; **not at all** überhaupt nicht; **not yet** noch nicht ▷ *Have you finished?* — *Not yet.* Bist du fertig? — Noch nicht. ▷ *They haven't arrived yet.* Sie sind noch nicht angekommen. ❷ nein ▷ *Can you lend me ten pounds?* — *I'm afraid not.* Können Sie mir zehn Pfund leihen? — Leider nein.

note n ❶ Notiz f; **to take notes** sich Notizen machen [48] ❷ (*letter*) Brief m (pl Briefe); **I'll write her a note.** Ich werde ihr schreiben. ❸ (*banknote*) Schein m (pl Scheine) ▷ *a five-pound note* ein Fünfpfundschein

note down vb aufschreiben [61] (imperf schrieb auf, perf hat aufgeschrieben)

notebook n ① Notizbuch nt (pl Notizbücher) ② (computer) Notebookcomputer m (pl Notebookcomputer)

notepad n Notizblock m (pl Notizblöcke)

nothing n nichts ▷ *What's wrong? — Nothing.* Was ist los? — Nichts. ▷ *nothing special* nichts Besonderes ▷ *He does nothing.* Er tut nichts. ▷ *He ate nothing for breakfast.* Er hat nichts zum Frühstück gegessen.

notice n (sign) Notiz f ▷ *to put up a notice* eine Notiz aushängen ▷ *Don't take any notice of him!* Nimm keine Notiz von ihm!; **a warning notice** ein Warnschild nt ▷ vb bemerken [7] (perf hat bemerkt)

notice board n Anschlagbrett nt (pl Anschlagbretter)

nought n Null f

noun n Substantiv nt (pl Substantive)

novel n Roman m (pl Romane)

novelist n Romanautor m (pl Romanautoren), Romanautorin f

November n November m ▷ *in November* im November

now adv, conj jetzt ▷ *What are you doing now?* Was tust du jetzt?; **just now** gerade; **by now** inzwischen; **now and then** ab und zu

nowhere adv nirgends ▷ *nowhere else* sonst nirgends

nuclear adj nuklear; **nuclear power** die Kernkraft; **a nuclear power station** ein Kernkraftwerk nt

nuisance n *It's a nuisance.* Es ist sehr lästig.; **Sorry to be a nuisance.** Tut mir leid, dass ich schon wieder ankomme.

numb adj taub ▷ *numb with cold* taub vor Kälte

number n ① (total amount) Anzahl f ▷ *a large number of people* eine große Anzahl von Menschen ② (of house, telephone, bank account) Nummer f ▷ *They live at number five.* Sie wohnen in der Nummer fünf. ▷ *What's your phone number?* Wie ist Ihre Telefonnummer?; **You've got the wrong number.** Sie sind falsch verbunden. ③ (figure, digit) Zahl f ▷ *I can't read the second number.* Ich kann die zweite Zahl nicht lesen.

number plate n Nummernschild nt (pl Nummernschilder)
* The first letters of a German number
* plate allow you to tell where the car's
* owner lives. Thus L stands for Leipzig,
* LB for Ludwigsburg, LU for
* Ludwigshafen, etc.

nun n Nonne f ▷ *She's a nun.* Sie ist Nonne.

nurse n Krankenpfleger m, Krankenschwester f ▷ *He's a nurse.* Er ist Krankenpfleger. ▷ *She's a nurse.* Sie ist Krankenschwester.

nursery n ① (for children) Kindergarten m (pl Kindergärten) ② (for plants) Baumschule f

nursery school n Kindergarten m (pl Kindergärten)
* German children go to **Kindergarten**
* from the age of 3 to 6.

nut n ① Nuss f (pl Nüsse) ② (made of metal) Mutter f

nuts adj *He's nuts.* (informal) Er spinnt.

nylon n Nylon nt

O

oak n Eiche f ▷ *an oak table* ein Eichentisch m
oar n Ruder nt (pl Ruder)
oats npl Hafer m
obedient adj gehorsam
obey vb gehorchen [**48**] (perf hat gehorcht) ▷ *She didn't obey her mother.* Sie hat ihrer Mutter nicht gehorcht.; **to obey the rules** die Regeln befolgen [**7**]
object n Gegenstand m (pl Gegenstände) ▷ *a familiar object* ein vertrauter Gegenstand
objection n Einspruch m (pl Einsprüche)
oboe n Oboe f ▷ *I play the oboe.* Ich spiele Oboe.
obsessed adj besessen ▷ *He's completely obsessed with trains.* Er ist von Zügen ganz besessen.
obsession n Leidenschaft f ▷ *Football's an obsession of mine.* Fußball ist meine Leidenschaft.
obtain vb erhalten [**33**] (imperf erhielt, perf hat erhalten)

obvious adj offensichtlich
obviously adv ❶ (of course) natürlich ▷ *Do you want to pass the exam? — Obviously!* Willst du die Prüfung bestehen? — Natürlich! ▷ *Obviously not!* Natürlich nicht! ❷ (visibly) offensichtlich ▷ *She was obviously exhausted.* Sie war offensichtlich erschöpft.
occasion n Gelegenheit f ▷ *a special occasion* eine besondere Gelegenheit; **on several occasions** mehrmals
occasionally adv ab und zu
occupation n Beschäftigung f
occupy vb besetzen [**7**] (perf hat besetzt) ▷ *That seat is occupied.* Der Platz ist besetzt.
occur vb (happen) passieren [**76**] (perf ist passiert) ▷ *The accident occurred yesterday.* Der Unfall ist gestern passiert.; **It suddenly occurred to me that ...** Plötzlich ist mir eingefallen, dass ...
OCD abbr (= obsessive compulsive disorder) Zwangsstörung f
ocean n Ozean m (pl Ozeane)
o'clock adv **at four o'clock** um vier Uhr; **It's five o'clock.** Es ist fünf Uhr.
October n Oktober m ▷ *in October* im Oktober
octopus n Tintenfisch m (pl Tintenfische)
odd adj ❶ eigenartig ▷ *That's odd!* Das ist eigenartig! ❷ ungerade ▷ *an odd number* eine ungerade Zahl
of prep von ▷ *some photos of my holiday* Fotos von meinen Ferien ▷ *three of us* drei von uns ▷ *a friend of mine* ein Freund von mir ▷ *That's very kind of you.* Das ist sehr nett von Ihnen. ▷ *Can I have half of that?* Kann ich die Hälfte davon haben?

▌ 'of' is not translated when specifying a quantity of something.
▷ *a kilo of oranges* ein Kilo Orangen

ENGLISH > GERMAN

'of' is often expressed by using the genitive.
▷ *the end of the film* das Ende des Films ▷ *the top of the stairs* das obere Ende der Treppe ▷ *the front of the house* die Vorderseite des Hauses; **a boy of ten** ein zehnjähriger Junge; **the fourteenth of September** der vierzehnte September; **It's made of wood.** Es ist aus Holz.

off *adv, prep, adj*

For other expressions with 'off', see the verbs 'get', 'take', 'turn' etc.

❶ *(heater, light, TV)* aus ▷ *All the lights are off.* Alle Lichter sind aus. **❷** *(tap, gas)* zu ▷ *Are you sure the tap is off?* Bist du sicher, dass der Hahn zu ist? **❸** *(cancelled)* abgesagt ▷ *The match is off.* Das Spiel wurde abgesagt.; **to be off sick** krank sein [**65**]; **a day off** ein freier Tag; **to take a day off work** sich einen Tag freinehmen [**52**]; **She's off school today.** Sie ist heute nicht in der Schule.; **I must be off now.** Ich muss jetzt gehen.; **I'm off.** Ich gehe jetzt.

offence *n (crime)* Vergehen *nt (pl* Vergehen)

offer *n* Angebot *nt (pl* Angebote) ▷ *a good offer* ein günstiges Angebot; **'on special offer'** 'im Sonderangebot'
▶ *vb* anbieten [**8**] *(imperf* bot an, *perf* hat angeboten) ▷ *He offered to help me.* Er bot mir seine Hilfe an. ▷ *I offered to go with them.* Ich habe ihnen angeboten mitzugehen.

office *n* Büro *nt (pl* Büros) ▷ *She works in an office.* Sie arbeitet in einem Büro.; **doctor's office** die Arztpraxis

officer *n (in army)* Offizier *m (pl* Offiziere); **a police officer** ein Polizist/ eine Polizistin

official *adj* offiziell

off-licence *n* Wein- und Spirituosenhandlung *f*

offside *adj (in football)* im Abseits

olive oil

often *adv* oft ▷ *It often rains.* Es regnet oft. ▷ *How often do you go to church?* Wie oft gehst du in die Kirche? ▷ *I'd like to go skiing more often.* Ich würde gern öfter Ski fahren.

oil *n* **❶** *(for lubrication, cooking)* Öl *nt (pl* Öle); **an oil painting** ein Ölgemälde *nt* **❷** *(petroleum)* Erdöl *nt* ▷ *North Sea oil* Erdöl aus der Nordsee
▶ *vb* ölen [**38**]

oil rig *n* Bohrinsel *f* ▷ *He works on an oil rig.* Er arbeitet auf einer Bohrinsel.

ointment *n* Salbe *f*

okay *excl, adj* okay ▷ *Could you call back later?* — *Okay!* Kannst du später anrufen? — Okay! ▷ *I'll meet you at six o'clock, okay?* Ich treffe dich um sechs Uhr, okay? ▷ *Is that okay?* Ist das okay? ▷ *How was your holiday?* — *It was okay.* Wie waren die Ferien? — Okay.; **I'll do it tomorrow, if that's okay with you.** Ich mache das morgen, wenn du einverstanden bist.; **Are you okay?** Bist du in Ordnung?

old *adj* alt ▷ *an old dog* ein alter Hund ▷ *old people* alte Menschen ▷ *my old English teacher* mein alter Englischlehrer ▷ *How old are you?* Wie alt bist du? ▷ *He's ten years old.* Er ist zehn Jahre alt. ▷ *my older brother* mein älterer Bruder ▷ *my older sister* meine ältere Schwester ▷ *She's two years older than me.* Sie ist zwei Jahre älter als ich. ▷ *He's the oldest in the family.* Er ist der Älteste der Familie.

old age pensioner *n* Rentner *m (pl* Rentner), Rentnerin *f* ▷ *She's an old age pensioner.* Sie ist Rentnerin.

old-fashioned *adj* altmodisch ▷ *She wears old-fashioned clothes.* Sie trägt altmodische Kleidung. ▷ *My parents are rather old-fashioned.* Meine Eltern sind ziemlich altmodisch.

olive *n* Olive *f*

olive oil *n* Olivenöl *nt (pl* Olivenöle)

Olympic® *adj* olympisch; **the Olympics** die Olympischen Spiele
omelette *n* Omelett *nt* (*pl* Omeletts)
on *prep, adv*

> There are several ways of translating 'on'. Scan the examples to find one that is similar to what you want to say. For other expressions with 'on' see the verbs 'go', 'put', 'turn' etc.

❶ **auf**

> Use the accusative to express movement or a change of place. Use the dative when there is no change of place.

▷ *It's on the table.* Es ist auf dem Tisch. ▷ *Please, put it on the table.* Stell es bitte auf den Tisch. ▷ *on an island* auf einer Insel ▷ *on the left* auf der linken Seite
❷ **an** ▷ *on Friday* am Freitag ▷ *on Christmas Day* am ersten Weihnachtsfeiertag ▷ *on the twentieth of June* am zwanzigsten Juni ▷ *on my birthday* an meinem Geburtstag; **on Fridays** freitags

> Use the accusative to express movement or a change of place. Use the dative when there is no change of place.

▷ *There was not a single picture on the wall.* An der Wand hing kein einziges Bild. ▷ *She hung a picture up on the wall.* Sie hängte ein Bild an die Wand. ❸ **in** ▷ *on the second floor* im zweiten Stock ▷ *on TV* im Fernsehen ▷ *What's on TV?* Was kommt im Fernsehen? ▷ *I heard it on the radio.* Ich habe es im Radio gehört.; **on the bus (1)** *(by bus)* mit dem Bus ▷ *I go into town on the bus.* Ich fahre mit dem Bus in die Stadt. **(2)** *(inside)* im Bus ▷ *There was no empty seats on the bus.* Es gab keinen freien Platz im Bus.; **I go to school on my bike.** Ich fahre mit dem Fahrrad zur Schule.; **on holiday** in den Ferien ▷ *They're on holiday.* Sie sind in den Ferien.; **They are on strike.** Sie streiken.

▶ *adj* ❶ *(heater, light, TV)* **an** ▷ *I left the light on.* Ich habe das Licht angelassen. ▷ *Is the dishwasher on?* Ist die Spülmaschine an? ❷ *(tap, gas)* **auf** ▷ *Leave the tap on.* Lass den Hahn auf.; **What's on at the cinema?** Was gibt's im Kino?

once *adv* einmal ▷ *once a week* einmal pro Woche ▷ *once more* noch einmal ▷ *I've been to Germany once before.* Ich war schon einmal in Deutschland.; **Once upon a time ...** Es war einmal ...; **at once** sofort; **once in a while** ab und zu

one *num, pron*

> Use **ein** for masculine and neuter nouns, **eine** for feminine nouns.

❶ **ein** ▷ *one man* ein Mann ▷ *one child* ein Kind ▷ *We stayed there for one day.* Wir sind einen Tag dortgeblieben. ❷ **eine** ▷ *one minute* eine Minute ▷ *Do you need a stamp? — No thanks, I've got one.* Brauchst du eine Briefmarke? — Nein danke, ich habe eine. ▷ *I've got one brother and one sister.* Ich habe einen Bruder und eine Schwester. ❸ **eins**

> Use **eins** when counting.

▷ *one, two, three* eins, zwei, drei
❹ *(impersonal)* **man** ▷ *One never knows.* Man kann nie wissen.; **this one (1)** *(masculine)* dieser ▷ *Which foot hurts? — This one.* Welcher Fuß tut weh? — Dieser. **(2)** *(feminine)* diese ▷ *Which is your cup? — This one.* Welche ist deine Tasse? — Diese. **(3)** *(neuter)* dieses ▷ *Which is the best photo? — This one.* Welches ist das beste Foto? — Dieses.; **that one (1)** *(masculine)* der da ▷ *Which pen did you use? — That one.* Welchen Schreiber hast du benützt? — Den da. **(2)** *(feminine)* die da ▷ *Which bag is yours? — That one.* Welche ist deine Tasche? — Die da. **(3)** *(neuter)* das da ▷ *Which is*

ENGLISH > GERMAN

your car? — That one. Welches ist Ihr Auto? — Das da.

oneself pron ① sich ▷ *to hurt oneself* sich wehtun ② selbst ▷ *It's quicker to do it oneself.* Es geht schneller, wenn man es selbst macht.

one-way adj *a one-way street* eine Einbahnstraße

onion n Zwiebel f ▷ *onion soup* die Zwiebelsuppe

online adj, adv online

only adv, adj, conj ① einzig ▷ *Monday is the only day I'm free.* Montag ist mein einziger freier Tag. ▷ *German is the only subject I like.* Deutsch ist das einzige Fach, das ich mag. ② nur ▷ *How much was it? — Only twenty euros.* Wie viel hat es gekostet? — Nur zwanzig Euro. ▷ *We only want to stay for one night.* Wir wollen nur eine Nacht bleiben. ▷ *the same sweater, only in black* der gleiche Pullover, nur in Schwarz; **an only child** ein Einzelkind nt

onwards adv ab ▷ *from July onwards* ab Juli

open adj offen ▷ *The window was open.* Das Fenster war offen.; **The baker's is open on Sunday morning.** Die Bäckerei hat am Sonntagmorgen auf.; **in the open air** im Freien
▶ vb ① aufmachen [4] (perf hat aufgemacht) ▷ *Can I open the window?* Kann ich das Fenster aufmachen? ▷ *What time do the shops open?* Um wie viel Uhr machen die Geschäfte auf? ② aufgehen [29] (imperf ging auf, perf ist aufgegangen) ▷ *The door opens automatically.* Die Tür geht automatisch auf. ▷ *The door opened and in came Jim.* Die Tür ging auf und Jim kam herein.

opening hours npl Öffnungszeiten fpl

opera n Oper f

operate vb (machine) bedienen [7] (perf hat bedient); **to operate on someone** jemanden operieren [76]

operation n Operation f ▷ *a major operation* eine größere Operation; **to have an operation** operiert werden [91]

opinion n Meinung f ▷ *He asked me my opinion.* Er fragte mich nach meiner Meinung. ▷ *What's your opinion?* Was ist deine Meinung?; **in my opinion** meiner Meinung nach

opinion poll n Meinungsumfrage f

opponent n Gegner m (pl Gegner), Gegnerin f

opportunity n Gelegenheit f; **to have the opportunity to do something** die Gelegenheit haben [32], etwas zu tun

opposed adj *to be opposed to something* gegen etwas sein [65]

opposite adj, adv, prep
① entgegengesetzt ▷ *It's in the opposite direction.* Es ist in der entgegengesetzten Richtung.
② gegenüber ▷ *They live opposite.* Sie wohnen gegenüber. ▷ *the girl sitting opposite me* das Mädchen, das mir gegenüber saß; **the opposite sex** das andere Geschlecht

opposition n Opposition f

optician n Optiker m (pl Optiker), Optikerin f ▷ *She's an optician.* Sie ist Optikerin.

optimistic adj optimistisch

option n ① (choice) Wahl f ▷ *I've got no option.* Ich habe keine andere Wahl. ② (optional subject) Wahlfach nt (pl Wahlfächer) ▷ *I'm doing geology as my option.* Ich habe Geologie als Wahlfach.

or conj ① oder ▷ *Tea or coffee?* Tee oder Kaffee?

Use **weder ... noch** in negative sentences.

▷ *I don't eat meat or fish.* Ich esse weder Fleisch noch Fisch. ② (otherwise) sonst ▷ *Hurry up or you'll miss the bus.* Beeil dich, sonst verpasst du den Bus.; **Give me the money, or else!** Gib mir das Geld, sonst gibt's was!

oral adj mündlich ▷ *an oral exam* eine mündliche Prüfung
▶ n mündliche Prüfung f ▷ *I've got my German oral soon.* Ich habe bald meine mündliche Prüfung in Deutsch.

orange n Orange f; **an orange juice** ein Orangensaft m
▶ adj (colour) orangerot

orchard n Obstgarten m (pl Obstgärten)

orchestra n ❶ Orchester nt (pl Orchester) ▷ *I play in the school orchestra.* Ich spiele im Schulorchester. ❷ (stalls) Parkett nt ▷ *We sat in the orchestra.* Wir saßen im Parkett.

order n ❶ (sequence) Reihenfolge f ▷ *in alphabetical order* in alphabetischer Reihenfolge ❷ (at restaurant, in shop) Bestellung f ▷ *The waiter took our order.* Der Ober nahm unsere Bestellung auf. ❸ (instruction) Befehl m (pl Befehle) ▷ *That's an order.* Das ist ein Befehl.; **in order to** um zu; **'out of order'** 'außer Betrieb'
▶ vb bestellen [7] (perf hat bestellt) ▷ *We ordered steak and chips.* Wir haben Steak mit Pommes frites bestellt. ▷ *Are you ready to order?* Möchten Sie bestellen?

order about vb herumkommandieren [15] (perf hat herumkommandiert)

ordinary adj ❶ gewöhnlich ▷ *an ordinary day* ein gewöhnlicher Tag ❷ (people) normal ▷ *an ordinary family* eine normale Familie ▷ *He's just an ordinary guy.* Er ist ein ganz normaler Mensch.

organ n (instrument) Orgel f ▷ *I play the organ.* Ich spiele Orgel.

organic adj (fruit) biologisch angebaut; **organic vegetables** das Biogemüse sg

organization n Organisation f

organize vb organisieren [76] (perf hat organisiert)

original adj originell ▷ *It's a very original idea.* Das ist eine sehr originelle Idee.; *Our original plan was to go camping.* Ursprünglich wollten wir zelten.

originally adv ursprünglich

Orkney n Orkneyinseln fpl; **in Orkney** auf den Orkneyinseln

ornament n Vezierung f

orphan n Waisenkind nt (pl Waisenkinder) ▷ *She's an orphan.* Sie ist ein Waisenkind.

other adj, pron andere ▷ *Have you got these jeans in other colours?* Haben Sie diese Jeans in anderen Farben? ▷ *on the other side of the street* auf der anderen Straßenseite; **the other day** neulich; **the other one (1)** (masculine) der andere ▷ *This hat?* — *No, the other one.* Dieser Hut? — Nein, der andere. **(2)** (feminine) die andere ▷ *This cup?* — *No, the other one.* Diese Tasse? — Nein, die andere. **(3)** (neuter) das andere ▷ *This photo?* — *No, the other one.* Dieses Foto? — Nein, das andere.; **the others** die anderen ▷ *The others are going but I'm not.* Die anderen gehen, ich nicht.

otherwise adv, conj sonst ▷ *Note down the number, otherwise you'll forget it.* Schreib dir die Nummer auf, sonst vergisst du sie. ▷ *Put some sunscreen on, you'll get burned otherwise.* Creme dich ein, sonst bekommst du einen Sonnenbrand. ▷ *I'm tired, but otherwise I'm fine.* Ich bin müde, aber sonst geht's mir gut.

ought vb

> If you want to say that you feel obliged to do something, use the conditional tense of **sollen**.

▷ *I ought to phone my parents.* Ich sollte meine Eltern anrufen. ▷ *You ought not to do that.* Du solltest das nicht tun.

> If you want to say that something is likely, use the conditional tense of **müssen**.

▷ *He ought to win.* Er müsste gewinnen.

our adj unser ▷ *Our boss is quite nice.* Unser Chef ist ganz nett. ▷ *Our company*

ENGLISH > GERMAN

is going to expand. Unsere Firma wird expandieren. ▷ *Our house is quite big.* Unser Haus ist ziemlich groß. ▷ *Our neighbours are very nice.* Unsere Nachbarn sind sehr nett.

Do not use **unser** with parts of the body.

▷ *We had to shut our eyes.* Wir mussten die Augen zumachen.

ours pron ❶ unserer ▷ *Your garden is very big, ours is much smaller.* Euer Garten ist sehr groß, unserer ist viel kleiner.

unsere ▷ *Your school is very different from ours.* Eure Schule ist ganz anderes als unsere.

unseres ▷ *Your house is bigger than ours.* Euer Haus ist größer als unseres.

❷ unsere ▷ *Our teachers are strict. — Ours are too.* Unsere Lehrer sind streng. — Unsere auch.; **Is this ours?** Gehört das uns? ▷ *This car is ours. Whose is this? — It's ours.* Wem gehört das? — Uns.

ourselves pron ❶ uns ▷ *We really enjoyed ourselves.* Wir haben uns wirklich amüsiert. ❷ selbst ▷ *We built our garage ourselves.* Wir haben die Garage selbst gebaut.

out adv

There are several ways of translating 'out'. Scan the examples to find one that is similar to what you want to say. For other expressions with 'out', see the verbs 'go', 'put', 'turn' etc.

❶ (*outside*) draußen ▷ *It's cold out.* Es ist kalt draußen. ❷ (*light, fire*) aus ▷ *All the lights are out.* Alle Lichter sind aus.; **She's out.** Sie ist weg.; **She's out shopping.** Sie ist zum Einkaufen.; **out there** da draußen [29]; **to go out with somebody** mit jemandem gehen [29]; **out of** (1) aus ▷ *to drink out of a glass* aus einem Glas trinken (2) von ▷ *in nine cases out of ten* in neun von zehn Fällen (3) außerhalb ▷ *He lives out of town.* Er wohnt außerhalb der Stadt.; **out of town** drei Kilometer außerhalb der Stadt; **out of curiosity** aus Neugier; **out of work** arbeitslos; **That is out of the question.** Das kommt nicht infrage.; **You're out!** (*in game*) Du bist draußen!; **'way out'** 'Ausgang'

outdoor adj im Freien ▷ *outdoor activities* Aktivitäten im Freien; **an outdoor swimming pool** ein Freibad nt

outdoors adv im Freien

outfit n Outfit nt (pl Outfits) ▷ *a cowboy outfit* ein Cowboyoutfit

outing n Ausflug m (pl Ausflüge) ▷ *to go on an outing* einen Ausflug machen

outline n ❶ (*summary*) Grundriss m (gen Grundrisses, pl Grundrisse) ▷ *This is an outline of the plan.* Das ist der Grundriss des Plans. ❷ (*shape*) Umriss m (gen Umrisses, pl Umrisse) ▷ *We could see the outline of the mountain.* Wir konnten den Umriss des Berges erkennen.

outside n Außenseite f
▶ adj, adv, prep ❶ äußere ▷ *the outside walls* die äußeren Mauern ❷ draußen ▷ *It's very cold outside.* Draußen ist es sehr kalt. ❸ außerhalb ▷ *outside the school* außerhalb der Schule ▷ *outside school hours* außerhalb der Schulzeit

outskirts npl Stadtrand msg ▷ *on the outskirts of the town* am Stadtrand

outstanding adj bemerkenswert

oval adj oval

oven n Backofen m (pl Backöfen)

over prep, adv, adj ❶ über

Use the accusative to express movement or a change of place. Use the dative when there is no change of place.

▷ *The ball went over the wall.* Der Ball flog über die Mauer. ▷ *There's a mirror over the washbasin.* Über dem Becken ist ein Spiegel. ❷ (*more than*) über ▷ *It's over* twenty kilos. Es ist über zwanzig Kilo schwer. ▷ *The temperature was over thirty degrees.* Die Temperatur lag über dreißig Grad. ❸ *(finished)* vorbei ▷ *I'll be happy when the exams are over.* Ich bin froh, wenn die Prüfungen vorbei sind.; **over the holidays** die Ferien über; **over Christmas** über Weihnachten; **over here** hier; **over there** dort; **all over Scotland** in ganz Schottland

overcast *adj* bedeckt ▷ *The sky was overcast.* Der Himmel war bedeckt.

overdose *n (of drugs)* Überdosis f *(pl* Überdosen*)* ▷ *to take an overdose* eine Überdosis nehmen

overdraft *n* Überziehungskredit *m*

overseas *adv* ❶ im Ausland ▷ *I'd like to work overseas.* Ich würde gern im Ausland arbeiten. ❷ ins Ausland ▷ *His company has sent him overseas.* Seine Firma hat ihn ins Ausland geschickt.

overtake *vb* überholen **[18]** *(perf* hat überholt*)* ▷ *He overtook me.* Er hat mich überholt.

overtime *n* Überstunden *fpl* ▷ *to work overtime* Überstunden machen

overtook *vb see* **overtake**

overweight *adj* **to be overweight** Übergewicht haben **[32]**

owe *vb* schulden **[54]**; **to owe somebody something** jemandem etwas schulden **[54]**

owing to *prep* wegen ▷ *owing to bad weather* wegen des schlechten Wetters

owl *n* Eule *f*

own *adj* eigen ▷ *I've got my own bathroom.* Ich habe mein eigenes Badezimmer.; **I'd like a room of my own.** Ich hätte gern ein eigenes Zimmer.; **on one's own** allein
▶ *vb* besitzen **[68]** *(imperf* besaß, *perf* hat besessen*)* ▷ *My father owns a small business.* Mein Vater besitzt ein kleines Geschäft.

own up *vb* zugeben **[28]** *(pres* gibt zu, *imperf* gab zu, *perf* hat zugegeben*)*

owner *n* Besitzer *m (pl* Besitzer*)*, Besitzerin *f*

oxygen *n* Sauerstoff *m*

oyster *n* Auster *f*

ozone layer *n* Ozonschicht *f*

P

Pacific n Pazifik m
pack vb packen [**38**] ▷ I'll help you pack. Ich helfe dir packen. ▷ I've packed my case. Ich habe meinen Koffer gepackt.; **Pack it in!** (stop it) Lass es!
▶ n ❶ (packet) Packung f ▷ a pack of cigarettes eine Packung Zigaretten ❷ (of yoghurts, cans) Pack m (pl Packs) ▷ a six-pack ein Sechserpack; **a pack of cards** ein Spiel Karten nt
package n Paket nt (pl Pakete); **a package holiday** eine Pauschalreise
packed adj gerammelt voll ▷ The cinema was packed. Das Kino war gerammelt voll.
packed lunch n Lunchpaket nt (pl Lunchpakete); **I take a packed lunch to school.** Ich nehme für mittags etwas zum Essen in die Schule mit.
packet n Packung f ▷ a packet of cigarettes eine Packung Zigaretten
pad n (notepad) Notizblock m (pl Notizblöcke)
paddle vb ❶ (canoe) paddeln [**34**] ❷ (in water) planschen [**48**]
▶ n (for canoe) Paddel nt (pl Paddel); **to go for a paddle** planschen gehen [**29**]
padlock n Vorhängeschloss nt (gen Vorhängeschlosses, pl Vorhängeschlösser)
page n (of book) Seite f
▶ vb **to page somebody** jemanden per Pager benachrichtigen [**7**]
pain n Schmerz m (gen Schmerzes, pl Schmerzen) ▷ a terrible pain ein furchtbarer Schmerz; **I've got pains in my stomach.** Ich habe Bauchschmerzen.; **to be in pain** Schmerzen haben [**32**]; **He's a real pain.** (informal) Er geht einem echt auf die Nerven.
painful adj schmerzhaft; **to suffer from painful periods** starke Periodenschmerzen haben [**32**]; **to be painful** wehtun [**81**]
painkiller n Schmerzmittel nt (pl Schmerzmittel)
paint n Farbe f
▶ vb ❶ streichen (imperf strich, perf hat gestrichen) ▷ to paint something green etwas grün streichen ❷ (pictures) malen [**38**] ▷ She painted a picture of the house. Sie hat von dem Haus ein Bild gemalt.
paintbrush n Pinsel m (pl Pinsel)
painter n Maler m (pl Maler), Malerin f; **a painter and decorator** ein Anstreicher m
painting n ❶ Malen nt ▷ My hobby is painting. Malen ist mein Hobby. ❷ (picture) Bild nt (pl Bilder) ▷ a painting by Picasso ein Bild von Picasso
pair n Paar nt (pl Paare) ▷ a pair of shoes ein Paar Schuhe; **a pair of scissors** eine Schere; **a pair of trousers** eine Hose; **a pair of jeans** eine Jeans; **in pairs** paarweise
Pakistan n Pakistan nt; **from Pakistan** aus Pakistan; **to Pakistan** nach Pakistan

Pakistani n Pakistani m (pl Pakistani), Pakistani f
▶ adj pakistanisch; **He's Pakistani.** Er ist Pakistani.
palace n Palast m (pl Paläste)
pale adj blass ▷ *You're very pale.* Du bist sehr blass.; **a pale blue shirt** ein hellblaues Hemd
Palestine n Palästina nt; **from Palestine** aus Palästina; **to Palestine** nach Palästina
Palestinian adj palästinensisch; **He's Palestinian.** Er ist Palästinenser.
▶ n Palästinenser m (pl Palästinenser), Palästinenserin f
palm n (of hand) Handteller m (pl Handteller); **a palm tree** eine Palme
pan n ❶ (saucepan) Topf m (pl Töpfe) ❷ (frying pan) Pfanne f
pancake n Pfannkuchen m (pl Pfannkuchen)
panic n Panik f
▶ vb in Panik geraten (pres gerät in Panik, imperf geriet in Panik, perf ist in Panik geraten) ▷ *She panicked.* Sie geriet in Panik.; **Don't panic!** Nur keine Panik!
panther n Panther m (pl Panther)
pantomime n Weihnachtsmärchen nt (pl Weihnachtsmärchen)
pants npl ❶ (underwear) Unterhose f ▷ *a pair of pants* eine Unterhose ❷ (trousers) Hose f ▷ *a pair of pants* eine Hose
pantyhose npl (US) Strumpfhose f
paper n ❶ Papier nt (pl Papiere) ▷ *a piece of paper* ein Stück Papier ▷ *a paper towel* ein Papierhandtuch ❷ (newspaper) Zeitung f ▷ *an advert in the paper* eine Anzeige in der Zeitung; **an exam paper** eine Klausur
paperback n Taschenbuch nt (pl Taschenbücher)
paper clip n Büroklammer f
paper round n to do a paper round Zeitungen austragen [**77**]

parachute n Fallschirm m (pl Fallschirme)
parade n Parade f
paradise n Paradies nt (gen Paradieses, pl Paradiese)
paragraph n Paragraf m (gen Paragrafen, pl Paragrafen)
parallel adj parallel
paralyzed adj gelähmt
paramedic n Sanitäter m (pl Sanitäter), Sanitäterin f
parcel n Paket nt (pl Pakete)
pardon n Pardon? Wie bitte?
parent n ❶ (father) Vater m ❷ (mother) Mutter f; **my parents** meine Eltern
Paris n Paris nt
park n Park m (pl Parks); **a national park** ein Nationalpark; **a theme park** ein Themenpark; **a car park** ein Parkplatz m
▶ vb parken [**38**] ▷ *Where can I park my car?* Wo kann ich mein Auto parken?; **We couldn't find anywhere to park.** Wir haben nirgends einen Parkplatz gefunden.
parking n Parken nt ⊳ 'no parking' 'Parken verboten'
parking lot n (US) Parkplatz m (gen Parkplatzes, pl Parkplätze)
parking meter n Parkuhr f
parking ticket n Strafzettel m (pl Strafzettel)
parliament n Parlament nt (pl Parlamente)
parole n on parole auf Bewährung
parrot n Papagei m (pl Papageien)
parsley n Petersilie f
part n ❶ (section) Teil m (pl Teile) ▷ *The first part of the film was boring.* Der erste Teil des Films war langweilig. ❷ (component) Teil nt (pl Teile) ▷ *spare parts* Ersatzteile ❸ (in play, film) Rolle f; **to take part in something** an etwas teilnehmen [**52**]
particular adj bestimmt ▷ *I am looking for a particular book.* Ich suche ein

bestimmtes Buch. ▷ *Are you looking for anything particular?* Suchen Sie nach etwas Bestimmtem?; **nothing in particular** nichts Bestimmtes
particularly *adv* besonders
partly *adv* zum Teil
partner *n* Partner *m* (*pl* Partner), Partnerin *f*
part-time *adj, adv* Teilzeit ▷ *a part-time job* eine Teilzeitarbeit ▷ *She works part-time.* Sie arbeitet Teilzeit.
party *n* ❶ Party *f* (*pl* Partys) ▷ *a birthday party* eine Geburtstagsparty ▷ *a Christmas party* eine Weihnachtsparty ▷ *a New Year party* eine Silvesterparty ❷ (*political*) Partei *f* ▷ *the Conservative Party* die Konservative Partei ❸ (*group*) Gruppe *f* ▷ *a party of tourists* eine Gruppe Touristen
pass *n* Pass *m* (*gen* Passes, *pl* Pässe) ▷ *The pass was blocked with snow.* Der Pass war zugeschneit. ▷ *That was a good pass by Ferguson.* Das war ein guter Pass von Ferguson.; **to get a pass** (*in exam*) bestehen [72]; **a bus pass (1)** (*monthly*) eine Monatskarte für den Bus **(2)** (*for old-age pensioners*) eine Seniorenkarte für den Bus

- Almost all German cities operate an integrated public transport system; you can buy a weekly (**Wochenkarte**), monthly (**Monatskarte**) or yearly (**Jahreskarte**) pass which is valid for that period on all buses, trams and light railway vehicles in a particular zone.

▷ *vb* ❶ (*give*) geben [28] (*pres* gibt, *imperf* gab, *perf* hat gegeben) ▷ *Could you pass me the salt?* Könntest du mir das Salz geben? ❷ (*go by*) vergehen [29] (*imperf* verging, *perf* ist vergangen) ▷ *The time has passed quickly.* Die Zeit ist schnell vergangen. ❸ (*on foot*) vorbeigehen [29] an (*imperf* ging vorbei, *perf* ist vorbeigegangen) ▷ *I pass his house on my way to school.* Auf dem Weg zur Schule

gehe ich an seinem Haus vorbei. ❹ (*in vehicle*) vorbeifahren [21] an (*pres* fährt vorbei, *imperf* fuhr vorbei, *perf* ist vorbeigefahren) ▷ *We passed the post office.* Wir sind an der Post vorbeigefahren. ❺ (*exam*) bestehen [72] (*imperf* bestand, *perf* hat bestanden) ▷ *Did you pass?* Hast du bestanden?; **to pass an exam** eine Prüfung bestehen [72]
pass out *vb* (*faint*) ohnmächtig werden [91] (*pres* wird ohnmächtig, *imperf* wurde ohnmächtig, *perf* ist ohnmächtig geworden)
passage *n* ❶ (*piece of writing*) Abschnitt *m* (*pl* Abschnitte) ▷ *Read the passage carefully.* Lest den Abschnitt sorgfältig durch. ❷ (*corridor*) Gang *m* (*pl* Gänge)
passenger *n* Passagier *m* (*pl* Passagiere), Passagierin *f*
passion *n* Leidenschaft *f*
passive *adj* passiv; **passive smoking** das Passivrauchen
Passover *n* Passahfest *nt*
passport *n* Pass *m* (*gen* Passes, *pl* Pässe); **passport control** die Passkontrolle
password *n* Passwort *nt* (*pl* Passwörter)
past *adv, prep* (*beyond*) nach ▷ *It's on the right, just past the station.* Es ist auf der rechten Seite, gleich nach dem Bahnhof. ▷ *It's quarter past nine.* Es ist Viertel nach neun. ▷ *It's past midnight.* Es ist nach Mitternacht.; **It's half past ten.** Es ist halb elf.; **to go past (1)** (*vehicle*) vorbeifahren [21] an ▷ *The bus went past without stopping.* Der Bus ist vorbeigefahren, ohne anzuhalten. ▷ *The bus goes past our house.* Der Bus fährt an unserem Haus vorbei. **(2)** (*on foot*) vorbeigehen [29] ▷ *He went past without saying hello.* Er ging vorbei, ohne Hallo zu sagen. ▷ *I went past your house yesterday.* Ich bin gestern an eurem Haus vorbeigegangen.

▸ n Vergangenheit f ▷ *She lives in the past.* Sie lebt in der Vergangenheit.; **in the past** *(previously)* früher ▷ *That was common in the past.* Das war früher üblich.

pasta n Teigwaren fpl ▷ *Pasta is easy to cook.* Teigwaren sind leicht zu kochen.

pasteurized adj pasteurisiert

pastry n Teig m; **pastries** *(cakes)* das Gebäck sg

pat vb *(dog, cat)* streicheln [**88**] *(perf* hat gestreichelt)

patch n ❶ Stück nt *(pl* Stücke) ▷ *a patch of material* ein Stück Stoff ❷ *(for flat tyre)* Flicken m *(pl* Flicken); **He's got a bald patch.** Er hat eine kahle Stelle.

path n Weg m *(pl* Wege)

pathetic adj schrecklich schlecht ▷ *Our team was pathetic.* Unsere Mannschaft war schrecklich schlecht.

patience n ❶ Geduld f ▷ *He hasn't got much patience.* Er hat nicht viel Geduld. ❷ *(card game)* Patience f ▷ *to play patience* Patience spielen

patient n Patient m *(gen* Patienten, *pl* Patienten), Patientin f
▸ adj geduldig

patio n Terrasse f

patrol n ❶ *(military)* Patrouille f ❷ *(of police)* Streife f

patrol car n Streifenwagen m *(pl* Streifenwagen)

pattern n Muster nt *(pl* Muster) ▷ *a geometric pattern* ein geometrisches Muster ▷ *a sewing pattern* ein Nähmuster

pause n Pause f

pavement n Bürgersteig m *(pl* Bürgersteige)

paw n Pfote f

pay n Bezahlung f
▸ vb bezahlen [**7**] *(perf* hat bezahlt) ▷ *They pay me more on Sundays.* Sie bezahlen mir sonntags mehr. ▷ **to pay by cheque** mit Scheck bezahlen ▷ **to pay by credit card** mit Kreditkarte bezahlen; **to pay for something** für etwas bezahlen [**7**]; **to pay extra for something** für etwas extra bezahlen [**7**]; **to pay attention** aufpassen [**31**]; **Don't pay any attention to him.** Beachte ihn einfach nicht.; **to pay somebody a visit** jemanden besuchen [**7**]; **to pay somebody back** *(money)* es jemandem zurückzahlen [**15**]

payment n Bezahlung f

payphone n Münzfernsprecher m *(pl* Münzfernsprecher)

PC n *(= personal computer)* PC m *(pl* PCs) ▷ *She typed the report on her PC.* Sie hat den Bericht am PC erfasst.

PE n *(= physical education)* Sportunterricht m

pea n Erbse f

peace n ❶ *(after war)* Frieden m ❷ *(quietness)* Stille f

peaceful adj ❶ *(calm)* ruhig ▷ *a peaceful afternoon* ein ruhiger Nachmittag ❷ *(not violent)* friedlich ▷ *a peaceful protest* ein friedlicher Protest

peach n Pfirsich m *(pl* Pfirsiche)

peacock n Pfau m *(pl* Pfauen)

peak n *(of mountain)* Gipfel m *(pl* Gipfel); **the peak rate** der Spitzentarif; **in peak season** in der Hochsaison

peanut n Erdnuss f *(pl* Erdnüsse) ▷ *a packet of peanuts* eine Packung Erdnüsse

peanut butter n Erdnussbutter f ▷ *a peanut-butter sandwich* ein Brot mit Erdnussbutter

pear n Birne f

pearl n Perle f

pebble n Kieselstein m *(pl* Kieselsteine); **a pebble beach** ein Kieselstrand m

peculiar adj eigenartig ▷ *He's a peculiar person.* Er ist ein eigenartiger Mensch. ▷ *It tastes peculiar.* Es schmeckt eigenartig.

pedal n Pedal nt *(pl* Pedale)

ENGLISH > GERMAN

pedestrian n Fußgänger m (pl Fußgänger), Fußgängerin f
pedestrian crossing n Fußgängerüberweg m (pl Fußgängerüberwege)
pee n to have a pee (informal) pinkeln [88]
peel n (of orange) Schale f
▶ vb ❶ schälen [38] ▷ Shall I peel the potatoes? Soll ich die Kartoffeln schälen? ❷ sich schälen [38] ▷ My nose is peeling. Meine Nase schält sich.
peg n ❶ (for coats) Haken m (pl Haken) ❷ (clothes peg) Wäscheklammer f ❸ (tent peg) Hering m (pl Heringe)
pelican crossing n Fußgängerampel f
pelvis n Becken nt (pl Becken)
pen n Schreiber m (pl Schreiber)
penalty n ❶ (punishment) Strafe f ▷ the death penalty die Todesstrafe ❷ (in football) Elfmeter m (pl Elfmeter) ❸ (in rugby) Strafstoß m (gen Strafstoßes, pl Strafstöße); **a penalty shoot-out** ein Elfmeterschießen nt
pence npl Pence mpl
pencil n Bleistift m (pl Bleistifte); **in pencil** mit Bleistift
pencil case n Federmäppchen nt (pl Federmäppchen)
pencil sharpener n Bleistiftspitzer m (pl Bleistiftspitzer)
pendant n Anhänger m (pl Anhänger)
pen friend n Brieffreund m (pl Brieffreunde), Brieffreundin f
penguin n Pinguin m (pl Pinguine)
penicillin n Penizillin n
penis n Penis m (gen Penis, pl Penisse)
penknife n Taschenmesser nt (pl Taschenmesser)
penny n Penny m (pl Pennys or Pence)
pension n Rente f
pensioner n Rentner m (pl Rentner), Rentnerin f
people npl ❶ Leute pl ▷ The people were nice. Die Leute waren nett. ▷ a lot of people viele Leute ❷ (individuals)

429 | **perhaps**

Menschen mpl ▷ six people sechs Menschen ▷ several people mehrere Menschen; **German people** die Deutschen; **People say that ...** Man sagt, dass ...
pepper n ❶ (spice) Pfeffer m ▷ Pass the pepper, please. Gib mir mal bitte den Pfeffer. ❷ (vegetable) Paprikaschote f ▷ a green pepper eine grüne Paprikaschote
peppermill n Pfeffermühle f
peppermint n (sweet) Pfefferminzbonbon nt (pl Pfefferminzbonbons); **peppermint chewing gum** der Kaugummi mit Pfefferminzgeschmack
per prep pro ▷ per day pro Tag ▷ per week pro Woche; **thirty miles per hour** dreißig Meilen in der Stunde
per cent adv Prozent nt ▷ fifty per cent fünfzig Prozent
percentage n Prozentsatz m (gen Prozentsatzes, pl Prozentsätze)
percussion n Schlagzeug nt (pl Schlagzeuge) ▷ I play percussion. Ich spiele Schlagzeug.
perfect adj perfekt ▷ He speaks perfect English. Er spricht perfekt Englisch.
perfectly adv ❶ ganz ▷ You know perfectly well what happened. Du weißt ganz genau, was passiert ist. ❷ (very well) perfekt ▷ The system worked perfectly. Das System hat perfekt funktioniert.
perform vb (act, play) spielen [38]
performance n ❶ (show) Vorstellung f ▷ The performance lasts two hours. Die Vorstellung dauert zwei Stunden. ❷ (acting) Darstellung f ▷ his performance as Hamlet seine Darstellung des Hamlet ❸ (results) Leistung f ▷ the team's poor performance die schwache Leistung der Mannschaft
perfume n Parfüm nt (pl Parfüms)
perhaps adv vielleicht ▷ a bit boring, perhaps etwas langweilig vielleicht

period | 430

▷ *Perhaps he's ill.* Vielleicht ist er krank. ▷ *perhaps not* vielleicht nicht

period n ❶ Zeit f ▷ *for a limited period* für eine begrenzte Zeit ❷ *(in history)* Epoche f ▷ *the Victorian period* die viktorianische Epoche ❸ *(menstruation)* Periode f ▷ *I'm having my period.* Ich habe meine Periode. ❹ *(lesson time)* Stunde f ▷ *Each period lasts forty minutes.* Jede Stunde dauert vierzig Minuten.

permanent adj ❶ *(damage, solution, relationship)* dauerhaft ▷ *a permanent solution* eine dauerhafte Lösung ❷ *(difficulties, tension)* dauernd ▷ *a permanent headache* dauernde Kopfschmerzen ❸ *(job, address)* fest ▷ *a permanent job* eine feste Arbeit

permission n Erlaubnis f (pl Erlaubnisse) ▷ *to ask somebody's permission* jemanden um Erlaubnis bitten; **Could I have permission to leave early?** Darf ich früher gehen?

permit n Schein m (pl Scheine) ▷ *a fishing permit* ein Angelschein

persecute vb verfolgen [**84**] (perf hat verfolgt)

person n ❶ Mensch m (gen Menschen, pl Menschen) ▷ *She's a very nice person.* Sie ist ein netter Mensch. ❷ *(in grammar)* Person f ▷ *first person singular* erste Person Singular; **in person** persönlich

personal adj persönlich

personality n Persönlichkeit f

personally adv persönlich ▷ *I don't know him personally.* Ich kenne ihn nicht persönlich. ▷ *Personally I don't agree.* Ich persönlich bin nicht einverstanden.

perspiration n Schweiß m

persuade vb überreden [**54**] (perf hat überredet); **to persuade somebody to do something** jemanden überreden [**54**], etwas zu tun

Peru n Peru nt

Peruvian adj peruanisch

ENGLISH > GERMAN

pessimistic adj pessimistisch

pest n *(person)* Nervensäge f ▷ *He's a real pest!* Er ist eine echte Nervensäge!

pester vb belästigen [**7**] (perf hat belästigt) ▷ *Stop pestering me!* Hör auf, mich zu belästigen!; **The children pestered me to take them to the zoo.** Die Kinder ließen ihr keine Ruhe, mit ihnen in den Zoo zu gehen.

pesticide n Pestizid nt

pet n Haustier nt (pl Haustiere) ▷ *Have you got a pet?* Hast du ein Haustier?; **She's the teacher's pet.** Sie ist das Schätzchen der Lehrerin.

petrol n Benzin nt (pl Benzine)

petrol station n Tankstelle f

pharmacy n Apotheke f

pheasant n Fasan m (pl Fasane)

philosophy n Philosophie f

phobia n Phobie f

phone n ❶ Telefon nt (pl Telefone) ▷ *Where's the phone?* Wo ist das Telefon? ▷ *Is there a phone here?* Gibt es hier ein Telefon?; **by phone** telefonisch ❷ *(mobile)* Handy nt (pl Handys) ▷ *I've got a new phone.* Ich habe ein neues Handy.; **to be on the phone** *(speaking)* telefonieren [**76**]; **Can I use the phone, please?** Kann ich mal bitte telefonieren? ▶ vb anrufen [**56**] (imperf rief an, perf hat angerufen) ▷ *I tried to phone you yesterday.* Ich habe gestern versucht, dich anzurufen.

phone bill n Telefonrechnung f

phone book n Telefonbuch nt (pl Telefonbücher)

phone box n Telefonzelle f

phone call n Anruf m (pl Anrufe) ▷ *There's a phone call for you.* Da ist ein Anruf für Sie.; **to make a phone call** telefonieren [**76**]

phonecard n Telefonkarte f

phone number n Telefonnummer f

photo n Foto nt (pl Fotos) ▷ *to take a photo* ein Foto machen ▷ *to take a photo*

ENGLISH > GERMAN

of somebody ein Foto von jemandem machen

photocopier n Fotokopierer m (pl Fotokopierer)

photocopy n Fotokopie f
▶ vb fotokopieren [**76**] (perf hat fotokopiert)

photograph n Foto nt (pl Fotos) ▷ to take a photograph ein Foto machen ▷ to take a photograph of somebody ein Foto von jemandem machen

> Be careful not to translate **photograph** by Fotograf.

▶ vb fotografieren [**76**] (perf hat fotografiert)

photographer n Fotograf m (gen Fotografen, pl Fotografen), Fotografin f ▷ She's a photographer.

photography n Fotografie f ▷ My hobby is photography. Mein Hobby ist die Fotografie.

phrase n Wendung f

phrase book n Sprachführer m (pl Sprachführer)

physical adj (of the body) körperlich ▷ physical exercise körperliche Bewegung; **physical education** der Sportunterricht; **physical therapist** (man) der Krankengymnast
▶ n (US) ärztliche Untersuchung f

physicist n Physiker m (pl Physiker), Physikerin f ▷ He's a physicist. Er ist Physiker.

physics n Physik f ▷ She teaches physics. Sie unterrichtet Physik.

physiotherapist n Krankengymnast m (gen Krankengymnasten, pl Krankengymnasten), Krankengymnastin f

physiotherapy n Krankengymnastik f

pianist n Pianist m (gen Pianisten, pl Pianisten), Pianistin f

piano n Klavier nt (pl Klaviere) ▷ I play the piano. Ich spiele Klavier. ▷ I have piano lessons. Ich nehme Klavierstunden.

431 | piece

pick n Take your pick! Du hast die Wahl!
▶ vb ❶ (choose) auswählen [**4**] (perf hat ausgewählt) ▷ I picked the biggest piece. Ich habe das größte Stück ausgewählt. ❷ (fruit, flowers) pflücken [**48**]; **to pick on somebody** auf jemandem herumhacken [**15**] ▷ She's always picking on me. Sie hackt dauernd auf mir herum.; **to pick out** auswählen [**4**] ▷ I like them all – it's difficult to pick one out. Sie gefallen mir alle – es ist schwierig, eins auszuwählen.; **to pick up** (1) (collect) abholen [**4**] ▷ We'll come to the airport to pick you up. Wir holen dich am Flughafen ab. (2) (from floor) aufheben ▷ Could you help me pick up the toys? Kannst du mir helfen, die Spielsachen aufzuheben? (3) (informal: learn) aufschnappen [**4**] ▷ I picked up some Spanish during my holiday. Ich habe während der Ferien etwas Spanisch aufgeschnappt.

pickpocket n Taschendieb m (pl Taschendiebe), Taschendiebin f

picnic n Picknick nt (pl Picknicke); **to have a picnic** picknicken [**48**]

picture n ❶ Bild nt (pl Bilder) ▷ The books has lots of pictures. Das Buch ist voller Bilder.; **to draw a picture of something** etwas zeichnen [**53**] ❷ Foto nt (pl Fotos) ▷ My picture was in the paper. Mein Foto war in der Zeitung. ❸ (painting) Gemälde nt (pl Gemälde) ▷ a famous picture ein berühmtes Gemälde; **to paint a picture of something** etwas malen [**38**]; **the pictures** (cinema) das Kino ▷ Shall we go to the pictures? Sollen wir ins Kino gehen?

pie n ❶ (savoury) Pastete f ❷ (sweet) Obstkuchen m (pl Obstkuchen);
an apple pie ein gedeckter Apfelkuchen

piece n Stück nt (pl Stücke) ▷ A small piece, please. Ein kleines Stück, bitte.;

a piece of furniture ein Möbelstück nt; **a piece of advice** ein Ratschlag m

pier n Pier m (pl Piere)

pierced adj ❶ durchstochen ▷ I've got pierced ears. Ich habe durchstochene Ohrläppchen. ❷ gepierct ▷ She's got a pierced nose. Sie hat eine gepiercte Nase.

piercing adj (cry) durchdringend

pig n Schwein nt (pl Schweine)

pigeon n Taube f

piggy bank n Sparschwein nt (pl Sparschweine)

pigtail n Zopf m (pl Zöpfe)

pile n ❶ (tidy) Stapel m (pl Stapel) ❷ (untidy) Haufen m (pl Haufen)

pill n Pille f; **to be on the pill** die Pille nehmen [52]

pillow n Kopfkissen nt (pl Kopfkissen)

pilot n ❶ Pilot m (pl Piloten), Pilotin f ▷ He's a pilot. Er ist Pilot.

pimple n Pickel m (pl Pickel)

PIN n (= personal identification number) PIN-Nummer f

pin n Stecknadel f; **I've got pins and needles in my foot.** Mein Fuß ist eingeschlafen.

pinball n Flipper m (pl Flipper); **to play pinball** flippern [34]; **a pinball machine** ein Flipper

pinch vb ❶ kneifen (imperf kniff, perf hat gekniffen) ▷ He pinched me! Er hat mich gekniffen! ❷ (informal: steal) klauen [38] ▷ Who's pinched my pen? Wer hat meinen Schreiber geklaut?

pine n Kiefer f ▷ a pine table ein Kieferntisch m

pineapple n Ananas f (pl Ananas)

pink adj rosa

 rosa is invariable.

▷ a pink shirt ein rosa Hemd

pint n Pint nt (pl Pints)
- In Germany measurements are in
- litres and centilitres. A pint is about
- 0.6 litres. German people don't drink
- pints of beer, they are more likely to
- order ein großes Bier.

to have a pint ein Bier trinken [80]

pipe n ❶ (for water, gas) Rohr nt (pl Rohre) ▷ The pipes froze. Die Rohre sind eingefroren. ❷ (for smoking) Pfeife f ▷ He smokes a pipe. Er raucht Pfeife.; **the pipes** (bagpipes) der Dudelsack sg ▷ He plays the pipes. Er spielt Dudelsack.

pirate n Pirat m (gen Piraten, pl Piraten)

pirated adj **a pirated video** ein Raubvideo nt

Pisces nsg Fische mpl ▷ I'm Pisces. Ich bin Fisch.

pistol n Pistole f

pitch n Platz m (gen Platzes, pl Plätze) ▷ a football pitch ein Fußballplatz
▶ vb (tent) aufschlagen [59] (pres schlägt auf, imperf schlug auf, perf hat aufgeschlagen) ▷ We pitched our tent near the beach. Wir haben unser Zelt in der Nähe des Strandes aufgeschlagen.

pity n Mitleid nt; **What a pity!** Wie schade!
▶ vb bemitleiden [7] (perf hat bemitleidet)

pizza n Pizza f (pl Pizzas)

place n ❶ (location) Ort m (pl Orte) ▷ It's a quiet place. Es ist ein ruhiger Ort. ▷ interesting places interessante Orte ❷ (space) Platz m (gen Platzes, pl Plätze) ▷ a parking place ein Parkplatz ▷ a university place ein Studienplatz; **to change places** die Plätze tauschen [48]; **to take place** stattfinden [24]; **at your place** bei dir; **to my place** zu mir
▶ vb legen [38] ▷ He placed his hand on hers. Er legte seine Hand auf ihre.; **He was placed third.** Er wurde Dritter.

plain n Ebene f
▶ adj, adv ❶ (self-coloured) einfarbig ▷ a plain carpet ein einfarbiger Teppich ❷ (not fancy) einfach ▷ a plain white blouse eine einfache weiße Bluse

plain chocolate n bittere Schokolade f
plait n Zopf m (pl Zöpfe) ▷ She wears her hair in a plait. Sie trägt einen Zopf.
plan n Plan m (pl Pläne) ▷ What are your plans for the holidays? Welche Ferienpläne habt ihr? ▷ to make plans Pläne machen ▷ a plan of the campsite ein Plan des Zeltplatzes; **Everything went according to plan.** Alles lief nach Plan.; **my essay plan** das Konzept für meinen Aufsatz
▶ vb planen [38] ▷ We're planning a trip to Germany. Wir planen eine Reise nach Deutschland. ▷ Plan your revision carefully. Plant eure Stoffwiederholung sorgfältig.; **to plan to do something** vorhaben [32], etwas zu tun ▷ I'm planning to get a job in the holidays. Ich habe vor, mir einen Ferienjob zu suchen.
plane n Flugzeug nt (pl Flugzeuge) ▷ by plane mit dem Flugzeug
planet n Planet m (gen Planeten, pl Planeten)
plant n ① Pflanze f ▷ to water the plants die Pflanzen gießen ② (factory) Fabrik f
▶ vb pflanzen [36]
plant-based adj pflanzlich
plaster n ① (sticking plaster) Pflaster nt (pl Pflaster) ▷ Have you got a plaster? Hast du ein Pflaster? ② (for fracture) Gips m (gen Gipses, pl Gipse) ▷ Her leg's in plaster. Sie hat das Bein in Gips.
plastic n Plastik nt ▷ It's made of plastic. Es ist aus Plastik.
▶ adj aus Plastik ▷ a plastic mac ein Regenmantel aus Plastik; **a plastic bag** eine Plastiktüte
plate n (for food) Teller m (pl Teller)
platform n ① (at station) Bahnsteig m (pl Bahnsteige) ▷ on platform seven auf Bahnsteig sieben ② (for performers) Podium nt (pl Podien)
play n Stück nt (pl Stücke) ▷ a play by Shakespeare ein Stück von Shakespeare ▷ to put on a play ein Stück aufführen
▶ vb ❶ spielen [38] ▷ He's playing with his friends. Er spielt mit seinen Freunden. ▷ What sort of music do they play? Welche Art von Musik spielen sie? ▷ I play hockey. Ich spiele Hockey. ▷ I play the guitar. Ich spiele Gitarre. ▷ She's always playing that record. Sie spielt dauernd diese Platte. ❷ (against person, team) spielen [38] gegen ▷ Germany are playing Scotland. Deutschland spielt gegen Schottland.
play down vb herunterspielen [15] (perf hat heruntergespielt)
player n Spieler m (pl Spieler), Spielerin f ▷ a football player ein Fußballspieler
playground n ① (at school) Schulhof m (pl Schulhöfe) ② (in park) Spielplatz m (gen Spielplatzes, pl Spielplätze)
playgroup n Spielgruppe f
playing card n Spielkarte f
playing field n Sportplatz m (gen Sportplatzes, pl Sportplätze)
playtime n Pause f
pleasant adj angenehm
please excl bitte ▷ Two coffees, please. Zwei Kaffee bitte.
pleased adj ❶ (happy) erfreut ▷ My mother's not going to be very pleased. Meine Mutter wird nicht sehr erfreut sein. ❷ (satisfied) zufrieden ▷ It's beautiful, she'll be pleased with it. Es ist wunderschön, sie wird damit sehr zufrieden sein.; **to be pleased about something** sich über etwas freuen [38]; **Pleased to meet you!** Angenehm!
pleasure n Vergnügen nt (pl Vergnügen) ▷ I read for pleasure. Ich lese zum Vergnügen.
plenty n mehr als genug ▷ I've got plenty. Ich habe mehr als genug. ▷ That's plenty, thanks. Danke, das ist mehr als genug.; **I've got plenty to do.** Ich habe viel zu tun.; **plenty of** ① viele ▷ plenty of

pliers | 434

opportunities viele Möglichkeiten **(2)** *(more than enough)* genügend ▷ *I've got plenty of money.* Ich habe genügend Geld. ▷ *We've got plenty of time.* Wir haben genügend Zeit.

pliers *npl* Zange *fsg*; **a pair of pliers** eine Zange

plot *n* ❶ *(of story, play)* Handlung *f* ❷ *(against somebody)* Verschwörung *f* ▷ *a plot against the president* eine Verschwörung gegen den Präsidenten; **a plot of land** ein Stück Land *nt*; **a vegetable plot** ein Gemüsebeet *nt*
▶ *vb* planen **[38]** ▷ *They were plotting to kill him.* Sie planten, ihn zu töten.

plough *n* Pflug *m* (*pl* Pflüge)
▶ *vb* pflügen **[38]**

plug *n* ❶ *(electrical)* Stecker *m* (*pl* Stecker) ▷ *The plug is faulty.* Der Stecker ist kaputt. ❷ *(for sink)* Stöpsel *m* (*pl* Stöpsel)

plug in *vb* einstecken **[4]** *(perf* hat eingesteckt)

plum *n* Pflaume *f* ▷ *plum jam* die Pflaumenmarmelade

plumber *n* Klempner *m* (*pl* Klempner), Klempnerin *f* ▷ *He's a plumber.* Er ist Klempner.

plump *adj* rundlich

plural *n* Plural *m* (*pl* Plurale)

plus *prep, adj* plus ▷ *four plus three equals seven.* Vier plus drei macht sieben. ▷ *I got a B plus.* Ich habe eine Zwei plus bekommen.
  • In Germany, grades are given from
  • 1 to 6, with 1 being the best.
three children plus a dog drei Kinder und ein Hund

p.m. *abbr* **at eight p.m.** um acht Uhr abends
  • In Germany times are often given
  • using the 24-hour clock.

pneumonia *n* Lungenentzündung *f*

poached *adj* **a poached egg** ein verlorenes Ei *nt*

ENGLISH > GERMAN

pocket *n* Tasche *f*; **pocket money** das Taschengeld

podcast *n* Podcast *m* (*pl* Podcasts) ▷ *to download a podcast* einen Podcast herunterladen

poem *n* Gedicht *nt* (*pl* Gedichte)

poet *n* Dichter *m* (*pl* Dichter), Dichterin *f*

poetry *n* Gedichte *ntpl* ▷ *to write poetry* Gedichte schreiben

point *n* ❶ *(spot, score)* Punkt *m* (*pl* Punkte) ▷ *a point on the horizon* ein Punkt am Horizont ▷ *They scored five points.* Sie machten fünf Punkte. ❷ *(comment)* Bemerkung *f* ▷ *He made some interesting points.* Er machte ein paar interessante Bemerkungen.
❸ *(tip)* Spitze *f* ▷ *a pencil with a sharp point* ein Bleistift mit einer scharfen Spitze ❹ *(in time)* Zeitpunkt *m* ▷ *At that point, we were three one up.* Zu dem Zeitpunkt lagen wir mit drei zu eins in Führung.; **a point of view** ein Gesichtspunkt *m*; **to get the point** begreifen; **That's a good point!** Da hast du recht.; **There's no point.** Das hat keinen Wert.; **What's the point?** Wozu?; **Punctuality isn't my strong point.** Pünktlichkeit ist nicht meine Stärke.; **two point five (2.5)** zwei Komma fünf (2,5)
▶ *vb* mit dem Finger zeigen **[38]** ▷ *Don't point!* Man zeigt nicht mit dem Finger!; **to point at somebody** auf jemanden zeigen **[38]**; **to point a gun at somebody** auf jemanden mit der Waffe zielen **[38]**; **to point something out (1)** *(show)* auf etwas zeigen **[38]** ▷ *The guide pointed out Big Ben.* Unser Führer zeigte auf Big Ben. **(2)** *(mention)* auf etwas hinweisen ▷ *I should point out that ...* Ich möchte darauf hinweisen, dass ...

pointless *adj* nutzlos ▷ *It's pointless to argue.* Es ist nutzlos zu streiten.

poison *n* Gift *nt* (*pl* Gifte)
▶ *vb* vergiften **[2]** *(perf* hat vergiftet)

ENGLISH > GERMAN

poisonous adj giftig

poke vb He poked me in the eye. Er stieß mir ins Auge.

poker n Poker nt ▷ I play poker. Ich spiele Poker.

Poland n Polen nt; **from Poland** aus Polen; **to Poland** nach Polen

polar bear n Eisbär m (gen Eisbären, pl Eisbären)

Pole n (Polish person) Pole m (gen Polen, pl Polen), Polin f

pole n Mast m (pl Masten) ▷ a telegraph pole ein Telegrafenmast; **a tent pole** eine Zeltstange; **a ski pole** ein Skistock m; **the North Pole** der Nordpol; **the South Pole** der Südpol

police npl Polizei f ▷ We called the police. Wir haben die Polizei gerufen.

> Note that 'police' is used with a plural verb and **Polizei** with a singular verb.

▷ The police haven't arrived yet. Die Polizei ist noch nicht da.; **a police car** ein Polizeiwagen m; **a police station** ein Polizeirevier nt

policeman n Polizist m (gen Polizisten, pl Polizisten) ▷ He's a policeman. Er ist Polizist.

police officer n Polizist m (gen Polizisten, pl Polizisten), Polizistin (gen Polizistinnen) ▷ She's a police officer. Sie ist Polizistin.

policewoman n Polizistin f ▷ She's a policewoman. Sie ist Polizistin.

Polish adj polnisch; **He's Polish.** Er ist Pole.; **She's Polish.** Sie ist Polin.
▶ n (language) Polnisch nt (pl Polnischen)

polish n ❶ (for shoes) Schuhcreme f (pl Schuhcremes) ❷ (for furniture) Politur f
▶ vb ❶ (shoes) eincremen [4] (perf hat eingecremt) ❷ (glass, furniture) polieren [76] (perf hat poliert)

polite adj höflich

politely adv höflich

political adj politisch

politician n Politiker m (pl Politiker), Politikerin f

politics n pl Politik f ▷ I'm not interested in politics. Ich interessiere mich nicht für Politik.

pollute vb verschmutzen [7] (perf hat verschmutzt)

polluted adj verschmutzt

pollution n Umweltverschmutzung f; **air pollution** die Luftverschmutzung

polythene bag n Plastiktüte f

pond n Teich m (pl Teiche) ▷ We've got a pond in our garden. Wir haben einen Teich in unserem Garten.

pony n Pony nt (pl Ponys)

ponytail n Pferdeschwanz m (gen Pferdeschwanzes, pl Pferdeschwänze) ▷ He's got a ponytail. Er hat einen Pferdeschwanz.

pony trekking n to go pony trekking Pony reiten gehen [29]

poodle n Pudel m (pl Pudel)

pool n ❶ (puddle) Pfütze f ❷ (pond) Teich m (pl Teiche) ❸ (for swimming) Schwimmbecken nt (pl Schwimmbecken) ❹ (game) Poolbillard nt ▷ Shall we have a game of pool? Sollen wir eine Partie Poolbillard spielen?; **the pools** (football) das Toto

poor adj ❶ arm ▷ a poor family eine arme Familie ▷ They are poorer than we are. Sie sind ärmer als wir. ▷ Poor David! Der arme David!; **the poor** die Armen mpl ❷ (bad) schlecht ▷ a poor mark eine schlechte Note

pop adj pop music die Popmusik; **a pop star** ein Popstar m; **a pop group** eine Popgruppe; **a pop song** ein Popsong m

pop in vb vorbeikommen [40] (imperf kam vorbei, perf ist vorbeigekommen)

pop out vb kurz weggehen [29] (imperf ging weg, perf ist weggegangen)

pop round vb I'm just popping round to John's. Ich gehe nur mal kurz zu John.

popcorn n Popcorn nt

pope n Papst m (pl Päpste)
poppy n Mohn m
popular adj beliebt ▷ She's a very popular girl. Sie ist sehr beliebt.
population n Bevölkerung f
porch n Veranda f (pl Veranden)
pork n Schweinefleisch nt ▷ I don't eat pork. Ich esse kein Schweinefleisch.; **a pork chop** ein Schweinekotelett nt
porridge n Haferbrei m
port n ❶ (harbour) Hafen m (pl Häfen) ❷ (wine) Portwein m ▷ a glass of port ein Glas Portwein
portable adj tragbar ▷ a portable TV ein tragbarer Fernseher
porter n ❶ (in hotel) Portier m (pl Portiers) ❷ (at station) Gepäckträger m (pl Gepäckträger)
portion n Portion f ▷ a large portion of chips eine große Portion Pommes frites
portrait n Porträt nt (pl Porträts)
Portugal n Portugal nt; **from Portugal** aus Portugal; **to Portugal** nach Portugal
Portuguese adj portugiesisch; **She's Portuguese.** Sie ist Portugiesin.
▶ n ❶ (person) Portugiese m (gen Portugiesen, pl Portugiesen), Portugiesin f ❷ (language) Portugiesisch nt (gen Portugiesischen)
posh adj vornehm ▷ a posh hotel ein vornehmes Hotel
position n Stellung f ▷ an uncomfortable position eine unbequeme Stellung
positive adj ❶ (good) positiv ▷ a positive attitude eine positive Einstellung ❷ (sure) ganz sicher ▷ I'm positive. Ich bin ganz sicher.
possession n **Have you got all your possessions?** Hast du all deine Sachen?
possibility n Möglichkeit f ▷ It's a possibility. Das ist eine Möglichkeit.
possible adj möglich ▷ as soon as possible sobald wie möglich

possibly adv (perhaps) vielleicht ▷ Are you coming to the party? — Possibly. Kommst du zur Party? — Vielleicht.; **... if you possibly can.** ... wenn du irgend kannst.; **I can't possibly come.** Ich kann unmöglich kommen.
post n ❶ (letters) Post f ▷ Is there any post for me? Ist Post für mich da? ❷ (pole) Pfosten m (pl Pfosten) ▷ The ball hit the post. Der Ball traf den Pfosten. ❸ (on forum, blog) Beitrag m (pl Beiträge)
▶ vb ❶ aufgeben [28] (pres gibt auf, imperf gab auf, perf hat aufgegeben) ▷ I've got some cards to post. Ich muss ein paar Karten aufgeben. ❷ (on website) posten [2]
postbox n Briefkasten m (pl Briefkästen)
postcard n Postkarte f
postcode n Postleitzahl f
  * German postcodes consist of a
  * 5-figure number which precedes the
  * name of the city.
poster n ❶ Poster nt (pl Poster) ▷ I've got posters on my bedroom walls. Ich habe in meinem Zimmer Poster an den Wänden. ❷ (advertising) Plakat nt (pl Plakate) ▷ There are posters all over town. In der ganzen Stadt hängen Plakate.
postman n Briefträger m (pl Briefträger) ▷ He's a postman. Er ist Briefträger.
post office n Postamt nt (pl Postämter) ▷ Where's the post office, please? Wo ist das Postamt, bitte?; **She works for the post office.** Sie arbeitet bei der Post.
postpone vb verschieben (imperf verschob, perf hat verschoben) ▷ The match has been postponed. Das Spiel wurde verschoben.
postwoman n Briefträgerin f ▷ She's a postwoman. Sie ist Briefträgerin.
pot n ❶ Topf m (pl Töpfe) ▷ a pot of jam ein Marmeladentopf ❷ (for hot drinks) Kanne f ❸ (marijuana) Gras nt ▷ to smoke

pot Gras rauchen; **pots and pans** Töpfe und Pfannen

potato n Kartoffel f ▷ *a baked potato* eine gebackene Kartoffel ▷ *potato salad* der Kartoffelsalat; **mashed potatoes** der Kartoffelbrei; **potato chips** die Kartoffelchips mpl

pottery n Keramik f

pound n *(weight, money)* Pfund nt (pl Pfunde or Pfund)

> When talking about an amount of money or specifying a quantity of something use the plural form **Pfund**.

▷ *two pounds of carrots* zwei Pfund Karotten ▷ *How many euros do you get for a pound?* Wie viel Euro bekommt man für ein Pfund? ▷ *a pound coin* eine Pfundmünze
▶ vb pochen [**48**] ▷ *My heart was pounding.* Mein Herz hat gepocht.

pour vb *(liquid)* gießen [**31**] (imperf goss, perf hat gegossen) ▷ *She poured some water into the pan.* Sie goss etwas Wasser in den Topf. ▷ *It's pouring.* Es gießt.; **She poured him a drink.** Sie goss ihm einen Drink ein.; **Shall I pour you a cup of tea?** Soll ich Ihnen eine Tasse Tee einschenken?; **in the pouring rain** im strömenden Regen

poverty n Armut f

powder n ❶ Pulver nt ❷ *(face powder)* Puder m (pl Puder)

power n ❶ *(electricity)* Strom m ▷ *The power's off.* Es gibt keinen Strom.; **a power cut** ein Stromausfall m; **a power point** eine Steckdose; **a power station** ein Kraftwerk nt ❷ *(energy)* Energie f ▷ *nuclear power* die Kernenergie ▷ *solar power* die Sonnenenergie ❸ *(authority)* Macht f (pl Mächte) ▷ *to be in power* an der Macht sein

powerful adj ❶ mächtig ▷ *a powerful man* ein mächtiger Mann ❷ *(physically)* kräftig ❸ *(machine)* leistungsstark

practical adj praktisch ▷ *a practical suggestion* ein praktischer Vorschlag ▷ *She's very practical.* Sie ist sehr praktisch.

practically adv praktisch ▷ *It's practically impossible.* Es ist praktisch unmöglich.

practice n ❶ *(for sport)* Training nt ▷ *football practice* das Fußballtraining ❷ Übung f ▷ *You need more practice.* Du brauchst mehr Übung.; **I've got to do my piano practice.** Ich muss Klavier üben.; **It's normal practice in our school.** Das ist in unserer Schule so üblich.; **in practice** in der Praxis; **a medical practice** eine Arztpraxis

practise vb ❶ *(music, hobby, language)* üben [**38**] ▷ *I ought to practise more.* Ich sollte mehr üben. ▷ *I practise the flute every evening.* Ich übe jeden Abend Flöte. ▷ *I practised my German when we were on holiday.* Ich habe in den Ferien mein Deutsch geübt. ❷ *(sport)* trainieren [**76**] (perf hat trainiert) ▷ *The team practises on Thursdays.* Die Mannschaft trainiert donnerstags. ▷ *I don't practise enough.* Ich trainiere nicht genug.

praise vb loben [**38**] ▷ *The teacher praised her work.* Der Lehrer lobte ihre Arbeit.

pram n Kinderwagen m (pl Kinderwagen)

prawn n Garnele f

pray vb beten [**2**] ▷ *to pray for something* für etwas beten

prayer n Gebet nt (pl Gebete)

precious adj kostbar

precise adj genau ▷ *at that precise moment* genau in diesem Augenblick

precisely adv genau ▷ *Precisely!* Genau!; **at ten o'clock precisely** um Punkt zehn Uhr

predict vb vorhersagen [**15**] (perf hat vorhergesagt)

prefect | 438 — ENGLISH > GERMAN

prefect n
• German schools do not have prefects. **My sister's a prefect.** Meine Schwester ist im letzten Schuljahr und führt die Aufsicht bei den Jüngeren.

prefer vb lieber mögen [**50**] (pres mag lieber, imperf mochte lieber, perf hat lieber gemocht) ▷ **Which would you prefer?** Was magst du lieber? ▷ **I prefer German to chemistry.** Ich mag Deutsch lieber als Chemie.; **I preferred the first version.** Die erste Version hat mir besser gefallen.

pregnant adj schwanger ▷ **She's six months pregnant.** Sie ist im siebten Monat schwanger.

prejudice n ❶ Vorurteil nt (pl Vorurteile) ▷ **That's just a prejudice.** Das ist ein Vorurteil. ❷ Vorurteil ntpl ▷ **There's a lot of racial prejudice.** Es gibt viele Rassenvorurteile.

prejudiced adj voreingenommen; **to be prejudiced against somebody** gegen jemanden voreingenommen sein [**65**]

premature adj verfrüht; **a premature baby** eine Frühgeburt

Premier League n erste Liga f ▷ **in the Premier League** in der ersten Liga
• The 'Premier League' is the direct
• equivalent of the German
• **Bundesliga**.

premises npl Geschäftsräume mpl ▷ **They're moving to new premises.** Sie ziehen in neue Geschäftsräume um.

prep n (homework) Hausaufgaben fpl ▷ **history prep** die Hausaufgaben in Geschichte

preparation n Vorbereitung f

prepare vb vorbereiten [**2**] (perf hat vorbereitet) ▷ **She prepares lessons in the evening.** Abends bereitet sie Stunden vor.; **to prepare for something** Vorbereitungen für etwas treffen [**78**]

prepared adj **to be prepared to do something** bereit sein [**65**], etwas zu tun

prep school n private Grundschule f

prescribe vb (medicine) verschreiben [**61**] (imperf verschrieb, perf hat verschrieben) ▷ **He prescribed me a course of antibiotics.** Er hat mir eine Antibiotikakur verschrieben.

prescription n Rezept nt (pl Rezepte) ▷ **You can't get it without a prescription.** Das bekommt man nicht ohne Rezept.

present adj ❶ (in attendance) anwesend ▷ **He wasn't present at the meeting.** Er war bei der Besprechung nicht anwesend. ❷ (current) gegenwärtig ▷ **the present situation** die gegenwärtige Situation; **the present tense** die Gegenwart
▶ n ❶ (gift) Geschenk nt (pl Geschenke) ▷ **I'm going to buy presents.** Ich kaufe Geschenke.; **to give somebody a present** jemandem etwas schenken [**38**] ❷ (time) Gegenwart f ▷ **She was living in the past not the present.** Sie lebte in der Vergangenheit, nicht in der Gegenwart.; **up to the present** bis heute; **for the present** momentan; **at present** im Augenblick; **the present tense** das Präsens
▶ vb **to present somebody with something** (prize, medal) jemandem etwas verleihen

presenter n (on TV) Moderator m (pl Moderatoren), Moderatorin f

president n Präsident m (gen Präsidenten, pl Präsidenten), Präsidentin f

press n Presse f; **a press conference** eine Pressekonferenz
▶ vb ❶ drücken [**38**] ▷ **Don't press too hard!** Nicht zu fest drücken! ❷ treten [**79**] auf (pres tritt auf, imperf trat, perf hat getreten) ▷ **He pressed the accelerator.** Er trat aufs Gaspedal.

press-up n Liegestütz m (gen Liegestützes, pl Liegestütze) ▷ **I do twenty press-ups every morning.** Ich mache jeden Morgen zwanzig Liegestütze.

pressure n Druck m ▷ He's under a lot of pressure. Er steht unter viel Druck.; **a pressure group (1)** (small-scale, local) eine Bürgerinitiative **(2)** (large-scale, more political) eine Pressure-Group ▶ vb Druck ausüben [4] auf (perf hat Druck ausgeübt) ▷ They are pressuring me. Sie üben Druck auf mich aus.

presume vb annehmen [1] (pres nimmt an, imperf nahm an, perf hat angenommen) ▷ I presume so. Das nehme ich an.

pretend vb to pretend to do something so tun [81], als ob man etwas täte

Note that **als ob** is followed by the subjunctive.

pretty adj, adv ❶ hübsch ▷ She's very pretty. Sie ist sehr hübsch. ❷ (rather) ziemlich ▷ That film was pretty bad. Der Film war ziemlich schlecht.; **It's pretty much the same.** Das ist mehr oder weniger dasselbe.

prevent vb verhindern [88] (perf hat verhindert); **to prevent somebody from doing something** jemanden davon abhalten [33], etwas zu tun

previous adj vorherig

previously adv früher

price n Preis m (gen Preises, pl Preise)

price list n Preisliste f

prick vb stechen (pres sticht, imperf stach, perf hat gestochen) ▷ I've pricked my finger. Ich habe mir in den Finger gestochen.

pride n Stolz m (gen Stolzes)

priest n Priester m (pl Priester) ▷ He's a priest. Er ist Priester.

primarily adv vor allem

primary adj hauptsächlich

primary school n Grundschule f
- Children in Germany begin **Grundschule** at the age of 6. The **Grundschule** provides primary education in school years 1 to 4.

▷ She's still at primary school. Sie ist noch in der Grundschule.

prime minister n Premierminister m (pl Premierminister), Premierministerin f

prince n Prinz m (pl Prinzen, gen Prinzen) ▷ the Prince of Wales der Prinz von Wales

princess n Prinzessin f ▷ Princess Anne Prinzessin Anne

principal adj hauptsächlich; **the principal reason** der Hauptgrund; **my principal concern** mein Hauptanliegen nt
▶ n (of college) Direktor m (pl Direktoren), Direktorin f

principle n Prinzip nt (pl Prinzipien); **on principle** aus Prinzip

print n ❶ (photo) Abzug m (pl Abzüge) ▷ colour prints Farbabzüge ❷ (letters) Schrift f; **in small print** klein gedruckt ❸ (fingerprint) Fingerabdruck m (pl Fingerabdrücke) ❹ (picture) Kunstdruck m (pl Kunstdrucke) ▷ a framed print ein gerahmter Kunstdruck

printer n (machine) Drucker m (pl Drucker)

printout n Ausdruck m (pl Ausdrucke)

priority n Priorität f

prison n Gefängnis nt (gen Gefängnisses, pl Gefängnisse); **in prison** im Gefängnis

prisoner n Gefangene m (gen Gefangenen, pl Gefangenen), Gefangene f (gen Gefangenen) ▷ a prisoner (man) ein Gefangener

private adj privat; **a private school** eine Privatschule; **private property** das Privateigentum; **'private'** (on envelope) 'persönlich'; **a private bathroom** ein eigenes Badezimmer; **I have private lessons.** Ich bekomme Nachhilfestunden.

prize n Preis m (gen Preises, pl Preise) ▷ to win a prize einen Preis gewinnen

prize-giving n Preisverleihung f

prizewinner n Preisträger m (pl Preisträger), Preisträgerin f

pro n Profi m (pl Profis)
- der Profi is also used for women. ▷ *This was her first year as a pro.* Dies war ihr erstes Jahr als Profi.; **the pros and cons** das Für und Wider

probability n Wahrscheinlichkeit f

probable adj wahrscheinlich

probably adv wahrscheinlich ▷ *probably not* wahrscheinlich nicht

problem n Problem nt (pl Probleme) ▷ *No problem!* Kein Problem!

process n Prozess m (gen Prozesses, pl Prozesse) ▷ *the peace process* der Friedensprozess; **to be in the process of doing something** gerade dabei sein [65], etwas zu tun

procession n (religious) Prozession f

produce vb ① (manufacture) herstellen [4] (perf hat hergestellt) ② (play, show) inszenieren [76] (perf hat inszeniert) ③ (film) produzieren [76] (perf hat produziert)

producer n ① (of play, show) Regisseur m (pl Regisseure), Regisseurin f ② (of film) Produzent m (gen Produzenten, pl Produzenten), Produzentin f

product n Produkt nt (pl Produkte)

production n ① Produktion f ▷ *They're increasing production.* Sie erhöhen die Produktion. ② (play, show) Inszenierung f ▷ *a production of 'Hamlet'* eine Hamletinszenierung

profession n Beruf m (pl Berufe)

professional n Profi m (pl Profis)
- der Profi is also used for women. ▷ *She now plays as a professional.* Sie spielt jetzt als Profi.
▶ adj (player) professionell ▷ *a very professional piece of work* eine sehr professionelle Arbeit; **a professional musician** ein Berufsmusiker m

professor n Professor m (pl Professoren), Professorin f; **He's the German professor.** Er hat den Lehrstuhl für Deutsch inne.

profit n Gewinn m (pl Gewinne)

profitable adj gewinnbringend

program n Programm nt (pl Programme) ▷ *a computer program* ein Computerprogramm
▶ vb programmieren [76] (perf hat programmiert) ▷ *to program a computer* einen Computer programmieren

programme n Programm nt (pl Programme)

programmer n Programmierer m (pl Programmierer), Programmiererin f ▷ *She's a programmer.* Sie ist Programmiererin.

progress n Fortschritt m (pl Fortschritte) ▷ *You're making progress!* Du machst Fortschritte!

prohibit vb verbieten [8] (imperf verbat, perf hat verboten) ▷ *Smoking is prohibited.* Das Rauchen ist verboten.

project n ① (plan) Projekt nt (pl Projekte) ② (at school) Referat nt (pl Referate) ▷ *I'm doing a project on Berlin.* Ich schreibe ein Referat über Berlin.

projector n Projektor m (pl Projektoren)

promise n Versprechen nt (pl Versprechen) ▷ *You didn't keep your promise.* Du hast dein Versprechen nicht gehalten.; **That's a promise!** Versprochen!
▶ vb versprechen [70] (pres verspricht, imperf versprach, perf hat versprochen) ▷ *She promised to write.* Sie hat versprochen zu schreiben. ▷ *I'll write, I promise!* Ich schreibe, das verspreche ich!

promote vb **to be promoted** befördert werden [91]

promotion n ① (in job) Beförderung f ② (advertising) Werbung f

prompt adj, adv schnell ▷ *a prompt reply* eine schnelle Antwort; **at eight o'clock prompt** genau um acht Uhr

pronoun n Pronomen nt (pl Pronomen)

pronounce vb aussprechen [70] (pres spricht aus, imperf sprach aus, perf hat

ENGLISH > GERMAN

ausgesprochen) ▷ *How do you pronounce that word?* Wie spricht man das Wort aus?

pronunciation n Aussprache f

proof n Beweis m (gen Beweises, pl Beweise)

proper adj ❶ (genuine) echt ▷ *proper German bread* echtes deutsches Brot ❷ (decent) ordentlich ▷ *We didn't have a proper lunch.* Wir hatten kein ordentliches Mittagessen. ▷ *It's difficult to get a proper job.* Es ist schwierig, einen ordentlichen Job zu bekommen. ▷ *We need proper training.* Wir brauchen eine ordentliche Ausbildung. ❸ (appropriate) richtig ▷ *You have to have the proper equipment.* Sie brauchen die richtige Ausrüstung.; **If you had come at the proper time ...** Wenn du zur rechten Zeit gekommen wärst ...

properly adv ❶ (correctly) richtig ▷ *You're not doing it properly.* Du machst das nicht richtig. ❷ (appropriately) anständig ▷ *Dress properly for your interview.* Zieh dich zum Vorstellungsgespräch anständig an.

property n Eigentum nt; **'private property'** 'Privateigentum'; **stolen property** das Diebesgut

propose vb vorschlagen [59] (pres schlägt vor, imperf schlug vor, perf hat vorgeschlagen) ▷ *I propose a new plan.* Ich schlage einen neuen Plan vor.; **to propose to do something** vorhaben [32], etwas zu tun; **to propose to somebody** (for marriage) jemandem einen Heiratsantrag machen [48]

prosecute vb strafrechtlich verfolgen [84] (perf hat verfolgt) ▷ *They were prosecuted for murder.* Sie wurden wegen Mordes strafrechtlich verfolgt.; **'Shoplifters will be prosecuted'** 'Jeder Diebstahl wird zur Anzeige gebracht'

prostitute n Prostituierte f (gen Prostituierten); **a male prostitute** ein Prostituierter

441 | psychologist

protect vb schützen [36]

protection n Schutz m (gen Schutzes)

protein n Protein nt (pl Proteine)

protest n Protest m (pl Proteste) ▷ *He ignored their protests.* Er hat ihre Proteste ignoriert.; **a protest march** ein Protestmarsch m
▶ vb protestieren [76] (perf hat protestiert)

Protestant n Protestant m (gen Protestanten, pl Protestanten), Protestantin f ▷ *She's a Protestant.* Sie ist Protestantin.
▶ adj protestantisch ▷ *a Protestant church* eine protestantische Kirche

protester n Demonstrant m (gen Demonstranten, pl Demonstranten), Demonstrantin f

proud adj stolz ▷ *Her parents are proud of her.* Ihre Eltern sind stolz auf sie.

prove vb beweisen (imperf bewies, perf hat bewiesen) ▷ *The police couldn't prove it.* Die Polizei konnte es nicht beweisen.

proverb n Sprichwort nt (pl Sprichwörter)

provide vb stellen [38] ▷ *We'll provide the food.* Wir stellen das Essen.; **to provide somebody with something** jemandem etwas zur Verfügung stellen [38]

provide for vb versorgen [7] (perf hat versorgt)

provided conj vorausgesetzt, dass ▷ *He'll play provided he's fit.* Er spielt, vorausgesetzt, dass er fit ist.

prune n Backpflaume f

psychiatrist n Psychiater m (pl Psychiater), Psychiaterin f ▷ *She's a psychiatrist.* Sie ist Psychiaterin.

psychological adj psychologisch

psychologist n Psychologe m (gen Psychologen, pl Psychologen), Psychologin f ▷ *He's a psychologist.* Er ist Psychologe.

psychology n Psychologie f
PTO abbr (= please turn over) b. w. (= bitte wenden)
pub n Kneipe f
public n Öffentlichkeit f ▷ open to the public der Öffentlichkeit zugänglich; **in public** in der Öffentlichkeit
▶ adj öffentlich ▷ public opinion die öffentliche Meinung ▷ public transport öffentliche Verkehrsmittel ntpl; **a public holiday** ein gesetzlicher Feiertag; **the public address system** die Lautsprecheranlage
publicity n Publicity f
public school n Privatschule f
publish vb veröffentlichen [84] (perf hat veröffentlicht)
publisher n (company) Verlag m (pl Verlage)
pudding n Nachtisch m ▷ What's for pudding? Was gibt's zum Nachtisch?; **rice pudding** der Milchreis; **black pudding** die Blutwurst
puddle n Pfütze f
puff pastry n Blätterteig m
pull vb ziehen [96] (imperf zog, perf hat gezogen) ▷ Pull! Zieh!; **He pulled the trigger.** Er drückte ab.; **to pull a muscle** sich einen Muskel zerren [38]; **You're pulling my leg!** (informal) Du willst mich wohl auf den Arm nehmen!; **to pull down** abreißen [48]; **to pull out (1)** (tooth, weed) herausziehen [96] **(2)** (car) ausscheren [4] ▷ The car pulled out to overtake. Das Auto scherte aus, um zu überholen. **(3)** (withdraw) aussteigen [74] ▷ She pulled out of the tournament. Sie ist aus dem Turnier ausgestiegen.; **to pull through** (survive) durchkommen [40]; **to pull up** (car) anhalten [33]
pullover n Pullover m (pl Pullover)
pulse n Puls m (gen Pulses, pl Pulse) ▷ The nurse felt his pulse. Die Schwester fühlte ihm den Puls.
pump n ❶ Pumpe f ▷ a bicycle pump eine Fahrradpumpe; **a petrol pump** eine Zapfsäule ❷ (shoe) Sportschuh m (pl Sportschuhe)
▶ vb pumpen [38]; **to pump up** (tyre) aufpumpen [4]
pumpkin n Kürbis m (gen Kürbisses, pl Kürbisse)
punch n ❶ (blow) Schlag m (pl Schläge) ▷ a violent punch ein heftiger Schlag ❷ (drink) Punsch m
▶ vb ❶ (hit) schlagen [59] (pres schlägt, imperf schlug, perf hat geschlagen) ▷ He punched me! Er hat mich geschlagen! ❷ (in ticket machine) entwerten [18] (perf hat entwertet) ▷ Punch your ticket before you get on the train. Entwerten Sie Ihre Fahrkarte, bevor Sie in den Zug steigen. ❸ (by ticket inspector) knipsen [48] ▷ He forgot to punch my ticket. Er hat vergessen, meine Fahrkarte zu knipsen.
punctual adj pünktlich
punctuation n Zeichensetzung f
puncture n Reifenpanne f ▷ to have a puncture eine Reifenpanne haben
punish vb bestrafen [7] (perf hat bestraft) ▷ The teacher punished him. Der Lehrer bestrafte ihn.
punishment n Strafe f
punk n (person) Punker m (pl Punker), Punkerin f; **a punk rock band** eine Punkband
pupil n Schüler m (pl Schüler), Schülerin f
puppet n Marionette f
purchase vb erwerben [90] (pres erwirbt, imperf erwarb, perf hat erworben)
pure adj rein ▷ pure orange juice reiner Orangensaft; **He's doing pure maths.** Er macht rein theoretische Mathematik.
purple adj lila
purpose n Zweck m (pl Zwecke) ▷ What is the purpose of these changes? Welchen

Zweck haben diese Veränderungen?; **his purpose in life** sein Lebensinhalt; **on purpose** absichtlich

purr vb schnurren [48]

purse n ① (for money) Geldbeutel m (pl Geldbeutel) ② (US: handbag) Handtasche f

pursue vb verfolgen [84] (perf hat verfolgt)

push n to give somebody a push jemanden stoßen
▶ vb ① (button) drücken [38] ② drängeln [34] ▷ *Don't push!* Nicht drängeln!; **to push somebody to do something** jemanden drängen [38], etwas zu tun; **to push drugs** mit Drogen handeln [34]; **to push around** herumkommandieren [76]; **Push off!** (informal) Hau ab!; **I pushed my way through.** Ich drängelte mich durch.

pushchair n Sportwagen m (pl Sportwagen)

push-up n Liegestütz m (gen Liegestützes, pl Liegestütze) ▷ *I do twenty push-ups every morning.* Ich mache jeden Morgen zwanzig Liegestütze.

put vb

Use **legen** when you're putting something down flat, use **stellen** when you're standing something upright.

① legen [38] ▷ *Where shall I put my things?* Wohin soll ich meine Sachen legen? ▷ *She's putting the baby to bed.* Sie legt das Baby ins Bett. ② stellen [38] ▷ *Put the vase on the table.* Stell die Vase auf den Tisch.; **Don't forget to put your name on the paper.** Vergiss nicht, deinen Namen auf das Papier zu schreiben.

put aside vb zurücklegen [15] (perf hat zurückgelegt)

put away vb wegräumen [4] (perf hat weggeräumt)

put back vb ① zurücklegen [15] (perf hat zurückgelegt) ② zurückstellen [15] (perf hat zurückgestellt)

put down vb ① abstellen [4] (perf hat abgestellt) ② (in writing) aufschreiben [61] (imperf schrieb auf, perf hat aufgeschrieben)

put forward vb vorstellen [4] (perf hat vorgestellt)

put in vb (install) einbauen [4] (perf hat eingebaut)

put off vb ① (switch off) ausmachen [48] (perf hat ausgemacht) ② (postpone) verschieben (imperf verschob, perf hat verschoben) ③ (distract) stören [38] ④ (discourage) entmutigen [18] (perf hat entmutigt)

put on vb ① (clothes) anziehen [96] (imperf zog an, perf hat angezogen) ② (lipstick) auftragen [77] (pres trägt auf, imperf trug auf, perf hat aufgetragen) ③ (record) auflegen [4] (perf hat aufgelegt) ④ (light, heater, TV) anmachen [4] (perf hat angemacht) ⑤ (play, show) aufführen [4] (perf hat aufgeführt) ⑥ aufstellen [4] (perf hat aufgestellt)

put out vb ① (light, cigarette) ausmachen [48] (perf hat ausgemacht) ② (fire) löschen [48]

put through vb verbinden (imperf verband, perf hat verbunden)

put up vb ① (pin up) aufhängen [35] (perf hat aufgehängt) ② (tent) aufschlagen [59] (pres schlägt auf, imperf schlug auf, perf hat aufgeschlagen) ③ (price) erhöhen [19] (perf hat erhöht) ④ (accommodate) übernachten lassen [42] (pres lässt übernachten, imperf ließ übernachten, perf hat übernachten lassen)

puzzle n (jigsaw) Puzzle nt (pl Puzzles)

puzzled adj verdutzt ▷ *You look puzzled!* Du siehst verdutzt aus!

pyjamas npl Schlafanzug m (pl Schlafanzüge) ▷ *my pyjamas* mein

Schlafanzug; **a pair of pyjamas** ein Schlafanzug; **a pyjama top** ein Schlafanzugoberteil nt
pyramid n Pyramide f
Pyrenees npl **the Pyrenees** die Pyrenäen pl

q

quad bike n Quad nt (pl Quads)
qualification n Qualifikation f
▷ *vocational qualifications* die beruflichen Qualifikationen; **to leave school without any qualifications** die Schule ohne einen Abschluss verlassen [**42**]
qualified adj ausgebildet ▷ *a qualified driving instructor* ein ausgebildeter Fahrlehrer ▷ *a qualified nurse* eine ausgebildete Krankenschwester
qualify vb ❶ *(for job)* seinen Abschluss machen [**48**] ▷ *She qualified as a teacher last year.* Sie hat letztes Jahr ihren Abschluss als Lehrerin gemacht. ❷ *(in competition)* sich qualifizieren [**76**] (perf hat sich qualifiziert) ▷ *Our team didn't qualify.* Unsere Mannschaft konnte sich nicht qualifizieren.
quality n ❶ Qualität f ▷ *a good quality of life* eine gute Lebensqualität; **good-quality ingredients** qualitativ hochwertige Zutaten ❷ *(of person)* Eigenschaft f ▷ *good qualities* gute Eigenschaften

ENGLISH > GERMAN

quantity n Menge f
quarantine n Quarantäne f ▷ *in quarantine* in Quarantäne
quarrel n Streit m (pl Streite)
▶ vb sich streiten (imperf stritt sich, perf hat gestritten)
quarry n (for stone) Steinbruch m (pl Steinbrüche)
quarter n Viertel nt (pl Viertel) ▷ *three quarters* drei Viertel ▷ *a quarter of an hour* eine viertel Stunde; **three quarters of an hour** eine Dreiviertelstunde; **a quarter past ten** Viertel nach zehn; **a quarter to eleven** Viertel vor elf
quarter final n Viertelfinale nt (pl Viertelfinale)
quartet n Quartett nt (pl Quartette) ▷ *a string quartet* ein Streichquartett
quay n Kai m (pl Kais)
queen n ❶ Königin f ▷ *Queen Elizabeth* Königin Elisabeth ❷ (playing card) Dame f ▷ *the queen of hearts* die Herzdame
query n Frage f
▶ vb infrage stellen [38] ▷ *No one queried my decision.* Niemand hat mein Entscheidung infrage gestellt.; **They queried the bill.** Sie reklamierten die Rechnung.
question n Frage f ▷ *That's a difficult question.* Das ist eine schwierige Frage.; **Can I ask a question?** Kann ich etwas fragen?; **It's out of the question.** Das kommt nicht infrage.
▶ vb befragen [7] (perf hat befragt); **He was questioned by the police.** Die Polizei hat ihn vernommen.
question mark n Fragezeichen nt (pl Fragezeichen)
questionnaire n Fragebogen m (pl Fragebögen)
queue n Schlange f
▶ vb Schlange stehen [72] (imperf stand Schlange, perf hat Schlange gestanden) ▷ *We queued for an hour.* Wir haben eine Stunde lang Schlange gestanden.; **to**

445 | quotation

queue for something für etwas anstehen [72]
quick adj, adv schnell ▷ *a quick lunch* ein schnelles Mittagessen ▷ *Quick, phone the police!* Schnell, rufen Sie die Polizei! ▷ *It's quicker by train.* Mit dem Zug geht es schneller.; **Be quick!** Beeil dich!; **She's a quick learner.** Sie lernt schnell.
quickly adv schnell ▷ *It was all over very quickly.* Es war alles sehr schnell vorbei.
quiet adj ❶ (not talkative, peaceful) ruhig ▷ *You're very quiet today.* Du bist heute sehr ruhig. ▷ *a quiet little town* eine ruhige, kleine Stadt ❷ (not noisy) leise ▷ *The engine's very quiet.* Der Motor ist sehr leise.; **Be quiet!** Sei still!; **Quiet!** Ruhe!
quietly adv leise ▷ *He quietly opened the door.* Er öffnete leise die Tür.
quilt n (duvet) Steppdecke f
quit vb ❶ gibt auf, [28] (pres gibt auf, imperf gab auf, perf hat aufgegeben) ▷ *I quit my job last week.* Ich habe meine Stelle letzte Woche aufgegeben.
❷ aufhören [4] ▷ *I quit smoking.* Ich habe mit dem Rauchen aufgehört.
quite adv ❶ (rather) ziemlich ▷ *It's quite warm today.* Heute ist es ziemlich warm. ▷ *I've been there quite a lot.* Ich war schon ziemlich oft da. ▷ *quite a lot of money* ziemlich viel Geld ▷ *quite a few people* ziemlich viele Leute ▷ *It costs quite a lot.* Es ist ziemlich teuer. ▷ *It's quite a long way.* Es ist ziemlich weit. ▷ *It was quite a shock.* Es war ein ziemlicher Schock.; **I quite liked the film, but ...** Der Film hat mir ganz gut gefallen, aber ... ❷ (entirely) ganz ▷ *I'm not quite sure.* Ich bin mir nicht ganz sicher. ▷ *It's not quite the same.* Das ist nicht ganz das Gleiche.; **quite good** ganz gut
quiz n Quiz nt (gen Quiz, pl Quiz)
quotation n Zitat nt (pl Zitate) ▷ *a quotation from Shakespeare* ein Shakespearezitat

quotation marks npl
Anführungszeichen ntpl
quote n Zitat nt (pl Zitate) ▷ a Shakespeare quote ein Shakespearezitat; **quotes** (quotation marks) die Anführungszeichen
▶ vb zitieren [**76**] (perf hat zitiert)

r

rabbi n Rabbiner m (pl Rabbiner)
rabbit n Kaninchen nt (pl Kaninchen); **a rabbit hutch** ein Kaninchenstall m
race n ❶ (sport) Rennen nt (pl Rennen) ▷ a cycle race ein Radrennen ❷ (species) Rasse f ▷ the human race die Menschheit; **race relations** Rassenbeziehungen fpl
▶ vb ❶ rennen [**55**] (imperf rannte, perf ist gerannt) ▷ We raced to catch the bus. Wir sind gerannt, um den Bus zu erreichen. ❷ (have a race) um die Wette laufen [**43**] mit (pres läuft um die Wette, imperf lief um die Wette, perf ist um die Wette gelaufen) ▷ I'll race you! Ich laufe mit dir um die Wette!
racecourse n Pferderennbahn f
racer n (bike) Rennrad nt (pl Rennräder)
racetrack n Rennbahn f
racial adj **racial discrimination** die Rassendiskriminierung
racing car n Rennwagen m (pl Rennwagen)
racing driver n Rennfahrer m (pl Rennfahrer), Rennfahrerin f

racism n Rassismus m (gen Rassismus)
racist adj rassistisch; **He's racist.** Er ist ein Rassist.
▶ n Rassist m (gen Rassisten, pl Rassisten), Rassistin f
rack n (for luggage) Gepäckträger m (pl Gepäckträger)
racket n ❶ (for sport) Schläger m (pl Schläger) ▷ my tennis racket mein Tennisschläger ❷ (noise) Krach m ▷ a terrible racket ein furchtbarer Krach
racquet n Schläger m (pl Schläger)
radar n Radar nt
radiation n Strahlung f
radiator n Heizkörper m (pl Heizkörper)
radio n Radio nt (pl Radios); **on the radio** im Radio; **a radio station** ein Rundfunksender m
radioactive adj radioaktiv
radish n ❶ (small red) Radieschen nt (pl Radieschen) ❷ (long white) Rettich m (pl Rettiche)
RAF n (= Royal Air Force) britische Luftwaffe f ▷ He's in the RAF. Er ist bei der britischen Luftwaffe.
raffle n Tombola f (pl Tombolas) ▷ a raffle ticket ein Tombolalos nt
raft n Floß nt (gen Floßes, pl Flöße)
rag n Lumpen m (pl Lumpen) ▷ dressed in rags in Lumpen gekleidet; **a piece of rag** ein Lappen m
rage n Wut f ▷ mad with rage wild vor Wut; **to be in a rage** wütend sein [**65**]; **It's all the rage.** Es ist große Mode.
rail n ❶ (on stairs, bridge, balcony) Geländer nt (pl Geländer) ❷ (on railway line) Schiene f; **by rail** mit dem Zug
railcard n Bahncard® f (pl Bahncards)
railroad n (US) Eisenbahn f
railway n Eisenbahn f; **a railway line** eine Eisenbahnlinie; **a railway station** ein Bahnhof m
rain n Regen m ▷ **in the rain** im Regen
▶ vb regnen [**53**] ▷ It rains a lot here. Hier regnet es viel.; **It's raining.** Es regnet.

rainbow n Regenbogen m (pl Regenbogen)
raincoat n Regenmantel m (pl Regenmäntel)
rainfall n Niederschlag m (pl Niederschläge)
rainforest n Regenwald m (pl Regenwälder)
rainy adj regnerisch
raise vb ❶ (lift) hochheben (imperf hob hoch, perf hat hochgehoben) ▷ He raised his hand. Er hob die Hand hoch.
❷ (improve) heben (imperf hob, perf hat gehoben) ▷ They want to raise standards in schools. Sie wollen das Niveau in den Schulen heben.; **to raise money** Spenden sammeln [**34**]
raisin n Rosine f
rake n Rechen m (pl Rechen)
rally n ❶ (of people) Kundgebung f
❷ (sport) Rallye f (pl Rallyes) ▷ a rally driver ein Rallyefahrer m ❸ (in tennis) Ballwechsel m (pl Ballwechsel)
rambler n Wanderer m (pl Wanderer), Wanderin f
ramp n (for wheelchairs) Rampe f
ran vb see **run**
rang vb see **ring**
range n Auswahl f ▷ a wide range of colours eine große Auswahl an Farben; **a range of subjects** verschiedene Themen; **a mountain range** eine Bergkette
▶ vb **to range from ... to** gehen [**29**] von ... bis; **Tickets range from two to twenty pounds.** Karten kosten von zwei bis zwanzig Pfund.
rap n (music) Rap m
rape n Vergewaltigung f
▶ vb vergewaltigen [**7**] (perf hat vergewaltigt)
rapids npl Stromschnellen fpl
rare adj ❶ (unusual) selten ▷ a rare plant eine seltene Pflanze ❷ (steak) blutig

raspberry n Himbeere f ▷ *raspberry jam* die Himbeermarmelade

rat n Ratte f

rather adv ziemlich ▷ *I was rather disappointed.* Ich war ziemlich enttäuscht. ▷ *Twenty pounds! That's rather a lot!* Zwanzig Pfund! Das ist aber ziemlich viel!; **rather a lot of** ziemlich viel; **rather than** statt; **I'd rather ...** Ich würde lieber ...

rattlesnake n Klapperschlange f

rave vb schwärmen [**38**] ▷ *They raved about the film.* Sie schwärmten von dem Film.
▶ n *(party)* Raveparty f (pl Ravepartys); **rave music** die Ravemusik

ravenous adj **to be ravenous** einen Riesenhunger haben [**32**]

raw adj *(food)* roh; **raw materials** die Rohstoffe mpl

razor n Rasierapparat m (pl Rasierapparate); **a razor blade** eine Rasierklinge

RE n (= *religious education*) Religionsunterricht m

reach n **out of reach** außer Reichweite; **within easy reach of** leicht zu erreichen
▶ vb ① ankommen [**40**] in ▷ *We reached the hotel at ten o'clock.* Wir sind um zehn Uhr im Hotel angekommen.; **We hope to reach the final.** Wir wollen ins Endspiel kommen. ② *(decision)* treffen [**78**] ▷ *Eventually they reached a decision.* Sie haben schließlich eine Entscheidung getroffen.; **He reached for his gun.** Er griff nach seiner Pistole.

reaction n Reaktion f

reactor n Reaktor m (pl Reaktoren) ▷ *a nuclear reactor* ein Kernreaktor

read vb lesen [**45**] (pres liest, imperf las, perf hat gelesen) ▷ *I don't read much.* Ich lese nicht viel. ▷ *Have you read it?* Hast du es gelesen? ▷ *Read the text out loud.* Lies den Text laut.

reading n Lesen nt ▷ *Reading is one of my hobbies.* Lesen ist eines meiner Hobbies.

ready adj fertig ▷ *She's nearly ready.* Sie ist fast fertig.; **He's always ready to help.** Er ist immer bereit zu helfen.; **a ready meal** ein Fertiggericht nt; **to get ready** sich fertig machen [**48**]; **to get something ready** etwas machen [**48**]

real adj ① *(not fake)* echt ▷ *He wasn't a real police officer.* Er war kein echter Polizist. ▷ *It's real leather.* Es ist echtes Leder. ② wirklich ▷ *Her real name is Cordelia.* Ihr wirklicher Name ist Cordelia. ▷ *in real life* im wirklichen Leben; **It was a real nightmare.** Es war wirklich ein Albtraum.

realistic adj realistisch

reality n Wirklichkeit f

realize vb **to realize that ...** bemerken [**7**], dass ...

really adv wirklich ▷ *She's really nice.* Sie ist wirklich nett. ▷ *I'm learning Italian.* — *Really?* Ich lerne Italienisch. — *Wirklich?* ▷ *Do you really think so?* Meinst du wirklich?; **Do you want to go?** — **Not really.** Willst du gehen? — Eigentlich nicht.

realtor n *(US)* Immobilienhändler m (pl Immobilienhändler), Immobilienhändlerin f

reason n Grund m (pl Gründe) ▷ *There's no reason to think that ...* Es gibt keinen Grund zu meinen, dass ...; **for security reasons** aus Sicherheitsgründen; **That was the main reason I went.** Das war der Hauptgrund, warum ich gegangen bin.

reasonable adj ① *(sensible)* vernünftig ▷ *Be reasonable!* Sei vernünftig! ② *(not bad)* ganz ordentlich ▷ *He wrote a reasonable essay.* Er hat einen ganz ordentlichen Aufsatz geschrieben.

reasonably adv ziemlich ▷ *reasonably well* ziemlich gut; **reasonably priced**

ENGLISH > GERMAN

accommodation preiswerte Unterbringung
reassure vb beruhigen [18] (perf hat beruhigt)
reassuring adj beruhigend
rebel n Rebell m (pl Rebellen), Rebellin f
▸ vb rebellieren [76] (perf hat rebelliert)
rebellious adj aufmüpfig
receipt n Quittung f
receive vb erhalten [33] (pres erhält, imperf erhielt, perf hat erhalten)
receiver n (of phone) Hörer m (pl Hörer) ▷ to pick up the receiver den Hörer abnehmen
recent adj neueste ▷ the recent developments in … die neuesten Entwicklungen in …; **in recent years** in den letzten Jahren
recently adv in letzter Zeit ▷ I've been doing a lot of training recently. Ich habe in letzter Zeit viel trainiert.
reception n ❶ (in hotel) Rezeption f ▷ Please leave your key at reception. Bitte geben Sie Ihren Schlüssel an der Rezeption ab. ❷ (party) Empfang m (pl Empfänge) ▷ The reception will be at a hotel. Der Empfang findet in einem Hotel statt.
receptionist n Empfangschef m (pl Empfangschefs), Empfangsdame f
recipe n Rezept nt (pl Rezepte)
reckon vb meinen [38] ▷ What do you reckon? Was meinst du?
recognize vb erkennen [39] (imperf erkannte, perf hat erkannt) ▷ You'll recognize me by my red hair. Du wirst mich an meinen roten Haaren erkennen.
recommend vb empfehlen [17] (pres empfiehlt, imperf empfahl, perf hat empfohlen) ▷ What do you recommend? Was können Sie empfehlen?
reconsider vb to reconsider something sich etwas noch einmal überlegen [82]

record n ❶ (recording) Schallplatte f ▷ my favourite record meine Lieblingsschallplatte ❷ (sport) Rekord m (pl Rekorde) ▷ the world record der Weltrekord; **in record time** in Rekordzeit; **He's got a criminal record.** Er ist vorbestraft.; **records** (of police, hospital) die Akten; **There is no record of your booking.** Ihre Buchung ist nirgends belegt.
▸ vb (on film, tape) aufnehmen [52] (pres nimmt auf, imperf nahm auf, perf hat aufgenommen) ▷ They've just recorded their new album. Sie haben eben ihr neues Album aufgenommen.
recorded delivery n **to send something recorded delivery** etwas per Einschreiben senden
recorder n (instrument) Blockflöte f ▷ She plays the recorder. Sie spielt Blockflöte
recording n Aufnahme f
record player n Plattenspieler m (pl Plattenspieler)
recover vb sich erholen [19] (perf hat sich erholt) ▷ He's recovering from a knee injury. Er erholt sich von einer Knieverletzung.
recovery n Erholung f; **Best wishes for a speedy recovery!** Gute Besserung!
rectangle n Rechteck nt (pl Rechtecke)
rectangular adj rechteckig
recycle vb wiederverwerten [7] (perf hat wiederverwertet)
recycling n Recycling nt
red adj rot ▷ a red rose eine rote Rose ▷ red meat rotes Fleisch ▷ Peter's got red hair. Peter hat rote Haare.; **to go through a red light** bei Rot über die Ampel fahren [21]
redcurrant n Rote Johannisbeere f
redecorate vb renovieren [76] (perf hat renoviert)
redo vb noch einmal machen [48]

reduce vb ermäßigen [7] (perf hat ermäßigt) ▷ *at a reduced price* zu ermäßigtem Preis; **'reduce speed now'** 'Geschwindigkeit verringern'

reduction n Nachlass m (gen Nachlasses, pl Nachlässe) ▷ *a five per cent reduction* ein Nachlass von fünf Prozent; **'Huge reductions!'** 'Stark reduzierte Preise!'

redundant adj **to be made redundant** entlassen werden [91]

refer vb **to refer to** anspielen [4] auf

referee n Schiedsrichter m (pl Schiedsrichter), Schiedsrichterin f

reference n (for job application) Arbeitszeugnis nt (gen Arbeitszeugnisses, pl Arbeitszeugnisse) ▷ *Would you please give me a reference?* Können Sie mir bitte ein Arbeitszeugnis geben?; **With reference to your letter of ...** Mit Bezug auf Ihren Brief vom ...; **a reference book** ein Nachschlagewerk nt

refill vb nachfüllen [4] (perf hat nachgefüllt) ▷ *He refilled my glass.* Er füllte mein Glas nach.

reflect vb (light, image) reflektieren [76] (perf hat reflektiert)

reflection n (in mirror) Spiegelbild nt (pl Spiegelbilder)

reflex n Reflex m (gen Reflexes, pl Reflexe)

reflexive adj reflexiv ▷ *a reflexive verb* ein reflexives Verb

refreshing adj erfrischend

refreshments npl Erfrischungen fpl

refrigerator n Kühlschrank m (pl Kühlschränke)

refuge n Zuflucht f

refugee n Flüchtling m (pl Flüchtlinge)
  der Flüchtling is also used for women.

refund n Rückvergütung f
  ▶ vb zurückerstatten [2] (perf hat zurückerstattet)

refuse vb sich weigern [88]
  ▶ n Müll m; **refuse collection** die Müllabfuhr

regain vb **to regain consciousness** wieder zu Bewusstsein kommen [40]

regard n **Give my regards to Alice.** Grüße an Alice.; **Martin sends his regards.** Martin lässt grüßen.; **'with kind regards'** 'mit freundlichen Grüßen'
  ▶ vb **to regard something as** etwas betrachten [7] als; **as regards** was ... betrifft

regiment n Regiment nt (pl Regimenter)

region n Gegend f

regional adj regional

register n (in school) Klassenbuch nt (pl Klassenbücher)
  ▶ vb (at school, college) sich einschreiben [61] (imperf schrieb sich ein, perf hat sich eingeschrieben)

registered adj **a registered letter** ein eingeschriebener Brief

registration n (in school) Namensaufruf m (pl Namensaufrufe)

regret n Bedauern nt; **I've got no regrets.** Ich bedaure nichts.
  ▶ vb bedauern [88] (perf hat bedauert) ▷ *You'll regret it!* Du wirst es bedauern!; **to regret doing something** es bedauern [88], etwas getan zu haben

regular adj ❶ regelmäßig ▷ *at regular intervals* in regelmäßigen Abständen ▷ *a regular verb* ein regelmäßiges Verb; **to take regular exercise** regelmäßig Sport machen [48] ❷ (average) normal ▷ *a regular portion of fries* eine normale Portion Pommes frites

regularly adv regelmäßig

regulation n Bestimmung f

rehearsal n Probe f

rehearse vb proben [38]

rein n Zügel m (pl Zügel) ▷ *the reins* die Zügel

reindeer n Rentier nt (pl Rentiere)

reject vb (idea, suggestion) verwerfen [92] (pres verwirft, imperf verwarf, perf hat verworfen) ▷ We rejected the idea. Wir haben die Idee verworfen.; **I applied but they rejected me.** Ich habe mich beworben, wurde aber abgelehnt.

related adj (people) verwandt ▷ Are you related to her? Bist du mit ihr verwandt? ▷ We're related. Wir sind miteinander verwandt.; **The two events were not related.** Es bestand kein Zusammenhang zwischen den beiden Ereignissen.

relation n ❶ (person) Verwandte m (gen Verwandten, pl Verwandten), Verwandte f (gen Verwandten) ▷ He's a distant relation. Er ist ein entfernter Verwandter. ▷ I've got relations in London. Ich habe Verwandte in London. ▷ my close relations meine engsten Verwandten ❷ (connection) Bezug m (pl Bezüge) ▷ It has no relation to reality. Es hat keinen Bezug zur Wirklichkeit.; **in relation to** im Verglichen mit

relationship n Beziehung f ▷ We have a good relationship. Wir haben eine gute Beziehung. ▷ I'm not in a relationship at the moment. Ich habe im Moment keine Beziehung.

relative n Verwandte m (gen Verwandten, pl Verwandten), Verwandte f (gen Verwandten) ▷ a relative (man) ein Verwandter ▷ my close relatives meine engsten Verwandten; **all her relatives** ihre ganze Verwandtschaft

relatively adv relativ

relax vb sich entspannen [18] (perf hat sich entspannt) ▷ I relax listening to music. Ich entspanne mich beim Musikhören.; **Relax! Everything's fine.** Immer mit der Ruhe! Alles ist in Ordnung.

relaxation n Entspannung f ▷ I don't have much time for relaxation. Ich habe nicht viel Zeit für Entspannung.

relaxed adj entspannt

relaxing adj entspannend ▷ I find cooking relaxing. Ich finde Kochen entspannend.

relay n a relay race ein Staffellauf m

release vb ❶ (prisoner) freilassen [42] (pres lässt frei, imperf ließ frei, perf hat freigelassen) ❷ (report, news) veröffentlichen [84] (perf hat veröffentlicht) ❸ (record, video) herausbringen [13] (imperf brachte heraus, perf hat herausgebracht)
▶ n (from prison) Freilassung f ▷ the release of Nelson Mandela die Freilassung Nelson Mandelas; **the band's latest release** die neueste Platte der Band

relevant adj (documents) entsprechend; **That's not relevant.** Das ist nicht relevant.; **to be relevant to something** einen Bezug zu etwas haben [32]

reliable adj zuverlässig ▷ a reliable car ein zuverlässiges Auto ▷ He's not very reliable. Er ist nicht sehr zuverlässig.

relief n Erleichterung f ▷ That's a relief! Das ist eine Erleichterung!

relieved adj erleichtert ▷ I was relieved to hear … Ich war erleichtert zu hören …

religion n Religion f ▷ What religion are you? Welche Religion hast du?

religious adj religiös ▷ I'm not religious. Ich bin nicht religiös.; **my religious beliefs** mein Glaube m

reluctant adj to be reluctant to do something etwas nur ungern tun [81]

reluctantly adv ungern ▷ She reluctantly accepted. Sie hat ungern angenommen.

rely on vb sich verlassen [42] auf (pres verlässt sich, imperf verließ sich, perf hat sich verlassen) ▷ I'm relying on you. Ich verlasse mich auf dich.

remain vb bleiben [10] (imperf blieb, perf ist geblieben); **to remain silent** schweigen

remaining adj restlich ▷ *the remaining ingredients* die restlichen Zutaten

remark n Bemerkung f

remarkable adj bemerkenswert

remarkably adv bemerkenswert

remember vb sich erinnern [88] (perf hat sich erinnert) ▷ *I can't remember his name.* Ich kann mich nicht an seinen Namen erinnern. ▷ *I don't remember.* Ich erinnere mich nicht.

> In German you often say 'don't forget' rather than 'remember' when reminding somebody about something.

▷ *Remember your passport!* Vergiss deinen Pass nicht! ▷ *Remember to write your name on the form.* Vergiss nicht, deinen Namen auf das Formular zu schreiben.

remind vb erinnern [88] (perf hat erinnert) ▷ *It reminds me of Scotland.* Es erinnert mich an Schottland. ▷ *I'll remind you tomorrow.* Ich werde dich morgen daran erinnern. ▷ *Remind me to speak to Daniel.* Erinnere mich, dass ich mit Daniel sprechen will.

remote adj abgelegen ▷ *a remote village* ein abgelegenes Dorf

remote control n Fernbedienung f

remotely adv entfernt ▷ *There was nobody remotely resembling this description.* Niemand sah dieser Beschreibung auch nur entfernt ähnlich.; **It's remotely possible that ...** Es ist gerade eben noch möglich, dass ...; **to work remotely** im Homeoffice arbeiten

remove vb entfernen [18] (perf hat entfernt) ▷ *Did you remove the stain?* Hast du den Fleck entfernt?

renew vb (passport, licence) verlängern lassen [42] (pres lässt verlängern, imperf ließ verlängern, perf hat verlängern lassen) ▷ *You'll need to renew your passport.* Du musst deinen Pass verlängern lassen.; **to renew a contract** einen Vertrag verlängern [88]

renewable adj (energy, resource, passport) erneuerbar

renovate vb renovieren [76] (perf hat renoviert) ▷ *The building's been renovated.* Das Gebäude ist renoviert worden.

rent n Miete f

> Be careful not to translate **rent** by **Rente**.

▶ vb mieten [2] ▷ *We rented a car.* Wir haben ein Auto gemietet.

reoffend vb erneut straffällig werden [91]

reorganize vb umorganisieren [4] (perf hat umorganisiert)

rep n (= representative) Vertreter m (pl Vertreter), Vertreterin f

repaid vb see **repay**

repair vb reparieren [76] (perf hat repariert); **to get something repaired** etwas reparieren lassen [42]
▶ n Reparatur f

repay vb (money) zurückzahlen [15] (perf hat zurückgezahlt)

repeat vb wiederholen [4] (perf hat wiederholt)
▶ n Wiederholung f ▷ *There are too many repeats on TV.* Es gibt zu viele Wiederholungen im Fernsehen.

repeatedly adv wiederholt

repetitive adj (movement, work) monoton

replace vb ersetzen [36] (perf hat ersetzt)

replay n *There will be a replay on Friday.* Das Spiel wird am Freitag wiederholt.
▶ vb (match) wiederholen [4] (perf hat wiederholt)

reply n Antwort f
▶ vb antworten [2]

report vb ❶ (of event) Bericht m (pl Berichte) ▷ *a report in the paper* ein Zeitungsbericht ❷ (at school) Zeugnis nt (gen Zeugnisses, pl Zeugnisse) ▷ *I got*

a good report. Ich habe ein gutes Zeugnis bekommen.; **report card** das Zeugnis
▶ vb melden [**54**] ▷ *I've reported the theft.* Ich habe den Diebstahl gemeldet.
❷ **sich melden** [**54**] ▷ *Report to reception when you arrive.* Melden Sie sich bei Ihrer Ankunft am Empfang.

reporter n Reporter m (pl Reporter), Reporterin f ▷ *She'd like to be a reporter.* Sie möchte gern Reporterin werden.

represent vb (person) vertreten [**79**] (pres vertritt, imperf vertrat, perf hat vertreten) ▷ *My lawyer represented me in court.* Mein Anwalt hat mich vor Gericht vertreten.

representative adj repräsentativ

reptile n Reptil nt (pl Reptilien)

republic n Republik f

reputation n Ruf m

request n Bitte f
▶ vb bitten [**9**] um (imperf bat, perf hat gebeten) ▷ *He requested information.* Er bat um Informationen.

require vb erfordern [**19**] (perf hat erfordert) ▷ *Her job requires a lot of patience.* Ihre Arbeit erfordert viel Geduld.

resat vb *see* **resit**

rescue vb retten [**2**]
▶ n Rettung f ▷ *a rescue operation* eine Rettungsaktion; **a mountain rescue team** ein Team der Bergwacht; **the rescue services** der Rettungsdienst sg; **to come to somebody's rescue** jemandem zu Hilfe kommen [**40**]

research n (experimental) Forschung f ▷ *He's doing research.* Er ist in der Forschung tätig.; **Research has shown that ...** Forschungen haben ergeben, dass ...; **She's doing some research in the library.** Sie sammelt in der Bibliothek Material.

resemblance n Ähnlichkeit f

resent vb übel nehmen [**52**] (pres nimmt übel, imperf nahm übel, perf hat übel genommen) ▷ *I really resent your criticism.* Ich nehme Ihnen Ihre Kritik wirklich übel.; **I resent being dependent on her.** Ich ärgere mich darüber, von ihr abhängig zu sein.

resentful adj verärgert ▷ *He was resentful about the way they were treated.* Er war verärgert darüber, wie sie behandelt wurden.

reservation n ❶ (at restaurant) Reservierung f; **I'd like to make a reservation for this evening.** Ich möchte für heute Abend einen Tisch reservieren. ❷ (for journey, at hotel) Buchung f; **I've got a reservation for two nights.** Ich habe für zwei Nächte gebucht.

reserve n ❶ (place) Schutzgebiet nt (pl Schutzgebiete) ▷ *a nature reserve* ein Naturschutzgebiet ❷ (person) Reservespieler m (pl Reservespieler), Reservespielerin f ▷ *She was reserve in the game last Saturday.* Sie war beim Spiel letzten Samstag Reservespielerin.
▶ vb reservieren [**76**] (perf hat reserviert) ▷ *I'd like to reserve a table for tomorrow evening.* Ich möchte für morgen Abend einen Tisch reservieren.

reserved adj reserviert ▷ *a reserved seat* ein reservierter Platz ▷ *He's quite reserved.* Er ist ziemlich reserviert.

resident n Bewohner m (pl Bewohner), Bewohnerin f

residential adj **a residential area** ein Wohngebiet nt

resign vb ❶ zurücktreten [**79**] (pres tritt zurück, imperf trat zurück, perf ist zurückgetreten) ▷ *The minister resigned.* Der Minister ist zurückgetreten.
❷ (employee) kündigen [**38**] ▷ *She resigned to take up a post abroad.* Sie kündigte, um einen Posten im Ausland zu übernehmen.

resit vb wiederholen [**4**] (perf hat wiederholt) ▷ *I'm resitting the exam in May.* Ich wiederhole die Prüfung im Mai.

resolution n (decision) Beschluss m (gen Beschlusses, pl Beschlüsse); **Have you made a New Year's resolution?** Hast du zum neuen Jahr gute Vorsätze gefasst?

resort n (at seaside) Badeort m (pl Badeorte) ▷ *It's a resort on the Costa del Sol.* Es ist ein Badeort an der Costa del Sol.; **a ski resort** ein Skiort; **as a last resort** als letzter Ausweg

resources npl (financial) Mittel ntpl ▷ *We haven't the resources to build a swimming pool.* Wir haben nicht die Mittel, um ein Schwimmbad zu bauen.; **natural resources** Bodenschätze mpl

respect n Respekt m
▶ vb respektieren [76] (perf hat respektiert)

respectable adj ❶ anständig ▷ *respectable people* anständige Leute pl ❷ (standard, marks) ordentlich

responsibility n Verantwortung f

responsible adj ❶ verantwortlich ▷ *to be responsible for something* für etwas verantwortlich sein; **It's a responsible job.** Es ist ein verantwortungsvoller Posten. ❷ (mature) verantwortungsbewusst ▷ *You should be more responsible.* Du solltest verantwortungsbewusster sein.

rest n ❶ (relaxation) Pause f ▷ *five minutes' rest* eine fünfminütige Pause; **to have a rest** sich ausruhen [4] ❷ (remainder) Rest m (pl Reste) ▷ *I'll do the rest.* Ich mache den Rest. ▷ *the rest of the money* der Rest des Geldes; **the rest of them** die anderen
▶ vb ❶ (relax) sich ausruhen [4] (perf hat sich ausgeruht) ▷ *She's resting in her room.* Sie ruht sich in ihrem Zimmer aus. ❷ (not overstrain) schonen [38] ▷ *He has to rest his knee.* Er muss sein Knie schonen. ❸ (lean) lehnen [38] ▷ *I rested my bike against the window.* Ich habe mein Fahrrad ans Fenster gelehnt.

restaurant n Restaurant nt (pl Restaurants) ▷ *We don't often go to restaurants.* Wir gehen nicht oft ins Restaurant.; **a restaurant car** ein Speisewagen m

restless adj unruhig

restore vb (building, picture) restaurieren [76] (perf hat restauriert)

restrict vb beschränken [18] (perf hat beschränkt)

rest room n (US) Toilette f

result n Ergebnis nt (gen Ergebnisses, pl Ergebnisse) ▷ *my exam results* meine Prüfungsergebnisse; **What was the result? — One nil.** Wie ist das Spiel ausgegangen? — Eins zu null.

résumé n ❶ Zusammenfassung f ▷ *a résumé of her speech* eine Zusammenfassung ihrer Rede ❷ (US: CV) Lebenslauf m (pl Lebensläufe)

retire vb in Rente gehen [29] (imperf ging in Rente, perf ist in Rente gegangen) ▷ *He retired last year.* Er ist letztes Jahr in Rente gegangen.

retired adj im Ruhestand ▷ *She's retired.* Sie ist im Ruhestand. ▷ *a retired teacher* ein Lehrer im Ruhestand

retirement n Ruhestand m

return n ❶ Rückkehr f ▷ *after our return* nach unserer Rückkehr; **the return journey** die Rückfahrt; **a return match** ein Rückspiel nt ❷ (ticket) Rückfahrkarte f ▷ *A return to Freiburg, please.* Eine Rückfahrkarte nach Freiburg, bitte.; **in return** dafür; **in return for** für; **Many happy returns!** Herzlichen Glückwunsch zum Geburtstag!
▶ vb ❶ (come back) zurückkommen [40] (imperf kam zurück, perf ist zurückgekommen) ▷ *I've just returned from holiday.* Ich bin gerade aus den Ferien zurückgekommen.; **to return home** wieder nach Hause kommen [40] ❷ (go back) zurückkehren [15] (perf

ist zurückgekehrt.) ▷ *He returned to Germany.* Er ist nach Deutschland zurückgekehrt. ❸ *(give back)* zurückgeben [**28**] *(pres* gibt zurück, *imperf* gab zurück, *perf* hat zurückgegeben) ▷ *She borrows my things and doesn't return them.* Sie leiht sich meine Sachen aus und gibt sie dann nicht zurück.

retweet *n* Retweet *m (pl* Retweets)

reunion *n* Treffen *nt (pl* Treffen)

reveal *vb (truth, facts)* ans Licht bringen [**13**] *(imperf* brachte ans Licht, *perf* hat ans Licht gebracht) ▷ *The survey reveals that many people are overweight.* Die Untersuchung bringt ans Licht, dass viele Menschen Übergewicht haben.; **She refused to reveal the whereabouts of her daughter.** Sie weigerte sich, den Aufenthaltsort ihrer Tochter preiszugeben.; **It was revealed that ...** Es wurde bekannt gegeben, dass ...

revenge *n* Rache *f* ▷ *in revenge* aus Rache; **to take revenge** sich rächen [**48**]

reverse *vb (car)* rückwärtsfahren [**21**] *(pres* fährt rückwärts, *imperf* fuhr rückwärts, *perf* ist rückwärtsgefahren) ▷ *He reversed without looking.* Er fuhr rückwärts ohne zu sehen.; **to reverse the charges** *(telephone)* ein R-Gespräch führen [**38**]
▶ *adj* umgekehrt ▷ *in reverse order* in umgekehrter Reihenfolge; **in reverse gear** im Rückwärtsgang

review *n* ❶ *(of policy, salary)* Überprüfung *f* ❷ *(of subject)* Prüfung *f*; **to be under review** überprüft werden [**91**]

revise *vb* den Stoff wiederholen [**38**] ▷ *I haven't started revising yet.* Ich habe noch nicht angefangen, den Stoff zu wiederholen.; **I've revised my opinion.** Ich habe meine Meinung geändert.

revision *n* Wiederholung des Stoffes *f*; **Have you done a lot of revision?** Hast du schon viel Stoff wiederholt?

revolting *adj* ekelhaft

revolution *n* Revolution *f* ▷ *the French Revolution* die Französische Revolution

reward *n* Belohnung *f*

rewarding *adj* dankbar ▷ *a rewarding job* eine dankbare Arbeit

rewind *vb* zurückspulen [**15**] *(perf* hat zurückgespult) ▷ *to rewind a cassette* eine Kassette zurückspulen

Rhine *n* Rhein *m*

rhinoceros *n* Nashorn *nt (pl* Nashörner)

rhubarb *n* Rhabarber *m* ▷ *a rhubarb tart* ein Rhabarberkuchen

rhythm *n* Rhythmus *m (gen* Rhythmus, *pl* Rhythmen)

rib *n* Rippe *f*

ribbon *n* Band *nt (pl* Bänder)

rice *n* Reis *m*; **rice pudding** der Milchreis

rich *adj* reich; **the rich** die Reichen *mpl*

rid *vb* **to get rid of** loswerden [**91**]

ride *n* **to go for a ride (1)** *(on horse)* reiten gehen [**29**] **(2)** *(on bike)* mit dem Fahrrad fahren [**21**]; **We went for a bike ride.** Wir haben eine Fahrt mit dem Fahrrad gemacht.; **It's a short bus ride to the town centre.** Die Stadtmitte ist nur eine kurze Busfahrt entfernt.
▶ *vb (on horse)* reiten *(imperf* ritt, *perf* ist geritten) ▷ *I'm learning to ride.* Ich lerne reiten.; **to ride a bike** Fahrrad fahren [**21**] ▷ *Can you ride a bike?* Kannst du Fahrrad fahren?

rider *n* ❶ *(on horse)* Reiter *m (pl* Reiter), Reiterin *f* ▷ *She's a good rider.* Sie ist eine gute Reiterin. ❷ *(on bike)* Fahrradfahrer *m (pl* Fahrradfahrer), Fahrradfahrerin *f*

ridiculous *adj* lächerlich ▷ *Don't be ridiculous!* Mach dich nicht lächerlich!

riding *n* Reiten *nt*; **to go riding** reiten gehen [**29**]; **a riding school** eine Reitschule

rifle n Gewehr nt (pl Gewehre) ▷ *a hunting rifle* ein Jagdgewehr

right adj, adv

There are several ways of translating 'right'. Scan the examples to find one that is similar to what you want to say.

❶ (correct, suitable) richtig ▷ *the right answer* die richtige Antwort ▷ *Am I pronouncing it right?* Spreche ich das richtig aus? ▷ *It isn't the right size.* Es ist nicht die richtige Größe. ▷ *We're on the right train.* Wir sind im richtigen Zug. ▷ *It's not right to behave like that.* Es ist nicht richtig, sich so zu benehmen.; **Is this the right road for Hamburg?** Sind wir hier richtig nach Hamburg?; **I think you did the right thing.** Ich glaube, du hast das Richtige getan.; **to be right (1)** (person) recht haben [32] ▷ *You were right!* Du hattest recht! **(2)** (statement, opinion) richtig sein [65] ▷ *That's right!* Das ist richtig! ❷ (accurate) genau ▷ *Do you have the right time?* Haben Sie die genaue Zeit? ❸ (not left) rechte ▷ *the right foot* der rechte Fuß ▷ *my right arm* mein rechter Arm ▷ *your right hand* deine rechte Hand ▷ *her right eye* ihr rechtes Auge ❹ (turn) rechts ▷ *Turn right at the lights.* Biegen Sie an der Ampel rechts ab.; **Look right!** Sehen Sie nach rechts!; **Right! Let's get started.** Okay! Fangen wir an.; **right away** sofort
▶ n ❶ Recht nt (pl Rechte) ▷ *You've got no right to do that.* Du hast kein Recht, das zu tun. ❷ (not left) rechte Seite f; **on the right;** rechts; **right of way** die Vorfahrt

right-hand adj **the right-hand side** die rechte Seite; **It's on the right-hand side.** Es liegt rechts.

right-handed adj rechtshändig

rightly adv richtig ▷ *If I remember rightly, ...* Wenn ich mich richtig erinnere, ... ▷ *She rightly decided that he was lying.* Sie kam zu dem richtigen Schluss, dass er log.

ring n ❶ Ring m (pl Ringe) ▷ *a gold ring* ein goldener Ring ▷ *a diamond ring* ein Diamantring; **a wedding ring** ein Ehering ❷ (circle) Kreis m (gen Kreises, pl Kreise) ▷ *to stand in a ring* im Kreis stehen ❸ (of bell) Klingeln nt; **There was a ring at the door.** Es klingelt.; **to give somebody a ring** jemanden anrufen [56]
▶ vb ❶ anrufen [56] (imperf rief an, perf hat angerufen) ▷ *Your mother rang.* Deine Mutter hat heute früh angerufen.; **to ring somebody** jemanden anrufen [56]; **to ring somebody up** jemanden anrufen [56]. ❷ klingeln [34] ▷ *The phone's ringing.* Das Telefon klingelt.; **to ring the bell** (doorbell) klingeln [34]; **to ring back** zurückrufen [56]

ring binder n Ringheft nt (pl Ringhefte)

ringtone n Klingelton m (pl Klingeltöne)

rinse vb spülen [38]

riot n Krawalle mpl
▶ vb randalieren [76] (perf hat randaliert)

rip vb zerreißen (imperf zerriss, perf hat zerrissen) ▷ *I've ripped my jeans.* Ich habe meine Jeans zerrissen. ▷ *My skirt's ripped.* Mein Rock ist zerrissen.

rip off vb (informal) ausnehmen [52] (pres nimmt aus, imperf nahm aus, perf hat ausgenommen)

rip up vb zerreißen (imperf zerriss, perf hat zerrissen)

ripe adj reif

rip-off n **It's a rip-off!** (informal) Das ist Nepp!

rise n ❶ (in prices, temperature) Anstieg m (pl Anstiege) ▷ *a sudden rise in temperature* ein plötzlicher Temperaturanstieg ❷ (pay rise) Gehaltserhöhung f
▶ vb ❶ (increase) steigen [74] (imperf

ENGLISH > GERMAN

stieg. *perfist gestiegen*) ▷ *Prices are rising.* Die Preise steigen. ❷ **aufgehen** [**29**] (*imperf* ging auf, *perf* ist aufgegangen) ▷ *The sun rises early in June.* Die Sonne geht im Juni früh auf.

risk n Risiko nt (pl Risiken); **to take risks** Risiken eingehen [**29**]; **It's at your own risk.** Auf eigene Gefahr.
▶ vb riskieren [**76**] (*perf* hat riskiert) ▷ *You risk getting a fine.* Du riskierst einen Strafzettel. ▷ *I wouldn't risk it.* Das würde ich an deiner Stelle nicht riskieren.

rival n Rivale m (gen Rivalen, pl Rivalen), Rivalin f
▶ adj rivalisierend ▷ *a rival gang* eine rivalisierende Bande; **a rival company** ein Konkurrenzunternehmen nt

river n Fluss m (gen Flusses, pl Flüsse); **the river Rhine** der Rhein

road n Straße f ▷ *There's a lot of traffic on the roads.* Es herrscht viel Verkehr auf den Straßen.; **They live across the road.** Sie wohnen gegenüber.

road map n Straßenkarte f

road rage n Aggressivität im Straßenverkehr f

road sign n Verkehrsschild nt (pl Verkehrsschilder)

roadworks npl Bauarbeiten fpl

roast adj roast chicken das Brathähnchen; **roast potatoes** die Röstkartoffeln; **roast pork** der Schweinebraten; **roast beef** der Rindsbraten

rob vb **to rob somebody** jemanden berauben [**7**]; **to rob a bank** eine Bank ausrauben [**4**]; **to rob somebody of something** jemandem etwas rauben [**38**]

robber n Räuber m (pl Räuber), Räuberin f; **a bank robber** ein Bankräuber

robbery n Raub m (pl Raube); **a bank robbery** ein Bankraub; **armed robbery** der bewaffnete Raubüberfall

457 | Roman

robin n Rotkehlchen nt (pl Rotkehlchen)

robot n Roboter m (pl Roboter)

rock n ❶ (*substance*) Fels m (gen Fels) ▷ *They tunnelled through the rock.* Sie gruben einen Tunnel durch den Fels. ❷ (*boulder*) Felsbrocken m (pl Felsbrocken) ▷ *I sat on a rock.* Ich saß auf einem Felsbrocken. ❸ (*stone*) Stein m (pl Steine) ▷ *The crowd threw rocks.* Die Menge fing an, Steine zu werfen. ❹ (*music*) Rock m ▷ *a rock concert* ein Rockkonzert ▷ *He's a rock star.* Er ist ein Rockstar. ❺ (*sweet*) Zuckerstange f ▷ *a stick of rock* eine Zuckerstange; **rock and roll** Rock 'n' Roll
▶ vb erschüttern [**19**] (*perf* hat erschüttert) ▷ *The explosion rocked the building.* Die Explosion erschütterte das Gebäude.

rocket n (*firework, spacecraft*) Rakete f

rocking horse n Schaukelpferd nt (pl Schaukelpferde)

rod n (*for fishing*) Angel f

rode vb see **ride**

role n Rolle f

role play n Rollenspiel nt (pl Rollenspiele) ▷ *to do a role play* ein Rollenspiel machen

roll n ❶ Rolle f ▷ *a roll of tape* eine Rolle Klebestreifen ▷ *a toilet roll* eine Rolle Toilettenpapier ❷ (*bread*) Brötchen nt (pl Brötchen)
▶ vb rollen [**38**]; **to roll out the pastry** den Teig ausrollen [**4**]

Rollerblade® n Rollerblade® m (pl Rollerblades)

roller coaster n Achterbahn f

roller skates npl Rollschuhe mpl

roller-skating n Rollschuhlaufen nt; **to go roller-skating** Rollschuh laufen [**43**]

Roman adj, n (*ancient*) römisch ▷ *a Roman villa* eine römische Villa ▷ *the Roman empire* das Römische Reich; **the Romans** die Römer mpl

Roman Catholic n Katholik m (gen Katholiken, pl Katholiken), Katholikin f ▷ He's a Roman Catholic. Er ist Katholik.

romance n (novels) Liebesroman m (pl Liebesromane) ▷ I read a lot of romances. Ich lese viele Liebesromane.; **a holiday romance** ein Ferienflirt m

Romania n Rumänien nt; **from Romania** aus Rumänien; **to Romania** nach Rumänien

Romanian adj rumänisch

romantic adj romantisch

roof n Dach nt (pl Dächer)

roof rack n Dachträger m (pl Dachträger)

room n ❶ (at junction) Zimmer nt (pl Zimmer) ▷ the biggest room in the house das größte Zimmer des Hauses ▷ She's in her room. Sie ist in ihrem Zimmer. ▷ the music room das Musikzimmer; **a single room** ein Einzelzimmer; **a double room** ein Doppelzimmer ❷ (space) Platz m (gen Platzes) ▷ There's no room for that box. Es ist kein Platz für diese Schachtel.

root n Wurzel f

rope n Seil nt (pl Seile)

rose vb see **rise**
▶ n (flower) Rose f

rot vb verfaulen [7] (perf ist verfault)

rotten adj ❶ (decayed) faulig ▷ a rotten apple ein fauliger Apfel; **rotten weather** (informal) das Mistwetter; **That's a rotten thing to do.** Das ist gemein.; **to feel rotten** (informal) sich mies fühlen [38]

rough adj ❶ rau ▷ My hands are rough. Meine Hände sind rau. ▷ It's a rough area. Das ist eine raue Gegend. ❷ (game) hart ▷ Rugby's a rough sport. Rugby ist ein harter Sport. ❸ (water) stürmisch ▷ The sea was rough. Das Meer war stürmisch. ❹ ungefähr ▷ I've got a rough idea. Ich habe eine ungefähre Vorstellung.; **to feel rough** sich nicht wohlfühlen [4]

roughly adv ungefähr ▷ It weighs roughly twenty kilos. Es wiegt ungefähr zwanzig Kilo.

round adj, adv, prep ❶ rund ▷ a round table ein runder Tisch ❷ (around) um ▷ We were sitting round the table. Wir saßen um den Tisch herum. ▷ She wore a scarf round her neck. Sie trug einen Schal um den Hals.; **It's just round the corner.** (very near) Es ist gleich um die Ecke.; **to go round to somebody's house** bei jemandem vorbeigehen [29]; **to have a look round** sich umsehen [64]; **to go round a museum** sich ein Museum ansehen [64]; **round here** hier in der Gegend; **all round** ringsherum; **all year round** das ganze Jahr über; **round about** (roughly) etwa
▶ n (of tournament, boxing match) Runde f ▷ a round of golf eine Runde Golf; **a round of drinks** eine Runde

roundabout n ❶ (at junction) Kreisverkehr m (pl Kreisverkehre) ❷ (at funfair) Karussell nt (pl Karussells)

rounders nsg Schlagball m

round trip n (US) Hin- und Rückfahrt f; **a round-trip ticket** eine Rückfahrkarte

route n Route f ▷ We're planning our route. Wir planen unsere Route.

route planner n Routenplaner m (pl Routenplaner)

routine n Routine f

row (1) n Reihe f ▷ a row of houses eine Reihe Häuser ▷ Our seats are in the front row. Unsere Plätze sind in der ersten Reihe.; **five times in a row** fünfmal hintereinander

row (2) n ❶ (noise) Krach m ▷ What's that terrible row? Was ist das für ein furchtbarer Krach? ❷ (quarrel) Streit m (pl Streite); **to have a row** Streit haben [32]

row vb rudern [88] ▷ We took turns to row. Wir haben abwechselnd gerudert.

rowboat n (US) Ruderboot nt (pl Ruderboote)

ENGLISH > GERMAN

rowing n (sport) Rudern nt ▷ My hobby is rowing. Rudern ist mein Hobby.; **a rowing boat** ein Ruderboot nt

royal adj königlich ▷ the royal family die königliche Familie

rub vb ① (stain) reiben (imperf rieb, perf hat gerieben) ② (part of body) sich reiben ▷ Don't rub your eyes! Reib dir nicht die Augen!; **I rubbed myself with a towel.** Ich rieb mich mit einem Handtuch trocken.; **to rub something out** etwas ausradieren [76]

rubber n ① Gummi m (pl Gummis) ▷ rubber soles die Gummisohlen ② (eraser) Radiergummi m (pl Radiergummis) ▷ Can I borrow your rubber? Kann ich deinen Radiergummi ausleihen?; **a rubber band** ein Gummiband nt

rubbish n ① (refuse) Müll m ▷ When do they collect the rubbish? Wann wird der Müll abgeholt? ② (junk) Krempel m ▷ They sell a lot of rubbish at the market. Sie verkaufen eine Menge Krempel auf dem Markt. ③ (nonsense) Unsinn m ▷ Don't talk rubbish! Red keinen Unsinn!; **That's a load of rubbish!** (informal) Das ist doch Unsinn!; **This magazine is rubbish!** (informal) Die Zeitschrift ist Schrott!; **a rubbish bin** ein Mülleimer m; **a rubbish dump** eine Müllkippe
▶ adj (informal) miserabel ▷ They're a rubbish team! Sie sind eine miserable Mannschaft!

rucksack n Rucksack m (pl Rucksäcke)

rude adj ① (impolite) unhöflich ▷ It's rude to interrupt. Es ist unhöflich dazwischenzureden. ▷ He was very rude to me. Er war sehr unhöflich zu mir. ② (offensive) unanständig ▷ a rude joke ein unanständiger Witz; **a rude word** ein Schimpfwort nt

rug n ① Teppich m (pl Teppiche) ▷ a Persian rug ein Perserteppich ② (blanket) Decke f ▷ a tartan rug eine karierte Decke

459 | **run**

rugby n Rugby nt ▷ I play rugby. Ich spiele Rugby.

ruin n Ruine f ▷ the ruins of the castle die Ruine der Burg; **My life is in ruins.** Mein Leben ist ruiniert.
▶ vb ruinieren [76] (perf hat ruiniert) ▷ You'll ruin your shoes. Du ruinierst dir deine Schuhe. ▷ That's far too expensive. You are ruining me! Das ist viel zu teuer. Du ruinierst mich noch!; **It ruined our holiday.** Es hat uns den Urlaub verdorben.

rule n ① Regel f ▷ the rules of grammar die Grammatikregeln; **as a rule** in der Regel ② (regulation) Vorschrift f ▷ It's against the rules. Das ist gegen die Vorschriften.
▶ vb regieren [76] (perf hat regiert)

rule out vb (possibility) ausschließen (imperf schloss aus, perf hat ausgeschlossen)

ruler n Lineal nt (pl Lineale) ▷ Can I borrow your ruler? Kann ich dein Lineal ausleihen?

rum n Rum m

rumour n Gerücht nt (pl Gerüchte) ▷ It's just a rumour. Es ist nur ein Gerücht.

run n (in cricket) Lauf m (pl Läufe) ▷ to score a run einen Lauf machen; **to go for a run** einen Dauerlauf machen [48]; **I did a ten-kilometre run.** Ich bin zehn Kilometer gelaufen.; **on the run** auf der Flucht; **in the long run** auf Dauer
▶ vb ① laufen [43] (pres läuft, imperf lief, perf ist gelaufen) ▷ I ran five kilometres. Ich bin fünf Kilometer gelaufen.; **to run a marathon** an einem Marathonlauf teilnehmen [52] ② (manage) leiten [2] ▷ He runs a large company. Er leitet ein großes Unternehmen. ③ (organize) veranstalten [2] (perf hat veranstaltet) ▷ They run music courses in the holidays. Sie veranstalten Musikkurse während der Ferien. ④ (water) laufen [43] ▷ Don't leave the tap running. Lass das Wasser nicht laufen.; **to run a bath** ein Bad

einlaufen lassen [**42**] ❶ (by car) fahren [**21**] (pres fährt, imperf fuhr, perf hat gefahren) ▷ I can run you to the station. Ich kann dich zum Bahnhof fahren.; **to run away** weglaufen [**43**]; **Time is running out.** Die Zeit wird knapp.; **We ran out of money.** Uns ist das Geld ausgegangen.; **to run somebody over** jemanden überfahren [**21**]; **to get run over** überfahren werden [**91**]

rung vb see **ring**

runner n Läufer m (pl Läufer), Läuferin f

runner-up n Zweite m (gen Zweiten, pl Zweiten), Zweite f (gen Zweiten)

running n Laufen nt ▷ Running is my favourite sport. Laufen ist mein Lieblingssport.

run-up n **in the run-up to Christmas** in der Zeit vor Weihnachten

runway n Startbahn f

rush n Eile f; **in a rush** in Eile
▶ vb ❶ (run) rennen [**55**] (imperf rannte, perf ist gerannt) ▷ Everyone rushed outside. Alle rannten hinaus. ❷ (hurry) sich beeilen [**7**] (perf hat sich beeilt) ▷ There's no need to rush. Wir brauchen uns nicht zu beeilen.

rush hour n Hauptverkehrszeit f ▷ in the rush hour in der Hauptverkehrszeit

Russia n Russland nt; **from Russia** aus Russland; **to Russia** nach Russland

Russian adj russisch; **He's Russian.** Er ist Russe.; **She's Russian.** Sie ist Russin.
▶ n ❶ (person) Russe m (gen Russen, pl Russen), Russin f ❷ (language) Russisch nt (gen Russischen)

rust n Rost m

rusty adj rostig ▷ a rusty bike ein rostiges Fahrrad; **My German is very rusty.** Mein Deutsch ist ziemlich eingerostet.

rye n Roggen m; **rye bread** das Roggenbrot

S

Sabbath n ❶ (Christian) Sonntag m (pl Sonntage) ❷ (Jewish) Sabbat m (pl Sabbate)

sack n Sack m (pl Säcke); **to get the sack** gefeuert werden [**91**]
▶ vb **to sack somebody** jemanden feuern [**34**]

sacred adj heilig

sacrifice n Opfer nt (pl Opfer)

sad adj traurig

saddle n Sattel m (pl Sättel)

saddlebag n Satteltasche f

safe n Safe m (pl Safes) ▷ She put the money in the safe. Sie tat das Geld in den Safe.
▶ adj ❶ sicher ▷ It's perfectly safe. Es ist völlig sicher. ▷ This car isn't safe. Das Auto ist nicht sicher. ❷ (out of danger) in Sicherheit ▷ You're safe now. Sie sind jetzt in Sicherheit.; **to feel safe** sich sicher fühlen [**38**]; **safe sex** Safer Sex

safety n Sicherheit f; **a safety belt** ein Sicherheitsgurt m; **a safety pin** eine Sicherheitsnadel

ENGLISH > GERMAN

Sagittarius n Schütze m (gen Schützen) ▷ *I'm Sagittarius.* Ich bin Schütze.
said vb see **say**
sail n Segel nt (pl Segel)
▶ vb ❶ (travel) segeln [**34**] (perf ist gesegelt) ❷ (set off) abfahren [**21**] (pres fährt ab, imperf fuhr ab, perf ist abgefahren) ▷ *The boat sails at eight o'clock.* Das Schiff fährt um acht Uhr ab.
sailing n Segeln nt ▷ *His hobby is sailing.* Segeln ist sein Hobby.; **to go sailing** segeln gehen [**29**]; **a sailing boat** ein Segelboot nt; **a sailing ship** ein Segelschiff nt
sailor n Matrose m (gen Matrosen, pl Matrosen), Matrosin f ▷ *He's a sailor.* Er ist Matrose.
saint n Heilige m (gen Heiligen, pl Heiligen), Heilige f (gen Heiligen) ▷ *a saint (man)* ein Heiliger
sake n **for the sake of** um ... willen
salad n Salat m (pl Salate); **salad cream** die Salatmayonnaise; **salad dressing** die Salatsoße
salami n Salami f (gen Salamis, pl Salamis)
salary n Gehalt nt (pl Gehälter)
sale n (end of season reductions) Schlussverkauf m (pl Schlussverkäufe) ▷ *There's a sale on at Harrods.* Bei Harrods ist Schlussverkauf.; **on sale** erhältlich; **'for sale'** "zu verkaufen"
sales assistant n Verkäufer m (pl Verkäufer), Verkäuferin f ▷ *She's a sales assistant.* Sie ist Verkäuferin.
salesman n ❶ (sales rep) Vertreter m (pl Vertreter) ▷ *He's a salesman.* Er ist Vertreter.; **a double-glazing salesman** ein Vertreter für Doppelfenster ❷ (sales assistant) Verkäufer m (pl Verkäufer)
saleswoman n ❶ (sales rep) Vertreterin f ▷ *She's a saleswoman.* Sie ist Vertreterin. ❷ (sales assistant) Verkäuferin f
salmon n Lachs m (gen Lachses, pl Lachse)

461 | **sat nav**

salon n Salon m (pl Salons) ▷ *a hair salon* ein Friseursalon ▷ *a beauty salon* ein Kosmetiksalon
salt n Salz nt (gen Salzes, pl Salze)
salty adj salzig
Salvation Army n Heilsarmee f
same adj gleiche ▷ *The same coat is cheaper elsewhere.* Der gleiche Mantel ist anderswo billiger. ▷ *He asked me the same question.* Er hat mir die gleiche Frage gestellt. ▷ *I have the same car.* Ich habe das gleiche Auto. ▷ *We obviously have the same problems.* Wir haben offensichtlich die gleichen Probleme.; **at the same time** zur gleichen Zeit; **It's not the same.** Das ist nicht das Gleiche.; **They're exactly the same.** Sie sind genau gleich.
sample n Probe f ▷ *a free sample of perfume* eine kostenlose Parfümprobe
sand n Sand m
sandal n Sandale f ▷ *a pair of sandals* ein Paar Sandalen
sand castle n Sandburg f
sandwich n Sandwich nt ▷ *I normally have a sandwich for lunch.* Zu Mittag esse ich meistens ein belegtes Brot.; **a cheese sandwich** ein Käsebrot
sang vb see **sing**
sanitary towel n Damenbinde f
sank vb see **sink**
Santa Claus n Weihnachtsmann m (pl Weihnachtsmänner)
sarcastic adj sarkastisch
sardine n Sardine f
sat vb see **sit**
satchel n Schulranzen m (pl Schulranzen)
satellite n Satellit m (gen Satelliten, pl Satelliten); **a satellite dish** eine Satellitenschüssel; **satellite television** das Satellitenfernsehen
satisfactory adj befriedigend
satisfied adj zufrieden
sat nav n GPS nt (pl GPS)

Saturday n Samstag m (pl Samstage) ▷ *on Saturday* am Samstag ▷ *every Saturday* jeden Samstag ▷ *last Saturday* letzten Samstag ▷ *next Saturday* nächsten Samstag; **on Saturdays** samstags; **a Saturday job** ein Samstagsjob

sauce n Soße f

saucepan n Kochtopf m (pl Kochtöpfe)

saucer n Untertasse f

Saudi Arabia n Saudi-Arabien nt; **to Saudi Arabia** nach Saudi-Arabien

sausage n Wurst f (pl Würste); **a sausage roll** eine Wurst im Blätterteig

save vb ❶ *(money, time)* sparen [38] ▷ *I've saved fifty pounds.* Ich habe fünfzig Pfund gespart. ▷ *I saved money by waiting for the sales.* Ich habe Geld gespart, weil ich bis zum Schlussverkauf gewartet habe. ▷ *We took a taxi to save time.* Wir haben ein Taxi genommen, um Zeit zu sparen. ❷ *(rescue)* retten [2] ▷ *Luckily, all the passengers were saved.* Zum Glück wurden alle Passagiere gerettet. ❸ *(on computer)* speichern [88] ▷ *I saved the file onto the hard drive.* Ich habe die Datei auf der Festplatte gespeichert.; **to save up** sparen [38]

savings npl Ersparnisse fpl ▷ *She spent all her savings on a computer.* Sie gab all ihre Ersparnisse für einen Computer aus.

savoury adj *(not sweet)* salzig

saw vb see **see**
▷ n Säge f

saxophone n Saxofon nt (pl Saxofone) ▷ *I play the saxophone.* Ich spiele Saxofon.

say vb sagen [38] ▷ *What did he say?* Was hat er gesagt? ▷ *Did you hear what she said?* Hast du gehört, was sie gesagt hat? ▷ *Could you say that again?* Können Sie das noch einmal sagen?; **That goes without saying.** Das ist selbstverständlich.

saying n Redensart f ▷ *It's just a saying.* Das ist so eine Redensart.

scale n ❶ *(of map)* Maßstab m (pl Maßstäbe) ▷ *a large-scale map* eine Karte großen Maßstabs ❷ *(size, extent)* Ausmaß nt (gen Ausmaßes, pl Ausmaße) ▷ *a disaster on a massive scale* eine Katastrophe von riesigem Ausmaß ❸ *(in music)* Tonleiter f

scales npl *(in kitchen, shop)* Waage fsg; **bathroom scales** die Personenwaage

scampi n Scampi pl

scandal n ❶ *(outrage)* Skandal m (pl Skandale) ▷ *It caused a scandal.* Es hat einen Skandal verursacht. ❷ *(gossip)* Tratsch ▷ *It's just scandal.* Das ist nur Tratsch.

Scandinavia n Skandinavien nt; **from Scandinavia** aus Skandinavien; **to Scandinavia** nach Skandinavien

Scandinavian adj skandinavisch; **He's Scandinavian.** Er ist Skandinavier.

scar n Narbe f

scarce adj ❶ knapp ▷ *scarce resources* knappe Geldmittel ❷ rar ▷ *Jobs are scarce.* Jobs sind rar.

scarcely adv kaum ▷ *I scarcely knew him.* Ich kannte ihn kaum.

scare n Schrecken m (pl Schrecken); **a bomb scare** ein Bombenalarm m
▷ vb **to scare somebody** jemandem Angst machen [48]

scarecrow n Vogelscheuche f

scared adj **to be scared** Angst haben [32]; **to be scared of** Angst haben [32] vor

scarf n ❶ *(long)* Schal m (pl Schals) ❷ *(square)* Halstuch nt (pl Halstücher)

scary adj furchterregend ▷ *It was really scary.* Es war wirklich furchterregend.

scene n ❶ *(place)* Ort m (pl Orte) ▷ *The police were on the scene.* Die Polizei war schnell vor Ort. ▷ *the scene of the crime* der Ort des Verbrechens ❷ *(event, sight)* Spektakel nt (pl Spektakel) ▷ *It was an amazing scene.* Es war ein erstaunliches Spektakel.; **to make a scene** eine Szene machen [48]

ENGLISH > GERMAN   463 | **screen**

scenery n (landscape) Landschaft f

schedule n Programm nt (pl Programme) ▷ a busy schedule ein volles Programm; **on schedule** planmäßig; **to be behind schedule** Verspätung haben **[32]**

scheduled flight n Linienflug m (pl Linienflüge)

scheme n ❶ (idea) Plan m (pl Pläne) ▷ a crazy scheme ein verrückter Plan ❷ (project) Projekt nt (pl Projekte) ▷ a council road-widening scheme ein Straßenverbreiterungsprojekt der Gemeinde

scholarship n Stipendium nt (pl Stipendien)

school n Schule f; **to go to school** in die Schule gehen **[29]**

schoolbook n Schulbuch nt (pl Schulbücher)

schoolboy n Schuljunge m (gen Schuljungen, pl Schuljungen)

schoolchildren npl Schulkinder ntpl

schoolgirl n Schulmädchen nt (pl Schulmädchen)

science n Wissenschaft f

science fiction n Science-Fiction f

scientific adj wissenschaftlich

scientist n (doing research) Wissenschaftler m (pl Wissenschaftler), Wissenschaftlerin f ▷ She's a scientist. Sie ist Wissenschaftlerin.; **He trained as a scientist.** Er hat eine wissenschaftliche Ausbildung.

scissors npl Schere f ▷ a pair of scissors eine Schere

scooter n ❶ Motorroller m (pl Motorroller) ❷ (child's toy) Roller m (pl Roller)

score n Spielstand m (pl Spielstände); **What's the score?** Wie steht das Spiel?; **The score was three nil.** Es stand drei zu null.
▶ vb ❶ (goal) schießen (imperf schoss, perf hat geschossen) ▷ to score a goal ein Tor schießen ❷ (point) machen **[48]** ▷ to score six out of ten sechs von zehn Punkten machen ❸ (keep score) zählen **[38]**; **Who's going to score?** Wer zählt?

Scorpio n Skorpion m ▷ I'm Scorpio. Ich bin Skorpion.

Scot n Schotte m (gen Schotten, pl Schotten), Schottin f

Scotch tape® n (US) Tesafilm® m

Scotland n Schottland nt; **from Scotland** aus Schottland; **in Scotland** in Schottland; **to Scotland** nach Schottland

Scots adj schottisch ▷ a Scots accent ein schottischer Akzent

Scotsman n Schotte m (gen Schotten, pl Schotten)

Scotswoman n Schottin f

Scottish adj schottisch ▷ a Scottish accent ein schottischer Akzent; **He's Scottish.** Er ist Schotte.; **She's Scottish.** Sie ist Schottin.

scout n Pfadfinder m (pl Pfadfinder) ▷ I'm in the Scouts. Ich bin bei den Pfadfindern.; **girl scout** die Pfadfinderin

scrambled eggs npl Rührei ntpl

scrap n ❶ Stück nt (pl Stücke) ▷ a scrap of paper ein Stück Papier ❷ (fight) Schlägerei f; **scrap iron** das Alteisen
▶ vb (plan, idea) verwerfen **[92]** (pres verwirft, imperf verwarf, perf hat verworfen) ▷ The plan was scrapped. Der Plan wurde verworfen.

scrapbook n Album nt (pl Alben)

scratch vb kratzen **[36]** ▷ Stop scratching! Hör auf zu kratzen!
▶ n (on skin) Kratzer m (pl Kratzer); **to start from scratch** von vorn anfangen **[23]**

scream n Schrei m (pl Schreie)
▶ vb schreien **[62]** (imperf schrie, perf hat geschrien)

screen n ❶ (cinema) Leinwand f (pl Leinwände) ❷ (television, computer) Bildschirm m (pl Bildschirme) ▷ An error *message appeared on the screen.* Auf dem Bildschirm erschien eine Fehlermeldung.

screen saver n (computer) Bildschirmschoner m (pl Bildschirmschoner)

screw n Schraube f

screwdriver n Schraubenzieher m (pl Schraubenzieher)

scribble vb kritzeln [**34**]

scrub vb schrubben [**48**] ▷ *He scrubbed the floor.* Er schrubbte den Boden.

sculpture n Skulptur f

sea n Meer nt (pl Meere)

seafood n Meeresfrüchte fpl ▷ *I don't like seafood.* Ich mag Meeresfrüchte nicht.

seagull n Möwe f

seal n ❶ (animal) Seehund m (pl Seehunde) ❷ (on container) Siegel nt (pl Siegel)
▶ vb ❶ (container) versiegeln [**84**] (perf hat versiegelt) ❷ (letter) zukleben [**4**] (perf hat zugeklebt)

seaman n Seemann m (pl Seeleute)

search vb durchsuchen [**18**] (perf hat durchsucht) ▷ *They searched the woods for her.* Sie haben den Wald nach ihr durchsucht.; **to search for something** nach etwas suchen [**48**]
▶ n Suche f

search party n Suchtrupp m (pl Suchtrupps)

seashore n Strand m (pl Strände) ▷ *on the seashore* am Strand

seasick adj seekrank ▷ *to be seasick* seekrank sein

seaside n **at the seaside** am Meer; **We're going to the seaside.** Wir fahren ans Meer.

season n Jahreszeit f ▷ *What's your favourite season?* Welche Jahreszeit hast du am liebsten?; **out of season** außerhalb der Saison; **during the holiday season** während der Ferienzeit; **a season ticket** eine Dauerkarte

seat n Platz m (gen Platzes, pl Plätze)

seat belt n Sicherheitsgurt m (pl Sicherheitsgurte); **Fasten your seat belt!** Schnalle dich an!

seaweed n Alge f

second adj zweite ▷ *the second man from the right* der zweite Mann von rechts ▷ *her second husband* ihr zweiter Mann ▷ *on the second page* auf der zweiten Seite ▷ *my second child* mein zweites Kind; **to come second** (in race) Zweiter werden [**91**]; **the second of August** der zweite August
▶ n Sekunde f ▷ *It'll only take a second.* Es dauert nur eine Sekunde.

secondary school n ❶ Gymnasium nt (pl Gymnasien) ❷ Realschule f
* Germans always specify the type
* of secondary school. **Gymnasium**
* takes nine years and leads to **Abitur**,
* **Realschule** takes six years and leads
* to **mittlere Reife**.

second-class adj, adv ❶ (ticket, compartment) zweiter Klasse ▷ *to travel second-class* zweiter Klasse fahren ❷ (stamp, letter) normal
* In Germany there is no first-class or
* second-class post. However, letters
* cost more to send than postcards, so
* you have to remember to say what
* you are sending when buying stamps.
* There is also an express service.
▷ *to send something second-class* etwas mit normaler Post schicken

second-hand adj gebraucht; **a second-hand car** ein Gebrauchtwagen m

secondly adv zweitens ▷ *firstly ... secondly ...* erstens ... zweitens ...

secret adj geheim ▷ *a secret mission* eine geheime Mission
▶ n Geheimnis nt (gen Geheimnisses, pl Geheimnisse) ▷ *It's a secret.* Es ist ein Geheimnis. ▷ *Can you keep a secret?* Kannst du ein Geheimnis für dich behalten?; **in secret** heimlich

ENGLISH > GERMAN

secretary n Sekretär m (pl Sekretäre), Sekretärin f ▷ *She's a secretary.* Sie ist Sekretärin.

secretly adv heimlich

section n ❶ Teil m (pl Teile) ▷ *I passed the written section of the exam.* Ich habe den schriftlichen Teil der Prüfung bestanden. ❷ *(in shop)* Abteilung f ▷ *the food section* die Lebensmittelabteilung

security n Sicherheit f ▷ *airport security* die Sicherheit auf den Flughäfen; **to have no job security** keinen sicheren Job haben [32]; **a security guard** ein Sicherheitsbeamter

security guard n Wächter m (pl Wächter), Wächterin f; **She's a security guard.** Sie ist beim Sicherheitsdienst.

see vb sehen [64] ▷ *I can't see.* Ich kann nichts sehen. ▷ *I saw him yesterday.* Ich habe ihn gestern gesehen. ▷ *Have you seen him?* Hast du ihn gesehen?; **See you!** *(informal)* Tschüss!; **See you soon!** Bis bald!; **to see to something** sich um etwas kümmern [38]

seed n Samen m (pl Samen); **sunflower seeds** die Sonnenblumenkerne mpl

seem vb scheinen [57] (*imperf* schien, *perf* hat geschienen) ▷ *The shop seemed to be closed.* Das Geschäft schien geschlossen zu haben. ▷ *That seems like a good idea.* Das scheint eine gute Idee zu sein.; **She seems tired.** Sie wirkt müde.; **It seems that ...** Es sieht so aus, dass ...; **There seems to be a problem.** Anscheinend gibt's ein Problem.

seen vb see **see**

seesaw n Wippe f

seldom adv selten

select vb auswählen [4] (*perf* hat ausgewählt)

selection n Auswahl f

self-catering adj **a self-catering apartment** eine Wohnung für Selbstversorger

self-confidence n Selbstvertrauen nt ▷ *He hasn't got much self-confidence.* Er hat nicht viel Selbstvertrauen.

self-conscious adj gehemmt

self-defence n Selbstverteidigung f ▷ *self-defence classes* der Selbstverteidigungskurs; **She killed him in self-defence.** Sie hat ihn in Notwehr getötet.

self-employed adj **to be self-employed** selbstständig sein [65]; **the self-employed** die Selbstständigen mpl

selfish adj egoistisch ▷ *Don't be so selfish.* Sei nicht so egoistisch.

self-service adj **It's self-service.** *(café, shop)* Da ist Selbstbedienung.; **a self-service restaurant** ein Selbstbedienungsrestaurant nt

sell vb verkaufen [84] (*perf* hat verkauft) ▷ *He sold it to me.* Er hat es mir verkauft.; **to sell off** verkaufen [84]; **The tickets are all sold out.** Alle Karten sind ausverkauft.; **The tickets sold out in three hours.** Die Karten waren in drei Stunden ausverkauft.

sell-by date n Verfallsdatum nt (pl Verfallsdaten)

Sellotape® n Tesafilm® m

semi n Doppelhaushälfte f ▷ *We live in a semi.* Wir wohnen in einer Doppelhaushälfte.

semicircle n Halbkreis m (gen Halbkreises, pl Halbkreise)

semicolon n Strichpunkt m (pl Strichpunkte)

semi-detached house n Doppelhaushälfte f ▷ *We live in a semi-detached house.* Wir wohnen in einer Doppelhaushälfte.

semi-final n Halbfinale nt (pl Halbfinale)

semi-skimmed milk n fettarme Milch f

send vb schicken [48] ▷ *She sent me money.* Sie hat mir Geld geschickt.; **to send back** zurückschicken [4]; **to send off**

(1) (goods, letter) abschicken [4] **(2)** (in sports match) vom Platz schicken [48] ▷ He was sent off. Er wurde vom Platz geschickt.; **to send off for something (1)** (free) etwas kommen lassen [42] ▷ I've sent off for a brochure. Ich habe mir eine Broschüre kommen lassen. **(2)** (paid for) etwas bestellen [7] ▷ She sent off for a new passport. Sie hat einen neuen Pass beantragt.; **to send out** verschicken [7]

senior adj leitend ▷ senior management die leitenden Angestellten; **senior school** die weiterführende Schule; **senior pupils** die Oberstufenschüler

senior citizen n Senior m (pl Senioren), Seniorin f

sensational adj sensationell

sense n ① (faculty) Sinn m (pl Sinne) ▷ the five senses die fünf Sinne ▷ the sixth sense der sechste Sinn; **the sense of touch** der Tastsinn; **the sense of smell** der Geruchsinn; **sense of humour** der Sinn für Humor ② (wisdom) Verstand m; **Use your common sense!** Benutze deinen gesunden Menschenverstand!; **It makes sense.** Das macht Sinn.; **It doesn't make sense.** Das macht keinen Sinn.

sensible adj vernünftig ▷ Be sensible! Sei vernünftig! ▷ It would be sensible to check first. Es wäre vernünftig, zuerst nachzusehen.

> Be careful not to translate **sensible** by sensibel.

sensitive adj sensibel ▷ She's very sensitive. Sie ist sehr sensibel.

sent vb see **send**

sentence n ① Satz m (gen Satzes, pl Sätze) ▷ What does this sentence mean? Was bedeutet dieser Satz? ② (judgment) Urteil nt (pl Urteile) ▷ The court will pass sentence tomorrow. Das Gericht wird morgen das Urteil verkünden. ③ (punishment) Strafe f ▷ the death sentence die Todesstrafe; **He got a life sentence.** Er hat lebenslänglich bekommen.
▶ vb verurteilen [84] (perf hat verurteilt) ▷ to sentence somebody to life imprisonment jemanden zu einer lebenslangen Gefängnisstrafe verurteilen ▷ to sentence somebody to death jemanden zum Tode verurteilen

sentimental adj sentimental

separate adj getrennt ▷ separate rooms getrennte Zimmer; **I wrote it on a separate sheet.** Ich habe es auf ein extra Blatt geschrieben.; **on separate occasions** bei verschiedenen Gelegenheiten; **on two separate occasions** zweimal
▶ vb ① trennen [38] ② (married couple) sich trennen [38]

separately adv extra

separation n Trennung f

September n September m ▷ in September im September

sequel n (book, film) Fortsetzung f

sergeant n ① (army) Feldwebel m (pl Feldwebel), Feldwebelin f ② (police) Polizeimeister m (pl Polizeimeister), Polizeimeisterin f

serial n Fernsehserie f

series nsg ① Sendereihe f ▷ a TV series eine Sendereihe im Fernsehen ② (of numbers) Reihe f

serious adj ① ernst ▷ You look very serious. Du siehst sehr ernst aus.; **Are you serious?** Ist das dein Ernst? ② (illness, mistake) schwer

> Be careful not to translate **serious** by seriös.

seriously adv im Ernst ▷ No, but seriously ... Nein, aber im Ernst ...; **to take somebody seriously** jemanden ernst nehmen [52]; **seriously injured** schwer verletzt; **Seriously?** Im Ernst?

servant n Diener m (pl Diener), Dienerin f

serve vb ① servieren [76] (perf hat serviert) ▷ Dinner is served. Das Essen ist

ENGLISH > GERMAN

serviert. ❷ **aufschlagen** [59] (pres schlägt auf, imperf schlug auf, perf hat aufgeschlagen) ▷ *It's Paolini's turn to serve.* Paolini schlägt auf. ❸ (prison sentence) **absitzen** [68] (imperf saß ab, perf hat abgesessen); **to serve time** im Gefängnis sein [65]; **It serves you right.** Das geschieht dir recht.
▶ n ❶ (tennis) Aufschlag m (pl Aufschläge); **It's your serve.** Du hast Aufschlag.

service vb (car, washing machine) überholen [18] (perf hat überholt)
▶ n ❶ Bedienung f ▷ *Service is included.* Die Bedienung ist inklusive. ❷ (of car) Inspektion f ❸ (church service) Gottesdienst m (pl Gottesdienste); **the Fire Service** die Feuerwehr; **the armed services** die Streitkräfte

service charge n Bedienung f ▷ *There's no service charge.* Die Bedienung wird nicht extra berechnet.

service station n Tankstelle f

serviette n Serviette f

session n Sitzung f

set n Satz m (gen Satzes, pl Sätze) ▷ *a set of keys* ein Satz Schlüssel ▷ *Williams won the set.* (tennis) Williams hat den Satz gewonnen.; **a chess set** ein Schachspiel nt; **a train set** eine Spielzeugeisenbahn
▶ vb ❶ (alarm clock) stellen [38] ▷ *I set the alarm for seven o'clock.* Ich habe den Wecker auf sieben Uhr gestellt. ❷ (record) aufstellen [4] (perf hat aufgestellt) ▷ *The world record was set last year.* Der Weltrekord wurde letztes Jahr aufgestellt. ❸ (sun) untergehen [29] (imperf ging unter, perf ist untergegangen) ▷ *The sun was setting.* Die Sonne ging unter.; **The film is set in Morocco.** Der Film spielt in Marokko.; **to set off** aufbrechen [11]; **to set out** aufbrechen [11]; **to set the table** den Tisch decken [38]

settee n Sofa nt (pl Sofas)

467 | shade

settle vb ❶ (problem) lösen [38] ❷ (argument) beilegen [4] (perf hat beigelegt); **to settle an account** eine Rechnung begleichen; **to settle down** (calm down) ruhiger werden [91]; **Settle down!** Beruhige dich!; **to settle in** sich einleben [4]; **to settle on something** sich für etwas entscheiden

seven num sieben ▷ *She's seven.* Sie ist sieben.

seventeen num siebzehn ▷ *He's seventeen.* Er ist siebzehn.

seventeenth adj siebzehnte ▷ *the seventeenth of August* der siebzehnte August

seventh adj siebte ▷ *the seventh floor* der siebte Stock ▷ *the seventh of August* der siebte August

seventy num siebzig ▷ *She's seventy.* Sie ist siebzig.

several adj, pron einige ▷ *several schools* einige Schulen ▷ *several of them* einige von ihnen

sew vb nähen [38]; **to sew up** (tear) flicken [48]

sewing n Nähen nt; **I like sewing.** Ich nähe gern.; **a sewing machine** eine Nähmaschine

sewn vb see **sew**

sex n Geschlecht nt (pl Geschlechter); **to have sex with somebody** mit jemandem Verkehr haben [32]; **sex education** der Aufklärungsunterricht

sexism n Sexismus m (gen Sexismus)

sexist adj sexistisch

sexual adj sexuell ▷ *sexual harassment* die sexuelle Belästigung; **sexual discrimination** die Diskriminierung aufgrund des Geschlechts

sexuality n Sexualität f

sexy adj sexy

shabby adj schäbig

shade n ❶ Schatten m (pl Schatten) ▷ *in the shade* im Schatten ❷ (colour) Ton m (pl Töne) ▷ *a shade of blue* ein Blauton

shadow n Schatten m (pl Schatten)

shake vb ❶ ausschütteln [4] (perf hat ausgeschüttelt) ▷ She shook the rug. Sie hat den Teppich ausgeschüttelt. ❷ schütteln [34] ▷ She shook the bottle. Sie hat die Flasche geschüttelt. ❸ (tremble) zittern [88] ▷ He was shaking with fear. Er zitterte vor Angst.; **to shake one's head** (in refusal) den Kopf schütteln [34]; **to shake hands with somebody** jemandem die Hand geben [28]

shaken adj mitgenommen ▷ I was feeling a bit shaken. Ich war etwas mitgenommen.

shall vb Shall I shut the window? Soll ich das Fenster zumachen?; **Shall we ask him to come with us?** Sollen wir ihn fragen, ob er mitkommt?

shallow adj (water, pool) flach

shambles nsg Chaos nt (gen Chaos) ▷ It's a complete shambles. Es ist ein völliges Chaos.

shame n Schande f ▷ The shame of it! Diese Schande!; **What a shame!** Wie schade!; **It's a shame that …** Es ist schade, dass …

shampoo n Shampoo nt (pl Shampoos) ▷ a bottle of shampoo eine Flasche Shampoo

shape n Form f

share n ❶ (in company) Aktie f ▷ They've got shares in BT. Sie haben Aktien von BT. ❷ (portion) Anteil m (pl Anteile)
▶ vb teilen [38] ▷ to share a room with somebody mit jemandem im Zimmer teilen; **to share out** verteilen [84]

shark n Hai m (pl Haie)

sharp adj ❶ (razor, knife) scharf ▷ I need a sharper knife. Ich brauche ein schärferes Messer. ❷ (spike, point) spitz ❸ (clever) gescheit ▷ She's very sharp. Sie ist sehr gescheit.; **at two o'clock sharp** Punkt zwei Uhr

shave vb (have a shave) sich rasieren [76] (perf hat sich rasiert); **to shave one's legs** sich die Beine rasieren [76]

shaver n an electric shaver ein Elektrorasierer m

shaving cream n Rasiercreme f (pl Rasiercremes)

shaving foam n Rasierschaum m

she pron sie ▷ She's very nice. Sie ist sehr nett.

shed n Schuppen m (pl Schuppen)

she'd = **she had**; **she would**

sheep n Schaf nt (pl Schafe) ▷ dozens of sheep Dutzende von Schafen

sheepdog n Schäferhund m (pl Schäferhunde)

sheer adj rein ▷ It's sheer greed. Das ist die reine Gier.

sheet n (on bed) Leintuch nt (pl Leintücher); **a sheet of paper** ein Blatt Papier nt

shelf n Regal nt (pl Regale)

shell n ❶ (on beach) Muschel f ❷ (of egg, nut) Schale f ❸ (explosive) Granate f

she'll = **she will**

shellfish n Schalentier nt (pl Schalentiere)

shelter n to take shelter sich unterstellen [4]; **a bus shelter** eine überdachte Bushaltestelle

shelves npl see **shelf**

shepherd n Schäfer m (pl Schäfer), Schäferin f

sherry n Sherry m (pl Sherrys)

she's = **she is**; **she has**

Shetland Islands npl Shetlandinseln fpl

shift n Schicht f ▷ His shift starts at eight o'clock. Seine Schicht fängt um acht Uhr an. ▷ the night shift die Nachtschicht; **to do shift work** Schicht arbeiten [2]
▶ vb (move) verschieben (imperf verschob, perf hat verschoben) ▷ I couldn't shift the wardrobe. Ich konnte den Schrank nicht verschieben.; **Shift yourself!** (informal) Jetzt aber los!

shin n Schienbein nt (pl Schienbeine)

shine vb scheinen [57] (imperf schien, perf hat geschienen) ▷ The sun was shining. Die Sonne schien.

shiny adj glänzend
ship n Schiff nt (pl Schiffe)
shirt n ❶ (man's) Hemd nt (pl Hemden) ❷ (woman's) Bluse f
shiver vb zittern [88]
shock n Schock m (pl Schocks); **to get a shock (1)** (surprise) einen Schock bekommen [40] **(2)** (electric) einen Schlag bekommen [40]; **an electric shock** ein elektrischer Schlag ▶ vb (upset) schockieren [76] (perf hat schockiert) ▷ I was shocked by the tragedy. Ich war über die Tragödie schockiert. ▷ Nothing shocks me any more. Mich schockiert nichts mehr.
shocked adj schockiert ▷ He'll be shocked if you say that. Wenn du das sagst, wird er schockiert sein.
shocking adj schockierend ▷ It's shocking! Es ist schockierend! ▷ a shocking waste eine schockierende Verschwendung
shoe n Schuh m (pl Schuhe)
shoelace n Schnürsenkel m (pl Schnürsenkel)
shoe polish n Schuhcreme f (pl Schuhcremes)
shoe shop n Schuhgeschäft nt (pl Schuhgeschäfte)
shone vb see **shine**
shook vb see **shake**
shoot vb ❶ (gun, in football) schießen (imperf schoss, perf hat geschossen) ▷ Don't shoot! Nicht schießen!; **to shoot at somebody** auf jemanden schießen; **He was shot in the leg.** Er wurde ins Bein getroffen.; **to shoot an arrow** einen Pfeil abschießen ❷ (kill) erschießen (imperf erschoss, perf hat erschossen) ▷ He was shot by a sniper. Er wurde von einem Heckenschützen erschossen.; **to shoot oneself** (dead) sich erschießen ❸ (film) drehen [38] ▷ The film was shot in Prague. Der Film wurde in Prag gedreht.

shooting n ❶ Schüsse mpl ▷ They heard shooting. Sie hörten Schüsse.; **a shooting** eine Schießerei ❷ (hunting) Jagd f ▷ to go shooting auf die Jagd gehen
shop n Geschäft nt (pl Geschäfte) ▷ a sports shop ein Sportgeschäft
shop assistant n Verkäufer m (pl Verkäufer), Verkäuferin f ▷ She's a shop assistant. Sie ist Verkäuferin.
shopkeeper n Ladenbesitzer m (pl Ladenbesitzer), Ladenbesitzerin f ▷ He's a shopkeeper. Er ist Ladenbesitzer.
shoplifting n Ladendiebstahl m (pl Ladendiebstähle)
shopping n (purchases) Einkäufe mpl ▷ Can you get the shopping from the car? Kannst du die Einkäufe aus dem Auto holen?; **I love shopping.** Ich gehe gern einkaufen.; **to go shopping** einkaufen gehen [29]; **a shopping bag** eine Einkaufstasche; **a shopping centre** ein Einkaufszentrum nt
shop window n Schaufenster nt (pl Schaufenster)
shore n Küste f; **on shore** an Land
short adj ❶ kurz ▷ a short skirt ein kurzer Rock ▷ short hair kurze Haare ▷ a short break eine kurze Pause ▷ a short walk ein kurzer Spaziergang; **too short** zu kurz ❷ (person) klein ▷ She's quite short. Sie ist ziemlich klein.; **to be short of something** knapp an etwas sein [65]; **In short, the answer's no.** Kurz, die Antwort ist nein.; **at short notice** kurzfristig
shortage n Mangel m ▷ a water shortage ein Wassermangel
short cut n Abkürzung f ▷ I took a short cut. Ich habe eine Abkürzung genommen.
shortly adv ❶ bald ▷ He'll be arriving shortly. Er kommt bald. ❷ kurz ▷ shortly after the accident kurz nach dem Unfall
shorts npl Shorts pl ▷ a pair of shorts ein Paar Shorts

short-sighted adj kurzsichtig
shot vb see **shoot**
▶ n ❶ (gunshot) Schuss m (gen Schusses, pl Schüsse) ❷ (photo) Foto nt (pl Fotos) ▷ a shot of the church ein Foto der Kirche ❸ (injection) Spritze f
shotgun n Flinte f
should vb sollen [69] ▷ You should take more exercise. Du solltest mehr Sport machen.; **He should be there by now.** Er müsste jetzt da sein.; **That shouldn't be too hard.** Das dürfte nicht zu schwer sein.; **I should have told you before.** Ich hätte es dir vorher sagen sollen.

> When 'should' means 'would' use **würde**.

▷ I should go if I were you. Ich würde gehen, wenn ich du wäre.; **I should be so lucky!** Das wäre ja schön!
shoulder n Schulter f; **a shoulder bag** eine Umhängetasche
shouldn't = **should not**
shout vb schreien [62] (imperf schrie, perf hat geschrien) ▷ Don't shout! Schrei doch nicht so! ▷ 'Go away!' he shouted. 'Geh weg!' schrie er.
▶ n Schrei m (pl Schreie)
shovel n Schaufel f
show n ❶ (performance) Show f (pl Shows) ❷ (programme) Sendung f ❸ (exhibition) Ausstellung f
▶ vb ❶ zeigen [38]; **to show somebody something** jemandem etwas zeigen [38] ❷ beweisen (imperf bewies, perf hat bewiesen) ▷ She showed great courage. Sie hat großen Mut bewiesen.; **It shows.** Das sieht man.; **to show off** (informal) angeben [28]; **to show up** (turn up) aufkreuzen [4]
shower n ❶ Dusche f; **to have a shower** duschen [48] ❷ (of rain) Schauer m (pl Schauer)
shown vb see **show**
show-off n Angeber m (pl Angeber), Angeberin f

shrank vb see **shrink**
shriek vb kreischen [38]
shrimps npl Krabben fpl
shrink vb (clothes, fabric) einlaufen [43] (pres läuft ein, imperf lief ein, perf ist eingelaufen)
Shrove Tuesday n Fastnachtsdienstag m
shrug vb **He shrugged his shoulders.** Er zuckte mit den Schultern.
shrunk vb see **shrink**
shuffle vb **to shuffle the cards** die Karten mischen [48]
shut vb zumachen [4] (perf hat zugemacht) ▷ What time do you shut? Wann machen Sie zu? ▷ What time do the shops shut? Wann machen die Geschäfte zu?; **to shut down** schließen ▷ The cinema shut down last year. Das Kino hat letztes Jahr geschlossen.; **to shut up (1)** (close) verschließen **(2)** (be quiet) den Mund halten [33] ▷ Shut up! Halt den Mund!
shuttle n ❶ (plane) Pendelflugzeug nt (pl Pendelflugzeuge) ❷ (train) Pendelzug m (pl Pendelzüge) ❸ (bus) Pendelbus m (gen Pendelbusses, pl Pendelbusse)
shuttlecock n (badminton) Federball m (pl Federbälle)
shy adj schüchtern
Sicily n Sizilien nt; **from Sicily** aus Sizilien; **to Sicily** nach Sizilien
sick adj ❶ (ill) krank ▷ He was sick for four days. Er war vier Tage krank. ❷ (joke, humour) übel ▷ That's really sick! Das war wirklich übel!; **to be sick** (vomit) sich übergeben [28]; **I feel sick.** Mir ist schlecht.; **to be sick of something** etwas leid sein [65]
sickness n Krankheit f
side n ❶ Seite f ▷ He was driving on the wrong side of the road. Er fuhr auf der falschen Straßenseite. ▷ He's on my side. Er ist auf meiner Seite.; **side by side**

ENGLISH > GERMAN

nebeneinander; **the side entrance** der Seiteneingang; **to take sides** Partei ergreifen ❷ *(edge)* Rand m *(pl* Ränder*)* ▷ **by the side of the road** am Straßenrand ❸ *(of pool, river)* Ufer nt *(pl* Ufer*)* ▷ **by the side of the lake** am Ufer des Sees

sideboard n Anrichte f

side effect n Nebeneffekt m *(pl* Nebeneffekte*)*

sidewalk n *(US)* Bürgersteig m *(pl* Bürgersteige*)*

sideways adv ❶ *(look)* von der Seite ❷ *(move, be facing)* zur Seite; **sideways on** von der Seite

sieve n Sieb nt *(pl* Siebe*)*

sigh n Seufzer m *(pl* Seufzer*)*
▶ vb seufzen [**36**]

sight n Anblick m ▷ **an amazing sight** ein irrer Anblick; **in sight** in Sicht; **out of sight** nicht zu sehen; **to have poor sight** schlechte Augen haben [**32**]; **to know somebody by sight** jemanden vom Sehen kennen [**39**]; **the sights** *(tourist spots)* die Sehenswürdigkeiten

sightseeing n Sightseeing nt; **to go sightseeing** Sightseeing machen [**48**]

sign n ❶ *(notice)* Schild nt *(pl* Schilder*)* ▷ There was a big sign saying 'private'. Da war ein großes Schild, auf dem 'privat' stand.; **a road sign** ein Verkehrsschild ❷ *(gesture, indication)* Zeichen nt *(pl* Zeichen*)* ▷ There's no sign of improvement. Es gibt kein Zeichen einer Besserung.; **What sign are you?** *(star sign)* Was für ein Sternzeichen sind Sie?
▶ vb unterschreiben [**61**] *(imperf* unterschrieb*, perf* hat unterschrieben*)*; **to sign on** (1) *(as unemployed)* sich arbeitslos melden [**54**] (2) *(for course)* sich einschreiben [**61**]

signal n Signal nt *(pl* Signale*)*
▶ vb **to signal to somebody** jemandem ein Zeichen geben [**28**]

signature n Unterschrift f

significance n Bedeutung f

471 | **singing**

significant adj bedeutend

sign language n Zeichensprache f

signpost n Wegweiser m *(pl* Wegweiser*)*

silence n Stille f ▷ There was absolute silence. Es herrschte absolute Stille.

silent adj still

silk n Seide f
▶ adj seiden ▷ **a silk scarf** ein seidener Schal

silky adj seidig

silly adj dumm ▷ That's the silliest excuse I've ever heard. Das ist die dümmste Ausrede, die ich je gehört habe.

silver n Silber nt ▷ **a silver medal** eine Silbermedaille

similar adj ähnlich ▷ My sister is very similar to me. Meine Schwester ist mir sehr ähnlich.

simple adj ❶ einfach ▷ It's very simple. Das ist sehr einfach. ❷ *(simple-minded)* einfältig ▷ He's a bit simple. Er ist etwas einfältig.

simply adv einfach ▷ It's simply not possible. Es ist einfach nicht möglich.

sin n Sünde f
▶ vb sündigen [**84**]

since prep, adv, conj ❶ seit ▷ since Christmas seit Weihnachten ▷ I haven't seen her since she left. Ich habe sie nicht gesehen, seit sie weggezogen ist.; **since then** seither; **ever since** seitdem ❷ *(because)* da ▷ Since you're tired, let's stay at home. Da du müde bist, bleiben wir doch zu Hause.

sincere adj aufrichtig

sincerely adv **Yours sincerely ...** Mit freundlichen Grüßen ...

sing vb singen [**66**] *(imperf* sang*, perf* hat gesungen*)* ▷ He sang out of tune. Er hat falsch gesungen. ▷ **Have you ever sung this tune before?** Hast du die Melodie schon mal gesungen?

singer n Sänger m *(pl* Sänger*)*, Sängerin f

singing n Singen nt

single adj (unmarried) alleinstehend; **a single room** ein Einzelmmer nt; **not a single thing** absolut nichts ▶ n ❶ (ticket) einfache Fahrkarte f ▷ A single to Bonn, please. Eine einfache Fahrkarte nach Bonn, bitte. ❷ (record) Single f (pl Singles); **a CD single** eine CD-Single

single parent n She's a single parent. Sie ist alleinerziehende Mutter.; **a single parent family** eine Einelternteilfamilie

singular n Singular m (pl Singulare) ▷ in the singular im Singular

sink n Spüle f
▶ vb sinken [67] (imperf sank, perf ist gesunken)

sir n
  In German no form of address is normally used apart from **Sie**.
  ▷ Would you like to order, Sir? Möchten Sie bestellen?; **Yes sir.** Ja.

siren n Sirene f

sister n Schwester f ▷ my little sister meine kleine Schwester ▷ I wanted to speak to the sister on the ward. Ich wollte die Stationsschwester sprechen.

sister-in-law n Schwägerin f

sit vb ❶ (be sitting) sitzen [68] (imperf saß, perf hat gesessen) ▷ She was sitting on the floor. Sie saß auf dem Boden. ❷ (sit down) sich setzen [36] ▷ Sit on that chair. Setz dich auf den Stuhl.; **to sit down** sich setzen [36]; **to be sitting** sitzen [68]; **to sit an exam** eine Prüfung machen [48]

site n ❶ Stätte f ▷ an archaeological site eine archäologische Stätte; **the site of the accident** der Unfallort ❷ (campsite) Campingplatz m (gen Campingplatzes, pl Campingplätze); **a building site** eine Baustelle

sitting room n Wohnzimmer nt (pl Wohnzimmer)

situation n Situation f

six num sechs ▷ He's six. Er ist sechs.

sixteen num sechzehn ▷ He's sixteen. Er ist sechzehn.

sixteenth adj sechzehnte ▷ the sixteenth of August der sechzehnte August

sixth adj sechste ▷ the sixth floor der sechste Stock ▷ the sixth of August der sechste August

sixty num sechzig ▷ She's sixty. Sie ist sechzig.

size n
  Germany uses the European system
  for clothing and shoe sizes.
❶ (of object, clothing) Größe f ▷ What size do you take? Welche Größe haben Sie?; **I'm a size ten.** Ich habe Größe achtunddreißig. ❷ (of shoes) Schuhgröße f ▷ I take size six. Ich habe Schuhgröße neununddreißig.

skate vb ❶ (ice-skate) Schlittschuh laufen [43] (pres läuft Schlittschuh, imperf lief Schlittschuh, perf ist Schlittschuh gelaufen) ❷ (roller-skate) Rollschuh laufen [43] (pres läuft Rollschuh, imperf lief Rollschuh, perf ist Rollschuh gelaufen)

skateboard n Skateboard nt (pl Skateboards)

skateboarding n Skateboardfahren nt; **to go skateboarding** Skateboard fahren [21]

skates npl ❶ Schlittschuhe mpl ❷ (roller skates) Rollschuhe mpl

skating n ❶ Schlittschuhlaufen nt; **to go skating** Schlittschuh laufen [43] ❷ (roller-skating) Rollschuhlaufen nt; **to go skating** Rollschuh laufen [43]; **a skating rink** eine Rollschuhbahn

skeleton n Skelett nt (pl Skelette)

sketch n (drawing) Skizze f
▶ vb skizzieren [76] (perf hat skizziert)

ski vb Ski fahren [21] (pres fährt Ski, imperf fuhr Ski, perf ist Ski gefahren) ▷ Can you ski? Kannst du Ski fahren?

▶ n Ski m (pl Skier); **ski boots** die Skistiefel; **a ski lift** ein Skilift m; **ski pants** die Skihose sg; **a ski pole** ein Skistock m; **a ski slope** eine Skipiste; **a ski suit** ein Skianzug m

skid vb schleudern [88] (perf ist geschleudert)

skier n Skifahrer m (pl Skifahrer), Skifahrerin f

skiing n Skifahren nt; **to go skiing** Ski fahren [21]; **to go on a skiing holiday** in den Skiurlaub fahren [21]

skilful adj geschickt

skill n Können nt ▷ *a lot of skill* viel Können

skilled adj; **a skilled worker** ein Facharbeiter m

skimmed milk n Magermilch f

skin n Haut f (pl Häute); **skin cancer** der Hautkrebs

skinhead n Skinhead m (pl Skinheads)

    der Skinhead is also used for women.

skinny adj mager

skip n (container) Container m (pl Container)
▶ vb ① (with rope) seilspringen [71] (perf ist seilgesprungen) ② auslassen [42] (pres lässt aus, imperf ließ aus, perf hat ausgelassen) ▷ *to skip a meal* eine Mahlzeit auslassen; **I skipped the maths lesson.** Ich habe die Mathestunde geschwänzt.

skirt n Rock m (pl Röcke)

skive vb (be lazy) faulenzen [36]; **to skive off** (informal) schwänzen [36]

skull n Schädel m (pl Schädel)

sky n Himmel m (pl Himmel)

Skype® n Skype®

skyscraper n Wolkenkratzer m (pl Wolkenkratzer)

slam vb zuknallen [4] (perf hat/ist zugeknallt)

    For the perfect tense use **haben** when the verb has an object and **sein** when there is no object.

▷ *The door slammed.* Die Tür ist zugeknallt. ▷ *She slammed the door.* Sie hat die Tür zugeknallt.

slang n Slang m (pl Slangs)

slap n Ohrfeige f
▶ vb **to slap somebody** jemandem einen Klaps geben [28]

slate n ① Schiefer m (pl Schiefer) ② (for roof) Schieferziegel m (pl Schieferziegel)

sledge n Schlitten m (pl Schlitten)

sledging n **to go sledging** Schlitten fahren [21]

sleep n Schlaf m ▷ *I need some sleep.* Ich brauche Schlaf.; **to go to sleep** einschlafen [58]
▶ vb schlafen [58] (pres schläft, imperf schlief, perf hat geschlafen) ▷ *I couldn't sleep.* Ich konnte nicht schlafen.; **to sleep with somebody** mit jemandem schlafen [58]; **to sleep together** miteinander schlafen [58]; **to sleep around** mit jedem schlafen [58]; **to sleep in** verschlafen [58]

sleeping bag n Schlafsack m (pl Schlafsäcke)

sleeping pill n Schlaftablette f

sleepover n Übernachtung f; **to have a sleepover** bei Freunden übernachten [2]

sleepy adj schläfrig; **to feel sleepy** schläfrig sein [65]; **a sleepy little village** ein verschlafenes kleines Dorf

sleet n Schneeregen m ▶ vb **It's sleeting.** Es fällt Schneeregen.

sleeve n ① Ärmel m (pl Ärmel) ▷ *long sleeves* lange Ärmel ▷ *short sleeves* kurze Ärmel ② (record sleeve) Hülle f

slept vb see **sleep**

slice n Scheibe f
▶ vb aufschneiden [60] (imperf schnitt auf, perf hat aufgeschnitten)

slide n ① (in playground) Rutschbahn f ② (photo) Dia nt (pl Dias) ③ (hair slide) Klemme f
▶ vb rutschen [48] (perf ist gerutscht)

slight adj klein ▷ *a slight problem* ein kleines Problem ▷ *a slight improvement* eine kleine Verbesserung

slightly adv etwas

slim adj schlank
▶vb (be on a diet) abnehmen [52] (pres nimmt ab, imperf nahm ab, perf hat abgenommen) ▷ *I'm slimming.* Ich nehme gerade ab.

sling n Schlinge f ▷ *She had her arm in a sling.* Sie hatte den Arm in der Schlinge.

slip n ❶ (mistake) Schnitzer m (pl Schnitzer) ❷ (underskirt) Unterrock m (pl Unterröcke); **a slip of paper** ein Zettel m; **a slip of the tongue** ein Versprecher m
▶vb ausrutschen [4] (perf ist ausgerutscht) ▷ *He slipped on the ice.* Er ist auf dem Eis ausgerutscht.; **to slip up** (make a mistake) einen Fehler machen [48]

slipper n Hausschuh m (pl Hausschuhe) ▷ *a pair of slippers* ein Paar Hausschuhe

slippery adj glatt

slip-up n Schnitzer m (pl Schnitzer); **There's been a slip-up.** Da ist etwas schiefgelaufen.

slope n Abhang m (pl Abhänge)

slot n Schlitz m (gen Schlitzes, pl Schlitze)

slot machine n ❶ (for gambling) Geldspielautomat m (gen Geldspielautomaten, pl Geldspielautomaten) ❷ (vending machine) Automat m (gen Automaten, pl Automaten)

slow adj, adv langsam ▷ *He's a bit slow.* Er ist etwas langsam.; **to go slow** (1) (person) langsam gehen [29] (2) (car) langsam fahren [21] ▷ *Drive slower!* Fahr langsamer!; **My watch is slow.** Meine Uhr geht nach.

slow down vb verlangsamen [84] (perf hat verlangsamt)

slowly adv langsam

slug n (animal) Nacktschnecke f

slum n Slum m (pl Slums)

smack n (slap) Klaps m (gen Klapse)
▶vb **to smack somebody** jemandem einen Klaps geben [28]

small adj klein; **small change** das Kleingeld

> Be careful not to translate **small** by **schmal**.

smart adj ❶ (elegant) schick ❷ (clever) intelligent ▷ *a smart idea* eine intelligente Idee

smartphone n Smartphone nt (pl Smartphones)

smashing adj (informal) klasse ▷ *I think he's smashing.* Ich finde, er ist klasse.

> **klasse** is invariable.

▷ *a smashing film* ein klasse Film

smell n Geruch m (pl Gerüche); **the sense of smell** der Geruchssinn
▶vb ❶ stinken (imperf stank, perf hat gestunken) ▷ *That old dog really smells!* Der alte Hund stinkt!; **to smell of something** nach etwas riechen ❷ (detect) riechen (imperf roch, perf hat gerochen) ▷ *I can't smell anything.* Ich kann nichts riechen.

smelly adj stinkend; **He's got smelly feet.** Seine Füße stinken.

smelt vb see **smell**

smile n Lächeln nt
▶vb lächeln [34]

smiley n Smiley m (pl Smileys)

smoke n Rauch m
▶vb rauchen [48] ▷ *I don't smoke.* Ich rauche nicht. ▷ *He smokes cigars.* Er raucht Zigarren.

smoker n Raucher m (pl Raucher), Raucherin f

smoking n Rauchen nt ▷ *to give up smoking* mit dem Rauchen aufhören ▷ *Smoking is bad for you.* Rauchen schadet der Gesundheit.; **'no smoking'** 'Rauchen verboten'

ENGLISH > GERMAN

smooth adj ❶ (surface) glatt ❷ (person) aalglatt
smoothie n Smoothie m (pl Smoothies)
SMS n (= short message service) SMS f
smudge n Dreck m
smuggle vb schmuggeln [34]
smuggler n Schmuggler m (pl Schmuggler), Schmugglerin f
smuggling n Schmuggeln nt
snack n Snack m (pl Snacks) ▷ to have a snack einen Snack zu sich nehmen
snack bar n Imbissstube f
snail n Schnecke f
snake n Schlange f
snap vb (break) brechen [11] (pres bricht, imperf brach, perf ist gebrochen) ▷ The branch snapped. Der Zweig brach.; **to snap one's fingers** mit dem Finger schnipsen [48]
snatch vb **to snatch something from somebody** jemandem etwas entreißen; **My bag was snatched.** Man hat mir meine Handtasche entrissen.
sneak vb **to sneak in** sich hineinschleichen; **to sneak out** sich hinausschleichen; **to sneak up on somebody** an jemanden heranschleichen
sneeze vb niesen [38]
sniff vb ❶ schniefen [38] ▷ Stop sniffing! Hör auf zu schniefen! ❷ schnüffeln [88] an ▷ The dog sniffed my hand. Der Hund schnüffelte an meiner Hand.; **to sniff glue** schnüffeln [88]
snob n Snob m (pl Snobs)

   ■ der Snob is also used for women.
▷ She is such a snob. Sie ist ein furchtbarer Snob.
snooker n Snooker nt ▷ to play snooker Snooker spielen
snooze n Nickerchen nt (pl Nickerchen) ▷ to have a snooze ein Nickerchen machen
snore vb schnarchen [48]

475 | soak

snow n Schnee m
▷ vb schneien [38] ▷ It's snowing. Es schneit.
snowball n Schneeball m (pl Schneebälle)
snowboarding n Snowboarding nt
snowflake n Schneeflocke f
snowman n Schneemann m (pl Schneemänner) ▷ **to build a snowman** einen Schneemann machen
so conj, adv ❶ also ▷ The shop was closed, so I went home. Das Geschäft war zu, also ging ich nach Hause. ▷ It rained, so I got wet. Es hat geregnet, also bin ich nass geworden. ▷ So, have you always lived in London? Also, hast du schon immer in London gewohnt?; **So what?** Na und? ❷ so ▷ It was so heavy! Es war so schwer! ▷ It's not so heavy! Es ist nicht so schwer! ▷ He was talking so fast I couldn't understand. Er hat so schnell geredet, dass ich nichts verstanden habe. ▷ How's your father? — Not so good. Wie geht's deinem Vater? — Nicht so gut. ▷ He's like his sister but not so clever. Er ist wie seine Schwester, aber nicht so klug.; **so much** (a lot) so sehr ▷ I love you so much. Ich liebe dich so sehr!; **so much ...** so viel ... ▷ I've got so much work. Ich habe so viel Arbeit.; **so many ...** so viele ... ▷ I've got so many things to do today. Ich muss heute so viele Dinge erledigen.; **so do I** ich auch ▷ I love horses. — So do I. Ich mag Pferde. — Ich auch.; **so have we** wir auch ▷ I've been to Hamburg. — So have we. Ich war schon einmal in Hamburg. — Wir auch.; **I think so.** Ich glaube schon.; **I hope so.** Hoffentlich.; **That's not so.** Das ist nicht so.; **so far** bis jetzt ▷ It's been easy so far. Bis jetzt war es einfach.; **so far so good** so weit, so gut.; **ten or so people** so etwa zehn Leute; **at five o'clock or so** so gegen fünf Uhr
soak vb einweichen [4] (perf hat eingeweicht)

soaking adj völlig durchnässt ▷ *We were soaking. Wir waren völlig durchnässt.*; **soaking wet** patschnass

soap n Seife f

soap opera n Seifenoper f

soap powder n Waschpulver nt (pl Waschpulver)

sob vb schluchzen [36] ▷ *She was sobbing. Sie schluchzte.*

sober adj nüchtern

sober up vb nüchtern werden [91] (pres wird nüchtern, imperf wurde nüchtern, perf ist nüchtern geworden)

soccer n Fußball m ▷ **to play soccer** Fußball spielen; **a soccer player** ein Fußballspieler m

social adj sozial ▷ *social problems* soziale Probleme; **a social class** eine gesellschaftliche Schicht; **I have a good social life.** Ich komme viel unter Leute.; **social media** Social Media npl

socialism n Sozialismus m (gen Sozialismus)

socialist adj sozialistisch
▶ n Sozialist m (gen Sozialisten, pl Sozialisten), Sozialistin f ▷ *She's a Socialist. Sie ist Sozialistin.*

social security n ❶ (money) Sozialhilfe f; **to be on social security** Sozialhilfe bekommen [40] ❷ (organization) Sozialversicherung f

social worker n Sozialarbeiter m (pl Sozialarbeiter), Sozialarbeiterin f ▷ *She's a social worker. Sie ist Sozialarbeiterin.*

society n ❶ Gesellschaft f ▷ *We live in a multicultural society. Wir leben in einer multikulturellen Gesellschaft.* ❷ Verein m (pl Vereine) ▷ *the Royal Society for the Prevention of Cruelty to Animals* der Tierschutzverein; **a drama society** eine Theatergruppe

sociology n Soziologie f

sock n Socke f

socket n Steckdose f

sofa n Sofa nt (pl Sofas)

soft adj weich; **soft cheese** der Weichkäse; **to be soft on somebody** (be kind to) nachsichtig mit jemandem sein [65]; **a soft drink** ein alkoholfreies Getränk; **soft drugs** weiche Drogen; **a soft option** eine bequeme Lösung

software n Software f

soil n Boden m (pl Böden)

solar adj solar; **solar eclipse** die Sonnenfinsternis

solar power n Sonnenenergie f

sold vb see **sell**

soldier n Soldat m (gen Soldaten, pl Soldaten), Soldatin f ▷ *He's a soldier. Er ist Soldat.*

solicitor n ❶ (for lawsuits) Rechtsanwalt m (pl Rechtsanwälte), Rechtsanwältin f ▷ *He's a solicitor. Er ist Rechtsanwalt.* ❷ (for property, wills) Notar m (pl Notare), Notarin f ▷ *She's a solicitor. Sie ist Notarin.*

solid adj ❶ stabil ▷ *a solid wall* eine stabile Wand ❷ massiv ▷ *solid gold* massives Gold; **for three hours solid** drei geschlagene Stunden lang

solo n Solo nt (pl Soli) ▷ *a guitar solo* ein Gitarrensolo

solution n Lösung f

solve vb lösen [38]

some adj, pron ❶ ein paar
▫ Use **ein paar** with plural nouns.
▷ *some nice pictures* ein paar nette Bilder ▷ *I only sold some of them.* Ich habe nur ein paar verkauft.; **Some people say that ...** Manche Leute sagen, dass ...; **some day** eines Tages; **some day next week** irgendwann nächste Woche ❷ (some but not all) einige ▷ *Are these mushrooms poisonous? — Only some.* Sind diese Pilze giftig? — Nur einige.; **I only took some of it.** Ich habe nur etwas davon genommen.; **I'm going to buy some stamps. Do you want some too?** Ich kaufe Briefmarken. Willst du auch welche?; **Would you like some**

coffee? — No thanks, I've got some. Möchten Sie Kaffee? — Nein danke, ich habe schon welchen.

▪ 'some' is frequently not translated. ▷ *Would you like some bread?* Möchtest du Brot? ▷ *Have you got some mineral water?* Haben Sie Mineralwasser?

somebody pron jemand ▷ *Somebody stole my bag.* Jemand hat meine Tasche gestohlen.

somehow adv irgendwie ▷ *I'll do it somehow.* Ich mache es irgendwie. ▷ *Somehow I don't think he believed me.* Irgendwie hat er mir anscheinend nicht geglaubt.

someone pron jemand

something pron etwas ▷ *something special* etwas Besonderes ▷ *Wear something warm.* Zieh etwas Warmes an.; **That's really something!** Das ist echt toll!; **It cost a hundred pounds, or something like that.** Es kostet hundert Pfund, oder so in der Gegend.; **His name is Phil or something.** Er heißt Phil oder so ähnlich.

sometime adv mal ▷ *You must come and see us sometime.* Du musst uns mal besuchen.; **sometime last month** irgendwann letzten Monat

sometimes adv manchmal ▷ *Sometimes I think she hates me.* Manchmal denke ich, sie hasst mich.

somewhere adv irgendwo ▷ *I've left my keys somewhere.* Ich habe irgendwo meine Schlüssel liegen lassen. ▷ *I'd like to live somewhere sunny.* Ich würde gern irgendwo leben, wo es sonnig ist.

son n Sohn m (pl Söhne)

song n Lied nt (pl Lieder)

son-in-law n Schwiegersohn m (pl Schwiegersöhne)

soon adv bald ▷ *very soon* sehr bald; **soon afterwards** kurz danach; **as soon as possible** sobald wie möglich

sooner adv früher ▷ *a bit sooner* etwas früher ▷ *sooner or later* früher oder später

soprano n Sopran m (pl Soprane)

sore adj **It's sore.** Es tut weh.; **That's a sore point.** Das ist ein wunder Punkt. ▶ n Wunde f

sorry adj **I'm really sorry.** Es tut mir wirklich leid.; **Sorry!** Entschuldigung!; **I feel sorry for her.** Sie tut mir leid.

sort n Art f ▷ *There are different sorts of mushrooms.* Es gibt verschiedene Arten von Pilzen.; **what sort of ... (1)** was für ein ... ▷ *What sort of cake is that?* Was für ein Kuchen ist das? ▷ *What sort of bike have you got?* Was für ein Fahrrad hast du? **(2)** was für eine ... ▷ *What sort of school do you go to?* In was für eine Schule gehst du?

sort out vb ❶ (objects) sortieren [76] (perf hat sortiert) ❷ (problems) lösen [38]

soul n ❶ (spirit) Seele f ❷ (music) Soul m

sound n ❶ (noise) Geräusch nt (pl Geräusche); **Don't make a sound!** Still!; **I heard the sound of footsteps.** Ich hörte Schritte. ❷ Lautstärke f ▷ *Can I turn the sound down?* Kann ich die Lautstärke runterdrehen?
▶ vb klingen (imperf klang, perf hat geklungen) ▷ *That sounds interesting.* Das klingt interessant.; **It sounds as if she's doing well at school.** Dem Anschein nach ist sie gut in der Schule.; **That sounds like a good idea.** Das scheint eine gute Idee zu sein.
▶ adj, adv gut ▷ *That's sound advice.* Das ist ein guter Rat.; **to be sound asleep** fest schlafen [58]

soundtrack n Soundtrack m (pl Soundtracks)

soup n Suppe f ▷ *vegetable soup* die Gemüsesuppe

sour adj sauer

south adj, adv nach Süden ▷ *We were travelling south.* Wir sind nach Süden

South Africa gefahren.; **the south coast** die Südküste; **a south wind** ein Südwind m; **south of** südlich von ▸ n Süden m ▹ **in the south** im Süden; **in the South of Germany** in Süddeutschland

South Africa n Südafrika nt; **from South Africa** aus Südafrika; **to South Africa** nach Südafrika

South America n Südamerika nt; **from South America** aus Südamerika; **to South America** nach Südamerika

South American n Südamerikaner m (pl Südamerikaner), Südamerikanerin f ▸ adj südamerikanisch

southeast n Südosten m; **southeast England** Südostengland nt

southern adj südlich ▹ the southern part of the island der südliche Teil der Insel; **Southern England** Südengland nt

South Pole n Südpol m

southwest n Südwesten m; **southwest Germany** Südwestdeutschland nt

souvenir n Souvenir nt (pl Souvenirs) ▹ a souvenir shop ein Souveniergeschäft nt

soya n Soja f

soy sauce n Sojasoße f

space n ❶ Platz m (gen Platzes) ▹ There's enough space. Es ist genug Platz da.; **a parking space** ein Parkplatz ❷ (outer space) Raum m

spacecraft n Raumschiff nt (pl Raumschiffe)

spade n Spaten m (pl Spaten); **spades** (in cards) das Pik

Spain n Spanien nt; **from Spain** aus Spanien; **in Spain** in Spanien; **to Spain** nach Spanien

Spaniard n Spanier m (pl Spanier), Spanierin f

spaniel n Spaniel m (pl Spaniels)

Spanish adj spanisch; **He's Spanish.** Er ist Spanier.; **She's Spanish.** Sie ist Spanierin.

▸ n (language) Spanisch nt (gen Spanischen); **the Spanish** die Spanier mpl

spanner n Schraubenschlüssel m (pl Schraubenschlüssel)

spare vb **Can you spare a moment?** Hast du mal einen Moment Zeit?; **I can't spare the time.** Ich habe die Zeit nicht.; **There's no room to spare.** Es ist kein Platz übrig.; **We arrived with time to spare.** Wir waren zu früh da.

Be careful not to translate **to spare** by sparen.

▸ n Ersatzteil nt (pl Ersatzteile); **I've lost my key. — Have you got a spare?** Ich habe meinen Schlüssel verloren. — Hast du einen Ersatzschlüssel?

▸ adj **spare batteries** die Ersatzbatterien fpl; **a spare part** ein Ersatzteil nt; **a spare room** ein Gästezimmer nt; **spare time** die Freizeit f ▹ What do you do in your spare time? Was machen Sie in Ihrer Freizeit?; **spare wheel** das Reserverad

sparkling adj (water) mit Kohlensäure; **sparkling wine** der Sekt

sparrow n Spatz m (gen Spatzen, pl Spatzen)

spat vb see **spit**

speak vb sprechen [70] (pres spricht, imperf sprach, perf hat gesprochen) ▹ Do you speak English? Sprechen Sie Englisch?; **to speak to somebody** mit jemandem reden [54]; **spoken German** gesprochenes Deutsch

speak up vb lauter sprechen [70] (pres spricht, imperf sprach, perf hat gesprochen)

speaker n ❶ (loudspeaker) Lautsprecher m (pl Lautsprecher) ❷ (in debate) Redner m (pl Redner), Rednerin f

special adj besondere ▸ a special occasion ein besonderer Anlass

specialist n Fachmann m (pl Fachleute), Fachfrau f

speciality n Spezialität f

specialize vb sich spezialisieren [76] (perf hat sich spezialisiert) ▷ *We specialize in skiing equipment.* Wir haben uns auf Skiausrüstung spezialisiert.

specially adv ❶ besonders ▷ *It can be very cold here, specially in winter.* Es kann hier sehr kalt werden, besonders im Winter. ❷ speziell ▷ *It's specially designed for teenagers.* Das ist speziell für Teenager gedacht.; **not specially** nicht besonders

species nsg Art f

specific adj ❶ (*particular*) speziell ▷ *certain specific issues* gewisse spezielle Fragen ❷ (*precise*) genau ▷ *Could you be more specific?* Könnten Sie sich etwas genauer ausdrücken?

specs npl Brille fsg ▷ *a pair of specs* eine Brille

spectacles npl Brille fsg ▷ *a pair of spectacles* eine Brille

spectacular adj spektakulär

spectator n Zuschauer m (pl Zuschauer), Zuschauerin f

speech n Rede f ▷ *to make a speech* eine Rede halten

speechless adj sprachlos ▷ *speechless with admiration* sprachlos vor Bewunderung ▷ *I was speechless.* Ich war sprachlos.

speed n ❶ Gang m (pl Gänge); **a three-speed bike** ein Dreigang rad nt ❷ Geschwindigkeit f ▷ *at top speed* mit Höchstgeschwindigkeit; **to speed up** schneller werden [91]

speedboat n Schnellboot nt (pl Schnellboote)

speed limit n Geschwindigkeitsbegrenzung f ▷ *to break the speed limit* die Geschwindigkeitsbegrenzung überschreiten

spell vb ❶ (*in writing*) schreiben [61] (imperf schrieb, perf hat geschrieben) ▷ *How do you spell that?* Wie schreibt man das? ❷ (*out loud*) buchstabieren [76] (perf hat buchstabiert) ▷ *Can you spell that please?* Können Sie das bitte buchstabieren?; **I can't spell.** Ich kann keine Rechtschreibung.
▶ n **to cast a spell on somebody** jemanden verhexen [7]; **to be under somebody's spell** wie verzaubert sein [65]

spelling n Rechtschreibung f ▷ *My spelling is terrible.* Meine Rechtschreibung ist furchtbar.; **a spelling mistake** ein Rechtschreibfehler m

spelt vb see **spell**

spend vb ❶ (*money*) ausgeben [28] (pres gibt aus, imperf gab aus, perf hat ausgegeben) ❷ (*time*) verbringen [13] (imperf verbrachte, perf hat verbracht) ▷ *He spent a month in Italy.* Er verbrachte einen Monat in Italien.

Be careful not to translate **to spend** by *spenden*.

spice n Gewürz nt (gen Gewürzes, pl Gewürze)

spicy adj scharf ▷ *Indian food's much spicier than German food.* Indisches Essen ist viel schärfer als deutsches.

spider n Spinne f

spill vb (*tip over*) verschütten [7] ▷ *He spilled his coffee.* Er hat seinen Kaffee verschüttet.; **to get spilt** verschüttet werden [91]

spinach n Spinat m

spine n Rückgrat nt (pl Rückgrate)

spire n Kirchturm m (pl Kirchtürme)

spirit n ❶ (*courage*) Mut m ❷ (*energy*) Energie f; **to be in good spirits** gut gelaunt sein [65]

spirits npl Spirituosen pl

spiritual adj geistlich ▷ *the spiritual leader of Tibet* der geistliche Führer Tibets

spit vb spucken [38]; **to spit something out** etwas ausspucken [4]; **It's spitting.** Es tröpfelt.

spite n **in spite of** trotz; **out of spite** aus Gehässigkeit
▶ vb ärgern [88] ▷ *He just did it to spite me.* Er tat es nur, um mich zu ärgern.

spiteful adj ❶ *(action)* gemein ❷ *(person)* gehässig

splash vb bespritzen [7] *(perf* hat bespritzt*)* ▷ *Don't splash me!* Bespritz mich nicht!
▶ n Platsch m ▷ *I heard a splash.* Ich hörte einen Platsch.; **a splash of colour** ein Farbfleck m

splendid adj wunderbar

splinter n Splitter m *(pl* Splitter*)*

split vb ❶ zerteilen [95] *(perf* zerteilt*)* ▷ *He split the wood with an axe.* Er zerteilte das Holz mit einer Axt. ❷ zerbrechen [11] *(pres* zerbricht, *imperf* zerbrach, *perf* ist zerbrochen*)* ▷ *The ship hit a rock and split in two.* Das Schiff lief auf einen Fels und zerbrach in zwei Teile. ❸ *(divide up)* teilen [38] ▷ *They split the profits.* Sie teilten den Gewinn.; **to split up (1)** *(couple)* sich trennen [38] **(2)** *(group)* sich auflösen [4]

spoil vb ❶ verderben *(pres* verdirbt, *imperf* verdarb, *perf* hat verdorben*)* ▷ *It spoiled our evening.* Es hat uns den Abend verdorben. ❷ *(child)* verwöhnen [84] *(perf* hat verwöhnt*)*

spoiled adj verwöhnt ▷ *a spoiled child* ein verwöhntes Kind

spoilsport n Spielverderber m *(pl* Spielverderber*)*, Spielverderberin f

spoilt adj verwöhnt ▷ *a spoilt child* ein verwöhntes Kind
▶ vb see **spoil**

spoken vb see **speak**

spokesman n Sprecher m *(pl* Sprecher*)*

spokesperson n Sprecher m *(pl* Sprecher*)*, Sprecherin f

spokeswoman n Sprecherin f

sponge n Schwamm m *(pl* Schwämme*)*; **a sponge bag** ein Kulturbeutel m; **a sponge cake** ein Rührkuchen m

sponsor n Sponsor m *(pl* Sponsoren*)*, Sponsorin f
▶ vb sponsern [88] ▷ *The festival was sponsored by ...* Das Festival wurde gesponsert von ...

spontaneous adj spontan

spooky adj ❶ *(eerie)* gruselig ▷ *a spooky story* eine gruselige Geschichte ❷ *(strange)* komisch ▷ *a spooky coincidence* ein komischer Zufall

spoon n Löffel m *(pl* Löffel*)* ▷ *a spoon of sugar* ein Löffel Zucker

spoonful n **a spoonful of soup** ein Löffel Suppe

sport n Sport m ▷ *What's your favourite sport?* Was ist dein Lieblingssport?; **a sports bag** eine Sporttasche; **a sports car** ein Sportwagen m; **a sports jacket** eine Sportjacke; **Go on, be a sport!** Nun komm schon, sei kein Frosch!

sportsman n Sportler m *(pl* Sportler*)*

sportswear n Sportkleidung f

sportswoman n Sportlerin f

sporty adj sportlich ▷ *I'm not very sporty.* Ich bin nicht besonders sportlich.

spot n ❶ *(mark)* Fleck m *(pl* Flecke*)* ▷ *There's a spot of blood on your shirt.* Du hast einen Blutfleck auf dem Hemd. ❷ *(in pattern)* Punkt m *(pl* Punkte*)* ▷ *a red dress with white spots* ein rotes Kleid mit weißen Punkten ❸ *(pimple)* Pickel m *(pl* Pickel*)* ▷ *I've got a big spot on my chin.* Ich habe einen großen Pickel am Kinn. ❹ *(place)* Platz m *(gen* Platzes, *pl* Plätze*)* ▷ *It's a lovely spot for a picnic.* Es ist ein herrlicher Platz für ein Picknick.; **on the spot (1)** *(immediately)* sofort ▷ *They gave her the job on the spot.* Sie haben ihr den Job sofort gegeben. **(2)** *(at the same place)* an Ort und Stelle ▷ *They were able to mend the car on the spot.* Sie konnten das Auto an Ort und Stelle reparieren.
▶ vb entdecken [18] *(perf* hat entdeckt*)* ▷ *I spotted Jack.* Ich habe Jack entdeckt.

ENGLISH > GERMAN

spotless adj makellos
spotlight n Scheinwerferlicht nt
spotty adj (pimply) pickelig
sprain vb **I've sprained my ankle.** Ich habe mir den Fuß verstaucht.
▶ n Verstauchung f ▷ *It's just a sprain.* Es ist nur eine Verstauchung.
spray n Spray nt (pl Sprays) ▷ *hair spray* das Haarspray
▶ vb sprühen [38] ▷ *to spray perfume on one's hand* sich Parfüm auf die Hand sprühen ▷ *Somebody had sprayed graffiti on the wall.* Irgendjemand hatte Graffiti auf die Wand gesprüht.
spread n *cheese spread* der Streichkäse; **chocolate spread** der Schokoladenaufstrich
▶ vb ① streichen (imperf strich, perf hat gestrichen) ▷ *to spread butter on a cracker* Butter auf einen Cracker streichen ② (disease, news) sich verbreiten [2] (perf hat sich verbreitet) ▷ *The news spread rapidly.* Die Nachricht verbreitete sich schnell.; **to spread out** (people) sich verteilen [84]
spreadsheet n (computer program) Tabellenkalkulation f
spring n ① (season) Frühling m (pl Frühlinge) ▷ *in spring* im Frühling ② (metal coil) Feder f ③ (water hole) Quelle f
springtime n Frühjahr nt (pl Frühjahre) ▷ *in springtime* im Frühjahr
sprint n Sprint m (pl Sprints); **a hundred-metre sprint** ein Einhundertmeterlauf m
▶ vb rennen [55] (imperf rannte, perf ist gerannt) ▷ *She sprinted for the bus.* Sie rannte, um den Bus zu erreichen.
sprouts npl **Brussels sprouts** der Rosenkohl sg
spy n Spion m (pl Spione), Spionin f
▶ vb **to spy on somebody** jemanden nachspionieren [4]
spying n Spionage f

481 | stain

square n ① Quadrat nt (pl Quadrate) ▷ *a square and a triangle* ein Quadrat und ein Dreieck ② Platz m (gen Platzes, pl Plätze) ▷ *the town square* der Rathausplatz
▶ adj **two square metres** zwei Quadratmeter; **It's two metres square.** Es misst zwei mal zwei Meter.
squash n (sport) Squash nt ▷ *I play squash.* Ich spiele Squash.; **a squash court** ein Squashcourt m; **a squash racket** ein Squashschläger m; **orange squash** der Orangensaft
▶ vb zerdrücken [95] (perf hat zerdrückt) ▷ *You're squashing me.* Du zerdrückst mich.
squeak vb ① (mouse, child) quieksen [48] ② (creak) quietschen [48]
squeeze vb ① (fruit, toothpaste) pressen [31] ② (hand, arm) drücken [38] ▷ *to squeeze somebody's arm* jemandem den Arm drücken; **to squeeze into tight jeans** sich in enge Jeans quetschen [48]
squirrel n Eichhörnchen nt (pl Eichhörnchen)
stab vb **to stab somebody** (1) (wound) jemanden mit dem Messer verletzen [36] (2) (kill) jemanden erstechen
stable n Stall m (pl Ställe)
▶ adj stabil ▷ *a stable relationship* eine stabile Beziehung
stack n Stapel m (pl Stapel) ▷ *a stack of books* ein Stapel Bücher
stadium n Stadion nt (pl Stadien)
staff n ① (in company) Belegschaft f ② (in school) Lehrerschaft f
stage n ① (in plays) Bühne f ② (for speeches, lectures) Podium nt (pl Podien); **at this stage** (1) an diesem Punkt ▷ *at this stage in the negotiations* an diesem Punkt der Verhandlungen (2) im Augenblick ▷ *At this stage, one can't tell.* Im Augenblick kann man das noch nicht sagen.; **to do something in stages** etwas in Etappen machen [48]
stain n Fleck m (pl Flecke)
▶ vb beflecken [7] (perf hat befleckt)

stainless steel n Edelstahl m
stair n (step) Stufe f
staircase n Treppe f
stairs npl Treppe fsg
stale adj (bread) altbacken
stalemate n (in chess) Patt nt (pl Patts)
stall n Stand m (pl Stände) ▷ He's got a market stall. Er hat einen Marktstand.; **the stalls** (in cinema, theatre) das Parkett sg
stammer n Stottern nt; **He's got a stammer.** Er stottert.
stamp vb (passport) abstempeln [4] (perf hat abgestempelt); **to stamp one's foot** mit dem Fuß aufstampfen [4]
▶ n ❶ Briefmarke f ▷ I need a stamp. Ich brauche eine Briefmarke. ▷ a stamp album ein Briefmarkenalbum ▷ a stamp collection eine Briefmarkensammlung ❷ (rubber stamp) Stempel m (pl Stempel)
stand vb ❶ (be standing) stehen [72] (imperf stand, perf hat gestanden) ▷ He was standing by the door. Er stand an der Tür. ❷ (stand up) aufstehen [72] (perf ist aufgestanden) ❸ (tolerate, withstand) aushalten [33] (pres hält aus, imperf hielt aus, perf hat ausgehalten) ▷ I can't stand all this noise. Ich halte diesen Lärm nicht aus.; **to stand for (1)** (be short for) stehen [72] für ▷ 'BT' stands for 'British Telecom'. 'BT' steht für 'British Telecom'. **(2)** (tolerate) dulden [54] ▷ I won't stand for it! Ich dulde das nicht!; **to stand in for somebody** jemanden vertreten [79]; **to stand out** herausragen [15]; **to stand up** (get up) aufstehen [72]; **to stand up for** eintreten [79] für ▷ Stand up for your rights! Tretet für eure Rechte ein!
standard adj normal ▷ the standard procedure die normale Vorgehensweise; **standard German** das Hochdeutsch; **standard equipment** die Standardausrüstung
▶ n Niveau nt (pl Niveaus) ▷ The standard is very high. Das Niveau ist sehr hoch.;

the standard of living der Lebensstandard; **She's got high standards.** Sie hat hohe Ansprüche.
stands npl (at sports ground) Tribüne fsg
stank vb see **stink**
staple n Heftklammer f
▶ vb zusammenheften [4] (perf hat zusammengeheftet)
stapler n Heftmaschine f
star n ❶ (in sky) Stern m (pl Sterne) ❷ (celebrity) Star m (pl Stars)
  der Star is also used for women.
▷ She's a TV star. Sie ist ein Fernsehstar.; **the stars** (horoscope) die Sterne
▶ vb die Hauptrolle spielen [38] ▷ The film stars Nicole Kidman. Nicole Kidman spielt in dem Film die Hauptrolle.; ... **starring Viola Davis** ... mit Viola Davis in der Hauptrolle
stare vb **to stare at something** etwas anstarren [4]
start n ❶ Anfang m (pl Anfänge) ▷ It's not much, but it's a start. Es ist nicht viel, aber es ist immerhin ein Anfang.; **Shall we make a start on the washing-up?** Sollen wir den Abwasch in Angriff nehmen? ❷ (of race) Start m (pl Starts)
▶ vb ❶ anfangen [23] (pres fängt an, imperf fing an, perf hat angefangen) ▷ What time does it start? Wann fängt es an?; **to start doing something** anfangen [23], etwas zu tun ❷ (organization) gründen [54] ▷ He wants to start his own business. Er möchte ein eigenes Geschäft gründen. ❸ (campaign) ins Leben rufen [56] (imperf rief ins Leben, perf hat ins Leben gerufen) ▷ She started the campaign. Sie hat die Kampagne ins Leben gerufen. ❹ (car) anlassen [42] (pres lässt an, imperf ließ an, perf hat angelassen) ▷ He couldn't start the car. Er konnte das Auto nicht anlassen.; **The car wouldn't start.** Das Auto ist nicht angesprungen.; **to start off** (leave) aufbrechen [11]

starter n (first course) Vorspeise f

starve vb (die) verhungern [**88**] (perf ist verhungert) ▷ *People were literally starving.* Die Menschen sind förmlich verhungert.; **I'm starving!** Ich bin am Verhungern!; **They starved us in prison.** Sie ließen uns im Gefängnis hungern.

state n ❶ (upset) Zustand m (pl Zustände); **He was in a real state.** Er ist fast durchgedreht. ❷ (government) Staat m; **the States** (USA) die Staaten
▶ vb ❶ (say) erklären [**19**] (perf hat erklärt) ▷ *He stated his intention to resign.* Er erklärte seine Absicht zurückzutreten. ❷ (give) angeben [**28**] (pres gibt an, imperf gab an, perf hat angegeben) ▷ *Please state your name and address.* Geben Sie bitte Ihren Namen und Ihre Adresse an.

statement n Erklärung f

station n ❶ (railway) Bahnhof m (pl Bahnhöfe); **the bus station** der Busbahnhof; **a police station** eine Polizeiwache; **a radio station** ein Rundfunksender m

stationer's n Schreibwarengeschäft nt (pl Schreibwarengeschäfte)

statue n Statue f

stay vb ❶ (remain) bleiben [**10**] (imperf blieb, perf ist geblieben) ▷ *Stay here!* Bleiben Sie hier!; **to stay in** (not go out) zu Hause bleiben [**10**]; **to stay up** aufbleiben [**10**] ❷ (spend the night) übernachten [**2**] (perf hat übernachtet) ▷ *to stay with friends* bei Freunden übernachten; **Where are you staying?** Wo wohnen Sie?; **to stay the night** über Nacht bleiben [**10**]; **We stayed in Belgium for a few days.** Wir waren ein paar Tage in Belgien.
▶ n Aufenthalt m (pl Aufenthalte) ▷ *my stay in Bonn* mein Aufenthalt in Bonn

steady adj ❶ stetig ▷ *steady progress* stetiger Fortschritt ❷ fest ▷ *a steady job* eine feste Arbeit ❸ (voice, hand) ruhig ❹ (person) solide; **a steady boyfriend** ein fester Freund; **a steady girlfriend** eine feste Freundin; **Steady on!** Immer mit der Ruhe!

steak n (beef) Steak nt (pl Steaks) ▷ *steak and chips* Steak mit Pommes frites

steal vb stehlen [**73**] (pres stiehlt, imperf stahl, perf hat gestohlen)

steam n Dampf m (pl Dämpfe) ▷ *a steam engine* eine Dampflokomotive

steel n Stahl m ▷ *a steel door* eine Stahltür

steep adj (slope) steil

steeple n Kirchturm m (pl Kirchtürme)

steering wheel n Lenkrad nt (pl Lenkräder)

step n ❶ (pace) Schritt m (pl Schritte) ▷ *He took a step forward.* Er machte einen Schritt nach vorn. ❷ (stair) Stufe f ▷ *She tripped over the step.* Sie stolperte über die Stufe.
▶ vb **to step aside** zur Seite treten [**79**]; **to step back** zurücktreten [**79**]

stepbrother n Stiefbruder m (pl Stiefbrüder)

stepchild n Stiefkind nt (pl die Stiefkinder)

stepdaughter n Stieftochter f (pl Stieftöchter)

stepfather n Stiefvater m (pl Stiefväter)

stepladder n Trittleiter f

stepmother n Stiefmutter f (pl Stiefmütter)

stepsister n Stiefschwester f

stepson n Stiefsohn m (pl Stiefsöhne)

stereo n Stereoanlage f

sterling adj **five pounds sterling** fünf britische Pfund

stew n Eintopf m (pl Eintöpfe)

steward n Steward m (pl Stewards)

stewardess n Stewardess f (pl Stewardessen)

stick n Stock m (pl Stöcke)
▶ vb (with adhesive) kleben [**38**]; **I can't stick it any longer.** Ich halte das nicht mehr aus.

stick out | 484

stick out vb herausstrecken [**15**] (perf hat herausgestreckt)

sticker n Aufkleber m (pl Aufkleber)

stick insect n Gespenstheuschrecke f (pl Gespenstheuschrecken)

sticky adj klebrig ▷ to have sticky hands klebrige Hände haben; **a sticky label** ein Aufkleber m

stiff adj, adv (rigid) steif; **to have a stiff neck** einen steifen Hals haben [**32**]; **to feel stiff (1)** steif sein [**65**] ▷ I feel stiff after the long journey. Ich bin nach der langen Reise ganz steif. **(2)** Muskelkater haben [**32**] ▷ I feel stiff after playing football yesterday. Ich habe gestern Fußball gespielt und habe jetzt Muskelkater.; **to be bored stiff** sich zu Tode langweilen [**38**]; **to be frozen stiff** total durchgefroren sein [**65**]; **to be scared stiff** furchtbare Angst haben [**32**]

still adv ❶ immer noch ▷ I still haven't finished. Ich bin immer noch nicht fertig. ▷ Are you still in bed? Bist du immer noch im Bett?; **better still** noch besser ❷ (even so) trotzdem ▷ She knows I don't like it, but she still does it. Sie weiß, dass sie das nicht mag, sie macht es aber trotzdem. ❸ (after all) immerhin ▷ Still, it's the thought that counts. Es war immerhin gut gemeint.
▶ adj still ▷ Keep still! Halt still! ▷ Sit still! Sitz still!

sting n Stich m (pl Stiche) ▷ a wasp sting ein Wespenstich
▶ vb stechen (pres sticht, imperf stach, perf hat gestochen) ▷ I've been stung. Ich bin gestochen worden.

stink vb stinken (imperf stank, perf hat gestunken) ▷ It stinks! Es stinkt!
▶ n Gestank m

stir vb umrühren [**4**] (perf hat umgerührt)

stitch vb (cloth) nähen [**38**]
▶ n Stich m (pl Stiche) ▷ I had five stitches. Ich wurde mit fünf Stichen genäht.

ENGLISH > GERMAN

stock n ❶ (supply) Vorrat m (pl Vorräte) ❷ (in shop) Lager nt (pl Lager) ▷ in stock auf Lager; **out of stock** ausverkauft ❸ Brühe f ▷ chicken stock die Hühnerbrühe
▶ vb (shop: have in stock) führen [**38**] ▷ Do you stock camping stoves? Führen Sie Campingkocher?; **to stock up** sich eindecken [**4**]

stock cube n Brühwürfel m (pl Brühwürfel)

stocking n Strumpf m (pl Strümpfe)

stomach n ❶ Magen m (pl Mägen) ▷ on a full stomach mit vollem Magen ❷ Bauch m (pl Bäuche) ▷ to lie on one's stomach auf dem Bauch liegen

stomachache n **to have a stomachache** Bauchschmerzen haben [**32**]

stone n (rock) Stein m (pl Steine) ▷ a stone wall eine Steinmauer ▷ a peach stone ein Pfirsichstein
• In Germany weight is expressed in
• kilos. A stone is about 6.3 kg.
▷ I weigh eight stone. Ich wiege fünfzig Kilo.

stood vb see **stand**

stool n Hocker m (pl Hocker)

stop vb ❶ aufhören [**4**] (perf hat aufgehört) ▷ He stopped crying. Er hörte auf zu weinen. ▷ I think the rain's going to stop. Ich glaube, es hört auf zu regnen.
▷ You should stop smoking. Du solltest aufhören zu rauchen.; **to stop somebody doing something** jemanden daran hindern [**88**], etwas zu tun; **Stop it!** Hör auf! ❷ (bus, train, car) halten [**33**] (pres hält, imperf hielt, perf hat gehalten) ▷ The bus doesn't stop here. Der Bus hält hier nicht. ❸ stoppen [**48**] ▷ a campaign to stop whaling eine Kampagne, um den Walfang zu stoppen; **Stop!** Halt!
▶ n Haltestelle f ▷ a bus stop eine Bushaltestelle.; **This is my stop.** Ich muss jetzt aussteigen.

stopwatch n Stoppuhr f

store n ① (shop) Geschäft nt (pl Geschäfte) ▷ a furniture store ein Möbelgeschäft ② (stock, storeroom) Lager nt (pl Lager)
▶ vb ① lagern [88] ▷ They store potatoes in the cellar. Sie lagern Kartoffeln im Keller. ② (information) speichern [88]

storey n Stock m (pl Stock) ▷ the first storey der erste Stock; **a three-storey building** ein dreistöckiges Gebäude

storm n ① (gale) Sturm m (pl Stürme) ② (thunderstorm) Gewitter nt (pl Gewitter)

stormy adj stürmisch

story n Geschichte f

stove n ① (in kitchen) Herd m (pl Herde) ② (camping stove) Kocher m (pl Kocher)

straight adj ① gerade ▷ a straight line eine gerade Linie ② glatt ▷ a straight hair glatte Haare ③ (heterosexual) hetero; **straight away** sofort; **straight on** geradeaus

straightforward adj einfach

strain n (stress) Anstrengung f; **It was a strain.** Es war anstrengend.
▶ vb sich verrenken [7] (perf hat sich verrenkt) ▷ I strained my back. Ich habe mir den Rücken verrenkt.; **I strained a muscle.** Ich habe mir einen Muskel gezerrt.

strange adj sonderbar ▷ That's strange! Das ist sonderbar!

stranger n Fremde m (gen Fremden, pl Fremden), Fremde f (gen Fremden) ▷ a stranger (man) ein Fremder; **Don't talk to strangers.** Sprich nicht mit fremden Menschen.; **I'm a stranger here.** Ich bin hier fremd.

strangle vb erwürgen [19] (perf hat erwürgt)

strap n ① (of bag, camera, shoe, suitcase) Riemen m (pl Riemen) ② (of bra, dress) Träger m (pl Träger) ③ (of watch) Armband nt (pl Armbänder)

straw n Stroh nt; **That's the last straw!** Jetzt reicht's aber!

strawberry n Erdbeere f ▷ strawberry jam die Erdbeermarmelade ▷ a strawberry ice cream ein Erdbeereis

stray n a stray cat eine streunende Katze

stream n Bach m (pl Bäche)

street n Straße f ▷ in the street auf der Straße

streetlamp n Straßenlampe f

street plan n Stadtplan m (pl Stadtpläne)

streetwise adj (informal) gewieft

strength n Kraft f (pl Kräfte)

stress vb betonen [7] (perf hat betont) ▷ I would like to stress that ... Ich möchte betonen, dass ...
▶ n Stress m (gen Stresses)

stretch vb ① (person, animal) sich strecken [48] ▷ The dog woke up and stretched. Der Hund wachte auf und streckte sich. ② (get bigger) ausleiern [4] (perf ist ausgeleiert) ▷ My sweater stretched when I washed it. Mein Pullover ist in der Wäsche ausgeleiert. ③ (stretch out) spannen [38] ▷ They stretched a rope between the trees. Sie spannten ein Seil zwischen den Bäumen.; **to stretch out one's arms** die Arme ausbreiten [4]

stretcher n Trage f

stretchy adj elastisch

strict adj streng

strike n Streik m (pl Streiks); **to be on strike** streiken [38]; **to go on strike** in den Streik treten [79]
▶ vb ① schlagen [59] (pres schlägt, imperf schlug, perf hat geschlagen) ▷ The clock struck three. Die Uhr schlug drei. ▷ She struck him across the mouth. Sie schlug ihm auf den Mund. ② (go on strike) streiken [38]; **to strike a match** ein Streichholz anzünden [54]

striker n ① (person on strike) Streikende m (pl Streikenden), Streikende f (gen Streikenden) ▷ a striker (man) ein Streikender ② (footballer)

string | 486   **ENGLISH > GERMAN**

Torschütze m (gen Torschützen, pl Torschützen)
string n ❶ (string) Schnur f (pl Schnüre) ▷ *a piece of string* eine Schnur ❷ (of violin, guitar) Saite f
strip vb (get undressed) sich ausziehen [96] (imperf zog sich aus, perf hat sich ausgezogen)
▶ n Streifen m (pl Streifen); **a strip cartoon** ein Comicstrip m
stripe n Streifen m (pl Streifen)
striped adj gestreift ▷ *a striped skirt* ein gestreifter Rock
stroke vb streicheln [88]
▶ n Schlag m (pl Schläge) ▷ *to have a stroke* einen Schlag bekommen
stroll n **to go for a stroll** einen Spaziergang machen [48]
stroller n (US) (for child) Sportwagen m (pl Sportwagen)
strong adj stark ▷ *She's very strong.* Sie ist sehr stark. ▷ *Gerry is stronger than Robert.* Gerry ist stärker als Robert.
strongly adv dringend ▷ *We strongly recommend that ...* Wir empfehlen dringend, dass ...; **He smelt strongly of tobacco.** Er roch stark nach Tabak.; **strongly built** solide gebaut; **I don't feel strongly about it.** Das ist mir ziemlich egal.
struck vb see **strike**
struggle vb (physically) sich wehren [38] ▷ *He struggled, but he couldn't escape.* Er wehrte sich, aber er konnte sich nicht befreien.; **to struggle to do something** (1) (fight) kämpfen [38], um etwas zu tun ▷ *He struggled to get custody of his daughter.* Er kämpfte, um das Sorgerecht für seine Tochter zu bekommen. (2) (have difficulty) Mühe haben [32], etwas zu tun ▷ *She struggled to pay the bill.* Sie hatte Mühe, die Rechnung zu bezahlen.
▶ n (for independence, equality) Kampf m (pl Kämpfe) ▷ *It was a struggle.* Es war ein Kampf.

stubborn adj stur
stuck vb see **stick**
▶ adj **It's stuck.** Es klemmt.; **to get stuck** stecken bleiben [10]
stuck-up adj (informal) hochnäsig
stud n ❶ (earring) Ohrstecker m (pl Ohrstecker) ❷ (on football boots) Stollen m (pl Stollen)
student n Student m (gen Studenten, pl Studenten), Studentin f
studio n Studio nt (pl Studios) ▷ *a TV studio* ein Fernsehstudio; **a studio flat** eine Einzimmerwohnung
study vb ❶ (at university) studieren [76] (perf hat studiert) ▷ *I plan to study biology.* Ich habe vor, Biologie zu studieren. ❷ (do homework) lernen [38] ▷ *I've got to study tonight.* Ich muss heute Abend lernen.
stuff n ❶ (things) Sachen fpl ▷ *There's some stuff on the table for you.* Auf dem Tisch stehen Sachen für dich. ❷ (possessions) Zeug nt ▷ *Have you got all your stuff?* Hast du all dein Zeug?
stuffy adj (room) stickig ▷ *It's really stuffy in here.* Hier drin ist es wirklich stickig.
stumble vb stolpern [88] (perf ist gestolpert)
stung vb see **sting**
stunk vb see **stink**
stunned adj (amazed) sprachlos ▷ *I was stunned.* Ich war sprachlos.
stunning adj umwerfend
stunt n (in film) Stunt m (pl Stunts)
stuntman n Stuntman m (pl Stuntmen)
stupid adj blöd ▷ *a stupid joke* ein blöder Witz; **Me, go jogging? Don't be stupid!** Ich und joggen? Du spinnst wohl!
stutter vb stottern [88]
▶ n **He's got a stutter.** Er stottert.
style n Stil m (pl Stile) ▷ *That's not his style.* Das ist nicht sein Stil.
subject n ❶ Thema nt (pl Themen) ▷ *The subject of my project was the internet.* Das Thema meines Referats war das Internet. ❷ (at school) Fach nt

(pl Fächer) ▷ What's your favourite subject? Was ist dein Lieblingsfach?
subjunctive n Konjunktiv m
submarine n U-Boot nt (pl U-Boote)
subscription n (to paper, magazine) Abonnement nt (pl Abonnements) ▷ to take out a subscription to something etwas abonnieren [76]
subsidy n Subvention f
substance n Substanz f
substitute n (player) Ersatzspieler m (pl Ersatzspieler), Ersatzspielerin f ▶ vb ersetzen [36] (perf hat ersetzt) ▷ to substitute wine for beer Bier durch Wein ersetzen
subtitled adj mit Untertiteln
subtitles npl Untertitel mpl ▷ an English film with German subtitles ein englischer Film mit deutschen Untertiteln
subtle adj fein ▷ a subtle difference ein feiner Unterschied
subtract vb abziehen [96] (imperf zog ab, perf hat abgezogen) ▷ to subtract three from five drei von fünf abziehen
suburb n Vorstadt f (pl Vorstädte) ▷ a suburb of Berlin eine Vorstadt von Berlin ▷ They live in the suburbs. Sie wohnen in der Vorstadt.
subway n ❶ (underpass) Unterführung f ❷ (underground) U-Bahn f
succeed vb Erfolg haben [32] (pres hat Erfolg, imperf hatte Erfolg, perf hat Erfolg gehabt) ▷ He succeeded in his plan. Er hatte mit seinem Plan Erfolg.; **I succeeded in convincing him.** Es ist mir gelungen, ihn zu überzeugen.
success n Erfolg m (pl Erfolge) ▷ The play was a great success. Das Stück war ein großer Erfolg.
successful adj erfolgreich ▷ a successful attempt ein erfolgreicher Versuch ▷ He's a successful businessman. Er ist ein erfolgreicher Geschäftsmann.; **to be successful in doing something** etwas mit Erfolg tun [81]

successfully adv mit Erfolg
such adj, adv so ▷ such nice people so nette Leute ▷ such a long journey eine so lange Reise; **such a lot of (1)** (so much) so viel ▷ such a lot of work so viel Arbeit **(2)** (so many) so viele ▷ such a lot of mistakes so viele Fehler; **such as** (like) wie zum Beispiel; **not as such** nicht eigentlich; **There's no such thing.** So was gibt es nicht.
such-and-such adj der und der ▷ such-and-such a place der und der Ort die und die ▷ such-and-such a time die und die Zeit das und das ▷ such-and-such a problem das und das Problem
suck vb (sweets) lutschen [48] ▷ to suck one's thumb am Daumen lutschen
sudden adj plötzlich ▷ a sudden change eine plötzliche Änderung; **all of a sudden** plötzlich
suddenly adv plötzlich ▷ Suddenly, the door opened. Plötzlich ging die Tür auf.
suede n Wildleder nt ▷ a suede jacket eine Wildlederjacke
suffer vb leiden [44] (imperf litt, perf hat gelitten) ▷ She was really suffering. Sie hat wirklich gelitten.; **to suffer from a disease** an einer Krankheit leiden [44]
suffocate vb ersticken [19] (perf ist erstickt)
sugar n Zucker m (pl Zucker)
suggest vb vorschlagen [59] (pres schlägt vor, imperf schlug vor, perf hat vorgeschlagen) ▷ I suggested they set off early. Ich habe vorgeschlagen, dass sie früh aufbrechen sollen.
suggestion n Vorschlag m (pl Vorschläge)
suicide n Selbstmord m (pl Selbstmorde) ▷ to commit suicide Selbstmord begehen
suicide bomber n Selbstmordattentäter m (pl Selbstmordattentäter), Selbstmordattentäterin f

suicide bombing n Selbstmordattentat nt (pl Selbstmordattentate)

suit n ❶ (man's) Anzug m (pl Anzüge) ❷ (woman's) Kostüm nt (pl Kostüme) ▷ vb ❶ (be convenient for) passen [31] ▷ What time would suit you? Welche Zeit würde Ihnen passen? ▷ That suits me fine. Das passt mir gut.; **Suit yourself!** Wie du willst! ❷ (look good on) stehen [72] (imperf stand, perf hat gestanden) ▷ That dress really suits you. Das Kleid steht dir wirklich.

suitable adj ❶ passend ▷ a suitable time eine passende Zeit ❷ (clothes) angemessen ▷ suitable clothing angemessene Kleidung

suitcase n Koffer m (pl Koffer)

suite n (of rooms) Suite f; **a bedroom suite** eine Schlafzimmereinrichtung

sulk vb schmollen [48]

sultana n Sultanine f

sum n ❶ (calculation) Rechnen nt; **She's good at sums.** Sie kann gut rechnen. ❷ (amount) Summe f ▷ a sum of money eine Geldsumme

sum up vb zusammenfassen [15] (perf hat zusammengefasst)

summarize vb zusammenfassen [15] (perf hat zusammengefasst)

summary n Zusammenfassung f

summer n Sommer m (pl Sommer) ▷ in summer im Sommer; **summer clothes** die Sommerkleidung sg; **the summer holidays** die Sommerferien

summertime n Sommer m (pl Sommer) ▷ in summertime im Sommer

summit n Gipfel m (pl Gipfel)

sun n Sonne f ▷ in the sun in der Sonne

sunbathe vb sonnenbaden [54] (perf hat sonnengebadet)

sunblock n Sonnenschutzmittel nt (pl Sonnenschutzmittel)

sunburn n Sonnenbrand m (pl Sonnenbrände)

sunburnt adj I got sunburnt. Ich habe einen Sonnenbrand bekommen.

Sunday n Sonntag m (pl Sonntage) ▷ every Sunday jeden Sonntag ▷ last Sunday letzten Sonntag ▷ next Sunday nächsten Sonntag ▷ on Sunday am Sonntag; **on Sundays** sonntags

Sunday school n Sonntagsschule f

sunflower n Sonnenblume f

sung vb see **sing**

sunglasses npl Sonnenbrille f sg ▷ a pair of sunglasses eine Sonnenbrille

sunk vb see **sink**

sunlight n Sonnenlicht nt

sunny adj sonnig ▷ a sunny morning ein sonniger Morgen; **It's sunny.** Die Sonne scheint.

sunrise n Sonnenaufgang m (pl Sonnenaufgänge)

sunroof n Schiebedach nt (pl Schiebedächer)

sunscreen n Sonnenschutzcreme f (pl Sonnenschutzcremes)

sunset n Sonnenuntergang m (pl Sonnenuntergänge)

sunshine n Sonnenschein m

sunstroke n Hitzschlag m (pl Hitzschläge) ▷ to get sunstroke einen Hitzschlag bekommen

suntan n to have a suntan braun sein [65]; **suntan lotion** die Sonnenmilch; **suntan oil** das Sonnenöl

super adj klasse
▌ klasse is invariable.
▷ a super film ein klasse Film

supermarket n Supermarkt m (pl Supermärkte)

supernatural adj übernatürlich

superstitious adj abergläubisch

supervise vb beaufsichtigen [84] (perf hat beaufsichtigt)

supervisor n ❶ (in factory) Vorarbeiter m (pl Vorarbeiter), Vorarbeiterin f ❷ (in department store) Abteilungsleiter m (pl Abteilungsleiter), Abteilungsleiterin f

supper n Abendessen nt (pl Abendessen)

supplement n ❶ (of newspaper, magazine) Beilage f ❷ (money) Zuschlag m (pl Zuschläge)

supplies npl (food) Vorräte mpl

supply vb ❶ (goods, material) liefern [88] ▷ The farm supplied us with food. Der Bauernhof lieferte uns die Lebensmittel. ❷ (put at somebody's disposal) stellen [38] ▷ The centre supplied all the necessary equipment. Das Zentrum hat die ganze notwendige Ausrüstung gestellt.
▶ n Vorrat m (pl Vorräte) ▷ a supply of paper ein Papiervorrat; **the water supply** (to town) die Wasserversorgung

supply teacher n Aushilfslehrer m (pl Aushilfslehrer), Aushilfslehrerin f

support vb ❶ unterstützen [36] ▷ My mum has always supported me. Meine Mutti hat mich immer unterstützt.; **What team do you support?** Für welche Mannschaft bist du? ❷ (financially) sorgen [38] für ▷ She had to support five children on her own. Sie musste allein für ihre fünf Kinder sorgen.
▶ n (backing) Unterstützung f

supporter n ❶ Fan m (pl Fans)
der Fan is also used for women.
▷ a Liverpool supporter ein Liverpool-Fan ❷ Anhänger m (pl Anhänger), Anhängerin f ▷ She's a supporter of the Labour Party. Sie ist Anhängerin der Labour-Party.

suppose vb annehmen [1] (pres nimmt an, imperf nahm an, perf hat angenommen) ▷ I suppose he's late. Ich nehme an, er kommt zu spät. ▷ Suppose you won the lottery. Nimm mal an, du gewinnst im Lotto. ▷ I suppose so. Das nehme ich an.; **to be supposed to do something** etwas tun sollen [69]; **You're supposed to show your passport.** Sie müssen Ihren Pass zeigen.

supposing conj angenommen ▷ Supposing you won the lottery ... Angenommen, du gewinnst im Lotto ...;
Sure! Klar!; **to make sure that ...** sich vergewissern [88], dass ...

surely adv sicherlich ▷ Surely you've been to London? Du warst doch sicherlich schon in London? ▷ The church is open on Sundays, surely? Die Kirche ist sonntags doch sicherlich geöffnet?

surf n Brandung f
▶ vb surfen [38] (perf hat gesurft); **to surf the Net** im Internet surfen [38]

surface n Oberfläche f

surfboard n Surfbrett nt (pl Surfbretter)

surfing n Surfen nt; **to go surfing** surfen gehen [29]

surgeon n Chirurg m (gen Chirurgen, pl Chirurgen), Chirurgin f ▷ She's a surgeon. Sie ist Chirurgin.

surgery n (doctor's surgery) Arztpraxis f (pl Arztpraxen); **surgery hours** die Sprechstunden

surname n Nachname m (gen Nachnamens, pl Nachnamen)

surprise n Überraschung f

surprised adj überrascht ▷ I was surprised to see him. Ich war überrascht, ihn zu sehen.

surprising adj überraschend

surrender vb sich ergeben [28] (pres ergibt sich, imperf ergab sich, perf hat sich ergeben)

surrogate mother n Leihmutter f (pl Leihmütter)

surround vb umstellen [4] (perf hat umstellt) ▷ The police surrounded the house. Die Polizei hat das Haus umstellt. ▷ You're surrounded! Sie sind umstellt!; **surrounded by** umgeben von

surroundings npl Umgebung fsg ▷ a hotel in beautiful surroundings ein Hotel in wunderschöner Umgebung

survey n (research) Umfrage f

sure adj sicher ▷ Are you sure? Bist du sicher?;

survive vb überleben [**18**] (perf hat überlebt)

survivor n Überlebende m (gen Überlebenden, pl Überlebenden), Überlebende f (gen Überlebenden) ▷ *There were no survivors.* Es gab keine Überlebenden.

suspect vb verdächtigen [**84**] (perf hat verdächtigt)
▶ n Verdächtige m (gen Verdächtigen, pl Verdächtigen), Verdächtige f (gen Verdächtigen) ▷ *a suspect (man)* ein Verdächtiger

suspend vb ❶ (from school) verweisen (imperf verwies, perf hat verwiesen) ▷ *He was suspended.* Er wurde von der Schule verwiesen. ❷ (from team) sperren [**38**] ❸ (from job) suspendieren [**76**] (perf hat suspendiert)

suspense n ❶ (waiting) Ungewissheit f ▷ *The suspense was terrible.* Die Ungewissheit war furchtbar. ❷ (in story) Spannung f; **a film with lots of suspense** ein sehr spannender Film

suspicious adj ❶ argwöhnisch ▷ *He was suspicious at first.* Zuerst war er argwöhnisch. ❷ (suspicious-looking) verdächtig ▷ *a suspicious person* eine verdächtige Person

swallow vb schlucken [**48**]

swam vb see **swim**

swan n Schwan m (pl Schwäne)

swap vb tauschen [**48**] ▷ *Do you want to swap?* Willst du tauschen?; **to swap an apple for a sweet** einen Apfel für ein Bonbon eintauschen [**4**]

swear vb ❶ (make an oath) schwören (imperf schwor, perf hat geschworen) ❷ (curse) fluchen [**38**]

swearword n Kraftausdruck m (pl Kraftausdrücke)

sweat n Schweiß m (gen Schweißes)
▶ vb schwitzen [**36**]

sweater n Pullover m (pl Pullover)

sweaty adj ❶ (person, face) verschwitzt ▷ *I'm all sweaty.* Ich bin ganz verschwitzt. ❷ (hands) feucht

Swede n (person) Schwede m (gen Schweden, pl Schweden), Schwedin f

Sweden n Schweden nt; **from Sweden** aus Schweden; **to Sweden** nach Schweden

Swedish adj schwedisch; **He's Swedish.** Er ist Schwede.; **She's Swedish.** Sie ist Schwedin.
▶ n (language) Schwedisch nt (gen Schwedischen)

sweep vb fegen [**38**] ▷ *to sweep the floor* den Boden fegen

sweet n ❶ (candy) Bonbon m (pl Bonbons) ▷ *a bag of sweets* eine Tüte Bonbons ❷ (pudding) Nachtisch m ▷ *What sweet did you have?* Was für einen Nachtisch hattest du?
▶ adj ❶ süß ▷ *Isn't she sweet?* Ist sie nicht süß? ❷ (kind) nett ▷ *That was really sweet of you.* Das war wirklich nett von dir.; **sweet and sour pork** Schweinefleisch süß-sauer

sweetcorn n Mais m

swept vb see **sweep**

swerve vb ausscheren [**4**] (perf ist ausgeschert) ▷ *He swerved to avoid the cyclist.* Er scherte aus, um dem Fahrradfahrer auszuweichen.

swim n to go for a swim schwimmen gehen [**29**]
▶ vb schwimmen [**63**] (imperf schwamm, perf ist geschwommen) ▷ *Can you swim?* Kannst du schwimmen? ▷ *She swam across the river.* Sie schwamm über den Fluss.

swimmer n Schwimmer m (pl Schwimmer), Schwimmerin f ▷ *She's a good swimmer.* Sie ist eine gute Schwimmerin.

swimming n Schwimmen nt; **to go swimming** schwimmen gehen [**29**]; **Do you like swimming?** Schwimmst du gern?; **a swimming cap** eine

swimsuit n Badeanzug m (pl Badeanzüge); **a swimming costume** ein Badeanzug m; **a swimming pool** ein Schwimmbad nt; **swimming trunks** die Badehose sg

swimsuit n Badeanzug m (pl Badeanzüge)

swing n (in playground, garden) Schaukel f
▶ vb schaukeln [34]

swipe vb ❶ klauen [38] (informal) ▷ The pickpocket swiped my wallet. Der Taschendieb klaute mir die Brieftasche. ❷ wischen [48] (on phone) ▷ Swipe the screen to unlock. Zum Entsperren über den Screen wischen.

Swiss adj Schweizer ▷ I like Swiss cheese. Ich mag Schweizer Käse.; **Andreas is Swiss.** Andreas ist Schweizer.; **Claudie is Swiss.** Claudie ist Schweizerin.
▶ n (person) Schweizer m (pl Schweizer), Schweizerin f; **the Swiss** die Schweizer

switch n (for light, radio etc) Schalter m (pl Schalter)
▶ vb tauschen [48] ▷ to switch A for B A gegen B tauschen

switch off vb ausschalten [2] (perf hat ausgeschaltet)

switch on vb anschalten [2] (perf hat angeschaltet)

Switzerland n Schweiz f (gen Schweiz)

Note that the definite article is used in German for countries which are feminine.

from Switzerland aus der Schweiz; **in Switzerland** in der Schweiz; **to Switzerland** in die Schweiz

swollen adj (arm, leg) geschwollen

swop vb tauschen [48] ▷ Do you want to swop? Willst du tauschen?; **to swop an apple for a sweet** einen Apfel für ein Bonbon eintauschen [4]

sword n Schwert nt (pl Schwerter)

swore vb see swear

sworn vb see swear

swot vb (informal) pauken [38] ▷ I'll have to swot for the maths exam. Ich muss für die Matheprüfung pauken.
▶ n (informal) Streber m (pl Streber), Streberin f

swum vb see swim

swung vb see swing

syllabus n Lehrplan m (pl Lehrpläne)
▷ on the syllabus auf dem Lehrplan

symbol n Symbol nt (pl Symbole)

sympathetic adj verständnisvoll

Be careful not to translate **sympathetic** by sympathisch.

sympathize vb **to sympathize with somebody** (pity) Mitgefühl mit jemandem haben [32]

sympathy n Mitleid nt

symptom n Symptom nt

syringe n Spritze f

system n System nt (pl Systeme)

table n Tisch m (pl Tische) ▷ *to lay the table* den Tisch decken
tablecloth n Tischdecke f
tablespoon n Esslöffel m (pl Esslöffel) ▷ *a tablespoon of sugar* ein Esslöffel Zucker
tablespoonful n a tablespoonful of sugar ein Esslöffel Zucker
tablet n ❶ (medicine) Tablette f ❷ (computer) Tablet nt (pl Tablets)
table tennis n Tischtennis nt (gen Tischtennis) ▷ *to play table tennis* Tischtennis spielen
tact n Takt m
tactful adj taktvoll
tactics npl Taktik f sg
tadpole n Kaulquappe f
tag n (label) Etikett nt (pl Etiketts)
tail n Schwanz m (gen Schwanzes, pl Schwänze); **Heads or tails?** Kopf oder Zahl?
tailor n Schneider m (pl Schneider), Schneiderin f ▷ *He's a tailor.* Er ist Schneider.

take vb ❶ nehmen [52] (pres nimmt, imperf nahm, perf hat genommen) ▷ *He took a plate from the cupboard.* Er nahm einen Teller aus dem Schrank. ▷ *We took a taxi.* Wir haben ein Taxi genommen. ❷ (take along) mitnehmen [52] (pres nimmt mit, imperf nahm mit, perf hat mitgenommen) ▷ *Are you taking your camera?* Nimmst du deine Kamera mit? ▷ *Don't take anything valuable with you.* Nehmen Sie nichts Wertvolles mit. ▷ *He goes to London every week, but he never takes me.* Er fährt jede Woche nach London, aber er nimmt mich nie mit. ▷ *Do you take your exercise books home?* Nehmt ihr eure Hefte mit nach Hause? ❸ (to a certain place) bringen [13] (imperf brachte, perf hat gebracht) ▷ *She always takes him to school.* Sie bringt ihn immer zur Schule. ▷ *I'm taking my coat to the cleaner's.* Ich bringe meinen Mantel in die Reinigung. ❹ (require) brauchen [48] ▷ *She always takes hours to get ready.* Sie braucht immer Stunden, bis sie fertig ist. ▷ *It takes five people to do this job.* Für diese Arbeit braucht man fünf Leute. ▷ *That takes a lot of courage.* Dazu braucht man viel Mut.; **It takes a lot of money to do that.** Das kostet viel Geld. ❺ (last) dauern [88] ▷ *The journey took three hours.* Die Fahrt dauerte drei Stunden. ▷ *It won't take long.* Das dauert nicht lange. ❻ (tolerate) ertragen [77] (pres erträgt, imperf ertrug, perf hat ertragen) ▷ *He can't take being criticized.* Er kann es nicht ertragen, kritisiert zu werden. ❼ (exam, test, subject) machen [48] ▷ *Have you taken your driving test yet?* Hast du deine Fahrprüfung schon gemacht? ▷ *I'm taking German instead of French.* Ich mache Deutsch statt Französisch.
take after vb nachschlagen [59] (pres schlägt nach, imperf schlug nach, perf hat nachgeschlagen)

ENGLISH > GERMAN

take apart vb to take something apart etwas auseinandernehmen [52]
take away vb ❶ (object) wegnehmen [52] (pres nimmt weg, imperf nahm weg, perf hat weggenommen)
❷ (person) wegbringen [13] (imperf brachte weg, perf hat weggebracht)
take back vb zurückbringen [13] (imperf brachte zurück, perf hat zurückgebracht)
take down vb herunternehmen [52] (pres nimmt herunter, imperf nahm herunter, perf hat heruntergenommen)
take in vb (understand) verstehen [72] (imperf verstand, perf hat verstanden)
take off vb ❶ (plane) abfliegen [25] (imperf flog ab, perf ist abgeflogen)
❷ (clothes) ausziehen [96] (imperf zog aus, perf hat ausgezogen)
take out vb (from container, pocket) herausnehmen [52] (pres nimmt heraus, imperf nahm heraus, perf hat herausgenommen)
take over vb übernehmen [52] (pres übernimmt, imperf übernahm, perf hat übernommen)
takeaway n ❶ (meal) Essen zum Mitnehmen nt (pl Essen zum Mitnehmen) ❷ (shop) Imbissstube f ▷ a Chinese takeaway eine chinesische Imbissstube
takeoff n (of plane) Abflug m (pl Abflüge)
tale n (story) Geschichte f
talent n Talent nt (pl Talente) ▷ She's got lots of talent. Sie hat sehr viel Talent.; **to have a talent for** something eine Begabung für etwas haben [32]; **He's got a real talent for languages.** Er ist wirklich sprachbegabt.
talented adj begabt
talk n ❶ (speech) Vortrag m (pl Vorträge) ▷ She gave a talk on rock climbing. Sie hielt einen Vortrag über das Klettern.
❷ (conversation) Gespräch nt (pl Gespräche) ▷ We had a talk about her problems. Wir hatten ein Gespräch über ihre Probleme.; **I had a talk with my Mum about it.** Ich habe mit meiner Mutti darüber gesprochen. ❸ (gossip) Gerede nt ▷ It's just talk. Das ist nur Gerede.
▶ vb reden [54] ▷ We talked about the weather. Wir haben über das Wetter geredet.; **to talk something over with somebody** etwas mit jemandem besprechen [70]
talkative adj redselig
tall adj ❶ (person, tree) groß ▷ They've cut down the tallest tree in the park. Sie haben den größten Baum im Park gefällt. ▷ He's two metres tall. Er ist zwei Meter groß. ❷ (building) hoch

> Before a noun or after an article, use **hohe**.

▷ a tall building ein hohes Gebäude
tame adj (animal) zahm
tampon n Tampon m (pl Tampons)
tan n She's got a lovely tan. Sie ist schön braun.
tangerine n Mandarine f
tank n ❶ (for water, petrol) Tank m (pl Tanks) ❷ (military) Panzer m (pl Panzer); **a fish tank** ein Aquarium nt
tanker n ❶ (ship) Tanker m (pl Tanker) ▷ an oil tanker ein Öltanker ❷ (truck) Tankwagen m (pl Tankwagen) ▷ a petrol tanker ein Benzintankwagen
tap n ❶ (water tap) Wasserhahn m (pl Wasserhähne) ❷ (gentle blow) Klaps m (pl Klapse)
tap-dancing n Stepptanzen nt; **I do tap-dancing.** Ich mache Stepptanz.
tape n (sticky tape) Klebstreifen m (pl Klebstreifen)
tape measure n Maßband nt (pl Maßbänder)
target n Ziel nt (pl Ziele)
tart n Kuchen m (pl Kuchen) ▷ an apple tart ein Apfelkuchen

tartan adj im Schottenkaro ▷ *a tartan scarf* ein Schal im Schottenkaro

task n Aufgabe f

taste n Geschmack m (pl Geschmäcke) ▷ *It's got a really strange taste.* Es hat einen sehr eigenartigen Geschmack. ▷ *She has good taste.* Sie hat einen guten Geschmack.; **a joke in bad taste** ein geschmackloser Witz; **Would you like a taste?** Möchtest du mal probieren?
▶ vb ❶ probieren [76] (perf hat probiert) ▷ *Would you like to taste it?* Möchtest du mal probieren? ❷ schmecken [48] ▷ *You can taste the garlic in it.* Man kann den Knoblauch schmecken.; **to taste of something** nach etwas schmecken [48]

tasty adj schmackhaft

tattoo n Tätowierung f

taught vb see **teach**

Taurus n Stier m ▷ *I'm Taurus.* Ich bin Stier.

tax n (on goods, income) Steuer f

taxi n Taxi nt (pl Taxis) ▷ *a taxi driver* ein Taxifahrer

taxi rank n Taxistand m (pl Taxistände)

TB n (= tuberculosis) TB f (= Tuberkulose)

tea n ❶ Tee m (pl Tees) ▷ *a cup of tea* eine Tasse Tee

* Usually, tea is not drunk with milk
* and sugar in Germany, but is served
* with lemon, and is referred to as
* **Schwarztee**. Fruit teas and herbal
* teas are also very widespread.

a tea bag ein Teebeutel m ❷ (evening meal) Abendessen nt (pl Abendessen) ▷ *We were having tea.* Wir saßen beim Abendessen.

teach vb ❶ beibringen [13] (imperf brachte bei, perf hat beigebracht) ▷ *My sister taught me to swim.* Meine Schwester hat mir das Schwimmen beigebracht.; **That'll teach you!** Das wird dir eine Lehre sein! ❷ (in school) unterrichten [2] (perf hat unterrichtet) ▷ *She teaches physics.* Sie unterrichtet Physik.

teacher n Lehrer m (pl Lehrer), Lehrerin f ▷ *a maths teacher* ein Mathelehrer ▷ *She's a teacher.* Sie ist Lehrerin. ▷ *He's a primary school teacher.* Er ist Grundschullehrer.

team n Mannschaft f ▷ *a football team* eine Fußballmannschaft ▷ *She was in my team.* Sie war in meiner Mannschaft.

teapot n Teekanne f

tear n Träne f ▷ *She was in tears.* Sie war in Tränen aufgelöst.
▶ vb zerreißen (imperf zerriss, perf hat/ist zerrissen) ▷ *Mind you don't tear the page.* Pass auf, dass du die Seite nicht zerreißt.

> For the perfect tense use **haben** when the verb has an object and **sein** when there is no object.

▷ *You've torn your shirt.* Du hast dein Hemd zerrissen. ▷ *Your shirt is torn.* Dein Hemd ist zerrissen. ▷ *It won't tear, it's very strong.* Es zerreißt nicht, es ist sehr stark.; **to tear up** zerreißen

tease vb ❶ (unkindly) quälen [38] ▷ *Stop teasing that poor animal!* Hör auf, das arme Tier zu quälen! ❷ (jokingly) necken [48] ▷ *He's teasing you.* Er neckt dich nur.; **I was only teasing.** Ich habe nur einen Scherz gemacht.

teaspoon n Teelöffel m (pl Teelöffel) ▷ *a teaspoon of sugar* ein Teelöffel Zucker

teaspoonful n **a teaspoonful of sugar** ein Teelöffel Zucker

teatime n (in evening) Abendessenszeit f ▷ *It was nearly teatime.* Es war fast Abendessenszeit.; **Teatime!** Abendessen!

tea towel n Geschirrtuch nt (pl Geschirrtücher)

technical adj technisch; **a technical college** eine Fachhochschule

technician n Techniker m (pl Techniker), Technikerin f

ENGLISH > GERMAN

technological adj technologisch

technology n Technologie f

teddy bear n Teddybär m (gen Teddybären, pl Teddybären)

teenage adj ❶ für Teenager ▷ *a teenage magazine* eine Zeitschrift für Teenager ❷ (boys, girls) heranwachsend ▷ *She has two teenage daughters.* Sie hat zwei heranwachsende Töchter.

teenager n Teenager m (pl Teenager) ▪ der Teenager is also used for girls.

teens npl *She's in her teens.* Sie ist ein Teenager.

tee-shirt n T-Shirt nt (pl T-Shirts)

teeth see tooth

teleconferencing n Telekonferenzen fpl

telephone n Telefon nt (pl Telefone) ▷ *on the telephone* am Telefon; **a telephone box** eine Telefonzelle; **a telephone call** ein Anruf m; **the telephone directory** das Telefonbuch; **a telephone number** eine Telefonnummer

telescope n Teleskop nt (pl Teleskope)

television n Fernsehen nt; **on television** im Fernsehen; **a television programme** eine Fernsehsendung

tell vb sagen [38]; **to tell somebody something** jemandem etwas sagen [38]; **to tell somebody to do something** jemandem sagen [38], er solle etwas tun; **to tell lies** lügen [47]; **to tell a story** eine Geschichte erzählen [19]; **I can't tell the difference between them.** Ich kann sie nicht unterscheiden.

tell off vb schimpfen [38]

telly n Fernseher m (pl Fernseher); **to watch telly** fernsehen [64]; **on telly** im Fernsehen

temper n **to be in a temper** wütend sein [65]; **to lose one's temper** wütend werden [91]; **He's got a terrible temper.** Er ist furchtbar jähzornig.

495 | terminally

temperature n (of oven, water, person) Temperatur f; **The temperature was thirty degrees.** Es waren dreißig Grad.; **to have a temperature** Fieber haben [32]

temple n Tempel m (pl Tempel)

temporary adj vorläufig

temptation n Versuchung f

tempting adj verlockend

ten num zehn ▷ *She's ten.* Sie ist zehn.

tend vb **to tend to do something** dazu neigen [38], etwas zu tun

tennis n Tennis nt (gen Tennis) ▷ *Do you play tennis?* Spielst du Tennis?; **a tennis ball** ein Tennisball m; **a tennis court** ein Tennisplatz m

tennis player n Tennisspieler m (pl Tennisspieler), Tennisspielerin f ▷ *He's a tennis player.* Er ist Tennisspieler.

tenor n Tenor m (pl Tenöre)

tenpin bowling n Bowling nt; **to go tenpin bowling** Bowling spielen [38]

tense adj angespannt ▷ *a tense situation* eine angespannte Situation ▶ n **the present tense** das Präsens; **the future tense** das Futur

tension n Spannung f

tent n Zelt nt (pl Zelte)

tenth adj zehnte ▷ *the tenth floor* der zehnte Stock ▷ *the tenth of August* der zehnte August

term n (at school) Trimester nt (pl Trimester)

⁃ In Germany the school and university
⁃ year is divided into two semesters
⁃ rather than three terms.

to come to terms with something sich mit etwas abfinden [24]

terminal adj (illness, patient) unheilbar ▶ n (of computer) Terminal nt (pl Terminals); **an oil terminal** ein Ölterminal m; **an air terminal** ein Terminal m

terminally adv **to be terminally ill** unheilbar krank sein [65]

terrace n ❶ (patio) Terrasse f ❷ (row of houses) Häuserreihe f; **the terraces** (at stadium) die Ränge

terraced adj **a terraced house** ein Reihenhaus nt

terrible adj furchtbar ▷ My German is terrible. Mein Deutsch ist furchtbar.

terribly adv furchtbar ▷ He suffered terribly. Er litt furchtbar. ▷ I'm terribly sorry. Es tut mir furchtbar leid.

terrific adj (wonderful) super

■ super is invariable.

▷ That's terrific! Das ist super! ▷ You look terrific! Du siehst super aus!

terrified adj **I was terrified!** Ich hatte furchtbare Angst!

terrorism n Terrorismus m (gen Terrorismus)

terrorist n Terrorist m (gen Terroristen, pl Terroristen), Terroristin f; **a terrorist attack** ein Terrorangriff m

test n ❶ (at school) Arbeit f ▷ I've got a test tomorrow. Ich schreibe morgen eine Arbeit. ❷ (trial, check) Test m (pl Tests) ▷ nuclear tests Atomtests ❸ (medical) Untersuchung f ▷ a blood test eine Blutuntersuchung f ▷ They're going to do some more tests tomorrow. Sie machen morgen noch weitere Untersuchungen.; **driving test** die Fahrprüfung

▶ vb ❶ probieren [76] (perf hat probiert); **to test something out** etwas ausprobieren [4] ❷ (class) abfragen [4] (perf hat abgefragt) ▷ He tested us on the new vocabulary. Er hat uns die neuen Wörter abgefragt.; **She was tested for drugs.** Man hat bei ihr einen Drogentest gemacht.

test tube n Reagenzglas nt (gen Reagenzglases, pl Reagenzgläser)

text n ❶ (text message) SMS f (pl SMS)

▶ vb eine SMS schicken [48] ▷ I'll text you. Ich schicke dir eine SMS.

textbook n Lehrbuch nt (pl Lehrbücher); **a German textbook** ein Deutschbuch

textiles npl Textilien fpl; **a textiles factory** eine Textilfabrik

text message n SMS f (pl SMS)

text messaging n Versenden von SMS nt

Thames n Themse f

than conj als ▷ She's taller than me. Sie ist größer als ich. ▷ I've got more books than him. Ich habe mehr Bücher als er. ▷ **more than ten years** mehr als zehn Jahre ▷ **more than once** mehr als einmal

thank vb sich bedanken [7] bei (perf hat sich bedankt) ▷ Don't forget to write and thank them. Vergiss nicht, ihnen zu schreiben und dich bei ihnen zu bedanken.; **thank you** danke; **thank you very much** vielen Dank

thanks excl danke; **thanks to** dank

that adj, pron, conj ❶ dieser ▷ that man dieser Mann; diese ▷ that woman diese Frau; dieses ▷ that book dieses Buch; **that one (1)** (masculine) der da ▷ This man? — Nein, der da. **(2)** (feminine) die da ▷ This woman? — No, that one. Diese Frau? — Nein, die da. **(3)** (neuter) das da ▷ Do you like this photo? — No, I prefer that one. Gefällt dir dieses Foto? — Nein, das da gefällt mir besser. ❷ das ▷ Did you see that? Hast du das gesehen? ▷ What's that? Was ist das? ▷ Who's that? Wer ist das? ▷ Is that you? Bist du das?; **That's ...** Das ist ... ▷ That's my German teacher. Das ist meine Deutschlehrerin.; **That's what he said.** Das hat er gesagt.

■ In relative clauses use **der**, **die** or **das**, depending on the gender of the noun 'that' refers to.

❸ der ▷ the man that saw us der Mann, der uns sah; die ▷ the woman that saw us die Frau, die uns sah; das ▷ the child that saw us das Kind, das uns sah; die ▷ the people that helped us die Leute, die uns geholfen haben ❹ dass ▷ He thought that Henry was ill. Er dachte, dass Henry krank war. ▷ *I know that she likes chocolate.* Ich weiß, dass sie Schokolade mag. ❸ so ▷ *It was that big.* Es war so groß. ▷ *It's about that high.* Es ist etwa so hoch. ▷ *It's not that difficult.* Es ist nicht so schwierig.

the *art*

> Use **der** with a masculine noun, **die** with a feminine noun, and **das** with a neuter noun. For plural nouns always use **die**.

❶ der ▷ *the boy* der Junge; die ▷ *the orange* die Orange; das ▷ *the girl* das Mädchen ❷ die ▷ *the children* die Kinder

theatre *n* Theater *nt* (*pl* Theater)

theft *n* Diebstahl *m* (*pl* Diebstähle)

their *adj* ihr ▷ *their father* ihr Vater ▷ *their mother* ihre Mutter ▷ *their child* ihr Kind ▷ *their parents* ihre Eltern

> Do not use **ihr** with parts of the body.

▷ *They can't bend their arms.* Sie können die Arme nicht bewegen.

theirs *pron* ❶ ihrer ▷ *This is our computer, not theirs.* Das ist unser Computer, nicht ihrer.
ihre ▷ *It's not our garage, it's theirs.* Das ist nicht unsere Garage, sondern ihre.
ihres ▷ *It's not our car, it's theirs.* Das ist nicht unser Auto, sondern ihres. ❷ ihre ▷ *These are not our ideas, they're theirs.* Das sind nicht unsere Ideen, sondern ihre.; **Is this theirs?** Gehört das ihnen?

them *pron* ❶ sie ▷ *I didn't see them.* Ich habe sie nicht gesehen.

> Use **sie** after prepositions which take the accusative.

▷ *It's for them.* Es ist für sie. ❷ ihnen

> Use **ihnen** when 'them' means 'to them'.

▷ *I gave them some brochures.* Ich habe ihnen ein paar Broschüren gegeben. ▷ *I told them the truth.* Ich habe ihnen die Wahrheit gesagt.

> Use **ihnen** after prepositions which take the dative.

▷ *Ann and Sophie came. Graham was with them.* Ann und Sophie sind gekommen. Graham war bei ihnen.

themselves *pron* ❶ sich ▷ *Did they hurt themselves?* Haben sie sich verletzt?
❷ selbst ▷ *They did it themselves.* Sie haben es selbst gemacht.

then *adv, conj* ❶ dann ▷ *I get dressed. Then I have breakfast.* Ich ziehe mich an. Dann frühstücke ich. ▷ *My pen's run out.* — *Use a pencil then!* Mein Kugelschreiber ist leer. — Dann nimm einen Bleistift!
❷ (*at that time*) damals ▷ *There was no electricity then.* Damals gab es keinen Strom.; **now and then** ab und zu ▷ *Do you play chess?* — *Now and then.* Spielst du Schach? — Ab und zu.; **By then it was too late.** Da war es schon zu spät.

there *adv*

> Use **dort** when something is in a fixed position, **dorthin** when there is movement involved.

❶ dort ▷ *Can you see that house there? Siehst du das Haus dort?* ▷ *Berlin? I've never been there.* Berlin? Ich war noch nie dort.; **over there** dort drüben; **in there** dort drin; **on there** darauf; **up there** dort oben; **down there** dort unten ❷ dorthin ▷ *Put it there.* Stell es dorthin. ▷ *He went there on Friday.* Er ging am Freitag dorthin.; **There he is!** Da ist er ja!; **There is …** (1) Es ist … ▷ *There's a factory near my house.* In der Nähe von meinem Haus ist eine Fabrik.
(2) Es gibt … ▷ *There is a lot of poverty in the world.* Es gibt viel Armut auf der Welt.; **There are …** (1) Es sind … ▷ *There are five people in my family.* In meiner Familie sind fünf Leute. (2) Es gibt … ▷ *There are many schools in this city.* In dieser Stadt gibt es viele Schulen.; **There has been an accident.** Es hat einen Unfall gegeben.

therefore adv deshalb
there's = there is; there has
thermometer n Thermometer nt (pl Thermometer)
Thermos® n Thermosflasche® f
these adj, pron ❶ diese ▷ these shoes die Schuhe; THESE ones diese Schuhe hier ❷ die hier ▷ I want these! Ich möchte die hier! ▷ I'm looking for some sandals. Can I try these? Ich suche Sandalen. Kann ich die hier anprobieren?
they pron sie ▷ Are there any tickets left? — No, they're all sold. Gibt es noch Karten? — Nein, sie sind schon alle verkauft. ▷ Do you like those shoes? — No, they're horrible. Gefallen dir die Schuhe? — Nein, sie sind furchtbar.; **They say that ...** Man sagt, dass ...
they'd = they had; they would
they'll = they will
they're = they are
they've = they have
thick adj ❶ (not thin) dick ▷ one metre thick einen Meter dick ❷ (stupid) dumm
thief n Dieb m (pl Diebe), Diebin f
thigh n Schenkel m
thin adj dünn
thing n Ding nt (pl Dinge) ▷ beautiful things schöne Dinge ▷ What's that thing called? Wie heißt das Ding da?; **my things** (belongings) meine Sachen; **You poor thing!** (1) (man) Du Armer! (2) (woman) Du Arme!
think vb ❶ denken [14] (imperf dachte, perf hat gedacht) ▷ I think you're wrong. Ich denke, du hast unrecht. ▷ What are you thinking about? Woran denkst du?; **What do you think about the suggestion?** Was halten Sie von dem Vorschlag? ❷ glauben [38] ▷ I don't think I can come. Ich glaube nicht, dass ich kommen kann.; **I think so.** Ich glaube schon.; **I don't think so.** Ich glaube nicht. ❸ (spend time thinking) nachdenken [14] (perf hat nachgedacht) ▷ Think carefully before you reply. Denk gut nach, bevor du antwortest. ▷ I'll think about it. Ich denke darüber nach. ❹ (imagine) sich vorstellen [4] (perf hat sich vorgestellt) ▷ Think what life would be like without cars. Stell dir vor, wie es wäre, wenn es keine Autos gäbe.; **I'll think it over.** Ich werde es mir überlegen.

third adj dritte ▷ the third day der dritte Tag ▷ the third time das dritte Mal ▷ the third of August der dritte August; **He came third.** Er wurde Dritter.
▶ n Drittel nt (pl Drittel) ▷ a third of the population ein Drittel der Bevölkerung
thirdly adv drittens
Third World n Dritte Welt f
thirst n Durst m
thirsty adj to be thirsty Durst haben [32]
thirteen num dreizehn ▷ I'm thirteen. Ich bin dreizehn.
thirteenth adj dreizehnte ▷ the thirteenth of August der dreizehnte August
thirty num dreißig ▷ She's thirty. Sie ist dreißig.
this adj, pron ❶ dieser ▷ this man dieser Mann; diese ▷ this woman diese Frau; dieses ▷ this child dieses Kind; **this one** (1) (masculine) der hier ▷ That man over there? — No, this one. Der Mann dort? — Nein, der hier. (2) (feminine) die hier ▷ That woman over there? — No, this one. Die Frau dort? — Nein, die hier. (3) (neuter) das hier ▷ I don't like that picture over there, I prefer this one. Das Bild dort gefällt mir nicht, das hier gefällt mir besser. ❷ das ▷ You see this? Siehst du das? ▷ What's this? Was ist das? ▷ This is my mother. (introduction) Das ist meine Mutter.; **This is Gavin speaking.** (on the phone) Hier spricht Gavin.
thistle n Distel f
thorough adj gründlich ▷ She's very thorough. Sie ist sehr gründlich.

those adj, pron ❶ diese ▷ *those shoes* diese Schuhe.; **THOSE shoes** diese Schuhe dort ❷ die da ▷ *I want those!* Ich möchte die da! ▷ *I'm looking for some sandals. Can I try those?* Ich suche Sandalen. Kann ich die da anprobieren?

though conj, adv obwohl ▷ *It's warm, though it's raining.* Es ist warm, obwohl es regnet.; **He's nice, though not very clever.** Er ist nett, aber nicht besonders klug.

thought vb see **think**
▶ n (idea) Gedanke m (gen Gedankens, pl Gedanken) ▷ *I've just had a thought.* Mir ist eben ein Gedanke gekommen.; **It was a nice thought, thank you.** Das war nett, vielen Dank.; **It's the thought that counts.** Es war gut gemeint.

thoughtful adj ❶ (deep in thought) nachdenklich ▷ *You look thoughtful.* Du siehst nachdenklich aus. ❷ (considerate) aufmerksam ▷ *She's very thoughtful.* Sie ist sehr aufmerksam.

thoughtless adj gedankenlos

thousand num a **thousand** eintausend; **two thousand pounds** zweitausend Pfund; **thousands of people** Tausende von Menschen

thousandth adj tausendste

thread n Faden m (pl Fäden)

threat n Drohung f

threaten vb drohen [38] ▷ *He threatened me.* Er hat mir gedroht. ▷ *to threaten to do something* drohen, etwas zu tun

three num drei ▷ *She's three.* Sie ist drei.

three-piece suite n dreiteilige Polstergarnitur f

threw vb see **throw**

thrilled adj **I was thrilled.** (pleased) Ich habe mich unheimlich gefreut.

thriller n Thriller m (pl Thriller)

thrilling adj spannend

throat n Hals m (gen Halses, pl Hälse); **to have a sore throat** Halsweh haben [32]

through prep, adj, adv durch ▷ *through the window* durch das Fenster ▷ *to go through Leeds* durch Leeds fahren ▷ *to go through a tunnel* durch einen Tunnel fahren; **I know her through my sister.** Ich kenne sie über meine Schwester.; **The window was dirty and I couldn't see through.** Das Fenster war schmutzig, und ich konnte nicht durchsehen.; **a through train** ein durchgehender Zug; **'no through road'** 'keine Durchfahrt'

throughout prep **throughout Britain** in ganz Großbritannien; **throughout the year** das ganze Jahr über

throw vb werfen [92] (pres wirft, imperf warf, perf hat geworfen) ▷ *He threw the ball to me.* Er warf mir den Ball zu.; **to throw a party** eine Party machen [48]; **That really threw him.** Das hat ihn aus der Fassung gebracht.; **to throw away (1)** (rubbish) wegwerfen [92] **(2)** (chance) vergeben [28]; **to throw out (1)** (throw away) wegwerfen [92] **(2)** (person) rauswerfen [92] ▷ *I threw him out.* Ich habe ihn rausgeworfen.; **to throw up** sich übergeben [28]

thumb n Daumen m (pl Daumen)

thumb tack n (US) Reißzwecke f

thump vb **to thump somebody** (informal) jemandem eine verpassen [7]

thunder n Donner m (pl Donner)

thunderstorm n Gewitter nt (pl Gewitter)

Thursday n Donnerstag m (pl Donnerstage) ▷ *on Thursday* am Donnerstag ▷ *every Thursday* jeden Donnerstag ▷ *last Thursday* letzten Donnerstag ▷ *next Thursday* nächsten Donnerstag; **on Thursdays** donnerstags

tick n ❶ (mark) Häkchen nt (pl Häkchen) ❷ (of clock) Ticken nt; **in a tick** in einer Sekunde
▶ vb ❶ ankreuzen [36] (perf hat

angekreuzt) ▷ *Tick the appropriate box.* Kreuzen Sie das entsprechende Kästchen an. ❷ *(clock)* ticken [**48**]; **to tick off (1)** *(on list)* abhaken [**4**] **(2)** *(scold)* ausschimpfen [**4**]

ticket *n* ❶ *(for bus, tube, train)* Fahrkarte *f* ▷ *an underground ticket* eine Fahrkarte für die U-Bahn ❷ *(for plane)* Ticket *nt (pl* Tickets) ❸ *(for theatre, concert, cinema, museum)* Eintrittskarte *f*; **a parking ticket** ein Strafzettel *m*

ticket inspector *n* Fahrscheinkontrolleur *m (pl* Fahrscheinkontrolleure), Fahrscheinkontrolleurin *f*

ticket office *n* ❶ *(for travel)* Fahrkartenschalter *m (pl* Fahrkartenschalter) ❷ *(for theatre, cinema)* Kasse *f*

tickle *vb* kitzeln [**34**]

tide *n* **high tide** die Flut; **low tide** die Ebbe

tidy *adj* ordentlich ▷ *Your room is very tidy.* Dein Zimmer ist sehr ordentlich. ▷ *She's very tidy.* Sie ist sehr ordentlich.
▶ *vb* aufräumen [**4**] *(perf* hat aufgeräumt) ▷ *Go and tidy your room.* Geh und räum dein Zimmer auf.; **to tidy up** aufräumen [**4**]

tie *n (necktie)* Krawatte *f*; **It was a tie.** *(in sport)* Es gab ein Unentschieden.
▶ *vb* ❶ *(ribbon, shoelaces)* zubinden *(imperf* band zu, *perf* hat zugebunden); **I tied a knot in the rope.** Ich machte einen Knoten in das Seil. ❷ *(in sport)* unentschieden spielen [**38**]; **They tied three all.** Sie haben drei zu drei gespielt.; **to tie up (1)** *(parcel)* zuschnüren [**4**] **(2)** *(dog, boat)* anbinden **(3)** *(prisoner)* fesseln [**34**]

tiger *n* Tiger *m (pl* Tiger)

tight *adj* ❶ *(tight-fitting)* eng ▷ *tight jeans* enge Jeans ❷ *(too tight)* zu eng ▷ *This dress is a bit tight.* Das Kleid ist etwas zu eng.

tighten *vb* ❶ *(rope)* spannen [**38**] ❷ *(screw)* anziehen [**96**] *(imperf* zog an, *perf* hat angezogen)

tightly *adv (hold)* fest

tights *npl* Strumpfhose *fsg* ▷ *a pair of tights* eine Strumpfhose

tile *n* ❶ *(on roof)* Dachziegel *m (pl* Dachziegel) ❷ *(on wall, floor)* Fliese *f*

till *n* Kasse *f*
▶ *prep, conj* ❶ bis ▷ *I waited till ten o'clock.* Ich habe bis zehn Uhr gewartet.; **till now** bis jetzt; **till then** bis dann ❷ vor

Use **vor** if the sentence you want to translate contains a negative such as 'not' or 'never'.

▷ *It won't be ready till next week.* Vor nächster Woche wird es nicht fertig.
▷ *Till last year I'd never been to Germany.* Vor letztem Jahr war ich nie in Deutschland.

time *n* ❶ Zeit *f* ▷ *It's time to get up.* Es ist Zeit zum Aufstehen. ▷ *It was two o'clock, German time.* Es war zwei Uhr, deutsche Zeit. ▷ *I'm sorry, I haven't got time.* Ich habe leider keine Zeit.; **What time is it?** Wie viel Uhr ist es?; **What time do you get up?** Um wie viel Uhr stehst du auf?; **on time** pünktlich; **from time to time** von Zeit zu Zeit; **in time** rechtzeitig; **just in time** gerade noch rechtzeitig; **in no time** im Nu ❷ *(moment)* Moment *m (pl* Momente) ▷ *This isn't a good time to ask him.* Das ist kein guter Moment, um ihn zu fragen.; **for the time being** momentan ❸ *(occasion)* Mal *nt (pl* Male) ▷ *next time* nächstes Mal; **this time** diesmal; **two at a time** jeweils zwei; **How many times?** Wie oft?; **at times** manchmal; **a long time** lange; **in a week's time** in einer Woche; **Come and see us any time.** Besuchen sie uns, wann Sie wollen.; **to have a good time** sich amüsieren [**76**]; **two times two** zwei mal zwei

ENGLISH > GERMAN

time off n Freizeit f

timetable n ① (for train, bus) Fahrplan m (pl Fahrpläne) ② (at school) Stundenplan m (pl Stundenpläne)

tin n ① Dose f ▷ a tin of beans eine Dose Bohnen ▷ a biscuit tin eine Keksdose ② (type of metal) Zinn nt

tin opener n Dosenöffner m (pl Dosenöffner)

tiny adj winzig

tip n ① (money) Trinkgeld nt (pl Trinkgelder) ▷ Shall I give him a tip? Soll ich ihm ein Trinkgeld geben? ② (advice) Tipp m (pl Tipps) ▷ a useful tip ein guter Tipp ③ (end) Spitze f; **It's on the tip of my tongue.** Es liegt mir auf der Zunge.; **a rubbish tip** eine Müllkippe; **This place is a complete tip!** (informal) Was für ein Saustall!

▶ vb **to tip somebody** jemandem ein Trinkgeld geben [28]

tipsy adj beschwipst ▷ I'm feeling a bit tipsy. Ich bin etwas beschwipst.

tiptoe n on tiptoe auf Zehenspitzen

tired adj müde ▷ I'm tired. Ich bin müde.; **to be tired of something** etwas leid sein [65]

tiring adj ermüdend

tissue n Papiertaschentuch nt (pl Papiertaschentücher) ▷ Have you got a tissue? Hast du ein Papiertaschentuch?

title n Titel m (pl Titel)

to prep ① nach ▷ to go to Munich nach München fahren ▷ We went to Italy. Wir sind nach Italien gefahren. ▷ the train to London der Zug nach London ▷ the road to Edinburgh die Straße nach Edinburgh ▷ to the left nach links; **I've never been to Munich.** Ich war noch nie in München. ② in ▷ to go to school in die Schule gehen ▷ to go to the theatre ins Theater gehen ③ zu

Use **zu** when you talk about going to a particular place or person.
▷ We drove to the station. Wir fuhren zum Bahnhof. ▷ to go to the doctor's zum Arzt gehen ▷ to go to the baker's zum Bäcker gehen ▷ Let's go to Anne's house. Lass uns zu Anne nach Hause gehen.; **a letter to his mother** ein Brief an seine Mutter; **It's hard to say.** Es ist schwer zu sagen.; **It's easy to criticize.** Es ist leicht zu kritisieren.; **something to drink** etwas zu trinken ④ (as far as, until) bis ▷ to count to ten bis zehn zählen ▷ It's ninety kilometres to the border. Es sind neunzig Kilometer bis zur Grenze.; **from ... to** von ... bis; **ten to nine** zehn vor neun

Use the dative when you say or give something to somebody.
▷ Give it to me! Gib es mir! ▷ That's what he said to me. Das ist, was er zu mir gesagt hat.; **to talk to somebody** mit jemandem reden [54]

When 'to' is used with the infinitive, it is often not translated.
▷ I'd like to go. Ich würde gern gehen. ⑤ (in order to) um ... zu

um ... zu is used with the infinitive.
▷ I did it to help you. Ich tat es, um dir zu helfen. ▷ She's too young to go to school. Sie ist noch zu jung, um in die Schule zu gehen.; **the key to the front door** der Schlüssel für die Haustür; **the answer to the question** die Antwort auf die Frage

toad n Kröte f

toast n ① Toast m (pl Toasts) ▷ a piece of toast eine Scheibe Toast ② (speech) Trinkspruch m (pl Trinksprüche) ▷ to drink a toast to somebody einen Trinkspruch auf jemanden ausbringen

toaster n Toaster m (pl Toaster)

toastie n Toast m (pl Toasts) ▷ a cheese toastie ein Käsetoast

tobacco n Tabak m

tobacconist's n Tabakladen m (pl Tabakläden)

today adv heute ▷ What did you do today? Was hast du heute gemacht?

toddler n Kleinkind nt (pl Kleinkinder)

toe n Zeh m (pl Zehen) ▷ my big toe mein großer Zeh

toffee n Karamell m

together adv ❶ zusammen ▷ Are they still together? Sind sie noch zusammen? ❷ (at the same time) gleichzeitig ▷ Don't all speak together! Redet nicht alle gleichzeitig!; **together with** (with person) zusammen mit

toilet n Toilette f

toilet paper n Toilettenpapier nt

toiletries npl Toilettenartikel mpl

toilet roll n Rolle Toilettenpapier f

told vb see **tell**

toll n (on bridge, motorway) Benutzungsgebühr f

tomato n Tomate f ▷ tomato soup die Tomatensuppe

tomorrow adv morgen ▷ tomorrow morning morgen früh ▷ tomorrow night morgen Abend; **the day after tomorrow** übermorgen

ton n Tonne f ▷ That old bike weighs a ton. Das alte Fahrrad wiegt ja eine Tonne.

tongue n Zunge f; **to say something tongue in cheek** etwas nicht so ernst meinen [38]

tonic n (tonic water) Tonic nt (pl Tonics); **a gin and tonic** ein Gin Tonic m

tonight adv ❶ (this evening) heute Abend ▷ Are you going out tonight? Gehst du heute Abend aus? ❷ (during the night) heute Nacht ▷ I'll sleep well tonight. Ich werde heute Nacht gut schlafen.

tonsillitis n Mandelentzündung f ▷ She's got tonsillitis. Sie hat eine Mandelentzündung.

tonsils npl Mandeln fpl

too adv, adj ❶ (as well) auch ▷ My sister came too. Meine Schwester ist auch mitgekommen. ❷ (excessively) zu ▷ The water's too hot. Das Wasser ist zu heiß. ▷ We arrived too late. Wir sind zu spät gekommen.; **too much** zu viel; **too many** zu viele; **Too bad!** Da kann man nichts machen!

took vb see **take**

tool n Werkzeug nt (pl Werkzeuge); **a tool box** ein Werkzeugkasten m

tooth n Zahn m (pl Zähne)

toothache n Zahnschmerzen mpl ▷ to have toothache Zahnschmerzen haben

toothbrush n Zahnbürste f

toothpaste n Zahnpasta f (pl Zahnpasten)

top n ❶ (of tree) Spitze f ❷ (of mountain) Gipfel m (pl Gipfel) ❸ (of garment) Oberteil nt (pl Oberteile) ▷ a bikini top ein Bikinioberteil ❹ (of table) Kopfende nt (pl Kopfenden) ❺ (of box, jar) Deckel m (pl Deckel) ❻ (of bottle) Verschluss m (gen Verschlusses, pl Verschlüsse); **at the top of the page** oben auf der Seite; **to reach the top of the ladder** oben auf der Leiter ankommen [**40**]; **on top of** (on) oben auf; **There's a surcharge on top of that.** Es kommt noch ein Zuschlag dazu.; **from top to bottom** von oben nach unten

▶ adj (first-class) erstklassig ▷ a top hotel ein erstklassiges Hotel; **a top surgeon** ein Spitzenchirurg m; **a top model** (fashion) ein Topmodel nt; **He always gets top marks.** Er bekommt immer Spitzennoten.; **the top floor** der oberste Stock

topic n Thema nt (pl Themen) ▷ The essay can be on any topic. Der Aufsatz kann über ein beliebiges Thema sein.

torch n Taschenlampe f

tortoise n Schildkröte f

torture n Folter f; **It was pure torture.** (informal) Es war die Hölle.

▶ vb quälen [**38**] ▷ Stop torturing that poor animal! Hör auf, das arme Tier zu quälen!

total adj gesamt ▷ the total amount der gesamte Betrag

▶ n ❶ (amount) Gesamtmenge f

ENGLISH > GERMAN

❷ *(money, figures)* Endsumme f; **the grand total** die Gesamtsumme

totally *adv* völlig ▷ *He's totally useless.* Er ist völlig unfähig.

touch *n* to get in touch with somebody sich mit jemandem in Verbindung setzen [**36**]; **to keep in touch with somebody** mit jemandem in Verbindung bleiben [**10**]; **Keep in touch!** Lass von dir hören!; **to lose touch** sich aus den Augen verlieren [**85**]; **to lose touch with somebody** jemanden aus den Augen verlieren [**85**] ▶ *vb* berühren [**18**] *(perf* hat berührt); 'Do not touch' 'Nicht berühren'; **Don't touch that!** Fass das nicht an!

tough *adj* ❶ hart ▷ *It was tough, but I managed OK.* Es war hart, aber ich habe es geschafft. ▷ *It's a tough job.* Das ist eine harte Arbeit. ▷ *He thinks he's a tough guy.* Er meint, er sei ein harter Bursche. ❷ *(meat)* zäh ▷ *The meat's tough.* Das Fleisch ist zäh. ❸ *(strong)* fest ▷ *tough leather gloves* feste Lederhandschuhe; **Tough luck!** Das ist Pech!

tour *n* ❶ *(of town, museum)* Besichtigung f; **We went on a tour of the city.** Wir haben die Stadt besichtigt.; **a guided tour** eine Führung; **a package tour** eine Pauschalreise ❷ *(by singer, group)* Tournee f ▷ *on tour* auf Tournee ▷ *to go on tour* auf Tournee gehen ▶ *vb* Beyoncé's touring Europe. *(singer, artiste)* Beyoncé ist auf Europatournee.

tourism *n* Tourismus m *(gen* Tourismus)

tourist *n* Tourist m *(gen* Touristen, *pl* Touristen), Touristin f; **tourist information office** das Verkehrsbüro

towards *prep* ❶ *(in the direction of)* auf ... zu ▷ *He came towards me.* Er kam auf mich zu. ❷ *(of attitude)* gegenüber ▷ *my feelings towards him* meine Empfindungen ihm gegenüber

towel *n* Handtuch *nt (pl* Handtücher)

tower *n* Turm m *(pl* Türme); **a tower block** ein Hochhaus *nt*

town *n* Stadt f *(pl* Städte); **a town plan** ein Stadtplan *m*; **the town centre** die Stadtmitte; **the town hall** das Rathaus

tow truck *n (US)* Abschleppwagen *m (pl* Abschleppwagen)

toy *n* Spielzeug *nt (pl* Spielzeuge); **a toy shop** ein Spielwarengeschäft *nt*; **a toy car** ein Spielzeugauto *nt*

trace *n* Spur f ▷ *There was no trace of him.* Von ihm fehlte jede Spur. ▶ *vb (draw)* nachziehen [**96**] *(imperf* zog nach, *perf* hat nachgezogen)

tracing paper *n* Pauspapier *nt*

track *n* ❶ *(dirt road)* Pfad *m (pl* Pfade) ❷ *(railway line)* Gleis *nt (gen* Gleises, *pl* Gleise) ❸ *(in sport)* Rennbahn f ▷ *two laps of the track* zwei Runden der Rennbahn ❹ *(song)* Stück *nt (pl* Stücke) ▷ *This is my favourite track.* Das ist mein Lieblingsstück. ❺ *(trail)* Spur f ▷ *They followed the tracks for miles.* Sie folgten der Spur meilenweit.

track down *vb* **to track somebody down** jemanden finden [**24**] ▷ *The police never tracked down the killer.* Die Polizei hat den Mörder nie gefunden.

tracksuit *n* Jogginganzug *m (pl* Jogginganzüge)

tractor *n* Traktor *m (pl* Traktoren)

trade *n (skill, job)* Handwerk *nt* ▷ **to learn a trade** ein Handwerk erlernen

trade union *n* Gewerkschaft f
- Unions in Germany are organized
- within the **Deutscher**
- **Gewerkschaftsbund (DGB)**.

tradition *n* Tradition f

traditional *adj* traditionell

traffic *n* Verkehr *m* ▷ *The traffic was terrible.* Es war furchtbar viel Verkehr.

traffic circle *n (US)* Kreisverkehr *m (pl* Kreisverkehre)

traffic jam *n* Stau *m (pl* Staus)

traffic lights *npl* Ampel *fsg*

traffic warden n ❶ (man) Hilfspolizist m (gen Hilfspolizisten, pl Hilfspolizisten) ❷ (woman) Politesse f

tragedy n Tragödie f

tragic adj tragisch

trailer n ❶ (vehicle) Anhänger m (pl Anhänger) ❷ (caravan) Wohnwagen m (pl Wohnwagen) ❸ (advert for film) Vorschau f

train n Zug m (pl Züge)
▶ vb (sport) trainieren [76] (perf hat trainiert) ▷ to train for a race für ein Rennen trainieren; **to train as a teacher** eine Lehrerausbildung machen [48]; **to train an animal to do something** ein Tier dressieren [76], etwas zu tun

trained adj gelernt ▷ She's a trained nurse. Sie ist gelernte Krankenschwester.

trainee n ❶ (in profession) Praktikant m (gen Praktikanten, pl Praktikanten), Praktikantin f ▷ She's a trainee. Sie ist Praktikantin. ❷ (old: apprentice) Lehrling m (pl Lehrlinge)

der Lehrling is also used for women.

▷ She's a trainee plumber. Sie ist Klempnerlehrling.

trainer n ❶ (sports coach) Trainer m (pl Trainer), Trainerin f ❷ (of animals) Dresseur m (pl Dresseure), Dresseuse f

trainers npl Turnschuhe mpl ▷ a pair of trainers ein Paar Turnschuhe

training n ❶ Ausbildung f ▷ a training course ein Ausbildungskurs m ❷ (sport) Training nt (pl Trainings)

tram n Straßenbahn f

tramp n Landstreicher m (pl Landstreicher), Landstreicherin f

trampoline n Trampolin nt (pl Trampoline)

transfer n (sticker) Abziehbild nt (pl Abziehbilder)

trans(gender) adj trans

transit lounge n Transithalle f

translate vb übersetzen [36] (perf hat übersetzt) ▷ to translate something into English etwas ins Englische übersetzen

translation n Übersetzung f

translator n Übersetzer m (pl Übersetzer), Übersetzerin f ▷ Anita's a translator. Anita ist Übersetzerin.

transparent adj durchsichtig

transplant n Transplantation f ▷ a heart transplant eine Herztransplantation

transport n Transport m (pl Transporte) ▶ vb transportieren [76] (perf hat transportiert)

trap n Falle f

trash n (US) Müll m

trash can n (US) Mülleimer m (pl Mülleimer)

travel n Reisen nt
▶ vb reisen [36] (perf ist gereist) ▷ I prefer to travel by train. Ich reise lieber mit dem Zug.; **I'd like to travel round the world.** Ich würde gern eine Weltreise machen.; **We travelled over eight hundred kilometres.** Wir haben über achthundert Kilometer zurückgelegt.; **News travels fast!** Neuigkeiten sprechen sich schnell herum!

travel agency n Reisebüro nt (pl Reisebüros)

travel agent n Reisebürokaufmann m (pl Reisebürokaufleute), Reisebürokauffrau f ▷ She's a travel agent. Sie ist Reisebürokauffrau.; **at the travel agent's** im Reisebüro

traveller n ❶ (on bus, train) Fahrgast m (pl Fahrgäste)

der Fahrgast is also used for women.

❷ (on plane) Passagier m (pl Passagiere), Passagierin f

traveller's cheque n (old) Reisescheck m (pl Reiseschecks)

travelling n I love travelling. Ich reise sehr gern.

travel sickness n Reisekrankheit f

ENGLISH > GERMAN

tray n Tablett nt (pl Tabletts)
tread vb treten [79] (pres tritt, imperf trat, perf ist getreten) ▷ to tread on something auf etwas treten ▷ He trod on her foot. Er ist ihr auf den Fuß getreten.
treasure n Schatz m (gen Schatzes, pl Schätze)
treat n ① (present) Geschenk nt (pl Geschenke) ② (food) Leckerbissen m (pl Leckerbissen); **to give somebody a treat** jemandem eine besondere Freude machen [48]
▶ vb (well, badly) behandeln [34] (perf hat behandelt); **to treat somebody to something** jemandem etwas spendieren [76]
treatment n Behandlung f
treble vb sich verdreifachen [7] (perf hat sich verdreifacht) ▷ The price has trebled. Der Preis hat sich verdreifacht.
tree n Baum m (pl Bäume)
tremble vb zittern [88]
tremendous adj ① fantastisch ▷ Gordon is a tremendous person. Gordon ist fantastisch. ② gewaltig ▷ a tremendous success ein gewaltiger Erfolg
trend n ① (tendency) Tendenz f ② (fashion) Trend m (pl Trends)
trendy adj modisch
trial n (in court) Prozess m (gen Prozesses, pl Prozesse)
triangle n Dreieck nt (pl Dreiecke)
tribe n Stamm m (pl Stämme)
trick n ① Streich m (pl Streiche) ▷ to play a trick on somebody jemandem einen Streich spielen ② (knack) Trick m (pl Tricks) ▷ It's not easy: there's a trick to it. Das ist nicht leicht: Da ist ein Trick dabei.
▶ vb **to trick somebody** jemanden reinlegen [4]
tricky adj knifflig
tricycle n Dreirad nt (pl Dreiräder)
trip n Reise f ▷ to go on a trip eine Reise machen ▷ Have a good trip! Gute Reise!;

trumpet

a day trip ein Tagesausflug m
▶ vb (stumble) stolpern [88]
triple adj dreifach
triplets npl Drillinge mpl
trivial adj trivial
troll n (internet) Troll m (pl Trolle)
trolley n ① (for shopping) Einkaufswagen m (pl Einkaufswagen) ② (for luggage) Kofferkuli m (pl Kofferkulis)
trolling n (internet) Trolling nt
trombone n Posaune f ▷ I play the trombone. Ich spiele Posaune.
troops npl Truppen fpl ▷ British troops die britischen Truppen
trophy n Trophäe f ▷ to win a trophy eine Trophäe gewinnen
tropical adj tropisch ▷ tropical plants tropische Pflanzen; **The weather was tropical.** Es war tropisch heiß.
trouble n Problem nt (pl Probleme) ▷ The trouble is ... Das Problem ist ...; **What's the trouble?** Was ist das Problem?; **to be in trouble** in Schwierigkeiten sein [65]; **stomach trouble** die Magenbeschwerden fpl; **to take a lot of trouble over something** sich mit etwas viel Mühe geben [28]; **Don't worry, it's no trouble.** Keine Sorge, das macht keine Mühe.
troublemaker n Unruhestifter m (pl Unruhestifter), Unruhestifterin f
trousers npl Hose fsg ▷ a pair of trousers eine Hose
trout n Forelle f
truant n **to play truant** die Schule schwänzen [36]
truck n Lastwagen m (pl Lastwagen); **He's a truck driver.** Er ist Lastwagenfahrer.
true adj wahr ▷ true love wahre Liebe ▷ That's true. Das ist wahr.; **to come true** wahr werden [91]
trumpet n Trompete f ▷ She plays the trumpet. Sie spielt Trompete.

trunk n ❶ (of tree) Stamm m (pl Stämme) ❷ (of elephant) Rüssel m (pl Rüssel) ❸ (luggage) Schrankkoffer m (pl Schrankkoffer) ❹ (boot of car) Kofferraum m (pl Kofferräume)

trunks npl **swimming trunks** die Badehose sg

trust n Vertrauen nt ▷ **to have trust in somebody** Vertrauen zu jemandem haben
▶ vb **to trust somebody** jemandem vertrauen [84]; **Trust me!** Glaub mir!

truth n Wahrheit f

try n Versuch m (pl Versuche) ▷ his third try ein dritter Versuch; **It's worth a try.** Der Versuch lohnt sich.; **to give something a try** etwas versuchen [84]
▶ vb ❶ (attempt) versuchen [84] (perf hat versucht) ▷ to try to do something versuchen, etwas zu tun; **to try again** es noch einmal versuchen [84] ❷ (taste) probieren [76] (perf hat probiert) ▷ Would you like to try some? Möchtest du etwas probieren?; **to try on** (clothes) anprobieren [76]; **to try something out** etwas ausprobieren [4]

T-shirt n T-Shirt nt (pl T-Shirts)

tube n Tube f; **the Tube** (underground) die U-Bahn

tuberculosis n Tuberkulose f

Tuesday n Dienstag m (pl Dienstage) ▷ on Tuesday am Dienstag ▷ every Tuesday jeden Dienstag ▷ last Tuesday letzten Dienstag ▷ next Tuesday nächsten Dienstag; **on Tuesdays** dienstags

tug of war n Tauziehen nt

tuition n ❶ Unterricht m; **extra tuition** die Nachhilfestunden fpl ❷ (tuition fees) Studiengebühren fpl

tulip n Tulpe f

tumble dryer n Wäschetrockner m (pl Wäschetrockner)

tummy n Bauch m (pl Bäuche) ▷ I've got a sore tummy. Ich habe Bauchschmerzen.

tuna n Thunfisch m (pl Thunfische)

tune n (melody) Melodie f; **to play in tune** richtig spielen [38]; **to sing out of tune** falsch singen [66]

Tunisia n Tunesien nt; **in Tunisia** in Tunesien

tunnel n Tunnel m (pl Tunnel); **the Tunnel** (Chunnel) der Kanaltunnel

Turk n Türke m (gen Türken, pl Türken), Türkin f

Turkey n Türkei f

> Note that the definite article is used in German for countries which are feminine.

from Turkey aus der Türkei; **in Turkey** in der Türkei; **to Turkey** in die Türkei

turkey n Truthahn m (pl Truthähne)

Turkish adj türkisch
▶ n (language) Türkische nt (gen Türkischen)

turn n (in road) Abbiegung f; **'no left turn'** 'links abbiegen verboten'; **Whose turn is it?** Wer ist an der Reihe?; **It's my turn!** Ich bin an der Reihe!
▶ vb ❶ abbiegen (imperf bog ab, perf ist abgebogen) ▷ Turn right at the lights. Biegen Sie an der Ampel rechts ab. ❷ (become) werden [91] (pres wird, imperf wurde, perf ist geworden) ▷ to turn red rot werden; **to turn into something** sich in etwas verwandeln [34]

turn back vb umkehren [4] (perf ist umgekehrt)

turn down vb ❶ (offer) ablehnen [4] (perf hat abgelehnt) ❷ (radio, TV) leiser stellen [38] ❸ (heating) herunterdrehen [15] (perf hat heruntergedreht)

turn off vb ❶ (light, radio) ausmachen [48] (perf hat ausgemacht) ❷ (tap) zudrehen [15] (perf hat zugedreht) ❸ (engine) ausschalten [2] (perf hat ausgeschaltet)

turn on vb ❶ (light, radio) anmachen [4] (perf hat angemacht) ❷ (tap) aufdrehen [15] (perf hat aufgedreht) ❸ (engine)

ENGLISH > GERMAN

anlassen [42] (pres lässt an, imperf ließ an, perf hat angelassen)
turn out vb It turned out to be a mistake. Es stellte sich heraus, dass das ein Fehler war.
turn round vb ❶ (car) umkehren [4] (perf ist umgekehrt) ❷ (person) sich umdrehen [4] (perf hat sich umgedreht)
turn up vb ❶ (arrive) aufkreuzen [4] (perf ist aufgekreuzt) ❷ (heater) höherstellen [15] ❸ (radio, TV) lauter machen [48]
turning n It's the third turning on the left. Es ist die dritte Straße links.; We took the wrong turning. Wir sind falsch abgebogen.
turnip n Steckrübe f
turquoise adj (colour) türkis
turtle n Meeresschildkröte f
tutor n (private teacher) Lehrer m (pl Lehrer), Lehrerin f
TV n Fernsehen nt
tweet vb (internet) twittern [88]
tweezers npl Pinzette fsg ▷ a pair of tweezers eine Pinzette
twelfth adj zwölfte ▷ the twelfth floor der zwölfte Stock ▷ the twelfth of August der zwölfte August
twelve num zwölf ▷ She's twelve. Sie ist zwölf. ▷ at twelve o'clock um zwölf Uhr
twentieth adj zwanzigste ▷ the twentieth of August der zwanzigste August
twenty num zwanzig ▷ He's twenty. Er ist zwanzig.
twice adv zweimal; twice as much doppelt so viel
twin n Zwilling m (pl Zwillinge)
▪ der Zwilling is also used for women.
my twin brother mein Zwillingsbruder m; her twin sister ihre Zwillingsschwester; identical twins eineiige Zwillinge; a twin room ein Doppelzimmer mit zwei Betten
twinned adj Oxford is twinned with Bonn. Oxford und Bonn sind Partnerstädte.

twist vb ❶ (bend) biegen (imperf bog, perf hat gebogen); I've twisted my ankle. Ich habe mir den Fuß vertreten. ❷ (distort) verdrehen [84] (perf hat verdreht) ▷ You're twisting my words. Sie verdrehen meine Worte.
Twitter® n Twitter® nt
two num zwei ▷ She's two. Sie ist zwei.
type n Art f ▷ What type of camera have you got? Welche Art von Fotoapparat hast du?
▶ vb Schreibmaschine schreiben [61] ▷ Can you type? Kannst du Schreibmaschine schreiben?; to type a letter einen Brief tippen [38]
typewriter n Schreibmaschine f
typical adj typisch ▷ That's just typical! Das ist typisch!
tyre n Reifen m (pl Reifen) ▷ the tyre pressure der Reifendruck

u

UFO n (= unified flying object) UFO nt (pl UFOs) (= unbekanntes Flugobjekt)
ugly adj hässlich
UK n (= United Kingdom) **the UK** das Vereinigte Königreich; **from the UK** aus dem Vereinigten Königreich; **in the UK** im Vereinigten Königreich; **to the UK** in das Vereinigte Königreich
ulcer n Geschwür nt (pl Geschwüre)
Ulster n Ulster nt; **from Ulster** aus Ulster; **in Ulster** in Ulster; **to Ulster** nach Ulster
umbrella n ❶ Regenschirm m (pl Regenschirme) ❷ (for sun) Sonnenschirm m (pl Sonnenschirme)
umlaut n Umlaut m ▷ The plural of 'Haus' is written with an umlaut. Der Plural von 'Haus' wird mit Umlaut gebildet.; **a umlaut** ä; **o umlaut** ö; **u umlaut** ü
umpire n Schiedsrichter m (pl Schiedsrichter), Schiedsrichterin f
UN n (= United Nations) UN pl
unable adj **to be unable to do something** etwas nicht tun können [**41**]

unanimous adj einstimmig ▷ a unanimous decision ein einstimmiger Beschluss
unavoidable adj unvermeidlich
unbearable adj unerträglich
unbelievable adj unglaublich
unbreakable adj unzerbrechlich
uncertain adj ungewiss ▷ The future is uncertain. Die Zukunft ist ungewiss.; **to be uncertain about something** sich über etwas nicht im Klaren sein [**65**]
uncle n Onkel m (pl Onkel) ▷ my uncle mein Onkel
uncomfortable adj unbequem ▷ The seats are rather uncomfortable. Die Sitze sind ziemlich unbequem.
unconscious adj bewusstlos
uncontrollable adj unkontrollierbar
under prep unter

> Use the accusative to express movement or a change of place. Use the dative when there is no change of place.

▷ The ball rolled under the table. Der Ball rollte unter den Tisch. ▷ The cat's under the table. Die Katze ist unter dem Tisch. ▷ children under ten Kinder unter zehn; **under there** da drunter; **under twenty people** weniger als zwanzig Leute
underage adj minderjährig
underdog n Underdog m (pl Underdogs) ▷ We were the underdogs on this occasion. Wir waren diesmal die Underdogs.
underground adj, adv ❶ unterirdisch ▷ underground water pipes unterirdische Wasserrohre; **an underground car park** eine Tiefgarage ❷ **unter der Erde** ▷ Moles live underground. Maulwürfe leben unter der Erde.
▶ n U-Bahn f ▷ Is there an underground in Bonn? Gibt es in Bonn eine U-Bahn?
underline vb unterstreichen (imperf unterstrich, perf hat unterstrichen)

ENGLISH > GERMAN

underneath prep, adv ❶ unter
> Use the accusative to express movement or a change of place. Use the dative when there is no change of place.

▷ I put it underneath that pile. Ich habe es unter diesen Stapel gelegt. ▷ It was hidden underneath the carpet. Es war unter dem Teppich versteckt.
❷ darunter ▷ I got out of the car and looked underneath. Ich stieg aus dem Auto aus und sah darunter.

underpants npl Unterhose fsg ▷ a pair of underpants eine Unterhose

underpass n Unterführung f

undershirt n (US) Unterhemd nt (pl Unterhemden)

understand vb verstehen [72] (imperf verstand, perf hat verstanden) ▷ Do you understand? Verstehst du? ▷ I don't understand this word. Ich verstehe dieses Wort nicht. ▷ Is that understood? Ist das verstanden?

understanding adj verständnisvoll ▷ She's very understanding. Sie ist sehr verständnisvoll.

understood vb see **understand**

undertaker n Beerdigungsunternehmer m (pl Beerdigungsunternehmer), Beerdigungsunternehmerin f

underwater adj, adv unter Wasser ▷ It was filmed underwater. Es wurde unter Wasser gefilmt.; **an underwater camera** eine Unterwasserkamera

underwear n Unterwäsche f

undo vb aufmachen [4] (perf hat aufgemacht)

undress vb (get undressed) sich ausziehen [96] (imperf zog sich aus, perf hat sich ausgezogen) ▷ The doctor told me to get undressed. Der Arzt bat mich, mich auszuziehen.

unemployed adj arbeitslos ▷ He's unemployed. Er ist arbeitslos. ▷ He's been unemployed for a year. Er ist seit einem Jahr arbeitslos.; **the unemployed** die Arbeitslosen mpl

unemployment n Arbeitslosigkeit f

unexpected adj unerwartet ▷ an unexpected visitor ein unerwarteter Gast

unexpectedly adv überraschend ▷ They arrived unexpectedly. Sie sind überraschend gekommen.

unfair adj unfair ▷ It's unfair to girls. Es ist Mädchen gegenüber unfair.

unfamiliar adj unbekannt ▷ I heard an unfamiliar voice. Ich hörte eine unbekannte Stimme.

unfashionable adj unmodern

unfit adj nicht fit ▷ I'm rather unfit at the moment. Ich bin im Moment nicht sehr fit.

unfold vb auseinanderfalten [15] (perf hat auseinandergefaltet) ▷ She unfolded the map. Sie faltete die Karte auseinander.

unforgettable adj unvergesslich

unfortunately adv leider ▷ Unfortunately, I arrived late. Ich bin leider zu spät gekommen.

unfriendly adj unfreundlich ▷ They're a bit unfriendly. Sie sind etwas unfreundlich.

ungrateful adj undankbar

unhappy adj unglücklich ▷ He was very unhappy as a child. Er war als Kind sehr unglücklich. ▷ to look unhappy unglücklich aussehen

unhealthy adj ungesund

uni n Uni f (pl Unis) ▷ to go to uni zur Uni gehen

uniform n Uniform f ▷ the school uniform die Schuluniform
* School uniforms are virtually nonexistent in Germany.

uninhabited adj unbewohnt

union n (trade union) Gewerkschaft f

Union Jack n britische Flagge f

unique adj einzigartig

unit n Einheit f ▷ *a unit of measurement* eine Maßeinheit; **a kitchen unit** ein Kücheneinbauschrank m

United Kingdom n the United Kingdom das Vereinigte Königreich; **from the United Kingdom** aus dem Vereinigten Königreich; **in the United Kingdom** im Vereinigten Königreich; **to the United Kingdom** in das Vereinigte Königreich

United Nations npl The United Nations are extremely important. Die Vereinten Nationen sind äußerst wichtig.

United States n The United States play a big role. Die Vereinigten Staaten spielen eine große Rolle.; **from the United States** aus den Vereinigten Staaten; **in the United States** in den Vereinigten Staaten; **to the United States** in die Vereinigten Staaten

universe n Universum nt

university n Universität f ▷ *Do you want to go to university?* Möchtest du auf die Universität gehen? ▷ *Lancaster University* die Universität von Lancaster; **She's at university.** Sie studiert.

unless conj es sei denn ▷ *unless he leaves* es sei denn, er geht ▷ *I won't come unless you phone me.* Ich komme nicht, es sei denn, du rufst an.

unlikely adj unwahrscheinlich ▷ *It's possible, but unlikely.* Es ist möglich, aber unwahrscheinlich.

unload vb ausladen (pres lädt aus, imperf lud aus, perf hat ausgeladen) ▷ *We unloaded the car.* Wir haben das Auto ausgeladen.; **The lorries go there to unload.** Die Lastwagen fahren dorthin um abzuladen.

unlock vb aufschließen (imperf schloss auf, perf hat aufgeschlossen) ▷ *He unlocked the door.* Er schloss die Tür auf.

unlucky adj **to be unlucky (1)** (number, object) Unglück bringen [13] ▷ *They say thirteen is an unlucky number.* Es heißt, dass die Zahl dreizehn Unglück bringt. **(2)** (person) kein Glück haben [32] ▷ *Did you win?* — *No, I was unlucky. Hast du gewonnen?* — Nein, ich habe kein Glück gehabt.

unmarried adj (person) unverheiratet ▷ *an unmarried couple* ein unverheiratetes Paar; **an unmarried mother** eine ledige Mutter

unnatural adj unnatürlich

unnecessary adj unnötig

unpack vb (clothes, case) auspacken [4] (perf hat ausgepackt) ▷ *I went to my room to unpack.* Ich ging auf mein Zimmer, um auszupacken.

unpleasant adj unangenehm

unplug vb ausstecken [4] (perf hat ausgesteckt) ▷ *She unplugged the TV.* Sie hat den Fernseher ausgesteckt.

unpopular adj unbeliebt

unrealistic adj unrealistisch

unreasonable adj unmöglich ▷ *Her attitude was completely unreasonable.* Ihre Haltung war völlig unmöglich.

unreliable adj unzuverlässig ▷ *He's completely unreliable.* Er ist total unzuverlässig.

unroll vb aufrollen [4] (perf hat aufgerollt)

unscrew vb aufschrauben [4] (perf hat aufgeschraubt) ▷ *She unscrewed the top of the bottle.* Sie schraubte den Flaschenverschluss auf.

unskilled adj ungelernt ▷ *an unskilled worker* ein ungelernter Arbeiter

unsuccessful adj (attempt) erfolglos ▷ *an unsuccessful artist* ein erfolgloser Künstler; **to be unsuccessful in doing something** keinen Erfolg bei etwas haben [32]

unsuitable adj (clothes, equipment) ungeeignet

untidy adj unordentlich

untie vb ❶ (knot, parcel) aufmachen [4] (perf hat aufgemacht) ❷ (animal)

losbinden (*imperf* band los, *perf* hat losgebunden)
until *prep*, *conj* ❶ bis ▷ *I waited until ten o'clock.* Ich habe bis zehn Uhr gewartet.; **until now** bis jetzt; **until then** bis dahin ❷ vor

> Use **vor** if the sentence you want to translate contains a negative, such as 'not' or 'never'.

▷ *It won't be ready until next week.* Es wird nicht vor nächster Woche fertig sein. ▷ *Until last year I'd never been to Germany.* Vor letztem Jahr war ich noch nie in Deutschland.

unusual *adj* ungewöhnlich ▷ *an unusual shape* eine ungewöhnliche Form ▷ *It's unusual to get snow at this time of year.* Es ist ungewöhnlich, dass es um diese Jahreszeit schneit.

unwilling *adj* **to be unwilling to do something** nicht gewillt sein [65], etwas zu tun

unwrap *vb* auspacken [4] (*perf* hat ausgepackt) ▷ *Let's unwrap the presents.* Packen wir die Geschenke aus.

up *prep*, *adv* auf

> Use the accusative to express movement or a change of place. Use the dative when there is no change of place.

▷ *He drove me up the hill.* Er hat mich den Berg hinaufgefahren. ▷ *the chapel up on the hill* die Kapelle auf dem Berg; **up here** hier oben; **up there** dort oben; **up north** oben im Norden; **to be up** (*out of bed*) auf sein [65]; **What's up?** Was gibt's?; **What's up with her?** Was ist los mit ihr?; **to get up** (*in the morning*) aufstehen [72]; **to go up** (1) hinauffahren [4] ▷ *The bus went up the hill.* Der Bus ist den Berg hinaufgefahren. (2) (*on foot*) hinaufgehen [29] ▷ *We went up the hill.* Wir sind den Berg hinaufgegangen.; **to go up to somebody** auf jemanden zugehen

[29]; **She came up to me.** Sie kam auf mich zu.; **up to** (*as far as*) bis; **It's up to you.** Das ist dir überlassen.

> For other expressions with 'up', see the verbs 'go', 'come', 'put', 'turn' etc.

uphill *adv* bergauf
upper sixth *n* **the upper sixth** die dreizehnte Klasse
upright *adj* **to stand upright** aufrecht stehen [72]
upset *n* **a stomach upset** eine Magenverstimmung
▶ *adj* ❶ (*hurt*) gekränkt ▷ *She was upset when he said that.* Sie fühlte sich gekränkt, als er das sagte. ❷ (*sad*) betrübt ▷ *I was very upset when my father died.* Ich war sehr betrübt, als mein Vater starb.; **an upset stomach** eine Magenverstimmung
▶ *vb* aufregen [4] (*perf* hat aufgeregt) ▷ *Don't say anything to upset her!* Sag nichts, was sie aufregen könnte.
upside down *adv* verkehrt herum ▷ *It's upside down.* Es ist verkehrt herum.
upstairs *adv* oben ▷ *Where's your coat?* — *It's upstairs.* Wo ist dein Mantel? — Er ist oben.; **the people upstairs** die Leute von oben; **to go upstairs** hinaufgehen [29]
up-to-date *adj* ❶ (*car, stereo*) modern ❷ (*information*) aktuell ▷ *an up-to-date timetable* ein aktueller Fahrplan; **to bring something up to date** etwas auf den neuesten Stand bringen [13]; **to keep somebody up to date** jemanden auf dem Laufenden halten [33]
upwards *adv* hinauf ▷ *to look upwards* hinaufsehen
urgent *adj* dringend ▷ *Is it urgent?* Ist es dringend?
US *nsg* USA *pl*; **from the US** aus den USA; **in the US** in den USA; **to the US** in die USA
us *pron* uns ▷ *They saw us.* Sie haben uns gesehen. ▷ *They gave us a map.* Sie gaben

uns eine Karte.; **Who is it? — It's us!** Wer ist da? — Wir sind's!
USA n USA pl; **from the USA** aus den USA; **in the USA** in den USA; **to the USA** in die USA
use n It's no use. Es hat keinen Zweck.; **to make use of something** etwas benützen [**7**]
▶ vb benützen [**7**] (perf hat benützt) ▷ Can we use a dictionary in the exam? Können wir in der Prüfung ein Wörterbuch benützen?; **Can I use your phone?** Kann ich mal telefonieren?; **to use the toilet** auf die Toilette gehen [**29**]; **to use up** aufbrauchen [**4**]; **I used to live in London.** Ich habe früher mal in London gelebt.; **I used not to like maths, but now ...** Früher habe ich Mathe nicht gemocht, aber jetzt ...; **to be used to something** an etwas gewöhnt sein [**65**]; **a used car** ein Gebrauchtwagen m
useful adj nützlich
useless adj nutzlos ▷ This map is just useless. Diese Karte ist echt nutzlos.; **You're useless!** Du bist zu nichts zu gebrauchen!; **It's useless asking her!** Es ist zwecklos, sie zu fragen!
user n Benutzer m (pl Benutzer), Benutzerin f
user-friendly adj benutzerfreundlich
usual adj üblich ▷ as usual wie üblich
usually adv normalerweise ▷ I usually get to school at half past eight. Ich bin normalerweise um halb neun in der Schule.

V

vacancy n (job) freie Stelle f; **'Vacancies'** 'Zimmer frei'; **'No vacancies'** 'Belegt'
vacant adj ❶ (seat, job) frei ❷ (building) leer stehend ❸ (look) leer ▷ a vacant look ein leerer Blick
vacation n (US) ❶ (from school) Ferien pl ▷ They went on vacation to Mexico. Sie haben in Mexiko Ferien gemacht. ❷ (from work) Urlaub m (pl Urlaube) ▷ I have thirty days' vacation a year. Ich habe dreißig Tage Urlaub im Jahr.
vaccinate vb impfen [**38**]
vacuum vb staubsaugen [**38**] (imperf staubsaugte, perf hat gestaubsaugt) ▷ to vacuum the hall den Flur staubsaugen
vacuum cleaner n Staubsauger m (pl Staubsauger)
vagina n Vagina f (pl Vaginen)
vague adj vage
vain adj eitel ▷ He's so vain! Er ist so eitel!; **in vain** umsonst

ENGLISH > GERMAN

Valentine card n Valentinskarte f
* Germans celebrate Valentine's Day by giving flowers rather than sending cards.

Valentine's Day n Valentinstag m (pl Valentinstage)

valid adj gültig ▷ *This ticket is valid for three months.* Dieser Fahrschein ist drei Monate lang gültig.

valley n Tal nt (pl Täler)

valuable adj wertvoll ▷ *a valuable picture* ein wertvolles Bild ▷ *valuable help* wertvolle Hilfe

value n Wert m (pl Werte)

van n Lieferwagen m (pl Lieferwagen)

vandal n Vandale m (gen Vandalen, pl Vandalen), Vandalin f

vandalism n Vandalismus m (gen Vandalismus)

vandalize vb mutwillig zerstören [95] (perf hat mutwillig zerstört)

vanilla n Vanille f; **vanilla ice cream** das Vanilleeis

vape vb dampfen [48]

vaping n Dampfen nt

vanish vb verschwinden [86] (imperf verschwand, perf ist verschwunden)

variety n ❶ Abwechslung f ▷ *She likes variety in her life.* Sie hat gern Abwechslung im Leben. ❷ (kind) Sorte f ▷ *a new variety of rose* eine neue Rosensorte; **a variety of CDs** eine Vielzahl von CDs

various adj verschieden ▷ *We visited various villages.* Wir haben verschiedene Dörfer besucht.

vary vb schwanken [38] ▷ *It varies between two and four per cent.* Es schwankt zwischen zwei und vier Prozent.; **It varies.** Das ist unterschiedlich.

vase n Vase f

VAT n (= value added tax) Mehrwertsteuer f

VCR n (= video cassette recorder) Videorekorder m (pl Videorekorder)

513 | vicious

VDU n (= visual display unit) Bildschirm m (pl Bildschirme)

veal n Kalbfleisch nt

vegan n Veganer m (pl Veganer), Veganerin f ▷ *I'm a vegan.* Ich bin Veganerin.

vegetable n Gemüsesorte f; **vegetables** das Gemüse sg; **vegetable soup** die Gemüsesuppe

vegetarian adj vegetarisch ▷ *vegetarian lasagne* die vegetarische Lasagne; **He's vegetarian.** Er ist Vegetarier.
▶ n Vegetarier m (pl Vegetarier), Vegetarierin f ▷ *She's a vegetarian.* Sie ist Vegetarierin.

vehicle n Fahrzeug nt (pl Fahrzeuge)

vein n Vene f

velvet n Samt m

vending machine n Automat m (gen Automaten, pl Automaten)

verb n Verb nt (pl Verben)

verdict n Urteil nt (pl Urteile)

vertical adj senkrecht

vertigo n Schwindelgefühl nt; **He had an attack of vertigo.** Ihm wurde schwindlig.

very adv sehr ▷ *very tall* sehr groß ▷ *not very interesting* nicht sehr interessant; **very much (1)** sehr viel ▷ *He didn't eat very much.* Er hat nicht sehr viel gegessen. **(2)** (like, love, respect) sehr ▷ *I love her very much.* Ich liebe sie sehr.; **Thank you very much.** Vielen Dank.

vest n ❶ Unterhemd nt (pl Unterhemden) ❷ (waistcoat) Weste f

vet n Tierarzt m (gen Tierärzte, pl Tierärzte), Tierärztin f ▷ *She's a vet.* Sie ist Tierärztin.

via prep über ▷ *We went to Munich via Ulm.* Wir sind über Ulm nach München gefahren.

vicar n Pastor m (pl Pastoren), Pastorin f ▷ *He's a vicar.* Er ist Pastor.

vicious adj ❶ brutal ▷ *a vicious attack* ein brutaler Überfall ❷ (dog) bissig

victim ❸ (person) bösartig; **a vicious circle** ein Teufelskreis m

victim n Opfer nt (pl Opfer) ▷ He was the victim of a mugging. Er wurde das Opfer eines Straßenüberfalls.

victory n Sieg m (pl Siege)

video vb auf Video aufnehmen [**52**] (pres nimmt auf Video auf, imperf nahm auf Video auf, perf hat auf Video aufgenommen)
▶ n (film) Video nt (pl Videos) ▷ to watch a video ein Video ansehen ▷ a video of my family on holiday ein Video von meiner Familie in den Ferien; **a video call** ein Videoanruf m; **a video game** ein Videospiel nt

Vienna n Wien nt; **to Vienna** nach Wien

Vietnamese n Vietnamese m (pl Vietnamesen), Vietnamesin f
▶ adj vietnamesisch

view n ❶ Aussicht f ▷ There's an amazing view. Man hat dort eine tolle Aussicht. ❷ (opinion) Meinung f ▷ in my view meiner Meinung nach

viewer n Fernsehzuschauer m (pl Fernsehzuschauer), Fernsehzuschauerin f

viewpoint n Standpunkt m (pl Standpunkte)

vile adj (smell, food) ekelhaft

villa n Villa f (pl Villen)

village n Dorf nt (pl Dörfer)

vine n Weinrebe f

vinegar n Essig m

vineyard n Weinberg m (pl Weinberge)

viola n Bratsche f ▷ I play the viola. Ich spiele Bratsche.

violence n Gewalt f

violent adj ❶ (person, film) gewalttätig; **a violent crime** ein Gewaltverbrechen nt ❷ (explosion) gewaltig

violin n Geige f ▷ I play the violin. Ich spiele Geige.

violinist n Geigenspieler m (pl Geigenspieler), Geigenspielerin f

viral adj viral; **a viral video** ein virales Video

virgin n Jungfrau f ▷ to be a virgin Jungfrau sein

Virgo n Jungfrau f ▷ I'm Virgo. Ich bin Jungfrau.

virtual reality n virtuelle Realität f

virus n Virus nt (gen Virus, pl Viren)

visa n Visum nt (pl Visa)

visible adj sichtbar

visit n ❶ Besuch m (pl Besuche) ▷ my last visit to her mein letzter Besuch bei ihr ❷ (to country) Aufenthalt m (pl Aufenthalte) ▷ Did you enjoy your visit to Germany? Hat euer Deutschlandaufenthalt Spaß gemacht?
▶ vb ❶ (person) besuchen [**7**] (perf hat besucht) ❷ (place) besichtigen [**18**] (perf hat besichtigt) ▷ We'd like to visit the castle. Wir würden gern die Burg besichtigen.

visitor n Besucher m (pl Besucher), Besucherin f; **to have a visitor** Besuch haben [**32**]

visual adj visuell

vital adj äußerst wichtig ▷ It's vital for you to take these tablets. Es ist äußerst wichtig, dass du diese Tabletten nimmst.; **of vital importance** äußerst wichtig

vitamin n Vitamin nt (pl Vitamine)

vivid adj lebhaft ▷ to have a vivid imagination eine lebhafte Fantasie haben

vocabulary n Wortschatz m (gen Wortschatzes, pl Wortschätze)

vocational adj beruflich ▷ vocational training die berufliche Ausbildung; **a vocational college** eine Berufsschule

vodka n Wodka m (pl Wodkas)

voice n Stimme f

voice mail n Voicemail f

volcano n Vulkan m (pl Vulkane)

volleyball n Volleyball m ▷ to play volleyball Volleyball spielen

voluntary adj (contribution, statement) freiwillig; **to do voluntary work** ehrenamtlich tätig sein [**65**]

volunteer n Freiwillige m (gen Freiwilligen, pl Freiwilligen), Freiwillige f (gen Freiwilligen) ▷ a volunteer (man) ein Freiwilliger
▶ vb **to volunteer to do something** sich freiwillig melden [**54**], etwas zu tun

vomit vb sich übergeben [**28**] (pres übergibt sich, imperf übergab sich, perf hat sich übergeben)

vote n Stimme f
▶ vb wählen [**38**] ▷ to vote Labour Labour wählen [**38**]; **to vote for somebody** für jemanden stimmen [**38**]

voucher n Gutschein m (pl Gutscheine) ▷ a gift voucher ein Geschenkgutschein

vowel n Vokal m (pl Vokale)

vulgar adj vulgär

wage n Lohn m (pl Löhne) ▷ He collected his wages. Er hat seinen Lohn abgeholt.

waist n Taille f

waistcoat n Weste f

wait vb warten [**2**]; **to wait for something** auf etwas warten [**2**]; **to wait for somebody** auf jemanden warten [**2**]; **Wait a minute!** Einen Augenblick!; **to keep somebody waiting** jemanden warten lassen [**42**]; **I can't wait for the holidays.** Ich kann die Ferien kaum erwarten.; **I can't wait to see him again.** Ich kann's kaum erwarten, bis ich ihn wiedersehe.

wait up vb aufbleiben [**10**] (imperf blieb auf, perf ist aufgeblieben)

waiter n Kellner m (pl Kellner)

waiting list n Warteliste f

waiting room n Wartezimmer nt (pl Wartezimmer)

waitress n Kellnerin f

wake up vb aufwachen [**4**] (perf ist aufgewacht) ▷ I woke up at six o'clock. Ich bin um sechs Uhr aufgewacht.; **to wake somebody up** jemanden wecken [38]

Wales n Wales nt ▷ *the Prince of Wales* der Prinz von Wales; **from Wales** aus Wales; **in Wales** in Wales; **to Wales** nach Wales

walk vb ❶ gehen [29] (imperf ging, perf ist gegangen) ▷ *He walks fast.* Er geht schnell. ❷ (go on foot) zu Fuß gehen ▷ *Are you walking or going by bus?* Geht ihr zu Fuß oder nehmt ihr den Bus? ▷ *We walked ten kilometres.* Wir sind zehn Kilometer zu Fuß gegangen.; **to walk the dog** mit dem Hund spazieren gehen [29]
▶ n Spaziergang m (pl Spaziergänge) ▷ *to go for a walk* einen Spaziergang machen; **It's ten minutes' walk from here.** Von hier ist es zehn Minuten zu Fuß.

walking n Wandern nt; **I did some walking in the Alps last summer.** Ich habe letzten Sommer in den Alpen gewandert.

walking stick n Spazierstock m (pl Spazierstöcke)

wall n ❶ Mauer f ▷ *There's a wall round the garden.* Um den Garten ist eine Mauer. ❷ Wand f (pl Wände) ▷ *They have lots of pictures on the wall.* Sie haben viele Bilder an der Wand.

wallet n Brieftasche f

wallpaper n Tapete f

walnut n Walnuss f (pl Walnüsse)

wander vb **to wander around** herumlaufen

want vb möchten (pres mag, imperf mochte, perf hat gemocht) ▷ *Do you want some cake?* Möchtest du Kuchen?; **to want to do something** etwas wollen [94] ▷ *What do you want to do?* Was willst du machen?

war n Krieg m (pl Kriege)

ward n (room in hospital) Krankensaal m (pl Krankensäle)

wardrobe n (piece of furniture) Kleiderschrank m (pl Kleiderschränke)

warehouse n Lagerhaus nt (gen Lagerhauses, pl Lagerhäuser)

warm adj ❶ warm ▷ *warm water* warmes Wasser ▷ *It's warm in here.* Hier drin ist es warm. ▷ *It's warmer in the kitchen.* In der Küche ist es wärmer.

> When you talk about a person being 'warm', you use the impersonal construction.

▷ *I'm warm.* Mir ist warm. ▷ *I'm too warm.* Mir ist zu warm. ❷ herzlich ▷ *a warm welcome* ein herzlicher Empfang; **to warm up (1)** (for sport) sich aufwärmen **(2)** (food) aufwärmen ▷ *I'll warm up some lasagne for you.* Ich wärme dir etwas Lasagne auf.; **to warm over** aufwärmen

warn vb warnen [38] ▷ *Well, I warned you!* Ich habe dich ja gewarnt.; **to warn somebody not to do something** jemanden davor warnen, etwas zu tun [81]

warning n Warnung f

wart n Warze f

was vb see **be**

wash n **to have a wash** sich waschen [89]; **to give something a wash** etwas waschen [89]
▶ vb ❶ waschen [89] (pres wäscht, imperf wusch, perf hat gewaschen) ▷ *to wash something* etwas waschen [89] ❷ (have a wash) sich waschen [89] ▷ *Every morning I get up, wash and get dressed.* Jeden Morgen stehe ich auf, wasche mich und ziehe mich an.; **to wash one's hands** sich die Hände waschen [89]; **to wash one's hair** sich die Haare waschen [89]; **to wash up** abwaschen [89]

washbasin n Waschbecken nt (pl Waschbecken)

washcloth n (US) Waschlappen m (pl Waschlappen)

ENGLISH > GERMAN

washing n (clothes) Wäsche f; **Have you got any washing?** Hast du etwas zu waschen?; **to do the washing** Wäsche waschen [89]

washing machine n Waschmaschine f

washing powder n Waschpulver nt (pl Waschpulver)

washing-up n Abwasch m ▷ **to do the washing-up** den Abwasch machen

washing-up liquid n Spülmittel nt (pl Spülmittel)

wasn't = was not

wasp n Wespe f

waste n ① Verschwendung f ▷ *It's such a waste!* Es ist so eine Verschwendung! ▷ *It's a waste of time.* Es ist Zeitverschwendung! ② (rubbish) Müll m ▷ *nuclear waste* der Atommüll
▶ vb verschwenden [7] (perf hat verschwendet) ▷ *I don't like wasting money.* Ich verschwende nicht gerne Geld. ▷ *There's no time to waste.* Wir haben keine Zeit zu verschwenden.

wastepaper basket n Papierkorb m (pl Papierkörbe)

watch n Uhr f
▶ vb ① (film, video) ansehen [64] (pres sieht an, imperf sah an, perf hat angesehen) ▷ *Did you watch that film last night?* Hast du dir gestern Abend den Film angesehen?; **to watch television** fernsehen [64] ② zusehen [64] (pres sieht zu, imperf sah zu, perf hat zugesehen) ▷ *Watch me!* Sieh mir zu! ③ (keep a watch on) beobachten [2] (perf hat beobachtet) ▷ *The police were watching the house.* Die Polizei beobachtete das Haus.; **to watch out** aufpassen [31]; **Watch out!** Pass auf!

water n Wasser nt (pl Wasser)
▶ vb ① (plant) gießen (imperf goss, perf hat gegossen) ▷ *He was watering his tulips.* Er goss seine Tulpen. ② (garden) sprengen ▷ *We should water the lawn.* Wir sollten den Rasen sprengen.

waterfall n Wasserfall m (pl Wasserfälle)

watering can n Gießkanne f

watermelon n Wassermelone f

waterproof adj wasserdicht ▷ *Is this jacket waterproof?* Ist die Jacke wasserdicht?

water-skiing n Wasserskifahren nt; **to go water-skiing** Wasserski fahren [21]

wave n (in water) Welle f; **We gave him a wave.** Wir haben ihm zugewinkt.
▶ vb winken [38]; **to wave to somebody** jemandem zuwinken; **to wave goodbye** zum Abschied winken [38]

wax n Wachs nt (gen Wachses)

way n ① (manner) Art und Weise f ▷ *That's no way to talk to your mother!* Das ist keine Art und Weise, mit deiner Mutter zu reden!; **She looked at me in a strange way.** Sie sah mich sonderbar an.; **This book tells you the right way to do it.** Dieses Buch erklärt, wie man es machen muss.; **You're doing it the wrong way.** Du machst das falsch.; **In a way you're right.** In gewisser Weise hast du recht.; **a way of life** eine Art zu leben ② (route) Weg m ▷ *I don't know the way.* Ich kenne den Weg nicht.; **on the way** unterwegs; **It's a long way.** Es ist weit.; **Which way is it?** In welcher Richtung ist es?; **The supermarket is this way.** Zum Supermarkt geht es in diese Richtung.; **Do you know the way to the hotel?** Wissen Sie, wie man zum Hotel kommt?; **'way in'** 'Eingang'; **'way out'** 'Ausgang'; **by the way ...** übrigens ...

we pron wir ▷ *We're staying here for a week.* Wir sind eine Woche lang hier.

weak adj schwach ▷ *Maths is my weakest subject.* In Mathe bin ich am schwächsten.

wealthy adj reich

weapon n Waffe f

wear vb (clothes) tragen [77] (pres trägt, imperf trug, perf hat getragen) ▷ She was wearing a hat. Sie trug einen Hut. ▷ She was wearing black. Sie trug Schwarz.

weather n Wetter nt ▷ What was the weather like? Wie war das Wetter? ▷ The weather was lovely. Das Wetter war herrlich.

weather forecast n Wettervorhersage f

Web n the Web das Web

web address n Internetadresse f

webcam n Webcam f (pl Webcams)

web page n Webseite f

website n Website f (pl Websites)

we'd = we had; we would

wedding n Hochzeit f; **wedding anniversary** der Hochzeitstag; **wedding dress** das Brautkleid; **wedding ring** der Ehering

Wednesday n Mittwoch m (pl Mittwoche) ▷ on Wednesday am Mittwoch ▷ every Wednesday jeden Mittwoch ▷ last Wednesday letzten Mittwoch ▷ next Wednesday nächsten Mittwoch; **on Wednesdays** mittwochs

weed n Unkraut nt ▷ The garden's full of weeds. Der Garten ist voller Unkraut.

week n Woche f ▷ last week letzte Woche ▷ every week jede Woche ▷ next week nächste Woche ▷ in a week's time in einer Woche; **a week on Friday** Freitag in einer Woche

weekday n on weekdays wochentags

weekend n Wochenende nt (pl Wochenenden) ▷ at the weekend am Wochenende ▷ at weekends am Wochenende ▷ last weekend letztes Wochenende ▷ next weekend nächstes Wochenende

weigh vb wiegen (imperf wog, perf hat gewogen) ▷ How much do you weigh? Wie viel wiegst du? ▷ First, weigh the flour. Wiegen Sie zuerst das Mehl.; **to weigh oneself** sich wiegen

weight n Gewicht nt (pl Gewichte); **to lose weight** abnehmen [52]; **to put on weight** zunehmen [52]

weightlifting n Gewichtheben nt

weird adj sonderbar

welcome n They gave her a warm welcome. Sie haben sie herzlich empfangen.; **Welcome!** Herzlich willkommen! ▷ Welcome to Germany! Herzlich willkommen in Deutschland!
▶ vb **to welcome somebody** jemanden begrüßen [31]; **Thank you! — You're welcome!** Danke! — Bitte!

well adj, adv ① gut ▷ You did that really well. Das hast du wirklich gut gemacht.; **to do well** gut sein [65]; **to be well** (in good health) gesund sein [65]; **Get well soon!** Gute Besserung!; **Well done!** Gut gemacht! ② na ja ▷ It's enormous! Well, quite big anyway. Es ist riesig! Na ja, jedenfalls ziemlich groß.; **as well** auch
▶ n Brunnen m (pl Brunnen)

we'll = we will

well-behaved adj artig

wellingtons npl Gummistiefel mpl

well-known adj bekannt ▷ a well-known film star ein bekannter Filmstar

well-off adj gut situiert

Welsh adj walisisch; **He's Welsh.** Er ist Waliser.; **She's Welsh.** Sie ist Waliserin.; **Welsh people** die Waliser mpl
▶ n (language) Walisisch nt (gen Walisischen)

Welshman n Waliser m (pl Waliser)

Welshwoman n Waliserin f

went vb see go

were vb see be

we're = we are

weren't = were not

west n Westen m ▷ in the west im Westen
▶ adj, adv nach Westen ▷ We were travelling west. Wir fuhren nach

Westen.; **the west coast** die Westküste; **a west wind** ein Westwind m; **west of** westlich von; **the West Country** der Südwesten Englands

western n (film) Western m (gen Western, pl Western)
▶ adj westlich; **the western part of the island** der westliche Teil der Insel; **Western Europe** Westeuropa nt

West Indian adj westindisch; **He's West Indian.** Er ist aus Westindien.
▶ n (person) Westinder m (pl Westinder), Westinderin f

wet adj nass ▷ **wet clothes** nasse Kleider ▷ **to get wet** nass werden; **wet weather** regnerisches Wetter; **dripping wet** klatschnass; **It was wet all week.** Es hat die ganze Woche geregnet.

wet suit n Neoprenanzug m (pl Neoprenanzüge)

we've = we have

whale n Wal m (pl Wale)

what adj, pron ❶ was ▷ **What are you doing?** Was tust du? ▷ **What did you say?** Was hast du gesagt? ▷ **What is it?** Was ist das? ▷ **What's the matter?** Was ist los? ▷ **What happened?** Was ist passiert? ▷ **I saw what happened.** Ich habe gesehen, was passiert ist. ▷ **I heard what he said.** Ich habe gehört, was er gesagt hat.; **What?** Was? ❷ **welcher** ▷ **What name?** Welcher Name?
welche ▷ **What colour is it?** Welche Farbe hat es?
welches ▷ **What book do you want?** Welches Buch möchten Sie?
welche ▷ **What subjects are you studying?** Welche Fächer studierst du?; **What's the capital of Finland?** Wie heißt die Hauptstadt von Finnland?; **What a mess!** So ein Chaos!

wheat n Weizen m

wheel n Rad nt (pl Räder); **the steering wheel** das Lenkrad

wheelchair n Rollstuhl m (pl Rollstühle)

when adv, conj ❶ wann ▷ **When did he go?** Wann ist er gegangen? ❷ als ▷ **She was reading when I came in.** Sie las, als ich hereinkam.

where adv, conj wo ▷ **Where's Emma today?** Wo ist Emma heute? ▷ **Where do you live?** Wo wohnst du? ▷ **a shop where you can buy gardening tools** ein Geschäft, wo man Gartengeräte kaufen kann; **Where are you from?** Woher sind Sie?; **Where are you going?** Wohin gehst du?

> Be careful not to translate **where** by **wer**.

whether conj ob ▷ **I don't know whether to go or not.** Ich weiß nicht, ob ich gehen soll oder nicht.

which adj, pron ❶ welcher ▷ **Which coat is yours?** Welcher Mantel ist deiner?
welche ▷ **Which CD did you buy?** Welche CD hast du gekauft?
welches ▷ **Which book do you want?** Welches Buch willst du?
welche ▷ **Which shoes should I wear?** Welche Schuhe soll ich anziehen?

> When asking 'which one' use **welcher** or **welche** or **welches**, depending on whether the noun is masculine, feminine or neuter.

I know his brother. — Which one? Ich kenne seinen Bruder. — Welchen?; **I know his sister. — Which one?** Ich kenne seine Schwester. — Welche?; **I took one of your books. — Which one?** Ich habe eines deiner Bücher genommen. — Welches?; **Which would you like?** Welches möchtest du?; **Which of these are yours?** Welche davon gehören dir?

> In relative clauses use **der**, **die** or **das**, depending on the gender of the noun 'which' refers to.

❷ der ▷ **the film which is on now** der Film, der gerade läuft
die ▷ **the CD which is playing now** die CD, die gerade läuft

das ▷ *the book which I am reading* das Buch, das ich lese die ▷ *the sweets which I ate* die Süßigkeiten, die ich gegessen habe

while *conj* während ▷ *You hold the torch while I look inside.* Halt du die Taschenlampe, während ich hineinsehe. ▷ *She's dynamic, while he's more laid-back.* Sie ist dynamisch, während er eher lässig ist.
▶ *n* Weile *f* ▷ *after a while* nach einer Weile; **a while ago** vor einer Weile; **for a while** eine Zeit lang; **quite a while** ziemlich lange

whip *n* Peitsche *f*
▶ *vb* **❶** peitschen ▷ *She whipped her horse.* Sie peitschte ihr Pferd. **❷** (*eggs*) schlagen [59] (*pres* schlägt, *imperf* schlug, *perf* hat geschlagen)

whipped cream *n* Schlagsahne *f*
whiskers *npl* Schnurrhaare *ntpl*
whisky *n* Whisky *m* (*pl* Whiskys)
whisper *vb* flüstern [88]
whistle *n* Pfeife *f*; **The referee blew her whistle.** Die Schiedsrichterin hat gepfiffen.
▶ *vb* pfeifen (*imperf* pfiff, *perf* hat gepfiffen)

White *adj* (*person*) weiß; **a White man** ein Weißer
white *adj* weiß ▷ *He's got white hair.* Er hat weiße Haare.; **white wine** der Weißwein; **white bread** das Weißbrot; **white coffee** der Kaffee mit Milch
whiteboard *n* Weißwandtafel *f* ▷ *an interactive whiteboard* eine interaktive Weißwandtafel
Whitsun *n* Pfingsten *nt* (*gen* Pfingsten, *pl* Pfingsten)
who *pron* **❶** wer ▷ *Who said that?* Wer hat das gesagt? ▷ *Who's he?* Wer ist er?

> In relative clauses use **der**, **die** or **das**, depending on the gender of the noun 'who' refers to.

❷ der ▷ *the man who saw us* der Mann, der uns gesehen hat ▷ *the man who we* saw der Mann, den wir gesehen haben die ▷ *the woman who saw us* die Frau, die uns gesehen hat ▷ *the woman who we saw* die Frau, die wir gesehen haben das ▷ *the child who saw us* das Kind, das uns gesehen hat ▷ *the child who we saw* das Kind, das wir gesehen haben die ▷ *the people who saw us* die Leute, Pdie uns gesehen haben

> Be careful not to translate **who** by **wo**.

whole *adj* ganz ▷ *the whole class* die ganze Klasse ▷ *the whole day* den ganzen Tag ▷ *the whole world* die ganze Welt
▶ *n* **The whole of Wales was affected.** Ganz Wales war davon betroffen.; **on the whole** im Großen und Ganzen
wholemeal *adj* **wholemeal bread** das Vollkornbrot; **wholemeal flour** das Vollkornmehl
wholewheat *adj* (US) **wholewheat bread** das Vollkornbrot
whom *pron* wen ▷ *Whom did you see?* Wen hast du gesehen?; **the man to whom I spoke** der Mann, mit dem ich gesprochen habe; **the woman to whom I spoke** die Frau, mit der ich gesprochen habe
whose *pron*, *adj* wessen ▷ *Whose book is this?* Wessen Buch ist das?; **Whose is this?** Wem gehört das?; **I know whose it is.** Ich weiß, wem das gehört.; **the man whose picture was in the paper** der Mann, dessen Bild in der Zeitung war; **the woman whose picture was in the paper** die Frau, deren Bild in der Zeitung war; **the girl whose picture was in the paper** das Mädchen, dessen Bild in der Zeitung war
why *adv* warum ▷ *Why did you do that?* Warum hast du das getan? ▷ *Tell me why.* Sag mir warum. ▷ *Why not?* Warum nicht? ▷ *All right, why not?* Also gut, warum auch nicht?; **That's why he did it.** Deshalb hat er es getan.

ENGLISH > GERMAN

wicked adj ❶ (evil) böse ❷ (informal: really great) geil

wide adj, adv breit ▷ a wide road eine breite Straße; **wide open** weit offen; **wide awake** hellwach

widow n Witwe f ▷ She's a widow. Sie ist Witwe.

widower n Witwer m (pl Witwer) ▷ He's a widower. Er ist Witwer.

width n Breite f

wife n Frau f ▷ his wife seine Frau

Wi-Fi n Wi-Fi nt

wig n Perücke f

wild adj ❶ wild ▷ a wild animal ein wildes Tier ❷ (crazy) verrückt ▷ She's a bit wild. Sie ist ein bisschen verrückt.

wild card n Wildcard f (pl Wildcards)

wildlife n Tierwelt f ▷ I'm interested in wildlife. Ich interessiere mich für die Tierwelt.

will n Testament nt (pl Testamente) ▷ He left me some money in his will. Er hat mir in seinem Testament Geld vermacht.; **He came of his own free will.** Er ist freiwillig gekommen.
▷ vb

In German the present tense is often used to express somebody's intention to do something.

▷ I'll show you your room. Ich zeige Ihnen Ihr Zimmer. ▷ I'll give you a hand. Ich helfe dir.; **Will you help me?** Hilfst du mir?; **Will you wash up? — No, I won't.** Wäschst du ab? — Nein.

Use the German future tense when referring to the more distant future.

▷ I will come back one day. Ich werde eines Tages zurückkommen. ▷ It won't take long. Es wird nicht lange dauern.; **That'll be Dave.** Das wird Dave sein.; **Will you be quiet!** Werdet ihr wohl still sein!

willing adj **to be willing to do something** bereit sein, etwas zu tun [81]

win vb gewinnen [30] (imperf gewann, perf hat gewonnen) ▷ Did you win? Hast du gewonnen?; **to win a prize** einen Preis bekommen [40]
▷ n Sieg m (pl Siege)

wind vb ❶ (rope, wool, wire) wickeln ▷ He wound the rope round the tree. Er wickelte das Seil um den Baum. ❷ (river, path) sich schlängeln ▷ The road winds through the valley. Die Straße schlängelt sich durch das Tal.
▷ n Wind m (pl Winde) ▷ a strong wind ein starker Wind; **a wind farm** eine Windfarm; **a wind instrument** ein Blasinstrument nt; **wind power** die Windkraft

window n Fenster nt (pl Fenster) ▷ to break a window ein Fenster kaputt machen ▷ a broken window ein kaputtes Fenster; **a shop window** ein Schaufenster

windscreen n Windschutzscheibe f

windscreen wiper n Scheibenwischer m (pl Scheibenwischer)

windshield n (US) Windschutzscheibe f

windy adj (place) windig ▷ It's windy. Es ist windig.

wine n Wein m (pl Weine) ▷ a bottle of wine eine Flasche Wein ▷ a glass of wine ein Glas Wein; **white wine** der Weißwein; **red wine** der Rotwein; **a wine bar** eine Weinstube; **a wine glass** ein Weinglas nt; **the wine list** die Getränkekarte

wing n Flügel m (pl Flügel)

wink vb **to wink at somebody** jemandem zublinzeln

winner n Sieger m (pl Sieger), Siegerin f

winning adj **the winning team** die Siegermannschaft; **the winning goal** das entscheidende Tor

winter n Winter m (pl Winter) ▷ in winter im Winter

wipe vb abwischen [4] (perf hat abgewischt); **to wipe one's feet** sich die Füße abstreifen; **to wipe up** aufwischen

wire n Draht m (pl Drähte)

wisdom tooth n Weisheitszahn m (pl Weisheitszähne)

wise adj weise

wish vb **to wish for something** sich etwas wünschen [48]; **to wish to do something** etwas tun möchten; **I wish you were here!** Ich wünschte, du wärst da!; **I wish you'd told me!** Wenn du mir das doch nur gesagt hättest!
▶ n Wunsch m (pl Wünsche); **to make a wish** sich etwas wünschen [48]; **'best wishes'** (on greetings card) 'Alles Gute'; **'with best wishes, Jo'** 'alles Liebe, Jo'

with prep ❶ mit ▷ *Come with me.* Komm mit mir. ❷ *a woman with blue eyes* eine Frau mit blauen Augen; **Fill the jug with water.** Tu Wasser in den Krug.; **He walks with a stick.** Er geht am Stock. ❷ (at the home of) bei ▷ *We stayed with friends.* Wir haben bei Freunden übernachtet. ❸ vor ▷ *green with envy* grün vor Neid ▷ *to shake with fear* vor Angst zittern

without prep ohne ▷ *without a coat* ohne einen Mantel ▷ *without speaking* ohne etwas zu sagen

witness n Zeuge m (gen Zeugen, pl Zeugen), Zeugin f ▷ *There were no witnesses.* Es gab keine Zeugen.; **witness box** der Zeugenstand; **witness stand** der Zeugenstand

witty adj geistreich

wives npl see **wife**

woken up vb see **wake up**

woke up vb see **wake up**

wolf n Wolf m (pl Wölfe)

woman n Frau f; **a woman doctor** eine Ärztin

won vb see **win**

wonder vb sich fragen [38] ▷ *I wonder why she said that.* Ich frage mich, warum sie das gesagt hat. ▷ *I wonder what that means.* Ich frage mich, was das bedeutet.; **I wonder where Caroline is.** Wo Caroline wohl ist?

wonderful adj wunderbar

won't = will not

wood n ❶ (timber) Holz nt (pl Hölzer) ▷ *It's made of wood.* Es ist aus Holz. ❷ (forest) Wald m (pl Wälder) ▷ *We went for a walk in the wood.* Wir sind im Wald spazieren gegangen.

wooden adj hölzern; **a wooden chair** ein Holzstuhl m

woodwork n Schreinern nt ▷ *Dieter's hobby is woodwork.* Schreinern ist Dieters Hobby.

wool n Wolle f ▷ *It's made of wool.* Es ist aus Wolle.

word n Wort nt (pl Wörter) ▷ *a difficult word* ein schwieriges Wort; **What's the word for 'shop' in German?** Wie heißt 'shop' auf Deutsch?; **in other words** mit anderen Worten; **to have a word with somebody** mit jemandem reden [54]; **the words** (lyrics) der Text sg

word processing n Textverarbeitung f

word processor n Textverarbeitungssystem nt (pl Textverarbeitungssysteme)

wore vb see **wear**

work n Arbeit f ▷ *She's looking for work.* Sie sucht Arbeit. ▷ *He's at work at the moment.* Er ist zurzeit bei der Arbeit. ▷ *It's hard work.* Das ist harte Arbeit.; **to be off work** (sick) krank sein [65]; **He's out of work.** Er ist arbeitslos.
▶ vb ❶ (person) arbeiten [2] ▷ *She works in a shop.* Sie arbeitet in einem Laden. ▷ *to work hard* hart arbeiten ❷ (machine, plan) funktionieren [76] (perf hat funktioniert) ▷ *The heating isn't working.* Die Heizung funktioniert nicht. ▷ *My plan worked perfectly.* Mein Plan hat prima funktioniert.; **to work from home** im Homeoffice arbeiten; **to**

ENGLISH > GERMAN

work out (1) (exercise) trainieren [**76**] ▷ *I work out twice a week.* Ich trainiere zweimal pro Woche. (2) (turn out) klappen [**48**] ▷ *In the end it worked out really well.* Am Ende hat es richtig gut geklappt.; **to work something out** (figure out) auf etwas kommen [**40**] ▷ *I just couldn't work it out.* Ich bin einfach nicht darauf gekommen.; **It works out at ten pounds each.** Das macht für jeden zehn Pfund.

worker n Arbeiter m (pl Arbeiter), Arbeiterin f ▷ *He's a factory worker.* Er ist Fabrikarbeiter.; **She's a good worker.** Sie macht gute Arbeit.

work experience n Praktikum nt (pl Praktika) ▷ *work experience in a factory* ein Praktikum in einer Fabrik

working-class adj Arbeiterklasse f ▷ *a working-class family* eine Familie der Arbeiterklasse

workman n Arbeiter m (pl Arbeiter)

worksheet n Arbeitsblatt nt (pl Arbeitsblätter)

workshop n Werkstatt f (pl Werkstätten); **a drama workshop** ein Theaterworkshop m

workspace n Arbeitsplatz m (gen Arbeitsplatzes, pl Arbeitsplätze)

workstation n Arbeitsplatzcomputer m (pl Arbeitsplatzcomputer)

world n Welt f; **He's the world champion.** Er ist der Weltmeister.

World Wide Web n the World Wide Web das World Wide Web

worm n Wurm m (pl Würmer)

worn vb see **wear**
▶ adj abgenutzt ▷ *The carpet is a bit worn.* Der Teppich ist etwas abgenutzt.; **worn out** (tired) erschöpft

worried adj besorgt ▷ *She's very worried.* Sie ist sehr besorgt.; **to be worried about something** sich wegen etwas Sorgen machen [**48**]; **to look worried** besorgt aussehen [**64**]

523 | **would**

worry vb sich Sorgen machen ▷ *You worry too much.* Du machst dir zu viele Sorgen.; **Don't worry!** Keine Sorge!

worse adj, adv schlechter ▷ *My results were bad, but his were even worse.* Meine Noten waren schlecht, aber seine waren noch schlechter.; **I'm feeling worse.** Mir geht es schlechter.; **It was even worse than that.** Es war sogar noch schlimmer.

worst adj the worst (1) der schlechteste ▷ *the worst student in the class* der schlechteste Schüler der Klasse (2) die schlechteste ▷ *He got the worst mark in the whole class.* Er hat von der ganzen Klasse die schlechteste Note bekommen. (3) das schlechteste ▷ *the worst report I've ever had* das schlechteste Zeugnis, das ich je hatte; **my worst enemy** mein schlimmster Feind; **Maths is my worst subject.** In Mathe bin ich am schlechtesten.
▶ n Schlimmste nt (gen Schlimmsten) ▷ *The worst of it is that ...* Das Schlimmste daran ist, dass ...; **at worst** schlimmstenfalls; **if the worst comes to the worst** schlimmstenfalls

worth adj to be worth wert sein [**65**]; **It's worth it.** Das lohnt sich.

would vb Would you like ...? Möchtest du ...? ▷ *Would you like a biscuit?* Möchtest du einen Keks? ▷ *Would you like to go and see a film?* Möchtest du ins Kino gehen?; **Would you close the door please?** Würden Sie bitte die Tür zumachen?; **I'd like ...** Ich würde gern ... ▷ *I'd like to go to America.* Ich würde gern nach Amerika fahren.; **Shall we go and see a film? — Yes, I'd like that.** Sollen wir ins Kino gehen? — Au ja!; **I said I'd do it.** Ich sagte, ich würde es tun.; **If you asked him he'd do it.** Wenn du ihn fragen würdest, würde er es tun.; **If you had asked him he would have done it.** Wenn du ihn gefragt hättest, hätte er es getan.

wouldn't = would not

wound vb see **wind**
▶ vb verwunden [7] (perf hat verwundet) ▷ He was wounded. Er wurde verwundet.
▶ n Wunde f

wrap vb einpacken [4] (perf hat eingepackt) ▷ She's wrapping the present. Sie packt das Geschenk ein.; **Can you wrap it for me please?** (in shop) Können Sie es mir bitte in Geschenkpapier einpacken?; **to wrap up** einpacken [4]

wrapping paper n Geschenkpapier nt

wreck n Wrack nt (pl Wracks) ▷ That car is a wreck! Das Auto ist ein Wrack. ▷ After the exam I was a complete wreck. Nach der Prüfung war ich ein totales Wrack.
▶ vb ❶ (building) zerstören [95] (perf hat zerstört) ▷ The explosion wrecked the whole house. Die Explosion hat das ganze Haus zerstört. ❷ (car) kaputt fahren (pres fährt kaputt, imperf fuhr kaputt, perf hat kaputt gefahren) ▷ He's wrecked his car. Er hat sein Auto kaputt gefahren. ❸ (plan, holiday) verderben (pres verdirbt, imperf verdarb, perf hat verdorben) ▷ Our trip was wrecked by bad weather. Das schlechte Wetter hat uns den Ausflug verdorben.

wrestler n Ringer m (pl Ringer), Ringerin f

wrestling n Ringen nt ▷ His hobby is wrestling. Ringen ist sein Hobby.

wrinkled adj faltig

wrist n Handgelenk nt (pl Handgelenke)

write vb schreiben [61] (imperf schrieb, perf hat geschrieben) ▷ to write a letter einen Brief schreiben; **to write to somebody** jemandem schreiben [61]; **to write down** aufschreiben [61]

writer n Schriftsteller m (pl Schriftsteller), Schriftstellerin f ▷ She's a writer. Sie ist Schriftstellerin.

writing n Schrift f ▷ I can't read your writing. Ich kann deine Schrift nicht lesen.; **in writing** schriftlich

written vb see **write**

wrong adj, adv ❶ (incorrect) falsch ▷ The information was wrong. Die Information war falsch. ▷ the wrong answer die falsche Antwort.; **You've got the wrong number.** Sie haben sich verwählt. ❷ (morally bad) unrecht ▷ I think fox hunting is wrong. Ich meine, dass Fuchsjagden unrecht sind.; **to be wrong** (mistaken) unrecht haben [32]; **to do something wrong** etwas falsch machen [48]; **to go wrong** (plan) schiefgehen [29]; **What's wrong?** Was ist los?; **What's wrong with her?** Was ist mit ihr los?

wrote vb see **write**

WWW abbr (= World Wide Web); **the WWW** das WWW

Xmas n (= Christmas) Weihnachten nt
X-ray vb röntgen [**54**] ▷ They X-rayed my arm. Sie haben meinen Arm geröntgt.
▶ n Röntgenaufnahme f; **to have an X-ray** geröntgt werden [**91**]

yacht n ❶ (sailing boat) Segelboot nt (pl Segelboote) ❷ (luxury motorboat) Jacht f
yawn vb gähnen [**38**]
year n Jahr nt (pl Jahre) ▷ last year letztes Jahr ▷ next year nächstes Jahr ▷ to be fifteen years old fünfzehn Jahre alt sein; **an eight-year-old child** ein achtjähriges Kind

- In German secondary schools, years
- are counted from the **fünfte Klasse**
- (youngest) to the **dreizehnte Klasse**
- (oldest).

He's a first-year. Er ist in der fünften Klasse.
yell vb schreien [**62**] (imperf schrie, perf hat geschrien)
yellow adj gelb
yes adv ❶ ja ▷ Do you like it? — Yes. Gefällt es dir? — Ja. ▷ Yes please. Ja bitte. ❷ doch

Use **doch** to contradict a negative statement or question.

▷ Don't you like it? — Yes! Gefällt es dir nicht? — Doch! ▷ You're not Swiss, are you? — Yes I am! Sie sind nicht Schweizer, oder?

— Doch, ich bin Schweizer. ▷ *That's not true.* — *Yes it is!* Das ist nicht wahr. — Doch!

yesterday *adv* gestern ▷ *yesterday morning* gestern früh ▷ *yesterday afternoon* gestern Nachmittag ▷ *yesterday evening* gestern Abend ▷ *all day yesterday* gestern den ganzen Tag; **the day before yesterday** vorgestern

yet *adv* **❶** noch ▷ *It has yet to be proved that ...* Es muss noch bewiesen werden, dass ... **❷** *(in questions)* schon ▷ *Has the murderer been caught yet?* Ist der Mörder schon gefasst worden?; **not yet** noch nicht; **not as yet** noch nicht; **Have you finished yet?** Bist du fertig?

yoga *n* Yoga *nt*
yoghurt *n* Joghurt *m (pl* Joghurts*)*
yolk *n* Eigelb *nt (pl* Eigelbe*)*
you *pron*

> Only use **du** when speaking to one person, and when the person is your own age or younger. Use **ihr** for several people of your own age or younger. If in doubt use the polite form **Sie**.

❶ *(polite form, singular and plural)* Sie ▷ *Do you like football?* Mögen Sie Fußball? ▷ *Can I help you?* Kann ich Ihnen behilflich sein? ▷ *I saw you yesterday.* Ich habe Sie gestern gesehen. ▷ *It's for you.* Das ist für Sie. **❷** *(familiar singular)* du ▷ *Do you like football?* Magst du Fußball? ▷ *She's younger than you.* Sie ist jünger als du. ▷ *I know you.* Ich kenne dich. ▷ *I gave it to you.* Ich habe es dir gegeben. ▷ *It's for you.* Es ist für dich. ▷ *I'll come with you.* Ich komme mit dir mit. **❸** *(familiar plural)* ihr ▷ *Do you two like football?* Mögt ihr beiden Fußball? ▷ *I told you to be quiet.* Ich habe euch gesagt, ihr sollt still sein. ▷ *This is for you two.* Es ist für euch beide. ▷ *Can I come with you?* Kann ich mit euch mitkommen?

young *adj* jung ▷ *young people* junge Leute

younger *adj* jünger ▷ *He's younger than me.* Er ist jünger als ich. ▷ *my younger brother* mein jüngerer Bruder ▷ *my younger sister* meine jüngere Schwester

youngest *adj* jüngste ▷ *his youngest brother* sein jüngster Bruder ▷ *She's the youngest.* Sie ist die Jüngste.

your *adj*

> Only use **dein** when speaking to one person, and when the person is your own age or younger. For several people of your own age or younger use **euer**. If in doubt use the polite form **Ihr**.

❶ *(polite form, singular and plural)* Ihr ▷ *your father* Ihr Vater ▷ *your mother* Ihre Mutter ▷ *your house* Ihr Haus ▷ *your seats* Ihre Plätze **❷** *(familiar singular)* dein ▷ *your brother* dein Bruder ▷ *your sister* deine Schwester ▷ *your book* dein Buch ▷ *your parents* deine Eltern **❸** *(familiar plural)* euer ▷ *your father* euer Vater ▷ *your mother* eure Mutter ▷ *your car* euer Auto ▷ *your teachers* eure Lehrer

> Do not use **Ihr, dein** or **euer** with parts of the body.

▷ *Would you like to wash your hands?* Möchten Sie sich die Hände waschen? ▷ *Do you want to wash your hair?* Möchtest du dir die Haare waschen? ▷ *You two, go upstairs and brush your teeth.* Ihr beide geht nach oben und putzt euch die Zähne.

yours *pron*

> Only use **deiner/deine/deines** when talking to one person of your own age or younger. Use **euer/eure/eures** when talking to several people of your own age or younger. If in doubt use the polite form **Ihrer/Ihre/Ihres**.

❶ *(polite form, singular and plural)* Ihrer ▷ *That's a nice coat. Is it yours?* Das ist ein hübscher Mantel. Ist es Ihrer?; Ihre

▷ *What a pretty jacket. Is it yours?* Was für eine Hübsche Jacke. Ist das Ihre?; Ihres ▷ *I like that car. Is it yours?* Das Auto gefällt mir. Ist es Ihres?; Ihre ▷ *my parents and yours* meine Eltern und Ihre; **Is this yours?** Gehört das Ihnen?; **Yours sincerely, ...** Mit freundlichen Grüßen ... ❷ *(familiar singular)* deiner ▷ *I've lost my pen. Can I use yours?* Ich habe meinen Schreiber verlegt. Kann ich deinen benützen?; deine ▷ *Nice jacket. Is it yours?* Hübsche Jacke. Ist das deine?; deines ▷ *I like that car. Is it yours?* Das Auto gefällt mir. Ist das deines?; deine ▷ *my parents and yours* meine Eltern und deine ▷ *My hands are dirty, yours are clean.* Meine Hände sind schmutzig, deine sind sauber.; **Is this yours?** Gehört das dir? ❸ *(familiar plural)* euer ▷ *My computer is broken. Can I use yours?* Mein Computer ist kaputt. Kann ich euren benutzen?; eure ▷ *I haven't got a torch. Can I use yours?* Ich habe keine Taschenlampe. Kann ich eure benutzen?; eures ▷ *Our house is bigger than yours.* Unser Haus ist größer als eures.; eure ▷ *our parents and yours* unsere Eltern und eure; **Is this yours?** Gehört das euch?

yourself *pron*

> Only use **dich/dir** when talking to one person of your own age or younger. If in doubt use the polite form **sich**.

❶ *(polite form)* sich ▷ *Have you hurt yourself?* Haben Sie sich verletzt? ▷ *Tell me about yourself!* Erzählen Sie etwas von sich! ❷ *(familiar form)* dich ▷ *Have you hurt yourself?* Hast du dich verletzt? ❸ *(familiar form)* dir ▷ *Tell me about yourself!* Erzähl mir etwas von dir! ▷ *If you are not happy with yourself ...* Wenn du mit dir selbst nicht zufrieden bist ... ❹ selbst; **Do it yourself! (1)** Machen Sie es selbst! **(2)** Mach's selbst!

yourselves *pron*

> Only use **euch** when talking to people of your own age or younger. If in doubt use the polite form **sich**.

❶ *(polite form)* sich ▷ *Did you enjoy yourselves?* Haben Sie sich amüsiert? ❷ *(familiar form)* euch ▷ *Did you enjoy yourselves?* Habt ihr euch amüsiert? ❸ selbst; **Did you make it yourselves? (1)** Haben Sie es selbst gemacht? **(2)** Habt ihr es selbst gemacht?

youth club *n* Jugendzentrum *nt* (*pl* Jugendzentren)

youth hostel *n* Jugendherberge *f*

Z

zany *adj* irre komisch ▷ *a zany film* ein irre komischer Film
zebra *n* Zebra *nt* (*pl* Zebras)
zebra crossing *n* Zebrastreifen *m* (*pl* Zebrastreifen)
zero *n* Null *f*
Zimmer frame® *n* Rollator *m* (*pl* Rollatoren)
zip *n* Reißverschluss *m* (*gen* Reißverschlusses, *pl* Reißverschlüsse)
zip code *n* (US) Postleitzahl *f*
zip drive *n* Zip-Laufwerk *nt* (*pl* Zip-Laufwerke)
zipper *n* (US) Reißverschluss *m* (*gen* Reißverschlusses, *pl* Reißverschlüsse)
zodiac *n* Tierkreis *m* (*gen* Tierkreises); **the signs of the zodiac** die Sternzeichen
zone *n* Zone *f*
zoo *n* Zoo *m* (*pl* Zoos)
zoom lens *n* Zoomobjektiv *nt* (*pl* Zoomobjektive)
zucchini *npl* (US) Zucchini *pl*

VERB TABLES

Introduction

The verb tables in the following section contain 97 tables of German verbs (some regular and some irregular) in alphabetical order. Each table shows you the following forms:

Present	eg ich arbeite = I work or I'm working
Present Subjunctive	eg ich arbeite = I work
Perfect	eg ich habe gearbeitet = I worked or I have worked
Imperfect	eg ich arbeitete = I was working or I worked
Future	eg ich werde arbeiten = I will work
Conditional	eg ich würde arbeiten = I would work
Imperative	eg arbeite = work
Present Participle	eg arbeitend = working
Past Participle	eg gearbeitet = worked

On both sides of the dictionary, most of the German verbs are followed by a number (e.g. **holen** [38] vb <u>to fetch</u>). This number corresponds to a verb table number in this verbs section, where the pattern followed by the model verb is shown. When you come across **kämpfen** [38] vb <u>to fight</u>, for example, you will see that it follows the same pattern as that of model verb **holen**, shown in verb table **38**. For other verbs, a summary of the main forms is given after the word (eg **heben** (imperf **hob**, perf **hat gehoben**) vb to lift).

In the verb tables, you will find examples of **weak**, **strong** and **mixed** verb forms. **Weak** verbs follow regular patterns, **strong** verbs follow irregular patterns and **mixed** verbs follow a mixture of regular and irregular patterns.

In order to help you use the verbs shown in the verb tables correctly, there are also a number of example phrases at the bottom of each page to show the sense as it is used in context.

Remember:

ich	=	I
du	=	you (to one person you know well)
er	=	he/it
sie	=	she/it
es	=	it/he/she
wir	=	we
ihr	=	you (to more than one person you know well)
Sie	=	you (polite form, to one or more people)
sie	=	they

Table 1: annehmen *to accept*

strong, separable, formed with **haben**

PRESENT
ich	nehme an
du	nimmst an
er/sie/es	nimmt an
wir	nehmen an
ihr	nehmt an
sie/Sie	nehmen an

PRESENT SUBJUNCTIVE
ich	nehme an
du	nehmest an
er/sie/es	nehme an
wir	nehmen an
ihr	nehmet an
sie/Sie	nehmen an

PERFECT
ich	habe angenommen
du	hast angenommen
er/sie/es	hat angenommen
wir	haben angenommen
ihr	habt angenommen
sie/Sie	haben angenommen

IMPERFECT
ich	nahm an
du	nahmst an
er/sie/es	nahm an
wir	nahmen an
ihr	nahmt an
sie/Sie	nahmen an

FUTURE
ich	werde annehmen
du	wirst annehmen
er/sie/es	wird annehmen
wir	werden annehmen
ihr	werdet annehmen
sie/Sie	werden annehmen

CONDITIONAL
ich	würde annehmen
du	würdest annehmen
er/sie/es	würde annehmen
wir	würden annehmen
ihr	würdet annehmen
sie/Sie	würden annehmen

IMPERATIVE
nimm an! / nehmen wir an! / nehmt an! / nehmen Sie an!

PRESENT PARTICIPLE
annehmend

PAST PARTICIPLE
angenommen

EXAMPLE PHRASES

Ich **nehme an**, dass er heute nicht mehr kommt.
I assume that he isn't coming today.

Ich **habe** die neue Stelle **angenommen**.
I have accepted the new job.

weak,
formed with **haben**

to work **arbeiten**

Table 2

PRESENT
ich	arbeite
du	arbeitest
er/sie/es	arbeitet
wir	arbeiten
ihr	arbeitet
sie/Sie	arbeiten

PRESENT SUBJUNCTIVE
ich	arbeite
du	arbeitest
er/sie/es	arbeite
wir	arbeiten
ihr	arbeitet
sie/Sie	arbeiten

PERFECT
ich	habe gearbeitet
du	hast gearbeitet
er/sie/es	hat gearbeitet
wir	haben gearbeitet
ihr	habt gearbeitet
sie/Sie	haben gearbeitet

IMPERFECT
ich	arbeitete
du	arbeitetest
er/sie/es	arbeitete
wir	arbeiteten
ihr	arbeitetet
sie/Sie	arbeiteten

FUTURE
ich	werde arbeiten
du	wirst arbeiten
er/sie/es	wird arbeiten
wir	werden arbeiten
ihr	werdet arbeiten
sie/Sie	werden arbeiten

CONDITIONAL
ich	würde arbeiten
du	würdest arbeiten
er/sie/es	würde arbeiten
wir	würden arbeiten
ihr	würdet arbeiten
sie/Sie	würden arbeiten

IMPERATIVE
arbeite! / arbeiten wir! / arbeitet! / arbeiten Sie!

PRESENT PARTICIPLE
arbeitend

PAST PARTICIPLE
gearbeitet

EXAMPLE PHRASES

Er **hat** früher als Elektriker **gearbeitet**. — *He used to work as an electrician.*

Sie **arbeitete** wochenlang an dem Projekt. — *She worked for weeks on the project.*

Ich **würde** nicht gern sonntags **arbeiten**. — *I wouldn't like to work on Sundays.*

Table 3: **atmen** *to breathe* — weak, formed with **haben**

PRESENT
- ich atme
- du atmest
- er/sie/es atmet
- wir atmen
- ihr atmet
- sie/Sie atmen

PRESENT SUBJUNCTIVE
- ich atme
- du atmest
- er/sie/es atme
- wir atmen
- ihr atmet
- sie/Sie atmen

PERFECT
- ich habe geatmet
- du hast geatmet
- er/sie/es hat geatmet
- wir haben geatmet
- ihr habt geatmet
- sie/Sie haben geatmet

IMPERFECT
- ich atmete
- du atmetest
- er/sie/es atmete
- wir atmeten
- ihr atmetet
- sie/Sie atmeten

FUTURE
- ich werde atmen
- du wirst atmen
- er/sie/es wird atmen
- wir werden atmen
- ihr werdet atmen
- sie/Sie werden atmen

CONDITIONAL
- ich würde atmen
- du würdest atmen
- er/sie/es würde atmen
- wir würden atmen
- ihr würdet atmen
- sie/Sie würden atmen

IMPERATIVE
atme! / atmen wir! / atmet! / atmen Sie!

PRESENT PARTICIPLE
atmend

PAST PARTICIPLE
geatmet

EXAMPLE PHRASES

Sie **atmet** jetzt wieder etwas freier.
Wir **atmeten** tief ein und aus.
Dort **werden** wir frischere Luft **atmen**.

She is now breathing a bit more freely again.
We took deep breaths.
We'll breathe fresher air there.

weak, separable,
formed with **haben**

to be enough **ausreichen**

Table 4

PRESENT

ich	reiche aus
du	reichst aus
er/sie/es	reicht aus
wir	reichen aus
ihr	reicht aus
sie/Sie	reichen aus

PRESENT SUBJUNCTIVE

ich	reiche aus
du	reichest aus
er/sie/es	reiche aus
wir	reichen aus
ihr	reichet aus
sie/Sie	reichen aus

PERFECT

ich	habe ausgereicht
du	hast ausgereicht
er/sie/es	hat ausgereicht
wir	haben ausgereicht
ihr	habt ausgereicht
sie/Sie	haben ausgereicht

IMPERFECT

ich	reichte aus
du	reichtest aus
er/sie/es	reichte aus
wir	reichten aus
ihr	reichtet aus
sie/Sie	reichten aus

FUTURE

ich	werde ausreichen
du	wirst ausreichen
er/sie/es	wird ausreichen
wir	werden ausreichen
ihr	werdet ausreichen
sie/Sie	werden ausreichen

CONDITIONAL

ich	würde ausreichen
du	würdest ausreichen
er/sie/es	würde ausreichen
wir	würden ausreichen
ihr	würdet ausreichen
sie/Sie	würden ausreichen

IMPERATIVE

reiche(e) aus! / reichen wir aus! / reicht aus! / reichen Sie aus!

PRESENT PARTICIPLE

ausreichend

PAST PARTICIPLE

ausgereicht

---------- EXAMPLE PHRASES ----------

Er meint, das Geld **reiche** nicht **aus**.
Die Zeit **reichte** nie **aus**.
Das **wird** uns nicht **ausreichen**.

He thinks the money isn't enough.
There was never enough time.
That won't be enough for us.

Table 5: beginnen — to begin

strong, inseparable, formed with haben

PRESENT
ich	beginne
du	beginnst
er/sie/es	beginnt
wir	beginnen
ihr	beginnt
sie/Sie	beginnen

PRESENT SUBJUNCTIVE
ich	beginne
du	beginnest
er/sie/es	beginne
wir	beginnen
ihr	beginnet
sie/Sie	beginnen

PERFECT
ich	habe begonnen
du	hast begonnen
er/sie/es	hat begonnen
wir	haben begonnen
ihr	habt begonnen
sie/Sie	haben begonnen

IMPERFECT
ich	begann
du	begannst
er/sie/es	begann
wir	begannen
ihr	begannt
sie/Sie	begannen

FUTURE
ich	werde beginnen
du	wirst beginnen
er/sie/es	wird beginnen
wir	werden beginnen
ihr	werdet beginnen
sie/Sie	werden beginnen

CONDITIONAL
ich	würde beginnen
du	würdest beginnen
er/sie/es	würde beginnen
wir	würden beginnen
ihr	würdet beginnen
sie/Sie	würden beginnen

IMPERATIVE
beginn(e)! / beginnen wir! / beginnt! / beginnen Sie!

PRESENT PARTICIPLE
beginnend

PAST PARTICIPLE
begonnen

EXAMPLE PHRASES

Die Vorstellung **beginnt** gleich. — *The performance is about to begin.*
Er **hat** als Lehrling **begonnen**. — *He started off as an apprentice.*
Wir **würden** nicht ohne dich **beginnen**. — *We wouldn't start without you.*

strong, formed with **haben** — to bite **beißen** — Table 6

PRESENT
- ich beiße
- du beißt
- er/sie/es beißt
- wir beißen
- ihr beißt
- sie/Sie beißen

PRESENT SUBJUNCTIVE
- ich beiße
- du beißest
- er/sie/es beiße
- wir beißen
- ihr beißet
- sie/Sie beißen

PERFECT
- ich habe gebissen
- du hast gebissen
- er/sie/es hat gebissen
- wir haben gebissen
- ihr habt gebissen
- sie/Sie haben gebissen

IMPERFECT
- ich biss
- du bissest
- er/sie/es biss
- wir bissen
- ihr bisst
- sie/Sie bissen

FUTURE
- ich werde beißen
- du wirst beißen
- er/sie/es wird beißen
- wir werden beißen
- ihr werdet beißen
- sie/Sie werden beißen

CONDITIONAL
- ich würde beißen
- du würdest beißen
- er/sie/es würde beißen
- wir würden beißen
- ihr würdet beißen
- sie/Sie würden beißen

IMPERATIVE
beiß(e)! / beißen wir! / beißt! / beißen Sie!

PRESENT PARTICIPLE
beißend

PAST PARTICIPLE
gebissen

---- EXAMPLE PHRASES ----

Er versichert uns, sein Hund **beiße** nicht.
He assures us his dog doesn't bite.

Sie **biss** in den Apfel.
She bit into the apple.

Er **wird** dich schon nicht **beißen**!
He won't bite you!

Table 7: bestellen — to order

weak, inseparable, formed with haben

PRESENT
ich	bestelle
du	bestellst
er/sie/es	bestellt
wir	bestellen
ihr	bestellt
sie/Sie	bestellen

PRESENT SUBJUNCTIVE
ich	bestelle
du	bestellest
er/sie/es	bestelle
wir	bestellen
ihr	bestellet
sie/Sie	bestellen

PERFECT
ich	habe bestellt
du	hast bestellt
er/sie/es	hat bestellt
wir	haben bestellt
ihr	habt bestellt
sie/Sie	haben bestellt

IMPERFECT
ich	bestellte
du	bestelltest
er/sie/es	bestellte
wir	bestellten
ihr	bestelltet
sie/Sie	bestellten

FUTURE
ich	werde bestellen
du	wirst bestellen
er/sie/es	wird bestellen
wir	werden bestellen
ihr	werdet bestellen
sie/Sie	werden bestellen

CONDITIONAL
ich	würde bestellen
du	würdest bestellen
er/sie/es	würde bestellen
wir	würden bestellen
ihr	würdet bestellen
sie/Sie	würden bestellen

IMPERATIVE
bestelle(e)! / bestellen wir! / bestellt! / bestellen Sie!

PRESENT PARTICIPLE
bestellend

PAST PARTICIPLE
bestellt

EXAMPLE PHRASES

Ich **bestelle** uns schon mal ein Bier. — *I'll go and order a beer for us.*

Haben Sie schon **bestellt**? — *Have you ordered yet?*

Wir **bestellten** einen Tisch für zwei. — *We reserved a table for two.*

strong, formed with **haben** — to offer **bieten**

Table 8

PRESENT

ich	biete
du	bietest
er/sie/es	bietet
wir	bieten
ihr	bietet
sie/Sie	bieten

PRESENT SUBJUNCTIVE

ich	biete
du	bietest
er/sie/es	biete
wir	bieten
ihr	bietet
sie/Sie	bieten

PERFECT

ich	habe geboten
du	hast geboten
er/sie/es	hat geboten
wir	haben geboten
ihr	habt geboten
sie/Sie	haben geboten

IMPERFECT

ich	bot
du	bot(e)st
er/sie/es	bot
wir	boten
ihr	botet
sie/Sie	boten

FUTURE

ich	werde bieten
du	wirst bieten
er/sie/es	wird bieten
wir	werden bieten
ihr	werdet bieten
sie/Sie	werden bieten

CONDITIONAL

ich	würde bieten
du	würdest bieten
er/sie/es	würde bieten
wir	würden bieten
ihr	würdet bieten
sie/Sie	würden bieten

IMPERATIVE

biet(e)! / bieten wir! / bietet! / bieten Sie!

PRESENT PARTICIPLE

bietend

PAST PARTICIPLE

geboten

EXAMPLE PHRASES

Er **bot** ihm die Hand. — *He held out his hand to him.*
Was **werden** sie uns **bieten**? — *What will they offer us?*
Wir **würden** ihm gern mehr **bieten**. — *We would like to offer him more.*

Table 9: **bitten** *to ask (for)* — strong, formed with **haben**

PRESENT
- ich bitte
- du bittest
- er/sie/es bittet
- wir bitten
- ihr bittet
- sie/Sie bitten

PRESENT SUBJUNCTIVE
- ich bitte
- du bittest
- er/sie/es bitte
- wir bitten
- ihr bittet
- sie/Sie bitten

PERFECT
- ich habe gebeten
- du hast gebeten
- er/sie/es hat gebeten
- wir haben gebeten
- ihr habt gebeten
- sie/Sie haben gebeten

IMPERFECT
- ich bat
- du bat(e)st
- er/sie/es bat
- wir baten
- ihr batet
- sie/Sie baten

FUTURE
- ich werde bitten
- du wirst bitten
- er/sie/es wird bitten
- wir werden bitten
- ihr werdet bitten
- sie/Sie werden bitten

CONDITIONAL
- ich würde bitten
- du würdest bitten
- er/sie/es würde bitten
- wir würden bitten
- ihr würdet bitten
- sie/Sie würden bitten

IMPERATIVE
bitt(e)! / bitten wir! / bittet! / bitten Sie!

PRESENT PARTICIPLE
bittend

PAST PARTICIPLE
gebeten

--- EXAMPLE PHRASES ---

Ich **bitte** Sie, uns in Ruhe zu lassen.
I'm asking you to leave us alone.

Sie **bat** ihn um Hilfe.
She asked him for help.

strong, formed with sein — *to stay* **bleiben** — Table 10

PRESENT
ich	bleibe
du	bleibst
er/sie/es	bleibt
wir	bleiben
ihr	bleibt
sie/Sie	bleiben

PRESENT SUBJUNCTIVE
ich	bleibe
du	bleibest
er/sie/es	bleibe
wir	bleiben
ihr	bleibet
sie/Sie	bleiben

PERFECT
ich	bin geblieben
du	bist geblieben
er/sie/es	ist geblieben
wir	sind geblieben
ihr	seid geblieben
sie/Sie	sind geblieben

IMPERFECT
ich	blieb
du	bliebst
er/sie/es	blieb
wir	blieben
ihr	bliebt
sie/Sie	blieben

FUTURE
ich	werde bleiben
du	wirst bleiben
er/sie/es	wird bleiben
wir	werden bleiben
ihr	werdet bleiben
sie/Sie	werden bleiben

CONDITIONAL
ich	würde bleiben
du	würdest bleiben
er/sie/es	würde bleiben
wir	würden bleiben
ihr	würdet bleiben
sie/Sie	würden bleiben

IMPERATIVE
bleib(e)! / bleiben wir! / bleibt! / bleiben Sie!

PRESENT PARTICIPLE
bleibend

PAST PARTICIPLE
geblieben

--- EXAMPLE PHRASES ---

Hoffentlich **bleibt** das Wetter schön. — *I hope the weather stays fine.*

Dieses Erlebnis **blieb** in meiner Erinnerung. — *This experience stayed with me.*

Table 11: **brechen** *to break*

strong, formed with **haben/sein**°

PRESENT

ich	breche
du	brichst
er/sie/es	bricht
wir	brechen
ihr	brecht
sie/Sie	brechen

PRESENT SUBJUNCTIVE

ich	breche
du	brechest
er/sie/es	breche
wir	brechen
ihr	brechet
sie/Sie	brechen

PERFECT

ich	habe gebrochen
du	hast gebrochen
er/sie/es	hat gebrochen
wir	haben gebrochen
ihr	habt gebrochen
sie/Sie	haben gebrochen

IMPERFECT

ich	brach
du	brachst
er/sie/es	brach
wir	brachen
ihr	bracht
sie/Sie	brachen

FUTURE

ich	werde brechen
du	wirst brechen
er/sie/es	wird brechen
wir	werden brechen
ihr	werdet brechen
sie/Sie	werden brechen

CONDITIONAL

ich	würde brechen
du	würdest brechen
er/sie/es	würde brechen
wir	würden brechen
ihr	würdet brechen
sie/Sie	würden brechen

IMPERATIVE
brich! / brechen wir! / brecht! / brechen Sie!

PRESENT PARTICIPLE
brechend

PAST PARTICIPLE
gebrochen

°When **brechen** is used with no direct object, it is formed with **sein**.

EXAMPLE PHRASES

Sie **hat** ihr Versprechen **gebrochen**.	She broke her promise.
Der Sturz **brach** ihm fast den Arm.	The fall almost broke his arm.
Ich **würde** ihm nie die Treue **brechen**.	I would never break his trust.

mixed, *formed with* **haben**   *to burn* **brennen**

Table 12

PRESENT

ich	brenne
du	brennst
er/sie/es	brennt
wir	brennen
ihr	brennt
sie/Sie	brennen

PRESENT SUBJUNCTIVE

ich	brenne
du	brennest
er/sie/es	brenne
wir	brennen
ihr	brennet
sie/Sie	brennen

PERFECT

ich	habe gebrannt
du	hast gebrannt
er/sie/es	hat gebrannt
wir	haben gebrannt
ihr	habt gebrannt
sie/Sie	haben gebrannt

IMPERFECT

ich	brannte
du	branntest
er/sie/es	brannte
wir	brannten
ihr	branntet
sie/Sie	brannten

FUTURE

ich	werde brennen
du	wirst brennen
er/sie/es	wird brennen
wir	werden brennen
ihr	werdet brennen
sie/Sie	werden brennen

CONDITIONAL

ich	würde brennen
du	würdest brennen
er/sie/es	würde brennen
wir	würden brennen
ihr	würdet brennen
sie/Sie	würden brennen

IMPERATIVE

brenn(e)! / brennen wir! / brennet! / brennen Sie!

PRESENT PARTICIPLE

brennend

PAST PARTICIPLE

gebrannt

EXAMPLE PHRASES

Das Streichholz **brennt** nicht.
Das ganze Haus **brannte**.
Wir **werden** diese CD zuerst **brennen**.

The match won't light.
The entire house was on fire.
We'll burn this CD first.

Table 13: **bringen** *to bring* — mixed, formed with **haben**

PRESENT
- ich bringe
- du bringst
- er/sie/es bringt
- wir bringen
- ihr bringt
- sie/Sie bringen

PRESENT SUBJUNCTIVE
- ich bringe
- du bringest
- er/sie/es bringe
- wir bringen
- ihr bringet
- sie/Sie bringen

PERFECT
- ich habe gebracht
- du hast gebracht
- er/sie/es hat gebracht
- wir haben gebracht
- ihr habt gebracht
- sie/Sie haben gebracht

IMPERFECT
- ich brachte
- du brachtest
- er/sie/es brachte
- wir brachten
- ihr brachtet
- sie/Sie brachten

FUTURE
- ich werde bringen
- du wirst bringen
- er/sie/es wird bringen
- wir werden bringen
- ihr werdet bringen
- sie/Sie werden bringen

CONDITIONAL
- ich würde bringen
- du würdest bringen
- er/sie/es würde bringen
- wir würden bringen
- ihr würdet bringen
- sie/Sie würden bringen

IMPERATIVE
bring(e)! / bringen wir! / bringt! / bringen Sie!

PRESENT PARTICIPLE
bringend

PAST PARTICIPLE
gebracht

EXAMPLE PHRASES

Bringst du mich zum Flughafen? — *Can you take me to the airport?*
Max **hat** mir Blumen **gebracht**. — *Max brought me flowers.*
Das **brachte** mich auf eine Idee. — *It gave me an idea.*

mixed, *formed with* **haben**	*to think* **denken**

Table 14

PRESENT
ich	denke
du	denkst
er/sie/es	denkt
wir	denken
ihr	denkt
sie/Sie	denken

PRESENT SUBJUNCTIVE
ich	denke
du	denkest
er/sie/es	denke
wir	denken
ihr	denket
sie/Sie	denken

PERFECT
ich	habe gedacht
du	hast gedacht
er/sie/es	hat gedacht
wir	haben gedacht
ihr	habt gedacht
sie/Sie	haben gedacht

IMPERFECT
ich	dachte
du	dachtest
er/sie/es	dachte
wir	dachten
ihr	dachtet
sie/Sie	dachten

FUTURE
ich	werde denken
du	wirst denken
er/sie/es	wird denken
wir	werden denken
ihr	werdet denken
sie/Sie	werden denken

CONDITIONAL
ich	würde denken
du	würdest denken
er/sie/es	würde denken
wir	würden denken
ihr	würdet denken
sie/Sie	würden denken

IMPERATIVE
denk(e)! / denken wir! / denkt! / denken Sie!

PRESENT PARTICIPLE
denkend

PAST PARTICIPLE
gedacht

EXAMPLE PHRASES

Wie **denken** Sie darüber? — *What do you think about it?*
Er **hat** an sie **gedacht**. — *He thought of her.*
Es war das Erste, woran ich **dachte**. — *It was the first thing I thought of.*

Table 15: durchsetzen — to enforce

*weak, separable, formed with **haben***

PRESENT

ich	setze durch
du	setzt durch
er/sie/es	setzt durch
wir	setzen durch
ihr	setzt durch
sie/Sie	setzen durch

PRESENT SUBJUNCTIVE

ich	setze durch
du	setzest durch
er/sie/es	setze durch
wir	setzen durch
ihr	setzet durch
sie/Sie	setzen durch

PERFECT

ich	habe durchgesetzt
du	hast durchgesetzt
er/sie/es	hat durchgesetzt
wir	haben durchgesetzt
ihr	habt durchgesetzt
sie/Sie	haben durchgesetzt

IMPERFECT

ich	setzte durch
du	setztest durch
er/sie/es	setzte durch
wir	setzten durch
ihr	setztet durch
sie/Sie	setzten durch

FUTURE

ich	werde durchsetzen
du	wirst durchsetzen
er/sie/es	wird durchsetzen
wir	werden durchsetzen
ihr	werdet durchsetzen
sie/Sie	werden durchsetzen

CONDITIONAL

ich	würde durchsetzen
du	würdest durchsetzen
er/sie/es	würde durchsetzen
wir	würden durchsetzen
ihr	würdet durchsetzen
sie/Sie	würden durchsetzen

IMPERATIVE

setz(e) durch! / setzen wir durch! / setzt durch! / setzen Sie durch!

PRESENT PARTICIPLE

durchsetzend

PAST PARTICIPLE

durchgesetzt

EXAMPLE PHRASES

Er **setzte** sich mit seinem Plan **durch**.
He was successful with his plan.

Ich **würde** dieses Ziel gern bald **durchsetzen**.
I would like to achieve this aim soon.

modal, formed with **haben** — *to be allowed to* **dürfen**

Table 16

PRESENT
ich	darf
du	darfst
er/sie/es	darf
wir	dürfen
ihr	dürft
sie/Sie	dürfen

PRESENT SUBJUNCTIVE
ich	dürfe
du	dürfest
er/sie/es	dürfe
wir	dürfen
ihr	dürfet
sie/Sie	dürfen

PERFECT
ich	habe gedurft /dürfen
du	hast gedurft/dürfen
er/sie/es	hat gedurft/dürfen
wir	haben gedurft/dürfen
ihr	habt gedurft/dürfen
sie/Sie	haben gedurft/dürfen

IMPERFECT
ich	durfte
du	durftest
er/sie/es	durfte
wir	durften
ihr	durftet
sie/Sie	durften

FUTURE
ich	werde dürfen
du	wirst dürfen
er/sie/es	wird dürfen
wir	werden dürfen
ihr	werdet dürfen
sie/Sie	werden dürfen

CONDITIONAL
ich	würde dürfen
du	würdest dürfen
er/sie/es	würde dürfen
wir	würden dürfen
ihr	würdet dürfen
sie/Sie	würden dürfen

PRESENT PARTICIPLE
dürfend

PAST PARTICIPLE
gedurft / dürfen°

°This form is used when combined with another infinitive.

EXAMPLE PHRASES

Er meint, er **dürfe** das nicht. — *He thinks he isn't allowed to.*
Wir **durften** nicht ausgehen. — *We weren't allowed to go out.*
Das **würde** ich zu Hause nicht **dürfen**. — *I wouldn't be allowed to do that at home.*

Table 17: empfehlen — to recommend

*strong, inseparable, formed with **haben***

PRESENT
ich	empfehle
du	empfiehlst
er/sie/es	empfiehlt
wir	empfehlen
ihr	empfehlt
sie/Sie	empfehlen

PRESENT SUBJUNCTIVE
ich	empfehle
du	empfehlest
er/sie/es	empfehle
wir	empfehlen
ihr	empfehlet
sie/Sie	empfehlen

PERFECT
ich	habe empfohlen
du	hast empfohlen
er/sie/es	hat empfohlen
wir	haben empfohlen
ihr	habt empfohlen
sie/Sie	haben empfohlen

IMPERFECT
ich	empfahl
du	empfahlst
er/sie/es	empfahl
wir	empfahlen
ihr	empfahlt
sie/Sie	empfahlen

FUTURE
ich	werde empfehlen
du	wirst empfehlen
er/sie/es	wird empfehlen
wir	werden empfehlen
ihr	werdet empfehlen
sie/Sie	werden empfehlen

CONDITIONAL
ich	würde empfehlen
du	würdest empfehlen
er/sie/es	würde empfehlen
wir	würden empfehlen
ihr	würdet empfehlen
sie/Sie	würden empfehlen

IMPERATIVE
empfiehl! / empfehlen wir! / empfehlt! / empfehlen Sie!

PRESENT PARTICIPLE
empfehlend

PAST PARTICIPLE
empfohlen

EXAMPLE PHRASES

Was **empfiehlst** du mir zu tun? — *What would you recommend I do?*

weak, inseparable,
formed with **haben**

to discover **entdecken**

Table 18

PRESENT
ich	entdecke
du	entdeckst
er/sie/es	entdeckt
wir	entdecken
ihr	entdeckt
sie/Sie	entdecken

PRESENT SUBJUNCTIVE
ich	entdecke
du	entdeckest
er/sie/es	entdecke
wir	entdecken
ihr	entdecket
sie/Sie	entdecken

PERFECT
ich	habe entdeckt
du	hast entdeckt
er/sie/es	hat entdeckt
wir	haben entdeckt
ihr	habt entdeckt
sie/Sie	haben entdeckt

IMPERFECT
ich	entdeckte
du	entdecktest
er/sie/es	entdeckte
wir	entdeckten
ihr	entdecktet
sie/Sie	entdeckten

FUTURE
ich	werde entdecken
du	wirst entdecken
er/sie/es	wird entdecken
wir	werden entdecken
ihr	werdet entdecken
sie/Sie	werden entdecken

CONDITIONAL
ich	würde entdecken
du	würdest entdecken
er/sie/es	würde entdecken
wir	würden entdecken
ihr	würdet entdecken
sie/Sie	würden entdecken

IMPERATIVE
entdeck(e)! / entdecken wir! / entdeckt! / entdecken Sie!

PRESENT PARTICIPLE
entdeckend

PAST PARTICIPLE
entdeckt

EXAMPLE PHRASES

Sie **hat** das Versteck **entdeckt**. *She discovered the hide-out.*

Table 19: erzählen — to tell

*weak, inseparable, formed with **haben***

PRESENT
ich	erzähle
du	erzählst
er/sie/es	erzählt
wir	erzählen
ihr	erzählt
sie/Sie	erzählen

PRESENT SUBJUNCTIVE
ich	erzähle
du	erzählest
er/sie/es	erzähle
wir	erzählen
ihr	erzählet
sie/Sie	erzählen

PERFECT
ich	habe erzählt
du	hast erzählt
er/sie/es	hat erzählt
wir	haben erzählt
ihr	habt erzählt
sie/Sie	haben erzählt

IMPERFECT
ich	erzählte
du	erzähltest
er/sie/es	erzählte
wir	erzählten
ihr	erzähltet
sie/Sie	erzählten

FUTURE
ich	werde erzählen
du	wirst erzählen
er/sie/es	wird erzählen
wir	werden erzählen
ihr	werdet erzählen
sie/Sie	werden erzählen

CONDITIONAL
ich	würde erzählen
du	würdest erzählen
er/sie/es	würde erzählen
wir	würden erzählen
ihr	würdet erzählen
sie/Sie	würden erzählen

IMPERATIVE
erzähl(e)! / erzählen wir! / erzählt! / erzählen Sie!

PRESENT PARTICIPLE
erzählend

PAST PARTICIPLE
erzählt

EXAMPLE PHRASES

Er denkt, sie **erzähle** nur Lügen. — *He thinks all she tells is lies.*
Sie **erzählte** uns ihren Traum. — *She told us about her dream.*

strong, formed with **haben** — to eat **essen** — Table **20**

PRESENT
- ich esse
- du isst
- er/sie/es isst
- wir essen
- ihr esst
- sie/Sie essen

PRESENT SUBJUNCTIVE
- ich esse
- du essest
- er/sie/es esse
- wir essen
- ihr esset
- sie/Sie essen

PERFECT
- ich habe gegessen
- du hast gegessen
- er/sie/es hat gegessen
- wir haben gegessen
- ihr habt gegessen
- sie/Sie haben gegessen

IMPERFECT
- ich aß
- du aßest
- er/sie/es aß
- wir aßen
- ihr aßt
- sie/Sie aßen

FUTURE
- ich werde essen
- du wirst essen
- er/sie/es wird essen
- wir werden essen
- ihr werdet essen
- sie/Sie werden essen

CONDITIONAL
- ich würde essen
- du würdest essen
- er/sie/es würde essen
- wir würden essen
- ihr würdet essen
- sie/Sie würden essen

IMPERATIVE
iss! / essen wir! / esst! / essen Sie!

PRESENT PARTICIPLE
essend

PAST PARTICIPLE
gegessen

--- EXAMPLE PHRASES ---

Ich **esse** kein Fleisch. — *I don't eat meat.*
Ich **aß** den ganzen Kuchen. — *I ate the whole cake.*

Table 21: fahren — to drive; to go

strong, formed with **haben/sein**°

PRESENT
- ich fahre
- du fährst
- er/sie/es fährt
- wir fahren
- ihr fahrt
- sie/Sie fahren

PRESENT SUBJUNCTIVE
- ich fahre
- du fahrest
- er/sie/es fahre
- wir fahren
- ihr fahret
- sie/Sie fahren

PERFECT
- ich bin gefahren
- du bist gefahren
- er/sie/es ist gefahren
- wir sind gefahren
- ihr seid gefahren
- sie/Sie sind gefahren

IMPERFECT
- ich fuhr
- du fuhrst
- er/sie/es fuhr
- wir fuhren
- ihr fuhrt
- sie/Sie fuhren

FUTURE
- ich werde fahren
- du wirst fahren
- er/sie/es wird fahren
- wir werden fahren
- ihr werdet fahren
- sie/Sie werden fahren

CONDITIONAL
- ich würde fahren
- du würdest fahren
- er/sie/es würde fahren
- wir würden fahren
- ihr würdet fahren
- sie/Sie würden fahren

IMPERATIVE
fahr(e)! / fahren wir! / fahrt! / fahren Sie!

PRESENT PARTICIPLE
fahrend

PAST PARTICIPLE
gefahren

°When **fahren** is used with a direct object, it is formed with **haben**.

EXAMPLE PHRASES

In Deutschland **fährt** man rechts. — *In Germany they drive on the right.*

Ich **bin** mit der Familie nach Spanien **gefahren**. — *I went to Spain with my family.*

strong, formed with haben — *to fall* **fallen**

Table 22

PRESENT
ich	falle
du	fällst
er/sie/es	fällt
wir	fallen
ihr	fallt
sie/Sie	fallen

PRESENT SUBJUNCTIVE
ich	falle
du	fallest
er/sie/es	falle
wir	fallen
ihr	fallet
sie/Sie	fallen

PERFECT
ich	bin gefallen
du	bist gefallen
er/sie/es	ist gefallen
wir	sind gefallen
ihr	seid gefallen
sie/Sie	sind gefallen

IMPERFECT
ich	fiel
du	fielst
er/sie/es	fiel
wir	fielen
ihr	fielt
sie/Sie	fielen

FUTURE
ich	werde fallen
du	wirst fallen
er/sie/es	wird fallen
wir	werden fallen
ihr	werdet fallen
sie/Sie	werden fallen

CONDITIONAL
ich	würde fallen
du	würdest fallen
er/sie/es	würde fallen
wir	würden fallen
ihr	würdet fallen
sie/Sie	würden fallen

IMPERATIVE
fall(e)! / fallen wir! / fallt! / fallen Sie!

PRESENT PARTICIPLE
fallend

PAST PARTICIPLE
gefallen

EXAMPLE PHRASES

Er meint, der Euro **falle** im Wert. — *He thinks the euro is going down in value.*

Er **fiel** vom Fahrrad. — *He fell off his bike.*

Ihr **werdet** noch **fallen** und euch wehtun. — *You'll end up falling and hurting yourselves.*

Table 23: fangen — to catch

strong, formed with haben

PRESENT
- ich fange
- du fängst
- er/sie/es fängt
- wir fangen
- ihr fangt
- sie/Sie fangen

PRESENT SUBJUNCTIVE
- ich fange
- du fangest
- er/sie/es fange
- wir fangen
- ihr fanget
- sie/Sie fangen

PERFECT
- ich habe gefangen
- du hast gefangen
- er/sie/es hat gefangen
- wir haben gefangen
- ihr habt gefangen
- sie/Sie haben gefangen

IMPERFECT
- ich fing
- du fingst
- er/sie/es fing
- wir fingen
- ihr fingt
- sie/Sie fingen

FUTURE
- ich werde fangen
- du wirst fangen
- er/sie/es wird fangen
- wir werden fangen
- ihr werdet fangen
- sie/Sie werden fangen

CONDITIONAL
- ich würde fangen
- du würdest fangen
- er/sie/es würde fangen
- wir würden fangen
- ihr würdet fangen
- sie/Sie würden fangen

IMPERATIVE
fang(e)! / fangen wir! / fangt! / fangen Sie!

PRESENT PARTICIPLE
fangend

PAST PARTICIPLE
gefangen

EXAMPLE PHRASES

Ich fing den Ball.   *I caught the ball.*

strong, formed with **haben** — to find **finden** — Table 24

PRESENT
- ich finde
- du findest
- er/sie/es findet
- wir finden
- ihr findet
- sie/Sie finden

PRESENT SUBJUNCTIVE
- ich finde
- du findest
- er/sie/es finde
- wir finden
- ihr findet
- sie/Sie finden

PERFECT
- ich habe gefunden
- du hast gefunden
- er/sie/es hat gefunden
- wir haben gefunden
- ihr habt gefunden
- sie/Sie haben gefunden

IMPERFECT
- ich fand
- du fand(e)st
- er/sie/es fand
- wir fanden
- ihr fandet
- sie/Sie fanden

FUTURE
- ich werde finden
- du wirst finden
- er/sie/es wird finden
- wir werden finden
- ihr werdet finden
- sie/Sie werden finden

CONDITIONAL
- ich würde finden
- du würdest finden
- er/sie/es würde finden
- wir würden finden
- ihr würdet finden
- sie/Sie würden finden

IMPERATIVE
find(e)! / finden wir! / findet! / finden Sie!

PRESENT PARTICIPLE
findend

PAST PARTICIPLE
gefunden

---------- EXAMPLE PHRASES ----------

Sie sagt, sie **finde** ihn attraktiv. — *She says she finds him attractive.*
Hast du deine Brieftasche **gefunden**? — *Have you found your wallet?*
Wir **werden** dieses Dorf nie **finden**. — *We'll never find that village.*

Table 25: fliegen — to fly

strong, formed with **haben/sein**°

PRESENT
- ich fliege
- du fliegst
- er/sie/es fliegen
- wir fliegen
- ihr fliegt
- sie/Sie fliegen

PRESENT SUBJUNCTIVE
- ich fliege
- du fliegest
- er/sie/es fliege
- wir fliegen
- ihr flieget
- sie/Sie fliegen

PERFECT
- ich habe geflogen
- du hast geflogen
- er/sie/es hat geflogen
- wir haben geflogen
- ihr habt geflogen
- sie/Sie haben geflogen

IMPERFECT
- ich flog
- du flogst
- er/sie/es flog
- wir flogen
- ihr flogt
- sie/Sie flogen

FUTURE
- ich werde fliegen
- du wirst fliegen
- er/sie/es wird fliegen
- wir werden fliegen
- ihr werdet fliegen
- sie/Sie werden fliegen

CONDITIONAL
- ich würde fliegen
- du würdest fliegen
- er/sie/es würde fliegen
- wir würden fliegen
- ihr würdet fliegen
- sie/Sie würden fliegen

IMPERATIVE
flieg(e)! / fliegen wir! / fliegt! / fliegen Sie!

PRESENT PARTICIPLE
fliegend

PAST PARTICIPLE
geflogen

°When **fliegen** is used with no direct object, it is formed with **sein**.

EXAMPLE PHRASES

Wir **flogen** zusammen nach Spanien. — *We flew to Spain together.*

Es war, als **würde** ich **fliegen**. — *It was as if I was flying.*

strong,
formed with **haben/sein***

to flee **fliehen**

Table 26

PRESENT
ich	fliehe
du	fliehst
er/sie/es	flieht
wir	fliehen
ihr	flieht
sie/Sie	fliehen

PRESENT SUBJUNCTIVE
ich	fliehe
du	fliehest
er/sie/es	fliehe
wir	fliehen
ihr	fliehet
sie/Sie	fliehen

PERFECT
ich	bin geflohen
du	bist geflohen
er/sie/es	ist geflohen
wir	sind geflohen
ihr	seid geflohen
sie/Sie	sind geflohen

IMPERFECT
ich	floh
du	flohst
er/sie/es	floh
wir	flohen
ihr	floht
sie/Sie	flohen

FUTURE
ich	werde fliehen
du	wirst fliehen
er/sie/es	wird fliehen
wir	werden fliehen
ihr	werdet fliehen
sie/Sie	werden fliehen

CONDITIONAL
ich	würde fliehen
du	würdest fliehen
er/sie/es	würde fliehen
wir	würden fliehen
ihr	würdet fliehen
sie/Sie	würden fliehen

IMPERATIVE
flieh(e)! / fliehen wir! / flieht! / fliehen Sie!

PRESENT PARTICIPLE
fliehend

PAST PARTICIPLE
geflohen

*When **fliehen** is used with a direct object, it is formed with **haben**.

─────────── EXAMPLE PHRASES ───────────

Sie **floh** vor der Polizei. *She fled from the police.*

Table 27: **fließen** *to flow* — strong, formed with **sein**

PRESENT
- ich fließe
- du fließt
- er/sie/es fließt
- wir fließen
- ihr fließt
- sie/Sie fließen

PRESENT SUBJUNCTIVE
- ich fließe
- du fließest
- er/sie/es fließe
- wir fließen
- ihr fließet
- sie/Sie fließen

PERFECT
- ich bin geflossen
- du bist geflossen
- er/sie/es ist geflossen
- wir sind geflossen
- ihr seid geflossen
- sie/Sie sind geflossen

IMPERFECT
- ich floss
- du flossest
- er/sie/es floss
- wir flossen
- ihr flosst
- sie/Sie flossen

FUTURE
- ich werde fließen
- du wirst fließen
- er/sie/es wird fließen
- wir werden fließen
- ihr werdet fließen
- sie/Sie werden fließen

CONDITIONAL
- ich würde fließen
- du würdest fließen
- er/sie/es würde fließen
- wir würden fließen
- ihr würdet fließen
- sie/Sie würden fließen

IMPERATIVE
fließ(e)! / fließen wir! / fließt! / fließen Sie!

PRESENT PARTICIPLE
fließend

PAST PARTICIPLE
geflossen

EXAMPLE PHRASES

Welcher Fluss **fließt** durch Hamburg? — *Which river flows through Hamburg?*

strong, formed with **haben** — to give **geben** — Table 28

PRESENT

ich	gebe
du	gibst
er/sie/es	gibt
wir	geben
ihr	gebt
sie/Sie	geben

PRESENT SUBJUNCTIVE

ich	gebe
du	gebest
er/sie/es	gebe
wir	geben
ihr	gebet
sie/Sie	geben

PERFECT

ich	habe gegeben
du	hast gegeben
er/sie/es	hat gegeben
wir	haben gegeben
ihr	habt gegeben
sie/Sie	haben gegeben

IMPERFECT

ich	gab
du	gabst
er/sie/es	gab
wir	gaben
ihr	gabt
sie/Sie	gaben

FUTURE

ich	werde geben
du	wirst geben
er/sie/es	wird geben
wir	werden geben
ihr	werdet geben
sie/Sie	werden geben

CONDITIONAL

ich	würde geben
du	würdest geben
er/sie/es	würde geben
wir	würden geben
ihr	würdet geben
sie/Sie	würden geben

IMPERATIVE
gib! / geben wir! / gebt! / geben Sie!

PRESENT PARTICIPLE
gebend

PAST PARTICIPLE
gegeben

---------- EXAMPLE PHRASES ----------

Er **gab** mir das Geld für die Bücher.
He gave me the money for the books.

Wir **würden** alles dafür **geben**, ins Finale zu kommen.
We would give anything to reach the finals.

Table 29: **gehen** *to go*

strong, formed with **haben**

PRESENT
- ich gehe
- du gehst
- er/sie/es geht
- wir gehen
- ihr geht
- sie/Sie gehen

PRESENT SUBJUNCTIVE
- ich gehe
- du gehest
- er/sie/es gehe
- wir gehen
- ihr gehet
- sie/Sie gehen

PERFECT
- ich bin gegangen
- du bist gegangen
- er/sie/es ist gegangen
- wir sind gegangen
- ihr seid gegangen
- sie/Sie sind gegangen

IMPERFECT
- ich ging
- du gingst
- er/sie/es ging
- wir gingen
- ihr gingt
- sie/Sie gingen

FUTURE
- ich werde gehen
- du wirst gehen
- er/sie/es wird gehen
- wir werden gehen
- ihr werdet gehen
- sie/Sie werden gehen

CONDITIONAL
- ich würde gehen
- du würdest gehen
- er/sie/es würde gehen
- wir würden gehen
- ihr würdet gehen
- sie/Sie würden gehen

IMPERATIVE
geh(e)! / gehen wir! / geht! / gehen Sie!

PRESENT PARTICIPLE
gehend

PAST PARTICIPLE
gegangen

EXAMPLE PHRASES

Wir **sind** gestern schwimmen **gegangen**.
We went swimming yesterday.

Die Kinder **gingen** ins Haus.
The children went into the house.

In diesen Kleidern **würde** ich nicht ins Theater **gehen**.
I wouldn't go to the theatre in these clothes.

strong, inseparable,
formed with **haben**

to win **gewinnen**

Table **30**

PRESENT

ich	gewinne
du	gewinnst
er/sie/es	gewinnt
wir	gewinnen
ihr	gewinnt
sie/Sie	gewinnen

PRESENT SUBJUNCTIVE

ich	gewinne
du	gewinnest
er/sie/es	gewinne
wir	gewinnen
ihr	gewinnet
sie/Sie	gewinnen

PERFECT

ich	habe gewonnen
du	hast gewonnen
er/sie/es	hat gewonnen
wir	haben gewonnen
ihr	habt gewonnen
sie/Sie	haben gewonnen

IMPERFECT

ich	gewann
du	gewannst
er/sie/es	gewann
wir	gewannen
ihr	gewannt
sie/Sie	gewannen

FUTURE

ich	werde gewinnen
du	wirst gewinnen
er/sie/es	wird gewinnen
wir	werden gewinnen
ihr	werdet gewinnen
sie/Sie	werden gewinnen

CONDITIONAL

ich	würde gewinnen
du	würdest gewinnen
er/sie/es	würde gewinnen
wir	würden gewinnen
ihr	würdet gewinnen
sie/Sie	würden gewinnen

IMPERATIVE
gewinn(e)! / gewinnen wir! / gewinnt! / gewinnen Sie!

PRESENT PARTICIPLE
gewinnend

PAST PARTICIPLE
gewonnen

--- EXAMPLE PHRASES ---

Er **gewinnt** immer beim Kartenspielen.
He always wins at cards.

Er **hat** den ersten Preis **gewonnen**.
He won first prize.

grüßen *to greet*

weak, formed with **haben**

PRESENT
- ich grüße
- du grüßt
- er/sie/es grüßt
- wir grüßen
- ihr grüßt
- sie/Sie grüßen

PRESENT SUBJUNCTIVE
- ich grüße
- du grüßest
- er/sie/es grüße
- wir grüßen
- ihr grüßet
- sie/Sie grüßen

PERFECT
- ich habe gegrüßt
- du hast gegrüßt
- er/sie/es hat gegrüßt
- wir haben gegrüßt
- ihr habt gegrüßt
- sie/Sie haben gegrüßt

IMPERFECT
- ich grüßte
- du grüßtest
- er/sie/es grüßte
- wir grüßten
- ihr grüßtet
- sie/Sie grüßten

FUTURE
- ich werde grüßen
- du wirst grüßen
- er/sie/es wird grüßen
- wir werden grüßen
- ihr werdet grüßen
- sie/Sie werden grüßen

CONDITIONAL
- ich würde grüßen
- du würdest grüßen
- er/sie/es würde grüßen
- wir würden grüßen
- ihr würdet grüßen
- sie/Sie würden grüßen

IMPERATIVE
grüß(e)! / grüßen wir! / grüßt! / grüßen Sie!

PRESENT PARTICIPLE
grüßend

PAST PARTICIPLE
gegrüßt

EXAMPLE PHRASES

Sie **grüßte** mich mit einem Lächeln.   *She greeted me with a smile.*

strong, *formed with* **haben** — *to have* **haben** — Table 32

PRESENT

ich	habe
du	hast
er/sie/es	hat
wir	haben
ihr	habt
sie/Sie	haben

PRESENT SUBJUNCTIVE

ich	habe
du	habest
er/sie/es	habe
wir	haben
ihr	habet
sie/Sie	haben

PERFECT

ich	habe gehabt
du	hast gehabt
er/sie/es	hat gehabt
wir	haben gehabt
ihr	habt gehabt
sie/Sie	haben gehabt

IMPERFECT

ich	hatte
du	hattest
er/sie/es	hatte
wir	hatten
ihr	hattet
sie/Sie	hatten

FUTURE

ich	werde haben
du	wirst haben
er/sie/es	wird haben
wir	werden haben
ihr	werdet haben
sie/Sie	werden haben

CONDITIONAL

ich	würde haben
du	würdest haben
er/sie/es	würde haben
wir	würden haben
ihr	würdet haben
sie/Sie	würden haben

IMPERATIVE

hab(e)! / haben wir! / habt! / haben Sie!

PRESENT PARTICIPLE

habend

PAST PARTICIPLE

gehabt

EXAMPLE PHRASES

Hast du eine Schwester? — *Have you got a sister?*
Er sagt, er **habe** keine Zeit. — *He says he has no time.*
Er **hatte** Hunger. — *He was hungry.*

Table 33: halten *to hold*

strong, *formed with* **haben**

PRESENT
- ich halte
- du hältst
- er/sie/es hält
- wir halten
- ihr haltet
- sie/Sie halten

PRESENT SUBJUNCTIVE
- ich halte
- du haltest
- er/sie/es halte
- wir halten
- ihr haltet
- sie/Sie halten

PERFECT
- ich habe gehalten
- du hast gehalten
- er/sie/es hat gehalten
- wir haben gehalten
- ihr habt gehalten
- sie/Sie haben gehalten

IMPERFECT
- ich hielt
- du hielt(e)st
- er/sie/es hielt
- wir hielten
- ihr hieltet
- sie/Sie hielten

FUTURE
- ich werde halten
- du wirst halten
- er/sie/es wird halten
- wir werden halten
- ihr werdet halten
- sie/Sie werden halten

CONDITIONAL
- ich würde halten
- du würdest halten
- er/sie/es würde halten
- wir würden halten
- ihr würdet halten
- sie/Sie würden halten

IMPERATIVE
halt(e)! / halten wir! / haltet! / halten Sie!

PRESENT PARTICIPLE
haltend

PAST PARTICIPLE
gehalten

EXAMPLE PHRASES

Hältst du das mal für mich?   *Can you hold that for me?*

weak, formed with **haben** — to trade; to act **handeln** — Table **34**

PRESENT

ich	handle
du	handelst
er/sie/es	handelt
wir	handeln
ihr	handelt
sie/Sie	handeln

PRESENT SUBJUNCTIVE

ich	handle
du	handlest
er/sie/es	handle
wir	handeln
ihr	handlet
sie/Sie	handeln

PERFECT

ich	habe gehandelt
du	hast gehandelt
er/sie/es	hat gehandelt
wir	haben gehandelt
ihr	habt gehandelt
sie/Sie	haben gehandelt

IMPERFECT

ich	handelte
du	handeltest
er/sie/es	handelte
wir	handelten
ihr	handeltet
sie/Sie	handelten

FUTURE

ich	werde handeln
du	wirst handeln
er/sie/es	wird handeln
wir	werden handeln
ihr	werdet handeln
sie/Sie	werden handeln

CONDITIONAL

ich	würde handeln
du	würdest handeln
er/sie/es	würde handeln
wir	würden handeln
ihr	würdet handeln
sie/Sie	würden handeln

IMPERATIVE
handle! / handeln wir! / handelt! / handeln Sie!

PRESENT PARTICIPLE
handelnd

PAST PARTICIPLE
gehandelt

EXAMPLE PHRASES

Die Polizei **handelte** schnell. — *The police acted quickly.*
Er **würde** nie mit Drogen **handeln**. — *He would never deal drugs.*

Table 35: hängen — *to hang*

strong°, formed with **haben**

PRESENT
- ich hänge
- du hängst
- er/sie/es hängt
- wir hängen
- ihr hängt
- sie/Sie hängen

PRESENT SUBJUNCTIVE
- ich hänge
- du hängest
- er/sie/es hänge
- wir hängen
- ihr hänget
- sie/Sie hängen

PERFECT
- ich habe gehangen
- du hast gehangen
- er/sie/es hat gehangen
- wir haben gehangen
- ihr habt gehangen
- sie/Sie haben gehangen

IMPERFECT
- ich hing
- du hingst
- er/sie/es hing
- wir hingen
- ihr hingt
- sie/Sie hingen

FUTURE
- ich werde hängen
- du wirst hängen
- er/sie/es wird hängen
- wir werden hängen
- ihr werdet hängen
- sie/Sie werden hängen

CONDITIONAL
- ich würde hängen
- du würdest hängen
- er/sie/es würde hängen
- wir würden hängen
- ihr würdet hängen
- sie/Sie würden hängen

IMPERATIVE
häng(e)! / hängen wir! / hängt! / hängen Sie!

PRESENT PARTICIPLE
hängend

PAST PARTICIPLE
gehangen

°Conjugated as a weak verb when it has a direct object.

EXAMPLE PHRASES

Das Bild **hing** an der Wand.
Wir **werden** die Wäsche auf die Leine **hängen**.

The picture was hanging on the wall.
We'll hang the washing on the line.

weak, *formed with* **haben** — *to heat* **heizen** — Table 36

PRESENT
- ich heize
- du heizt
- er/sie/es heizt
- wir heizen
- ihr heizt
- sie/Sie heizen

PRESENT SUBJUNCTIVE
- ich heize
- du heizest
- er/sie/es heize
- wir heizen
- ihr heizet
- sie/Sie heizen

PERFECT
- ich habe geheizt
- du hast geheizt
- er/sie/es hat geheizt
- wir haben geheizt
- ihr habt geheizt
- sie/Sie haben geheizt

IMPERFECT
- ich heizte
- du heiztest
- er/sie/es heizte
- wir heizten
- ihr heiztet
- sie/Sie heizten

FUTURE
- ich werde heizen
- du wirst heizen
- er/sie/es wird heizen
- wir werden heizen
- ihr werdet heizen
- sie/Sie werden heizen

CONDITIONAL
- ich würde heizen
- du würdest heizen
- er/sie/es würde heizen
- wir würden heizen
- ihr würdet heizen
- sie/Sie würden heizen

IMPERATIVE
heiz(e)! / heizen wir! / heizt! / heizen Sie!

PRESENT PARTICIPLE
heizend

PAST PARTICIPLE
geheizt

EXAMPLE PHRASES

Der Ofen **heizt** gut.
An Ihrer Stelle **würde** ich das Haus besser **heizen**.

The stove gives off a good heat.
If I were you, I would heat the house better.

Table 37: **helfen** to help

*strong, dative, formed with **haben***

PRESENT
ich	helfe
du	hilfst
er/sie/es	hilft
wir	helfen
ihr	helft
sie/Sie	helfen

PRESENT SUBJUNCTIVE
ich	helfe
du	helfest
er/sie/es	helfe
wir	helfen
ihr	helfet
sie/Sie	helfen

PERFECT
ich	habe geholfen
du	hast geholfen
er/sie/es	hat geholfen
wir	haben geholfen
ihr	habt geholfen
sie/Sie	haben geholfen

IMPERFECT
ich	half
du	halfst
er/sie/es	half
wir	halfen
ihr	halft
sie/Sie	halfen

FUTURE
ich	werde helfen
du	wirst helfen
er/sie/es	wird helfen
wir	werden helfen
ihr	werdet helfen
sie/Sie	werden helfen

CONDITIONAL
ich	würde helfen
du	würdest helfen
er/sie/es	würde helfen
wir	würden helfen
ihr	würdet helfen
sie/Sie	würden helfen

IMPERATIVE
hilf! / helfen wir! / helft! / helfen Sie!

PRESENT PARTICIPLE
helfend

PAST PARTICIPLE
geholfen

EXAMPLE PHRASES

Sie sagt, sie **helfe** gern anderen.
She says she likes to help others.

Er **hat** mir dabei **geholfen**.
He helped me with it.

Er **wird** mir **helfen**, den Aufsatz zu schreiben.
He will help me write the essay.

weak, formed with **haben** — to fetch **holen**

Table 38

PRESENT

ich	hole
du	holst
er/sie/es	holt
wir	holen
ihr	holt
sie/Sie	holen

PRESENT SUBJUNCTIVE

ich	hole
du	holest
er/sie/es	hole
wir	holen
ihr	holet
sie/Sie	holen

PERFECT

ich	habe geholt
du	hast geholt
er/sie/es	hat geholt
wir	haben geholt
ihr	habt geholt
sie/Sie	haben geholt

IMPERFECT

ich	holte
du	holtest
er/sie/es	holte
wir	holten
ihr	holtet
sie/Sie	holten

FUTURE

ich	werde holen
du	wirst holen
er/sie/es	wird holen
wir	werden holen
ihr	werdet holen
sie/Sie	werden holen

CONDITIONAL

ich	würde holen
du	würdest holen
er/sie/es	würde holen
wir	würden holen
ihr	würdet holen
sie/Sie	würden holen

IMPERATIVE

hol(e)! / holen wir! / holt! / holen Sie!

PRESENT PARTICIPLE

holend

PAST PARTICIPLE

geholt

EXAMPLE PHRASES

Er **holt** jeden Tag frische Milch vom Supermarkt.
He gets fresh milk from the supermarket every day.

Ich **habe** mir eine Erkältung **geholt**.
I caught a cold.

Table 39: kennen — *to know (be acquainted with)*

*mixed, formed with **haben***

PRESENT
ich	kenne
du	kennst
er/sie/es	kennt
wir	kennen
ihr	kennt
sie/Sie	kennen

PRESENT SUBJUNCTIVE
ich	kenne
du	kennest
er/sie/es	kenne
wir	kennen
ihr	kennet
sie/Sie	kennen

PERFECT
ich	habe gekannt
du	hast gekannt
er/sie/es	hat gekannt
wir	haben gekannt
ihr	habt gekannt
sie/Sie	haben gekannt

IMPERFECT
ich	kannte
du	kanntest
er/sie/es	kannte
wir	kannten
ihr	kanntet
sie/Sie	kannten

FUTURE
ich	werde kennen
du	wirst kennen
er/sie/es	wird kennen
wir	werden kennen
ihr	werdet kennen
sie/Sie	werden kennen

CONDITIONAL
ich	würde kennen
du	würdest kennen
er/sie/es	würde kennen
wir	würden kennen
ihr	würdet kennen
sie/Sie	würden kennen

IMPERATIVE
kenn(e)! / kennen wir! / kennt! / kennen Sie!

PRESENT PARTICIPLE
kennend

PAST PARTICIPLE
gekannt

EXAMPLE PHRASES

Ich **kenne** ihn nicht.
I don't know him.

Er sprach von ihr, als **würde** er sie **kennen**.
He spoke of her as if he knew her.

Table 40

strong, *formed with* **sein** — *to come* **kommen**

PRESENT
ich	komme
du	kommst
er/sie/es	kommt
wir	kommen
ihr	kommt
sie/Sie	kommen

PRESENT SUBJUNCTIVE
ich	komme
du	kommest
er/sie/es	komme
wir	kommen
ihr	kommet
sie/Sie	kommen

PERFECT
ich	bin gekommen
du	bist gekommen
er/sie/es	ist gekommen
wir	sind gekommen
ihr	seid gekommen
sie/Sie	sind gekommen

IMPERFECT
ich	kam
du	kamst
er/sie/es	kam
wir	kamen
ihr	kamt
sie/Sie	kamen

FUTURE
ich	werde kommen
du	wirst kommen
er/sie/es	wird kommen
wir	werden kommen
ihr	werdet kommen
sie/Sie	werden kommen

CONDITIONAL
ich	würde kommen
du	würdest kommen
er/sie/es	würde kommen
wir	würden kommen
ihr	würdet kommen
sie/Sie	würden kommen

IMPERATIVE
komm(e)! / kommen wir! / kommt! / kommen Sie!

PRESENT PARTICIPLE
kommend

PAST PARTICIPLE
gekommen

EXAMPLE PHRASES

Ich **komme** zu deiner Party. — *I'm coming to your party.*
Er **kam** die Straße entlang. — *He was coming along the street.*

Table 41: **können** *to be able to*

modal, formed with **haben**

PRESENT

ich	kann
du	kannst
er/sie/es	kann
wir	können
ihr	könnt
sie/Sie	können

PRESENT SUBJUNCTIVE

ich	könne
du	könnest
er/sie/es	könne
wir	können
ihr	könnet
sie/Sie	können

PERFECT

ich	habe gekonnt/können
du	hast gekonnt/können
er/sie/es	hat gekonnt/können
wir	haben gekonnt/können
ihr	habt gekonnt/können
sie/Sie	haben gekonnt/können

IMPERFECT

ich	konnte
du	konntest
er/sie/es	konnte
wir	konnten
ihr	konntet
sie/Sie	konnten

FUTURE

ich	werde können
du	wirst können
er/sie/es	wird können
wir	werden können
ihr	werdet können
sie/Sie	werden können

CONDITIONAL

ich	würde können
du	würdest können
er/sie/es	würde können
wir	würden können
ihr	würdet können
sie/Sie	würden können

PRESENT PARTICIPLE

könnend

PAST PARTICIPLE

gekonnt / können*

*This form is used when combined with another infinitive.

EXAMPLE PHRASES

Er **kann** gut schwimmen.	He can swim well.
Sie sagt, ich **könne** jetzt noch nicht gehen.	She says I can't leave yet.
Morgen **werde** ich nicht kommen **können**.	I won't be able to come tomorrow.

strong, formed with **haben** — to leave; to allow **lassen**

Table 42

PRESENT

ich	lasse
du	lässt
er/sie/es	lässt
wir	lassen
ihr	lasst
sie/Sie	lassen

PRESENT SUBJUNCTIVE

ich	lasse
du	lassest
er/sie/es	lasse
wir	lassen
ihr	lasset
sie/Sie	lassen

PERFECT

ich	habe gelassen/lassen
du	hast gelassen/lassen
er/sie/es	hat gelassen/lassen
wir	haben gelassen/lassen
ihr	habt gelassen/lassen
sie/Sie	haben gelassen/lassen

IMPERFECT

ich	ließ
du	ließest
er/sie/es	ließ
wir	ließen
ihr	ließt
sie/Sie	ließen

FUTURE

ich	werde lassen
du	wirst lassen
er/sie/es	wird lassen
wir	werden lassen
ihr	werdet lassen
sie/Sie	werden lassen

CONDITIONAL

ich	würde lassen
du	würdest lassen
er/sie/es	würde lassen
wir	würden lassen
ihr	würdet lassen
sie/Sie	würden lassen

IMPERATIVE
lass! / lassen wir! / lasst! / lassen Sie!

PRESENT PARTICIPLE
lassend

PAST PARTICIPLE
gelassen / lassen°

°This form is used when combined with another infinitive.

EXAMPLE PHRASES

Ich **lasse** den Hund nicht auf das Sofa. *I won't let the dog on the sofa.*

Ich **würde** das Baby nie allein **lassen**. *I would never leave the baby alone.*

Table 43: laufen *to run*

strong, formed with **sein**

PRESENT
ich	laufe
du	läufst
er/sie/es	läuft
wir	laufen
ihr	lauft
sie/Sie	laufen

PRESENT SUBJUNCTIVE
ich	laufe
du	laufest
er/sie/es	laufe
wir	laufen
ihr	laufet
sie/Sie	laufen

PERFECT
ich	bin gelaufen
du	bist gelaufen
er/sie/es	ist gelaufen
wir	sind gelaufen
ihr	seid gelaufen
sie/Sie	sind gelaufen

IMPERFECT
ich	lief
du	liefst
er/sie/es	lief
wir	liefen
ihr	lieft
sie/Sie	liefen

FUTURE
ich	werde laufen
du	wirst laufen
er/sie/es	wird laufen
wir	werden laufen
ihr	werdet laufen
sie/Sie	werden laufen

CONDITIONAL
ich	würde laufen
du	würdest laufen
er/sie/es	würde laufen
wir	würden laufen
ihr	würdet laufen
sie/Sie	würden laufen

IMPERATIVE
lauf(e)! / laufen wir! / lauft! / laufen Sie!

PRESENT PARTICIPLE
laufend

PAST PARTICIPLE
gelaufen

EXAMPLE PHRASES

Er sagt, ihm **laufe** die Nase.   *He says he's got a runny nose.*
Er **lief** so schnell er konnte.   *He ran as fast as he could.*

strong, *formed with* **haben** *to suffer* **leiden**

Table 44

PRESENT
- ich leide
- du leidest
- er/sie/es leidet
- wir leiden
- ihr leidet
- sie/Sie leiden

PRESENT SUBJUNCTIVE
- ich leide
- du leidest
- er/sie/es leide
- wir leiden
- ihr leidet
- sie/Sie leiden

PERFECT
- ich habe gelitten
- du hast gelitten
- er/sie/es hat gelitten
- wir haben gelitten
- ihr habt gelitten
- sie/Sie haben gelitten

IMPERFECT
- ich litt
- du litt(e)st
- er/sie/es litt
- wir litten
- ihr littet
- sie/Sie litten

FUTURE
- ich werde leiden
- du wirst leiden
- er/sie/es wird leiden
- wir werden leiden
- ihr werdet leiden
- sie/Sie werden leiden

CONDITIONAL
- ich würde leiden
- du würdest leiden
- er/sie/es würde leiden
- wir würden leiden
- ihr würdet leiden
- sie/Sie würden leiden

IMPERATIVE
leid(e)! / leiden wir! / leidet! / leiden Sie!

PRESENT PARTICIPLE
leidend

PAST PARTICIPLE
gelitten

EXAMPLE PHRASES

Wir **leiden** sehr unter der Hitze. *We're suffering badly from the heat.*
Sie **litt** an Asthma. *She suffered from asthma.*

Table 45 — **lesen** to read

*strong, formed with **haben***

PRESENT
- ich lese
- du liest
- er/sie/es liest
- wir lesen
- ihr lest
- sie/Sie lesen

PRESENT SUBJUNCTIVE
- ich lese
- du lesest
- er/sie/es lese
- wir lesen
- ihr leset
- sie/Sie lesen

PERFECT
- ich habe gelesen
- du hast gelesen
- er/sie/es hat gelesen
- wir haben gelesen
- ihr habt gelesen
- sie/Sie haben gelesen

IMPERFECT
- ich las
- du lasest
- er/sie/es las
- wir lasen
- ihr last
- sie/Sie lasen

FUTURE
- ich werde lesen
- du wirst lesen
- er/sie/es wird lesen
- wir werden lesen
- ihr werdet lesen
- sie/Sie werden lesen

CONDITIONAL
- ich würde lesen
- du würdest lesen
- er/sie/es würde lesen
- wir würden lesen
- ihr würdet lesen
- sie/Sie würden lesen

IMPERATIVE
lies! / lesen wir! / lest! / lesen Sie!

PRESENT PARTICIPLE
lesend

PAST PARTICIPLE
gelesen

EXAMPLE PHRASES

Er sagt, er **lese** jeden Tag zwei Zeitungen.
He says he reads two newspapers every day.

Das **habe** ich in der Zeitung **gelesen**.
I read it in the newspaper.

Morgen **werde** ich Harry Potter **lesen**.
I'll read Harry Potter tomorrow.

strong, *formed with* **haben**

to lie **liegen**

Table 46

PRESENT
ich	liege
du	liegst
er/sie/es	liegt
wir	liegen
ihr	liegt
sie/Sie	liegen

PRESENT SUBJUNCTIVE
ich	liege
du	liegest
er/sie/es	liege
wir	liegen
ihr	lieget
sie/Sie	liegen

PERFECT
ich	habe gelegen
du	hast gelegen
er/sie/es	hat gelegen
wir	haben gelegen
ihr	habt gelegen
sie/Sie	haben gelegen

IMPERFECT
ich	lag
du	lagst
er/sie/es	lag
wir	lagen
ihr	lagt
sie/Sie	lagen

FUTURE
ich	werde liegen
du	wirst liegen
er/sie/es	wird liegen
wir	werden liegen
ihr	werdet liegen
sie/Sie	werden liegen

CONDITIONAL
ich	würde liegen
du	würdest liegen
er/sie/es	würde liegen
wir	würden liegen
ihr	würdet liegen
sie/Sie	würden liegen

IMPERATIVE
lieg(e)! / liegen wir! / liegt! / liegen Sie!

PRESENT PARTICIPLE
liegend

PAST PARTICIPLE
gelegen

EXAMPLE PHRASES

Wir **lagen** den ganzen Tag am Strand.   *We lay on the beach all day.*

Table 47

lügen *to (tell a) lie* — strong, formed with **haben**

PRESENT
ich	lüge
du	lügst
er/sie/es	lügt
wir	lügen
ihr	lügt
sie/Sie	lügen

PRESENT SUBJUNCTIVE
ich	lüge
du	lügest
er/sie/es	lüge
wir	lügen
ihr	lüget
sie/Sie	lügen

PERFECT
ich	habe gelogen
du	hast gelogen
er/sie/es	hat gelogen
wir	haben gelogen
ihr	habt gelogen
sie/Sie	haben gelogen

IMPERFECT
ich	log
du	logst
er/sie/es	log
wir	logen
ihr	logt
sie/Sie	logen

FUTURE
ich	werde lügen
du	wirst lügen
er/sie/es	wird lügen
wir	werden lügen
ihr	werdet lügen
sie/Sie	werden lügen

CONDITIONAL
ich	würde lügen
du	würdest lügen
er/sie/es	würde lügen
wir	würden lügen
ihr	würdet lügen
sie/Sie	würden lügen

IMPERATIVE
lüg(e)! / lügen wir! / lügt! / lügen Sie!

PRESENT PARTICIPLE
lügend

PAST PARTICIPLE
gelogen

EXAMPLE PHRASES

Er hat gelogen!
Ich würde lügen, wenn ich das sagen würde.

He told a lie!
I would be lying if I said that.

strong,
formed with **haben**

to do; to make **machen**

Table 48

PRESENT
ich	mache
du	machst
er/sie/es	macht
wir	machen
ihr	macht
sie/Sie	machen

PRESENT SUBJUNCTIVE
ich	mache
du	machest
er/sie/es	mache
wir	machen
ihr	machet
sie/Sie	machen

PERFECT
ich	habe gemacht
du	hast gemacht
er/sie/es	hat gemacht
wir	haben gemacht
ihr	habt gemacht
sie/Sie	haben gemacht

IMPERFECT
ich	machte
du	machtest
er/sie/es	machte
wir	machten
ihr	machtet
sie/Sie	machten

FUTURE
ich	werde machen
du	wirst machen
er/sie/es	wird machen
wir	werden machen
ihr	werdet machen
sie/Sie	werden machen

CONDITIONAL
ich	würde machen
du	würdest machen
er/sie/es	würde machen
wir	würden machen
ihr	würdet machen
sie/Sie	würden machen

IMPERATIVE
mach! / machen wir! / macht! / machen Sie!

PRESENT PARTICIPLE
machend

PAST PARTICIPLE
gemacht

EXAMPLE PHRASES

Was **machst** du?
Ich **habe** die Betten **gemacht**.
Ich **werde** es morgen **machen**.

What are you doing?
I made the beds.
I'll do it tomorrow.

Table 49: misstrauen — to mistrust

*weak, inseparable, formed with **haben***

PRESENT
ich	misstraue
du	misstraust
er/sie/es	misstraut
wir	misstrauen
ihr	misstraut
sie/Sie	misstrauen

PRESENT SUBJUNCTIVE
ich	misstraue
du	misstrauest
er/sie/es	misstraue
wir	misstrauen
ihr	misstrauet
sie/Sie	misstrauen

PERFECT
ich	habe misstraut
du	hast misstraut
er/sie/es	hat misstraut
wir	haben misstraut
ihr	habt misstraut
sie/Sie	haben misstraut

IMPERFECT
ich	misstraute
du	misstrautest
er/sie/es	misstraute
wir	misstrauten
ihr	misstrautet
sie/Sie	misstrauten

FUTURE
ich	werde misstrauen
du	wirst misstrauen
er/sie/es	wird misstrauen
wir	werden misstrauen
ihr	werdet misstrauen
sie/Sie	werden misstrauen

CONDITIONAL
ich	würde misstrauen
du	würdest misstrauen
er/sie/es	würde misstrauen
wir	würden misstrauen
ihr	würdet misstrauen
sie/Sie	würden misstrauen

IMPERATIVE
misstrau(e)! / misstrauen wir! / misstraut! / misstrauen Sie!

PRESENT PARTICIPLE
misstrauend

PAST PARTICIPLE
misstraut

EXAMPLE PHRASES

Er sagt, er **misstraue** allen Politikern.
He says he mistrusts all politicians.

Ich **habe** ihr von Anfang an **misstraut**.
I didn't trust her from the start.

modal, *formed with* **haben** — *to like* **mögen** — Table 50

PRESENT
- ich mag
- du magst
- er/sie/es mag
- wir mögen
- ihr mögt
- sie/Sie mögen

PRESENT SUBJUNCTIVE
- ich möge
- du mögest
- er/sie/es möge
- wir mögen
- ihr möget
- sie/Sie mögen

PERFECT
- ich habe gemocht/mögen
- du hast gemocht/mögen
- er/sie/es hat gemocht/mögen
- wir haben gemocht/mögen
- ihr habt gemocht/mögen
- sie/Sie haben gemocht/mögen

IMPERFECT
- ich mochte
- du mochtest
- er/sie/es mochte
- wir mochten
- ihr mochtet
- sie/Sie mochten

FUTURE
- ich werde mögen
- du wirst mögen
- er/sie/es wird mögen
- wir werden mögen
- ihr werdet mögen
- sie/Sie werden mögen

CONDITIONAL
- ich würde mögen
- du würdest mögen
- er/sie/es würde mögen
- wir würden mögen
- ihr würdet mögen
- sie/Sie würden mögen

PRESENT PARTICIPLE
mögend

PAST PARTICIPLE
gemocht / mögen°

°This form is used when combined with another infinitive.

EXAMPLE PHRASES

Ich **mag** gern Vanilleeis. — *I like vanilla ice cream.*
Er **mochte** sie nicht danach fragen. — *He didn't want to ask her about it.*

Table 51: müssen *to have to* — modal, formed with **haben**

PRESENT

ich	muss
du	musst
er/sie/es	muss
wir	müssen
ihr	müsst
sie/Sie	müssen

PRESENT SUBJUNCTIVE

ich	müsse
du	müssest
er/sie/es	müsse
wir	müssen
ihr	müsset
sie/Sie	müssen

PERFECT

ich	habe gemusst/müssen
du	hast gemusst/müssen
er/sie/es	hat gemusst/müssen
wir	haben gemusst/müssen
ihr	habt gemusst/müssen
sie/Sie	haben gemusst/müssen

IMPERFECT

ich	musste
du	musstest
er/sie/es	musste
wir	mussten
ihr	musstet
sie/Sie	mussten

FUTURE

ich	werde müssen
du	wirst müssen
er/sie/es	wird müssen
wir	werden müssen
ihr	werdet müssen
sie/Sie	werden müssen

CONDITIONAL

ich	würde müssen
du	würdest müssen
er/sie/es	würde müssen
wir	würden müssen
ihr	würdet müssen
sie/Sie	würden müssen

PRESENT PARTICIPLE
müssend

PAST PARTICIPLE
gemusst / müssen°

°This form is used when combined with another infinitive.

EXAMPLE PHRASES

Er meint, er **müsse** jetzt gehen. — *He thinks he'll have to leave now.*
Sie **hat** abwaschen **müssen**. — *She had to wash up.*

strong, *formed with* **haben** *to take* **nehmen**

Table 52

PRESENT
- ich nehme
- du nimmst
- er/sie/es nimmt
- wir nehmen
- ihr nehmt
- sie/Sie nehmen

PRESENT SUBJUNCTIVE
- ich nehme
- du nehmest
- er/sie/es nehme
- wir nehmen
- ihr nehmet
- sie/Sie nehmen

PERFECT
- ich habe genommen
- du hast genommen
- er/sie/es hat genommen
- wir haben genommen
- ihr habt genommen
- sie/Sie haben genommen

IMPERFECT
- ich nahm
- du nahmst
- er/sie/es nahm
- wir nahmen
- ihr nahmt
- sie/Sie nahmen

FUTURE
- ich werde nehmen
- du wirst nehmen
- er/sie/es wird nehmen
- wir werden nehmen
- ihr werdet nehmen
- sie/Sie werden nehmen

CONDITIONAL
- ich würde nehmen
- du würdest nehmen
- er/sie/es würde nehmen
- wir würden nehmen
- ihr würdet nehmen
- sie/Sie würden nehmen

IMPERATIVE
nimm / nehmen wir! / nehmt! / nehmen Sie!

PRESENT PARTICIPLE
nehmend

PAST PARTICIPLE
genommen

EXAMPLE PHRASES

Hast du den Bus in die Stadt **genommen**? — *Did you take the bus into town?*

Wir **werden** den Bus in die Stadt **nehmen**. — *We'll take the bus into town.*

Table 53: rechnen — to work out

weak, formed with **haben**

PRESENT
ich	rechne
du	rechnest
er/sie/es	rechnet
wir	rechnen
ihr	rechnet
sie/Sie	rechnen

PRESENT SUBJUNCTIVE
ich	rechne
du	rechnest
er/sie/es	rechne
wir	rechnen
ihr	rechnet
sie/Sie	rechnen

PERFECT
ich	habe gerechnet
du	hast gerechnet
er/sie/es	hat gerechnet
wir	haben gerechnet
ihr	habt gerechnet
sie/Sie	haben gerechnet

IMPERFECT
ich	rechnete
du	rechnetest
er/sie/es	rechnete
wir	rechneten
ihr	rechnetet
sie/Sie	rechneten

FUTURE
ich	werde rechnen
du	wirst rechnen
er/sie/es	wird rechnen
wir	werden rechnen
ihr	werdet rechnen
sie/Sie	werden rechnen

CONDITIONAL
ich	würde rechnen
du	würdest rechnen
er/sie/es	würde rechnen
wir	würden rechnen
ihr	würdet rechnen
sie/Sie	würden rechnen

IMPERATIVE
rechne! / rechnen wir! / rechnet! / rechnen Sie!

PRESENT PARTICIPLE
rechnend

PAST PARTICIPLE
gerechnet

EXAMPLE PHRASES

Ich **werde** mal schnell **rechnen**, wie viel das wird.

I'll work out quickly how much that's going to be.

| weak, formed with **haben** | to talk **reden** | Table 54 |

PRESENT
ich	rede
du	redest
er/sie/es	redet
wir	reden
ihr	redet
sie/Sie	reden

PRESENT SUBJUNCTIVE
ich	rede
du	redest
er/sie/es	rede
wir	reden
ihr	redet
sie/Sie	reden

PERFECT
ich	habe geredet
du	hast geredet
er/sie/es	hat geredet
wir	haben geredet
ihr	habt geredet
sie/Sie	haben geredet

IMPERFECT
ich	redete
du	redetest
er/sie/es	redete
wir	redeten
ihr	redetet
sie/Sie	redeten

FUTURE
ich	werde reden
du	wirst reden
er/sie/es	wird reden
wir	werden reden
ihr	werdet reden
sie/Sie	werden reden

CONDITIONAL
ich	würde reden
du	würdest reden
er/sie/es	würde reden
wir	würden reden
ihr	würdet reden
sie/Sie	würden reden

IMPERATIVE
red(e)! / reden wir! / redet! / reden Sie!

PRESENT PARTICIPLE
redend

PAST PARTICIPLE
geredet

EXAMPLE PHRASES

Er meint, ich **rede** Unsinn. *He thinks I'm talking nonsense.*
Ich **werde** mit deinem Vater **reden**. *I'll speak to your father.*

Table 55: **rennen** *to run*

mixed, formed with **sein**

PRESENT
ich	renne
du	rennst
er/sie/es	rennt
wir	rennen
ihr	rennt
sie/Sie	rennen

PRESENT SUBJUNCTIVE
ich	renne
du	rennest
er/sie/es	renne
wir	rennen
ihr	rennet
sie/Sie	rennen

PERFECT
ich	bin gerannt
du	bist gerannt
er/sie/es	ist gerannt
wir	sind gerannt
ihr	seid gerannt
sie/Sie	sind gerannt

IMPERFECT
ich	rannte
du	ranntest
er/sie/es	rannte
wir	rannten
ihr	ranntet
sie/Sie	rannten

FUTURE
ich	werde rennen
du	wirst rennen
er/sie/es	wird rennen
wir	werden rennen
ihr	werdet rennen
sie/Sie	werden rennen

CONDITIONAL
ich	würde rennen
du	würdest rennen
er/sie/es	würde rennen
wir	würden rennen
ihr	würdet rennen
sie/Sie	würden rennen

IMPERATIVE
renn(e)! / rennen wir! / rennt! / rennen Sie!

PRESENT PARTICIPLE
rennend

PAST PARTICIPLE
gerannt

EXAMPLE PHRASES

Sie **rannte** schnell weg.
Ich **werde** die 100 Meter nicht **rennen**.

She ran away fast.
I won't run the 100 metres.

| strong, formed with **haben** | to shout; to call **rufen** |

PRESENT
ich	rufe
du	rufst
er/sie/es	ruft
wir	rufen
ihr	ruft
sie/Sie	rufen

PRESENT SUBJUNCTIVE
ich	rufe
du	rufest
er/sie/es	rufe
wir	rufen
ihr	rufet
sie/Sie	rufen

PERFECT
ich	habe gerufen
du	hast gerufen
er/sie/es	hat gerufen
wir	haben gerufen
ihr	habt gerufen
sie/Sie	haben gerufen

IMPERFECT
ich	rief
du	riefst
er/sie/es	rief
wir	riefen
ihr	rieft
sie/Sie	riefen

FUTURE
ich	werde rufen
du	wirst rufen
er/sie/es	wird rufen
wir	werden rufen
ihr	werdet rufen
sie/Sie	werden rufen

CONDITIONAL
ich	würde rufen
du	würdest rufen
er/sie/es	würde rufen
wir	würden rufen
ihr	würdet rufen
sie/Sie	würden rufen

IMPERATIVE
ruf(e)! / rufen wir! / ruft! / rufen Sie!

PRESENT PARTICIPLE
rufend

PAST PARTICIPLE
gerufen

--- EXAMPLE PHRASES ---

Sie **ruft** um Hilfe. — *She is shouting for help.*
Ich **habe** dir ein Taxi **gerufen**. — *I called you a taxi.*

Table 57

scheinen *to shine; to seem*

strong, formed with **haben**

PRESENT
ich	scheine
du	scheinst
er/sie/es	scheint
wir	scheinen
ihr	scheint
sie/Sie	scheinen

PRESENT SUBJUNCTIVE
ich	scheine
du	scheinest
er/sie/es	scheine
wir	scheinen
ihr	scheinet
sie/Sie	scheinen

PERFECT
ich	habe geschienen
du	hast geschienen
er/sie/es	hat geschienen
wir	haben geschienen
ihr	habt geschienen
sie/Sie	haben geschienen

IMPERFECT
ich	schien
du	schienst
er/sie/es	schien
wir	schienen
ihr	schient
sie/Sie	schienen

FUTURE
ich	werde scheinen
du	wirst scheinen
er/sie/es	wird scheinen
wir	werden scheinen
ihr	werdet scheinen
sie/Sie	werden scheinen

CONDITIONAL
ich	würde scheinen
du	würdest scheinen
er/sie/es	würde scheinen
wir	würden scheinen
ihr	würdet scheinen
sie/Sie	würden scheinen

IMPERATIVE
schein(e)! / scheinen wir! / scheint! / scheinen Sie!

PRESENT PARTICIPLE
scheinend

PAST PARTICIPLE
geschienen

EXAMPLE PHRASES

Gestern **hat** die Sonne nicht **geschienen**.
The sun wasn't shining yesterday.

Sie **schienen** glücklich zu sein.
They seemed to be happy.

strong, *formed with* **haben** to sleep **schlafen**

Table 58

PRESENT
ich	schlafe
du	schläfst
er/sie/es	schläft
wir	schlafen
ihr	schlaft
sie/Sie	schlafen

PRESENT SUBJUNCTIVE
ich	schlafe
du	schlafest
er/sie/es	schlafe
wir	schlafen
ihr	schlafet
sie/Sie	schlafen

PERFECT
ich	habe geschlafen
du	hast geschlafen
er/sie/es	hat geschlafen
wir	haben geschlafen
ihr	habt geschlafen
sie/Sie	haben geschlafen

IMPERFECT
ich	schlief
du	schliefst
er/sie/es	schlief
wir	schliefen
ihr	schlieft
sie/Sie	schliefen

FUTURE
ich	werde schlafen
du	wirst schlafen
er/sie/es	wird schlafen
wir	werden schlafen
ihr	werdet schlafen
sie/Sie	werden schlafen

CONDITIONAL
ich	würde schlafen
du	würdest schlafen
er/sie/es	würde schlafen
wir	würden schlafen
ihr	würdet schlafen
sie/Sie	würden schlafen

IMPERATIVE
schlaf(e)! / schlafen wir! / schlaft! / schlafen Sie!

PRESENT PARTICIPLE
schlafend

PAST PARTICIPLE
geschlafen

EXAMPLE PHRASES

Sie **schläft** immer noch.   *She's still asleep.*
Hast du gut **geschlafen**?   *Did you sleep well?*

Table 59: schlagen *to beat* — strong, formed with **haben**

PRESENT
ich	schlage
du	schlägst
er/sie/es	schlägt
wir	schlagen
ihr	schlagt
sie/Sie	schlagen

PRESENT SUBJUNCTIVE
ich	schlage
du	schlagest
er/sie/es	schlage
wir	schlagen
ihr	schlaget
sie/Sie	schlagen

PERFECT
ich	habe geschlagen
du	hast geschlagen
er/sie/es	hat geschlagen
wir	haben geschlagen
ihr	habt geschlagen
sie/Sie	haben geschlagen

IMPERFECT
ich	schlug
du	schlugst
er/sie/es	schlug
wir	schlugen
ihr	schlugt
sie/Sie	schlugen

FUTURE
ich	werde schlagen
du	wirst schlagen
er/sie/es	wird schlagen
wir	werden schlagen
ihr	werdet schlagen
sie/Sie	werden schlagen

CONDITIONAL
ich	würde schlagen
du	würdest schlagen
er/sie/es	würde schlagen
wir	würden schlagen
ihr	würdet schlagen
sie/Sie	würden schlagen

IMPERATIVE
schlag(e)! / schlagen wir! / schlagt! / schlagen Sie!

PRESENT PARTICIPLE
schlagend

PAST PARTICIPLE
geschlagen

EXAMPLE PHRASES

Mein Herz **schlägt** schneller.
England **hat** Deutschland **geschlagen**.

My heart is beating faster.
England beat Germany.

strong, *formed with* **haben** — *to cut* **schneiden** — Table 60

PRESENT
- ich schneide
- du schneidest
- er/sie/es schneidet
- wir schneiden
- ihr schneidet
- sie/Sie schneiden

PRESENT SUBJUNCTIVE
- ich schneide
- du schneidest
- er/sie/es schneide
- wir schneiden
- ihr schneidet
- sie/Sie schneiden

PERFECT
- ich habe geschnitten
- du hast geschnitten
- er/sie/es hat geschnitten
- wir haben geschnitten
- ihr habt geschnitten
- sie/Sie haben geschnitten

IMPERFECT
- ich schnitt
- du schnittst
- er/sie/es schnitt
- wir schnitten
- ihr schnittet
- sie/Sie schnitten

FUTURE
- ich werde schneiden
- du wirst schneiden
- er/sie/es wird schneiden
- wir werden schneiden
- ihr werdet schneiden
- sie/Sie werden schneiden

CONDITIONAL
- ich würde schneiden
- du würdest schneiden
- er/sie/es würde schneiden
- wir würden schneiden
- ihr würdet schneiden
- sie/Sie würden schneiden

IMPERATIVE
schneid(e)! / schneiden wir! / schneidet! / schneiden Sie!

PRESENT PARTICIPLE
schneidend

PAST PARTICIPLE
geschnitten

---— EXAMPLE PHRASES —---

Ich **habe** mir in den Finger **geschnitten**. — *I've cut my finger.*
Ich **werde** das Brot in Scheiben **schneiden**. — *I'll slice the bread.*

Table 61: schreiben — to write

strong, formed with haben

PRESENT
- ich schreibe
- du schreibst
- er/sie/es schreibt
- wir schreiben
- ihr schreibt
- sie/Sie schreiben

PRESENT SUBJUNCTIVE
- ich schreibe
- du schreibest
- er/sie/es schreibe
- wir schreiben
- ihr schreibet
- sie/Sie schreiben

PERFECT
- ich habe geschrieben
- du hast geschrieben
- er/sie/es hat geschrieben
- wir haben geschrieben
- ihr habt geschrieben
- sie/Sie haben geschrieben

IMPERFECT
- ich schrieb
- du schriebst
- er/sie/es schrieb
- wir schrieben
- ihr schriebt
- sie/Sie schrieben

FUTURE
- ich werde schreiben
- du wirst schreiben
- er/sie/es wird schreiben
- wir werden schreiben
- ihr werdet schreiben
- sie/Sie werden schreiben

CONDITIONAL
- ich würde schreiben
- du würdest schreiben
- er/sie/es würde schreiben
- wir würden schreiben
- ihr würdet schreiben
- sie/Sie würden schreiben

IMPERATIVE
schreib(e)! / schreiben wir! / schreibt! / schreiben Sie!

PRESENT PARTICIPLE
schreibend

PAST PARTICIPLE
geschrieben

EXAMPLE PHRASES

Sie **hat** mir einen Brief **geschrieben**. — *She wrote me a letter.*

Er **schrieb** das Wort an die Tafel. — *He wrote the word on the blackboard.*

strong, *formed with* **haben** | *to shout* **schreien** | Table 62

PRESENT
ich	schreie
du	schreist
er/sie/es	schreit
wir	schreien
ihr	schreit
sie/Sie	schreien

PRESENT SUBJUNCTIVE
ich	schreie
du	schreiest
er/sie/es	schreie
wir	schreien
ihr	schreiet
sie/Sie	schreien

PERFECT
ich	habe geschrien
du	hast geschrien
er/sie/es	hat geschrien
wir	haben geschrien
ihr	habt geschrien
sie/Sie	haben geschrien

IMPERFECT
ich	schrie
du	schriest
er/sie/es	schrie
wir	schrieen
ihr	schriet
sie/Sie	schrieen

FUTURE
ich	werde schreien
du	wirst schreien
er/sie/es	wird schreien
wir	werden schreien
ihr	werdet schreien
sie/Sie	werden schreien

CONDITIONAL
ich	würde schreien
du	würdest schreien
er/sie/es	würde schreien
wir	würden schreien
ihr	würdet schreien
sie/Sie	würden schreien

IMPERATIVE
schrei(e)! / schreien wir! / schreit! / schreien Sie!

PRESENT PARTICIPLE
schreiend

PAST PARTICIPLE
geschrien

EXAMPLE PHRASES

Sie sagt, er **schreie** zu laut.
Wir **haben geschrien**, er hat uns aber nicht gehört.

She says he's shouting too loud.
We shouted but he didn't hear us.

schwimmen *to swim*

*strong, formed with **sein***

PRESENT

ich	schwimme
du	schwimmst
er/sie/es	schwimmt
wir	schwimmen
ihr	schwimmt
sie/Sie	schwimmen

PRESENT SUBJUNCTIVE

ich	schwimme
du	schwimmest
er/sie/es	schwimme
wir	schwimmen
ihr	schwimmet
sie/Sie	schwimmen

PERFECT

ich	bin geschwommen
du	bist geschwommen
er/sie/es	ist geschwommen
wir	sind geschwommen
ihr	seid geschwommen
sie/Sie	sind geschwommen

IMPERFECT

ich	schwamm
du	schwammst
er/sie/es	schwamm
wir	schwammen
ihr	schwammt
sie/Sie	schwammen

FUTURE

ich	werde schwimmen
du	wirst schwimmen
er/sie/es	wird schwimmen
wir	werden schwimmen
ihr	werdet schwimmen
sie/Sie	werden schwimmen

CONDITIONAL

ich	würde schwimmen
du	würdest schwimmen
er/sie/es	würde schwimmen
wir	würden schwimmen
ihr	würdet schwimmen
sie/Sie	würden schwimmen

IMPERATIVE

schwimm(e)! / schwimmen wir! / schwimmt! / schwimmen Sie!

PRESENT PARTICIPLE

schwimmend

PAST PARTICIPLE

geschwommen

--- EXAMPLE PHRASES ---

Er **ist** über den Fluss **geschwommen**. — *He swam across the river.*

Ich **würde** gern öfter **schwimmen**. — *I'd like to swim more often.*

strong, *formed with* **haben** — *to see* **sehen** — Table 64

PRESENT

ich	sehe
du	siehst
er/sie/es	sieht
wir	sehen
ihr	seht
sie/Sie	sehen

PRESENT SUBJUNCTIVE

ich	sehe
du	sehest
er/sie/es	sehe
wir	sehen
ihr	sehet
sie/Sie	sehen

PERFECT

ich	habe gesehen
du	hast gesehen
er/sie/es	hat gesehen
wir	haben gesehen
ihr	habt gesehen
sie/Sie	haben gesehen

IMPERFECT

ich	sah
du	sahst
er/sie/es	sah
wir	sahen
ihr	saht
sie/Sie	sahen

FUTURE

ich	werde sehen
du	wirst sehen
er/sie/es	wird sehen
wir	werden sehen
ihr	werdet sehen
sie/Sie	werden sehen

CONDITIONAL

ich	würde sehen
du	würdest sehen
er/sie/es	würde sehen
wir	würden sehen
ihr	würdet sehen
sie/Sie	würden sehen

IMPERATIVE

sieh(e)! / sehen wir! / seht! / sehen Sie!

PRESENT PARTICIPLE

sehend

PAST PARTICIPLE

gesehen

EXAMPLE PHRASES

Ich **habe** diesen Film noch nicht **gesehen**. — *I haven't seen this film yet.*

Wir **werden sehen**, wie sich die Dinge entwickeln. — *We'll see how things develop.*

Table 65: **sein** *to be*

strong, formed with **sein**

PRESENT
ich	bin
du	bist
er/sie/es	ist
wir	sind
ihr	seid
sie/Sie	sind

PRESENT SUBJUNCTIVE
ich	sei
du	sei(e)st
er/sie/es	sei
wir	seien
ihr	seiet
sie/Sie	seien

PERFECT
ich	bin gewesen
du	bist gewesen
er/sie/es	ist gewesen
wir	sind gewesen
ihr	seid gewesen
sie/Sie	sind gewesen

IMPERFECT
ich	war
du	warst
er/sie/es	war
wir	waren
ihr	wart
sie/Sie	waren

FUTURE
ich	werde sein
du	wirst sein
er/sie/es	wird sein
wir	werden sein
ihr	werdet sein
sie/Sie	werden sein

CONDITIONAL
ich	würde sein
du	würdest sein
er/sie/es	würde sein
wir	würden sein
ihr	würdet sein
sie/Sie	würden sein

IMPERATIVE
sei! / seien wir! / seid! / seien Sie!

PRESENT PARTICIPLE
seiend

PAST PARTICIPLE
gewesen

EXAMPLE PHRASES

Er **ist** zehn Jahre.
Wir **waren** gestern im Theater.
Morgen **werde** ich in Berlin **sein**.

He's ten years old.
We were at the theatre yesterday.
I'll be in Berlin tomorrow.

strong, *formed with* **haben** — *to sing* **singen**

Table 66

PRESENT
ich	singe
du	singst
er/sie/es	singt
wir	singen
ihr	singt
sie/Sie	singen

PRESENT SUBJUNCTIVE
ich	singe
du	singest
er/sie/es	singe
wir	singen
ihr	singet
sie/Sie	singen

PERFECT
ich	habe gesungen
du	hast gesungen
er/sie/es	hat gesungen
wir	haben gesungen
ihr	habt gesungen
sie/Sie	haben gesungen

IMPERFECT
ich	sang
du	sangst
er/sie/es	sang
wir	sangen
ihr	sangt
sie/Sie	sangen

FUTURE
ich	werde singen
du	wirst singen
er/sie/es	wird singen
wir	werden singen
ihr	werdet singen
sie/Sie	werden singen

CONDITIONAL
ich	würde singen
du	würdest singen
er/sie/es	würde singen
wir	würden singen
ihr	würdet singen
sie/Sie	würden singen

IMPERATIVE
sing(e)! / singen wir! / singt! / singen Sie!

PRESENT PARTICIPLE
singend

PAST PARTICIPLE
gesungen

EXAMPLE PHRASES

Er **singt** nicht gut.
Wir **werden** jetzt die Nationalhymne **singen**.

He's a bad singer.
We will sing the national anthem now.

Table 67: **sinken** *to sink*

*strong, formed with **sein***

PRESENT
ich	sinke
du	sinkst
er/sie/es	sinkt
wir	sinken
ihr	sinkt
sie/Sie	sinken

PRESENT SUBJUNCTIVE
ich	sinke
du	sinkest
er/sie/es	sinke
wir	sinken
ihr	sinket
sie/Sie	sinken

PERFECT
ich	bin gesunken
du	bist gesunken
er/sie/es	ist gesunken
wir	sind gesunken
ihr	seid gesunken
sie/Sie	sind gesunken

IMPERFECT
ich	sank
du	sankst
er/sie/es	sank
wir	sanken
ihr	sankt
sie/Sie	sanken

FUTURE
ich	werde sinken
du	wirst sinken
er/sie/es	wird sinken
wir	werden sinken
ihr	werdet sinken
sie/Sie	werden sinken

CONDITIONAL
ich	würde sinken
du	würdest sinken
er/sie/es	würde sinken
wir	würden sinken
ihr	würdet sinken
sie/Sie	würden sinken

IMPERATIVE
sink(e)! / sinken wir! / sinkt! / sinken Sie!

PRESENT PARTICIPLE
sinkend

PAST PARTICIPLE
gesunken

EXAMPLE PHRASES

Die Preise für Handys **sinken**.
Wann **ist** die Titanic **gesunken**?

Prices of mobile phones are falling.
When did the Titanic sink?

strong, formed with **haben**   *to sit* **sitzen**

Table 68

PRESENT
ich	sitze
du	sitzt
er/sie/es	sitzt
wir	sitzen
ihr	sitzt
sie/Sie	sitzen

PRESENT SUBJUNCTIVE
ich	sitze
du	sitzest
er/sie/es	sitze
wir	sitzen
ihr	sitzet
sie/Sie	sitzen

PERFECT
ich	habe gegessen
du	hast gegessen
er/sie/es	hat gegessen
wir	haben gegessen
ihr	habt gegessen
sie/Sie	haben gegessen

IMPERFECT
ich	saß
du	saßest
er/sie/es	saß
wir	saßen
ihr	saßt
sie/Sie	saßen

FUTURE
ich	werde sitzen
du	wirst sitzen
er/sie/es	wird sitzen
wir	werden sitzen
ihr	werdet sitzen
sie/Sie	werden sitzen

CONDITIONAL
ich	würde sitzen
du	würdest sitzen
er/sie/es	würde sitzen
wir	würden sitzen
ihr	würdet sitzen
sie/Sie	würden sitzen

IMPERATIVE
sitz(e)! / sitzen wir! / sitzt! / sitzen Sie!

PRESENT PARTICIPLE
sitzend

PAST PARTICIPLE
gesessen

EXAMPLE PHRASES

Er **saß** auf meinem Stuhl.
Wo **wird** der Präsident **sitzen**?
Wir **würden** gern in der ersten Reihe **sitzen**.

He was sitting on my chair.
Where will the president be sitting?
We'd like to sit in the front row.

Table 69

sollen *to be supposed to*

modal, formed with **haben**

PRESENT
ich	soll
du	sollst
er/sie/es	soll
wir	sollen
ihr	sollt
sie/Sie	sollen

PRESENT SUBJUNCTIVE
ich	solle
du	sollest
er/sie/es	solle
wir	sollen
ihr	sollet
sie/Sie	sollen

PERFECT
ich	habe gesollt/sollen
du	hast gesollt/sollen
er/sie/es	hat gesollt/sollen
wir	haben gesollt/sollen
ihr	habt gesollt/sollen
sie/Sie	haben gesollt/sollen

IMPERFECT
ich	sollte
du	solltest
er/sie/es	sollte
wir	sollten
ihr	solltet
sie/Sie	sollten

FUTURE
ich	werde sollen
du	wirst sollen
er/sie/es	wird sollen
wir	werden sollen
ihr	werdet sollen
sie/Sie	werden sollen

CONDITIONAL
ich	würde sollen
du	würdest sollen
er/sie/es	würde sollen
wir	würden sollen
ihr	würdet sollen
sie/Sie	würden sollen

PRESENT PARTICIPLE
sollend

PAST PARTICIPLE
gesollt / sollen*

*This form is used when combined with another infinitive.

EXAMPLE PHRASES

Ich **soll** um 5 Uhr dort sein. — *I'm supposed to be there at 5 o'clock.*
Ich **sollte** draußen bleiben. — *I was supposed to stay outside.*

strong, *formed with* **haben**   *to speak* **sprechen**

Table 70

PRESENT
ich	spreche
du	sprichst
er/sie/es	spricht
wir	sprechen
ihr	sprecht
sie/Sie	sprechen

PRESENT SUBJUNCTIVE
ich	spreche
du	sprechest
er/sie/es	spreche
wir	sprechen
ihr	sprechet
sie/Sie	sprechen

PERFECT
ich	habe gesprochen
du	hast gesprochen
er/sie/es	hat gesprochen
wir	haben gesprochen
ihr	habt gesprochen
sie/Sie	haben gesprochen

IMPERFECT
ich	sprach
du	sprachst
er/sie/es	sprach
wir	sprachen
ihr	spracht
sie/Sie	sprachen

FUTURE
ich	werde sprechen
du	wirst sprechen
er/sie/es	wird sprechen
wir	werden sprechen
ihr	werdet sprechen
sie/Sie	werden sprechen

CONDITIONAL
ich	würde sprechen
du	würdest sprechen
er/sie/es	würde sprechen
wir	würden sprechen
ihr	würdet sprechen
sie/Sie	würden sprechen

IMPERATIVE
sprich! / sprechen wir! / sprecht! / sprechen Sie!

PRESENT PARTICIPLE
sprechend

PAST PARTICIPLE
gesprochen

EXAMPLE PHRASES

Er **spricht** kein Italienisch.
Sie sagt, sie **spreche** aus Erfahrung.
Ich **werde** mit ihm darüber **sprechen**.

He doesn't speak Italian.
She says she's speaking from experience.
I'll speak to him about it.

springen *to jump*

strong, formed with **sein**

PRESENT
ich	springe
du	springst
er/sie/es	springt
wir	springen
ihr	springt
sie/Sie	springen

PRESENT SUBJUNCTIVE
ich	springe
du	springest
er/sie/es	springe
wir	springen
ihr	springet
sie/Sie	springen

PERFECT
ich	bin gesprungen
du	bist gesprungen
er/sie/es	ist gesprungen
wir	sind gesprungen
ihr	seid gesprungen
sie/Sie	sind gesprungen

IMPERFECT
ich	sprang
du	sprangst
er/sie/es	sprang
wir	sprangen
ihr	sprangt
sie/Sie	sprangen

FUTURE
ich	werde springen
du	wirst springen
er/sie/es	wird springen
wir	werden springen
ihr	werdet springen
sie/Sie	werden springen

CONDITIONAL
ich	würde springen
du	würdest springen
er/sie/es	würde springen
wir	würden springen
ihr	würdet springen
sie/Sie	würden springen

IMPERATIVE
spring(e)! / springen wir! / springt! / springen Sie!

PRESENT PARTICIPLE
springend

PAST PARTICIPLE
gesprungen

--- EXAMPLE PHRASES ---

Er **sprang** über den Zaun.   *He jumped over the fence.*

| strong, *formed with* **haben** | to stand **stehen** |

PRESENT

ich	stehe
du	stehst
er/sie/es	steht
wir	stehen
ihr	steht
sie/Sie	stehen

PRESENT SUBJUNCTIVE

ich	stehe
du	stehest
er/sie/es	stehe
wir	stehen
ihr	stehet
sie/Sie	stehen

PERFECT

ich	habe gestanden
du	hast gestanden
er/sie/es	hat gestanden
wir	haben gestanden
ihr	habt gestanden
sie/Sie	haben gestanden

IMPERFECT

ich	stand
du	stand(e)st
er/sie/es	stand
wir	standen
ihr	standet
sie/Sie	standen

FUTURE

ich	werde stehen
du	wirst stehen
er/sie/es	wird stehen
wir	werden stehen
ihr	werdet stehen
sie/Sie	werden stehen

CONDITIONAL

ich	würde stehen
du	würdest stehen
er/sie/es	würde stehen
wir	würden stehen
ihr	würdet stehen
sie/Sie	würden stehen

IMPERATIVE
steh(e)! / stehen wir! / steht! / stehen Sie!

PRESENT PARTICIPLE
stehend

PAST PARTICIPLE
gestanden

--- EXAMPLE PHRASES ---

Die Vase **steht** auf dem Tisch.	*The vase is on the table.*
Wir **standen** an der Bushaltestelle.	*We stood at the bus stop.*
Dieses Kleid **würde** dir gut **stehen**.	*This dress would suit you.*

Table 73: **stehlen** *to steal* — strong, *formed with* **haben**

PRESENT
- ich stehle
- du stiehlst
- er/sie/es stiehlt
- wir stehlen
- ihr stehlt
- sie/Sie stehlen

PRESENT SUBJUNCTIVE
- ich stehle
- du stehlest
- er/sie/es stehle
- wir stehlen
- ihr stehlet
- sie/Sie stehlen

PERFECT
- ich habe gestohlen
- du hast gestohlen
- er/sie/es hat gestohlen
- wir haben gestohlen
- ihr habt gestohlen
- sie/Sie haben gestohlen

IMPERFECT
- ich stahl
- du stahlst
- er/sie/es stahl
- wir stahlen
- ihr stahlt
- sie/Sie stahlen

FUTURE
- ich werde stehlen
- du wirst stehlen
- er/sie/es wird stehlen
- wir werden stehlen
- ihr werdet stehlen
- sie/Sie werden stehlen

CONDITIONAL
- ich würde stehlen
- du würdest stehlen
- er/sie/es würde stehlen
- wir würden stehlen
- ihr würdet stehlen
- sie/Sie würden stehlen

IMPERATIVE
stiehl! / stehlen wir! / stehlt! / stehlen Sie!

PRESENT PARTICIPLE
stehlend

PAST PARTICIPLE
gestohlen

EXAMPLE PHRASES

Er **hat** das ganze Geld **gestohlen**. — *He stole all the money.*
Ich **würde** euch nichts **stehlen**. — *I wouldn't steal anything from you.*

strong, *formed with* **sein** — *to climb* **steigen**

PRESENT
ich	steige
du	steigst
er/sie/es	steigt
wir	steigen
ihr	steigt
sie/Sie	steigen

PRESENT SUBJUNCTIVE
ich	steige
du	steigest
er/sie/es	steige
wir	steigen
ihr	steiget
sie/Sie	steigen

PERFECT
ich	bin gestiegen
du	bist gestiegen
er/sie/es	ist gestiegen
wir	sind gestiegen
ihr	seid gestiegen
sie/Sie	sind gestiegen

IMPERFECT
ich	stieg
du	stiegst
er/sie/es	stieg
wir	stiegen
ihr	stiegt
sie/Sie	stiegen

FUTURE
ich	werde steigen
du	wirst steigen
er/sie/es	wird steigen
wir	werden steigen
ihr	werdet steigen
sie/Sie	werden steigen

CONDITIONAL
ich	würde steigen
du	würdest steigen
er/sie/es	würde steigen
wir	würden steigen
ihr	würdet steigen
sie/Sie	würden steigen

IMPERATIVE
steig(e)! / steigen wir! / steigt! / steigen Sie!

PRESENT PARTICIPLE
steigend

PAST PARTICIPLE
gestiegen

EXAMPLE PHRASES

Sie **ist** auf die Leiter **gestiegen**. *She climbed up the ladder.*
Die Temperatur **stieg** auf 28 Grad. *The temperature rose to 28 degrees.*

Table 75: **sterben** to die

*strong, formed with **sein***

PRESENT
ich	sterbe
du	stirbst
er/sie/es	stirbt
wir	sterben
ihr	sterbt
sie/Sie	sterben

PRESENT SUBJUNCTIVE
ich	sterbe
du	sterbest
er/sie/es	sterbe
wir	sterben
ihr	sterbet
sie/Sie	sterben

PERFECT
ich	bin gestorben
du	bist gestorben
er/sie/es	ist gestorben
wir	sind gestorben
ihr	seid gestorben
sie/Sie	sind gestorben

IMPERFECT
ich	starb
du	starbst
er/sie/es	starb
wir	starben
ihr	starbt
sie/Sie	starben

FUTURE
ich	werde sterben
du	wirst sterben
er/sie/es	wird sterben
wir	werden sterben
ihr	werdet sterben
sie/Sie	werden sterben

CONDITIONAL
ich	würde sterben
du	würdest sterben
er/sie/es	würde sterben
wir	würden sterben
ihr	würdet sterben
sie/Sie	würden sterben

IMPERATIVE
stirb! / sterben wir! / sterbt! / sterben Sie!

PRESENT PARTICIPLE
sterbend

PAST PARTICIPLE
gestorben

EXAMPLE PHRASES

Ich **sterbe** hier vor Langeweile.
Er **starb** eines natürlichen Todes.
Daran **wirst** du nicht **sterben**!

I'm dying of boredom here.
He died a natural death.
It won't kill you!

weak, *formed with* **haben** — *to study* **studieren** — Table **76**

PRESENT
ich	studiere
du	studierst
er/sie/es	studiert
wir	studieren
ihr	studiert
sie/Sie	studieren

PRESENT SUBJUNCTIVE
ich	studiere
du	studierest
er/sie/es	studiere
wir	studieren
ihr	studieret
sie/Sie	studieren

PERFECT
ich	habe studiert
du	hast studiert
er/sie/es	hat studiert
wir	haben studiert
ihr	habt studiert
sie/Sie	haben studiert

IMPERFECT
ich	studierte
du	studiertest
er/sie/es	studierte
wir	studierten
ihr	studiertet
sie/Sie	studierten

FUTURE
ich	werde studieren
du	wirst studieren
er/sie/es	wird studieren
wir	werden studieren
ihr	werdet studieren
sie/Sie	werden studieren

CONDITIONAL
ich	würde studieren
du	würdest studieren
er/sie/es	würde studieren
wir	würden studieren
ihr	würdet studieren
sie/Sie	würden studieren

IMPERATIVE
studiere! / studieren wir! / studiert! / studieren Sie!

PRESENT PARTICIPLE
studierend

PAST PARTICIPLE
studiert

--- EXAMPLE PHRASES ---

Mein Bruder **studiert** Deutsch. — *My brother is studying German.*
Sie **hat** in Köln **studiert**. — *She was a student at Cologne University.*

Table 77

tragen *to wear; to carry*

strong, formed with **haben**

PRESENT
ich	trage
du	trägst
er/sie/es	trägt
wir	tragen
ihr	tragt
sie/Sie	tragen

PRESENT SUBJUNCTIVE
ich	trage
du	tragest
er/sie/es	trage
wir	tragen
ihr	traget
sie/Sie	tragen

PERFECT
ich	habe getragen
du	hast getragen
er/sie/es	hat getragen
wir	haben getragen
ihr	habt getragen
sie/Sie	haben getragen

IMPERFECT
ich	trug
du	trugst
er/sie/es	trug
wir	trugen
ihr	trugt
sie/Sie	trugen

FUTURE
ich	werde tragen
du	wirst tragen
er/sie/es	wird tragen
wir	werden tragen
ihr	werdet tragen
sie/Sie	werden tragen

CONDITIONAL
ich	würde tragen
du	würdest tragen
er/sie/es	würde tragen
wir	würden tragen
ihr	würdet tragen
sie/Sie	würden tragen

IMPERATIVE
trag(e)! / tragen wir! / tragt! / tragen Sie!

PRESENT PARTICIPLE
tragend

PAST PARTICIPLE
getragen

EXAMPLE PHRASES

Er sagt, er **trage** nie neue Kleider.	*He says he never wears new clothes.*
Ich **trug** ihren Koffer zum Bahnhof.	*I carried her case to the station.*
Ich **würde** meine Haare gern länger **tragen**.	*I'd like to wear my hair longer.*

strong, formed with **haben** — to meet **treffen**

PRESENT
- ich treffe
- du triffst
- er/sie/es trifft
- wir treffen
- ihr trefft
- sie/Sie treffen

PRESENT SUBJUNCTIVE
- ich treffe
- du treffest
- er/sie/es treffe
- wir treffen
- ihr treffet
- sie/Sie treffen

PERFECT
- ich habe getroffen
- du hast getroffen
- er/sie/es hat getroffen
- wir haben getroffen
- ihr habt getroffen
- sie/Sie haben getroffen

IMPERFECT
- ich traf
- du trafst
- er/sie/es traf
- wir trafen
- ihr traft
- sie/Sie trafen

FUTURE
- ich werde treffen
- du wirst treffen
- er/sie/es wird treffen
- wir werden treffen
- ihr werdet treffen
- sie/Sie werden treffen

CONDITIONAL
- ich würde treffen
- du würdest treffen
- er/sie/es würde treffen
- wir würden treffen
- ihr würdet treffen
- sie/Sie würden treffen

IMPERATIVE
triff! / treffen wir! / trefft! / treffen Sie!

PRESENT PARTICIPLE
treffend

PAST PARTICIPLE
getroffen

EXAMPLE PHRASES

Sie **trifft** sich zweimal pro Woche mit ihm. — *She meets with him twice a week.*

Wir **werden** uns am Bahnhof **treffen**. — *We'll meet at the station.*

Table 79: **treten** *to kick; to step*

strong, formed with **haben/sein***

PRESENT

ich	trete
du	trittst
er/sie/es	tritt
wir	treten
ihr	tretet
sie/Sie	treten

PRESENT SUBJUNCTIVE

ich	trete
du	tretest
er/sie/es	trete
wir	treten
ihr	tretet
sie/Sie	treten

PERFECT

ich	habe getreten
du	hast getreten
er/sie/es	hat getreten
wir	haben getreten
ihr	habt getreten
sie/Sie	haben getreten

IMPERFECT

ich	trat
du	trat(e)st
er/sie/es	trat
wir	traten
ihr	tratet
sie/Sie	traten

FUTURE

ich	werde treten
du	wirst treten
er/sie/es	wird treten
wir	werden treten
ihr	werdet treten
sie/Sie	werden treten

CONDITIONAL

ich	würde treten
du	würdest treten
er/sie/es	würde treten
wir	würden treten
ihr	würdet treten
sie/Sie	würden treten

IMPERATIVE
tritt! / treten wir! / tretet! / treten Sie!

PRESENT PARTICIPLE
tretend

PAST PARTICIPLE
getreten

*When **treten** is used with no direct object, it is formed with **sein**.

EXAMPLE PHRASES

Pass auf, wohin du **trittst**! — *Watch your step!*
Er **hat** mich **getreten**. — *He kicked me.*

strong, *formed with* **haben**

to drink **trinken**

Table **80**

PRESENT
ich	trinke
du	trinkst
er/sie/es	trinkt
wir	trinken
ihr	trinkt
sie/Sie	trinken

PRESENT SUBJUNCTIVE
ich	trinke
du	trinkest
er/sie/es	trinke
wir	trinken
ihr	trinket
sie/Sie	trinken

PERFECT
ich	habe getrunken
du	hast getrunken
er/sie/es	hat getrunken
wir	haben getrunken
ihr	habt getrunken
sie/Sie	haben getrunken

IMPERFECT
ich	trank
du	trankst
er/sie/es	trank
wir	tranken
ihr	trankt
sie/Sie	tranken

FUTURE
ich	werde trinken
du	wirst trinken
er/sie/es	wird trinken
wir	werden trinken
ihr	werdet trinken
sie/Sie	werden trinken

CONDITIONAL
ich	würde trinken
du	würdest trinken
er/sie/es	würde trinken
wir	würden trinken
ihr	würdet trinken
sie/Sie	würden trinken

IMPERATIVE
trink(e)! / trinken wir! / trinkt! / trinken Sie!

PRESENT PARTICIPLE
trinkend

PAST PARTICIPLE
getrunken

EXAMPLE PHRASES

Er **trank** die ganze Flasche leer.	*He drank the whole bottle.*
Ich **würde** gern ein Bier mit Ihnen **trinken**.	*I'd like to have a beer with you.*

Table 81: **tun** *to do*

strong, formed with **haben**

PRESENT
ich	tue
du	tust
er/sie/es	tut
wir	tun
ihr	tut
sie/Sie	tun

PRESENT SUBJUNCTIVE
ich	tue
du	tuest
er/sie/es	tue
wir	tuen
ihr	tuet
sie/Sie	tuen

PERFECT
ich	habe getan
du	hast getan
er/sie/es	hat getan
wir	haben getan
ihr	habt getan
sie/Sie	haben getan

IMPERFECT
ich	tat
du	tat(e)st
er/sie/es	tat
wir	taten
ihr	tatet
sie/Sie	taten

FUTURE
ich	werde tun
du	wirst tun
er/sie/es	wird tun
wir	werden tun
ihr	werdet tun
sie/Sie	werden tun

CONDITIONAL
ich	würde tun
du	würdest tun
er/sie/es	würde tun
wir	würden tun
ihr	würdet tun
sie/Sie	würden tun

IMPERATIVE
tu(e)! / tun wir! / tut! / tun Sie!

PRESENT PARTICIPLE
tuend

PAST PARTICIPLE
getan

EXAMPLE PHRASES

Er **hat** den ganzen Tag nichts **getan**. *He hasn't done anything all day.*

Ich **werde** das auf keinen Fall **tun**. *There is no way I'll do that.*

weak, inseparable, reflexive, formed with **haben**   to think about **sich überlegen**

Table 82

PRESENT

ich	überlege mir
du	überlegst dir
er/sie/es	überlegt sich
wir	überlegen uns
ihr	überlegt euch
sie/Sie	überlegen sich

PRESENT SUBJUNCTIVE

ich	überlege mir
du	überlegest dir
er/sie/es	überlege sich
wir	überlegen uns
ihr	überleget euch
sie/Sie	überlegen sich

PERFECT

ich	habe mir überlegt
du	hast dir überlegt
er/sie/es	hat sich überlegt
wir	haben uns überlegt
ihr	habt euch überlegt
sie/Sie	haben sich überlegt

IMPERFECT

ich	überlegte mir
du	überlegtest dir
er/sie/es	überlegte sich
wir	überlegten uns
ihr	überlegtet euch
sie/Sie	überlegten sich

FUTURE

ich	werde mir überlegen
du	wirst dir überlegen
er/sie/es	wird sich überlegen
wir	werden uns überlegen
ihr	werdet euch überlegen
sie/Sie	werden sich überlegen

CONDITIONAL

ich	würde mir überlegen
du	würdest dir überlegen
er/sie/es	würde sich überlegen
wir	würden uns überlegen
ihr	würdet euch überlegen
sie/Sie	würden sich überlegen

IMPERATIVE
überleg(e) dir! / überlegen wir uns! / überlegt euch! / überlegen Sie sich!

PRESENT PARTICIPLE
überlegend

PAST PARTICIPLE
überlegt

---- EXAMPLE PHRASES ----

Er **überlegte sich** einen schlauen Plan.   *He thought of a clever plan.*

Das **werde** ich **mir überlegen**.   *I'll have a think about it.*

Table 83

vergessen *to forget*

strong, inseparable, formed with **haben**

PRESENT
ich	vergesse
du	vergisst
er/sie/es	vergisst
wir	vergessen
ihr	vergesst
sie/Sie	vergessen

PRESENT SUBJUNCTIVE
ich	vergesse
du	vergessest
er/sie/es	vergesse
wir	vergessen
ihr	vergesset
sie/Sie	vergessen

PERFECT
ich	habe vergessen
du	hast vergessen
er/sie/es	hat vergessen
wir	haben vergessen
ihr	habt vergessen
sie/Sie	haben vergessen

IMPERFECT
ich	vergaß
du	vergaßest
er/sie/es	vergaß
wir	vergaßen
ihr	vergaßt
sie/Sie	vergaßen

FUTURE
ich	werde vergessen
du	wirst vergessen
er/sie/es	wird vergessen
wir	werden vergessen
ihr	werdet vergessen
sie/Sie	werden vergessen

CONDITIONAL
ich	würde vergessen
du	würdest vergessen
er/sie/es	würde vergessen
wir	würden vergessen
ihr	würdet vergessen
sie/Sie	würden vergessen

IMPERATIVE
vergiss! / vergessen wir! / vergesst! / vergessen Sie!

PRESENT PARTICIPLE
vergessend

PAST PARTICIPLE
vergessen

EXAMPLE PHRASES

Er sagt, er **vergesse** nie ein Gesicht.

He says he never forgets a face.

Ich **habe** seinen Namen vergessen.

I've forgotten his name.

weak, inseparable, formed with **haben**

to demand **verlangen**

Table 84

PRESENT
ich	verlange
du	verlangst
er/sie/es	verlangt
wir	verlangen
ihr	verlangt
sie/Sie	verlangen

PRESENT SUBJUNCTIVE
ich	verlange
du	verlangest
er/sie/es	verlange
wir	verlangen
ihr	verlanget
sie/Sie	verlangen

PERFECT
ich	habe verlangt
du	hast verlangt
er/sie/es	hat verlangt
wir	haben verlangt
ihr	habt verlangt
sie/Sie	haben verlangt

IMPERFECT
ich	verlangte
du	verlangtest
er/sie/es	verlangte
wir	verlangten
ihr	verlangtet
sie/Sie	verlangten

FUTURE
ich	werde verlangen
du	wirst verlangen
er/sie/es	wird verlangen
wir	werden verlangen
ihr	werdet verlangen
sie/Sie	werden verlangen

CONDITIONAL
ich	würde verlangen
du	würdest verlangen
er/sie/es	würde verlangen
wir	würden verlangen
ihr	würdet verlangen
sie/Sie	würden verlangen

IMPERATIVE
verlang(e)! / verlangen wir! / verlangt! / verlangen Sie!

PRESENT PARTICIPLE
verlangend

PAST PARTICIPLE
verlangt

EXAMPLE PHRASES

Wie viel **hat** er dafür **verlangt**? — *How much did he want for it?*
Sie **verlangten**, dass man sie anhört. — *They demanded to be heard.*

Table 85 — **verlieren** *to lose*

*strong, inseparable, formed with **haben***

PRESENT
ich	verliere
du	verlierst
er/sie/es	verliert
wir	verlieren
ihr	verliert
sie/Sie	verlieren

PRESENT SUBJUNCTIVE
ich	verliere
du	verlierest
er/sie/es	verliere
wir	verlieren
ihr	verlieret
sie/Sie	verlieren

PERFECT
ich	habe verloren
du	hast verloren
er/sie/es	hat verloren
wir	haben verloren
ihr	habt verloren
sie/Sie	haben verloren

IMPERFECT
ich	verlor
du	verlorst
er/sie/es	verlor
wir	verloren
ihr	verlort
sie/Sie	verloren

FUTURE
ich	werde verlieren
du	wirst verlieren
er/sie/es	wird verlieren
wir	werden verlieren
ihr	werdet verlieren
sie/Sie	werden verlieren

CONDITIONAL
ich	würde verlieren
du	würdest verlieren
er/sie/es	würde verlieren
wir	würden verlieren
ihr	würdet verlieren
sie/Sie	würden verlieren

IMPERATIVE
verlier(e)! / verlieren wir! / verliert! / verlieren Sie!

PRESENT PARTICIPLE
verlierend

PAST PARTICIPLE
verloren

EXAMPLE PHRASES

Wenn du **verlierst**, musst du mir 10 Euro zahlen.
If you lose, you'll have to pay me 10 euros.

Wir **haben** drei Spiele hintereinander **verloren**.
We lost three matches in a row.

strong, inseparable, formed with **sein** *to disappear* **verschwinden**

Table 86

PRESENT

ich	verschwinde
du	verschwindest
er/sie/es	verschwindet
wir	verschwinden
ihr	verschwindet
sie/Sie	verschwinden

PRESENT SUBJUNCTIVE

ich	verschwinde
du	verschwindest
er/sie/es	verschwinde
wir	verschwinden
ihr	verschwindet
sie/Sie	verschwinden

PERFECT

ich	bin verschwunden
du	bist verschwunden
er/sie/es	ist verschwunden
wir	sind verschwunden
ihr	seid verschwunden
sie/Sie	sind verschwunden

IMPERFECT

ich	verschwand
du	verschwand(e)st
er/sie/es	verschwand
wir	verschwanden
ihr	verschwandet
sie/Sie	verschwanden

FUTURE

ich	werde verschwinden
du	wirst verschwinden
er/sie/es	wird verschwinden
wir	werden verschwinden
ihr	werdet verschwinden
sie/Sie	werden verschwinden

CONDITIONAL

ich	würde verschwinden
du	würdest verschwinden
er/sie/es	würde verschwinden
wir	würden verschwinden
ihr	würdet verschwinden
sie/Sie	würden verschwinden

IMPERATIVE

verschwind(e)! / verschwinden wir! / verschwindet! / verschwinden Sie!

PRESENT PARTICIPLE

verschwindend

PAST PARTICIPLE

verschwunden

EXAMPLE PHRASES

Er **ist** seit Sonntag **verschwunden**. *He has been missing since Sunday.*

Unsere Sorgen **werden** bald **verschwinden**. *Our worries will soon disappear.*

Table 87: wachsen — to grow

strong, formed with **sein**

PRESENT
ich	wachse
du	wächst
er/sie/es	wächst
wir	wachsen
ihr	wachst
sie/Sie	wachsen

PRESENT SUBJUNCTIVE
ich	wachse
du	wachsest
er/sie/es	wachse
wir	wachsen
ihr	wachset
sie/Sie	wachsen

PERFECT
ich	bin gewachsen
du	bist gewachsen
er/sie/es	ist gewachsen
wir	sind gewachsen
ihr	seid gewachsen
sie/Sie	sind gewachsen

IMPERFECT
ich	wuchs
du	wuchsest
er/sie/es	wuchs
wir	wuchsen
ihr	wuchst
sie/Sie	wuchsen

FUTURE
ich	werde wachsen
du	wirst wachsen
er/sie/es	wird wachsen
wir	werden wachsen
ihr	werdet wachsen
sie/Sie	werden wachsen

CONDITIONAL
ich	würde wachsen
du	würdest wachsen
er/sie/es	würde wachsen
wir	würden wachsen
ihr	würdet wachsen
sie/Sie	würden wachsen

IMPERATIVE
wachs(e)! / wachsen wir! / wachst! / wachsen Sie!

PRESENT PARTICIPLE
wachsend

PAST PARTICIPLE
gewachsen

EXAMPLE PHRASES

Der Baum **wächst** nicht mehr.
Ich **bin** im letzten Jahr 10 Zentimeter **gewachsen**.
Meine Probleme **werden** weiter **wachsen**.

The tree has stopped growing.
I've grown 10 centimetres in the past year.
My problems will keep on growing.

weak, formed with **sein** — to hike **wandern**

Table **88**

PRESENT

ich	wand(e)re
du	wanderst
er/sie/es	wandert
wir	wandern
ihr	wandert
sie/Sie	wandern

PRESENT SUBJUNCTIVE

ich	wand(e)re
du	wandrest
er/sie/es	wand(e)re
wir	wandern
ihr	wandert
sie/Sie	wandern

PERFECT

ich	bin gewandert
du	bist gewandert
er/sie/es	ist gewandert
wir	sind gewandert
ihr	seid gewandert
sie/Sie	sind gewandert

IMPERFECT

ich	wanderte
du	wandertest
er/sie/es	wanderte
wir	wanderten
ihr	wandertet
sie/Sie	wanderten

FUTURE

ich	werde wandern
du	wirst wandern
er/sie/es	wird wandern
wir	werden wandern
ihr	werdet wandern
sie/Sie	werden wandern

CONDITIONAL

ich	würde wandern
du	würdest wandern
er/sie/es	würde wandern
wir	würden wandern
ihr	würdet wandern
sie/Sie	würden wandern

IMPERATIVE
wandre! / wandern wir! / wandert! / wandern Sie!

PRESENT PARTICIPLE
wandernd

PAST PARTICIPLE
gewandert

EXAMPLE PHRASES

Im Urlaub **werden** wir jeden Tag **wandern**.

On our holiday we'll go hiking every day.

Table 89: **waschen** to wash

strong, formed with haben

PRESENT
- ich wasche
- du wäschst
- er/sie/es wäscht
- wir waschen
- ihr wascht
- sie/Sie waschen

PRESENT SUBJUNCTIVE
- ich wasche
- du waschest
- er/sie/es wasche
- wir waschen
- ihr waschet
- sie/Sie waschen

PERFECT
- ich habe gewaschen
- du hast gewaschen
- er/sie/es hat gewaschen
- wir haben gewaschen
- ihr habt gewaschen
- sie/Sie haben gewaschen

IMPERFECT
- ich wusch
- du wuschest
- er/sie/es wusch
- wir wuschen
- ihr wuscht
- sie/Sie wuschen

FUTURE
- ich werde waschen
- du wirst waschen
- er/sie/es wird waschen
- wir werden waschen
- ihr werdet waschen
- sie/Sie werden waschen

CONDITIONAL
- ich würde waschen
- du würdest waschen
- er/sie/es würde waschen
- wir würden waschen
- ihr würdet waschen
- sie/Sie würden waschen

IMPERATIVE
wasche(e)! / waschen wir! / wascht! / waschen Sie!

PRESENT PARTICIPLE
waschend

PAST PARTICIPLE
gewaschen

EXAMPLE PHRASES

Ich **habe** mir die Hände **gewaschen**.
I washed my hands.

Die Katze **wusch** sich in der Sonne.
The cat was washing itself in the sunshine.

Ich **werde** mir jetzt die Haare **waschen**.
I'll go and wash my hair now.

strong, *formed with* **haben** — *to recruit; to advertise* **werben**

Table 90

PRESENT
- ich werbe
- du wirbst
- er/sie/es wirbt
- wir werben
- ihr werbt
- sie/Sie werben

PRESENT SUBJUNCTIVE
- ich werbe
- du werbest
- er/sie/es werbe
- wir werben
- ihr werbet
- sie/Sie werben

PERFECT
- ich habe geworben
- du hast geworben
- er/sie/es hat geworben
- wir haben geworben
- ihr habt geworben
- sie/Sie haben geworben

IMPERFECT
- ich warb
- du warbst
- er/sie/es warb
- wir warben
- ihr warbt
- sie/Sie warben

FUTURE
- ich werde werben
- du wirst werben
- er/sie/es wird werben
- wir werden werben
- ihr werdet werben
- sie/Sie werden werben

CONDITIONAL
- ich würde werben
- du würdest werben
- er/sie/es würde werben
- wir würden werben
- ihr würdet werben
- sie/Sie würden werben

IMPERATIVE
wirb! / werben wir! / werbt! / werben Sie!

PRESENT PARTICIPLE
werbend

PAST PARTICIPLE
geworben

EXAMPLE PHRASES

Die Partei **wirbt** zur Zeit Mitglieder.
The party is currently recruiting members.

Wir **werden** für unser neues Produkt **werben**.
We will advertise our new product.

werden *to become*

strong, formed with **sein**

PRESENT
ich	werde
du	wirst
er/sie/es	wird
wir	werden
ihr	werdet
sie/Sie	werden

PRESENT SUBJUNCTIVE
ich	werde
du	werdest
er/sie/es	werde
wir	werden
ihr	werdet
sie/Sie	werden

PERFECT
ich	bin geworden
du	bist geworden
er/sie/es	ist geworden
wir	sind geworden
ihr	seid geworden
sie/Sie	sind geworden

IMPERFECT
ich	wurde
du	wurdest
er/sie/es	wurde
wir	wurden
ihr	wurdet
sie/Sie	wurden

FUTURE
ich	werde werden
du	wirst werden
er/sie/es	wird werden
wir	werden werden
ihr	werdet werden
sie/Sie	werden werden

CONDITIONAL
ich	würde werden
du	würdest werden
er/sie/es	würde werden
wir	würden werden
ihr	würdet werden
sie/Sie	würden werden

IMPERATIVE
werde! / werden wir! / werdet! / werden Sie!

PRESENT PARTICIPLE
werdend

PAST PARTICIPLE
geworden

EXAMPLE PHRASES

Mir **wird** schlecht. — *I feel ill.*
Ich **werde** Lehrerin **werden**. — *I'll become a teacher.*

| strong, *formed with* **haben** | *to throw* **werfen** |

PRESENT

- ich werfe
- du wirfst
- er/sie/es wirft
- wir werfen
- ihr werft
- sie/Sie werfen

PRESENT SUBJUNCTIVE

- ich werfe
- du werfest
- er/sie/es werfe
- wir werfen
- ihr werfet
- sie/Sie werfen

PERFECT

- ich habe geworfen
- du hast geworfen
- er/sie/es hat geworfen
- wir haben geworfen
- ihr habt geworfen
- sie/Sie haben geworfen

IMPERFECT

- ich warf
- du warfst
- er/sie/es warf
- wir warfen
- ihr warft
- sie/Sie warfen

FUTURE

- ich werde werfen
- du wirst werfen
- er/sie/es wird werfen
- wir werden werfen
- ihr werdet werfen
- sie/Sie werden werfen

CONDITIONAL

- ich würde werfen
- du würdest werfen
- er/sie/es würde werfen
- wir würden werfen
- ihr würdet werfen
- sie/Sie würden werfen

IMPERATIVE

wirf! / werfen wir! / werft! / werfen Sie!

PRESENT PARTICIPLE

werfend

PAST PARTICIPLE

geworfen

EXAMPLE PHRASES

Er drohte ihm, er **werfe** ihn aus dem Haus.
Am liebsten **würde** ich das Handtuch **werfen**.

He threatened to throw him out of the house.
I feel like throwing in the towel.

Table 93: wissen *to know*

mixed, formed with **haben**

PRESENT
ich	weiß
du	weißt
er/sie/es	weiß
wir	wissen
ihr	wisst
sie/Sie	wissen

PRESENT SUBJUNCTIVE
ich	wisse
du	wissest
er/sie/es	wisse
wir	wissen
ihr	wisset
sie/Sie	wissen

PERFECT
ich	habe gewusst
du	hast gewusst
er/sie/es	hat gewusst
wir	haben gewusst
ihr	habt gewusst
sie/Sie	haben gewusst

IMPERFECT
ich	wusste
du	wusstest
er/sie/es	wusste
wir	wussten
ihr	wusstet
sie/Sie	wussten

FUTURE
ich	werde wissen
du	wirst wissen
er/sie/es	wird wissen
wir	werden wissen
ihr	werdet wissen
sie/Sie	werden wissen

CONDITIONAL
ich	würde wissen
du	würdest wissen
er/sie/es	würde wissen
wir	würden wissen
ihr	würdet wissen
sie/Sie	würden wissen

IMPERATIVE
wisse! / wissen wir! / wisset! / wissen Sie!

PRESENT PARTICIPLE
wissend

PAST PARTICIPLE
gewusst

EXAMPLE PHRASES

Ich **weiß** nicht.
Er **hat** nichts davon **gewusst**.
Morgen **werden** wir **wissen**, wer gewonnen hat.

I don't know.
He didn't know anything about it.
Tomorrow we'll know who has won.

modal, *formed with* **haben**   *to want* **wollen**

Table 94

PRESENT

ich	will
du	willst
er/sie/es	will
wir	wollen
ihr	wollt
sie/Sie	wollen

PRESENT SUBJUNCTIVE

ich	wolle
du	wollest
er/sie/es	wolle
wir	wollen
ihr	wollet
sie/Sie	wollen

PERFECT

ich	habe gewollt/wollen
du	hast gewollt/wollen
er/sie/es	hat gewollt/wollen
wir	haben gewollt/wollen
ihr	habt gewollt/wollen
sie/Sie	haben gewollt/wollen

IMPERFECT

ich	wollte
du	wolltest
er/sie/es	wollte
wir	wolten
ihr	wolltet
sie/Sie	wollten

FUTURE

ich	werde wollen
du	wirst wollen
er/sie/es	wird wollen
wir	werden wollen
ihr	werdet wollen
sie/Sie	werden wollen

CONDITIONAL

ich	würde wollen
du	würdest wollen
er/sie/es	würde wollen
wir	würden wollen
ihr	würdet wollen
sie/Sie	würden wollen

IMPERATIVE
wolle! / wollen wir! / wollt! / wollen Sie!

PRESENT PARTICIPLE
wollend

PAST PARTICIPLE
gewollt / wollen°

°This form is used when combined with another infinitive.

EXAMPLE PHRASES

Er **will** nach London gehen.   *He wants to go to London.*
Sie **wollten** nur mehr Geld.   *All they wanted was more money.*

Table 95: zerstören *to destroy*

*weak, inseparable, formed with **haben***

PRESENT
ich	zerstöre
du	zerstörst
er/sie/es	zerstört
wir	zerstören
ihr	zerstört
sie/Sie	zerstören

PRESENT SUBJUNCTIVE
ich	zerstöre
du	zerstörest
er/sie/es	zerstöre
wir	zerstören
ihr	zerstöret
sie/Sie	zerstören

PERFECT
ich	habe zerstört
du	hast zerstört
er/sie/es	hat zerstört
wir	haben zerstört
ihr	habt zerstört
sie/Sie	haben zerstört

IMPERFECT
ich	zerstörte
du	zerstörtest
er/sie/es	zerstörte
wir	zerstörten
ihr	zerstörtet
sie/Sie	zerstörten

FUTURE
ich	werde zerstören
du	wirst zerstören
er/sie/es	wird zerstören
wir	werden zerstören
ihr	werdet zerstören
sie/Sie	werden zerstören

CONDITIONAL
ich	würde zerstören
du	würdest zerstören
er/sie/es	würde zerstören
wir	würden zerstören
ihr	würdet zerstören
sie/Sie	würden zerstören

IMPERATIVE
zerstör(e)! / zerstören wir! / zerstört! / zerstören Sie!

PRESENT PARTICIPLE
zerstörend

PAST PARTICIPLE
zerstört

EXAMPLE PHRASES

Er **hat** ihr Selbstvertrauen **zerstört**.	*He has destroyed her self-confidence.*
Das **würde** unsere Freundschaft **zerstören**.	*It would destroy our friendship.*

strong, formed with **sein/haben**°   *to go; to pull* **ziehen**

Table 96

PRESENT
ich	ziehe
du	ziehst
er/sie/es	zieht
wir	ziehen
ihr	zieht
sie/Sie	ziehen

PRESENT SUBJUNCTIVE
ich	ziehe
du	ziehest
er/sie/es	ziehe
wir	ziehen
ihr	ziehet
sie/Sie	ziehen

PERFECT
ich	bin/habe gezogen
du	bist/hast gezogen
er/sie/es	ist/hat gezogen
wir	sind/haben gezogen
ihr	seid/habt gezogen
sie/Sie	sind/haben gezogen

IMPERFECT
ich	zog
du	zogst
er/sie/es	zog
wir	zogen
ihr	zogt
sie/Sie	zogen

FUTURE
ich	werde ziehen
du	wirst ziehen
er/sie/es	wird ziehen
wir	werden ziehen
ihr	werdet ziehen
sie/Sie	werden ziehen

CONDITIONAL
ich	würde ziehen
du	würdest ziehen
er/sie/es	würde ziehen
wir	würden ziehen
ihr	würdet ziehen
sie/Sie	würden ziehen

IMPERATIVE
zieh(e)! / ziehen wir! / zieht! / ziehen Sie!

PRESENT PARTICIPLE
ziehend

PAST PARTICIPLE
gezogen

°When **ziehen** is used with a direct object, it is formed with **haben**.

EXAMPLE PHRASES

Sie **zog** mich am Ärmel. — *She pulled at my sleeve.*
Ich **würde** nie nach Bayern **ziehen**. — *I would never move to Bavaria.*

Table 97: zwingen *to force*

strong, formed with **haben**

PRESENT
- ich zwinge
- du zwingst
- er/sie/es zwingt
- wir zwingen
- ihr zwingt
- sie/Sie zwingen

PRESENT SUBJUNCTIVE
- ich zwinge
- du zwingest
- er/sie/es zwinge
- wir zwingen
- ihr zwinget
- sie/Sie zwingen

PERFECT
- ich habe gezwungen
- du hast gezwungen
- er/sie/es hat gezwungen
- wir haben gezwungen
- ihr habt gezwungen
- sie/Sie haben gezwungen

IMPERFECT
- ich zwang
- du zwangst
- er/sie/es zwang
- wir zwangen
- ihr zwangt
- sie/Sie zwangen

FUTURE
- ich werde zwingen
- du wirst zwingen
- er/sie/es wird zwingen
- wir werden zwingen
- ihr werdet zwingen
- sie/Sie werden zwingen

CONDITIONAL
- ich würde zwingen
- du würdest zwingen
- er/sie/es würde zwingen
- wir würden zwingen
- ihr würdet zwingen
- sie/Sie würden zwingen

IMPERATIVE
zwing(e)! / zwingen wir! / zwingt! / zwingen Sie!

PRESENT PARTICIPLE
zwingend

PAST PARTICIPLE
gezwungen

EXAMPLE PHRASES

Ich **zwinge** mich dazu. — *I force myself to do it.*
Er **hat** ihn **gezwungen**, das zu tun. — *He forced him to do it.*